THE ROUGH GUIDE TO

Great Britain

This ninth edition updated by

Jules Brown, Tim Burford, Samantha Cook, Keith Drew,
Matthew H........
Phil Lee, N
Ann-Marie
Stewart, M

ROUGH
GUIDES

roughguides.com

Contents

Introduction to
Great Britain

If you didn't know that the "Great" in Great Britain was strictly a geographical term (it refers to the largest island – containing England, Scotland and Wales – of the British Isles), you'd be tempted to give Britain the accolade anyway. It's hard to think of another country that's given so much to the world – railways to royalty, shipbuilding to Shakespeare, football to fish and chips – and there are few holiday destinations suffused with as much history, based on more than five thousand years of settlement and a proud record of stability, democracy and invention. From dynamic London to misty Scottish mountains, fishing villages to futuristic cityscapes – and whether you're looking for urban adventures, pagan festivals, cutting-edge galleries, world-class museums, wilderness hikes or majestic buildings – Britain is undoubtedly best.

Of course, the kind of time you have here depends on which Britain you visit – which sounds odd until you take on board that we're talking about three different countries and three distinct national identities, all wrapped up in a relatively modest-sized "United Kingdom" on the western edge of Europe. England, Scotland and Wales have had centuries to get used to each other, but even so there are sharp reminders of past conflicts and present politics at every turn – from mighty border castles to proud, devolved parliaments – while you'll find separate "national" cultural collections in the three very different capital cities of London, Cardiff and Edinburgh. You're not walking into any kind of vicious separatist clamour, but it's as well to remember that England (by far the dominant country) is not the same thing as Britain (even if the English sometimes act that way).

As well as the national variations that spice up any visit, there's also huge regional diversity in Britain – from the myriad accents and dialects that puzzle foreigners to the dramatically diverse landscapes. Bucolic Britain is still easy to find, be it in gentle rolling farmland or alpine peaks and lakes, and tradition and heritage still underpins much that is unique about the great British countryside. But increasingly it's Britain's urban culture

ABOVE NOTTING HILL CARNIVAL; TARTAN; DAFFODILS **RIGHT** WORCESTER & BIRMINGHAM CANAL

– innovative arts and music, challenging architecture, trend-setting nightlife – that the tourist authorities choose to promote.

The Empire may be long gone, and Westminster might be uncertain about its political role in the modern world, but in recent years Britain has showcased its international hosting skills with gusto. The London 2012 Olympics and Glasgow 2014 Commonwealth Games each went above and beyond the nation's ever-modest expectations – in terms of both execution and medal count – and placed the British Isles on the podium of global attention once again.

After a flurry of national pride, only exacerbated by the Queen's Diamond Jubilee celebrations in 2012 and the dawning of a new generation of Windsors in 2013, the United Kingdom was on the brink of a shake-up when the Scottish public voted in the 2014 independence referendum, opting to remain part of the union by an unexpectedly fine margin. Still united as one, and emerging from the grips of a long recession, it's business as usual in Blighty, and there has never been a better time to visit.

Where to go

There's enough to see and do in Britain to swallow up months of travel. The rundown of country-by-country highlights over the following pages will help you plan an itinerary – or remind you of how much you've yet to see.

FACT FILE

- Britain is a **constitutional monarchy**, whose head of state is Queen Elizabeth II. **Parliament** is composed of the directly elected House of Commons and the unelected House of Lords. The **Prime Minister** is the head of the largest political party represented in the House of Commons.
- The **lowest point** is in the Fens of eastern England, at 13ft below sea level; the **highest mountain** is Ben Nevis, in Scotland, at 4406ft. The **longest river** is the Severn (220 miles), which flows through England and Wales.
- The **population** of Britain is about 61 million: 53 million in England, 5 million in Scotland and 3 million in Wales. The biggest city is London, with over 8 million inhabitants.
- The **longest distance** between two points on the British mainland – a journey beloved of charity fundraisers – is the 874 miles from Land's End (Cornwall, England) to John O'Groats (in the Scottish Highlands).
- You can always plan a day out at the **seaside** – nowhere in Britain is more than 75 miles from the coast.
- Cary Grant, Stan Laurel, Robert Pattinson, Christian Bale and Guy Pearce? They're all **Brits** – oh, and Gregory House, MD (Hugh Laurie) too. But London-girl Bridget Jones (Renée Zellweger) and Mary Poppins' Cockney chimney sweep Bert (Dick van Dyke)? Definitely not.

England

London is emphatically the place to start. Nowhere in the country can match the scope and innovation of the capital. It's a colossal, dynamic city that is perhaps not as immediately pretty as some of its European counterparts, but does have Britain's – arguably Europe's – best spread of nightlife, cultural events, museums, pubs, galleries and restaurants.

The other large **English cities** – Birmingham, Newcastle, Leeds, Manchester and Liverpool – each have their strengths and admirers. Birmingham has a resurgent arts scene, Leeds is the north's prime shopping city, and Newcastle's nightlife is legendary. Manchester can match the capital for glamour in terms of bars, clubbing and indie shopping, and also boasts two of the world's best-known football teams, while its near-neighbour Liverpool is successfully reinventing itself as a top cultural destination.

History runs deepest in England's oldest urban settlements. The glorious **cathedral cities**, like Lincoln, York, Salisbury, Durham and Winchester, form a beautiful national backbone of preserved churches, houses and buildings, while you're never more than a few miles from a spectacular castle, a majestic country house, or a ruined monastery. There are world-famous, UNESCO-recognized sites galore, from Blenheim Palace to Canterbury Cathedral, but all English towns can rustle up an example of bygone glory, whether medieval chapel, Georgian mansion or Victorian mill. Meanwhile, reminders of more **ancient times** are ubiquitous – and reveal quite how central England has been to thousands of years of European development. In the southwest there are remnants of an indigenous Celtic culture that was all but eradicated elsewhere by the Romans, who in turn left their mark from Hadrian's Wall in the north to Colchester in the south. Even more dramatic are the surviving traces of the very earliest **prehistoric** settlers – most famously the megalithic circles of Stonehenge and Avebury.

For many visitors, it's not the towns or monuments that are most beguiling, but the long-established **villages** of England, hundreds of which amount to nothing more

than a pub, a shop, a gaggle of cottages and a farmhouse or two. Traditional rural life may well be on the wane – though that's been said of England since the Industrial Revolution, over two hundred years ago – but in places like Devon, Cornwall, the Cotswolds, Cumbria and Yorkshire there are still villages, traditions and festivals that seem to spring straight from a Constable canvas or a Wordsworth poem. Indeed, the English **countryside** has been an extraordinarily fecund source of inspiration for writers and artists, and the English themselves have gone to great length to protect their natural heritage. Exmoor, Dartmoor, the North York Moors, the Lake District and the Peak District are the most dramatic of the country's ten **national parks**, each offering a mix of picturesque villages, wild landscapes and wonderful walks.

Scotland

The Scottish capital, **Edinburgh**, is – whisper it to the English – a far more handsome city than London, famous for its magnificent setting, majestic castle and ancient royal quarter of Holyrood, not to mention an acclaimed international arts festival and some excellent museums. A short journey west is the larger city of **Glasgow**, a sprawling postindustrial metropolis on the banks of the River Clyde that's an upbeat destination with great bars, clubs and restaurants. Its museums and galleries are some of the best in Britain, while the city's impressive architecture reflects the wealth of its eighteenth- and nineteenth-century heyday.

Author picks

Our indefatigable authors are always on the lookout for the best in Britain – start here for some truly wonderful British travel experiences...

Glorious gardens No one tends their gardens like the British, whether it's the Lost Gardens of Heligan in Cornwall (p.321), the intriguing "poison garden" at Alnwick in Northumberland (p.604), or the recently discovered historic walled gardens at Aberglasney (p.642).

Remote beaches Head to the extremities: to Par Beach, Isles of Scilly (p.332), the lonely beaches of North Uist (p.943) or Barafundle Bay, Pembrokeshire (p.647).

Wacky festivals The Welsh "capital of wackiness", Llanwrtyd Wells (p.669), combines festive fun and British idiosyncrasy, as does Hastings' Jack in the Green shindig (p.159).

Best views We simply can't choose – London from the Shard (p.90), dramatic Hartland Point in Devon (p.316), the stunning Scottish coast from Wester Ross (p.910) or the River Wye at Tintern Abbey (p.616).

Incredible industry From Ironbridge (p.398) to Manchester (p.454), Rhondda (p.622) to the Clyde (p.804), Britain invented the stuff the world wanted.

Modern masterpieces Visit one of the superb Tate Modern galleries in London (p.88), St Ives (p.330) and Liverpool (p.476), or rub shoulders with Lichtenstein and Warhol in the Scottish National Gallery of Modern Art in Edinburgh (p.743).

Classic journeys The Settle-to-Carlisle Railway (p.541) and the West Highland Railway (p.892) take some beating; walkers, meanwhile, should make for the newly opened Wales Coast Path (p.616), Britain's longest footpath.

Proper pubs You can't beat an evening by the fire in a crooked-ceilinged British pub. *Y Mochyn Du* in Cardiff (p.631), *The Bitter End* in Cockermouth (p.513) and the remote *Old Forge* in Knoydart (p.909) are a few of our favourite spots for a tipple.

> Our author recommendations don't end here. We've flagged up our favourite places – a perfectly sited hotel, an atmospheric café, a special restaurant – throughout the Guide, highlighted with the ★ symbol.

OPPOSITE FAIRY POOLS, ISLE OF SKYE
FROM TOP BARAFUNDLE BAY; *THE OLD FORGE* IN KNOYDART;
JACK IN THE GREEN, HASTINGS

THE CALL OF THE WILD

Despite the crowded motorways and urban sprawl, Britain can still be an astonishingly wild place. Natural habitats are zealously guarded in fifteen national parks, from the far southwest to the distant north – a jaw-dropping number of protected areas for a nation of Britain's size.

Even in the most popular parks – the almost Alpine **Lake District** (p.492), say, or the rugged **Peak District** (p.413) – it's never a problem to escape the day-tripper crowds, while true wilderness awaits in the **Cairngorms** of Scotland (p.896) or **Snowdonia** in Wales (p.697).

Outside the parks, too, every corner of Britain has its own wild charm – whether it's tracking Northumberland's **wild cattle** (p.602), seal-spotting at **Blakeney Point** (p.365), dolphin-watching on the **Moray Firth** (p.895) or hiking across windswept **Lundy Island** (p.316) to see its famous puffins.

Scotland's other towns and cities are only fitfully enticing, though central destinations like **Stirling**, **Perth** and **Dundee**, and **Aberdeen** in the northeast, make a valiant tilt at tourists, and, in the university town of **St Andrew's** (Prince William and Kate Middleton's alma mater) Scotland has a college town to rank with Oxford and Cambridge. However, what usually resonates most with visitors is Scotland's great outdoors, whether it's the well-walked hills of the **Trossachs** in central Scotland – home of Loch Lomond – or the **Highlands**, whose mountains, sea cliffs, shadowy glens and deep lochs cover the entire northern two-thirds of the country. In Highland Scotland in particular, famous destinations trip off the tongue – Loch Ness, Culloden, Cape Wrath and John O'Groats – while Ben Nevis has Britain's highest mountain.

Some of the most fascinating journeys are to be had on the **Scottish islands**, the most accessible of which extend in a long rocky chain off the Atlantic coast. Whether it's mooching around Mull, investigating the early Christian heritage of Iona, whisky-tasting on Islay, or touring the Isle of Arran – the most visited of the Hebrides – there are unique experiences on every inch of the Inner Hebridean archipelago. The outer Western Isles, meanwhile – from Lewis and Harris in the north to Barra in the south – feature some of Britain's most dramatic scenery, from towering sea cliffs to sweeping sandy beaches.

At Britain's northern extreme lie the sea- and wind-buffeted **Orkney** and **Shetland** islands, whose rich Norse heritage makes them distinct in dialect and culture from mainland Scotland, while their wild scenery offers some of Britain's finest birdwatching and some stunning Stone Age archeological remains.

ABOVE RED DEER STAG, CAIRNGORMS **OPPOSITE** HOLY ISLAND, ANGLESEY

Wales

It's **Cardiff**, of course, the vibrant capital, that boasts most of Wales's major institutions – the National Assembly, Millennium Stadium, Millennium Centre, National Museum and Gallery – and is the best place to get the feel of an increasingly confident country. Second city, **Swansea**, is grittier by far, a handy base for the sandy bays, high cliffs and pretty villages of the wonderful **Gower peninsula**. Meanwhile, in the postindustrial **Valleys** – once a byword for coal mining – a superb sequence of heritage parks, memorials and museums illuminates the period when South Wales produced a third of the world's coal.

Castles are everywhere in Wales, from the little stone keeps of the early Welsh princes to Edward I's ring of doughty fortresses, including Beaumaris, Conwy and Harlech. Religion played its part too – the cathedral at **St Davids** was founded as early as the sixth century AD, and the quiet charms of the later, medieval monastic houses, like ruined **Tintern Abbey**, are richly rewarding. Much older relics also loom large – **stone circles** offer a link to the pre-Roman era when the priestly order of Druids ruled over early Celtic peoples.

If England glories in its villages, perhaps it's the **small towns** of Wales that appeal most – New Age Machynlleth and lively Llangollen, the foodie centre of Abergavenny and festival-fuelled Llanwrtyd Wells. You could concoct a delightful tour that goes from one attractive, idiosyncratic town to another, but even so, you wouldn't want to miss Wales's

BRITAIN ON A PLATE

You might think of roast beef or fish and chips – but, only half-jokingly, Britain's national dish was recently proclaimed to be **chicken tikka masala**, a reflection of the extent to which Britain's postwar immigrant communities have contributed to the country's dining scene. Even the smallest town will have an Indian restaurant (more properly, Bangladeshi or Pakistani), with Chinese (largely Cantonese) and Thai restaurants common too – not to mention countless Italian trattorias and pizza places and Spanish tapas bars. For the most authentic food, there are a few ethnic enclaves you need to know about – **Chinatown** in London (p.72) and Manchester's "curry mile" in **Rusholme** (p.464) are probably the best-known, but there are all kinds of treats in store in the lesser-touristed parts of the country. Pakistani grills, Turkish meze or Polish pierogi in London's unheralded suburbs, a Kashmiri balti in **Birmingham** (p.405) or **Bradford** (p.533), or South Indian snacks in **Leicester** (p.433) – all are as British as can be.

other great glory – the wild countryside. The Cambrian mountains form the country's backbone, between the soaring peaks of **Snowdonia National Park** and the angular ridges of the **Brecon Beacons**. These are the two best places for a walking holiday – though you can get up Snowdon, Wales's highest mountain, by railway if you prefer. Mountainous Wales also offers world-class mountain biking – Coed-y-Brenin in Mid-Wales is the name all bikers know. As for the Welsh seaside, don't miss the magnificent clifftops of the rippling **Pembrokeshire** coast or the sandy beaches of the western **Cambrian** shore. Most of the coast remains unspoiled, and even where the long sweeps of sand have been developed they are often backed by enjoyable, traditional **seaside resorts**, such as Llandudno in the north, Aberystwyth in the west or Tenby in the south.

When to go

Considering the temperate nature of the **British climate** (see p.46), it's amazing how much mileage the locals get out of the subject: a two-day cold snap is discussed as if it were the onset of a new Ice Age, and a week in the upper 70s starts rumours of a drought. The fact is that summers rarely get very hot and the winters don't get very cold, except in the north of Scotland and the highest points of the English, Welsh and Scottish uplands. **Rainfall** is fairly even, though again mountainous areas get higher quantities throughout the year (the west coast of Scotland is especially damp, and Llanberis, at the foot of Snowdon, gets more than twice as much rainfall as Caernarfon, seven miles away).

In general, the south is warmer and sunnier than the north, but the bottom line is that it's impossible to say with any degree of certainty what the weather will be like when you visit. May might be wet and grey one year and gloriously sunny the next; November stands an equal chance of being crisp and clear or foggy and grim. If you're planning to lie on a beach, or camp in the dry, you'll want to visit **between June and September** – though don't blame us if it pours down all August, as it might well do. Otherwise, if you're balancing the clemency of the weather against the density of the crowds, the best months to explore are April, May, September and October.

OPPOSITE FROM TOP LEFT CLEY WINDMILL, NORFOLK; ON THE SEAFRONT AT WESTON-SUPER-MARE; GLOUCESTER CATHEDRAL; REGENT'S PARK, LONDON

32

things not to miss

It's not possible to see everything that Britain has to offer in one trip – and we don't suggest you try. What follows, in no particular order, is a selective taste of the highlights of England, Wales and Scotland, including stunning scenery, awe-inspiring architecture, thrilling activities and incomparable urban experiences. Each entry has a page reference that will take you straight to the Guide where you can find out more.

Coloured numbers refer to chapters in the Guide section.

1

1 THE GOWER PENINSULA
Page 637
A stunning stretch, fringed by glorious bays and dramatic cliffs, and dotted with prehistoric remains and castle ruins.

2 HAMPTON COURT PALACE
Page 106
With its yew-hedge maze and restored State Apartments, Henry VIII's extravagant Thames-side palace is the most revered of England's royal abodes.

3 STONEHENGE
Page 216
An ancient, still unexplained, ring of monoliths, Stonehenge attracts sun-worshippers in their thousands over the summer solstice.

4 THE LAKE DISTRICT
Page 492
England's largest national park is also one of its favourites, with sixteen lakes, scores of mountains and strong literary connections.

5

12

13

14

15

16

17

18

19 SURFING IN NORTH DEVON
Page 315
The beaches along the north coast of Devon offer some truly great breaks.

20 MANCHESTER'S NORTHERN QUARTER
Pages 460
Manchester's bohemian Northern Quarter is a hive of music venues, cutting-edge street art and lively bars.

21 HADRIAN'S WALL PATH, NORTHUMBERLAND
Page 597
You can walk or cycle the length of this atmospheric Roman wall, once the frontier against Britain's northern tribes.

22 CURRY IN BRADFORD
Page 533
Bradford's famed curry houses offer everything from cheap-and-cheerful baltis to slick contemporary dining.

23 KINLOCH CASTLE, RÙM
Page 936
Spend the night in a Scottish island hideaway – either in the old servants' quarters or in a four-poster bed.

24 SHOPPING IN THE LANES, BRIGHTON
Page 166
A warren of pedestrianized thoroughfares, Brighton's Lanes are lined with antiques shops, designer outlets and intimate pubs.

25 HAY-ON-WYE LITERARY FESTIVAL
Page 667
The prestigious literary festival at this bibliophile border town brings in all the bookish great and good.

22

23

24

25

29

30

31

32

Itineraries

The following itineraries plan routes through Britain in all its huge variety, from the wave-lashed Cornish coast to the misty hills of northern Scotland. Whether you want to survey the remnants of ancient cultures *in situ*, follow in the footsteps of some of the world's most famous writers, or feast on the best of British dining, these will point the way.

A HERITAGE TOUR

If there's one thing the Brits do brilliantly, it's heritage. Take a couple of weeks to travel back through the millennia.

❶ **Hampton Court Palace, London** You could spend days exploring this Tudor palace, famously pinched from Cardinal Wolsey by Henry VIII. Head straight for the State Apartments, and try not to lose yourself in the yew-hedge maze. **See p.106**

❷ **Salisbury Plain, Wiltshire** Salisbury Plain is littered with the remnants of Stone, Bronze and Iron Age settlements. Stonehenge is the most famous, but you should also make time for nearby Avebury, another stone circle built soon after 2500 BC. **See pp.216–218**

❸ **Blenheim Palace, Oxfordshire** This sumptuous residence is England's grandest example of Baroque civic architecture, more a monument than a house. **See p.238**

❹ **Ironbridge Gorge, Shropshire** The gorge, home to the world's first iron bridge (1781), is now a UNESCO World Heritage Site, with an array of fascinating museums and industrial attractions. **See p.398**

❺ **Conwy Castle, North Wales** The most spectacular of Edward I's Iron Ring of monumental fortresses is in a lovely town on the Conwy Estuary. **See p.716**

❻ **Chatsworth House, Derbyshire** Chatsworth House, built in the seventeenth century, is one of Britain's finest – and most familiar – stately homes, in a lovely Peak District location. **See p.421**

❼ **Holy Island, Northumberland** Atmospheric tidal island where the illuminated Lindisfarne Gospels were created. **See p.607**

❽ **Edinburgh Castle** Perched imposingly atop an extinct volcanic crag, Edinburgh Castle dominates not only the city but the history of Scotland itself. **See p.730**

THE LITERARY TRAIL

You could spend two or three weeks on this tour, which takes in visits to birth- and burial places and dedicated museums, and allows you to explore the landscapes that inspired so many great books.

❶ **Thomas Hardy country, Dorset** Dorset will be forever linked with the wildly romantic works of Thomas Hardy. The town of Dorchester (or "Casterbridge") is the obvious focus, but the surrounding countryside and the coast to the south feature heavily in his novels too. **See p.205**

❷ **Chawton, Hampshire** The modest but elegant home where Jane Austen lived and wrote her most celebrated works is a delight; you can also visit her brother's house, which now holds a library of women's writing. **See p.193**

ABOVE AFTERNOON TEA AT *THE RITZ*; HAMPTON COURT

❸ Stratford-upon-Avon, the Midlands Britain's most celebrated playwright defines this otherwise unextraordinary market town; don't miss Anne Hathaway's Cottage, and be sure to catch an RSC performance. **See p.385**

❹ Laugharne, South Wales Laugharne is saturated with the spirit of Welsh poet, Dylan Thomas; visit his boathouse and his grave, and have a drink in his favourite boozer, *Brown's Hotel*. **See p.643**

❺ Hay-on-Wye, Mid-Wales Browse antiquarian bookshops and join fellow bibliophiles at the literary festival at this appealing Welsh/English border town. **See p.667**

❻ Haworth, Yorkshire Get a glimpse of the Brontë sisters' lives in the pretty Yorkshire village of Haworth, and take a romantic *Wuthering Heights*-style stroll on the wild surrounding moors. **See p.535**

❼ The Lake District The Lake District has had a huge influence on writers as diverse as Beatrix Potter, William Wordsworth and John Ruskin – tour their homes, but be sure to explore the stunning natural surroundings that inspired them, too. **See p.492**

❽ Dumfries and Alloway, Southern Scotland Born in Alloway and laid to rest in Dumfries, Robert Burns is Scotland's most treasured poet. Both towns have a number of Burns-related sights. **See p.772 & p.779**

A FOODIE ODYSSEY

Long having lurked in the shadow of its more flamboyant European neighbours, British food is no longer the poor relation – this two-week-long trail focuses on offbeat destinations that offer memorable gastronomic experiences.

❶ Islay's whisky distilleries, Inner Hebrides Sample a wee dram and get behind the scenes at Islay's fascinating whisky distilleries. **See p.858**

❷ Baltis in Brum This delicious sizzling curry, which travelled with Pakistani immigrants to Birmingham, is an unmissable Brummy treat. **See p.411**

❸ Abergavenny, Mid-Wales Some of Britain's finest restaurants are to be found in and around the appealing market town of Abergavenny, along with a mouthwatering food festival in mid-September. **See p.666**

❹ Michelin-starred dining in Bray Splash out on a gastronomic experience at one of the two triple-Michelin-starred restaurants in Bray – Heston Blumenthal's *The Fat Duck* and Michael Roux Jr's *The Waterside Inn*. **See p.240**

❺ Street food in London From food trucks and pop-up stalls to traditional farmers' markets, the capital's streets offer an eclectic introduction to flavours from around the world. **See p.115**

❻ Oysters in Whitstable, Kent Kent's most bohemian seaside town has been farming oysters since classical times. July's Oyster Festival is a grand time to come, but you can tuck into freshly shucked bivalves at Wheeler's year-round. **See p.139**

❼ Seafood feasts in Padstow, Cornwall A stay on the Cornish coast warrants a fresh seafood extravaganza. Head to one of Rick Stein's restaurants for the very best in fish suppers. **See p.335**

A HERITAGE TOUR
THE LITERARY TRAIL
A FOODIE ODYSSEY

NORTH SEA

SCOTLAND

NORTHERN IRELAND

IRISH SEA

REPUBLIC OF IRELAND

WALES

ENGLAND

FULLER'S BEER ON TAP, LONDON

Basics

Getting there

London is one of the world's busiest transport hubs, and there are good deals from around the world on flights into the British capital. However, if you're planning to tour the north of England, North Wales or Scotland, consider flying directly instead to more convenient international airports like Birmingham, Manchester or Glasgow.

London's biggest and best-known airports – **Heathrow** and **Gatwick** – take the bulk of transatlantic and long-haul flights into the UK, though there are also three smaller London airports (**Stansted**, **Luton** and **City**) and a host of useful regional British airports, many of which are served by low-cost flights from mainland Europe and Ireland. Principally, in England these are **Manchester** and **Liverpool** in the northwest; **Birmingham** in the West Midlands; **Bristol**, Newquay and Exeter in the West Country; **Leeds-Bradford** and Doncaster Sheffield in Yorkshire; **Newcastle** and Durham Tees Valley in the northeast; **East Midlands**; and Bournemouth and Southampton in the south. There are also airports at Blackpool, Humberside, Nottingham and Norwich, plus at **Edinburgh**, **Glasgow** and **Aberdeen** in Scotland, and **Cardiff** and **Swansea** in Wales. The cheapest deals need to be booked well in advance and tend to have little or no flexibility, and taxes and fees can add significantly to any quoted price.

Overland routes from Europe include high-speed trains into London (with onward connections) through the Channel Tunnel – either passenger-only **Eurostar** services or the drive-on, drive-off **Eurotunnel** shuttle train. There's also a range of useful ferry routes offering direct access to various regions.

Flights from the US and Canada

Many airlines fly nonstop to London, Manchester and other British airports – flight time from the east coast is around seven hours, ten hours from the west. Flights on European airlines might be cheaper but tend to route through their respective European hubs, adding to the journey time.

Low-season round-trip **fares** from New York, Boston and Washington to London range from US$650–800, and in summer you can expect to pay more than US$1000 (add US$100–200 from other eastern cities). Low-season fares from the west coast can start at a little under US$1000, rising to more like US$1400 in summer and around Christmas. In **Canada**, the best deals involve flying to London from Toronto or Montreal (around Can$1000–1200 return). British Airways flies direct to Heathrow from Vancouver and Calgary while Air Canada has nonstop links from Vancouver, Calgary, Edmonton and Ottawa. From the west, fares range from Can$1200 to Can$1650.

There are nonstop flights from North America to Glasgow and Edinburgh. The majority of cheap fares, however, route through London or Manchester – or a European city. Return fares start from around US$850/Can$1000. There are no direct flights to Wales from outside Europe, so you're best off flying to England and continuing overland from there.

Flights from Australia, New Zealand and South Africa

Flight time from **Australia** and **New Zealand** to England or Scotland is at least 22 hours. Flights via Southeast Asia or the Middle East to London are generally the cheapest. Average **return fares** from eastern Australian cities to London are Aus$1500–2500 depending on the season; from Perth or Darwin you'll pay around Aus$200 less. Return fares from Auckland to London range from NZ$2000–3000.

There are direct flights from **South Africa** to London Heathrow with South African Airways (Jo'burg and Cape Town), British Airways (Jo'burg and Cape Town) and Virgin Atlantic (Jo'burg). You might get a cheaper deal on indirect routes with Emirates (from Cape Town, Durban and Jo'burg), Ethiopian Airlines (from Jo'burg), KLM (from Jo'burg) and Lufthansa (from Jo'burg). Return fares are generally around ZAR7000–8000. There are no direct flights from South Africa to Scotland or Wales.

A BETTER KIND OF TRAVEL

At Rough Guides we are passionately committed to travel. We believe it helps us understand the world we live in and the people we share it with – and of course tourism is vital to many developing economies. But the scale of modern tourism has also damaged some places irreparably, and climate change is accelerated by most forms of transport, especially flying. All Rough Guides' flights are carbon-offset, and every year we donate money to a variety of environmental charities.

Flights from Ireland

You can get a one-way flight between **Ireland** and England for around €50–80. There are routes out of Dublin, Cork, Knock, Kerry and Shannon to more than a dozen English, Scottish and Welsh airports; airlines include Stobart Air (previously Aer Arann), Ryanair, Aer Lingus and British Airways. The cheapest options **from Belfast** and Derry are usually easyJet, flybe and Ryanair.

Ferries

There are many ferry routes from mainland Europe and Ireland to Britain. The quickest, cheapest services to England are on the traditional cross-Channel routes **from the French ports** of Calais, Boulogne, Dieppe and Dunkerque to **Dover** and Folkestone in Kent. There are many other routes from elsewhere in France, plus Spain (Gijon, Santander and Bilbao), Belgium (Ostend and Zeebrugge) and the Netherlands (Hook of Holland, Amsterdam and Rotterdam) and Denmark (Esbjerg) into ports around the southern and eastern coasts of England, from Plymouth to Newcastle.

Ferry services from **Ireland** mainly run to England's northwest (Liverpool and the Isle of Man) and **Wales** (Holyhead, Fishguard and Pembroke). Northern Ireland has connections to **Scotland's western coast** (Stranraer, Troon and Cairnryan).

Fares on all routes vary considerably, according to time of year, and time and type of crossing – some high-speed ferry services can cut journey times on the same route by up to half – while accommodation is often obligatory (and welcome) on night crossings from the continent.

For up-to-date **information** on routes and operators, check ⓦdiscoverferries.com; to book direct, try ⓦaferry.com.

Trains

Direct **Eurostar trains** (ⓦeurostar.com) run roughly hourly to London St Pancras International from Calais (1hr 10min), Lille (1hr 20min), Brussels (2hr) and Paris (2hr 20min), with connections into those cities from across Europe and direct seasonal services from southern France (Avignon in summer; Bourg St Maurice and Moutiers in winter). Fares start from around €75 one way, though these special rates come with restrictions and you'll have to book well in advance. There are discounts on standard fares for travellers under 26 and over 60.

For drivers, the fastest and most convenient cross-Channel option is the **Eurotunnel** (ⓦeurotunnel.com) drive-on, drive-off shuttle train from Calais to Folkestone (around 75 miles southeast of London), which runs 24 hours and takes 35–45 minutes. Booking is advised, especially at weekends or if you want the best prices. The standard fare for a car and all its passengers is €60–95 one way; more if booked at short notice. **Irish Ferries** (ⓦirishferries.com) offer a very good "Rail Sail" deal, where you can book integrated train and ferry services from almost any station in Ireland to almost any station in Britain. Dublin to London, for example, takes under seven hours, with one-way fares starting at €55. For the best train information online, check the **Man in Seat 61** at ⓦseat61.com.

Buses

Eurolines (ⓦeurolines.co.uk) coordinates international bus services to London (with connections onwards) from dozens of **European cities**. This is the cheapest way of travelling, but you really do have to ask yourself how long you want to spend cooped up in a bus. Only routes from northern European cities are anything like bearable: the journey from Paris, for example, which takes around six hours to London Victoria Coach Station and costs from €25 one way.

Tours and organized holidays

Package tours of Britain, where all flights, accommodation and ground transport are arranged for you, can sometimes be cheaper than organizing things yourself. Many companies, for example, offer **coach tours** of Britain's historic highlights, or help you explore some aspect of the country's heritage, such as art and architecture, or gardens and stately homes. Other operators specialize in **activity holidays** (see box, p.43) either escorted (ie, guide-led) or self-guided, the latter usually being slightly cheaper.

AIRLINES

Aer Lingus ⓦaerlingus.com
Air Canada ⓦaircanada.com
British Airways ⓦba.com
easyJet ⓦeasyjet.com
Emirates ⓦemirates.com
Ethiopian Airlines ⓦethiopianairlines.com
flybe ⓦflybe.com
KLM ⓦklm.com
Lufthansa ⓦlufthansa.com

Ryanair Ⓦ ryanair.com
South African Airways Ⓦ flysaa.com
Stobart Air Ⓦ aerarann.com
Virgin Atlantic Ⓦ virgin-atlantic.com

AGENTS AND OPERATORS

North South Travel UK ☎ 01245 608 291, Ⓦ northsouthtravel
.co.uk. Friendly, competitive travel agency, offering discounted fares
worldwide. Profits are used to support projects in the developing world,
especially the promotion of sustainable tourism.
STA Travel UK ☎ 0333 321 0099, US ☎ 1800 781 4040, Australia
☎ 134 782, New Zealand ☎ 0800 474 400, South Africa ☎ 0861
701 781, Ⓦ statravel.co.uk. Worldwide specialists in independent
travel; also student IDs, travel insurance, car rental, rail passes, and more.
Good discounts for students and under-26s.
Trailfinders UK ☎ 0207 368 1200, Ireland ☎ 021 464 8800,
Ⓦ trailfinders.com. One of the best-informed and most efficient agents
for independent travellers.
Travel CUTS Canada ☎ 1800 667 2887, US ☎ 1800 592 2887,
Ⓦ travelcuts.com. Canadian youth and student travel firm.

PACKAGE TOURS

We have listed operators offering walking, cycling
and activity holidays in our "Sports and outdoor
activities" section (see box, p.43).
Abercrombie & Kent US ☎ 1800 554 7016, Ⓦ abercrombiekent
.com. Classy travel specialist, with no-expense-spared escorted and
independent trips, from a seven-night River Thames cruise to nine-day
tours of English gardens.
Contiki Holidays UK ☎ 0845 075 0990, Ⓦ contiki.com. Lively,
reasonably priced, budget-accommodation adventure tours for 18–35s,
including 5-day London trips or a nine-day England and Scotland trip.
Martin Randall Travel UK ☎ 020 8742 3355, Ⓦ martinrandall
.com. Wide-ranging all-inclusive historical and cultural tours led by
experts – for example, 7 days walking Hadrian's Wall, 4 days exploring
the Arts and Crafts heritage of the Cotswolds or 6 days visiting Snowdonia
and Anglesea.
Maupintour US ☎ 1800 255 4266, Ⓦ maupintour.com. Quality,
all-inclusive, themed escorted tours – from week-long jaunts around
Scotland to a trip to London and southwest England.

Getting around

**Almost every town and many villages in
Britain can be reached by train or – if you
have time and flexibility – bus, but public
transport costs are among the highest in
Europe and travel can eat up a large part
of your budget. It pays to investigate all
the special deals and passes, some of
which are only available outside Britain
and must be bought before you arrive. It
may be cheaper to drive, though fuel and**
**car rental rates are expensive and traffic
can be bad in the cities and on the
motorways.**

By plane

For longer journeys across Britain such as London–
Inverness or Manchester–Newquay, you might
consider **flying**, using airlines such as British Airways
(Ⓦ ba.com), easyJet (Ⓦ easyjet.com), Ryanair (Ⓦ ryan
air.com), flybe (Ⓦ flybe.com), Cityjet (Ⓦ cityjet.com)
and – in Scotland – Loganair (Ⓦ loganair.co.uk). Fares
on popular routes such as London or Birmingham to
Edinburgh and Glasgow, with journey times of
around just 1hr, can cost as little as £60 return –
which can be less than the equivalent train fares,
especially if you book early enough. That said, if you
factor in travel to the airport and check-in proce-
dures you won't always save much on total door-to-
door journey time. The time saving really comes into
play when considering flights to places like the Isle
of Man or the Scottish islands, where flying can save
a day of travel by local bus and ferry. The more
remote parts of Scotland have numerous minor
airports – some little more than gravel strips – and
fares are pretty reasonable.

By train

Despite grumbles about the rail network, and the
high cost of travel compared to other European rail
systems, getting around Britain by train is still the
best, most scenic and – usually – most painless way
to travel. Most major towns in **England** have rail
links, and mainline routes out of London in particular
are fast and frequent – the 200-mile trips to York and
Exeter, for instance, are covered in two hours. The
fastest journeys head north from London on east-
and west-coast mainline routes (to Birmingham,
Manchester, Leeds and Newcastle, among others),
and there are high-speed services to Kent from King's
Cross St Pancras; other journeys, however, can be
more complicated, particularly if you're travelling
east–west across the country, which might involve a
train change or two. **Scotland** has a more modest
rail network, at its densest in the central belt
between Edinburgh and Glasgow, and at its most
skeletal in the Highlands. **ScotRail** (Ⓦ scotrail.co.uk)
runs the majority of train services, sometimes on
lines rated among the great scenic routes of the
world. One appealing option is the overnight
Caledonian Sleeper from London to Edinburgh.
Travelling to **Wales**, most use the fast, frequent
service from London Paddington to **Newport**,

TOP 5 TRAIN JOURNEYS

North Yorkshire Moors Railway
See p.563
Ravenglass and Eskdale Railway
See p.512
Settle–Carlisle Railway See p.541
Snowdon Mountain Railway See p.703
West Highland Railway See p.892

Cardiff and **Swansea**. From other cities in England and Scotland, you'll probably need to change en route – at Bristol for the south coast, at Crewe for the north coast. Within Wales, services cover all the main cities and many rural towns and wayside halts.

Britain's trains are run by a myriad of **operators**, but all are required to work as a single network with integrated ticketing. The **National Rail Enquiries** website (ⓦ nationalrail.co.uk) is a useful first call for timetable, route and fare information; it lists all the regional operators and offers ticket-buying links from its journey planner. For an exhaustive rundown of train travel in the UK, check the excellent website **Man in Seat 61** (ⓦ seat61.com).

Buying tickets

As a rule, the earlier you book, the less you will pay. Always look out for **online offers** with **booking sites** like ⓦ thetrainline.com or ⓦ megatrain.com – the latter, in particular, offers a limited number of ridiculously low fares on certain popular routes. That said, it's also worth checking the websites of the individual operators, as occasionally their fares will trump those offered by the booking sites. A **seat reservation** is usually included with the ticket. Just turning up and buying a ticket at the station is always the most expensive way to go (sometimes phenomenally so); it's always worth asking at the ticket desk about the cheapest option for your journey, as you may get discounts on groups or couples travelling together. If the ticket office is closed, or the automatic machines aren't working, you may buy your ticket on board from the inspector. In some cases, though, buying a ticket on the train when you had the opportunity to buy one beforehand could lead to a penalty of £20 – the stations from which penalty fares apply will have large posters advertising that fact.

Cheapest, wherever you buy them, are advance tickets, which are only available several weeks in advance and sell out quickly. They are restricted to use only on the specified train – miss it, and you pay a surcharge or have to buy another ticket. Off-peak fares can be bought in advance or on the day of travel, but are only valid for travel at quieter times (generally outside 5–10am and 3–8pm Mon–Fri). Most expensive are the fully flexible Anytime tickets.

Rail passes

For overseas visitors planning to travel widely by train, a **BritRail pass** could be a wise investment (ⓦ britrail.net). It gives unlimited travel throughout England, Scotland and Wales (there are also separate England and Scotland passes) and is valid for varied periods of up to one month (consecutive days travel) or two months (flexi-travel). There are first- and second-class versions, discounted Youth Passes, Senior Passes (first-class only), and for every adult buying a full-priced ticket one child (ages 5 to 15) receives the same pass for free. Note that BritRail passes have to be bought before you enter the UK.

If you've been resident in a European country other than the UK for at least six months, an **InterRail pass** (ⓦ interrail.eu), allowing unlimited train travel in England, Wales and Scotland (for 3, 4, 6 or 8 days within one month), might be worth it – but note that you can't use the pass for travel in your own country of residence. **Eurail** passes are not valid in the UK, though they do provide discounts on Eurostar trains to England and on some ferry routes.

ⓦ nationalrail.co.uk details the many regional rail passes that can be bought by both locals and visitors. **Rover and Ranger passes** offer unlimited travel in single, multi-day or flexi-day formats – the Scottish Highland Rover, for example, which costs £81.50 for four out of eight consecutive days, or the Ride Cornwall Ranger, £10 for a day's worth of train travel in that county. There are numerous options when it comes to **annual railcards**, including the 16–25 Railcard, for full-time students and people between 16 and 25; the Senior Railcard for travellers over 60; the Two Together card for a couple travelling together (they don't have to be related); and the Family & Friends Railcard for groups of up to four adults and four children travelling together. Each costs £30 for the year and gives up to a third off most adult fares in Britain (more for children's fares).

By bus

Travel by bus – long-distance services are known as "coaches" – is usually much cheaper than by train, though less comfortable, and traffic congestion can make the same journey much longer. The biggest **inter-city** bus operators in England and Wales are **National Express** (ⓦ nationalexpress.com) and Megabus (ⓦ megabus.com); north of the border, routes are largely covered by Megabus and **Scottish Citylink** (ⓦ citylink.co.uk). On busy routes, and on any route at weekends and holidays, it's advisable to book ahead to get the best deal. Fares are very reasonable, with discounts for under-26s, over-60s and families, plus various advance-purchase fares, passes and special deals available. **Regional and urban** bus services are run by a huge array of companies. Check the official service **Traveline** (@traveline.info), for information and routes. In many cases, timetables and routes are well integrated, but operators tend to duplicate the busiest services, leaving the more remote spots neglected. As a rule, the further away from urban areas you get, the less frequent services become.

By car

Your British driving experience will depend very much on where you drive. Slogging through the traffic from major city to major city is rarely an illuminating way to see the nation – motorways ("M" roads) and main "A" roads may have up to four lanes in each direction, but even these can get very congested, with long tailbacks a regular occurrence, especially at peak travel times and on public holidays. Driving in the countryside, on the other hand, is far more agreeable, though on "B" roads and minor roads there might only be one lane (single track) in both directions. Keep your speed down, and be prepared for abrupt encounters with tractors, sheep and other hazards in remote spots. Don't underestimate the British **weather**, either. Snow, ice, fog and wind can cause havoc – and there has been major flooding in the past few years – and driving conditions, on motorways as much as in rural areas, can deteriorate quickly. Local radio stations feature regularly updated traffic bulletins, as does the **Highways Agency** (@highways.gov.uk).

Britain currently just has two **toll roads**, the M4 in Wales and the M6 in England, but **congestion charging** applies in London (see box, p.110). **Fuel** is pricey – unleaded petrol (gasoline) and diesel in particular. Out-of-town supermarkets usually have the lowest prices, while the highest prices are charged by motorway service stations.

Parking in towns, cities and popular tourist spots can be a nightmare and often costs a small fortune. A yellow line along the edge of the road indicates **parking restrictions**; check the nearest sign to see what they are. A double-yellow line means no parking at any time, though you can stop briefly to unload or pick up people or goods, while red lines signify no stopping at all. Fines for parking illegally are high – as much as £60 – and if you're wheel-clamped it will cost you £200 or so to get it released.

Rules and regulations

Drive on the left. **Seatbelts** must be worn by everyone in a vehicle, front and back, while motor-cyclists and their passengers must wear a helmet. You are not permitted to make a kerbside turn against a red light and must always give way to traffic (circulating clockwise) on a **roundabout** – this applies even for mini-roundabouts, which may be no more than a white circle painted on the road. **Speed limits** are 20 miles/hr in many residential streets, 30 miles/hr in built-up areas, 70 miles/hr on dual carriageways and motorways (freeways) and 60 miles/hr on most other roads – as a rule, assume that in any area with street lighting the speed limit is 30 miles/hr unless otherwise stated. Be alert to the signs, as **speed cameras** are everywhere.

Most foreign nationals can get by with their **driving licence** from home, but if you're in any doubt, obtain an **international driving permit** from a national motoring organization. Anyone bringing their own vehicle into the country should also carry vehicle registration, ownership and insurance documents.

The AA (@theaa.com), RAC (@rac.co.uk) and Green Flag (@greenflag.com) all operate **24-hour emergency breakdown** services, and offer online route planners. You may be entitled to free assistance through a reciprocal arrangement with a motoring organization in your home country – check before setting out. You can make use of these emergency services if you are not a member, but you will need to join on the spot and pay a hefty surcharge.

Vehicle rental

Car rental is best booked online through one of the large multinational chains (Avis, Budget, easyCar, Hertz or National, for example) or through a site such as @auto-europe.co.uk. **North Americans** might want to contact the independently owned Europe by Car (@1 800 223 1516, @europebycarblog.com), which has good deals on short- and longer-term rentals.

If you rent a car from a company in the UK, expect to pay around £30 per day, £50 for a weekend, or £120–200 per week. Few companies will rent to drivers with less than one year's experience and most will only rent to people between 21 or 23 and 70 years of age. Rental cars will be manual (stick shift) unless you specify otherwise – if you want an **automatic transmission**, book well ahead and expect to pay at least £170 a week. **Motorbike rental** is even more expensive – around £350 a week. Try London-based Raceways

(Ⓦraceways.net) or Manchester-based New Horizons (Ⓦnewhorizonsbikehire.co.uk).

By bike

Cycling around Britain can be a pleasant option, as long as you stick to the quieter "B" roads and country lanes – or, best of all, follow one of the **traffic-free trails** of the extensive National Cycle Network (see p.45).

Cycle helmets are not compulsory – but if you're hell-bent on tackling the congestion, pollution and aggression of city traffic, you're well advised to wear one. You do have to have a **rear reflector** and front and back **lights** when riding at night, and you are not allowed to carry children without a special **child seat**. It is also illegal to cycle on pavements and in most public parks, while **off-road** cyclists must stick to bridleways and by-ways designated for their use.

Bike rental is available at cycle shops in most large towns, and at villages within national parks and other scenic areas. Expect to pay around £20–25 per day, or more for specialist mountain bikes and less for multi-day rents; you may need to provide credit card details or leave a passport as a deposit.

Accompanied bikes are allowed free on mainline trains, but you usually need to book the space in advance; check Ⓦnationalrail.co.uk for individual company regulations. Bus and coach companies rarely accept cycles and even then only if they are dismantled and boxed.

Accommodation

Accommodation in Britain ranges from corporate chain hotels to crumbling castles, from budget backpacker hostels to chic boutique hotels. Characterful old buildings – former coaching inns, converted mansions and manor houses – also offer heaps of historic atmosphere. It also tends to be quite expensive, though there are bargains to be had.

Although booking online is your best bet, many tourist offices will **reserve rooms** for you if you turn up without having done so. Using this service might incur a deposit that's deducted from your first night's bill (usually ten percent); in others the office will take a percentage or flat-rate commission of a few quid. If you turn up at a hotel or guesthouse on spec, don't be afraid to ask to see your room before committing – any place worth its salt, be it designer hotel or humble B&B, should have no objection.

A nationwide **grading system**, annually upgraded, awards **stars** to hotels, guesthouses and B&Bs. There's no hard and fast correlation between rank and price, but the system does lay down minimum levels of standards and service. However, not every establishment participates, and you shouldn't assume that a particular place is no good simply because it doesn't. In the rural backwaters in particular some of the best accommodation is to be found in **farmhouses** and other simple properties whose facilities may technically fall short of official standards.

Hotels

British hotels vary wildly in size, style, comfort and price. The starting price for a basic hotel is around £80 per night for a double or twin room, breakfast usually included; anything more upmarket, or with a bit of boutique styling, will be around £100, while at the top-end the sky's the limit, especially in London or in resort or country-house hotels. Many city hotels in particular charge a room rate only.

Budget hotel chains – including Premier Inn (Ⓦpremierinn.com), Holiday Inn Express (Ⓦhiexpress.com), Jurys Inn (Ⓦjurysinns.com), Travelodge (Ⓦtravelodge.co.uk), Ibis (Ⓦibishotel.com) and Comfort/Quality/Sleep Inns (Ⓦchoicehotelsuk.co.uk) – have properties across the country. With no frills (and with breakfast charged extra), they are not always automatically the cheapest option, but they can be a good deal for families and small groups, and rates can get down to a bargain £40–50 per night if booked well in advance. Tune Hotels (Edinburgh and London; Ⓦtunehotels.com) and easyHotel (Edinburgh, Glasgow and London; Ⓦeasyhotel.com) can be even cheaper, offering a simple "add-on" system whereby you book a minimal room online with the option of adding niceties including cleaning, windows, TVs, towels…

B&Bs, guesthouses and pubs

At its most basic, the typical British **bed-and-breakfast** (**B&B**) is an ordinary private house with a couple of bedrooms set aside for paying guests.

TOP 5 QUIRKY HOTELS

Belle Tout Beachy Head. See p.162
Cley Mill B&B Norfolk. See p.366
Hotel Portmeirion North Wales.
 See p.707
Kinloch Castle Hostel Rùm. See p.936
Rough Luxe London. See p.113

ACCOMMODATION PRICES

Throughout this guide we give a headline price for every accommodation reviewed, which indicates the lowest price you could expect to pay per night for a **double or twin room in high season** (basically, from Easter to the end of September, though local variations apply). We also give the high-season price for a dorm bed (and a double room, where available) in a **hostel** – note that for YHA hostels, prices quoted are for nonmembers (members get a £3 discount per night) – and per pitch or per person prices for **campsites**. For **self catering**, we quote the minimum you might pay, for a night or a week, depending on the establishment, in high season. **Single occupancy** rates vary widely. Though they're typically around three-quarters of the price of a double, some places charge almost the full double rate and others charge only a little over half that. Rates in hotels and B&Bs may well drop between Sunday and Thursday, or if you stay more than one night, and some places will require a two-night minimum at the weekend and/or in high season.

Larger establishments with more rooms, particularly in resorts, style themselves as **guesthouses**, but they are pretty much the same thing.

At the extreme budget end of the scale – basic B&Bs under £60 a night, a little less in Wales – you'll normally experience small rooms, fairly spartan facilities and shared bathrooms (though there are some fantastic exceptions). You'll pay a few pounds more for en-suite shower and toilet, while at the top end of the range you can expect real style, fresh flowers, gourmet breakfasts, king-sized beds and luxurious bathrooms. Many top-notch B&Bs – say around £100 and up – offer more luxury and far better value pound for pound than more impersonal hotels. In this category you can also count **pubs** (or inns), and the increasingly popular "**restaurants with rooms**". Both will often have only a handful of rooms, but their atmosphere – and the lazy option of laying your head in the same place that you eat and drink – make them a good option.

Hostels

Between them, the **Youth Hostels Association** (Ⓦyha.org.uk) of England and Wales, and the **Scottish Youth Hostels Association** (Ⓦsyha.org.uk), have hundreds of hostels across Britain, ranging from lakeside mansions to thatched country cottages. There are still shared bathrooms and traditional single-sex bunk-bed dormitories in most, though the majority also now offer smaller rooms (sometimes en-suite) of two to six beds for couples, families and groups. Some hostels have been purpose-built, or have had expensive refurbishments, and in cities, resorts and national park areas the facilities are often every bit as good as budget hotels. Most offer self-catering kitchens, laundry facilities and lounges, while wi-fi access, cafés, bars, tour bookings and bike rental are common. The hostel will usually provide bed linen, pillows and duvet; towels and other necessities can often be rented.

You don't have to be a member to stay at a YHA hostel but nonmembers are charged an extra £3 a night. One year's membership, which is open only to residents of the EU, costs £15 per year for England and Wales, £10 for Scotland, and can be bought online or at any YHA hostel. Members gain automatic membership of the hostelling associations of the ninety countries affiliated to Hostelling International (HI; Ⓦhihostels.com).

Prices are calculated according to season, location and demand, with adult dorm beds costing from £15–30 per night – prices can get higher than that in London and at peak holiday periods. A private twin room in a hostel goes for around £40–70, and family rooms sleeping four from around £70. **Meals** are good value – breakfast or a packed lunch for around £5, or £10–13 for dinner. Advance **booking** is recommended, and essential at Easter, Christmas and from May to August.

A large number of **independent hostels** offer similar prices. With no membership fees, more relaxed rules, mixed dorms and no curfew, many of them, in the cities at least, tend to attract a predominantly young, keen-to-party crowd, but there are family-friendly options, too. For news and reviews, check Ⓦindependenthostelguide.co.uk or

---

TOP 5 HOSTELS

Grasmere Independent Hostel.
    See p.504
Lazy Crofter Bunkhouse Scottish
    Highlands. See p.916
NosDa Cardiff. See p.630
YHA Boscastle. See p.337
YHA Whitby See p.568

Ⓦ hostel-scotland.co.uk, which also list primitive bunkhouses, bunk barns and camping barns in the most rural locations.

Camping

There are hundreds of **campsites**, ranging from small, family-run places to large sites with laundries, shops and sports facilities. Costs start at around £5 per adult in the simplest sites, though at larger, more popular locations you can pay far more, and sometimes there are separate charges per car and tent. Many campsites also have accommodation in permanently fixed, fully equipped caravans, or in wooden cabins or similar. Perhaps in part to the unreliable weather, Brits have taken **glamping** to their hearts, with more tipis, yurts, bell tents and camping "pods" than you could shake a billycan at. Some are downright lavish (with beds, plump duvets, private loos and wood-burners) and are priced accordingly.

In Britain's wilder places you will find **camping barns** and **bunkhouses** (known as bothies in Scotland), many administered by the YHA and SYHA, though with plenty of others operated by individual farmers and families. They are pretty basic – often in converted agricultural buildings, old crofters' cottages and the like – but they are weatherproof and cheap (from around £8–10 a night). **Farmers** may offer field-and-tap pitches for around £3 per night, but setting up a tent without asking first is counted as trespassing and seriously frowned upon. Camping wild is illegal in most national parks and nature reserves – Dartmoor is one exception – but there are places in Scotland where you can camp wild in open country; check Ⓦ outdooraccess-scotland.com for the current situation.

The Rough Guide to Camping in Britain has detailed **reviews** of the best campsites, while Ⓦ coolcamping .co.uk, Ⓦ campingandcaravanningclub.co.uk and Ⓦ ukcampsite.co.uk are useful online resources.

Self-catering

Holiday self-catering properties range from city penthouses to secluded cottages. **Studios and apartments**, available by the night in an increasing number of cities, offer an attractive alternative to hotels, with prices from around £90 a night (more in London). Rural **cottages and houses** work out cheaper, though the minimum rental period may be a week. Depending on the season and location, expect to pay from around £350 for a week in a small cottage, perhaps three or four times that for a larger property in a popular tourist spot.

ACCOMMODATION CONTACTS

B&BS, HOTELS, FARMS AND STUDENT ROOMS

Bed&Fed Ⓦ bedandfed.co.uk. Informal "homes from home", with your hosts providing a simple supper, bed and a light breakfast.

CouchSurfing Ⓦ couchsurfing.org. Huge worldwide directory listing people willing to let other members stay with them for free.

Distinctly Different Ⓦ distinctlydifferent.co.uk. B&B or self-catering in converted buildings across Britain, from cow sheds to lighthouses.

Farm Stay Ⓦ farmstay.co.uk. The UK's largest network of farm-based accommodation – B&B, self-catering and camping.

LateRooms.com Ⓦ laterooms.com. Thousands of rooms across Britain available at up to fifty percent discount.

University rooms Ⓦ universityrooms.co.uk. Student halls of residence in university towns from Cornwall to Aberdeen, offering good-value rooms (mostly single) or self-catering apartments over the summer (July–Sept), Easter and Christmas holidays.

Wolsey Lodges Ⓦ wolseylodges.com. Superior B&B in grand properties throughout Britain, from Elizabethan manor houses to Victorian rectories.

SELF-CATERING

Airbnb Ⓦ airbnb.com. Cool self-catering, with a huge variety of properties – seaside cottages to farmhouses, canal barges to warehouse apartments.

Cottages4You Ⓦ cottages4you.co.uk. A wide range of properties all over the UK.

Landmark Trust Ⓦ landmarktrust.org.uk. A preservation charity that lists pricey, rather special accommodation in Britain's most distinctive historic properties – castles, ruins, follies, towers and cottages.

National Trust Holiday Cottages Ⓦ nationaltrustcottages.co.uk and Ⓦ nts.org.uk. Self-catering holiday cottages, houses and farmhouses, most of which are set in the gardens or grounds of National Trust (in England and Wales) and National Trust for Scotland properties.

Rural Retreats Ⓦ ruralretreats.co.uk. Upmarket accommodation in restored historic buildings from Cornwall to Scotland.

Scottish Country Cottages Ⓦ scottish-country-cottages.co.uk. Superior cottages with character scattered across Scotland.

Under the Thatch ☎ 0844 500 5101, Ⓦ underthethatch.co.uk. A select choice of self-catering cottages and cabins, from traditional thatched cottages in Wales to Romany caravans and yurts.

Wales Holidays Ⓦ wales-holidays.co.uk. A varied selection of hundreds of properties all over Wales.

Food and drink

Britain no longer has to feel ashamed of its culinary offerings – Cool Britannia is now a gourmet destination. Over the last twenty years, changing tastes have transformed supermarket shelves, restaurant menus and pub blackboards, with an increasing importance placed on

"ethical" and sustainable eating – not only sourcing products locally, but also using free-range, organic, humanely produced ingredients. London continues to be the main centre for all things foodie and fashionable, though great restaurants, gastropubs, farmers' markets and interesting local food suppliers can be found across Britain, often in surprisingly out-of-the-way places.

British cuisine

For some visitors the quintessential British meal is **fish and chips** (known in Scotland as a "fish supper", even at lunchtime), a dish that can vary from the succulently fresh to the indigestibly greasy: local knowledge is the key, as most towns, cities and resorts have at least one first-rate fish-and-chip shop ("chippie") or restaurant. Other **traditional British dishes** (steak and kidney pie, liver and onions, bacon sandwiches, roast beef, sausage and mash, pork pies) have largely discarded their stodgy image and been poshed up to become restaurant, and particularly gastropub, staples – comfort food still, but often cooked with the best ingredients and genuinely tasty. Many hitherto neglected or previously unfashionable British foods – from brawn to brains – are finding their way into top-end restaurants, too, as inventive restaurateurs, keen on using good, seasonal produce, reinvent the classics. The principles of this "nose to tail" eating crosses over with the increasingly modish **Modern British** cuisine, which marries local produce with ingredients and techniques from around the world. **Vegetarians** need not worry, either, despite all this emphasis on meat – veggie restaurants are fairly easy to find in towns and cities, and practically every restaurant and pub will have at least one vegetarian option, be it just a cheese sandwich or a plate of tomato pasta. As a failsafe, Italian, Indian and Chinese restaurants usually provide a decent choice of meat-free dishes.

The wealth of **fresh produce** varies regionally, from hedgerow herbs to fish landed from local boats, and, of course, seasonally. Restaurants are increasingly making use of seasonal ingredients – and in rural areas many farms offer "Pick Your Own" sessions, when you can come away with armfuls of delicious berries, orchard fruits, beetroot and the like. Year-round you'll find superlative seafood – from crabs to cockles, oysters to lobster – fine cheeses and delicious free-range meat. Check out the growing profusion of farmers'

> ### TOP 5 CAFÉS
> **Bar Italia** London. See p.115
> **Betty's** York. See p.547
> **Madame Fromage** Cardiff. See p.631
> **Turl Street Kitchen** Oxford. See p.236
> **Willow Tea Rooms** Glasgow. See p.791

markets (see ⓦ localfoods.org.uk) and farm shops, usually signposted by the side of the road in rural areas, to enjoy the best local goodies and artisan products.

Cafés, tearooms and coffee shops

Though still a nation of tea-heads, Brits have become bona fide **coffee** addicts, and international chain outlets, such as Starbucks, Costa and Caffè Nero line every high street. However, there will usually be at least one independent coffee shop, even in the smallest places, and artisan coffee, brewed with obsessive care by super-cool baristas, can be found in London, especially, along with some of the bigger cities. Despite the encroaching grip of the coffee chains, every town, city and resort in Britain should also have a few cheap **cafés** offering nonalcoholic drinks, all-day breakfasts, snacks and meals. Most are only open during the daytime, and have few airs and graces; the quality is not guaranteed, however. A few more genteel **teashops** or **tearooms** serve sandwiches, cakes and light meals throughout the day, as well, of course, as tea – the best of them will offer a full afternoon tea, including sandwiches, cakes, and scones with cream and jam.

Pubs and gastropubs

The old-fashioned British **pub** remains an enduring social institution, and is often the best introduction to town or village life. In some places, it might be your only choice for food. While occasionally the offerings can be terrible, heavily reliant on frozen meals, microwaves and deep-fat fryers, Britain's foodie renaissance, and a commercial need to diversify, means that many have had to up their game. A new breed of **gastropubs** serve restaurant-quality food in country inns and city pubs alike. Some are really excellent and just as expensive as a regular restaurant, though usually with a more informal feel – while others simply provide a relaxed place in which to enjoy a gourmet pork pie or cheese platter with your pint.

Restaurants

Partly by dint of its size, London has the broadest selection of **top-class restaurants**, and the widest choice of cuisines, but there are some seriously fine dining options in most major cities. Indeed, wherever you are in the UK you're rarely more than half an hour's drive from a really good meal – and some of the very best dining experiences are just as likely to be found in a suburban backstreet or sleepy village than a metropolitan hotspot. Heston Blumenthal's Michelin-star-studded *Fat Duck*, for example, touted as one of the world's best restaurants, is in the small Berkshire village of Bray, where you will also find the equally lauded *Waterside Inn* – while the best Indian food outside the Asian subcontinent is found in unsung cities like Bradford and Leicester.

While a great curry in Birmingham's Balti Triangle or a Cantonese feast in Manchester's Chinatown might **cost** you just £17 a head, the going rate for a meal with drinks in most modest restaurants is more like £27 per person. If a restaurant has any sort of reputation, you can expect to be spending £40–60 each, and much, much more for the services of a top chef – tasting menus (excluding drinks) at the best-known Michelin-starred restaurants cost upwards of £80 per person. However, **set meals** can be a steal, even at the poshest of restaurants, where a limited-choice two- or three-course lunch or a "pre-theatre" menu might cost less than half the usual price.

Drinking

Originating as wayfarers' hostelries and coaching inns, **pubs** – "public houses" – have outlived the church and marketplace as the focal points of many a British town and village. They are as varied as the townscapes: in larger market towns you'll find huge oak-beamed inns with open fires and polished brass fittings; in remoter upland villages there are

TOP 5 DESTINATION RESTAURANTS

Medlar London. See p.120
L'Enclume Cartmel. See p.498
The Kitchin Edinburgh. See p.752
The Foxhunter Nr Abergavenny. See p.667
Waterside Inn Bray. See p.240

stone-built pubs no larger than a two-bedroomed cottage. In towns and cities corner pubs still cater to local neighbourhoods, while chain bars with cheap drinks, and cooler, more offbeat cocktail bars, offer sociable nights out. Most pubs and bars now serve food, in some shape or form (see p.37).

Most pubs are officially open from 11am to 11pm, though cities and resorts have a growing number of places with extended licenses, especially at weekends. The legal **drinking age** is 18 and though many places will have a family room or a beer garden, young children may not always be welcome.

Beer

Beer, sold by the pint (generally £2.50–4) and half pint (half the price), is Britain's staple drink, but ask simply for a "beer" and you'll cause no end of confusion. While lager is sold everywhere, Britain's unique glory is its **real ale**, a refreshing, uncarbonated beer brewed with traditional ingredients, pumped by hand from a cask and served at cellar temperature (not "warm", as foreign jibes have it). If it comes out of an electric pump (and especially if it's labelled "smoothflow" or similar), it isn't the real thing. The most common ale is known as **bitter**, with a colour ranging from straw-yellow to dark brown, depending on the brew. Other real ales include golden or **pale ales**, plus darker and maltier milds, stouts and porters. Controversy exists over the head of foam on top: in southern England, people prefer their pint without a head, and

THE GREAT BRITISH BREAKFAST

The traditional **British breakfast** (aka the "Full English", "Full Scottish", etc) will keep you going all day. It kicks off with a choice of cereals, followed by any combination of eggs, bacon, sausage, tomatoes, mushrooms, baked beans and toast – all fried, though you can have your eggs scrambled or poached. Especially in northern England, it may also include "black pudding" (ie, blood sausage). Veggie alternatives are commonly available. A traditional **Scottish breakfast** includes oatmeal porridge (eaten with salt or sugar), oatcakes (plain savoury biscuits) and potato scones. Breakfasting anywhere in Britain, you may also be served kippers (smoked herring) or haddock with a poached egg on top. A "continental" breakfast usually means cereal, toast and preserves, though often croissants, fruit and yoghurt too. The staple early-morning drink is still tea, though **coffee** is readily available everywhere.

brimming to the top of the glass; in the north and Scotland, flat beer is frowned on and drinkers prefer a short head of foam. Traditional Scottish beer is a thick, dark ale known as **heavy**, graded by a shilling mark (/-) and served with a full head. Quite different in taste from English "bitter", heavy is a more robust, sweeter beer with less of an edge. You will also find "real" cider, made from fermented apple juice, and – particularly in England's West Country and Shropshire – **scrumpy**, a potent and cloudy beverage, usually flat, dry and very apple-y.

Many pubs are owned by large breweries who favour their own beers, though there should also be one or two "guest ales" available. For the best choice, however, you generally need to find a **free house** – an independently run pub that can sell whichever beer it pleases. There are some fantastic choices since Britain's small- and medium-sized microbreweries are flourishing – every region has its own independent outfits, brewing beers that are confined to one particular area or even just one pub. For more on British beer and pubs, check the website of the influential **Campaign for Real Ale** (Ⓦ camra.org.uk).

Whisky

Scotland's national drink is **whisky** – *uisge beatha*, the "water of life" in Gaelic (and almost never referred to as "scotch") – traditionally drunk in pubs with a half-pint of beer on the side, a combination known as a "nip and a hauf". Despite the dominance of the blended whiskies such as Johnnie Walker, Bell's, Teacher's and The Famous Grouse, single malt whisky is infinitely superior and, as a result, a great deal more expensive. Single malts vary in character enormously depending on the amount of peat used for drying the barley, the water used for mashing and the type of oak cask used in the maturing process. Malt whisky is best drunk with a splash of water to release its distinctive flavours.

Wine

English – and to a lesser extent Welsh – **wine** is fast shucking off its image as inferior to its longer-established European counterparts, with a number of small-scale, award-winning vineyards producing delicious tipples. Around four hundred vineyards across England, about twenty in Wales and a few in Scotland produce more than four million bottles a year between them. The speciality is sparkling wines, the best of which have beaten French Champagnes in tasting competitions. For more, see Ⓦ englishwineproducers.com which, despite its name, covers the whole of Britain.

The media

The British remain fond of their newspapers, from national dailies to local weeklies, while there are hundreds of TV and radio stations, both terrestrial and digital.

Newspapers and magazines

From Monday to Saturday, four **daily newspapers** occupy the "quality" end of the English market: the Rupert Murdoch-owned *Times*, the staunchly conservative *Daily Telegraph*, the left-of-centre *The Guardian* and the centrist *Independent*. Among the high-selling **tabloid titles**, the most popular is *The Sun*, a muck-raking right-wing Murdoch paper whose chief rival is the traditionally left-leaning *Daily Mirror*. The middlebrow daily tabloids – the *Daily Mail* and the *Daily Express* – are equally muck-raking and noticeably xenophobic. England's oldest **Sunday newspaper** is *The Observer*, in the same stable as *The Guardian*, while most other major papers publish their own Sunday editions.

The **Scottish press** produces two major daily papers, the liberal-left tabloid *The Scotsman*, based in Edinburgh, and the *Herald*, a broadsheet published in Glasgow; both have Sunday editions, *Scotland on Sunday* and the *Sunday Herald*. More wholesome and uniquely Scottish is the *Sunday Post*, published in Dundee. The biggest-selling dailies are the downmarket *Daily Record*, a tabloid from the same stable as the *Daily Mirror*, and the local edition of *The Sun*. Most of the main UK newspapers produce specific Scottish editions, but the "quality" press, be it the *Daily Telegraph* or *The Guardian*, are justifiably seen in Scotland as being "London" papers.

In **Wales**, where again English papers are widely available (though Welsh news is barely covered), the only quality Welsh daily is the *Western Mail*, a mix of local, Welsh, British and international news; Wales's national **Sunday paper**, *Wales on Sunday*, comes from the same group. In north Wales the *Daily Post* has a decent spectrum of news and features.

Of the range of **specialist magazines and periodicals** covering just about every subject, *The Economist* is a sober business magazine; the left-leaning *New Statesman* concentrates on social issues, and the satirical bi-weekly *Private Eye* prides itself on printing the stories the rest of the press won't touch. In Wales, *Planet* is an English-language, politically irreverent bimonthly combining Welsh interest with a wider cultural and international outlook, while

Scotland's *Scots Magazine* gives a good insight into old-fashioned, middle-of-the-road, Scottish values.

Television

UK **terrestrial television channels** are divided between the state-funded BBC (ⓦbbc.co.uk), and the commercial channels ITV (ⓦitv.com), Channel 4 (ⓦchannel4.com) and Channel 5 (ⓦchannel5 .com). Despite periodic mutterings about the licence fee (paid by all British viewers), there's still more than enough quality to keep the **BBC** in good repute both at home and abroad. The commercial channels are united by a more tabloid approach to programme-making – if they don't get the advertising they don't survive.

The UK's **satellite** and **cable** TV companies are mounting a strong challenge to the erstwhile dominance of the terrestrial channels. Live sport, in particular, is increasingly in the hands of Rupert Murdoch's Sky, the major satellite provider.

Most British homes and hotels get around forty "freeview" channels spread across the networks, including dedicated news, film, sports, arts and entertainment channels.

Radio

The BBC's **radio network** (ⓦbbc.co.uk/radio) has five nationwide stations: **Radio 1** (almost exclusively devoted to chart and dance music); **Radio 2** (light pop and rock for an older audience); **Radio 3** (classical and jazz); **Radio 4** (current affairs, arts and drama); and **5 Live** (sports, news, live discussions and phone-ins). BBC Radio Scotland and BBC Radio Wales offer their own perspective on news, politics, arts and sport; **BBC Radio Cymru** is exclusively Welsh-language. **Digital-only** BBC stations include the alternative-music 6 Music, and the BBC Asian Network, while Scotland, Wales, Shetland and Orkney have their own dedicated BBC news, music, talk and sport stations. In addition, there are other national stations – like TalkSport and Classic FM – as well as a whole host of local stations in every region, both BBC and commercial.

Festivals and events

Many British festivals date back centuries, but the majority of the showpiece events marketed to tourists – from the military pageant of the Trooping of the Colour to the jolly bombast of the Proms – say little about the country's folk history and even less about contemporary Britain. For a more instructive idea of what makes the British tick, you'd do better to catch some grassroots festivities, like London's exuberant Notting Hill Carnival or a wacky village celebration.

WEIRD AND WONDERFUL FESTIVALS

National nuttiness and general British barminess is displayed at dozens of local festivals every year. The Highlands and Islands of Scotland offer rich pickings when it comes to ancient traditions: at New Year, for example, when the **Kirkwall Boys' and Men's Ba' Games**, in Orkney, sees a mass, drunken football game through the streets of the town, with the players jumping into the harbour as a grand finale. In **Whuppity Scourie** (March 1), local children race round Lanark church beating each other with home-made paper weapons – a representation (it's thought) of the chasing away of winter. **Easter** is also big on eccentricity, from the blacked-up Lancashire clog dancers doing the **Bacup Nutters Dance** (Easter Saturday; ⓦcoconutters.co.uk) to the **Hare Pie Scramble** and **Bottle-Kicking** (Easter Monday), a chaotic village bottle-kicking contest at Hallaton, Leicestershire. Meanwhile, Gawthorpe in Yorkshire sees the **World Coal-Carrying Championship** (Easter Monday; ⓦgawthorpemaypole.org.uk), an annual race to carry 50kg of coal a mile through the village. There's more odd racing at the **Brockworth Cheese Rolling** (late May, bank holiday Monday; ⓦcheese-rolling.co.uk) when crowds of daredevils chase a large cheese wheel down a murderous Gloucestershire incline. Later in the year, thousands flock to Ashton, Northamptonshire, to watch modern-day gladiators fight for glory armed only with a nut and twelve inches of string, in the **World Conker Championship** (mid-October; ⓦworldconkerchampionships.com). Perhaps the British capital of bonkers festivities is Wales's Llanwrtyd Wells (ⓦgreen-events.co.uk). Among other events you can get covered in muck in the **World Bog Snorkelling Championships** (August bank holiday Sunday), or try your luck at the **Real Ale Wobble,** a mountain-biking and real-ale-drinking event in November.

JANUARY–MARCH

London Parade (Jan 1) Ⓦ londonparade.co.uk. Floats, marching bands, clowns, cheerleaders and classic cars wend their way through the centre of London.

Celtic Connections (last 2 weeks Jan) Ⓦ celticconnections.com. A major celebration of Celtic, folk and world music, held in venues across Glasgow.

Burns Night (Jan 25). Scots worldwide get stuck into haggis, whisky and vowel-grinding poetry to commemorate Scotland's greatest poet.

Up-Helly-Aa, Lerwick, Shetland (last Tues in Jan) Ⓦ uphellyaa .org. Spectacular Norse festival culminating in the burning of a Viking longship.

Chinese New Year (Feb 19, 2015; Feb 8, 2016; Jan 28, 2017). Processions, fireworks and festivities in the region's three main Chinatowns – London, Liverpool and Manchester.

Shrove Tuesday (47 days before Easter Sunday). The last day before Lent is also known as "Pancake Day" – it's traditional to eat thin pancakes, usually with sugar and lemon.

Shrovetide Football (Shrove Tuesday & Ash Wednesday) Ⓦ ashbourne-town.com. The world's oldest, largest, longest, craziest football game takes place in and around Ashbourne, Derbyshire.

Rye Bay Scallop Week (10 days end Feb/early March) Ⓦ scallop .org.uk. Ten days of foodie events in the pretty Sussex town of Rye: scallop tastings, cookery demos, barrow races and special menus.

Six Nations Rugby tournament Feb & March (Ⓦ rbs6nations .com). Tournament between Scotland, England, Wales, Ireland, France and Italy.

St David's Day (March 1) Wales's national day, with *hwyrnos* (late nights) and celebrations nationwide.

APRIL–JUNE

St George's Day (April 23) Ⓦ stgeorgesholiday.com. England's national day is also, by chance, the birthday of William Shakespeare, so in addition to Morris dancing and other traditional festivities in towns and villages, there are also Bard-related events at Stratford-upon-Avon (Ⓦ shakespeare.org.uk).

Padstow 'Obby 'Oss (May 1) Ⓦ padstowlive.com. Processions, music and May Day dancing in Padstow, Cornwall, centering on the 'oss itself, a curious costumed and masked figure with obscure origins. See p.335

Helston Furry Dance (May 8). Ancient custom involving a courtly procession and "Floral Dance" through the Cornish town. See p.324

Glyndebourne Opera Festival (mid-May to late Aug) Ⓦ glyndebourne.com. One of the classiest arts festivals in the country, in East Sussex. See p.163

Spirit of Speyside Scotch Whisky Festival (end April–early May) Ⓦ spiritofspeyside.com. Five-day binge with pipe bands, gigs, dancing and distillery crawls.

Bath International Music Festival (mid- to late June) Ⓦ bathmusicfest.org.uk. Top-class, ten-day arts and music jamboree, ranging from orchestral music to jazz and world music. See p.275

Hay Festival (last week) Ⓦ www.hayfestival.com. Bibliophiles descend on this Welsh border town for a big literary shindig and its offshoot HowTheLightGetsIn, a festival of philosophy and music. See p.667

Highland Games (end May to mid-Sept) Ⓦ shga.co.uk. Celebrating a tradition dating back over a thousand years, more than sixty Games take place across the Scottish Highlands, northeast Scotland and Argyll – all including traditional sports, cycling, running and wrestling, plus piping and Highland dance.

Great Welsh Beer & Cider Festival (early June) Ⓦ gwbcf.org.uk. Huge three-day event highlighting hundreds of ales and ciders (the majority from Welsh breweries) in Cardiff.

Trooping the Colour (a Sat in June) Ⓦ royal.gov.uk. Massed bands, equestrian pageantry, gun salutes and fly-pasts for the Queen's Official Birthday on Horse Guards Parade, London.

Aldeburgh Festival (mid- to end June) Ⓦ aldeburgh.co.uk. Suffolk jamboree of classical music, established by Benjamin Britten. See p.354

Cardiff Singer of the World competition (mid-June) Ⓦ bbc .co.uk/cardiffsinger. Huge, week-long festival of music and song held in odd-numbered years, with a star-studded list of international opera and classical singers.

JULY–SEPTEMBER

T in the Park (early/mid-July) Ⓦ tinthepark.com. Scotland's biggest outdoor music event, held near Kinross, with a party atmosphere and star-studded line-up of contemporary bands.

Llangollen International Eisteddfod (early July) Ⓦ international-eisteddfod.co.uk. "The world's greatest folk festival" attracts more than twelve thousand international participants, including choirs, dancers, folk singers, groups and instrumentalists. See p.696

Pride London (end June/early July) Ⓦ prideinlondon.org. Britain's biggest LGBT event, with parades, music and general gaiety. Brighton (Ⓦ brighton-pride.org) and Manchester (Ⓦ manchesterpride.com) have big Gay Pride events of their own in August.

The Proms (mid-July to mid-Sept) Ⓦ bbc.co.uk/proms. Top-flight international classical music festival at the Royal Albert Hall, London, ending in the famously patriotic Last Night of the Proms. See p.129

Whitstable Oyster Festival (last week) Ⓦ whitstableoysterfestival .com. Street parades and music, and a beachside "blessing of the oysters" and heaps of fresh bivalves to snack on, of course. See p.139

WOMAD (late July) Ⓦ womad.org. Renowned four-day world music festival outside Malmesbury, Wiltshire.

Edinburgh Festival (Aug) Ⓦ eif.co.uk, Ⓦ edfringe.com. One of the world's great arts festivals, with an "official" festival and a "fringe" that runs for a month combined. See pp.746–747

Royal National Eisteddfod (1st week) Ⓦ eisteddfod.org.uk. The "National Eisteddfod of Wales" is Wales's leading festival and the largest travelling cultural festival in Europe – a week-long annual culture, music and arts bash.

TOP 5 MUSIC FESTIVALS

Green Man Crickhowell, Wales. See p.665
Liverpool International Music Festival
See p.480
Glastonbury See p.281
Cambridge Folk Festival See p.379
Latitude Southwold. See p.357

Cowes Week (1st week) W cowesweek.co.uk. Sailing extravaganza in the Isle of Wight, with partying and star-studded entertainment. See p.189

Broadstairs Folk Week (mid-Aug) W broadstairsfolkweek.org.uk. Excellent folk and world music festival, with workshops, kids' events and a torchlight parade.

Great British Beer Festival (mid-Aug) W gbbf.org.uk. Colossal booze-fest in London, featuring more than nine hundred real ales and ciders from around the world.

Notting Hill Carnival (last Sun & bank holiday Mon) W thenottinghillcarnival.com. Vivacious celebration led by London's Caribbean community but including everything from Punjabi drummers to Brazilian salsa, plus music, food and floats. See p.124

Whitby Folk Week (last week) W whitbyfolk.co.uk. A week's worth of Morris and sword dancing, finger-in-your-ear singing, storytelling and more. See p.569

Abbots Bromley Horn Dance (early Sept) W abbotsbromley .com. Vaguely pagan mass dance in mock-medieval costume – one of the most famous of England's ancient customs, in Staffordshire.

Heritage Open Days (2nd week Sept) W heritageopendays.org .uk. Annual opportunity to peek inside hundreds of buildings in England that don't normally open their doors to the public, from factories to Buddhist temples. Scotland's **Doors Open Days** (W doorsopendays .org.uk) and Wales's **Open Doors** (W wales.gov.uk) offer the same, every weekend in Sept.

Ludlow Food Festival (mid-Sept) W foodfestival.co.uk. High-profile fest in this foodie Shropshire town, with local producers, Michelin chefs, and scores of events and masterclasses.

St Ives September Festival (last 2 weeks) W stivesseptember festival.co.uk. Eclectic Cornish festival of art, poetry, literature, jazz, folk, rock and world music.

Abergavenny Food Festival (2 days, mid-Sept) W abergavennyfoodfestival.com. High-profile weekend of tastings, tours, foraging, quaffing and general guzzling at Wales's pre-eminent foodie town.

Wigtown Book Festival (end Sept–early Oct) W wigtownbook festival.com. Scotland's "national book town" celebrates its literary leanings with a ten-day book fest.

OCTOBER–DECEMBER

Swansea Festival of Music and the Arts (early to mid-Oct) W swanseafestival.org. Two superb weeks of concerts, drama, opera, ballet and art.

Glenfiddich Piping Championships (late Oct) W blairatholl .co.uk. Held at Blair Castle for the world's top-ten solo pipers.

Halloween (Oct 31). Last day of the Celtic calendar and All Hallows Eve: pumpkins, plus a lot of ghoulish dressing-up, trick-or-treating and parties.

Battle of Hastings re-enactment (Weekend in mid-Oct) W english-heritage.org.uk. Annual re-enactment of the famous 1066 battle in Battle, featuring over 1000 soldiers and living history encampments. .

Guy Fawkes Night/Bonfire Night (Nov 5). Nationwide fireworks and bonfires commemorating the foiling of the Gunpowder Plot in 1605 – atop every bonfire is hoisted an effigy known as the "guy" after Guy

Fawkes, one of the conspirators. Most notable events are at York (Fawkes' birthplace), Ottery St Mary in Devon and Lewes, East Sussex.

Lord Mayor's Show (2nd Sat) W lordmayorsshow.org. Held annually in the City of London since 1215, and featuring a daytime cavalcade and night-time fireworks to mark the inauguration of the new Lord Mayor.

Hogmanay and Ne'er Day (Dec 31 & Jan 1). Traditionally more important to the Scots than Christmas and known for the custom of "first-footing," when revellers visit neighbours at midnight bearing gifts. More popular these days are huge, organized street parties, most notably in Edinburgh, but also in Aberdeen, Glasgow and other Scottish cities.

New Year's Eve (Dec 31). Big parties all over Britain; in London, there's a massive fireworks display over the Thames, and thousands of inebriates crowding Trafalgar Square.

Sports and outdoor activities

As the birthplace of football, cricket, rugby and tennis, Britain boasts a series of sporting events that attract a world audience. If you prefer participating to spectating, the UK caters for just about every outdoor activity, too: we've concentrated below on walking, cycling and watersports, but there are also opportunities for anything from rock climbing to pony trekking.

Spectator sports

Football (soccer) is the national game in both Scotland and England, with a wide programme of professional league matches taking place every Saturday afternoon from early August to mid-May, with plenty of Sunday and midweek fixtures too. It's very difficult to get tickets to Premier League matches involving the most famous teams (Chelsea, Arsenal, Manchester United, Liverpool and Celtic), but tours of their grounds are feasible. You could also try one of the lower-league games.

Rugby comes in two codes – 15-a-side **Rugby Union** and 13-a-side **Rugby League**, both fearsomely brutal contact sports that can make entertaining viewing even if you don't understand the rules. In England, rugby is much less popular than football, but Rugby League has a loyal and dedicated fan base in the north – especially Yorkshire and Lancashire – while Union has traditionally been popular with the English middle class. Rugby League has never taken off in Wales and Scotland, but Rugby Union is popular in the Scottish Borders and is effectively the **national sport in**

Wales. Key Rugby Union and League games are sold out months in advance, but ordinary fixtures present few ticketing problems. The Rugby Union season runs from September to just after Easter, Rugby League February to September.

Cricket is British idiosyncrasy at its finest. Foreigners – and most Britons for that matter – marvel at a game that can last several days and still end in a draw, while many people are unfamiliar with its rules. International, five-day "Test" matches, pitting the English national side against visiting countries, are played most summers at grounds around the country, and tickets are usually fairly easy to come by. The domestic game traditionally centres on four-day County Championship matches between English county teams, though there's far bigger interest – certainly for casual watchers – in the "Twenty20" (T20) format, designed to encourage flamboyant, decisive play in short, three-hour matches.

Finally, if you're in England at the end of June and early July, you won't be able to miss the country's annual fixation with **tennis** in the shape of the Wimbledon championships. No one gives a hoot about the sport for the other fifty weeks of the year, but as long as one plucky Brit endures, the entire country gets caught up in tennis fever.

Walking

Walking routes track across many of Britain's wilder areas, amid landscapes varied enough to suit any taste. Turn up in any national park area and local information offices will be able to advise on anything from a family stroll to a full day out on the mountains. For shorter walks, you could check out the **National Trust** website (Ⓦ nationaltrust.org.uk), which details picturesque routes, of varying lengths, that weave through or near their properties, or if you are travelling on public transport, consult the user-generated site **Car Free Walks** (Ⓦ carfreewalks.org), which details hundreds of routes that set off and finish at train stations and bus stops, providing OS map links and elevation profiles for each. Various **membership associations**, including the Ramblers Association (Ⓦ ramblers.org.uk) and Walkers are Welcome

ACTIVITY TOUR OPERATORS

There are numerous activity tours available taking in the best of British outdoors. We've listed some of the best below.

BOATING AND SAILING

Blakes Holiday Boating UK Ⓣ 0844 856 7060, Ⓦ blakes. co.uk. Cruisers, yachts and narrowboats on the Norfolk Broads, the River Thames and various English and Scottish canals.

Classic Sailing UK Ⓣ 01872 580022, Ⓦ classic-sailing.co.uk. Hands-on sailing holidays on traditional wooden boats and tall ships, including Cornwall, Scotland and the Isles of Scilly

CYCLING

The Carter Company UK Ⓣ 01296 631671, Ⓦ the-carter-company.com. Gentle self-guided cycling and walking tours, including in London, Kent, Oxford and the Cotswolds, Devon, Cornwall, Dorset and Scotland, in simple or luxury accommodation.

Saddle Skedaddle UK Ⓣ 0191 265 1110, Ⓦ skedaddle.co.uk. Biking adventures and classic road rides – including guided, self-guided and tailor-made tours in Cornwall, the Cotswolds, Northumberland, the New Forest, Wales and Scotland, lasting from a weekend to a week.

SURFING

Big Friday UK Ⓣ 01637 872512, Ⓦ bigfriday.com. Surfing packages – some women-only – in England, with accommodation, travel and tuition laid on.

Surfers World UK Ⓣ 07540 022 1089, Ⓦ surfersworld.co.uk. Short breaks with surfing courses in Woolacombe, Croyde, and on the north Cornwall coast.

WALKING

Classic Journeys US Ⓣ 1800 200 3887, Ⓦ classicjourneys. com. Upmarket guided "cultural walking adventures" in classic English and Scottish destinations, including the Cotswolds, the Cornish coast, Edinburgh and the Highlands.

Contours Walking Holidays UK Ⓣ 01629 821900, Ⓦ contours.co.uk. Excellent short breaks or longer walking holidays and self-guided hikes in every region of England, Scotland and Wales, from famous trails to lesser-known local routes.

English Lakeland Ramblers US Ⓣ 1800 724 8801, Ⓦ ramblers.com. Escorted walking tours in the Lake District and the Cotswolds, as well as the Welsh Borders and the Scottish Highlands and islands, either inn-to-inn or based in a country hotel.

Ramblers Worldwide Holidays UK Ⓣ 01707 331133, Ⓦ ramblersholidays.co.uk. Sociable guided walking tours all over the UK, on a variety of themes, from dog-friendly via archeology to Nordic walking, and for various fitness levels.

Walkabout Scotland UK Ⓣ 0845 686 1344, Ⓦ walkaboutscotland.com. Hiking in Scotland, with guided hillwalking holidays, tours and day-trips.

Walkabout Wales UK Ⓣ 07775 444176, Ⓦ walkabout-wales.com. Though they focus on day-walks, this outfit also offers a varied programme of guided treks – from half-days to multi-day trips.

BRITAIN'S NATIONAL PARKS

Britain has fifteen national parks (ⓦ www.nationalparks.gov.uk), ranging from Dartmoor in the southwest to the Cairngorms in the north. Check out the round-up below for the best things to do and see in each.

- **Brecon Beacons** See p.662. In southern Wales, this range of grassy hills covers 520 square miles, with a striking sandstone scarp at the head of the South Wales coalfield, and cave-riddled limestone valleys to the south. Don't miss: the climb up Pen y Fan (see p.662).

- **Cairngorms** See p.896. In the Scottish Highlands, this is Britain's biggest national park, which includes its highest mountain massif. It includes some marvellous walking around Aviemore, and a gamut of sports and recreational facilities, not least skiing. Don't miss: the RSPB Reserve at Loch Garten (see p.899).

- **Dartmoor** See p.306. England's largest wilderness attracts back-to-nature hikers and tripped-out stone-chasers to Devon in equal measure – the open moorland walking can be pretty hard core, and Dartmoor is famous for its standing stones, Stone Age hut circles and hillforts. Don't miss: Grimspound Bronze Age village (see p.308).

- **Exmoor** See p.284. Exmoor straddles the Somerset–Devon border and on its northern edge overlooks the sea from high, hogback hills. Crisscrossed by trails and also accessible from the South West Coast Path, it's ideal for walking and pony trekking. Don't miss: the four-mile hike to Dunkery Beacon, Exmoor's highest point (see p.285).

- **Lake District** See p.492. Many people's favourite national park, the Lake District (in Cumbria, in northwest England) is an almost alpine landscape of glacial lakes and rugged mountains. It's great for hiking, rock climbing and watersports, but also has strong literary connections and thriving cultural traditions. Don't miss: Honister's hard-hat mine tour and mountain traverse (see p.510).

- **Loch Lomond and the Trossachs** See p.818. Scotland's first national park incorporates a stretch of the West Highland Way along the loch itself, the park's centrepiece. The wild glens of the Trossach range – a sort of miniature Highlands – are also highly scenic. Don't miss: the ascent of Ben Lomond (see box, p.821).

- **New Forest** See p.194. In the predominantly domesticated landscape of Hampshire, the country's best surviving example of a medieval hunting forest can be surprisingly wild. The majestic woodland is interspersed by tracts of heath, and a good network of paths and bridleways offers plenty of scope for biking and pony rides. Don't miss: camping in one of the stunning New Forest sites (see p.196).

(ⓦ walkersarewelcome.org.uk) also provide information and route ideas online.

Even for short hikes you need to be **properly equipped**, follow local advice and listen out for local weather reports – British weather is notoriously changeable and increasingly extreme. You will also need a good **map** – in most cases one of the excellent and reliable Ordnance Survey (OS) series (see p.49), usually available from local tourist offices, the best of which, along with outdoor shops, can also supply local maps, safety advice and guidebooks/leaflets.

Hiking trails

England's finest **walking areas** are the granite moorlands and spectacular coastlines of Devon and Cornwall in the southwest, and the highlands of the north – notably the Yorkshire Dales, the North York Moors and the Lake District. Keen hikers might want to tackle one of England and Wales's fifteen **National Trails** (ⓦ nationaltrail.co.uk), which amount to some 2500 miles of waymarked path and track. The most famous – certainly the toughest – is the **Pennine Way** (268 miles; usual walking time 16–19 days), stretching from the Derbyshire Peak District to the Scottish Borders (see box, p.420), while the challenging **South West Coast Path** (630 miles; from 30 days) through Cornwall, Devon, Somerset and Dorset tends to be tackled in shorter sections (see box, p.286). Other English trails are less gung-ho in character, like the **South Downs Way** (100 miles; 8 days) following the chalk escarpment and ridges of the South Downs (see box, p.161) or the fascinating **Hadrian's Wall Path** (84 miles; 7 days). In Wales, the spectacular **Pembrokeshire Coast Path** (186 miles; 10–15 days) reveals some of the most beautiful coastal scenery in Britain (see box, p.646), while **Glyndŵr's Way** (135 miles; 9

- **The Norfolk Broads** See p.363. The best place for a boating holiday – the rivers, marshes, fens and canals of Norfolk make up one of the important wetlands in Europe, and are also ideal for birdwatching. It's the one park where a car isn't much use – cyclists and walkers have the best of it. Don't miss: the long-distance footpath, Weaver's Way (see p.363).
- **Northumberland** See p.600. Where England meets Scotland, remote Northumberland in England's northeast is adventure country. The long-distance Pennine Way runs the length of the park, and the Romans left their mark in the shape of Hadrian's Wall, along which you can hike or bike. Don't miss: the Chillingham cattle wildlife safari (see p.602).
- **North York Moors** See p.559. A stunning mix of heather moorland, gentle valleys, ruined abbeys and wild coastline. Walking and mountain biking are the big outdoor activities here, but you can also tour the picturesque stone villages or hangout with Goths in Whitby. Don't miss: a day out at Ryedale Folk Museum (see p.562).
- **Peak District** See p.413. England's first national park (1951) is also the most visited, because it sits between the major population centres of the Midlands and the northwest. It's rugged outdoors country, with some dramatic underground caverns, tempered by stately homes and spa and market towns. Don't miss: a trip down Treak Cliff Cavern (see p.418).
- **Pembrokeshire Coast** See p.646. Some 170 miles of Wales's southwestern peninsula make up this park, best explored along the Pembrokeshire Coast Path that traverses the clifftops, often dipping down into secluded coves. Don't miss: the hike round St Bride's Bay (see p.640).
- **Snowdonia National Park** See p.697. Occupying almost the whole of the northwestern corner of Wales, this park incorporates a dozen of the country's highest peaks separated by dramatic glacial valleys and laced with hundreds of miles of ridge and moorland paths. Don't miss: a ride on the Snowdon Mountain Railway (see p.703).
- **South Downs** See p.161. Britain's newest national park (established 2010) might not be as wild as the others – about 85 percent is farmland – but it offers a rural escape into West and East Sussex from one of the most densely populated parts of the country. Don't miss: a walk along the South Downs Way, which covers over a hundred miles of the chalk uplands between Winchester and Beachy Head (see p.161).
- **Yorkshire Dales** See p.535. The best choice for walking, cycling and pony trekking, Yorkshire's second national park spreads across twenty dales, or valleys, at the heart of the Pennines. England's most scenic railway – the Settle-Carlisle line – is another great draw, while caves, waterfalls and castles provide the backdrop. Don't miss: the walk to dramatic Malham Cove (see p.539).

days) takes you through the moorland, farmland, woods and forests of Mid-Wales and **Offa's Dyke Path** (177 miles; 12 days) traces the England–Wales border (see p.675).

Scotland is covered by 26 "**Great Trails**" (W scotlandsgreattrails.org.uk), which cover more than 1700 miles between them. Of these, the **Southern Upland Way** crosses the country from coast to coast in the south, and is the longest at 212 miles (12–20 days). Probably the best known is the **West Highlandway** (see box, p.818), a 96-mile hike from Glasgow to Fort William via Loch Lomond and Glen Coe (7–10 days).

Cycling

The **National Cycle Network** is made up of 14,500 miles of signed cycle route, mainly on traffic-free paths (including disused railways and canal towpaths) and country roads. You're never far from one of the numbered routes, all of which are detailed on the **Sustrans** website (W sustrans.org .uk, plus W routes2ride.org.uk for Scotland), a charitable trust devoted to the development of environmentally sustainable transport. Sustrans also publishes an excellent series of waterproof cycle maps (1:100,000) and regional guides.

Major routes include the **C2C** (Sea-to-Sea), 140 miles between Whitehaven/Workington on the English northwest coast and Tynemouth/Sunderland on the northeast; the **Cornish Way** (123 miles), from Bude to Land's End; the **Celtic Trail** (220 miles) across South Wales and the Pembrokeshire coast, and the classic cross-Britain route from Land's End, in the far southwest of England, to John O'Groats, on the northeast tip of Scotland – roughly a thousand miles, which can be covered in two to three weeks, depending on which route you choose.

Britain's biggest cycling organization, the **Cycle Touring Club** (Ⓦctc.org.uk), provides lists of tour operators and rental outlets, and supplies members with touring and technical advice, plus insurance.

Watersports

Sailing and **windsurfing** in England are especially popular along the south coast (particularly the Isle of Wight and Solent) and in the Southwest (around Falmouth in Cornwall, and around Salcombe and Dartmouth in Devon). Here, and in the Lake District, you'll be able to rent dinghies, boats and kayaks, either by the hour or for longer periods of instruction – from around £30 for a couple of hours of kayaking to around £150 for a two-day nonresidential sailing course. Opportunities for sailing around Scotland (Ⓦsailscotland.co.uk) are great, but changeable conditions combined with tricksy tides and rocky shores demand good skills. If you want to learn to sail in Wales, contact Plas Menai: The National Watersports Centre (Ⓦplasmenai.co.uk), which offers sailing, windsurfing, kayaking and jet-skiing courses in a beautiful location on the Menai Strait.

Newquay in Cornwall is England's undisputed **surfing** centre, whose main break, Fistral, regularly hosts international contests. But there are quieter spots all along the north coast of Cornwall and Devon, as well as a growing scene on the more isolated northeast coast from Yorkshire up to Northumberland, with lots of action at the pretty seaside Teesside town of Saltburn. Scotland is fast gaining a reputation for the high quality of its breaks, with many people heading for Thurso on the north coast. Other good breaks lie within easy reach of large cities (eg Pease Bay, near Edinburgh, and Fraserburgh, near Aberdeen), while the west coast has numerous possibilities. Top spots for windsurfing and kitesurfing include Troon on the Ayrshire coast, St Andrews and Tiree. Surfing in Wales (Ⓦwsfsurfschool.co.uk) tends to be concentrated on the south coast, around the Gower Peninsula, which boasts a good variety of beach and reef breaks; key centres are Rhosneigr on Anglesey, Aberdyfi along the Cambrian Coast, Whitesands Bay (Porth-Mawr) near St Davids and Rhossili on the Gower Peninsula. For more **information** on surfing in Britain, including a directory of surf schools and an events calendar, check Ⓦsurfinggb.com.

Wales has led the way in terms of **coasteering**, a thrilling extreme sport that involves climbing, swimming, scrambling and cliff-jumping – with a guide – along the more spectacular stretches of rocky coast; other coasteering hotspots include Cornwall and the Scottish Highlands. Finally, if you can brave the often chilly temperatures, **wild swimming** has taken off in a big way in Britain, a wonderful way to experience its many beautiful rivers, lakes, lochs, waterfall pools and sea caves – check Ⓦwildswimming.co.uk for a rundown of good places.

Travel essentials

Climate

Though it has seen some extreme storms, flooding and snowfall in recent years, overall Britain has a generally temperate, maritime climate, which means largely moderate temperatures and a decent chance of at least some rain whenever you visit. If you're attempting to balance the clemency

AVERAGE DAILY MAXIMUM TEMPERATURES

CARDIFF

	Jan	Feb	Mar	Apr	May	Jun	Jul	Aug	Sep	Oct	Nov	Dec
°F	45	45	50	56	60	68	69	69	64	58	51	46
°C	7	7	10	13	16	20	21	21	18	14	11	8

EDINBURGH

	Jan	Feb	Mar	Apr	May	Jun	Jul	Aug	Sep	Oct	Nov	Dec
°F	42	43	46	51	56	64	65	64	61	54	48	44
°C	5	6	8	11	13	18	18	18	16	12	9	7

LONDON

	Jan	Feb	Mar	Apr	May	Jun	Jul	Aug	Sep	Oct	Nov	Dec
°F	43	44	50	56	62	69	71	71	65	58	50	45
°C	6	7	10	13	17	21	22	22	19	14	10	7

TIPPING

Although there are no fixed rules for **tipping**, a ten to fifteen percent tip is anticipated by restaurant waiters. Tipping taxi drivers 10 percent or so is optional, but most people at the very least round the fare up to the nearest pound. Some restaurants levy a "discretionary" or "optional" **service charge** of 10 or 12.5 percent, which must be clearly stated on the menu and on the bill. However, you are not obliged to pay it, and certainly not if the food or service wasn't what you expected. It is not normal to leave tips in pubs, though more swanky cocktail bars will present their bills on a saucer, where some people choose to leave a few coins. The only other occasions when you'll be expected to tip are at the hairdressers, and in upmarket hotels where porters and bell boys expect and usually get a pound or two per bag or for calling a taxi.

of the weather against the density of the crowds, even given regional variations and microclimates the best months to come to Britain are April, May, September and October.

Costs

Faced with another £4 pint, a £30 theatre ticket and a £20 taxi ride back to your £100-a-night hotel, Britain might seem like the most expensive place in Europe – in the cities, at least. Even if you're camping or hostelling, using public transport, buying picnic lunches and eating in pubs and cafés your minimum expenditure will be around £40 per person per day. Couples staying in B&Bs, eating at unpretentious restaurants and sightseeing should expect to splash out £70 per person, while if you're renting a car, staying in hotels and eating at fancier places, budget for at least £120 each. Double that last figure if you choose to stay in stylish city or grand country-house hotels, while on any visit to London work on the basis that you'll need an extra £30 per day.

Discounts and admission charges

Many of Britain's **historic attractions** – from castles to stately homes – are owned and/or operated by either the **National Trust** (wnationaltrust.org.uk; denoted as NT in the Guide), covering England and Wales, or the **National Trust for Scotland** (wnts.org.uk; NTS). Many other historic sites are operated by **English Heritage** (wenglish-heritage.org.uk; EH), **Historic Scotland** (whistoric-scotland.gov.uk; HS), and **CADW Welsh Historic Monuments** (wcadw.wales.gov.uk; CADW). All these organizations usually charge entry fees, though some sites are free. If you plan to visit more than half a dozen places owned by any of them, it's worth considering an annual membership (£40–60) – you can join on your first visit to any attraction. US members of the Royal Oak Foundation (wroyal-oak.org) get free admission to all National Trust properties.

Municipal art galleries and museums across the UK often have free admission, as do the world-class **state museums** in London, Cardiff, Edinburgh and elsewhere, from the British Museum (London) and the National Gallery of Scotland (Edinburgh) to York's National Railway Museum. Private and municipal museums and other collections rarely charge more than £6 admission. Some **cathedrals** and churches either charge admission or ask for voluntary donations.

The admission charges given in the Guide are the full adult rate, unless otherwise stated. Concessionary rates – **generally half-price** – for **senior citizens** (over 60), under-26s and **children** (from 5 to 17) apply almost everywhere, from tourist attractions to public transport. Family tickets are often available, and children under 5 are usually free.

Full-time students can benefit from an International Student ID Card (ISIC; wisic.org), and those under 26 from an International Youth Travel Card (IYTC), while **teachers** qualify for the International Teacher Identity Card (IITC). Available from STA Travel (see p.31), all cost £12 and are valid for special air, rail and bus fares, and discounts at museums and other attractions.

Crime and personal safety

Terrorist attacks and street riots in Britain – primarily England – may have changed the general perception of how safe it feels, but it's still extremely unlikely that you'll be at any risk as you travel around. There's heightened **security** in place at airports and major train stations, and as a holiday-maker you can avoid the toughest urban areas where crime flourishes. You can walk more or less anywhere without fear of harassment, though all the big cities have their edgy districts and it's always better to err on the side of caution, especially late at night. Leave your passport and valuables in a hotel or hostel safe (carrying **ID** is not compulsory; though if you look particularly youthful and intend to drink in a pub it can be a good idea to carry it), and exercise the usual caution on public transport. If you're taking a taxi, always make sure it's officially licensed and never pick one up in the street – unless it's an official black taxi in London (see p.109). Bar or restaurant staff can usually provide a reliable recommendation or direct you to the nearest taxi rank.

Other than asking for directions, most visitors rarely come into contact with the British **police**, who as a rule are approachable and helpful. Most wear chest guards and carry batons, though street officers do not normally carry guns. If you are robbed, report it straight away to the police; your insurance company will require a **crime report number**.

For **police**, **fire** and **ambulance** services phone ☎999.

Electricity

The **current** is 240V AC. North American appliances will need a transformer and adaptor; those from Europe, South Africa, Australia and New Zealand only need an adaptor.

Entry requirements

Citizens of all European countries – except Albania, Bosnia and Herzegovina, Macedonia, Montenegro, Serbia and all the former Soviet republics (other than the Baltic states) – can enter Britain with just a **passport**, for up to three months (and indefinitely if you're from the EU). Americans, Canadians, Australians and New Zealanders can stay for up to six months, providing they have a return ticket and funds to cover their stay. Citizens of most other countries require a **visa**, obtainable from their British consulate or mission office. Check with the **UK Border Agency** (Ⓦukvisas.gov.uk) for up-to-date information about visa applications, extensions and all aspects of residency.

Gay and lesbian travellers

Britain offers one of the most diverse and accessible **lesbian** and **gay** scenes anywhere in Europe. Nearly every sizeable town has some kind of organized gay life – from bars and clubs to community groups – with the major scenes found in London, Manchester, Brighton, Edinburgh, Glasgow, Cardiff and Swansea. Listings, news and reviews can be found at *Gay Times* (Ⓦgaytimes.co.uk), while for more information and useful links see Ⓦgaybritain .co.uk. The age of consent is 16.

Health

No vaccinations are required for entry into Britain. Citizens of all EU and EEA countries are entitled to free medical treatment within the National Health Service (NHS), which includes the vast majority of hospitals and doctors, on production of their **European Health Insurance Card** (EHIC) or, in extremis, their passport or national identity card. The same applies to those Commonwealth countries that have reciprocal healthcare arrangements with the UK – for example Australia and New Zealand. If you don't fall into either of these categories, you will be charged for all medical services – except those administered by accident and emergency units at National Health Service hospitals – so health insurance is strongly advised.

Pharmacists (known as **chemists** in Britain) can advise you on minor conditions but can dispense only a limited range of drugs without a doctor's prescription. Most are open standard shop hours, though there are also late-night branches in large cities and at 24-hour supermarkets. For generic pain-relief, cold remedies and the like, the local supermarket is usually the cheapest option.

Minor complaints and injuries can be dealt with at a **doctor's (GP's) surgery** – your hotel should be able to point you in the right direction, though you may not be seen immediately. For serious injuries, go to the 24-hour **Accident and Emergency (A&E)** department of the nearest **hospital**, and in an **emergency**, call an ambulance on ☎999. If you need medical help fast but it's not a 999 emergency you can also get free advice from NHS 111, the health service's 24-hour helpline (☎111).

Insurance

Even though EU healthcare privileges apply in the UK, it's a good idea to take out an **insurance policy** before travelling to cover against theft, loss and illness or injury. Most exclude so-called dangerous sports unless an extra premium is paid: in Britain this can mean most watersports, rock climbing and mountaineering, though hiking, kayaking and jeep safaris would probably be covered. For non-EU citizens, it's worth checking whether you are already covered.

Mail

Stamps are sold at post offices, as well as some supermarkets, newsagents and other stores. "First class" theoretically guarantees next-day UK

ROUGH GUIDES TRAVEL INSURANCE

Rough Guides has teamed up with WorldNomads.com to offer great **travel insurance** deals. Policies are available to residents of over 150 countries, with cover for a wide range of adventure sports, 24-hour emergency assistance, high levels of medical and evacuation cover and a stream of travel safety information. Roughguides.com users can take advantage of their policies online 24/7, from anywhere in the world – even if you're already travelling. And since plans often change when you're on the road, you can extend your policy and even claim online. Roughguides.com users who buy travel insurance with WorldNomads.com can also leave a positive footprint and donate to a community development project. For more information go to ⓦroughguides.com/travel-insurance.

delivery; "second class" delivery within three working days. Airmail to European destinations should arrive within three working days, and to countries outside Europe within five. A stamp for a first-class letter to anywhere in the British Isles currently costs 62p; second-class letters cost 53p. Note, though, that there are size restrictions: letters over 240 x 165 x 5mm are designated as "Large letters" and are correspondingly more expensive to send. To get an idea of international postage prices check the Royal Mail website (ⓦroyalmail.com/price-finder).

Maps

Petrol stations in Britain stock large-format **road atlases** produced by the AA, RAC, Collins, Ordnance Survey and others, which cover all of Britain, at a scale of around 1:250,000 and include larger-scale plans of major towns. The best of these is the Ordnance Survey road atlas, which handily uses the same grid reference system as their folding maps. Overall the Ordnance Survey (OS; ⓦordnancesurvey.co.uk) produces the most comprehensive maps, renowned for their accuracy and clarity. Their 1:50,000 (pink) Landranger series shows enough detail to be useful for most walkers and cyclists, and there's more detail still in the full-colour 1:25,000 (orange) Explorer series – both cover the whole of Britain. The full OS range is only available at a few big-city stores or online, but you can download high-res maps via the OS MapFinder app.

Money

Britain's currency is the **pound sterling** (£), divided into 100 pence (p). Coins come in denominations of 1p, 2p, 5p, 10p, 20p, 50p and £1 and £2. Bank of England notes are in denominations of £5, £10, £20 and £50. Scottish and Northern Irish banknotes are legal tender throughout Britain, though some traders may be unwilling to accept them. For current **exchange rates**, consult ⓦxe.com.

The easiest way to get hold of cash is to use your **debit card** in an **ATM**; there's usually a daily withdrawal limit, which varies depending on the money issuer, but starts at around £250. You'll find ATMs outside banks, at all major points of arrival and motorway service areas, at large supermarkets, petrol stations and even inside some pubs, rural post offices and village shops (though a charge of a few pounds may be levied on cash withdrawals at small, stand-alone ATMs – the screen will tell you and give you an option to cancel the operation). Depending on your bank and your debit card, you may also be able to ask for "cash back" when you shop at supermarkets.

Credit cards are widely accepted in hotels, shops and restaurants – MasterCard and Visa are almost universal, charge cards like American Express and Diners Club less so. Smaller establishments, such as B&Bs and some shops, may accept cash only. Remember that cash advances from ATMs using your credit card are treated as loans, with interest accruing daily from the date of withdrawal.

Paying by plastic involves inserting your credit or debit card into a "chip-and-pin" terminal, beside the till in shops, or brought to your table in restaurants, and then keying in your PIN to authorize the transaction; the only person handling your card is you. **Contactless** – or "wave and go" – payments, where you simply hold your credit or debit card on or near a card reader

DISTANCES, WEIGHTS AND MEASURES

Distances (and speeds) on British signposts are in miles, and beer is still served in pints. For everything else – money, weights and measures – a confusing mixture of metric and imperial systems is used: fuel is dispensed by the litre, while meat, milk and vegetables may be sold in either or both systems.

without having to key in a PIN, are increasingly available for transactions of up to £20. Contactless cards are marked with a little radio-waves icon, similar to the wi-fi symbol, which you'll also see at establishments that accept this kind of payment. Note that the same overseas transaction fees will apply to contactless payments as to those made with a PIN. See ⓦcontactless.info for more details and a list of businesses that accept wave and go.

You cannot use **travellers' cheques** as cash – you'll always have to cash them first, making them an unreliable source of funds in an emergency or in remote areas. Outside banking hours, you can change currency or cheques at **post offices** and **bureaux de change** – the former charge no commission, while the latter tend to be open longer hours and are found in most city centres and at major airports and train stations. Avoid changing cash or cheques in hotels, where the rates are poor.

Opening hours and public holidays

Though traditional office hours are Monday to Saturday from around 9am to 5.30 or 6pm, many businesses, shops and restaurants throughout Britain will open earlier – or later – and close later. The majority of shops are open daily, and, in the towns at least might stay open late on a Thursday evening, but some places – even the so-called "24hr supermarkets" – are closed on Sunday, and businesses in remote areas and villages might even have an "early closing day" – often Wednesday – when they close at 1pm. Banks are not open at the weekend. We have given full **opening hours** for everything we review – museums, galleries and

---

PUBLIC HOLIDAYS

Jan 1 (New Year's Day)
Jan 2 Scotland only
Good Friday
Easter Monday Not in Scotland
First Mon in May ("May Day")
Last Mon in May
Last Mon in Aug
Nov 30 (St Andrew's Day) Or nearest Mon if weekend; Scotland only
Dec 25 (Christmas Day)
Dec 26 (Boxing Day)
Note that if January 1, December 25 or December 26 falls on a Saturday or Sunday, the next weekday becomes a public holiday.

CALLING ABROAD FROM BRITAIN

Australia ☏0061 + area code minus the initial zero + number.
New Zealand ☏0064 + area code minus the initial zero + number.
US and Canada ☏001 + area code + number.
Republic of Ireland ☏00353 + area code minus the initial zero + number.
South Africa ☏0027 + area code + number.

---

tourist attractions, cafés, restaurants, pubs and shops – throughout the Guide.

While many local shops and businesses close on **public holidays**, few tourist-related businesses observe them, particularly in summer. However, nearly all museums, galleries and other attractions are closed on Christmas Day and New Year's Day, with many also closed on Boxing Day (Dec 26). Several of Britain's public holidays are usually referred to as **bank holidays** (though it's not just the banks who have a day off).

Phones

Every British landline number has a prefix, which, if beginning ☏01 or 02 represents an **area code**. The prefix ☏07 is for mobile phones/cellphones. A variety of ☏08 prefixes relate to the cost of calls – some, like ☏0800, are free to call from a landline, others (like ☏0845 and ☏0870) are more expensive than landlines, the actual price depending on your phone or phone operator. Beware, particularly, **premium-rate ☏09 numbers**, common for pre-recorded information services (including some tourist authorities), which can be charged at anything up to £1.50 a minute.

The cheapest way to make calls on any landline is to buy a **phonecard**, available from many newsagents or online in denominations of £5, £10 and upwards. You dial the company's local access number, key in the pin number on the card and then make your call. Most hotel rooms have telephones, but there is almost always an exorbitant surcharge for their use. Public **payphones** – telephone boxes – are still found, though with the ubiquity of mobile phones, they're seldom used.

Mobile phone access is universal in towns and cities, and rural areas are well served too, though coverage can be patchy. To use your own phone, check with your provider that international roaming is activated – and that your phone will work in the UK (unless you have a tri-band phone, it's unlikely that a mobile bought for use in the US, for example, will work outside the States and vice versa). If you do bring your own phone, note that you are likely to be charged extra for incoming calls or texts when abroad. The cost of calls within the EU has decreased within recent years, but calls to destinations further afield are still unregulated and can be prohibitively expensive. If you're staying in Britain for any length of time, it's often easiest to **buy a mobile** and local SIM card in the UK – basic pre-pay ("pay as you go") models start at around £30, usually including some calling credit.

Dial ✆ 100 for the **operator**, ✆ 155 for the international operator.

Smoking

Smoking is banned in all public buildings and offices, restaurants and pubs, and on all public transport.

Time

Greenwich Mean Time (GMT) – equivalent to Co-ordinated Universal Time (UTC) – is used from the end of October to the end of March; for the rest of the year Britain switches to **British Summer Time** (BST), one hour ahead of GMT.

Tourist information

Britain's tourism authority, VisitBritain (Ⓦ visitbritain .com), has offices worldwide, while regional tourism boards within the UK concentrate on particular areas. The official national websites, Ⓦ enjoyengland .com, Ⓦ visitscotland.com and Ⓦ visitwales.com are particularly useful, covering everything from local accommodation to festival dates, and there are many regional and other specialist websites dedicated to the UK that are worth consulting.

Tourist offices (also called Tourist Information Centres, or "TICs") exist in many British towns, though local cuts have led to some closures over recent years. They tend to follow standard shop hours (roughly Mon–Sat 9am–5.30pm), though are sometimes also open on Sundays, with hours curtailed during the winter season (Nov–Easter). We've listed opening hours in the Guide. Depending on the size of the office, staff will nearly always be able to book accommodation, reserve space on guided tours, and sell guidebooks, maps and walk leaflets.

Travellers with disabilities

On the whole, Britain has good facilities for travellers with disabilities. All new public buildings – including museums, galleries and cinemas – are obliged to provide **wheelchair access**; train stations and airports are accessible; many buses have easy-access boarding ramps; and dropped kerbs and signalled crossings are the rule in every city and town. The number of accessible hotels and restaurants is also growing, and reserved parking bays are available almost everywhere, from shopping malls to museums. If you have specific requirements, it's always best to talk first to your travel agent, chosen hotel or tour operator.

Wheelchair-users and blind or partially sighted people are given thirty to forty percent reductions on train fares, and people with other disabilities are eligible for the Disabled Persons Railcard (£20/year; Ⓦ disabledpersons-railcard.co.uk), which gives a third off the price of most tickets. There are no bus discounts for disabled tourists. In addition to the resources listed below, for detailed reviews of some of Britain's leading attractions – museums, markets, theatres – written by and for disabled people, download the *Rough Guide to Accessible Britain* (Ⓦ accessibleguide.co.uk).

USEFUL CONTACTS

Access-Able Ⓦ access-able.com. Online resource for travellers with disabilities, with links to UK operators and organizations.
Open Britain Ⓦ openbritain.net. Accessible-travel-related information, from accommodation to attractions.
Tourism For All Ⓦ www.tourismforall.org.uk. Listings, guides and advice for access throughout Britain.

Travelling with children

Facilities in Britain for travellers with children are similar to those in the rest of Europe. Breast-feeding is legal in all public places, including restaurants and cafés, and **baby-changing** rooms are widely available, including in shopping centres and train stations. Children aren't allowed in certain **licensed (ie, alcohol-serving) premises**, though this doesn't apply to restaurants, and many pubs and inns have family rooms or beer gardens where children are welcome. Some **B&Bs and hotels** won't accept children under a certain age (usually 12). Under-5s generally travel free on public transport and get in free to attractions; 5–16-year-olds are usually entitled to concessionary rates of up to half the adult rate/fare.

London

TOWER BRIDGE

1

London

For the visitor, London is a thrilling place. Monuments from the capital's glorious past are everywhere, from medieval banqueting halls and the great churches of Christopher Wren to eclectic Victorian architecture. You can relax in the city's quiet Georgian squares, explore the narrow alleyways of the City of London, wander along the riverside walkways, and uncover the quirks of what is still identifiably a collection of villages. The largest capital in the European Union, stretching for more than thirty miles from east to west, and with a population of over eight million, London is also incredibly diverse, ethnically and linguistically, offering cultural and culinary delights from right across the globe.

The capital's great historical **landmarks** – Big Ben, Westminster Abbey, Buckingham Palace, St Paul's Cathedral, the Tower of London and so on – draw in millions of tourists every year. Things change fast, though, and the regular emergence of new attractions ensures there's plenty to do even for those who've visited before. With Tate Modern and the Shard, the city boasts the world's most popular modern art museum and Western Europe's tallest building. And thanks to the 2012 Olympics, even the East End – not an area previously on most tourists' radar – has had a major overhaul.

You could spend days just **shopping** in London, mixing with the upper classes in the "tiara triangle" around Harrods, or sampling the offbeat weekend markets of Portobello Road, Brick Lane and Camden. The city's **pubs** have always had heaps of atmosphere, and **food** is now a major attraction too, with more than fifty Michelin-starred restaurants and the widest choice of cuisines on the planet. The **music**, **clubbing** and **gay and lesbian** scenes are second to none, and mainstream **arts** are no less exciting, with regular opportunities to catch outstanding theatre companies, dance troupes, exhibitions and opera.

London's special atmosphere comes mostly, however, from the life on its streets. A cosmopolitan city since at least the seventeenth century, when it was a haven for Huguenot immigrants escaping persecution in Louis XIV's France, today it is truly **multicultural**, with over half its permanent population originating from overseas. The last hundred years has seen the arrival of thousands from the Caribbean, the Indian subcontinent, the Mediterranean, the Far East and Eastern Europe, all of whom play an integral part in defining a metropolis that is unmatched in its sheer diversity.

THE LONDON EYE AND HOUSES OF PARLIAMENT

Highlights

❶ British Museum Quite simply one of the world's greatest museums. **See p.79**

❷ London Eye The universally loved observation wheel is a key London landmark. **See p.87**

❸ Tate Modern London's huge modern art gallery is housed in a spectacularly converted power station. **See p.88**

❹ Shakespeare's Globe Theatre Catch a show in this amazing reconstructed outdoor Elizabethan theatre. **See p.89**

❺ Highgate Cemetery The steeply sloping terraces of the West Cemetery's overgrown graves are the last word in Victorian Gothic gloom. **See p.101**

❻ Greenwich Picturesque riverside spot, with a weekend market, the National Maritime Museum and old Royal Observatory. **See p.102**

❼ Kew Gardens Stroll amid the exotic trees and shrubs, or head for the steamy glasshouses. **See p.105**

❽ Hampton Court Palace Tudor interiors, architecture by Wren and vast gardens make this a great day out. **See p.106**

❾ East End markets Best visited on a Sunday – start at Spitalfields, head towards Brick Lane and end up at Columbia Road. **See p.130 & p.131**

HIGHLIGHTS ARE MARKED ON THE MAP ON PP.56–57

GREATER LONDON

N

Luton Airport

HARROW

FINCHLEY

RAF Museum

HENDON

Kenwood House

Hampstead Heath

BRENT

NEASDEN

Keats' House

HAMPSTEAD

Wembley Stadium

Neasden Temple

Freud Museum

WEMBLEY

WILLESDEN

Regent Park

GREENFORD

Grand Union Canal

A40 (M)

EALING

Hyde Park

ACTON

Heathrow Airport & Windsor

Osterley Park & House

London Museum of Water & Steam

HAMMERSMITH

KENSINGTON

Chiswick House

Battersea Park

HOUNSLOW

Syon Park & House

7 KEW Kew Gardens

Old Deer Park

London Wetland Centre

PUTNEY

FULHAM

RICHMOND

TWICKENHAM

Marble Hill House

Ham House

Richmond Park

WANDSWORTH

Wimbledon Common

TEDDINGTON

Thames

Bushy Park

KINGSTON UPON THAMES

Hampton Court Palace **8**

MERTON

Morden Hall Park

0 2
miles

1

A brief history

The Romans founded **Londinium** in 47 AD as a stores depot on the marshy banks of the Thames. Despite frequent attacks – not least by Queen Boudica, who razed it in 61 AD – the port became secure in its position as capital of Roman Britain by the end of the century. London's expansion really began, however, in the eleventh century, when it became the seat of the last successful invader of Britain, the Norman duke who became **King William I of England** (aka "the Conqueror"). Crowned in Westminster Abbey, William built the White Tower – centrepiece of the Tower of London – to establish his dominance over the merchant population, the class that was soon to make London one of Europe's mightiest cities.

Little is left of medieval or Tudor London. Many of the finest buildings were wiped out in the course of a few days in 1666 when the **Great Fire of London** annihilated more than thirteen thousand houses and nearly ninety churches, completing a cycle of destruction begun the year before by the Great Plague, which killed as many as a hundred thousand people. Chief beneficiary of the blaze was Christopher Wren, who was commissioned to redesign the city and rose to the challenge with such masterpieces as St Paul's Cathedral and the Royal Naval Hospital in Greenwich.

Much of the public architecture of London was built in the Georgian and Victorian periods of the eighteenth and nineteenth centuries, when grand structures were raised to reflect the city's status as the financial and administrative hub of the **British Empire**. And though postwar development peppered the city with some undistinguished modernist buildings, more recent experiments in high-tech architecture, such as the Gherkin, the Walkie Talkie and the Shard, have given the city a new gloss.

Westminster

Political, religious and regal power has emanated from **Westminster** for almost a millennium. It was Edward the Confessor (1042–66) who first established Westminster as London's royal and ecclesiastical power base, some three miles west of the City of London. The embryonic English parliament used to meet in the abbey and eventually took over the old royal palace of Westminster. In the nineteenth century, Westminster – and Whitehall in particular – became the "heart of the Empire", its ministries ruling over a quarter of the world's population. Even now, though the UK's world status has diminished, the institutions that run the country inhabit roughly the same geographical area: Westminster for the politicians, Whitehall for the civil servants.

The monuments and buildings in and around Westminster also span the millennium, and include some of London's most famous landmarks – **Nelson's Column**, **Big Ben** and the **Houses of Parliament**, **Westminster Abbey**, plus two of the city's finest permanent art collections, the **National Gallery** and **Tate Britain**. This is a well-trodden tourist circuit since it's also one of the easiest parts of London to walk round, with all the major sights within a mere half-mile of each other, linked by one of London's most majestic streets, **Whitehall**.

Trafalgar Square

Despite the persistent noise of traffic, **Trafalgar Square** is still one of London's grandest architectural set pieces. John Nash designed the basic layout in the 1820s, but died long before the square took its present form. The Neoclassical National Gallery filled up the northern side of the square in 1838, followed five years later by the central focal point, **Nelson's Column**, topped by the famous admiral; the very large bronze lions didn't arrive until 1868, and the fountains – a real rarity in a London square – didn't take their present shape until the late 1930s.

As one of the few large public squares in London, Trafalgar Square has been both a tourist attraction and a focus for **political demonstrations** since the Chartists assembled

LONDON ORIENTATION: WHERE TO GO

Although the majority of the city's sights are situated north of the **River Thames**, which loops through the centre of the city from west to east, there is no single focus of interest. That's because London hasn't grown through centralized planning but by a process of agglomeration. Villages and urban developments that once surrounded the core are now lost within the amorphous mass of Greater London.

    Westminster, the country's royal, political and ecclesiastical power base for centuries, was once a separate city. The grand streets and squares to the north of Westminster, from **St James's** to **Covent Garden**, were built as residential suburbs after the Restoration in 1660, and are now the city's shopping and entertainment zones known collectively as the **West End**. To the east is the original City of London – known simply as **The City** – founded by the Romans, with more history than any other patch of the city, and now one of the world's great financial centres.

    The **East End**, east of the City, is not conventional tourist territory, but has recently emerged as a bolt hole for artists and a destination for clubbers – and of course, in its far eastern reaches, the East End is now home to the **Olympic Park**. It's worth exploring the south bank of the Thames, too, from the **London Eye**, in the west, to **Tate Modern** and beyond. The **museums** of South Kensington are a must, as is Portobello Road market in trendy Notting Hill, literary Hampstead and Highgate, in north London, either side of half-wild **Hampstead Heath**, and **Greenwich**, downstream of central London, with its nautical associations, royal park and observatory. Finally, there are plenty of rewarding day-trips in west London along the Thames from **Chiswick** to **Windsor**, most notably to Hampton Court Palace and Windsor Castle.

here in 1848 before marching to Kennington Common. Since then, countless demos and rallies have taken place, and nowadays various free events, commemorations and celebrations are staged here.

    Stranded on a traffic island to the south of the column, and pre-dating the entire square, is an **equestrian statue of Charles I**, erected shortly after the Restoration on the very spot where eight of those who had signed the king's death warrant were disembowelled. Charles's statue also marks the original site of the thirteenth-century **Charing Cross**, from where all distances from the capital are measured – a Victorian imitation now stands outside Charing Cross train station.

St Martin-in-the-Fields

Trafalgar Square • Mon, Tues, Thurs & Fri 8.30am–1pm & 2–6pm, Wed 8.30am–1.15pm & 2–5pm, Sat 9.30am–6pm, Sun 3.30–5pm; concerts Mon, Tues & Fri lunchtime • Free • ☎ 020 7766 1100, ⊛ stmartin-in-the-fields.org • ⊖ Charing Cross

The northeastern corner of Trafalgar Square is occupied by James Gibbs's church of **St Martin-in-the-Fields**, fronted by a magnificent Corinthian portico. Designed in 1721, the interior is purposefully simple, though the Italian plasterwork on the barrel vaulting is exceptionally rich; it's best appreciated while listening to one of the church's free lunchtime **concerts**. There's a licensed café (see p.115) in the roomy **crypt**, along with a shop, gallery and brass-rubbing centre.

National Gallery

Trafalgar Square • Daily 10am–6pm, Fri 10am–9pm • Guided tours daily 11.30am & 2.30pm, plus Fri 7pm, Sat & Sun 4pm • Free • ☎ 020 7747 2885, ⊛ nationalgallery.org.uk • ⊖ Charing Cross

The **National Gallery** was begun in 1824 by the British government. The gallery's canny acquisition policy has resulted in more than 2300 paintings, but the collection's virtue is not so much its size, but its range, depth and sheer quality. To view the collection chronologically, begin with the **Sainsbury Wing**, to the west. With more than one thousand paintings on permanent display in the main galleries, you'll need real stamina to see everything in one day, so if time is tight your best bet is to home in on your areas of special interest, having picked up a gallery plan at one of the information desks. **Audioguides**, with a brief audio commentary on each of the paintings on display are

1

● SHOPS
Camden Market	1/2
Greenwich Market	3

0   500
yards

■ ACCOMMODATION
B&B Belgravia	7
Clink 261	3
Clink 78	4
Luna Simone Hotel	8
Rough Luxe	2
St Pancras Renaissance Hotel	1
YHA St Pancras	5
YHA Thameside	6

◆ RESTAURANTS
Beagle	6
Caravan	5
Manna	3
Namaaste Kitchen	4
Sông Quê	8
Tonkotsu East	1
Zucca	10

Dalston, 1, 1 & 2

CENTRAL LONDON

N

CAFÉS & SNACKS

Fabrique	7
Hubbub	9
Maltby Street Market	11
Voodoo Ray's	2

PUBS & BARS

Edinboro Castle	10
Lock Tavern	3
Prince Alfred	13

GAY BARS AND CLUBS

Area	15
BarCode	14
The Black Cap	8
Duckie	16
The Eagle	17
Fire	18

CLUBS & LIVE MUSIC VENUES

Dalston Superstore	1
Green Note	9
Jazz Café	7
Kings Place	12
KOKO	5
Proud	4
Roundhouse	6
Underworld	2
Union Chapel	2

Lambeth

1

available (£4). Much better are the gallery's free **guided tours**, which set off from the Sainsbury Wing foyer.

Italian, Spanish and Dutch paintings

Among the National's **Italian** masterpieces are Leonardo's melancholic *Virgin of the Rocks*, Uccello's *Battle of San Romano*, Botticelli's *Venus and Mars* (inspired by a Dante sonnet) and Piero della Francesca's beautifully composed *Baptism of Christ*, one of his earliest works. The fine collection of Venetian works includes Titian's colourful early masterpiece *Bacchus and Ariadne*, his very late, much gloomier *Death of Acteon*, and Veronese's lustrous *Family of Darius before Alexander*. Later Italian works to look out for include a couple by Caravaggio, a few splendid examples of Tiepolo's airy draughtsmanship and glittering vistas of Venice by Canaletto and Guardi.

From **Spain** there are dazzling pieces by El Greco, Goya, Murillo and Velázquez, among them the provocative *Rokeby Venus*. From the **Low Countries**, standouts include van Eyck's *Arnolfini Marriage*, Memlinc's perfectly poised *Donne Triptych*, and a couple of typically serene Vermeers. There are numerous genre paintings, such as Frans Hals' *Family Group in a Landscape*, and some superlative landscapes, most notably Hobbema's *Avenue, Middleharnis*. An array of Rembrandt paintings that features some of his most searching portraits – two of them self-portraits – is followed by abundant examples of Rubens' expansive, fleshy canvases.

British and French paintings

Holbein's masterful *Ambassadors* and several of van Dyck's portraits were painted for the English court; and there's home-grown **British** art, too, represented by important works such as Hogarth's satirical *Marriage à la Mode*, Gainsborough's translucent *Morning Walk*, Constable's ever-popular *Hay Wain*, and Turner's *Fighting Temeraire*. Highlights of the **French** contingent include superb works by Poussin, Claude, Fragonard, Boucher, Watteau and David.

Impressionism and Post-Impressionism

Finally, there's a particularly strong showing of **Impressionists** and **Post-Impressionists** in rooms 43–46 of the East Wing. Among the most famous works are Manet's unfinished *Execution of Maximilian*, Renoir's *Umbrellas*, Monet's *Thames below Westminster*, Van Gogh's *Sunflowers*, Seurat's pointillist *Bathers at Asnières*, a Rousseau junglescape, Cézanne's proto-Cubist *Bathers* and Picasso's Blue Period *Child with a Dove*.

National Portrait Gallery

St Martin's Place • Daily 10am–6pm, Thurs & Fri till 9pm • Free; audioguide £3.50 • ☎ 020 7306 0055, ⓦ npg.org.uk • ⊖ Leicester Square

Around the east side of the National Gallery lurks the **National Portrait Gallery**, founded in 1856 to house uplifting depictions of the good and the great. Though it undoubtedly has some fine works among its collection of ten thousand portraits, many of the studies are of less interest than their subjects. Nevertheless, it's fascinating to trace who has been deemed worthy of admiration at any one time: aristocrats and artists in previous centuries, warmongers and imperialists in the early decades of the twentieth century, writers and poets in the 1930s and 1940s, and, latterly, retired footballers, and film and pop stars. The NPG's **audioguide** gives useful biographical background information.

Whitehall

Whitehall, the unusually broad avenue connecting Trafalgar Square to Parliament Square, is synonymous with the faceless, pinstriped bureaucracy charged with the day-to-day running of the country, who inhabit the governmental ministries which line the street. During the sixteenth and seventeenth centuries, however, Whitehall was the permanent residence of the kings and queens of England, and was actually synonymous with royalty.

The statues dotted about recall the days when Whitehall stood at the centre of an empire on which the sun never set. Halfway down, in the middle of the road, stands Edwin Lutyens' **Cenotaph**, a memorial to the war dead, erected after World War I and the centrepiece of the Remembrance Sunday ceremony in November. Close by are the gates of Downing Street, home to London's most famous address, **Number 10 Downing Street**, the seventeenth-century terraced house that has been the residence of the prime minister since it was presented to Sir Robert Walpole, Britain's first PM, by George II in 1732.

Banqueting House

Whitehall • Mon–Sat 10am–5pm • £5 • ☎ 020 3166 6000, ⓦ hrp.org.uk • ⊖ Charing Cross

Whitehall Palace was originally the London seat of the Archbishop of York, confiscated and greatly extended by Henry VIII after a fire at Westminster forced him to find alternative accommodation. The chief section of the old palace to survive the 1698 fire was the **Banqueting House** begun by Inigo Jones in 1619 and the first Palladian building to be built in England. The one room open to the public has no original furnishings, but is well worth seeing for the superlative Rubens ceiling paintings glorifying the Stuart dynasty, commissioned by Charles I in the 1630s. Charles himself walked through the room for the last time in 1649 when he stepped onto the executioner's scaffold from one of its windows.

Horse Guards: Household Cavalry Museum

Whitehall • Daily. March–Sept 10am–6pm; Oct–Feb 10am–5pm • £6 • ☎ 020 7930 3070, ⓦ householdcavalrymuseum.co.uk • ⊖ Charing Cross or Westminster

Two mounted sentries of the Queen's Household Cavalry and two horseless colleagues are posted to protect **Horse Guards**, originally the main gateway to St James's Park and Buckingham Palace. Round the back of the building, you'll find the **Household Cavalry Museum** where you can try on a trooper's elaborate uniform, complete a horse quiz and learn about the regiments' history. With the stables immediately adjacent, it's a sweet-smelling place, and – horse-lovers will be pleased to know – you can see the beasts in their stalls through a glass screen. Don't miss the pocket riot act on display, which ends with the wise warning: "must read correctly: variance fatal".

Churchill War Rooms

King Charles St • Daily 9.30am–6pm • £17.50 • ☎ 020 7930 6961, ⓦ iwm.org.uk • ⊖ Westminster

In 1938, in anticipation of Nazi air raids, the basements of the civil service buildings on the south side of King Charles Street, south of Downing Street, were converted into the **Cabinet War Rooms**. It was here that Winston Churchill directed operations and held Cabinet meetings for the duration of World War II and the

---

THE CHANGING OF THE GUARD

The Queen is Colonel-in-Chief of the seven **Household Regiments**: the Life Guards and the Blues and Royals are the two Household Cavalry regiments; while the Grenadier, Coldstream, Scots, Irish and Welsh Guards make up the Foot Guards.

The **Changing of the Guard** takes place at two London locations: the Foot Guards march with a band to Buckingham Palace (May–Aug daily 11.30am; Sept–April alternate days) – they're best sighted coming down the Mall around 11.15am, but remember there's no ceremony if it rains. The Household Cavalry have a ceremony at Horse Guards on Whitehall (Mon–Sat 11am, Sun 10am, with an elaborate inspection at 4pm), and they don't care if it rains or shines. A ceremony also takes place regularly at Windsor Castle (see p.239).

1

THE WEST END AND WESTMINSTER

1

● **RESTAURANTS**
Dehesa	10
Dishoom	17
Flesh & Buns	5
Kopapa	7
Mildred's	11
Mr Kong	18
Polpo	14
Tonkotsu	12

● **CAFÉS & SNACKS**
Bar Italia	6
Beatroot	8
Breakfast Club	21
Café in the Crypt	15
Claridges	13
Fernandez & Wells	4
Food for Thought	22
Fortnum & Mason	9
Homeslice	3
Maison Bertaux	20
Misato	19
Momo	24
The Ritz	1
Rock & Sole Place	23
The Wolseley	2
Yalla Yalla	16

■ **ACCOMMODATION**
Dean Street Townhouse	6
The Fielding Hotel	5
Hazlitt's	4
Nadler Soho	3
Sanctuary House	7
Seven Dials Hotel	2
YHA Oxford Street	1

■ **CLUBS & LIVE MUSIC VENUES**
12 Bar Club	1
Borderline	4
Ronnie Scott's	10

■ **GAY BARS & CLUBS**
Comptons	13
Freedom	12
Heaven	22
The King's Arms	8
Ku Bar	11/15
Retro Bar	21
She Bar	9
Star at Night	3
The Yard	15

■ **PUBS & BARS**
Argyll Arms	5
The Chandos	20
Cross Keys	6
Dog & Duck	7
Gordon's	23
Guinea	19
ICA Bar	24
LAB	8
Lamb & Flag	17
Red Lion	25
St Stephen's Tavern	26
The Salsbury	18
The Windmill	14

● **SHOPS**
Fortnum & Mason	5
Foyles	2
Hatchard's	4
John Lewis	1
Liberty	3

1

rooms have been left pretty much as they were when they were finally abandoned on VJ Day 1945, making for an atmospheric underground trot through wartime London. Also in the basement is the excellent **Churchill Museum**, where you can hear snippets of Churchill's most famous speeches and check out his trademark bowler, spotted bow tie and half-chewed Havana, not to mention his wonderful burgundy zip-up "romper suit".

Houses of Parliament

Parliament Square • ☎ 020 7219 3000, ⓦ parliament.uk • ⊖ Westminster

Clearly visible at the south end of Whitehall is one of London's best-known monuments, the Palace of Westminster, better known as the **Houses of Parliament**. The city's finest Victorian Gothic Revival building and symbol of a nation once confident of its place at the centre of the world, it's distinguished above all by the ornate, gilded clocktower popularly known as **Big Ben**, after the thirteen-tonne main bell that strikes the hour (and is broadcast across the world by BBC radio).

The original medieval palace burned down in 1834, and everything you see now – save for Westminster Hall – is the work of **Charles Barry**, who created an orgy of honey-coloured pinnacles, turrets and tracery that attempts to express national greatness through the use of Gothic and Elizabethan styles. You get a glimpse of the eleventh-century **Westminster Hall** en route to the public galleries, its huge oak hammer-beam roof making it one of the most magnificent secular medieval halls in Europe.

INFORMATION AND TOURS   HOUSES OF PARLIAMENT

Public galleries To watch proceedings in either the House of Commons – the livelier of the two – or the House of Lords, simply join the queue for the public galleries outside St Stephen's Gate. The public are let in slowly from about 4pm onwards on Mondays and Tuesdays, from around 1pm Wednesdays, noon on Thursdays, and 10am on Sitting Fridays. Security is tight and the whole procedure can take an hour or more, so to avoid the queues, turn up an hour or so later on or on a Sitting Friday.

Question Time UK citizens can attend Question Time – when the House of Commons is at its liveliest – which

takes place in the first hour (Mon 2.30pm, Tues–Thurs 11.30am) and Prime Minister's Question Time (Wed only), but they must book in advance with their local MP (☎ 020 7219 3000).

Guided tours Saturday year-round (9am–4.15pm; 1hr 15min; £25), plus Mon–Fri during school holidays. In both cases it's a good idea to book in advance (☎ 0844 847 1672). UK residents are entitled to a free guided tour of the palace, as well as up Big Ben (no under-11s); both need to be organized through your local MP.

Westminster Abbey

Abbey Mon–Fri 9.30am–4.30pm, Wed till 6pm, Sat 9.30am–2.30pm • £18 **Verger tours** Mon–Fri times vary • £3 **Great Cloisters** Daily 9am–6pm • Free **Chapter House & Abbey Museum** Daily 10am–4pm • Free **College Garden** Tues–Thurs: April–Sept 10am–6pm; Oct–March 10am–4pm • Free • ☎ 020 7222 5152, ⓦ westminster-abbey.org • ⊖ Westminster

The Houses of Parliament dwarf their much older neighbour, **Westminster Abbey**, yet this single building embodies much of the history of England: it has been the venue for all coronations since the time of William the Conqueror, and the site of more or less every royal burial for some five hundred years between the reigns of Henry III and George II. Scores of the nation's most famous citizens are honoured here, too (though many of the stones commemorate people buried elsewhere), and the interior is crammed with hundreds of monuments and statues.

Entry is via the north transept, cluttered with monuments to politicians and traditionally known as **Statesmen's Aisle**, from which you gain access to the main **nave**: narrow, light and, at over 100ft in height, one of the tallest in the country. The most famous monument in this section is the **Tomb of the Unknown Soldier**, near the west door. Passing through the choir, you reach the central sanctuary, site of the coronations,

1

and the wonderful **Cosmati floor mosaic**, constructed in the thirteenth century by Italian craftsmen.

Lady Chapel

The abbey's most dazzling architectural set piece, the **Lady Chapel**, was added by Henry VII in 1503 as his future resting place. With its intricately carved vaulting and fan-shaped gilded pendants, the chapel represents the final spectacular gasp of English Perpendicular Gothic.

Poets' Corner

Nowadays, the abbey's royal tombs are upstaged by **Poets' Corner**, in the south transept, though the first occupant, Geoffrey Chaucer, was in fact buried here not because he was a poet, but because he lived nearby. By the eighteenth century this zone had become an artistic pantheon, and since then, the transept has been filled with tributes to all shades of talent.

Great Cloisters and Coronation Chair

Doors in the south choir aisle (plus a separate entrance from Dean's Yard) lead to the **Great Cloisters**. On the east side lies the octagonal Chapter House, where the House of Commons met from 1257, boasting thirteenth-century apocalyptic wall paintings. Also worth a look is the **Abbey Museum**, filled with generations of lifelike (but bald) royal funereal effigies. After exploring the cloisters you can either exit via Dean's Yard, or via the West Door of the main nave, where you'll see Edward I's **Coronation Chair**, a decrepit oak throne dating from around 1300 and used for every coronation since.

Tate Britain

Millbank • Daily 10am–6pm; first Fri bi-monthly until 10pm • Free • ☏ 020 7887 8888, ⓦ tate.org.uk • ⊖ Pimlico

A purpose-built gallery half a mile south of Parliament, founded in 1897 with money from Henry Tate, inventor of the sugar cube, **Tate Britain** is devoted to British art. As well as the collection covering 1500 to the present, the gallery also puts on large-scale temporary exhibitions (for which there is a charge) that showcase British artists.

The pictures have recently been rehung chronologically, so you begin with the richly bejewelled portraits of the Elizabethan nobility, before moving on to Britain's most famous artists – Hogarth, Constable, Gainsborough, Reynolds and Blake – plus foreign-born artists like Van Dyck who spent much of their career in Britain. The ever-popular **Pre-Raphaelites** are always well represented, as are established twentieth-century greats such as Stanley Spencer and Francis Bacon alongside living artists such as David Hockney and Bridget Riley. Lastly, don't miss the Tate's outstanding **Turner collection**, displayed in the Clore Gallery.

Westminster Cathedral

Victoria St • **Cathedral** Mon–Fri 7am–7pm, Sat 8am–7pm, Sun 8am–8pm • Free **Campanile** Mon–Fri 9.30am–5pm, Sat & Sun 9.30am–6pm • £5 • ☏ 020 7798 9055, ⓦ westminstercathedral.org.uk • ⊖ Victoria

Begun in 1895, the stripey neo-Byzantine concoction of the Roman Catholic **Westminster Cathedral** was one of the last and wildest monuments to the Victorian era. It's constructed from more than twelve million terracotta-coloured bricks, decorated with hoops of Portland stone – "blood and bandages" style, as it's known – and culminates in a magnificent tapered campanile which rises to 274ft, served by a lift. The **interior** is only half finished, so to get an idea of what the place will look like when it's finally completed, explore the series of **side chapels** whose rich, multicoloured decor makes use of more than one hundred different marbles from around the world.

1

St James's

St James's, the exclusive little enclave sandwiched between St James's Park and Piccadilly, was laid out in the 1670s close to St James's Palace. Regal and aristocratic residences overlook Green Park, gentlemen's clubs cluster along Pall Mall and St James's Street, while jacket-and-tie restaurants and expense-account gentlemen's outfitters line Jermyn Street. Hardly surprising then that most Londoners rarely stray into this area. Plenty of folk, however, frequent **St James's Park**, with large numbers heading for the Queen's chief residence, **Buckingham Palace**, and the adjacent Queen's Gallery and Royal Mews.

The Mall

Laid out as a memorial to Queen Victoria, the tree-lined sweep of **The Mall** is at its best on Sundays, when it's closed to traffic. The bombastic **Admiralty Arch** was erected to mark the entrance at the Trafalgar Square end of The Mall, while at the Buckingham Palace end stands the ludicrous **Victoria Memorial**, Edward VII's overblown 2300-ton marble tribute to his mother, which is topped by a gilded statue of Victory. Four outlying allegorical groups in bronze confidently proclaim the great achievements of her reign.

St James's Park

Daily 5am–midnight • Free • ☎ 0300 061 2350, ⓦ royalparks.org.uk

Flanking nearly the whole length of the Mall, **St James's Park** is the oldest of the royal parks, having been drained and enclosed for hunting purposes by Henry VIII. It was landscaped by Nash in the 1820s, and today its lake is a favourite picnic spot. Pelicans – originally a gift from the Russians to Charles II – can still be seen at the eastern end of the lake, and there are exotic ducks, swans and geese aplenty.

Buckingham Palace

Daily: Aug 9.30am–7pm; Sept 9.30am–6pm • £20 • ☎ 020 7766 7300, ⓦ royalcollection.org.uk • ⊖ Green Park or Victoria

The graceless colossus of **Buckingham Palace** has served as the monarch's permanent London residence only since the accession of Victoria. Bought by George III in 1762, the building was overhauled in the late 1820s by Nash and again in 1913, producing a palace that's as bland as it's possible to be.

For two months of the year, the hallowed portals are grudgingly nudged open. The interior, however, is a bit of an anticlimax: of the palace's 750 rooms you're permitted to see twenty or so, and there's little sign of life, as the Queen decamps to Scotland every summer. For the rest of the year there's little to do here – not that this deters the crowds who mill around the railings, and gather in some force to watch the **Changing of the Guard** (see box, p.63), in which a detachment of the Queen's Foot Guards marches to appropriate martial music from St James's Palace and Wellington Barracks to the palace forecourt (unless it rains, that is).

Queen's Gallery

Buckingham Palace Rd • Daily 10am–5.30pm • £9.50 • ☎ 020 7766 7300, ⓦ royalcollection.org.uk • ⊖ Victoria

A Doric portico on the south side of Buckingham Palace forms the entrance to the **Queen's Gallery**, which puts on temporary exhibitions drawn from the **Royal Collection**, a superlative array of art that includes works by Michelangelo, Raphael, Holbein, Reynolds, Gainsborough, Vermeer, Van Dyck, Rubens, Rembrandt and Canaletto, as well as the world's largest collection of Leonardo drawings, the odd Fabergé egg and heaps of Sèvres china.

TOP 5 QUIRKY MUSEUMS

Dennis Severs' House East End.
See p.85
Horniman Museum Forest Hill. See p.103
Hunterian Museum Holborn. See p.77

**Old Operating Theatre and Herb
Garret** Southwark. See p.90
Sir John Soane's Museum Holborn.
See p.77

Royal Mews

Buckingham Palace Rd • Feb, March & Nov Mon–Sat 10am–4pm; April–Oct daily 10am–5pm; • £8.75 • ☎ 020 7766 7302,
ⓦ royalcollection.org.uk • ⊖ Victoria

Royal carriages are the main attraction at the Nash-built **Royal Mews**, in particular the
Gold State Coach, made for George III in 1762 and used in every coronation since,
smothered in 22-carat gilding and weighing four tonnes, its axles supporting four
life-size figures.

St James's Palace

Chapel Royal Oct to Good Friday services 8.30am & 11.15am Queen's Chapel Easter Sun–July Sun 8.30am & 11.15am • ⊖ Green Park

St James's Palace's main red-brick gate-tower is pretty much all that remains of the
Tudor palace erected here by Henry VIII. When Whitehall Palace burned down in
1698, St James's became the principal royal residence and, in keeping with tradition,
every ambassador to the UK is still accredited to the "Court of St James's", even though
the court has since moved down the road to Buckingham Palace. The modest,
rambling, crenellated complex is off-limits to the public, with the exception of the
Chapel Royal, situated within the palace, and the **Queen's Chapel**, on the other side of
Marlborough Road; both are open for services only.

Clarence House

Stable Yard Rd • Aug Mon–Fri 10am–4pm, Sat & Sun 10am–5.30pm; visits (by guided tour) must be booked in advance • £9.50 •
☎ 020 7766 7303, ⓦ royalcollection.org.uk • ⊖ Green Park

Clarence House, connected to the palace's southwest wing, was home to the Queen
Mother, and now serves as the official London home of Charles and his second wife
Camilla, but a handful of rooms can be visited over the summer when the royals are in
Scotland. The interior is pretty unremarkable, so apart from a peek behind the scenes
in a working royal palace, or a few mementos of the Queen Mum, the main draw is the
twentieth-century British paintings on display by the likes of Walter Sickert and
Augustus John.

Mayfair

Piccadilly, which forms the southern border of swanky **Mayfair**, may not be the
fashionable promenade it started out as in the eighteenth century, but a whiff of
exclusivity still pervades **Bond Street** and its tributaries, where designer clothes emporia
jostle for space with jewellers, bespoke tailors and fine art dealers. **Regent Street** and
Oxford Street, meanwhile, are home to the flagship branches of the country's most
popular chain stores.

Piccadilly Circus

Anonymous and congested it may be, but **Piccadilly Circus** is, for many Londoners, the
nearest their city comes to having a centre. A much-altered product of Nash's grand
1812 Regent Street plan and now a major traffic interchange, it may not be a

1

picturesque place, but thanks to its celebrated aluminium statue, popularly known as **Eros**, it's prime tourist territory.

The fountain's archer is one of the city's top attractions, a status that baffles all who live here. Despite the bow and arrow, it's not the god of love at all but his lesser-known brother, Anteros, god of requited love, commemorating the selfless philanthropic love of the Earl of Shaftesbury, a Bible-thumping social reformer who campaigned against child labour.

Regent Street

Regent Street, drawn up by John Nash in 1812 as both a luxury shopping street and a triumphal way between George IV's Carlton House and Regent's Park, was the city's earliest attempt at dealing with traffic congestion, slum clearance and planned social segregation, something that would later be perfected by the Victorians. The increase in the purchasing power of the city's middle classes in the last century brought the tone of the street "down" and heavyweight stores now predominate. Among the best known are **Hamley's**, reputedly the world's largest toyshop, and **Liberty**, the upmarket department store that popularized Arts and Crafts designs.

Piccadilly

Piccadilly apparently got its name from the ruffs or "pickadills" worn by the dandies who used to promenade here in the late seventeenth century. It's not much of a place for promenading today, however, with traffic nose to tail most of the day and night. Infinitely more pleasant places to window-shop are the various **nineteenth-century arcades** that shoot off to the north and south, originally built to protect shoppers from the mud and horse dung on the streets, but now equally useful for escaping exhaust fumes.

Royal Academy of Arts

Piccadilly • Daily 10am–6pm, Fri till 10pm • £10–15 • ☎ 020 7300 8000, ⓦ royalacademy.org.uk • ⊖ Green Park

The **Royal Academy of Arts** occupies one of the few surviving aristocratic mansions that once lined the north side of Piccadilly. Rebuilding in the nineteenth century destroyed the original curved colonnades beyond the main gateway, but the complex has kept the feel of a Palladian *palazzo*. The country's first-ever formal art school, founded in 1768, the RA hosts a wide range of art exhibitions, and an annual **Summer Exhibition** that remains an essential stop on the social calendar of upper-middle-class England. Anyone can enter paintings in any style, and the lucky winners get hung, in rather close proximity, and sold. RA "Academicians" are allowed to display six of their own works – no matter how awful. The result is a bewildering display, which gets panned annually by highbrow critics, but enjoyed happily by everyone else.

OXFORD STREET: THE BUSIEST STREET IN EUROPE

As wealthy Londoners began to move out of the City in the eighteenth century in favour of the newly developed West End, so **Oxford Street** – the old Roman road to Oxford – gradually became London's main shopping thoroughfare. Today, despite successive recessions and sky-high rents, Oxford Street remains Europe's busiest street, simply because this two-mile hotchpotch of shops is home to (often several) flagship branches of Britain's major retailers. The street's only real architectural landmark is **Selfridges** (see p.130) opened in 1909 with a facade featuring the Queen of Time riding the ship of commerce and supporting an Art Deco clock.

Bond Street

While Oxford Street, Regent Street and Piccadilly have all gone downmarket, **Bond Street**, which runs parallel with Regent Street, has carefully maintained its exclusivity. It is, in fact, two streets rolled into one: the southern half, laid out in the 1680s, is known as Old Bond Street; its northern extension, which followed less than fifty years later, is known as New Bond Street. They are both pretty unassuming streets architecturally, yet the shops that line them are among the flashiest in London, dominated by perfumeries, jewellers and designer clothing stores. In addition to fashion, Bond Street is also renowned for its fine art galleries and its **auction houses**, the oldest of which is Sotheby's, 34–35 New Bond St, whose viewing galleries are open free of charge.

Marylebone

Marylebone, which lies to the north of Oxford Street, is, like Mayfair, another grid-plan Georgian development – a couple of social and real-estate leagues below its neighbour, but a wealthy area nevertheless. It boasts a very fine art gallery, the **Wallace Collection**, and, in its northern fringes, one of London's biggest tourist attractions, **Madame Tussauds**, the oldest and largest wax museum in the world, plus the ever popular **Sherlock Holmes Museum**.

Wallace Collection

Manchester Square • Daily 10am–5pm • Free • ☎ 020 7563 9500, Ⓦ wallacecollection.org • ⊖ Bond Street

Housed in a miniature eighteenth-century chateau, the splendid **Wallace Collection** is best known for its eighteenth-century French paintings, Franz Hals' *Laughing Cavalier*, Titian's *Perseus and Andromeda*, Velázquez's *Lady with a Fan* and Rembrandt's affectionate portrait of his teenage son, Titus. The museum has preserved the feel of a grand stately home, its exhibits piled high in glass cabinets, and paintings covering almost every inch of wall space. The fact that these exhibits are set amid priceless Boulle furniture – and a bloody great armoury – makes the place even more remarkable.

Madame Tussauds

Marylebone Rd • Mon–Fri 9.30am–5.30pm, Sat & Sun 9am–6pm • Online tickets from £22.50 • ☎ 0871 894 3000, Ⓦ madametussauds .com • ⊖ Baker Street

Madame Tussauds has been pulling in the crowds ever since the good lady arrived in London from Paris in 1802 bearing the sculpted heads of guillotined aristocrats. The entrance fee might be extortionate, the waxwork likenesses of the famous occasionally dubious and the attempts to relieve you of yet more cash relentless, but you can still rely on finding London's biggest queues here (book online to avoid waiting). You can choose to opt out of the Chamber of Horrors Live show, a piece of hokum designed to frighten the living daylights out of tourists.

Sherlock Holmes Museum

239 Baker St • Daily 9.30am–6pm • £8 • ☎ 020 7224 3688, Ⓦ sherlock-holmes.co.uk • ⊖ Baker Street

Baker Street is synonymous with Sherlock Holmes, the fictional detective who lived at no. 221b (the actual number on the door of the museum). Unashamedly touristy, the **Sherlock Holmes Museum** is stuffed full of Victoriana and life-size models of characters from the books. It's an atmospheric and very competent exercise in period reconstruction – you can even don a deerstalker to have your picture taken by the fireside, looking like the great detective himself.

1

Soho

Bounded by Regent Street to the west, Oxford Street to the north and Charing Cross Road to the east, **Soho** is very much the heart of the West End. It's been the city's premier red-light district for centuries and retains an unorthodox and slightly raffish air that's unique for central London. It has an immigrant history as rich as that of the East End and a louche nightlife that has attracted writers and revellers of every sexual persuasion since the eighteenth century. Today it's London's most high-profile gay quarter, especially around **Old Compton Street**. Conventional sights are few, yet there's probably more street life here than anywhere in the city centre, whatever the hour. Most folk head to Soho to go the cinema or theatre, and to have a drink or a bite to eat in the innumerable bars, cafés and restaurants that pepper the area.

Leicester Square

When the big cinemas and nightclubs are doing good business, and the buskers are entertaining the crowds, **Leicester Square** is one of the most crowded places in London, particularly on a Friday or Saturday when huge numbers of tourists and half the youth of the suburbs seem to congregate here. It wasn't until the mid-nineteenth century that the square actually began to emerge as an entertainment zone; cinema moved in during the 1930s, a golden age evoked by the sleek black lines of the Odeon on the east side.

Chinatown

Chinatown, hemmed in between Leicester Square and Shaftesbury Avenue, is a self-contained jumble of shops, cafés and restaurants. Only a minority of London's Chinese live in these three small blocks, but it remains a focus for the community, a place to do business or the weekly shop, celebrate a wedding, or just meet up for meals, particularly on Sundays, when the restaurants overflow with Chinese families tucking into *dim sum*. **Gerrard Street** is the main drag, with telephone kiosks rigged out as pagodas and fake oriental gates or *paifang*.

Old Compton Street

If Soho has a main road, it would be **Old Compton Street**, which runs parallel with Shaftesbury Avenue. The shops, boutiques and cafés here are typical of the area and a good barometer of the latest fads. Soho has been a permanent fixture on the **gay scene** for the better part of a century, and you'll find a profusion of gay bars, clubs and cafés jostling for position here and round the corner in Wardour Street.

Covent Garden

More sanitized and commercial than neighbouring Soho, the shops and restaurants of **Covent Garden** today are a far cry from the district's heyday when the piazza was the great playground (and red-light district) of eighteenth-century London. The buskers in front of St Paul's Church, the theatres round about, and the **Royal Opera House** on Bow Street are survivors of this tradition, and on a balmy summer evening, **Covent Garden Piazza** is still an undeniably lively place to be.

Covent Garden Piazza

London's oldest planned square, laid out in the 1630s by Inigo Jones, **Covent Garden Piazza** was initially a great success, its novelty value alone attracting a rich and

1

aristocratic clientele, but over the next century the tone of the place fell as the fruit and vegetable market expanded, and theatres, coffee houses and brothels began to take over the peripheral buildings. When the market closed in 1974, the piazza narrowly survived being turned into an office development. Instead, the elegant Victorian market hall and its environs were restored to house shops, restaurants and arts-and-crafts stalls. Of Jones's original piazza, the only remaining parts are the two rebuilt sections of north-side arcading, and **St Paul's Church**, to the west.

London Transport Museum

Covent Garden Piazza • Mon–Thurs, Sat & Sun 10am–6pm, Fri 11am–6pm • Adults £15, under-16s free • ☎ 020 7379 6344, ⓦ ltmuseum.co.uk • ⊖ Covent Garden

A former flower-market shed on Covent Garden Piazza's east side is home to the **London Transport Museum**, a sure-fire hit for families with kids under 10. To follow the displays chronologically, head for Level 2, where you'll find a reconstructed 1829 Shillibeer's Horse Omnibus, which provided the city's first regular horse-bus service. Level 1 tells the story of the world's first underground system and contains a lovely 1920s Metropolitan Line carriage in burgundy and green with pretty, drooping lamps. On the ground floor, one double-decker **tram** is all that's left to pay tribute to the world's largest tram system, dismantled in 1952. Look out, too, for the first **tube** train, from the 1890s, whose lack of windows earned it the nickname "the padded cell".

Royal Opera House

Bow St • **Floral Hall** Daily 10am–3.30pm • Free **Backstage tours** Mon–Fri 10.30am, 12.30pm & 2.30pm, Sat hourly 10.30am–2.30pm • £12 • ☎ 020 7304 4000, ⓦ roh.org.uk • ⊖ Covent Garden

The arcading on the northeast side of the piazza was rebuilt as part of the redevelopment of the **Royal Opera House**, whose main Neoclassical façade dates from 1811 and opens onto Bow Street. Now, however, you can reach the opera house from a passageway in the corner of the arcading. The spectacular wrought-iron **Floral Hall** serves as the opera house's main foyer, and is open to the public, as is the *Amphitheatre* bar/restaurant (from 90min before performance to the end of the last interval), which has a glorious terrace overlooking the piazza.

Strand

Once famous for its riverside mansions, and later its music halls, the **Strand** – the main road connecting Westminster to the City – is a shadow of its former self. One of the few vestiges of glamour is **The Savoy**, London's first modern luxury hotel, built in 1889 on the site of the medieval Savoy Palace on the south side of the street. As its name suggests, the Strand once lay along the riverbank until the Victorians shored up the banks of the Thames to create the Embankment.

Somerset House

Strand • **Courtyard** Daily 7.30am–11pm • Free **Riverside terrace** Daily 8am–6pm • **Embankment galleries** Daily 10am–6pm • £6 • ☎ 020 7845 4600, ⓦ somersethouse.org.uk • ⊖ Temple or Covent Garden

Somerset House is the sole survivor of the grandiose river palaces that once lined the Strand. Although it looks like an old aristocratic mansion, the present building was purpose-built in 1776 to house government offices. Nowadays, Somerset House's granite-paved courtyard, which has a 55-jet **fountain** that spouts little syncopated dances straight from the cobbles, is used for open-air performances, concerts, installations and, in winter, an ice rink.

The south wing has a lovely riverside terrace with a café/restaurant and the **Embankment Galleries**, which host innovative special exhibitions on contemporary

1

art and design. You can also admire the Royal Naval Commissioners' superb gilded eighteenth-century barge in the **King's Barge House**, below ground level in the south wing.

Courtauld Gallery

Daily 10am–6pm • £6, £3 on Mon • ☎ 020 7848 2526, ⓦ courtauld.ac.uk • ⊖ Temple or Covent Garden

In the north wing of Somerset House is the **Courtauld Gallery**, chiefly known for its dazzling collection of Impressionist and Post-Impressionist paintings. Among the most celebrated is a small-scale version of Manet's *Déjeuner sur l'herbe*, Renoir's *La Loge*, and Degas' *Two Dancers*, plus a whole heap of Cézanne's canvases, including one of his series of *Card Players*. The Courtauld also boasts a fine selection of works by the likes of Rubens, Van Dyck, Tiepolo and Cranach the Elder, and has recently been augmented by the long-term loan of a hundred top-notch twentieth-century paintings and sculptures by, among others, Kandinksy, Matisse, Dufy, Derain, Rodin and Henry Moore.

Bloomsbury

Bloomsbury was built over in grid-plan style from the 1660s onwards, and the formal bourgeois Georgian squares laid out then remain the area's main distinguishing feature. In the twentieth century, Bloomsbury acquired a reputation as the city's most learned quarter, dominated by the dual institutions of the **British Museum** and **London University**, but perhaps best known for its literary inhabitants, among them T.S. Eliot and Virginia Woolf. Today, the British Museum is clearly the star attraction, but there are other minor sights, such as the **Charles Dickens Museum**. Only in its northern fringes does the character of the area change dramatically, as you near the hustle and bustle of **Euston**, **St Pancras** and **King's Cross** train stations.

British Museum

Great Russell St • Daily 10am–5.30pm, Fri till 8.30pm • Free • ☎ 020 7323 8299, ⓦ britishmuseum.org • ⊖ Tottenham Court Road, Russell Square or Holborn

The **British Museum** is one of the great museums of the world. With more than seventy thousand exhibits ranged over several miles of galleries, it boasts a huge collection of antiquities, prints and drawings – more than thirteen million objects (and growing). Its assortment of Roman and Greek art is unparalleled, its Egyptian collection is the most significant outside Egypt and, in addition, there are fabulous treasures from Anglo-Saxon and Roman Britain, from China, Japan, India and Mesopotamia.

The building itself, begun in 1823, is the grandest of London's Greek Revival edifices, dominated by the giant Ionian colonnade and portico that forms the main entrance. At the heart of the museum is the **Great Court**, with its remarkable, curving glass-and-steel roof, designed by Norman Foster. At the centre stands the copper-domed former **Round Reading Room**, built in the 1850s to house the British Library, where Karl Marx penned *Das Kapital*. More recently, it has been used for special exhibitions, which now take place in the new World Conservation and Exhibitions Centre.

The highlights

The most famous of the **Roman and Greek antiquities** are the Parthenon sculptures, better known as the **Elgin Marbles**, after the British aristocrat who acquired the reliefs in 1801. The **Egyptian collection** of monumental sculptures is impressive, but it's the ever-popular **mummies** that draw the biggest crowds. Also on display is the **Rosetta Stone**, which finally unlocked the secret of Egyptian hieroglyphs. There's a splendid

BLOOMSBURY AND AROUND

0 — 250 yards

■ **ACCOMMODATION**
Arosfa Hotel	2
Generator	1
Grange Langham Court Hotel	5
Ridgemount	3
YHA Central	4

● **RESTAURANTS & CAFÉS**
Cigala	2
Dawna Bhel Poori House	1
Hummus Bros	3

■ **PUBS & BARS**
The Duke	1
The Lamb	2
Museum Tavern	3
Princess Louise	4
The Social	5

● **SHOPS**
London Review Bookshop	2
Persephone Books	1

1

series of **Assyrian reliefs**, depicting events such as the royal lion hunts of Ashurbanipal, in which the king slaughters one of the cats with his bare hands.

The leathery half-corpse of the 2000-year-old **Lindow Man**, discovered in a Cheshire bog, and the Anglo-Saxon treasure from the **Sutton Hoo** ship burial, are among the highlights of the prehistoric and Romano-British section. The medieval and modern collections, meanwhile, range from the twelfth-century **Lewis chessmen**, carved from walrus ivory, to twentieth-century exhibits such as a copper vase by Frank Lloyd Wright.

The dramatically lit Mexican and North American galleries, plus the African galleries in the basement, represent just a small fraction of the museum's **ethnographic collection**, while select works from the BM's enormous collection of **prints and drawings** can be seen in special exhibitions. Among fabulous **Oriental treasures** in the north wing, closest to the back entrance on Montague Place, are ancient Chinese porcelain, ornate snuffboxes, miniature landscapes and a bewildering array of Buddhist and Hindu gods.

Charles Dickens Museum

48 Doughty St • Daily 10am–5pm • £8 • ☎ 020 7405 2127, ⓦ dickensmuseum.com • ⊖ Russell Square

Charles Dickens moved to Doughty Street in 1837, shortly after his marriage to Catherine Hogarth, and they lived here for two years, during which time he wrote *Nicholas Nickleby* and *Oliver Twist*. Catherine gave birth to two children in the bedroom here, and her youngest sister died tragically in Dickens's arms. Much of the house's furniture belonged to Dickens, at one time or another, and there's an early portrait miniature painted by his aunt in 1830. The museum puts on special exhibitions in the adjacent house, no. 49, where you'll also find a café.

British Library

96 Euston Rd • Mon & Wed–Fri 9.30am–6pm, Tues 9.30am–8pm, Sat 9.30am–5pm, Sun 11am–5pm • Free • ☎ 0843 208 1144, ⓦ bl.uk • ⊖ King's Cross

As one of the country's most expensive public buildings, the **British Library** took flak from all sides during its protracted construction, completed in 1997. Yet while it's true that the building's red-brick brutalism is resolutely unfashionable, and compares unfavourably with its cathedralesque Victorian neighbour, St Pancras Station, the library's interior has met with general approval, and the exhibition galleries are superb.

With the exception of the reading rooms, the library is open to the public and puts on a wide variety of exhibitions and events, and has several cafés, a restaurant and free wi-fi. In the John Ritblat Gallery a selection of the BL's ancient manuscripts, maps, documents and precious books, including the richly illustrated Lindisfarne Gospels, is on display. You can also turn the pages of various texts – from the Mercator's 1570s atlas of Europe to Leonardo da Vinci's notebook – on touch-screen computers.

King's Cross Station

Euston Rd • ⊖ King's Cross

King's Cross Station, opened in 1852, is a mere shed, compared with St Pancras Station, albeit one which has been recently beautifully restored. It is, of course, the station from which Harry Potter and his wizarding chums leave for school aboard the Hogwarts Express from platform 9¾. The film scenes were shot between platforms 4 and 5, and a station trolley is now embedded in the new concourse wall, providing a perfect photo opportunity for passing Potter fans.

Holborn

1

Holborn, on the periphery of the financial district of the City, has long been associated with the law, and its **Inns of Court** make for an interesting stroll, their archaic, cobbled precincts exuding the rarefied atmosphere of an Oxbridge college, and sheltering one of the city's oldest churches, the twelfth-century **Temple Church**. Holborn's gem, though, is the **Sir John Soane's Museum**, one of the most memorable and enjoyable of London's small museums, packed with architectural illusions and an eclectic array of curios.

Temple

Temple is the largest and most complex of the Inns of Court, where every barrister in England must study (and eat) before being called to the Bar. A few very old buildings survive here and the maze of courtyards and passageways is fun to explore.

Middle Temple Hall

Mon–Fri 10–11.30am & 3–4pm, phone to check access • Free • ☎ 020 7427 4800 • ⊖ Temple or Blackfriars

Medieval students ate, attended lectures and slept in the **Middle Temple Hall**, across the courtyard, still the Inn's main dining room. The present building, constructed in the 1560s, provided the setting for many great Elizabethan masques and plays – probably including Shakespeare's *Twelfth Night*, which is believed to have been premiered here in 1602. The hall is worth a visit for its fine hammer-beam roof, wooden panelling and decorative Elizabethan screen.

Temple Church

Mon, Tues, Thurs & Fri 11am–4pm, Wed 2–4pm • £4 • ☎ 020 7353 3470, ⓦ templechurch.com • ⊖ Temple or Blackfriars

The complex's oldest building is **Temple Church**, built in 1185 by the Knights Templar, and modelled on the Church of the Holy Sepulchre in Jerusalem. The interior features striking Purbeck marble piers, recumbent marble effigies of medieval knights and tortured grotesques grimacing in the spandrels of the blind arcading. The church makes an appearance in both the book and the film of Dan Brown's *The Da Vinci Code*.

Hunterian Museum

35–43 Lincoln's Inn Fields • Tues–Sat 10am–5pm • Free • ☎ 020 7869 6660, ⓦ www.rcseng.ac.uk • ⊖ Holborn

The **Hunterian Museum**, on the first floor of the Royal College of Surgeons, contains the unique specimen collection of the surgeon-scientist John Hunter (1728–93). The centrepiece is the Crystal Gallery, a wall of jars of pickled skeletons and body pieces – from the gall bladder of a puffer fish to the thyroid of a dromedary – prepared by Hunter himself. Among the most prized exhibits are the skeleton of the "Irish giant", Charles Byrne (1761–83), who was 7ft 10 inches tall, and the Sicilian dwarf Caroline Crachami (1815–24), who stood at just over 1ft 10 1/2 inches when she died at the age of nine.

Sir John Soane's Museum

13 Lincoln's Inn Fields • Tues–Sat 10am–5pm, first Tues of the month candle-lit 6–9pm • Free • Guided tour Sat 11am, £10 • ☎ 020 7405 2107, ⓦ soane.org • ⊖ Holborn

A group of buildings on the north side of Lincoln's Inn Fields houses the fascinating **Sir John Soane's Museum**. Soane (1753–1837), a bricklayer's son who rose to be architect of the Bank of England, was an avid collector who designed this house not only as a home and office, but also as a place to stash his large collection of art and antiquities. Arranged much as it was in his lifetime, the ingeniously planned house has an informal, treasure-hunt atmosphere, with surprises in every alcove. Note that the

1

museum is very popular and you may have to queue to get in – and get here early if you want to go on a guided tour or on a candle-lit evening.

The City

Stretching from Temple Bar in the west to the Tower of London in the east **The City** is where London began. It was here, nearly two thousand years ago, that the Romans first established a settlement on the Thames; later the medieval City emerged as the country's most important trading centre and it remains one of the world's leading financial hubs. However, in this Square Mile (as the City is sometimes referred to), you'll find few leftovers of London's early days, since four-fifths burnt down in the Great Fire of 1666. Rebuilt in brick and stone, the City gradually lost its centrality as London swelled westwards. What you see now is mostly the product of three fairly recent building phases: the Victorian construction boom; the postwar reconstruction following World War II; and the building frenzy that began in the 1980s and has continued ever since.

When you consider what has happened here, it's amazing that anything has survived to pay witness to the City's 2000-year history. Wren's spires still punctuate the skyline and his masterpiece, **St Paul's Cathedral**, remains one of London's geographical pivots. At the City's eastern edge, the **Tower of London** still boasts some of the best-preserved medieval fortifications in Europe. Other relics, such as Wren's **Monument** to the Great Fire and London's oldest synagogue and church, are less conspicuous, and even locals have problems finding modern attractions like the **Museum of London** and the **Barbican** arts complex.

Fleet Street

Fleet Street's associations with the printed press began in 1500, when Wynkyn de Worde, William Caxton's apprentice, moved the Caxton presses here from Westminster to be close to the lawyers of the Inns of Court (his best customers) and to the clergy of St Paul's. In 1702, the world's first daily newspaper, the now defunct **Daily Courant**, began publishing here, and by the nineteenth century, all the major national and provincial dailies had moved their presses to the area. Then in 1985, Britain's first colour tabloid, *Today*, appeared, using computer technology that rendered the Fleet Street presses obsolete. It was left to media tycoon Rupert Murdoch to take on the printers' unions in a bitter year-long dispute that changed the newspaper industry for ever. The press headquarters that once dominated the area have all now relocated, leaving just a handful of small publications and a few architectural landmarks to testify to 500 years of printing history.

St Bride's Church

Fleet St • Mon–Fri 9am–6pm, Sat 11am–3pm, Sun 10am–6.30pm • Free • ☎ 020 7427 0133, ⓦ stbrides.com • ⊖ St Paul's

To find out more about Fleet Street's history, check out the exhibition in the crypt of **St Bride's Church**, the "journalists' and printers' cathedral", situated behind the former Reuters building. The church also features Wren's tallest, and most exquisite, spire (said to be the inspiration for the traditional tiered wedding cake).

St Paul's Cathedral

Mon–Sat 8.30am–4.30pm • from £15 online • ☎ 020 7246 8348, ⓦ stpauls.co.uk • ⊖ St Paul's

Designed by Christopher Wren and completed in 1710, **St Paul's Cathedral** remains a dominating presence in the City, despite the encroaching tower blocks. Topped by an enormous lead-covered dome, its showpiece west facade is particularly magnificent.

1

TOP 5 CITY CHURCHES

The City of London is crowded with **churches** (🖥london-city-churches.org.uk), the majority of them built or rebuilt by Wren after the Great Fire. Weekday lunchtimes are a good time to visit, when many put on free concerts of classical and chamber music.

St Bartholomew-the-Great Cloth Fair; ⊖ Barbican. The oldest surviving pre-Fire church in the City and by far the most atmospheric.

St Mary Abchurch Abchurch Lane; ⊖ Cannon Street or Bank. Unique among Wren's City churches for its huge, painted, domed ceiling, plus the only authenticated reredos by Grinling Gibbons.

St Mary Aldermary Queen Victoria St; ⊖ Mansion House. Wren's most successful stab at Gothic, with fan vaulting in the aisles and a panelled ceiling in the nave.

St Mary Woolnoth Lombard St; ⊖ Bank. Hawksmoor's only City church, sporting an unusually broad, bulky tower and a Baroque clerestory that floods the church with light from its semicircular windows.

St Stephen Walbrook Walbrook; ⊖ Bank. Wren's dress rehearsal for St Paul's, with a wonderful central dome and plenty of original woodcarving.

The best place from which to appreciate St Paul's is beneath the **dome**, decorated (against Wren's wishes) with Thornhill's trompe-l'oeil frescoes. The most richly decorated section of the cathedral, however, is the **chancel**, where the gilded mosaics of birds, fish, animals and greenery, dating from the 1890s, are spectacular. The intricately carved oak and limewood **choir stalls**, and the imposing organ case, are the work of Wren's master carver, Grinling Gibbons.

The galleries

A series of stairs, beginning in the south aisle, lead to the dome's three **galleries**, the first of which is the internal **Whispering Gallery**, so called because of its acoustic properties – words whispered to the wall on one side are distinctly audible over 100ft away on the other, though the place is often so busy you can't hear much above the hubbub. The other two galleries are exterior: the wide **Stone Gallery**, around the balustrade at the base of the dome, and ultimately the tiny **Golden Gallery**, below the golden ball and cross which top the cathedral.

The crypt

Although the nave is crammed full of overblown monuments to military types, burials in St Paul's are confined to the whitewashed **crypt**, reputedly the largest in Europe. Immediately to your right is Artists' Corner, which boasts as many painters and architects as Westminster Abbey has poets, including Christopher Wren himself, who was commissioned to build the cathedral after its Gothic predecessor, Old St Paul's, was destroyed in the Great Fire. The crypt's two other star tombs are those of **Nelson** and **Wellington**, both occupying centre stage and both with even more fanciful monuments upstairs.

Museum of London

150 London Wall • Daily 10am–6pm • Free • ☎ 020 7001 9844, 🖥 museumoflondon.org.uk • ⊖ Barbican or St Paul's

Over the centuries, numerous Roman, Saxon and medieval remains have been salvaged or dug up and are now displayed in the **Museum of London**, whose permanent galleries provide an educational and imaginative trot through London's past, from prehistory to the present day. Specific exhibits to look out for include the Bucklersbury Roman mosaic and the model of Old St Paul's, but the prize possession is the **Lord Mayor's Coach**, built in 1757 and rivalling the Queen's in sheer weight of gold decoration. Look out, too, for the museum's excellent temporary exhibitions, gallery tours, lectures, walks and videos it organizes throughout the year.

PUBS & BARS

The Black Friar	16
The Counting House	14
Jerusalem Tavern	9
The Lamb Tavern	15
Loungelover	6
The Owl & Pussycat	5
Ten Bells	10
The Three Kings	7
Worship Street Whistling Shop	8
Ye Olde Cheshire Cheese	13
Ye Olde Mitre	12

GAY BAR

George & Dragon	1

CLUBS & LIVE MUSIC VENUES

Cargo	3
Fabric	11
Plastic People	2
XOYO	4

ACCOMMODATION

Apex City of London Hotel	7
Hoxton Hotel	1
The King's Wardrobe	4
The Rookery	4
Shoreditch Rooms	2
YHA St Paul's	5
The Zetter Hotel & Townhouse	3

RESTAURANTS

Duck and Waffle	8
The Hawksmoor	5
Lahore Kebab House	10
Moro	1
Quality Chop House	3
St John Bread and Wine	6
Tayyab's	9

1

● **SHOPS**
Brick Lane Market 2
Columbia Road Flower Market 1
Spitalfields Market 3

0 — 200
yards

● **CAFÉS & SNACKS**
Brick Lane Beigel Bake 2
Café 1001 4
Café Below 11
Prufrock Coffee 7

– – – City boundary

THE CITY AND AROUND

1

Guildhall

Gresham St • May–Sept daily 10am–5pm; Oct–April Mon–Sat 10am–5pm • Free • ☎ 020 7606 3030, ⓦ cityoflondon.gov.uk • ⊖ Bank

Despite being the seat of the City governance for over 800 years, **Guildhall** doesn't exactly exude municipal wealth. Nevertheless, it's worth popping inside the **Great Hall**, which miraculously survived both the Great Fire and Blitz. The hall is still used for functions, though only the walls survive from the original fifteenth-century building, which was the venue for several high-treason trials, including that of Lady Jane Grey.

Guildhall Art Gallery

Mon–Sat 10am–5pm, Sun noon–4pm • Free • ⊖ Bank

The purpose-built **Guildhall Art Gallery** contains one or two exceptional works, such as Rossetti's *La Ghirlandata*, and Holman Hunt's *The Eve of St Agnes*, plus a massive painting depicting the 1782 Siege of Gibraltar, commissioned by the Corporation, and a marble statue of Margaret Thatcher. In the basement, you can view the remains of a **Roman amphitheatre**, dating from around 120 AD, which was discovered when the gallery was built in 1988.

Clockmakers' Museum

Aldermanbury • Mon–Sat 9.30am–4.45pm • Free • ☎ 020 7332 1868, ⓦ clockmakers.org • ⊖ Bank

The **Clockmakers' Museum** has a collection of more than six hundred timepieces, from Tudor pocket watches to grandfather clocks, which ring out in unison on the hour. Of particular interest is H5, a marine chronometer that looks like an oversized pocket watch and was tested by George III himself. H4 had won John Harrison the Longitude Prize (see p.103) and he was required to produce H5 to prove it wasn't a fluke. The collection has been slated to move to the Science Museum (see p.96) in 2015.

Bank

Bank is the finest architectural arena in the City. Heart of the finance sector and the busy meeting point of eight streets, it's overlooked by a handsome collection of Neoclassical buildings – among them, the **Bank of England**, the **Royal Exchange** (now a shopping mall) and **Mansion House** (the Lord Mayor's official residence) – each one faced in Portland stone.

Bank of England

Threadneedle St • Mon–Fri 10am–5pm • Free • ☎ 020 7601 5545, ⓦ bankofengland.co.uk • ⊖ Bank

Established in 1694 by William III to raise funds for the war against France, the **Bank of England** wasn't erected on its present site until 1734. All that remains of the building on which Sir John Soane spent the best part of his career from 1788 onwards is the windowless, outer curtain wall. However, you can view a reconstruction of Soane's Bank Stock Office, with its characteristic domed skylight, read about the history, and touch a real gold bar, in the **museum**, which has its entrance on Bartholomew Lane.

LONDON BRIDGE

Until 1750, **London Bridge** was the only bridge across the Thames. The medieval bridge achieved world fame: built of stone and crowded with timber-framed houses, a palace and a chapel, it became one of the great attractions of London – there's a model in the nearby church of **St Magnus the Martyr** (Tues–Fri 10am–4pm). The houses were finally removed in the mid-eighteenth century, and a new stone bridge erected in 1831; that one now stands in the Arizona desert, having been bought in the 1960s by a man who, so the story goes, thought he'd purchased Tower Bridge. The present concrete structure, without doubt the ugliest yet, dates from 1972.

THE CITY **LONDON** | 83

AIMING HIGH: CITY SKYSCRAPERS

Throughout the 1990s, most people's favourite modern building in the City was Richard Rogers' **Lloyd's Building**, on Leadenhall Street – a vertical version of his Pompidou Centre in Paris – an inside-out array of glass and steel piping. Lloyd's was upstaged in 2003 by Norman Foster's 590ft-high glass diamond-clad **Gherkin**, which endeared itself to Londoners with its cheeky shape. Despite the economic recession, the City skyline continues to sprout yet more skyscrapers, with **The Cheesegrater**, Richard Rogers' 737ft wedge-shaped office block, opposite the Lloyd's Building, leading the charge. Still to rise, close by, is the Scalpel, a 620ft twisted angular shard of glass due for completion in 2017. More controversial has been the rise of Rafael Viñoly's 525ft **Walkie Talkie**, on Fenchurch Street, which features a public "sky garden" on the top floor. Meanwhile, on the other side of the river, of course, is the tallest of the lot, Renzo Piano's 1016ft **Shard**, by London Bridge (see p.90).

Bevis Marks Synagogue

Bevis Marks • Mon, Wed & Thurs 10.30am 2pm, Tues & Fri 10.30am–1pm, Sun 10.30am–12.30pm • Guided tours Wed & Fri noon, Sun 11am • £5 • ☎ 020 7626 1274, ⓦ bevismarks.org.uk • ⊖ Aldgate

Hidden away behind a red-brick office block in a little courtyard off Bevis Marks is the **Bevis Marks Synagogue**. Built in 1701 by Sephardic Jews who had fled the Inquisition in Spain and Portugal, this is the country's oldest surviving synagogue, and its roomy, rich interior gives an idea of just how wealthy the community was at the time. Nowadays, the Sephardic community has dispersed across London and the congregation has dwindled, though the magnificent array of chandeliers makes it popular for candlelit Jewish weddings.

Monument

Monument St • Daily 9.30am–5.30pm • £2 • ☎ 020 7626 2717, ⓦ themonument.info • ⊖ Monument

The **Monument** was designed by Wren to commemorate the Great Fire of 1666. Crowned with spiky gilded flames, this plain Doric column stands 202ft high; if it were laid out flat it would touch the bakery where the Fire started, east of Monument. The bas-relief on the base, now in very bad shape, depicts Charles II and the Duke of York in Roman garb conducting the emergency relief operation. Views from the gallery, accessed by 311 steps, are somewhat dwarfed nowadays by the buildings springing up around it.

Tower of London

March–Oct Sun & Mon 10am–5.30pm, Tues–Sat 9am–5.30pm; Nov–Feb closes 4.30pm • £20 • ☎ 0844 482 7799, ⓦ hrp.org.uk • ⊖ Tower Hill

One of Britain's main tourist attractions, the **Tower of London** overlooks the river at the eastern boundary of the old city walls. Despite all the hype, it remains one of London's most remarkable buildings, site of some of the goriest events in the nation's history, and somewhere all visitors and Londoners should explore at least once. Chiefly famous as a place of imprisonment and death, it has variously been used as a royal residence, armoury, mint, menagerie, observatory and – a function it still serves – a safe-deposit box for the Crown Jewels.

The lively free **guided tours** given by the Tower's **Beefeaters** (officially known as Yeoman Warders) are useful for getting your bearings. Visitors today enter the Tower along Water Lane, but in times gone by most prisoners were delivered through **Traitors' Gate**, on the waterfront. Immediately, they would have come to the **Bloody Tower**, which forms the main entrance to the Inner Ward, and which is where the 12-year-old Edward V and his 10-year-old brother were accommodated "for their own safety" in 1483 by their uncle, the future Richard III, and later murdered. It's also where **Walter Raleigh** was imprisoned on three separate occasions, including a thirteen-year stretch.

1

> ## HOXTON, SHOREDITCH AND DALSTON
>
> Since the 1990s, the northern fringe of the City has been colonized by artists, designers and architects and transformed itself into the city's most vibrant artistic enclave, peppered with contemporary art galleries and a whole host of very cool bars, restaurants and clubs. **Hoxton** (to the north of Old Street) and **Shoreditch** (to the south) kicked off the East End transformation, but they have since been upstaged by **Dalston** (up Kingsland Road). There are few conventional sights as such in all three areas, though each one is stuffed full of art galleries, and their hip nightlife and shopping scenes keep them lively.

Tower Green

At the centre of the Inner Ward is village-like **Tower Green**, where, over the years, seven highly placed but unlucky individuals have been beheaded, among them Anne Boleyn and her cousin Catherine Howard (Henry VIII's second and fifth wives). The **White Tower**, which overlooks the Green, is the original "Tower", begun in 1078, and now home to displays from the **Royal Armouries**. Even if you've no interest in military paraphernalia, you should at least pay a visit to the **Chapel of St John**, a beautiful Norman structure on the second floor that was completed in 1080 – making it the oldest intact church building in London.

Crown Jewels

The **Waterloo Barracks**, to the north of the White Tower, hold the **Crown Jewels**; queues can be painfully long, however, and you only get to view the rocks from moving walkways. The vast majority of exhibits post-date the Commonwealth (1649–60), when many of the royal riches were melted down for coinage or sold off. Among the jewels are some of the largest cut diamonds in the world, plus the legendary **Koh-i-Noor**, which was set into the Queen Mother's Crown in 1937.

Tower Bridge

Daily: April–Sept 10am–6pm; Oct–March 9.30am–5.30pm • £8 • ☏ 020 7403 3761, ⓦ towerbridge.org.uk • ⊖ Tower Hill

Tower Bridge ranks with Big Ben as the most famous of all London landmarks. Completed in 1894, its neo-Gothic towers are clad in Cornish granite and Portland stone, but conceal a steel frame, which, at the time, represented a considerable engineering achievement, allowing a road crossing that could be raised to give tall ships access to the upper reaches of the Thames. The raising of the bascules (from the French for "see-saw") remains an impressive sight – phone ahead or check the website to find out when the bridge is being raised. If you buy a ticket, you get to walk across the elevated walkways linking the summits of the towers and visit the Tower's Victorian Engine Rooms, on the south side of the bridge, where you can see the now defunct giant coal-fired boilers which drove the hydraulic system until 1976, and play some interactive engineering games.

The East End

Few places in London have engendered so many myths as the **East End** (a catch-all title which covers just about everywhere east of the City). Its name is synonymous with slums, sweatshops and crime, as epitomized by figures such as Jack the Ripper and the Kray Twins, but also with the rags-to-riches success stories of a whole generations of Jews who were born in these cholera-ridden quarters and then moved to wealthier pastures.

Despite the transformation of much of the East End, and the fanfare around the 2012 **Olympic Park**, it's still not an obvious place for sightseeing, and – for the most part – still no beauty spot. Most visitors come here for its famous **Sunday markets**:

clothes and crafts in trendy Spitalfields, hip vintage gear around Brick Lane and flowers on Columbia Road. As for the East End **Docklands**, including the vast and awesome **Canary Wharf** redevelopment, most of it can be gawped at from the driverless, overhead **Docklands Light Railway** or DLR (see p.109), or from one of the boats that course up and down the Thames.

Spitalfields

Spitalfields, within sight of the sleek tower blocks of the financial sector, lies at the old heart of the East End, where the French Huguenots settled in the seventeenth century, where the Jewish community was at its strongest in the late nineteenth century, and where today's Bengali community eats, sleeps, works and prays. If you visit just one area in the East End, it should be this, which preserves mementos from each wave of immigration. The focal point of the area is **Spitalfields Market**, the red-brick and green-gabled market hall built in 1893, which is busiest on Sundays.

Dennis Severs' House

18 Folgate St • Mon noon–2pm • £7 • Sun noon–4pm • £10 • Silent Nights Mon & Wed 6–9pm • £14 • ☎ 020 7247 4013, ⓦ dennissevershouse.co.uk • ⊖ Liverpool Street

You can visit one of Spitalfields' characteristic eighteenth-century terraced houses at 18 Folgate St, where the American artist **Dennis Severs** lived until 1999. Eschewing all modern conveniences, Severs lived under candlelight, decorating his house as it would have been two hundred years ago. The public were invited to share in the experience that he described as like "passing through a frame into a painting". Today visitors are free to explore the cluttered, candlelit rooms, which resonate with the distinct impression that the resident Huguenot family has just popped out: not least due to the smell of cooked food and the sound of horses' hooves on the cobbles outside.

V&A Museum of Childhood

Cambridge Heath Rd • Daily 10am–5.45pm • Free • ☎ 020 8983 5200, ⓦ www.museumofchildhood.org.uk • ⊖ Bethnal Green

The East End's most popular museum is the **V&A Museum of Childhood**. The open-plan, wrought-iron hall, originally part of (and still a branch of) the V&A (see p.93), was transported here in the 1860s to bring art to the East End. On the ground floor you'll see clockwork **toys** – everything from classic robots to a fully functioning model railway – marionettes and puppets, teddies and Smurfs and even Inuit dolls. The most famous exhibits are the remarkable antique **dolls' houses** dating back to 1673, now displayed upstairs, where you'll also find a play area for very small kids and the museum's special exhibitions.

QUEEN ELIZABETH OLYMPIC PARK

The focus of the 2012 Olympics was the **Olympic Park** laid out over a series of islands formed by the River Lee and various tributaries and canals. Since the Olympics, the whole area has been replanted with patches of grass, trees and flowers and peppered with cafés, making it a great new park in which to hangout on a sunny day. The centrepiece of the park is the **Olympic Stadium**, set to become home to West Ham United football club in 2015. Standing close to the stadium is the **Orbit** tower (daily: April–Sept 11am–6pm; Oct–March 11am–5pm; £15), a 377ft-high continuous loop of red recycled steel designed by Anish Kapoor. But the most eye-catching venue is Zaha Hadid's wave-like **Aquatics Centre**, four times over budget, but looking very cool and costing under £5 for a swim. Other venues to lok out for are the curvy **Velodrome**, with its banked, Siberian pine track and adjacent BMX circuit, and the Copper Box, used for handball during the games, now a multi-sports centre. The nearest **tube** is Stratford, near the Olympic Village (now renamed East Village) and the Westfield shopping centre.

1

Docklands

Built in the nineteenth century to cope with the huge volume of goods shipped along the Thames from all over the Empire, **Docklands** was once the largest enclosed cargo-dock system in the world. When the docks closed in the 1960s the area was generally regarded as having died forever, but regeneration in the 1980s brought luxury flats and, on the Isle of Dogs, a huge high-rise office development. Here, at **Canary Wharf**, Cesar Pelli's landmark stainless steel tower **One Canada Square** remains an icon on the city's eastern skyline. The excellent **Museum of London Docklands** (daily 10am–6pm; free), in an old warehouse in Canary Wharf, charts the history of the area from Roman times to the present day.

The South Bank

The **South Bank** has a lot going for it. As well as the massive waterside **Southbank Centre**, it's home to a host of tourist attractions including the enormously popular **London Eye**. With most of London sitting on the north bank of the Thames, the views from here are the best on the river, and thanks to the wide, traffic-free riverside boulevard, the whole area can be happily explored on foot. Just a short walk away lies the absorbing **Imperial War Museum**, which will be commemorating the First World War over the next few years and contains the country's only permanent exhibition devoted to the Holocaust.

Southbank Centre

Ⓦ southbankcentre.co.uk • ⊖ Waterloo or Embankment

In 1951, the South Bank Exhibition, on derelict land south of the Thames, formed the centrepiece of the national **Festival of Britain**, an attempt to revive morale postwar by celebrating the centenary of the Great Exhibition (when Britain really did rule over half the world). The most striking features of the site were the Ferris wheel (now reincarnated as the London Eye), the saucer-shaped Dome of Discovery (inspiration for the Millennium Dome), the Royal Festival Hall (which still stands) and the cigar-shaped steel-and-aluminium Skylon tower (yet to be revived).

The Festival of Britain's success provided the impetus for the creation of the **Southbank Centre**, home to artistic institutions such as the Royal Festival Hall, the Hayward Gallery, the BFI Southbank arts cinema, and the National Theatre (see p.127). Its unprepossessing concrete appearance is softened by its riverside location, its avenue of trees, its buskers and skateboarders, the weekend foodstalls behind the RFH and the busy secondhand bookstalls outside the BFI Southbank.

London Eye

Daily: 10am–8.30pm or later • From £17 online • ☎ 0871 781 3000, Ⓦ londoneye.com • ⊖ Waterloo or Westminster

Despite being little more than ten years old, the **London Eye** is one of the city's most famous landmarks. Standing an impressive 443ft high, it's the largest Ferris wheel in Europe, weighing over two thousand tonnes, yet as simple and delicate as a bicycle wheel. It's constantly in slow motion, which means a full-circle "circuit" in one of its 32 pods (one for each of the city's boroughs) should take around thirty minutes: that may seem a long time but in fact it passes incredibly quickly. Book online (to save money), but note that unless you've paid extra you'll still have to queue to get on. Tickets are also sold from the box office at the eastern end of County Hall.

London Aquarium

County Hall • Mon–Thurs 10am–6pm, Fri–Sun 10am–7pm • From £16 online • ☎ 08/1 663 1679, Ⓦ visitsealife.co.uk • ⊖ Waterloo or Westminster

The most popular attraction in County Hall – the giant building beside the London Eye – is the **Sea Life London Aquarium**, spread across three subterranean levels. With some super-large tanks, and everything from dog-face puffers and piranhas to robot fish (seriously) and crocodiles, this is an attraction that is almost guaranteed to please kids, albeit at a price (book online to save a few quid and to avoid queuing or save £5 by buying an after 3pm ticket). Impressive in scale, the aquarium boasts a thrilling Shark Walk, in which sharks swim beneath you, as well as a replica blue whale skeleton encasing an underwater walkway.

London Dungeon

County Hall • Mon & Wed–Fri 10am–5pm, Thurs 11am–5pm, Sat & Sun 10am–6pm; school holidays closes 7pm • from £22 online • ☎ 0871 423 2240, Ⓦ thedungeons.com • ⊖ Waterloo or Westminster

The latest venture to join in the shenanigans at County Hall is the **London Dungeon,** an orgy of Gothic horror and one of the city's major crowd-pleasers – to avoid queuing (and save money), buy your ticket online. Young teenagers and the credulous probably get the most out of the various ludicrous live-action scenarios through which visitors are herded, each one hyped up by the team of costumed ham-actors. These are followed by a series of fairly lame horror rides such as "Henry's Wrath Boat Ride" and a "Drop Dead Drop Ride", not to mention the latest "Jack the Ripper Experience".

1

Imperial War Museum

Lambeth Rd • Daily 10am–6pm • Free • ☎ 020 7416 5000, ⓦ london.iwm.org.uk • ⊖ Lambeth North or Elephant & Castle

Housed in a domed building that was once the infamous lunatic asylum "Bedlam", the superb **Imperial War Museum** holds by far the best military museum in the capital. The treatment of the subject is impressively wide-ranging and fairly sober, with the main hall's militaristic display offset by the lower-ground-floor array of documents and images attesting to the human damage of war. The museum also has a harrowing **Holocaust Exhibition** (not recommended for children under 14), which you enter from the third floor. Pulling few punches, this has made a valiant attempt to avoid depicting the victims of the Holocaust as nameless masses by focusing on individual cases, and interspersing the archive footage with eyewitness accounts from contemporary survivors.

Southwark

In Tudor and Stuart London, the chief reason for crossing the Thames to what is now **Southwark** was to visit the disreputable Bankside entertainment district around the south end of London Bridge. Four hundred years on, Londoners are heading to the area once more, thanks to a wealth of top attractions – led by the mighty **Tate Modern** – that pepper the traffic-free riverside path between Blackfriars Bridge and Tower Bridge. The area is conveniently linked to St Paul's and the City by the fabulous Norman Foster-designed **Millennium Bridge**, London's first pedestrian-only bridge.

Tate Modern

Bankside • Daily 10am–6pm, Fri & Sat till 10pm • Free; multimedia guides £4 • ☎ 020 7887 8888, ⓦ tate.org.uk • ⊖ Southwark or Blackfriars

Bankside is dominated by the awesome **Tate Modern**. Originally designed as an oil-fired power station by Giles Gilbert Scott, this austere, brick-built "cathedral of power" was converted into a splendid modern art gallery in 2000. The best way to enter is down the ramp from the west so that you get the full effect of the stupendously large turbine hall. It's easy enough to find your way around the galleries, with levels 2, 3 and 4 displaying the permanent collection, and levels 2 and 3 also putting on fee-paying special exhibitions – level 7 is home to a bar/restaurant with a great view over the

1

Thames. Along with the free guided tours and multimedia guides, various apps are available and the Tate has free wi-fi.

Works are grouped thematically and although the displays change every year or so, you're still pretty much guaranteed to see works by **Monet** and Bonnard, Cubist pioneers **Picasso** and Braque, Surrealists such as **Dalí**, abstract artists like **Mondrian**, Bridget Riley and Pollock, and Pop supremos **Warhol** and Lichtenstein. And such is the space here that several artists get whole rooms to themselves, among them Joseph Beuys, with his shamanistic wax and furs, and **Mark Rothko**, whose abstract "Seagram Murals", originally destined for a posh restaurant in New York, have their own shrine like room in the heart of the collection.

Shakespeare's Globe

21 New Globe Walk · Exhibition daily 9am–5.30pm · £13.50 · ☎ 020 7902 1400, ⓦ shakespearesglobe.com · ⊖ Southwark or London Bridge

Dwarfed by Tate Modern, but equally remarkable in its own way, **Shakespeare's Globe Theatre** is a reconstruction of the open-air polygonal playhouse where most of the Bard's later works were first performed. The theatre, which boasts the first new thatched roof in central London since the Great Fire of 1666 – and the first candle-lit indoor theatre since the advent of electricity – puts on plays by Shakespeare and his contemporaries, both outside and in the indoor Sam Wanamaker Playhouse. To find out more about Shakespeare and the history of Bankside, the Globe's stylish **exhibition** is well worth a visit. You can have a virtual play on medieval instruments such as the crumhorn or sackbut, prepare your own edition of Shakespeare, and feel the thatch, hazelnut-shell and daub used to build the theatre. There's also an informative **guided tour** round the two theatres – during the summer season, in afternoons, you get to visit the exhibition and the remains of the nearby Rose Theatre instead.

Golden Hinde

St Mary Overie Dock · Mon–Sat 10am–5.30pm, Sun 10am–5pm, but phone ahead · £6 · ☎ 020 7403 0123, ⓦ goldenhinde.com · ⊖ London Bridge

An exact replica of the **Golden Hinde**, the galleon in which Francis Drake sailed around the world from 1577 to 1580, nestles in St Mary Overie Dock, at the

1

eastern end of Clink Street. The ship is surprisingly small, and its original crew of eighty-plus must have been cramped to say the least. There's a lack of interpretive panels, so it's worth paying the little bit extra and getting a guided tour from one of the folk in period costume – ring ahead to check that a group hasn't booked the place up.

Southwark Cathedral

Mon–Fri 8am–6pm, Sat & Sun 11am–5pm • Free • ☎ 020 7367 6734, ⓦ southwarkcathedral.org.uk • ⊖ London Bridge

Close by the *Golden Hinde* stands **Southwark Cathedral**, built as the medieval Augustinian priory church of St Mary Overie, and given cathedral status only in 1905. Of the original thirteenth-century church, only the choir and retrochoir now remain, separated by a tall and beautiful stone Tudor screen, making them probably the oldest Gothic structures left in London. The nave was entirely rebuilt in the nineteenth century, but the cathedral contains numerous interesting monuments, from a thirteenth-century oak effigy of a knight to an early twentieth-century memorial to Shakespeare.

Borough Market

8 Southwark St • Mon–Wed 10am–3pm, Thurs 11am–5pm, Fri noon–6pm, Sat 8am–5pm • ☎ 020 7407 1002, ⓦ boroughmarket.org.uk • ⊖ London Bridge

Borough Market is tucked beneath the railway arches between Borough High Street and Southwark Cathedral. The early-morning wholesale fruit and vegetable market winds up around 8am and is one of the few still trading under its original Victorian wrought-iron shed. But the market is best known nowadays for its busy specialist food market, with stalls selling top-quality and pricey produce from around the world – it's very popular so get there early on Friday and Saturday.

The Shard

32 London Bridge • Daily 9am–10pm• From £25 online • ☎ 0844 499 7111, ⓦ theviewfromtheshard.com • ⊖ London Bridge

It's hard to justify the hubristic (Qatari-funded) Shard, London's – and the country's – tallest building. Even less justifiable are the ticket prices to reach the top floors of Renzo Piano's 1016ft-high, tapered, glass-clad skyscraper. Still, once you're there, if you can ignore the New Age muzak, the views are sublime, making everything else in London look small, from the unicycle of the London Eye to the tiny box that is St Paul's Cathedral, while the model railway of London Bridge is played out below you.

Old Operating Theatre Museum and Herb Garret

St Thomas St • Daily 10.30am–5pm; closed mid-Dec to early Jan • £6.50 • ☎ 020 7188 2679, ⓦ thegarret.org.uk • ⊖ London Bridge

By far the most educative and the strangest of Southwark's museums is the **Old Operating Theatre Museum and Herb Garret**. Built in 1821 up a spiral staircase at the top of a church tower, where the hospital apothecary's herbs were stored, this women's operating theatre was once adjacent to the women's ward of St Thomas' Hospital (now in Lambeth). Despite being gore-free, the museum is as stomach-churning as the nearby London Dungeon (see p.87). The surgeons who used this room would have concentrated on speed and accuracy (most amputations took less than a minute), but there was still a thirty percent mortality rate, with many patients simply dying of shock, and many more from bacterial infection.

London Bridge Experience

2–4 Tooley St • Mon–Fri & Sun 10am–5pm, Sat 10am–6pm • from £18 online • ☎ 0800 043 4666, ✆ thelondonbridgeexperience.com • ⊖ London Bridge

With the London Dungeon now in County Hall (see p.87), Gothic horror fans should head instead to this slightly more historically pertinent scarefest. First off, it's a theatrical trot through the history of London Bridge, with guides in period garb hamming up the gory bits. Then, in case you're not scared enough yet, in the **London Tombs** section (no under 11s), more actors, dressed as zombies and murderers, leap out of the fog to frighten the wits out of you.

HMS Belfast

The Queen's Walk • Daily: March–Oct 10am–6pm; Nov–Feb 10am–5pm • £14 • ☎ 020 7940 6300, ✆ iwm.org.uk • ⊖ London Bridge

HMS Belfast, a World War II cruiser, is permanently moored between London Bridge and Tower Bridge. Armed with six torpedoes, and six-inch guns with a range of more than fourteen miles, the *Belfast* spent over two years of the war in the Royal Naval shipyards after being hit by a mine in the Firth of Forth at the beginning of hostilities. It later saw action in the Barents Sea during World War II and during the Korean War, before being decommissioned. The maze of cabins is fun to explore but if you want to find out more about the *Belfast*, head for the exhibition rooms in zone 5.

City Hall

The Queen's Walk • Mon–Thurs 8.30am–6pm, Fri 8.30am–5.30pm • Free • ☎ 020 7983 4000, ✆ london.gov.uk • ⊖ London Bridge

East of the *Belfast*, overlooking the river, Norman Foster's startling glass-encased **City Hall** looks like a giant car headlight or fencing mask, and serves as the headquarters for the Greater London Authority and the Mayor of London. Visitors are welcome to stroll up the helical walkway, visit the café and watch proceedings from the second floor.

Kensington and Chelsea

Hyde Park and **Kensington Gardens** cover a distance of a mile and a half from Oxford Street in the northeast to Kensington Palace, set in the Royal Borough of **Kensington** and **Chelsea**. Other districts go in and out of fashion, but this area has been in vogue ever since royalty moved into **Kensington Palace** in the late seventeenth century.

The most popular tourist attractions lie in **South Kensington**, where three of London's top **museums** – the Victoria and Albert, Natural History and Science museums – stand on land bought with the proceeds of the 1851 Great Exhibition. Chelsea, to the south, has a slightly more bohemian pedigree. In the 1960s, the **King's Road** carved out its reputation as London's catwalk, while in the late 1970s it was the epicentre of the punk explosion. Nothing so rebellious goes on in Chelsea now, though its residents like to think of themselves as rather more artistic and intellectual than the purely moneyed types of Kensington.

Hyde Park and Kensington Gardens

Hyde Park Daily 5am–midnight **Kensington Gardens** Daily 6am–dusk • ☎ 0300 061 2000, ✆ royalparks.gov.uk • ⊖ Hyde Park Corner, Marble Arch, Knightsbridge or Lancaster Gate

Hangings, muggings, duels and the 1851 Great Exhibition are just some of the public events that have taken place in **Hyde Park**, which remains a popular spot for political demonstrations and pop concerts. For most of the time, however, the park is simply a lazy leisure ground – a wonderful open space that allows you to lose all sight of the city beyond a few persistent tower blocks.

1

The park is divided in two by the **Serpentine**, which has a pretty upper section known as the **Long Water**, which narrows until it reaches a group of four fountains. In the southern section, you'll find the popular **Lido** (mid-June to mid-Sept daily 10am–6pm; £4.50) on its south bank and the **Diana Memorial Fountain** (daily: March & Oct 10am–6pm; April–Aug 10am–8pm; Sept 10am–7pm; Nov–Feb 10am–4pm), less of a fountain and more of a giant oval-shaped mini-moat. The western half of the park is, in fact, officially known as **Kensington Gardens**; its two most popular attractions are the **Serpentine Gallery**, which puts on contemporary art exhibitions, and the overblown **Albert Memorial**.

Marble Arch

At Hyde Park's treeless northeastern corner is **Marble Arch**, erected in 1828 as a triumphal entry to Buckingham Palace, but now stranded on a busy traffic island at the west end of Oxford Street. This is a historically charged piece of land, as it marks the site of **Tyburn gallows**, the city's main public execution spot until 1783. It's also the location of **Speakers' Corner**, a peculiarly English Sunday morning tradition, featuring an assembly of ranters and hecklers.

Wellington Arch

Hyde Park Corner • Daily: April–Sept 10am–6pm; Oct 10am–5pm; Nov–March 10am–4pm • £4.20; EH • ⊖ Hyde Park Corner

At the southeast corner of Hyde Park, the **Wellington Arch** stands in the midst of **Hyde Park Corner**, one of London's busiest traffic interchanges. Erected in 1828, the arch was originally topped by an equestrian statue of the Duke himself, later replaced by Peace driving a four-horse chariot. Inside, you can view an exhibition on the history of the arch, and of London's outdoor sculpture, and take a lift to the top of the monument where the exterior balconies offer a bird's-eye view of the swirling traffic.

Apsley House

149 Piccadilly • Wed–Sun: April–Oct 11am–5pm; Nov–March 11am–4pm • EH • £6.90 • ⊖ Hyde Park Corner

Overlooking the traffic whizzing round Hyde Park Corner is **Apsley House**, Wellington's London residence and now a museum to the "Iron Duke". The highlight is the **art collection**, much of which used to belong to the King of Spain. Among the best pieces, displayed in the Waterloo Gallery on the first floor, are works by de Hooch, Van Dyck, Velázquez, Goya, Rubens and Correggio. The famous, more than twice life-size, nude statue of Napoleon by Antonio Canova stands at the foot of the main staircase.

Serpentine Gallery

Daily 10am–6pm; Teahouse mid-June to mid-Oct • Free • ⊖ Knightsbridge or South Kensington

In the southeast corner of Kensington Gardens stands the **Serpentine Gallery** built as a tearoom in 1908, but used as an a contemporary art gallery since the 1960s – and, more recently, the gallery has commissioned a leading architect to design a summer tea pavilion extension each year. A second exhibition space, the **Serpentine Sackler Gallery**, is housed in a former munitions depot nearby, with a permanent tearoom on the side, designed by Zaha Hadid.

Albert Memorial

Guided tours March–Dec first Sun of month 2pm & 3pm; 45min; £7 • ☎ 020 7495 0916 • ⊖ Knightsbridge or South Kensington

Erected in 1876, the richly decorated, High Gothic **Albert Memorial** is as much a hymn to the glorious achievements of Britain as to its subject, Queen Victoria's husband, who died of typhoid in 1861. Albert occupies the central canopy, gilded from head to toe and clutching a catalogue for the 1851 Great Exhibition that he helped to organize.

Royal Albert Hall

Kensington Gore • Guided tours from door 12 daily except Wed 10.30am–3.30pm; £8.50 • ☎ 020 7838 3105, ⓦ royalalberthall.com •
⊖ South Kensington or High Street Kensington

The 1851 Exhibition's most famous feature – the gargantuan glasshouse of the Crystal
Palace – no longer exists, but the profits were used to buy a large tract of land south of
the park, now home to South Kensington's remarkable cluster of museums and
colleges, plus the vast **Royal Albert Hall**, a splendid iron-and-glass-domed concert hall
with an exterior of red brick, terracotta and marble that became the hallmark of South
Ken architecture. The hall is the venue for Europe's most democratic music festival, the
Henry Wood Promenade Concerts, better known as the **Proms** (see box, p.129).

Kensington Palace

Kensington Gardens • Daily: Easter–Oct 10am–6pm; Nov–Easter 10am–5pm • £15.40 • ☎ 020 3166 6000, ⓦ hrp.org.uk • ⊖ Queensway
or High Street Kensington

Bought by William and Mary in 1689, the modestly proportioned Jacobean brick
mansion of **Kensington Palace** was the chief royal residence for the next fifty years. KP,
as it's fondly known in royal circles, is best known today as the place where Princess
Diana lived from her marriage until her death in 1997. Today, it's the official residence
of a number of royals including Prince William and Kate Middleton.

The palace is home to the **Royal Ceremonial Dress Collection**, which means you
usually get to see a few of the frocks worn by Diana, as well as several of the Queen's
dresses. The highlights of the King's state apartments are the trompe-l'oeil ceiling
paintings by William Kent, particularly those in the Cupola Room, and the paintings
in the King's Gallery by, among others, Tintoretto. Also of interest in the King's Gallery
is the wind dial above the fireplace, connected to the palace weather vane, which was
built for William III and is still fully functioning.

In the more modest Queen's state apartments, the curators have stepped up the
multimedia theatrics to tell the sad story of Queen Anne, whose eighteen children
all predeceased her. On the ground floor, you can learn about **Queen Victoria**, who
spent an unhappy childhood in the palace, under the steely gaze of her strict
German mother. According to her diary, her best friends were the palace's numerous
"black beetles".

Leighton House

12 Holland Park Rd • Daily except Tues 10am–5.30pm • £7 • ⓦ rbkc.gov.uk/museums • ⊖ High Street Kensington

Several wealthy Victorian artists rather self-consciously founded an artists' colony in
the streets that lay to the west of Kensington Gardens. "It will be opulence, it will be
sincerity", Lord Leighton opined before starting work on the remarkable **Leighton
House** in the 1860s – he later became President of the Royal Academy and was
ennobled on his deathbed. The big attraction is the domed **Arab Hall**, decorated with
Saracen tiles, gilded mosaics and latticework drawn from all over the Islamic world.
The other rooms are hung with paintings by Lord Leighton and his Pre-Raphaelite
chums – there's even a Tintoretto.

Victoria and Albert Museum (V&A)

Cromwell Rd • Daily 10am–5.45pm, Fri till 10pm • Free • ☎ 020 7942 2000, ⓦ vam.ac.uk • ⊖ South Kensington

For sheer variety and scale, the **Victoria and Albert Museum** is the greatest museum of
applied arts in the world. Beautifully but haphazardly displayed across a seven-mile,
four-storey maze of rooms, the V&A's treasures are impossible to survey in a single
visit; get hold of a floor plan to help you decide which areas to concentrate on, and
look out for the various free tours that set off from the main information desk in the

1

CHELSEA TO NOTTING HILL

1

■ ACCOMMODATION

Aster House	9
Lincoln House	1
Meininger	6
Morgan House	11
Nadler Kensington	7
Portobello Gold	2
Twenty Nevern Square	8
Vancouver Studios	3
Vicarage Hotel	4
YHA Earl's Court	10
YHA Holland Park	5

● RESTAURANTS

Le Café Anglais	6
Dinner by Heston Blumenthal	8
Hereford Road	10
Medlar	1
The Providores and Tapa Room	2

● CAFÉS & SNACKS

Books for Cooks	3
Capote y Toros	9
Comptoir Libanais	7
Lisboa Patisserie	1
Patisserie Valerie at Sagne	4

■ PUBS & BARS

Churchill Arms	3
Cooper's Arms Bar	6
The Elgin	1
Grenadier	4
The Nag's Head	5
The Pig's Ear	7

■ LIVE MUSIC VENUE

Notting Hill Arts Club	2

● SHOPS

Daunt Books	3
Harrods	7
Harvey Nichols	6
Honest Jon's	2
Portobello Road Market	1
Rough Trade	4
Selfridges	5

1

Grand Entrance. And if you're flagging, head for the edifying café in the museum's period-piece Morris, Gamble & Poynter Rooms.

Whatever your taste, there's bound to be something to grab your attention: the finest collection of Italian sculpture outside Italy, the world's largest collection of Indian art outside India, plus extensive Chinese, Islamic and Japanese galleries; a gallery of twentieth-century objets d'art; and more Constable paintings than Tate Britain. Among the other highlights are the justifiably popular Jewellery section, the beautifully designed British Galleries, the Costume rooms and the fascinating Theatre & Performance rooms which house the collection of the former Covent Garden Theatre Museum. In addition, the V&A's temporary shows on art, photography and fashion – some of which you have to pay for – are among the best in Britain.

Science Museum

Exhibition Rd • Daily 10am–6pm • Free • ☏ 0870 870 4868, ⓦ sciencemuseum.org.uk • ⊖ South Kensington

Established as a technological counterpart to the V&A, the **Science Museum** is undeniably impressive, filling seven floors with items drawn from every conceivable area of science, with hands-on galleries that appeal to adults and kids.

Stop first at the **information desk**, pick up a museum plan and check the daily events schedule; you can also sign up for a free **guided tour** on a specific subject. Most people will want to head for the **Wellcome Wing**, full of state-of-the-art interactive computers and an IMAX cinema (tickets £10), and geared to appeal to even the most museum-phobic teenager. To get there, you must pass through the Making of the Modern World, a display of iconic inventions from Robert Stephenson's *Rocket* train of 1829 to the Ford Model T, the world's first mass-produced car.

Those with kids should head for the popular Launchpad, the museum's busiest interactive gallery on Floor 3. The Challenge of Materials gallery, on Floor 1, is aimed more at adults, and is an extremely stylish exhibition covering the use of materials ranging from aluminium to zerodur (used for making laser gyroscopes), while Energy, on Floor 2, has a great "do not touch" electric-shock machine that absolutely fascinates kids.

Natural History Museum

Cromwell Rd • Daily 10am–5.50pm • Free • ☏ 020 7942 5000, ⓦ nhm.ac.uk • ⊖ South Kensington

Alfred Waterhouse's purpose-built mock-Romanesque colossus ensures the status of the **Natural History Museum** as London's most handsome museum, both an important resource for serious zoologists and a major tourist attraction.

The main entrance leads to the **Blue Zone**, which includes the ever-popular Dinosaur gallery, with its grisly life-sized **animatronic dinosaurs**. Popular sections over in the **Green Zone** include the Creepy-Crawlies, and the excellent **Investigate** gallery, where children aged 7 to 14 get to play at being scientists (you need to obtain a timed ticket).

Little visited, compared to the rest of the museum, the **Darwin Centre** – also known as the **Orange Zone** – is dominated by the giant concrete **Cocoon**, home to more than twenty million specimens. Visitors can take the lift to the seventh floor and enter the Cocoon to learn more about the history of the collection, about taxonomy and the research and field trips the museum funds. In the nearby **Zoology spirit building**, you can view a small selection of bits and bobs pickled in glass jars, but if you want to join one of the **guided tours** that take you behind the scenes, you need to book on the day.

If the queues for the museum are long (as they can be at weekends and during school holidays), head for the side entrance on Exhibition Road, which leads into the former Geology Museum, now known as the **Red Zone**, a visually exciting romp through the

1

earth's evolution. The most popular sections are the slightly tasteless Kobe earthquake simulator, and the spectacular display of gems and crystals in the Earth's Treasury.

Chelsea

From the Swinging Sixties up until the era of Punk, **Chelsea** had a slightly bohemian pedigree; these days, it's just another wealthy west London suburb. Among the most nattily attired of all those parading down the King's Road nowadays are the scarlet- or navy-blue-clad Chelsea Pensioners, army veterans from the nearby **Royal Hospital**.

Saatchi Gallery

King's Rd • Daily 10am–6pm • Free • ☎ 020 7811 3070, ⊚ saatchi-gallery.co.uk • ⊖ Sloane Square

On the south side of the King's Road, a short stroll from Sloane Square, the former **Duke of York's HQ**, built in 1801, is now the unlikely home of the **Saatchi Gallery**, which puts on changing exhibitions of contemporary art in its whitewashed rooms. Charles Saatchi, the collector behind the gallery, was the man who introduced Young British Artists (YBAs) like Damien Hirst, Sarah Lucas, Tracey Emin and Rachel Whiteread to the world in the 1990s.

Royal Hospital

Royal Hospital Rd • Mon–Sat 11am–noon & 2–4pm, Sun 2–4pm • Free • ☎ 020 7881 5200, ⊚ chelsea-pensioners.co.uk • ⊖ Sloane Square

Founded as a retirement home for army veterans by Charles II in 1682, and designed by Christopher Wren, the **Royal Hospital**'s majestic red-brick wings and grassy courtyards became a blueprint for institutional and collegiate architecture all over the English-speaking world. The public are welcome to view the austere hospital chapel, and the equally grand, wood-panelled dining hall, opposite, where three hundred or so Pensioners still eat under the royal portraits and the vast allegorical mural of Charles II. On the east side of the hospital, a small **museum** displays Pensioners' uniforms, medals and two German bombs.

National Army Museum

Royal Hospital Rd • Daily 10am–5.30pm • Free • ☎ 020 7881 6606, ⊚ nam.ac.uk • ⊖ Sloane Square

The concrete bunker next door to the Royal Hospital, on Royal Hospital Road, houses the **National Army Museum**. There are plenty of interesting historical artefacts, a top-class art gallery, plus an impressive array of uniforms and medals, a model of Waterloo and the skeleton of Napoleon's horse, Marengo, but for a more nuanced exploration of war, you're better off visiting the Imperial War Museum (see p.88).

North London

Almost all of **North London**'s suburbs are easily accessible by tube from the centre, though just a handful of these satellite villages, now subsumed into the general mass of the city, are worth bothering with. First off, you should explore one of London's finest parks, **Regent's Park**, home to London Zoo; **Camden Town**, famous for its huge weekend market, is nearby. The highlights, however, are the village-like suburbs of **Hampstead** and **Highgate**, on the edge of London's wildest patch of greenery, **Hampstead Heath**.

Regent's Park

Daily from 5am • Free • ☎ 0300 061 2300, ⊚ royalparks.org.uk • ⊖ Regent's Park, Baker Street, Great Portland Street, St John's Wood or Camden Town

Regent's Park is one of London's smartest parks, with a boating lake, ornamental ponds, waterfalls and some lovely gardens. Under the reign of the Prince Regent (later George

1

IV), the park was to be girded by a continuous belt of terraces, and sprinkled with a total of 56 villas, including a magnificent royal palace. Inevitably, the plan was never fully realized, but enough was built to create something of the idealized garden city that Nash and the Prince Regent had envisaged. Within the Inner Circle, the **Queen Mary's Gardens** are by far the prettiest section of the park. Prominent on the skyline is the shiny copper dome of **London Central Mosque** at 146 Park Road, an entirely appropriate addition given the Prince Regent's taste for the Orient.

London Zoo

Daily: March–Oct 10am 6pm; Nov–Feb 10am–4pm • £22 • ☎ 0844 225 1826, ⓦ zsl.org • ⊖ Camden Town

The northeastern corner of the park is occupied by **London Zoo**. Founded in 1826 with the remnants of the royal menagerie, the enclosures here are as humane as any inner-city zoo could make them, and kids usually enjoy themselves. The invertebrate house, now known as BUGS, the Gorilla Kingdom, the African Bird Safari, and the walk-through rainforest and monkey enclosure are guaranteed winners.

Camden Town

For all its tourist popularity, **Camden Market** remains a genuinely offbeat place. The sheer variety of what's on offer – from cheap CDs to furniture, along with a mass of street fashion and clubwear, and plenty of food stalls – is what makes **Camden Town** so special. More than 100,000 shoppers turn up here each weekend, and most parts of the market now stay open week-long, alongside a crop of shops, cafés and bistros.

Jewish Museum

129 Albert St • Sat–Thurs 10am–5pm, Fri 10am–2pm • £7.50 • ☎ 020 7284 7384, ⓦ jewishmuseum.org.uk • ⊖ Camden Town

Despite having no significant Jewish associations, Camden is home to London's purpose-built **Jewish Museum**. On the first floor, there's an engaging exhibition explaining Jewish practices, illustrated by cabinets of Judaica. On the second floor, there's a special Holocaust gallery which tells the story of Leon Greenman (1920–2008), one of only two British Jews who suffered and survived Auschwitz. The museum also puts on a lively programme of special exhibitions, discussions and concerts, and has a café on the ground floor.

Hampstead

Perched on a hill to the west of Hampstead Heath, **Hampstead** village developed into a fashionable spa in the eighteenth century, and was not much altered thereafter. Later, it became one of the city's most celebrated literary *quartiers* and even now it retains its reputation as a bolt hole of the high-profile intelligentsia and discerning pop stars. Proximity to **Hampstead Heath** is, of course, the real joy of Hampstead; this mixture of

---

REGENT'S CANAL BY BOAT

Three companies run daily **boat services** between Camden and Little Venice, passing through the Maida Hill tunnel. The narrowboat *Jenny Wren* (March Sat & Sun; April–Oct daily; ☎ 020 7485 4433, ⓦ walkersquay.com) starts off at Camden, goes through a canal lock (the only company to do so) and heads for Little Venice (with live commentary), while *Jason's* narrowboats (April–Oct daily; ☎ 020 7286 3428, ⓦ jasons.co.uk) start off at Little Venice (live commentary); the London Waterbus Company (April–Sept daily; Oct Thurs–Sun only; Nov–March Sat & Sun only, weather permitting; ☎ 020 7482 2550, ⓦ londonwaterbus.com) sets off from both places and calls at London Zoo. Whichever you choose, you can board at either end; **tickets** cost around £12 return, and journey time is 45 minutes one-way.

1

woodland, smooth pasture and landscaped garden is quite simply the most exhilarating patch of greenery in London.

Keats' House

Keats Grove • March–Oct Tues–Sun 1–5pm; Nov–Feb Fri–Sun 1–5pm • £5.50 • ☎ 020 7332 3868, Ⓦ cityoflondon.gov.uk • ⊖ Hampstead or Hampstead Heath Overground

Hampstead's most illustrious figure is celebrated at **Keats' House**, an elegant, whitewashed Regency double villa off Downshire Hill at the bottom of the High Street. Inspired by the tranquillity of Hampstead and by his passion for girl-next-door Fanny Brawne (whose house is also part of the museum), Keats wrote some of his most famous works here before leaving for Rome, where he died of consumption in 1821, aged just 25. The neat, rather staid interior contains books and letters, Fanny's engagement ring and the four-poster bed in which the poet first coughed up blood, confiding to his companion, Charles Brown, "that drop of blood is my death warrant".

2 Willow Road

March–Oct Wed–Sun 11am–5pm • £6 • ☎ 020 7435 6166, Ⓦ nationaltrust.org.uk • ⊖ Hampstead or Hampstead Heath Overground

An unassuming red-brick terraced house built in the 1930s by the Hungarian-born architect **Ernö Goldfinger** (1902–87), 2 Willow Road gives a fascinating insight into the modernist mindset. This was a state-of-the-art pad when Goldfinger moved in, and as he changed little during the following fifty years, what you see today is a 1930s avant-garde dwelling preserved in aspic, a house at once both modern and old-fashioned. An added bonus is that the rooms are packed with works of art by the likes of Bridget Riley, Duchamp, Henry Moore and Man Ray. Before 3pm, visits are by guided tour only (noon, 1 & 2pm); after 3pm, the public has unguided access.

Freud Museum

20 Maresfield Gardens • Wed–Sun noon–5pm • £7 • Ⓦ freud.org.uk • ⊖ Finchley Road

The **Freud Museum** is one of the most poignant of London's house museums. Having lived in Vienna for his entire adult life, the psychotherapist, by now semi-disabled and with only a year to live, was forced to flee the Nazis, arriving in London in the summer of 1938. The ground-floor study and library look exactly as they did when Freud lived here; the collection of erotic antiquities and the famous couch, sumptuously draped in Persian rugs, were all brought here from Vienna. Upstairs, home movies of family life are shown continually, and a small room is dedicated to his daughter, Anna, herself an influential child analyst, who lived in the house until her death in 1982.

Hampstead Heath

Daily 24hr • Free • ☎ 020 7332 3322, Ⓦ cityoflondon.gov.uk • Hampstead tube and Hampstead Heath or Gospel Oak Overground. Bus #210 from ⊖ Hampstead or Golders Green or Bus #24 from central London

Hampstead Heath may not have much of its original heathland left, but it packs a wonderful variety of bucolic scenery into its eight hundred acres. At its southern end are the rolling green pastures of **Parliament Hill**, north London's premier spot for kite flying. On either side are numerous ponds, three of which – one for men, one for women and one mixed – you can swim in. The thickest woodland is to be found in the **West Heath**, beyond Whitestone Pond, also the site of the most formal section, **Hill Garden**, a secretive and romantic little gem with eccentric balustraded terraces and a ruined pergola. Beyond lies **Golders Hill Park**, where you can gaze at pygmy goats and fallow deer, and inspect the impeccably maintained aviaries, home to flamingos, cranes and other exotic birds.

Kenwood House

Daily 10am–5pm • Free • ☎ 020 8348 1286, Ⓦ english-heritage.org.uk • Bus #210 from ⊖ Archway or Golders Green

Don't miss the landscaped grounds of Kenwood, in the north of the Heath, which are focused on the whitewashed Neoclassical mansion of **Kenwood House**. The house is

1

now home to a collection of seventeenth- and eighteenth-century art, including a handful of real masterpieces by Vermeer, Rembrandt, Boucher, Gainsborough and Reynolds. Of the period interiors, the most spectacular is Robert Adam's sky-blue and pink library.

Highgate Cemetery

Swain's Lane • **East Cemetery** April–Oct Mon–Fri 10am–5pm, Sat & Sun 11am–5pm; Nov–March closes 4pm • £4 **West Cemetery** March–Nov Mon–Fri 1.45pm, Sat & Sun every 30min 11am–4pm • £12 • No under-8s • ☎ 020 8340 1834, ⓦ highgate cemetery.org • ⊖ Highgate

Highgate Cemetery, ranged on both sides of Swain's Lane, is London's best-known graveyard. The most illustrious incumbent of the **East Cemetery** is **Karl Marx**. Marx himself asked for a simple grave topped by a headstone, but by 1954 the Communist movement decided to move his grave to a more prominent position and erect the hulking bronze bust that now surmounts a granite plinth. To visit the more atmospheric and overgrown **West Cemetery**, with its spooky Egyptian Avenue and sunken catacombs, you must take a guided tour. Among the prominent graves usually visited are those of artist Dante Gabriel Rossetti, and lesbian novelist Radclyffe Hall.

RAF Museum

Grahame Park Way • Daily 10am–6pm • Free • ☎ 020 8205 2266, ⓦ rafmuseum.org.uk • ⊖ Colindale

A world-class assembly of historic military aircraft can be seen at the **RAF Museum**, in the former Hendon Aerodrome beside the M1 motorway. Enthusiasts won't be disappointed, but anyone looking for a balanced account of modern aerial warfare should probably go to the Imperial War Museum (see p.88). Those with children should head for the hands-on Aeronauts gallery; those without might prefer to explore the often overlooked display galleries, ranged around the edge of the Main Aircraft Hall, which contain an art gallery and an exhibition on the history of flight, accompanied by replicas of some of the deathtraps of early aviation.

Neasden Temple

105–119 Brentfield Rd • Daily 9am–6pm • Temple (with audioguide) • Free; exhibition £2 • ☎ 020 8965 2651, ⓦ londonmandir.baps.org • ⊖ Neasden

Perhaps the most remarkable building in the whole of London lies just off the North Circular, in the glum suburb of Neasden. Here, rising majestically above the surrounding semi-detached houses, is the **Shri Swaminarayan Mandir**, a traditional Hindu temple topped with domes and *shikharas*, erected in 1995 in a style and scale unseen outside of India for over a millennium. You enter through the Haveli (cultural complex) and, after taking off your shoes, proceed to the Mandir (temple) itself, carved entirely out of Carrara marble, with every possible surface transformed into a honeycomb of arabesques, flowers and seated gods. Beneath the Mandir, an **exhibition** explains the basic tenets of Hinduism and details the life of Lord Swaminarayan, and includes a video about the history of the building.

South London

Now largely built up into a patchwork of Victorian terraces, **South London** nevertheless includes one outstanding area for sightseeing, and that is **Greenwich**, with its fantastic ensemble of the Royal Naval College and the Queen's House, the National Maritime Museum, the Royal Observatory, and the beautifully landscaped royal park. The only

1

other suburban sights that stand out are the **Dulwich Picture Gallery**, a public art gallery even older than the National Gallery, and the eclectic **Horniman Museum**, in neighbouring Forest Hill.

Greenwich

Greenwich draws tourists out from the centre in considerable numbers. At its heart is the outstanding architectural set piece of the **Old Royal Naval College** and the **Queen's House**, courtesy of Christopher Wren and Inigo Jones respectively. Most visitors, however, come to see the **Cutty Sark**, the **National Maritime Museum** and Greenwich Park's **Royal Observatory**. With the added attractions of its riverside pubs and walks – plus startling views across to Canary Wharf and Docklands – it makes for one of the best weekend trips in the capital. To reach Greenwich, you can take a **train** from London Bridge (every 30min), a **boat** from one of the piers in central London (every 20–30min), or the **DLR** to Cutty Sark station (every 4–10min).

Cutty Sark

King William Walk • Daily 10am–5pm • £12 • ☎ 020 8858 6608, ⓦ rmg.co.uk • Cutty Sark DLR

Wedged in a dry dock by the river is the majestic **Cutty Sark**, the world's last surviving tea clipper. Launched in 1869, the *Cutty Sark* was actually more famous in its day as a wool clipper, returning from Australia in just 72 days. The vessel's name comes from Robert Burns' *Tam O'Shanter*, in which Tam, a drunken farmer, is chased by Nannie, an angry witch in a short Paisley linen dress, or "cutty sark"; the clipper's figurehead shows her clutching the hair from the tail of Tam's horse. After a devastating fire in 2007, the ship has been beautifully restored and now includes a museum beneath the ship's copper-lined keel displaying a collection of more than eighty ships' figureheads.

Old Royal Naval College

Daily 10am–5pm • Free • ☎ 020 8269 4747, ⓦ ornc.org • Cutty Sark DLR

It's appropriate that the one London building that makes the most of its riverbank location should be the **Old Royal Naval College**, a majestic Baroque ensemble designed, for the most part, by Wren. Initially built as a royal palace, but eventually converted into the Royal Hospital for Seamen, the complex was later home to the Royal Naval College, but now houses the University of Greenwich and the Trinity College of Music. The two grandest rooms, situated underneath Wren's twin domes, are open to the public and well worth visiting. The **Chapel**, in the east wing, has exquisite pastel-shaded plasterwork and spectacular, decorative detailing on the ceiling, all designed by James "Athenian" Stuart after a fire in 1799 destroyed the original interior. Opposite the chapel is the magnificent **Painted Hall** in the west wing, which is dominated by James Thornhill's gargantuan allegorical ceiling painting, and his trompe-l'oeil fluted pilasters. Over in the Pepys Building, you can get a good overview of Greenwich's history in **Discover Greenwich**. The building also contains a tourist information office and the Royal Hospital's old brewhouse, which used to supply a ration of three pints to each seaman, and has now been revived and turned into a café/microbrewery.

National Maritime Museum

Romney Rd • Daily 10am–5pm • Free • ☎ 020 8858 4422, ⓦ rmg.co.uk • Cutty Sark DLR

The main building of the excellent **National Maritime Museum** is centred on a spectacular glass-roofed courtyard, which houses the museum's largest artefacts, among them the splendid 63ft-long gilded **Royal Barge**, designed in Rococo style by William Kent for Prince Frederick, the much unloved eldest son of George II. The various themed galleries are superbly designed to appeal to visitors of all ages, but if you have kids, head for Floor Two, where the **Children's Gallery** gives kids a taste of life on the sea, loading miniature cargo, firing a cannon, learning to use Morse Code and so forth.

Older children and adults alike will enjoy honing their ship-handling skills on the **Ship Simulator** next door.

Inigo Jones's **Queen's House**, originally built amid a rambling Tudor royal palace, is now the focal point of the Greenwich ensemble, and is an integral part of the Maritime Museum. As royal residences go, it's an unassuming country house, but as the first Neoclassical building in the country, it has enormous architectural significance. The interior currently houses the museum's **art collection** including works by painters as diverse as Reynolds and Lowry. Off the Great Hall, a perfect cube, lies the beautiful **Tulip Staircase**, Britain's earliest cantilevered spiral staircase – its name derives from the floral patterning in the wrought-iron balustrade.

Royal Observatory

Blackheath Ave · **Astronomy Centre** Daily 10am–5pm · Free **Flamsteed House** Daily 10am–5pm · £7 **Planetarium** Mon–Fri 12.45–3.45pm; Sat & Sun & school holidays noon–4pm · £6.50 · ☎ 020 8312 6565, ⓦ rmg.co.uk · Greenwich DLR/train station

Perched on the crest of Greenwich Park's highest hill, the **Royal Observatory** was established by Charles II in 1675. It's housed in a rather dinky Wren-built red-brick building, whose northeastern turret sports a bright-red time-ball that climbs the mast at 12.58pm and drops at 1pm GMT precisely; it was added in 1833 to allow ships on the Thameslink to set their clocks.

Greenwich's greatest claim to fame, of course, is as the home of **Greenwich Mean Time** (GMT) and the **Prime Meridian**. Since 1884, Greenwich has occupied zero longitude – hence the world sets its clocks by GMT. The observatory housed the first Astronomer Royal, John Flamsteed, whose chief task was to study the night sky in order to discover an astronomical method of finding the longitude of a ship at sea. Beyond the Octagon Room, where the king used to show off to his guests, are the Time galleries, which display four of the clocks designed by **John Harrison**, including "H4", which helped win the Longitude Prize in 1763.

The **Astronomy Centre** houses high-tech galleries giving a brief rundown of the Big Bang theory of the universe and invites you to consider the big questions of astronomy today. You can also watch one of the thirty-minute presentations in the state-of-the-art **Planetarium**, introduced by a Royal Observatory astronomer.

Dulwich Picture Gallery

Gallery Rd · Tues–Fri 10am–5pm, Sat & Sun 11am–5pm · £6 · ☎ 020 8693 5254, ⓦ dulwichpicturegallery.org.uk · West Dulwich (from Victoria) or North Dulwich (from London Bridge) train stations

Dulwich Picture Gallery, the nation's oldest public art gallery, was designed by John Soane in 1814. Soane created a beautifully spacious building, awash with natural light and crammed with superb paintings – elegiac landscapes by Cuyp, one of the world's finest Poussin series, and splendid works by Hogarth, Gainsborough, Van Dyck, Canaletto and Rubens, plus **Rembrandt**'s tiny *Portrait of a Young Man*, a top-class portrait of poet, playwright and Royalist, the future Earl of Bristol. At the centre of the museum is a tiny mausoleum designed by Soane for the sarcophagi of the gallery's founders.

Horniman Museum

100 London Rd · Daily 10.30am–5.30pm · Free, aquarium £3.30 · ☎ 020 8699 1872, ⓦ horniman.ac.uk · Forest Hill train station from Victoria or London Bridge

The wonderful **Horniman Museum** was purpose-built in 1901 by Frederick Horniman, a tea trader with a passion for collecting. In addition to the museum's natural history collection of stuffed birds and animals, there's an eclectic ethnographic collection, and a music gallery with more than 1500 instruments from Chinese gongs to electric guitars. The state-of-the-art aquarium in the basement is definitely worth the entrance fee, as are the special ethnographic exhibitions the museum puts on.

1 West London

Most visitors experience **West London** en route to or from Heathrow Airport, either from the confines of the train or tube (which runs overground at this point), or the motorway. The city and its satellites seem to continue unabated, with only fleeting glimpses of the countryside. However, in the five-mile stretch from Chiswick to Osterley there are several former country retreats, now surrounded by suburbia.

The Palladian villa of **Chiswick House** is perhaps the best known. However, it draws nothing like as many visitors as **Syon House**, most of whom come for the gardening centre and the indoor adventure playground rather than for the house itself, a showcase for the talents of Robert Adam, who also worked at **Osterley House**, another Elizabethan conversion.

Running through much of the area is the **River Thames**, once the "Great Highway of London" and still the most pleasant way to travel in these parts during summer. Boats plough up the Thames all the way from central London via the **Royal Botanic Gardens** at **Kew** and the picturesque riverside at **Richmond**, as far as **Hampton Court**.

Chiswick House

Great Chertsey Rd • **House** April–Oct Mon–Wed & Sun 10am–6pm; Oct closes 5pm • £6.10; EH • **Gardens** Daily 7am–dusk • Free • ☎ 020 8995 0508, ⓦ chgt.org.uk • Chiswick train station from Waterloo or ⊖ Turnham Green

Chiswick House is a perfect little Neoclassical villa, designed in the 1720s by the Earl of Burlington, and set in one of the most beautifully landscaped gardens in London. Like its prototype, Palladio's Villa Rotonda near Vicenza, the house was created as a "temple to the arts" where, amid his fine art collection, Burlington could entertain artistic friends such as Swift, Handel and Pope. Entertaining took place on the **upper floor**, a series of cleverly interconnecting rooms, each enjoying a wonderful view out onto the gardens – all, that is, except the Tribunal, the domed octagonal hall at the centre of the villa, where the earl's finest paintings and sculptures would have been displayed.

London Museum of Water & Steam

Corner of Kew Bridge Road and Green Dragon Lane • Daily 11am–4pm • £11.50 • ☎ 020 8568 4757, ⓦ waterandsteam.org.uk • Bus #237 or #267 from ⊖ Gunnersbury or Kew Bridge train station from Waterloo

Difficult to miss, thanks to its stylish Italianate standpipe tower, the **Museum of Water & Steam** occupies a former Victorian pumping station, 100yd west of Kew Bridge. At the heart of the museum is the Steam Hall, which contains a triple expansion steam engine and four gigantic nineteenth-century Cornish beam engines. The museum also has a hands-on **Waterworks** gallery in the basement, devoted to the history of the capital's water supply, and **Splash Zone** ideal for younger kids. The best time to visit is at weekends, when each of the museum's industrial dinosaurs is put through its paces, and the small narrow-gauge steam **Waterworks Railway** runs back and forth round the yard.

Syon House

London Rd • **House** Mid-March to Oct Wed, Thurs & Sun 11am–5pm • £11.50 • **Gardens only** Mid-March to Oct daily 10.30am–5pm • £6.50 • ☎ 020 8560 0882, ⓦ syonpark.co.uk • Bus #237 or #267 from ⊖ Gunnersbury or Kew Bridge train station

From its rather plain castellated exterior, you'd never guess that **Syon House** contains the most opulent eighteenth-century interiors in London. The splendour of Robert Adam's refurbishment is immediately revealed, however, in the pristine **Great Hall**, an apsed double cube with a screen of Doric columns at one end and classical statuary

RIVER TRANSPORT: HEADING WEST
From April to October **Westminster Passenger Services** runs a scheduled service
from Westminster Pier to Kew, Richmond and Hampton Court (3hr one-way; £15 single,
£22.50 return; ☎ 020 7930 2062, ⓦ wpsa.co.uk). In addition, **Turks** runs a regular service
from Richmond to Hampton Court (April to mid-Sept Tues–Sun; £8 single, £9.50 return;
☎ 020 8546 2434, ⓦ turks.co.uk). For the latest on boat services on the Thames, see
ⓦ tfl.gov.uk.

dotted around the edges. There are several more Adam-designed rooms to admire in
the house, in particular the **Long Gallery** – 136ft by just 14ft – plus a smattering of
works by Lely, Van Dyck and others.

While Adam beautified Syon House, Capability Brown laid out its **gardens** around
an artificial lake, surrounding it with oaks, beeches, limes and cedars. The gardens'
chief focus now, however, is the crescent-shaped **Great Conservatory**, an early
nineteenth-century addition which is said to have inspired Joseph Paxton, architect of
the Crystal Palace.

Osterley House

Jersey Rd · **House** March & Oct Wed–Sun noon–4pm; April–Sept Wed–Sun 11am–5pm; Dec Sat & Sun noon–4pm · **Gardens** Daily
March & Oct–Dec noon–4pm; April–Sept 11am–5pm · £8.25; NT · ☎ 020 8232 5050, ⓦ nationaltrust.org.uk · ⊖ Osterley

Home to a colossal Elizabethan mansion redesigned by Robert Adam, **Osterley** is one
of London's largest surviving estate parks, which still gives the impression of being in
the countryside, despite the M4 motorway to the north. Osterley House boasts a
characteristically cool **Entrance Hall**, followed by the so-called State Rooms of the south
wing. Highlights include the **Drawing Room**, with Reynolds portraits on the damask
walls and a coffered ceiling centred on a giant marigold, and the **Etruscan Dressing
Room**, in which every surface is covered in delicate painted trelliswork, sphinxes and
urns; Adam (and Wedgwood) dubbed the style "Etruscan", though it is in fact derived
from Greek vases found at Pompeii.

Kew Gardens

Kew Rd · Daily 9.30am–6.30pm or dusk · £15 · ☎ 020 8332 5655, ⓦ kew.org · ⊖ Kew Gardens

Established in 1759, Kew's **Royal Botanic Gardens** manage the extremely difficult task
of being both a world leader in botanic research and an extraordinarily beautiful and
popular public park. There's always something to see, whatever the season, but to get
the most out of the place come sometime between spring and autumn, bring a picnic
and stay for the day.

Of all the glasshouses, by far the most celebrated is the **Palm House**, a curvaceous
mound of glass and wrought iron, designed by Decimus Burton in the 1840s. Its
drippingly humid atmosphere nurtures most of the known palm species, while in the
basement there's a small, excellent tropical aquarium. Elsewhere in the gardens, you'll
find the **Treetop Walkway**, which lifts you 60ft off the ground, and gives you a novel
view of the tree canopy.

The three-storey red-brick mansion of **Kew Palace** (April–Oct only), to the northwest
of the Palm House, was bought by George II as a nursery and schoolhouse for his
umpteen children. Later, George III was confined to the palace and subjected to the
dubious attentions of doctors who attempted to find a cure for his "madness". There
are one or two bits and bobs belonging to the royals, like the much-loved dolls' house,
on the ground floor, which belonged to George III's daughters. Upstairs, you can view
the chair in which Queen Charlotte passed away in 1818, while the top floor has been
left pretty much untouched since those days.

1

Richmond

Richmond, upriver from Kew, basked for centuries in the glow of royal patronage, with Plantagenet kings and Tudor monarchs frequenting the riverside palace. Although most of the courtiers and aristocrats have gone, it is still a wealthy district, with two theatres and highbrow pretensions.

Richmond Park

Daily: March–Sept 7am–dusk; Oct–Feb 7.30am–dusk • Free • ☎ 0300 061 2200, ⓦ royalparks.gov.uk • Bus #371 or #65 from ↔ Richmond to Petersham Gate

Richmond's greatest attraction is the enormous **Richmond Park**, at the top of Richmond Hill – 2500 acres of undulating grassland and bracken, dotted with coppiced woodland and as wild as anything in London. Eight miles across at its widest point, this is Europe's largest city park, famed for its red and fallow deer, which roam freely, and for its ancient oaks. For the most part untamed, the park does have a couple of deliberately landscaped plantations that feature splendid springtime azaleas and rhododendrons.

Ham House

Ham St • **House** March–Oct daily except Fri noon–4pm • £10 • **Gardens** Daily: March–Oct 10am–5pm; Nov–Feb 10am–4pm • £4; NT • ☎ 020 8940 1950, ⓦ nationaltrust.org.uk • Bus #371 or #65 from ↔ Richmond

Leave the rest of London far behind at **Ham House**, home to the earls of Dysart for nearly three hundred years. Expensively furnished in the seventeenth century, but little altered since then, the house is blessed with one of the finest Stuart interiors in the country, from the stupendously ornate Great Staircase to the Long Gallery, featuring six "Court Beauties" by Peter Lely. Elsewhere, there are several fine Verrio ceiling paintings, some exquisite parquet flooring and works by Van Dyck and Reynolds. Also glorious are the formal seventeenth-century **gardens**, especially the Cherry Garden, laid out with a pungent lavender parterre. The Orangery, overlooking the original kitchen garden, serves as a tearoom.

Strawberry Hill

268 Waldegrave Rd • Mon–Wed 2–6pm, Sat & Sun noon–6pm (last admission 4.20pm) • £10.80 • ☎ 020 8744 1241, ⓦ strawberryhillhouse.org.uk • Strawberry Hill train station from Waterloo

In 1747 writer, wit and fashion queen Horace Walpole, youngest son of former prime minister Robert Walpole, bought this "little play-thing house…the prettiest bauble you ever saw…set in enamelled meadows, with filigree hedges", renamed it **Strawberry Hill** and set about inventing the most influential building in the Gothic Revival. Walpole appointed a "Committee of Taste" to embellish his project with details from other Gothic buildings: screens from Old St Paul's and Rouen cathedrals, and fan vaulting from Henry VII's Chapel in Westminster Abbey. Walpole wanted visits of Strawberry Hill to be a theatrical experience, and, with its eccentric Gothic decor, it remains so to this day.

Hampton Court

Daily: April–Oct 10am–6pm; Nov–March 10am–4.30pm • Palace, gardens & maze £16.50, free guided tours available (45min); gardens only £5.20; maze only £4 • ☎ 020 3166 6000, ⓦ hrp.org.uk • Hampton Court train station from Waterloo

Hampton Court Palace, a sprawling red-brick ensemble on the banks of the Thames thirteen miles southwest of London, is the finest of England's royal abodes. Built in 1516 by the upwardly mobile **Cardinal Wolsey**, Henry VIII's Lord Chancellor, it was purloined by Henry himself after Wolsey fell from favour. In the second half of the seventeenth century, Charles II laid out the gardens, inspired by what he had seen at

Versailles, while William and Mary had large sections of the palace remodelled by Wren a few years later.

There's not a lot of information in any of the rooms, but audioguides are available and free guided tours are led by period-costumed historians who bring the place to life. If your energy is lacking – and Hampton Court is huge – the most rewarding sections are: **Henry VIII's Apartments**, which feature the glorious double-hammer-beamed Great Hall; **William III's Apartments**; and **Henry VIII's Kitchens**.

Tickets to the Royal Apartments cover entry to the rest of the sites in the grounds. Those who don't wish to visit the apartments are free to wander around the gardens and visit the curious **Royal Tennis Courts** (April–Oct), but have to pay to try out the palace's famously tricky yew-hedge **Maze**, and visit the **Privy Garden**, where you can view Andrea Mantegna's colourful, heroic canvases, *The Triumphs of Caesar*, housed in the Lower Orangery, and the celebrated **Great Vine**, whose grapes are sold at the palace each year in September.

ARRIVAL AND DEPARTURE LONDON

BY PLANE

The capital's five international airports – Heathrow, Gatwick, Stansted, Luton and City Airport – are all less than an hour from the city centre.

HEATHROW

Fifteen miles west of central London, Heathrow (W heathrowairport.com) has five terminals and three train/tube stations: one for terminals 1, 2 and 3, and separate ones for terminals 4 and 5. All stations are in Travelcard Zone 6.

Heathrow Express High-speed (W heathrowexpress.com) trains travel nonstop to Paddington Station (daily 5am–midnight; every 15min; 15min; online tickets £21 single/£34 return).

Heathrow Connect Less pricey trains (W heathrowconnect.com) travel to Paddington with several stops on the way (Mon–Sat 5am–midnight, Sun 6am–11pm; every 30min; 30–40min; £10 single).

Underground An even cheaper alternative is to take the tube (Piccadilly line) into central London (Mon–Sat 5am–11.45pm, Sun 6am–11.30pm; every 5min; 50min; £5.70 single/£8.90 for a One Day Off-Peak Travelcard).

National Express National Express bus services (W nationalexpress.com) run direct to Victoria Coach Station (daily every 15–30min; 40–55min; £6 single, £11 return).

Night buses From midnight, you can take night bus #N9 (every 20min; 1hr 10min; £1.45). Heathrow to Trafalgar Square, with several other stops in West London en route.

GATWICK

Around 30 miles south of London, Gatwick Airport (W gatwickairport.com) has good transport connections with the city.

Gatwick Express The nonstop Gatwick Express (W gatwickexpress.com) runs between the airport's South Terminal and Victoria Station (daily 4.30am–1.30am; every 15min; 30min; £20 single, £35 return).

Overground trains Other train options include Southern services to Victoria (every 15min–hourly; 35min) or Govia Thameslink services to various stations (every 15–hourly; journey 30–45min), including London Bridge and St Pancras, tickets for either cost around £10 single.

Buses easyBus (W easybus.co.uk) runs buses to West Brompton tube (daily 4.30am–midnight; every 20min; 1hr 10min), with online tickets from £2 single (£10 if you buy on board). National Express buses run from Gatwick direct to central London (daily 5am–9.30pm; hourly; 1hr 30min); tickets cost around £7 single, £13.50 return.

STANSTED

Roughly 35 miles northeast of the capital, Stansted (W stanstedairport.com) is commonly used by the budget airlines.

Stansted Express The most convenient way to get into town is by train on the Stansted Express (W stanstedexpress.com) to Liverpool Street (daily 5.30am–12.30am; every 15–30min; 45min; £24 single, £33 return).

Buses All year round, 24 hours a day, Green Line and easyBus runs buses to Baker Street tube (daily 7am–1am; every 20min; 1hr 15min; online tickets from £2 single, £10 if you buy on board). National Express runs buses to Golders Green and Victoria Coach Station (24hr; every 30min; 1hr 30min–1hr 45min; £9 single).

LUTON

Around 30 miles north of London, Luton (W london-luton.co.uk) handles mostly charter flights.

Luton Airport Parkway A free shuttle bus (every 10min; 5min) transports passengers to Luton Airport Parkway train station, connected to St Pancras (every 15min–hourly; 25–35min; £15 single) and other central London stations.

Buses All year round, 24 hours a day, Green Line and easyBus run the #757 coach from Luton Airport to Baker Street and Victoria Coach Station (every 20–30min; 1hr 20min; from £2 online, or as much as £10).

1

CITY AIRPORT

London's smallest airport, used primarily by business people, City Airport (wlondoncityairport.com) is in Docklands, 10 miles east of central London. Docklands Light Railway (DLR) will take you straight to Bank in the City (Mon–Sat 5.30am–12.15am, Sun 7am–11.15pm every 8–15min; 20min; around £5), where you can change to the Tube.

BY TRAIN

From Europe Eurostar (weurostar.com) trains arrive at St Pancras International, next door to King's Cross.

From Britain Arriving by train from elsewhere in Britain, you'll come into one of London's numerous mainline stations, all of which have adjacent Underground stations linking into the city centre's tube network. As a rough guide, Charing Cross handles services to Kent; Euston to the Midlands, northwest England and Glasgow; Fenchurch Street to south Essex; King's Cross to northeast England and Scotland; Liverpool Street to eastern England; Marylebone to the Midlands; Paddington to southwest England; St Pancras for Eurostar and the southeast, plus trains to East Midlands and South Yorkshire; and Victoria and Waterloo to southeast England.

Information National Rail Enquiries (☎0845 748 4950, wnationalrail.co.uk).

DESTINATIONS

London Charing Cross to: Canterbury West (hourly; 1hr 40min); Dover Priory (Mon–Sat every 30min; 1hr 40min–1hr 50min); Hastings (every 30min; 1hr 30min); Rochester (every 30min; 1hr 10min).

London Euston to: Birmingham New Street (every 20min; 1hr 25min); Carlisle (every 2hr; 3hr 15min); Lancaster (hourly; 2hr 30min); Liverpool Lime Street (hourly; 2hr 10min); Manchester Piccadilly (every 20min; 2hr 10min).

London King's Cross to: Brighton (Mon–Sat 4 hourly, Sun 2 hourly; 1hr); Cambridge (every 30min; 45min); Durham (hourly; 2hr 40min–3hr); Leeds (hourly; 2hr 25min); Newcastle (every 30min; 3hr); Peterborough (every 30min; 45min); York (every 30min; 2hr).

London Liverpool Street to: Cambridge (every 30min; 1hr 15min); Norwich (every 30min; 1hr 55min).

London Paddington to: Bath (every 30min–hourly; 1hr 30min); Bristol (every 30–45min; 1hr 40min); Cheltenham (every 2hr; 2hr 15min); Exeter (hourly; 2hr 15min); Gloucester (every 2hr; 2hr); Oxford (every 30min; 55min); Penzance (every 1–2hr; 5hr 30min); Plymouth (every 3hr 15min–3hr 40min); Windsor (change at Slough; Mon–Fri every 20min; Sat & Sun every 30min; 30–40min); Worcester (hourly; 2hr 20min).

London St Pancras to: Brighton (every 20min; 1hr 20min); Canterbury (every 30min; 1hr); Dover Priory (hourly; 1hr 5min); Leicester (every 30min; 1hr 10min); Nottingham (every 30min; 1hr 40min–2hr); Rochester (every 30min; 40min); Sheffield (every 30min; 2hr 10min–2hr 30min).

London Victoria to: Arundel (Mon–Sat every 30min, Sun hourly; 1hr 30min); Brighton (every 30min; 50min); Canterbury East (every 30min–hourly; 1hr 25min); Chichester (Mon–Sat 2 hourly; 1hr 35min); Dover Priory (Mon–Sat every 30min; 1hr 40min–1hr 55min); Lewes (Mon–Sat every 30min, Sun hourly; 1hr 10min); Rochester (every 30min; 45min).

London Waterloo to: Portsmouth Harbour (every 30min; 1hr 35min); Southampton Central (every 30min; 1hr 15min); Winchester (every 30min; 1hr); Windsor (Mon–Sat every 30min, Sun hourly; 50min).

BY BUS

Victoria Coach Station Coming into London by coach (☎0870 580 8080, wnationalexpress.com), you're most likely to arrive at Victoria Coach Station, a couple of hundred yards south down Buckingham Palace Road from the train and Underground stations of the same name.

Information Traveline (☎0871 200 2233, wtravel ine.info).

Destinations Bath (hourly to every 1hr 30min; 3hr 30min); Birmingham (every 30min–hourly; 2hr 35min); Brighton (hourly; 2hr 10min); Bristol (hourly; 2hr 30min); Cambridge (hourly; 2hr); Canterbury (hourly; 2hr); Dover (hourly; 2hr 30min–3hr); Exeter (every 2hr; 4hr 15min); Gloucester (hourly; 3hr 20min); Liverpool (6 daily; 4hr 50min–5hr 30min); Manchester (9 daily; 4hr 50min–5hr 30min); Newcastle (5 daily; 6hr 25min–7hr 55min); Oxford (every 15min; 1hr 50min); Plymouth (6 daily; 5hr 20min); Stratford (4 daily; 3hr).

GETTING AROUND

London's **transport network** is among the most complex and expensive in the world, but on the bright side you should be able to get to wherever you want, most hours of the day or night. Avoid travelling during the **rush hour** (Mon–Fri 8–9.30am & 5–7pm), when tubes become unbearably crowded, and some buses get so full that they won't let you on. Transport for London (TfL) provides excellent free maps and details of bus and tube services from its six **Travel Information Centres**: the most central is at Piccadilly Circus tube station (Mon–Fri 7.45am–7pm, Sat 9.15am–7pm, Sun 9.15am–6pm); there are other desks at the arrivals at Heathrow (terminals 1, 2 & 3) and various tube/train stations. There's also a 24-hour helpline and an excellent website for information on all bus and tube services (☎0843 222 1234, wtfl.gov.uk/plan-a-journey).

BY TUBE

Except for very short journeys, the Underground – or tube – is by far the quickest way to get about.

Tube lines Eleven different lines cross much of the metropolis, although London south of the river is not very well covered. Each line has its own colour and name – all you need to know is which direction you're travelling in: northbound, eastbound, southbound or westbound, and the final destination.

Zones London is divided into six concentric zones, with the vast majority of the city's accommodation, pubs, restaurants and sights in zones 1 and 2.

Services Services are frequent (Mon–Sat 5.30am–12.30am, Sun 7.30am–11.30pm), and you rarely have to wait more than five minutes for a train between central stations.

Fares Single fares are expensive – a journey in the central zone costs nearly £5 – so if you're intending to make more than one journey, an Oyster card or a Travelcard is by far your best option (see box below).

BY BUS

London's red buses – most, but not all, of them, double-deckers – tend to get stuck in traffic jams, which prevents their running to a regular timetable. You must signal to get the bus to stop, and press the bell in order to get off.

Services Some buses run a 24-hour service, but most run between about 5am and midnight, with a network of Night Buses (prefixed with the letter "N") operating outside this period (every 20–30min).

Fares The standard walk-on fare is £1.45, but you cannot pay by cash, only with a card or pass (see box below).

BY TRAIN

Large areas of London's outskirts are best reached by the suburban (overground) train network. Wherever a sight can only be reached by overground train, we've indicated in the guide the nearest train station and the central terminus from which you can depart.

BY DLR

The Docklands Light Railway sets off from Bank, or from Tower Gateway, close to Tower Hill tube. The train, which cuts right through the middle of the office Canary Wharf buildings under a parabolic steel-and-glass canopy, is also a great way to get to Greenwich (see p.102).

BY BOAT

Unfortunately, boat services on the Thames are not fully integrated into the public transport system. If you have a valid Travelcard (either in paper or Oyster form), you're entitled to a third off, but if you have a pay-as-you-go Oyster card, you get just ten percent off.

Services Timetables and services are complex, and there are numerous companies and small charter operators – for a full list pick up a booklet from a TfL information centre (see opposite) or visit ⓦ tfl.gov.uk. One of the largest companies is Thames Clippers (ⓦ thamesclippers.com), who run a regular commuter service (every 20–30min; around £6.50 single) between Waterloo and Greenwich; an off-peak hop-on, hop-off River Roamer on their services costs £15.

BY TAXI

Black cabs Compared to most capital cities, London's metered black cabs are an expensive option unless there are three or more of you. The minimum fare is £2.40, and a ride from Euston to Victoria, for example, costs around £12–15 (Mon–Fri 6am–8pm). After 8pm on weekdays and all day during the weekend, a higher tariff applies, and after 10pm it's higher still. A yellow light over the windscreen tells you if the cab is available – just stick your arm out to hail it. To order a black cab in advance, phone

---

GETTING ABOUT: OYSTER CARDS AND PASSES

The cheapest, easiest way to get about London is to use an **Oyster card**, London's transport smartcard, available from all tube stations and TfL Travel Information Centres, and valid on almost all networks .Use it either to store a weekly/monthly/yearly **Travelcard**, or as a pay-as-you-go deal; you can top it up at all tube stations and many newsagents. As you enter the tube or bus, simply touch in your card at the card reader – if you're using pay-as-you-go, the fare will be taken off. If you're using the tube or train, you need to touch out again, or a maximum cash fare of up to £8.60 will be deducted. A pay-as-you-go Oyster operates daily price-capping; you will stop being charged when you've paid the equivalent of a Day Travelcard, but you still need to touch in (and out). Oyster cards are free for those buying monthly or yearly tickets; everyone else needs to hand over a £5 refundable deposit.

   Children under 11 travel for free; children aged 11–15 travel free on all buses and at child-rate on the tube; children aged 16 or 17 can travel at half the adult rate on all forms of transport. However, all children over 10 must have an Oyster photocard to be eligible for free travel – these should be applied for in advance online.

   Various other travelcards and bus passes are available, too; check ⓦ tfl.gov.uk for details.

1

THE CONGESTION CHARGE

All vehicles entering central London on weekdays between 7am and 6pm are liable to a **congestion charge** of £11.50 per vehicle. Drivers can pay the charge online, over the phone and at garages and shops, and must do so before midnight the same day or incur a £2.50 surcharge – 24 hours later, you'll be liable for a £130 Penalty Charge Notice (reduced to £65 if you pay within 14 days). Disabled travellers, motorcycles, minibuses and some alternative-fuel vehicles are exempt from the charge, and local residents get a ninety percent discount, but you must register in order to qualify. For more details, visit ⓦ tfl.gov.uk.

ⓣ 0871 871 8710, and be prepared to pay an extra £2.

Minicabs Private minicabs are considerably cheaper than black cabs, but they cannot be hailed from the street. All minicabs must be licensed and able to produce a TfL ID on demand, but the best way to pick a company is to take the advice of the place you're at, unless you want to be certain of a woman driver, in which case call Lady Mini Cabs (ⓣ 020 7272 3300), or a gay/lesbian-friendly driver, in which case call London Cabs (ⓣ 020 7205 2677). If saving money (and time) is your main priority, then you might consider using the Uber app where the price varies according to supply and you can see which cabs are close by.

BY BIKE

Boris bikes The easiest way to cycle round London is to use the city's cycle hire scheme – or Boris bikes, as they're universally known, after Boris Johnson, the Mayor of London at the time they were introduced. There are over 700 docking stations across central London. With a credit or debit card, you can buy 24 hours' access to the bikes for just £2, after which you get the first 30min free, so if you hop from station to station, you don't pay another penny. Otherwise, it's £1 for the first hour, increasing rapidly after that to £15 for three hours. If you're going to use the scheme a lot, you may be best off becoming a member and getting a key – for more details see ⓦ tfl.gov.uk.

Bike rental Bikes can also be rented from the London Bicycle Tour Company, 1a Gabriel Wharf on the South Bank (ⓣ 020 7923 6838, ⓦ londonbicycle. com), costing around £20 a day or £50 a week.

INFORMATION

City of London Information Centre The City has the most central information office, situated on the south side of St Paul's Cathedral (Mon–Sat 9.30am–5.30pm, Sun 10am–4pm; ⓣ 020 7332 1456, ⓦ visitthecity.co.uk; ⊖ St Paul's).

Maps If you want to find your way around every nook and cranny of the city you'll need to invest in either an *A–Z Atlas* or a *Nicholson Streetfinder*, both of which have a street index covering every street in the capital. You can get them at most bookshops and newsagents for around £5. Stanfords, in Covent Garden at 12–14 Long Acre, WC2 (ⓣ 020 7836 1321, ⓦ stanfords.co.uk) is a good map shop.

Listings magazines The most useful listings magazine for visitors is *Time Out*, a free weekly which comes out on Tuesday. It carries news and consumer features, along with critical appraisals of all the week's theatre, film, music, exhibitions, children's events and more; listings themselves are much more comprehensive on its website (ⓦ timeout.com).

ACCOMMODATION

London **accommodation** is undeniably expensive, and will be by far your major outlay when visiting the city. The hostels are among the most costly in the world, while venerable institutions such as the *Ritz*, the *Dorchester* and the *Savoy* charge the very top international prices – from £300 per luxurious night. For a decent **hotel** room, you shouldn't expect much change out of £100 a night, and even the most basic **B&Bs** struggle to bring their tariffs down to £80 for a double with shared facilities. If you're not bothered about atmosphere or local flavour then the **chain hotels** are a safe bet – but they'll offer far less character than the places that we've reviewed below. *Premier Inn* (ⓦ premierinn.com), *Travelodge* (ⓦ travelodge.co.uk), *easyHotel* (ⓦ easyhotel.com) and *Tune* (ⓦ tunehotels.com) all have hotels in central locations. Whatever the time of year, you should book as far in advance as you can if you want to stay within a couple of tube stops of the West End.

BOOKING

British Hotel Reservation Centre (BHRC) If you arrive without having made plans (which is *not* a good idea), head for the BHRC (24hr helpline ⓣ 020 7592 3055, ⓦ bhrc.co.uk) desks at Heathrow airport, Victoria bus station and St Pancras and Victoria train stations. BHRC offices are open daily from early till late, and there's no booking fee.

Useful websites You can book accommodation for free at ⓦ londontown.com; payment is made directly to the hotel

CLOCKWISE FROM TOP LEFT AFTERNOON TEA AT THE RITZ (P.116); PORTOBELLO ROAD MARKET (P.131); THE LAMB PUB (P.121); BAR ITALIA, SOHO (P.115) >

1

and they offer good discounts. ⓦcouchsurfing.org puts young travellers in touch with people to stay with for free, while ⓦairbnb.co.uk offers rooms and flats in interesting locations and properties, and ⓦonefinestay.com offers a very luxurious version of the same.

HOTELS

When choosing your area, bear in mind that as a rule the West End – Soho, Covent Garden, St James's, Mayfair and Marylebone – and the western districts of Knightsbridge and Kensington are dominated by expensive, upmarket hotels, whereas Bloomsbury is both less expensive and very central. For rock-bottom rooms, the widest choice is close to the main train termini of Victoria and Paddington, and among the budget B&Bs of Earl's Court.

VICTORIA

B&B Belgravia 64–66 Ebury St, SW1 ☎020 7259 8570, ⓦbb-belgravia.com; ⊖Victoria; map pp.60–61. A B&B with flair, close to the train and bus stations. The rooms are comfy and all en suite, with sash windows and modern touches; those on the ground floor can be noisy. They also have nearby studios for similar rates. Free wi-fi and bike loan. **£120**

Luna Simone Hotel 47–49 Belgrave Rd, SW1 ☎020 7834 5897, ⓦlunasimonehotel.com; ⊖Victoria; map pp.60–61. Good-value B&B with friendly staff and plain, well-maintained en-suite rooms, including triples and quads. Big English breakfasts are included, and there's free wi-fi on the ground floor and in the lobby. **£140**

★**Morgan House** 120 Ebury St, SW1 ☎020 7730 2384, ⓦmorganhouse.co.uk; ⊖Victoria; map pp.94–95. A well above-average B&B in a comfortable Georgian building in a pretty street on the Chelsea/Victoria borders. Rooms are mostly en suite; the family room (£158) crams in a double and a bunk bed. Full breakfasts, and free wi-fi in the lobby. **£84**

WESTMINSTER

Sanctuary House 33 Tothill St, SW1 ☎020 7799 4044, ⓦsanctuaryhousehotel.com; ⊖St James's Park; map pp.64–65. Run by Fuller's Brewery, above a Fuller's pub, with uncontroversial modernish decor. Breakfast is extra, and served in the pub, but the location, right by St James's Park, is terrific. Ask about special deals. Free wi-fi. **£160**

MARYLEBONE

Lincoln House 33 Gloucester Place, W1 ☎020 7486 7630, ⓦlincoln-house-hotel.com; ⊖Marble Arch or BakerSt; map pp.94–95. Dark wood panelling and nautical paraphernalia give this large Georgian guesthouse a quirky feel, and the rooms are en suite and comfortable, with tea and coffee facilities. Rates vary according to the size of the bed and length of stay; there are good online discounts. Breakfast costs extra. Free wi-fi. **£105**

SOHO

Dean Street Townhouse 69–71 Dean St, W1 ☎020 7341775, ⓦdeanstreettownhouse.com; ⊖Tottenham Court Road or Leicester Square; map pp.64–65. One of a chic set of hotels owned by the trendy Soho House members' club, this 1730s house offers "tiny" (at 160 square feet it's no exaggeration) "small", "medium" and "bigger" rooms – all of them doubles. Luxury details come with real style – handpainted wallpaper, funky toiletries and clawfoot tubs, some of which are in the bedrooms themselves. Free wi-fi. **£260**

★**Hazlitt's** 6 Frith St, W1 ☎020 7434 1771, ⓦhazlittshotel.com; ⊖Tottenham Court Road; map pp.64–65. An early eighteenth-century building hiding a hotel of real character and charm, with en-suite, wonky-floored rooms decorated and furnished as close to period style as convenience and comfort allow. Breakfast (served in the rooms) is not included. Free wi-fi. **£210**

Nadler Soho 10 Carlisle St, W1 ☎020 3697 3697, ⓦthenadler.com; ⊖Tottenham Court Road; map pp.64–65. Glossy hotel offering good value for its excellent location. The rooms are modern and high-tech, if unexciting (the cheapest are pretty small), and each has a mini-kitchen – with espresso machine – which means you could effectively self-cater. **£170**

COVENT GARDEN

The Fielding Hotel 4 Broad Court, Bow St, WC2 ☎020 7836 8305, ⓦwww.thefieldinghotel.co.uk; ⊖Covent Garden; map pp.64–65. Quietly situated on a pedestrianized court, this simple hotel is a hidden gem. Its en-suite rooms are a firm favourite with visiting performers, since it's just a few yards from the Royal Opera House. No breakfast. Free wi-fi. **£140**

Seven Dials Hotel 7 Monmouth St, WC2 ☎020 7681 0791, ⓦsevendialshotellondon.com; ⊖Covent

LONDON POSTCODES

A brief word on **London postcodes**: the name of each street is followed by a letter giving the geographical location (E for "east", WC for "west central" and so on) and a number that specifies the postal area. However, this is not a reliable indication of the remoteness of the locale – W5, for example, lies beyond the more remote sounding NW10 – so it's always best to check a map before taking a room in what may sound like a fairly central area.

Garden; map pp.64–65. Pleasant, family-run B&B in an attractive Covent Garden street. Rooms (singles to quads) are small, but all are clean and simple and most are en suite. Free wi-fi. **£105**

BLOOMSBURY AND KING'S CROSS

Arosfa Hotel 83 Gower St, WC1 ☎020 7636 2115, ⓦarosfalondon.com; ⊖Goodge Street or Euston Square; map p.75. Fifteen en-suite B&B rooms. Some are tiny, but this is a clean, comfy and reliable option. Full breakfast, and free wi-fi in the lounge. **£120**

Grange Langham Court Hotel 31–35 Langham St, W1 ☎020 7436 6622, ⓦgrangehotels.com; ⊖Oxford Circus; map p.75. The rooms are small, but they're clean and comfortable, and the price, for this location – in a quiet spot near Regent Street – is reasonable. **£130**

★**Ridgemount** 65–67 Gower St, WC1 ☎020 7636 1141, ⓦridgemounthotel.co.uk; ⊖Goodge Street; map p.75. Old-fashioned, cosy, family-run guesthouse, with small, clean rooms (15 of the 32 have shared facilities – which are spotless). A reliable, basic Bloomsbury bargain. Full breakfast and free wi-fi. **£82**

Rough Luxe 1 Birkenhead St, WC1 ☎020 7837 5338, ⓦroughluxe.co.uk; ⊖King's Cross; map pp.60–61. This funky six room guesthouse offers comfort and shabby chic style. Each room is different, and the aesthetic – peeling plaster, original artworks – is stronger in some than others. Free wi-fi. **£190**

St Pancras Renaissance Hotel Euston Rd, NW1 ☎020 7841 3540, ⓦmarriott.co.uk; ⊖King's Cross; map pp.60–61. The old St Pancras station, George Gilbert Scott's Gothic Revival masterpiece, is now a glamorous *Marriott*. The lofty public spaces and colossal lobby evoke the golden era of railway travel, but not all the rooms are in the main building and the others, in an annexe, aren't worth the price. Check online for dramatic deals. **£275**

CLERKENWELL AND THE CITY

Apex City of London Hotel 1 Seething Lane, EC3 ☎0845 365 0000, ⓦapexhotels.co.uk; ⊖Tower Hill; map pp.80–81. Swish business hotel on a secluded street near the Tower of London. Room rates vary according to availability, so book early. Free gym, sauna and steam room, and free wi-fi. The nearby *Apex London Wall* (7–9 Copthall Ave, EC2; Moorgate tube) has more of a boutique feel but similar rates. **£160**

The King's Wardrobe 6 Wardrobe Place, Carter Lane, EC4 ☎020 7792 2222, ⓜbridgestreet.com; ⊖St Paul's; map pp.80–81. In a quiet courtyard just behind St Paul's Cathedral, this place is part of an international chain that caters largely for a business clientele – the apartments offer fully equipped kitchens and workstations, concierge service and housekeeping. Though housed in a

fourteenth-century building that once contained Edward III's royal regalia, the interior is modern. **£185**

The Rookery 12 Peter's Lane, Cowcross St, EC1 ☎020 7336 0931, ⓦrookeryhotel.com; ⊖Farringdon; map pp.80–81. Rambling Georgian townhouse on the edge of the City, in trendy Clerkenwell, that makes a delightful little hideaway. Rooms offer faded Baroque glam, with antique fittings, characterful bathrooms and creaky floorboards. **£185**

★**The Zetter Hotel & Townhouse** 86–88 Clerkenwell Rd, EC1 ☎020 7324 4567, ⓦthezetter.com; ⊖Farringdon; map pp.80–81. Glamorous warehouse conversion with a laidback edge, with gorgeous, colourful rooms with lots of eco touches; the on-site *Bruno Loubet* brasserie is a popular spot. The Georgian *Townhouse*, across the square, is more whimsical, with thirteen boudoirish rooms and a cosy cocktail bar. Free wi-fi. **£150**

THE EAST END

Hoxton Hotel 81 Great Eastern St, EC2 ☎020 7550 1000, ⓦhoxtonhotels.com; ⊖Old Street; map pp.80–81. "The Hox" remains a youthful stalwart in this once edgy (but hurtling rapidly towards the mainstream) neighbourhood, with exposed brick and contemporary art in the public spaces, and simple, modern rooms. Rates include a light breakfast, free wi-fi and an hour's local calls a day, and there's a bar and popular brasserie. Rates depend on availability and vary wildly. **£90**

Shoreditch Rooms Shoreditch House, Ebor St, E1 ☎020 7739 5040, ⓦshoreditchrooms.com; Shoreditch High St Overground; map pp.80–81. From the same stable as the *Dean Street Townhouse* (see opposite) this hip little place has the same no nonsense room-naming policy, with 26 options from "Tiny" up to "Small-plus". Rooms may be small but they're lovely, with lots of fresh, sun-bleached colours and vintage style. Staying here also allows you to hangout with the beautiful people in the members' club next door. Free wi-fi. **£165**

SOUTH BANK AND SOUTHWARK

Southwark Rose Ibis Styles London 43–47 Southwark Bridge Rd, SE1 ☎020 7015 1480, ⓦibis .com; ⊖London Bridge; map pp.88–89. The *Southwark Rose* is a good central, budget option with design touches that raise the rooms a little above the bland chain hotels in this area. Rooms are generally comfortable and clean, and a buffet breakfast is included in rates, which vary widely depending on availability. Free wi-fi. **£120**

★**Tune Westminster** 118–120 Westminster Bridge Rd, London SE1 ⓦtunehotels.com; ⊖Lambeth North or Waterloo; map p.86. Doing away with fuss like tables, chairs and closets keeps rates low at this London outpost of the Asian cheapie chain. The pricing policy is smart – simply

1

opt to pay for extras, including towels, TV, hairdryers or wi-fi, on the booking site. Rooms are small and modern. **£70**

KENSINGTON AND EARL'S COURT

★**Aster House** 3 Sumner Place, SW7 ☎020 7581 5888, ⊛asterhouse.com; ⊖South Kensington; map pp.94–95. Pleasant, award-winning B&B, in a luxurious South Ken white-stuccoed street; one of the rooms opens out onto the lovely garden, and there's a large conservatory where a buffet breakfast is served. **£200**

Nadler Kensington 25 Courtfield Gardens, SW5 ☎020 7244 2255, ⊛thenadler.com; ⊖Earl's Court; map pp.94–95. Good-value accommodation, with no fussy extras. Rooms range from "bijou singles" to "deluxe"; all are comfortable, clean and quiet, modern and attractive, with mini-kitchens and free wi-fi. A good choice for groups and families. **£130**

Twenty Nevern Square 20 Nevern Square, SW5 ☎020 7565 9555, ⊛20nevernsquare.com; ⊖Earl's Court; map pp.94–95. In an area of bog-standard B&Bs, this is an inexpensive boutique hotel with some style. Rooms are en suite; some, however, are teensy. Buffet breakfast included. Free wi-fi. **£90**

Vicarage Hotel 10 Vicarage Gate, W8 ☎020 7229 4030, ⊛londonvicaragehotel.com; ⊖Notting Hill Gate or High Street Kensington; map pp.94–95. Nicely located B&B on a residential street a step away from Kensington Gardens. Clean rooms; some have shared facilities and quads are available. A full English breakfast is included. Free wi-fi. **£112**

PADDINGTON, BAYSWATER AND NOTTING HILL

Portobello Gold 95–97 Portobello Rd, W1 ☎020 7460 4910, ⊛portobellogold.com; ⊖Notting Hill Gate or Holland Park; map pp.94–95. A friendly option with five basic rooms and a small apartment above a lively pub-restaurant. Rooms are plain, and some are tiny, with miniature en suites; the apartment sleeps six – at a pinch – and has a little roof terrace. Breakfast not included. Free wi-fi. **£75**

Vancouver Studios 30 Prince's Square, W2 ☎020 7243 1270, ⊛vancouverstudios.co.uk; ⊖Bayswater; map pp.94–95. Self-contained, smallish self-catering studios in a grand old Victorian townhouse with maid service and a pretty walled garden. They also have a couple of apartments, sleeping up to six. Free wi-fi. **£140**

NORTH LONDON

Hampstead Village Guesthouse 2 Kemplay Rd, NW3 ☎020 7435 8679, ⊛hampsteadguesthouse.com; ⊖Hampstead. Prettily located on a quiet residential street between Hampstead Village and the Heath, this is an unconventional guesthouse in a family home. Rooms

(most en suite) are full of character, crammed with books, pictures and personal mementos. Breakfast costs extra. Free wi-fi. **£105**

HOSTELS

London's official Youth Hostel Association (YHA) hostels (⊛yha.org.uk) are generally the cleanest, most efficiently run in the capital. However, they often charge more than private hostels, and tend to get booked up months in advance. Independent hostels are cheaper and more relaxed, but can be less reliable in terms of facilities – some are noisy, not that clean, and essentially little more than places to flop after partying all night. A good website for booking independent places online is ⊛hostellondon.com.

YHA HOSTELS

★**Central** 104 Bolsover St, W1 ☎0845 371 9154, ⊛yha.org.uk; ⊖Great Portland Street; map p.75. Excellent 300-bed hostel in a quiet West End spot, with a kitchen and café-bar. Free wi-fi for members. Dorms only (mostly en suite). No groups. Dorms **£33**

Earl's Court 38 Bolton Gardens, SW5 ☎0845 371 9114, ⊛yha.org.uk; ⊖Earl's Court; map pp.94–95. Better than a lot of accommodation in Earl's Court, this 186-bed hostel has a kitchen and café and patio garden. Single-sex dorms and private rooms. Dorms **£24**, doubles **£80**

Holland Park Holland Walk, W8 ☎0845 371 9122, ⊛yha.org.uk; ⊖Holland Park or High Street Kensington; map pp.94–95. Idyllically situated in Holland Park and fairly convenient for the centre. Kitchen and café. Popular with groups. Dorms **£22**

Oxford Street 14 Noel St, W1 ☎0845 371 9133, ⊛yha.org.uk; ⊖Oxford Circus or Tottenham Court Road; map pp.64–65. The Soho location and relatively modest size mean this hostel tends to fill quickly. The atmosphere is party central rather than family-friendly. Private rooms available. Free wi-fi for members. Dorms **£36**, doubles **£80**

St Pancras 79–81 Euston Rd, NW1 ☎0845 371 9344, ⊛yha.org.uk; ⊖King's Cross St Pancras; map pp.60–61. Modern hostel on a busy road, popular with families. Rooms are clean, bright, double-glazed and en suite. No kitchen, but there is a café. No groups. Dorms **£28**, doubles **£80**

St Paul's 36 Carter Lane, EC4 ☎0845 371 9012, ⊛yha.org.uk; ⊖St Paul's; map pp.80–81. A 215-bed hostel in a superb location opposite St Paul's Cathedral. No kitchen, but it has a café for breakfast (included in rates) and dinner. Small groups only. Dorms **£32**, doubles **£65**

Thameside 20 Salter Rd, SE16 ☎0845 371 9756, ⊛yha.org.uk; ⊖Rotherhithe; map pp.60–61. London's largest YHA hostel, with 320 beds, is in a quiet spot near the river. It can feel a bit of a trek from the centre, but it's near the O2, has a good pub next door and often has space. Self-catering available, and a restaurant serving breakfast and dinner. Dorms £25, doubles £50

INDEPENDENT HOSTELS

Clink 78 78 King's Cross Rd, WC1 ☎020 7183 9400, ⓦclinkhostels.com; ⊖King's Cross; map pp.60–61. This huge party hostel is run by the same folk as *Clink 261*, with funky decor, a lively bar, and plenty of features from the days when it was a Victorian courthouse – you can even stay in an old cell. Dorms (4–16 beds) can be cramped, though partitions on the "pod" bunks increase privacy; special girls-only dorms include mirrors and clothes hangers. Plus private rooms, some en suite. Kitchen. Breakfast included. Dorms £17, doubles £65

Clink 261 261–265 Gray's Inn Rd, WC1 ☎020 7833 9400, ⓦclinkhostels.com; ⊖King's Cross; map pp.60–61. Clean, smallish hostel in a converted office block near King's Cross Station, with laundry and kitchen

facilities. Mostly 4–10 beds, with some private rooms that sleep up to three. Breakfast included. Dorms £17, doubles £60

Generator 37 Tavistock Place, WC1 ☎020 7388 7666, ⓦgeneratorhostels.com; ⊖Russell Square or Euston; map p.75. A huge, funky party hostel, with more than 850 beds and bright, clubby decor. Dorms (some women-only) have 4–12 beds, and there are singles, twins, triples and quads – some of which are en suite. There's a late-night bar, a café and a laundry, but no kitchen. Free wi-fi. Groups welcome. Dorms £20, doubles £75

★**Meininger** 65–67 Queen's Gate, SW7 ☎020 3318 1407, ⓦmeininger-hostels.com; ⊖Gloucester Road; map pp.94–95. Cheery, secure 48-room modern hostel near the South Ken museums, run by a German chain. Dorms (4–12 beds), some women-only, plus singles and doubles. No kitchen; breakfast costs £6. There's a laundry. You can save a lot of money by booking early online. Dorms £33, doubles £125

EATING

London is a great city for eating out. You can sample any kind of **cuisine** here, from Georgian to Peruvian, Modern British to fusion. And it needn't be expensive – even in the fanciest restaurants, set menus (most often served at lunch) can be a great deal, and modish "sharing plates" can be a godsend if you want to cut costs. The city's dynamic **street food** scene, meanwhile, with food trucks, carts and pop-up stalls dishing up artisan food at low prices, offers an amazing diversity. Keep track of the ever-shifting scene on ⓦkerbfood.com

CAFÉS AND SNACKS

While the old-fashioned London caffs are a dying breed, the city has plenty of great little places where you can get quick, filling and inexpensive meals – especially good at lunchtime, most of them are open in the evenings too. Bear in mind also that many pubs (see p.120) serve food, from simple pub grub to haute cuisine.

WESTMINSTER

Café in the Crypt St Martin-in-the-Fields, Duncannon St, WC2 ☎020 7766 1158, ⓦstmartin-in-the-fields .org; ⊖Charing Cross; map pp.64–65. Comfort food, with lots of veggie dishes, in a handy (and atmospheric) location – below the church in the eighteenth-century crypt. On sunny summer days you might want to have a drink or light lunch in the separate *Café in the Courtyard*, in the terrace behind the church. Mon & Tues 8am–8pm, Wed 8am–10.30pm (live jazz after 8pm), Thurs–Sat 8am–9pm, Sun 11am–6pm.

MAYFAIR AND MARYLEBONE

★**Comptoir Libanais** 65 Wigmore St, W1 ☎020 7935 1110, ⓦlecomptoir.co.uk; ⊖Bond Street; map pp.94–95. This cheap and cheerful, kitsch and stylish Middle Eastern deli/diner serves crunchy falafels, herby Lavosh breads, tagines and patisserie. The home-made lemonades are delicious. Mains from around £6.

Mon–Sat 8am–11.30pm, Sun 9am–10.30pm.

Momo 25 Heddon St, W1 ☎020 7434 4040, ⓦmomoresto.com; ⊖Piccadilly Circus; map pp.64–65. Reasonably priced, tasty snacks, honey-soaked pastries and aromatic mint tea in a wonderful Arabic tearoom/terrace stuffed with Moroccan memorabilia. The attached restaurant is good fun, too. Mon–Fri 8am–1am, Sat 10am–1am, Sun noon–1am.

Patisserie Valerie at Sagne 105 Marylebone High St, W1 ☎020 7935 6240, ⓦpatisserie-valerie.co .uk; ⊖Bond Street; map pp.94–95. Opened in 1926, this café – one of the best in the chain – is among Marylebone's finest. You can get light lunches and snacks, but it's the cakes that are to die for. There's another good branch on Old Compton Street in Soho. Mon–Fri 7am–8pm, Sat 8am–8pm, Sun 8.30am–7pm.

★**The Wolseley** 160 Piccadilly, W1 ☎020 7499 6996, ⓦthewolseley.com; ⊖Green Park; map pp.64–65. The European brasserie-style food is delicious, though pricey – come for breakfast or afternoon tea – in this grand old café/restaurant with a stunning 1920s interior. Mon–Fri 7am–midnight, Sat 8am–midnight, Sun 8am–11pm.

SOHO AND CHINATOWN

★**Bar Italia** 22 Frith St, W1 ☎020 7437 4520, ⓦbaritaliasoho.co.uk; ⊖Leicester Square; map pp.64–65. Tiny espresso bar that's been a Soho institution

1

MORE THAN JUST A CUPPA: AFTERNOON TEA

The classic English **afternoon tea** – assorted sandwiches, scones and cream, cakes and tarts, and, of course, lashings of leaf tea – is available all over London. The most popular venues are the top hotels and swanky department stores; you should count on spending around £40 a head and book well in advance. Most hotels will expect "smart casual attire"; only *The Ritz* insists on jacket and tie. Prices quoted here are for the standard teas; most places offer champagne teas, or more substantial high teas, for a higher price.

Claridges Brook St, W1 ☎020 7629 8860, ⓦ claridges.co.uk; ⊖ Bond Street; map pp.64–65. Daily 3pm, 3.30pm, 5pm & 5.30pm. £50.

Fortnum & Mason 181 Piccadilly, W1 ☎0845 602 5694, ⓦ fortnumandmason.com; ⊖ Green Park or Piccadilly Circus; map pp.64–65. Mon–Sat noon–9pm, Sun noon–8pm. £40.

The Ritz Piccadilly, W1 ☎020 7300 2345, ⓦ theritz london.com; ⊖ Green Park; map pp.64–65. Daily 11.30am, 1.30pm, 3.30pm, 5.30pm & 7.30pm. £47.

The Wolseley 160 Piccadilly, W1 ☎020 7499 6996, ⓦ thewolseley.com; ⊖ Green Park; map pp.64–65. Mon–Fri 3–6.30pm, Sat 3.30–5.30pm, Sun 3.30–6.30pm. £23.75.

since the 50s, keeping many of its original features (including the Gaggia coffee machine) and its iconic neon sign. Daily 7am–5am.

Beatroot 92 Berwick St, W1 ☎020 7437 8591, ⓦ beatroot.org.uk; ⊖ Piccadilly Circus, Oxford Circus or Tottenham Court Road; ; map pp.64–65. Great little veggie/vegan café by the market, doling out savoury bakes, stews and salads (plus good cakes) in boxes of varying sizes, from around a fiver. Mon–Fri 9am–9pm, Sat 11am–9pm.

 Breakfast Club 33 D'Arblay St, W1 ☎020 7434 2571, ⓦ thebreakfastclubcafes.com; ⊖ Oxford Circus; map pp.64–65. Comfy, battered, cheery and tattily retro, this laidback place is a fun (and popular) spot to linger over big all-day breakfasts, brunches, wraps, burgers, burritos and the like. Other branches around town. Mon–Sat 8am–10pm, Sun 8am–7pm.

Fernandez & Wells 73 Beak St, W1 ☎020 287 8124, ⓦ fernandezandwells.com; ⊖ Piccadilly Circus or Oxford Circus; map pp.64–65. Fabulous, freshly prepared sandwiches, artisan coffee and tempting cakes – most people take away, but there are one or two tables. Other branches around town. Mon–Fri 7.30am–6pm, Sat & Sun 9am–6pm.

★**Maison Bertaux** 28 Greek St, W1 ☎020 7437 6007, ⓦ maisonbertaux.com; ⊖ Leicester Square; map pp.64–65. Long-standing, old-fashioned and *très* French patisserie, with two floors and some outdoor seating. The decor is pretty, the cakes are out of this world, and a loyal, lingering clientele keeps the place bustlling. Mon–Sat 9.30am–10pm, Sun 9.30am–8pm.

Misato 11 Wardour St, W1 ☎020 7734 0808; ⊖ Leicester Square; map pp.64–65. Simple, canteen-style Japanese place serving filling rice and noodle dishes, plus hearty bento boxes and sushi, for low prices. Daily noon–10.30pm.

Yalla Yalla 1 Greens Court, W1 ☎020 7287 7663, ⓦ yalla-yalla.co.uk; ⊖ Piccadilly Circus; map pp.64–65. The name is Arabic for "hurry, hurry!", and the ambience in this hole-in-the-wall is buzzy and fast. The Beirut street food includes good-value veggie meze and plenty of nicely spiced skewered meats. Meze from £3. Branches in Shoreditch and Fitzrovia. Mon–Fri 10am–11.30pm, Sat 11am–11pm.

COVENT GARDEN

★**Food for Thought** 31 Neal St, WC2 ☎020 7836 0239, ⓦ foodforthought-london.co.uk; ⊖ Covent Garden; map pp.64–65. This minuscule veggie restaurant and takeaway has been dishing up hearty veggie/vegan soups, salads, hot dishes and desserts for some forty years, from a menu that changes twice daily. It's a crush at peak times. Mon–Sat noon–8.30pm, Sun noon–5.30pm.

Homeslice 13 Neal's Yard, WC2 ☎020 7836 4604, ⓦ homeslicepizza.co.uk; ⊖ Covent Garden; map pp.64–65. Funky little spot, which started its days as a streetfood truck, offering wood-fired thin-crust gourmet pizzas plus Prosecco on tap. £4 per slice, £20 for a 20" pizza. Mon–Sat noon–11pm, Sun noon–6pm.

Rock & Sole Plaice 47 Endell St, WC2 ☎020 7836 3785; ⊖ Covent Garden; map pp.64–65. A rare survivor; a traditional fish-and-chip shop in central London. The fish is tasty, though not cheap. Eat in or at a pavement table, or take away. Daily noon–10.30pm.

BLOOMSBURY

★**Diwana Bhel Poori House** 121–123 Drummond St, NW1 ☎020 7387 5556; ⊖ Euston; map p.75. On a street lined with good Indian restaurants, this South Indian vegetarian diner wins for its scrumptious all-you-can-eat lunchtime buffets (daily; £6.95) and huge, fresh thalis (from £7). BYOB. Mon–Sat noon–10.30pm, Sun noon–9.30pm.

1

Hummus Bros 37–63 Southampton Row, WC1 ☎020 7404 7079, ⓦhbros.co.uk; ⊖Holborn; map p.75. Tiny "hummus bar"/takeaway, with a couple of benches and formica tables, offering hummus with warm pitta and toppings from guacamole to chunky beef, plus salads and falafels. From £4. Mon–Fri 11am–9pm.

THE EAST END AND DALSTON

Brick Lane Beigel Bake 159 Brick Lane, E1 ☎020 7729 0616; ⊖Shoreditch High Street Overground; map pp.80–81. Classic bagel takeaway in the heart of the East End – very cheap, even for your top-end filling, smoked salmon and cream cheese. Daily 24hr.

Café 1001 91 Brick Lane, E1 ☎020 7247 6166, ⓦcafe1001.co.uk; ⊖Whitechapel or Shoreditch High Street Overground; map pp.80–81. This café-bar/club has kept going right through the East End's gentrification, and still keeps its laidback atmosphere, with sofas to crash on, used books to read and simple snacks and fattening cakes to sample. Frequent DJ sets and comedy nights. Daily 6am–midnight.

Fabrique Arch 385, Geffrye St, E2 ☎020 7033 0268, ⓦfabrique.co.uk; Hoxton Overground; map pp.60–61. Come to this simple, pretty Scandinavian bakery for spicy cinnamon buns, stone oven-baked sourdough breads, cream cakes and Johan & Nyström coffee. Mon–Fri 8am–6pm, Sat & Sun 10am–6pm.

Prufrock Coffee 23–25 Leather Lane, EC1 ☎020 7242 0467, ⓦprufrockcoffee.com; ⊖Chancery Lane or Farringdon; map pp.80–81. This pared-down shrine to the coffee bean, brainchild of world barista champion Gwilym Davies, pioneered London's artisan coffee craze and still outdoes its rivals. Mon–Fri 8am–6pm, Sat & Sun 10am–5pm.

Voodoo Ray's 95 Kingsland High St, E8 ☎020 7249 7865, ⓦvoodoorays.co.uk; Dalston Junction Overground; map pp.60–61. Grungy late-night joints come and go in Dalston, but *Voodoo Ray's* seems set to stay – a post-party pizza/Margarita joint where the pizzas (from £3.50/slice) are huge and the Margaritas – usually being necked by a crowd who've had quite enough already – are strong. Mon–Wed & Sun 5pm–midnight, Thurs 5pm–1am, Fri 5pm–3am, Sat noon–3pm.

THE CITY, DOCKLANDS AND THE EAST END

★Café Below Church of St Mary-le-Bow, Cheapside, EC2 ☎020 7329 0789, ⓦcafebelow.co.uk; ⊖St Paul's or Bank; map pp.80–81. A City gem: a cosy, good-value café in a Norman church crypt, serving modern Mediterranean food, with lots of veggie choices, and sticky breakfast pastries. Mains from £6. Mon–Fri 7.30am–2.30pm.

Hubbub 269 Westferry Rd, E14 ☎020 7515 5577, ⓦhubbubcafebar.com; Mudchute DLR; map pp.60–61. A real find in the otherwise drab Docklands eating scene,

this café-bar is housed in a former Victorian church, now an arts centre, and does decent burgers, sandwiches and tapas. Mon–Wed noon–11pm, Thurs & Fri noon–midnight, Sat 10am–midnight, Sun 10am–10.30pm.

THE SOUTH BANK AND SOUTHWARK

Maltby Street Market Maltby St ⓦmaltby.st; ⊖London Bridge; map pp.60–61. Edgier and less expensive than nearby Borough Market, this street-food hot spot huddles under the railway arches south of Tower Bridge, with stalls, food carts and pop-ups serving everything from Mozambique sauces to artisan gin. Most action is on the lively Ropewalk. Sat 9am–4pm, Sun 11am–4pm.

Marsh Ruby 30 Lower Marsh, SE1 ☎020 7620 0593, ⓦmarshruby.com; ⊖Waterloo; map p.86. Terrific filling lunchtime curries for around a fiver: the food, on seasonally changing menus, is mostly organic/free range and the communal dining is basic but cheery. Mon–Fri 11.30am–3pm.

KENSINGTON, CHELSEA AND NOTTING HILL

Books for Cooks 4 Blenheim Crescent, W11 ☎020 7221 1992, ⓦwww.booksforcooks.com; ⊖Ladbroke Grove or Notting Hill Gate; map pp.94–95. Tiny café within London's top cookery bookshop. Get there in time to grab a table for the set-menu lunch (noon–1.30pm). Tues–Sat 10am–6pm.

Capote y Toros 157 Old Brompton Rd, SW5 ☎020 7373 0567, ⓦcambiodetercio.co.uk; ⊖Gloucester Rd or South Kensington; map pp.94–95. The emphasis at this sunny bar is on Spain's wonderful sherries, with more than forty available by the glass, along with interesting tapas (£5–12). Tues–Sat 6–11.30pm.

★Lisboa Patisserie 57 Golborne Rd, W10 ☎020 8968 5242; ⊖Westbourne Park; map pp.94–95. Friendly, bustling Portuguese *pastelaria* selling the best custard tarts this side of Lisbon – along with coffee and a variety of cakes. *Café Oporto* at 62a Golborne Road is a good fallback if this place is full. Daily 7.30am–7.30pm.

NORTH LONDON

Brew House Kenwood House, Hampstead Lane, NW3; ⊖Highgate. Handy café serving everything from full English breakfasts to gourmet sandwiches, cakes and teas, either in the house's old servants' wing or in the huge, sunny garden courtyard. Daily: spring & summer 9am–6pm; rest of year 9am–4pm.

★Louis Patisserie 32 Heath St, NW3 ☎020 7435 9908; ⊖Hampstead. For more than fifty years now this tiny, understated, and gloriously old-fashioned Hungarian tearoom/patisserie has been serving sticky cakes, tea and coffee to Heath-bound hordes and elderly locals. Daily 9am–6pm.

1

WEST LONDON

Pembroke Lodge Richmond Park, Richmond TW10 ☎ 020 8940 8207, ⓦ pembroke-lodge.co.uk; ⊖ Richmond. In a gorgeous Georgian mansion in Richmond Park, this café has one of the best views in London and nice outdoor seating – there are some hot dishes, plus sandwiches and cakes. Daily 9am–5.30pm or 30min before dusk.

RESTAURANTS
MAYFAIR AND MARYLEBONE

★**Dehesa** 25 Ganton St, W1 ☎ 020 7494 4170, ⓦ dehesa.co.uk; ⊖ Oxford Circus or Piccadilly Circus; map pp.64–65. Very classy Spanish-Italian charcuterie and tapas bar serving rustic, robust food – try deep-fried courgette flowers with goat's cheese and honey, or salt cod croquettes, or just enjoy a plate of *jamón Ibérico* and a glass of Albariño. Tapas £5–10. Mon–Fri noon–3pm & 5–11pm, Sat noon–11pm, Sun noon–10pm.

The Providores and Tapa Room 109 Marylebone High St, W1 ☎ 020 7935 6175, ⓦ theprovidores.co.uk; ⊖ Baker Street or Bond Street; map pp.94–95. Outstanding fusion restaurant, co-helmed by New Zealand celeb chef Peter Gordon, with the more casual, cheaper *Tapa Room* café downstairs. Mon–Fri 9am–10.30pm, Sat 9am–3pm & 4–10.30pm, Sun 9am–3pm & 4–10pm.

SOHO AND CHINATOWN

Mildred's 45 Lexington St, W1 ☎ 020 7494 1634, ⓦ mildreds.co.uk; ⊖ Oxford Circus or Piccadilly Circus; map pp.64–65. *Mildred's* has a fresher and more contemporary feel than many veggie restaurants, and serves creative global cuisine. It's petite, and can get very busy, but takes no bookings. Mains £8–12. Mon–Sat noon–11pm.

★**Mr Kong** 21 Lisle St, WC2 ☎ 020 7437 7341, ⓦ mrkongrestaurant.com; ⊖ Leicester Square; map pp.64–65. Chinatown stalwart, with a very long menu of Cantonese food – don't miss the mussels in black bean sauce – and a good range of veggie dishes. Mains £7–25. Mon–Sat noon–2.45am, Sun noon–1.45am.

Polpo 41 Beak St, W1 ☎ 020 7734 4479, ⓦ polpo.co.uk; ⊖ Piccadilly Circus; map pp.64–65. Warm, well-established restaurant modelled on a Venetian *bacaro*. Small plates from £3 – try grilled fennel with white anchovy, *pizzette* or any of the *polpette* (meatballs). Reservations for lunch only. Mon–Sat noon–11pm, Sun noon–4pm.

Tonkotsu 63 Dean St, W1 ☎ 020 7437 0071, ⓦ tonkotsu.co.uk; ⊖ Tottenham Court Road; map pp.64–65. Slurpable, silky home-made ramen noodles in rich, savoury stocks, with pork belly, smoked haddock or veggie options. From £9. Mon–Fri noon–3pm & 5–10.30pm, Sat noon–10.30pm, Sun noon–10pm.

COVENT GARDEN

Dishoom 12 Upper St Martin's Lane, WC2 ☎ 020 7420 9320, ⓦ dishoom.com; ⊖ Leicester Square or Covent Garden; map pp.64–65. Recreating the atmosphere of the Persian cafés of Old Bombay, *Dishoom* is witty and stylish, but most importantly, serves delicious food – don't miss the black dhal. Mains from £6.50, small dishes for less. Mon–Thurs 8am–11pm, Fri 8am–midnight, Sat 9am–midnight, Sun 9am–11pm.

Flesh & Buns 41 Earlham St, WC2 ☎ 020 7632 9500, ⓦ fleshandbuns.com; ⊖ Covent Garden; map pp.64–65. The boozy, hipster rock'n'roll vibe at this noisy Japanese izakaya-style basement restaurant belies the superlative quality of the food: the rice buns of the name are the stars here, served with succulent meat or delicious fish – perfect to soak up huge quantities of sake. Mon & Tues noon–3pm & 5–10.30pm, Wed–Fri noon–3pm & 5–11.30pm, Sat noon–11.30pm, Sun noon–9.30pm.

Kopapa 32–34 Monmouth St, WC2 ☎ 020 7240 6076, ⓦ kopapa.co.uk; ⊖ Covent Garden; map pp.64–65. Fusion food from the Kiwi team behind *Providores* (see above). Dishes like tempura spicy dahl-stuffed inari pocket on caramelised coconut with pickled green papaya offer fresh, complex flavours; many are designed to share. Small plates from £6. Good breakfasts and brunches, too. Mon–Fri 8.30–11.30am & noon–11pm, Sat 9.30am–4pm & 4.30–11pm, Sun 9.30am–4pm & 4.30–9.45pm.

BLOOMSBURY

★**Caravan** 1 Granary Square, N1C ☎ 020 7101 7661, ⓦ caravankingscross.co.uk; ⊖ King's Cross St Pancras; map pp.60–61. A trailblazer on the burgeoning King's Cross scene, this buzzy spot, occupying a huge old grain store, serves tempting Modern European/fusion breakfasts, brunches, small plates and coffee to a lively crowd, many of them from the next-door St Martin's School of Art. Small plates from £5. Mon & Tues 8am–10.30pm, Wed & Thurs 8am–11pm, Fri 8am–midnight, Sat 10am–midnight, Sun 10am–4pm.

Cigala 54 Lamb's Conduit St, WC1 ☎ 020 7405 1717, ⓦ cigala.co.uk; ⊖ Russell Square; map p.75. Simple dishes, robust flavours and Spanish flair at this sophisticated Iberian restaurant with daily changing menus. Mains from £12; two-/three-course set lunch menus £17.50/£19.50; tapas from £4. Mon–Fri noon–10.45pm, Sat 12.30–10.45pm, Sun 12.30–9.45pm.

THE CITY AND CLERKENWELL

Duck and Waffle Heron Tower, 110 Bishopsgate, EC2 ☎ 020 3640 7310, ⓦ duckandwaffle.com; ⊖ Aldgate; map pp.80–81. Forty floors up, this smart place offers amazing City views and hipster comfort food (the signature dish features waffles, duck confit, fried duck egg and mustard maple syrup; £17). Small plates from £9. Daily 24hr.

★**Moro** 34–36 Exmouth Market, EC1 ☎020 7833 8336, ⓦmoro.co.uk; ⊖Farringdon or Angel; map pp.80–81. Gorgeous, welcoming restaurant that's a place of pilgrimage for disciples of Sam and Sam Clark's Moorish/Iberian cookbooks. The lamb dishes and the yoghurt cake are perennial hits, but all of it is tremendous, prepared with unusual ingredients. Booking essential. Mains £16 21, with tapas (around £5) served all day; they also have a tiny tapas bar, *Morito*, next door (where reservations are taken for lunch only). Mon–Sat noon–10.30pm, Sun 12.30–2.45pm.

Quality Chop House 88–94 Farringdon Rd, EC1 ☎020 7278 1452, ⓦthequalitychophouse.com; ⊖Farringdon; map pp.80–81. Beautiful old dining room, butcher's and slightly more casual wine bar with a daily changing menu focusing on the best cuts of British meat and freshest British produce. It's not cheap (weekday lunch mains from £13), but you can get set menus at dinner (£35) and Sun lunch (£28). Mon–Sat noon–3pm & 6–10.30pm. Sun noon–4pm; wine bar Mon–Sat noon–midnight.

St John Bread and Wine 94 96 Commercial St, E1 ☎020 7251 0848, ⓦstjohnbreadandwine.com; ⊖Liverpool Street; map pp.80–81. A simpler offshoot of the famed *St John*, with the same superlative British food on a regularly changing menu – featuring offal, pig's cheek and the like, but also wonderful veg and fish dishes, and simple breakfasts. Dishes £5–18. Mon–Fri 9–11am, noon–3pm & 6–11pm, Sat 9–11am, noon 4pm & 6–11pm, Sun 9–11am, noon–4pm & 6–9pm.

THE EAST END AND DALSTON

Beagle 397–400 Geffrye St, E2 ☎020 7613 2967, ⓦbeaglelondon.co.uk; ⊖Hoxton; map pp.60–61. Occupying three railway arches, this Hoxton restaurant buzzes with a young crowd enjoying robust Modern British food and fashionable cocktails. Mains from £10. Mon & Tues 6–10.30pm, Wed–Fri noon–3pm & 6–10.30pm, Sat 11am–3pm & 6–10.30pm, Sun 11am–5pm.

The Hawksmoor 157 Commercial St, E1 ☎020 7426 4850, ⓦthehawksmoor.com; ⊖Liverpool Street or Shoreditch High Street Overground; map pp.80–81. Carnivores drool at the mention of this steakhouse, where the charcoal-grilled cuts of meat, impeccably sourced, are huge and succulent. A full meal could set you back well over £50, but the two-/three-course menu (Mon–Sat noon–3pm & 5–6pm) cuts costs at £23/£26. Mon–Sat noon–2.30pm & 5–10.30pm, Sun noon–4.30pm.

Lahore Kebab House 2–10 Umberston St, E1 ☎020 7481 9737, ⓦlahore-kebabhouse.com; ⊖Aldgate East; map pp.80–81. Famed Punjabi kebab house, just off Commercial Road. Go for the lamb cutlets and roti, and arrive hungry. BYOB. Mains £7–11. Daily noon–1am.

Sông Quê 134 Kingsland Rd, E2 ☎020 7613 3222, ⓦsongque.co.uk; ⊖Hoxton station; map pp.60–61. In a street crammed with budget Vietnamese restaurants, this simple place offers good *phô* (£8.50) and spicy seafood dishes. Mon–Fri noon–3pm & 5.30–11pm, Sat noon–11pm, Sun noon–10.30pm.

★**Tayyab's** 83–89 Fieldgate St, E1 ☎020 7247 9543, ⓦtayyabs.co.uk; ⊖Whitechapel; map pp.80–81. For more than forty years *Tayyab's* has been offering straightforward Punjabi food: good, freshly cooked and served without pretension. Prices have remained low (mains from £7) and booking is essential. BYOB. Daily noon–11.30pm.

Tonkotsu East Arch 334, 1a Dunston St, E8 ☎020 7254 2478, ⓦtonkotsu.co.uk; ⊖Haggerston; map pp.60–61. The Dalston branch of Soho's favourite Japanese noodle joint serves the same rich, silky home-made noodles in oily, savoury stocks, plus dumplings and *gyoza*, to a local hipster crowd sipping cocktails to while away what can be a long wait for a table. Mon 5–10pm, Tues–Fri noon–3pm & 5–10pm, Sat noon–10pm, Sun noon–9.30pm.

SOUTHBANK AND SOUTHWARK

The Laughing Gravy 154 Blackfriars Rd, SE1 ☎020 7998 1701, ⓦthelaughinggravy.co.uk; ⊖Southwark; map p.86. Welcoming, cosy brasserie serving robust Modern English and Mediterranean food in a brick-lined dining room; a great find in this neck of the woods. Mon–Thurs noon–3pm & 5–10pm, Fri noon–3pm & 5–10.30pm, Sat noon 4pm & 5 10.30pm, Sun noon–4.30pm.

Zucca 184 Bermondsey St, SE1 ☎020 7378 6809, ⓦzuccalondon.com; ⊖London Bridge; map pp.60–61. Prices for the elegant modern Italian food in this lovely restaurant – fresh pasta, creamy risottos, grilled shellfish, all made with the freshest, simplest ingredients – are surprisingly low. Mains from £11. Tues–Fri noon–3pm & 6–10pm, Sat noon–3.30pm & 6–10pm, Sun noon–4pm.

KENSINGTON AND CHELSEA

★**Dinner by Heston Blumenthal** Mandarin Oriental Hotel, 66 Knightsbridge, SW1 ☎020 7201 3833, ⓦdinnerbyheston.com; ⊖Knightsbridge; map pp.94–95. Blumenthal doesn't actually cook here – the head chef worked with him at the *Fat Duck* – and there is less emphasis on flashy molecular cuisine, but the creative food, using old English recipes, is as intriguing as you would expect – try the spiced pigeon and the tipsy cake. Mains from £28; the three-course weekday lunch menu (£38) is a bargain. Daily noon–2.30pm & 6.30–10.30pm.

1

★**Medlar** 438 Kings Rd, SW10 ☎020 7349 1900, ⓦmedlarrestaurant.co.uk; ⊖Fulham Broadway; map pp.94–95. Lovely Michelin-starred place offering French-influenced Modern British food – duck breast and confit with puy lentils, beetroot, mustard fruits and paysanne salad, for example – in a relaxed dining room. It's all prix fixe, and good value, with three-course lunches (£27 Mon–Fri, £30 Sat, £35 Sun) and dinners (£45 Mon–Sat, £35 Sun). Daily noon–3pm & 6.30–10.30pm.

BAYSWATER AND NOTTING HILL

Le Café Anglais 8 Porchester Gardens, W2 ☎020 7221 1415, ⓦlecafeanglais.co.uk; ⊖Bayswater; map pp.94–95. Splendid Modern British/European brasserie and oyster bar in an airy, vaguely Art Deco space – hard to believe you're in the bland Whiteley's shopping mall. Mains £14–28; set lunch menus (two/three courses) from £10. Mon–Thurs noon–3.30pm & 6.30–10.30pm, Fri noon–3.30pm & 6.30–11pm, Sat 11am–3.30pm & 6.30–11pm, Sun noon–3.30pm & 6.30–10pm.

Hereford Road 3 Hereford Rd, W2 ☎020 7727 1144, ⓦherefordroad.org; ⊖Queensway/Notting Hill Gate; map pp.94–95. *St John* alumni Tom Pemberton brings highly accomplished English cooking to West London, with the focus on old-fashioned excellence and the best produce. Mains from £11.50, and bargain set meals, from £9.50, on weekday lunchtimes. Mon–Sat noon–3pm & 6–10.30pm, Sun noon–4pm & 6–10pm.

NORTH LONDON

Jin Kichi 73 Heath St, NW3 ☎020 7794 6158, ⓦwww.jinkichi.com; ⊖Hampstead. Tiny, homely and very busy neighbourhood Japanese diner specializing in charcoal-grilled *yakitori* (skewers): lots of chicken, of course, but also quails' eggs or ox tongue, among others. Tues–Sat 12.30–2pm & 6–10.45pm, Sun 12.30–2pm & 6–10pm.

Manna 4 Erskine Rd, NW3 ☎020 7722 8028, ⓦmannav.com; ⊖Chalk Farm; map pp.60–61. Upscale veggie restaurant, full of Primrose Hill yoga bunnies, serving large portions of mostly organic food, much of it vegan, from around the world. Mains £12–14. Tues–Fri noon–3pm & 6.30–10pm, Sat noon–3pm & 6–10pm, Sun noon–8.30pm.

Namaaste Kitchen 64 Parkway ☎020 7485 5977, ⓦnamaastekitchen.co.uk; ⊖Camden Town; map pp.60–61. Superb contemporary Indian and Pakistani restaurant, presenting unusual dishes from spicy crab-and-cod cakes to wild rabbit *achari*, plus a gluten-free menu. Mains £9–17, set menu £10. Mon–Thurs noon–2.30pm & 5.30–11.30pm, Fri & Sat noon–11.30pm, Sun noon–11pm.

SOUTH LONDON

Old Brewery Pepys Building, Old Royal Naval College, SE10 ☎0203 327 1280, ⓦoldbrewerygreenwich.com; Cutty Sark DLR. The café of the Meantime craft brewery serves light meals during the day before transforming into a more expensive Modern British brasserie in the evening. Daily 11am–11pm.

WEST LONDON

Chez Lindsay 11 Hill Rise, Richmond TW10 ☎020 8948 7473, ⓦchezlindsay.co.uk; ⊖Richmond. Small, bright Breton restaurant, serving *galettes*, crêpes and more formal French main courses, including lots of fresh fish and shellfish. *Galettes* from £4, mains £11–23. Mon–Sat noon–11pm, Sun noon–10pm.

DRINKING

WESTMINSTER

The Chandos 29 St Martin's Lane, W1 ☎020 7836 1401; ⊖Charing Cross; map pp.64–65. If you can get one of the booths downstairs, or the leather sofas upstairs in the more relaxed Opera Room Bar, then you'll find it difficult to leave, especially given the cheap Sam Smith's beer. Mon–Sat 11am–11pm, Sun noon–10.30pm.

★**St Stephen's Tavern** 10 Bridge St, SW1 ☎020 7925 2286, ⓦststephenstavern.co.uk; ⊖Westminster; map pp.64–65. Opulent Victorian pub, built in 1867, wall to wall with civil servants and MPs, and serving good real ales. Mon–Fri 11am–11pm, Sat 11am–8pm, Sun noon–6pm.

ST JAMES'S, MAYFAIR AND MARYLEBONE

Guinea 30 Bruton Place, W1 ☎020 7409 1728, ⓦtheguinea.co.uk; ⊖Bond Street or Oxford Circus; map pp.64–65. Pretty, old-fashioned, flower-strewn back-lane pub, serving good Young's bitter and excellent steak-and-kidney pies. Invariably packed to its tiny rafters. There's a traditional steak restaurant attached. Mon–Fri 11am–11pm, Sat 6–11pm.

ICA Bar The Mall, SW1 ☎020 7930 8619, ⓦica.org.uk; ⊖Piccadilly Circus or Charing Cross; map pp.64–65. Cool drinking venue in the contemporary gallery, popular with an arty crowd. Tues evenings (6–7.30pm) see buy-one-get-one-free deals on cocktails. Tues–Sun 11am–11pm.

Red Lion 23 Crown Passage, SW1 ☎020 7930 4141; ⊖Green Park; map pp.64–65. Hidden away in a passageway off Pall Mall, this is a genuinely warm and cosy local, with super-friendly bar staff, well-kept beer and above-average sandwiches. Mon–Sat 11.30am–11pm.

The Windmill 6–8 Mill St, W1 ☎020 7491 8050, ⓦwindmillmayfair.co.uk; ⊖Oxford Circus; map pp.64–65. Convivial pub just off Regent St, a perfect retreat for exhausted shoppers. The Young's beers are good, as are the pies, for which the pub has won numerous awards. Mon–Fri 11am–11pm, Sat noon–5pm.

SOHO

Argyll Arms 18 Argyll St, W1 ☎020 7734 6117, ⊕nicholsonspubs.co.uk; ⊖Oxford Circus; map pp.64–65. Mobbed by shoppers and tourists alike, but this Nicholson's pub has preserved many features of its Victorian interior and offers a good range of real ales. Mon–Thurs 10am–11.30pm, Fri & Sat 10am–midnight, Sun 10am–11pm.

Dog & Duck 18 Bateman St, W1 ☎020 7494 0697, ⊕nicholsonspubs.co.uk; ⊖Tottenham Court Road; map pp.64–65. Tiny Nicholson's corner pub that retains much of its old character, beautiful Victorian tiling and mosaics, a choice of real ales and typically mixed Soho clientele. If it gets too busy downstairs, head upstairs to the George Orwell Bar (he used to drink here). Daily 10am–11pm.

LAB 12 Old Compton St, W1 ☎020 7437 7820, ⊕labbaruk.com; ⊖Leicester Square; map pp.64–65. Two-floor bar with a clubby feel where cocktail-school graduates serve up classics and new concoctions. DJs Thurs–Sat. Mon–Sat 4pm–midnight, Sun 4–10.30pm.

★**The Social** 5 Little Portland St, W1 ☎020 7636 4992, ⊕thesocial.com; ⊖Oxford Circus; map p.75. Retro club/bar and diner, with DJs playing everything from afro to electronica, and a genuinely hedonistic, hard-partying crowd. Mon–Wed noon–midnight, Thurs & Fri 9am–1am, Sat 6pm–1am.

COVENT GARDEN AND STRAND

★**Cross Keys** 31 Endell St, WC2 ☎020 7836 5185, ⊕crosskeyscoventgarden.com; ⊖Covent Garden; map pp.64–65. Stuffed with copper pots, and memorabilia, and fronted with a profusion of flowers, this most welcoming of West End pubs attracts an appealing blend of older Covent Garden residents, young workers and tourists. Mon–Sat 11am–11pm, Sun noon–10.30pm.

★**Gordon's** 47 Villiers St, WC2 ☎020 7930 1408, ⊕gordonswinebar.com; ⊖Charing Cross or Embankment; map pp.64–65. Cavernous, shabby, atmospheric wine bar specializing in ports, sherries and Madeiras. The genial atmosphere makes this a favourite with local office workers, who spill outdoors in the summer. Mon–Sat 11am–11pm, Sun noon–10pm.

Lamb & Flag 33 Rose St, WC2 ☎020 7497 9504, ⊕lambandflagcoventgarden.co.uk; ⊖Leicester Square; map pp.64–65. Over 300 years old, this agreeably tatty Fuller's pub, tucked away down an alley between Garrick and Floral streets, is invariably packed. Mon–Thurs 11am–11pm, Fri & Sat 11am–11.30pm, Sun noon–10.30pm.

The Salisbury 90 St Martin's Lane, WC2 ☎020 7836 5863, ⊕taylor-walker.co.uk; ⊖Leicester Square; map pp.64–65. Beautifully preserved Victorian pub, run by Taylor Walker, with etched and engraved windows, bronze figurines and Art Nouveau fittings. Mon–Wed 11am–11pm, Thurs 11am–11.30pm, Fri 11am–midnight, Sat noon–midnight, Sun noon–10.30pm.

BLOOMSBURY

The Duke 7 Roger St, WC1 ☎020 7242 7230, ⊕dukepub.co.uk; ⊖Russell Square; map p.75. Lovely little neighbourhood gastropub, without the pretensions often associated with the breed, and an authentic Art Deco bent to the decor. Its discreet location keeps the crowd in the small bar manageable. Mon–Sat noon–11pm.

The Lamb 94 Lamb's Conduit St, WC1 ☎020 7405 0713, ⊕youngs.co.uk; ⊖Russell Square; map p.75. This marvellously well-preserved Victorian pub, serving Young's ales, is packed with atmosphere with its old mirrors, gleaming dark wood and etched glass "snob" screens. Check out the intriguing old sepia photos lining the walls. Mon–Wed noon–11pm, Thurs & Fri noon–midnight, Sat 11am–midnight, Sun noon–10.30pm.

Museum Tavern 49 Great Russell St, WC1 ☎020 7242 8987, ⊕taylor-walker.co.uk; ⊖Tottenham Court Road or Russell Square; map p.75. Karl Marx's erstwhile drinking hole is a handsome old Taylor Walker pub opposite the main entrance to the British Museum. Mon–Thurs 11am–11.30pm, Fri & Sat 11am–midnight, Sun 10am–10pm.

HOLBORN

Princess Louise 209 High Holborn, WC1 ☎020 7405 8816, ⊕princesslouisepub.co.uk; ⊖Holborn; map p.75. Architecturally, one of London's most impressive Victorian pubs, featuring gold-trimmed mirrors, gorgeous mosaics and a fine moulded ceiling. Even the toilets are listed. The Sam Smith's beer is reasonably priced, too. Mon–Fri 11am–11pm, Sat noon–11pm, Sun noon–6.45pm.

Ye Olde Mitre 1 Ely Court, EC1 ☎020 7405 4751, ⊕yeoldemitreholborn.co.uk; ⊖Farringdon; map pp.80–81. Hidden down a tiny alleyway off Hatton Garden, this atmospheric Fuller's pub dates back to 1546; the low-ceilinged, wood-panelled rooms are packed with history and the ales are good. Mon–Fri 11am–11pm.

CLERKENWELL

★**Jerusalem Tavern** 55 Britton St, EC1 ☎020 7490 4281, ⊕stpetersbrewery.co.uk; ⊖Farringdon; map pp.80–81. Something special: a tiny, converted Georgian coffee house – the frontage dates from 1810 – that has retained much of its original character. Better still, the excellent draught beers are from St Peter's Brewery in Suffolk. Mon–Fri 11am–11pm.

1

The Three Kings 7 Clerkenwell Close, EC1 ☎ 020 7253 0483; ⊖ Farringdon; map pp.80–81. This Clerkenwell favourite is tucked away just north of Clerkenwell Green, with a delightful eclectic interior and two small rooms upstairs perfect for long occupation. Right next to *The Crown*, on Clerkenwell Green itself, which is also well worth a trip. Mon–Fri noon–11pm, Sat 5.30–11pm.

THE CITY

★ **The Black Friar** 174 Queen Victoria St, EC4 ☎ 020 7236 5474, ⓦ nicholsonspubs.co.uk; ⊖ Blackfriars; map pp.80–81. Quirky old Nicholson's pub with Art Nouveau marble friezes of boozy monks and a highly decorated alcove – all original, dating from 1905. A lovely fireplace and an unhurried atmosphere make this a relaxing place to drink. Mon–Sat 10am–11pm, Sun noon–10.30pm.

The Counting House 50 Cornhill, EC2 ☎ 020 7283 7123, ⓦ the-counting-house.com; ⊖ Bank; map pp.80–81. Inspired Fuller's conversion, of an old bank, with a magnificent interior featuring high ceilings, marble pillars, mosaic flooring and a large, oval island bar. Mon–Fri 11am–11pm.

The Lamb Tavern 10–12 Leadenhall Market, EC3 ☎ 020 7626 2454, ⓦ lambtavernleadenhall.com; ⊖ Monument; map pp.80–81. In the heart of beautiful Leadenhall Market, this Young's pub offers almost exclusively standing room only (both inside and out). The tiled *Tom's Bar* downstairs can be cosier, and offers cheese and sausage platters. Mon–Fri 11am–11pm.

★ **Ye Olde Cheshire Cheese** Wine Office Court, 145 Fleet St, EC4 ☎ 020 7353 6170; ⊖ Temple or Blackfriars; map pp.80–81. This seventeenth-century watering hole – the haunt of eminent historical figures including Dickens and Dr Johnson – has several snug, dark-panelled bars and real fires. Popular with tourists, but by no means exclusively so. Mon–Fri 11.30am–11pm, Sat noon–11pm.

THE EAST END AND DOCKLANDS

The Gun 27 Coldharbour, E14 ☎ 020 7515 5222, ⓦ thegundocklands.com; ⊖ Canary Wharf, South Quay or Blackwall DLR. Legendary dockers' pub, once the haunt of Lord Nelson, *The Gun* is now a classy gastropub, with unrivalled views over the O2. Mon–Sat 11am–midnight, Sun 11am–11pm.

Loungelover 1 Whitby St, E1 ☎ 020 7012 1234, ⓦ loungelover.co.uk; ⊖ Shoreditch High Street Overground; map pp.80–81. Behind the unprepossessing facade of this former meat-packing factory lies a opulently camp bar with a nice line in creative cocktails. It's been around a while on the Shoreditch scene and seems set to stay, despite the occasionally too-cool-for-school service. Mon–Thurs 6pm–midnight, Fri & Sat 5pm–1am.

The Owl & Pussycat 34 Redchurch St, E2 ☎ 020 3487 0088, ⓦ owlandpussycatshoreditch.com; ⊖ Shoreditch High Street Overground; map pp.80–81. One of many old boozers in the area to have been gussied up and hipsterfied, this backstreet pub has managed to keep a generally mellow vibe. It can get hectic at the weekends, but that comes with the territory. Sun & Mon noon–11pm, Tues–Sat noon–midnight.

Ten Bells 84 Commercial St, E1 ☎ 020 7366 1721, ⓦ tenbells.com; ⊖ Shoreditch High Street Overground; map pp.80–81. Historic pub, with Jack the Ripper associations, with some beautiful Victorian tiling and a fantastic Modern British restaurant upstairs (booking essential; closed Mon). Mon–Wed & Sun noon–midnight, Thurs–Sat noon–1am.

Town of Ramsgate 62 Wapping High St, EW1 ☎ 020 7481 8000, ⓦ townoframsgate.co.uk; ⊖ Wapping Overground. Dark, narrow, medieval pub near what used to be Execution Dock. Captain Blood was discovered here with the Crown Jewels under his cloak, "Hanging" Judge Jeffreys was arrested here trying to flee, and Captain Bligh and Fletcher Christian were regulars. The beer garden, overlooking the river, is a big draw. Daily noon–midnight.

Worship Street Whistling Shop 63 Worship St, EC2 ☎ 020 7247 0015, ⓦ whistlingshop.com; ⊖ Old Street; map pp.80–81. Theatrical, shabbily opulent cocktail bar that set the bar high when it spearheaded London's gin palace craze. The drinks, composed with unusual ingredients, are wildly creative. Tues 5pm–midnight, Wed & Thurs 5pm–1am, Fri & Sat 5pm–2am.

SOUTH BANK AND SOUTHWARK

Anchor & Hope 36 The Cut, SE1 ☎ 020 7928 9898, ⓦ anchorandhopepub.co.uk; ⊖ Southwark; map p.86. The *Anchor* gastropub dishes up excellent, simple grub: Modern European and creative, with mouth-watering puds. Bookings are only taken for Sunday lunch. Mon 5–11pm, Tues–Sat 11am–11pm, Sun 12.30–5pm.

The Anchor 34 Park St, SE1 ☎ 020 7407 1577; ⊖ London Bridge; map pp.88–89. Built in 1770, this sprawling pub retains only a few vestiges of the past, but has one of the city's few riverside terraces – inevitably it's often crowded with tourists. Mon–Wed 11am–11pm, Thurs–Sat 11am–midnight, Sun noon–11pm.

George Inn 77 Borough High St, SE1 ☎ 020 7407 2056, ⓦ nationaltrust.org.uk/george-inn; ⊖ Borough or London Bridge; map pp.88–89. London's only surviving galleried coaching inn, dating from the seventeenth century and now owned by the National Trust; mobbed by tourists, but it does serve a good range of real ales. Daily 11am–11pm.

★ **King's Arms** 25 Roupell St, SE1 ☎ 020 7207 0784, ⓦ windmilltaverns.com; ⊖ Waterloo; map p.86. Terrific

1

local divided into two sections; a traditional drinking area in the front, with a tastefully cluttered, conservatory-style dining space at the rear, where good Thai food is served at long wooden tables. Mon–Fri 11am–11pm, Sat noon–11pm, Sun noon–10.30pm.

KENSINGTON AND CHELSEA

★ **Churchill Arms** 119 Kensington Church St, W8 ☎ 020 7727 4242, ⊛ churchillarmskensington.co.uk; ⊖ Notting Hill Gate; map pp.94–95. Justifiably popular, flower-festooned pub serving Fuller's beers, Guinness, and good Thai food. Mon–Wed 11am–11pm, Thurs–Sat 11am–midnight, Sun noon–10.30pm.

Cooper's Arms Bar 87 Flood St, SW3 ☎ 020 7376 3120, ⊛ coopersarms.co.uk; ⊖ Sloane Square; map pp.94 95. Decent, spacious neighbourhood pub, which may not be more than the sum of its parts – reasonable gastropub food, a range of beers, plenty of spots to choose from – but is still a good find so close to the King's Road. Daily noon–11pm.

The Elgin 96 Ladbroke Grove, W11 ☎ 020 7229 5663, ⊛ geronimo-inns.co.uk; ⊖ Ladbroke Grove; map pp.94–95. Capacious pub where the buzzy vibe, lovely original features, funky decor and fancy gastropub menu bring in the cool Portobello crowd. Mon–Thurs 11am–11pm, Fri & Sat 11am–midnight, Sun noon–10.30pm.

Grenadier 18 Wilton Row, SW1 ☎ 020 7235 3074, ⊛ taylor-walker.co.uk; ⊖ Hyde Park Corner or Knightsbridge; map pp.94–95. Located in a cobbled mews, this quaint little Taylor Walker pub was Wellington's local (his horse block still stands outside) and his officers' mess; the original pewter bar survives, as does a cosy, old-fashioned ambience. Real ales and pricey bar food. Mon–Sat noon–11pm, Sun noon–10.30pm.

★ **The Nag's Head** 53 Kinnerton St, SW1 ☎ 020 7235 1135; ⊖ Hyde Park Corner or Knightsbridge; map pp.94–95. Convivial, quirky little pub in a posh mews, with eclectic, raffish memorabilia plastered over the walls, real ales, occasional live jazz and a mobile phone ban. Like going back in time – and only in a good way. Mon–Sat 11am–11pm, Sun noon–10.30pm.

The Pig's Ear 35 Old Church St, SW3 ☎ 020 7352 2908, ⊛ thepigsear.info; ⊖ Sloane Square; map pp.94–95. Charming, locally adored gastropub serving the best craft ales and classy Modern British food. Daily noon–11pm.

NORTH LONDON

Edinboro Castle 57 Mornington Terrace, NW1 ☎ 020 7255 9651, ⊛ www.edinborocastlepub.co.uk; ⊖ Camden Town; map pp.60–61. A large pub with an unfussy interior and an enormous beer garden which hosts summer weekend barbecues. Above-average selection of

draught continental lagers and a couple of real ales, plus a not-bad gastro menu. Mon–Sat noon–11pm, Sun noon–10.30pm.

The Flask 77 Highgate West Hill, N6 ☎ 020 8348 7346, ⊛ theflaskhighgate.com; bus #210 from ⊖ Archway. Ideally situated at the heart of Highgate village green – with a rambling, low-ceilinged interior and a summer terrace – and, as a result, very, very popular at the weekend. Mon–Sat noon–11pm, Sun noon–10.30pm.

The Holly Bush 22 Holly Mount, off Holly Hill, NW3 ☎ 020 7435 2892, ⊛ hollybushhampstead.co.uk; ⊖ Hampstead. A lovely, creaky old Fuller's pub, with a real fire in winter, tucked away in the steep backstreets of Hampstead village. Some fine real ales on offer, as well as decent food (particularly the sausages and pies), though it can get mobbed at weekends. Mon–Sat noon–11pm, Sun noon–10.30pm.

Lock Tavern 35 Chalk Farm Rd, NW1 ☎ 020 7482 7163, ⊛ lock-tavern.com; ⊖ Chalk Farm; map pp.60–61. Rambling pub with comfy sofas, a leafy roof terrace and a beer garden, street food-style pub grub and DJs playing anything from punk funk and electro to avant-country. Mon–Thurs noon–midnight, Fri & Sat noon–1am, Sun noon–11pm.

Prince Alfred 5a Formosa St, W9 ☎ 020 7286 3287, ⊛ theprincealfred.com; ⊖ Warwick Ave; map pp.60–61. A Victorian pub with all its original 1862 fittings intact, right down to the glazed "snob screens" that divide the bar into a series of "snugs". There's a pricey Modern European restaurant at the back. Mon–Thurs noon–11pm, Fri & Sat noon–midnight, Sun noon–10.30pm.

SOUTH LONDON

Crown & Greyhound 73 Dulwich Village, SE21 ☎ 020 8299 4976, ⊛ www.thecrownandgreyhound.co.uk; North Dulwich station from London Bridge. Large Victorian pub, convenient for the Picture Gallery, with a big beer garden. Mon–Wed 11am–11pm, Thurs–Sat 11am–midnight, Sun noon–10.30pm.

Cutty Sark Ballast Quay, off Lassell St, SE10 ☎ 020 8858 3146, ⊛ cuttysarkse10.co.uk; Cutty Sark DLR or Maze Hill station from Charing Cross or London Bridge. This Georgian pub is a good place for a riverside pint and can often be less touristy than the nearby *Trafalgar Tavern*. Mon–Sat 11am–11pm, Sun noon–10.30pm.

WEST LONDON

★ **Dove** 19 Upper Mall, W6 ☎ 020 8748 9474, ⊛ dovehammersmith.co.uk; ⊖ Ravenscourt Park. Wonderful low-beamed, old riverside pub with the smallest bar in the UK (4ft by 7ft), a terrace and a very popular Sunday roasts. Mon–Sat 11am–11pm, Sun noon–10.30pm.

1

White Cross Hotel Water Lane, Richmond, TW9 ☎020 8940 6844, ⓦthewhitecrossrichmond.com; ⊖Richmond. With a longer pedigree and more character than its rivals, the *White Cross* has a very popular, large garden overlooking the river and a lounge with an open fire. Mon–Sat 11am–11pm, Sun 11am–10.30pm.

NIGHTLIFE

LIVE MUSIC VENUES

London's live music scene is extremely diverse, encompassing all variations of rock, blues, roots and world music, and, along with impressive homegrown talent, the city's media spotlight makes it pretty much the place for young bands to break into the global mainstream.

GENERAL VENUES

★**Academy Brixton** 211 Stockwell Rd, SW9 ☎0844 477 2000, ⓦo2academybrixton.co.uk; ⊖Brixton. The Academy has seen them all, from mods and rockers to Snoop Dogg. The 5000-capacity Art Deco hall doesn't always deliver perfect sound quality, but remains a cracking place to see bands.

Cargo 83 Rivington St, EC2 ☎020 7739 3440, ⓦcargo-london.com; ⊖Old Street or Shoreditch High Street Overground; map pp.80–81. Small, popular venue in what was once a railway arch, with a restaurant and chilled garden area. Hosts a variety of live acts, including jazz, hip-hop, indie and folk, and excellent club nights.

Forum 9–17 Highgate Rd, NW5 ☎020 7428 4099, ⓦmamacolive.com/theforum; ⊖Kentish Town. Decent mid-sized venue, with a large stage hosting a mix of successful and underground new acts and groups inching their way onto the nostalgia circuit.

Hammersmith Apollo 45 Queen Caroline St, W6 ☎020 8563 3800, ⓦeventimapollo.com; ⊖Hammer-smith. The former Hammersmith Odeon is a cavernous space (downstairs is seating or standing, depending on the occasion), featuring everyone from Jack White to James Blunt, plus stand-up and popular theatre.

★**O2 Shepherds Bush Empire** Shepherd's Bush Green, W12 ☎0844 477 2000, ⓦo2shepherdsbush empire.co.uk; ⊖Shepherd's Bush. Yet another grand old theatre, the 2000-capacity Empire now hosts a fine cross-section of interesting UK and international bands. There's often a great atmosphere at the front downstairs, while the vertigo-inducing upstairs balconies provide great stage views.

★**Roundhouse** Chalk Farm Rd, NW1 ☎0844 482 8008, ⓦroundhouse.org.uk; ⊖Chalk Farm; map pp.60–61. This magnificent listed Victorian steam engine shed is one of London's premier performing arts centres; alongside circus, comedy and spoken word, its programme includes artier rock acts and world music.

ROCK, BLUES, INDIE AND FOLK

★**12 Bar Club** Denmark St, WC2 ☎020 7240 2622, ⓦ12barclub.com; ⊖Tottenham Court Road; map pp.64–65. Tiny, atmospheric bar and venue offering up-and-coming, cheap and often pleasantly eccentric indie, blues and folk gigs.

Borderline Orange Yard, Manette St, W1 ☎0844 847 2465, ⓦmamacolive.com/theborderline; ⊖Tottenham Court Road; map pp.64–65. Small and slightly ramshackle basement joint with awkward pillars but good sound and a diverse musical policy.

Green Note 106 Parkway, NW1 ☎020 7485 9899, ⓦgreennote.co.uk; ⊖Camden Town; map pp.60–61. Intimate music venue that punches way above its weight with its excellent line-up of roots, folk, acoustic and world music, and has a little veggie café to boot.

KOKO 1a Camden High St, NW1 ⓦkoko.uk.com; ⊖Mornington Crescent; map pp.60–61. An institution since its days as the Camden Palace, this venue's grand interior hosts popular club nights and gigs – and has historically been a favourite venue for superstars doing "secret" shows.

Underworld 174 Camden High St, NW1 ☎020 7482 1932, ⓦtheunderworldcamden.co.uk; ⊖Camden Town; map pp.60–61. Shouty, scruffy warren under the *World's End* pub – a great place to check out metal, metalcore and nu-metal bands.

★**Union Chapel** Compton Terrace, N1 ☎020 7226 1686, ⓦunionchapel.org.uk; ⊖Highbury & Islington; map pp.60–61. Intimate venue in a beautiful old church (seating is on pews); the line-up ranges from contemporary folk via comedy to world music, R'n'B and indie legends.

NOTTING HILL CARNIVAL

The two-day free **festival** (ⓦthenottinghillcarnival.com) in Notting Hill is the longest-running, best-known and biggest street party in Europe. Dating back more than fifty years, the Caribbean carnival is a tumult of imaginatively decorated parade floats, eye-catching costumes, thumping sound systems, live bands, irresistible food and huge crowds. It takes place on the Sunday and Monday of the last weekend of August.

JAZZ AND WORLD MUSIC

Jazz Café 5 Parkway, NW1 ☎020 7485 6834, ⓦmamacolive.com/thejazzcafe; ⊖Camden Town; map pp.60–61. A combination of big names (at big prices) and acts from the clubbier end of jazz – along with Latin, funk and urban – keep the dancefloor and balcony buzzing. You can dine, too, if you book in advance – though the service gets mixed reports.

Kings Place 90 York Way, N1 ☎020 7520 1490, ⓦkingsplace.co.uk; ⊖King's Cross; map pp.60–61. Excellent classical, jazz and world music gigs at this rather swish development, with great acoustics, beside the *Guardian* newspaper's offices.

Ronnie Scott's 47 Frith St, W1 ☎020 7439 0747, ⓦronniescotts.co.uk; ⊖Leicester Square; map pp.64–65. The most famous jazz club in London, this small, smart and atmospheric Soho stalwart features all the jazz greats, with some gigs from up-and-coming stars.

★**The Vortex** 11 Gillett Square, N16 ☎020 7254 4097, ⓦvortexjazz.co.uk; Dalston Kingsland or Dalston Junction Overground. This small, purpose-built venue is a serious player on the live jazz scene, combining a touch of urban style with a cosy, friendly atmosphere – it's a good place to check out free and improvised jazz.

CLUBS

Disco tunnels, sticky-floored indie clubs and epic house nights – London has it all. Many clubs keep going until 6am or later; some are open all week, others sporadically; and very often a venue will host a different club each night of the week. Admission charges vary enormously, with small midweek nights starting at around £3–5 and large weekend events charging as much as £30; around £10–15 is the average. For the latest, check flyers in the city's record stores and bars or log on to ⓦtimeout.com and ⓦresidentadvisor.net.

Bethnal Green Working Men's Club 44–46 Pollard Row, E2 ☎020 7739 7170, ⓦworkersplaytime.net; ⊖Bethnal Green. Old school decor and postwar kitsch set the backdrop for some serious playtime: fifties dress-up, burlesque, disco, rock'n'roll, cheese and a whole lot more. Thurs–Sat 9pm–2am, check listings

for other days.

★**Dalston Superstore** 177 Kingsland High St, E8 ☎020 7254 2273, ⓦdalstonsuperstore.com; Dalston Junction Overground; map pp.60–61. Starting its days as a gay club, this hedonistic Dalston stalwart brings in the hipster crowds with its savvy hipster mix of electronica, house in all its forms, old-school disco pop and indie. Good food, too. Usually Wed–Sat; plus some Sun nights.

Fabric 77a Charterhouse St, EC1 ☎020 7336 8898, ⓦfabriclondon.com; ⊖Farringdon; map pp.80–81. Despite long queues (book online to speed things up) and a mazelike layout that means you may take hours to find friends, jackets and some of its numerous rooms, this huge club remains one of the world's finest, focusing on drum'n'bass and dubstep, hip-hop, techno and house, with live bands and quality DJ line-ups. Usually Fri–Sat 11pm–5.30am or 8am.

★**Notting Hill Arts Club** 21 Notting Hill Gate, W11 ☎020 7460 4459, ⓦnottinghillartsclub.com; ⊖Notting Hill Gate; map pp.94–95. Groovy, arty, dressed-down basement club/bar that's popular for everything from Latin-inspired funk, jazz and hip-hop through to disco, house and indie. Usually Tues–Sat.

Plastic People 147–149 Curtain Rd, EC2 ☎020 7739 6471, ⓦplasticpeople.co.uk; ⊖Old Street; map pp.80–81. Thumping basement club whose broad booking policy stretches through techno and Afro-pop to reggae and dubstep. Usually Thurs 9.30/10pm–2am, Fri & Sat until 4am.

Proud Camden Stables Market, Chalk Farm Rd, NW1 ☎0207 482 3867, ⓦproudcamden.com; ⊖Camden Town; map pp.60–61. Indie, rave, live bands, costume parties, exhibitions and more – *Proud Camden*, in a former horse hospital, also offers decent food during the day and an outdoor terrace in summer. Hours vary – clubs usually till 2.30am.

XOYO 32–37 Cowper St, EC2 ☎020 7354 9993, ⓦxoyo.co.uk; ⊖Old Street; map pp.80–81. Huge Shoreditch club whose legendary weekend club nights and regular live gigs pull in the biggest names in everything from EDM to indie rock. Usually Tues–Sat.

GAY AND LESBIAN NIGHTLIFE

London's **lesbian and gay scene** is so huge, diverse and well established that it's easy to forget just how much – and how fast – it has grown over the last couple of decades. **Soho** remains its spiritual heart, with a mix of traditional gay pubs, designer café-bars and a range of gay-run services, while Vauxhall and Shoreditch/Dalston are also good stomping grounds. Details of most events appear at ⓦtimeout.com. The major **outdoor event** of the year is **Pride in London** (ⓦprideinlondon.org) in late June/early July, a colourful, noisy march through the city streets and various entertainment events.

BARS AND CLUBS

London's gay club nights appear and disappear with alarming frequency, so always check the listings to see what's happening (see above). Entry prices can be as low as

£5, but you're looking at more like £12–20 for all-nighters. Most places welcome most people, and the scene tends to be friendly.

MIXED BARS

The Black Cap 171 Camden High St, NW1 ☎020 7485 0538, ⓦtheblackcap.com; ⊖ Camden Town; map pp.60–61. Venerable north London establishment offering cabaret, drag and dancing almost every night. The upstairs *Shufflewick* bar is quieter and more pub-like, and there's a terrace. Mon & Tues noon–12.30am, Wed & Thurs noon–2am, Fri noon–3am, Sun noon–1am.

Freedom 66 Wardour St, W1 ☎020 7734 0071, ⓦfreedombarsoho.com; ⊖ Piccadilly Circus; map pp.64–65. Established gay place, long popular with a straight/gay/metrosexual Soho crowd. The basement becomes an intimate club later on, hosting regular cabaret and club nights. Mon–Thurs 4pm–3am, Fri & Sat 2pm–3am, Sun 2–10.30pm.

George & Dragon 2–4 Hackney Rd, E2 ☎020 7012 1100; ⊖ Old Street; map pp.80–81. Dandies, fashionistas and locals meet in this lively, often rammed Shoreditch hangout. The interior setup is traditional, but the attitudes – and the club nights ("Cockabilly", anyone?) are not. Daily 6pm–midnight.

Ku Bar 30 Lisle St, WC2 ☎020 7437 4303, ⓦku -bar.co.uk; ⊖ Leicester Square; map pp.64–65. The Lisle Street original, with a downstairs club open late, is one of Soho's largest and best-loved gay bars, serving a scene-conscious yet low-on-attitude clientele. It has a stylish sibling bar on Frith Street. Mon–Sat noon–3am, Sun noon–midnight.

★**Retro Bar** 2 George Court (off Strand), WC2 ☎020 7839 8760, ⓦretrobarlondon.co.uk; ⊖ Charing Cross or Embankment; map pp.64–65. Indie/retro bar playing 1970s, 80s, rock, pop, rockabilly and alternative sounds, and featuring regular DJ nights. Mon–Fri noon–11pm, Sat 2–11pm, Sun 2–10.30pm.

The Yard 57 Rupert St, W1 ☎020 7437 2652, ⓦyardbar.co.uk; ⊖ Piccadilly Circus; map pp.64–65. The courtyard often heaves with a mixed, post-work crowd at this laidback, sociable bar – in fine weather it's one of the best spots in Soho for alfresco drinking. Mon–Wed 4–11.30pm, Thurs 3–11.30pm, Fri & Sat 2pm–midnight, Sun 2–10.30pm.

LESBIAN BARS

She Bar 23 Old Compton St, W1 ☎020 7437 4303, ⓦshe-soho.com; ⊖ Tottenham Court Road; map pp.64–65. Rather swish lesbian bar from the *Ku Bar* stable (see above) in the heart of Soho, with occasional DJ nights. Mon–Thurs 4–11.30pm, Fri & Sat 4pm–12.30am, Sun 4–10.30pm.

Star at Night 22 Great Chapel St, W1 ☎020 7494 2488,

ⓦthestaratnight.com; ⊖ Tottenham Court Road; map pp.64–65. Comfortable, mixed but female-led, venue. It's popular with a slightly older crowd who want somewhere to sit, a decent glass of wine (or gin) and good conversation. Tues–Sat 6–11.30pm.

GAY MEN'S BARS

★**BarCode** Arch 69, Albert Embankment, SE11 ☎020 7582 4180, ⓦbarcode-london.com; ⊖ Vauxhall; map pp.60–61. Slick, spacious cruisey gay men's bar in the heart of Vauxhall's clubbing quarter. Thurs 10pm–4am, Fri 8pm–8am, Sat 10pm–midnight.

Comptons 53 Old Compton St, W1 ☎0203 238 0163, ⓦfaucetinn.com; ⊖ Leicester Square or Piccadilly Circus; map pp.64–65. This large, friendly pub attracts a butch, cruising yet relaxed 25-plus crowd. DJs at weekends. Mon–Thurs noon–11.30pm, Fri & Sat noon–midnight, Sun noon–10.30pm.

The King's Arms 23 Poland St, W1 ☎020 7734 5907; ⊖ Oxford Circus; map pp.64–65. London's best-known and perennially popular bear bar, with a traditional London pub atmosphere, with a karaoke night on Sun. Mon–Thurs noon–11pm, Fri & Sat noon–midnight, Sun 1pm–10.30pm.

CLUBS

Area 67–68 Albert Embankment, SE1 ☎020 3242 0040, ⓦarealondon.net; ⊖ Vauxhall; map pp.60–61. With two dancefloors and impressive laser and light displays, *Area* hosts big-name international DJs and the after-hours club *Beyond* on Sunday mornings (from 3am). Nights vary.

★**Duckie** Royal Vauxhall Tavern, 372 Kennington Lane, SE11 ☎020 7737 4043, ⓦduckie.co.uk; ⊖ Vauxhall; map pp.60–61. *Duckie*'s decadent mix of performance art and skewed theme nights, as well as cult DJs The Readers Wifes playing everything from Kim Wilde to the Velvet Underground, has kept this splendid club night going strong for more than fifteen years. Sat 9pm–2am.

★**The Eagle** 349 Kennington Lane, SE11 ☎020 7793 0903, ⓦeaglelondon.com; ⊖ Vauxhall; map pp.60–61. Home to the excellent Sunday-nighter Horse Meat Disco, with a vibe that loosely evokes late 1970s New York, complete with facial hair, checked shirts and a pool table. Nightly.

Fire South Lambeth Rd, SW8 ☎020 3242 0040, ⓦfirelondon.net; ⊖ Vauxhall; map pp.60–61. *Fire* is London's superclub of choice for a mixed though mostly male crowd of disco bunnies and hardboyz. Fri, Sat & occasionally Sun.

Heaven Villiers St, WC2 ☎0844 847 2351, ⓦheavennightclub-london.com; ⊖ Charing Cross or Embankment; map pp.64–65. Said to be the UK's most popular gay club, this 2000-capacity venue is home

to G-A-Y (Thurs–Sat), the queen of London's scene nights, with big-name DJs, PAs and shows. Thurs–Sat & Mon.
Popstarz Various locations ⓦpopstarz.org. The unusual, long-established and winning formula of indie, pop and R&B, plus cheap beer and no attitude attracts a mixed, studenty crowd. Usually Fri 10pm–5am.
★**Sink the Pink** Bethnal Green Working Men's Club, 42 Pollard Row, E2 ☎020 7739 7170, ⓦsinkthe pinklondon.com; ⊖Bethnal Green. Theatrical, youthful and glamorous fun – attracting a decadent, mixed and inclusive crowd. Various Sat nights.

THEATRE AND COMEDY

London has enjoyed a reputation for quality **theatre** since the time of Shakespeare and, despite the continuing dominance of blockbuster musicals and revenue-spinning star vehicles, still provides platforms for innovation and new writing. The **West End** is the heart of "Theatreland", with Shaftesbury Avenue its most congested drag, but the term is more of a conceptual pigeon-hole than a geographical term. Some of the most exciting work is performed in what have become known as the **Off-West End** theatres, while further down the financial ladder still are the **fringe** theatres, often pub venues, where ticket prices are lower, and quality more variable. As for **comedy**, you're never too far from a gig in London, whether it's a big-name stadium show, an old favourite like the Comedy Store – at the heart of the alternative comedy movement of the 1980s – or a neighbourhood pub hosting new young hopefuls. Check ⓦchortle.co.uk and ⓦtimeout.com for listings.

COSTS

Prices Tickets for £15 are restricted to the fringe; the box-office average is closer to £35–40 with £50–110 the usual top price. The cheapest way to get a ticket is to go to the theatre box office in person; you will probably be charged a booking fee if you buy over the phone or online. Keep an eye on the websites, however, for special deals including cheap Monday seats, or standby "on-the-day" tickets – even for the big musicals and well-reviewed plays. Students, senior citizens and the unemployed can get concessionary rates for most shows, and many theatres offer reductions on standbys to these groups. Whatever you do, avoid the touts and the unofficial ticket agencies that abound in the West End – there's no guarantee that the tickets are genuine.
Discount tickets The Society of London Theatre runs a useful booth, tkts (Mon–Sat 10am–7pm, Sun 11am–4.30pm; ⓦtkts.co.uk), in Leicester Square, which sells on-the-day tickets for all the West End shows at discounts of up to fifty percent, though they tend to be in the top end of the price range, are limited to four per person, and carry a service charge of £3 per ticket.

THEATRES

Almeida Almeida St, N1 ☎020 7359 4404, ⓦalmeida .co.uk; ⊖Angel or Highbury & Islington. Popular little Islington venue that premieres excellent new plays and excitingly reworked classics, and has attracted some big Hollywood names.
Arcola Theatre 24 Ashwin St, E8 ☎020 7503 1646, ⓦarcolatheatre.com; Dalston Kingsland or Dalston Junction Overground. Exciting fringe theatre in an old Dalston factory. Challenging plays – classics and modern works – include shows from young, international companies. Some "Pay what you can" tickets on Tuesday nights.

Barbican Centre Silk St, EC2 ☎020 7638 8891, ⓦbarbican.org.uk; ⊖Barbican or Moorgate. A wide variety of productions from puppetry and musicals to new and classical drama.
Battersea Arts Centre 176 Lavender Hill, SW11 ☎020 7223 2223, ⓦbac.org.uk; Clapham Junction train station from Victoria or Waterloo. A multistage building, housed in an old town hall, renowned for excellent contemporary drama, physical theatre, comedy and cabaret.
Bush 7 Uxbridge Rd, W12 8LJ ☎020 8743 5050, ⓦbushtheatre.co.uk; ⊖Shepherd's Bush Market. This lively local theatre is second only to the Royal Court as a reliable venue for new writing.
Donmar Warehouse 41 Earlham St, WC2 ☎0844 871 7624, ⓦdonmarwarehouse.com; ⊖Covent Garden. A small, central performance space, noted for new writing and interesting reappraisals of the classics.
Menier Chocolate Factory 53 Southwark St, SE1 ☎020 7378 1713, ⓦwww.menierchocolatefactory .com; ⊖London Bridge. Great fringe producing house in a former Victorian factory, with a decent bar and restaurant attached. Shows – musical revivals, old classics, new writing – are consistently good.
National Theatre South Bank, SE1 ☎020 7452 3000, ⓦnationaltheatre.org.uk; ⊖Waterloo. The country's top actors and directors produce shows ranging from Greek tragedies via experimental new writing to Broadway musicals in three theatres. Some productions sell out months in advance, but day tickets, for the lowest-priced seats available, go on sale on the morning of each performance – get there by 8am I ook out, too, for special "Travelex" performances, when half the seats go for £15.
Open Air Theatre Regent's Park, Inner Circle, NW1 ☎0844 826 4242, ⓦopenairtheatre.com;

1

Baker Street. Lovely alfresco space in Regent's Park hosting a tourist-friendly summer programme of Shakespeare, musicals, plays and concerts, many of which are geared towards children.

★ **Roundhouse** Chalk Farm Rd, NW1 ☎ 0844 482 8008, ⓦ roundhouse.org.uk; ⊖ Chalk Farm. Camden's most exciting cultural venue, in an old – round – engine repairs shed, puts on cutting-edge theatre, circus, cabaret and live gigs.

Royal Court Sloane Square, SW1 ☎ 020 7565 5000, ⓦ royalcourttheatre.com; ⊖ Sloane Square. The Royal Court is one of the best places in London to catch radical new writing, either in the proscenium arch Theatre Downstairs, or the smaller Theatre Upstairs.

Sam Wanamaker Playhouse New Globe Walk, SE1 ☎ 020 7401 9919, ⓦ shakespearesglobe.com; ⊖ London Bridge, Blackfriars or Southwark. Indoor Jacobean-style theatre, lit by candles and with bench seating, on the Globe site. Some Shakespearean plays, plus Jacobean productions and the occasional opera.

Shakespeare's Globe New Globe Walk, SE1 ☎ 020 7401 9919, ⓦ shakespearesglobe.com; ⊖ London Bridge, Blackfriars or Southwark. This open-roofed replica Elizabethan theatre uses only natural light and the minimum of scenery, and puts on fun Shakespearean shows – along with works from the Bard's contemporaries, including Christopher Marlowe, and modern works on Elizabethan themes – from May to September. Seats from around £15, with "Yard" tickets (standing-room only) for around a fiver.

Soho Theatre 21 Dean St, W1 ☎ 020 7478 0100, ⓦ sohotheatre.com; ⊖ Tottenham Court Road. Very central venue that specializes in new writing from around the globe, as well as regular comedy and cabaret.

Tricycle Theatre 269 Kilburn High Rd, NW6 ☎ 020 7328 1000, ⓦ tricycle.co.uk; ⊖ Kilburn. One of London's most dynamic venues, showcasing a mixed bag of new plays, often with a multicultural bent, and usually with a sharp political focus.

CINEMA

There are a lot of cinemas in London, especially the **West End**, with the biggest on and around Leicester Square. A few classy independent chains show more offbeat screenings, in various locations – check out the **Picturehouse** (ⓦ picturehouses.co.uk), **Curzon** (ⓦ curzoncinemas.com) and **Everyman** (ⓦ everymancinema.com). **Tickets** at the major screens cost at least £13, although concessionary rates are offered for some shows at virtually all cinemas, usually at off-peak times. Anyone with an Orange phone can make use of the two-for-one "Orange Wednesday" tickets.

BFI Southbank Belvedere Rd, South Bank, SE1 ☎ 020 7928 3232, ⓦ bfi.org.uk; ⊖ Waterloo. Splendid themed seasons, showing between eight and fourteen films daily on four screens. The BFI also runs the IMAX (☎ 033 0333 7878), a huge glazed drum in the middle of Waterloo roundabout. The colossal screen is not recommended for anyone with vertigo.

Electric 191 Portobello Rd, W11 ☎ 020 7908 9696, ⓦ electriccinema.co.uk; ⊖ Notting Hill Gate or Ladbroke Grove. One of the oldest cinemas in the country (opened 1911), the Electric keeps much of its lovely old interior, but has added the requisite indie armchairs, footstools and two-seater sofas, along with a glam bar, to

create a luxury experience. The programme concentrates on the quirkiest mainstream hits and offbeat offerings.

ICA Cinema Nash House, The Mall, SW1 ☎ 020 7930 3647, ⓦ ica.org.uk; ⊖ Piccadilly Circus or Charing Cross. One of the capital's most cutting-edge programmes – offering world, documentary and underground movies in the Institute of Contemporary Arts.

Prince Charles 7 Leicester Place, WC2 ☎ 020 7494 3654, ⓦ princecharlescinema.com; ⊖ Leicester Square or Piccadilly Circus. Two screens in the heart of the West End, with good prices (starting at just £5, less for members) and a daily changing programme of newish movies, classics and cult favourites, plus participatory "singalong" romps.

CLASSICAL MUSIC

On most days you should be able to catch a concert by one of the major **orchestras** based in the capital or a more specialized ensemble. Unless a glamorous guest conductor is wielding the baton, or one of the world's high-profile orchestras is giving a performance, full houses are a rarity, so even at the biggest concert halls you should be able to pick up a ticket for around £15 (the usual range is about £12–50). During the week there are also numerous **free concerts**, often at lunchtimes, in London's churches or given by the city's two leading conservatoires, the Royal College of Music (ⓦ rcm.ac.uk) and Royal Academy of Music (ⓦ ram.ac.uk).

CONCERT VENUES

Barbican Centre Silk St, EC2 ☎ 020 7638 8891, ⓦ barbican.org.uk; ⊖ Barbican or Moorgate. With the outstanding resident London Symphony

Orchestra (ⓦ lso.co.uk), the BBC Symphony Orchestra (ⓦ bbc.co.uk/orchestras) as associate orchestra, and top foreign orchestras and big-name soloists in regular attendance, the Barbican is an outstanding venue for classical music.

1

THE PROMS

The **London Proms** (Royal Albert Hall ☎0845 401 5040, ⊛bbc.co.uk/proms; ⊖South Kensington) provide a summer-season feast of classical music, much of it at bargain-basement prices; uniquely, there are five hundred **standing places** available each night, which cost just £5, even on the famed last night. Standing tickets are made available only on the day itself and must be bought on the door. Seated **tickets** cost between £12 and £95; those for the last night are allocated by ballot and start at £57. The acoustics may not be the world's best, but the calibre of the performers is unbeatable, the atmosphere superb, and the programme a creative mix of standards and new or obscure works. And the hall is so vast that even if you turn up an hour or so before the show starts you are unlikely to be turned away.

Southbank Centre Belvedere Rd, South Bank, SE1 ☎020 7960 4200, ⊛southbankcentre.co .uk; ⊖Waterloo or Embankment. The SBC has three spaces, none of which is exclusively used for classical music. The 2500-seat Royal Festival Hall (RFH), home to the Philharmonia (⊛philharmonia.co.uk) and the London Philharmonic (⊛lpo.co.uk), is tailor-made for large scale choral and orchestral works, while the Queen Elizabeth Hall (QEH) and intimate Purcell Room are used for chamber concerts, solo recitals, opera and choirs.

Wigmore Hall 36 Wigmore St, W1 ☎020 7935 2141, ⊛wigmore-hall.org.uk; ⊖Bond Street or Oxford Circus. With its near-perfect acoustics, the Wigmore Hall – built in 1901 as a hall for the adjacent Bechstein piano showroom – is a firm favourite, so book well in advance. Piano recitals and chamber music are superb, as are the recitals by some of the world's greatest singers.

OPERA

English National Opera Coliseum, St Martin's Lane, WC2 ☎020 7845 9300, ⊛eno.org; ⊖Leicester Square or Charing Cross. Operas sung in English, an adventurous repertoire, modern productions and reasonable pricing (£16–130, with standbys for concessions from £15 and various special deals available).

Opera Up Close King's Head, 115 Upper St, N1 ☎020 7478 0160, ⊛kingsheadtheatre.com; ⊖Angel or Highbury & Islington. New writing and classics with a twist from superb resident company Opera Up Close, who sing in English with the most basic of accompaniment in this tiny pub theatre and regularly appear at other venues too.

Royal Opera House Bow St, WC2 ☎020 7304 4000, ⊛roh.org.uk; ⊖Covent Garden. This beautiful old opera house puts on lavish operas, most of them, but not all, fairly traditonal productions. All are performed in the original language with subtitles. Ticket prices can reach £900, but the restricted-view seating (or standing room) from around £15 is perfectly good. Get in line early for one of the day seats, which are released from 10am on the day of a performance.

DANCE

The biggest dance festival is **Dance Umbrella** (⊛danceumbrella.co.uk), a season (Oct/Nov) of new and cutting-edge work. For a **roundup** of all the major dance events in town, check ⊛londondance.com.

The Place 17 Duke's Rd, WC1 ☎020 7121 1100, ⊛theplace.org.uk; ⊖Euston. A small theatre that presents the work of contemporary choreographers and student performers.

Royal Opera House Bow St, WC2 ☎020 7304 4000, ⊛roh.org.uk; ⊖Covent Garden. Based at the Opera House, the Royal Ballet is a world-renowned classical company with some outstanding principals. Tickets for the main house are cheaper than for opera (£7–200), with more experimental, generally less expensive, productions in the smaller Linbury Studio Theatre. Sell-outs are frequent so book early.

Sadler's Wells Rosebery Ave, EC1 ☎0844 412 4300, ⊛sadlerswells.com; ⊖Angel. Sadler's Wells hosts Britain's best contemporary dance companies and many of the finest international companies are regular visitors. The Lilian Baylis Theatre, tucked around the back, puts on smaller-scale shows, while the Peacock Theatre near Covent Garden adds some populist shows, including street dance, to the mix.

SHOPPING

DEPARTMENT STORES

Fortnum & Mason 181 Piccadilly, W1 ☎0845 300 1707, ⊛fortnumandmason.com; ⊖Green Park or Piccadilly Circus; map pp.64–65. Beautiful 300-year-old store with murals, cherubs, chandeliers and fountains as a backdrop to its perfectly English offerings. Famous for its

1

fabulous, pricey food, it also specializes in upmarket designer clothes, furniture, luggage and jewellery. Mon–Sat 10am–9pm, Sun noon–6pm.

Harrods 87–135 Brompton Rd, Knightsbridge, SW1 ☎0845 605 1234, ⓦharrods.com; ⊖Knightsbridge; map pp.94–95. Harrods has everything, including pretension in spades – a "clean and presentable" dress code is enforced, and backpacks either have to be carried or placed in the store's left luggage. Check out the life-size bronze statue of Princess Diana and Dodi Al Fayed, who was the son of previous owner Mohamed Al Fayed, dancing on a beach. Shopping-wise, it is most notable for its huge toy department, designer labels and sumptuous food hall, with exquisite Arts and Crafts tiling. Mon–Sat 10am–8pm, Sun noon–6pm.

Harvey Nichols 109–125 Knightsbridge, SW1 ☎020 7201 8088, ⓦharveynichols.com; ⊖Knightsbridge; map pp.94–95. "Harvey Nicks" has all the latest designer collections, luxury items and cosmetics ranges, and a food hall offering frivolous goodies at high prices. Mon–Sat 10am–8pm, Sun noon–6pm.

John Lewis 300 Oxford St, W1 ☎020 7629 7711, ⓦjohnlewis.co.uk; ⊖Oxford Circus; map pp.64–65. Famous for being "never knowingly undersold", this much loved institution can't be beaten for basics, including well-made clothes, furniture and household goods. Mon–Sat 10am–8pm, Sun noon–6pm.

★**Liberty** 210–220 Regent St, W1 ☎020 7734 1234, ⓦliberty.co.uk; ⊖Oxford Circus; map pp.64–65. A fabulous emporium of luxury, this exquisite store, with its mock-Tudor exterior, is most famous for its fabrics, design and accessories, but is also great for mainstream and high fashion. Mon–Sat 10am–8pm, Sun noon–6pm.

★**Selfridges** 400 Oxford St, W1 ☎0800 123 400, ⓦselfridges.com; ⊖Bond Street; map pp.94–95. This huge, airy palace of clothes, food and furnishings was London's first great department store. The vast mens- and womenswear departments offer mainstream designers and casual lines alongside hipper, younger labels. The food hall is superb, too. Hours vary; usually Mon–Sat 9.30am–9pm, Sun noon–6pm.

BOOKS

Daunt Books 83 Marylebone High St, W1 ☎020 7224 2295, ⓦdauntbooks.co.uk; ⊖Bond Street or Baker Street; map pp.94–95. Inspirational range of travel literature and guidebooks, with lots of novels and nonfiction too, in a handsome, galleried interior. Other branches. Mon–Sat 9am–7.30pm, Sun 11am–6pm.

Foyles 107 Charing Cross Rd, WC2 ☎020 7437 5660, ⓦfoyles.co.uk ⊖Tottenham Court Road; map pp.64–65. This venerable old bookstore has moved down the road and given itself a revamp, with huge departments devoted to fiction, nonfiction, kids books and more. Mon–Sat

9.30am–9pm, Sun noon–6pm.

Hatchards 187 Piccadilly, W1 ☎020 7439 9921, ⓦwww.hatchards.co.uk; ⊖Piccadilly Circus; map pp.64–65. A little overshadowed by the colossal Waterstones down the road, and actually part of the Waterstones group, the venerable Hatchards holds its own when it comes to quality fiction, biography, history and travel. Mon–Sat 9.30am–7pm, Sun noon–6pm.

London Review Bookshop 14 Bury Place, WC1 ☎020 7269 9030, ⓦlrbshop.co.uk; ⊖Holborn; map p.75. All the books reviewed in the august literary journal and many, many more in this tranquil Bloomsbury bookstore. Mon–Sat 10am–6.30pm, Sun noon–6pm.

★**Persephone Books** 59 Lamb's Conduit St, WC1 ☎020 7242 9292, ⓦpersephonebooks.co.uk; ⊖Russell Square or Holborn; map p.75. Lovely offspring of a publishing house that specializes in neglected twentieth-century writing by women. Mon–Fri 10am–6pm, Sat noon–5pm.

MUSIC

Gramex 104 Lower Marsh, SE1 ☎020 7401 3830, ⓦgramex.co.uk; ⊖Lambeth North; map p.86. A splendid find for classical-music and jazz-lovers, this new and secondhand record store features CDs and vinyl, and comfy leather armchairs. Mon–Sat 11am–7pm.

Honest Jon's 278 Portobello Rd, W10 ☎020 8969 9822, ⓦhonestjons.com; ⊖Ladbroke Grove; map pp.94–95. Jazz, soul, funk, R&B, rare groove, reggae, world music and more in this West London stalwart, with current releases, secondhand finds and reissues. Mon–Sat 10am–6pm, Sun 11am–5pm.

Rough Trade 130 Talbot Rd, W11 ☎020 7229 8541, ⓦroughtrade.com; ⊖Ladbroke Grove; map pp.94–95. This historic indie specialist has knowledgeable, friendly staff and a dizzying array of CDs and vinyl from electronica via reggae to indie and beyond. There's another branch, Rough Trade East, in the Old Truman Brewery (91 Brick Lane, E1). Mon–Sat 10am–6.30pm, Sun 11am–5pm.

MARKETS

★**Borough Market** 8 Southwark St, SE1 ☎020 7407 1002, ⓦboroughmarket.org.uk; ⊖London Bridge or Borough; map pp.88–89. Foodie heaven with suppliers from all over the UK converging to sell organic and artisan goodies. Wed & Thurs 10am–5pm, Fri 10am–6pm, Sat 8am–5pm.

Brick Lane Brick Lane, Cygnet and Sclater streets, E1; Bacon, Cheshire and Chilton streets, E2; ⊖Aldgate East or Liverpool Street; map pp.80–81. Huge, sprawling, cheap and frenzied, this famous East End market has become a fixture on the hipster circuit, with great vintage clothes and good food stalls. It would be hard to say what you *can't* find here. Sun 9am–5pm.

Camden Market Camden High St to Chalk Farm Rd, NW1 ⓦcamdenlock.net; ⊖ Camden Town or Chalk Farm; map pp.60–61. Once beloved of hippies, punks and Goths, and now a firm favourite with European tourists, Camden is actually a gaggle of markets, segueing into each other and supplemented by lively stores and restaurants in the surrounding streets. Don't miss the fantastic food stalls down by the canal. Daily 9.30am–6.30pm, but most action Thurs–Sun.

★ **Columbia Road Flower Market** Columbia Rd, E2 ⓦcolumbiaroad.Info; map pp.80–81. This pretty East End street spills over in a profusion of blooms and resounds with the bellows of Cockney barrow boys during its glorious Sunday market. Come late for the best bargains, or early to enjoy a coffee and brunch in one of the groovy local cafés. It's an excellent shopping area, abounding in indie, arty and vintage stores. Sun 8am–around 3pm.

Greenwich Market Greenwich High Rd, SE10 ⓦgreenwichmarketlondon.com; Greenwich train station from Charing Cross or London Bridge, or Greenwich or Cutty Sark DLR; map pp.60–61. Sprawling

flea markets with some 120 stalls. Tues, Wed & Fri–Sun are best for arts, crafts and food; for antiques and vintage come on Tues, Thurs and Fri. Tues–Sun 10am–5.30pm.

Portobello Road Market Portobello and Golborne rds, W10 and W11 ⓦshopportobello.co.uk; ⊖ Ladbroke Grove or Notting Hill Gate; map pp.94–95. Approach this enormous market, or rather markets, from the Notting Hill end, winding your way through the antiques and bric-a-brac down to the fruit and veg, and then via the fashion stalls under the Westway to the thriving vintage scene at Portobello Green. The Golborne Road market is cheaper and less crowded, with antique and retro furniture on Fri and Sat (food and bric-à-brac Mon–Thurs). Antique market: Sat 8am–6pm. Portobello Green: Fri–Sun. Golborne Rd: Mon–Sat.

Spitalfields Commercial St, E1 ⓦvisitspitalfields .com; ⊖ Liverpool St; map pp.80–81. The East End's historic Victorian fruit and veg hall houses a fashionable food, crafts and vintage market, with rotating themed markets each Sat Mon–Fri 10am–5pm, Sun 9am–5pm.

DIRECTORY

Hospitals For 24hr accident and emergency phone ☎ 999 or turn up at St Mary's Hospital, Praed St, W2 (☎ 020 3312 6666; ⊖ Paddington) or University College London Hospital, 235 Euston Rd, NW1 (☎ 020 3456 7890; ⊖ Euston Square or Warren Street).

Left luggage Left luggage is available at all airports and major train terminals.

Police Phone ☎ 999 in emergencies, otherwise ☎ 0101 (ⓦmet.police.uk). Central police stations include: Charing Cross, Agar St, WC2 (⊖ Charing Cross); Holborn, 10 Lambs Conduit St, WC1 (⊖ Holborn); Marylebone, 1–9 Seymour

Street W1 (⊖ Marble Arch); and West End Central, 27 Savile Row, W1 (⊖ Oxford Circus). The City of London has its own police force, 182 Bishopsgate, EC2 (☎ 020 7601 2222, ⓦcityoflondon.police.uk; ⊖ Liverpool Street).

Post offices The only (vaguely) late-opening post office is at 24–28 William IV St, WC2N 4DL, near Trafalgar Square (Mon–Fri 8.30am–6.30pm, Tues opens 9.15am, Sat 9am–5.30pm); it's also the city's poste restante collection point. For general postal enquiries phone ☎ 0345 611 2970 (Mon–Fri 8.15am–6pm, Sat 8.30am–2pm), or visit ⓦroyalmail.com.

The Southeast

POPPIES ON THE SOUTH DOWNS, SUSSEX

The Southeast

The southeast corner of England was traditionally where London went on holiday. In the past, trainloads of East Enders were shuttled to the hop fields and orchards of Kent for a working break from the city; boats ferried people down the Thames to the beaches of north Kent; while everyone from royalty to cuckolding couples enjoyed the seaside at Brighton, a blot of decadence in the otherwise sedate county of Sussex. Although many of the old seaside resorts have struggled to keep their tourist custom in the face of ever more accessible foreign destinations, the region still has considerable charm, its narrow country lanes and verdant meadows appearing, in places, almost untouched by modern life.

The proximity of Kent and Sussex to the continent has dictated the history of this region, which has served as a gateway for an array of invaders. **Roman** remains dot the coastal area – most spectacularly at **Bignor** and **Fishbourne** in Sussex and **Lullingstone** in Kent – and many roads, including the main A2 London to Dover, follow the arrow-straight tracks laid by the legionaries. When **Christianity** spread through Europe, it arrived in Britain on the **Isle of Thanet** – the northeast tip of Kent, since rejoined to the mainland by silting. In 597 AD Augustine moved inland and established a monastery at **Canterbury**, still the home of the Church of England and the county's prime historic attraction.

The last successful invasion of England took place in 1066, when the **Normans** overran King Harold's army near **Hastings**, on a site now marked by **Battle Abbey**. The Normans left their mark all over this corner of the kingdom, and Kent remains unmatched in its profusion of medieval castles, among them **Dover**'s sprawling cliff-top fortress guarding against continental invasion and **Rochester**'s huge, box-like citadel, close to the old dockyards of **Chatham**, power base of the formerly invincible British navy.

Away from the great historic sites, you can spend unhurried days in elegant old towns such as **Royal Tunbridge Wells**, **Rye** and **Lewes**, or enjoy the less elevated charms of the traditional resorts, of which fashionable **Brighton** is by far the best, combining the buzz of a university town with a good-time atmosphere. The picturesque **South Downs Way**, which winds its way through the South Downs National Park, offers an expanse of rolling chalk uplands that, as much as anywhere can in the crowded southeast, gets you away from it all. Kent and Sussex also harbour some of the country's finest **gardens** – ranging from the lush flowerbeds of **Sissinghurst** to the great landscaped estate of **Petworth House** – and a string of excellent **art galleries**, among them the Pallant Gallery in **Chichester**, the Turner Contemporary in **Margate**, the Towner in **Eastbourne** and the tiny Ditchling Museum of Art and Craft just outside Brighton.

GETTING AROUND   THE SOUTHEAST

By car Outside of the main towns, driving is the easiest way to get around, although commuter traffic in this corner of England is very heavy. The A2, M2 and M20 link the capital with Dover and Ramsgate, while the M23/A23 provides a quick run to Brighton. The A27 runs west–east across the Sussex coast, giving access to Chichester,

Highlights

❶ Whitstable Oyster Festival Scoff fresh oysters and quaff dark oyster ale in this week-long festival of food, music and beer by the sea. **See p.139**

❷ Margate With its quirky Old Town, its broad sandy beach and the fabulous Turner Contemporary art gallery, this brash old resort is an increasingly hip destination. **See p.140**

❸ Canterbury Cathedral The destination of the pilgrims in Chaucer's *Canterbury Tales*, with a magnificent sixteenth-century interior that includes a shrine to the murdered Thomas à Becket. **See p.143**

❹ The White Cliffs of Dover Immortalized in song, art and literature, the famed chalky cliffs offer walks and vistas over the Channel. **See p.150**

❺ Rye Ancient hilltop town of picturesque cobbled streets, with some great places to eat, shop and sleep. **See p.156**

❻ Walking the South Downs Way Experience the best walking in the southeast – and some fantastic views – on this national trail, which spans England's newest National Park. **See p.161**

❼ The Lanes and North Laine, Brighton Explore the café- and shop-crammed streets of the maze-like Lanes and the buzzy, hip North Laine: Brighton at its best. **See p.166**

HIGHLIGHTS ARE MARKED ON THE MAP ON PP.136–137

Arundel, Brighton, Lewes, Eastbourne and Hastings, but can be slow-going.

By train Southeastern (w southeasternrailway.co.uk) covers Kent and the easternmost part of Sussex, and runs the high-speed services from London St Pancras to the North Kent coast and Chichester. The rest of Sussex, and parts of Surrey, are served by Southern Railways (w southernrailway.com). Surrey is mainly served by South West Trains (w southwesttrains.co.uk).

By bus National Express services from London and other main towns are pretty good, though local bus services are less impressive, and tend to dry up completely on Sundays outside of the major towns. Traveline (w travelinesoutheast .org.uk) has route details and timetables.

North Kent

North Kent has a good share of appealing destinations, all easily accessible from London. The attractive town of **Rochester** boasts both historic and literary interest, while the old-fashioned seaside resorts of **Whitstable** and **Broadstairs** are favourites with weekenders from the capital. **Margate**, meanwhile, offers a dash of offbeat bucket-and-spade charm with the presence of the Tate Modern and a thriving vintage scene.

Rochester and around

The handsome Medway town of **ROCHESTER** was first settled by the Romans, who built a fortress on the site of the present castle; some kind of fortification has remained here ever since. The town's most famous son is **Charles Dickens**, who spent his youth and final years near here – mischievously, it appears as "Mudfog" in *The Mudfog Papers*, and "Dullborough" in *The Uncommercial Traveller* as well as featuring in Pickwick Papers and much of his last, unfinished novel, *The Mystery of Edwin Drood*. Many of the town's buildings feature in his novels.

THE SOUTHEAST

HIGHLIGHTS

1. Whitstable Oyster Festival
2. Margate
3. Canterbury Cathedral
4. The White Cliffs of Dover
5. Rye
6. Walking the South Downs Way
7. The Lanes and North Laine, Brighton

In neighbouring Chatham, the colossal **Chatham Historic Dockyard** records more than four hundred years of British maritime history, and is well worth a trip even if ships don't rock your boat.

Rochester castle

Northwest end of High St • Daily: April–Sept 10am–6pm; Oct–March 10am–4pm • £6; EH • ☎ 01634 335882, ⓦ english-heritage.org.uk

In 1077, William I gave Gundulf – architect of the White Tower at the Tower of London – the job of improving defences on the River Medway's northernmost bridge on Watling Street. The resulting **Rochester castle**, now ruined, remains one of England's best-preserved examples of a Norman fortress, with the stark 100ft-high ragstone keep glowering over the town and the interior all the better for having lost its floors, allowing clear views up and down the dank shell. The outer walls and two of the towers retain their corridors and spiral stairwells, allowing access to the uppermost battlements.

Rochester Cathedral

Boley Hill • Mon–Fri & Sun 7.30am–6pm, Sat 7.30am–5pm; tours Mon–Fri & Sun 10am–4.30pm, Sat 10am–2pm • Free; tours £4 • ☎ 01634 843366, ⓦ rochestercathedral.org

Built on Anglo-Saxon foundations, Rochester's **cathedral** dates back to the eleventh century – though the building itself has been much modified over the past thousand years. Plenty of Norman touches have endured, however, particularly in the nave and on the cathedral's west front, with its pencil-shaped towers and richly carved portal and tympanum. Some fine paintings survived the Dissolution; look out for the thirteenth-century depiction of the Wheel of Fortune on the walls of the choir (only half of which survives).

Guildhall Museum

High St • Tues–Sun 10am–4.30pm • Free • ☎ 01634 332900, ⓦ medway.gov.uk

At the northwest end of Rochester's pleasant High Street, the **Guildhall Museum** holds a very good, chilling exhibition on the prison ships – or hulks – used to house convicts and prisoners of war in the late eighteenth century. Among other exhibits, the **Dickens Discovery Rooms**, in the adjoining building, include a wordy display about his life, and a short film about the locations that feature in his work.

Chatham Historic Dockyard

Chatham • Daily: mid-Feb to March & Nov 10am–4pm; April–Oct 10am–6pm; last entry 2hr before closing • £18.50, children £11.50 • ☎ 01634 823800, ⓦ thedockyard.co.uk • Bus #140 or #141 from Rochester, or from Chatham train station, which is a 30min walk or a £7 taxi ride from the docks

Two miles east of Rochester, the **Chatham Historic Dockyard**, founded by Henry VIII, was by the time of Charles II the major base of the Royal Navy. The dockyards were closed in 1984, with the end of the shipbuilding era, but reopened soon afterwards as a tourist attraction. The eighty-acre site, with its array of historically and architecturally fascinating ships and buildings, is too big to explore in one trip. Highlights include the Victorian sloop **HMS Gannet**, the 400yd-long **Victorian Ropery**, the **No 1 Smithery** exhibition and the **Ocelot submarine**, the last warship built at the yard.

ARRIVAL AND INFORMATION   ROCHESTER

By train Rochester train station is at the southeastern end of High Street.

Destinations Canterbury (every 30–45min; 50min); Chatham (every 5–25min; 3min); London Charing Cross (Mon–Sat every 30min; 1hr 10min); London St Pancras (every 30min–hourly; 35–40min); London Victoria (every 20–40min; 45min–1hr).

By bus Regular local buses to and from Chatham depart from Corporation Street, which runs parallel to High Street.

Tourist office 95 High Street (Mon–Sat 10am–5pm, Sun 10.30am–5pm; ☎ 01634 338141, ⓦ visitmedway.org).

ACCOMMODATION

Salisbury House 29 Watts Ave ☎01634 400182. Pleasant Victorian guesthouse with large rooms, friendly owners and a great location on a quiet leafy street, just a 10min walk up the hill behind the castle. **£70**

Ship & Trades Maritime Way, Chatham Maritime ☎01634 895200, ⊛shipandtradeschatham.co.uk. This lively waterside pub-restaurant near the dockyards offers contemporary, nautically themed B&B rooms, some with great views. Rates include breakfast. **£80**

EATING AND DRINKING

The Deaf Cat 83 High St ⊛thedeafcat.com. Opposite the cathedral, this boho coffee shop and gallery, dedicated to the memory of Dickens' deaf cat, serves good coffee, veggie sandwiches and simple home-made cakes to a laidback crowd. Mon–Sat 9am–5pm, Sun 10am–5pm.

Topes 60 High St ☎01634 845270, ⊛topesrestaurant .com. Rochester's nicest restaurant, around the corner from the cathedral, serves Modern British dishes such as guinea fowl, wild garlic and radicchio risotto in a wood-panelled dining room with sloping ceilings. Wed–Sat noon–2.30pm & 6.30–9pm, Sun noon–2.30pm.

Whitstable

Fishermen, artists, yachties and foodies rub along in **WHITSTABLE**, where the sense of community, and tradition, is strong. The **oysters** for which the town is famed have been farmed here since classical times, when the Romans feasted on the region's marine delicacies, and today the annual **Oyster Festival** (end July, ⊛whitstableoysterfestival.co.uk) sees the place come alive with a parade, performances, the "Landing of the Oysters" ceremony and raucous oyster-eating competitions.

Follow the signs from the vibrant **High Street** and **Harbour Street**, with its delis, restaurants and indie stores, to reach the **seafront**, a quiet shingle beach punctuated by weathered groynes and backed for most of its length by seaside houses and colourful beach huts in varying states of repair.

Whitstable Harbour

The Victorian **harbour**, a mix of pretty and gritty that defines Whitstable to a tee, bustles with a fish market, whelk stalls and a couple of seafood restaurants, and offers plenty of places to sit outside and watch the activity. The handsome 1892 Thames sailing barge, **Greta** (☎07711 657919, ⊛greta1892.co.uk), offers boat trips around the estuary.

ARRIVAL AND INFORMATION WHITSTABLE

By train From the train station it's a 15min walk to the centre, along Cromwell Road to Harbour St, the northern continuation of High Street.
Destinations Broadstairs (Mon–Sat every 30min; 25min); London Victoria (every 30min–1hr; 1hr 30min); Margate (Mon–Sat every 30min; 23min); Ramsgate (Mon–Sat every 30min; 35min).

By bus Buses #4, #4A, #4B and #5 shuttle between Whitstable town centre and Canterbury (every 15min; 30min).
Tourist information The Whitstable Shop, 34 Harbour Street (Mon–Fri 10am–4pm, Sat 10am–3pm, Sun 11am–2pm; ☎01227 770060, ⊛canterbury.co.uk).

GETTING AROUND

By bike Local cycle routes include the picturesque Crab and Winkle Way, a disused railway line linking the town to Canterbury, 6 miles away, and the coastal Oyster Bay Trail.
Bike rental Kent Cycle Hire, 61 Harbour Street (book in advance; ☎01227 388058, ⊛kentcyclehire.com), rents bikes from £18/day to £77/week, with tandems and child seats available. You can also pick up here and drop off in Canterbury.

ACCOMMODATION

Copeland House 4 Island Wall ☎01227 266207, ⊛copelandhouse.co.uk. Georgian B&B in a great location, with a garden backing onto the beachside walk. The six rooms – two with sea views – are cosy and comfortable; some bathrooms are private but not en suite (gowns are provided). No credit cards. **£85**

★**Fishermen's Huts** Near the harbour ☎01227 280280, ⊛whitstablefishermanshuts.com. Thirteen two-storey

2

weatherboard cockle-farmers' huts (sleeping two to six) offering cute, characterful accommodation near the harbour. Most have sea views, and some have basic self-catering

EATING AND DRINKING

Old Neptune Marine Terrace ☎ 01227 272262, ⓦ neppy .co.uk. Standing alone in its white weatherboards on the beach, this atmospheric pub is the perfect spot to enjoy a sundowner at a picnic table on the shingle, or to hunker down with a pint after a bracing beach walk. Some real ales, plus occasional live music. Mon–Wed & Sun noon– 10.30pm, Thurs noon–11pm, Fri & Sat noon–11.30pm.

★**The Sportsman** Faversham Rd, Seasalter ☎ 01227 273370, ⓦ thesportsmanseasalter.co.uk. The drab exterior belies the Michelin-starred experience inside this fabulous gastropub, in a lonesome spot between marshes and beach four miles west of town. The faultless, deceptively simple food takes local sourcing to the extreme: fresh seafood, marsh lamb, veg from a farm down the road, seaweed from the beach, bread and butter made

facilities. Rates include full breakfast, served at the nearby *Continental Hotel*; weekday rates soar during school holidays. Sun–Thurs £95, Fri & Sat (two-night min) £195

right here – even the salt comes from the sea outside. Mains from £18; reservations advised. Food served Tues– Sat noon–2pm & 7–9pm, Sun noon–2.30pm.

★**Wheeler's Oyster Bar** 8 High St ☎ 01227 273311, ⓦ wheelersoysterbar.com. A Whitstable institution dating back to 1856, this is one of the best restaurants in Kent. It's an informal, friendly little place, with just four tables in a tiny back parlour and a few stools at the fish counter, but the inventive, super-fresh seafood is stunning, whether you choose fresh oysters, a "light plate" or more substantial mains (from £16) like halibut roasted with a chorizo crust. Takeout from the counter includes tasty crab sandwiches for a couple of quid. BYO; cash only; reservations advised. Mon & Tues 10.30am–9pm, Thurs 10.15am–9pm, Fri 10.15am– 9.30pm, Sat 10am–10pm, Sun 11.30am–9pm.

Margate

The seaside town of **MARGATE** may not be the prettiest on the Kent coast, but its offbeat combination of eccentricity, nostalgia and cheery seaside fun give it a definite appeal. With the splendid **Turner Contemporary**, a cluster of funky cafés, **vintage shops** and indie galleries in the old town, and a couple of excellent places to stay – not to mention the golden sandy **beach** – a stopover in Margate has plenty to recommend it.

Turner Contemporary

Rendezvous • Tues–Sun 10am–6pm • Free • ☎ 01843 233000, ⓦ turnercontemporary.org

Rearing up on the east side of the harbour, the stunning, opalescent **Turner Contemporary** dominates the seafront. Named for J.M.W. Turner, who went to school in the Old Town in the 1780s, and who returned frequently as an adult to take advantage of the dazzling light, the gallery is built on the site of the lodging house where he painted some of his famous seascapes. Offering fantastic views of the ever-changing seascape through its enormous windows, the tranquil space hosts temporary exhibitions of high-profile contemporary art.

Shell Grotto

Grotto Hill • Easter–Oct daily 10am–5pm; Nov–Easter Sat & Sun 11am–4pm • £3.50 • ☎ 01843 220008, ⓦ shellgrotto.co.uk

Discovered, or so the story goes, in 1835, Margate's bizarre **Shell Grotto** has been captivating visitors ever since. Accessed via a damp subterranean passageway, the grotto's hallways and chambers are completely covered with mosaics made entirely from shells – more than 4.5 million of them, tinted silvery grey and black by the fumes of Victorian gas lamps. The origins of the grotto remain a mystery – some believe it to be an ancient pagan temple, others a more recent Regency folly – which only adds to its offbeat charm.

ARRIVAL AND INFORMATION

MARGATE

By train The station is near the seafront on Station Road. Destinations Broadstairs (every 5–30min; 5min); Canterbury (hourly; 30min); London Street Pancras (hourly; 1hr 30min); London Victoria (Mon–Sat every 30min; 1hr

50min); Ramsgate (every 5–20min; 10min); Whitstable (Mon–Sat every 30min; 23min).
By bus Buses pull in at the clocktower on Marine Parade. Destinations Broadstairs (every 5–15min; 25min);

Canterbury (every 20–30min; 50min); London Victoria (4 daily; 2hr 30min); Ramsgate (every 5–15min; 30min).

Tourist office The Droit House, Harbour Arm (April–Oct daily 10am–5pm; Nov–March Tues–Sat 10am–5pm; ☎01843 577577, ⓦ visitthanet.co.uk).

ACCOMMODATION

Reading Rooms 31 Hawley Square ☎01843 225166, ⓦ thereadingroomsmargate.co.uk. Stunning boutique B&B in a handsome Georgian townhouse. The three artfully distressed guest rooms have huge, luxurious bathrooms; breakfast is served in your room. No children. **£150**

★**Walpole Bay Hotel** Fifth Ave, Cliftonville ☎01843 221703, ⓦ walpolebayhotel.co.uk. This family-run hotel has changed little since Edwardian times, and exudes an air of shabby gentility from its pot-plant-cluttered dining room to its clanky vintage elevator. Don't miss the living museum and collection of napery art; with its eccentric charm, the *Walpole* is a favourite of many artists and writers. Rooms vary considerably, but most have sea views, and all are comfy, clean and well equipped. **£85**

EATING AND DRINKING

BeBeached Harbour Arm ☎01843 226008, ⓦ bebeached.co.uk. Irresistible on a sunny day, this colourful café – spot the kitsch pink parasols – offers cheery, creative comfort food. Brunches are particularly popular, and there are some great veggie options. Service can be slow when it's busy, so take your time, relax on a deckchair and drink in the sea view. Mains from £7. Wed, Thurs & Sun 11am–4.30pm, Fri & Sat 11am–4.30pm & 7.30–9.30pm.

★**GB Pizza Co** 14a Marine Drive ☎01843 297700, ⓦ greatbritishpizza.com. Phenomenally good, thin-crust gourmet pizzas on the seafront – try the Margate-rita, or pear and blue cheese – plus fab coffee, cakes and organic wine. Gluten-free bases available. Mon–Sat noon–9pm, Sun noon–3pm.

★**The Lifeboat** 1 Market St ☎07837 024259, ⓦ thelifeboat-margate.com. Cosy tavern on the Old Town's main square with a friendly, rustic interior, a great range of local drinks – ales, wines, ciders, perries and juices – and artisan cheeses, sausages and pies from Kentish producers. Live folk music, too. Daily noon–midnight or earlier.

Broadstairs

Overlooking its golden sandy beach – Viking Bay – from its cliff-top setting, unspoiled **BROADSTAIRS** is the smallest and most immediately charming of the resort towns in northeast Kent. A fishing village turned Victorian resort, it's within walking distance of several sandy **bays** and is renowned for its excellent **folk festival**. It also has strong **Charles Dickens** connections: the author stayed in various hotels here, and eventually rented an "airy nest" overlooking the sea, where he finished writing *David Copperfield*. A small **museum** and, in June, the **Dickens Festival** (ⓦ broadstairsdickensfestival.co.uk), play up the associations.

Dickens House Museum

2 Victoria Parade • Daily: Easter to mid-June, Sept & Oct 1–4.30pm; mid-June to Aug 10am–5pm • £3.75 • ☎01843 861232, ⓦ dickensfellowship.org/broadstairs

The broad balconied cottage that now houses the **Dickens House Museum** was once the home of Miss Mary Pearson Strong, on whom Dickens based the character of Betsey Trotwood in *David Copperfield*. Inside you'll find Victorian posters, photography and costumes, Dickens' correspondence, illustrations from the original novels and a reconstruction of Betsey Trotwood's parlour.

ARRIVAL AND DEPARTURE   BROADSTAIRS

By train Broadstairs station is on Lloyd Road, a 10min walk along the High Street to the seafront.
Destinations Canterbury (hourly; 25min); London St Pancras (hourly; 1hr 20min); London Victoria (every 30min–hourly; 1hr 55min); Margate (every 5–30min; 5min); Ramsgate (every 20min–hourly; 7min); Whitstable (Mon–Sat every 30min; 25min).

By bus Buses stop along the High Street.
Destinations Canterbury (every 20–30min; 1hr 30min); London Victoria (4 daily; 2hr 45min); Margate (every 5–15min; 25min); Ramsgate (every 10–20min; 10min).

Tourist information The nearest tourist office is in Margate (see opposite); ⓦ visitbroadstairs.co.uk is a useful website.

2

ACCOMMODATION

★**Belvidere Place** Belvedere Rd ☎01843 579850, ⓦbelvidereplace.co.uk. This stylish, quirky boutique B&B earns extra points for its warm, friendly management and gourmet breakfasts. The five lovely rooms feature sleek bathrooms, contemporary art and one-off vintage furniture finds. **£130**

East Horndon Hotel 4 Eastern Esplanade ☎01843 868306, ⓦeasthorndonhotel.com. Comfortable B&B in a spacious Victorian house overlooking Stone Bay, just a 5min seaside stroll from the centre of Broadstairs. Rooms are large, spruce and well equipped, some with sea views. **£80**

EATING AND DRINKING

Morelli's 14 Victoria Parade ☎01843 862500 ⓦmorellis gelato.com/stores/broadstairs. Deliciously old-fashioned 1930s ice-cream parlour, with vintage formica, leatherette and wicker decor and a free jukebox featuring Sinatra and Rat Pack classics. Scoops of delicious home-made gelato cost from £2. Mon–Fri 8am–5.30pm, Sat & Sun 8am–6pm.

Tartar Frigate Harbour St ☎01843 862013, ⓦtartar frigate.co.uk. In an unbeatable location right on the harbour, this eighteenth-century flint pub is a relaxed, friendly place to hangout, with regular folk bands and jam sessions. There's a popular seafood restaurant upstairs, too (for which you should

book ahead). Pub Mon–Sat 11am–11pm, Sun 11am–10.30pm; restaurant Mon–Sat noon–1.45pm & 7–9.45pm, Sun seatings 12.30pm & 3.30pm.

★**Wyatt & Jones** 23–27 Harbour St ☎01843 865126, ⓦwyattandjones.co.uk. Stylish, airy restaurant a pebble's throw from the beach, dishing up super-fresh Modern British food – smoked cod in a wild garlic and mussel chowder, duck breast with herb potato cake and braised chicory – using the best seasonal, mainly Kentish ingredients. Mains from £12. Mon–Sat 9–11am, noon–3pm & 6–10pm, Sun 9–11am & 12.30–5pm.

Ramsgate

RAMSGATE, the largest of the Thanet towns, is rich in robust Victorian red brick and elegant Georgian squares. It has a handsome location, set high on a cliff that's linked to the seafront and **Royal Harbour** by broad, sweeping ramps. Down by the bustling harbour a collection of cafés and bars overlooks the bobbing yachts, while the town's small, popular **beach** lies just a short stroll away.

Ramsgate Maritime Museum

Clock House, Royal Harbour • May–Sept Tues–Sun 10am–5.30pm • £1.50 • ☎01843 570662, ⓦramsgatemaritimemuseum.org

The **Ramsgate Maritime Museum** chronicles the seafaring history of the area from Roman times. One illuminating section focuses on the Goodwin Sands sandbanks, six miles southeast of Ramsgate – the occasional playing pitch of the eccentric Goodwin Sands Cricket Club.

ARRIVAL AND DEPARTURE

RAMSGATE

By train Ramsgate's station lies about a mile northwest of the centre, at the end of Wilfred Road, at the top of the High Street.

Destinations Broadstairs (every 20min–hourly; 7min); Canterbury (hourly; 22min); Faversham (Mon–Sat every 30min; 40min); London Street Pancras (hourly; 1hr 15min); London Charing Cross (every 20–40min; 2hr 15min);

London Victoria (Mon–Sat every 30min–hourly; 2hr); Margate (every 5–20min; 10min); Whitstable (Mon–Sat every 30min; 35min).

By bus Buses pull in at the harbour.

Destinations Broadstairs (every 10–20min; 10min); Canterbury (Mon–Sat hourly; 45min); London Victoria (4 daily; 3hr); Margate (every 5–15min; 30min).

ACCOMMODATION, EATING AND DRINKING

Age & Sons Charlotte Court ☎01843 851515, ⓦageandsons.co.uk. Three options, occupying a Victorian warehouse on a shady square, accessed by an alley: a relaxed ground-floor café with comfy outdoor seating, a restaurant offering creative Kentish cuisine (mains from £11), and a basement bar. Café: Tues–Sun 10am–5pm (kitchen closes 3.30pm); restaurant: Tues–Sat noon–3.30pm & 7–9.30pm, Sun noon–3.30pm; bar: Fri & Sat 7pm–late.

Belgian Café 98 Royal Parade ☎01843 587925, ⓦwww.belgiancafe.co.uk. Big, informal brasserie-style place near the seafront, its outside tables spilling over with an eclectic crowd enjoying great breakfasts and brunches, Belgian beers, real ales and marina views. Occasional live music. Sun–Thurs 7am–2am, Fri & Sat 7am–3am.

Caboose Café and Bar 18 Queen St ☎01843 570984, ⓦcaboosecafe.co.uk. Casual coffee bar that's both friendly and cool, with gourmet coffee and an inexpensive light menu – sandwiches, salads, Mediterranean-style snacks – plus big breakfasts and brunches, with a Mexican menu in the evening. Regular live events. Mon & Tues 9am–5pm, Wed–Fri 9am–11pm, Sat 10am–11pm, Sun 10am–5pm.

Royal Harbour Hotel 10–12 Nelson Crescent ☎01843 591514, ⓦroyalharbourhotel.co.uk. Two interconnecting Georgian townhouses with 27 quirky, nautically themed rooms, from tiny "cabins" to four-posters with sea views, and a cosy lounge with real fire, newspapers and an honesty bar. **£120**

Canterbury

2

The fine old city of **CANTERBURY** offers a rich slice through two thousand years of English history, with Roman and early Christian remains, a ruined Norman castle and a famous cathedral that looms over a medieval warren of time-skewed Tudor buildings. Its compact centre, partly ringed by ancient **walls**, is virtually car-free, but this doesn't stop the High Street seizing up in high summer with the milling crowds.

Brief history

The city that began as a Belgic settlement was known as **Durovernum Cantiacorum** to the Romans, who established a garrison and supply base here, and renamed **Cantwarabyrig** by the Saxons. In 597 the Saxon King Ethelbert welcomed the monk Augustine, despatched by the pope to convert England to Christianity; one of the two Benedictine monasteries founded by Augustine – Christ Church, raised on the site of the Roman basilica – was to become England's first cathedral.

After the Norman invasion, a power struggle ensued between the archbishops, the abbots from the nearby monastery – now **St Augustine's Abbey** – and King Henry II. This culminated in the assassination of Archbishop **Thomas à Becket** in the cathedral in 1170, a martyrdom that created one of Christendom's greatest shrines and made Canterbury one of the country's richest cities. Geoffrey Chaucer's **Canterbury Tales**, written towards the end of the fourteenth century, portrays the festive, ribald nature of medieval pilgrimages to Becket's tomb, which was later plundered and destroyed on the orders of Henry VIII.

With its pilgrimage days effectively over, the next couple of centuries saw a downturn in Canterbury's fortunes. In 1830, however, a pioneering passenger railway service, linking the city to the seaside at Whitstable, resulted in another bout of growth. Canterbury suffered extensive damage from German bombing in 1942 during one of the "**Baedeker Raids**" – a Nazi campaign to destroy Britain's most treasured historic sites as identified in the eponymous German travel guides. The cathedral survived, however, and today, along with St Augustine's Abbey and the venerable St Martin's Church (at the corner of B. Holmes Road and St Martin's Lane), has been designated by UNESCO as a **World Heritage Site**.

Canterbury Cathedral

Buttermarket • April–Oct Mon–Sat 9am–5.30pm, Sun 12.30–2.30pm; Nov–March Mon–Sat 9am–5pm, Sun 12.30–2.30pm; last entry 30min before closing; tours Mon–Fri 10.30am (not in Jan), noon & 2pm (2.30pm in summer), Sat 10.30am, noon & 1pm • £10.50, guided tours £5, audio tours £4 • ☎ 01227 762862, ⓦ www.canterbury-cathedral.org

Mother Church of the Church of England, **Canterbury Cathedral** fills the northeast quadrant of the city with a sense of authority, even if architecturally it's not the country's most impressive. A cathedral has stood here since 602, but the building you see today owes most to a Norman archbishop, Lanfranc, who in 1070 rebuilt the place after a huge fire. It was modified over successive centuries, and today the puritanical lines of the late medieval Perpendicular style dominate.

The interior

In the magnificent interior, look for the tomb of Henry IV and his wife, Joan of Navarre, and for the gilt bronze effigy of Edward III's son, the Black Prince,

2

CANTERBURY

all of them in the **Trinity Chapel** beyond the Gothic Quire. Vivid medieval **stained-glass windows** here depict the life and miraculous works of Thomas à Becket. The spot where Becket died, known as "The Martyrdom", is in the northwest transept by the **Altar of the Sword's Point**, where a jagged modern sculpture of the assassins' weapons is suspended on the wall. Steps from here descend to the low, Romanesque arches of the **crypt**, one of the few remaining relics of the Norman cathedral and considered the finest such structure in the country, with some amazingly well-preserved carvings on the capitals of the sturdy columns.

Roman Museum

Butchery Lane • Daily 10am–5pm • £8 • ☎ 01227 785575, ⊕ canterbury.co.uk/museums

Following the devastating German bombings of 1942, excavations of the destroyed Longmarket area, off the High Street, exposed the foundations of a Roman townhouse complete with mosaic floors. These are now preserved *in situ* in the subterranean **Roman Museum**, but it's the rich haul of **artefacts**, domestic and military, that prove to be the big attraction.

Canterbury Tales

St Margaret's St • Daily: Jan, Feb, Nov & Dec 10am–4.30pm; March–June, Sept & Oct 10am–5pm; July & Aug 9.30am–5pm • £8.75, children £6.75 • ☎ 01227 479227, ⓦ canterburytales.org.uk

Based on Geoffrey Chaucer's book, the **Canterbury Tales** is a quasi-educational, fun, attraction. Costumed guides set you on your way through odour-enhanced galleries depicting a series of fourteenth-century tableaux as you follow the progress of a group of pilgrims (or rather, suitably scrofulous mannequins) from London to Becket's fabulously ornate shrine. Each new space provides a setting for one of the famous tales.

Beaney House of Art and Knowledge

18 High St • Mon–Wed, Fri & Sat 9am–5pm, Thurs 9am–7pm, Sun 10am–5pm • Free • ☎ 01227 378100, ⓦ thebeaney.co.uk

With its stuffed animals, pinned beetles and intriguing cases of **antiquities and archeological finds**, the **Beaney House of Art and Knowledge**, a sturdy terracotta, brick and mock-Tudor ensemble built in 1898, has the not unlikeable feel of a Victorian collection. Don't miss the **paintings**, including the Van Dyck portrait of Kent MP Sir Basil Dixwell (1638), a Walter Sickert landscape (1937), painted during his four-year stay on the Kent coast, and the vigorous images of 1930s Kentish hop-pickers and gypsies by English Impressionist Dame Laura Knight.

Canterbury Heritage Museum

Stour St • Daily 10am–5pm • £8 • ☎ 01227 475202, ⓦ canterbury.co.uk/museums

The **Canterbury Heritage Museum** provides an excellent jaunt through local history, with particularly strong sections on the Roman city, the medieval pilgrimage era and the Tudors and Stuarts – and interesting sections on local literary figures Christopher Marlowe, Joseph Conrad and Oliver Postgate (originator, in the 1970s, of *Bagpuss* and *The Clangers*).

St Augustine's Abbey

Monastery St • April–Sept daily 10am–6pm; Oct Wed–Sun 10am–5pm; Nov–March Sat & Sun 10am–4pm • £5.20; EH • ☎ 01227 767345, ⓦ english-heritage.org.uk

Ruined **St Augustine's Abbey**, founded as a monastery by Augustine in 598, was vastly altered and enlarged by the Normans before being destroyed in the Dissolution. Today, it is an atmospheric site, with more to see than its ruinous state might suggest. Ground plans, clearly delineated in stone on soft carpets of grass, along with scattered semi-intact chapels, altar slabs and tombstones, evoke the original buildings almost as powerfully as if they were still standing, while information panels admirably recount the abbey's changing fortunes.

ARRIVAL AND INFORMATION   CANTERBURY

By train Canterbury has two train stations: Canterbury East (in the south) and Canterbury West (in the north), each a 15min walk from the cathedral. Canterbury West is used by the high-speed train from London St Pancras.

Destinations from Canterbury East Chatham (every 30min; 45min); Dover Priory (Mon–Sat every 30min, Sun hourly; 30min); London Victoria (every 30min; 1hr 35min); Rochester (every 30–45min; 50min).

Destinations from Canterbury West Ashford (every 10–30min; 15–25min); Broadstairs (hourly; 25min); London Bridge (Mon–Sat every 30min; 1hr 40min); London Charing Cross (Mon–Sat every 30min; 1hr 45min); London St Pancras (Mon–Sat hourly; 55min); Margate

(hourly; 30min); Ramsgate (hourly; 22min).

By bus National Express services and local Stagecoach East Kent buses use the station just inside the city walls on St George's Lane beside the Whitefriars shopping complex.

Destinations Broadstairs (every 20–30min; 1hr 30min); Deal (Mon–Sat 1–3 hourly, Sun 5 daily; 1hr 5min); Dover (every 30min–6 daily; 35min); London Victoria (hourly; 1hr 50min); Margate (every 20–30min; 50min); Ramsgate (hourly; 45min); Sandwich (every 20min–5 daily; 40min); Whitstable (every 15min; 30min).

Tourist office In the Beaney, 18 High Street (Mon–Wed 9am–5pm, Thurs 9am–7pm, Fri & Sat 9am–5pm, Sun 10am–5pm; ☎ 01227 861162, ⓦ canterbury.co.uk).

2

ACCOMMODATION

Canterbury accommodation consists mostly of B&Bs and small hotels and can be difficult to secure in July and August, when prices increase – book well in advance if possible.

HOTELS AND B&BS

ABode 30 High St ☎01227 766266, ⓦabodehotels .co.uk/canterbury. Standard rooms are rather ordinary, while the priciest suite comes with a rooftop terrace and cathedral views. Various, good-value online packages are available. *Michael Caines'* restaurant and his less expensive tavern are on site. **£130**

Arthouse B&B 24 London Rd ☎07976 725457, ⓦarthousebandb.com. You get a variety of options, and wonderful seclusion in this funky B&B situated in an old fire station, a 10min walk from Westgate. The main Victorian house has two doubles (each with private bathroom) sharing a lounge and kitchen – you can rent both and have the place completely to yourself. There's also a sunny self-contained double and a modern Scandinavian-style timber studio in the back garden. A DIY continental breakfast is optional. **£65**

Cathedral Gate 36 Burgate ☎01227 464381, ⓦcathgate.co.uk. Built in 1438 and with a fantastic location next to the cathedral, this ancient pilgrims' hostelry – all crooked, creaking floors and narrow, steep staircases – is in no way fancy, but it's comfortable, with cathedral views from many of the rooms and a simple continental breakfast. The cheapest rooms share toilets and (tiny) showers, but have basins and tea- and coffee-making facilities. **£81.50**

House of Agnes 71 St Dunstan's St ☎01227 472185, ⓦhouseofagnes.co.uk. You can't fail but be charmed by the crooked exterior of this quirky B&B near Westgate, which has eight individually themed and designed rooms in the main fourteenth-century house (mentioned in *David Copperfield*), and another eight, less characterful, options in the large walled garden at the back. There's a guest lounge with an honesty bar. **£90**

★No. 7 Longport 7 Longport ☎01227 455367, ⓦ7longport.co.uk. This fabulous little hideaway – a tiny, luxuriously decorated fifteenth-century cottage with a double bedroom, wet room and lounge – is tucked away in the courtyard garden of the friendly owners' home, opposite St Augustine's Abbey. Breakfasts are wonderful, with lots of locally sourced ingredients, and can be eaten in the main house or the courtyard. **£90**

HOSTELS

★Kipps 40 Nunnery Fields ☎01227 786121, ⓦkipps -hostel.com. This excellent self-catering hostel, a 10min walk from Canterbury East Station, is clean and very friendly with homely touches and a nice walled garden. Nightly events mean you can be sociable, but it's more a home from home than a party hostel. No curfew. Single-sex and mixed en-suite dorms plus single, double and triple rooms. Dorms **£19.50**, doubles **£65**

YHA Canterbury 54 New Dover Rd ☎0845 371 9010, ⓦyha.org.uk/hostel/canterbury. Half a mile out of town, 15min on foot from Canterbury East Station, this seventy-bed hostel is set in a Victorian villa. There's a café and self-catering facilities. It's closed during the day, with an 11pm curfew. Dorms **£19**, doubles **£52**

CAMPSITE

Neals Place Farm Neals Place Rd ☎01227 765632, ⓦnealsplacefarmcampsite.co.uk. On a working farm off the A290, a mere 20min walk from the city, this is a peaceful campsite, with eighteen spacious pitches in an orchard. Closed Oct–March. Pitches **£10** (plus £2.50 per person), caravan **£20** (plus £2.50 per person)

EATING

Boho Café 27 High St ☎01227 458931. This funky café-bar, with its paintbox-bright, mismatched decor, has a cheerful neighbourhood feel. The menu (around £5–10) ranges from big breakfasts via tapas and coffee and cake to home-made burgers. There's seating on the street, and a pretty suntrap garden at the back. Free wi-fi. Mon–Sat 9am–6pm, Sun 10am–5pm.

Café des Amis 93–95 St Dunstan's St ☎01227 464390, ⓦcafedez.com. Very popular, lively Mexican/Tex-Mex place with eclectic, carnivalesque decor and delicious food. Try the paella (£26.50 for two) followed by a bubbling chocolate *fundido*. Mon–Thurs noon–10pm, Fri noon–10.30pm, Sat 10am–10.30pm, Sun 9am–9.30pm.

Deeson's 25–26 Sun St ☎01227 767854, ⓦdeesons restaurant.co.uk. With its fresh flowers, linocuts and local art, this is an appealing setting in which to enjoy creative Modern British cuisine. Based on local produce, the menu changes regularly, but mains (from £13) such as roast loin of saltmarsh lamb with salsify are typical. Good-value set lunch and early evening menus. Mon–Sat noon–3pm & 5–10pm, Sun noon–10pm.

★The Goods Shed Station Rd West ☎01227 459153, ⓦthegoodsshed.co.uk. It doesn't get any more locally sourced than this – a buzzing, shabby-chic Modern British restaurant in the excellent Goods Shed farmers' market, where most of the ingredients are provided by the stalls themselves. The regularly changing menu might feature dishes such as scallops with bean purée and chorizo (£8.50), or pork chop with black pudding and apple and quince puree (£14). Tues–Fri 8–10.30am, noon–2.30pm & 6–9.30pm, Sat 8–10.30am, noon–3pm & 6–9.30pm, Sun 9–10.30am & noon–3pm.

Tiny Tim's 34 St Margaret's St ☎01227 450793, ⓦtinytimstearoom.com. Despite the name there's nothing twee about this elegant, 1930s-inspired tearoom, which offers more than twenty blends of tea as well as luxurious afternoon teas (all day, from £16.50), breakfasts and light lunches. In good weather you can sit in the cute back garden. Tues–Sat 9.30am–5pm, Sun 10.30am–4pm.

DRINKING

Canterbury is a nice place for a drink, with a number of pubs serving **real ales** in cosy, historic buildings. The local Shepherd Neame-owned places are in the majority, but look out, too, for beers from Canterbury's own Wantsum and Canterbury breweries.

Dolphin 17 St Radigund's St ☎01227 455963, ⓦthedolphincanterbury.co.uk. Likeable 1930s-built pub with a good selection of local real ales, a log fire in winter and a big, grassy beer garden in summer. Tasty food, too; the Sunday lunch (not available in summer) is a local favourite. Daily noon–late.

Parrot Radigund's Hall, 1–9 Church Lane ☎01227 762355, ⓦtheparrotonline.com. Ancient hostelry – one of the oldest in Canterbury – in a quiet location, with loads of character, a decent selection of ales and a not-quite-gastro gastropub menu. There's a beer terrace at the back. Daily noon–late.

ENTERTAINMENT

Taking place over two weeks in October, the **Canterbury Festival** (ⓦcanterburyfestival.co.uk) offers an international mix of music, theatre and performance. **Lounge on the Farm** (ⓦloungeonthefarm.co.uk), meanwhile, in early July, is a family-friendly and relatively chilled contender on the music festival calendar, staging a smart range of nostalgia bands, big names and up-and-coming local artists. Its location, on a working farm 10min south of Canterbury, is due to change in 2015, so check the website for news.

Gulbenkian Theatre Kent University ☎01227 769075, ⓦthegulbenkian.co.uk. Various cultural events, including contemporary drama, dance, comedy and film, are hosted at this excellent theatre-cum-cinema.

Marlowe Theatre The Friars ☎01227 787787, ⓦmarlowetheatre.com. This modern theatre, named after the sixteenth century Canterbury-born playwright, is the city's main venue for mainstream music, drama and shows.

Sandwich and around

Tiny **SANDWICH**, one of the best-preserved medieval towns in the country, is a sleepy, picturesque place, with some fine half-timbered buildings lining its narrow lanes, a peaceful **quayside** and a lovely location on the willow-lined banks of the River Stour. It also boasts one of England's best golf courses, the **Royal St George's Golf Course** (ⓦroyalstgeorges.com), less than a mile east of town.

The quayside

Sandwich's riverfront **quayside**, peaceful today, was once the heart of a great medieval port. Thanks to silting up of the estuary the sea is now miles away, but the waterfront gives the place a breezily nautical atmosphere, with small boats moored by the toll bridge, open countryside stretching out across the river, and the cry of seagulls raking the air. **Boat trips** (£7–35; ☎07958 376183, ⓦsandwichriverbus.co.uk) run from the toll bridge over the Stour up to Richborough Roman Fort and down to the estuary to spot seals and birds.

ARRIVAL AND INFORMATION   SANDWICH

By train Sandwich station is off St George's Road, from where it's a 10min walk north to the town centre and the quay. Destinations Deal (every 30min–1hr; 6min); Dover (every 30min–1hr; 25min); London Charing Cross (hourly; 2hr 20min); Ramsgate (hourly; 15min).

By bus Buses pull in and depart from outside the tourist office.

Destinations Canterbury (every 20min–1hr; 45min); Deal (Mon–Sat every 20min–1hr; 25–35min); Dover (Mon–Sat every 45min–1hr; 45min–1hr); Ramsgate (Mon–Sat hourly; 30min).

Tourist office In the Guildhall, Cattle Market, in the town centre (April–Oct Mon–Sat 10am–4pm; ☎01304 613565, ⓦwhitecliffscountry.org.uk).

THE CINQUE PORTS

In 1278 Dover, Hythe, Sandwich, Romney and Hastings – already part of a long-established but unofficial confederation of defensive coastal settlements – were formalized under a charter by Edward I as the **Cinque Ports** (pronounced "sink", despite the name's French origin). In return for providing England with maritime support, the five ports were granted trading privileges and other liberties – including self-government, exemption from taxes and tolls and "possession of goods thrown overboard" – that enabled them to prosper while neighbouring ports struggled.

Rye, Winchelsea and seven other **"limb" ports** on the southeast coast were later added to the confederation. The ports' privileges were eventually revoked in 1685; their maritime services had become increasingly unnecessary after Henry VIII had founded a professional navy and, due to a shifting coastline, several of their harbours had silted up anyway, stranding some of them miles inland. Today, of all the Cinque Ports, only Dover is still a major working port.

ACCOMMODATION

Bell Hotel The Quay ☎01304 613388, ⓦbellhotel sandwich.co.uk. Rambling nineteenth-century hostelry that has stood on this site since Tudor times. Rooms are comfy, in an uncontroversial, contemporary style; the priciest have balconies overlooking the Stour. There's a good in-house restaurant, and service throughout is great. **£110**

EATING AND DRINKING

George and Dragon 24 Fisher St ☎01304 613106, ⓦgeorgeanddragon-sandwich.co.uk. A fifteenth-century inn and popular, unpretentious gastropub, with good Modern British food (mains average £13), well-kept cask ales, roaring real fires in winter and a courtyard for alfresco dining. Booking advised in the evening. Mon–Fri 11am–3pm & 6–11pm, Sat 11am–11pm, Sun 11am–4.30pm; food served Mon–Sat noon–2pm & 6–9pm, Sun noon–2pm.

No Name 1 No Name St ☎01304 612626, ⓦnonameshop.co.uk. For picnic supplies, including hot baguettes, look no further than this excellent French deli opposite the Guildhall. During the day you can also choose from a seasonally changing menu of light French dishes – tartines, soups, quiche – and heartier mains such as baked mussels, duck confit and thyme-roasted chicken. Dishes around £5–10. Deli Mon–Sat 8am–5pm, Sun 9am–4pm; bistro daily 9am–3pm.

Deal

The low-key seaside town of **DEAL**, six miles southeast of Sandwich, was the site of Julius Caesar's first successful landfall in Britain in 55 BC. Today it's an appealing place, with a broad, steeply shelving shingle **beach** backed by a jumble of faded Georgian townhouses, a picturesque **old town** redolent with maritime history, and a striking concrete **pier** lined with hopeful anglers casting their lines. Henry VIII's two seafront **castles**, linked by a seaside path, are the main attractions, and there are enough nice **places to eat**, drink and stay to make the town an appealing weekend destination.

Deal Castle

Marine Rd • April–Sept daily 10am–6pm; Oct daily 10am–5pm; Nov–March Sat & Sun 10am–4pm • £5.20; EH • ☎01304 372762, ⓦenglish-heritage.org.uk

Diminutive **Deal Castle**, at the south end of town, is one of the most striking of Henry VIII's forts. Its distinctive shape – viewed from the air it looks like a Tudor rose – is owed less to aesthetics than to sophisticated military engineering: squat rounded walls would be better at deflecting missiles. Self-guided **audio-tours** outline every detail of the design, with the bare rooms revealing how the castle changed over the years and giving a good sense of how the soldiers lived.

Walmer Castle

Kingsdown Rd, one mile south of Deal • April–Sept daily 10am–6pm; Oct daily 10am–5pm • £7.90; EH • ☎ 01304 364288, ⓦ english
-heritage.org.uk • Hourly Stagecoach buses from Deal; also accessible on foot along the seafront (30min)

South of Deal Castle, **Walmer Castle** is another of Henry VIII's rotund Tudor-rose-
shaped defences, built to protect the coast from its enemies across the Channel. Like
Deal Castle it saw little fighting, and changed use when it became the official residence
of the Lords Warden of the Cinque Ports in 1708 (which it remains, though the title
itself is now strictly ceremonial). Adapted over the years, today the castle resembles a
heavily fortified stately home more than a military stronghold. The best-known
resident was the Duke of Wellington, who was given the post of Lord Warden in 1828
and who died here in 1852; not surprisingly, the house is packed with memorabilia
such as the armchair in which he expired and a pair of original Wellington boots.

ARRIVAL AND INFORMATION   DEAL

By train The station is on Queen St, 10min from the sea.
Destinations Dover (every 30min–1hr; 15min); London
Charing Cross (every 30min 1hr; 2hr 10min); Ramsgate
(every 30min–1hr; 20min); Sandwich (every 30min–1hr;
6min).
By bus Buses run from South Street in the town centre.

Destinations Canterbury (Mon–Sat 1–3 hourly, Sun 5
daily; 1hr 5min); Dover (every 20min–1hr; 50min); London
Victoria (2 daily; 2hr 35min–3hr 25min).
Tourist office Town Hall, High Street (Mon–Fri
9.30am–1pm & 2–4.30pm, Sat 10am–2pm; ☎ 01304
369576, ⓦ whitecliffscountry.org.uk).

ACCOMMODATION AND EATING

81 Beach St 81 Beach St ☎ 01304 368136, ⓦ 81beach
street.co.uk. Unfussy, contemporary beachfront brasserie.
Mains might include slow-cooked pork belly (£16) or baked
skate with saffron rice (£15.50); weekday lunches are less
expensive (two courses £12.80, three courses £15.90).
Mon–Sat noon–3pm & 6–10pm, Sun noon–4pm.
★ **Black Douglas Coffee House** 82 Beach St ☎ 01304
365486, ⓦ blackdouglas.co.uk. Funky, cosily informal
little spot on the blustery seafront, with scrubbed wooden
tables, local art on the walls, newspapers and books for

browsing, and a focus on good, locally sourced home-made
food. Mon–Thurs & Sat 9am–5pm, Fri 9am–5pm &
7–10pm, Sun 10am–4pm.
Number 1 B&B 1 Ranelagh Rd ☎ 01304 364459,
ⓦ numberonebandb.co.uk. This friendly, popular B&B is
the nicest place to stay in town. The handsome Victorian
townhouse is in a great spot, near Deal Castle and the
beach, and the four rooms are stylish and contemporary,
with luxurious extras. Good breakfasts, too. Two-night
minimum stay on summer weekends. £87

Dover and around

Given its importance as a travel hub – it's the busiest ferry port in Europe – **DOVER** is
surprisingly small, and, badly bombed during World War II, its town centre and
seafront don't inspire many travellers to linger. The main attractions, however, are big
ones: **Dover Castle**, looming proudly above town, and the iconic **White Cliffs**, flanking
the town on both sides.

Dover Castle

Castle Hill • April–July & Sept daily 10am–6pm; Aug daily 9.30am–6pm; Oct daily 10am–6pm; Nov to mid-Feb Sat & Sun 10am–4pm •
£17.50; children £10.50; EH • ☎ 01304 211067, ⓦ english-heritage.org.uk

No historical stone goes unturned at **Dover Castle**, an astonishingly imposing defensive
complex that has protected the English coast for more than two thousand years. In 1068
William the Conqueror, following the Battle of Hastings, built over the earthworks of an
Iron Age hillfort here; a century later, Henry II constructed the handsome **keep**, or Great
Tower, that now presides over the heart of the complex. The grounds also include a **Roman
lighthouse**, a **Saxon church** – with motifs graffitied by irreverent Crusaders still visible near
the pulpit – and all manner of later additions, including a network of **Secret Wartime
Tunnels** dug during the Napoleonic Wars and extended during World War II.

Ideally you should allow a **full day** for a visit. If time is short, head first for the **Operation Dynamo tunnel tours**, affecting immersive experiences that, accompanied by the muffled sound of anti-aircraft guns and screaming Spitfires, shed light on the build-up to the war and the Dunkirk evacuation. From there, make your way to Henry's **Great Tower**. Here the opulent medieval royal court has been painstakingly recreated; everything from the pots and pans in the kitchen to the richly coloured furniture and wall hangings in the King's Chamber.

2

The White Cliffs of Dover

Stretching sixteen miles along the coast, a towering 350ft high in places, the vast **White Cliffs of Dover** are composed of chalk – plus traces of quartz, shells and flint. Much of the cliffs lie within the Kent Downs Area of Outstanding Natural Beauty, and with their chalk grasslands home to rare plants, butterflies and migrant birds, have been designated a Site of Special Scientific Interest. A **walk** along the cliffs affords you amazing views of the Straits of Dover – and on a clear day you may well even see France.

ARRIVAL AND INFORMATION
DOVER

By train Dover Priory station is off Folkestone Road, a 10min walk west of the centre.
Destinations Canterbury (every 30min–1hr; 30min); London Charing Cross (every 30min–1hr; 1hr 55min); London St Pancras (hourly; 1hr 10min); London Victoria (Mon–Sat every 20–40min; 2hr).
By bus Buses from London run to the ferry terminal, and then on to the town-centre bus station on Pencester Road.

Destinations Canterbury (every 30min–6 daily; 35min); Deal (every 20min–1hr; 50min); Hastings (every 1–2hr; 2hr 40min); London Victoria (every 30min–1hr; 2hr 5min–3hr); Sandwich (Mon–Sat every 45min–1hr; 45min–1hr).
Tourist office In the Dover Museum, Market Square (April–Sept Mon–Sat 9.30am–5pm, Sun 10am–3pm; Oct–March Mon–Sat 9.30am–5pm; ☏01304 201066, ⓦ whitecliffscountry.org.uk).

ACCOMMODATION

Maison Dieu 89 Maison Dieu Rd ☏01304 204033, ⓦ maisondieu.com. Very welcoming, central guesthouse with seven spotless single, double, twin and family rooms, most of which are en suite. A few have views over the garden to Dover Castle. Good breakfasts, but they cost extra. **£70**
Marquis at Alkham Alkham, 5 miles west of Dover ☏01304 873410, ⓦ themarquisatalkham.co.uk. This

swanky restaurant-with-rooms offers luxury accommodation behind the exterior of a 200-year-old inn. The ten chic rooms have huge windows, many with picture-perfect views across the Downs, and the award-winning *Marquis* restaurant is superb. Rates include breakfast; staying during the week, when you can choose a room-only tariff, is cheaper. **£149**

EATING AND DRINKING

★Allotment 9 High St ☏01304 214467, ⓦ the allotmentdover.co.uk. A light-filled oasis on Dover's unremarkable High Street, this simple, shabby-chic bistro is by far the best place to eat in town. The daily-changing menu concentrates on the best seasonal produce, with many ingredients sourced from local allotments and lots of delicious veggie options (don't miss the goat's cheese and asparagus tart). Mains £8.50–16. Tues–Sat 8.30am–11pm.

The Coastguard St Margaret's Bay, four miles goat's east of Dover ☏01304 851019, ⓦ www.thecoastguard .co.uk. This beachside pub, at the bottom of the White Cliffs in the seaside village of St Margaret's Bay, is a great spot for a summer lunch, with a large seasalty terrace and small beer garden that stretches practically down to the shingle. Creative local dishes, with lots of fresh fish and seafood. Mains £10–20. Daily 10.30am–11pm; food 12.30–2.45pm & 6.30–8.45pm.

Romney Marsh

In Roman times, what is now the southernmost chunk of Kent was submerged beneath the English Channel. The lowering of the sea levels in the Middle Ages and later reclamation created a hundred-square-mile area of shingle and marshland, now known

CLOCKWISE FROM TOP LEFT LEEDS CASTLE (P.154); OYSTERS AT WHITSTABLE (P.139); BEACHY HEAD (P.161) >

2

as **Romney Marsh**. Once home to important Cinque and limb ports (see box, p.148), and villages made wealthy from the wool trade, this now rather forlorn expanse presents a melancholy aspect, given over to agriculture and with few sights – unless you count the sheep, the birdlife and several curious medieval **churches**. While this flat, depopulated area makes good walking and cycling country, its salt-speckled, big-skied strangeness can also be appreciated on the dinky **Romney, Hythe & Dymchurch Railway** (RH&DR; April–Oct daily; Nov–March occasional weekends, plus special events and tours; £16 Hythe–Dungeness return, less for shorter journeys; ☎01797 362353, ⊕rhdr .org.uk), a fifteen-inch-gauge line whose miniature steam trains run the 13.5 miles between the loneseome shingle spit of **Dungeness** and seaside town of **Hythe**. The latter has an eerie medieval **ossuary** in the Norman church of St Leonard's, high on a hill on the north side of town (May–Sept Mon–Sat 11am–1pm & 2–4pm, Sun 2–4pm; ☎01303 262370, ⊕stleonardschurchhythekent.org).

Port Lympne Wild Animal Park

Lympne, 3 miles west of Hythe • Daily: April–Oct 9.30am–6.30pm, last admission 3pm; Nov–March 9.30am–5pm, last admission 2.30pm • £23.95, children £19.95 (save 20 percent by booking online); valid for a year • ☎ 0844 842 4647, ⊕ aspinallfoundation.org/port-lympne

An incongruous sight in this quiet corner of Kent, **Port Lympne Wild Animal Park** is home to more than six hundred beasts, including lemurs, gorillas, African elephants, Barbary lions (now extinct in the wild) and the largest breeding herd of black rhinos outside Africa. Visits are safari-style, on bone-rattling trucks. The best way to see the park can be outside opening hours: **dusk safaris** including dinner are available in summer (£45), while **accommodation** options range from glamping to self-catering.

Dungeness

An end-of-the-earth eeriness pervades **DUNGENESS**, the windlashed shingle headland at the marsh's southernmost tip. Dominated by two hulking nuclear power stations (one of them disused), "the Ness" is not conventionally pretty, but there's a strange beauty to this lost-in-time spot, where a scattering of weatherboard shacks and disused railway carriages houses fishermen, artists and recluses drawn to the area's bleak, otherworldly allure. The late Derek Jarman, artist and filmmaker, made his home here, at **Prospect Cottage** – on Dungeness Road, a twenty-minute walk from the RH&DR station – and the shingle garden he created from beachcombed treasures and tough little plants remains a poignant memorial. Panoramic views over the headland can be had from the decommissioned **Old Lighthouse** (May & mid-Sept to end Oct Sat & Sun 10.30am–4.30pm; June Wed–Sun 10.30am–4.30pm; July to mid-Sept daily 10.30am–4.30pm; £3.50; ☎01797 321300, ⊕dungenesslighthouse.com), built in 1904.

The unique ecology around here attracts huge colonies of gulls, terns, smews and gadwalls; you can see them, and all manner of waterbirds, waders and wildfowl, from the excellent **RSPB visitor centre** (daily: March–Oct 10am–5pm; Nov–Feb 10am–4pm; £3; ☎01797 320558, ⊕rspb.org.uk) on the Lydd road three miles from Dungeness.

The High Weald

The Weald stretches across a large area between the North and South Downs and includes parts of both Kent and Sussex. The central part, the High Weald, is epitomized by gentle hills, sunken country lanes and somnolent villages as well as some of England's most beautiful gardens, including **Sissinghurst**. The bracken and gorse-speckled heathland that makes up nearby **Ashdown Forest** – setting for the Winnie-the-Pooh stories – is a lovely spot for longer walks. The Weald also offers a wealth of picturesque historical sites, foremost among them a trio of picture-book castles – **Leeds Castle**, **Hever Castle** and

Bodiam Castle – as well as stately homes at **Penshurst** and **Knole**, a well-preserved Roman villa at **Lullingstone**, the fascinating home of wartime leader Winston Churchill at **Chartwell** and Rudyard Kipling's countryside retreat at **Bateman's**. **Tunbridge Wells**, set in the heart of the beautiful High Weald countryside, makes a good base.

Royal Tunbridge Wells

The handsome spa town of **ROYAL TUNBRIDGE WELLS** was established after a bubbling ferrous **spring** discovered here in 1606 was claimed to have curative properties, and reached its height of popularity during the Regency period when restorative cures were in vogue. It remains an elegant place, with some smart places to stay and eat and three lovely urban parks: the **Grove** and, to the north, **Calverley Grounds** offer formal gardens, paths and splendid views, while the wilder **Common**, spreading out to the west, is laced with historic pathways.

The Pantiles

Tucked off the southernmost end of the High Street, the colonnaded **Pantiles** – named for the clay tiles, shaped in wooden pans, that paved the street in the seventeenth century – is a pedestrianized parade of independent shops, delis and cafés that exudes a faded elegance. Here, at the original **Chalybeate Spring**, outside the 1804 Bath House, a costumed "dipper" will serve you a cup of the iron rich waters (Easter–Sept Wed–Sun 10.30am–3.30pm; 50p), a tradition dating back to the eighteenth century.

ARRIVAL AND INFORMATION

ROYAL TUNBRIDGE WELLS

By train The train station stands where the High Street becomes Mount Pleasant Road.
Destinations Hastings (via Battle; every 30min–1hr; 40–50min); London Bridge (every 15–30min; 45min); London Charing Cross (every 15–30min; 55min).
By bus Buses set down and pick up along the High Street and Mount Pleasant Road.

Destinations Brighton (every 30min–1hr; 1hr 40min); Hever (Mon–Sat 2 daily; 35–45min); Lewes (every 30min–1hr; 1hr 10min); London Victoria (1 daily; 1hr 40min).
Tourist office The Corn Exchange, The Pantiles (April–Sept Mon–Sat 10am–3pm; Oct–March Tues–Sat 10am–3pm; ☏01892 515675, ⓦvisittunbridgewells. com)

ACCOMMODATION

★**Hotel du Vin** Crescent Rd ☏0844 748 9266, ⓦhotelduvin.com. Elegantly set in a Georgian mansion overlooking Calverley Grounds, this member of the luxe *Hotel du Vin* chain is mellow and quietly classy with a cosy bar and lounge and a sloping old staircase leading up to the rooms. **£125**

The Victorian B&B 22 Lansdowne Rd ☏01892 533633, ⓦthevictorianbandb.com. Bursting with authentic High Victoriana, to the point of fabulous kitsch, this comfortable, characterful and friendly B&B offers three rooms. There's a pretty garden, where you can take the rather good breakfast in summer. **£100**

EATING AND DRINKING

The Black Pig 18 Grove Hill Rd ☏01892 523030, ⓦthe blackpig.net. Excellent gastropub, where locally sourced, free-range and organic dishes on the daily changing menu might include venison bresaola or pan-roasted hake, plus snacks including delicious home-made Scotch eggs. The terrace is lovely in summer. Daily noon–11pm; food served Mon–Thurs noon–2.30pm & 7–9.30pm, Fri noon–2.30pm & 7–10pm, Sat noon–4pm & 6–10pm, Sun noon–9pm.

Mount Edgcumbe The Common ☏01892 618854, ⓦthemountedgcumbe.com. An offbeat place for a drink, a coffee or a Modern British meal. Hidden on the Common, this Georgian house has a deliciously rural feel, with a very nice garden. Regular live jazz and blues. Mon–Wed 11am–11pm,

Thurs–Sat 11am–11.30pm, Sun noon–10.30pm; food served Mon–Thurs noon–3pm & 6–9.30pm, Fri & Sat noon–9.30pm, Sun bar menu noon–8pm.

★**Sankey's** 39 Mount Ephraim ☏01892 511422, ⓦsankeys.co.uk. Appealing brasserie and oyster bar serving top-notch seafood from £11, along with fish and chips. You can also get food – and lots of craft beers – in the cosy pub upstairs, decked out with enamel signs and brewery mirrors. There's a sunny deck. Restaurant: Tues–Sat noon–3pm & 6–10pm; pub: Mon–Wed & Sun noon–midnight, Thurs noon–1am, Fri & Sat noon–3am; food served Mon–Thurs noon–3pm & 6–8pm, Fri noon–3pm, Sat noon–5pm, Sun noon–4pm & 6–8pm.

Sissinghurst

Biddenden Rd, 15 miles east of Tunbridge Wells • Mid-March to mid-May & July–Oct daily 11am–5.30pm; mid-May to end June Mon, Wed & Fri 11am–7pm, Tues, Thurs, Sat & Sun 11am–5.30pm; Nov & Dec daily 11am–3pm • £11.20; NT • ☎ 01580 710700, ⓦ nationaltrust.org.uk/sissinghurst

When she and her husband took it over in 1930, the writer Vita Sackville-West described the neglected Tudor estate of **Sissinghurst** as "a garden crying out for rescue". Over the following thirty years they transformed the five-acre plot into one of England's greatest country gardens, the romantic abundance of flowers, spilling over onto narrow brick pathways, defying the formality of the great gardens that came before. Don't miss the **White Garden**, with its pale blooms and silvery-grey foliage, and, in season, the lush, overblown **Rose Garden**. In the Tudor **tower** that Vita used as her quarters you can climb 78 steep stairs to get a bird's-eye view of the gardens and the ancient surrounding woodlands; halfway up, peep into Vita's study, which feels intensely personal still, with rugs on the floor and a photo of her lover, Virginia Woolf, on her desk.

Bodiam Castle

Bodiam, near Robertsbridge, 20 miles southeast of Tunbridge Wells • Jan to mid-Feb Sat & Sun 11am–4pm; mid-Feb to Oct daily 10.30am–5pm • £7.20; NT • ☎ 01580 830196, ⓦ nationaltrust.org.uk/bodiam-castle/ • Steam train from Tenterden (April–Sept up to 5 services a day; ☎ 01580 765155, ⓦ kesr.org.uk)

One of the country's most picturesque castles, **Bodiam** is a classically stout square block with rounded corner turrets, battlements and a wide moat. When it was built in 1385 to guard what were the lower reaches of the River Rother, Bodiam was state-of-the-art military architecture, but during the Civil War, a company of Roundheads breached the fortress and removed its roof to reduce its effectiveness as a possible stronghold for the king. Over the next 250 years Bodiam fell into neglect until restoration in the last century. The extremely steep spiral staircases, leading to the crenellated battlements, will test all but the strongest of thighs.

Bateman's

Bateman's Lane, Burwash, off the A265, 20 miles southeast of Tunbridge Wells • Daily: mid-March to Oct 11am–5pm; Nov & Dec 11.30am–3.30pm • £8.95; NT • ☎ 01435 882302, ⓦ nationaltrust.org.uk/batemans

Half a mile south of the picturesque village of Burwash, **Bateman's** was the idyllic home of the writer and journalist Rudyard Kipling from 1902 until his death in 1936. The house was built by a local ironmaster in the seventeenth century and is set amid attractive gardens, which feature a still-working watermill converted by Kipling to generate electricity (it grinds corn most Wednesdays and Saturdays at 2pm). Inside, the house displays Kipling's letters, early editions of his work and mementos from his travels.

Leeds Castle

30 miles northeast of Tunbridge Wells • Daily: April–Sept 10.30am–4.30pm; Oct–March 10.30am–3pm • £19, children £11 • ☎ 01622 765400, ⓦ leeds-castle.com

Its reflection shimmering in a lake, the enormous **Leeds Castle** resembles a fairy-tale palace. Beginning life around 1119, it has had a chequered history and is now run as a commercial concern, with a range of paying attractions including golf, hot-air ballooning, Segway tours and jousting, plus a branch of the zip-lining treetop adventure experience **Go Ape** (ⓦ goape.co.uk). The castle's interior fails to match the stunning exterior and the grounds, and though you can see a set of royal apartments, overall the twentieth-century renovations have tended to quash any historical charm; if you're happy to forego the paying attractions, you could simply wander around the five hundred acres of beautifully landscaped grounds for free on one of the **public footpaths**.

Penshurst Place

Penshurst, 7 miles northwest of Tunbridge Wells • April–Oct daily noon–4pm, grounds 10.30am–6pm • £10, grounds only £8 • ☎ 01892 870307, ⓦ penshurstplace.com • Trains from London Bridge or Charing Cross to Penshurst Station, then a 2.5-mile walk)

Tudor timber-framed houses line the main street of the attractive village of **PENSHURST**. Presiding over it all is fourteenth-century **Penshurst Place**, home to the Sidney family since 1552 and birthplace of the Elizabethan soldier and poet, Sir Philip Sidney. The jaw-dropping Barons Hall is the glory of the interior, with its 60ft-high chestnut-beamed roof still in place. The 48 acres of grounds offer good parkland walks, while the eleven-acre walled **garden** is a beautiful example of Elizabethan garden design.

Hever Castle

10 miles northwest of Tunbridge Wells • April–Oct daily 10.30am–6pm; March, Nov & Dec Wed–Sun 10.30am–4pm • £15.50, children £8.70, gardens only £13/£8.20 • ☎ 01732 865224, ⓦ hevercastle.co.uk • Trains from London Bridge or Victoria to Hever (1.5 miles from castle)

The moated **Hever Castle** was the childhood home of Anne Boleyn, second wife of Henry VIII, and where Anne of Cleves, Henry's fourth wife, lived after their divorce. In 1903, having fallen into disrepair, the castle was bought by William Waldorf Astor, American millionaire-owner of *The Observer*, who had the house assiduously restored in mock Tudor style. Today, Hever has an intimate feel, and though it does display some intriguing Elizabethan and Jacobite artefacts it tells you more overall about the

---

ENGLISH WINE: A SPARKLING SUCCESS STORY

The **English wine** industry is booming. Around four hundred vineyards across the country produce about four million bottles a year (more than fifty percent of it sparkling), and the best of the harvest more than rivals the more famous names over the Channel – indeed, many sparkling wines from the southeast have beaten the best Champagnes in international blind-tasting competitions. With almost identical soil and geology to the Champagne region, and increased temperatures due to global warming, the southeast is home to many of the country's best vineyards, several of which now offer **tours and tastings**. In the southeast these include:

KENT

Biddenden Gribble Bridge Lane, Biddenden ☎ 01580 291726, ⓦ biddendenvineyards.com. Kent's oldest commercial vineyard, producing wines from eleven varieties of grape, as well as traditional ciders and juices. Free themed vineyard tours run once or twice a month, but you can take a self-guided tour any time, and there is a shop/café on site. Mon–Sat 10am–5pm, Sun 11am–5pm (Jan & Feb closed Sun).

Chapel Down Small Hythe, Tenterden ☎ 01580 763033, ⓦ chapeldown.com. Multi-award-winning winemaker, suppliers to Jamie Oliver and Gordon Ramsay – they do a great lager, too – with a wine and English produce store on site, as well as a lovely terrace restaurant overlooking the vines. Guided tours and tastings (£10) daily April–Oct.

SUSSEX

Bolney Wine Estate Foxhole Lane, Bolney ☎ 01444 881894, ⓦ bolneywineestate.co.uk. This small, family run vineyard has a lovely setting and offers a variety of tours, some finishing up at the on-site café. The vineyard has won awards for its sparkling wines, but is also known – unusually for the UK – for its red

wines. Shop Mon–Sat 9am–5pm; café closed Mon. Tours £16–39.50 (Fri, Sat & Sun – see website for dates).

Ridgeview Wine Estate Ditchling Common, off the B2112 ☎ 01444 241441, ⓦ ridgeview.co.uk. Long-established, multi-award-winning vineyard, known for its sparkling wines, produced using traditional Champagne grape varieties and methods. Tours (1hr 30min–2hr; pre-booking essential) run a couple of times a month, or you can just turn up at the cellar door and taste before you buy. Mon–Sat 11am–4pm, closed Sat in Jan & Feb; tours £15.

SURREY

Denbies Wine Estate London Rd, Dorking ☎ 01306 876616, ⓦ denbies.co.uk. Vast commercial vineyard specializing in sparkling wines and whites – on a good year, they can produce up to 400,000 bottles. Tours include a "train" (truck) ride through the surrounding estate, which also has public footpaths. Mon–Sat 9.30am–5.30pm, Sun 10am–5.30pm, Nov–March closes 5pm; indoor tours £9.95, £14 with sparkling wines, £16 with food; "train" tours £6, £10.50 with sparkling wine.

aspirations of American plutocrats than the lifestyle of Tudor nobles. **Anne Boleyn's room** is the most affecting; you can see the prayer book she carried to the executioner's block, inscribed in her own writing and with references to the Pope crossed out. Outside is Waldorf Astor's beautiful **Italian Garden**, decorated with statuary, some more than two thousand years old, as well as a traditional yew-hedge maze, adventure playground, splashy water maze and boating lakes.

2 Chartwell

Mapleton Rd, Westerham, 17.5 miles northwest of Tunbridge Wells • March–Oct daily 11am–5pm • £12.50; gardens and studio only £6.25; NT • ☎ 01732 868381, ⓦ nationaltrust.org.uk/chartwell

Packed with the wartime Prime Minister's possessions – including his rather contemplative paintings – there is something touchingly intimate and rather fascinating about **Chartwell**, the country residence of **Winston Churchill** from 1924 until his death in 1965. In the rolling **grounds**, dotted with lakes and ponds and shaded by mature fruit trees, you can see his **studio**, lined ceiling to floor with more than one hundred canvases; the works are of varying quality, however, and some of the best can be seen in the house itself.

Knole

Sevenoaks, entered from the south end of Sevenoaks High St • **House** Mid-March to Oct Tues–Sun noon–4pm • £10.40; NT **Grounds** Daily dawn–dusk • Free; NT • ☎ 01732 462100, ⓦ nationaltrust.org.uk/knole • Trains from London Bridge or Charing Cross to Sevenoaks station, from where it is about a 20min walk to the Knole entrance

Covering a whopping four acres and designed to echo the calendar – with 365 rooms, 52 staircases, twelve entrances and seven courtyards – **Knole** palace, in the commuter town of **Sevenoaks**, is an astonishingly handsome ensemble. Built in 1456 as a residence for the archbishops of Canterbury, it was appropriated in 1538 by Henry VIII, who loved to hunt in its thousand acres of **parkland** (still today home to several hundred wild deer). Elizabeth I gave the estate to her Lord Treasurer, Thomas Sackville, who remodelled the house in Renaissance style in 1605; it has remained in the family's hands ever since, with its Jacobean exterior preserved. Writer and gardener Vita Sackville-West was brought up here, and her lover Virginia Woolf derived inspiration for her novel *Orlando* from frequent visits. Highlights of this evocatively decaying treasure trove include the lustrous **Venetian Ambassador's Room** with its staggering carved and gilded bed, once belonging to James II; it, and its hangings of sea-green, blue and gold velvet, are literally crumbling away.

Rye and around

Perched on a hill overlooking the Romney Marshes, the pretty, ancient town of **RYE** was added as a "limb" to the original Cinque Ports (see box, p.148), but was subsequently marooned two miles inland by the retreat of the sea and the silting-up of the River Rother. It is now one of the most visited places in East Sussex – half-timbered, skew-roofed and quintessentially English, with plenty of interesting independent shops to poke around in and some excellent places to eat.

Rye's most picturesque street – and the most photographed – is the sloping cobbled **Mermaid Street**, the town's main thoroughfare in the sixteenth century. At the top of Mermaid Street, just around the corner in West Street, lies **Lamb House** (end March–Oct Tues & Sat 2–6pm; £5; NT; ☎ 01580 762334, ⓦ nationaltrust.org.uk/lamb-house), home of the authors Henry James and (subsequently) E.F. Benson. Just a few cobbled yards away is the peaceful oasis of Church Square, where **St Mary's Church** boasts the oldest functioning pendulum clock in the country; the ascent of the church tower (£3) offers fine views over the clay-tiled roofs.

Rye's acclaimed **literary festival** (Ⓦ ryefestival.co.uk) takes place over two weeks in September and also features a wide range of musical and visual arts events. The other big annual event is **Rye Bay Scallop Week** (Ⓦ scallop.org.uk), held at the end of February.

Rye Castle Museum

Ypres Tower Church Square • Daily: April–Oct 10.30am–4.30pm; Nov–March 10.30am–3.30pm • £3 **East St Museum** 3 East St • Normally April–Oct Sat, Sun & bank hols 10.30am–4.30pm, but call ahead to check • Free • ☎ 01797 227798, Ⓦ ryemuseum.co.uk

In the far corner of Church Square stands the **Ypres** (pronounced "Wipers") **Tower**, built to keep watch for cross-Channel invaders and now a part of the **Rye Castle Museum**; the other museum site is on nearby East Street. Both buildings house a number of relics from Rye's past, including an eighteenth-century fire engine and plenty of paraphernalia from the town's smuggling heyday.

Camber Sands

Around three miles east of Rye, on the other side of the River Rother estuary, **Camber Sands** is a two-mile stretch of gorgeous dune-backed sandy beach that has become a renowned centre of wind- and watersports. The nicest way to reach it from Rye is by bike, on the three mile dedicated cycle path.

ARRIVAL AND GETTING AROUND

By train Rye's train station is at the bottom of Station Approach, off Cinque Ports St; it's a 5min walk up to the High Street. Regular trains run to Hastings (hourly; 20min) and London St Pancras (hourly; 1hr 10min).
By bus Bus #100 runs into the centre of town from Hastings (Mon–Sat hourly, Sun every 2hr; 40min), passing

through Winchelsea en route. Buses #711 and #100 run from Rye station to Camber Sands (Mon–Sat hourly, Sun every 2hr; 15min).
Bike rental You can rent bicycles from Rye Hire, 1 Cyprus Place (Mon–Fri 8am–5pm, Sat 8am–noon; £10/half day, £15/day; ☎ 01797 223033, Ⓦ ryehire.co.uk).

INFORMATION

Tourist office 4–5 Lion Street (daily: April–Sept 10am–5pm; Oct–March 10am–4pm; ☎ 01797 229049, Ⓦ visit1066country.com).
Heritage and Information Centre Strand Quay (daily:

April–Oct 10am–5pm; Nov, Feb & March 10am–4pm; Dec & Jan call to check opening hours; ☎ 01797 226696, Ⓦ ryeheritage.co.uk). Privately run.

ACCOMMODATION

★**The George** 98 High St ☎ 01797 222114, Ⓦ thegeorgeinrye.com. This luxurious small hotel manages to get everything just right, from the cosy, wood-beamed bar and excellent restaurant to the tasteful, individually furnished rooms: there are 34 to choose from, ranging from an Arts and Crafts-styled room decked out in William Morris textiles to a hip Art Deco hangout with a circular bed. **£135**
Rye Windmill Off Ferry Rd ☎ 01797 224027, Ⓦ rye windmill.co.uk. Great-value for Rye, this 300-year-old Grade

II-listed smock windmill contains ten spotless contemporary en-suite rooms. Splash out on the Windmill Suite (£150) at the top of the mill for panoramic views over Rye. **£85**
Ship Inn The Strand ☎ 01797 222233, Ⓦ theshipinnrye .co.uk. Ten quirky rooms above an equally characterful quayside pub. Despite being on the small side, rooms are funky, cheerful and charming, featuring bright prints and wallpaper, with fun touches such as rubber ducks in the bathroom and teabags stored in retro tins. **£100**

EATING AND DRINKING

★**Ambrette** In the White Vine House hotel, 24 High St ☎ 01797 222043, Ⓦ theambrette.co.uk. The oak-panelled dining room of the *White Vine House hotel* provides a suitably stunning backdrop to fabulous contemporary Indian cuisine – the likes of pan-grilled steak of Kentish mutton in a Kashmiri-style sauce, or local fish served with mung lentil kedgeree (mains £11–17). For

the full experience opt for the Tasting menu (£50). Mon–Thurs 11.30am–2.30pm & 6–9.30pm, Fri–Sun 11.30am–2.30pm & 5.30–10pm.
Knoops Tower Forge, Hilders Cliff, Landgate ☎ 01797 225838, Ⓦ knoops.co.uk. This little place only offers one thing – hot chocolate – but it does it with style. Choose your chocolate (from 27% to 80% solids; £3), add your

extras (various spices, peppers, fruits, even flowers – all 50p, or a shot of something stronger for £1) and wait to be presented with your own bowl of made-to-order chocolately loveliness. Daily 10am–6pm.

Tuscan Kitchen 8 Lion St ☎01797 223269, ⓦ tuscankitchenrye.co.uk. The delicious, authentic Tuscan cuisine on offer at this beamed, low-ceilinged restaurant has won it a lot of fans; pasta dishes are around £10–12, while mains such as *pollo alla cacciatora* or fillet steak range from £14 to £23. Book well ahead. Wed &

Thurs 6–10pm, Fri & Sat noon–3pm & 6–10pm, Sun noon–3pm & 6–9.30pm.

★**Ship Inn** The Strand ☎01797 222233, ⓦ theshipinnrye.co.uk. Fabulous, laidback quayside pub, with quirky decor, well-worn sofas and plenty of cosy nooks, plus board games (including a Rye-themed Monopoly) to while away a rainy afternoon. There's a good selection of local ales on tap, and excellent seasonal food. Daily 11am–11pm; food served Mon–Fri noon–3pm & 6.30–10pm, Sat & Sun noon–3.30pm & 6.30–10.30pm.

Hastings

Once an influential Cinque Port (see box, p.148), **HASTINGS** is a curious mixture of unpretentious fishing port, tatty seaside resort and bohemian retreat popular with artists. The town is best known, however, for the eponymous **battle** which took place nearby; in 1066, William, Duke of Normandy, landed at Pevensey Bay, a few miles west of town, and marched to meet Harold's army at nearby Battle (see p.160).

Old Town

The pretty **Old Town**, east of the pier, is by far the nicest part of Hastings. **High Street** and pedestrianized **George Street** are the focus, both lined with antiques shops, galleries, restaurants and pubs. Running parallel to the High Street is **All Saints Street**, punctuated with the odd, rickety, timber-framed dwelling from the fifteenth century.

West Hill

The quickest way up **West Hill**, which separates the Old Town from the less interesting modern quarter, is to hop on the **West Hill Cliff Railway**, which climbs up from George Street (April–Oct daily 10am–5.30pm; Nov–Feb Sat & Sun 11am–4pm; £2.50 return; ☎01424 451111).

Hastings Castle

West Hill • Hours vary but generally mid-Feb to Easter Sat & Sun 10am–3pm; Easter–Oct daily 10am–4pm • £4.50 • ☎01424 422964, ⓦ smuggersadventure.co.uk & ⓦ visit1066country.com

Very little remains of **Hastings Castle**, erected by William the Conqueror in 1066: storms in the thirteenth century caused the cliffs to subside, tipping most of it into the sea. The ruins, however, offer an excellent prospect of the town, and an audiovisual show, **The 1066 Story**, describes the events of the last successful invasion of the British mainland.

The Stade

Down by the seafront, the area known as **The Stade** is characterized by its tall, black weatherboard **net shops**, most dating from the mid-nineteenth century, and still in use today. The Stade is home to the town's fishing fleet – the largest beach-launched fleet in Europe – and many of the net shops sell fresh fish.

Jerwood Gallery

Rock-a-Nore Rd • Tues–Fri 11am–5pm, Sat & Sun 11am–6pm; first Tues of month open until 8pm; extended hours during school holidays • £8, free on first Tues of month 4–8pm • ☎01424 728377, ⓦ jerwoodgallery.org

HASTINGS JACK-IN-THE-GREEN

The biggest weekend of the year is the **Jack-in-the-Green Festival** (May Day weekend; ⊚hastingsjack.co.uk), three days of festivities culminating in a riotous parade of dancers, drummers and leaf-bedecked revellers through the streets of the Old Town up to Hastings' hilltop castle, where "the Jack" – a garlanded leaf-covered figure whose origins date back to the eighteenth century – is ritually slain and the spirit of summer released.

2

Adjacent to the fishing quarter, the sleek **Jerwood Gallery**, covered in shimmering dark-glazed tiles, provides a home for the Jerwood Foundation's modern art collection, which includes works by Stanley Spencer, Walter Sickert and Augustus John. A café up on the first floor overlooks the fishing boats on the beach.

East Hill

Just behind the net shops, the venerable **East Hill Cliff Railway** (April–Oct daily 10am–5.30pm; Nov–Feb Sat & Sun 11am–4pm; £2.50 return; ☎01424 451111), the steepest funicular in the country, climbs up to **East Hill**, for wonderful views over the town and access to **Hastings County Park**, a beautiful expanse of heathland, woodland and sandstone cliffs, which spreads east for three miles.

Hastings Pier

West of The Stade, **Hastings Pier** (⊚hpcharity.co.uk), which was burnt down in an arson attack in 2010, is due to reopen in 2015 after an ambitious multi-million pound refurbishment, with open-air film screenings, funfair rides and seasonal events planned.

ARRIVAL AND INFORMATION   HASTINGS

By train The train station is a 10min walk from the seafront along Havelock Road.
Destinations Brighton (every 30min; 1hr 5min); Eastbourne (every 20min; 25min); Lewes (every 30min; 55min); London Charing Cross (every 30min; 1hr 30min–1hr 45min); London St Pancras (hourly; 1hr 45min); Rye (hourly; 20min); Tunbridge Wells (every 30min; 35–50min)
By bus National Express coach services operate from the station at the junction of Havelock and Queen's roads.
Destinations Battle (Mon–Sat hourly, Sun every 2–3 hrs; 15min); Dover (hourly; 2hr 50min); Eastbourne (Mon–Sat every 20–30min, Sun hourly; 1hr 15min); London Victoria (1 daily; 2hr 35min); Rye (Mon–Sat hourly, Sun every 2hr; 40min).
Tourist office On the seafront midway between the pier and the Old Town, at Aquila House on Breeds Place (hours may change but currently April–Oct Mon–Fri 9am–5pm, Sat 9.30am–5.30pm, Sun 10.30am–4pm; Nov–March Mon–Fri 9am–5pm, Sat 10am–4pm, Sun 10.30am–1pm; ☎01424 451111, ⊚visit1066country.com).

ACCOMMODATION

Senlac Guesthouse 47 Cambridge Gardens ☎01424 435767, ⊚senlacguesthouse.co.uk. Stylish yet affordable, this friendly guesthouse near the station is fantastic value. Smart, contemporary rooms come with i-Phone docking stations, DVD players and wi-fi. The cheapest rooms share bathrooms. Breakfast costs £8.50 extra. **£55**
★**Swan House** 1 Hill St ☎01892 430014, ⊚swanhousehastings.co.uk. Beautiful B&B in a half-timbered fifteenth-century building on one of the Old Town's most picturesque streets. Rooms are luxurious and tasteful, and there's a pretty decked patio garden in which to enjoy the gourmet breakfast on sunny days. The owners also run the quirkier but similarly elegant *Old Rectory* nearby. **£120**

EATING, DRINKING AND ENTERTAINMENT

There's no shortage of great **restaurants** in Hastings, many serving fresh fish from the town's fishing fleet. There's also a thriving **live music** scene; pick up the *Ultimate Alternative* listings magazine (⊚ua1066.co.uk), available in pubs and clubs throughout town, for a comprehensive guide to what's on.

Dragon 71 George St ☎01424 423688. Hip hangout – part restaurant, part bar – with tasty food (the locally sourced menu changes weekly), art exhibitions and a nice assortment of squishy sofas. Mon–Sat noon–11pm, Sun noon–10.30pm.

Maggies Above the fish market, Rock-a-Nore Rd ☎ 01424 430205. The best fish and chips in town can be found at this first-floor café, right on the beach. It's open for lunch only, and is very popular, so you'll need to book ahead. Mon–Sat noon–2pm.

Porter's Wine Bar 56 High St ☎ 01424 427000,

ⓦ porterswinebar.com. Friendly, family-run wine bar, with jazz and acoustic music on Wednesday and Thursday nights and Sunday afternoons, including a regular spot by acclaimed jazz pianist and local resident Lianne Carroll. Good, home-cooked, bistro-style food also on offer. Mon–Fri noon–3pm & 7pm–midnight, Sat noon–midnight, Sun 12.30–11pm.

Battle Abbey and Battlefield

At the south end of High St, Battle • April–Sept daily 10am–6pm; Oct daily 10am–5pm; Nov–March Sat & Sun 10am–4pm • £8; EH • ☎ 01424 775705, ⓦ english-heritage.org.uk • Buses #304 and #305 from Hastings , or regular trains from Hastings and London Charing Cross to Battle station, a 10min walk away

Six miles inland from Hastings in the small town of Battle, the remains of **Battle Abbey** claim to occupy the site of the most famous land battle in British history. Here, or hereabouts, on October 14, 1066, the invading Normans swarmed up the hillside from Senlac Moor and overcame the army of King Harold, spelling an end to Anglo-Saxon England. Before the battle took place, William vowed that, should he win, he would build a religious foundation on the very spot of Harold's slaying to atone for the bloodshed, and, true to his word, Battle Abbey was built four years later and subsequently occupied by a fraternity of Benedictines.

The abbey, once one of the richest in the country, was partially destroyed in the Dissolution and much rebuilt and revised over the centuries. The magnificent 1330s gatehouse still survives, along with the thirteenth-century rib-vaulted dormitory range, but all that remains of William's original abbey church is an outline on the grass, with the site of the high altar – the spot where Harold was supposedly killed – marked by a memorial stone. An excellent **visitor centre** shows a film about the battle and the events leading up to it.

Eastbourne

Like so many of the southeast's seaside resorts, **EASTBOURNE** was kick-started into life in the 1840s, when the Brighton, Lewes and Hastings Rail Company built a branch line from Lewes to the sea. Nowadays Eastbourne has a solid reputation as a retirement town by the sea, and though the contemporary **Towner Gallery** has introduced a splash of modernity, the town's charms remain for the most part sedate and old-fashioned. The focus of the elegant seafront is the Victorian **pier**, partly destroyed by fire in 2014; just to the west is the splendid **bandstand** (ⓦ www.eastbournebandstand.co.uk), which hosts various musical events throughout the year. The real draw, however, is the town's proximity to one of the scenic highlights of the South Downs National Park: the stunning coastal scenery of **Beachy Head** and the **Seven Sisters Country Park**.

Towner Art Gallery and Museum

Devonshire Park • Tues–Sun & bank hol Mon 10am–6pm • Tours daily at 11.30am • Free • ☎ 01323 434670, ⓣ townereastbourne.org.uk

Housed in a sleek modern edifice by Devonshire Park, the excellent **Towner Art Gallery and Museum** puts on four or five exhibitions a year, which are shown alongside rotating displays of modern and contemporary art from its own permanent collection. On the second floor there's a café-bar with a small terrace overlooking the rooftops of Eastbourne to the South Downs beyond.

ARRIVAL AND INFORMATION   EASTBOURNE

By train Eastbourne's train station is a splendid Italianate terminus, just a 10min walk from the seafront

up Terminus Road.

Destinations Brighton (every 20min; 35min); Hastings

(every 20min; 30min); Lewes (every 20min; 30min); London Victoria (Mon–Sat every 30min, Sun hourly; 1hr 35min).
By bus The bus station is on Junction Road, by the train station.
Destinations Brighton (every 10–15min; 1hr 15min); Hastings (Mon–Sat every 20min, Sun hourly; 1hr 10min); London Victoria (2 daily; 3–4hr); Tunbridge Wells (Mon–

Sat hourly; 50min).
Tourist office 3 Cornfield Road, just off Terminus Road (March, April & Oct Mon–Fri 9.15am–5.30pm, Sat 9.15am–4pm; May–Sept Mon–Fri 9.15am–5.30pm, Sat 9.15am–5pm, Sun 10am–1pm; Nov–Feb Mon–Fri 9.15am–4.30pm, Sat 9.15am–1pm; 0871 663 0031, www.visiteastbourne.com)

2

ACCOMMODATION AND EATING

Dolphin 14 South St 01323 746622, thedolphin eastbourne.co.uk. One of the town's nicest pubs, this laid-back hangout has locally brewed beers on tap (including Harveys and Dark Star) and serves good home-cooked food including burgers and local fish (£7.50–9.50). Mon–Thurs 11am–11pm, Fri & Sat 11am–midnight, Sun noon–10.30pm; food served Mon–Thurs noon–2.30pm & 6–9.30pm, Fri & Sat noon–9.30pm, Sun noon–8pm.
Fusciardi's 30 Marine Parade 01323 722128 fusciardiicecreams.co.uk. This fabulous ice-cream parlour is an Eastbourne institution, with piled-high sundaes that are a work of art. Cash only. Daily 9am–7pm,

later in summer.
Pebble Beach 53 Royal Parade 01323 431240, pebblebeacheastbourne.com. Boutique B&B at the eastern end of town, with six stylish, good-value rooms set across three floors of a Victorian seafront townhouse. The nicest room is up on the first floor, with floor-to-ceiling windows and a private balcony looking out to sea. **£80**
Urban Ground 2a Bolton Rd 01323 410751, urbanground.co.uk. The best coffee shop in Eastbourne by a long chalk, with hip decor, great coffee and a range of tasty sandwiches, charcuterie boards and cakes. Mon–Sat 7.30am–6pm, Sun 9am–6pm.

Beachy Head and the Seven Sisters Country Park

A short walk west from Eastbourne – or a short bus ride – takes you out along the most dramatic stretch of coastline in the South Downs National Park, where the chalk uplands are cut by the sea into a sequence of splendid cliffs that stretch for nine pristine miles. The most spectacular of these, **Beachy Head** (575ft high) is a two-mile uphill slog from Eastbourne. A couple of miles to the west of here the cliffs dip down to **Birling Gap**, where's there's access to the beach, and a National Trust-run café and information centre. Birling Gap marks the eastern end of a series of magnificent undulating chalk cliffs known as the **Seven Sisters**, which end three miles further west at the meandering River Cuckmere. The Seven Sisters Country Park provides some of the most impressive walks in the county, taking in the cliff-top path and the lower valley of the River Cuckmere. Head up to

---

SOUTH DOWNS NATIONAL PARK AND THE SOUTH DOWNS WAY

The fifteenth and newest member of Britain's National Park family, the **South Downs National Park** came into being in 2010. Covering over six hundred square miles, it stretches for seventy miles from eastern Hampshire to the white chalk cliffs of East Sussex. The park is located in one of the most densely populated parts of the country, and in contrast to other "wilder" National Parks, it contains a high proportion of farmland – about 85 percent of the park.

There are **visitor centres** in East Sussex at the Seven Sisters Country Park, at Beachy Head and at Birling Gap (see p.162 for all). The **South Downs National Park Authority** website (southdowns.gov.uk) is another useful source of information about the area.

THE SOUTH DOWNS WAY

One of the best ways to explore the park is to strike off into the countryside on the **South Downs Way**, which rises and dips over one hundred miles along the chalk uplands between the city of Winchester and the spectacular cliffs at Beachy Head, and offers the southeast's finest walks. The OS *Landranger* **maps** #198 and #199 cover the eastern end of the route; you'll need #185 and #197 as well to cover the lot. Several **guidebooks** are available (some covering the route in just one direction); you can also check out the **website** nationaltrail.co.uk/southdowns.

Seaford Head, on the western side of the Cuckmere estuary, for the iconic view of the cliffs you'll see on every postcard, with the picturesque coastguard's cottages in the foreground.

ARRIVAL AND INFORMATION

By bus Bus #13X runs from Eastbourne and Brighton via Beachy Head, Birling Gap and the Seven Sisters Country Park Visitor Centre (late April to late June Sat & Sun only; late June to mid-Sept daily; every 30min).

By car There are pay-and-display car parks at Beachy Head, Birling Gap (NT) and at Exceat (access point for the Cuckmere Valley) on the A259 between Brighton and Eastbourne.

Tourist information Beachy Head Countryside Centre,

BEACHY HEAD AND SEVEN SISTERS

Beachy Head (April–Oct daily 10am–4pm; call to check winter hours; ☎ 01323 737273, ⊛ beachyhead.org.uk). Seven Sisters Country Park Visitor Centre, Exceat, on the A259 (April–Oct daily 10.30am–4.30pm; Nov–March Sat & Sun 11am–4pm; ☎ 01323 870280, ⊛ www .sevensisters.org.uk). Birling Gap Information Centre, Birling Gap (daily 10am–4pm; ☎ 01323 423197, ⊛ nationaltrust.org.uk/birling-gap-and-the-seven -sisters).

ACCOMMODATION

★ **Belle Tout** Beachy Head ☎ 01323 423185, ⊛ belletout.co.uk. For a real treat book into this fabulous lighthouse, perched high up on the dramatic cliffs just west of Beachy Head. The cosy rooms boast stupendous

views, there's a snug residents' lounge and – best of all – there's unrestricted access to the lamproom at the top of the lighthouse, where you can sit and watch the sun go down. **£185**

Lewes

LEWES, the county town of East Sussex, straddles the River Ouse as it carves a gap through the South Downs on its final stretch to the sea. Though there's been some rebuilding, the core of Lewes remains remarkably good-looking: replete with crooked older dwellings, narrow lanes – or "twittens" – and Georgian houses. With numerous traces of its long history still visible (not least a medieval castle), plus a lively cultural scene, plenty of independent and antiques shops, and some of England's most appealing chalkland on its doorstep, Lewes makes a great Sussex base. Nearby, the Bloomsbury Group's country home at **Charleston** and the newly opened **Ditchling Museum of Art and Craft** are both a short hop by car.

Lewes Castle

169 High St • March–Oct Mon & Sun 11am–5.30pm, Tues–Sat 10am–5.30pm; Nov–Feb Mon & Sun 11am–4.30pm, Tues–Sat 10am–4.30pm, closed Mon in Jan • £7, combined ticket with Anne of Cleves House £10.50 • ☎ 01273 486290, ⊛ sussexpast.co.uk

Both **Lewes Castle** and St Pancras Priory (see opposite) were the work of William de Warenne, who was given the land by his father-in-law, William I, following the Norman Conquest. Inside the castle complex – unusual for being built on two mottes, or mounds – the shell of the eleventh-century keep remains, and can be climbed for excellent views over the town to the surrounding Downs. Tickets include admission to the **museum** (same hours as castle) by the entrance, where exhibits include archeological artefacts, a town model and a tapestry of the Battle of Lewes stitched to commemorate the battle's 750th anniversary in 2014.

Southover

From the High Street, the steep, cobbled and much photographed **Keere Street** leads to **Southover**, the southern part of town. At the foot of Keere Street, tranquil **Grange Gardens** (daily dawn–dusk; free) sprawl around Southover Grange, once the childhood home of the diarist John Evelyn. Nearby on Southover High Street is the timber-framed **Anne of Cleves House** (Feb–Nov Tues–Sat 10am–5pm, Mon &

GLYNDEBOURNE

Founded in 1934, **Glyndebourne**, three miles east of Lewes, off the A27 (☎01273 812321, ⓦglyndebourne.com), is Britain's only unsubsidized opera house, and the Glyndebourne season (mid-May to Aug) is an indispensable part of the high-society calendar. Tickets are pricey, but there are cheaper, standing-room-only ones available at reduced prices, and discounts for under-30s if you register first.

2

Sun 11am–5pm; £5.20, combined ticket with the castle £10.50; ☎01273 474610, ⓦsussexpast.org.uk), a fifteenth-century hall house laid out as it would have looked in Tudor times. Cross the road and head down Cockshut Lane to reach the evocative ruins of **St Pancras Priory** (open access; free); in its heyday it was one of Europe's principal Cluniac institutions, with a church the size of Westminster Abbey.

ARRIVAL AND INFORMATION | LEWES

By train The train station is south of High Street down Station Road.

Destinations Brighton (every 10–20min; 15min); Eastbourne (every 20 30min; 20 30min); London Victoria (Mon–Sat every 30min, Sun hourly; 1hr 10min)

By bus The bus station is on Eastgate St, near the foot of School Hill.

Destinations Brighton (Mon–Sat every 15min, Sun hourly; 30min); Tunbridge Wells (Mon–Sat every 30min, Sun hourly; 1hr 10min).

Tourist office At the junction of High Street and Fisher Street (April–Sept Mon–Sat 9.30am–4.30pm, Sun 10am–2pm; Oct–March Mon–Fri 9.30am–4.30pm, Sat 10am–2pm; ☎01273 483448, ⓦlewes.gov.uk); they hold copies of the free monthly magazine *Viva Lewes* (ⓦvivalewes.co.uk).

ACCOMMODATION

The Corner House 14 Cleve Terrace ☎01273 567138, ⓦlewescornerhouse.co.uk. Super-friendly B&B on a quiet Edwardian terrace, close to Grange Gardens. The two en-suite rooms have lovely homely touches such as patchwork quilts and plenty of books, and the owner is a great source of information on the town and area. **£90**

Monty's Broughton House, 16 High St ☎01273 476750, ⓦmontysaccommodation.co.uk. Stylish, contemporary open-plan room on the top floor of a townhouse on the High Street, complete with a modern four-poster, freestanding bath (and separate swish shower room) and a small kitchenette. Breakfast isn't included, but you're right in the thick of things here, with plenty of nearby cafés to choose from. **£130**

YHA South Downs Itford Farm, Beddingham, 5 miles from Lewes ☎0870 371 9574. The nearest hostel to Lewes is a gem, newly renovated from a characterful old farm, and in a fabulous location right on the South Downs Way footpath, with great transport connections (Southease station – with regular connections to Lewes – is just 200yd away). There's a café and licensed bar too. Dorms **£15**, doubles **£32**

EATING AND DRINKING

Bill's 56 Cliffe High St ☎01273 476918, ⓦbillsproducestore.co.uk. No visit to Lewes would be complete without a leisurely weekend brunch at this always buzzing café, which started life as a greengrocer's here in Lewes and now has branches across the country. Mon–Thurs 8am–10.30pm, Fri & Sat 8am–11pm, Sun 9am–10.30pm.

★**Buttercup Café** In Pastorale Antiques, 15 Malling St ☎01273 477664, ⓦthebuttercupcafe.co.uk. Tucked away at the end of Cliffe High Street, this cosy, quirky café is a hidden gem, with plenty of outdoor seating in a tranquil sun-trap courtyard, and a simple daily-changing seasonal menu. The salad plates (£6.50) are fabulous. Mon–Sat 9.30am–4pm.

★**Famiglia** 17 Market St ☎01273 479539, ⓦfamiglia-lazzati.co.uk. Small family-run Italian restaurant that's a local favourite for its great home-cooked, locally sourced food (pizzas from £7, pastas £8–10, mains from £13). Make sure you leave room for the lip-smackingly good "Trio" of puds. Mon–Fri noon–2.30pm & 5–10pm, Sat & Sun noon–10pm.

Lewes Arms Mount Place ☎01273 473252, ⓦlewesarms.co.uk. This characterful local is a good spot to sample a pint of Sussex Best, produced down the road at Harveys brewery. Great-value, home-cooked food too (jerk chicken, burgers, home-made pasties and more, all under £9). Mon–Thurs 11am–11pm, Fri & Sat 11am–midnight, Sun noon–11pm; food served Mon–Fri noon–8.30pm, Sat noon–9pm, Sun noon–8.30pm.

Charleston Farmhouse

6 miles east of Lewes, signposted off the A27 • April–Oct: Sun & bank hol Mon 1–5.30pm; Wed–Sat visit by 1hr tours only 1–6pm (July, Aug & Sept from noon); last entry 1hr before closing • £11, garden only £4.50 • ☎ 01323 811626, ⓦ charleston.org.uk

Charleston Farmhouse was the country home and gathering place of the writers, intellectuals and artists known as the Bloomsbury Group. Virginia Woolf's sister Vanessa Bell, Vanessa's husband, Clive Bell, and her lover, Duncan Grant, moved here during World War I so that the men, both conscientious objectors, could work on local farms. Almost every surface of the farmhouse interior is painted and the walls are hung with paintings by Picasso, Renoir and Augustus John, alongside the work of the residents. The guided tours give a fascinating insight into the lives of the unconventional group of friends and lovers; try to visit on a day when a tour is running if you can.

Brighton

Vibrant, quirky and cool, **BRIGHTON** (or Brighton and Hove, to give it its official name) is one of the country's most popular seaside destinations. The essence of the city's appeal is its faintly bohemian vitality, a buzz that comes from a mix of holiday-makers, foreign-language students, a thriving gay community, and an energetic local student population from the art college and two universities.

Any trip to Brighton inevitably begins with a visit to its two most famous landmarks – the exuberant **Royal Pavilion** and the wonderfully tacky **Brighton Pier** – followed by a stroll along the seafront promenade or the pebbly beach. Just as interesting, though, is an exploration of Brighton's car-free **Lanes** – the maze of narrow alleys marking the old town – or a meander through the more bohemian streets of **North Laine**. Brighton's other great draw is its **cultural life**: you're spoilt for choice when it comes to live music, theatre, comedy and concerts, especially if you coincide your visit with the **Brighton Festival** (May), the largest arts festival in England.

The Royal Pavilion

4/5 Pavilion Buildings • Daily: April–Sept 9.30am–5.45pm; Oct–March 10am–5.15pm; last entry 45min before closing • £11 • ☎ 03000 290900, ⓦ www.brighton-hove-rpml.org.uk

In any survey to find England's most loved building, there's always a bucketful of votes for Brighton's exotic extravaganza, the **Royal Pavilion**. The building was the south-coast pied-à-terre of the fun-loving Prince Regent (the future George IV), who first visited the seaside resort in 1783 and spent much of the next forty years partying, gambling and frolicking with his mistress here. The building you see today is the work of John Nash, architect of London's Regent Street, who in 1815 redesigned the Prince's original modest dwelling into an extraordinary confection of slender minarets, twirling domes, pagodas, balconies and miscellaneous motifs imported from India and China. The result defined a genre of its own – Oriental Gothic.

Inside, the **Banqueting Room** erupts with ornate splendour and is dominated by a one-tonne chandelier hung from the jaws of a massive dragon cowering in a plantain tree. The stunning **Music Room**, the first sight of which reduced George to tears of joy, has a huge dome lined with more than 26,000 individually gilded scales and hung with exquisite umbrella-like glass lamps. After climbing the famous cast-iron staircase with its bamboo-look banisters, you can go into Victoria's sober and seldom-used bedroom and the North Gallery where the king's portrait hangs, along with a selection of satirical cartoons. More notable, though, is the **South Gallery**, decorated in sky-blue with trompe-l'oeil bamboo trellises and a carpet that appears to be strewn with flowers.

BRIGHTON

■ ACCOMMODATION	
Cavalaire House	4
Drakes Hotel	8
Guest and the City	5
Kemp Townhouse	9
KIPPS	2
MyHotel	1
Pelirocco	7
A Room With a View	3
Snooze	6

● SHOPS	
Hope and Harlequin	3
Ink'd Gallery	6
Lavender Room	7
Pecksniffs	2
Resident	5
She Said	1
Snoopers Paradise	4

THE LANES

● RESTAURANTS	
64 Degrees	4
Bom-Bane's	12
Chilli Pickle	9
Food for Friends	5
Gingerman	11
Melrose	13
Plateau	6
Riddle and Finns	1
Terre-à-Terre	7

● CAFÉS & SNACKS	
Café Coho	3
Gelato Gusto	10
Jack and Linda's Smokehouse	8
Marwood	2
Metrodeco	14

● PUBS & BARS	
Bee's Mouth	7
Craft Beer Co.	8
The Cricketers	5
The Greys	2
Mesmerist	6
Northern Lights	3
OHSO Social	1
Oki-Nami	9

● CLUBS & LIVE MUSIC VENUES	
Audio	3
Concorde 2	10
FunFair	13
Green Door Store	4
Proud Cabaret	6
	11

Churchill Square Shopping Centre

The Brighton Centre

Clock Tower

Train Station

Police Station

Jubilee Library

Komedia

Theatre Royal

Museum and Art Gallery

Brighton Dome

Royal Pavilion

Pavilion Gardens

Brighton Fishing Museum

Sea Life Centre

Brighton Wheel

Volk's Electric Railway

West Pier

Booth Museum of Natural History ▲

Duke of York's Picturehouse ▲

Hospital ▲

Yellowave & ▲

HOVE

KEMP TOWN

NORTH LAINE

THE LANES

0   250 yards

SEE "THE LANES" INSET MAP

Brighton Museum and Art Gallery

Royal Pavilion Gardens • Tues–Sun 10am–5pm • Free • ☎ 03000 290900, ⓦ www.brighton-hove-rpml.org.uk

Across the gardens from the Pavilion stands the **Brighton Museum and Art Gallery** – once part of the royal stable block – which houses a wonderful and eclectic mix of modern fashion and design, archeology, painting and local history. Among the highlights are Dalí's famous sofa (1938) based on Mae West's lips, the 13,000-object ethnographic collection, and the mummified animals and painted coffins of the Ancient Egypt galleries.

The Lanes

Tucked between the Pavilion and the seafront is a warren of narrow, pedestrianized alleyways known as **The Lanes** – the core of the old fishing village from which Brighton evolved. Long-established antiques shops and jewellers', designer outlets and several cafés, pubs and restaurants make this a great place to wander.

North Laine

Vibrant, buzzy **North Laine** (ⓦ northlaine.co.uk), which spreads north of North Street along Kensington Gardens and Sydney, Gardner and Bond streets, is more offbeat than the Lanes. Here the eclectic shops, selling secondhand records, vintage gear, homeware, upmarket fashion and New Age objects, mingle with cool coffee shops and pavement cafés and bars.

The seafront

To soak up the tackier side of Brighton, head down to the **seafront** and take a stroll along **Brighton Pier** (daily: April–Oct 10am–10pm; Nov–March 11am–5pm; ☎ 01273 609361, ⓦ brightonpier.co.uk), completed in 1899, its every inch devoted to cacophonous fun and money-making. The busiest section of the seafront lies between Brighton Pier and the derelict **West Pier**, half a mile west along the seafront; here, down at beach level underneath the old fishermen's arches, the **Lower Esplanade** is lined with cafés, giftshops, galleries (ⓦ theartistquarter.co.uk), bars and clubs. The Lower Esplanade is also home to the **Brighton Fishing Museum** (daily 9am–5pm; free; ☎ 01273 723064, ⓦ brightonfishingmuseum.org.uk), which displays old photos and video footage of the golden days of the local fishing industry and houses a large Sussex clinker, a boat once common on Brighton beach.

East of Brighton Pier, the 165ft **Brighton Wheel** (Mon–Thurs & Sun 10am–9pm; Fri & Sat 10am–11pm; £8 for 12–15min ride; ☎ 01273 722822, ⓦ brightonwheel.com), in place until 2016, offers panoramic views of the city. Opposite, on Marine Parade, the **Sea Life Centre** (daily 10am–5/6/7pm; £17.50; ☎ 01273 604234, ⓦ visitsealife.com/Brighton) is the world's oldest operating aquarium, opened in 1872; its wonderfully atmospheric Victorian aquarium hall is the main attraction. Just east of the Brighton Wheel, the antiquated locomotives of **Volk's Electric Railway** (Easter–Sept Mon & Fri 11.15am–5pm, Tues–Thurs 10.15am–5pm, Sat & Sun 10.15am–6pm; every 15min; £3.60 return; ⓦ volkselectricrailway.co.uk) – the first electric train in the country – run eastward towards **Brighton Marina** (ⓦ brightonmarina.co.uk), stopping off en route at the fabulous **Yellowave** beach sports venue (May–Sept Mon–Fri 10am–10pm, Sat & Sun 10am–8pm; Oct–April Tues–Thurs 11am–9pm, Fri 11am–5pm, Sat & Sun 10am–5pm; court rental £21/hr; ☎ 01273 672222, ⓦ yellowave.co.uk), the perfect spot for a taster of beach volleyball on a sunny day, with six courts, plus a bouldering wall and an excellent café.

Hove

West of the city centre, **Hove** – which started life as a separate resort in the 1820s and only merged with Brighton in 1997 – is an elegant neighbourhood, with a much quieter beachfront, some beautiful Regency architecture and plenty of good shops and places to eat. The main sight is **Hove Museum**, 19 Church Street (Mon, Tues & Thurs–Sat 10am–5pm, Sun & bank hol Mon 2–5pm; free; ☎03000 290900, ⓦwww.brighton -hove-rpml.org.uk; bus #1, #1A, #6, #49 or #49A), which houses a fascinating and eclectic collection that covers everything from contemporary crafts to a 3500-year-old Bronze Age cup. A six-seater cinema shows early silent films made in Hove.

ARRIVAL AND DEPARTURE
BRIGHTON

By train Brighton train station is at the top of Queen's Road, which descends to the Clocktower and then becomes West St, eventually leading to the seafront, a 10min walk away.
Destinations Arundel (Mon–Sat every 30min, Sun hourly; 1hr 20min); Chichester (every 30min; 45–55min); Eastbourne (every 20min; 35min); Hastings (every 30min; 1hr 5min); Lewes (every 10–20min; 15min); London Bridge (Mon–Sat 4 hourly, Sun every 30min; 1hr); London King's Cross (2–4 hourly; 1hr 15min); London Victoria (1–2 hourly; 55min–1hr 20min); Portsmouth Harbour (Mon–

Sat every 30min, Sun hourly; 1hr 30min).
By bus The long-distance bus station is just in from the seafront on the south side of the Old Steine.
Destinations Arundel (Mon–Fri every 30min; 2hr); Chichester (Mon–Sat every 15min, Sun every 30min; 1hr 45min); Eastbourne (every 10–15min; 1hr 15min); Lewes (Mon–Sat every 15min, Sun hourly; 30min); London Victoria (hourly; 2hr 20min); Portsmouth (Mon–Sat every 30min, Sun hourly; 3hr 30min); Tunbridge Wells (Mon–Sat every 30min, Sun hourly; 1hr 35min).

GETTING AROUND

By bus A one-day CitySaver ticket (£4.70) allows you unlimited travel on the city bus network. Short-hop journeys cost £1.80. The website ⓦjourneyon.co.uk has a journey planner.
By taxi For a city taxi, call ☎01273 202020 or ☎01273 204060. There are central ranks at Brighton station, East St, Queens Square near the clocktower and outside St Peter's Church.
By tour For details of city tours, which range from ghost walks to bike tours to a "Piers and Queers" tour, see

ⓦvisitbrighton.com/things-to-do/walking-guides. The website also has downloadable PDF walking tours and podcasts.
By bike The website ⓦjourneyon.co.uk has a journey planner, and a downloadable cycling map of the city.
Bike rental Amsterdammers, Unit 8, under the station, off Trafalgar Street (£7/3hr, £10/24hr; ☎01273 571555, ⓦbrightoncyclehire.com); Brighton Beach Bike Hire, Madeira Drive, by Yellowave (£6 for 1hr, £12 for 3hr, £16 for 4+ hours; ☎07917 753794, ⓦbrightonsports.co.uk).

INFORMATION

Visitor information There are ten staffed Visitor Information points (VIPs) throughout the city, including at Brighton Pier, the Royal Pavilion shop and Jubilee Library in the North Laine.
Useful apps, magazines and websites VisitBrighton

produces a free app for smartphones (ⓦvisitbrighton.com /apps). The best listing magazine is *Source* (ⓦbrighton source.co.uk), but *XYZ* (ⓦxyzmagazine.co.uk) and *BN1* (ⓦbn1magazine.co.uk) are also worth a look.

ACCOMMODATION

Brighton's **accommodation** is pricey, with rates often rising substantially at weekends. The listings below quote weekend, high-season rates; at many places these prices will fall dramatically out of season and midweek, so it pays to check around. Note that at weekends there's generally a two-night-minimum stay. Much of the city's nicest B&B accommodation is found in **Kemp Town**, east of the city centre, either off St James's Street (the city's "Gay Village") or around Kemp Town Village, with its cool cafés, delis and antique shops.

HOTELS AND B&BS
Cavalaire House 34 Upper Rock Gardens ☎01273 696899, ⓦcavalaire.co.uk. Warm and welcoming B&B, with artwork from Brighton artists on the walls, fresh flowers in the cheery breakfast room, and a friendly resident dog. Rooms vary: the cheapest are cosy and traditional, while the more expensive deluxe rooms have a bit more style. **£149**
Drakes Hotel 33–34 Marine Parade ☎01273 696934, ⓦdrakesofbrighton.com. The unbeatable seafront location

is the big draw at this chic, minimalist boutique hotel. All the luxuries you'd expect are here, and the most expensive rooms come with freestanding baths by floor-to-ceiling windows. There's an excellent in-house restaurant too. Room only **£160**
★ **Guest and the City** 2 Broad St ☎01273 698289, ⓦguestandthecity.co.uk. Lovely B&B in a great central location a minute from the pier, with stylish rooms (the two feature rooms – £140 – come with stained-glass windows of classic Brighton scenes), and super-friendly owners who

2

couldn't be more helpful. **£90**

★**Kemp Townhouse** 21 Atlingworth St ☎01273 681400, ⓦkemptownhouse.com. Stylish Regency townhouse – the city's only five-star guesthouse – with excellent service, chic rooms and great breakfasts. Seaview rooms come with binoculars for gazing out to sea, and all rooms come have a carafe of complimentary port. **£115**

MyHotel 17 Jubilee St ☎01273 900300, ⓦmyhotels .com/my-hotel-brighton. Hip boutique hotel in the heart of North Laine, with rooms designed along feng shui lines, and a great bar, *Merkaba*, downstairs. Rates fluctuate with demand, so check online for last-minute bargains. **£140**

★**Pelirocco** 10 Regency Square ☎01273 327055, ⓦhotelpelirocco.co.uk. "England's most rock'n'roll hotel" is a real one-off, featuring extravagantly themed rooms inspired by pop culture and pin-ups. There's a Fifties-style boudoir, a Pop Art "Modrophenia" room featuring bedside tables made from scooters, and even a twin room styled as Lord Vader's Quarters, complete with light sabre, Darth Vader costume and Star Wars DVDs. **£115**

A Room With A View 41 Marine Parade ☎01273 682885, ⓦaroomwithaviewbrighton.com. This boutique guesthouse, right on the seafront, offers some of the best views in town. All rooms come with Nespresso machines and bathrobes; some have free-standing baths, others power showers. Pick of the bunch is the first-floor balcony room (£255). **£135**

Snooze 25 St George's Terrace ☎01273 605797, ⓦsnoozebrighton.com. Quirky, characterful guesthouse in Kemp Town Village, with six funky rooms that range from a 1970s-style penthouse suite to a room decked out with vintage black-and-white photos of topless pin-ups. **£140**

HOSTELS

KIPPS 76 Grand Parade ☎01273 604182, ⓦkipps -brighton.com. Quiet, friendly hostel in a great spot opposite the Royal Pavilion, with comfy rooms (some en suite) and dorms, a licensed bar and good-value breakfasts (£2.50 for dorms, included for rooms). Dorms **£30**, doubles **£82**

EATING

Brighton has the greatest concentration of **restaurants** in the southeast after London – including one of the country's best vegetarian restaurants – and a thriving **café** culture, especially in the buzzy North Laine area. There are plenty of good **coffee shops** in the city, including those belonging to Brighton-based chains Ground and the Small Batch Coffee Company; the latter has its own roastery in Hove.

CAFÉS AND SNACKS

Café Coho 53 Ship St ☎01273 747777, ⓦcafecoho .co.uk. Stylish café, with exposed brick walls, a counter piled high with pastries, salads and sandwiches, and tables outside for people-watching; it's a great spot for a lazy weekend brunch. The house coffee is Union's Revelation blend, and there's always a guest coffee available too. Mon–Fri 8am–6pm, Sat 8am–7pm, Sun 8.30am–6.30pm.

Gelato Gusto 2 Gardner St ☎01273 673402, ⓦgelato gusto.com. Fabulous *gelateria*, with regularly-changing flavours that run from Sea Salt Caramel to Syrup Sponge Pudding. Mon–Fri 11.30am–6pm, Sat & Sun 11am–6pm.

★**Jack and Linda's Smokehouse** 197 Kings Arches. This tiny beachfront smokehouse is run by a lovely couple who've been traditionally smoking fish here for over a decade. Grab a fresh crab sandwich or hot mackerel roll (£3–4) to eat on the beach for a perfect summer lunch. April–Sept daily 10am–5pm.

★**Marwood** 52 Ship St ☎01273 382063, ⓦthemarwood .com. Quirky, laidback café with great coffee and food (mains around £7) and splendidly bonkers decor that runs from stuffed animals and skateboards on the walls to Star Wars spaceships dangling from the ceiling. Mon & Tues 8am–8pm, Wed–Fri 8am–11pm, Sat 9am–11pm, Sun 10am–8pm.

Metrodeco 38 Upper St James St ☎01273 677243, ⓦmetro-deco.com. The place to come for afternoon tea, this Parisian-style tea salon in Kemp Town serves over twenty bespoke blends of tea, dainty sandwiches, scones and fancies (£16 Mon–Fri, £18 weekend), all presented on vintage crockery; splash out on a "tea cocktail" for the full experience. Great breakfasts and lunches too. Mon–Thurs & Sun 9.30am–6pm, Fri & Sat 9.30am–9pm.

RESTAURANTS

64 Degrees 53 Meeting House Lane ☎01273 770115, ⓦ64degrees.co.uk. The best seats in the house at this tiny restaurant in the Lanes are up at the counter of the open kitchen: the idea is that you choose several small plates of food (£5–12.50) and share them, to create your own tasting menu. The food's inventive, delicious and prepared in front of you, and the whole experience is brilliant fun. Mon–Thurs noon–2.30pm & 5–9.45pm, Fri & Sat noon–3.30pm & 6–9.45pm.

Bom-Bane's 24 George St ☎01273 606400, ⓦbom -banes.com. Fun little café/restaurant run by musician Jane Bom-Bane. The decor is decidedly eccentric – each of the individually designed tables holds a surprise in store – and the hearty Belgium-influenced food is delicious (*stoemp* and sausage £10.25). There are weekly film nights (Wed; £5.50) and occasional live music nights. Tues, Thurs & Fri 5–11.30pm, Wed & Sat 12.30–11.30pm.

★**Chilli Pickle** 17 Jubilee St ☎01273 900383, ⓦthechillipickle.com. Stylish, buzzing restaurant in North Laine serving sophisticated, authentic Indian food – everything from masala dosas to Chennai seafood stew (mains £10–17). At lunchtimes they offer a range of thalis and "street food". Mon–Sat noon–3pm & 6–10.30pm, Sun noon–3pm & 6–10pm.

Food for Friends 18 Prince Albert St ☎01273 202310, ⊕foodforfriends.com. Brighton's original vegetarian restaurant – on this spot for over thirty years – serves up sophisticated veggie dishes that are imaginative enough to please die-hard meat-eaters too: mains (£12–14) might include spicy Asian tofu salad, or saffron ravioli in a blue cheese sauce. Mon–Thurs & Sun noon–10pm, Fri & Sat noon–10.30pm.

Gingerman 21a Norfolk Square ☎01273 326688, ⊕gingermanrestaurant.com. Small but perfectly formed one-room restaurant serving up some of the best food in Brighton. The weekly-changing set menus cost £15 for 2 courses at lunch, £30 at dinner. Tues–Sun 12.30–2pm & 7–10pm.

Melrose 132 King's Rd ☎01273 326520, ⊕melrose restaurant.co.uk. Traditional seafront establishment that's been serving up tasty, excellent value fish and chips (£6.75), local seafood, roasts and custard-covered puddings for over forty years. The next door *Regency Restaurant* is smaller and similar. Daily 11.30am–10.30pm.

Plateau 1 Bartholomews ☎01273 733085, ⊕plateau

brighton.co.uk. Laidback little restaurant-cum-wine bar serving cocktails, organic beers and wine, and food that ranges from small "bites" (£5–9) to bigger "plats" (from £11), so you can stop by for a nibble and a drink, or a full-blown meal. Mon–Fri 11am–late, Sat & Sat 10am–late.

★ **Riddle and Finns** 12b Meeting House Lane ☎01273 721667, ⊕riddleandfinns.co.uk. Bustling champagne and oyster bar in the Lanes, where you can tuck into a huge range of shellfish and fish (mains £13–19) at communal marble-topped tables in a white-tiled, candle-lit dining room with an open kitchen. It's very popular, and they don't take bookings, so expect to wait at busy times. Their sister restaurant, the beachfront *Riddle & Finns The Beach*, is equally good. Mon–Thurs & Sun noon–10pm, Fri & Sat noon–11pm, plus Sat & Sun 9.15–11.15am.

★ **Terre-à-Terre** 71 East St ☎01273 729051, ⊕terreaterre.co.uk. One of the country's best vegetarian restaurants, this award winning place serves up fabulous, inventive global veggie cuisine (mains around £15), in a modern arty setting. The taster plate for two (£23) is a good place to start if you're befuddled by the weird and wonderful creations on offer. Mon–Fri noon–10.30pm, Sat 11am–11pm, Sun 11am–10pm.

NIGHTLIFE AND ENTERTAINMENT

As well as its mainstream **theatre** and **concert** venues, Brighton has a fantastic art-house **cinema**, myriad **clubs** and plenty of **live music venues** alongside its hip bars and traditional boozers. For up-to-date details of **what's on**, there's an array of free listings magazines available from the tourist office (see p.167).

PUBS AND BARS

Bee's Mouth 10 Western Rd ☎01273 770083. Quirky, sumptuously decorated pub on the Brighton/Hove border, with a good range of bottled beers, and three subterranean levels hosting live music, film nights and life drawing. Mon–Thurs 4.30pm–12.30am, Fri 4.30pm–1.30am, Sat 2.30pm–1.30am, Sun 3.30pm–12.30am.

Craft Beer Co. 22–23 Upper North St ⊕thecraftbeerco .com. One for beer lovers, this friendly pub has nine daily-changing cask ales and over 200 bottled varieties. The house Craft Pale Ale is brewed for them by Kent Brewery. Mon–Wed 3–11pm, Thurs 3–11.30pm, Fri noon–midnight, Sat noon–1am, Sun noon–10.30pm.

The Cricketers 15 Black Lion St ☎01273 329472, ⊕cricketersbrighton.co.uk. Brighton's oldest pub, immortalized by Graham Greene in *Brighton Rock*, has a traditional feel, with good daytime pub grub, real ales and a cosy courtyard bar. Mon–Thurs 11am–midnight, Fri & Sat 11am–1am, Sun noon–11pm.

The Greys 105 Southover St ☎01273 680734, ⊕greyspub.com. Friendly, laidback pub with an open fire and a great menu. Frequent live music (especially country, bluegrass and Americana), comedy and talks. Mon–Wed 4–11pm, Thurs 4–11.30pm, Fri 3pm–12.30am, Sat noon–12.30am, Sun noon–11pm.

Mesmerist 1–3 Prince Albert St ☎01273 328542, ⊕drinkinbrighton.co.uk/mesmerist. Large, lively and welcoming bar inspired by 1930s gin palaces, burlesque and the steampunk movement: cheap drinks, free entry and rock'n'roll and swing tunes make this a good pre-club choice. Mon–Thurs & Sun noon–1am, Fri & Sat noon–2am.

★ **Northern Lights** 6 Little East St ☎01273 747096, ⊕northernlightsbrighton.co.uk. Laidback, ever-popular bar with a Scandinavian theme: choose from two dozen different flavoured vodkas, aquavit, and beers from Denmark, Sweden and Finland. The Nordic menu features reindeer, Smörgåsbord and pickled herring. Mon–Thurs 5pm–midnight, Fri & Sat noon–2am, Sun noon–midnight.

OHSO Social 250a Kings Road Arches ☎01273 746067, ⊕ohsosocial.co.uk. Get the full Brighton experience on the terrace of this late-night beachfront bar, with great cocktails and uninterrupted views of Brighton pier. Daily 9am–late.

Oki-Nami 6 New Rd ☎01273 773777, ⊕okinami.com. Small, one-room cocktail bar upstairs from the Japanese restaurant of the same name, co-owned by Norman Cook (aka Fatboy Slim), with a balcony overlooking New Road that's perfect for people-watching. Daily 5pm–late.

2

CLUBS AND LIVE MUSIC VENUES

Audio 10 Marine Parade ☎01273 606 906, ⓦaudio brighton.com. Trendy seafront hangout that boasts a terrace with sea views and a large bar on the first floor. The basement club is always packed, playing everything from indie to house and drum 'n' bass.

Concorde 2 Madeira Shelter, Madeira Drive ☎01273 673311, ⓦconcorde2.co.uk. A Victorian tearoom in a former life, Brighton's trendiest live music venue features up-and-coming acts, big names (from The White Stripes to Jarvis Cocker) and varied club nights.

Funfair 12–15 King's Rd ☎01273 757447. Quirky funfair-themed club with exotic performers, a ball pit, distortion mirrors and fun music that runs from motown to disco.

★**Green Door Store** Trafalgar Arches, Lower Goods Yard ⓦthegreendoorstore.co.uk. Über-cool club and live music venue in the arches under the train station, playing anything from psych to blues, punk or powerdisco. The bar is free entry; live gig entry varies.

Proud Cabaret Brighton 83 St Georges Rd ☎01273 605789, ⓦproudcabaretbrighton.com. Opulent venue in a former ballroom hosting dinner and cabaret/burlesque shows, plus diverse club nights.

ARTS CENTRES, THEATRES AND CINEMAS

Brighton Dome 29 New Rd ☎01273 709709, ⓦbrightondome.org. Home to three venues – Pavilion Theatre, Concert Hall and Corn Exchange – offering mainstream theatre, concerts, dance and performance.

★**Duke of Yorks Picturehouse** Preston Circus ☎0871 704 2056, ⓦpicturehouses.co.uk. Grade II-listed cinema with a licensed bar showing art-house, independent and classic films. Dukes at Komedia is its sister cinema based at the Komedia arts centre (see below).

★**Komedia** 44–47 Gardner St ☎0845 293 8480, ⓦkomedia.co.uk/brighton. A Brighton institution, this highly regarded arts venue hosts stand-up comedy, live music and cabaret, as well as fun club nights.

Theatre Royal New Rd ☎01273 764400, ⓦambassadortickets.com/theatreroyal. Venerable old theatre – going since 1807 – offering predominantly mainstream plays, opera and musicals.

SHOPPING

Most of Brighton's high street chains are found in and around **Churchill Square** (ⓦchurchillsquare.co.uk). The best areas for independent shops are the **Lanes** and **North Laine** (ⓦnorthlaine.co.uk); it's also worth wandering over to **Kemp Town** for a browse around its antiques shops.

Hope and Harlequin 31 Sydney St ☎01273 675222, ⓦhopeandharlequin.com. Upmarket vintage shop, stocking clothes and collectables up to the 1970s, with a special emphasis on the 1930s and 40s. Mon & Wed–Sat 10.30am–6pm, Tues noon–5pm, Sun 11am–5pm.

Ink'd Gallery 96 North Rd ☎01273 645299, ⓦink-d .co.uk. Excellent contemporary art gallery, with frequent rehangs and a great mix of artists and mediums, from paintings and ceramics to street art. Mon–Sat 10am–6pm, Sun noon–4pm.

Lavender Room 16 Bond St ☎01273 220380, ⓦlavender-room.co.uk. Stylish boutique selling fragrances, lingerie, jewellery and vintage-inspired home accessories. Mon–Sat 10am–6pm, Sun 11am–5pm.

Pecksniffs 45–46 Meeting House Lane ☎01273 723292, ⓦpecksniffs.com. Independent British fragrance house in the Lanes, selling a range of perfumes, bespoke blends and body products. Mon–Sat 10am–5pm, Sun 10.30am–4pm.

Resident 28 Kensington Gardens ☎01273 606312, ⓦresident-music.com. Award-winning independent record shop in North Laine; it also sells tickets for local venues. Mon–Sat 9am–6.30pm, Sun 10am–6pm.

She Said 32 Ship St ☎01273 777811, ⓦshesaidboutique .com. The city that gave rise to the "dirty weekend" has its fair share of erotic emporiums, but this one is the classiest – it's even been featured in *Vogue*. Mon–Sat 10am–6pm, Sun 11am–5pm, plus occasional late-night openings.

Snoopers Paradise 7–8 Kensington Gardens ☎01273 602558. You can't visit Brighton without popping into this huge North Laine flea market. It contains over ninety different stalls over two floors; Snoopers Attic (ⓦsnoopersattic.co.uk), a "vintage makers' boutique" up on the first floor, is worth a special mention. Mon–Sat 10am–6pm, Sun 11am–4pm.

Arundel and around

The hilltop town of **ARUNDEL**, eighteen miles west of Brighton, has for seven centuries been the seat of the dukes of Norfolk, whose fine **castle** looks over the valley of the River Arun. The medieval town's well-preserved appearance and picturesque setting draws in the crowds on summer weekends, but at any other time a visit reveals one of West Sussex's least spoilt old towns. The two main attractions are the castle and the towering Gothic **cathedral**, but the rest of Arundel is pleasant to wander round, especially the antique-shop-lined Maltravers and Arun streets. North of Arundel lie a couple more attractions: **Bignor Roman Villa**, with some outstanding Roman mosaics; and the grand, seventeenth-century **Petworth House**, which has a notable art collection.

At the end of August, Arundel's **festival** (ⓦarundelfestival.co.uk) features everything from open-air theatre to salsa bands.

Arundel Castle

Mill Rd • April–Oct Tues–Sun & Mon in Aug & bank hol Mon: keep 10am–4.30pm; Fitzalan Chapel & grounds 10am–5pm; castle rooms noon–5pm • Castle, keep, grounds & chapel £16; keep, grounds & chapel £11; grounds & chapel £9 • ☎ 01903 882173, ⓦ arundelcastle.org

Despite its medieval appearance, much of what you see of **Arundel Castle** is comparatively new, the result of a series of lavish reconstructions from 1718 onwards, after the original Norman structure was badly damaged during the Civil War. One of the oldest parts is the twelfth-century **keep**, from which you can peer down onto the current duke's spacious residence and the pristine castle grounds. Inside the main castle, the highlights include the impressive **Barons Hall** and the **library**, which has paintings by Gainsborough, Holbein and Van Dyck.

Arundel Cathedral

Corner of Parson's Hill & London Rd • Daily 9am–6pm or dusk • Free • ☎ 01903 882297, ⓦ www.arundelcathedral.org

The flamboyant **Arundel Cathedral** was constructed in the 1870s by the fifteenth duke of Norfolk over the town's former Catholic church; its spire was designed by John Hansom, inventor of the hansom cab. Inside are the enshrined remains of St Philip Howard, the canonized thirteenth earl, who was sentenced to death in 1585, accused of Catholic conspiracy against Elizabeth I's Protestant court. He died of dysentery in the Tower of London ten years later.

Bignor Roman Villa

6 miles north of Arundel, Bignor • March–Oct daily 10am–5pm, last entry 4pm • £6 • ☎ 01798 869259, ⓦ bignorromanvilla.co.uk

The excavated third-century ruins of the **Bignor Roman Villa** are famed for their spectacular Roman mosaics. The site is superbly situated at the base of the South Downs and features the longest extant section of mosaic in England, as well as the remains of a hypocaust, the Romans' underfloor heating system.

Petworth House

11 miles north of Arundel • **House** Mid-March to Oct Mon–Wed, Sat & Sun 11am–5pm, also Thurs & Fri for 45min guided snapshot tours only • **Pleasure Ground** Daily: mid-Jan to mid-March 10.30am–3.30pm; mid-March to Oct 10.30am–5pm; Nov to mid-Dec 10.30am–3.30pm • **Park** Daily 8am–dusk • House £12.50, snapshot tours £5, Pleasure Ground and park free; NT • ☎ 01798 342207, ⓦ nationaltrust.org.uk/petworth • Train to Pulborough, then Stagecoach Coastline #1 bus (Mon–Sat hourly, Sun every 2hr)

Petworth House, adjoining the pretty little town of **PETWORTH**, is one of the southeast's most impressive stately homes. Built in the late seventeenth century, the house is stuffed with treasures – including the 1592 Molyneux globe, believed to be the earliest terrestrial globe in existence – and contains an outstanding art collection, with paintings by Van Dyck, Titian, Gainsborough, Bosch, Reynolds, Blake and Turner (the last a frequent guest here). The 700-acre **grounds**, home to a large herd of fallow deer, were landscaped by Capability Brown and are considered one of his finest achievements.

ARRIVAL AND INFORMATION **ARUNDEL**

By train Arundel's station is half a mile south of the town centre over the river on the A27.

Destinations Brighton (Mon–Sat every 30min, Sun hourly;

1hr 20min); Chichester (Mon–Sat every 30min, Sun hourly; 20min); London Victoria (Mon–Sat every 30min, Sun hourly; 1hr 30min); Portsmouth Harbour (every 30min; 55min).

2

By bus Buses pull in either on High Street or River Road. Destinations Brighton (Mon–Fri every 30min; 2hr); Chichester (Mon–Sat every 2hr; 35min).

Tourist information There's a self-service Visitor Information Point at Arundel Museum, opposite the castle entrance on Mill Road (daily 10am–4pm; ⓦ sussexbythesea.com).

ACCOMMODATION

Amberley Castle Amberley ☎ 01798 831992, ⓦ amberleycastle.co.uk. For a real splurge, indulge in an overnight stay at this 600-year-old castle, complete with portcullis, 60ft curtain walls, gardens, lakes, croquet lawn and nineteen luxurious bedrooms, many with four-poster beds. **£265**

Swan Hotel 27–29 High St ☎ 01903 882314, ⓦ swanarundel.co.uk. Fourteen smart rooms above a pub, decked out in shabby chic style, with shutters and bare boards or coir carpets, and seaside prints on the wall. **£115**

EATING AND DRINKING

Bay Tree 21 Tarrant St ☎ 01903 883679, ⓦ thebaytree arundel.co.uk. Cosy and relaxed little restaurant squeezed into three low-beamed rooms, with a small terrace out the back. Mains such as pheasant breast wrapped in bacon cost £16–18 at dinner; lunch features simpler dishes. Mon–Fri 11.30am–2.45pm & 6.30–9.15pm, Sat 10.30am–4pm & 6.30–9.30pm, Sun 10.30am–4pm & 6.30–9.15pm.

George and Dragon Inn Burpham ☎ 01903 883131, ⓦ georgeatburpham.co.uk. Three miles from Arundel (a lovely walk up the east bank of the river), this seventeenth-century pub has bags of character, real ales from the Arundel Brewery and a foodie-friendly à la carte menu (mains £11–20). Mon–Fri 10.30am–3pm & 6–11pm, Sat 10.30am–11pm, Sun 10.30am–10pm; food served Mon–Fri 10.30am–2.30pm & 6–9pm, Sat 10.30am–3pm & 6–9.30pm, Sun noon–5pm & 6–9pm.

Chichester and around

The handsome city of **CHICHESTER** has plenty to recommend it: a splendid twelfth-century **cathedral**, a thriving cultural scene and an outstanding collection of modern British art on show at the **Pallant House Gallery**. The city began life as a Roman settlement, and its Roman cruciform street plan is still evident in the four-quadrant symmetry of the town centre. The main streets lead off from the Gothic **Market Cross**, a bulky octagonal rotunda topped by ornate finials and a crown lantern spire, built in 1501 to provide shelter for the market traders. The big attraction outside Chichester is **Fishbourne Roman Palace**, the largest excavated Roman site in Britain, though for families a day at dune-backed **West Wittering beach** will be hard to beat.

Chichester Festivities (☎ 01243 528356, ⓦ chifest.org.uk) is Chichester's annual arts festival, taking place at a range of venues over two weeks in late June, and featuring music, talks, theatre, comedy and other events.

Chichester Cathedral

West St • Daily: mid-April to mid-Oct 7.15am–7pm; mid-Oct to mid-April 7.15am–6pm; drop-in 45min guided tours Mon–Sat 11.15am & 2.30pm • Free • ☎ 01243 782595, ⓦ chichestercathedral.org.uk

Chichester's chief attraction is its fine Gothic **Cathedral**. Building began in 1076, but the church was extensively rebuilt following a fire a century later and has been only minimally modified since about 1300, except for the slender spire and the unique, freestanding fifteenth-century bell tower. The **interior** is renowned for its modern devotional art, which includes a stained-glass window by Marc Chagall and an altar-screen tapestry by John Piper. Older treasures include a sixteenth-century painting in the north transept of the past bishops of Chichester, and the fourteenth-century Fitzalan tomb that inspired Philip Larkin to write *An Arundel Tomb*. However, the highlight is a pair of carvings created around 1140, the **Chichester Reliefs**, which show the raising of Lazarus and Christ at the gate of Bethany; originally brightly coloured, with semiprecious stones set in the figures' eyes, the reliefs are among the finest Romanesque stone carvings in England.

Pallant House Gallery

9 North Pallant • Tues, Wed, Fri & Sat 10am–5pm, Thurs 10am–8pm, Sun & bank hols 11am–5pm; highlights tours Sat 2pm, themed tours Thurs 5.15pm • £8, Tues £4, Thurs 5–8pm free (£4 for main exhibition) • ☎ 01243 774557, ⓦ pallant.org.uk

Off South Street, in the well-preserved Georgian quadrant of the city known as the Pallants, you'll find **Pallant House Gallery**, a superlative collection of twentieth-century British art housed in a Queen Anne townhouse and award-winning contemporary extension. Artists on display from the permanent collection include Henry Moore, Lucian Freud, Walter Sickert, Barbara Hepworth and Peter Blake, and there are also excellent temporary exhibitions.

Fishbourne Roman Palace

Salthill Rd, Fishbourne • Feb & Nov to mid-Dec daily 10am–4pm; March–Oct daily 10am–5pm; mid-Dec to Jan Sat & Sun 10am–4pm • £8.70 • ☎ 01243 789829, ⓦ sussexpast.co.uk • Train from Chichester to Fishbourne (hourly; 3min); turn right from the station and the palace is a few minutes' walk away

Fishbourne, two miles west of Chichester, is the largest and best-preserved Roman dwelling in the country. Roman relics have long been turning up hereabouts, and in 1960 a workman unearthed their source — the site of a depot constructed by the invading Romans in 43 AD, which is thought later to have become the vast, hundred-room palace of a Romanized Celtic aristocrat. The one surviving wing, the north wing, displays floor mosaics depicting Fishbourne's famous dolphin riding cupid as well as the more usual geometric patterns. An audiovisual programme portrays the palace as it would have been in Roman times, and the extensive gardens attempt to recreate the palace grounds.

ARRIVAL AND DEPARTURE   CHICHESTER

By train Chichester's train station lies on Stockbridge Rd; it's a 10min walk north to the Market Cross.
Destinations Arundel (Mon–Sat every 30min, Sun hourly; 20–30min); Brighton (every 30min; 45–55min); London Victoria (every 30min; 1hr 35min).

By bus The bus station is across the road from the train station on Southgate.
Destinations Arundel (Mon–Sat hourly; 30min); Brighton (Mon–Sat every 15min, Sun every 30min; 1hr 45min); Portsmouth (hourly; 55min).

INFORMATION AND GETTING AROUND

Tourist office At the Novium, Tower Street (Mon–Sat 10am–5pm, Sun 10am–4pm; ☎ 01243 775888, ⓦ visitchichester.org).

By tour Guided tours are bookable through the tourist office (April–Sept Tues & Wed at 11am, Sat at 2pm; Oct–March Tues at 11am, Sat at 2pm; £4.50).

ACCOMMODATION

★**Chichester Apartments** 230 Oving Rd ☎ 01243 771464, ⓦ chichesterapartments.co.uk. Six beautiful, stylish serviced apartments, with underfloor heating, fresh flowers and quality linen. Everything you might need is provided, from top-notch toiletries to breakfast supplies and cooking essentials. Super-friendly owners too. Three-

night mini-break (per night) £99, weekly rate £500
★**Musgrove House B&B** 63 Oving Rd ☎ 01243 790179, ⓦ musgrovehouse.co.uk. This smart, friendly boutique B&B, a short walk for the centre, is fantastic value: the three impeccably tasteful rooms come with iPod docks, silk duvets and local art on the walls. £80

EATING AND DRINKING

Amelie and Friends 31 North St ☎ 01243 771444, ⓦ amelieandfriends.com. Buzzy little restaurant with a strikingly designed wood-and-white interior and a peaceful walled garden at the back, perfect for lazy alfresco lunches or afternoon tea (offered daily 3–4pm; book in advance). Mains such as sea bream or apple and cheddar potato latkes cost £10–17, with lighter dishes available at lunchtime. Mon–Fri noon–2.30pm, 3–4pm & 5.30–9pm, Sat noon–4pm & 5–9pm, Sun noon–2.30pm & 3–4pm.

★**Richmond Arms** Mill Rd, West Ashling ☎ 01243 572046, ⓦ therichmondarms.co.uk. Five miles from Chichester, West Ashling's village pub is a real find, with heaps of style and great food that runs from roast duck with pomegranate molasses and pickled rhubarb, to BBQ Cornish squid with spicy coleslaw (£15–22). On Friday and Saturday evenings a pizza wagon serves up artisan-style pizzas. Wed–Sat noon–2pm & 6–9pm, Sun noon–3pm.

2

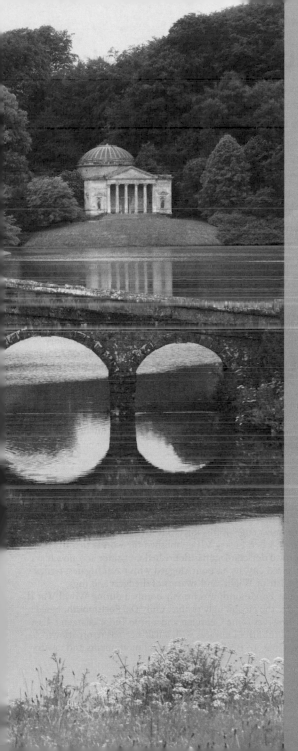

Hampshire, Dorset and Wiltshire

STOURHEAD, WILTSHIRE

Hampshire, Dorset and Wiltshire

The distant past is perhaps more tangible in Hampshire (often abbreviated to "Hants"), Dorset and Wiltshire than in any other part of England. Predominantly rural, these three counties overlap substantially with the ancient kingdom of Wessex, whose most famous ruler, Alfred, repulsed the Danes in the ninth century and came close to establishing the first unified state in England. And even before Wessex came into being, many earlier civilizations had left their stamp on the region. The chalky uplands of Wiltshire boast several of Europe's greatest Neolithic sites, including Stonehenge and Avebury, while in Dorset you'll find Maiden Castle, the most striking Iron Age hillfort in the country, and the Cerne Abbas Giant, source of many a legend.

The Romans tramped all over these southern counties, leaving the most conspicuous signs of their occupation at the amphitheatre of **Dorchester** – though that town is more closely associated with the novels of Thomas Hardy and his vision of Wessex. None of the landscapes of this region could be described as grand or wild, but the countryside is consistently seductive, not least the crumbling fossil-bearing cliffs around **Lyme Regis**, the managed woodlands of the **New Forest** and the gentle, open curves of **Salisbury Plain**. Its towns are also generally modest and slow-paced, with the notable exceptions of the two great maritime bases of **Portsmouth** and **Southampton**, a fair proportion of whose visitors are simply passing through on their way to the more genteel pleasures of the **Isle of Wight**. The two great cathedral cities in these parts, **Salisbury** and **Winchester**, and the seaside resort of **Bournemouth** see most tourist traffic, and the great houses of **Wilton**, **Stourhead**, **Longleat** and **Kingston Lacy** also attract the crowds: you don't have to wander far off the beaten track, however, to find pretty medieval churches, manor houses, rolling landscapes and unspoilt country inns.

Portsmouth

Britain's foremost naval station, **PORTSMOUTH** occupies the bulbous peninsula of Portsea Island, on the eastern flank of a huge, easily defended harbour. The ancient Romans raised a fortress on the northernmost edge of this inlet, but this strategic location wasn't fully exploited until Tudor times, when Henry VII established the world's first dry dock here and made Portsmouth a royal dockyard. It has flourished ever since and nowadays Portsmouth is a large industrialized city, its harbour clogged with naval frigates, ferries bound for the continent or the Isle of Wight, and swarms of dredgers and tugs.

Due to its military importance, Portsmouth was heavily bombed during World War II, and bland tower blocks now give the city an ugly profile. Only **Old Portsmouth**, based around the original harbour, preserves some Georgian and a little Tudor character. East of here is **Southsea**, a residential suburb of terraces with a half-hearted resort strewn along its shingle beach, where a mass of B&Bs face stoic naval monuments and tawdry seaside amusements.

Boats to Gosport p.181	**Lyme's Jurassic coast** p.213
The Real Downton Abbey p.192	**Stonehenge – a brief history** p.218
The Watercress Line p.193	

STONEHENGE

Highlights

❶ Osborne House Wander around the stunning gardens and get an insight into royal family life at Queen Victoria's former seaside home. **See p.189**

❷ The New Forest William the Conqueror's old hunting ground, home to wild ponies and deer, is ideal for walking, biking and riding. **See p.194**

❸ Square and Compass, Worth Matravers A pub straight from a Thomas Hardy novel, with wonky rooms, a tiny hatch of a bar, real ales and stunning views. **See p.204**

❹ Sea kayaking in Studland View the rugged Old Harry Rocks up close on a guided kayak tour through sea arches and below towering chalk cliffs. **See p.204**

❺ Durdle Door Famous natural arch at the end of a splendid beach, accessed by a steep cliff path – a great place for walkers and swimmers alike. **See p.205**

❻ Hive Beach Café, Burton Bradstock Sit right on the beach and sample some of Dorset's freshest local seafood, washed down with an ice-cold glass of wine. **See p.212**

❼ Stonehenge Marvel at one of Britain's most iconic sites, which is now much enhanced by an informative environmentally-friendly visitor centre. **See p.216**

HIGHLIGHTS ARE MARKED ON THE MAP ON P.178 ❶❷❸❹❺❻❼

HAMPSHIRE, DORSET AND WILTSHIRE

HIGHLIGHTS

1. Osborne House
2. The New Forest
3. Square and Compass, Worth Matravers
4. Sea kayaking in Studland
5. Durdle Door
6. Hive Beach Café, Burton Bradstock
7. Stonehenge

Portsmouth Historic Dockyard

Queen St • Daily: April–Oct 10am–6pm; Nov–March 10am–5.30pm; last entry 1hr 30min before closing • All-inclusive ticket £26, for unlimited visits to all attractions; individual attraction tickets £17 except Action Stations and National Museum, £11; all tickets valid for one year • ☎ 023 9283 9766, ⓦ historicdockyard.co.uk

For most visitors, a trip to Portsmouth begins and ends at the **Historic Dockyard**, in the **Royal Naval Base** at the end of Queen Street. The complex comprises three ships and several museums, with the main attractions being HMS *Victory*, HMS *Warrior*, the National Museum of the Royal Navy, the Mary Rose Museum, and a boat tour around the harbour. In addition, the Dockyard Apprentice exhibition gives insights into the working of the docks in the early twentieth century, while Action Stations provides interactive activities and simulators, plus the UK's tallest indoor climbing tower.

HMS Warrior

Portsmouth Historic Dockyard's youngest ship, **HMS Warrior**, dates from 1860. It was Britain's first armoured (iron-clad) battleship, complete with sails and steam engines, and was the pride of the fleet in its day. The ship displays a wealth of weaponry, including rifles, pistols and sabres, though the *Warrior* was never challenged nor even fired a cannon in her 22 years at sea.

Mary Rose Museum

The impressive, new boat-shaped **Mary Rose Museum** was built around Henry VIII's flagship, the **Mary Rose**, and houses not only the ship itself, but also thousands of objects retrieved from or near the wreck including guns, gold and the crew's personal effects. The ship capsized before the king's eyes off Spithead in 1545 while engaging French intruders, sinking swiftly with almost all her seven-hundred-strong crew. In 1982 a massive conservation project successfully raised the remains of the hull, which silt had preserved beneath the seabed, and you can now view the world's only remaining sixteenth-century warship through protective glass windows.

HMS Victory

HMS Victory was already forty years old when she set sail from Portsmouth for Trafalgar on September 14, 1805, returning in triumph three months later, but bearing the corpse of Admiral Nelson. Shot by a sniper from a French ship at the height of the battle, Nelson expired below deck three hours later, having been assured that victory was in sight. A plaque on the deck marks the spot where Nelson was fatally wounded and you can also see the wooden cask in which his body was preserved in brandy for the return trip to Britain. Although badly damaged during the battle, the *Victory* continued in service for a further twenty years, before being retired to the dry dock where she rests today.

National Museum of the Royal Navy

Opposite the *Victory*, various buildings house the exhaustive **National Museum of the Royal Navy**. Tracing naval history from Alfred the Great's fleet to the present day, the collection includes some jolly figureheads, Nelson memorabilia, including the only surviving sail from HMS *Victory*, and nautical models, though coverage of more recent conflicts is scantily treated. The Trafalgar Experience is a noisy, vivid recreation of the battle itself, with gory bits to thrill the kids.

Royal Navy Submarine Museum

Haslar Jetty, Gosport • Daily: April–Oct 10am–5.30pm; Nov–March 10am–4.30pm, last tour 1hr before closing • £12.50, joint ticket with Explosion! including Waterbus £15 • ☎ 023 9251 0354, ⓦ submarine-museum.co.uk

Portsmouth's naval theme persists throughout otherwise humdrum Gosport, where the **Royal Navy Submarine Museum** displays, unsurprisingly, submarines – six in total, some of which you can enter. Allow a couple of hours to explore these slightly creepy vessels – a guided tour inside HMS *Alliance* gives you a gloomy insight into how cramped life was on board, and the museum elaborates evocatively on the history of submersible craft.

Explosion! The Museum of Naval Firepower

Priddy's Hard, Gosport • April–Oct daily 10am–5pm; Nov–March Sat & Sun 10am–4pm, last entry 1hr before closing • £10, joint ticket with Submarine Museum including Waterbus £15 • ☎ 023 9250 5600, ⓦ explosion.org.uk

Near the Royal Submarine Museum, housed in an old armaments depot, **Explosion!** tells the story of naval warfare from the days of gunpowder to the present, with

BOATS TO GOSPORT

Gosport can be reached by taking the **passenger ferry** from Harbour train station jetty between the historic dockyard and Gunwharf Quays (daily 5.30am–midnight every 10–15min; 5min; £2.90 return; ☎ 023 9252 4551, ⓦ gosportferry.co.uk). If you're planning to visit both Gosport's museums, however, it's worth taking the **Waterbus** (ⓦ portsmouth-boat-trips.co.uk /waterbus/portsmouth_harbour_waterbus.html), which shuttles hourly (10am–4pm) between the Historic Dockyard, Gunwharf Quays, the Submarine Museum and Explosion!, since its fare is included in the joint Gosport Museums' ticket.

weapons of all descriptions, including mines, big guns and torpedoes, all backed up by vivid computer animations.

The Spinnaker Tower

Gunwharf Quays • Sept–July daily 10am–5.30pm; Aug Mon–Thurs & Sun 9.30am–6pm, Fri & Sat 9.30am–5.30pm • £8.95 • ☎ 023 9285 7520, ⓦ spinnakertower.co.uk

From Portsmouth Harbour train station, it's a short walk along the historic waterfront to the sleek modern **Gunwharf Quays** development, with a multitude of cafés, restaurants, nightspots and shops. Here you'll find the **Spinnaker Tower**, an elegant, 557ft-high sail-like structure, offering **views** of up to twenty miles over land and sea. Its three viewing decks can be reached by a high-speed lift, the highest one being open to the elements, though most people stick to View Deck 1, which has one of Europe's largest glass floors.

Old Portsmouth

It's a well-signposted fifteen-minute walk south of Gunwharf Quays to what remains of **Old Portsmouth**. Along the way, you pass the simple **Cathedral of St Thomas** on the High Street, whose original twelfth-century features have been obscured by rebuilding after the Civil War and again in the twentieth century. The High Street ends at a maze of cobbled Georgian streets huddling behind a fifteenth-century wall protecting the **Camber**, or old port, where Walter Raleigh landed the first potatoes and tobacco from the New World. Nearby, the Round and Square towers, which punctuate the Tudor fortifications, are popular vantage points for observing the comings and goings of the boats.

D-Day Museum

Clarence Esplanade, Southsea • Daily: April–Sept 10am–5.30pm; Oct–March 10am–5pm; last entry 30min before closing • £6.50 • ☎ 023 9282 6722, ⓦ ddaymuseum.co.uk

In the suburb of **Southsea**, south and west of Old Portsmouth, the **D-Day Museum** focuses on Portsmouth's role as the principal assembly point for the Normandy beach landings in World War II, code-named "Operation Overlord". The museum's most striking exhibit is the 295ft-long Overlord Embroidery, a sort of twentieth-century equivalent of the Bayeux Tapestry, which took five years to complete.

Southsea Castle

Clarence Esplanade, Southsea • March–Oct Tues–Sun & bank hol Mons 10am–5pm • Free • ☎ 023 9282 6722, ⓦ southseacastle.co.uk

Next door to the D-Day Museum, Southsea's most historic building, marked by a little lighthouse, is the squat **Southsea Castle**, built from the remains of Beaulieu Abbey (see p.196). You can go inside the keep and learn about Portsmouth's military history, and can climb up to the spot from where Henry VIII is said to have watched the *Mary Rose* sink in 1545 (see p.179), though in fact you can get just as good views by climbing along the adjacent seafront ramparts.

Charles Dickens' Birthplace

393 Old Commercial Rd • April–Sept Tues–Sun & bank hol Mons 10am–5.30pm, plus sporadic days in winter; check website for details • £4 • **☎** 023 9282 6722, **ⓦ** charlesdickensbirthplace.co.uk

Just over a mile northeast of Old Portsmouth, **Charles Dickens' Birthplace** is set up to look much as it would have looked when the famous novelist was born here in 1812. Charles's father, John, moved to Portsmouth in 1809 to work for the Navy Pay Office before he was recalled to London in 1815, so Charles only lived here for three years, but nevertheless he is said to have returned often and set parts of *Nicholas Nickleby* in the city. The modest house not only contains period furniture but also a wealth of information about the time when Dickens lived here, and the influences on his novels.

Portchester Castle

Church Rd, Portchester • April–Sept daily 10am–6pm; Oct daily 10am–5pm; Nov–March Sat & Sun 10am–4pm, but Feb half-term daily 10am–4pm • £5.20; EH

Six miles northwest of the city centre, just past the marina development at Port Solent, **Portchester Castle** was built by the Romans in the third century, and boasts the finest surviving example of Roman walls in northern Europe – still over 20ft high and incorporating some twenty bastions. The Normans felt no need to make any substantial alterations when they moved in, but a keep was later built within Portchester's precincts by Henry II, which Richard II extended and Henry V used as his garrison when assembling the army that was to fight the Battle of Agincourt.

ARRIVAL AND INFORMATION

PORTSMOUTH

By train Portsmouth's main train station is in the city centre, but the line continues to Harbour Station, the most convenient stop for the dockyard sights and old town.
Destinations Brighton (every 30min; 1hr 20min–1hr 30min); London Waterloo (every 15–20min; 1hr 35min–2hr 10min); Salisbury (hourly; 1hr 15min); Southampton (every 15–20min; 45min–1hr); Winchester (hourly; 1hr 10min).
By bus National Express buses stop at The Hard Interchange, right by Harbour Station.
Destinations London Victoria (hourly; 1hr 45min–2hr 20min); Southampton (hourly; 50min–1hr).
By ferry Wightlink passenger catamarans leave from the

jetty at Harbour Station for Ryde, on the Isle of Wight (see p.184), while car ferries depart from the ferry port off Gunwharf Road, just south of Gunwharf Quays, for Fishbourne on the Isle of Wight (see p.184). Hovercraft link Southsea with Ryde, while ferries run regularly from the Harbour Station to Gosport, on the other side of Portsmouth Harbour (see box, p.181).
Tourist offices There are two tourist offices in Portsmouth (**☎** 023 9282 6722, **ⓦ** visitportsmouth.co.uk), one in the City Museum, 2 Museum Road (Tues–Sun 10am–5pm), the other in the D-Day Museum on Clarence Esplanade in Southsea (April–Sept daily 10am–5pm; Oct–March daily 10am–4pm).

ACCOMMODATION

Florence House 2 Malvern Rd, Southsea **☎** 023 9275 1666, **ⓦ** florencehousehotel.co.uk. Tasteful boutique B&B in an Edwardian townhouse with a range of rooms over three floors, all spick and span and with flatscreen TVs. There's a tiny downstairs bar and communal lounge, and parking permits can be provided. If it's full, the same group runs three other boutique-style hotels in the same area. **£86**
Holiday Inn Express The Plaza, Gunwharf Quays **☎** 023 9289 4240, **ⓦ** hiexpress.co.uk. It may be part of a

chain, but it's clean and contemporary, and Portsmouth's most central option. The rooms are compact, but its location, right on Gunwharf Quays, can't be faulted. There's a large, airy breakfast room and bar too. **£136**
Sailmaker's Loft 5 Bath Square **☎** 023 9282 3045, **ⓦ** sailmakersloft.org.uk. This modern B&B is just back from the waterfront, right opposite *The Still* pub, with top-floor rooms overlooking the water. It's worth paying the extra £5 to have your own bathroom. **£65**

EATING AND DRINKING

Abarbistro 58 White Hart Rd **☎** 023 9281 1585, **ⓦ** abarbistro.co.uk. Lively bar/restaurant with an outside terrace on the edge of Old Portsmouth. The menu features bistro-style classics such as moules (£13) and steaks (£19),

plus a daily-changing menu of fish and pasta dishes. Mon–Sat 11am–11pm, Sun noon–11pm.
Aspex Gallery Café The Vulcan Building, Gunwharf Quays **☎** 023 9277 8080, **ⓦ** aspex.org.uk. Cosy café on

the ground floor of the Aspex Gallery in a historic former naval building near the waterfront. The menu features simple dishes such as delicious home-made soups with focaccia (£4), vast ploughman's for two (£8), plus some daily specials, all eaten surrounded by installations and artworks: there's a great children's corner too. Daily 11am–4pm.

The Still and West 2 Bath Square, Old Portsmouth

023 9282 1567, stillandwest.co.uk. A waterfront terrace and cosy interior with views over the harbour make this pub worth stopping by: the food ranges from the traditional fish and chips (£10.50) to whole sea bream (£14.50) and Hampshire lamb chops (£16). Mon–Sat 10am–11pm, Sun 11am–10.30pm; food served Mon–Fri noon–9pm, Sat noon–10pm, Sun noon–8pm.

Southampton

A glance at the map gives some idea of the strategic maritime importance of SOUTHAMPTON, which stands on a triangular peninsula formed at the place where the rivers Itchen and Test flow into Southampton Water, an eight-mile inlet from the Solent. Sure enough, Southampton has figured in numerous stirring events: it witnessed the exodus of Henry V's Agincourt-bound army, the Pilgrim Fathers' departure in the *Mayflower* in 1620 and the maiden voyages of such ships as the *Queen Mary* and the *Titanic*. Despite its pummelling by the Luftwaffe and some disastrous postwar urban sprawl, the thousand-year-old city has retained some of its medieval charm in parts and reinvented itself as a twenty-first century shopping centre in others, with the giant glass-and-steel **West Quay** as its focus. A short stroll north of here, Southampton's new **Cultural Quarter** is worth a visit, with its open squares, excellent art gallery and the superb Sea City Museum.

City Art Gallery

Civic Centre, Commercial Rd • Mon–Fri 10am–3pm, Sat 10am–5pm • Free • 023 8083 3000, southampton.gov.uk/art

Core of the modern town is the Civic Centre, a short walk east of the train station and home to the excellent **Southampton City Art Gallery**. Its collection is particularly strong on contemporary British artists with works by Gilbert and George, Anthony Gormley and Andy Goldsworthy. Older paintings are also on show, among them works by Gainsborough, Joshua Reynolds and the Impressionists – Monet and Pissarro included.

The Sea City Museum

Civic Centre, Havelock Rd • Daily 10am–5pm • £6, children free • 023 8083 3007, seacitymuseum.co.uk

The purpose-built **Sea City Museum** is a triumph of design that succeeds in being both moving and fun. Opened on April 10, 2012, the hundredth anniversary of the day that the *Titanic* sailed from Southampton's Town Quay on its maiden voyage, the museum provides a fascinating insight into the history of the ship, its crew, its significance to Edwardian Southampton and, of course, an account of the fateful journey, which started in high excitement to end only four days later in tragedy.

| **ARRIVAL AND INFORMATION** | **SOUTHAMPTON** |

By train Southampton's central station is in Blechynden Terrace, west of the Civic Centre.

Destinations Bournemouth (every 15–20min; 30–50min); London Waterloo (every 15–20min; 1hr 20min–1hr 30min); Portsmouth (every 15–20min; 50min–1hr); Salisbury (every 30min; 30–40min); Weymouth (every 30min; 1hr 20min–1hr 35min); Winchester (every 15min; 15–30min).

By bus National Express buses run from the coach station on Harbour Parade.

Destinations Bournemouth (12 daily; 45min–1hr); London Victoria (15 daily; 2hr–2hr 30min); Portsmouth (13 daily; 50min–1hr); Salisbury (1 daily; 40min); Weymouth (3 daily; 2hr 40min) and Winchester (every 20–30min; 25–45min).

Tourist information There is no tourist office in Southampton, though *Oceans* tearoom, at 13 High St, acts as a basic Information Point (Mon–Sat 9am–5pm, Sun 10am–4pm; 023 8178 1017, discoversouthampton .co.uk), where you can pick up leaflets, maps and guides to the city.

3

ACCOMMODATION

Ennios Town Quay Rd ☎023 8022 1159, ⊛ennios -boutique-hotel.co.uk. In a former warehouse right on the waterfront, this boutique-style hotel has plush rooms with comfortable beds and smart bathrooms. The stylishly decorated rooms come with L'Occitane toiletries, and there's an excellent Italian restaurant downstairs. £95

★**Pig in the Wall** 8 Western Esplanade, ☎0238 063 6900, ⊛thepighotel.com. Built into the city walls,

Southampton's most stylish boutique hotel has been cleverly renovated and beautifully decorated in a shabby-chic style. All the rooms have powerful showers and top-of-the range coffee machines – the large (pricier) rooms boast glamorous roll top baths in the room itself. There's a great bar/lounge/deli downstairs, or you can jump in one of the hotel Land Rovers which will take you to their sister hotel/restaurant in the New Forest for dinner (see p.198). £130

EATING AND DRINKING

The Arthouse Gallery Café 178 Above Bar St ☎023 8023 8582, ⊛thearthousesouthampton. co.uk. Friendly community-run café, which serves delicious home-made vegan and vegetarian dishes, such as a "global" hotpot and Greek meze with hummus, pitta and stuffed vine leaves (both £8), as well as organic ciders and beers. The café also hosts workshops, art exhibitions, knitting circles and live music; upstairs, there's a piano, comfy sofas and plenty of board games. Tues & Sun noon–5pm, Wed, Thurs & Fri 11am–9.30pm, Sat noon–10pm.

Kuti's Royal Thai Gate House, Royal Pier ☎023 8033 9211, ⊛kutisroyalthaipier.com. Choose from the à la carte menu or an excellent all-you-can-eat Thai buffet (Mon–Thurs £16, Fri & Sat £18) at this superbly ornate

waterside restaurant that was once the terminal for ocean liners including the *Titanic*. There are fine views over the water from the upstairs restaurant, as well as an outside deck for summer evenings. Mon 6–10.30pm, Tues–Sun noon–2.30pm & 6pm–midnight.

Red Lion 55 High St ☎023 8033 3595. One of the oldest and most atmospheric pubs in Southampton, dating from the twelfth century, complete with its own minstrels' gallery. The half-timbered apartment known as Henry V's "Court Room" was used for the famous trial of a group of hapless lords who had conspired to murder Henry V, in 1415. They serve fine real ales and traditional British dishes. Mon–Sat 11am–11pm, Sun noon–10.30pm; food served daily noon–2pm & 6–9pm.

The Isle of Wight

The lozenge-shaped **ISLE OF WIGHT** has begun to shake off its old-fashioned image and attract a younger, livelier crowd, with a couple of major annual **rock festivals** and a scattering of fashionable hotels. Despite measuring less than 23 miles at its widest point, the island packs in a surprising variety of landscapes and coastal scenery. Its **beaches** have long attracted holiday-makers, and the island was a favourite of such eminent Victorians as Tennyson, Dickens, Swinburne, Julia Margaret Cameron and Queen Victoria herself, who made **Osborne House**, near Cowes, her permanent home after Albert died.

ARRIVAL AND DEPARTURE   ISLE OF WIGHT

There are three **ferry** departure points from the mainland to the Isle of Wight – Portsmouth, Southampton and Lymington. **Wightlink** (⊛wightlink.co.uk) runs car ferries from Lymington to Yarmouth (40min) and from Gunwharf Terminal in Portsmouth to Fishbourne (45min), as well as a high-speed catamaran from Portsmouth Harbour to Ryde Pier (passengers only; 20min). **Hovertravel** (⊛hovertravel.co.uk), meanwhile, runs hovercraft from Clarence Esplanade in Southsea to Ryde (passengers only; 10min). From Southampton, **Red Funnel** (⊛redfunnel.co.uk) operates a high-speed catamaran to West Cowes (passengers only; 25min) and a car ferry to East Cowes (1hr). **Fare** structures and **schedules** on all routes are labyrinthine, from £16 for a day-return foot passenger ticket on the Southampton to West Cowes route in low season to over £100 for a high-season return for a car and four passengers on the Lymington to Yarmouth route: check the ferry companies' websites for full details of current fares.

INFORMATION

Tourist information There are no walk-in tourist offices on the island, but general tourist information is

available on ⊛islandbreaks.co.uk or ☎01983 813813.

GETTING AROUND

By bus Local buses are run by Southern Vectis (☎ 0871 200 2233, ⓦ islandbuses.info), who sell good-value tickets offering unlimited travel on their network (£10/day, £15/2 days, £24/week).

By train There are two train lines on the island: the seasonal Isle of Wight Steam Railway (☎ 01983 882204, ⓦ iwsteamrailway.co.uk) runs from Wootton Bridge to Smallbrook Junction, where it connects with the east-coast

Island line from Ryde to Shanklin (every 20–40min; 25min; ☎ 0345 600 0650, ⓦ islandlinetrains.co.uk).

By bike Cycling is a popular way of getting around the island, though in summer the narrow lanes can get very busy. For bike rental, contact Wight Cycle Hire (☎ 01983 761800, ⓦ wightcyclehire.co.uk): its office is in Yarmouth, but it can deliver bikes anywhere on the island (£10/half-day, £14/day).

Ryde

As a major ferry terminal, **RYDE** is the first landfall many visitors make on the island, but one where few choose to linger, despite some grand nineteenth-century architecture and a fine sandy town beach.

Postcard Museum

The Royal Victoria Arcade, Union St • Mon–Fri noon–5pm, Sat 11am–5pm, also Sun 11am–5pm in Aug • £3.50 • ☎ 01983 717435, ⓦ donaldmcgill.info

Ryde's quirky little **Postcard Museum** crams in a good proportion of the twelve thousand saucy postcards created by artist Donald McGill. The cards, produced throughout the first half of the twentieth century, reached their peak of popularity in the 1930s. Packed with daft double entendres, the collection here also shows how far things have moved since the Obscene Publications Act regularly tried to have McGill's cards banned.

ARRIVAL AND DEPARTURE   RYDE

The **bus station**, **Hovercraft terminal** and **Esplanade train station** are all near the base of the pier, while **catamarans** from Portsmouth dock at the Pier Head.

ACCOMMODATION AND EATING

The Boathouse Springvale Rd, Seaview, 2 miles east of Ryde ☎ 01983 810616, ⓦ theboathouseiow.co.uk. It's a pleasant 2-mile walk along the coast to this classy gastropub, whose garden boasts fantastic views across the Solent. A great spot for a drink, it also serves fish and chips (£11.50) and more upmarket fare such as lobster salad (£18) and fresh fish of the day. It also has spacious en-suite rooms decorated in a contemporary style with iPod docks: superior rooms have sea views. Mon–Thurs & Sun 9am–10.30pm, Fri–Sat 9am–11pm; food served daily 9–11am, noon–2.30pm & 6–9.30pm. **£125**

Kasbah 76 Union St ☎ 01983 810088. Lively Moroccan-themed café-bar where you can chill out to world music and play chess. Also has a friendly, laidback B&B upstairs with clean and cosy rooms, some with sea views – it can be noisy at weekends, but is great value. Mon & Tues 11.30am–11pm, Wed–Sat 11.30am–2am, Sun noon–12.30am. **£70**

Olivos 32–33 Union St, Ryde ☎ 01983 611118, ⓦ olivorestaurant.co.uk/ryde. Tasty Italian dishes in a buzzy, stylish restaurant with bare-brick walls and an open kitchen. There are decent pizzas (£9–11) and pasta dishes (£10–13), plus some less usual main courses, such as venison with meatballs (£16) and chicken drumsticks stuffed with chorizo and mozzarella (£13). Daily 8am–11pm.

★**The Priory Bay Hotel** Priory Drive, Seaview ☎ 01983 613146, ⓦ priorybay.com. Three miles east of Ryde, this elegant country house hotel has a wonderful setting with lawns leading down to the sands of Priory Bay. It's smart but unstuffy, child-friendly and has a great restaurant, where many of the ingredients are foraged from the grounds or caught in the local seas. There's also an outdoor pool, plus some self-catering cottages and luxurious yurts in the grounds. **£200**

Brading Roman Villa

Morton Old Road • Daily 9.30am–5pm • £6.50 • ☎ 01983 406223, ⓦ bradingromanvilla.org.uk • Buses #2 & #3 from Ryde or Sandown

Just south of the ancient village of **Brading**, on the busy Ryde to Sandown A3055, the remains of **Brading Roman Villa** are renowned for their **mosaics**. This is the more impressive of two such villas on the island, both of which were probably sites of bacchanalian worship. The Brading site is housed in an attractive modern museum and its superbly preserved mosaics include intact images of Medusa and depictions of Orpheus.

Sandown

The traditional seaside resort of **SANDOWN** merges with its neighbour Shanklin across the sandy reach of Sandown Bay, representing the island's holiday-making epicentre. Sandown, a traditional 1960s bucket-and-spade resort, appropriately enough possesses the island's only surviving pleasure **pier**, bedecked with various traditional amusements and a large theatre with nightly entertainment in season.

ARRIVAL AND DEPARTURE   SANDOWN

By train The Island Line train station, served by trains from Ryde and Shanklin, is on Station Ave, about a 10min walk inland from the pier.

By Bus Buses #2, #3 & #8 between Ryde and Newport stop in Sandown.

ACCOMMODATION AND EATING

The Lawns 72 Broadway ☎ 01983 402549, ⓦ lawnshotel isleofwight.co.uk. Friendly, comfortable, non-smoking guesthouse with attractive gardens, a bar and free wi-fi; the plush rooms have flatscreen TVs, and the breakfasts are good. Minimum stay of three nights in the summer. **£88**

The Reef The Esplanade ☎ 01983 403219, ⓦ thereefsan

down.co.uk. A bright bar/restaurant right on the seafront with great views. It serves up a range of mid-priced dishes including pizzas, pasta, steaks and fresh fish: prices start at around £9 for a pizza, £10 for burgers, up to £20 for a 10oz fillet steak. Food served summer daily 11am–10pm; winter Sun–Thurs 11am–9pm, Fri & Sat 11am–9.30pm.

Shanklin

SHANKLIN, with its auburn cliffs, Old Village and scenic Chine, has a marginally more sophisticated aura than its northern neighbour. The rose-clad, thatched **Old Village** may be syrupy, but the adjacent **Shanklin Chine** (daily: April to late May & mid-Sept to Oct 10am–5pm; late May to mid-Sept 10am–10pm; £3.90, ☎ 01983 866432, ⓦ shanklinchine.co.uk), a twisting pathway descending a mossy ravine and decorated on summer nights with fairy lights, is undeniably picturesque; former local resident John Keats once drew inspiration from the environs.

ARRIVAL AND DEPARTURE   SHANKLIN

By train The final stop on the Island Line from Ryde, Shanklin train station is about half a mile inland at the top of Regent Street.

By bus The bus station (buses #2 & #3 from Ryde and Newport) is a little south of the train station.

ACCOMMODATION

Rylstone Manor Rylstone Gardens ☎ 01983 862806, ⓦ rylstone-manor.co.uk. This superb Victorian pile, with period decor, sits right in the middle of the leafy public

gardens at the top of the cliff. It has its own bar and dining room, though children under 16 are not allowed and in high season there is a 3-night minimum let. **£145**

EATING AND DRINKING

Fisherman's Cottage Southern end of the Esplanade, at the bottom of Shanklin Chine ☎ 01983 863882, ⓦ shanklinchine.co.uk/index.php/fishermans-cottage -welcome. An atmospheric nineteenth-century thatched pub right on the seafront, with outside tables: it's child-friendly and serves wholesome pub food, such as fish pie and cod and chips. Opening times vary, but generally March–Oct Mon–Sat 11am–midnight, Sun 11am–10.30pm; food

served Mon–Sat noon–8pm, Sun noon–5pm.

★**Old Thatch Teashop** 4 Church Rd ☎ 01983 865587, ⓦ oldthatchteashop.co.uk. There's a warren of rooms in this friendly and efficient teahouse, with pretty gardens at the back. It serves lunches – soup and sandwiches – and is highly regarded for its delicious home-made scones and cakes. Mon–Sat 10am–5pm, Sun 11am–5pm, but sometimes stays open later in summer.

Ventnor

The seaside resort of **VENTNOR** and its two village suburbs of **Bonchurch** and **St Lawrence** sit at the foot of St Boniface Down, the island's highest point at 787ft. The Down periodically disintegrates into landslides, creating the jumbled terraces known locally as the **Undercliff**, whose sheltered, south-facing aspect, mild winter temperatures and thick carpet of undergrowth have contributed to the former fishing village becoming a fashionable health spa. Thanks to these unique factors, the town possesses rather more character than the island's other resorts, its Gothic Revival buildings clinging dizzily to zigzagging bends.

The floral terraces of the Cascade curve down to the slender Esplanade and narrow beach, where some of the former boat-builders' cottages now house shops, cafés and restaurants. From the Esplanade, it's a pleasant mile-long stroll to Ventnor's rolling **Botanical Gardens**, filled with exotic plants and impressive glasshoues (daily 10am–4pm, £6 75; ☎01983 855397, ⓦbotanic.co.uk).

ACCOMMODATION   VENTNOR

Hambrough Hotel Hambrough Rd ☎01983 856333, ⓦthehambrough.com. Small, stylish, modern hotel above the top-quality *Hambrough* restaurant. The comfortable rooms come with all the luxuries, including flatscreen TV and espresso machines; most have sea views, and some have balconies. **£170**

The Lake Hotel Shore Rd, Lower Bonchurch ☎01983 852613, ⓦlakehotel.co.uk. Family-run hotel in a nineteenth-century country manor with lovely grounds. It has an attractive sun lounge, a bar and terrace and twenty large, comfortable rooms, all en suite. Free wi-fi. **£98**

EATING AND DRINKING

El Toro Contento 2 Pier St ☎01983 857600, ⓦeltoro contento.co.uk. A cosy restaurant dishing up home-made tapas, such as chorizo in cider, and spicy mussels, most for under a fiver. Also serves Spanish hams and cheeses and will cook paella for £10.40 a head (min 4 people) with 24hr notice. Summer daily 5–10pm; winter Thurs–Sun 4–10pm.

★**The Pond Café** Bonchurch Village Rd, Bonchurch ☎01983 855666, ⓦthehambrough.com/the-pond -cafe. Cheaper and less formal than its sister restaurant in Ventnor, *The Hambrough*, this small, smart restaurant

overlooking the village pond is nevertheless very well-regarded. It serves rustic Italian-style cuisine, with a short menu of good-value dishes, such as roast pigeon (£15) and beetroot risotto (£12.50), plus tasty stone-baked pizzas (9.50). Thurs–Mon 10.30am–3pm & 6–9.30pm.

★**Wheelers Crab Shed** Steephill Cove ☎01983 852177. Delicious home-made crab pasties, sandwiches and ciabattas served from a pretty shack on the seashore. Also tasty local lobster salads and daily fish specials. May–Sept daily except Tues (plus sunny weekends & hols in other months) 11am–3.30pm.

The southwest coast

The western Undercliff begins to recede at the village of Niton, where a footpath continues to the most southerly tip of the island, **St Catherine's Point**, marked by a modern lighthouse. A prominent landmark on the downs behind is **St Catherine's Oratory**, known locally as the "Pepper Pot": originally a lighthouse, it reputedly dates from 1325.

Seven miles northwest along the coast, Military Road ascends the flank of Compton Down before descending into Freshwater Bay. If you're walking this way, you might stop off at the National Trust-owned **Compton Bay**, a splendid spot for a swim or a picnic, frequented by local surfers and accessed by a steep path leading down from the cliffs.

Dimbola Lodge

Terrace Lane, Freshwater Bay • Nov–March Tues–Sun plus bank hol Mons 10am–4pm; April–Oct daily 10am–5pm • £5 • ☎01983 756814, ⓦdimbola.co.uk

On the coastal road at Freshwater Bay, **Dimbola Lodge** was the home of pioneer photographer Julia Margaret Cameron, who settled here after visiting local resident Tennyson in 1860. The building now houses a gallery of her work plus changing exhibitions, as well as a room devoted to memorabilia from the Isle of Wight festival. There's also a bookshop and tearoom/restaurant.

3

ACCOMMODATION

Tom's Eco Lodge Tapnell Farm, Newport Rd ☎07717 666346, ⓦtomsecolodge.com. Set on a lovely farm with stunning views over the distant Solent, these ready erected, upmarket tents are the ultimate in glamping – they come complete with fridges, electricity, private hot-water showers and flushing toilets. Great for families. Three-night weekend **£671**, per week **£1560**

The Needles and Alum Bay

The breezy four-mile ridge of **Tennyson Down** running from Freshwater Bay to **The Needles** is one of the island's most satisfying walks, with vistas onto rolling downs and vales. On top of the Down, there's a monument to the eponymous poet, who lived on the island for forty years from 1853 until his death. At its western tip sits the **Needles Old Battery**, a gun emplacement built 250ft above the sea in 1863 (April–Oct daily 10.30am–5pm; fort may be closed in bad weather; £5; NT; ☎01983 754772, ⓦnationaltrust.org.uk). There are fabulous views from here over the three tall chalk stacks known as **The Needles**, which jut out into the English Channel. Needles Pleasure Cruises runs **boat trips** round the Needles (April–Oct; £5.50; ☎01983 761587; ⓦwww .needlespleasurecruises.co.uk) from **Alum Bay**, a twenty-minute walk away. To catch the boat, you can walk down the cliff path or take the chairlift (£4 return), which descends the polychrome cliffs to ochre-hued sands.

Yarmouth

Four miles east of the Needles and linked to Lymington in the New Forest by car ferry, the pleasant town of **YARMOUTH**, on the northern coast of the Isle of Wight, makes a lovely entrance to the island and is the best base for exploring its western tip. Although razed by the French in 1377, the port prospered after **Yarmouth Castle** (Easter–Sept Mon–Thurs & Sun 11am–4pm; £4; EH), tucked between the quay and the pier, was commissioned by Henry VIII. Inside, some of the rooms have recreated life in a sixteenth-century castle, and there's also a display on the many wrecks that floundered here in the Solent, while the battlements afford superb views over the estuary. Yarmouth's only other real sight is the Grade II listed **pier**, England's longest wooden pier still in use.

ACCOMMODATION   YARMOUTH

The George Hotel Quay St ☎01983 760331, ⓦthegeorge.co.uk. In a great position right by the ferry dock, with a lovely garden overlooking the Solent, this seventeenth-century hotel has hosted the likes of Charles II in its time. The rooms are comfortable and elegantly furnished, some with balconies looking out over the water, and there's an excellent restaurant downstairs, specializing in local and organic produce. **£190**

EATING AND DRINKING

The Blue Crab High St ☎01983 760014, ⓦthebluecrab.co.uk. A simply decorated restaurant, with cosy booths, that offers fish and shellfish dishes such whole Cornish sole (£17). Also does top-quality fresh fish and chips to take away for £7. Tues, Wed & Sun 11am–3pm, Thurs 10am–3pm & 6–11pm, Fri & Sat 11am–3pm & 6–11pm.

Gossips Café The Square, on the pier ☎01983 760646,

ⓦthegossipscafe.co.uk. A great place for lunch or a snack – it does a huge selection of sandwiches (most around £4) and tortilla wraps, as well as hot dishes, such as pizzas (from £5) and daily specials, including seafood chowder (£7) and Thai prawn curry (£8). The real selling point, however, is the superb view of the comings and goings of the boats. Summer Mon–Fri 8.45am–6pm, Sat & Sun 8.30am–6.30pm; winter daily 8.45am–4.30/5pm.

Cowes

COWES, at the island's northern tip, is associated with sailing craft and boat building: Henry VIII installed a castle to defend the Solent's expanding naval dockyards from the French and Spanish, and in the 1950s the world's first hovercraft made its test runs here. In 1820 the Prince Regent's patronage of the yacht club gave the port its cachet with the Royal Yacht Squadron, now one of the world's most exclusive sailing clubs. The first week of August sees the international yachting festival **Cowes Week** (ⓦaamcowesweek.co.uk), where serious sailors mingle with visiting royalty; most summer weekends see some form of nautical event taking place in or around town.

The town is bisected by the River Medina, with **West Cowes** being the older, more interesting half. At the bottom of the meandering High Street, **boat trips** around the harbour and the Solent leave from Thetis Wharf, near the Parade (☎01983 564602, ⓦsolentcruises.co.uk). The more industrial **East Cowes**, where you'll find Osborne House, is connected to West Cowes by a "floating bridge", or chain ferry (every 10–15min, Mon–Sat 5.35am–12.30am, Sun 6.40am–12.30am; pedestrians free, cars £2).

Osborne House

East Cowes • April–Sept daily 10am–6pm; Oct daily 10am–4pm; Nov–March Sat & Sun 10am–4pm • £13.40; EH • ☎ 01983 200022, ⓦ englishheritage.org.uk • Bus #4 from Ryde or #5 from Newport, or either from East Cowes

The only place of interest in East Cowes is Queen Victoria's family home, **Osborne House**, signposted one mile southeast of town. The house was built in the late 1840s by Prince Albert and Thomas Cubitt in the style of an Italianate villa, with balconies and large terraces overlooking the landscaped gardens towards the Solent. The **state rooms**, used for entertaining visiting dignitaries, exude formality as one would expect – the Durbar Room, clad almost entirely in ivory, is particularly impressive – while the **private apartments** feel homely in a manner appropriate to an affluent family holiday residence that Osborne was. Following Albert's death, the desolate Victoria spent much of her time here, and it's where she eventually died in 1901. Since then, according to her wishes, the house has remained virtually unaltered, allowing an intimate glimpse into Victoria's family life. In the **grounds**, you can see the remains of a barracks with its own drawbridge, built by Prince Albert as a place where the boys could play soldiers, and Queen Victoria's original bathing machine, next to her private beach.

ACCOMMODATION	COWES

WEST COWES

Villa Rothsay Baring Rd, West Cowes ☎01983 295178, ⓦvilla-rothsay.co.uk. Upmarket boutique hotel that's maintained its Victorian roots with period decor throughout – think drapes, ornate stairways and stained-glass windows. Some of the rooms have sea views and balconies (£10 extra) and there are great views from the grounds and raised patio area. **£145**

EAST COWES AND AROUND

Albert Cottage York Ave, East Cowes ☎01983 299309, ⓦalbertcottagehotel.com. Adjacent to and once part of the Osborne estate, this lovely mansion, set in its own

grounds, has a country house feel to it. Rooms are very comfortable, and have flatscreen TVs; it has its own highly rated restaurant, too. **£125**

★ **Into the Woods** Lower Westwood, Brocks Copse Rd, Wootton ☎07769 696464, ⓦisleofwighttreehouse .com. Lovely, luxury treehouse (sleeps 4) and shepherds' huts (sleep 6) to rent on a farm in a secluded wood, three miles south of East Cowes. Both are beautifully finished and eco-friendly complete with wood-burning stoves, en-suite showers, and even wi-fi. The location is peaceful, with chickens and geese, rope swings to play on and woods to run around in – the perfect combination of nature and home comforts. Two nights from **£300**

EATING AND DRINKING

WEST COWES

The Coast Bar & Dining Room 15 Shooters Hill ☎01983 298574, ⓦthecoastbar.co.uk. Light and airy bar/restaurant with wooden floors and a lively, informal vibe. The menu features wood-fired pizzas (£8–12), plus the likes of seafood bouillabaisse (£14.50), mushroom risotto (£11) and a good selection of steaks (£17.50). Daily 9am–midnight.

Lugleys The Parade, West Cowes, ☎01983 299618, ⓦlugleysofcowes.com. In a great position facing the sea, this fashionable bar/restaurant is a good spot for a coffee, evening drink or quality meal, with a menu featuring salmon and prawn linguine (£12) and fresh fish from around £14. There are also good-value set menus (three courses for £19). Mon–Fri 10am–3pm & 6–11pm, Sat 10am–11pm, Sun 10am–4pm.

3

Moocows 55 Cross St ☎ 01983 200750, ⓦ moocowstuff .com. It may overlook a car park, but this lively, stylish café-bar is a great place to hangout. It hosts arts and crafts workshops, quiz and poetry evenings and serves imaginative meze, such as local wild mushrooms and goats cheese on toast (£8), stuffed courgettes (£7), chorizo with melon and mint (£9) and venison on ciabatta (£9) – and the cocktails are delicious too. Tues–Sat 10.30am–late.

Carisbrooke Castle

Castle Hill, southwest of Newport • Daily: April–Sept 10am–4.45pm; Oct–Easter 10am–3.45pm • £7.70; EH • ☎ 01983 523112, ⓦ englishheritage.org.uk • Buses #6, #12 or #38 from Newport

NEWPORT, the capital of the Isle of Wight, sits at the centre of the island at a point where the River Medina's commercial navigability ends. The town isn't particularly engaging, but is worth a visit for the hilltop fortress of **Carisbrooke Castle**. The most famous resident of this austere Norman pile was Charles I, detained here (and caught one night ignominiously jammed between his room's bars while attempting escape) before his execution in London. The **museum** features relics from his incarceration, as well as those of the last royal resident, Princess Beatrice, Queen Victoria's youngest daughter. There's also a sixteenth-century well-house, where you can watch donkeys trudge around a huge treadmill to raise a barrel 160ft up the well shaft.

Winchester and around

Nowadays a tranquil, handsome market town, **WINCHESTER** was once one of the mightiest settlements in England. Under the Romans it was Venta Belgarum, the fifth largest town in Britain, but it was **Alfred the Great** who really put Winchester on the map when he made it the capital of his Wessex kingdom in the ninth century. For the next two hundred years or so Winchester ranked alongside London, its status affirmed by William the Conqueror's coronation in both cities and by his commissioning of the local monks to prepare the **Domesday Book**. It wasn't until after the Battle of Naseby in 1645, when Cromwell took the city, that Winchester began its decline into provinciality.

Hampshire's county town now has a scholarly and slightly anachronistic air, embodied by the ancient almshouses that still provide shelter for senior citizens of "noble poverty" – the pensioners can be seen walking round the town in medieval black or mulberry-coloured gowns with silver badges. It also makes a good base from which to explore the nearby towns of **Chawton** and **Selborne**, homes, respectively, to Jane Austen and the eminent naturalist, Gilbert White.

Winchester Cathedral

9 The Close • Mon–Sat 9.30am–5pm, Sun 12.30–3pm • £7.50, including a guided tour (ticket valid for one year); tower tour £6 • ☎ 01962 857275, ⓦ winchester-cathedral.org.uk

The first minster to be built in Winchester was raised by Cenwalh, the Saxon king of Wessex in the mid-seventh century, and traces of this building have been unearthed near the present **cathedral**, which was begun in 1079 and completed some three hundred years later. The exterior is not its best feature – squat and massive, it crouches stumpily over the tidy lawns of the Cathedral Close. The interior is rich and complex, however, and its 556ft **nave** makes this Europe's longest medieval church. Outstanding features include the carved Norman font of black Tournai marble, the fourteenth-century misericords (the choir stalls are the oldest complete set in the country) and some amazing monuments – **William of Wykeham's Chantry**, halfway down the nave on the right, is one of the most ornate.

Jane Austen, who died in Winchester, is commemorated close to the font by a memorial brass and slab beneath which she's interred, though she's recorded simply as the daughter of a local clergyman. Above the high altar lie the mortuary chests of pre-Conquest kings, including **Canute** (though the bones were mixed up after Cromwell's Roundheads broke up the chests in 1645); **William Rufus**, killed while hunting in the New Forest in 1100, lies in the presbytery.

Behind the impressive Victorian screen at the end of the presbytery, look out for the memorial shrine to **St Swithun**. Originally buried outside in the churchyard, his remains were later interred inside where the "rain of heaven" could no longer fall on him, whereupon he took revenge and the heavens opened for forty days – hence the legend that if it rains on St Swithun's Day (July 15) it will do so for another forty. His exact burial place is unknown.

Accessible from the north transept, the Norman **crypt** – often flooded – is home to Anthony Gormley's contemplative figure *Sound II*, reflected in the waters. The cathedral's original foundations were dug in marshy ground, and at the beginning of the last century a steadfast diver, William Walker, spent five years replacing the rotten timber foundations with concrete.

Great Hall

At the top of the High St on Castle Ave • Daily 10am–5pm • Free, £3 donation requested • ☎ 01962 846476, ⓦ hants.gov.uk/greathall

The **Great Hall** is all that remains of a thirteenth-century castle destroyed by Cromwell. Sir Walter Raleigh heard his death sentence here in 1603, though he wasn't finally dispatched until 1618, and Judge Jeffreys held one of his Bloody Assizes (see p.983) in the castle after Monmouth's rebellion in 1685. The main interest now is a large, brightly painted disc slung on one wall like some curious antique dartboard. This is alleged to be King Arthur's Round Table, but the woodwork is probably fourteenth-century, later repainted as a PR exercise for the Tudor dynasty – the portrait of Arthur at the top of the table bears an uncanny resemblance to Henry VIII.

College Street

College Street is home to the buildings of **Winchester College**, the oldest public school in England – established in 1382 by William of Wykeham for "poor scholars", it now educates few but the wealthy and privileged. You can look round the medieval college buildings, its cloisters and Gothic chapel on a **guided tour** (Mon, Wed, Fri & Sat 10.45am, noon, 2.15pm & 3.30pm; Tues & Thurs 10.45am & noon; Sun 2.15pm & 3.30pm; £6; ☎01962 621100, ⓦwinchestercollege.org).

At no.8 College Street stands the house where **Jane Austen** died. She moved here from Chawton in 1817 (see opposite), when she was already ill with Addison's Disease, and died later the same year, aged 42. The house is privately owned, though, so you can't look round. At the top of the street, the thirteenth-century **Kings Gate** is one of the city's original medieval gateways, housing the tiny St Swithun's Church.

Wolvesey Castle

Entrance off College St • April–Sept daily 10am–5pm • Free • EH • ⓦ englishheritage.org.uk

East of the cathedral, the remains of Winchester's Saxon walls bracket the ruins of the twelfth-century **Wolvesey Castle** – actually the palace for the Bishops of Winchester, who once wielded great clout over England's religious and political affairs. As a result, this was once one of the most important buildings in Winchester, encompassing its own stables, prison, chapel and gardens. Today, the castle ruins remain impressive, dwarfing the current dwelling place of the Bishop of Winchester, a relatively modest house built in 1680, which sits alongside it.

ARRIVAL AND INFORMATION   WINCHESTER

By train Winchester train station is about a mile northwest of the cathedral on Stockbridge Road.

Destinations Bournemouth (every 15–20min; 45min–1hr); London Waterloo (every 15–20min; 1hr–1hr 10min); Portsmouth (hourly; 1hr); Southampton (every 15–20min; 15–20min).

By bus National Express buses pull in and depart from the conveniently located bus station on the Broadway, opposite the tourist office.

Destinations Bournemouth (5 daily; 1hr 15min–1hr 35min); London (8 daily; 1hr 50min–2hr); Southampton (approx every hour; 25–45min).

Tourist office In the imposing Guildhall (May–Sept Mon–Sat 10am–5pm, Sun & bank hols 11am–4pm; Oct–April Mon–Sat 10am–5pm; ☎01962 840500, ⓦ visitwinchester.co.uk).

ACCOMMODATION

29 Christchurch Rd 29 Christchurch Rd ☎01962 868 661, ⓦ fetherstondilke.com. Well-furnished, comfortable B&B in a charming Regency house located in a quiet residential part of town. No smoking. **£95**

★Hotel du Vin Southgate St ☎01962 841414, ⓦ hotelduvin.com. The first in the classy hotel chain, this lovely Georgian townhouse has been given a stylish makeover and now comprises plush rooms – some

---

THE REAL DOWNTON ABBEY

Tucked away in the northern reaches of Hampshire, 20 miles north of Winchester, **Highclere Castle** (castle, exhibition and gardens £20, castle and gardens £13, gardens only £5; ☎01635 253210, ⓦ highclerecastle.co.uk) will be very familiar to fans of ITV's hit period drama, **Downton Abbey**, which is filmed here. Home to Lord Carnarvon and his family, the house is approached via a long drive that winds through a stunning 5000-acre estate, and is surrounded by beautiful **gardens** designed by Capability Brown. Inside the house, *Downton Abbey* aficionados will enjoy loitering in the **Drawing Room** and the **Library**, scene of many a drama and quivering stiff-upper-lip of Lord Grantham and his family, while upstairs you can peer into the bedrooms of the Crawley girls. In the castle cellars, an **Egyptian Exhibition** celebrates the real-life fifth Earl of Carnarvon, who, in 1922, discovered the tomb of Tutankhamun with Howard Carter, and who funded many of Carter's expeditions. Since the house is still a family home and is also sometimes closed for filming, its opening hours vary from month to month and year to year; call or check the website for details.

THE WATERCRESS LINE

ALRESFORD, six miles east of Winchester, is the departure-point for the **Mid-Hants Watercress Line** (Aug & school hols daily; Feb–July, Sept & Oct days vary, call or check website for details; £16; ☎ 01962 733810, ⓦ watercressline.co.uk), a steam-powered railway so named because it passes through the former watercress beds that once flourished here. The train chuffs ten miles to **Alton**, with gourmet dinners served on board on Saturday evenings, plus real ales from local breweries and traditional Sunday lunches.

---

cottage-style, with their own private entrances and terraces – a lovely patio garden, chic bar and great restaurant (see below). This is the first choice for accommodation in Winchester, especially if you can bag one of their periodic special offers. **£155**

The Old Vine 8 Great Minster St ☎ 01962 854616, ⓦ oldvinewinchester.com. Lovely, big rooms that combine period decor with modern touches such as widescreen TVs, above a fine bar/restaurant, and right opposite the cathedral. The street can be noisy at night. **£120**

EATING AND DRINKING

The Black Boy Wharf Hill ☎ 01962 861754, ⓦ the blackboypub.com. Fantastic old pub with log fires in winter, walls lined with books and low ceilings hung with old coins and miniature bottles. Good cask ales from local breweries are on draught and there's reasonable pub grub from £8.50, as well as a small outdoor terrace. Mon–Thurs noon–11pm, Fri & Sat noon–midnight, Sun noon–11.30pm.

Ginger Two For Tea 28–29 St Thomas St ☎ 01962 877733, ⓦ gingertwofortea.co.uk. Small teashop tucked away in the backstreets, serving tasty lunches – the smoked salmon stack (£6) is delicious – home-made cakes, coffees and a huge array of herbal and fruit teas. Mon–Fri 7.30am–6pm, Sat 8.30am–6pm, Sun 9.30am–5pm.

★**Hotel du Vin** Southgate St ☎ 01962 841414, ⓦ hotelduvin.com. Buzzy bistro-style restaurant in a series of attractive dining rooms, some with open fireplaces. The food is excellent, much of it locally sourced, and reasonably priced, with main courses such as beef bourguignon (£19), and starters such as baked figs with gorgonzola and Serrano ham for £9.50. The wine list, as you would expect, is impressive, with many wines available by the half bottle. Mon–Sat noon–2.30pm & 5.30–10pm, Sun noon–4pm & 6–9pm.

Wykeham Arms 75 Kingsgate St ☎ 01962 853834, ⓦ wykehamarmswinchester.co.uk. This highly atmospheric eighteenth-century pub has a warren of cosy rooms, with open fireplaces, good bar snacks and decent beers. Daily 11am–11pm.

Chawton

A mile southwest of Alton and sixteen miles northeast of Winchester, the village of **CHAWTON** was home to Jane Austen from 1809 to 1817, during the last and most prolific years of her life – it was here that she wrote or revised almost all of her six books, including *Sense and Sensibility* and *Pride and Prejudice*. A plain red-brick building in the centre of the village, **Jane Austen's House** (Jan to mid-Feb Sat & Sun 10.30am–4.30pm; mid-Feb to May & Sept–Dec daily 10.30am–4.30pm; June–Aug daily 10am–5pm; £7.50; ☎ 01420 83262, ⓦ www.jane-austens-house-museum.org.uk) contains first editions of some of her greatest works and provides a fascinating insight into the daily life of the author.

Chawton House

House Tours (£7) take place Jan–March Tues at 2.30pm; April–Dec Tues & Thurs at 2.30pm; June–Sept also Wed at 10.30am; book ahead on ☎ 01420 541010 as places are limited • **Gardens** Mon–Fri 10.30am–4.30pm • £3.50

A short walk from Jane Austen's house is **Chawton House**, which belonged to Jane's brother, Edward Austen Knight. It remained in the Austen family until 1987, when it was bought by American IT millionairess Sandy Lerner who opened the **Chawton House Library**, containing an impressive collection of women's writing in English from 1600–1830. The house, which has now been fully restored, can be visited on a guided **tour**, or you can look round the **gardens** independently. The **library** is open by appointment only (Mon–Fri 10am–5pm).

By bus From Winchester bus station, take the hourly #X64 to Alton Butts then it's a 12min walk.

By train The village is accessible on the "Watercress line" steam train (see box, p.193).

The New Forest

Covering about 220 square miles, the **NEW FOREST** is one of southern England's favourite rural playgrounds, attracting some 13.5 million day-visits annually. The land was requisitioned by William the Conqueror in 1079 as a hunting ground, and the rights of its inhabitants soon became subservient to those of his precious deer. Fences to impede their progress were forbidden and terrible punishments were meted out to those who were caught poaching – hands were lopped off, eyes put out. Later monarchs less passionate about hunting than the Normans gradually restored the commoners' rights, and today the New Forest enjoys a unique patchwork of ancient laws and privileges alongside the regulations applying to its National Park status.

The **trees** here are now much more varied than they were in pre-Norman times, with birch, holly, yew, Scots pine and other conifers interspersed with the ancient oaks and beeches. One of the most venerable trees is the much-visited **Knightwood Oak**, just a few hundred yards north of the A35, three miles southwest of Lyndhurst, which measures about 22ft in circumference at shoulder height. The most conspicuous species of **fauna** is the New Forest **pony** – you'll see them grazing nonchalantly by the roadsides and ambling through some villages. The local deer are less visible now that some of the faster roads are fenced, although several species still roam the woods, including the tiny **sika deer**, descendants of a pair that escaped from nearby Beaulieu in 1904.

ARRIVAL AND DEPARTURE

THE NEW FOREST

By train The main London to Weymouth train line passes through the New Forest, with fast trains stopping at Brockenhurst (see p.198): slower trains also stop at Ashurst, Sway and New Milton. From Brockenhurst a branch line runs to Lymington (every 30min; 10min) to link with the Isle of Wight ferry.

GETTING AROUND

Though the southern Forest stretches have a reasonably efficient bus network, to get the best from the New Forest, you need to walk or ride through it, avoiding the places cars can reach.

By bus Useful routes through the Forest include bus #6 from Southampton to Lymington via Lyndhurst and Brockenhurst; the coastal routes #X1 and #X2 from Bournemouth and Christchurch to Lymington; and in summer the hop-on hop-off open-top New Forest Tour bus which runs on three different circular routes around the Forest, taking in all the main settlements, and can carry up to four bikes free (mid-June to mid-Sept; £13 for a one-day ticket, which is valid on all three routes; ⓦ thenewforesttour.info). Services are run by More Buses (ⓣ 0845 072 7093, ⓦ morebus.co.uk) and Blue Star (ⓣ 01280 618233, ⓦ bluestarbus.co.uk).

By bike There are 150 miles of car-free gravel roads in the Forest, making cycling an appealing prospect – pick up a book of route maps from tourist offices or bike rental shops. Bikes can be rented at several places in the Forest: for details of cycle routes and bike hire outfits, check ⓦ new-forest-national-park.com/bike-hire-in-the-new -forest.html.

INFORMATION

Information offices There are two information centres in the Forest, one in Lyndhurst (see p.196), and the other in Lymington (see p.197), in the St Barbe Museum, on New St, off the High Street (daily 10am–4pm; ⓣ 01590 689000, ⓦ lymington.org).

Maps The Ordnance Survey Leisure Map 22 of the New Forest is best for exploring. Shops in Lyndhurst sell specialist walking books and natural history guides.

ACCOMMODATION

Camping There are ten campsites throughout the Forest run by Camping in the Forest (☎ 0845 130 8224, ⓦ campingintheforest.co.uk); all are open from mid-April to early Sept, and some are open year-round. Some are very simple, with few or no facilities, others have electricity and hot shower blocks, but they all have open access to the Forest, many have streams and fords running through them, with ponies and donkeys wandering freely.

Lyndhurst

LYNDHURST, its town centre skewered by an agonizing one-way system, isn't a particularly interesting place, though the brick **parish church** is worth a glance for its William Morris glass and the grave of Mrs Reginald Hargreaves, better known as Alice Liddell, Lewis Carroll's model for Alice. The town is of most interest to visitors for the **New Forest Museum and Visitor Centre** in the central car park off the High Street (daily 10am–5pm; ☎ 023 8028 2269, ⓦ newforestcentre.org.uk), and the adjoining **museum** (£4), which focuses on the history, wildlife and industries of the Forest. The Forest's most visited site, the **Rufus Stone**, stands three miles northwest of Lyndhurst. Erected in 1745, it marks the putative spot where the Conqueror's son and heir, **William II** – aka William Rufus after his ruddy complexion – was killed by a crossbow bolt in 1100.

ACCOMMODATION
LYNDHURST

Limewood Hotel Beaulieu Road ☎ 023 8028 7177, ⓦ limewoodhotel.co.uk. About a mile outside Lyndhurst, this luxurious hotel has smart, spacious designer-style rooms in a country-house atmosphere, with its own restaurant. The grounds are beautiful and the Herb House spa with its outdoor hot tub is to die for. **£315**

Rufus House Southampton Rd ☎ 023 8028 2930, ⓦ rufushouse.co.uk. A couple of mins out of town on the Ashurst road, opposite some fine New Forest countryside, this good-value place has plenty of character. Its tower room has a four-poster bed, though front rooms face a busy road. **£98**

EATING AND DRINKING

★ **The Oak Inn** Pinkney Lane, Bank ☎ 023 8028 2350, ⓦ oakinnlyndhurst.co.uk. Fantastic little country pub a mile out of Lyndhurst, with low wooden ceilings and a roaring fire in winter and a garden for the summer. It's popular with walkers and cyclists and there's decent food, featuring local ingredients – it's best to book in advance. Mon–Fri 11.30am–3pm & 5.30–11pm, Sat 11.30am–11pm, Sun noon–10.30pm; food served

Mon–Fri noon–2.30pm & 6–9.30pm, Sat noon–9.30pm, Sun noon–9pm.

La Pergola Southampton Rd ☎ 023 8028 4184, ⓦ la -pergola.co.uk. Lively Italian restaurant in an attractive building with its own garden. Sizzling meat dishes cost around £15–18, and there's tasty pasta and pizza from £9 and superb home-made desserts, as well as daily specials. Tues–Sun & bank hols 11am–2.30pm & 6–10.30pm.

Beaulieu

The village of **BEAULIEU** (pronounced "Bewley"), in the southeast corner of the New Forest, was the site of one of England's most influential monasteries, a Cistercian house founded in 1204 by King John – in remorse, it is said, for ordering a group of supplicating monks to be trampled to death. Built using stone ferried from Caen in northern France and Quarr on the Isle of Wight, the **abbey** managed a self-sufficient estate of ten thousand acres, but was dismantled soon after the Dissolution. Its refectory now forms the parish church, which, like everything else in Beaulieu, has been subsumed by the Montagu family who have owned a large chunk of the New Forest since one of Charles II's illegitimate progeny was created duke of the estate.

Beaulieu Palace and the Motor Museum

Daily: June–Sept 10am–6pm; Oct–May 10am–5pm • £20 • ☎ 01590 612435, ⓦ beaulieu.co.uk

Beaulieu estate comprises **Palace House**, the attractive if unexceptional family home of the Montagus, a ruined Cistercian **Abbey** and the main attraction, the **National Motor Museum**, all set in fine grounds. The Motor Museum's collections of 250 vehicles includes spindly antiques, recent classics and Formula I cars rubbing shoulders with land-speed racers, vintage Rolls-Royces, Ferraris and a Sinclair C5, as well as some of *Top Gear*'s more outlandish vehicles. A monorail runs through the museum and round the grounds, towards the Palace House, formerly the abbey's gatehouse, which ccontains masses of Montagu-related memorabilia, while the undercroft of the abbey houses an exhibition depicting medieval monastic life.

EATING AND DRINKING   BEAULIEU

The Terrace The Montagu Arms, Lyndhurst Rd ☎ 01590 612324, ⓦ montaguarmshotel.co.uk. The New Forest's only Michelin-starred restaurant, in an attractive dining room overlooking a pretty garden where you can eat in the summer. The menu uses local, seasonal ingredients, some grown in the hotel's own

kitchen garden, and features dishes such as monkfish with asparagus or Lymington sea bass with watercress. The two-course lunch menu is good value at £22.50, while the three-course evening menu will set you back £70. Wed & Thurs noon–2.30pm & 7–9pm, Fri & Sat noon–2.30pm & 6.30–9pm.

Buckler's Hard

The hamlet of **BUCKLER'S HARD**, a couple of miles downstream from Beaulieu, has a wonderful setting. A row of picturesque thatched shipwrights' cottages, some of which are inhabited, leads down to the Beaulieu River; it doesn't look much like a **shipyard** now, but from Elizabethan times onwards dozens of men o' war were assembled here from giant New Forest oaks. Several of Nelson's ships were launched here, to be towed carefully by rowing boats past the sandbanks and across the Solent to Portsmouth. The largest house in the hamlet, which forms part of the Montagu estate, belonged to Henry Adams, the master builder responsible for most of the Trafalgar fleet; it's now a hotel, pub and restaurant (see below). At the top of the village is the **Maritime Museum**, which traces the history of the great ships and incorporates buildings preserved in their eighteenth-century form. The hamlet is also the starting point for a bucolic **river cruise** down the Beaulieu River (Easter to Oct daily roughly every hour 11am–4.30pm; 30min; £4.50).

ARRIVAL AND INFORMATION   BUCKLERS HARD

Entry The site is open daily: April–Sept 10am–5.30pm; Oct–March 10am–4.30pm. Tickets (£6.20) include entrance to the museum and parking.

Tourist information For more information call ☎ 01590 616203 or check ⓦ bucklershard.co.uk.

ACCOMMODATION

The Master Builder's Hotel ☎ 0844 815 3399, ⓦ themasterbuilders.co.uk. Picturesque and peaceful, this wonderful quirky hotel is in a sixteenth-century building with open fires and a superb location overlooking the river; the

rooms are a mixed bunch, some have oriental flourishes and individually designed furniture, and some have views of the river. There's also a decent restaurant and pub – you can take your drink outside onto the lawns in nice weather. **£140**

Lymington

The most pleasant point of access for ferries to the Isle of Wight (see p.184) is **LYMINGTON**, a sheltered haven that's become one of the busiest leisure harbours on the south coast. Rising from the quay area, the cobbled street of the old town is lined with Georgian houses. At the top of the High Street (opposite Church Lane) is the partly thirteenth-century church of **St Thomas the Apostle**, with a cupola-topped tower built in 1670.

ARRIVAL AND DEPARTURE   LYMINGTON

By train A branch line runs from the main line at Brockenhurst to Lymington (every 30min; 10min). Trains call first at Lymington Town station, a short walk from the high street, then run onto Lymington Pier to link with the

Isle of Wight ferry.
By bus Bus #6 runs from Southampton to Lymington via Lyndhurst and Brockenhurst; the coastal routes #X1 and #X2 run here from Christchurch and Bournemouth.

ACCOMMODATION, EATING AND DRINKING

Britannia House Mill Lane ☎01590 672091, ⓦ britannia-house.com. A well-kept, friendly and central B&B, right by the train station. The comfortable rooms are on the small side but there's a fine sitting room commanding views over the waterfront. **£90**

Lanes Ashley Lane ☎01590 672777, ⓦ lanesof lymington.com. Set in an old chapel and former school, with some tables on an internal balcony, this bright buzzy restaurant and bar serves locally sourced fish and meats (£17–25) including sea bass and duck breast, and less pricey burgers and steaks (£11–19). Tues–Sat 11.30–2.30pm & 6.30–9.30pm, also open Sun 6.30–9.30pm in July & Aug.

The Ship Inn The Quay ☎01590 676903, ⓦ theshiplymington.co.uk. With a terrace facing the water, this classy, friendly pub has a stylish nautical interior

of bleached wood and chrome. It also offers a superior restaurant menu featuring Modern British seasonal dishes such as pork belly with scallops (£18), along with pub classics like beef and Guinness pie (£12). Daily 11am–11pm; food served Mon–Sat noon–10pm, Sun noon–9pm.

Stanwell House High St ☎01590 677123, ⓦ stanwellhouse.com. The most upmarket choice in town, this handsome boutique-style hotel has an array of individually designed rooms boasting rolltop baths, flatscreen TVs and the like. Its seafood restaurant is also the top spot to eat, in a dining room with a distinctly colonial feel (mains from around £17); there is also a less formal bistro serving modern European cuisine, and light snacks and afternoon teas are also available. Daily 7am–9pm. **£140**

Brockenhurst

You'll frequently find New Forest ponies strolling down the high street of **BROCKENHURST**, undoubtedly the most attractive and liveliest town in the forest. Surrounded by idyllic heath and woodland and with a ford at one end of its High Street, it's a picturesque spot and a useful travel hub.

ARRIVAL AND DEPARTURE

BROCKENHURST

By train The train station is on the eastern edge of town – from here, turn left and left again into the main Brookley Road, where you'll find the bulk of shops, banks and places to eat and drink. Mainline services run every 15–20min

from/to London Waterloo (1hr 30min), Southampton (15–20min) and Winchester (30min). In addition, a branch line runs to Lymington (every 30min; 10min) to link with the Isle of Wight ferry.

ACCOMMODATION, EATING AND DRINKING

★**New Park Manor** Lyndhurst Rd ☎0844 482 2152, ⓦ luxuryfamilyhotels.co.uk. This lovely family-friendly country house hotel in the middle of the New Forest pulls off the difficult trick of being both stylish and luxurious as well as relaxed and efficient. The staff are friendly and helpful and there's a fantastic spa, with an outdoor hot tub where you can sip champagne while watching the deer in the neighbouring fields. There are plenty of rooms that sleep families as well as inter-connecting rooms (childcare in the hotel crèche is free) and the hotel restaurant specializes in local produce. Family suites **£345**; doubles **£115**

★**The Pig** Beaulieu Rd ☎01590 622354, ⓦ thepighotel.co.uk. Brockhenhurst's best restaurant by a mile is in a fabulous New Forest country house, set in stunning grounds. The innovative menu uses ingredients from its gardens or from the surrounding area – fish is smoked on site, eggs come from its own chickens, and the

herbs and vegetables are all home-grown. All the ingredients are sourced from within 25 miles and the results are delicious, such as New Forest wood pigeon with locally foraged mushrooms (around £14). Daily 12.30–2.30pm & 6.30–9.30pm. **£140**

Rose and Crown Lyndhurst Rd ☎01590 622225, ⓦ rosecrownpubbrockenhurst.co.uk. A traditional Forest inn dating from the thirteenth century with a pleasant garden and a skittle alley. It serves large portions of good-value pub grub (most mains from £9–15), a selection of real ales and also has en-suite rooms (£90). Daily 11am–11pm.

Thatched Cottage Hotel 16 Brookley Rd ☎01590 623090, ⓦ thatched-cottage.co.uk. Dating from 1627, this is indeed an ancient thatched cottage, with tiny, low-beamed rooms as crammed with character as they are with furniture. There are just five rooms in the original building, along with newer "garden rooms"; the cream teas are divine, too. **£90**

Bournemouth and around

Renowned for its pristine sandy beach (one of southern England's cleanest) and its gardens, the resort of **BOURNEMOUTH** dates from 1811, when a local squire, Louis

Tregonwell, built a summerhouse on the wild, unpopulated heathland that once occupied this stretch of coast, and planted the first of the pine trees that now characterize the area. The mild climate, sheltered site and glorious beach encouraged the rapid growth of a full-scale family-holiday resort, complete with piers, cliff railways and boat trips. Today Bournemouth has a rather genteel, slightly geriatric image, counterbalanced by burgeoning numbers of language students, clubbers and a low-key surfing scene in the neighbouring suburb of **Boscombe**.

In the centre of town, the graveyard of **St Peter's** church is where **Mary Shelley**, author of the Gothic horror tale *Frankenstein*, is buried, together with the heart of her husband, the Romantic poet Percy Bysshe Shelley. The tombs of Mary's parents – radical thinker William Godwin and early feminist Mary Wollstonecraft – are also in the graveyard.

Russell-Cotes Art Gallery and Museum

Russell-Cotes Rd, East Cliff • Tues–Sun & bank hols 10am–5pm • Oct–March free; April–Sept £5 • ☎ 01202 451858, ⓦ russell-cotes
.bournemouth.gov.uk

Surrounded by lovely gardens on a clifftop, the **Russell-Cotes Art Gallery and Museum** has one of the UK's best collections of Victoriana, collected from around the world by the wealthy Russell-Cotes family. The quirky assortment of artworks, Oriental souvenirs and curios, such as the axe that allegedly beheaded Mary Queen of Scots, are displayed in an ornately decorated mansion, once the family home. Highlights of the collection are Rossetti's *Venus Verticordia* (1864) and England's most important collection of Victorian nudes, which scandalized much of society at the time.

| ARRIVAL AND INFORMATION | BOURNEMOUTH |

The **train station** and **bus station** lie opposite each other about a mile inland. They're connected to the town centre and seafront by frequent buses, or you can walk there in around 15–20min.

By train Destinations Brockenhurst (every 15–20min; 15–25min); Dorchester (every 30min–1hr; 45min); London Waterloo (every 30min; 2hr); Poole (every 20min; 10min); Southampton (every 15–20min; 30–50min); Weymouth (hourly; 55min); Winchester (every 15–20min; 45min–1hr). **By bus** Destinations Direct National Express buses run to London (hourly; 2hr 30min); Salisbury (Mon–Sat every 30min, Sun 7 daily; 1hr 10min); Southampton (12 daily; 45min–1hr); Weymouth (4 daily; 1hr 15min–1hr 30min); and Winchester (5 daily; 1hr 15min–1hr 35min).

Tourist office Westover Road (June–Aug Mon–Sat 9.30am–5pm, Sun 11am–3pm; Sept–Oct & April–June Mon–Sat 10am–4.30pm; ☎ 0845 051 1700, ⓦ bournemouth.co.uk).

ACCOMMODATION

The Cumberland East Overcliff Drive, East Cliff ☎ 01202 290722, ⓦ cumberlandbournemouth.co.uk. This sumptuous Art Deco building is right on the seafront and has its own substantial outdoor pool in the front garden. It also has a leisure club and stylish bar. Rooms are more standard, though bag one with a sea view and you won't be disappointed. **£190**

★ **The Greenhouse Hotel** 4 Grove Rd ☎ 01202 498900, ⓦ thegreenhousehotel.co.uk. Boutique-style, eco-friendly hotel in a Grade II-listed Victorian villa a short walk from the town centre. The stylish rooms come with all the latest mod cons, ultra-comfy beds, plus free home-made biscuits. The environmental standards are very high – water is solar-heated, and much of the electricity generated on site. There's also an excellent bar and restaurant. **£130**

Urban Beach Hotel 23 Argyll Rd, Boscombe ☎ 01202 301509, ⓦ urbanbeachhotel.co.uk. A short (but steep) walk from Boscombe's surf beach, and close to the shops, this old Victorian townhouse has been given a boutique makeover. There are a variety of rooms, all of which are stylish with designer furniture, comfy beds and DVDs. The downstairs bar/restaurant serves great cocktails. **£100**

EATING AND DRINKING

Kino Lounge 39 Bourne Ave ☎ 01202 552588. Small, fashionable wood-and-chrome restaurant just off Bournemouth's main square. It serves good-value and very tasty pizzas plus a Mediterranean-influenced menu which includes meze and pasta. Most mains £5–8. Mon–Thurs 11am–10pm, Fri & Sat 11am–11pm.

Koh Thai Tapas Daimler House, 38-40 Poole Hill ☎ 01202 294723, ⓦ koh-thai.co.uk. Lively restaurant

3

done out with stylish Thai decor – all dark wood furniture, comfy sofas and fresh orchids. The Thai food is beautifully presented and can be ordered in tapas size (£5–7) or full portions. Mains (£9–17) include Thai curries, stir fries and noodles. The cocktails are great too. Mon 5.30–10pm, Tues–Thurs & Sun 12.30–3pm & 5.30–10pm, Fri & Sat 12.30–3pm & 5.30–10.30pm.

★ **Urban Reef** Undercliff Drive, Boscombe ☎ 01202 443960, ⓦ urbanreef.com. Art Deco-style restaurant/ bar/café in a fabulous position on Boscombe seafront. Designed to give great sea views from both floors, its quirky decor features a mock-up beach hut hanging on the wall, and there's a large deck for drinks on the front. Food varies from eggs Florentine (£7.25) and cooked breakfast (£7.50), through ciabattas and wraps (£8) to mains such as lamb meatballs (£8) and line-caught sea bass (£18). Mon & Tues 9am–6pm, Wed–Fri 9am–11pm, Sat 8am–11pm, Sun 8am–6pm.

NIGHTLIFE AND ENTERTAINMENT

Flirt 21 The Triangle ☎ 01202 553999, ⓦ flirtcafebar .com. Quirky, gay-friendly café by day, serving good-value buffet lunches, which turns into a buzzy bar/restaurant at night. Sit on one of the old airline seats and enjoy a beer, and look out for various themed evenings from cabaret and quiz nights to book clubs and open mic sessions. Daily 9am–11pm.

O2 Academy 570 Christchurch Rd, Boscombe ☎ 01202 399922, ⓦ o2academybournemouth.co.uk. Big name acts play in this atmospheric venue that used to be Boscombe's old Opera House. Also hosts regular club nights with top DJs.

★ **Sixty Million Postcards** 19–21 Exeter Rd ☎ 01202 292697, ⓦ sixtymillionpostcards.com. One of Bourne- mouth's best bars, attracting an unpretentious but trendy student crowd. There are board games, various alcoves for cosy chats and comfy sofas. Offers a good range of beers, drinks and good-value burgers, with occasional live music. Mon–Thurs & Sun noon–midnight, Fri & Sat noon–2am.

Wimborne Minster

An ancient town on the banks of the River Stour, just a few minutes' drive north from the suburbs of Bournemouth, **WIMBORNE MINSTER** is an attractive little town, worth an hour or two's wander around its narrow alleys, or along the riverbank. It's home to southern England's largest covered **market** (Fri–Sun; ⓦ wimbornemarket.co.uk), though its main point of interest is the great church, the Minster of St Cuthberga.

Minster of St Cuthberga

High St • Mon–Sat 9.30am–5.30pm, Sun 2.30–5.30pm; Chained Library Easter–Oct daily 10.30am–12.30pm & 2–4pm; phone for winter opening times • Free • ☎ 01202 884753, ⓦ wimborneminster.org.uk

Built on the site of an eighth-century monastery, the **Minster of St Cuthberga**'s massive twin towers of mottled grey and tawny stone dwarf the rest of town. At one time the church was even more imposing – its spire crashed down during morning service in 1602. What remains today is basically Norman with later additions, such as the Perpendicular west tower; this bears a figure dressed as a grenadier of the Napoleonic era, who strikes every quarter-hour with a hammer. The **Chained Library** above the choir vestry, dating from 1686, is Wimborne's most prized possession and one of the oldest public libraries in the country. Its collection of ancient books includes a manuscript written on lambskin dating from 1343.

Kingston Lacy

2 miles northwest of Wimborne Minster • **House** Mid-March to Oct Wed–Sun 11am–5pm • £12.50 (includes grounds); NT • **Grounds** Daily: mid-March to Oct 10.30am–5.30pm; Nov to mid-March 10.30am–4pm • £7 • ☎ 01202 883402, ⓦ nationaltrust.org.uk/kingston-lacy

The glorious seventeenth-century mansion of **Kingston Lacy** stands in 250 acres of parkland grazed by a herd of Red Devon cattle. Designed for the Bankes family, who were exiled from Corfe Castle (see p.203) after the Roundheads reduced it to rubble, the brick building was clad in grey stone during the nineteenth century by Sir Charles Barry, co-architect of the Houses of Parliament. William Bankes, then owner of the house, was a great traveller and collector, and the **Spanish Room** is a superb scrapbook of his Grand Tour souvenirs. Kingston Lacy's **picture collection** is also outstanding, featuring Titian, Rubens, Velázquez and many other old masters.

Christchurch

CHRISTCHURCH, five miles east of Bournemouth, is best known for **Christchurch Priory** (April–Oct Mon–Sat 9.30am–5pm, Sun 2.15–5.30pm; Nov–March Mon–Sat 9.30am–4pm, Sun 2.15–5.30pm; £3 donation requested; ☎01202 485804, ☜christchurchpriory.org), which, at 311ft, is England's longest parish church. The oldest parts of the current church date back to 1094, and its fan-vaulted North Porch is the country's biggest. Fine **views** can be gained from the top of the 120ft-high **tower** (£2.50; book on ☎01202 485804).

The area round the old town quay has a carefully preserved charm, with the **Red House Museum and Gardens** on Quay Road (Tues–Fri 10am–5pm, Sat 10am–4pm; free; ☎0845 603 5635, ☜www3.hants.gov.uk/redhouse.htm) containing an affectionate collection of local memorabilia. **Boat trips** (Easter–Oct daily; ☎01202 429119) leave from the grassy banks of the riverside quay east to the sandspit at Mudeford (30min; £7.50 return) or upriver to Tuckton (15min; £3 return).

ARRIVAL AND INFORMATION   CHRISTCHURCH

By train Christchurch is on the main London to Weymouth line; the train station is on Stour Road, about a mile north of the town centre.

By bus Local buses from Bournemouth in the east,

Lymington in the west and Ringwood in the north, pull up at the bus stop close to the tourist office on the high street.

Tourist office 49 High Street (Mon 9am–4.30pm, Tues–Sat 10am–4.30pm; ☎01202 471780, ☜visitchristchurch.info).

Poole

West of Bournemouth, **POOLE** is an ancient seaport on a huge, almost landlocked harbour. The town developed in the thirteenth century and was successively colonized by pirates, fishermen and timber traders. The old quarter by the quayside contains more than one hundred historic buildings, as well as the contemporary Poole Museum.

Poole Museum

4 Old High St · Easter–Oct Mon–Sat 10am–5pm, Sun noon–5pm; Nov–Easter Tues–Sat 10am–4pm, Sun noon–4pm · Free · ☎01202 262600, ☜boroughofpoole.com/museums

Poole Museum traces the town's development through the centuries, with displays of local ceramics and tiles and a rare Iron Age log boat that was dug out of the harbour in 1964: carved out of a single tree trunk, the 33ft-long boat dates from around 300 BC. Look out, too, for the fascinating footage of the flying boats that took off from Poole harbour during the 1940s for the Far East and Australia.

Brownsea Island

Feb & March boats from Sandbanks only (Sat & Sun 10am–4pm, every 30min); April–Oct boats from Sandbanks and Poole Quay (daily 10am–5pm, every 30min) · Boats from Sandbanks £6 return; boats from Poole Quay £10 return · Entrance to island £6.60; NT · ☎01202 707744, ☜nationaltrust.org.uk/brownsea-island

Brownsea Island is famed for its red squirrels, wading birds and other **wildlife**, which you can spot along themed trails. The landscape is surprisingly diverse for such a small island – much of it is heavily wooded, though there are also areas of heath and marsh, and narrow, shingly beaches – and it's pretty easy to escape from the boat-trippers and find a peaceful corner to picnic.

Compton Acres

164 Canford Cliffs Rd · Daily: Easter–Oct 10am–6pm; Nov–Easter 10am–4pm; last entry 1hr before closing · £7.95 · ☎01202 700778, ☜comptonacres.co.uk · Bus #50 from Bournemouth and #52 from Poole

One of the area's best-known gardens, **Compton Acres** lies on the outskirts of Poole, signposted off the A35 Poole Road towards Bournemouth. Spectacularly sited over ten acres on steep slopes above Poole Harbour, each of the seven gardens here has a different international theme, including a formal Italian garden and the elegantly understated Japanese Garden, its meandering streams crossed by stone steps and wooden bridges.

3

ARRIVAL AND INFORMATION

By train Poole's train station is on Serpentine Road, about a 15min walk from the waterfront along the high street.

Destinations Bournemouth (every 20min; 10min); London Waterloo (every 30min; 2hr–2hr 10min); Weymouth (every 30min; 35–45min).

By bus The bus station is in front of the Dolphin Centre on

POOLE

Kingland Road, with regular National Express services to London Victoria (13 daily; 2hr 55min–3hr 45min).

Tourist office Poole Quay (April–June, Sept & Oct daily 10am–5pm; July & Aug daily 10am–6pm; Nov–March Mon–Fri 10am–5pm, Sat 10am–4pm; ☎ 0845 234 5560, ⊚ pooletourism.com).

ACCOMMODATION

Corkers 1 High St ☎ 01202 681393, ⊚ corkers.co.uk. Above a lively café/restaurant, this B&B offers some of the best-value rooms in town – the two superb front rooms, one of which sleeps three, have harbour-facing balconies. Parking offered for a small fee. **£85**

★**Hotel du Vin** Thames St ☎ 01202 685666,

⊚ hotelduvin.com. Inside a fine old mansion house with a double staircase, this stylish hotel has plush, comfortable, rooms, an atmospheric restaurant and wine cellar, and a very cosy bar with its own log fire – great in winter. The location is great, in the pretty old town, a minute's walk from the Quay. **£135**

EATING AND DRINKING

Da Vinci's 7 The Quay ☎ 01202 667528, ⊚ da-vincis .co.uk. Set in an old warehouse on Poole Quay, this is an old-fashioned Italian restaurant with friendly service and harbour views. The menu features inexpensive pizza and pasta (£8–14), as well as pricier traditional dishes, such as vitello Milanese (£17), and daily fish specials. Mon–Fri noon–2pm & 5.30–10pm, Sat & Sun noon–10.30pm.

★**Deli on the Quay** D17 Dolphin Quays, The Quay ☎ 01202 660022, ⊚ delionthequay.com. Bright, light harbourfront café-deli stacked with delicious preserves, wines and the like. The café serves fresh croissants, sandwiches and decent coffee. Mon & Wed–Fri 9am–5pm, Tues 9am–8.30pm, Sat & Sun 10am–5pm;

Nov–March closes 4pm Mon–Fri, Aug open until 10pm.

Poole Arms The Quay ☎ 01202 673450. Completely covered with green tiles, this wonderfully atmospheric historic pub is reassuringly old-fashioned, with decent beers and fresh fish daily. There's outdoor seating on the waterfront too. Mon–Sat 11am–11pm, Sun noon–11pm; food served daily noon–2.30pm & 6–8.30pm.

Storm 16 High St ☎ 01202 674970. Owned by a chef/fisherman, this restaurant, unsurprisingly, specializes in locally caught seafood. The menu changes daily according to what is available, but expect such delights as local pollack (£18) or sea bass with curly kale (£20). Mon–Fri & Sun 6–11pm, Sat 5.30–11pm, phone for irregular lunchtime hours.

The Isle of Purbeck

Though not actually an island, the **ISLE OF PURBECK** – a promontory of low hills and heathland jutting out beyond Poole Harbour – does have an insular and distinctive feel. Reached from the east by the ferry from Sandbanks at the narrow mouth of Poole Harbour, or by a long and congested landward journey via the bottleneck of **Wareham**, Purbeck can be a difficult destination to reach, but its villages are immensely pretty, none more so than **Corfe Castle**, with its majestic ruins. From **Swanage**, a low-key seaside resort, the Dorset Coast Path provides access to the oily shales of Kimmeridge Bay, the spectacular cove at **Lulworth** and the much-photographed natural arch of **Durdle Door**.

The whole coast from Purbeck to Exmouth in Devon – dubbed the **Jurassic Coast** (⊚ jurassiccoast.com) – is a World Heritage Site on account of its geological significance and fossil remains; walkers can access it along the South West Coast Path.

ARRIVAL AND GETTING AROUND

By ferry There are regular ferries from Sandbanks (7am–11pm every 20min; pedestrians & bikes £1, cars £3.50; ☎ 01929 450203, ⊚ sandbanksferry.co.uk).

By bike Cycling is a great way to get around, though be prepared for steep hills; bikes can be rented from Cycle Experience at Wareham Station (☎ 01929 556601, ⊚ purbeck

ISLE OF PURBECK

cyclehire.co.uk) and Charlie the Bikemonger, 5 Queen's Rd, in Swanage (☎ 01929 475833, ⊚ charliethebikemonger.com).

By bus The Purbeck Breezer runs two services around the Purbecks – route #40 from Poole to Swanage via Wareham and Corfe Castle, and route #50 from Bournemouth to Swanage via the Sandbanks ferry and Studland. In summer, some services are open-top.

By train Wareham is the only place served by mainline trains, though a restored steam train service also runs between Swanage and Norden (see p.204).

Wareham

The grid pattern of its streets indicates the Saxon origins of **WAREHAM**, and the town is surrounded by even older earth ramparts known as the Walls. A riverside setting adds greatly to its charms, though the place gets fairly overrun in summer. Nearby lies an enclave of quaint houses around **Lady St Mary's Church**, which contains the marble coffin of Edward the Martyr, murdered at Corfe Castle in 978 by his stepmother, to make way for her son Ethelred. **St Martin's Church**, at the north end of town, dates from Saxon times and holds a faded twelfth-century mural of St Martin offering his cloak to a beggar. The church's most striking feature, however, is a romantic effigy of T.E. Lawrence in Arab dress, which was originally destined for Salisbury Cathedral, but was rejected by the dean there who disapproved of Lawrence's sexual proclivities. Lawrence was killed in 1935 in a motorbike accident on the road from Bovington (six miles west); his simply furnished cottage is at **Clouds Hill**, seven miles northwest of Wareham (mid-March to Oct Wed–Sun 11am–5pm or dusk; £5.50; NT; ☎01929 405616, ⓦnationaltrust.org.uk/clouds-hill). The small **museum** next to Wareham's town hall in East Street (Easter–Oct Mon–Sat 10am–4pm; free, ☎01929 553448, ⓦgreenacre.info/WTM) focuses on local history and Lawrence memorabilia.

ARRIVAL AND INFORMATION WAREHAM

By train Wareham station, a 15min walk north of the town, sees regular trains from London (every 30min; 2hr 20min) and Weymouth (every 20–40min; 25–35min).

Tourist office Trinity Church, South Street (Easter–Oct Mon–Sat 9.30am–5pm; Nov–Easter Mon 10am–4pm, Tues–Sat 9.30am–4pm; ☎01929 552740, ⓦpurbeck.gov.uk).

Corfe Castle

The romantic **castle ruins** (daily: March & Oct 10am–5pm; April–Sept 10am–6pm; Nov–Feb 10am–4pm; £8, NT, ☎01929 481294, ⓦnationaltrust.org.uk/corfe-castle) crowning the hill behind the village of **CORFE CASTLE** are perhaps the most evocative in England. The family seat of Sir John Bankes, Attorney General to Charles I, this Royalist stronghold withstood a Cromwellian siege for six weeks, gallantly defended by Lady Bankes. One of her own men, Colonel Pitman, eventually betrayed the castle to the Roundheads, after which it was reduced to its present gap-toothed state by gunpowder. Apparently the victorious Roundheads were so impressed by Lady Bankes' courage that they allowed her to take the keys to the castle with her – they can still be seen in the library at the Bankes' subsequent home, Kingston Lacy (see p.200).

ACCOMMODATION CORFE CASTLE

Mortons House East St, Corfe Castle ☎01929 480988, ⓦmortonshouse.co.uk. A sixteenth-century manor house with a beautiful walled garden and log fires in winter, this award-winning small hotel has snug rooms, some with four-poster beds and stone fireplaces. The restaurant offers top local cuisine. **£160**

Norden Farm Norden ☎01929 480098, ⓦnordenfarm .com. Tucked into a tranquil valley, this working farm has extensive fields for tents and caravans, good facilities, its own shop and a menagerie of animals. Closed Nov–Feb. Pitches from **£13**

Norden House Norden Farm, Norden ☎01929 480177, ⓦnordenhouse.com. If you don't fancy camping, you can stay in Norden House, a Georgian building in the grounds of the farm, which has a range of comfortable rooms, a lovely garden and its own slightly pricey restaurant. **£90**

EATING AND DRINKING

The Greyhound The Square, Corfe Castle ☎01929 480205, ⓦgreyhoundcorfe.co.uk. One of England's oldest coaching inns, with frequent live music and a pleasant garden at the back with views of the castle. The food is good, with local specialities such as venison casserole (£14.50), as well as a good range of hearty sandwiches – the steak sandwich comes with chips and salad for £8.50. Daily 11am–11pm; food daily noon–9pm.

★ **The Scott Arms** West St, Kingston ☎ 01929 480270, ⊕ thescottarms.com. In the neighbouring village, a steep climb above Corfe Castle, this is a wonderful old inn with a warren of cosy rooms at the front and a large, modern-looking back room that doubles as its restaurant. The

biggest draw is its garden, which commands a stupendous view over Corfe Castle in the valley below. The food is substantial and in summer the *Jerk Shak* sells fantastic Caribbean food in the garden. Daily 11am–11pm; food served Mon–Thurs noon–2.30pm & 6.30–8.30pm, Fri noon–2.30pm & 6–8.45pm, Sat noon–2.45pm & 6–8.45pm, Sun noon–3.45pm & 6–8.30pm.

Swanage

Purbeck's largest town, **SWANAGE**, is a traditional seaside resort with a pleasant sandy beach and an ornate town hall. The town's station is the southern terminus of the **Swanage Steam Railway** (April–Oct daily; Nov– March Sat & Sun plus school hols; £11.50 return; ☎ 01929 425800, ⊕ swanagerailway.co.uk), which runs for six miles to Norden, just north of Corfe Castle. West of Swanage, you can pick up the coastal path to **Durlston Country Park**, around a mile out of town. Set in 280 acres of coastal woodland and crisscrossed with cliff-top paths, it is a great place for a picnic or for wind-blown walks.

ACCOMMODATION — SWANAGE AND AROUND

The Swanage Haven 3 Victoria Rd ☎ 01929 423088, ⊕ swanagehaven.com. Good-value boutique-style guesthouse: the smart rooms have flatscreen TVs and the decked garden has a great outdoor hot tub. Breakfasts are good, made from locally sourced ingredients. No children. **£150**

★ **Tom's Field Campsite** Langton Matravers, a couple of miles west of Swanage ☎ 01929 427110, ⊕ tomsfield camping.co.uk. Wonderfully sited and well-run, this is the best campsite in the region, with sea views from some of the pitches and direct access to the coast path. It also lets out bunks in a converted Nissen hut – The Walker's Barn – or a converted pigsty called The Stone Room. The campsite has a well-stocked shop, but only takes reservations for longer stays – for short stays, especially on sunny weekends, you'll need to turn up early to bag a pitch. Stone Room **£25**; Walker's Barn per person **£12**; camping pitches **£14**

EATING AND DRINKING

Gee Whites The Old Stone Quay, 1 High St ☎ 01929 425720, ⊕ geewhites.co.uk. Completely rebuilt in 2014, this superb open-air seafood bar and ice-cream parlour is right on the quay serving local lobster, crabs, mussels and oysters. The menu changes daily according to what's been caught, but a bowl of mussels with bread and tempura prawns costs a very reasonable £6. Summer daily 9am–9.30pm; outside summer hours are weather dependent.

★ **Seventh Wave** Durlston Castle & Country Park, Lighthouse Rd ☎ 01929 421111, ⊕ 7eventhwave.com. Inside Durlston Castle with stunning views over the coast, this is an unmissable stop – either for a coffee, drink or full meal. There are tapas-like snacks from around £4, fresh fish or mains from £14–18. April–Sept Mon–Fri 10am–5pm,

Sat & Sun 10am–5pm & 6–9pm; Oct–March daily 9.30am–4pm.

★ **Square and Compass** Worth Matravers, 4 miles west of Swanage ☎ 01929 439229, ⊕ squareand compasspub.co.uk. In a quintessential Purbeck village, with stunning views over the surrounding downs and sea, this is one of England's finest pubs: the bar is a tiny hatch, the interior is a winter fug of log fires, walkers, families and dogs (and the occasional live band), while outside there's a motley collection of stone seats and wooden benches. Regularly winning CAMRA awards for its local ales and ciders, and with its own little fossil museum, it also serves delicious home-made pies and pasties. Mon–Thurs noon–3pm & 6–11pm, Fri–Sun noon–11pm.

Studland

East of Swanage, you can follow the Southwest Coast path over Ballard Down to descend into the pretty village of **STUDLAND** at the southern end of **Studland Bay**. The most northerly stretch of the beach, **Shell Bay**, is a magnificent strand of icing-sugar sand backed by a remarkable heathland ecosystem that's home to all six British species of reptile – adders are quite common, so be careful. On Middle Beach, you can **hire kayaks** from the **Studland Sea School** (☎ 01929 450430, ⊕ studlandseaschool.co.uk) or take one of their excellent guided kayak or snorkelling tours round Old Harry Rocks, through cliff arches and sea caves.

★**Bankes Arms** Manor Rd ☎01929 450225, ⓦbankesarms.com. Lovely location, good food, and a great range of real ales, some from local independent breweries and others from its own on-site Isle of Purbeck Brewery. The pub food costs slightly more than average, but the portions are big, and frankly it's worth it for the joy of sitting in the grassy front garden with fantastic bay views, or by the roaring log fire in the cosy Purbeck stone interior. Daily 11am–11pm; food served noon–9.30pm (Sun to 9pm).

Lulworth Cove and around

The quaint thatch-and-stone villages of **EAST LULWORTH** and **WEST LULWORTH** form a prelude to **Lulworth Cove**, a perfect shell-shaped bite formed when the sea broke through a weakness in the cliffs and then gnawed away at them from behind, forming a circular cave that eventually collapsed to leave a bay enclosed by sandstone cliffs. West of the cove, **Stair Hole** is a roofless sea cave riddled with arches that will eventually collapse to form another Lulworth Cove. The mysteries of local geology are explained at the **Lulworth Heritage Centre** (daily 10am–4/6pm; free) by the car park at the top of the lane leading down to the cove.

Durdle Door

A mile west of Lulworth Cove, the iconic limestone arch of **Durdle Door** can be reached via the steep uphill path that starts from Lulworth Cove's car park. The arch itself sits at the end of a long shingle beach (which can be accessed via steep steps), a lovely place for catching the sun and swimming in fresh, clear water. There are further steps to a bay just east of Durdle Door, **St Oswald's Bay**, with another shingle beach and offshore rocks that you can swim out to.

Castle Inn Main Rd, West Lulworth ☎01929 400311, ⓦthecastleinn-lulworthcove.co.uk. Up in the village, this sixteenth-century thatched pub has a lovely terraced garden, a good range of local real ales and a selection of traditional pub games. High-quality pub grub features home made steak and ale pie and beef bourguignon. It's also very dog-friendly. Mon–Fri noon–2.30pm & 6–10.30pm, Sat & Sun noon–10.30pm; food served daily noon–9pm.

Durdle Door Holiday Park ☎01929 400200, ⓦlulworth.com. Superbly positioned up on the cliffs above Durdle Door, this campsite has fabulous views from its touring field, while tents can be pitched in the more sheltered wooded field. It's a 20min walk across fields to Lulworth Cove and there's also a shop and café-bar on site. Pitches **£33**

Lulworth Cove Inn Main Rd, Lulworth Cove ☎01929 400333, ⓦlulworth-coveinn.co.uk. With a great location right on the main street leading down to the cove and overlooking the duck pond, this is the first choice in Lulworth itself, especially if you can bag one of the front rooms that come with their own cove-view terraces (£10 extra). The pub downstairs offers local Blandford ales, real fires, a pleasant garden and decent food, including citrus salmon skewer (£10.50) and haddock smokie (£14.50) among the usual pub staples. Daily 11am–11pm; food served noon–9pm. **£100**

Dorchester and around

For many, **DORCHESTER**, county town of Dorset, is essentially **Thomas Hardy**'s town; he was born at Higher Bockhampton, three miles east, his heart is buried in Stinsford, a couple of miles northeast (the rest of him is in Westminster Abbey), and he spent much of his life in Dorchester itself, where his statue now stands on High West Street. The town appears in his novels as Casterbridge, and the local countryside is evocatively depicted, notably the wild heathland of the east (Egdon Heath) and the eerie yew forest of Cranborne Chase. The real Dorchester has a pleasant central core of mostly seventeenth-century and Georgian buildings, though the town's origins go back to the Romans, who founded "Durnovaria" in about 70 AD. The Roman walls were replaced in the eighteenth century by tree-lined avenues called "Walks", but some traces of the Roman period have survived. On the southeast edge of town, **Maumbury Rings** is where the Romans held vast gladiatorial combats in an amphitheatre adapted from a Stone Age site.

In addition to its Hardy connections, Dorchester is also associated with the notorious **Judge Jeffreys**, who, after the ill-fated rebellion of the Duke of Monmouth (one of Charles II's illegitimate offspring) against James II, held his "**Bloody Assizes**" in the Oak Room of the former Antelope Hotel (now offices) on Cornhill in 1685. A total of 292 men were sentenced to death, though most got away with a flogging and transportation to the West Indies, while 74 were hung, drawn and quartered, their heads stuck on pikes throughout Dorset and Somerset. Judge Jeffreys lodged just round the corner in High West Street, in what are now offices.

Old Crown Courts

58–60 High St • Mon–Thurs 10am–4.30pm • £2 • ☎ 01305 267992

The **Old Crown Courts**, also known as Shire Hall, are of interest principally as the place where six men from the nearby village of Tolpuddle, now known as the **Tolpuddle Martyrs** (see opposite), were sentenced to transportation for forming what was in effect Britain's first trade union. Although the council buildings are still in use, the room in which the Martyrs were tried has been preserved as a memorial; you can sit behind the judge's desk and bang his gavel, or ponder their fate from the jurors' bench.

Dorset County Museum

High West St • April–Oct Mon–Sat 10am–5pm; Nov–March Mon–Sat 10am–4pm • £6.50 • ☎ 01305 262735, ⊛ dorsetcountymuseum.org

The best place to find out about Dorchester's history is the engrossing **Dorset County Museum**, where archeological and geological displays trace Celtic and Roman history, including a section on nearby Maiden Castle (see below). Pride of place goes to the recreation of Thomas Hardy's study, where his pens are inscribed with the names of the books he wrote with them.

Maiden Castle

Around 2 miles southwest of Dorchester • Open access • Free

One of southern England's finest prehistoric sites, **MAIDEN CASTLE** stands on a hill southwest of Dorchester. Covering about 115 acres, it was first developed around 3000 BC by a Stone Age farming community and then used during the Bronze Age as a funeral mound. Iron Age dwellers expanded it into a populous settlement and fortified it with a daunting series of ramparts and ditches, just in time for the arrival of Vespasian's Second Legion. The ancient Britons' slingstones were no match for the more sophisticated weapons of the Roman invaders, however, and Maiden Castle was stormed in a massacre in 43 AD. What you see today is a massive series of grassy concentric ridges about 60ft high, creasing the surface of the hill. The main finds from the site are displayed in the Dorset County Museum (see above).

Cerne Abbas giant

Cerne Abbas, 7 miles north of Dorchester, just off the A352 • Open access • Free; NT • ☎ 01297 489481, ⊛ nationaltrust.org.uk/cerne-giant

The village of **CERNE ABBAS** has bags of charm, with gorgeous Tudor cottages and abbey ruins, but its main attraction is the enormously priapic **giant** carved in the chalk hillside just north of the village, standing 180ft high and brandishing a club over his disproportionately small head. The age of the monument is disputed, though it is likely that the giant originated as some primeval fertility symbol. Folklore has it that lying on the outsize member will induce conception, but the National Trust, who now own the site, do their best to stop people wandering over it and damaging the 2ft-deep trenches that form the outlines. Although you can walk round the giant, the carving itself is fenced off to avoid erosion and you don't get the full impact of the giant when you are so close – for the best view, follow signs to the car park and **viewpoint** on the hillside opposite.

Tolpuddle Martyrs Museum

Tolpuddle, 8 miles east of Dorchester, off the A3 • April–Oct Tues–Sat 10am–5pm, Sun 11am–5pm; Nov–March Thurs–Sat 10am–4pm, Sun 11am–4pm • Free • ☎ 01305 848237, ⓦ tolpuddlemartyrs.org.uk

The delightful Dorset village of **TOLPUDDLE** is of interest principally because of the **Tolpuddle Martyrs**. In 1834, six villagers, George and James Loveless, Thomas and John Standfield, John Brine and James Hammett, were sentenced to transportation for banding together to form the Friendly Society of Agricultural Labourers, in order to petition for a small wage increase on the grounds that their families were starving. After a public outcry the men were pardoned, and the Martyrs passed into history as founders of the trade union movement. Six memorial cottages were built in 1934 to commemorate the centenary of the Martyrs' conviction. The middle one has been turned into the little **Tolpuddle Martyrs Museum**, which charts the story of the men, from their harsh rural lives before their conviction to the horrors of transportation in a convict ship and the brutal conditions of the penal colonies in Australia.

ARRIVAL AND INFORMATION

By train Dorchester has two train stations, Dorchester South and Dorchester West, both south of the centre.
Destinations from Dorchester South Bournemouth (every 30min; 40–45min); London (every 30min; 2hr 35min–2hr 50min); Weymouth (every 15–20min; 10–15min).
Destinations from Dorchester West Bath (7 daily; 2hr); Bristol (7 daily; 2hr 30min).
By bus Most local buses stop around the car park on

DORCHESTER AND AROUND

Acland Rd, to the east of South St, though long-distance buses pull in next to Dorchester South train station.
Destinations Bournemouth (4 daily; 1hr–1hr 40min); London (1 daily; 3hr 50min); Weymouth (roughly every 15min; 30min).
Tourist office 11 Antelope Walk (April–Oct Mon–Sat 9am–5pm; Nov–March Mon–Sat 9am–4pm; ☎ 01305 267992, ⓦ visit-dorset.com).

ACCOMMODATION

The Old Rectory Winterbourne Steepleton, 4 miles west of Dorchester ☎ 01305 889468, ⓦ theoldrectorybandb .co.uk. A lovely former rectory in a tiny, pretty village. Dating from 1850, the B&B has four comfortable en-suite rooms, one with a four-poster, and attractive well-kept gardens. **£70**

Westwood House 29 High West St ☎ 01305 268018, ⓦ westwoodhouse.co.uk. Comfortable Georgian townhouse on the busy high street, with well-furnished rooms, all with wi-fi and flatscreen TVs. The breakfasts are great, and include options such as smoked haddock with poached egg. **£95**

EATING AND DRINKING

★**Café Jagos** 8 High West St ☎ 01305 266056, ⓦ cafejagos.com. Good-value salads and sandwiches come in large portions at this pleasant café with contemporary decor – the panninis (£5) and main courses such as local rabbit and cider stew (£8), are all tasty. On Fri and Sat nights the bar area comes into its own with frequent live music and DJs. Mon–Thurs 10am–4pm, Fri–Sat 10am–4pm & 10pm–4am.
Potters Café 19 Durngate St ☎ 01305 260312. Very appealing café/restaurant with a log fire in winter and a

small garden. It serves a range of inexpensive dishes such as fish soup, tiger prawns and curries from £7 to £9. Mon–Sat 9.30am–4pm, Sun 10am–2.30pm.
Sienna 36 High West St ☎ 01305 250022, ⓦ siennarestaurant.co.uk. Dorset's only Michelin-starred restaurant, this tiny, upmarket place specializes in locally sourced Modern British cuisine such as West Country venison with celeriac and pear. Prices start at around £26 for the two-course lunch menu, up to £65 a head for the evening tasting menu. Tues 7–9pm, Wed–Sat 12.30–2pm & 7–9.30pm.

Sherborne

Tucked away in the northwest corner of Dorset, ten miles north of Cerne Abbas, the pretty town of **SHERBORNE** was once the capital of Wessex, its church having cathedral status until Old Sarum (see p.216) usurped the bishopric in 1075.

Abbey Church

3 Abbey Close • Daily: April–Oct 8am–6pm; Nov–March 8am–4pm • Suggested donation £3.50 • ☎ 01935 812452,
Ⓦ sherborneabbey.com

Sherborne's former historical glory is embodied by the magnificent **Abbey Church** founded in 705 and later becoming a Benedictine abbey. Most of its extant parts date from a rebuilding in the fifteenth century. Among the abbey church's many tombs are those of Alfred the Great's two brothers, Ethelred and Ethelbert, and the Elizabethan poet Thomas Wyatt, all in the northeast corner.

The castles

Sherborne boasts no fewer than two "castles", both associated with Sir Walter Raleigh. Queen Elizabeth I first leased, then gave, Raleigh the twelfth-century **Old Castle**, on Castletom (April–June, Sept & Oct daily 10am–5pm; July & Aug daily 10am–6pm; £3.70; EH; ☎ 01935 812730, Ⓦ english-heritage.org.uk/daysout/properties/sherborne -old-castle) but it seems that he despaired of feudal accommodation and built himself a more comfortably domesticated house, **Sherborne Castle**, in adjacent parkland, accessed from New Road (April–Oct Tues–Thurs, Sat & Sun 11am–4.30pm; castle interior closed on Sat until 2pm; castle and gardens £11, gardens only £6; ☎ 01935 812072, Ⓦ sherbornecastle.com). When Sir Walter fell from the queen's favour by seducing her maid of honour, the Digby family acquired the house and have lived here ever since. The Old Castle fared less happily, and was pulverized by Cromwellian cannon fire for the obstinately Royalist leanings of its occupants.

ARRIVAL AND INFORMATION
SHERBORNE

By train The station is 5min south of the town centre, and is served by hourly trains between London and Exeter, with some services continuing on to Plymouth.

By bus Buses from Dorchester, Yeovil and Blandford Forum pull in outside the train station.

Tourist office 3 Tilton Court, Digby Road (Mon–Sat: April–Oct 9am–5pm; Oct & Nov 9.30am–4pm; Dec–March 10am–3pm; ☎ 01935 815341, Ⓦ sherbornetown.com).

ACCOMMODATION AND EATING

The Eastbury Long St ☎ 01935 813131, Ⓦ theeastbury hotel.co.uk. In a fine Georgian house, with its own highly regarded restaurant, bar and lovely walled gardens. The front rooms are on the small side and it's worth paying extra for an executive room, which are spacious and boutique in feel, overlooking the gardens. The restaurant specializes in dishes made from seasonal and locally sourced ingredients. **£150**

★ **Oliver's** 19 Cheap St ☎ 01935 815005, Ⓦ olivers coffeehouse.co.uk. With long wooden benches laid out in a former butcher's, adorned with the original tiles, this friendly café-deli serves great cakes and coffee, accompanied by oodles of atmosphere. Mon–Fri 9am–5pm, Sat 9.30am–5pm, Sun 10–4pm.

Shaftesbury

Fifteen miles east of Sherborne on the A30, **SHAFTESBURY** perches on a spur of lumpy hills, with severe gradients on three sides of the town. On a clear day, views from the town are terrific – one of the best vantage points is **Gold Hill**, quaint, cobbled and very steep. At its crest, the **Gold Hill Museum and Garden** (April–Oct daily 10.30am–4pm; free; ☎ 01747 852157, Ⓦ goldhillmuseum.org.uk) displays items ranging from locally made buttons, for which the area was once renowned, to a mummified cat.

Pilgrims used to flock to Shaftesbury to pay homage to the bones of Edward the Martyr, which were brought to the **Abbey** in 978, though now only the footings of the abbey church survive, just off the main street on Park Walk (April–Oct daily 10am–5pm; £3; ☎ 01747 852910, Ⓦ shaftesburyabbey.org.uk). **St Peter's Church** on the marketplace is one of the few reminders of Shaftesbury's medieval grandeur, when it boasted a castle, twelve churches and four market crosses.

ARRIVAL AND INFORMATION
SHAFTESBURY

By bus Shaftesbury has services from Salisbury (Mon–Sat 8 daily; 1hr 15min) and Blandford Forum (Mon–Sat 7 daily; 40min).

Tourist office 8 Bell Street (April–Sept Mon–Sat 10am–5pm; Oct–March Mon–Sat 10am–3pm; ☎01747 853514, ⓦ shaftesburydorset.com).

ACCOMMODATION

The Grosvenor Arms The Commons ☎01747 850580, ⓦthegrosvenorarms.co.uk. This former coaching inn in the centre of town has had a successful makeover into a buzzy, boutique-style hotel. The rooms are stylish with comfy beds, coffee machines and flat-screen TVs, and the downstairs restaurant is good too, with a wood-fired pizza oven, plus local fish and meat dishes. **£150**

La Fleur de Lys Bleke St ☎01747 853717, ⓦlafleurdelys.co.uk. Long-established hotel, with a range of comfortable rooms above a highly rated if pricey restaurant; the back rooms have the best views, while those at the front are on a busy through-road. **£135**

EATING AND DRINKING

The Mitre 23 High St ☎01747 853002, ⓦyoungs .co.uk. A traditional pub with a terrace at the back giving lovely views; inside, there's a cosy dining room with a wood-burning stove and reasonably priced pub grub including steak and ale pie (£10). Mon–Thurs 10.30am–11pm, Fri & Sat 10.30am–midnight, Sun noon–10.30pm; food served summer noon 9pm)

winter noon–3pm & 6–9pm.

★**The Salt Cellar** Gold Hill ☎01747 851838. Right at the top of the hill itself and with great views, this place serves inexpensive snacks and daily specials from around £8, including home-made pies, in the pillar-lined interior or at outdoor tables on the cobbles. Mon–Sat 9am–5pm, Sun 10am–5pm

Weymouth and around

Whether George III's passion for sea bathing was a symptom of his eventual madness is uncertain, but it was at **WEYMOUTH** that in 1789 he became the first reigning monarch to follow the craze. Sycophantic gentry rushed into the waves behind him, and soon the town, formerly a busy port, took on the elegant Georgian stamp that it bears today.

A lively family holiday destination in summer, Weymouth reverts to a more sedate rhythm out of season. The highlight, of course, is its long sandy beach, but there are also a number of "all-weather" attractions in town. A few buildings survive from pre-Georgian times: the restored **Tudor House** at 3 Trinity Street (May to mid-Oct Tues–Fri 1–3.45pm; Nov, Dec & Feb–April first Sun of month 2–4pm; £3.50; ☎01305 779711) and the ruins of **Sandsfoot Castle** (free access), built by Henry VIII, overlooking Portland Harbour. But Weymouth's most imposing architectural heritage stands along the **Esplanade**, a dignified range of bow-fronted and porticoed buildings gazing out across the graceful bay. At the far end of the Esplanade, the Quay juts out into the sea, housing the town's ferry terminals and its newest attraction, the 173ft-high **Sea Life Tower** (April–July & Sept–Oct daily 11am–5pm; Aug daily 11am–6pm; Nov–March Mon & Thurs–Sun 11am–3pm; from £5.40 or combined ticket with Sea Life Adventure Park £22.85, £15.50 online; ☎03333 212001, ⓦsealifeweymouth .com), which provides stunning views over the town and coastline. Beyond here, the more intimate quayside of the **Old Harbour** is linked to the Esplanade by the pedestrianized **St Mary's Street**. At the other end of the promenade, in Lodmoor Country Park, the excellent **Sea Life Park** (daily March–Oct 10am–5pm, Nov–Feb 10am–4pm; last admission 1hr before closing; combined ticket with Sea Life Tower £22.85, £15.50 online; ☎03333 212001, ⓦsealifeweymouth.com) is home to turtles, penguins, otters and seals, as well as a sea-horse breeding centre, and the crocodile creek log flume ride.

Just south of the town stretch the giant arms of Portland Harbour, and a long causeway links Weymouth to the **Isle of Portland**. The causeway stands on the easternmost section of the eighteen-mile bank of pebbles known as Chesil Beach (see p.211), running northwest towards the fishing port of **West Bay**.

3

By train Weymouth is served at least hourly by trains from London (2hr 45min), Southampton (1hr 25min–1hr 40min), Bournemouth (50min) and Poole (35–45min), with less regular services from Bristol (2hr 30min) and Bath (2hr 10min); trains arrive at the station on King St, a couple of mins' walk back from the seafront.

By bus Buses from Dorchester (3–4 hourly; 30min) pull in at the stops by King George III's statue.

Tourist office A volunteer-run information service is based in Weymouth Pavilion, The Esplanade (daily 10am–6pm; ☎01305 783225, ⓦvisitweymouth.co.uk).

ACCOMMODATION

★**Bay View House** 35 The Esplanade ☎01305 782083, ⓦbayview-weymouth.co.uk. Clean, friendly and well-kept guesthouse. The comfortable room at the front with a bay window overlooking the sea is great value (it's just a little bit costlier than the others). Also has family rooms and free private garage parking. **£60**

Old Harbour View 12 Trinity Rd ☎01305 774633, ⓦoldharbourview.co.uk. Cosy guesthouse in a great location right on the harbourfront. It consists of just two

rooms in a Georgian townhouse, but it's worth paying a few pounds extra for the one at the front with a harbour view. The breakfasts are great, using locally sourced and free-range ingredients. **£86**

The Seaham 3 Waterloo Place ☎01305 782010, ⓦthe seahamweymouth.co.uk. Attractive Georgian terraced house at the quieter end of town. The rooms are comfortable and well furnished and some have sea views; breakfast includes a good choice of local free-range products. **£80**

EATING AND DRINKING

Enzos 110 The Esplanade ☎01305 778666, ⓦenzo -ristorante.co.uk. Traditional Italian restaurant, but with clean, contemporary decor, tiled floors and modern furnishings; it's right on the seafront, but slightly away from the hubbub of the main drag. It serves a range of pasta dishes (£8–10), as well as daily local specials, such as linguine lobster (£15). Excellent value. Daily 12.30–2.30pm & 5.30–10.30pm.

Floods Bistro 19 Custom House Quay ☎01305 772270, ⓦfloodsrestaurant.co.uk. Small harbourfront restaurant

with a few outside tables, serving top-quality fresh fish – try the skate wing with mussels and herb sauce (£13), or they may even have lobster or John Dory depending on the catch of the day. Daily noon–2.30pm & 7–11pm.

Phoenix Bakery Cafe 6–7 Coburg ☎01305 767894, ⓦphoenixbakery.co.uk. This artisan bakery is a great place to pick up supplies for a picnic, including warm pastries, cakes and savouries straight from the oven – or check out the delicious mushroom and cheese bruschettas for lunch, while watching the bakers at work. Daily 9am–4pm.

Isle of Portland

Stark, wind-battered and treeless, the **Isle of Portland** is famed above all for its hard white limestone, which has been quarried here for centuries – Wren used it for St Paul's Cathedral, and it clads the UN headquarters in New York. It was also used for the 6000ft breakwater that protects Portland Harbour – the largest artificial harbour in Britain, built by convicts in the nineteenth century and the main centre for the 2012 Olympic Games sailing events. It is still surveyed by **Portland Castle** (daily: April–Sept 10am–6pm; Oct & Nov 10am–5pm; £4.90; EH; ☎01305 820539, ⓦenglishheritage .org.uk/daysout/properties/portland-castle), which was commissioned by Henry VIII. Southeast of here, the craggy limestone of the Isle rises to 496ft at Verne Hill. At **Portland Bill**, the southern tip of the island, you can climb the 153 steps of **Portland Lighthouse** (Easter–June Sun–Thurs 11am–5pm; July–Sept Sun–Fri 11am–5pm; £4; ☎01305 820495), which dates from 1906, for superb views in all directions.

By bus First Bus runs bus #1 every 10 min from Commercial Road in Weymouth to Portland (30–40min).

EATING AND DRINKING

Cove House Inn 91 Chiswell ☎01305 820895, ⓦthecovehouseinn.co.uk. A good spot for food or a quick drink, with pub staples, such as burgers (£8), as well as a daily local fish menu, featuring such treats as scallops with

chilli, garlic and cream (£11). It's cosy inside with a wood-burner and big windows with sea views, while the outside tables look over Chesil Beach. Mon–Sat 11am–11pm, Sun noon–10.30pm.

Crab House Café Ferrymans Way, Portland Rd at the entrance to the Portland causeway ☎ 01305 788867, ⓦ crabhousecafe.co.uk. In a great location overlooking Chesil Beach, this upmarket beach shack is renowned for its superb, locally caught fresh fish and seafood, including oysters from its own beds. The menu changes daily according to the catch, but expect dishes such as turbot steak poached in saffron cream with mussels (£22). There are tables outside, and reservations are advised for the restaurant, though you may be lucky to squeeze into the café area. Wed & Thurs noon–2pm & 6–9pm, Fri & Sat noon–2.30pm & 6–9.30pm, Sun noon–3.30pm.

Chesil Beach

Chesil Beach is the strangest feature of the Dorset coast, a 200yd-wide, 50ft-high bank of pebbles that extends for eighteen miles, its component stones gradually decreasing in size from fist-like pebbles at Portland to "pea gravel" at Burton Bradstock in the west. This sorting is an effect of the powerful coastal currents, which make this one of the most dangerous beaches in Europe – churchyards in the local villages display plenty of evidence of wrecks and drownings. Though not a swimming beach, Chesil is popular with sea anglers, and its wild, uncommercialized atmosphere makes an appealing antidote to the south coast resorts. Behind the beach, **The Fleet**, a brackish lagoon, was the setting for J. Meade Faulkner's classic smuggling tale, *Moonfleet*.

ACCOMMODATION

★ **East Shilvinghampton Farm** Portesham ☎ 01420 80804, ⓦ featherdown.co.uk. A lovely farm in a beautiful valley, a couple of miles inland from the Fleet Lagoon. It has seven spacious, luxurious tents to rent – ready-erected, with running water, a toilet, a wood-burning stove and comfortable beds – in an idyllic field that looks down the valley, with horses, goats and chickens in the paddock next door. From **£200** for three nights

Abbotsbury

At the point where Chesil Beach attaches itself to the shore is the pretty village of **ABBOTSBURY**, all tawny ironstone and thatch. The village has three main attractions, which can be visited individually or on a combined Passport ticket for £17.

The most absorbing is the **Swannery** (daily mid-March to Oct 10am–5pm; £10.95, ☎ 01305 871130), a wetland reserve for mute swans dating back to medieval times, when presumably it formed part of the abbot's larder. If you visit in late May or June, you'll see baby cygnets waddling around and squabbling at your feet. The eel-grass reeds through which the swans paddle were once harvested to thatch roofs throughout the region. One example can be seen on the fifteenth-century Tithe Barn, the last remnant of the abbey and today housing the **Children's Farm**, whose highlights include goat-racing and pony rides (mid-March to Aug & Oct half-term daily 10am–5pm; Sept & Oct Sat & Sun 10am–5pm; £9.50; ☎ 01305 871130). Lastly, in the **Subtropical Gardens** (daily: Nov–March 10am–4pm, April–Oct 10am–5pm; closed over Christmas period; £10.95; ☎ 01305 871387) delicate species thrive in the microclimate created by Chesil's stones, which act as a giant radiator to deter all but the worst frosts.

INFORMATION   ABBOTSBURY

Tourist office West Yard Barn, West Street (☎ 01305 871130, ⓦ abbotsbury-tourism.co.uk).

Bridport

Ten miles west of Abbotsbury is the pretty town of **BRIDPORT**, mentioned in the Domesday Book of 1086 and an important port before the rivers silted up in the early 1700s, leaving it stranded a mile or so inland today. It's a pleasant old town of solid brick buildings with very wide streets, a hangover from its days as a major rope-making centre when cords were stretched between the houses to be twisted and dyed. Today, it's a lively **market** town (Wed & Sat) with an arty, alternative vibe. The town's harbour lies a mile or so south at **West Bay**, which has a fine sandy beach sheltered below majestic red cliffs – the sheer East Cliffs are a tempting challenge for intrepid walkers – and made a suitably brooding location for the ITV murder series, *Broadchurch*.

ACCOMMODATION, EATING AND DRINKING

The Bull 34 East St ☎01308 422878, ⊛thebullhotel .co.uk. Friendly, boutique-style hotel in a former seventeenth-century coaching inn in the centre of town. The rooms are comfortable and modern, with Neal's Yard toiletries: there are some family rooms, too. The restaurant and bar are good, too: try the Lyme Bay scallops (£9.50) to start, followed by a 12oz rib-eye steak (£21). Daily noon–3pm & 6.30–9.30pm. **£100**

★ **Hive Beach Café** Beach Rd, Burton Bradstock, 3 miles east of Bridport ☎01308 897070, ⊛hivebeachcafe .co.uk. Laidback café/restaurant on the beach, serving top-quality seafood, such as baked halibut (£17) and grilled Cornish sardines (£11). If your budget can stretch to it, splash out on the fabulous seafood platter featuring local lobster, crab and scallops (£60 for two). Also delicious home-made cakes, excellent coffee, good breakfasts and very friendly service. Hours vary according to the season, but if it's a

BRIDPORT AND AROUND

nice day they will almost certainly be open.

★ **Norburton Hall** Shipton Lane, Burton Bradstock ☎01308 897007, ⊛norburtonhall.com. The Edwardian *Norburton Hall* is a great place to stay, with six acres of rolling grounds close to the beach at Burton Bradstock. It has three beautifully furnished en-suite bedrooms, one with a four-poster bed: grand without being too formal, it also has several self-catering cottages to rent in the outbuildings. Cottages from **£420**/week; B&B **£130**

The Riverside West Bay ☎01308 422011, ⊛thefishrestaurant-westbay.co.uk. Reservations are recommended for this renowned restaurant which offers fresh, sumptuous fish and seafood and fine river views. There is a daily changing menu, but expect the likes of grilled John Dory with chargrilled peppers (£22). The two-course mid-week lunch menu is good value at around £20. Tues–Sat noon–2.30pm 6.30–9pm, Sun noon–2.30pm.

Lyme Regis

LYME REGIS, Dorset's most westerly town, shelters snugly between steep, fossil-filled cliffs. Its intimate size and photogenic qualities make this a popular and congested spot in high summer, with some upmarket literary associations – Jane Austen summered in a seafront cottage and set part of *Persuasion* in Lyme (the town appears in the 1995 film version), while novelist John Fowles lived here until his death in 2005 (the film adaptation of his book, *The French Lieutenant's Woman*, was shot here).

Colourwashed cottages and elegant Regency and Victorian villas line its seafront and flanking streets, but Lyme's best-known feature is a practical reminder of its commercial origins: **the Cobb**, a curving harbour wall originally built in the thirteenth century. It has suffered many alterations since, most notably in the nineteenth century, when its massive boulders were clad in neater blocks of Portland stone.

On Bridge Street, the excellent **Lyme Regis Museum** (Easter–Oct Mon–Sat 10am–5pm, Sun 11am–5pm; Nov–Easter Wed–Sun, plus Mon & Tues in school hols 11am–4pm; £3.95; ☎01297 443370, ⊛lymeregismuseum.co.uk) displays artefacts related to the town's literary connections, including John Fowles' office chair, and provides a crash course in local history and geology, while **Dinosaurland** on Coombe Street (late Feb to late Oct daily 10am–4pm; sporadic openings at other times; £5; ☎01297 443541, ⊛dinosaurland.co.uk), fills out the story of ammonites and other local fossils. The town is also something of a foodie destination, with lots of superb fish restaurants and good pubs, plus the **Town Mill Complex** (⊛townmill.org.uk) in Mill Lane, just off Coombe Street, where there's a fantastic cheese shop, local brewery and café, as well as a working mill, pottery and art gallery.

ARRIVAL AND INFORMATION

LYME REGIS

By train Lyme's nearest station is in Axminster, 5 miles north, served by regular trains from London Waterloo and Exeter: bus #31 runs from the station to Lyme, then on to

Weymouth.
By bus First Buses (⊛firstgroup.com) runs a daily bus service from Exeter (1hr 40min), Bridport (35min), Weymouth (1hr

LYME'S JURASSIC COAST

The cliffs around Lyme are made up of a complex layer of limestone, greensand and unstable clay, a perfect medium for preserving **fossils**, which are exposed by landslips of the waterlogged clays. In 1811, after a fierce storm caused parts of the cliffs to collapse, 12-year-old Mary Anning, a keen fossil-hunter, discovered an almost complete dinosaur skeleton, a 30ft ichthyosaurus now displayed in London's Natural History Museum.

Hands-off inspection of the area's complex **geology** can be enjoyed all around the town: as you walk along the seafront and out towards The Cobb, look for the outlines of ammonites in the walls and paving stones. To the west of Lyme, the **Undercliff** is a fascinating jumble of overgrown landslips, now a nature reserve, where a great path wends its way through the undergrowth for around seven miles to neighbouring Seaton in Devon. East of Lyme, a huge landslip in 2008 closed the Dorset Coast Path to **Charmouth** (Jane Austen's favourite resort), as well as blocking the two-mile beach route to the resort, which was previously walkable at low tide. At Charmouth, you can take the coastal path leading to the headland of **Golden Cap**, whose brilliant outcrop of auburn sandstone is crowned with gorse.

3

40min) and Poole every couple of hours (3hr 20min).
Tourist office Church Street (April–Oct Mon–Sat

10am–5am, Sun 10am–4pm; Nov–March Mon–Sat 10am–3pm; ☎ 01297 442138, ⓦ lymeregis.org)

ACCOMMODATION

Alexandra Hotel Pound St ☎ 01297 442010, ⓦ hotelalexandra.co.uk. Popular with honeymooners, this is the town's top hotel, located inside an eighteenth-century manor house with bleached wood floors and lovely gardens overlooking the sea. Many of the comfortable rooms have sea views, and there is also a highly rated restaurant. **£177**

Old Lyme 29 Coombe St ☎ 01297 442929, ⓦ oldlymeguesthouse.co.uk. Central guesthouse right in the town centre in a lovely 300-year-old stone former post office. There are six smallish but spruce bedrooms – one is a triple room and all are en suite, or with a private bathroom. **£80**

EATING AND DRINKING

Hix Oyster and Fish House Cobb Rd ☎ 01297 446910, ⓦ hixoysterandfishhouse.co.uk. In a lovely location overlooking the town and sea, this airy restaurant, owned by acclaimed chef Mark Hix, specializes in local fish and seafood: sublime main courses include Portland black bream (£20), though there are cheaper options, like fish pie (£15). April–Oct daily noon–10pm; Nov–March Tues–Sat noon–10pm, Sun noon–6pm.

Royal Standard 25 Marine Parade ☎ 01297 442637, ⓦ theroyalstandardlymeregis.co.uk. Beachside inn dating back four hundred years, with a log fire inside, and a great sea-facing beer garden that leads onto the beach. There are real ales on tap, brewed by Palmers in nearby Bridport, and decently priced pub grub (from £9). Daily 10am–11pm; food served noon–9pm.

Tierra Kitchen 1a Coombe St ☎ 01297 445189,

ⓦ tierrakitchen.co.uk. Overlooking the mill stream, *Tierra Kitchen* is a bright vegetarian restaurant serving a range of tasty seasonal dishes such as butternut squash and cheddar sausages, meze and vegetable tagine (£7–9) or evening meals like pistachio tortilla and pumpkin gnocchi (around £14). It also serves coffees, cakes and pastries. Thurs–Sat 11am–3pm & 6–10pm, Sun 11am–3pm.

Town Mill Bakery 2 Coombe St ☎ 01297 444754, ⓦ townmillbakery.com. A wonderful bakery/café serving a superb array of breads, cakes and muffins all freshly baked on the premises. The ingredients are mostly local and largely organic, with sublime breakfasts of home-made jam, boiled eggs and local honey – choose your bread and toast it yourself, then sit at the long wooden communal tables. Lunch includes home-made soup and pizzas (from £7). Tues–Sun 8.30am–4pm, til 8pm in summer.

Salisbury and around

SALISBURY, huddled below Wiltshire's chalky plain in the converging valleys of the Avon and Nadder, sprang into existence in the early thirteenth century, when the bishopric was moved from nearby **Old Sarum** (see p.216). Today, it looks from a distance very much as it did when Constable painted his celebrated view of it, and though traffic may clog its centre, this prosperous and well-kept city is designed on a pleasantly human scale, with no sprawling suburbs or high-rise buildings to challenge the supremacy of the cathedral's immense spire. The city's inspiring silhouette is best admired by taking a twenty-minute walk through the water meadows southwest of the centre to the suburb of **Harnham**.

North of Salisbury stretches a hundred thousand acres of chalky upland, known as **Salisbury Plain**; it's managed by the Ministry of Defence whose presence has protected it from development and intensive farming, thereby preserving species that are all but extinct elsewhere in England. Though largely deserted today, in previous times Salisbury Plain positively throbbed with communities. Stone Age, Bronze Age and Iron Age settlements left hundreds of burial mounds scattered over the chalklands, as well as major complexes at Danebury, Badbury, Figsbury, **Old Sarum**, and, of course, the great circle of **Stonehenge**, England's most famous historical monument. To the west, Salisbury's hinterland also includes one of Wiltshire's great country mansions, **Wilton House**, as well as Stourhead and Longleat Safari Park.

Salisbury Cathedral

Daily Mon–Sat 9am–5pm, Sun noon–4pm • **Chapter House** April–Oct Mon–Sat 9.30am–4.30pm, Sun 12.45–3.45pm; Nov–March Mon–Sat 10am–4.30pm, Sun 12.45–3.45pm • £6.50 suggested donation • **Tower tours** April–Sept Mon–Sat at least one daily, usually at 1.15pm, up to 5 a day at busy times; advance booking recommended on ☏ 01722 555120 • £10 • ⊛ salisburycathedral.org.uk

Begun in 1220, **Salisbury Cathedral** was mostly completed within forty years and is thus unusually consistent in its style, with one prominent exception – the **spire**, which was added a century later and, at 404ft, is the highest in England. Its survival is something of a miracle, for the foundations penetrate only about 6ft into marshy ground, and when Christopher Wren surveyed it he found the spire to be leaning almost 2.5ft out of true. He added further tie rods, which finally arrested the movement.

The interior is over-austere, but there's an amazing sense of space and light in its high nave, despite the sombre pillars of grey Purbeck marble, which are visibly bowing beneath the weight they bear. Monuments and carved tombs line the walls. Don't miss the octagonal **chapter house**, which displays a rare original copy of the Magna Carta, and whose walls are decorated with a frieze of scenes from the Old Testament.

The Close

Surrounding the cathedral is the **Close**, a peaceful precinct of lawns and mellow old buildings. Most of the houses have seemly Georgian facades, though some, like the Bishop's Palace and the deanery, date from the thirteenth century. **Mompesson House** (mid-March to Oct Mon–Wed, Sat & Sun 11am–5pm; £5.70, garden only £1; NT; ☏ 01722 420980, ⊛ nationaltrust.org.uk/mompesson-house), built by a wealthy merchant in 1701, contains some beautifully furnished eighteenth-century rooms and a superbly carved staircase. Also in the Close is the **King's House**, home to the **Salisbury and South Wiltshire Museum** (Oct–May Mon–Sat 10am–5pm; June–Sept Mon–Sat 10am–5pm & Sun noon–5pm; £5; ☏ 01722 332151, ⊛ salisburymuseum.org.uk) – an absorbing account of local history.

Around the Market Square

The Close's **North Gate** opens onto the centre's older streets, where narrow pedestrianized alleyways bear names like Fish Row and Salt Lane, indicative of their trading origin. Many half-timbered houses and inns have survived, and the last of four market crosses, **Poultry Cross**, stands on stilts in Silver Street, near the Market Square. The market, held on Tuesdays and Saturdays, still serves a large agricultural area, as it did in earlier times when the city grew wealthy on wool. Nearby, the church of **St Thomas** – named after Thomas à Becket – is worth a look inside for its carved timber roof and "Doom painting" over the chancel arch, depicting Christ presiding over the Last Judgment. Dating from 1475, it's the largest of its kind in England.

ARRIVAL AND DEPARTURE
SALISBURY

By train Trains from London arrive half a mile west of Salisbury's centre, on South Western Road.

Destinations Bath (hourly; 55min); Bristol (hourly; 1hr 10min); London Waterloo (every 30min; 1hr 30min); Portsmouth (hourly; 1hr 20min); Southampton (every 30min; 30min–50min).

By bus Buses stop at various sites around the city centre.

Destinations Bournemouth (Mon–Sat every 30min, Sun hourly; 1hr 15min); London (1 daily; 3hr 15min); Southampton (Mon–Sat hourly; 1hr 10min).

INFORMATION AND TOURS

Tourist office Fish Row, just off Market Square (Mon–Fri 9am–5pm, Sat 10am–4pm, Sun & bank hols 10am–2pm; 📞 01722 3428606, 🌐 visitwiltshire.co.uk) and is the starting point for informative and inexpensive guided walks of the city.

Bus tours Tours to Stonehenge and Old Sarum depart from the train station (bus only £14, with entry to Old Sarum and Stonehenge £28; 📞 01722 336855, 🌐 thestonehengetour.info) every 30min in summer, and hourly in winter.

ACCOMMODATION

★**Old Mill** Town Path, Harnham 📞 01722 327517, 🌐 signature-hospitality.com. The fully equipped rooms of this riverside pub have great views across the meadows to the cathedral. The location feels really rural but is just a short walk from the city centre. Real ales are on tap in the bar, and there's an adjoining restaurant serving good local food. **£110**

St Anns House 32–34 St Ann St ☎01722 335657, ⓦstannshouse.co.uk. A well-restored Georgian townhouse with stylish, comfortable rooms in a quiet street a short walk from the cathedral. **£90**

★**Sarum College** 19 The Close ☎01722 424800, ⓦsarum.ac.uk. By no means luxurious but in the best location in Salisbury, this friendly ecumenical college rents out simple en-suite doubles with views over The Close and cathedral, plus others without private facilities. There's also a decent common room, and breakfast is included. **£100**

EATING AND DRINKING

★**Gallery Café at Fisherton Mill** 108 Fisherton St ☎01722 500200, ⓦfishertonmill.co.uk. Great café within a renovated mill/art gallery serving delicious soups (£4.50), sandwiches on stone-baked bread (£5.60) and main courses such as salmon with artichoke (£13). Upstairs, you can watch artists at work in their studios, weaving and making jewellery. Tues–Fri 10am–5pm, Sat 9.30am–5pm. Also open for dinner sporadically; check website.

★**Haunch of Venison** 1 Minster St ☎01722 411313. One of the city's most atmospheric and historic pubs, with a wonderful warren of rooms, and a fireplace dating from 1588. The quirky, sloping-floored restaurant serves interesting dishes such as venison and redcurrant sausages (£11) and crackled pork belly with cider mustard sauce (£17). Daily 11am–11pm.

The Mill 7 The Maltings ☎01722 412127, ⓦgkpubs .co.uk/pubs-in-salisbury/mill-pub. Large, lively, popular pub whose main attraction is its lovely riverside location, right in the city centre. Standard pub meals, such as sausage and mash and bbq ribs, and real ales are available, as well as tea and coffee until 9pm. Mon–Thurs & Sun 11am–11pm, Fri & Sat 11am–midnight ; food served daily 11am–9pm.

Salisbury Chocolate Shop and Patisserie 33 High St ☎01722 327422, ⓦchocolatesandpatisserie.com. Long-established and popular café/chocolate shop with tables outside on a pedestrianized street. It serves delicious cakes and croissants baked daily – the hot chocolate is particularly tasty, and there's a good range of coffees too. Mon–Sat 9.30am–5pm, Sun noon–5pm.

Old Sarum

2 miles north of Salisbury • Daily: July & Aug 9am–6pm; Sept–June 10am–5pm • £4; EH • ☎01722 335398, ⓦenglish-heritage.org.uk

The ruins of **Old Sarum** occupy a bleak hilltop site. Possibly occupied up to five thousand years ago, then developed as an Iron Age fort whose double protective ditches remain, it was settled by Romans and Saxons before the Norman bishopric of Sherborne was moved here in the 1070s. Within a couple of decades a new **cathedral** had been consecrated at Old Sarum, and a large religious community was living alongside the soldiers in the central castle. Old Sarum was an uncomfortable place, parched and windswept, and in 1220 the dissatisfied clergy – additionally at loggerheads with the castle's occupants – appealed to the pope for permission to decamp to Salisbury (still known officially as New Sarum). When permission was granted, the stone from the cathedral was commandeered for Salisbury's gateways, and once the church had gone the population waned. By the nineteenth century Old Sarum was deserted, and today the dominant features of the site are huge earthworks, banks and ditches, with a broad trench encircling the rudimentary remains of the Norman palace, castle and cathedral.

Stonehenge

9 miles north of Salisbury • Daily: mid-March to May & Sept to mid-Oct 9.30am–7pm; June–Aug 9am–8pm; mid-Oct to mid-March 9.30am–5pm; last entry 2hr before closing; advance booking of timed tickets essential • £14.90; EH • ☎0870 333 1181, ⓦenglish -heritage.org.uk/Stonehenge • Shuttle buses to the site leave every 10min from the visitor centre

No ancient structure in England arouses more controversy than **Stonehenge**, a mysterious ring of monoliths. While archeologists argue over whether it was a place of ritual sacrifice and sun-worship, an astronomical calculator or a royal palace, the guardians of the site have struggled for years to accommodate its year-round visitors, particularly during the summer **solstice**, when crowds of 35,000 or more gather to watch the sunrise.

Access to the stones themselves is via a **shuttle-bus service** from a smart new **visitor centre** that opened in 2013, after years of debate and planning. This low-rise, environmentally sensitive pair of buildings includes a shop, café and **exhibition** space combining archeological remains from the area with high-tech interactive displays explaining the significance and history of it all. Outside, you can look round a cluster of recreated Neolithic houses, and try your hand at pulling a life-size Preseli bluestone. Perhaps a more fitting way to approach to the site, however, is on foot – it's a pleasant, way-marked thirty-minute walk across fields to the stones.

Wilton House

5 miles west of Salisbury • **House** Easter & May–Aug Sun–Thurs & bank hol Sat 11.30am–5pm • £14.50 (includes grounds) • **Grounds** Middle two weeks of April plus May to mid-Sept daily 11am–5.30pm • £6

The splendid **Wilton House** dominates the village of Wilton, renowned for its carpet industry. The original Tudor house, built for the first earl of Pembroke on the site of a dissolved Benedictine abbey, was ruined by fire in 1647 and rebuilt by Inigo Jones, whose classic hallmarks can be seen in the sumptuous Single Cube and Double Cube rooms, so called because of their precise dimensions.

The easel **paintings** are what makes Wilton really special, however – the collection includes works by Van Dyck, Rembrandt, two of the Brueghel family, Poussin, Andrea del Sarto and Tintoretto. In the grounds, the famous **Palladian Bridge** has been joined by various ancillary attractions including an adventure playground and an audiovisual show on the colourful earls of Pembroke.

Stourhead

25 miles west of Salisbury • **House** Mid-Feb to mid-March Sat & Sun 11am–3pm; mid March to Oct daily 11am–4.30pm; Nov daily 11am–3.30pm; Dec Fri–Sun 11am–3pm • £8.80, £14.70 with garden; NT • **Gardens** mid-April to Sept daily 9am–7pm; Oct to mid-April daily 9am–5pm • £8.80, £14.70 with house • **King Alfred's Tower** March–Oct Sat & Sun noon–4pm • £3.60 • ☎ 01747 841152, ⓦ nationaltrust.org.uk/stourhead

Landscape gardening was a favoured mode of display among the grandest eighteenth-century landowners, and **Stourhead** is one of the most accomplished examples of the genre. The house itself is of minor interest, though it has some good Chippendale furniture, but it is the stunning **gardens** that are the highlight. At the entrance, you can pick up a map detailing a lovely two-mile walk around the lake. The estate itself is vast and includes a pub, a church, a farm shop (a good place to pick up a picnic), plus **King Alfred's Tower**, three miles or so from the main entrance (you can drive round the estate and park by the tower, if it's too far to walk). Built in 1772, it is one of England's oldest follies, and you can climb the two hundred or so steps up to the top for fine views across the estate and into neighbouring counties.

Longleat

27 miles west of Salisbury • Opening hours and closing days vary throughout the season, but are generally 10am–5pm, 6pm or 7pm; check website for exact times and days • House and grounds only £13.95, all attractions £26.77 • ☎ 01985 844400, ⓦ longleat.co.uk

The African savanna intrudes into the bucolic Wiltshire countryside at **Longleat** safari and adventure park. In 1946 the sixth marquess of Bath became the first stately-home owner to open his house to the paying public on a regular basis, and in 1966 he caused even more amazement when Longleat's Capability Brown landscapes were turned into England's first drive-through **safari park,** with lions, tigers, giraffes and rhinos on show, plus monkeys clambering all over your car. Other attractions followed, including a large hedge maze, a *Doctor Who* exhibition, high-tech simulators, and the seventh marquess's saucy murals (children not admitted). Beyond the razzmatazz, there's an exquisitely furnished Elizabethan house, with an enormous library and a fine collection of pictures, including Titian's *Holy Family*.

3

STONEHENGE – A BRIEF HISTORY

Some people may find **Stonehenge** underwhelming, but understanding a little of its history and ancient significance gives an insight into its mystical appeal. What exists today is only a small part of the original prehistoric complex, as many of the outlying stones were probably plundered by medieval and later farmers for building materials. The **construction** of Stonehenge is thought to have taken place in several stages. In about 3000 BC the outer circular bank and ditch were built, just inside which was dug a ring of 56 pits, which at a later date were filled with a mixture of earth and human ash. Around 2500 BC the first stones were raised within the earthworks, comprising approximately forty great blocks of dolerite (bluestone), whose ultimate source was Preseli in Wales. Some archeologists have suggested that these monoliths were found lying on Salisbury Plain, having been borne down from the Welsh mountains by a glacier in the last Ice Age, but the lack of any other glacial debris on the plain would seem to disprove this theory. It really does seem to be the case that the stones were cut from quarries in Preseli and dragged or floated here on rafts, a prodigious task that has defeated recent attempts to emulate it.

The crucial phase in the creation of the site came during the next six hundred years, when the incomplete bluestone circle was transformed by the construction of a circle of 25 **trilithons** (two uprights crossed by a lintel) and an inner horseshoe formation of five trilithons. Hewn from Marlborough Downs sandstone, these colossal stones (called sarsens), ranging from 13ft to 21ft in height and weighing up to thirty tons, were carefully dressed and worked – for example, to compensate for perspectival distortion the uprights have a slight swelling in the middle, the same trick as the builders of the Parthenon were to employ hundreds of years later. More bluestones were arranged in various patterns within the outer circle over this period. The purpose of all this work remains baffling, however. The symmetry and location of the site (a slight rise in a flat valley with even views of the horizon in all directions) as well as its alignment towards the points of sunrise and sunset on the summer and winter solstices tend to support the supposition that it was some sort of observatory or time-measuring device. The site ceased to be used at around 1600 BC, and by the Middle Ages it had become a "landmark". Recent excavations have revealed the existence of a much larger settlement here than had previously been thought – the most substantial Neolithic village of this period to be found on the British mainland in fact – covering a wide area.

Avebury

The village of **AVEBURY** stands in the midst of a **stone circle** (free access) that rivals Stonehenge – the individual stones are generally smaller, but the circle itself is much wider and more complex. A massive earthwork 20ft high and 1400ft across encloses the main circle, which is approached by four causeways across the inner ditch, two of them leading into wide avenues stretching over a mile beyond the circle. It was probably built soon after 2500 BC, and presumably had a similar ritual or religious function to Stonehenge. The structure of Avebury's diffuse circle is quite difficult to grasp, but there are plans on the site, and the nearby museum (see below) has further details and background on the site.

Alexander Keiller Museum

Daily: April–Oct 10am–6pm; Nov–March 10am–4pm • £4.90; NT • ☎ 01672 539250, ⓦ nationaltrust.org.uk/avebury

You can get an excellent overview of the Avebury stones and their significance at the nearby **Alexander Keiller Museum**, at the western entrance. The museum is housed in two separate buildings: the **Stables Gallery** houses some of Keiller's original finds, while the seventeenth-century **Barn Gallery** has exhibits on local archeology, interactive displays plus activities for children.

Silbury Hill and West Kennet Long Barrow

Just outside Avebury, the neat green mound of **Silbury Hill** is disregarded by the majority of drivers whizzing by on the A4. At 130ft it's no great height, but when you realize it's the largest prehistoric artificial mound in Europe, and was made using nothing more than primitive spades, it commands more respect. It was probably constructed around 2600 BC, and though no one knows quite what it was for, the likelihood is that it was a burial mound. You can't actually walk on the hill – having admired it briefly from the car park, cross the road to the footpath that leads half a mile to the **West Kennet Long Barrow** (free access; NT & EH). Dating from about 3250 BC, this was definitely a chamber tomb – nearly fifty burials have been discovered here.

ACCOMMODATION AND EATING | AVEBURY

Circles Next to the Barn Gallery ☎01672 539250. This National Trust café is your best bet for an inexpensive lunch, offering good meals and snacks, with plenty of veggie options and, of course, tasty cakes and cream teas. There's indoor seating in a converted farm building, and outdoor tables in the courtyard. Daily: April–Oct 10am–5.30pm; Nov–March 10am–4pm.

Manor Farm High St ☎01672 539294, ⓦmanor farmavebury.com. A comfortable B&B on a working farm right in the centre of the village. There are three rooms, two of which have views over the Avebury stones, and there's also a private guests' sitting room. **£100**

Lacock

LACOCK, twelve miles west of Avebury, is the perfect English feudal village, albeit one gentrified by the National Trust and besieged by tourists all summer, partly due to its fame as a location for several films and TV series – the recent *Harry Potter* films among others. The village's most famous son is photography pioneer **Henry Fox Talbot**, a member of the dynasty that has lived in the local abbey since it passed to Sir William Sharington on the Dissolution of the Monasteries in 1539. Fox Talbot was the first person to produce a photographic negative, and the **Fox Talbot Museum**, in a sixteenth-century barn by the abbey gates (daily: mid-Feb to Oct 10.30am–5.30pm; Nov to mid-Feb 11am–4pm; £12.50 including abbey, abbey garden and cloisters; NT; ☎01249 73045, ⓦnationaltrust.org.uk/lacock), captures something of the excitement he must have experienced as the dim outline of an oriel window in the abbey imprinted itself on a piece of silver nitrate paper.

The **abbey** itself (mid-Feb to Oct daily except Tues 11am–5pm; Nov to mid-Feb Sat & Sun noon–4pm; cloisters and grounds same hours as Fox Talbot museum; £12.50 including museum; NT; ☎01249 73045, ⓦnationaltrust.org.uk/lacock), preserves a few monastic fragments amid the eighteenth-century Gothic, while the church of **St Cyriac** (free access) contains the opulent tomb of Sir William Sharington himself, buried beneath a splendid barrel-vaulted roof.

ARRIVAL AND DEPARTURE | LACOCK

By bus The #234 runs hourly from Chippenham and Frome, stopping outside the *George Inn* (ⓦfirstgroup.com).

ACCOMMODATION AND EATING

Beechfield House Hotel Beanacre, 2 miles south of Lacock ☎01225 703700, ⓦbeechfieldhouse.co.uk. This lovely country house hotel has comfortable rooms, an excellent restaurant and a heated outdoor pool all set in attractive grounds. It has family rooms and the service is friendly but professional. **£150**

George Inn 4 West St ☎01249 730263. A rambling, attractive pub with roaring fires and a dog-wheel (the dog powered the wheel to turn a spit over the fire). Good for a drink, with a variety of guest ales, plus decent pub food,

such as home-made pie of the day (£11.50). Mon–Thurs 11am–3pm & 6–11pm, Fri & Sat 11am–11pm, Sun 11am–10.30pm; food served noon–2.30pm & 6–9pm (closes 8.30pm on Sun).

Lacock Pottery The Tanyard, Church St ☎01249 730266, ⓦlacockbedandbreakfast.com. Three comfortable B&B rooms in a lovely old building overlooking the church and the village. Breakfasts are good, featuring home-made bread and jams. **£90**, or **£100** at weekends

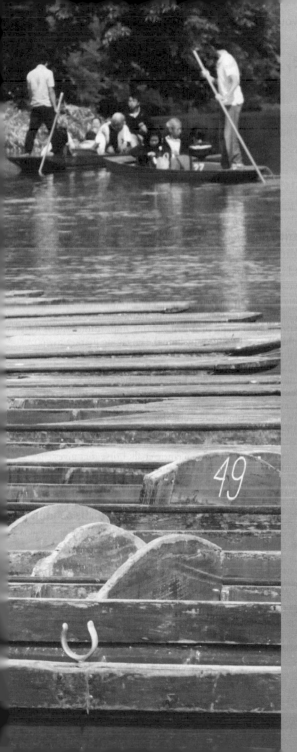

Oxfordshire, the Cotswolds and around

PUNTING IN OXFORD

Oxfordshire, the Cotswolds and around

About sixty miles northwest of London, the small university city of Oxford is one of England's great urban set-pieces, presenting as impressive a collection of Gothic, Classical and Revival architecture as anywhere in Europe. Oxford anchors a diverse swathe of terrain that reaches across central southern England straddling the Chiltern Hills, a picturesque band of chalk uplands on the fringes of the capital. Close to the orbital M25 motorway this is commuter country, but further out a rural spirit survives from England's pre-industrial past, felt most tangibly in the Cotswolds, rolling hills between Oxford and Cheltenham that encompass some of the country's most celebrated landscapes and photogenic villages.

Covering much of **Oxfordshire** and **Gloucestershire**, the picture-postcard **Cotswolds** region is dotted with glorious honey-coloured villages, old churches and handsome stone mansions, with scenic drives galore and plenty of walking opportunities, not least on the long-distance Cotswolds Way. Highlights include the engaging market town of **Chipping Campden**, the delightful village of **Northleach** and bustling **Cirencester**. Within striking distance of Oxford are handsome **Woodstock**, a little town that lies alongside one of England's most imposing country homes, **Blenheim Palace**, and further south, **Henley-on-Thames**, an attractive spot on the river, famous for its regatta. To the west lies **Cheltenham**, an appealing Regency spa town famous for its horse-racing that serves as a base for visits to **Gloucester** cathedral.

Striking west from the Chilterns across the North Wessex Downs is the 85-mile-long **Ridgeway**, a prehistoric track – and now a national trail possessing a string of prehistoric sites, the most extraordinary being the gigantic chalk horse that gives the **Vale of White Horse** its name. Bordering south Oxfordshire, **Berkshire** has the royal residence of **Windsor Castle** as its focus, but can also offer a fine gallery in the Thames-side village of **Cookham**.

GETTING AROUND OXFORDSHIRE, THE COTSWOLDS & AROUND

By train There are mainline train services from London's Paddington Station to Reading, Oxford, Cheltenham and Gloucester; trains from Paddington also stop at Cotswold villages including Kingham (midway between Burford and Stow-on-the-Wold) and Moreton-in-Marsh (between Stow-on-the-Wold and Chipping Campden). Oxford is also on the main cross-country line between Birmingham and Reading/Southampton. Chiltern line trains from London Marylebone also serve Oxford, as well as smaller stations in Buckinghamshire. Branch lines supplement the main routes.

By bus Long-distance buses stick mostly to the motorways, providing an efficient service to all the larger towns, but local services between the villages are patchy, sometimes nonexistent.

By car The Cotswolds are enclosed by the M5, M4 and M40, which, along with the M1 and A1(M) to the east, provide easy access.

STONE COTTAGES, CIRENCESTER

Highlights

❶ Oxford One of Britain's most captivating cities, with dozens of historic colleges, memorable museums and an enjoyably lively undergraduate atmosphere. See p.225

❷ Windsor Castle The oldest and largest inhabited castle in the world – still an important ceremonial residence of the Queen, in the Berkshire countryside outside London See p.239

❸ Chipping Campden Perfectly preserved medieval wool town, with honey-coloured houses lining its historic main street. See p.248

❹ Cirencester Self-styled "Capital of the Cotswolds", with a bustling marketplace overlooked by the superb Gothic church of St John the Baptist. **See p.250**

❺ Festivals in Cheltenham Cheltenham's three-day National Hunt Festival is one of the highlights of the British racing calendar, while the town also boasts lively festivals dedicated to folk, jazz, classical music, literature and science. **See p.253**

❻ Gloucester Cathedral The earliest – and one of the finest – examples of English Perpendicular architecture, topped by a magnificent tower. **See p.256**

HIGHLIGHTS ARE MARKED ON THE MAP ON P.224

OXFORDSHIRE, THE COTSWOLDS & AROUND

HIGHLIGHTS

1. Oxford
2. Windsor Castle
3. Chipping Campden
4. Cirencester
5. Festivals in Cheltenham
6. Gloucester Cathedral

Oxford

When visitors think of **OXFORD**, they almost always imagine its **university**, revered as one of the world's great academic institutions, inhabiting honey-coloured stone buildings set around ivy-clad quadrangles. The image is accurate enough, but although the university dominates central Oxford both physically and spiritually, the wider city has an entirely different character, its economy built chiefly on the **factories** of Cowley, south of the centre. It was here that Britain's first mass-produced cars were produced in the 1920s and, although there have been more downs than ups in recent years, the plants are still vitally important to the area.

Oxford should be high on anyone's itinerary, and can keep you occupied for several days. The **colleges** include some of England's finest architecture, and the city also has some excellent **museums** and a good range of bars and restaurants.

Christ Church College

St Aldates • Mon–Sat 10am–4.30pm, Sun 2–4.30pm • July & Aug £8.50, rest of year £7–8; discounts apply if you visit at times when the hall and/or cathedral are closed • ☎ 01865 276492, ⓦ chch.ox.ac.uk

Stretching along the east side of St Aldates is the main façade of **Christ Church College**, whose distinctive Tom Tower was added by Christopher Wren in 1681 to house the weighty "Great Tom" bell. The tower lords it over the main entrance of what is Oxford's largest and arguably most prestigious college, but visitors have to enter from the south, a signed five-minute walk away – just beyond the tiny War Memorial

4

OXFORD'S COLLEGES

So where, exactly, is **Oxford University**? Everywhere – and nowhere. The university itself is nothing more than an administrative body, setting examinations and awarding degrees. Although it has its own offices (on Wellington Square), they are of no particular interest. What draws all the attention are the university's constituent **colleges** – 38 of them (plus another six religious foundations known as Permanent Private Halls), most occupying historic buildings scattered throughout the city centre. It is they which hold the 800-year-old history of the university, and exemplify its spirit.

The origins of the university are obscure, but it seems that the reputation of **Henry I**, the so-called "Scholar King", helped attract students in the early twelfth century. The first **colleges**, founded mostly by rich bishops, were essentially ecclesiastical institutions and this was reflected in collegiate rules and regulations – until 1877 lecturers were not allowed to marry, and women were not granted degrees until 1920.

There are common **architectural features** among the colleges, with the students' rooms and most of the communal areas – chapels, halls (dining rooms) and libraries – arranged around quadrangles (**quads**). Each, however, has its own character and often a label, whether it's the richest (St John's), most left-wing (Wadham) or most public-school-dominated (Christ Church). Collegiate rivalries are long established, usually revolving around sports, and tension between the city and the university – "Town" and "Gown" – has existed as long as the university itself.

EXPLORING THE COLLEGES

All the more popular colleges have restricted **opening hours** – and may close totally during academic functions. Most now also impose an **admission charge**, while some (such as University and Queens) are out of bounds to outsiders. Regardless of published rules, it's always worth asking at the **porter's lodge**, at the main entrance of each college: porters have ultimate discretion and if you ask they may let you look around. One nice way to gain access is to attend choral evensong, held during term time and offering the chance to enjoy superb music in historic surroundings for free. New College Choir is generally reckoned to be the best, while Queens College and Merton are also good. Some colleges also **rent out student rooms** in the holidays (see p.234).

OXFORD

4

ACCOMMODATION

Bath Place	4
Buttery	5
Central Backpackers	8
Isis Guesthouse	11
Malmaison	10
Old Bank	9
Old Parsonage	1
Oxford Backpackers	6
Oxford Youth Hostel	7
The Randolph	3
Richmond	2

RESTAURANTS

Branca	1
Chiang Mai Kitchen	11
Edamame	3
Gee's	2
Pie Minister	7
Quod	10
Turf Street Kitchen	4

CAFÉS

Ben's Cookies	9
Missing Bean	8
News Café	5
Vaults & Garden	6

PUBS & BARS

The Bear	5
Eagle & Child	2
Lamb & Flag	3
Raoul's	1
Turf Tavern	4

CLUBS & LIVE MUSIC

| Café Tarifa | 6 |
| O2 Academy | 7 |

0   100
yards

Garden and at the top of Christ Church Meadow. Don't be surprised if you have to queue to get in. This is the most touristy of all the Oxford Colleges, particularly popular thanks to its Harry Potter connections: many scenes from the films were shot here, while a studio recreation of the college's Hall provided the set of Hogwarts Hall.

From the entrance it's a short step to the striking **Tom Quad**, the largest quad in Oxford – so large in fact that the Royalists penned up their mobile larder of cattle here during the Civil War. Guarded by the Tom Tower, the quad's soft, honey-coloured stone makes a harmonious whole, but it was actually built in two main phases with the southern side dating back to Wolsey, the north finally finished in the 1660s. A wide stone staircase in the quad's southeast corner beneath a stupendous fan-vaulted ceiling leads up to the **Hall**, the grandest refectory in Oxford with a fanciful hammer-beam roof and a set of stern portraits of past scholars by a roll call of famous artists, including Reynolds, Gainsborough and Millais. Albert Einstein, William Gladstone and no fewer than twelve other British prime ministers were educated here.

Oxford Cathedral

Christ Church's college chapel is otherwise known as **Oxford Cathedral**. The Anglo-Saxons built a church on this site in the seventh century as part of the priory of St Frideswide (Oxford's patron saint), although the present building dates mainly from 1120–80. The priory was suppressed in 1524, but the church survived. It's unusually discordant, with all sorts of bits and bobs from different periods, but fascinating all the same. The dominant features are the sturdy circular columns and rounded arches of the Normans, but there are also early Gothic pointed arches and the chancel ceiling is a particularly fine example of fifteenth-century stone vaulting.

Christ Church Picture Gallery

Canterbury Quad, Christ Church • July–Sept Mon–Sat 10.30am–5pm, Sun 2–5pm; June same times but closed Tues; Oct–May Mon & Wed–Sat 10.30am–1pm & 2–4.30pm, Sun 2–4.30pm • £4, or £2 with a Christ Church admission ticket • Free tour Mon 2.30pm • ☎ 01865 276172, ⓦ www.chch.ox.ac.uk/gallery

Hidden away in Christ Church's pocket-sized Canterbury Quad is the college's **Picture Gallery**. The extensive collection comprises around three hundred paintings and two thouand drawings, with fine works by artists from Italy and the Netherlands including paintings by Tintoretto, Van Dyck and Frans Hals and drawings by da Vinci, Dürer, Raphael and Michelangelo. A gateway off Canterbury Quad exits to Oriel Square.

Christ Church Meadow

Christ Church Meadow fills in the tapering gap between the rivers Cherwell and Thames. If you decide to delay visiting Christ Church College, you can take a stroll east along Broad Walk for the Cherwell or keep straight down tree-lined (and more appealing) New Walk for the Thames.

Merton College

Merton St • Mon–Fri 2–5pm, Sat & Sun 10am–5pm • £3 • ☎ 01865 276310, ⓦ merton.ox.ac.uk

Merton College is historically the city's most important. Balliol and University colleges may have been founded earlier, but it was Merton – opened in 1264 – which set the model for colleges in both Oxford and Cambridge, being the first to gather its students and tutors together in one place. Furthermore, unlike the other two, Merton retains some of its original medieval buildings, with the best of the thirteenth-century architecture clustered around **Mob Quad**, a charming courtyard with mullioned windows and Gothic doorways to the right of the Front Quad. From the Mob Quad, an archway leads through to the **Chapel**, dating from 1290, inside which you'll find the funerary plaque of Thomas Bodley, founder of Oxford's famous Bodleian Library (see p.230).

Magdalen College

High St • Daily: July–Sept noon–7pm, rest of year 1–6pm or dusk • £5 • ☎ 01865 276000, ⓦ magd.ox.ac.uk

At the east end of the High Street stands **Magdalen College** (pronounced mawdlin), whose gaggle of stone buildings is overshadowed by its chunky medieval bell tower. Steer right from the entrance and you reach the **Chapel**, which has a handsome reredos, though you have to admire it through the windows of an ungainly stone screen. The adjacent **cloisters** are adorned by standing figures, some biblical and others folkloric, most notably a tribe of grotesques. Magdalen also boasts better **grounds** than most other colleges, with a bridge – at the back of the cloisters – spanning the River Cherwell to join **Addison's Walk**. You can hire punts from beneath **Magdalen Bridge**, beside the college.

Botanic Garden

Rose Lane • Daily 9am–6pm; March, April, Sept & Oct closes 5pm; Nov–Feb closes 4pm • £4.50 • ⓦ www.botanic-garden.ox.ac.uk

Bounded by a curve of the River Cherwell, Oxford's **Botanic Garden** is the oldest of its kind in England, established in 1621. Still enclosed by its original high wall, it comprises several different zones, from a lily pond, a bog garden and a rock garden through to borders of bearded irises and variegated plants. There are also six large **glasshouses** housing tropical and carnivorous species.

New College

New College Lane • Daily: Easter–Oct 11am–5pm, rest of year 2–4pm • Easter–Oct £3, rest of year free • ☎ 01865 279555, ⓦ new.ox.ac.uk

Founded in 1379, **New College** is entered via the large but rather plain **Front Quad**. On the left side of the quad rises the magnificent Perpendicular **Chapel**, arguably the finest in Oxford. The ante-chapel contains some superb fourteenth-century stained glass and the west window – of 1778 – holds an intriguing Nativity scene based on a design by Sir Joshua Reynolds. Beneath it stands the wonderful 1951 sculpture *Lazarus* by Jacob Epstein. Immediately past the chapel lies the college's peaceful **cloisters**.

An archway on the east side of the Front Quad leads through to the modest **Garden Quad**, with the thick flowerbeds of the **College Garden** beckoning beyond. The north side of the garden is flanked by the largest and best preserved section of Oxford's medieval **city wall**. The conspicuous earthen **mound** in the middle is a later decorative addition, not medieval.

4

TAKING TO THE WATER

Punting is a favourite summer pastime among both students and visitors, but handling a punt – a flat-bottomed boat ideal for the shallow waters of the Thames and Cherwell rivers – requires some practice. The punt is propelled and steered with a long pole, which beginners inevitably get stuck in riverbed mud: if this happens, let go of it and paddle back, or you're likely to be dragged overboard.

There are two central **boat rental** places: Magdalen Bridge Boathouse (☎ 01865 202643, ⓦ oxfordpunting.co.uk), beside the Cherwell at the east end of the High Street; and Salter's Steamers (☎ 01865 243421, ⓦ salterssteamers.co.uk) at Folly Bridge, south of Christ Church. Opening times vary: call for details, or try and arrive early (around 10am) to avoid the queues which build up on sunny summer afternoons. At either expect to **pay** £20 per hour plus a deposit of about £50; ID is required. Punts can take a maximum of five people: four sitting and one punting.

Salter's Steamers also runs **passenger boats** along the Thames from Folly Bridge downstream to Abingdon, about eight miles south, between late May and mid-September. There are two boats daily (4hr return; £20). Oxford River Cruises (☎ 01865 987147, ⓦ oxfordrivercruises.com) also sets sail from Folly Bridge (April–Oct): details of their half-dozen cruises – including a "lunchtime picnic" trip – are online.

Bridge of Sighs

Spanning **New College Lane** a few paces off Catte Street, you can't miss the iconic **Bridge of Sighs**, an archway completed in 1914 to link two buildings of Hertford College. In truth it bears little resemblance to its Venetian namesake but nonetheless has a certain Italianate elegance. It was designed, so the story goes, to give residents of Hertford's older buildings to the south a way to reach the newfangled flushing toilets being installed across the road without having to venture outdoors.

Bodleian Library

Broad St • Closed to the public; some rooms accessible on tours (see below) • ☎ 01865 287400, ⓦ bodley.ox.ac.uk

Christopher Wren's pupil Nicholas Hawksmoor designed the **Clarendon Building**, a domineering, solidly symmetrical edifice at the east end of Broad Street, completed in 1713. It now forms part of the **Bodleian Library**. Founded by scholar Sir Thomas Bodley in 1602, the Bodleian is the UK's largest library after the British Library in London, with an estimated 117 miles of shelving. It includes the modernist 1930s **New Bodleian** (now known as the **Weston Library** after extensive renovation) directly opposite the Clarendon, designed by Sir Giles Gilbert Scott and linked to the main building by tunnels. As one of the UK and Ireland's six copyright libraries, the Bodleian must find room for a copy of every book, pamphlet, magazine and newspaper published in Britain.

4

TOURS
BODLEIAN LIBRARY

An **audioguide** is available for self-guided tours of the quad and Divinity School (40min; £2.50) — or there's a host of **guided tours** to those few areas of the Bodleian open to the public. It's always advisable to **book in advance** with the tours office (Mon–Sat 9am–4pm, Sun 11am–4pm; ☎ 01865 287400, ⓦ www.bodley.ox.ac.uk), located inside the Great Gate on Catte Street.

Mini tour 30min; £5. Divinity School and Duke Humfrey's Library. Mon–Sat 3.30pm, 4pm & 4.40pm, Sun 12.45pm, 2.15pm, 3.15pm, 4pm & 4.40pm.
Standard tour 1hr; £7. Divinity School, Duke Humfrey's Library and Convocation House. Mon–Sat 10.30am, 11.30am, 1pm & 2pm, Sun 11.30am, 2pm & 3pm.
Extended tour "Upstairs Downstairs" 1hr 30min;

£13. Divinity School, Duke Humfrey's Library, Convocation House, Gladstone Link, Radcliffe Camera. Wed & Sat 9.15am; booking essential.
Extended tour "Reading rooms" 1hr 30min; £13. Divinity School, Duke Humfrey's Library, Convocation House, Upper Reading Room. Sun 11.15am & 1.15pm; booking essential.

Old Schools Quadrangle

Mon–Fri 9am–5pm, Sat 9am–4.30pm, Sun 11am–5pm • Free

Behind the Clarendon Building you enter the Bodleian's beautifully proportioned **Old Schools Quadrangle**, completed in 1619 in an ornate Jacobean-Gothic style and offering access to all of the university's academic faculties, or schools: the name of each is lettered in gold above the doorways which ring the quad. On the east side rises the handsome **Tower of the Five Orders**, its tiers of columns in ascending order Tuscan, Doric, Ionic, Corinthian and Composite.

The Divinity School

Mon–Fri 9am–5pm, Sat 9am–4.30pm, Sun 11am–5pm • £1

Entered from the quad, the **Divinity School** is a highlight. Begun in 1424, this exceptional room is a masterpiece of late Gothic architecture, featuring an extravagant vaulted ceiling adorned with a riot of pendants and 455 decorative bosses. Built to house the university's theology faculty, it was, until the nineteenth century, also where degree candidates were questioned about their subject by two interlocutors, with a professor acting as umpire. Few interiors in Oxford are as impressive.

The Sheldonian Theatre

Broad St • Feb–Nov Mon–Sat 10am–4.30pm, July & Aug also Sun 10.30am–4pm; Dec & Jan Mon–Fri 10am–3.30pm • £3.50 • Ⓦ www.sheldon.ox.ac.uk

At the east end of Broad Street, the **Sheldonian Theatre** is ringed by railings topped with a line of glum-looking, pop-eyed classical busts. The Sheldonian was Christopher Wren's first major work, a reworking of the Theatre of Marcellus in Rome, semicircular at the back and rectangular at the front. It was conceived in 1663, when the 31-year-old Wren's main job was as professor of astronomy. Designed as a stage for university ceremonies, nowadays it also functions as a concert hall, but the interior lacks much sense of drama, and even the views from the cupola are disappointing.

Museum of the History of Science

Broad St • Tues–Fri noon–5pm, Sat 10am–5pm, Sun 2–5pm • Free • Ⓦ mhs.ox.ac.uk

The classical heads that shield the Sheldonian Theatre (see above) continue along the front of the fascinating **Museum of the History of Science**, whose two floors display an amazing clutter of antique microscopes and astrolabes, sundials, quadrants and sextants. The highlights are Elizabeth I's own astrolabe and a blackboard used by Einstein in 1931, still covered with his scribbled equations.

Trinity College

Broad St • Not set hours, usually Mon–Fri 9am–12.15pm & 1.30–4pm, Sat & Sun 1–4pm • £2 • ☎ 01865 279900, Ⓦ trinity.ox.ac.uk

Trinity College is fronted by three dinky lodge-cottages. Behind them the manicured lawn of the Front Quad stretches back to the richly decorated **Chapel**, awash with Baroque stucco work. Its high altar is flanked by an exquisite example of the work of Grinling Gibbons – a distinctive performance, with cherubs' heads peering out from delicate foliage. Behind the chapel stands **Durham Quad**, an attractive ensemble of old stone buildings begun at the end of the seventeenth century.

The Radcliffe Camera

Radcliffe Sq • Closed to the public; accessible only on Bodleian Library's extended tour: Wed & Sat 9.15am • £13 • booking essential • ☎ 01865 287400, Ⓦ bodley.ox.ac.uk

The mighty rotunda of the **Radcliffe Camera**, built between 1737 and 1748 by James Gibbs, architect of London's St Martin-in-the-Fields church, displays no false modesty. Dr John Radcliffe, royal physician (to William III), was, according to a contemporary diarist, "very ambitious of glory": when he died in 1714 he bequeathed a mountain of money for the construction of a library. Gibbs was one of the few British architects of the period to have been trained in Rome and his design is thoroughly Italian in style, its limestone columns ascending to a delicate balustrade, decorated with pin-prick urns and encircling a lead-sheathed dome. Taken over by the Bodleian Library in 1860, it now houses a reading-room, accessible to the public only on the Bodleian's "extended tour" (see opposite).

All Souls College

High St • Mon–Fri 2–4pm, closed Aug • Free • ☎ 01865 279379, Ⓦ all-souls.ox.ac.uk

Running the entire east side of Radcliffe Square, its immense chapel windows the epitome of the Perpendicular Gothic style, **All Souls College** is one of the quietest places in central Oxford: it has no undergraduates. Uniquely, it admits only "fellows" – that is, distinguished scholars – either by election of existing fellows, or by an exam reputed to be the hardest in the world. The result is that All Souls is generally silent. Sightseers gather at the elaborate gates on Radcliffe Square, wondering how to gain access to the lovely quad beyond: turn right and walk around the corner onto High Street to reach

4

the **college entrance**. This gives onto the modest Front Quad, location of the spectacular fifteenth-century **chapel**, with its gilded hammerbeam roof and neck-cricking reredos (though all its figures are Victorian replacements). Move through to the spacious **North Quad**, the object of all that admiration: Hawksmoor's soaring Gothic twin towers face the Radcliffe Square gates, while ahead, the Codrington Library – also Hawksmoor – sports a conspicuous, brightly decorated sundial designed by Wren.

Church of St Mary the Virgin

High St • Daily 9am–5pm, July & Aug until 6pm • Free; tower £3 • ⓦ www.university-church.ox.ac.uk

On the High Street behind Radcliffe Square, **St Mary the Virgin** is a hotchpotch of architectural styles, but mostly dates from the fifteenth century. The church's saving graces are its elaborate, thirteenth-century pinnacled spire and its distinctive Baroque **porch**, flanked by chunky corkscrewed pillars. The interior is disappointingly mundane, though the carved poppy heads on the choir stalls are of some historical interest: the tips were brusquely squared off when a platform was installed here in 1555 to stage the heresy trial of Cranmer, Latimer and Ridley, leading Protestants who had run foul of Queen Mary. The church's other diversion is the **tower**, with wonderful views.

Covered Market

High St • Mon–Sat 9am–5.30pm, Sun 10am–4pm • ⓦ oxford-coveredmarket.co.uk

For refreshment on the hoof – as well as a fascinating glimpse into the everyday life of Oxford away from the colleges – drop into the **Covered Market**, wedged between the High Street and Market Street. Opened in 1774, it remains full of atmosphere, home to butchers, bakers, fishmongers, greengrocers and cheese sellers as well as cafés, clothes boutiques and shoe shops.

Carfax Tower

Carfax • Daily 10am–5.30pm, Oct closes 4.30pm, March closes 4pm, Nov–Feb closes 3pm • £2.20

The busy **Carfax** crossroads is a fulcrum, where chiefly "gown" architecture along the High Street to the east is balanced by the distinctly "town" atmosphere of Cornmarket and Queen Street to the west. This has been a crossroads for more than a thousand years: roads met here in Saxon times, and the name "Carfax" derives from the Latin *quadrifurcus* ("four-forked"). The junction is overlooked by a square thirteenth-century **tower**, adorned by a pair of clocktower jacks. You can **climb** it for wide views over the centre, though other vantage points – principally St Mary's (see above) – have the edge.

St Michael-at-the-Northgate

Cornmarket • Daily 10.30am–5pm, Nov–March closes 4pm • Church free; tower £2.50 • ⓦ www.smng.org.uk

Storming north of Carfax, **Cornmarket** is now a busy pedestrianized shopping strip lined with familiar high-street stores. There's precious little here to fire the imagination until you reach **St Michael-at-the-Northgate**, a church recorded in the Domesday Book, with a late fourteenth-century font where Shakespeare's godson was baptized in 1606. The church's Saxon **tower**, built in 1050, is Oxford's oldest surviving building; enter for rooftop views and to see an eleventh-century sheela-na-gig.

Ashmolean Museum

Beaumont St • Tues–Sun 10am–5pm • Free • ☎ 01865 278000, ⓦ www.ashmolean.org

Second only to the British Museum in London, the **Ashmolean Museum** occupies a mammoth Neoclassical building on the corner of Beaumont Street and St Giles. It grew from the collections of the magpie-like **John Tradescant**, gardener to Charles I and an energetic traveller, and today it possesses a vast and far-reaching collection covering everything from Minoan vases to Stradivarius violins.

Light and airy modern galleries cover four floors (pick up a **plan** at reception). The "orientation" gallery in the basement provides a thematic overview of the museum, while the ground floor houses the museum's "ancient world" exhibits, including its superb Egyptology collection and an imposing room full of Greek sculptures. Floor 1 is dedicated to Mediterranean, Indian and Islamic artefacts (Hindu bronzes, Iranian pottery and so on) while floor 2 is mainly European, including the museum's wide-ranging collection of Dutch, Flemish and Italian paintings. Floor 3 focuses on European art since 1800, including works by Sickert, Pissarro and the Pre-Raphaelites.

Oxford University Museum of Natural History

Parks Road • Daily 10am–5pm • Free • ☎ 01865 272950, ⓦ www.oum.ox.ac.uk

From the Ashmolean, it's a brief walk north up St Giles to the *Lamb & Flag* pub, beside which an alley cuts east through to the **Oxford University Museum of Natural History**. The building, constructed under the guidance of John Ruskin, looks like a cross between a railway station and a church – and the same applies inside, where a High Victorian-Gothic fusion of cast iron and glass features soaring columns and capitals decorated with animal and plant motifs. Exhibits include some impressive dinosaur skeletons, models of exotic beasties, a four-billion-year-old meteorite, and so on.

Pitt Rivers Museum

Parks Road • Mon noon–4.30pm, Tues–Sun 10am–4.30pm • Free • ☎ 01865 270927, ⓦ www.prm.ox.ac.uk

Oxford's eye-popping **Pitt Rivers Museum** is housed in the same building as the University Museum of Natural History, accessed via a door at the rear of the ground-floor level. Founded in 1884, this is one of the world's finest ethnographic museums and an extraordinary relic of the Victorian age, arranged like an exotic junk shop with each intricately crammed cabinet labelled meticulously by hand. The exhibits – brought to England by, among others, Captain Cook – range from totem poles and mummified crocodiles to African fetishes and gruesome shrunken heads.

Modern Art Oxford

30 Pembroke St • Tues–Sat 11am–6pm, Sun noon–5pm • Free • ☎ 01865 722733, ⓦ www.modernartoxford.org.uk

Just south of Carfax, narrow Pembroke Street heads west to the outstanding **Modern Art Oxford** gallery, founded in 1965 and hosting an excellent changing programme of temporary exhibitions. It's worth stopping by, whatever happens to be showing.

Oxford Castle Unlocked

New Road • Daily 10am–5pm; tours every 20min, last at 4.20pm • £9.95; discount for booking online • ☎ 01865 260666, ⓦ oxfordcastleunlocked.co.uk

West of Carfax is the site of what was **Oxford Castle**, built in 1071. **Oxford Castle Unlocked** offers memorable forty-minute **guided tours**, during which costumed warders lead you up the Saxon-era **St George's Tower**, show you medieval prison cells and take you down into the Romanesque crypt beneath **St George's Chapel**, telling tales of wars, executions and hauntings along the way.

ARRIVAL AND DEPARTURE   OXFORD

By train Oxford station is on the west side of the city centre, a 10min walk from the centre along Hythe Bridge Street. Don't mix it up with the new Oxford Parkway station in the northern outskirts, served by direct buses into the centre.

Destinations Bath (2 hourly; 1hr 20min–1hr 40min); Birmingham (2 hourly; 1hr 10min); Bristol (hourly; 1hr 40min); Cheltenham (every 30min; 2hr–2hr 15min); Gloucester (every 30min; 1hr 40min–2hr 20min); London (2–3 hourly; 1hr); Winchester (2 hourly; 1hr 10min–1hr 30min); Worcester (2 hourly; 1hr 15min–1hr 35min).

By bus Most buses are operated by Oxford Bus (☎ 01865 785400, ⊚ oxfordbus.co.uk) or Stagecoach (☎ 01865 772250, ⊚ www.stagecoachbus.com/oxfordshire). Long-distance routes terminate at Gloucester Green bus station, in the city centre adjoining George Street; most county buses terminate on Magdalen Street, St Giles or St Aldates.

Destinations London Victoria coach station (Oxford Tube and X90 express coaches daily every 10–30min; 1hr 40min); Heathrow airport (Airline coach daily every 20–30min; 1hr 30min); Gatwick airport (Airline coach daily hourly; 2hr). Burford (45min), Northleach (1hr) and Cheltenham (1hr 30min) are served by the #853 (Mon–Sat 2–4 daily, Sun daily).

By car Five big park-and-ride sites (⊚ parkandride.net) are signposted around the ring road. All offer cheap parking (around £2 a day) as well as frequent buses into the centre (usually every 8–15min: Mon–Sat 6am–11pm, Sun 8am–7pm; £2.70 return). Central Oxford is not car-friendly: many streets are pedestrianized and parking is limited. The largest car park is at the Westgate shopping mall, accessed off Thames Street (around £28 for up to 24hrs).

GETTING AROUND

On foot From the rail station to Magdalen Bridge is roughly a mile and a quarter, and passes almost everything of interest on the way.

By bike Bainton Bikes at Walton Street Cycles, 78 Walton Street (☎ 01865 311610, ⊚ baintonbikes.com) rents bikes from £10/day.

By taxi There are taxi ranks at Carfax, Gloucester Green, St Giles and the railway station. Otherwise call Radio Taxis (☎ 01865 242424, ⊚ radiotaxisoxford.co.uk).

INFORMATION AND TOURS

Tourist office 15 Broad Street (Mon–Sat 9.30am–5.30pm, Sun 10am–4pm; Oct–March closes 30min earlier; ☎ 01865 252200, ⊚ visitoxfordand oxfordshire.com). Staff also sell discounted tickets for a range of nearby attractions, including Blenheim Palace, as well as tickets for coaches to London.

Listings information *Daily Info* (⊚ dailyinfo.co.uk) is the continually updated online version of Oxford's student newssheet. You'll spot the paper version (printed twice a week) pinned up in colleges and cafés around town.

Guided tours The tourist office offers excellent guided walking tours of the city centre (daily 10.45am & 2pm; extra slots if there's sufficient demand; 2hr; £8.50). Many walking guides tout for business along Broad Street, offering daytime walks and evening ghost tours, and Blackwell's bookshop, 48–53 Broad Street (☎ 01865 792792) also runs several literary-themed walking tours each week (April–Oct; £8).

ACCOMMODATION

As well as the places listed below, another good source of accommodation is the **university**. Outside term time, many colleges let out rooms on a B&B basis at often bargain rates. Expect little or no hotel-style service, but you are free to soak up the college ambience and may score with a view over a historic quad. For more information, visit ⊚ oxfordrooms.co.uk.

HOTELS

★**Bath Place** 4 Bath Place ☎ 01865 791812, ⊚ bath place.co.uk. This unusual hotel is tucked away down an old cobbled courtyard flanked by ancient buildings in an unbeatable central location. The sixteen creaky rooms are each individually decorated in attractive antique style with canopied beds and bare stone walls. **£120**

★**Malmaison** Oxford Castle, 3 New Rd ☎ 01865 268400, ⊚ malmaison.com. Classy designer hotel in what was a Victorian prison, part of the Oxford Castle complex. Rooms – which take up three cells, knocked through – are nothing short of glamorous, featuring contemporary bathrooms and hi-tech gadgets. Head through to C wing for bigger mezzanine suites. **£210**

Old Bank 92 High St ☎01865 799599, ☷oldbank -hotel.co.uk. Great location for a slick hotel in a shiny conversion of an old bank. All 42 bedrooms are decorated in crisp, modern style, some with great views over All Souls College opposite. **£220**

Old Parsonage 1 Banbury Rd ☎01865 310210, ☷oldparsonage-hotel.co.uk. Completely refurbished in 2014, this lovely hotel occupies a charming, wisteria-clad old building of 1660, with 35 tasteful, modern rooms. Free parking, and free walking tours for guests on request. **£235**

The Randolph 1 Beaumont St ☎01865 256400, ☷randolph-hotel.com. Oxford's most famous hotel, long the favoured choice of the well-heeled visitor, occupying a neo-Gothic brick building with a distinctive, nineteenth-century interior. Now part of the *Macdonald* chain, still with traditional service, well-appointed bedrooms and a distinguished club atmosphere. **£224**

GUESTHOUSES AND B&BS

Buttery 11 Broad St ☎01865 811950, ☷thebutteryhotel.co.uk. Slap-bang central location for this friendly sixteen-room guesthouse-cum-hotel, with modest rooms, plain but decent. Choose a back room to avoid the noise of carousing students. **£115**

Isis Guesthouse 45–53 Iffley Rd ☎01865 613700, ☷isisguesthouse.com. From July to September, this

college hall – within easy walking distance of Magdalen Bridge – becomes a guesthouse with 37 single and double rooms (about half en suite), decorated in a brisk if frugal modern style. **£90**

Richmond 25 Walton Crescent ☎01865 311777, ☷the -richmond-oxford.co.uk. Quiet B&B attached to the excellent *Al-Shami* Lebanese restaurant. Rooms are simple but prices are remarkably low – and you can opt for a delicious Lebanese breakfast (hummus, olives, white cheese, pitta bread etc). **£65**

HOSTELS

Central Backpackers 13 Park End St ☎01865 242288, ☷centralbackpackers.co.uk. Independent hostel with fifty beds (including female-only dorms), 24-hour access and a friendly attitude. On a busy street: expect noise from nearby bars. Dorms **£22–28**

Oxford Backpackers 9a Hythe Bridge St ☎01865 721761, ☷hostels.co.uk. Independent hostel with 120 beds in bright, modern dorms (including female-only) and 24-hour access – but just a touch scruffy. Dorms **£20–26**

Oxford Youth Hostel 2a Botley Rd ☎0845 371 9131, ☷yha.org.uk. In a modern block behind the train station, this popular YHA hostel has 187 beds in four- and six-bedded dorms, plus nine doubles, some en suite. There's 24-hour access, with good facilities and a decent café. Dorms **£18-23**, doubles **£45**

EATING

With so many students and tourists, Oxford has a wide choice of places to eat. Lunchtimes tend to be very busy, though there's no shortage of options. The **restaurant** scene ranges from fine dining to more affordable outlets offering seasonal cooking. The best choice lies on the edge of the centre, along Walton Street and Little Clarendon Street in easygoing Jericho, or southeast on the grungier Cowley Road, buzzing with after-work lounge bars.

CAFÉS

★**Ben's Cookies** 108 Covered Market ☎01865 247407, ☷benscookies.com. This hole in the wall – the first outlet in the Ben's Cookies chain – has been churning out the best cookies in Oxford, perhaps England (and some say the world) since 1984, from ginger to peanut butter to triple chocolate chunk. Mon–Sat 9.15am–5.30pm, Sun 10am–4pm.

Missing Bean 14 Turl St ☎01865 794886, ☷www .themissingbean.co.uk. Plate-glass windows look out onto this pleasant old street, as conversation swirls and reputedly the best coffee in Oxford goes down. Mon–Fri 8am–6.30pm, Sat 9am–6.30pm, Sun 10am–5.30pm.

News Café 1 Ship St ☎01865 242317. Breakfasts, bagels and daily specials, plus beer and wine in this brisk and efficient café. Plenty of local and international newspapers are on hand too. Sun–Thurs 9am–5pm, Fri & Sat 9am–6pm.

★**Vaults & Garden** Radcliffe Sq ☎01865 279112, ☷thevaultsandgarden.com. Occupying atmospheric

stone-vaulted chambers attached to St Mary's church, this always-busy café serves up good-quality organic, locally sourced wholefood, as well as coffee and cake. A small outside terrace area gazes up at the Radcliffe Camera. Cash only. Daily 8.30am–6pm.

RESTAURANTS

Branca 111 Walton St ☎01865 556111, ☷branca -restaurants.com. Large, buzzy bar-brasserie dishing up well-prepared Italian food, from simple pastas, pizzas and risottos through to more elaborate meat and fish mains (£10–16). Daily noon–11pm.

Chiang Mai Kitchen 130a High St ☎01865 202233, ☷chiangmaikitchen.co.uk. An authentically spicy blast of Thai cooking in a homely little timber-framed medieval building tucked down an alleyway off the High Street. All the traditional classics are done well, including a good vegetarian selection. Mains around £9. Reservations advised. Mon–Sat noon–10.30pm, Sun noon–10pm.

4

Edamame 15 Holywell St ☎01865 246916, ⓦedamame.co.uk. Voted one of the best Japanese restaurants in Britain, this tiny canteen-style place enjoys a flawless reputation. No bookings are taken, so you may have to queue (and then share a table). Tuck into ramen noodle soup with pork, chicken or tofu, for instance, or salmon *teriyaki*. There's plenty for vegetarians. Thursday night is sushi night. Mains £6–9. Cards not accepted at lunchtime. Wed 11.30am–2.30pm, Thurs–Sat 11.30am–2.30pm & 5–8.30pm, Sun noon–3.30pm.

Gee's 61 Banbury Rd ☎01865 553540, ⓦgees -restaurant.co.uk. Formal restaurant occupying chic Victorian conservatory premises. The inventive menu takes in British seasonal dishes such as asparagus and locally reared spring lamb, aided by steaks, fish dishes and more Continental cuisine – lobster linguine, bouillabaisse, duck confit. Mains £14–24; two-course early supper menu (Mon–Fri until 6pm) £13. Book ahead. Sun–Thurs 10am–10.30pm, Fri & Sat 10am–11pm.

★**Pie Minister** 56 Covered Market ☎01865 241613, ⓦpieminister.co.uk. Your nose will lead you to this pie shop inside the Covered Market. The wide choice includes deerstalker pie (venison and red wine), moo pie (beef and ale), heidi pie (goat's cheese and spinach), and so on, all accompanied by mashed potato, gravy and minty peas for around £5–6. Mon–Sat 10am–5pm, Sun 11am–4pm.

Quod 92 High St ☎01865 202505, ⓦquod.co.uk. Landmark brasserie in a central location. Once the solemn hall of a bank, the spacious interior now offers picture windows and contemporary art. Plump for the two-course set lunch (£13) – think devilled kidneys on toast or minty courgette soup, followed by steak *béarnaise* or mushroom tagliatelle. À la carte mains are £12–17. There's a nice bar, and live jazz on Sunday (5–7pm). Mon–Sat 7am–11pm, Sun 7am–10.30pm.

★**Turl Street Kitchen** 16 Turl St ☎01865 264171, ⓦturlstreetkitchen.co.uk. Much-loved hideaway on a charming backstreet, one of Oxford's top spots for a quiet battery-recharge over coffee and cake. Food is seasonal and hearty – parsnip soup, braised free-range chicken with chickpeas, fennel and wild garlic gratin – served in a cosy setting of sofas and grained wood. Mains £8–14. All profits support a local charity. Sun–Thurs 8am–midnight, Fri & Sat 8am–1am.

DRINKING

The Bear 6 Alfred St ☎01865 728164, ⓦbearoxford .co.uk. Tucked away down a narrow side street, this tiny old pub (the oldest in Oxford, founded roughly 800 years ago) offers a wide range of beers amid its traditional decor, which includes a collection of ties. Mon–Thurs 11am–11pm, Fri & Sat 11am–midnight, Sun 11.30am–10.30pm.

Eagle & Child 49 St Giles ☎01865 302925, ⓦnicholsonspubs.co.uk. Dubbed the "Bird & Baby", this was once the haunt of J.R.R. Tolkien and C.S. Lewis. The beer is still good and the old wood-panelled rooms at the front are great, but the pub is no longer independently owned – and feels a bit corporate. Mon–Thurs 11am–11pm, Fri & Sat 11am–midnight, Sun noon–10.30pm.

★**Lamb & Flag** 12 St Giles ☎01865 515787.

Generations of university types have relished this quiet old tavern, which comes with low-beamed ceilings and cramped but cosy rooms in which to enjoy hand-drawn ale and genuine pork scratchings. Cash only. Mon–Sat noon–11pm, Sun noon–10.30pm.

Raoul's 32 Walton St ☎01865 553732, ⓦraoulsbar .com. Famed Jericho cocktail bar, with a retro 70s theme, great tunes and a devoted clientele. Navigate the mammoth menu of cocktails to choose a fave or three. Sun–Tues 4pm–midnight, Wed–Sat 4pm–1am.

★**Turf Tavern** 4 Bath Place ☎01865 243235, ⓦtheturftavern.co.uk. Small, atmospheric medieval pub, reached via narrow passageways off Holywell Street, with a fine range of beers, and mulled wine in winter. Mon–Sat 11am–11.15pm, Sun 11am–10.30pm.

ENTERTAINMENT AND NIGHTLIFE

CLUBS AND LIVE MUSIC

Café Tarifa 56 Cowley Rd ☎01865 256091, ⓦfacebook .com/cafetarifaoxford. Atmospheric lounge bar decked out in Moorish/Arabian style, with cocktails and cushions, also hosting a variety of generally chilled live music and DJ nights and cult movie screenings. Mon–Thurs 5pm–midnight, Fri 5pm–12.30am, Sat noon–12.30am, Sun 5–11pm.

O2 Academy 190 Cowley Rd ☎01865 813500, ⓦo2academyoxford.co.uk. Oxford's liveliest indie and dance venue, with a fast-moving programme of live bands and guest DJs.

CLASSICAL MUSIC AND THEATRE

Holywell Music Room 32 Holywell St ☎01865 766266, ⓦwww.music.ox.ac.uk. This small, plain, Georgian building was opened in 1748 as the first public music hall in England. It offers a varied programme, from straight classical to experimental, with occasional bouts of jazz. Popular Sunday morning "coffee concerts" (ⓦcoffeeconcerts.co.uk) run year-round.

North Wall South Parade ☎01865 319450, ⓦthenorthwall.com. This much-loved arts centre located in posh Summertown, a mile or so north of the centre, hosts small-scale theatre, comedy and workshops.

Sheldonian Theatre Broad St ☎01865 277299,

Ⓦ www.sheldon.ox.ac.uk. Seventeenth-century edifice that is Oxford's top concert hall, despite rather dodgy

acoustics, with the Oxford Philomusica symphony orchestra in residence (Ⓦ oxfordphil.com).

DIRECTORY

Bookshops The leading university bookshop is Blackwell, 48 Broad Street (Ⓣ 01865 792792, Ⓦ blackwell.co.uk). The Albion Beatnik Bookstore, 34a Walton Street (Ⓣ 07737 876213, Ⓦ albionbeatnikbookstore.blogspot.com) stocks "interesting twentieth-century books", and hosts readings

and jazz evenings.

Markets Gloucester Green hosts a food market (Wed 9am–5pm) and arts and crafts market (Thurs 9am–5pm), as well as a great local farmers' market (1st & 3rd Thurs of month 9am–3pm).

Around Oxford

From Oxford, a short journey west brings you into the Cotswolds; your first stop could be Burford (see p.243) or Moreton-in-Marsh (see p.245). Even nearer to Oxford lie the charming little town of **Woodstock** and its imperious country-house neighbour **Blenheim Palace**, birthplace of Winston Churchill, while further south, at the edges of Oxfordshire, you could make for the pleasantly old-fashioned riverside haunt of **Henley-on-Thames** or the open walking country around the **Vale of White Horse**.

Woodstock

WOODSTOCK, eight miles northwest of Oxford, has royal associations going back to Saxon times, with a string of kings attracted by its excellent hunting. The Royalists used Woodstock as a base during the Civil War, but, after their defeat, Cromwell never got round to destroying either the town or its manor house: the latter was ultimately given to the Duke of Marlborough in 1704, who razed it to build Blenheim Palace (see p.238). Long dependent on royal and then ducal patronage, Woodstock is now both a well-heeled commuter town for Oxford and a base for visitors to Blenheim. It is also an extremely pretty little place, its handsome stone buildings gathered around the main square, at the junction of Market and High streets.

Oxfordshire Museum

Park St • Tues–Sat 10am–5pm, Sun 2–5pm • Free • Ⓣ 01993 811456, Ⓦ www.tomocc.org.uk

Occupying an eighteenth-century house in the centre of Woodstock, the rather good **Oxfordshire Museum** offers an engaging take on the county's archeology, social history and industry. Part of the rear garden shelters original megalosaurus footprints, recovered from a local quarry and displayed amid a Jurassic garden of ferns, pines and redwoods.

ARRIVAL AND INFORMATION

WOODSTOCK

By bus #S3 (hourly) to/from Oxford (30min) and Chipping Norton (20min); #233 (Mon–Sat hourly) to/from Burford (45min).

Useful websites Ⓦ wakeuptowoodstock.com & Ⓦ oxfordshirecotswolds.org

ACCOMMODATION AND EATING

The Bear Park St Ⓣ 01993 811124, Ⓦ bearhotel woodstock.co.uk. Behind the ivy-clad walls of this thirteenth-century coaching inn lurks a stylish, modern chain hotel – oak-carved four-poster beds, roaring log fires and all. Grab a table by the bay window for upscale, country-house food: Gressingham duck, Scottish beef and the like. Two-course menu £32. Food served Mon–Thurs noon–2.30pm & 7–9.30pm, Fri & Sat noon–2.30pm & 6.45–10pm, Sun noon–2.30pm & 7–9pm. **£100**

King's Arms Market St Ⓣ 01993 813636, Ⓦ www .kingshotelwoodstock.co.uk. Chic little hotel, with fifteen contemporary-styled rooms. The fine restaurant (mains £12–17) specializes in Modern British cuisine – leg of lamb or organic salmon. The bar/restaurant can remain busy until after 11pm: if you want an early night, choose a room at the back. Food served Mon–Fri noon–2.30pm & 6.30–9.30pm, Sat & Sun noon–9pm. **£150**

4

Blenheim Palace

Woodstock • **Palace** Mid-Feb to end Oct daily 10.30am–5.30pm; Nov to mid-Dec Wed–Sun same times **Park** Daily 9am–6pm or dusk • Palace, park and gardens £22; park and gardens £13 • ☎ 01993 810530, ⓦ blenheimpalace.com

In 1704, as a thank-you for his victory over the French at the Battle of Blenheim, Queen Anne gave John Churchill, **Duke of Marlborough** (1650–1722) the royal estate of Woodstock, along with the promise of enough cash to build himself a gargantuan palace.

Work started promptly on **Blenheim Palace** with Sir John Vanbrugh, who was also responsible for Castle Howard in Yorkshire (see p.553), as principal architect. However, the duke's formidable wife, Sarah Jennings, who had wanted Christopher Wren, was soon at loggerheads with Vanbrugh, while Queen Anne had second thoughts, stifling the flow of money. Construction work was halted and the house was only finished after the duke's death at the instigation of his widow, who ended up paying most of the bills and designing much of the interior herself. The end result is England's grandest example of Baroque civic architecture, an Italianate palace of finely worked yellow stone that is more a monument than a house – just as Vanbrugh intended.

The **interior** of the house is stuffed with paintings and tapestries, plus all manner of objets d'art, including furniture from Versailles and carvings by Grinling Gibbons. The **Churchill Exhibition** on the ground floor provides a fascinating introduction to Winston (1874–1965), born at Blenheim as grandson of the seventh Duke of Marlborough, and buried alongside his wife in the graveyard of Bladon church just outside the estate.

The gardens and park

Miniature train: March–Oct every 30min • 50p

Start your exploration of Blenheim's **gardens** by riding the narrow-gauge **miniature train** on a looping journey to the **Pleasure Gardens** a few hundred yards to the east (also an easy walk). Here, as well as a café, you'll find a butterfly house, lavender garden, maze and other diversions. On the west side of the house, fountains spout beside the terrace of the palace café and paths lead down to the lake past the vivid **Rose Garden**. A path from the front of the house leads you across Blenheim's open **park** down to Vanbrugh's **Grand Bridge** and up to the hilltop **Column of Victory**, topped by a heroic statue of the 1st Duke.

ARRIVAL AND DEPARTURE   BLENHEIM PALACE

Entrances The Blenheim Palace estate has two entrances: the Hensington Gate lies just south of Woodstock on the A44 Oxford Road, a few minutes' walk from the town centre, while the quieter Woodstock Gate is in the centre of

Woodstock, at the far end of Park Street.

By bus #S3 (hourly) stops at the Hensington Gate, on its route to/from Chipping Norton (20min) and Oxford (30min), as does #233 (Mon–Sat hourly) to/from Burford (45min).

TOURS

Blenheim Palace tours Free guided tours (35min) inside the palace depart about every quarter-hour, though you're free to opt out and stroll at your own pace. On

Sundays or when the palace is very busy, the tours are replaced by guides stationed in every room, who give details as you move through.

Henley-on-Thames

Three counties – Oxfordshire, Berkshire and Buckinghamshire – meet at **HENLEY-ON-THAMES**, long a favourite stopping place for travellers between London and Oxford. Nowadays, Henley is a good-looking, affluent commuter town at its prettiest among the old brick and stone buildings that flank the short main drag, **Hart Street**. At one end of Hart Street is the Market Place and its fetching **Town Hall**, at the other stand the easy Georgian curves of **Henley Bridge**. Overlooking the bridge is the parish church of **St Mary**, whose square tower sports a set of little turrets worked in chequerboard flint and stone.

HENLEY ROYAL REGATTA

Henley is best known for its **Royal Regatta**, established in 1839 and now the world's top amateur rowing tournament. The regatta, featuring past and potential Olympic rowers, begins on the Wednesday before the first weekend in July and runs for five days. Contact the Regatta Headquarters on the east side of Henley Bridge for ticket details (☎01491 572153, ⓦhrr.co.uk).

River and Rowing Museum

Mill Meadows • Daily 10am–5.30pm; Sept–April closes 5pm • £8.50 • ☎01491 415600, ⓦrrm.co.uk

A five-minute walk south along the riverbank from the foot of Hart Street lies Henley's imaginative **River and Rowing Museum**. Three galleries explore the wildlife and ecology of the Thames along with the history of rowing and the regatta, from ancient triremes to the modern Olympics. A fourth gallery is devoted to models illustrating scenes from the children's classic *Wind in the Willows* by Kenneth Grahame (1859–1932), set near Henley.

ARRIVAL AND DEPARTURE   HENLEY-ON-THAMES

By train Trains serve Henley (1–2 hourly, with 1 or 2 changes) from London Paddington (1hr) and Reading (30min). From the station, it's a 5min walk north to Hart Street.

By bus Buses, including services from Oxford (hourly, 50min) and London (every 30min; 45min direct or 1hr, changing at Twyford) stop on Hart Street or Bell Street in the centre.

INFORMATION AND TOURS

Tourist office In the Town Hall (Mon–Sat 10am–4pm; Oct–March 10.30am–3.30pm; ☎01491 578034, ⓜsouthernoxfordshire.com and ⓜvisitoxfordandoxfordshire.com).

Boat trips Just south of the bridge, Hobbs of Henley offers boat trips along the Thames (Easter–Sept; 1hr; £8.75; ☎01491 572035, ⓦhobbsofhenley.com), and has rowing boats and motor-launches for rent.

ACCOMMODATION AND EATING

★**The Angel** Thameside ☎01491 410678, ⓦtheangelhenley.com. Of Henley's many pubs, this one stands out for its prime riverside location, with a fine outside deck overlooking the water. Decent food, too: light bites £5–8, mains £10–14. Food served Mon–Fri noon–10pm, Sat 11.30am–10pm, Sun 11.30am–7pm.

Hotel du Vin New St ☎0844 736 4258, ⓦhotelduvin.com. This slick central hotel occupies the creatively revamped old Brakspear Brewery. Rooms are in contemporary boutique style; a few on the top floor have river views. The restaurant serves sumptuous modern European cuisine using local produce. Mains £13–19. Food served Mon–Sat noon–2.30pm & 5.30–10pm, Sun noon–4pm & 6–9.30pm. __£135__

Maison Blanc 1 Duke St ☎01491 577294, ⓦmaisonblanc.co.uk. Part of local celebrity chef Raymond Blanc's culinary empire, this busy little café does good food along with fancy cakes, sandwiches and freshly baked bread – perfect for a picnic. Mon–Sat 8am–6pm, Sun 9am–5.30pm.

Windsor

Every weekend trains from London Waterloo and Paddington are packed with people heading for **WINDSOR**, the royal enclave 21 miles west of London, where they join the human conveyor belt round **Windsor Castle**. If you've got the energy or inclination, it's also possible to cross the river to visit **Eton College**, which grew from a fifteenth-century free school for impoverished scholars and choristers to become one of the most elitist schools in the world (for guided tours contact ☎01752 671000, ⓦetoncollege.com).

Windsor Castle

Daily: March–Oct 9.45am–5.15pm; Nov–Feb 9.45am–4.15pm • £18.50 • ☎020 7766 7304, ⓦroyalcollection.org.uk

Towering above the town on a steep chalk bluff, **Windsor Castle** is an undeniably imposing sight, its chilly grey walls, punctuated by mighty medieval bastions, continuing as far as the eye can see. Inside, most visitors just gape in awe at the monotonous, gilded grandeur of the **State Apartments**, while the real highlights – the paintings from the Royal Collection that line the walls – are rarely given a second glance. More impressive is

St George's Chapel, a glorious Perpendicular structure ranking with Henry VII's chapel in Westminster Abbey (see p.66), and the second most important resting place for royal corpses after the Abbey. On a fine day, put aside some time for exploring **Windsor Great Park**, which stretches for several miles to the south of the castle.

ARRIVAL AND DEPARTURE
WINDSOR

By train London Paddington to Windsor & Eton Central station via Slough (every 30min; 40min) or London Waterloo to Windsor & Eton Riverside station (every 30min; 55min). From Oxford and Reading, change at Slough.

Cookham and around

Tiny **COOKHAM**, a prosperous Berkshire village five miles northwest of Windsor on the border with Buckinghamshire, was the former home of **Stanley Spencer** (1891–1959), one of Britain's greatest – and most eccentric – artists.

Stanley Spencer Gallery

High St • April–Oct daily 10.30am–5.30pm; Nov–March Thurs–Sun 11am–4.30pm • £5 • ☎ 01628 471885, ⓦ stanleyspencer.org.uk • 15min walk from Cookham station

The son of a local music teacher, Stanley Spencer spent much of his life in Cookham, which he once famously described as "a village in Heaven". Much of his work was inspired by the Bible, and many of his paintings depict biblical tales transposed into his Cookham surroundings. Much of Spencer's most acclaimed work is displayed in London's Tate Britain, but there's a fine sample here at the **Stanley Spencer Gallery**, which occupies the old Methodist Chapel on the High Street. Three prime exhibits are *View from Cookham Bridge*, the unsettling *Sarah Tubb and the Heavenly Visitors*, and the wonderful (unfinished) *Christ Preaching at Cookham Regatta*. The permanent collection is enhanced by regular exhibitions of Spencer's paintings and the gallery also contains incidental Spencer letters, documents and memorabilia. Download details of an hour-long walk round Cookham, visiting places with which Spencer is associated, from the gallery website.

Bray

About three miles south of Cookham, on the banks of the Thames south of Maidenhead, the even smaller village of **BRAY** has the unlikely distinction of hosting two of Britain's four triple-Michelin-starred restaurants (the other two are in London) – including, famously, Heston Blumenthal's *Fat Duck*.

ARRIVAL AND DEPARTURE
COOKHAM AND AROUND

By train First get to Maidenhead, served by trains every 15min from London Paddington (40min) and Reading (15min). Change at Maidenhead for hourly trains to Cookham (7min). Bray is a mile or so from Maidenhead station.

EATING AND DRINKING

COOKHAM

Bel & The Dragon High St ☎ 01628 521263, ⓦ belandthedragon-cookham.co.uk. Just across the street from the Spencer Gallery, this historic half-timbered pub is a nice place for a pint, while the airy modern restaurant offers excellent upmarket international cuisine (mains £10–27), with a more affordable bar menu, backed by an extensive wine list. Also five comfortable rustic-style rooms. Food served Mon–Fri noon–3pm & 6–10pm, Sat 10.30am–3pm & 6–10pm, Sun noon–9pm. <u>£114</u>

BRAY

Fat Duck High St ☎ 01628 580333, ⓦ thefatduck .co.uk. Regularly voted one of the world's top restaurants, showcasing chef Heston Blumenthal's uniquely inventive culinary style, with tasting menus (£195) featuring classic creations like snail porridge and egg-and-bacon ice cream, with whiskey wine gums to finish. Reservations (bookable up to two months in advance) are like gold dust. Tues–Sat noon–2pm & 7–9pm.

Waterside Inn Ferry Rd ☎ 01628 620691, ⓦ waterside -inn.co.uk. Part of the Roux family's culinary empire, this lovely restaurant has been wowing diners with its idiosyncratic

take on classical French cuisine since 1972. Signature dishes include the sumptuous soufflé Suissesse (cheese soufflé with double cream) and *tronçonnette de homard* (pan-fried lobster with white port sauce). Lunchtime menus are £50–80, while the main six-course tasting menu is £160. Reserve well in advance. Wed–Sun noon–2pm & 7–10pm.

Vale of White Horse

In the southwestern corner of Oxfordshire lies the pretty **Vale of White Horse**, a shallow valley whose fertile farmland is studded with tiny villages and dotted with a striking collection of prehistoric remains. The **Ridgeway National Trail**, running along – or near – the top of the downs, links several of these ancient sites and offers wonderful, breezy views. The Vale is easily visited as a day-trip from Oxford or elsewhere, but you might opt to stay locally in one of the Vale's quaint villages – tiny **Woolstone** is perhaps the most appealing.

The Uffington White Horse

Dawn to dusk • Free • ☎ 01793 762209, ⓦ nationaltrust.org.uk • 10mins walk from signposted car park • From Oxford, take a bus to Wantage (45min), then change for a Swindon-bound bus to Woolstone (35min), 15mins walk away

White Horse Hill, overlooking the B4507 six miles west of the unexciting market town of Wantage, follows close behind Stonehenge (see p.216) and Avebury (see p.218) in the hierarchy of Britain's ancient sites, though it attracts nothing like the same number of visitors. Carved into the north-facing slope of the downs, the 374ft-long **Uffington White Horse** looks like something created with a few swift strokes of an immense brush. The first written record of the horse's existence dates from the time of Henry II, but it was cut much earlier, probably in the first century BC, making it one of the oldest chalk figures in Britain. There's no lack of weird and wonderful theories concerning its origins, but burial sites excavated in the surrounding area point to the horse having some kind of sacred function, though no one knows quite what.

Just below the horse is **Dragon Hill**, a small flat-topped hillock that has its own legend. Locals long asserted that this was where St George killed and buried the dragon, a theory proved, so they argued, by the bare patch at the top and the channel down the side, where blood trickled from the creature's wounds. Here also, at the top of the hill, is the Iron Age earthwork of **Uffington Castle**, which provides wonderful views over the Vale.

ACCOMMODATION AND EATING — VALE OF WHITE HORSE

Fox and Hounds Uffington ☎ 01367 820680, ⓦ uffingtonpub.co.uk. Friendly local pub in this quiet village a mile and a half north of White Horse Hill, with two house-proud en-suite rooms for B&B and decent food (mains around £11). Food served Mon–Fri noon–2pm & 6–9pm, Sat noon–3pm & 6–9pm, Sun noon–3pm. **£75**

White Horse Inn Woolstone ☎ 01367 820726, ⓦ whitehorsewoolstone.co.uk. A mile north of White Horse Hill, this half-timbered, partly thatched old inn offers swanky accommodation, mostly in a modern annexe, and upmarket pub food (mains £13–20). Food served daily noon–2.30pm & 6–9pm. **£80**

THE RIDGEWAY NATIONAL TRAIL

The Iron Age inhabitants of Britain developed the **Ridgeway** (ⓦ nationaltrail.co.uk/ridgeway) as a major thoroughfare, a fast route that beetled across the chalky downs of modern-day Berkshire and Oxfordshire, negotiated the Thames and then traversed the Chiltern Hills. It was probably once part of a longer route extending from the Dorset coast to the Wash in Norfolk. Today, the Ridgeway is a National Trail, running from **Overton Hill**, near Avebury in Wiltshire, to **Ivinghoe Beacon**, 87 miles to the northeast near Tring. Crossing five counties, it keeps to the hills and avoids densely populated areas, except where the Thames slices through the trail at **Goring Gap**, marking the transition from the open Berkshire–Oxfordshire downs to the wooded valleys of the Chilterns.

It's fairly easy hiking, and most of the route is accessible to cyclists. The prevailing winds mean that it is best walked in a northeasterly direction. The trail is strewn with prehistoric monuments, though the finest archeological remains are on the downs edging the **Vale of White Horse** (see opposite) and around **Avebury** (see p.218).

The Cotswolds

The limestone hills that make up the **Cotswolds** are preposterously photogenic, dotted with a string of picture-book villages, many of them built by wealthy cloth merchants between the fourteenth and sixteenth centuries. Largely bypassed by the Industrial Revolution, which heralded the area's commercial decline, the Cotswolds is characterised by beautifully preserved traditional architecture. Numerous churches are decorated with beautiful carving, for which the local limestone was ideal: soft and easy to carve when first quarried, but hardening after long exposure to the sunlight.

For their beauty and ease of access the Cotswolds are a major tourist attraction, with many towns afflicted by plagues of tearooms, antiques shops and coach parties. To see the region at its best, avoid the main towns and instead escape into the countryside. If you have a car, almost any minor road between Oxford and Cheltenham will deliver views, thatched cottages and oodles of rural atmosphere; otherwise, plan day-walks from one of the more attractive centres – **Chipping Campden** is the number one choice, or opt for **Northleach**, foodie hub **Kingham** or the walkers' haven of **Winchcombe**.

This might be a tamed landscape, but there's good scope for exploring the byways, either in the gentler valleys that are most typical of the Cotswolds or along the dramatic escarpment that marks the western boundary with the Severn Valley. The **Cotswold Way** national trail runs for a hundred miles along the edge of the Cotswold escarpment from Chipping Campden in the northeast to Bath in the southwest, with a number of prehistoric sites providing added interest along the route. The section around **Belas Knap** is particularly rewarding, offering superb views over Cheltenham and the Severn Valley to the distant Malvern Hills.

GETTING AROUND   THE COTSWOLDS

By train Hourly trains from London Paddington (via Oxford) stop at Kingham (1hr 25min) and Moreton-in-Marsh (1hr 35min), access points for the central and northern Cotswolds between Stow and Chipping Campden. On a different line from Paddington via Swindon, hourly trains serve Kemble (1hr 15min), near Tetbury and Cirencester.

By bus Local buses do a reasonable job connecting the larger towns and villages, but few buses run on Sundays. Smaller villages are rarely served more than once a week, if at all. Local tourist offices will be able to advise on travel plans – or check the public transport info at ⓦ escapetothecotswolds.org.uk.

On foot The Cotswolds is prime walking country: at any point there's likely to be a marked trail nearby for anything from an hour's rural stroll to a multi-day epic. Loads of routes are downloadable for free (see below), with full descriptions and maps.

INFORMATION

Useful websites ⓦ cotswolds.com, ⓦ oxfordshirecotswolds.org & ⓦ escapetothecotswolds.org.uk

Burford

Twenty miles west of Oxford you get your first real taste of the Cotswolds at **BURFORD**, where the long and wide High Street, which slopes down to the bridge over the River Windrush, is simply magnificent, despite the traffic. The street is flanked by a remarkable line of old buildings that exhibit almost every type of classic Cotswolds feature, from wonky mullioned windows and half-timbered facades with bendy beams, through to spiky brick chimneys, fancy bow-fronted, stone houses and grand horse-and-carriage gateways.

FIVE COTSWOLDS CHURCHES

St James Chipping Campden. See p.248
St John the Baptist Burford. See p.244
St John the Baptist Cirencester.
See p.250
St Mary Tetbury. See p.252
St Peter and St Paul Northleach.
See p.247

Church of St John the Baptist

Church Green, near the river • ⓦ burfordchurch.org

Of all the Cotswold churches, **St John the Baptist** has the most historical resonance, with architectural bits and pieces surviving from every phase of its construction, beginning with the Normans and ending in the wool boom of the seventeenth century – the soaring Gothic spire built atop the old Norman tower is particularly eye-catching. Thereafter, it was pretty much left alone and, most unusually, its clutter of mausoleums, chapels and chantries survived the Reformation. A plaque outside commemorates three "Levellers" – a loose coalition of free-thinking radicals that blossomed during the English Civil War – who were executed here in 1649 and whose aims are commemorated on **Levellers Day** in May (ⓦlevellersday. wordpress.com).

ARRIVAL AND INFORMATION   BURFORD

By bus #853 (Mon–Sat 2–4 daily, Sun daily) stops by the A40 at the top of Burford from Northleach (15min), Cheltenham (45min) and Oxford (45min). Also #233 (Mon–Sat hourly) from Woodstock (50min) and #X10 from Chipping

Norton (Mon–Sat hourly; 30min) stop on the High Street.
Tourist office 33a High Street (Mon–Sat 9.30am–5pm, Sun 10am–4pm; ☎01993 823558, ⓦwww.oxford shirecotswolds.org).

ACCOMMODATION AND EATING

★**Angel** 14 Witney St ☎01993 822714, ⓦtheangel atburford.co.uk. This sixteenth-century inn is highly regarded for its lively, creative menu – a madeira *jus* enlivening roast chicken, coriander and chilli adding zip to crab linguine, and so on. Mains £14–18, or two-course menu £18. Also three ensuite rooms, tasteful and traditional. Food served Mon–Sat noon–3pm & 6–9.30pm, Sun noon–4pm & 6–8.30pm. £90

Bay Tree Sheep St ☎01993 822791, ⓦcotswold-inns -hotels.co.uk. First-class hotel in a lovely location off the High Street, occupying a wisteria-clad stone house dating from the sixteenth century. Its twenty-odd rooms, in the main house and a couple of annexes, are done up in a

distinctly lavish rendition of period character. Bar meals are excellent (from £12) featuring anything from oriental-style duck confit to local pork sausages. Food served daily noon–2pm & 7–9.30pm. £180

Bull 105 High St ☎01993 822220, ⓦbullatburford .co.uk. This venerable old inn has been hosting guests for more than three hundred years – Charles II dallied here with Nell Gwynne, as did Lord Nelson with Lady Hamilton. Traditionally styled rooms feature panelling and four-poster beds. The restaurant grafts French and Mediterranean influences onto local ingredients, with emphasis on fish and seafood. Mains £16–21. Food served Mon–Sat noon–3pm & 6–9.30pm, Sun noon–4pm & 6–9pm. £100

Kelmscott Manor

Kelmscott • April–Oct Wed & Sat 11am–5pm • £9 • Timed tickets: call ahead to confirm arrangements • ☎01367 252486,
ⓦ kelmscottmanor.org.uk • No public transport • The car park is a 10min walk from the house

Kelmscott Manor, amid the Thames-side water-meadows about eight miles south of Burford off the A361, is a place of pilgrimage for devotees of **William Morris**, who used this Tudor house as a summer home from 1871 to his death in 1896. The simple beauty of the house is enhanced by the furniture, fabrics and wallpapers created by Morris and his Pre-Raphaelite friends, including Burne-Jones and Rossetti.

Kingham

When *Country Life* magazine calls you "England's favourite village", it could easily prompt a downward spiral. But for **KINGHAM**, set in the Evenlode Valley between Chipping Norton (the highest town in Oxfordshire) and Stow-on-the-Wold (the highest town in the Cotswolds), everything's looking up. There's still nothing to do in this cheery, noticeably upmarket village, other than eat well, walk well and sleep well… but that's the point. The stroll in from the railway station – served by mainline trains from London and Oxford – is lovely, marked by the Perpendicular tower of **St Andrew's Church**.

ARRIVAL AND DEPARTURE

By train Kingham has hourly trains from London Paddington (1hr 25min), Oxford (25min), Moreton (10min) and Worcester (50min). The station is a mile west of the village.

By bus The only buses are sporadic local services.

ACCOMMODATION AND EATING

Daylesford Organic Daylesford ✆01608 731700, ⓦ daylesford.com. This super-sleek farm complex includes a spectacularly well-stocked deli and café, where light lunches (£10–14) are filled out by cream teas and informal suppers (Fri & Sat only; booking essential). Absurdly expensive, but very good. Mon–Wed 9am–5pm, Thurs–Sat 9am–6pm, Sun 10am–4pm, also Fri & Sat 7–9pm.

★**Kingham Plough** Kingham ✆01608 658327, ⓦ thekinghamplough.co.uk. The epitome of a Cotswold gastropub, book ahead for one of Oxfordshire's most atmospheric, upmarket and welcoming restaurants. Local, seasonal produce of all kinds, expertly prepared, is served off a short, daily-changing menu (mains £16–25). They also have seven country-style rooms. Food served Mon–Thurs noon–9pm, Fri & Sat noon–9.30pm, Sun noon–3pm & 6–8pm. **£95**

Kings Head Bledington ✆01608 658365, ⓦ thekingsheadinn.net. Just west of Kingham, this sixteenth-century inn hosts regulars supping pints at the bar, and also serves local, ethically sourced food – potted shrimps, steak-and-ale pie, Cotswold lamb – alongside Modern British fusion dishes (mains £13–15). The rooms, some floral, some designer-chic, are a snip. Food served Mon–Thurs noon–2pm & 6.30–9pm, Fri noon–2pm & 6.30–9.30pm, Sat noon–2.30pm & 6.30–9.30pm, Sun noon–2.30pm & 7–9pm. **£95**

Moreton-in-Marsh

A key transport hub and one of the Cotswolds' more sensible towns, **MORETON-IN-MARSH** is named for a now-vanished wetland nearby. It has always been an important access point for the countryside and remains so with its **railway station**, on the line between London, Oxford and Worcester. It also sits astride the A429 Fosse Way, the former Roman road that linked Exeter with Lincoln. On the broad, handsome **High Street**, enhanced with Jacobean and Georgian facades, stands the nineteenth-century **Redesdale Hall**, named for Lord Redesdale, father of the infamous Mitford sisters (among them Diana, wife of British wartime fascist leader Oswald Mosley; and Unity, a close companion of Adolf Hitler), who as children lived at Batsford House near the town.

ARRIVAL AND INFORMATION

By train Moreton has hourly trains from London Paddington (1hr 35min), Oxford (35min), Kingham (10min) and Worcester (40min). The station is a two-minute walk from the High Street.

By bus #21 (Mon–Sat 3 daily) from Broadway (25min), Chipping Campden (45min) and Stratford-upon-Avon (1hr 15min); #22 (Mon–Sat 5 daily) from Chipping Campden (30min) and Stratford-upon-Avon (1hr); #23 (Mon–Sat 2 daily) from Stratford-upon-Avon (1hr 5min); #801 (Mon–Sat hourly; June–Sept also 2 on Sun) from Stow-on-the-Wold (15min), Lower Slaughter (20min), Bourton-on-the-Water (25min), Northleach (40min) and Cheltenham (1hr 15min).

Tourist office High Street (Mon 8.45am–4pm, Tues–Thurs 8.45am–5.15pm, Fri 8.45am 4.45pm, Sat 10am–1pm; Nov–March Sat closes 12.30pm; ✆01608 650881, ⓦ cotswold.gov.uk & ⓦ cotswolds.com).

ACCOMMODATION AND EATING

Acacia Guest House 2 New Rd ✆01608 650130, ⓦ acaciainthecotswolds.co.uk. Decent little B&B on the short street connecting the station to the High Street – very handy for arrivals and departures by train or bus. **£60**

★**Horse and Groom** Bourton-on-the-Hill ✆01386 700413, ⓦ horseandgroom.info. Occupying a Georgian building of honey-coloured Cotswold stone two miles west of Moreton, this free house has a reputation for good beer and excellent food. The menu changes frequently, focused on meat sourced from local farmers and seasonal veg. It's popular; book ahead. Mains £10–20. Also five appealing rooms, one with French doors opening onto the garden. Mon–Fri 11am–2.30pm & 6–11pm, Sat 11am–3pm & 6–11pm, Sun noon–3.30pm. **£120**

Manor House High St ✆01608 650501, ⓦ cotswold -inns-hotels.co.uk. Pleasant four-star hotel occupying a sixteenth-century former coaching inn, with a nice garden and stylish rooms. Its posh restaurant, with muted contemporary styling, serves Modern British cuisine (three courses £39), with good vegetarian options available. Daily noon–2.30pm & 7–9.30pm. **£120**

4

Stow-on-the-Wold

Ambling over a steep hill seven hundred feet above sea level, **STOW-ON-THE-WOLD**, five miles south of Moreton, draws in a number of visitors disproportionate to its size and attractions, which essentially comprise an old **marketplace** surrounded by pubs, antique and souvenir shops, and an inordinate number of tearooms. The narrow walled alleyways, or "tchures", running into the square were designed for funnelling sheep into the market, which is itself dominated by an imposing Victorian hall. **St Edward's church** has a photogenic north porch, where two yew trees flanking the door appear to have grown into the stonework.

Cotswold Cricket Museum

Brewery Yard • Tues–Sat 9.30am–5pm, Sun 9.30am–3.30pm • £3.50 • ☎ 01451 870083, ⓦ cotswoldcricketmuseum.co.uk

Just off the square, the small **Cotswold Cricket Museum** is a labour of love: the owner Andy Collier has built up memorabilia over 25 years, from blazers to signed bats and photos galore. He's always around for a chat: cricket buffs could lose a day to this place.

ARRIVAL AND INFORMATION
STOW-ON-THE-WOLD

By bus Buses stop just off the main square, including #801 (Mon–Sat every 1–2hrs; May–Sept also twice on Sun) from Bourton-on-the-Water (10min), Lower Slaughter (5min), Moreton (15min), Northleach (30min) and Cheltenham (1hr).

Tourist office In the cricket museum, Brewery Yard (Tues–Sat 9.30am–5pm, Sun 9.30am–3.30pm; ☎ 01451 830341, ⓦ stowinfo.co.uk & ⓦ cotswolds.com).

ACCOMMODATION AND EATING

Number Nine 9 Park St ☎ 01451 870333, ⓦ number-nine.info. Pleasant old house offering quality B&B just down from the town square. The three bedrooms feature low beams but contemporary styling – and the rates are a bargain. **£65**

Porch House Digbeth St ☎ 01451 870048, ⓦ porch-house.co.uk. Purportedly the oldest inn in Britain, with parts of the building dated at 947 AD (though the interiors have been freshly modernized). The 13 hessian-floored rooms look good, but are on the small side. The restaurant is a comfortably posh affair (mains £12–17), with cheaper nosh in the wonky-beamed pub. Food served – pub Mon–Sat noon–9.30pm, Sun noon–8.30pm; restaurant Mon–Sat 6.30–9.30pm. **£100**

★**Queen's Head** The Square ☎ 01451 830563 ⓦ donnington-brewery.com. Traditional old pub that provides good beer, good service and a pleasant chatty atmosphere. Food is a level above standard pub grub (mains roughly £9–11). Mon–Sat 11am–11pm, Sun noon–10.30pm.

★**YHA hostel** The Square ☎ 0845 371 9540, ⓦ yha.org.uk. This good-looking Georgian townhouse is the Cotswolds' only youth hostel – an excellent choice for a budget stay, with small dorms and a choice of family rooms (4–6 beds) as well as kitchen facilities, a garden and a little café. Dorms **£19–23**, doubles **£50**

Bourton-on-the-Water

BOURTON-ON-THE-WATER is the epicentre of Cotswold tourism. Beside the village green – flanked by photogenic Jacobean and Georgian facades in yellow Cotswold stone – five picturesque little **bridges** span the shallow River Windrush, dappled by shade from overhanging trees. It looks lovely, but its proximity to main roads means that it's invariably packed with people: tourist coaches cram in all summer long and the little **High Street** now concentrates on souvenirs and teashops, interspersed with everything from a Model Village and Motoring Museum to a Dragonfly Maze and Bird Park.

Lower Slaughter

A mile outside Bourton-on-the-Water, **LOWER SLAUGHTER** (as in *slohtre*, Old English for a marshy place, cognate with "slough") is a more enticing prospect, though still on the day-trippers' circuit. Pop by to take in some of the most celebrated village scenery in the Cotswolds, as the River Eye snakes its way between immaculate honeystone cottages. There is a small **museum** (and souvenir shop) signposted in a former mill, but the main attraction of the stroll through the village is to stop in for a little something at one of the grand hotels occupying gated mansions on both sides of the street.

Northleach

Secluded in a shallow depression, **NORTHLEACH** is one of the most appealing and atmospheric villages in the Cotswolds – a great base to explore the area. Despite the fact that the A40 Oxford–Cheltenham road and A429 Fosse Way cross at a large roundabout nearby, virtually no tourist traffic makes its way into the centre. Rows of immaculate late medieval cottages cluster around the **Market Place** and adjoining **Green**.

The Old Prison

A429 • Daily 9.30am–4.30pm • Free • ☎ 01451 861563, ⓦ escapetothecotswolds.org.uk

Just outside town the old Georgian **prison** has interesting displays on the history of crime and punishment, along with "**Escape to the Cotswolds**", a visitor centre explaining the work of the Cotswolds Conservation Board in maintaining the Cotswolds Area of Outstanding Natural Beauty.

Church of St Peter and St Paul

Mill End • Daily 9am–5pm • Free • ☎ 01451 861432, ⓦ northleach.org

One of the finest of the Cotswolds wool churches, **St Peter and St Paul** is a classic example of the fifteenth-century Perpendicular style, with a soaring tower and beautifully proportioned nave lit by wide clerestory windows. The floors of the aisles are inlaid with an exceptional collection of memorial brasses, marking the tombs of the merchants whose endowments paid for the church. On several, you can make out the woolsacks laid out beneath the owner's feet – a symbol of wealth and power that survives today in the House of Lords in London, where a woolsack is placed on the Lord Chancellor's seat.

ARRIVAL AND DEPARTURE	**NORTHLEACH**
By bus Buses stop by the Green.	Moreton-in-Marsh (45min); #853 (Mon–Sat 2–4 daily, Sun
Destinations #801 (Mon–Sat every 2hrs) to Cheltenham	daily) to Burford (15min), Oxford (1hr) and Cheltenham
(35min), Bourton-on-the-Water (15min), Lower	(30min); #855 (Mon–Sat 5–6 daily) to Cirencester (20–
Slaughter (20min), Stow-on-the-Wold (30min) and	40min) and Bibury (20min).

ACCOMMODATION AND EATING

Cotswold Lion Café Old Prison ☎ 01451 861563, ⓦ escapetothecotswolds.org.uk. Friendly daytime café on the edge of the town, serving up teas, coffees, cakes and light lunches (under £10). Daily 9.30am–4.30pm.

Wheatsheaf West End ☎ 01451 860244, ⓦ cotswoldswheatsheaf.com. Excellent former coaching inn, remodelled in a bright modern style softened by period furniture, bookcases and etchings. Its restaurant has upscale Mediterranean-influenced cuisine – lamb shank with polenta, aubergine and apricot tagine, and so forth. Mains £13–18. Also 14 comfortable, en-suite guest rooms. Food served daily noon–3pm (Sun 3.30pm) & 6–9pm. **£140**

Bibury

A detour between Northleach and Cirencester passes through **BIBURY**, dubbed "the most beautiful village in England" by Victorian designer William Morris. Bibury draws attention for **Arlington Row**, originally built around 1380 as a wool store and converted in the seventeenth century into a line of cottages to house weavers. Their hound's-tooth gables, warm yellow stone and wonky windows stole William Morris's heart – and are now immortalised in the British passport as an image of England.

By bus #855 (Mon–Sat 5 daily) from Northleach (20min) and Cirencester (20min)

Chipping Campden

On the northern edge of the Cotswolds near Stratford-upon-Avon (see p.385), **CHIPPING CAMPDEN** gives a better idea than anywhere else in the area as to how a prosperous wool town might have looked in the Middle Ages. Its name derives from the Saxon term *campadene*, meaning cultivated valley, and the Old English *ceapen*, or market. The elegant **High Street** is hemmed in by mostly Tudor and Jacobean facades – an undulating line of weather-beaten roofs above twisted beams and mullioned windows. The evocative seventeenth-century **Market Hall** has survived too, an open-sided pavilion propped up on sturdy stone piers in the middle of the High Street, where farmers once gathered to sell their produce.

The Old Silk Mill

Sheep St • Daily 10am–5pm • **Hart Silversmiths** Mon–Fri 9am–5pm, Sat 9am–noon • ☎ 01386 841100, Ⓦ hartsilversmiths.co.uk

Just off the High Street is the **Old Silk Mill**, where designer Charles Ashbee relocated the London Guild of Handicraft in 1902, introducing the Arts and Crafts movement to the Cotswolds. Today, as well as housing galleries of local art, the building rings with the noise of chisels from the resident stone carvers. Upstairs, you're free to wander into the workshop of **Hart**, a silversmith firm – like stepping into an old photograph, with metalworking tools strewn everywhere under low ceilings, and staff perched by the windows working by hand on decorative pieces.

Court Barn Museum

Church St • Tues–Sun 10am–5pm; Oct–March closes 4pm • £4 • ☎ 01386 841951, Ⓦ courtbarn.org.uk

The history of the Guild of Handicraft, and its leading exponents, is explained at the superb **Court Barn museum**. Sited opposite a magnificent row of seventeenth-century Cotswold stone **almshouses**, the museum displays the work of Charles Ashbee and eight Arts and Crafts cohorts, placing it all in context with informative displays and short videos. Featured works include the bookbinding of Katharine Adams, stained-glass design of Paul Woodroffe and furniture by Gordon Russell.

St James' Church

Church St • March–Oct Mon–Sat 10am–5pm, Sun 2–6pm; Nov–Feb Mon–Sat 11am–4pm, Sun 2–4pm; closes 3pm in Dec & Jan • Free • Ⓦ stjameschurchcampden.co.uk

At the top of the village rises **St James' Church**. Built in the fifteenth century, the zenith of Campden's wool-trading days, this is the archetypal Cotswold wool church, beneath a magnificent 120ft tower. Inside, the airy nave is bathed in light from the clerestory windows. The South Chapel holds the ostentatious **funerary memorial** of the Hicks family, with fancily carved marble effigies lying on a table-tomb.

Dover's Hill

Panoramic views crown the short but severe hike up the first stage of the Cotswold Way, north from Chipping Campden to **Dover's Hill** (which is also accessible by car). The highest point, 740ft above sea level, affords breathtaking vistas to the Malvern Hills and beyond. This is where, in 1612, local lawyer Robert Dover organised competitions of running, jumping, wrestling and shin-kicking that rapidly became known as the **Cotswold Olimpicks**, still staged here annually (see Ⓦ olimpickgames.com).

ARRIVAL AND INFORMATION

By train Moreton-in-Marsh station (see p.245) is eight miles away, connected by bus #21 or #22 (Mon–Sat every 1–2hrs; 45min).

By bus Buses stop on the High Street, including the linked buses #21 & #22.

Destinations Broadway (Mon–Sat 3 daily; 20min),

Moreton-in-Marsh (Mon–Sat every 1–2hrs; 45min) and Stratford-upon-Avon (Mon–Sat every 1–2hrs; 35min).

Tourist office High Street (March–Oct daily 9.30am–5pm; Nov–Feb Mon–Thurs 9.30am–1pm, Fri–Sun 9.30am–4pm; ☎ 01386 841206, ⓦ campdenonline .org & ⓦ cotswolds.com).

ACCOMMODATION AND EATING

★ **Badgers Hall** High St ☎ 01386 840839, ⓦ hadgershall. com. This tearoom in an old stone house has won awards for its inch-perfect take on traditional English tea and cakes, all freshly made daily. Also light lunches (under £10). En-suite guest rooms upstairs feature period detail – beamed ceilings and antique pine furniture. Tearoom Mon–Sat 10am–4.30pm, Sun 11am–4.30pm. **£110**

★ **Eight Bells** Church St ☎ 01386 840371, ⓦ eight bellsinn.co.uk. Much-loved old inn with a first-rate restaurant – pheasant with mushrooms, pork with apricots and chestnuts, lamb's liver on bubble and squeak. Mains

£13–17. Also with seven individually done-up bedrooms, smartly modern without boutique pretension. Food served Mon–Thurs noon–2pm & 6.30–9pm, Fri & Sat noon–2.30pm & 6.30–9.30pm, Sun noon–9pm. **£115**

Volunteer Inn Lower High St ☎ 01386 840688, ⓦ the volunteerinn.net. Nine budget rooms at this lively pub, often used by walkers and cyclists (you can rent bikes here from £12/ day; see ⓦ cyclecotswolds.co.uk). The onsite *Maharaja* restaurant serves unusual Bangladeshi fish and chicken curries and fruity Kashmiri dishes (mains £8–17). Food served Sun–Thurs 5–10.30pm, Fri & Sat 5–11pm. **£60**

Broadway

BROADWAY, five miles west of Chipping Campden, is a particularly handsome little village at the foot of the steep escarpment that rolls along the western edge of the Cotswolds. It seems likely that the Romans were the first to settle here, but Broadway's high times were as a stagecoach stop on the route from London to Worcester. Its long, broad main street, framed by honeystone cottages and shaded by chestnut trees, attracts more visitors than is comfortable, but things do quieten down in the evening.

Gordon Russell Design Museum

Russell Sq • Tues–Sun 11am–5pm; Nov–Feb closes 4pm; closed Jan • £5 • ☎ 01386 854695, ⓦ gordonrussellmuseum.org

Just off the village green, the absorbing **Gordon Russell Design Museum** is dedicated to the work of this local furniture-maker (1892–1980), whose factory formerly stood next door. Influenced both by the Arts and Crafts movement but also by modern technology, Russell's stated aim was to "make decent furniture for ordinary people" through "a blend of hand and machine". The museum showcases many of his classic furniture designs, alongside other period artefacts ranging from metalware to mirrors.

Ashmolean Museum Broadway

65 High St • Tues–Sun 10am–5pm • £6 • ☎ 01386 859047, ⓦ www.ashmoleanbroadway.org

A former coaching inn now holds an annexe of Oxford's **Ashmolean Museum**. Objects across four floors of displays include embroidered tapestries and furniture in the panelled ground floor rooms, Worcester porcelain, glass, examples of William Morris tiles, and Cotswold pottery on the upper levels, as well as paintings by Gainsborough and Reynolds.

Broadway Tower

Fish Hill • Daily 10am–5pm; shorter hours in bad weather • £4.80 • ☎ 01386 852390, ⓦ broadwaytower.co.uk

A mile southeast of the village, **Broadway Tower**, a turreted folly built in 1798, has become an icon of the Cotswolds, perched at more than 1,000 feet above sea level with stupendous views that purportedly encompass thirteen counties. Now privately owned, it stands alongside a family activity park with an adventure playground, snack bar and picnic area. The historical displays inside are a bit limp: visit to climb the 71 steps to the roof, for those views. A circular **walk** (4 miles; 3hr) heads up to the tower.

4

ARRIVAL AND INFORMATION

By bus #21 (Mon–Sat 3 daily) from Chipping Campden (20min), Moreton-in-Marsh (25min) and Stratford-upon-Avon (50min); #606 (Mon–Sat 4 daily) from Winchcombe (35min) and Cheltenham (1hr).

Tourist office Russell Sq (April–Oct Mon–Sat 10am–5pm, Sun 11am–3pm; Feb, March, Nov & Dec closes 4pm; Jan closed; ☎01386 852937, ⱳ beautifulbroadway .com).

ACCOMMODATION AND EATING

Crown and Trumpet 14 Church St ☎01386 853202, ⱳ cotswoldholidays.co.uk. This cheery, historic local tavern has decent beers, a lively atmosphere, quality Sunday roasts and regular sessions of live blues and jazz. Mains £6–12. Also five simple en-suite rooms. Food served Mon–Fri 11am–3pm & 5–11pm, Sat 11am–11pm, Sun noon–4pm & 6–10.30pm. **£70**

Olive Branch 78 High St ☎01386 853440, ⱳ theolivebranch-broadway.com. Award-winning guesthouse in an old stone house – a touch

pastel-and-chintz, but cosy and well run. Some rooms have king-size beds and access to the garden. **£102**

Russell's 20 High St ☎01386 853555, ⱳ russellsofbroad way.co.uk. This relaxed, stylish restaurant serves Modern British cooking: Cotswold lamb chops with honey-roasted figs, lamb and sweetbreads, monkfish with bulghur wheat and pomegranate. Mains £17–24, or two-course set menu £17. Seven boutique rooms feature mood-lighting, designer furniture and huge stand-alone bathtubs and showers-for-two. Food served daily noon–2.30pm & 6–9.30pm. **£115**

Winchcombe and around

About eight miles southwest of Broadway – and nine miles northeast of Cheltenham – **WINCHCOMBE** has a long main street flanked by a fetching medley of stone and half-timbered buildings. Placid today, it was an important Saxon town and one-time capital of the kingdom of Mercia, and flourished during the medieval cloth boom, one of the results being **St Peter's** church, a mainly fifteenth-century structure distinguished by forty alarming gargoyles that ring the exterior. Rising amid a magnificent estate on Winchcombe's southern edge, **Sudeley Castle** combines ravishing good looks with a fascinating history.

Belas Knap

2 miles south of Winchcombe • Always open • Free; EH • ⱳ english-heritage.org.uk • On foot from Winchcombe, the path strikes off to the right near the entrance to Sudeley Castle. When you reach the country lane at the top, turn right and then left for the 10min hike to the barrow

The Neolithic long barrow of **Belas Knap** occupies one of the Cotswolds' wildest summits. Dating from around 3000 BC, this is the best-preserved burial chamber in England, stretched out like a strange sleeping beast cloaked in green velvet, more than fifty feet long. The best way to get there is to **walk**.

ARRIVAL AND INFORMATION

By bus #606 (Mon–Sat 4 daily) from Broadway (35min) and Cheltenham (25min).

Tourist office High Street (April–Oct daily 10am–4pm; ☎01242 602925, ⱳ winchcombe.co.uk & ⱳ cotswolds.com).

Cirencester

Self-styled "Capital of the Cotswolds", the affluent town of **CIRENCESTER** lies on the southern fringes of the region, midway between Oxford and Bristol. As Corinium, it became a provincial capital and a centre of trade under the **Romans**, in Britannia second in size and importance only to "Londinium" (London). The Saxons destroyed almost all of the Roman city, and the town only revived with the wool boom of the Middle Ages. Few medieval buildings have survived, however, and the houses along the town's most handsome streets – Park, Thomas and Coxwell – date mostly from the seventeenth and eighteenth centuries. Cirencester's heart is the delightful **Market Place**, packed with traders' stalls every Monday and Friday, and for the fortnightly Saturday farmers' market.

Church of St John the Baptist

Market Place • Daily 10am–5pm; Oct–March closes 4pm • Free • ☎01285 659317, ⱳ cirenparish.co.uk

The magnificent parish church of **St John the Baptist**, built during the fifteenth century, dominates the market place. The church's most notable feature is its huge **porch**, so big that it once served as the local town hall. The flying buttresses that support the tower had to be added when it transpired that the church had been built over the filled-in Roman ditch that ran beside the Gloucester–Silchester road, which passed this way. Inside the church is a colourful wineglass **pulpit**, carved in stone around 1450, and the **Boleyn Cup**, a gilded silver goblet made in 1535 for Anne Boleyn.

Corinium Museum

Park St · Mon–Sat 10am–5pm, Sun 2–5pm; Nov–March closes 4pm · £4.95 · ☎ 01285 655611, ⓦ coriniummuseum.org

West of the Market Place, the sleek **Corinium Museum** is devoted to the history of the town from Roman to Victorian times. The collection of Romano-British antiquities is particularly fine, including wonderful **mosaic pavements**. Other highlights include a trove of Bronze Age gold and an excellent video on Cotswold life in the Iron Age.

New Brewery Arts Centre

Brewery Court, off Cricklade St · Mon–Sat 9am–5pm, April–Dec also Sun 10am–4pm · Free · ☎ 01285 657181, ⓦ newbreweryarts.org.uk

Just south of the Market Place, the **New Brewery Arts Centre** is occupied by more than a dozen resident artists whose studios you can visit and whose work you can buy in the shop. It's worth popping by to see who is working and exhibiting – and, perhaps, to catch some live music.

ARRIVAL AND INFORMATION

By train From Kemble station, about 5 miles southwest – served by hourly trains from London Paddington (1hr 15min) and Cheltenham (1hr) – take bus #881 (Mon–Sat every 2hrs; 15min) or a taxi (about £10).

By bus National Express coaches from London and Heathrow Airport stop on London Rd, while local buses stop in or near Market Place.

Destinations #51 to Cheltenham (Mon–Sat hourly, 40min); #852 to Gloucester (Mon–Sat 4 daily; 1hr 10min); #855 to Bibury (Mon–Sat 4 daily; 15min); Moreton-in-Marsh (Mon–Sat daily, Northleach (Mon–Sat 5–6 daily, 20–40min); 1hr 20min), Stow-on-the-Wold (Mon–Sat daily; 1hr 10min); and #881 to Tetbury (Mon–Sat 5 daily; 40min); National Express to Heathrow airport (5 daily; 1hr 30min) and London Victoria (5–8 daily; 2hr 20min).

Tourist office At the Corinium Museum, Park Street (Mon–Sat 10am 5pm, Sun 2–5pm; Nov–March closes 4pm; ☎ 01285 654180, ⓦ cotswolds.com & ⓦ cotswold.gov.uk).

ACCOMMODATION

Corinium 12 Gloucester St ☎ 01285 659711, ⓦ coriniumhotel.com. Decent three-star family-run hotel in a historic property a short walk northwest of the centre. Only fifteen rooms, modestly priced and adequately furnished. **£105**

Fleece Market Place ☎ 01285 658507, ⓦ thefleece cirencester.co.uk. This old town-centre inn has been freshly updated to a smart, contemporary look. The 28 rooms, all beams and low ceilings, feature swanky en-suite bathrooms. **£94**

Ivy House 2 Victoria Rd ☎ 01285 656626, ⓦ ivyhousecotswolds.com. One of the more attractive of a string of B&Bs along this road, a high-gabled Victorian house with four en-suite rooms. **£80**

EATING AND DRINKING

Graze 3 Gosditch St ☎ 01285 658957, ⓦ bathales.com. Across from the church, this splendid old building – its neo-Gothic facade concealing what was a thirteenth-century tithe barn – is now a rather good gastropub, turning out locally sourced pork and lamb chops, steaks and burgers. Mon–Thurs 11am–11pm, Fri 11am–midnight, Sat 9am–midnight, Sun 9am–11pm.

★**Jesse's Bistro** The Stableyard, 14 Black Jack St ☎ 01285 641497, ⓦ jessesbistro.co.uk. Wonderful little hideaway, in a courtyard near the museum. The speciality here is fish and seafood, freshly caught and whisked over direct from Cornwall. Expect crab salad or *moules marinière*, oven-roasted mackerel or pepper-crusted bream alongside meaty favourites such as rump steak or calves' liver. Mains roughly £12–14. Mon noon–2.30pm, Tues–Sat noon–2.30pm & 7–9.30pm.

Made By Bob The Corn Hall, 26 Market Place ☎ 01285 641818, ⓦ foodmadebybob.com. Buzzy, hip daytime café/restaurant. Opens for breakfast (Bircher muesli, kippers, eggs Benedict, full English; £5–10), and stays open after lunch for posh tea. Watch the chefs prepare anything from fish soup with gruyère or red pepper tart to grilled squid or ribeye steak (mains £9–18) – or visit the deli section for swanky sandwiches (£5–6). Mon–Wed 7.30am–5.30pm, Thurs & Fri 7.30am–5.30pm & 7–9pm, Sat 8am–5.30pm.

Tetbury and around

With Prince Charles's Highgrove estate and Princess Anne's Gatcombe Park nearby, **TETBURY** is the Cotswolds' most royal town – but this attractive, engaging place has plenty going for it with or without the Windsors. Scenic countryside, good shopping and excellent food make a fine combination. Just down from the central crossroads, marked by the seventeenth-century **Market House**, Tetbury's **church** (daily 10am–4pm) – curiously dedicated to both St Mary the Virgin and St Mary Magdalene – is one of England's finest examples of **Georgian Gothic**.

Westonbirt: the National Arboretum

3 miles southwest of Tetbury • Daily 9am–8pm; Sept–March closes 5pm • Guided walks March–Oct Wed 11am, Sat & Sun 2pm • £5–9 depending on season; guided walks free • ☎ 01666 880220, ⓦ forestry.gov.uk/westonbirt • Bus #27 (Mon–Fri 5 daily, 3 on Sat; 8min from Tetbury)

Everything about **Westonbirt: The National Arboretum** relies on superlatives, from its role as protector of some of the oldest, biggest and rarest trees in the world to the display of natural colours it puts on in autumn. With seventeen miles of paths to roam, across six hundred acres, the best advice is to make a day of it. There are guided walks, **self-guided trails** and lots for kids and families.

ARRIVAL AND INFORMATION	TETBURY
By bus Buses drop off in the centre, including #881 from Cirencester (Mon–Sat every 2hrs; 40min). **Tourist office** 33 Church Street (March–Oct Mon–Sat	10am–4pm; Nov–Feb Mon–Sat 11am–2pm; ☎ 01666 503552, ⓦ visittetbury.co.uk & ⓦ cotswolds.com).

Painswick

PAINSWICK is a beautiful old Cotswolds wool town easily accessible from Cheltenham. The fame of Painswick's **church** stems not so much from the building itself as from the surrounding **graveyard**, where 99 yew trees, trimmed into bulbous lollipops, surround a collection of eighteenth-century table tombs unrivalled in the Cotswolds.

Rococo Garden

Half a mile north of Painswick, off Gloucester Rd (B4073) • Mid-Jan to Oct daily 11am–5pm • £6.50 • ☎ 01452 813204, ⓦ rococogarden.org.uk

Created in the early eighteenth century, the **Rococo Garden** has been restored to its original form with the aid of a painting from 1748. This is England's only example of Rococo garden design, a short-lived fashion typified by a mix of formal geometrical shapes and more naturalistic, curving lines. With a vegetable patch as an unusual centrepiece, it spreads across a sheltered gully – for the best views, walk around anticlockwise.

THAMES HEAD

Between Cirencester and Tetbury, **Kemble** is surrounded by water meadows regarded as the **source of the River Thames**. From Kemble station – served by hourly trains from London Paddington (1hr 15min) and Cheltenham (1hr) – walk half a mile north to the *Thames Head Inn* (☎ 01285 770259, ⓦ thamesheadinn.co.uk), by the railway bridge on the A433. At the pub, bar staff and a sketch-map hanging in the porch can point you onto the stroll of about fifteen minutes to **Thames Head**, a point by a copse in open fields, where a stone marker declares a shallow depression to be the river's source. However, the Thames is fed by groundwater, and since the water table rises and falls, the river's source shifts: don't be disappointed if Thames Head is dry when you visit. The **Thames Path** (ⓦ nationaltrail.co.uk) starts here: walk it direct to Greenwich in southeast London, 184 miles away.

ARRIVAL AND INFORMATION

By bus #46 runs from Cheltenham (hourly; 30min).

Tourist office Painswick's summer-only tourist office (April–Oct Mon–Wed 10am–1pm, Thurs & Fri 10am–4pm, Sat 10am–1pm; ☎ 07503 516924, ⓦ visitthecotswolds.

PAINSWICK

org.uk & ⓦ cotswolds.com) was, at the time of writing, temporarily housed in St Mary's Church ahead of a relocation to the gravedigger's hut in the churchyard.

ACCOMMODATION AND EATING

Cardynham House Tibbiwell St ☎ 01452 814006, ⓦ cardynham.co.uk. Lovely guesthouse with nine modern themed rooms, most with four-poster beds, all en suite. The bistro (closed Sun eve & Mon) has simple, well-cooked nosh – cod loin, lamb cutlets, beef stroganoff and the like (mains £12–16). **£90**

★**Olivas** Friday St ☎ 01452 814774, ⓦ olivas .moonfruit.com. Brilliant deli and café that does delicious Mediterranean-style lunches – Spanish soups and stews of chicken, chickpeas and chorizo, stuffed aubergines, loads of tapas including calamari, whitebait, olives, and more, all around £10. Daily 10am–5pm.

Cheltenham

Until the eighteenth century **CHELTENHAM** was a modest Cotswold town like any other, but the discovery of a spring in 1716 transformed it into Britain's most popular **spa**. During Cheltenham's heyday, a century or so later, royalty and nobility descended in droves to take the waters, which were said to cure anything from constipation to worms. These days, the town – still lively, still posh – has lots of good restaurants and some of England's best-preserved Regency architecture.

Cheltenham also has excellent **arts festivals** (ⓦ cheltenhamfestivals.com) – **jazz** (April), **science** (June), **classical music** (July) and **literature** (Oct), plus a separately run **folk** festival (Feb) – as well as world-class **horse-racing** (see box, p.255).

Promenade

Cheltenham's main street, **Promenade**, sweeps majestically south from the High Street, lined with some of the town's grandest houses and smartest shops. It leads into Imperial Square, whose greenery is surrounded by proud Regency terraces that herald the handsome terraces and squares of the Montpellier district, which stretches south in a narrow block to Suffolk Road, making for a pleasant urban stroll.

The Wilson (Cheltenham Art Gallery and Museum)

Clarence St • Daily 9.30am–5.15pm • Free • ☎ 01242 237431, ⓦ thewilson.org.uk

Just off the Promenade stands **The Wilson**, formerly known as the **Cheltenham Art Gallery and Museum**, now housing the tourist office, a shop selling beautiful work by the Gloucestershire Guild of Craftsmen (ⓦ guildcrafts.org.uk) and four floors of exhibitions. The rebranding honours Edward Wilson, a Cheltonian who was on Scott's ill-fated Antarctic expedition of 1912. Photographs and some of his Antarctic gear are displayed alongside a collection focused on the Arts and Crafts movement, ranging from superb furniture to ceramics, jewellery, pottery and exquisitely hand-illustrated books.

Holst Birthplace Museum

4 Clarence Rd • June–Sept Tues–Sat 10am–5pm, Sun 1.30–5pm; rest of year Tues–Sat 10am–4pm; closed Jan • £5 • ☎ 01242 524846, ⓦ holstmuseum.org.uk

Housed in a refined Regency terrace house, the **Holst Birthplace Museum** was where the composer of *The Planets* was born, in 1874. Its intimate rooms hold plenty of Holst memorabilia – including his piano in the ground-floor music room – and give a good insight into Victorian family life.

4

Pittville Pump Room

Pittville Park • Daily 10am–4pm • ☎ 01242 523852, ⓦ pittvillepumproom.org.uk

About ten minutes' walk north along handsome Evesham Road brings you into the **Pittville** district, where local chancer Joseph Pitt began work on a grand spa in the 1820s, soon afterwards running out of cash, though he did manage to complete the domed **Pump Room** before he hit the skids. A lovely Classical structure with an imposing colonnaded facade, it is now used mainly as a concert hall, but you can still sample the pungent **spa waters** from the marble fountain in the main auditorium for free.

ARRIVAL AND INFORMATION   CHELTENHAM

By train Cheltenham Spa station is on Queen's Rd, southwest of the centre; local buses run into town every 10min, otherwise it's a 20min walk.

Destinations Birmingham New Street (2–3 hourly; 40min); Bristol (every 30min; 40min); London Paddington (hourly, some change at Swindon; 2hr 15min).

By bus National Express coaches to and from London and Heathrow Airport stop on Royal Well Road. Local buses stop on Promenade.

Destinations #46 to Painswick (hourly; 30min); #51 to Cirencester (Mon–Sat hourly; 40min); #94 to Gloucester (every 10min; 35min); #606 to Winchcombe

(Mon–Sat approx hourly; 20min) and Broadway (Mon–Sat 2–3 daily; 45min); #801 to Northleach (Mon–Sat every 1–2hrs; 35min), Stow-on-the-Wold (Mon–Sat hourly; June–Sept also 2 on Sun; 1hr) and Moreton-in-Marsh (Mon–Sat hourly; June–Sept also 2 on Sun; 1hr 15min); #853 to Northleach (Mon–Sat 3 daily, Sun daily; 30min), Burford (Mon–Sat 3 daily, Sun daily; 45min) and Oxford (Mon–Sat 3 daily, Sun daily; 1hr 30min).

Tourist office In The Wilson gallery, Clarence Street (daily 9.30am–5.15pm; ☎ 01242 237431, ⓦ visitcheltenham .com & ⓦ cotswolds.com).

CHELTENHAM RACES

Cheltenham racecourse (☎01242 513014, ⍟cheltenham.co.uk), on the north side of town, is Britain's main venue for National Hunt racing, also known as "steeplechase" – where the horses jump hurdles or fences. The principal events are the four-day **Festival** in March, which attracts sixty thousand people each day, culminating in the famous **Cheltenham Gold Cup**, and the three-day **Open** in November, but there are smaller meetings throughout the season, which runs from late October to early May. For what many say is the best view, book ahead for entry to the pen opposite the main stand, known as Best Mate Enclosure (about £10–50, depending on event).

ACCOMMODATION

Cheltenham has plenty of **hotels** and **guesthouses**, many of them in fine Regency houses, but you should book well in advance during the races and festivals.

Abbey 14 Bath Parade ☎01242 516053, ⍟abbeyhotel -cheltenham.com. Thirteen individually furnished rooms at this centrally located B&B, with wholesome breakfasts taken overlooking the garden. **£87**

Big Sleep Wellington St ☎01242 696999, ⍟the bigsleephotel.com. Contemporary budget hotel with 59 rooms including family rooms and suites, all with a retro designer feel and hi-tech gadgetry but no frills – and unusually low prices. **£55**

Hotel du Vin Parabola Rd ☎01242 588450, ⍟hotelduvin.com. Occupying a splendid old Regency mansion, this glam boutique-style hotel in the sought-after Montpellier district has 49 stylish rooms and suites

and a reputation for excellence. **£105**

Lypiatt House Lypiatt Rd ☎01242 224994, ⍟lypiatt .co.uk. Splendid, four-square Victorian villa set in its own grounds a short walk from the centre, with spacious rooms, open fires and a conservatory with a small bar. **£98**

Montpellier Chapter Bayshill Rd ☎01242 527788, ⍟themontpellierchapterhotel.com. Gloriously grand villa hotel in the classy Montpellier neighbourhood. The restaurant is super-stylish, with its open kitchen and glassed terrace, and the same contemporary flair extends to the rooms, with their monsoon showers, feature walls, hi-tech gadgetry and some with in-room bathtubs and/or balconies. **£125**

EATING

★**Daffodil** 18–20 Suffolk Parade ☎01242 700055, ⍟www.thedaffodil.com. Eat in the circle bar or auditorium of this breathtakingly designed 1920s Art Deco ex-cinema, where the screen has been replaced with a hubbub of chefs. Great atmosphere and first-class British cuisine (mains £14–22), as well as cocktails and a swish of style. Live jazz Sat lunchtime & Mon night. Mon–Sat noon–11pm.

Le Champignon Sauvage 24 Suffolk Rd ☎01242 573449, ⍟lechampignonsauvage.co.uk. Cheltenham's highest-rated restaurant, its sensitively updated classic French cuisine awarded two Michelin stars among a welter of other awards. The ambience is chic and intimate, the presentation immaculately artistic. The full menu is £48 (two courses) or £59 (three courses), or opt for the smaller set menu at £26 (two courses). Book well ahead. Tues–Sat

12.30–1.15pm & 7.30–8.30pm.

Lumière Clarence Parade ☎01242 222200, ⍟www .lumiere.cc. Upscale, contemporary, seasonal British food in a genial ambience of informality. Cornish scallops or sexed-up corned beef prelude mains such as Gloucester Old Spot pork done two ways, partridge or local venison. Three-course menu £55 (or £28 at lunch). Tues 7–9pm, Wed–Sat noon–1.30pm & 7–9pm.

Red Pepper 13 Regent St ☎01242 253900, ⍟www .redpeppercheltenham.co.uk. Family-run deli, coffee lounge and bistro in the centre of town, with a friendly, informal vibe. Light lunches of pie and mash or fishcake and salad (£7–9), through to rack of lamb, gnocchi or sea bass in the evenings (mains £11–15). Downstairs coffee lounge daily 9am–6pm; upstairs bistro Tues–Fri 6–9.30pm, Sat noon–3pm & 6–9.30pm, Sun noon–3pm.

DRINKING AND NIGHTLIFE

Beehive 1–3 Montpellier Villas ☎01242 702270, ⍟thebeehivemontpellier.com. Popular, easygoing pub in Montpellier, under new management in 2014, with good beer, a friendly ambience and decent pub grub in the atmospheric restaurant upstairs. Mon–Sat 11am–11pm, Sun noon–10pm.

★**John Gordons** 11 Montpellier Arcade ☎01242

245985, ⍟johngordons.co.uk. Lovely little independent wine bar, hidden off Montpellier's fanciest street. Take a seat in the shop or outside in the old Victorian covered arcade to watch the world go by while sampling a glass or two of wine, alongside a plate of charcuterie, cheeses and/ or antipasti (£6–14). Mon–Wed 9.30am–11pm, Thurs–Sat 9.30am–midnight, Sun 11am–10pm.

Montpellier Wine Bar Bayshill Lodge, Montpellier St · ☎ 01242 527774, ⓦ montpellierwinebar.co.uk. Stylish wine bar and restaurant with lovely bow-fronted windows on a busy little corner. Hangout at the bar with glass of something smooth, or drop in mid-morning for brunch. Mon–Thurs 10am–3pm & 6–9.30pm, Fri–Sun 10am–9.30pm.

Gloucester

For centuries life was good for **GLOUCESTER**, ten miles west of Cheltenham. The Romans chose this spot for a garrison to guard the River Severn, while in Saxon and Norman times the Severn developed into one of Europe's busiest trade routes. The city became a major religious centre too, but from the fifteenth century onwards a combination of fire, plague, civil war and increasing competition from rival towns sent Gloucester into a decline from which it never recovered – even the opening of a new canal in 1827 between Gloucester and Sharpness to the south failed to revive the town's dwindling fortunes.

Today, the **canal** is busy once again, though this time with pleasure boats, and the Victorian **docks** have undergone a facelift, offering a fascinating glimpse into the region's industrial past. The main reason for a visit, however, remains Gloucester's magnificent **cathedral**, one of the finest in the country.

Gloucester Cathedral

College Green · Daily 7.30am–6pm · Free · ⓦ gloucestercathedral.org.uk

The superb condition of **Gloucester Cathedral** is striking in a city that has lost so much of its history. The Saxons founded an abbey here, but four centuries later Benedictine monks arrived intent on building their own church; work began in 1089. As a place of worship it shot to importance after the murder of King Edward II in 1327 at Berkeley Castle: Gloucester took his body, and the king's shrine became a major place of pilgrimage. The money generated helped finance the conversion of the church into the country's first and greatest example of the **Perpendicular style**: the magnificent 225ft tower crowns the achievement.

Beneath the reconstructions of the fourteenth and fifteenth centuries, some Norman aspects remain, best seen in the **nave**, which is flanked by sturdy pillars and arches adorned with immaculate zigzag carvings. The **choir** provides the best vantage point for admiring the **east window** completed in around 1350 and – at almost 80ft tall – the largest medieval window in Britain, a stunning cliff face of stained glass. Beneath it, to the left (as you're facing the east window) is the **tomb of Edward II**, immortalized in alabaster and marble. Below the east window lies the **Lady Chapel**, whose delicate carved tracery holds a staggering patchwork of windows. The innovative nature of the cathedral's design can also be appreciated in the beautiful **cloisters**, completed in 1367 and featuring the first fan vaulting in the country – used to represent the corridors of Hogwart's School in the *Harry Potter* films.

Gloucester Waterways Museum

Gloucester Docks • Daily: July & Aug 10.30am–5pm; rest of year 11am–4pm; boat trips May–Aug daily on the hour noon–3pm; April, Sept & Oct Sat & Sun only; 45min • £5.50; boat trip £6 • ☎01452 318200, ⓦ canalrivertrust.org.uk/gloucester-waterways-museum

Less than half a mile southwest of the city centre, **Gloucester Docks** holds fourteen warehouses built for storing grain following the opening of the Sharpness canal to the River Severn in 1827. Most have been turned into offices and shops, but the southernmost Llanthony Warehouse is now occupied by the **Gloucester Waterways Museum**, which delves into every nook and cranny of the area's watery history, from the engineering of the locks to the lives of the horses that trod the towpaths, along with plenty of interactive displays. The museum runs regular **boat trips** out onto the Sharpness canal, with commentary.

ARRIVAL AND INFORMATION

GLOUCESTER

By train Gloucester station is on Bruton Way, a 5min walk east of the centre.
Destinations Birmingham New Street (hourly; 50min); Bristol (hourly; 40min); London Paddington (hourly, some change at Swindon; 1hr 55min).
By bus National Express coaches to and from London and Heathrow Airport stop opposite the train station, as do local buses.

Destinations #94 to Cheltenham (every 10min; 35min), #852 to Cirencester (Mon–Sat 4 daily; 1hr 10min), #853 to Northleach (Mon–Sat 2 daily, Sun daily; 55min), Burford (Mon–Sat 2 daily, Sun daily; 1hr 20min) and Oxford (Mon–Sat 2 daily, Sun daily; 2hr).
Tourist office 28 Southgate Street (Mon 10am–5pm, Tues–Sat 9.30am–5pm; ☎01452 396572, ⓦ thecityofgloucester.co.uk & ⓦ cotswolds.com).

ACCOMMODATION AND EATING

Café René 31 Southgate St ☎01452 309340, ⓦ caferene.co.uk. This lively, fancifully decorated central pub serves decent burgers and steaks, with plenty for vegetarians (mains £9–14) and lighter lunches, as well as great Sunday barbecues in summer, and live blues, jazz and acoustic music twice a week. After 11pm on weekend nights, the cellar bar turns into a club (£2 admission), for loud local DJs. Sun–Thurs 11am–midnight, Fri & Sat 11am–4am.

Mulberry House 2a Heathville Rd ☎01452 720079, ⓦ the-mulberry-house.co.uk. Decent B&B in a modern family home roughly ten minutes' walk northeast. Two en-suite doubles are enhanced with quality breakfasts. Cash only. £55

New Inn 16 Northgate St ☎01452 522177, ⓦ newinn-hotel.co.uk. Pop into this fourteenth-century pub in the city centre to sup a pint of one of their several cask ales and have a gander at the preserved interior – this is Britain's most complete surviving medieval courtyard tavern, ringed by galleries (and, reputedly, haunted). Also 33 fairly basic rooms, with corporate furniture and swirly carpets. Mon–Thurs 11am–11pm, Fri & Sat 11am–midnight, Sun noon–10.30pm. £54

So Thai Longsmith St ☎01452 535185, ⓦ so-thai .co.uk. This Thai restaurant has rapidly gained a reputation for quality and authenticity. The decor takes in vaulted brickwork, service is attentive and the food – including unusual northern Thai pork curry with pineapple and lamb *massaman curry* – expertly prepared. Mains £9–16, two-course lunch menu £9. Tues–Sun 11am–10pm.

Bristol, Bath and Somerset

ST MICHAEL'S TOWER, GLASTONBURY TOR

5

Bristol, Bath and Somerset

The soft, undulating green swards of Somerset encapsulate rural England at its best. The scenery is always varied, with tidy cricket greens and well-kept country pubs contrasting with its wilder, more dramatic landscapes, from limestone gorges to windswept marshland. A world away from all of this, the main city hereabouts is Bristol, one of the most dynamic and cosmopolitan centres outside London. Its medieval old quarter and revitalized waterfront are supplemented by a superb range of pubs, clubs and restaurants. Just a few miles away, the graceful, Georgian, honey-toned terraces of Bath combine with beautifully preserved Roman baths, a clutch of first-class museums and a mellow café culture to make it an unmissable stop.

Within easy reach to the south lie the exquisite cathedral city of **Wells** and the ancient town of **Glastonbury**, a site steeped in Christian lore, Arthurian legend and New Age mysticism. The nearby **Mendip Hills** are fine walking territory and are pocked by cave systems, as at **Wookey Hole** and **Cheddar Gorge**. Beyond here, verdant **South Somerset**, with its pretty little hamstone villages and traditional cider farms, matches the county's bucolic ideal more than any other region. The county town of **Taunton** makes a useful base for exploring the **Quantocks**, while further west, straddling the border with Devon, the heathery slopes and wide-open spaces of **Exmoor** offer a range of hikes, with wonderful views from its cliffy seaboard.

Bristol

On the borders of Gloucestershire and Somerset, **BRISTOL** has harmoniously blended its mercantile roots with an innovative, modern culture, fuelled by technology-based industries, a large student population and a lively arts and music scene. As well as its vibrant **nightlife**, the city's sights range from medieval churches to cutting-edge attractions highlighting its maritime and scientific achievements.

Weaving through its centre, the River Avon forms part of a system of waterways that made Bristol a great inland port, in later years booming on the transatlantic trafficking of rum, tobacco and slaves. In the nineteenth century, the illustrious **Isambard Kingdom Brunel** laid the foundations of a tradition of engineering, creating two of Bristol's greatest monuments: the *ss Great Britain* and the lofty Clifton Suspension Bridge.

Bristol Cathedral

College Green · Mon–Fri 8am–6pm, Sat & Sun 8am–5pm · **Evensong** Mon–Fri 5.15pm, Sat & Sun 3.30pm · Free **Guided tours** usually Sat 11.30am, sometimes also 1.30pm · Free · ⓦ bristol-cathedral.co.uk

Founded as an abbey around 1140 on the supposed spot of St Augustine's convocation with Celtic Christians in 603, venerable **Bristol Cathedral** became a cathedral church with the Dissolution of the Monasteries in the mid-sixteenth century. The two towers

Beau Nash p.270	**Glastonbury Festival** p.281
Bath's festivals p.275	**The West Somerset Railway** p.283
Glastonbury Tales p.280	**The South West Coast Path** p.286

GLASTONBURY FESTIVAL

Highlights

❶ ss Great Britain, Bristol Moored in the dock in which she was built, the iconic ship is now an iconic museum, an interactive insight into life aboard a nineteenth-century steamer. **See p.265**

❷ Thermae Bath Spa Take the purifying waters at this cutting-edge facility in the UK's original spa town. **See p.270**

❸ Royal Crescent, Bath In a city famous for its graceful arcs of Georgian terraces, this is the granddaddy of them all, an architectural tour de force with a magnificent vista. **See p.272**

❹ Wells Cathedral A gem of medieval masonry, this richly ornamented Gothic

masterpiece is the centrepiece of England's smallest city. **See p.276**

❺ Cheddar Gorge Impressive rockscape with a network of illuminated caves at its base; it's an excellent starting point for wild walks in the Mendip Hills. **See p.277**

❻ Glastonbury Festival Pack your tent, dust off your welllies and enjoy the ride that is simply Britain's biggest, boldest and best music festival. **See p.281**

❼ Exmoor Whether you ride it, bike it or hike it, the rolling wilderness of Exmoor offers fine opportunities to experience the great outdoors. **See p.284**

HIGHLIGHTS ARE MARKED ON THE MAP ON P.262

HIGHLIGHTS

1 ss Great Britain, Bristol
2 Thermae Bath Spa
3 Royal Crescent, Bath
4 Wells Cathedral
5 Cheddar Gorge
6 Glastonbury Festival
7 Exmoor

WALES

Cardiff

Barry

Bridgend

Bristol Channel

Bridgwater Bay

River Severn

Portishead

Clevedon

Weston-super-Mare

Burnham-on-Sea

Uphill

Foreland Point

South West Coast Path

Lynmouth
Lynton

Watersmeet

Porlock Weir
Porlock
Selworthy

Minehead
Dunster
Dunster Castle

Holford

Simonsbath

EXMOOR NATIONAL PARK

Exford

Winsford

Tarr Steps

Dulverton

Tiverton

DEVON

South Molton

Chulmleigh

Bristol

Bath

Keynsham
Newton St Loe

Radstock

Frome

Gillingham

Stalbridge
Sturminster Newton

DORSET

Sherborne

Corton Denham

Wincanton

Bruton
Castle Cary

Haynes International Motor Museum

Lovington

Somerton

Yeovil

Montacute House

Fleet Air Arm Museum

Hinton St George

South Petherton

Perry's Cider Mills

Chard

Burrow Hill Cider Farm

SOMERSET

Shepton Mallet
Pilton

Wookey Hole

Wells

Ebbor Gorge

Glastonbury

Street

Wilkins

Cheddar Gorge
Cheddar

Thatchers

Bristol Airport

Ashbridge

Mendip Hills

Bridgwater

Fiddington

Nether Stowey
Aisholt
Crowcombe
Friscombe

Quantock Hills

Bishops Lydeard

Combe Florey

West Somerset Railway

Taunton

Sheppy's Cider

Wellington

Wales

Bristol

Avon

M4
M5
M32
M48

A46
A36
A37
A38
A39
A358
A361
A371
A372
A396
A399
A303
A30
A37
A303

N

0 miles 10

on the west front were erected in the nineteenth century in a faithful act of homage to Edmund Knowle, architect and abbot at the start of the fourteenth century. The interior offers a unique example among Britain's cathedrals of a German-style "hall church", in which the aisles, nave and choir rise to the same height. Abbot Knowle's immense **choir** offers one of the country's most exquisite illustrations of the early Decorated style of Gothic, while the adjoining thirteenth-century **Elder Lady Chapel** contains some fine tombs and eccentric carvings of animals, including (between the arches on the right) a monkey playing the bagpipes accompanied by a ram on the violin. The **Eastern Lady Chapel** has some of England's finest examples of heraldic glass. From the south transept, a door leads to the **Chapter House**, a richly carved piece of late Norman architecture.

City Museum and Art Gallery

Queen's Rd, at the top of Park St • Daily 10am–5pm, Sat & Sun till 6pm • Free • ☎ 0117 922 3571, ⓦ bristolmuseums.org.uk/bristol
-museum-and-art-gallery

Housed in a grandiose Edwardian-Baroque building, the **City Museum and Art Gallery** has sections on local archeology, geology and natural history, as well as an important collection of Chinese porcelain and some magnificent Assyrian reliefs carved in the eighth century BC. Art works by Banksy, the Bristol School and French Impressionists are mixed in with some choice older pieces, including a portrait of Martin Luther by Cranach the Elder and Giovanni Bellini's unusual *Descent into Limbo*.

St Stephen's

21 Stephen's St, off Corn St • Mon–Fri & Sun 8.45am–4pm • Free • ☎ 0117 927 7977, ⓦ saint-stephens.com

Surrounded by characterless modern buildings just east of The Centre, **St Stephen's** is one of Bristol's oldest and most graceful churches. It dates from the thirteenth century, was rebuilt in the fifteenth, and was thoroughly restored with plenty of neo-Gothic trimmings in 1875. The church has some flamboyant tombs inside, mainly of various members of the merchant class who were the church's main patrons.

Corn Exchange

The Georgian **Corn Exchange** was designed by John Wood of Bath and now contains the covered **St Nicholas Markets**, a lively spot for a wander or a bite to eat. The four engraved brass pillars outside the entrance date from the sixteenth and seventeenth centuries and originally served as trading tables – thought to be the "nails" that gave rise to the expression "pay on the nail".

The New Room

36 The Horsefair, Broadmead • Mon–Sat 10am–4pm • Free • ☎ 0117 926 4740, ⓦ newroombristol.org.uk

Hidden inside **Broadmead** shopping centre is England's first Methodist chapel, **the New Room**. Established by John Wesley in 1739, it looks very much as he left it, with a double-deck pulpit in the chapel, beneath a hidden upstairs window from which the evangelist could observe the progress of his trainee preachers.

King Street and around

King Street, a short walk southeast from The Centre, was laid out on marshland in 1663 and still holds a cluster of historic buildings, among them the **Theatre Royal**, the oldest working theatre in the country, opened in 1766 and preserving many of its original Georgian features. Further down, and in a very different architectural style, stands the timber-framed **Llandoger Trow** pub (see p.268), once the haunt of seafarers,

5

▲ ④ & A420 Chippenham

ACCOMMODATION
Brooks Guesthouse	5
Bristol Marriott Royal Hotel	6
Clifton House	1
Hotel du Vin	3
Number 9, PB	2
Rock & Bowl Motel	4
YHA Bristol	7

CAFÉS & RESTAURANTS
Bistro du Vin	5
Bordeaux Quay	10
Full Court Press	7
Kathmandu	6
Lido	1
Maitreya Social	4
Primrose Café & Bistro	2
riverstation	11
Severnshed	12
Source	8
Thali Café	3
Watershed	9

PUBS & BARS
Avon Gorge Hotel	2
Big Chill Bar	6
Browns	5
Canteen	1
The Coronation Tap	3
Goldbrick House	8
Grain Barge	14
Llandoger Trow	12
No. 1 Harbourside	13
Start the Bus	10

CLUBS & LIVE MUSIC
Colston Hall	7
Fiddlers	17
The Fleece	11
The Louisiana	16
St George's	9
Syndicate	4
Thekla	15

BRISTOL

0   200
yards

and reputed to have been the meeting place of Daniel Defoe and Alexander Selkirk, the model for Robinson Crusoe. South of King Street is the elegant, grassy **Queen Square**.

St Mary Redcliffe

Redcliffe Way, Redcliffe • Mon–Sat 8.30am–5pm, Sun 8am–8pm • Free • ☎ 0117 929 1487, ⊛ stmaryredcliffe.co.uk

Described by Elizabeth I as "the fairest, goodliest and most famous parish church in England", the richly decorated church of **St Mary Redcliffe**, across Redcliffe Bridge from The Centre, was largely paid for and used by merchants and mariners. The present building was begun at the end of the thirteenth century, though it was added to in subsequent centuries and its tall spire – a distinctive feature on the city's skyline – dates from 1872. Inside, memorials and tombs recall figures associated with the building, including the Handel Window, installed in 1859 on the centenary of the death of Handel, who composed on the magnificent organ here.

Above the church's north porch is the muniment room, where **Thomas Chatterton** claimed to have found a trove of medieval manuscripts; the poems, distributed as the work of a fifteenth-century monk named Thomas Rowley, were in fact dazzling fakes. The young poet committed suicide after his forgery was exposed, supplying English literature with one of its most glamorous stories of self-destructive genius. The "Marvellous Boy" (according to William Wordsworth) is remembered by a memorial stone in the south transept.

At Bristol

Anchor Rd • Daily 10am–5pm, Sat, Sun & hols till 6pm • £12.05, under-15s £7.70, under-3s free • ☎ 0845 345 1235, ⊛ at-bristol.org.uk

Occupying a corner of Harbourside's sleekly modern **Millennium Square**, marked out by the spherical, stainless-steel planetarium attached to one side, **At-Bristol** deals with all things science. It's chiefly aimed at children, but there's enough interactive wizardry here to entertain and inform everyone, with opportunities to view the blood in your veins, freeze your shadow and create your own short films (with input from Aardman Animations). The planetarium has up to eight shows daily, which should be booked when you buy your entry ticket (from £1 extra).

M-Shed

Princes Wharf, Wapping Rd • Tues–Fri 10am–5pm, Sat, Sun & bank hols 10am–6pm • Free, £2 donation suggested • Guided tours Tues & Thurs–Sat 11.30am, Wed 2.30pm; 1hr; £2 • Boat and railway rides on selected days throughout the year; £1–5 • ☎ 0117 352 6600, ⊛ bristolmuseums.org.uk/m-shed

Opened in 2011, the superb **M-Shed**, housed in an old harbourside transit shed, is Bristol's first museum dedicated to itself, past and present, and offers the best official insight into what makes the city tick. It's an enjoyable, unashamedly populist survey, full of memorabilia and anecdotes and casting light on everything from the city's mercantile history and its role in the transatlantic slave trade to its festivals and street-life. On the ground floor, Bristol Places charts the city's changing face, from the Bristol Dinosaur through its development as a port and the hardships of World War II. Bristol People, on the floor above, and the adjoining Bristol Life, look at the (often ordinary) folk who have shaped the city, whilst the latter includes an excellent – and long overdue – display on the slave trade in Bristol. Afetrwards, head out to the long terrace for fantastic harbour views.

ss Great Britain

Great Western Dockyard • Daily 10am–5.30pm, Nov–March till 4.30pm • £13.75 • ☎ 0117 926 0680, ⊛ ssgreatbritain.org

Harbourside's major draw, and one of Bristol's iconic sights, the **ss Great Britain** was the first propeller-driven, ocean-going iron ship in the world, built by **Isambard Kingdom Brunel** in 1843. She initially ran between Liverpool and New York, then between Liverpool

5

and Melbourne, circumnavigating the globe 32 times and chalking up over a million miles at sea. Her ocean-going days ended in 1886 when she was caught in a storm off Cape Horn, and she was eventually recovered and returned to Bristol in 1970. On board, you can see restored cabins and peer into the immense engine room, whilst the adjoining museum gives the background of the vessel and of Bristol's long shipbuilding history.

Clifton

On the western side of the city, **Clifton**, once an aloof spa resort, is now Bristol's stateliest neighbourhood. At the top of Blackboy Hill, the wide green expanses of **Durdham Down** and **Clifton Downs** stretch right up to the edge of the Avon Gorge, a popular spot for picnickers, joggers and kite-flyers. On the southern edge of the Downs is the select enclave of Clifton Village, centred on the Mall, where **Royal York Crescent**, the longest Georgian crescent in the country, offers splendid views over the steep drop to the River Avon below.

Clifton Suspension Bridge

Free, £1 for vehicles **Visitor Centre** Daily 10am–5pm • Free **Guided tours** Easter–Oct Sat & Sun 3pm • 45min • Free • ⓦ cliftonbridge.org.uk

A few minutes' walk from Clifton Village is Bristol's most famous symbol, **Clifton Suspension Bridge**, 702ft long and poised 245ft above high water. Money was first put forward for a bridge to span the Avon Gorge by a Bristol wine merchant in 1754, though it wasn't until 1829 that a competition was held for a design, won by **Isambard Kingdom Brunel** on a second round, and not until 1864 that the bridge was completed, five years after Brunel's death. Hampered by financial difficulties, the bridge never quite matched the engineer's original ambitious design, which included Egyptian-style towers topped by sphinxes at each end. You can see copies of his plans in the **Visitor Centre** at the far side of the bridge, alongside designs proposed by Brunel's rivals, some of them frankly bizarre.

ARRIVAL AND DEPARTURE   BRISTOL

By train Temple Meads train station is a 20min walk east of the city centre.
Destinations Bath (every 15–30min; 15min); Birmingham (every 30min–1hr; 1hr 25min); Bridgwater (every 30min–1hr; 50min); Cheltenham (every 30min–1hr; 40min–1hr); Exeter (every 30min–1hr; 1hr); Gloucester (every 30min–1hr; 50min); London Paddington (every 30min–1hr; 1hr 40min); Taunton (every 15–50min; 30min); Yeovil (7 daily; 1hr 10min).

By bus Bristol's bus station (ⓦ firstgroup.com) is centrally located off Marlborough Street; Megabus services to and from London stop opposite Colston Hall, off The Centre, the traffic-ridden nucleus of the city.
Destinations Bath (Mon–Sat every 15min, Sun every 30min; 50min); Glastonbury (every 30min; 1hr 30min); London (every 30min–1hr; 2hr 30min); Wells (every 30min; 1hr).

INFORMATION AND TOURS

Tourist office E-Shed, Canon's Road (Daily 11am–4pm, Sat from 10am; ☎ 0906 711 2191, ⓦ visitbristol.co.uk).
Tours City Sightseeing Bristol (☎ 07425 788123, ⓦ citysightseeingbristol.co.uk) runs a hop-on, hop-off,

open-top bus tour of the city's key sights (£13), while Bristol Packet (☎ 0117 926 8157, ⓦ bristolpacket.co.uk) offers cruises around the harbour and along the river to Bath (from £5.75).

GETTING AROUND

By ferry A ferry, setting off from the Quayhead, just south of The Centre, connects various parts of the Floating Harbour, including Temple Meads station and the ss *Great Britain* (every 20min; 10am–6.15pm; from £1.50 single;

£2.50 return; £6 all-day ticket; ⓦ bristolferry.com).
By bus Local buses are useful for getting to Clifton's upper reaches; take #8 or #9 from Temple Meads station or The Centre, which also connects the city's train and bus stations.

ACCOMMODATION

With a few notable exceptions, good accommodation in Bristol is surprisingly thin on the ground. Hotels and B&Bs in the centre can suffer from traffic noise and the sound of late-night drinkers; for quieter and more traditional lodgings, choose Clifton, with a range of pubs and restaurants on the main axis of Whiteladies Road.

5

★**Brooks Guesthouse** St Nicholas St, entrance on Exchange Ave ☎ 0117 930 0066, ⓦ brooksguesthouse bristol.com. Set in the midst of bustling St Nicholas Markets, this boutique B&B has small but comfortable rooms that come with iPod docks, DVD players and free wi-fi. The airy modern breakfast room gives onto a spacious courtyard for relaxing with a book or a drink. You can also stay in an airstream trailer on the roof (from £110). **£65**

Bristol Marriott Royal Hotel College Green ☎ 0117 925 5100, ⓦ bristolmarriottroyal.co.uk. Right next to Bristol Cathedral, this Italianate-style Victorian hotel is by far the more attractive of the city's two *Marriotts*, with spacious rooms, two restaurants and a Champagne bar, and a lovely swimming pool. **£105**

Clifton House 4 Tyndall's Park Rd ☎ 0117 973 5407, ⓦ cliftonhousebristol.com. This handily sited B&B at the bottom of Clifton and near the centre offers fairly plush rooms with big windows, modern bathrooms and plenty of space – superior rooms, costing £20 extra, are huge. There's free wi-fi and parking. **£75**

Hotel du Vin The Sugar House, Narrow Lewins Mead ☎ 0117 925 5577, ⓦ hotelduvin.co.uk. Chic conversion of an old dockside sugar factory, centrally located, with dark, contemporary decor. Rooms have big beds and grand bathrooms, and there's an excellent restaurant to boot (see below). **£149**

★**Number 9. PB** 9 Prince's Buildings ☎ 0117 973 4615, ⓦ 9pb.co.uk. A short walk from the Clifton Suspension Bridge and within staggering distance of several real-ale pubs, this five-storey Georgian B&B, lovingly cared for by its easy-going owners, enjoys a grand vista over the Avon Gorge from its antique-filled rooms. Great breakfasts, too. Singles from £60. No credit cards. **£85**

Rock & Bowl Motel 22 Nelson St ☎ 0117 325 1980, ⓦ rocknbowlmotel.com. Clean and efficiently run hostel in an ex-dole office above a busy bowling alley. Single- and mixed-sex dorms (4- to 12-person) and a few en-suite doubles and twins, plus a self-catering kitchen. Laundry and wi-fi. Dorms **£16**, doubles **£49**

YHA Bristol 14 Narrow Quay ☎ 0845 371 9726, ⓦ yha .org.uk. In a refurbished warehouse on the quayside, this warm and friendly hostel has mostly four-bed dorms, plus (smallish) private doubles. There's a decent kitchen, and prices include an abundant breakfast. Dorms **£20.50**, doubles **£49**

EATING

CAFÉS

Full Court Press 59 Broad St ☎ 07794 808552, ⓦ fcpcoffee.com. The select menu of superb speciality coffees at this dinky joint near St Nicks Markets have made it an instant hit with local connoisseurs. Try your single coffee served four ways (£8). Mon–Fri 7.30am–5pm, Sat 9am–5pm, Sun 10am–4pm.

Primrose Café & Bistro 1 Clifton Arcade, Boyces Ave ☎ 0117 946 6577, ⓦ primrosecafe.co.uk. Homely café in Clifton Village serving a good range of teas and organic fruit juices. Light-hearted lunchtime sandwiches include onion bhaji and mango chutney; evening fare (from £13.95) is more elaborate. Café Mon–Sat 9am–5pm, Sun 9.30am–3pm; bistro Tues–Thurs 6pm–late, Fri 7pm–late.

Watershed 1 Canon's Rd ☎ 0117 927 5101, ⓦ water shed.co.uk. Cool café-bar overlooking the boats in one of Bristol's longest-established arts complexes. Good coffee and local beers are supplemented by an appetizing menu, and there's free wi-fi and a small (non-smoking) terrace. Mon & Sat 10am–11pm, Tues–Fri 9.30am–11pm, Sun 10am–10.30pm.

RESTAURANTS

Bistro du Vin Hotel du Vin, The Sugar House, Narrow Lewins Mead ☎ 0117 925 5577, ⓦ hotelduvin.com. Fine French bistro-style dining in a former sugar factory, using good seasonal West Country produce in its Modern European menu; mains from £14. Mon–Sat noon–2.30pm & 5.30–10pm, Fri & Sat till 10.30pm, Sun noon–4pm & 6–9.30pm.

Bordeaux Quay V-Shed, Harbourside ☎ 0117 943 1200, ⓦ bordeaux-quay.co.uk. Housed in a former warehouse, with an elegantly minimalist restaurant upstairs offering harbour views (mains from £13), and a less formal downstairs brasserie (main dishes from £10.50). The food in both is mainly Mediterranean, and is steadfastly organic. There's also a bar and an excellent deli. Restaurant Tues–Sat 6–10pm, Sun noon–3pm; brasserie and bar Mon–Fri 8am–10.30pm, Sat 9am–10.30pm, Sun 9am–9pm.

Kathmandu Colston Tower, Colston St ☎ 0117 929 4455, ⓦ kathmandu-curry.com. This smart, family-run restaurant is a bastion of quality Nepalese cooking, though the menu also ventures south of the border as well. Tasty dishes, including *momo* (£7.95) and *chhoyla* (lamb cooked in a Tandoori oven with ginger and garlic; £9.95), are pepped up by spices imported from the owners' home village just outside Kathmandu. Mon–Thurs 5.45–11pm, Fri & Sat 5.45pm–midnight.

★**Lido** Oakfield Place, Clifton; restaurant entrance on Southleigh Rd ☎ 0117 933 9533, ⓦ lidobristol.com. Set-piece venue given a stylish new lease of life as a restaurant/bar and pool/spa complex. The glass-walled restaurant overlooks the outdoor pool, which makes dining on dishes like wood-roast chicken and chickpeas (£17.50) while others exercise a deliciously guilty affair. Restaurant daily noon–3pm & Mon–Sat 6–10pm, poolside bar Mon–Sat 8am–11pm, Sun 9am–6pm.

Maitreya Social 89 St Mark's Rd ☎ 0117 951 0100, ⓦ cafemaitreya.co.uk. Tucked away in the multicultural

5

but rundown neighbourhood of Easton, this easy-going place serves delicious, inventive vegetarian dishes – smoky roasted parsnip and cashew roulade (£10.95), for example, or warm samphire salad. Tues–Thurs 6–11.30pm, Fri & Sat 10am–11.30pm, Sun 10am–4pm.

riverstation The Grove ☎0117 914 4434, ⊚riverstation.co.uk. Two-storey former river-police station, with all-day brunches at the relaxed ground-floor bar and kitchen and more refined Modern European dining upstairs. Set lunches here cost around £13, while main courses in the evening start at £15.50. Try to bag a table by the window for the dockside views. Restaurant Mon–Sat noon–2.30pm & 6–10.30pm, Fri & Sat till 11pm, Sun noon–3pm; bar and kitchen Mon–Wed 9am–11pm, Thurs–Sat 9am–midnight, Sun 10am–5pm.

Severnshed The Grove ☎0117 925 1212, ⊚severnshedrestaurant.co.uk. With a waterside terrace, *Severnshed* serves pastas and pizzas (from £7) and grills, including firesticks – meat or fish kebabs (£17–21). DJs provide the soundtrack on Fri and Sat evenings. Daily 9am–11pm, Fri & Sat till 2am.

★**Source** 1–3 Exchange Ave, off St Nicholas St ☎0117 927 2998, ⊚source-food.co.uk. Almost all the food in this airy canteen next to St Nick's Markets is from the West Country, and much of it is organic and can be bought to take away – Cornish crab cakes, salt-marsh lamb, Somerset rosé veal (from £8), for example. Mon–Fri 8am–5pm, Sat 8am–6pm, first Sun of month 9am–4pm.

Thali Café 1 Regent St, Clifton ☎0117 974 3793, ⊚thethalicafe.co.uk. *Dhaba*-style South Asian food in vibrant surroundings. This Clifton branch – there are four others across Bristol – has the trademark deep-pink decor and range of tasty *thalis*, a balanced selection of dishes served on a stainless-steel platter (from £8.95). Daily noon–10pm, Sat & Sun from 10am.

DRINKING

Avon Gorge Hotel Sion Hill ☎0117 973 8955, ⊚theavongorge.com. Perched on the edge of the Gorge in Clifton Village, the hotel's modern bar draws in the crowds thanks to the magnificent views of the Suspension Bridge from its broad terrace. Daily 11am–11pm, Sun till 10.30pm.

Big Chill Bar 15 Small St ☎0117 930 4217, ⊚bigchill.net/bristol. Cool lounge and club for late-night drinking and dancing, connected to the festival of the same name. North American soul food comes courtesy of Mi Casa Cantina pop-up, but it's the quality live music and DJs (Wed–Sat) that make this place. Mon 5pm–1am, Tues & Wed noon–1am, Thurs noon–2am, Fri & Sat noon–3am.

Browns 38 Queen's Rd ☎0117 930 4777, ⊚browns-restaurants.com. Spacious and relaxed place for an evening drink, housed in the Venetian-style former university refectory. Wide choice of tipples includes 45 wines and Champagnes by the glass and some fine cocktails. Mon–Sat 8am–midnight, Mon & Tues till 11pm, Wed till 11.30pm, Sun 9am–11pm.

Canteen Hamilton House, 80 Stokes Croft ☎0117 923 2017, ⊚canteenbristol.co.uk. Overlooked by one of Banksy's most famous murals, a drab 1960s office block now accommodates this incredibly popular collective-style bar. Take a seat at a graffitied table for a coffee or a pint, or try something from the cheap, sustainable menu. Live music from 9.30pm most nights (from 4pm on Sun). Daily 10am–midnight, Fri & Sat till 1am.

★**The Coronation Tap** 8 Sion Place, Clifton ☎0117 973 9617, ⊚thecoronationtap.com. A proper cider house, The *Cori Tap* produces its own Exhibition "apple juice", which is sold by the half-pint only, and stocks a wide range of locally produced ciders. Excellent live music, too.

Daily 5.30pm–11.30pm, Sat & Sun from 7pm.

Goldbrick House 69 Park St ☎0117 945 1950, ⊚goldbrickhouse.co.uk. Stylish multi-level concept – café, restaurant (think cauliflower, hazelnut and gruyere pearl barley risotto; £13.25) and choice cocktail bar – housed in an old Georgian building, with original fireplaces and dark leather armchairs. Mon–Thurs 9am–midnight, Fri & Sat 9am–1am.

Grain Barge Mardyke Wharf, Hotwell Rd ☎0117 929 9347, ⊚grainbarge.com. Floating pub, café and restaurant near the mouth of the harbour, with a tranquil ambience and half a dozen real ales brewed at the Bristol Beer Factory. Interesting calendar of events, including live music on Fri evenings. Daily noon–11pm, Fri & Sat till 11.30pm.

Llandoger Trow 1–3 King St ☎0117 926 1650, ⊚brewersfayre.co.uk. Seventeenth-century drinking den full of historical associations (see p.263), with cosy nooks and armchairs, benches outside and a separate restaurant upstairs. Snacks and full meals available. Gets very busy on summer evenings. Mon–Sat 11am–11pm, Sun noon–10.30pm.

No.1 Harbourside 1 Canon's Rd ☎0117 929 1100, ⊚no1harbourside.co.uk. Laidback lounge bar for drinks and snacks all day until late, and live music (Wed–Sat). Meals (beetroot salad, ox-cheek ragu) are accompanied by free soup. Daily 10am–midnight, Mon & Sun till 11pm, Fri & Sat till 2am.

Start the Bus 7–9 Baldwin St ☎0117 930 4370, ⊚startthebus.tv. Mellow, slightly grungy bar/restaurant by day, buzzing music venue at night, with live bands most evenings. Food (including pulled-pork burgers and fishfinger sandwiches) served until 10pm. Daily noon–1am, Thurs till 2am, Fri & Sat till 3am.

NIGHTLIFE AND ENTERTAINMENT

Colston Hall Colston St ☎ 0844 887 1500, ⓦ colstonhall .org. Major names in the classical, jazz, rock and world genres appear in this stalwart mainstream venue. Hosts various Bristol music festivals throughout the year.

Fiddlers Willway St, Bedminster ☎ 0117 987 3403, ⓦ fiddlers.co.uk. Mainly live folk, world music and Afrobreat at this relaxed, family-run venue (formerly a prison) south of the river.

The Fleece 12 St Thomas St ☎ 0117 945 0996, ⓦ thefleece.co.uk. Stone-flagged ex-wool warehouse, now a loud, sweaty pub staging everything from acoustic blues and alt-country to punk and deathcore.

The Louisiana Wapping Rd ☎ 0117 926 5978, ⓦ thelouisiana.net. Established music pub with a well-earned reputation for helping break bands (The White Stripes, Florence and the Machine) and promoting local artists. It's a mite cramped, but the acoustics and atmosphere are excellent.

★**St George's** Great George St ☎ 0845 402 4001, ⓦ stgeorgesbristol.co.uk. Elegant Georgian church with superb acoustics, staging a packed programme of lunchtime and evening concerts covering classical, world, folk and jazz music.

Syndicate 15 Nelson St ☎ 0117 945 0325, ⓦ thesyndicate.com. A real super-club, the largest in Bristol, and home to various club nights dealing in house, garage, electro and R&B.

Thekla East Mud Dock, The Grove ☎ 0117 929 3301, ⓦ theklabristol.co.uk. Much-loved studenty riverboat venue, staging a varied line-up of live bands plus indie, house and pop club nights. Look out for the Banksy stencil of the Grim Reaper on its hull.

Bath

Just twelve miles from Bristol, **BATH** has a very different feel from its neighbour – more harmonious, compact, leisurely and complacent. The city's elegant crescents and Georgian buildings are studded with plaques naming Bath's eminent inhabitants from its heyday as a spa resort; it was here that Jane Austen set *Persuasion* and *Northanger Abbey*, and where Gainsborough established himself as a portraitist and landscape painter.

Bath owes its name and fame to its **hot springs** – the only ones in the country – which made it a place of reverence for the local Celtic population, though it took Roman technology to turn it into a fully fledged bathing establishment. The baths fell into decline with the departure of the Romans, but the town later regained its importance under the Saxons, its abbey seeing the coronation of the **first king of all England**, Edgar, in 973. A new bathing complex was built in the sixteenth century, popularized by the visit of Elizabeth I in 1574, and the city reached its fashionable zenith in the eighteenth century, when **Beau Nash** ruled the town's social scene (see box, p.270). It was at this time, Bath's "Golden Age", that the city acquired its ranks of Palladian mansions and Regency townhouses, all of them built in the local **Bath stone**. The legacy is a city whose greatest enjoyment comes simply from wandering its streets, with their pale gold architecture and sweeping vistas.

The Roman Baths

Abbey Churchyard • Daily: March–June, Sept & Oct 9am–6pm; July & Aug 9am–10pm; Nov–Feb 9.30am–5.30pm; last entry 1hr before closing • £13.50, £14 in July & Aug, £17 combined ticket with Fashion Museum • Free audioguides and hourly guided tours • ☎ 0225 477785, ⓦ romanbaths.co.uk

There are hours of entertainment in Bath's premier attraction, the **Roman Baths**, comprising the baths themselves and an informative museum – highlights include the Sacred Spring, part of the temple of the local deity Sulis Minerva, where water still bubbles up at a constant 46.5ºC; the open-air (but originally covered) Great Bath, its vaporous waters surrounded by nineteenth-century pillars, terraces and statues of famous Romans; the Circular Bath, where bathers cooled off; and the Norman King's Bath, where people were taking a restorative dip right up until 1978.

Among a quantity of coins, jewellery and sculpture exhibited are the bronze head of Sulis Minerva and a grand, Celtic-inspired gorgon's head from the temple's pediment.

5

Models of the complex at its greatest extent give some idea of the awe which it must have inspired, while the graffiti salvaged from the Roman era – mainly curses and boasts – offer a personal slant on this antique leisure centre.

You can get a free glimpse into the baths from the next-door **Pump Room**, the social hub of the Georgian spa community and still redolent of that era, which houses a formal tearoom and restaurant (see p.275).

Bath Abbey

Abbey Churchyard • April–Oct Mon 9.30am–5.30pm, Tues–Fri 9am–5.30pm, Sat 9am–6pm, Sun 1–2.30pm & 4.30–5.30pm (till 6pm in Aug); Nov–March Mon–Sat 9am–4.30pm, Sun 1–2.30pm & 4.30–5.30pm • Requested donation £2.50 • ⓦ bathabbey.org

Although there has been a church on the site since the seventh century, **Bath Abbey** did not take its present form until the end of the fifteenth century, when Bishop Oliver King began work on the ruins of the previous Norman building, some of which were incorporated into the new church. The bishop was said to have been inspired by a vision of angels ascending and descending a ladder to heaven, which the present facade recalls on the turrets flanking the central window. The west front also features the founder's signature in the form of carvings of olive trees surmounted by crowns, a play on his name.

The **interior** is in a restrained Perpendicular style, although it does boast splendid fan vaulting on the ceiling, which was not completed until the nineteenth century. The floor and walls are crammed with elaborate monuments and memorials, and traces of the grander Norman building are visible in the Gethsemane Chapel.

On most days, you can join a 45-minute tower tour (£6) to see the massive bells, clock and bell-pulling machinery, and can enjoy a bird's-eye view of Bath – but be prepared for the 212 spiral steps.

Thermae Bath Spa

Hot Bath St • **Baths** Daily: New Royal Bath 9am–9.30pm, last entry 7pm; Cross Bath 10am–8pm, last entry 6pm • £17 (1hr 30min) to £57 (full day) **Visitor centre** April–Sept Mon–Sat 10am–5pm, Sun 11am–4pm • Free • ☎ 0844 888 0844, ⓦ thermaebathspa.com

At the bottom of the elegantly colonnaded Bath Street, the fantastic **Thermae Bath Spa** allows you to take the waters in much the same way that visitors to Bath have done throughout the ages, but with state-of-the-art spa facilities. Heated by the city's thermal waters, the spa includes two open-air pools, one on the roof of its centrepiece, the New Royal Bath, Sir Nicholas Grimshaw's sleekly futuristic "glass cube". Various treatments are offered, from massages to hot-stone therapies and a small **visitor centre** has displays relating to Bath's thermal waters.

BEAU NASH

Bath's social renaissance in the eighteenth century was largely due to one man: **Richard "Beau" Nash** (1674–1761), an ex-army officer, ex-lawyer, dandy and gambler, who became Bath's Master of Ceremonies in 1704, conducting public balls of an unprecedented splendour. Wielding dictatorial powers over dress and behaviour, Nash orchestrated the social manners of the city and even extended his influence to cover road improvements and the design of buildings. In an early example of health awareness, he banned smoking in Bath's public rooms at a time when pipe-smoking was generally enjoyed among men, women and children. Less philanthropically, he also encouraged gambling and even took a percentage of the bank's takings. According to his rules, balls were always to begin at 6pm and end at 11pm and each one had to open with a minuet "danced by two persons of the highest distinction present". White aprons were banned, gossipers and scandalmongers were shunned, and, most radical of all, the wearing of swords in public places was forbidden. Nash's fortunes changed when gambling restrictions were introduced in 1739, greatly reducing his influence; he died in poverty aged 87, but was treated to a suitably lavish send-off.

BATH

▲ Warminster & A36

▲ at Chippenham
▲ at Bristol

ACCOMMODATION
Bath Paradise House	7
Belmont	6
Brindleys B&B	2
Harington's	4
Queensberry Hotel	1
Three Abbey Green	5
White Hart Inn	8
YMCA	3

CAFÉS & RESTAURANTS
Acorn Vegetarian Kitchen	10
Bistro La Barrique	7
The Circus	3
Colonna & Small's	8
Jazz Café	5
King William	11
The Mint Room	2
Olive Tree	9
Pump Room	4
Same Same But Different	6
Wild Café	12

PUBS
The Bell	2
Coeur de Lion	8
The Raven	7
The Salamander	6
The Star Inn	1

LIVE MUSIC VENUES
Chapel Arts Centre	10
Moles	5
Porter	4
Sub 13	3
Theatre Royal	9

5

Queen Square and around

North of Hot Bath Street, Sawclose is presided over by the **Theatre Royal**, opened in 1805 and one of the country's finest surviving Georgian theatres; Beau Nash had his first house in Bath here from 1743, in what is now the theatre's foyer. Barton Street leads north of Sawclose to **Queen Square**, the first Bath venture of the architect **John Wood the Elder** (1704–54), champion of Neoclassical Palladianism, who lived at no. 15 (not no. 24 as a tablet there asserts). East of the square, the wide shopping strand of **Milsom Street** was designed by Wood as the main thoroughfare of Georgian Bath.

Herschel Museum of Astronomy

19 New King St • Mid-Jan to mid-Dec Daily 1–5pm, Sat & Sun from 11am • £6 • ☎ 01225 446865, ⓦ bath-preservation-trust.org.uk

A few minutes west of the centre is the small **Herschel Museum of Astronomy**, the former home of the musician and astronomer Sir William Herschel and his sister Caroline, who together discovered the planet Uranus here in 1781. Among the furnishings, musical instruments and knick-knacks from the Herschels' era, you can see a replica of the telescope with which Uranus was identified.

Jane Austen Centre

40 Gay St • April–Oct daily 9.45am–5.30pm, July & Aug 9.30am–6pm; Nov–March Mon–Fri & Sun 11am–4.30pm, Sat 9.45am–5.30pm • £8 • ☎ 01225 443000, ⓦ janeausten.co.uk

The **Jane Austen Centre** provides a superficial overview of the author's connections with Bath, illustrated by extracts from her writings, contemporary costumes, furnishings and household items; visits start with a talk every twenty minutes. Austen lived just down the road at 25 Gay Street – one of a number of places the author inhabited while in Bath.

The Royal Crescent and around

No. 1 Royal Crescent Mid-Feb to Dec daily 10.30–5.30pm, Mon from noon • £8.50, or £10.50 with Building of Bath Collection • ☎ 01225 428126, ⓦ no1royalcrescent.org.uk

At the top of Gay Street, the elder John Wood's masterpiece, **The Circus**, consists of three crescents arranged in a tight circle of three-storey houses, with a carved frieze running round the entire circle. Wood died soon after laying the foundation stone, and the job was finished by his son, **John Wood the Younger** (1728–1782), who was as instrumental as his father in defining Bath's elegant Georgian appearance. The painter Thomas Gainsborough lived at no. 17 from 1760 to 1774.

The Circus is connected by Brock Street to the **Royal Crescent**, grandest of Bath's crescents, begun by the younger John Wood in 1767. The stately arc of thirty houses – said to be the country's first – is set off by a spacious sloping lawn from which a magnificent vista extends to green hills and distant ribbons of honey-coloured stone. The interior of **No. 1 Royal Crescent**, on the corner with Brock Street, has been restored to reflect as nearly as possible its original Georgian appearance at the end of the eighteenth century.

At the bottom of the Crescent, Royal Avenue leads onto **Royal Victoria Park**, the city's largest open space, containing an aviary and nine acres of botanical gardens.

The Fashion Museum

Assembly Rooms, Bennett St • Daily 10.30am–6pm, Nov–Feb till 5pm; last admission 1hr before closing • £8, or £17 with the Roman Baths; NT • ☎ 01225 477789, ⓦ fashionmuseum.co.uk

The younger John Wood's **Assembly Rooms**, east of the Circus, were, with the Pump Room, the centre of Bath's social scene. The building was virtually destroyed by bombing during World War II, but it has since been perfectly restored and houses the **Fashion Museum**, a collection of clothing from the Stuart era to the latest Milanese designs.

5

Building of Bath Collection

The Vineyards, The Paragon • Mid-Feb to Nov Tues–Fri 10am–5pm, Sat & Sun 10.30am–5pm • £5, or £10.50 with No. 1 Royal Crescent •
☎ 01225 333895, ⓦ buildingofbathcollection.org.uk

The Georgian-Gothic Countess of Huntingdon's Chapel houses the **Building of Bath Collection**, a fascinating exploration of the construction and architecture of the city and a great place to start your visit. Everything is covered, from the kind of facades associated with the two John Woods to balustrades, door designs and such aspects of interior ornamentation as marbling, stencilling and japanning.

Holburne Museum

Great Pulteney St • Daily 10am–5pm, Sun from 11am • Free • ☎ 01225 388569, ⓦ holburne.org

The River Avon is crossed by the graceful, shop-lined **Pulteney Bridge**, an Italianate structure designed by Robert Adam, from the other side of which a lengthy vista stretches along Great Pulteney Street to the imposing classical facade of the **Holburne Museum**. The building, with a startlingly modern extension at the back, holds an impressive range of decorative and fine art, mostly furniture, silverware, porcelain and paintings, including several works by Gainsborough, notably the famous *Byam Family*, his largest portrait. Look out, too, for works by Constable, Stubbs and Angelika Kauffman.

ARRIVAL AND INFORMATION   BATH

By train Bath Spa train station is a short walk south of the centre at the bottom of Manvers Street.
Destinations Bristol (every 15–30min; 15min); London Paddington (every 30min–1hr; 1hr 30min); Salisbury (every 30min–1hr; 1hr).

By bus The bus station (ⓦ firstgroup.com) lies next to the train station on Dorchester Street.
Destinations Bristol (Mon–Sat every 15min, Sun every 30min; 50min); London (12 daily; 2hr 30min–3hr 15min);

Salisbury (Mon–Sat every 30min with change; 2hr 35min–2hr 50min); Wells (Mon–Sat hourly, Sun 7 daily; 1hr 20min).

By bike If you're coming from Bristol, you can cycle all the way along a cycle-path that follows the route of a disused railway line and the course of the River Avon.

Tourist office Next to the abbey in Abbey Churchyard (Mon–Sat 9.30am–5.30pm, Sun 10am–4pm; ☎ 0906 711 2000, ⓦ visitbath.co.uk).

GETTING AROUND AND TOURS

Walking or biking are the best ways to enjoy Bath's Georgian terraces — cars are a hindrance and parking is expensive; drivers should use one of the Park-and-Ride car parks on the periphery of town.

Bike rental Bath Bike Hire, Sydney Wharf, Bathwick Hill (£10/day; ☎ 01225 447276, ⓦ bathbikehire.com). They also rent narrowboats (from £60/half-day).

Boat tours Hour-long river trips can be made from Pulteney Bridge; operators include Pulteney Cruisers (March–Nov 1–3 hourly; £8; ☎ 01225 312900, ⓦ bath boating.com) and Avon Cruising (April–Oct 5–7 daily; £8; ☎ 07791 910650, ⓦ pulteneyprincess.co.uk).

Walking tours Mayor's Guides run free 2hr walking tours, starting outside the Pump Room in Abbey Churchyard (ⓦ bathguides.org.uk; Mon–Fri & Sun 10.30am & 2pm, Sat 10.30am, May–Sept also Tues & Thurs 7pm), while the Jane Austen Centre arranges 1hr 30min walks in the author's footsteps, also leaving from Abbey Churchyard (☎ 01225 443000, ⓦ janeausten .co.uk; Sat & Sun 11am; £12).

ACCOMMODATION

Bath is chock-full of hotels and B&Bs, but most of the latter are small, and it's always worth booking early, especially at weekends, when most places demand a two-night minimum and prices rise; rates quoted below are midweek. There are also good-value, central hostels, though the nearest campsites are some distance outside town. Note that the centre can get noisy at night, so choose a room away from the street for an undisturbed sleep.

Bath Paradise House 86–88 Holloway ☎ 01225 317723, ⓦ paradise-house.co.uk. Georgian villa an uphill trudge from the centre, but with wonderful views. Open fires in winter, elegant four-posters in some of the

rooms, and three rooms opening straight onto the award-winning gardens. **£130**

Belmont 7 Belmont, Lansdown Rd ☎ 01225 423082, ⓦ belmontbath.co.uk. Large doubles, some with tiny, clean,

5

modern en-suite bathrooms, in a centrally located B&B in a house designed by John Wood. No credit cards. **£50**

Brindleys B&B 14 Pulteney Gardens ☎ 01225 461728, ⓦ brindleysbath.co.uk. Half a dozen light, airy and elegantly decorated bijoux en-suite rooms that have more than a hint of a French country manor house about them, a feeling that extends to the stylish communal areas. It's set in a quiet residential area but is just a 5min walk from the centre of town. **£130**

Harington's Queen St ☎ 01225 461728, ⓦ haringtons hotel.co.uk. Central hotel in a converted townhouse with friendly service and modern, well-equipped rooms, mostly quite small, and some at the top of steep steps. Breakfasts are superlative, food is available throughout the day and there's wi-fi. **£148**

Queensberry Hotel Russel St ☎ 01225 447928, ⓦ the queensberry.co.uk. Spread across four Georgian townhouses at the top end of town, the *Queensberry* has got quirky cool down to a "T", with tastefully minimalist rooms – each one

different and each one with a fabulous bathroom – stylish communal areas, a lovely walled garden, and a superb basement restaurant (see below) that means dinner-and-room offers can often prove to be a good deal. **£140**

★ **Three Abbey Green** 3 Abbey Green ☎ 01225 428558, ⓦ threeabbeygreen.com. Top-notch B&B in a superbly renovated Georgian house just steps from the abbey. The airy, spotless rooms are beautifully done; the larger ones overlooking a peaceful square are more expensive. **£120**

★ **White Hart Inn** Widcombe Hill ☎ 01225 313985, ⓦ whitehartbath.co.uk. The comfiest of Bath's hostels has a kitchen, a first-class bar/restaurant and a spacious courtyard. There are clean doubles and twins available, some en suite. Midnight curfew. Dorms **£15**, doubles **£50**

YMCA International House, Broad St ☎ 01225 325900, ⓦ bathymca.co.uk. Clean, central and spacious, this friendly place has dorms, singles and doubles. No curfew, but no kitchen, either. All rates include breakfast (cooked breakfast £3.50 extra). Dorms **£21**, doubles **£60**

EATING

CAFÉS

Colonna & Small's 6 Chapel Row ☎ 07766 808067, ⓦ colonnaandsmalls.co.uk. The high-browed but helpful brewmasters at this stripped-back coffee specialists serve a serious cup of Joe. Choose from a range of weekly changing single-origin espresso beans and filter coffees. Just don't ask for milk. Or sugar. Mon–Fri 8am–5.30pm, Sat 8.30am–5.30pm, Sun 10am–4pm.

Jazz Café 1 Kingsmead Square ☎ 01225 329002, ⓦ bathjazzcafe.co.uk. Big breakfasts, snack fodder and dishes such as shredded slow-cooked chilli beef (£8.75) are served at this boho hangout. There are beers and wines, newspapers are on hand, and outside seating to boot. Mon–Sat 8.30am–5pm, Sun10.30am–4pm.

★ **Wild Café** 10a Queen St ☎ 01225 448673, ⓦ wild cafe.co.uk. Tucked away down a cobbled sidestreet behind Queen Square, the open kitchen at this incredibly popular whitewashed café – look out for the blue bicycle outside – does a roaring trade in crispy risotto balls, rabbit pies (mains from £9.95), salads and sandwiches (including an excellent BLT; £5.75). Mon–Fri 8am–5pm, Sat 9am–6pm, Sun 10am–5pm.

RESTAURANTS

★ **Acorn Vegetarian Kitchen** 2 North Parade Passage ☎ 01225 446059, ⓦ acornvegetariankitchen.co.uk. Bath's favourite veggie and vegan restaurant offers original and delicious dishes in an unruffled, arty environment: think truffled broccoli and curried cauliflower fritter (mains from £15.75, £9.75 at lunch; "Little Plates" from £2.95). Beers and wines are organic. Mon–Fri & Sun noon–3pm & 5.30–9.30pm, Sat noon–3.30pm & 5.30–10pm.

Bistro La Barrique 31 Barton St ☎ 01225 463861,

ⓦ bistrolabarique.co.uk. This place has cornered the market in "French tapas", or *petits plats*, ideal for grazing on such dishes as mushroom flan, gratinated duck confit and boeuf bourguignon, most costing £6.50. The room is nothing special, but there's a nice walled garden where you can eat alfresco. Daily noon–2.30pm & 5pm–late.

The Circus 34 Brock St ☎ 01225 466020, ⓦ the circuscafeandrestaurant.co.uk. There's a refined but relaxed atmosphere at this little family-run brasserie, just a stroll from the Royal Crescent, which specializes in well-prepared Modern British dishes such as West Country rabbit (£16.90, £5 cheaper at lunch). Mon–Sat 10am–midnight.

★ **King William** 36 Thomas St ☎ 01225 428096, ⓦ kingwilliampub.com. North of the centre, beyond The Paragon/Bathwick Street but well worth the walk, the *King William* regularly receives accolades for its excellent, locally sourced food, such as slow-cooked pork belly (£15) and butterbean and leek crumble (£13), but the beer and wine list is top-drawer, too. Bar Mon–Fri noon–3pm & 5–11pm, Sat noon–midnight, Sun noon–11pm; restaurant Wed–Fri 6–9pm, Sat 6–10pm, Sun noon–3pm.

The Mint Room Longmead Gospel Hall, Lower Bristol Rd ☎ 01225 446656, ⓦ themintroom.co.uk. Indian food but not as you know it: innovative yet authentic regional cuisine ranging from *murgh palak paneer* (chicken breast stuffed with spinach and home-made cheese) to a South Indian seafood *moilee* (mains from £7.95). Daily noon–2.30pm & 6–11pm, Fri & Sat till 11.30pm.

Olive Tree Queensberry Hotel, Russel St ☎ 01225 447928, ⓦ olivetreebath.co.uk. This is one of Bath's top restaurants, offering French-inspired dishes, a contemporary ambience and discreetly attentive service. The menu might feature crab lasagne (£12.95) or beetroot and tarragon

BATH'S FESTIVALS

Bath hosts a great range of festivals throughout the year, notably the **Bath International Music Festival** (ⓦ bathfestivals.org.uk/music), held between mid-May and June and featuring jazz, classical and world music; the **Bath Fringe Festival** (late May to early June; ⓦ bathfringe.co.uk), with the accent on art and performance; and **Bath Literature Festival** (ten days in Feb/March; ⓦ bathfestivals.org.uk/literature). For further information on these and other festivals, contact the festivals office at Abbey Chambers, Kingston Buildings (ⓣ 01225 462231, ⓦ bathfestivals.org.uk).

risotto (£18), and the desserts are delectable. Set-price lunches from £18.50. Mon–Thurs 7–9.30pm, Fri & Sat 12.30–2pm & 6.30–10pm, Sun 12.30–2pm & 7–9.30pm.
Pump Room Abbey Churchyard ⓣ 01225 444477, ⓦ romanbaths.co.uk. Splash out on a Champagne breakfast, sample the excellent lunchtime menu (mains from £12.95) or succumb to a Bath bun or a range of cream teas, all accompanied by a classical trio. It's a bit hammy and overpriced, and you may have to queue, but you get a good view of the Baths. Daily 9.30am–4.30pm; July, Aug & Dec and during major festivals 9.30am–9pm.
Same Same But Different 7a Prince's Buildings, Bartlett

St ⓣ 01225 466856, ⓦ samesame.co.uk. Excellent café/restaurant that manages to mix a laidback ambience with quality food – unusual tapas dishes start at £4.50, or go for something a bit more substantial, such as finger-licking sticky pork with triple-cooked chips (£10.95). Mon 8am–6pm, Tues–Fri 8am–11pm, Sat 9am–11pm, Sun 10am–5pm.
Yak Yeti Yak 12 Pierrepont St ⓣ 01225 442299, ⓦ yakyetiyak.co.uk. Quality Nepalese restaurant in a series of cellar rooms with a choice of chairs or floor cushions. Meat dishes are stir-fried or spicily marinated, and there's a good vegetarian selection (dishes all £5.60–8.90). Daily noon–2pm & 6–10.30pm, Fri & Sat from 5pm.

DRINKING

★**The Bell** 103 Walcot St ⓣ 01225 460426, ⓦ thebellinnbath.co.uk. Easy-going, slightly grungy tavern with a great jukebox, live music (Mon & Wed eve, plus Sun lunchtime) and DJs (Fri, Sat & Sun). There's bar billiards and a beer garden with table footy. Mon–Sat 11.30am–11pm, Sun noon–10.30pm.
Coeur de Lion 17 Northumberland Place ⓣ 01225 463568, ⓦ coeur-de-lion.co.uk. Centrally located tavern on a flagstoned shopping alley, with a few tables outside (and more upstairs). It's Bath's smallest boozer (it serves local Abbey Ales) and a regular tourist stop, but has good lunchtime food (baguettes from £4.75). Daily 10am–11.30pm.
The Raven 6–7 Queen St ⓣ 01225 425045, ⓦ theravenofbath.co.uk. Civilized watering hole with first-rate local ales – it was CAMRA Pub of the Year in 2013 – served both

downstairs and in the less crowded upstairs room (unless one of the storytelling nights is being held there). Food available, including renowned pies (£8.80). Mon–Thurs 11.30am–11pm, Fri & Sat 11.30am–midnight, Sun noon–10.30pm.
The Salamander 3 John St ⓣ 01225 428889. Local brewer Bath Ales pub with a traditional, dark wood interior, a relaxed atmosphere and tasty dishes available at the bar or in the upstairs restaurant (mains from £11.95). Daily 10am–11.30pm.
▲**The Star Inn** 23 The Vineyards, The Paragon ⓣ 01225 425071. First licensed in 1760, this Abbey Ales pub has a classic Victorian interior, and beers that include the award-winning Bellringer and draught Bass served from a jug. Mon–Thurs noon–2.30pm & 5.30pm–midnight, Fri & Sat noon–1am, Sun noon–midnight.

NIGHTLIFE AND ENTERTAINMENT

Chapel Arts Centre St James' Memorial Hall, Lower Borough Walls ⓣ 01225 461700, ⓦ chapelarts.org. Nice little venue for all kinds of performing arts, with an emphasis on jazz, blues and folk. Arrive early to get one of the cabaret-style tables.
★**Moles** 14 George St ⓣ 01225 404445, ⓦ moles .co.uk. Currently being renovated following a fire in March 2014, this Bath institution should be up and running soon and featuring its much-loved mix of good live music, DJs and club nights. The cramped basement can get pretty hot and sweaty, though – not for claustrophobes. Normally Mon & Sun 11am–midnight, Tues & Wed 11am–2am, Thurs 11am–3am, Fri & Sat 11am–4am.
Porter 15A George St ⓣ 01225 585100, ⓦ theporter .co.uk. This multifaceted Georgian townhouse is home to a

mellow lounge-bar on the first floor, with over half a dozen craft beers, and a late-night basement bar, with live jazz every Thurs, DJs at the weekend, and a monthly comedy club (£3). Lounge bar daily 10am–midnight, Fri & Sat till 2am; basement bar Thurs 6pm–midnight, Fri & Sat 6pm–2am.
Sub 13 144 Edgar Buildings, George St ⓣ 01225 466667, ⓦ sub13.net. Settle into a white leather booth in the Champagne lounge or chill out in the backyard terrace at this edgy basement bar, boasting the best drinks list in town. Mon–Sat 5pm–midnight, Fri till 2am, Sat till 3am.
Theatre Royal Sawclose ⓣ 01225 448844, ⓦ theatre royal.org.uk. Theatre and ballet fans should check out what's showing at this historic venue, if only for the atmosphere. More experimental productions are staged in its Ustinov Studio, with family shows at the egg.

5

Wells

The miniature cathedral city of **WELLS**, 21 miles south of Bristol and the same distance southwest from Bath, has not significantly altered in eight hundred years. Charming and compact, it is eminently walkable, and a stroll around its tightly knit streets reveals a cluster of medieval buildings, archways and almshouses.

Wells Cathedral

Cathedral Green • Daily 7am–7pm, Oct–March till 6pm; tours Mon–Sat 10am, 11am, 1pm, 2pm & 3pm (Nov–March 11am, noon & 2pm); 1hr; free • Suggested donation £6 • ☎ 01749 674483, ⓦ wellscathedral.org.uk

Hidden from sight until you pass into its spacious close from central Market Place, **Wells Cathedral** presents a majestic spectacle, the broad lawn of the former graveyard providing a perfect foreground. The west front teems with some three hundred thirteenth-century figures of saints and kings, once brightly painted and gilded, though their present honey tint has a subtle splendour of its own. The sensational facade was constructed about fifty years after work on the main building was begun in 1180.

The **interior** is a supreme example of early English Gothic, the long nave punctuated by a dramatic and very modern-looking "scissor arch", one of three that were constructed in 1338 to take the extra weight of the newly built tower. Beyond the arches, there are some gnarled old tombs to be seen in the aisles of the **Quire**, at the end of which is the richly coloured stained glass of the fourteenth-century **Lady Chapel**. The **capitals and corbels** of the transepts hold some amusing narrative carvings, and in the north transept there's a 24-hour astronomical **clock** dating from 1390. Opposite the clock, a well-worn flight of steps leads to the **Chapter House**, an octagonal room elaborately ribbed in the Decorated style.

Wells & Mendip Museum

8 Cathedral Green • Easter–Oct Mon–Sat 10am–5pm; Nov–Easter Mon–Sat 11am–4pm • £3 • ☎ 01749 673477, ⓦ wellsmuseum.org.uk

The row of clerical houses on the north side of Cathedral Green mainly dates from the seventeenth and eighteenth centuries. The chancellor's house is now the **Wells & Mendip Museum**, displaying some of the cathedral's original statuary as well as a good geological section with fossils from the Mendip area and, until 2018, changing exhibitions on World War I – the Somme battlefield, a military field hospital – using artefacts donated by local residents.

Bishop's Palace

Daily: Mid-Feb–March, Nov & Dec 10am–4pm; April–Oct 10am–6pm; tours daily 11.30am, April–Oct also 2.30pm • £7.70 • ☎ 01749 988111, ⓦ bishopspalace.org.uk

The tranquil grounds of the **Bishop's Palace**, residence of the Bishop of Bath and Wells since 1206, are reachable through the Bishop's Eye archway from Market Place. The palace was walled and moated as a result of a rift with the borough in the fourteenth century, and the imposing gatehouse still features the grooves of the portcullis and a chute for pouring oil and molten lead on would-be assailants. The gardens contain the springs from which the city takes its name and the scant but impressive remains of the **Great Hall**, built at the end of the thirteenth century and despoiled during the Reformation. Across the lawn stand the square **Bishop's Chapel** and **Bishop Jocelyn's Hall**, a few state rooms holding displays relating to the history of the site and the Undercroft café.

ARRIVAL AND INFORMATION WELLS

By bus Buses (☎ 0845 602 0156, ⓦ firstgroup.com or ⓦ webberbus.com) pull in at the station off Market Street. Destinations Bath (Mon–Sat hourly, Sun 7 daily; 1hr 20min); Bridgwater (Mon–Sat 1–3 hourly; 1hr 20min);

Bristol (every 30min–1hr; 1hr 5min); Glastonbury (Mon–Sat every 15min, Sun hourly; 15min); Taunton (Mon–Sat 8 daily; 1hr 20min); Wookey Hole (Mon–Sat every 30min–1hr; 15min); Yeovil (1–3 hourly; 1hr 20min).

Tourist office There's an info desk in the Wells & Mendip Museum, 8 Cathedral Green (Easter–Oct Mon–Sat 10am–5pm; Nov–Easter Mon–Sat 11am–4pm; ☎01749 671770, ✉ visitwellsinfo@gmail.com).

ACCOMMODATION

Beryl Hawkers Lane, 1 mile northeast of Wells ☎01749 678738, �🌐 beryl-wells.co.uk. Luxury country-house B&B, a former hunting lodge, set in lovely gardens with a children's play area and pool (May–Sept). Decor varies between the 14 rooms – some are quite twee, others stylishly understated – though all enjoy views. **£100**

The Crown Market Place ☎01749 673457, �🌐 www .crownatwells.co.uk. Fifteenth-century coaching inn where William Penn was arrested in 1695 for illegal

preaching; it's got a suitably old-fashioned flavour that verges on the fusty and faded. Rooms can be noisy from the bar and bistro below and/or the Saturday market. **£95**

Swan Hotel Sadler St ☎01749 836300, �🌐 swan hotelwells.co.uk. A swankier choice than *The Crown*, this rambling inn has plenty of antique character, plus friendly service and a rated restaurant (for which booking is essential). Pricier rooms have cathedral views. **£122**

EATING AND DRINKING

★**The Good Earth** 4 Priory Rd ☎01749 678600. Lovely wholefood restaurant that was making a name for itself with its delicious home-made quiches long before eco food was in vogue. Soups, salads, veggie pizzas and other organic goodies (mains from £4.95) available to eat in or take away. Mon–Fri 9am–4.30pm, Sat 9am–6pm.

Old Spot 12 Sadler St ☎01749 689099, ⍟ theoldspot .co.uk. Spacious, easy-going place with Old Spot pork among other appetising items on the eclectic set-price two- and three-course lunches (£15.50/£18.50) and à la carte dinners (mains from £12.50). Wed–Sat 12.30–2.30pm & 7–9.30pm, Sun 12.30–2.30pm.

The Mendips

Northwest of Wells, the ancient woodland, exposed heaths and limestone crags of the **Mendip Hills** are chiefly famous for **Wookey Hole** – the most impressive of many caves in this narrow limestone chain – and for **Cheddar Gorge**, where a walk through the narrow cleft makes a starting point for more adventurous hikes across the Mendips.

Wookey Hole

Two miles northwest of Wells • Daily 10am–5pm, Nov–March till 4pm • £18, online £15.30 • ☎01749 672243, ⍟ wookey.co.uk

It's folklore rather than geology that takes precedence at **Wookey Hole**, a stunning cave complex of deep pools and intricate rock formations hollowed out by the River Axe. Highlight of the hour-long tour is the alleged petrified remains of the Witch of Wookey, a "blear-eyed hag" who was said to turn her evil eye on crops, young lovers and local farmers. To finish off, there's a functioning Victorian paper mill and rooms containing speleological exhibits, plus a melange of family "attractions".

Cheddar Gorge

Six miles west of Wookey on the A371, the nondescript village of **Cheddar** has given its name to Britain's best-known cheese – most of it now mass-produced far from here – and is also renowned for the **Cheddar Gorge**, lying about a mile to the north.

Cutting a jagged gash across the Mendip Hills, the limestone gorge is an amazing geological phenomenon, though its natural beauty is rather compromised by Lower Gorge's mile of trinket shops and parking areas. Few trippers venture further than the first few curves of the gorge, which holds its most dramatic scenery – at its narrowest, the road squeezes between cliffs towering almost 500ft above – though each turn of the two-mile length presents new, sometimes startling vistas.

5

Those fit enough can climb the 274 steps of **Jacob's Ladder** to a cliff-top tower with views towards Glastonbury Tor, with occasional glimpses of Exmoor and the sea (spring/autumn half-terms & Easter–Sept daily, also Feb–Easter & Oct weekends only: Easter, May, July & Aug 10am–5pm, other times from 10.30am; free to Cheddar Caves ticket-holders). From the tower, there's a circular three-mile cliff-top Gorge Walk, and you can branch off along marked paths to such secluded spots as **Black Rock** reserve, just two miles from Cheddar, or **Black Down** and Beacon Batch, at 1068ft the Mendips' highest point.

Cheddar Caves

Daily: Easter, May, July & Aug 10am–5pm, rest of year from 10.30am • £18.95, online £16.11 • ☏ 01934 742343, ⓦ cheddargorge.co.uk

Beneath the towering Cheddar Gorge, the **Cheddar Caves** were scooped out by underground rivers in the wake of the Ice Age, and subsequently occupied by primitive communities. Today, the caves are floodlit to pick out the subtle tones of the rock, and the array of rock formations that resemble organ pipes, waterfalls and giant birds.

ARRIVAL AND INFORMATION

By bus The Mendip Hills are most easily explored with your own wheels. Public transport (ⓦ firstgroup.com or ⓦ webberbus.com) is essentially limited to First Group's #126 (Mon–Sat hourly, 4 on Sun; 25min) and Webber Bus #67 (Mon–Sat every 30min–1hr; 15min), both from Wells.

THE MENDIPS

Tourist information There's a National Trust information centre in Cheddar Gorge (11am–5pm: mid-March–Oct daily except Thurs, mid-July to mid-Sept daily; ☏ 01934 844518, ⓦ nationaltrust.org.uk).

ACCOMMODATION AND EATING

Chedwell Cottage 59 Redcliffe St, Cheddar ☏ 01934 743268, ✉ info@chedwellcottage.co.uk. In a quiet lane a 10min walk from the gorge, the charming owners of this homely B&B provide three simply furnished en-suite rooms and delicious breakfasts including home-made bread. No credit cards. **£65**

The Wookey Hole Inn Wookey Hole ☏ 01749 676677, ⓦ wookeyholeinn.com. Very close to the caves, this is a great

place to stay the night, with funky, fully equipped guest rooms and a restaurant (booking essential) that offers a range of expensive but memorable dishes (mains from £12.95). Mon–Sat noon–2.30pm & 7–9.30pm, Sun noon–3pm. **£100**

YHA Cheddar Hillfield, Cheddar ☏ 0845 371 9730, ⓦ yha .org.uk. Clinically refurbished Victorian house with clean, spacious rooms – four- to six-bed dorms, en-suite doubles and family rooms – and a decent kitchen. Dorms **£19**, doubles **£39**

Glastonbury

On the southern edge of the Mendips and six miles south of Wells, **GLASTONBURY**, famed for its annual music festival, is built around the evocative set of ruins belonging to its former abbey. The town lies at the heart of the so-called **Isle of Avalon**, a region rich with mystical associations, and for centuries it has been one of the main Arthurian sites of the West Country – today, it's an enthusiastic centre for all manner of New Age cults.

Glastonbury Abbey

Abbey Gatehouse, Magdalene St • Daily 9am–6pm, June–Aug till 8pm, Nov–Feb till 4pm • £6 • ☏ 01458 832267, ⓦ glastonburyabbey.com

Aside from its mythological origins, **Glastonbury Abbey** can claim to be the country's oldest Christian foundation, dating back to the seventh century and possibly earlier. Enlarged by St Dunstan in the tenth century, it became the richest Benedictine abbey in the country; three Anglo-Saxon kings (Edmund, Edgar and Edmund Ironside) were buried here, and the library had a far-reaching fame. Further expansion took place under the Normans, though most of the additions were destroyed by fire in 1184. Rebuilt, the abbey was the longest in Europe when it was destroyed during the Dissolution of the Monasteries in 1539, and the ruins, now hidden behind walls and nestled among grassy parkland, can only hint at its former extent. The most complete set of remains is the shell

THE MILD MILD WEST...

BANKSY

5

> ## GLASTONBURY TALES
>
> At the heart of the complex web of **myths surrounding Glastonbury** is the early Christian legend that the young Jesus once visited this site, a story that is not as far-fetched as it sounds. The Romans had a heavy presence in the area, mining lead in the Mendips, and one of these mines was owned by **Joseph of Arimathea**, a well-to-do tin merchant said to have been related to Mary. It's not completely unfeasible that the merchant took his kinsman on one of his many visits to his property, in a period of Christ's life of which nothing is recorded – it was this possibility to which William Blake referred in his *Glastonbury Hymn*, better known as *Jerusalem*: "And did those feet in ancient times/Walk upon England's mountains green?"
>
> Another legend relates how Joseph was imprisoned for twelve years after the Crucifixion, miraculously kept alive by the **Holy Grail**, the chalice of the Last Supper, in which the blood was gathered from the wound in Christ's side. The Grail, along with the spear that had caused the wound, were later taken by Joseph to Glastonbury, where he built the "First Church", around which the abbey later grew, and commenced the conversion of Britain.
>
> Glastonbury is also popularly identified with the mythical **Avalon**; the story goes that King Arthur, having been mortally wounded in battle, sailed to Avalon where he was buried in the abbey's choir, alongside his queen – somehow Glastonbury was taken to be the best candidate for the place.

of the Lady Chapel, with its carved figures of the Annunciation, the Magi and Herod.

The abbey's **choir**, announced by the half-worn but striking transept piers, holds what is alleged to be the tomb of **Arthur and Guinevere**. The discovery of two bodies in an ancient cemetery outside the abbey in 1191 was taken to confirm that here was, indeed, the mystical Avalon; they were transferred here in 1278 but disappeared in the mid-sixteenth century. Elsewhere in the grounds, the fourteenth-century **abbot's kitchen** is the only monastic building to survive intact, with four huge corner fireplaces and a great central lantern above. Behind the main entrance to the grounds, look out for the thorn tree that is supposedly a descendant of the original **Glastonbury Thorn** on Wearyall Hill, said to have sprouted from the staff of Joseph of Arimathea. Big-name **concerts and drama productions** take place in the abbey grounds in summer – check the website for details.

Glastonbury Lake Villages Museum

9 High St • Mon–Sat 10am–4pm • £3; EH • ☎ 01458 832954, ⓦ english-heritage.org.uk

The fifteenth-century **Glastonbury Tribunal** provides an atmospheric setting for the small but interesting **Glastonbury Lake Villages Museum**, with displays from the Iron Age settlements that fringed the former marshland below the Tor. The villages' wattle houses were consistently rebuilt on layers of clay as they slowly submerged into the marshes, and the perfectly preserved finds include jewellery made from animal bones and a 3000-year-old wooden canoe.

Somerset Rural Life Museum

Abbey Farm, Chilkwell St • Previously Tues–Sat 10am–5pm • Free • ☎ 01823 2788057, ⓦ somersetrurallifemuseum.org.uk

Centred round the fourteenth-century Abbey Barn, the engaging **Somerset Rural Life Museum** has historically focused on a range of local rural occupations, from cider-making and peat-digging to the unusual practice of mud-horse fishing, named after the sledge shrimpers used to navigate the mud flats of Bridgwater Bay. It was closed for refurbishment at the time of writing but is expected to reopen in early 2016.

Glastonbury Tor

From Chilkwell St, turn left into Well House Lane and immediately right for the footpath that leads up to the Tor; the shorter, steeper path is accessed from the top of Well House Lane and is served by the Tor Bus (see opposite) • Free; NT • ⓦ nationaltrust.org.uk

Towering over the Somerset Levels, the 521ft-high conical hill of **Glastonbury Tor** commands stupendous views as far as the Welsh mountains on very clear days. It is topped by the dilapidated **St Michael's Tower**, sole remnant of a fourteenth-century church, and pilgrims once embarked on the stiff climb up here with hard peas in their shoes as penance – nowadays, people come to picnic, fly kites or feel the vibrations of crossing ley-lines.

ARRIVAL AND INFORMATION
GLASTONBURY

By bus Frequent buses (ⓦfirstgroup.com) #29, #375, #376 and #377 connect Glastonbury with Wells; #376 also goes to Bristol and #29 to Taunton.
Destinations Bristol (Mon–Sat every 30min, Sun hourly; 1hr 35min); Taunton (Mon–Sat 8 daily 1hr 5min); Wells (Mon–Sat every 15min, Sun hourly; 15min).

Tourist office The Tribunal, 9 High Street (Mon–Sat 10am–4pm; ☏01458 832954, ⓦglastonburytic.co.uk).
Internet There's internet access in the tourist office, and a relaxed internet café in Glastonbury's Assembly Rooms (Tues–Sat noon–6pm; ⓦassemblyrooms.org.uk), reached through a courtyard off the High Street.

GETTING AROUND

By bus The Glastonbury Tor Bus runs from the abbey car park to the base of the Tor every 30min, and stops at the Somerset Rural Life Museum (when open) and Chalice Well (April–Sept daily 10am–5pm; £3, valid all day).

By bike Glastonbury Cycles, 67 High Street (☏01458 830639, ✉glastonburycycles@live.co.uk) rents bikes for £10/15 per half-/full-day.

ACCOMMODATION

George & Pilgrim Hotel 1 High St ☏01458 831146, ⓦrelaxinnz.co.uk. This fifteenth-century oak-panelled inn with mullioned windows brims with medieval atmosphere. It's tired and worn in parts and some of the rooms are a bit ordinary – go for one of the older ones, which include frilly four-posters. **£85**
Glastonbury Backpackers 4 Market Place ☏01458 833353, ⓦglastonburybackpackers.com. Centrally located former coaching inn (it's in *The Crown*), a bit scuffed, but clean enough, with a kitchen, a games room, wi-fi access and no curfew. Also private 3-, 4- and 5-person rooms available (£22pp). Can get noisy from the lively bar

(closes 2.30am at weekends). Dorms **£15**
Mapleleaf Middlewick Cottages Wick Lane, 1.5 miles north of Glastonbury ☏01458 832351, ⓦmiddlewick holidaycottages.co.uk. A dozen self-catering cottages plus glamping cabins in rural surroundings, the former with stone walls, oak floors and, in some, cosy wood burners. There's a steam room, indoor pool, BBQ and pizza oven. **£92.50**
★ **White House** 21 Manor House Rd ☏01458 830886, ⓦtheglastonburywhitehouse.com. Lovely B&B with two en-suite rooms. Everything is eco-friendly and organic, including the optional veggie breakfast (from £5), which can be served in your room. **£75**

EATING AND DRINKING

Blue Note Café 4a High St ☏01458 832907. A relaxed place to hangout over coffees and cakes with some courtyard seating. It's vegetarian and mostly organic, with nourishing soups, salads and halloumi burgers (mains from £5.50). Daily 9am–5pm.

Hawthorns 8–12 Northload St ☏01458 831255. Homely bar and restaurant whose main draw is its eclectic menu: daily ethnic specials (from £12.50) and a variety of award-winning curries chalked up on the blackboard. Tues & Wed 6–11pm, Thurs noon–3pm & 6–11pm, Fri & Sat

---

GLASTONBURY FESTIVAL

Glastonbury Festival of Contemporary and Performing Arts (ⓦglastonburyfestivals .co.uk) takes place most years over four days in late June, with happy campers braving the predictable mudfest at Worthy Farm, outside Pilton, six miles east of Glastonbury itself. Having started as a small hippy affair in the 1970s, "Glastonbury" has become the biggest and best-organized festival in the country, without shedding too much of its alternative feel. Much more than just a music festival, large parts of the sprawling site are given over to themed "lifestyle" areas, from the meditation marquees of Green Fields to campfire-filled Strummerville and futuristic Arcadia. Bands cover all musical spectrums, from up-and-coming indie groups to international superstars – recent headliners have included Arcade Fire, Metallica and Kasabian. Despite the steep price (£210), tickets are invariably snapped up within hours of going on sale around October of the previous year.

5

noon–11pm, Sun noon–10pm.

★**Hundred Monkeys** 52 High St ☎01458 833386, ⓦhundredmonkeyscafe.com. Mellow contemporary café/restaurant whose wholesome snacks include a renowned seafood soup, as well as gourmet sarnies (from £6) and varied salads (from £7). Take-away available. Mon–Thurs 8am–8pm, Fri & Sat 8am–9pm, Sun 9am–5pm.

King Arthur 31–33 Benedict St ☎01458 831442. Wood-floored freehouse near St Benedict's Church, serving pricey salads (£10) and pies (£13) and with live music most nights. Drinks are reassuringly local: beer from Glastonbury Ales, cider from Wilkins. Mon 5pm–midnight, Tues–Sat noon–midnight, Sun noon–11pm.

Taunton

West of Glastonbury, the county town of **Taunton** makes a handy starting point for excursions into the Quantock Hills, and, as home to the worthwhile **Museum of Somerset**, is of more interest than nearby Bridgwater. While in town, take a look at the pinnacled and battlemented towers of its two most important churches – **St James** on Coal Orchard and **St Mary Magdalene** on Church Square – both fifteenth-century structures remodelled by the Victorians.

Museum of Somerset

Taunton Castle, Castle Green • Tues–Sat 10am–5pm • Free • ☎01823 255088, ⓦwww.somerset.gov.uk/museums

Started in the twelfth century, **Taunton Castle** staged the trial of royal claimant Perkin Warbeck, who in 1490 declared himself to be the Duke of York, the younger of the "Princes in the Tower" – the sons of Edward IV, who had been murdered seven years earlier. Parts of the structure were pulled down in 1662 and much of the rest has been altered, and it now houses the **Museum of Somerset**, a wide-ranging display that includes finds from Somerset's Lake Villages; the "Frome Hoard", the second largest collection of Roman coins ever discovered in Britain; and a superb fragment of Roman mosaic found near Langport in the Somerset Levels. Part of the castle houses the Great Hall where Judge Jeffreys held one of his "Bloody Assizes" following the Monmouth Rebellion of 1685, at which 144 prisoners were sentenced to be hanged, drawn and quartered.

ARRIVAL AND INFORMATION   TAUNTON

By train The train station lies a 20min walk north of town. There's also the West Somerset Railway (see box opposite), which terminates at Bishops Lydeard.

Destinations Bridgwater (1–2 hourly; 10min); Bristol (every 15–30min; 35min–1hr 5min); Dulverton (Mon–Sat hourly; 1hr 20min); Dunster (Mon–Sat every 30min, Sun hourly; 1hr 20min); Glastonbury (Mon–Sat 8 daily; 1hr 5min); London (9–10 daily; 3–4hr); Minehead (Mon–Sat every 30min, Sun hourly; 1hr 25min); Wells (Mon–Sat 8 daily; 1hr 20min); Yeovil (Mon–Sat hourly; 1hr 15min).

By bus Taunton's bus station (ⓦfirstgroup.com) is off Castle Green.

Destinations Bishops Lydeard (Mon–Sat every 30min, Sun hourly; 30min); Bridgwater (Mon–Sat every 30min, Sun hourly; 45min); Combe Florey (Mon–Sat every 30min,

Tourist office In the library building, Paul Street (Mon–Sat 9.30am–4.30pm; ☎01823 336344, ⓦtauntondeane .gov.uk). Provides information and publications on the whole area, including the Quantocks.

ACCOMMODATION AND EATING

The Castle Castle Green ☎01823 272671, ⓦthe -castle-hotel.com. The town's most atmospheric hotel is an upmarket choice, a wisteria-clad mansion next to Taunton Castle, exuding an appropriately old-fashioned baronial style. Breakfast costs from £6.50 on top of room rates. **£139**

The Cosy Club Hunts Court, Corporation St ☎01823 253476, ⓦcosyclub.co.uk. In a converted Victorian arts college, this bar has several rooms across two floors, with comfy chairs and quirky decor. Coffees, teas and meals are available; tapas are £11.50 for three, burgers from £7.95. Daily 9am–10pm.

The Old Mill Netherclay, Bishop's Hull, 2 miles west of Taunton ☎01823 289732, ⓦbandbtaunton.co.uk. Right on the River Tone, this peaceful B&B set in a former corn mill only has a couple of rooms, the larger one worth the slightly higher price for its river views. Restored pieces of the old mill machinery lend the place the air of a small museum. No credit cards. **£65**

The Quantock Hills

Extending for some twelve miles north of Taunton, the **Quantock Hills** are fairly off the beaten track, enclosed by a triangle of roads leading coastwards from Bridgwater and Taunton. Its snug villages, many of them boasting beautifully preserved churches, are connected by steep, narrow lanes and set in scenic wooded valleys or "combes" that are watered by clear streams and grazed by red deer.

Nether Stowey and around

Eight miles west of Bridgwater on the A39, on the edge of the hills, the pretty village of **NETHER STOWEY** is best known for its association with **Samuel Taylor Coleridge**, who in 1796 walked here from Bristol to join his wife and child at their new home. Coleridge drew inspiration for some of his best-known works whilst rambling through the surrounding countryside, and you can pick up a leaflet at his former abode for the **Coleridge Way** (⑩coleridgeway.co.uk), a walking route that supposedly follows the poet's footsteps between Nether Stowey and Lynmouth (see p.286) on the Exmoor coast; waymarked with quill signs, the 51-mile hike passes through some of the most scenic parts of the Quantocks and Exmoor.

Coleridge Cottage

35 Lime St • March–Oct Mon & Thurs–Sun 11am–5pm • £5.20; NT • ☎ 01278 732662, ⑩ nationaltrust.org.uk/coleridgecottage

At this "miserable cottage", as Sara Coleridge rather harshly called what is now **Coleridge Cottage**, you can see the poet's parlour and reading room, and, upstairs, his bedroom and an exhibition room containing various letters and first editions. Rooms, including the kitchen, are laid out as they would have been in the eighteenth century, filled with the family's personal belongings and mementos.

The western Quantocks

On the southwestern edge of the Quantocks, the village of **BISHOPS LYDEARD**, terminus of the West Somerset Railway, is worth a wander, not least for **St Mary's** church, with a splendid tower and carved bench-ends inside. A couple of miles north, pretty **COMBE FLOREY** is almost exclusively built of the pink-red sandstone characteristic of Quantock villages. For over fifteen years (1829–45), the local rector was the unconventional cleric Sydney Smith, called "the greatest master of ridicule since Swift" by the essayist Macaulay; more recently it was home to Evelyn Waugh.

A little over three miles further north along the A358, **CROWCOMBE** is another typical cob-and-thatch Quantock village, with a well-preserved Church House from 1515 and a lovely old church with a superb collection of pagan-looking carved bench-ends. A minor road from here winds up to **Triscombe Stone**, in the heart of the Quantocks, from where a footpath leads for about a mile to the range's highest point at **Wills Neck** (1260ft).

THE WEST SOMERSET RAILWAY

Fringing the western side of the Quantocks, the **West Somerset Railway** (☎ 01643 704996, ⑩ west-somerset-railway.co.uk) is a restored branch line that runs twenty miles between the station outside the village of Bishops Lydeard, five miles northwest of Taunton, to Minehead on the Somerset coast (see p.285; 1hr 15min; £11.40 one-way, £17 return). Between late March and October (plus some weekend and winter dates), up to seven steam and diesel trains depart daily from Bishops Lydeard, stopping at renovated stations on the way. Rover tickets, allowing multiple journeys, cost £17/day, £32/two days, £68/week, and bikes cost £2 extra. Bus #28 goes to Bishops Lydeard station from Taunton town centre and train station.

5

Stretching between Wills Neck and the village of Aisholt, the moorland plateau of **Aisholt Common** is best explored from **West Bagborough**, where a five-mile path starts at Birches Corner. Lower down the slopes, outside Aisholt, the banks of **Hawkridge Reservoir** make a lovely picnic stop.

GETTING AROUND
THE QUANTOCK HILLS

By public transport The West Somerset Railway (see box, p.283) stops near some of the villages along the west flank of the range, though you'll need your own wheels to reach the best spots, as public transport in is minimal.

ACCOMMODATION AND EATING

★**The Blue Ball Inn** Triscombe ☎01984 618242, ⓦblueballinn.info. This secluded inn below Wills Neck has two tastefully decorated B&B rooms, plus meals sourced from neighbouring farms (mains from £11), good local ales and a nice pub garden. Tues–Sat noon–3pm & 6–11pm (Sat noon–11pm in summer), Sun noon–6pm. **£75**

Carew Arms Crowcombe ☎01984 618631, ⓦthecarewarms.co.uk. Don't be put off by the stags' heads covering the walls and the riding boots by the fire – this is a delightful rustic pub with a skittles alley and a spacious garden. Local ales complement the top-notch nosh (from £12.95). Half a dozen rooms also available. Daily noon–2pm, Tues–Sat also 7–9pm. **£64**

Farmers Arms Combe Florey ☎01823 432267, ⓦfarmersarmsatcombeflorey.co.uk. Signposted off the A358 just north of the village, this tidily thatched old pub has log fires, an attractive garden and a menu strong on lamb and poultry (mains from £8.50 at lunch, £15 at dinner). Booking advisable at peak times. Mon–Sat noon–2pm & 7–9pm, Sun noon–2.30pm.

Mill Farm Caravan and Camping Park Fiddington, a couple of miles east of Nether Stowey ☎01278 732286, ⓦmillfarm.biz. This family-friendly site has indoor and outdoor pools, a boating lake, a gym and pony rides. Advance booking essential at peak times. There are cottages that can be rented by the week (£490). Closed Dec–Feb. Camping pitches **£20.50**

The Old House Castle St, Nether Stowey ☎01278 732392, ⓦtheoldhouse-quantocks.co.uk. This large house in the centre of the village once accommodated Samuel Coleridge. The two rooms – Sarah's Room and the huge Coleridge Suite – are period-furnished, and there's an acre of garden. Self-catering cottages also available (from £495/week). **£80**

★**Parsonage Farm** Over Stowey, a mile south of Nether Stowey ☎01278 733237, ⓦparsonfarm .co.uk. In the shadow of a lovely old Quantock church, this homely B&B with its own orchard and walled kitchen garden has stone floors, brick fireplaces and heaps of character. Run organically and sustainably by a native of Vermont, it offers a Vermont breakfast among other options, and simple candle-lit suppers (£11). **£65**

Exmoor

A high, bare plateau sliced by wooded combes and gurgling streams, **EXMOOR** (ⓦexmoor-nationalpark.gov.uk) can present one of the most forbidding landscapes in England, especially when shrouded in a sea mist. On clear days, though, the moorland of this National Park reveals rich bursts of colour and an amazing diversity of wildlife, from buzzards to the unique **Exmoor ponies**, a breed closely related to prehistoric horses and now on the endangered list. Much more elusive are the **red deer**, England's largest native wild animal, of which Exmoor supports the country's only wild population, currently around three thousand.

Endless **walking routes** are possible along a network of some six hundred miles of footpaths and bridleways, and **horseriding** is another option for getting the most out of Exmoor's desolate beauty. Inland, there are four obvious bases for walks, all on the Somerset side of the county border: **Dulverton** in the southeast, site of the main information facilities; **Simonsbath** in the centre; **Exford**, near Exmoor's highest point at Dunkery Beacon; and the attractive village of **Winsford**, close to the A396 on the east of the moor.

Exmoor's coastline offers an alluring alternative to the open moorland, all of it accessible via the **South West Coast Path**, which embarks on its long coastal journey at **Minehead**, though there is more charm to be found further west at the sister villages of **Lynton** and **Lynmouth**, just over the Devon border.

Dulverton and the eastern moor

The village of **DULVERTON**, on Exmoor's southern edge is the Park Authority's headquarters and, with its cafés and shops, makes a good entry point to Exmoor. Five miles north, just west of the A396, **WINSFORD** lays justified claim to being the moor's prettiest hamlet. A scattering of thatched cottages ranged around a sleepy green, it is watered by a confluence of streams and rivers, giving it no fewer than seven bridges.

Four miles northwest of Winsford, the village of **EXFORD**, an ancient crossing point on the River Exe, is popular with hunting folk as well as with walkers for the four-mile hike to **Dunkery Beacon**, Exmoor's highest point at 1704ft.

Exmoor Forest and Simonsbath

At the heart of the National Park lies **Exmoor Forest**, the barest (and wettest) part of the moor, scarcely populated except by roaming sheep and a few red deer – the word "forest" denotes simply that it was a king's hunting reserve. In the middle of it stands the village of **SIMONSBATH** (pronounced "Simmonsbath"), once home to the Knight family, who bought the forest in 1819 and, by introducing tenant farmers, building roads and importing sheep, brought systematic agriculture to an area that had never before produced any income.

Minehead

The Somerset port of **MINEHEAD** quickly became a favourite Victorian watering hole with the arrival of the railway, and it has preserved an upbeat holiday-town atmosphere ever since. Steep lanes link the two quarters of **Higher Town**, on the slopes of North Hill, containing some of the oldest houses, and **Quay Town**, the harbour area. Minehead is a terminus for the **West Somerset Railway**, which curves eastwards into the Quantocks as far as Bishops Lydeard (see p.283), and also for the South West Coast Path (see box, p.286), signposted beyond the harbour.

Dunster

Three miles southeast of Minehead, the old village of **DUNSTER** is the area's major attraction. Its impressive castle rears above its well-preserved High Street, where the octagonal **Yarn Market**, dating from 1609, recalls Dunster's wool-making heyday.

Dunster Castle

March to Oct daily 11am–5pm; Dec 6–21 Sat & Sun 11am–3pm; grounds early March to Oct daily 10am–5pm; Nov & Dec 11am–4pm • £9.30, grounds only £5.60; NT • ☎ 01643 821314, ⓦ nationaltrust.org.uk/dunstercastle

A landmark for miles around with its towers and turrets, **Dunster Castle** has parts dating back to the thirteenth century, but most of its fortifications were demolished following the Civil War. The structure was subjected to a thorough Victorian restoration in 1868–72, from which it emerged as something of an architectural showpiece, though its interior preserves much from its earlier incarnations. Tours take in a bedroom once occupied by Charles II, a fine seventeenth-century carved staircase, a richly decorated banqueting hall and various portraits of the Luttrells, owners of the house for six hundred years. The grounds include terraced gardens and riverside walks, all overlooked by a hilltop folly, **Conygar Tower**, dating from 1775.

Porlock

Six miles west of Minehead and cupped on three sides by the hogbacked hills of Exmoor, the thatch-and-cob houses and distinctive charm of **PORLOCK** draw armies of tourists. Many come in search of the village's literary links: according to Coleridge's own less-than-reliable testimony, it was a "man from Porlock" who broke the opium trance in

5

which he was composing *Kubla Khan*, while the High Street's fourteenth-century *Ship Inn* features prominently in the Exmoor romance *Lorna Doone* and, in real life, sheltered the poet Robert Southey. Just two miles west yet feeling refreshingly remote, the tiny harbour of **PORLOCK WEIR** is a tranquil spot for a breath of sea air and a drink.

Lynton

Eleven miles west of Porlock, just inside Devon, the Victorian resort of **LYNTON** perches above a lofty gorge with splendid views over the sea. Almost completely cut off from the rest of the country for most of its history, the village struck lucky during the Napoleonic Wars, when frustrated Grand Tourists – unable to visit their usual continental haunts – discovered in Lynton a domestic piece of alpine landscape, nicknaming the area "Little Switzerland". Samuel Taylor Coleridge and William Hazlitt trudged over to Lynton from the Quantocks, but the greatest spur to the village's popularity came with the publication in 1869 of R.D. Blackmore's Exmoor melodrama *Lorna Doone*, based on the outlaw clans who inhabited these parts in the seventeenth century.

Lynmouth and around

Some 500ft below Lynton, at the junction and estuary of the East and West Lyn rivers, **LYNMOUTH** – joined to Lynton by an ingenious **cliff railway** (mid-Feb to mid-Nov daily generally 10am–7pm, though closing times vary; £3.50 return; ⓦcliffrailwaylynton.co.uk), or walkable along an adjacent zigzagging path – was where the poet Percy Shelley spent his nine-week honeymoon with his 16-year-old bride Harriet Westbrook, writing his polemical *Queen Mab*. At the top of the village, you can explore the walks and waterfalls and an exhibition on the uses of waterpower in the wooded **Glen Lyn Gorge** (daily 10am–6pm, Nov–Easter till 3pm; £5), all the more poignant given that the village was almost washed away by flooding in August 1952, when 34 people lost their lives. **Boat trips** (Easter–Sept; £10; ☎01598 753207) depart from the harbour for Woody Bay and back – a great opportunity to view the cliffs and the birdlife that thrives on them.

ARRIVAL AND DEPARTURE   **EXMOOR**

By bus In addition to the bus services (ⓦfilers.co.uk, ⓦfirstgroup.com, ⓦquantockheritage.com & ⓦwebberbus.com) listed below, the Moor Rover provides a service to and from anywhere within the National Park (and along the Coleridge Way; see p.283) for walkers and bikers – bikes are hitched on the back; call to book a ride at least 24hr in advance (☎01643 709701, ⓦatwest.org.uk).

Destinations from Dulverton Taunton (Mon–Sat hourly; 1hr 20min).

Destinations from Dunster Bishops Lydeard (Mon–Sat every 30min, Sun hourly; 50min); Minehead (Mon–Sat every 30min, Sun hourly; 10min); Taunton (Mon–Sat every 30min, Sun hourly; 1hr 20min).

Destinations from Lynton/Lynmouth Barnstaple (Mon–Sat 4–9 daily; 55min–1hr 5min); Ilfracombe (April–Oct 3 daily, Nov–March weekends only; 55min–1hr); Minehead (Mon–Sat 2 daily; 55min); Porlock (3 daily; 40min).

Destinations from Minehead Bishops Lydeard (Mon–Sat every 30min, Sun hourly; 55min); Bridgwater (Mon–Fri daily; 1hr 25min); Dunster (Mon–Sat every 30min, Sun hourly; 10min); Lynmouth (Mon–Sat 2 daily; 55min); Nether Stowey (Mon–Sat 6 daily; 1hr 5min); Porlock

---

THE SOUTH WEST COAST PATH

Britain's longest national trail, the **South West Coast Path** (ⓦsouthwestcoastpath.com) starts at Minehead and tracks the coastline along the northern seaboard of Somerset and Devon, round Cornwall, back into Devon and on to Dorset, where it finishes close to the entrance to Poole Harbour. Much of the well-signposted **630-mile route** runs on land owned by the National Trust.

The relevant Ordnance Survey **maps** can be found at most village shops en route, while Aurum Press (ⓦaurumpress.co.uk) produces four *National Trail Guides* covering the route and the **South West Coast Path Association** (☎01752 896237, ⓦswp.org.uk) publishes an annual guide to the whole path, including accommodation lists, ferry timetables, tide times and transport details.

(Mon–Sat 11 daily; 15min); Porlock Weir (Mon–Sat 9 daily; 25min); Taunton (Mon–Sat every 30min, Sun hourly; 1hr 25min); Wells (Mon–Sat 8 daily; 1hr 20min).

INFORMATION

NATIONAL PARK VISITOR CENTRES

Dulverton 7–9 Fore Street (daily: April–Oct 10am–5pm; Nov–March 10.30am–3pm; ☎ 01398 323841).

Dunster At the top of Dunster Steep, by the main car park (Easter–Oct daily 10am–5pm; Nov & Feb half-term to Easter Sat & Sun 10.30am–3pm; ☎ 01643 821835).

Lynmouth Lynmouth Pavilion, The Esplanade (daily 10am–5pm; ☎ 01598 752509).

TOURIST OFFICES

Minehead The Beach Hotel, The Avenue (☎ 01643 702624, ⓦ minehead.co.uk).

Porlock The Old School Centre, West End, High Street (summer Mon–Fri 10am–1pm & 2–5pm, Sat 10am–5pm, Sun 10am–1pm; winter Tues–Fri 10am–1pm, Sat 10am–2pm; ☎ 01643 863150, ⓦ porlock.co.uk).

Lynton In the town hall, Lee Road (daily 10am–5pm, Sun till 2pm; ☎ 01598 752225, ⓦ lynton-lynmouth-tourism.co.uk).

TOURS AND ACTIVITIES

Exmoor Adventures (☎ 01643 863536, ⓦ exmoor adventures.co.uk). Rock-climbing, kayaking and other group activities (from £35pp).

Red Stag Safaris (☎ 01643 841831, ⓦ redstagsafari .co.uk). Small-group 4WD trips taking in wildlife and local history (from £25pp).

ACCOMMODATION AND EATING

Baytree 29 Blenheim Rd, Minehead ☎ 01643 703374, ⓦ baytreebandbminehead.co.uk. Victorian B&B offering roomy en-suites, including a family unit. The author Arthur C. Clarke was born a few doors along at no. 13. No credit cards. No children under-10. Closed Nov–March. **£60**

★ Glen Lodge Hawkcombe ☎ 01643 863371, ⓦ glenlodge.net. Beautifully furnished Victorian B&B offering perfect seclusion, comfort and character. There are distant sea views from the rooms and access to the moor right behind. No credit cards. **£90**

Hillside House 22 Watersmeet Rd, Lynmouth ☎ 01598 753836, ⓦ hillside-lynmouth.co.uk. Apart from the teddy bears, this simple but cosy B&B is refreshingly free of the tweeness that affects most of the guesthouses hereabouts. Most rooms are spacious, and all but one enjoy views over the East Lyn River. **£56**

Luttrell Arms 36 High St, Dunster ☎ 01643 821555, ⓦ luttrellarms.co.uk. Fifteenth-century inn with open fires and beamed rooms, some with four-posters. The bar and more formal restaurant (mains £14–19) offer decent food, and there's a pleasant garden. Bar daily 10am–11pm; restaurant daily 7–9.30pm. **£133**

★ Miller's at the Anchor Porlock Weir ☎ 01643 862753, ⓦ millersattheanchor.co.uk. This wonderfully unique, curio-stuffed hotel enjoys a superb setting on tranquil Porlock Weir's miniature harbourfront. The rooms are great, the staff courteous, and there's even a quirky mini-cinema. Light lunches and à la carte dinners are available in the equally atmospheric restaurant. Daily noon–3pm Wed–Sun also 7–8.30pm. **£88**

★ North Walk House North Walk, Lynton ☎ 01598 753372, ⓦ northwalkhouse.co.uk. Top-quality B&B in a stunning position overlooking the sea, and convenient for the coast path. The spacious, stylish rooms have wooden floors bedecked in rugs, and most have wrought-iron beds. Breakfasts are filling and delicious, and great organic dinners are available to guests for £28 per person. Garden studio (from £175 for 3nts) also available. **£120**

Rising Sun Harbourside, Lynmouth ☎ 01598 753223, ⓦ risingsunlynmouth.co.uk. The stylish rooms in this fourteenth-century inn all have the requisite beams and sloping floors. The pub and restaurant are equally atmospheric, serving classic English dishes plus plenty of seafood (from £12.25) and a few vegetarian options. Bar daily 11am–11pm, Sun till 10.30pm; food served daily noon 2.30pm & 6–9pm in bar, 7–8.30pm in restaurant. **£150**

Shelley's 8 Watersmeet Rd, Lynmouth ☎ 01598 753219, ⓦ shelleyshotel.co.uk. Right next to the Glen Lyn Gorge, this traditional hotel/B&B has friendly owners, a great location and literary credentials. You can sleep in the room supposed to have been occupied by the poet Shelley when he honeymooned here. No under-12s. **£89**

★ Simonsbath House Simonsbath ☎ 01643 831259, ⓦ simonsbathhouse.co.uk. Cosy bolt hole offering spacious and swanky rooms with glorious moorland views and a quality restaurant (three-course meals £22). Self-catering cottages in a converted barn are also available (from £200 for 2nts). **£120**

Tongdam 26 High St, Dulverton ☎ 01398 323397, ⓦ tongdam.com. Take a break from English country cooking at this quality Thai outpost (most dishes £12.50–16.50). There's also excellent, modern and tastefully furnished accommodation. Daily noon–3pm & 6–10.30pm. **£56**

Vanilla Pod 10–12 Queens St, Lynton ☎ 01598 753706. Good wholesome meals are served at this friendly place, which morphs from a café-bar by day into a Modern British restaurant come nightfall. Evening mains such as pork in cider start at £7.50. Daily 10am–9.30pm.

Devon and Cornwall

MOUSEHOLE, CORNWALL

Devon and Cornwall

At the western extremity of England, the counties of Devon and Cornwall encompass everything from genteel, cosy villages to vast Atlantic-facing strands of golden sand and wild expanses of granite moorland. The winning combination of rural peace and first-class beaches lends the peninsula a particular appeal to outdoors enthusiasts, and the local galleries, museums and restaurants provide plenty of rainy-day diversions. Together, these attractions have made the region perennially popular, so much so that tourism has replaced the traditional occupations of fishing and farming as the main source of employment and income. The authentic character of Devon and Cornwall may be obscured during the summer season, but avoid the peak periods and you can't fail to be seduced by their considerable charms.

If it's wilderness you're after, nothing can beat the remoter tracts of **Dartmoor**, the greatest of the West Country's granite massifs, much of which retains its solitude despite its proximity to the region's two major cities. Of these, **Exeter** is by far the more interesting, dominated by the twin towers of its medieval cathedral and offering a rich selection of restaurants and nightlife. As for **Plymouth**, much of this great naval port was destroyed by bombing during World War II, though some of the city's Elizabethan core has survived.

The coastline on either side of Exeter and Plymouth enjoys more hours of sunshine than anywhere else on the British mainland, and there is some justification in Devon's principal resort, **Torquay**, styling itself the capital of the "English Riviera". St Tropez it ain't, but there's no denying a certain glamour, alloyed with an old-fashioned charm that the seaside towns of **East Devon** and the cliff-backed resorts of the county's northern littoral share.

Cornwall too has its pockets of concentrated tourist development – chiefly at **Falmouth** and **Newquay**, the first of these a sailing centre, the second a major draw for surfers due to its fine west-facing beaches. **St Ives** is another crowd-puller, though the town has a separate identity as an arts centre. Further up Cornwall's long northern coast, the fortified site of **Tintagel** and the rock-walled harbour of **Boscastle** have an almost embattled character in the face of the turbulent Atlantic. However, the full elemental power of the ocean can best be appreciated on the western headlands of **Lizard Point** and **Land's End**, where the cliffs resound to the constant thunder of the waves, or, offshore, on **Lundy Island**, in the Bristol Channel, and the **Isles of Scilly**, 28 miles west of Land's End.

Inland, the mild climate has enabled a slew of gardens to flourish, none quirkier than the **Eden Project**, which imaginatively highlights the diversity of the earth's plant systems with the help of science-fiction-style "biomes".

DARTMOOR PONIES

Highlights

❶ Hiking on Dartmoor Experience this bleakly beautiful landscape along a good network of paths. **See p.306**

❷ Surfing in North Devon The endless ranks of rollers pounding Devon's west-facing northern coast – above all at Woolacombe, Croyde and Saunton – draw surfers of every ability. **See p.315**

❸ Eden Project, **Cornwall** Embark on a voyage of discovery around the planet's ecosystems at this disused clay pit, now home to a fantastic array of exotic plants and crops. **See p.320**

❹ Cornish beaches Cornwall has some of the country's best beaches, most of them in

fabulous settings. Beauties include Whitesand Bay, Newquay, the Isles of Scilly and Bude; and Porthcurno, overlooked by dramatic black crags. **See p.328, p.333, p.331, p.338 & p.328**

❺ St Ives Fine-sand beaches, a brace of renowned galleries and a maze of tiny lanes give this bustling harbour town a feel-good vibe. **See p.330**

❻ Seafood in Padstow The local catch goes straight into the excellent restaurants of the southwestern peninsula. Padstow, where celebrity chef Rick Stein owns a number of places, is a great culinary hotspot. **See p.335**

HIGHLIGHTS ARE MARKED ON THE MAP ON P.292

DEVON & CORNWALL

HIGHLIGHTS

1. Hiking on Dartmoor
2. Surfing in North Devon
3. Eden Project, Cornwall
4. Cornish beaches
5. St Ives
6. Seafood in Padstow

N

Getting around the West Country by public transport can be a convoluted and lengthy process, especially in remoter areas.

By train You can reach Exeter, Plymouth, Bodmin, Truro and Penzance by train on the main rail lines from London and the Midlands, with branch lines linking Falmouth (from Truro), Newquay (from Par) and St Ives (from St Erth). The frequent London Waterloo–Exeter service makes several useful stops in Devon, at Axminster, Feniton, Honiton and Pinhoe.

By bus Buses from the chief towns fan out along the coasts and into the interior, though the service can be rudimentary (or completely non-existent) for the smaller villages.
South West Coast Path The best way of exploring the coast of Devon and Cornwall is on foot along the South West Coast Path (ⓦ southwestcoastpath.com), England's longest waymarked trail.

Devon

With its verdant meadows, winding country lanes and cosy thatched cottages, **Devon** has long been idealized as a vision of a pre-industrial, "authentic" England. In fact much of the county is now inhabited largely by retired folk and urban refugees, but there is still tranquillity and sugar-free charm to be found here, from moorland villages to quiet coves on the cliff-hung coastline.

Reminders of Devon's leading role in the country's **maritime history** are never far away, particularly in the two cities of **Exeter** and **Plymouth**. These days it's the yachties who take advantage of the numerous creeks and bays, especially on Devon's southern coast, where ports such as **Dartmouth** and **Salcombe** are awash with amateur sailors. Landlubbers flock to the sandy beaches and seaside resorts, of which **Torquay**, on the south coast, and **Ilfracombe**, on the north, are the busiest. The most attractive are those that have preserved traces of their nineteenth-century elegance, such as **Sidmouth**, in east Devon. Inland, the county is characterized by swards of lush pasture and a scattering of sheltered villages, the population dropping to almost zero on **Dartmoor**, the wildest and bleakest of the West's moors.

Exeter

EXETER has more historical sights than any other town in Devon or Cornwall, legacies of an eventful existence dating from its Celtic foundation and the establishment here of the most westerly Roman outpost. After the Roman withdrawal, Exeter was refounded by Alfred the Great and by the time of the Norman Conquest had become one of the largest towns in England, profiting from its position on the banks of the River Exe. The expansion of the wool trade in the Tudor period sustained the city until the eighteenth century. Since then, Exeter has maintained its status as Devon's commercial and cultural hub, despite having much of its ancient centre gutted by World War II bombing.

Exeter Cathedral

The Cloisters, south of Cathedral Close • Mon–Sat 9am–4.45pm, Sun 11.30am–3.30pm • £6, or £8 including access to the North Tower; tours of the roof (1hr 30min) cost an additional £5 • ☎ 01392 255573, ⓦ exeter-cathedral.org.uk

The most distinctive feature of the city's skyline, **Exeter Cathedral** is a stately monument with two great Norman towers flanking the nave. Close up, it's the facade's ornate Gothic screen that commands attention: its three tiers of sculpted (and very weathered) figures – including Alfred, Athelstan, Canute, William the Conqueror and Richard II – were begun around 1360, part of a rebuilding programme which left only the towers from the original construction.

Entering the cathedral, you're confronted by the longest unbroken **Gothic ceiling** in the world, its **bosses** vividly painted – one, towards the west front, shows the murder of Thomas à Becket. The **Lady Chapel** and **Chapter House** – at the far end of the building and off the right transept respectively – are thirteenth-century, but the main part of the

EXETER

Exeter St David's
Train Station

ACCOMMODATION
Abode Exeter	3
Globe Backpackers	5
Raffles	1
Southernhay House	4
Town House	2

RESTAURANTS
Conservatory Restaurant	4
Harry's	1
Herbie's	6
Michael Caines	5

CAFÉS
Devon Coffee	3
The Exploding Bakery	2

PUBS & BARS
The Beer Cellar	5
Prospect Inn	6
Rusty Bike	1

CLUBS & LIVE MUSIC VENUES
Cavern Club	4
Exeter Phoenix	3
Timepiece	2

nave, including the lavish rib vaulting, dates from a century later. There are many fine examples of sculpture from this period, including, in the minstrels' gallery high up on the left side, angels playing musical instruments, and, below them, figures of Edward III and Queen Philippa. In the **Choir** don't miss the 60ft **bishop's throne** or the **misericords** – decorated with mythological figures and dating from around 1260, they are thought to be the oldest in the country. Outside, a graceful statue of the theologian Richard Hooker surveys the **Cathedral Close**, a motley mixture of architectural styles from Tudor to Regency, though most display Exeter's trademark red brickwork. For a glimpse of the cathedral's clock mechanism and spectacular views across the city, consider joining one of the guided tours of the roof.

The Guildhall

High St · Generally Mon–Fri 10.30am–1pm & 1.30–4pm, Sat 10.30am–12.30pm, but subject to change at short notice and sometimes closed for functions; call ahead · Free · ☎ 01392 665500

Some older structures still stand amid the banal concrete of the modern town centre, including, on the pedestrianized High Street, Exeter's finest civic building, the fourteenth-century **Guildhall**, claimed to be England's oldest municipal building in regular use. It's fronted by an elegant Renaissance portico, and merits a glance inside for its main chamber, whose arched roof timbers rest on carved bears holding staves, symbols of the Yorkist cause during the Wars of the Roses.

Royal Albert Memorial Museum

Queen St • Tues–Sun 10am–5pm • Free • ☎ 01392 265858, ⊛ rammuseum.org.uk

The **Royal Albert Memorial Museum** is the closest thing in Devon to a county museum. Exuding the Victorian spirit of wide-ranging curiosity, it includes everything from a menagerie of stuffed animals to mock-ups of the various building styles used at different periods in the city. The collections of silverware, watches and clocks contrast nicely with the colourful ethnography section, and the picture gallery has some good specimens of West Country art.

Underground passages

Paris St • June–Sept & school hols Mon–Sat 9.30am–5.30pm, Sun 10.30am–4pm; Oct–May Tues–Fri 11.30am–5.30pm, Sat 9.30am–5.30pm, Sun 11.30am–4pm • £6 • ☎ 01392 665887, ⊛ exeter.gov.uk/passages

Off the top end of the High Street, the Princesshay shopping precinct holds the entrance to a network of **underground passages**, first excavated in the fourteenth century to bring water to the cathedral precincts, and now visitable on a guided **tour** – not recommended for claustrophobes.

Around the River Exe

The **River Exe** marks the old city's southwestern boundary; today, the **Quayside** is mostly devoted to leisure activities. Pubs, shops and cafés share space with handsomely restored nineteenth-century warehouses and the smart **Custom House**, built in 1681, its opulence reflecting the former importance of the cloth trade. The area comes into its own at night, but is worth a wander at any time; you can rent bikes and canoes here, too (see below).

ARRIVAL AND DEPARTURE

EXETER

By plane Exeter's airport is around 6 miles east of the centre, just off the A30. Stagecoach buses #56A and #56B connect the airport with the bus station on Paris Street (roughly hourly; 20min).
Destinations London City (1–3 daily; 1hr 15min); Manchester (1–3 daily; 1hr 10min); St Mary's, Isles of Scilly (late April to Oct Mon–Sat 1–5 daily; 1hr).

By train Exeter has two main train stations, Exeter Central and St David's, the latter a 15min uphill walk or 10min bus ride from the city centre. South West trains from Salisbury stop at both, as do trains on the branch lines to Barnstaple and Exmouth, but most long-distance trains stop at St David's only.
Destinations Barnstaple (Mon–Sat hourly, Sun 7 daily;

1hr–1hr 30min); Bodmin (every 30min–1hr; 2hr–2hr 30min); Liskeard (every 1–2hr; 1hr 30min–2hr); London (every 30min–1hr; 2–3hr); Par (roughly hourly; 2hr); Penzance (roughly hourly; 3hr–3hr 10min); Plymouth (every 30min–1hr; 1hr); Torquay (every 30min–1hr; 35–55min); Totnes (every 30min–1hr; 35min); Truro (every 30min–1hr; 2hr 20min–2hr 40min).

By bus The bus station is on Paris St, one block north of the tourist office.
Destinations Newquay (2 daily; 3hr 30min); Penzance (2 daily; 4hr–4hr 40min); Plymouth (every 1–2hr; 50min–1hr 45min); Sidmouth (Mon–Sat every 20–30min, Sun every 30min–1hr; 40–50min); Torquay (roughly hourly; 1hr–1hr 10min); Truro (2 daily; 3hr 20min).

INFORMATION AND ACTIVITIES

Tourist office Dix's Field, off Princesshay (Mon–Sat 9.30am–4.30pm; ☎ 01392 665700, ⊛ heartofdevon .com).
Saddles & Paddles On the quayside (☎ 01392 424241,

⊛ sadpad.com). You can rent bikes here (£15/day); they also have canoes (£10 for the first hour and £5/hr thereafter), should you wish to explore the Exeter Canal, which runs 5 miles to Topsham and beyond.

ACCOMMODATION

Abode Exeter Cathedral Yard ☎ 01392 319955, ⊛ abodehotels.co.uk. Built in 1769 and reputedly the first

inn in England to be described as a "hotel", the former *Royal Clarence* is now part of a smart national chain. It's in a superb

6

location near the cathedral, with contemporary bedrooms (some small) and a swanky restaurant (see below). **£85**

Globe Backpackers 71 Holloway St ☎01392 215521, ⓦ exeterbackpackers.co.uk. Clean and central (though a bit of a hike from the stations), this hostel has a kitchen and free wi-fi. Dorms have six to ten beds and there are a few private rooms too. Closed noon–3.30pm. Dorms **£17.50**; doubles **£45**

Raffles 11 Blackall Rd ☎01392 270200, ⓦ raffles -exeter.co.uk. The rooms in this elegant Victorian B&B are furnished with Pre-Raphaelite etchings and other items from the owners' antiques business. Breakfasts make use of

the organic garden produce. Free wi-fi. **£78**

★**Southernhay House** 36 Southernhay East ☎01392 435324, ⓦ southernhayhouse.com. Attractive, individually themed rooms in a renovated nineteenth-century townhouse, with plush carpets and – in the best rooms – freestanding bathtubs. Breakfast is included as standard, but cheaper rates are available if you stay on a room-only basis. **£150**

Town House 54 St David's Hill ☎01392 494994, ⓦ townhouseexeter.co.uk. This Edwardian guesthouse midway between the train stations backs onto a churchyard and has a garden, wi-fi access and abundant breakfasts. Rooms are modern but some bathrooms are small. **£79**

EATING

Conservatory Restaurant 18 North St ☎01392 273858, ⓦ theconservatoryrestaurant.co.uk. Centrally located restaurant popular for its fresh fish dishes (including grilled sole from Cornwall) and wine from Devon. The two-course lunch is good value at £16.95. Tues–Sat noon–2pm & 5.30–9pm.

★**Devon Coffee** 88 Queen St ☎07796 678559, ⓦ facebook.com/devoncoffeeshop. Relaxed, independent coffee shop, where the decor is all stressed wood and chalkboards. The brownies here (£2.20) are exceedingly good and the coffee – as you'd expect from the name – isn't bad either. Mon–Sat 8am–6pm, Sun 10am–4pm.

★**The Exploding Bakery** 1b Central Crescent, Queen St ☎01392 427900, ⓦ explodingbakery.com. Slurp top-quality coffee (just £2 a cup) as you watch sweet-smelling cakes being pulled out of the ovens at this busy little wholesale bakery. If people-watching gets boring, there's plenty of art on the walls. Mon–Fri

8am–4pm, Sat 9am–4pm.

Harry's 86 Longbrook St ☎01392 202234, ⓦ harrys -exeter.co.uk. In a converted Victorian stonemason's workshop, this place attracts a cheery crowd with its good-value Mexican, Italian and American staples (most mains around £10). Daily 10am–2pm & 6–11pm.

★**Herbie's** 15 North St ☎01392 258473. Friendly, dimly lit place serving up great vegan, vegetarian and wholefood dishes (most mains under £10) plus organic beers, wines and ice cream. Mon 11am–2.30pm, Tues–Fri 11am–2.30pm & 6–9.30pm, Sat 10.30am–3.30pm & 6–9.30pm.

Michael Caines Abode Exeter Hotel, Cathedral Yard ☎01392 319955, ⓦ michaelcaines.com. Exeter's classiest restaurant offers sophisticated modern European cuisine in sleek surroundings. Prices are fairly high, but there are cheaper, two-course menus on offer at lunchtime and during the early evening (£14.95 and £16.95 respectively). Mon–Sat noon–2.30pm & 6–9pm (last orders).

DRINKING

The Beer Cellar 2 South St ☎01392 757570, ⓦ beer -cellar.co.uk. This friendly corner bar near the cathedral does great craft beer on tap and in bottles to take away. Look out for beers from the local Branscombe Vale Brewery. Daily 10am–10.30pm.

Prospect Inn The Quay ☎01392 273152, ⓦ heavitree brewery.co.uk. You can eat and drink sitting outside at this seventeenth-century riverside pub, which was the setting

for TV drama *The Onedin Line*. Mon–Thurs & Sun 10am–11pm, Fri & Sat 10am–midnight.

★**Rusty Bike** 67 Howell Rd ☎01392 214440, ⓦ rustybike-exeter.co.uk. There's an excellent vibe at this pub with vintage table-football and a range of malt whiskies and tequilas as well as local beers and ciders. Also offers good bar meals, a garden and occasional live music. Mon–Fri 5–11pm, Sat noon–midnight, Sun noon–11pm.

NIGHTLIFE AND ENTERTAINMENT

Cavern Club 83–84 Queen St ☎01392 495370, ⓦ exetercavern.com. A long-established hub of Exeter's music scene, this subterranean haunt is best known for its live bands (think indie, punk and metal) but it also has more diverse club nights and is open for daytime snacks. Daily 11.30am–5pm & 8pm–late.

Exeter Phoenix Bradlynch Place, Gandy St ☎01392 667080, ⓦ exeterphoenix.org.uk. Live music and comedy are among the cultural offerings at this arts centre, which also hosts films, exhibitions and readings and has a

nice café-bar. Mon–Sat 10am–11pm (and sometimes Sun for events).

Timepiece Little Castle St ☎01392 493096, ⓦ timepiecenightclub.co.uk. Occupying a former prison, this bar, club and performance venue hosts student nights (Mon in term time), salsa parties (Tues) and world music sessions (Sun in term time), plus big Indie, chart and house nights on Fri and Sat. Tues–Sat 7.30pm–1.30/2am, also Sun & Mon in term time.

A La Ronde

5 miles south of Exeter off the A376 • Mid-Feb to Oct daily 11am–5pm; Nov to mid-Feb Sat & Sun noon–4pm • £7.80; NT •
☎ 01395 265514, ⓦ nationaltrust.org.uk/a-la-ronde • Take bus #56 from Exeter's bus station and get off at the Courtlands Cross stop

The Gothic folly of **A La Ronde** was the creation of two spinster cousins, Jane and Mary Parminter, who in the 1790s were inspired by their European Grand Tour to build a **sixteen-sided house**, possibly based on the Byzantine basilica of San Vitale in Ravenna. The end product is filled with mementos of the Parminters' travels as well as a number of their more offbeat creations, such as a frieze made of feathers culled from game birds and chickens. In the upper rooms are a gallery and staircase completely covered in shells, too fragile to be visited, though part can be glimpsed from the completely enclosed octagonal room on the first floor. Superb views over the Exe estuary extend from the dormer windows on the second floor.

6

Sidmouth

Set amid a shelf of crumbling red sandstone, **SIDMOUTH** is the stately queen of east Devon's resorts. The cream-and-white town boasts nearly five hundred buildings listed as having special historic or architectural interest, among them the grand Georgian homes of **York Terrace** behind the Esplanade. Both the mile-long main town beach and **Jacob's Ladder**, a cliff-backed shingle and sand strip to the west of town, are easily accessible and well tended. To the east, the coast path climbs steep Salcombe Hill to follow cliffs that give sanctuary to a range of birdlife including yellowhammers, green woodpeckers and the rarer grasshopper warbler. Further on, the path descends to meet one of the most isolated and attractive beaches in the area, **Weston Mouth**.

ARRIVAL AND INFORMATION

By bus Sidmouth can be reached on bus #52A or #52B from Exeter's bus station (every 15–30min; 50min).

Tourist office The tourist office is on Ham Lane, off the eastern end of the Esplanade (Feb–March & Nov–Dec Mon–Sat 10am–1.30pm; April & Oct Mon–Sat 10am–4pm; Sun 10am–1.30pm; May–Sept daily 10am–5pm; ☎ 01395 516441, ⓦ visitsidmouth.co.uk). Head here for information on bay cruises and free guided walks around the area.

ACCOMMODATION

The Hollies Salcombe Rd ☎ 01395 514580, ⓦ holliesguesthouse.co.uk. Rooms in this Regency building blend contemporary and traditional styles, with the owner's watercolours on the walls. The seafront is less than a 10min walk away. **£70**

The Longhouse Salcombe Hill Rd ☎ 01395 577973, ⓦ holidaysinsidmouth.co.uk. It's about a mile from the seafront, but the hilltop views from this B&B – once part of the Norman Lockyer Observatory – compensate. The two rooms are large and comfortable, and there's a nice patio-garden. No credit cards. **£85**

EATING AND DRINKING

The Dairy Shop 5 Church St ☎ 01395 513018. Stacked wall to wall with chutneys, gooseberry wine, biscuits and the like, this café-cum-shop is a good spot for soups (£4.95), savoury crêpes (£5.25) or an ice cream. Mon–Sat 9am–5pm.

Swan Inn 37 York St ☎ 01395 512849, ⓦ youngs.co.uk. Close to the tourist office, this convivial but slightly run-down pub with a garden serves real ales, baguettes, plus meat and fish dishes (rump steak £11.25). Mon–Sat 11am–11pm, Sun noon–11pm; food served Mon–Sat noon–9.30pm, Sun noon–8pm.

Beer

Eight miles east of Sidmouth, the largely unspoiled fishing village of **BEER** lies huddled within a small sheltered cove between gleaming white headlands. A stream rushes along a deep channel dug into Beer's main street, and if you can ignore the crowds in high summer much of the village looks unchanged since the time when it was a smugglers' haven. While away a sunny afternoon here fishing for mackerel in the bay (around £6/person), or pull up a deckchair and tuck into a couple of fresh crab sandwiches on the beach.

Beer Quarry Caves

Quarry Lane, about a mile west of the village • Mid-April to Sept 10am–5.30pm; last tour 1hr before closing • £7 • ☎ 01297 680282, Ⓦ beerquarrycaves.co.uk.

The area around Beer is best known for its quarries, which were worked from Roman times until the nineteenth century: **Beer stone** was used in many of Devon's churches and houses, and as far afield as London. You can visit the underground **Beer Quarry Caves**, which includes an exhibition of pieces carved by medieval masons.

ARRIVAL AND DEPARTURE   BEER

By bus Beer is connected to Sidmouth by bus #899 (Mon–Sat 3–5 daily; 25–50min), which departs from Sidmouth Triangle.

ACCOMMODATION AND EATING

Bay View Fore St ☎ 01297 20489, Ⓦ bayviewbeer .com. Close to the beach and harbour, most of the rooms in this bright B&B overlook the sea. Abundant breakfasts in the attached café, which does crab sandwiches to take away (£6.50 with tea or coffee), include smoked haddock and waffles with maple syrup. Closed Nov– Easter. **£80**

Steamers New Cut ☎ 01297 22922, Ⓦ steamers restaurant.co.uk. Attractive, family-run restaurant on a quiet alley just up from the harbour. The fresh fish dishes are the main reason to come here, with locally caught hake, sole and sea bass (£15–20) all featuring on the menu. Tues–Sat 10.30am–2pm and 6.45–9pm, Sun 11.45am–2.15pm.

Torquay

Sporting a mini-corniche and promenades landscaped with flowerbeds, **TORQUAY** comes closest to living up to the self-styled "English Riviera" sobriquet. The much-vaunted palm trees and the coloured lights that festoon the harbour by night contribute to the town's unique flavour, a blend of the mildly exotic with classic English provincialism. Torquay's transformation from a fishing village began with its establishment as a fashionable haven for invalids, among them the consumptive Elizabeth Barrett Browning, who spent three years here.

The town centres on the small **harbour** and marina, separated by limestone cliffs from Torquay's main beach, **Abbey Sands**, which takes its name from Torre Abbey, behind the beachside road.

Torre Abbey

The King's Drive • Wed–Sun 10am–5pm • £7.50 • ☎ 01803 293593, Ⓦ torre-abbey.org.uk

The Norman church that once stood here was razed by Henry VIII, though a gatehouse, tithe barn, chapter house and tower escaped demolition. **Torre Abbey** now contains a good museum, set in pretty ornamental gardens, with collections of silver and glass, window designs by Edward Burne-Jones, illustrations by William Blake, and nineteenth-century and contemporary works of art.

Living Coasts

Beacon Quay • Daily: Easter–Sept 10am–5pm; Oct–Easter 10am–4pm; last entry 1hr before closing • £10.50, or £21.50 with Paignton Zoo (see opposite) • ☎ 01803 202470, Ⓦ livingcoasts.org.uk

At the northern end of Torquay harbour, **Living Coasts** is home to a variety of fauna and flora found on British shores, including puffins, penguins and seals. There are reconstructed beaches, cliff faces and an estuary, as well as underwater viewing areas and a huge meshed aviary. The rooftop café and restaurant have splendid panoramic views.

The beaches

East of Torquay's harbour, you can follow the shore round to some good sand beaches. **Meadfoot Beach**, one of the busiest, is reached by crossing Daddyhole Plain, named after a large chasm in the adjacent cliff caused by a landslide, but locally attributed to the devil ("Daddy"). North of the Hope's Nose promontory, the coast path leads to a string of less crowded beaches, including **Babbacombe Beach** and, beyond, **Watcombe** and **Maidencombe**.

ARRIVAL AND INFORMATION   TORQUAY

By train Torquay's main train station is off Rathmore Road, southwest of Torre Abbey Gardens. There are regular trains from/to Exeter (every 15–55min; 35–55min).

By bus Most buses stop on Lymington Road (a short walk north of the centre), or on The Strand, close to the marina.

Destinations Exeter (at least 12 daily; 1hr); Plymouth (Mon–Sat 9 daily, Sun 6 daily; 2hr–2hr 50min).

Tourist office The English Riviera Visitor Information Centre is on Vaughan Parade, by the harbour (daily 9.30am–5pm; ☎ 0844 474 2233, ⓦ englishriviera.co.uk).

ACCOMMODATION

Allerdale Hotel 21 Croft Rd ☎ 01803 292667, ⓦ allerdale hotel.co.uk. For glorious views and stately surroundings, head for this Victorian villa, a pleasingly old-fashioned place with a long garden and spacious rooms. Meals are available, and there's a bar, snooker and free wi-fi. **£80**

Exton House 12 Bridge Rd ☎ 01803 293561, ⓜ extonhotel.co.uk. Small, clean and quiet B&B a 10min walk from the train station (free pick-up is usually offered),

and just 15min from the centre. The guests' lounge has a balcony, and there's free wi-fi. Book direct for the best rates. **£60**

Torquay Backpackers 119 Abbey Rd ☎ 01803 299924, ⓦ torquaybackpackers.co.uk. Friendly hostel a 15min walk northeast of the train station, with free wi-fi, free tea and coffee, and nice common areas (including space outside for barbecues). Weekly rates available. Dorms **£17**; doubles **£38**

EATING AND DRINKING

Hole in the Wall Park Lane ☎ 01803 200755. This pub is supposed to be one of Torquay's oldest, and was Irish playwright Sean O'Casey's boozer when he lived here. There's a good range of beers, a separate restaurant (with mains around £10) and live music on Tues, Thurs and Sun. Daily noon–midnight; food served Mon–Sat noon–2.30pm & 5.30–9.30pm, Sun 12.30–2.30pm & 6–9.30pm.

Number 7 Fish Bistro Beacon Terrace ☎ 01803 295055, ⓦ no7-fish.com. Just above the harbour, this place is a must for seafood fans, covering everything from fresh whole crab to grilled turbot – or whatever else the boats have brought in. Most mains cost around £18. June–Oct Mon–Sat 12.15–1.45pm & 6–9.45pm; Nov–May Tues–Sat same hours.

Paignton

Lacking Torquay's gloss, **PAIGNTON** is the least attractive of the Riviera's resorts, though it is home to **Paignton Zoo** (daily: summer 10am–6pm; winter 10am–4.30pm or dusk; £14.45, or £21.50 with Living Coasts in Torquay; ⓦ paigntonzoo.org.uk), a mile out on Totnes Road. Near the seafront, Paignton's main train station is also the terminus of the **Dartmouth Steam Railway** (April–Oct daily, plus selected dates Nov–March; ☎ 01803 555872, ⓦ dartmouthrailriver.co.uk), which connects with **Goodrington Sands** beach before following the Dart to Kingswear, seven miles south. You could make a day of it by taking the ferry from Kingswear to Dartmouth (see p.302), then taking a riverboat up the Dart to Totnes, from where you can take any bus back to Paignton – a "Round Robin" ticket (£23.50) lets you do this.

ARRIVAL AND DEPARTURE   PAIGNTON

By train Trains from Exeter (every 30min–1hr; 40min–1hr 10min) and Torquay (every 30min–1hr; 5min) arrive at the main train station off Sands Road, 5mins from the harbour.

By bus The bus station is next to the train station,

off Sands Road.

Destinations Brixham (every 10–20min; 20min); Exeter (every 30min–1hr; 1hr 15min–1hr 30min); Torquay (every 5–10min; 20–35min).

Brixham

BRIXHAM is a major fishing port and the prettiest of the Torbay towns. Among the trawlers on the quayside is moored a full-size reconstruction of the **Golden Hind** (March–Oct daily 10am–4pm, £4; ☎ 01803 856223, ⓦ goldenhind.co.uk), the surprisingly small vessel in which Francis Drake circumnavigated the world. The harbour is overlooked by an unflattering statue of William III, who landed in Brixham to claim the crown of England in 1688.

From the harbour, climb King Street and follow Berry Head Road to reach the promontory at the southern limit of Torbay, **Berry Head**, now a conservation area attracting colonies of nesting seabirds. There are fabulous views, and you can see the remains of fortifications built during the Napoleonic Wars.

ARRIVAL AND INFORMATION   BRIXHAM

By bus Most buses arrive at and depart from Town Square and Bank Lane, in the upper town.
Destinations Exeter (2 daily; 1hr 40min); Paignton (every 10–20min; 25min); Torquay (every 10–20min; 40–50min).

Tourist office The tourist office (daily 10am–5pm; ☎ 0844 474 2233, ⊚ englishriviera.co.uk) is inside Hobb Nobs Gift Shop at 19 The Quay.

ACCOMMODATION

Harbour View King St ☎ 01803 853052, ⊚ harbourview brixhambandb.co.uk. As the name implies, its position is the best asset of this B&B, which has small but clean and modern en-suite rooms. The owners also take care of some self-catering accommodation; call for details. **£80**

Quayside Hotel King St ☎ 01803 855751, ⊚ quaysidehotel.co.uk. Handsome 29-room hotel with superb harbour views, two bars and a good restaurant where meat and seafood dishes are £15–17. It's worth paying extra for a harbour-facing room. **£102**

EATING AND DRINKING

Blue Anchor 83 Fore St ☎ 01803 859373. A great spot for a relaxed pint of local ale, with open fires and low beams. They also offer a full menu of (rather mediocre) bar food. Mon–Sat 11am–midnight, Sun 11am–11.30pm; food served daily noon–2.30pm & 6–9.30pm.
Poopdeck 14 The Quay ☎ 01803 858681, ⊚ poopdeck

restaurant.com. You'll find all manner of cockles, whelks and crab sticks at Brixham's harbourside stalls, but for a top-class seafood feast try this place, where a plate of grilled local fish costs £17.50 and a hot shellfish platter is £24.95 – book early for a table overlooking the harbour. Tues–Thurs 6–9.30pm, Fri & Sat noon–2.30pm & 6–10pm, Sun noon–2.30pm.

Greenway

4 miles west of Brixham, outside Galmpton • Early March to Oct Wed–Sun 10.30am–5pm, also Tues same hours during Easter and summer school hols • £9.40; NT • ☎ 01803 842382, ⊚ nationaltrust.org/greenway • Greenway Ferry (☎ 01803 882811, ⊚ greenwayferry.co.uk) offers services from Dartmouth (6–8/day; £8 return) and Totnes (1 daily; £8 return), as well as from Torquay (11am) and Brixham (11.30am) for £22/person including return journey by vintage bus; steam trains run from Paignton to Greenway Halt (up to 10 daily; 20min; £7.50), from where it's a 30min walk through woodland to the house; coming by car, parking is free but must be booked a day in advance

The birthplace of Walter Raleigh's three seafaring half-brothers, the Gilberts, and later rebuilt for Agatha Christie, **Greenway** stands high above the Dart amid steep wooded grounds (the ascent from the river landing is challenging). As well as arriving by ferry or steam train, you can reach the house on foot on the waymarked "**Greenway walk**" from Brixham (around 1hr 30min) or via the Dart Valley Trail from Dartmouth or Kingswear (both around 1hr 20min) – Dartmouth's tourist office can supply route maps (see p.302). Once here, you'll find a low-key collection of memorabilia belonging to the Christie family, including archeological scraps, silverware, ceramics and books, while the grounds afford lovely views over the river.

Totnes

On the west bank of the River Dart, **TOTNES** has an ancient pedigree, its period of greatest prosperity occurring in the sixteenth century when this inland port exported cloth to France and brought back wine. Some handsome sixteenth-century buildings survive from that era, and there is still a working port down on the river, but these days Totnes has mellowed into a residential market town, popular with the alternative and New Age crowd.

EXCURSIONS FROM TOTNES

The highest navigable point on the **River Dart** for seagoing vessels, Totnes is the starting point for **cruises to Dartmouth**, leaving from Steamer Quay (Feb–Oct 1–4 daily; 1hr 15min; £14 return; ☎01803 555872, ⍟dartmouthrailriver.co.uk). **Riverside walks** in either direction pass some congenial pubs and, near the railway bridge at Littlehempston, the station of the **South Devon Railway**, where you can board a steam train running along the Dart to Buckfastleigh, on the edge of Dartmoor (late March to Oct 4–9 daily; 30min; £12.40 return, ☎08453 451420, ⍟southdevonrailway.co.uk).

6

The town centres on the long main street that changes its name from Fore Street to the High Street at the **East Gate**, a much retouched medieval arch. On Fore Street, the town **museum**, occupying a four-storey Elizabethan house, illustrates how wealthy clothiers lived at the peak of Totnes's fortunes (April–Sept Mon–Sat 10.30am–4.30pm; last admission 3.30pm; £3; ☎01803 863821, ⍟totnesmuseum .org). From the East Gate, **Ramparts Walk** trails off along the old city walls, curving round the fifteenth-century church of **St Mary**, a red sandstone building containing an exquisitely carved rood screen. Looming over the High Street, the town's oldest monument, **Totnes Castle**, is a classic Norman structure of the motte and bailey design (daily: April–Sept 10am–6pm; Oct 10am–5pm; £3.70; EH; ☎1803 864406, ⍟englishheritage.org.uk).

ARRIVAL AND INFORMATION

TOTNES

By train Totnes train station lies just off Station Road, a 10min walk north from the centre; it's served by trains from/to Exeter (every 10–40min; 30min) and Plymouth (every 10min–1hr; 30min).

By bus Most buses stop on or around two central streets: The Plains and Coronation Road.

Destinations Exeter (up to 12 daily; 1hr 15min–1hr 35min);

Paignton (every 20min; 15–50min); Plymouth (Mon–Sat every 10min–1hr, Sun 8 daily; 1hr–1hr 15min); Torquay (Mon–Sat every 30min, Sun every 20min–1hr; 50min).

Tourist office At The Town Mill, near the Morrisons car park (April–Oct Mon–Fri 9.30am–5pm, Sat 10am–4pm; Nov–March Mon–Fri 10am–4pm, Sat 10am–1pm; ☎01803 863168, ⍟totnesinformation.co.uk)

ACCOMMODATION

Alison Fenwick's B&B 3 Plymouth Rd, off the High St ☎01803 866917, ⍟totnes-accommodation.co.uk. Central, great-value B&B run by a former tourist guide, with three simple rooms, one of them en suite. Wi-fi available. No credit cards. Closed Nov–Feb. **£50**

Great Grubb Fallowfields, Plymouth Rd ☎01803 849071, ⍟thegreatgrubb.co.uk. Leather sofas, restful colours, healthy breakfasts and a patio are the main appeal of this friendly B&B a short walk from the centre,

where work by local artists is displayed in the rooms. Free wi-fi. **£70**

Royal Seven Stars Hotel The Plains ☎01803 862125, ⍟royalsevenstars.co.uk. This seventeenth-century coaching inn has had a modern makeover, giving it contemporary bedrooms and a stylish bar alongside the traditional *Saloon Bar* and brasserie. The Sunday-night deal, including a carvery meal and breakfast for two, is great value at £80. **£118.75**

EATING AND DRINKING

The Barrel House 59 High St ☎01803 863000, ⍟barrelhousetotnes.co.uk. There's a café at street level and a former ballroom upstairs where you can eat salads, burgers and more for around £10. Occasional DJs, live music and comedy nights. Food served Mon–Sat 9am–11.30am & noon–4pm, Sun noon–3pm; shows usually Wed–Sat from 8pm.

Steam Packet Inn St Peter's Quay ☎01803 863880, ⍟steampacketinn.co.uk. This family-friendly inn reached by walking south along The Plains makes an excellent spot for a riverside drink or bite to eat.

There's a range of local ales, bar snacks and meals in the conservatory restaurant (most mains £11–13). Also has double rooms available on a bed and breakfast basis (£105). Mon–Sat 11am–11pm, Sun noon–10.30pm.

Willow 87 High St ☎01803 862605. Inexpensive vegetarian snacks, evening meals and organic drinks are served at this mellow café/restaurant. Main dishes are less than £10. There's a courtyard, and live acoustic music on Fri. No credit cards. Mon, Tues & Thurs 10am–5pm, Wed, Fri & Sat 10am–5pm & 6.30–9pm.

6

Dartmouth and around

South of Torbay, and eight miles downstream from Totnes, **DARTMOUTH** has thrived since the Normans recognized the trading potential of this deep-water port. Today its activities embrace fishing, freight and a booming leisure industry, as well as the education of the senior service's officer class at the Royal Naval College, on a hill overlooking the port.

Regular ferries shuttle across the River Dart between Dartmouth and **Kingswear**, terminus of the Dartmouth Steam Railway (see p.299). **Boat cruises** from Dartmouth are the best way to view the deep creeks and grand houses overlooking the river, among them Greenway (see p.300).

Dartmouth Museum

Duke St • April–Oct Mon & Sun 1–4pm, Tues–Sat 10am–4pm; Nov–March daily noon–3pm • £2 • ☎ 01803 832923, ⓦ dartmouthmuseum.org

Behind the enclosed boat basin at the heart of town, the four-storey **Butterwalk** at the top of Duke Street was built in the seventeenth century for a local merchant. The timber-framed construction, richly decorated with woodcarvings, was restored after bombing in World War II though still looks precarious as it overhangs the street on eleven granite columns. This arcade now holds shops and Dartmouth's small **museum**, mainly devoted to maritime curios, including old maps, prints and models of ships.

Dartmouth Castle

A mile southeast of town off Castle Rd • April–Sept daily 10am–6pm; Oct daily 10am–5pm; Nov–March Sat & Sun 10am–4pm • £5.50; EH • ☎ 01803 833588, ⓦ english-heritage.org.uk

A twenty-minute riverside walk southeast from **Bayard's Cove** – a short cobbled quay lined with eighteenth-century houses, where the Pilgrim Fathers stopped en route to the New World – brings you to **Dartmouth Castle**, one of two fortifications on opposite sides of the estuary dating from the fifteenth century. The castle was the first in England to be constructed specifically to withstand artillery, though was never tested in action, and consequently is excellently preserved.

If you don't fancy the walk back, you can take a **ferry** back to Dartmouth Quay (Easter–Oct continuous service 10am–4/5pm; £2; ⓦ dartmouthcastleferry.co.uk).

Blackpool Sands

Roughly two miles southwest of Dartmouth Castle, the coastal path brings you through the pretty hilltop village of **Stoke Fleming** to **Blackpool Sands**, the best beach in the area. The unspoilt cove, flanked by steep, wooded cliffs, was the site of a battle in 1404 in which Devon archers repulsed a Breton invasion force sent to punish the privateers of Dartmouth for their cross-Channel raiding.

ARRIVAL AND INFORMATION — DARTMOUTH

By ferry Coming from Torbay, visitors to Dartmouth can save time and a long detour through Totnes by using the frequent Higher Ferry (ⓦ dartmouthhigherferry.com) or Lower Ferry (southhams.gov.uk/DartmouthLowerFerry) across the Dart from Kingswear (50p–£1.50 foot passengers; £4.50–4.70 for cars); the last ones are at around 10.45pm.

Tourist office The Discover Dartmouth tourist office is on Mayor's Ave (March Mon–Sat 10am–4pm; April–Oct Mon–Sat 9.30am–4.30pm, Sun 10am–2pm; Nov–Feb Mon, Tues & Thurs–Sat 10am–4pm; ☎ 01803 834224, ⓦ discoverdartmouth.com).

ACCOMMODATION, EATING AND DRINKING

Avondale 5 Vicarage Hill ☎ 07968 026449, ⓦ avondaledartmouth.co.uk. On a steep hill west of the quay, this is a friendly, spacious and simply furnished B&B with terrific views over the town and river. Free wi-fi. **£88**
Browns 27–29 Victoria Rd ☎ 01803 832572, ⓦ brownshoteldartmouth.co.uk. Boutique-style hotel, with small, stylish rooms decorated with contemporary

paintings. Good Mediterranean dishes are served in the bar and restaurant. Mon–Thurs & Sun 10am–7/8pm, Fri & Sat 11am–11.30pm. **£145**
Café Alf Resco Lower St ☎ 01803 835880, ⓦ cafealfresco.co.uk. Funky snack bar that's good for all-day breakfasts, steaming coffees and occasional live music in summer. There's decent accommodation available above

the café. Daily 7am–2pm. **£90**

The Seahorse 5 South Embankment ☎01803 835147, ⓦseahorserestaurant.co.uk. Seafood restaurant facing the river, offering such Italian-inspired dishes as spaghetti with clams and flame-grilled sea bass. It's pricey, with mains costing £19 and up, but there's a two-course lunch menu (£20), and the same team also runs *Rockfish*, a couple of doors down, which serves first-class fish and chips (daily noon–9.30pm). Tues–Sat noon–3pm & 6–10pm, Sun 12.30–2.30pm.

Salcombe

The area between the Dart and Plym estuaries, the **South Hams**, holds some of Devon's comeliest villages and most striking coastline. The "capital" of the region, **Kingsbridge**, is a useful transport hub but lacks the appeal of **SALCOMBE**, reachable on a summer ferry from Kingsbridge. Once a nondescript fishing village, Devon's southernmost resort is now a full-blown sailing and holiday centre, its calm waters strewn with small pleasure craft.

You can swot up on boating and local history at **Salcombe Maritime Museum** on Market Street, off the north end of the central Fore Street (April–Oct daily 10.30am–12.30pm & 2.30–4.30pm; £1.50; ☎01548 843080, ⓦsalcombemuseum.org.uk) or take a ferry down to South Sands and climb up to the intriguing **Overbeck's Museum** at Sharpitor (mid-Feb to Oct daily 11am–5pm; £7.80; NT; ☎01548 842893, ⓦnationaltrust.org.uk/overbecks), which focuses on the area's natural history and nineteenth-century curiosities.

ARRIVAL AND INFORMATION   SALCOMBE

By bus Salcombe is served by regular buses from Kingsbridge (hourly; 30min), which is where you'll have to change if you're coming from Dartmouth and further afield.

Tourist office Market Street (late March to mid-July &

Sept–Nov daily 10am–5pm; late July to Aug Mon–Sat 9am–6pm, Sun 10am–5pm; Nov to mid-March Mon–Sat 10am–3pm; ☎01548 843927, ⓦsalcombeinformation.co.uk).

ACCOMMODATION AND EATING

Higher Rew Caravan and Camping Park 2 miles west of town, near Kingsbridge ☎01548 842681, ⓦhigherrew.co.uk. Large, grassy campsite on a slope near town, surrounded by attractive farmland. The on-site facilities are good, and there are plenty of places for kids to play. Closed Nov–March. Pitches **£20**

Waverley Devon Rd ☎01548 842633, ⓦwaverleybandb.co.uk. Rooms in this B&B are clean and the breakfasts are excellent, with lots of choice. It's less than a 10min walk to the centre. Self-catering also available. **£80**

Winking Prawn North Sands ☎01548 842326, ⓦwinkingprawn.co.uk. Right on the beach, this is an alluring stop for a cappuccino, baguette or ice cream by day, or a chargrilled steak or Cajun chicken salad in the evening, from around 6pm, when booking is advised (mains £15–20). You don't need to book for the summer barbecues (May–Sept 4–8.30pm; £16.95). Daily 8.45am–8.30pm.

Plymouth and around

PLYMOUTH's predominantly bland and modern face belies its great historic role as a naval base and, in the sixteenth century, the stamping ground of such national heroes as John Hawkins and Francis Drake. It was from here that Drake sailed to defeat the Spanish Armada in 1588, and 32 years later the port was the last embarkation point for the Pilgrim Fathers, whose New Plymouth colony became the nucleus for the English settlement of North America. The importance of the city's Devonport dockyards made the city a target in World War II, when the Luftwaffe reduced most of the old centre to rubble. Subsequent reconstruction has done little to improve the place, though it would be difficult to spoil the glorious vista over **Plymouth Sound**, the basin of calm water at the mouth of the combined Plym, Tavy and Tamar estuaries, largely unchanged since Drake played his famous game of bowls on the Hoe before joining battle with the Armada.

One of the best local excursions from Plymouth is to **Mount Edgcumbe**, where woods and meadows provide a welcome antidote to the urban bustle. East of Plymouth, the aristocratic opulence of **Saltram House** includes fine art and furniture, while to the north you can visit Francis Drake's old home at **Buckland Abbey**.

6

PLYMOUTH

The map includes labels:

▲ 1   ▲ Train Station   ▲ Buckland Abbey

■ ACCOMMODATION
Brittany Guest House	2
Globe Backpackers	3
Warleigh House	1

Mount Edgcumbe · Saltram House

CHARLES ST · CHARLES CROSS · EBRINGTON ST · NORTH ST · BEAUMONT RD · N

Drake Circus Shopping Centre · EXETER STREET · EXETER STREET · CORNWALL STREET · ARMADA WAY · NEW GEORGE STREET · WESTERN APP

Bus Station · BRETONSIDE · BRETONSIDE · SUTTON ROAD

Theatre Royal · ROYAL PARADE · ARMADA WAY · Guildhall · ST ANDREWS CROSS · HOW STREET · LOOE STREET · VAUXHALL ST · Plymouth Arts Centre · DERRYS CROSS

UNION STREET · CROSS · PRINCESS WAY · PRINCESS STREET · ATHERINE · PALACE ST

Plymouth Pavilions · THE CRESCENT · NOTTE STREET · PARADE QUAY · Sutton Harbour

CRESCENT AVE · ATHENAEUM STREET · ALFRED ST · ZION ST · HOE ST · HOE APPROACH RD · SOUTHSIDE ST · BARBICAN · National Marine Aquarium · MILLBAY RD · LOCKYER STREET · ARMADA WAY · CITADEL RD EAST · NEW ST · COXSIDE

CITADEL ROAD · CITADEL ROAD · Elizabethan House · THE BARBICAN

PROSPECT PLACE · LEIGHAM ST · HOLYROOD PL · INGE RD · HOE RD · LAMBHAY HILL · Mayflower Steps · Cattewater

Hoe Park · HOE ROAD · Royal Citadel

WALKER TERR · CLIFF ROAD · Smeaton's Tower · Plymouth Hoe

RADFORD ROAD · PIER STREET · HOE ROAD · MADEIRA ROAD

The Sound

■ PUB
The Dolphin	1

● CAFÉS & RESTAURANTS
Barbican Kitchen	2
Plymouth Arts Centre	1
West Hoe Fryer	3

Scale: 0 – 200 yards

Plymouth Hoe

A good place to start a tour of the city is **Plymouth Hoe**, an immense esplanade with glorious views over the water. Here, alongside various war memorials stands a rather portly statue of Sir Francis Drake, gazing grandly out to the sea. Appropriately, there's a bowling green back from the brow.

Smeaton's Tower

Plymouth Hoe • Jan & Dec Sat 10am–3pm; Feb–March Tues–Sun 10am–3pm; April–Sept Tues–Sun 10am–4.30pm; Oct & Nov Tues–Sat 10am–3pm • £2.60 • ☎ 01752 304774, ⊛ plymouth.gov.uk

One of the city's best-known landmarks, the red-and-white-striped **Smeaton's Tower** was erected in 1759 by John Smeaton on the treacherous Eddystone Rocks, fourteen miles out to sea. When replaced by a larger lighthouse in 1882, it was reassembled here, where it gives lofty views across Plymouth Sound.

Around the Barbican

At the old town's quay at **Sutton Harbour**, the **Mayflower Steps** commemorate the sailing of the Pilgrim Fathers, with a plaque listing the names and professions of the 102 Puritans on board. Edging the harbour, the **Barbican** district is the heart of old Plymouth: most of the buildings are now shops and restaurants.

Elizabethan House

32 New St • April–Sept Tues–Sat 10am–noon & 1–5pm • £2.60 • ☎ 01752 304774, ⊛ plymouth.gov.uk

New Street holds some of Plymouth's oldest buildings, among them the **Elizabethan House**, a captain's dwelling retaining most of the original architectural features, including a spiral staircase around what was probably a disused ship's mast. The three floors are crammed with fine sixteenth- and seventeenth-century furniture and textiles.

National Marine Aquarium

Rope Walk • Daily: April–Sept 10am–6pm; Oct–March 10am–5pm; last entry 1hr before closing • £13.75 • ☎ 0844 893 7938,
Ⓦ national-aquarium.co.uk

Across the footbridge from Sutton Harbour, the **National Marine Aquarium** has recreated a
range of marine environments, from moorland stream to coral reef and deep-sea ocean.
The most popular exhibits are the seahorses, the colourful reefs and the sharks, though
some of the smaller tanks hold equally compelling exhibits – the anemones, for example.

Mount Edgcumbe

2 miles southwest of the city, across the River Tamar • **House** April–Sept Sun–Thurs 11am–4.30pm (last admission 4pm) • £7.20 • **Park**
daily 8am–dusk • Free • ☎ 01752 822236, Ⓦ mountedgcumbe.gov.uk • Bus #34 from Royal Parade to Stonehouse, then passenger ferry
to Cremyll from Admiral's Hard (at least hourly; Ⓦ cremyll-ferry.co.uk); alternatively, in summer take the direct motor-launch from the
Mayflower Steps to Cawsand (Ⓦ cawsandferry.co.uk), then 2hr walk to house

Lying on the Cornish side of Plymouth Sound and visible from the Hoe is **Mount
Edgcumbe house**, a reconstruction of the bomb-damaged Tudor original, though inside
the predominant note is eighteenth-century, the rooms elegantly restored with authentic
Regency furniture. Far more enticing are the impeccable **gardens** divided into French,
Italian and English sections – the first two a blaze of flowerbeds adorned with classical
statuary, the last an acre of sweeping lawn shaded by exotic trees. The **park**, which is open
all year, gives access to the coastal path and the huge **Whitsand Bay**, the best bathing beach
for miles around, though subject to dangerous shifting sands and fierce currents.

Saltram House

Near Plympton, 2 miles east of Plymouth off the A38 • **House** Mid-March to Oct daily except Fri noon–4.30pm • £10 (includes garden); NT
• **Garden** Jan to mid-March & Nov–Dec daily 10am–4pm; mid-March to Oct daily 10am–5pm • £5.10 (or £10 with house) • Buses #19 or
#21 from Royal Parade to Cot Hill, from where it's a walk of a mile or so (signposted) • ☎ 01752 333500, Ⓦ nationaltrust.org.uk/saltram

The remodelled Tudor **Saltram House** is Devon's largest country house, featuring work by
architect Robert Adam and fourteen portraits by **Joshua Reynolds**, who was born in nearby
Plympton. The showpiece is the Saloon, a fussy but exquisitely furnished room dripping
with gilt and plaster, and set off by a huge Axminster carpet especially woven for it in
1770. Saltram's landscaped **garden** provides a breather from this riot of interior design.

Buckland Abbey

9 miles north of Plymouth • Mid-Feb to mid-March & early Dec to late Dec daily 11.30am–4.30pm; mid-March to Oct daily 10.30am–
5.30pm; Nov Fri–Sun 11.30am–4.30pm • £9.05, grounds only £5; NT • From Plymouth, take #83 or "Blue Flash" service #12 to Tavistock,
changing at Yelverton for #55 • ☎ 01822 853607, Ⓦ nationaltrust.org.uk/buckland-abbey

SIR FRANCIS DRAKE

Born around 1540 near Tavistock, **Francis Drake** worked in the domestic coastal trade from
the age of 13, but was soon taking part in the first English slaving expeditions between Africa
and the West Indies, led by his Plymouth kinsman John Hawkins. Later, Drake was active in the
secret war against Spain, raiding and looting merchant ships in actions unofficially sanctioned
by Elizabeth I. In 1572 he became the first Englishman to sight the Pacific, and soon afterwards,
on board the *Golden Hinde* (see p.89), became the first to **circumnavigate the world**, for
which he received a knighthood on his return in 1580. The following year Drake was made
mayor of Plymouth, settling in Buckland Abbey (see above), but was back in action before long
– in 1587 he "singed the king of Spain's beard" by entering Cadiz harbour and destroying 33
vessels that were to have formed part of Philip II's **armada**. When the replacement invasion
fleet appeared in the English Channel in 1588, Drake – along with Raleigh, Hawkins and
Frobisher – played a leading role in wrecking it. The following year he set off on an
unsuccessful expedition to help the Portuguese against Spain, but otherwise most of the next
decade was spent in relative inactivity in Plymouth, Exeter and London. Finally, in 1596 Drake
left with Hawkins for a raid on Panama, a venture that cost the lives of both captains.

6

Close to the River Tavy and on the edge of Dartmoor, **Buckland Abbey** was once the most westerly of England's Cistercian abbeys. After its dissolution, Buckland was converted to a family home by the privateer Richard Grenville (cousin of Walter Raleigh), from whom the estate was acquired by Francis Drake in 1582, the year after he became mayor of Plymouth. It remained Drake's home until his death, though the house reveals few traces of his residence. There are, however, numerous maps, portraits and mementos of his buccaneering exploits on show, most famous of which is Drake's Drum, which was said to beat a supernatural warning of impending danger to the country. More eye-catching are the oak-panelled **Great Hall**, previously the nave of the abbey, and, in the majestic grounds, a fine fourteenth-century **monastic barn**.

ARRIVAL AND INFORMATION   PLYMOUTH

By train Plymouth's train station is a mile north of the Hoe off Saltash Road. Frequent buses run between the station and the city centre.
Destinations Bodmin (every 30min–1hr; 45min); Exeter (every 20min–1hr; 1hr); Liskeard (every 30min–1hr; 30min); Par (every 30min–1hr; 50min); Penzance (every 30min–1hr; 2hr); Truro (every 30min–1hr; 1hr 20min).
By bus Buses pull in at the Bretonside bus station, just over St Andrew's Cross from Royal Parade.
Destinations Bodmin (hourly; 1hr 25min); Exeter (every

1–2hr; 1hr 15min–1hr 50min); Falmouth (2 daily; 2hr 30min); Newquay (hourly; 2hr); Penzance (5–6 daily; 3hr–3hr 30min); St Austell (4 daily; 1hr 20min); St Ives (3 daily; 3hr–3hr 30min); Torquay (Mon–Sat hourly; Sun 8 daily; 1hr 20min–2hr); Truro (5 daily; 2hr).
Tourist office The tourist office is off Sutton Harbour at 3–5 The Barbican (April–Oct Mon–Sat 9am–5pm, Sun 10am–4pm; Nov–March Mon–Fri 9am–5pm, Sat 10am–4pm; ☎ 01752 306330, ⓦ visitplymouth.co.uk).

ACCOMMODATION

Brittany Guest House 28 Athenaeum St ☎ 01752 262247, ⓦ brittanyguesthouse.co.uk. A good choice on this row close to the Barbican, with all rooms en suite. The easy-going owners offer a choice of breakfasts, and there's even a car park (a definite bonus in these parts). **£60**
Globe Backpackers 172 Citadel Rd ☎ 01752 225158, ⓦ plymouthbackpackers.co.uk. Relaxed hostel west of the Hoe, with kitchen, free tea and coffee, free wi-fi and a courtyard garden. It's a bit run-down, but clean enough.

Book ahead during the summer. Dorms **£16.50**; doubles **£38**
Warleigh House 5 miles northwest of the centre on Horsham Lane ☎ 07971 220152, ⓦ warleighhouse.co.uk. Beautifully furnished country house on the banks of the River Tavy, parts of which date back to the twelfth century, offering top-quality bed and breakfast accommodation. Two of the three rooms have four-poster beds, and all come with their own flatscreen TV and iPod dock. **£168**

EATING AND DRINKING

Barbican Kitchen 60 Southside St ☎ 01752 604448, ⓦ barbicankitchen.com. Modern decor, tasty food and a casual ambience draw the crowds at this bistro, housed in the ancient Black Friars Distillery. Choose from a varied menu that runs from sausage and mash to steak medallions (£10–19). There are some decent veggie options too. Mon–Thurs noon–2.30pm & 5–9.30pm, Fri & Sat noon–2.30pm & 5–10pm, Sun noon–3pm & 6–9pm.
The Dolphin 14 The Barbican ☎ 01752 660876. A local institution, this harbourside pub has an authentic atmosphere and Tribute and Bass ales straight from the barrel. Look out for the pictures by Beryl Cook, who used to drink here. Mon–Thurs 10am–11pm, Fri & Sat 10am–

midnight, Sun 11am–11.30pm.
Plymouth Arts Centre 38 Looe St ☎ 01752 206114, ⓦ plymouthartscentre.org. Exhibitions, films and performances are held here, and there's a very good restaurant run by one of Jamie Oliver's students, serving home-made burgers and fish dishes (from £10). Restaurant Tues–Sat 10am–11pm.
West Hoe Fryer 7 Radford Rd ☎ 01752 221409. It doesn't get much simpler than this: an old-style fish shop with a queue for takeaway orders on one side and tables on the other. Locals flock here for the chips (from £1.80), wrapped up with extras like pickled eggs and cockles. Mon–Sat noon–2pm & 5–9pm.

Dartmoor

Occupying the main part of the county between Exeter and Plymouth, **DARTMOOR** is southern England's greatest expanse of wilderness, some 368 square miles of raw granite, barren bogland, sparse grass and heather-grown moor. It was not always so desolate, as testified by the remnants of scattered Stone Age settlements and the ruined relics of the area's nineteenth-century tin-mining industry. Today desultory flocks of sheep and groups of ponies are virtually the only living creatures to be seen wandering over the central fastnesses of the National Park, with solitary birds – buzzards, kestrels, pipits, stonechats and wagtails – wheeling and hovering high above.

The core of Dartmoor, characterized by tumbling streams and high tors chiselled by the elements, is **Dartmoor Forest**, which has belonged to the Duchy of Cornwall since 1307, though there is almost unlimited public access. Networks of signposts or painted stones exist to guide **walkers**, but map-reading abilities are a prerequisite for any but the shortest walks, and considerable experience is essential for longer distances. Overnight parking is only allowed in authorized places, and no vehicles are permitted beyond fifteen yards from the road; camping should be out of sight of houses and roads, and fires are strictly forbidden. Information on **guided walks** and riding facilities is available from National Park visitor centres and tourist offices in Dartmoor's major towns and villages.

Postbridge and around

Northeast of Princetown, two miles north of the crossroads at **Two Bridges**, you can see

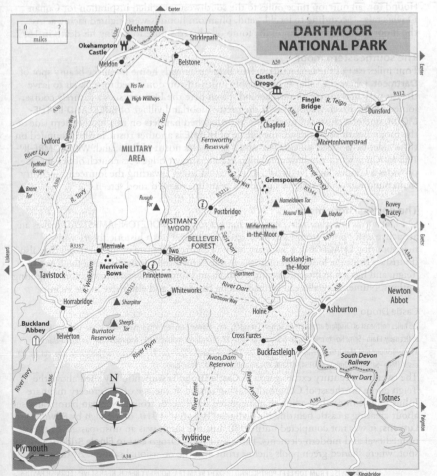

one of Dartmoor's **clapper bridges**: used by tin miners and farmers since medieval times, these simple structures consist of huge slabs of granite supported by piers of the same material. The largest and best preserved of these is three miles northeast at **POSTBRIDGE**. From here, you can head south through **Bellever Forest** to the open moor, where **Bellever Tor** (1453ft) affords outstanding views. North of Two Bridges, the dwarfed and misshapen oaks of **Wistman's Wood** are an evocative relic of the original Dartmoor Forest, cluttered with lichen-covered boulders and a dense undergrowth of ferns. The gnarled old trees are alleged to have been the site of druidic gatherings, a story unsupported by any evidence but quite plausible in this solitary spot.

Grimspound
3 miles northeast of Postbridge, off the B3212 • Open access • Free

The Bronze Age village of **Grimspound** lies below Hameldown Tor, about a mile off the road. Inhabited some three thousand years ago, this is the most complete example of Dartmoor's prehistoric settlements, consisting of 24 circular huts scattered within a four-acre enclosure. The site is thought to have been the model for the Stone Age settlement in which Sherlock Holmes camped in *The Hound of the Baskervilles*; while **Hound Tor**, an outcrop three miles to the southwest, provided inspiration for Conan Doyle's tale – according to local legend, phantom hounds were sighted racing across the moor to hurl themselves on the tomb of a hated squire following his death in 1677.

The southeastern moor
Four miles east of the crossroads at Two Bridges, crowds home in on the beauty spot of **Dartmeet**, where the valley is memorably lush and you don't need to walk far to leave the car park and ice-cream vans behind. From here the Dart pursues a leisurely course, joined by the River Webburn near the pretty moorland village of **BUCKLAND-IN-THE-MOOR**, one of a cluster of moorstone-and-thatched hamlets on this southeastern side of the moor. South of Buckland, the village of **HOLNE** is another rustic idyll surrounded on three sides by wooded valleys. Two and a half miles north of Buckland, **WIDECOMBE-IN-THE-MOOR** is set in a hollow amid high granite-strewn ridges. Its church of **St Pancras** provides a famous local landmark, its pinnacled tower dwarfing the fourteenth-century main building, whose interior includes a beautiful painted rood screen.

The northeastern moor
On Dartmoor's northeastern edge, the market town of **MORETONHAMPSTEAD** makes an attractive entry point from Exeter. Moretonhampstead has a historic rivalry with neighbouring **CHAGFORD**, a Stannary town (a chartered centre of the tin trade) that also flourished from the local wool industry. It stands on a hillside overlooking the River Teign, and has a fine fifteenth-century church and some good accommodation and eating options. Numerous **walks** can be made along the Teign and elsewhere in the vicinity.

Castle Drogo
2.5 miles northeast of Chagford across the A382, near Drewsteignton • **House** Late Feb to mid-March daily 11am–4pm; mid-March to Oct daily 11am–5pm; Nov to mid-Dec Sat & Sun noon–4pm • £8.70 (includes grounds); NT • **Grounds** Daily: Jan to mid-March 11am–4.30pm; mid-March to Oct 9am–5.30pm; Nov & Dec 11am–4.30pm • £5.50 • Bus #173 from Exeter's bus station stops outside the castle (Mon–Sat only; 50min) • ☎ 01647 433306, ⓦ nationaltrust.org.uk/castle-drogo

The twentieth-century extravaganza of **Castle Drogo** is stupendously sited above the Teign gorge northeast of Chagford. Having retired at the age of 33, grocery magnate Julius Drewe unearthed a link that suggested his descent from a Norman baron, and set about creating a castle befitting his pedigree. Begun in 1910, to a design by **Edwin Lutyens**, it was not completed until 1930, but the result was an unsurpassed synthesis of medieval and modern elements. Paths lead from Drogo east to **Fingle Bridge**, a lovely spot, where shaded green pools shelter trout and the occasional salmon. At the time of

FIRING RANGES ON DARTMOOR

A significant portion of northern Dartmoor, containing the moor's highest tors and some of its most famous beauty spots, is run by the **Ministry of Defence**, whose **firing ranges** are marked by red-and-white posts; when firing is in progress, red flags or red lights signify that entry is prohibited. Generally, if no warning flags are flying by 9am between April and Sept, or by 10am from Oct to March, there will be no firing on that day; alternatively, check at ☎0800 458 4868 or ⓦmod.uk/access.

6

writing, the castle was undergoing extensive renovation work but remained open to the public, giving visitors a rare chance to see rooms that had long been hidden from view.

Okehampton

The main centre on the northern fringes of Dartmoor, **OKEHAMPTON** grew prosperous as a market town for the medieval wool trade, and some fine old buildings survive between the two branches of the River Okement that meet here, among them the prominent fifteenth-century tower of the **Chapel of St James**. Across the road from the seventeenth-century town hall, a granite archway leads into the **Museum of Dartmoor Life** (April–Oct Mon–Fri 10.15am–4.15pm, Sat 10.15am–1pm; £2.50; ☎01837 52295, ⓦmuseumofdartmoorlife.org.uk), which offers an excellent overview of habitation on the moor since earliest times.

Okehampton Castle

A mile southwest of Okehampton • Daily: April–June & Sept–Oct 10am–5pm; July & Aug 10am–6pm • £4; EH • ☎01837 52844, ⓦenglish-heritage.org.uk

Perched above the West Okement, **Okehampton Castle** is the shattered hulk of a stronghold laid waste by Henry VIII. The tottering ruins include a gatehouse, Norman keep, and the remains of the Great Hall, buttery and kitchens. Woodland walks and riverside picnic tables invite a gentle exploration of what was once the deer park of the earls of Devon.

Lydford

Five miles southwest of Okehampton, the village of **LYDFORD** preserves the sturdy but small-scale **Lydford Castle** (daylight hours; free), a Saxon outpost, then a Norman keep and later used as a prison. The chief attraction here, though – apart from the hotels and restaurants – is the one-and-a-half-mile **Lydford Gorge** (March–Oct daily 10am–5pm; £6.90; NT; ☎01822 820320, ⓦnationaltrust.org.uk/lydford-gorge), overgrown with thick woods and alive with butterflies, spotted woodpeckers, dippers and herons.

Tavistock and around

The main town of the western moor, **TAVISTOCK** owes its distinctive Victorian appearance to the building boom that followed the discovery of copper deposits here in 1844. Originally, however, this market and Stannary town on the River Tavy grew around what was once the West Country's most important Benedictine abbey, established in the eleventh century. Some scant remnants survive in the churchyard of **St Eustace**, a mainly fifteenth-century building with stained glass from William Morris's studio in the south aisle.

North of Tavistock, a four-mile lane wanders up to **Brent Tor**, 1130ft high and dominating Dartmoor's western fringes. Access to its conical summit is easiest along a path gently ascending through gorse on its southwestern side, leading to the small church of St Michael at the top.

ARRIVAL AND DEPARTURE   **DARTMOOR**

BY TRAIN
Between mid-May and mid-Sept there's a Sunday

connection with Exeter (Sun 5 daily; 45min). The station is a 15min walk south of the centre.

BY BUS

Destinations from Princetown Exeter (late-May to mid-Sept Sat & Sun 1 daily; 1hr 30min); Moretonhampstead (late May to mid-Sept Sat & Sun 1 daily; 45min); Tavistock (Mon–Sat 1–3 daily; 30min).

Destinations from Moretonhampstead Chagford (Mon–Sat 3 daily; 15min); Exeter (5–7 daily; 50min); Okehampton (Mon–Sat 1 daily; 1hr); Princetown (late May to mid-Sept Sat & Sun 1 daily; 45min).

Destinations from Chagford Exeter (Mon–Sat 5 daily; 1hr); Moretonhampstead (Mon–Sat 3 daily; 15min); Okehampton (Mon–Sat 5 daily; 50min).

Destinations from Okehampton Exeter (every 30min–1hr; 50min–1hr 15min); Okehampton (Mon–Sat 1 daily; 1hr); Tavistock (7–9 daily; 45–55min).

Destinations from Tavistock Okehampton (7–9 daily; 45–55min); Plymouth (Mon–Sat every 15–30min, hourly on Sun; 1hr) and Princetown (Mon–Sat 1–3 daily; 30min).

6

GETTING AROUND

By bus Public transport is good to the main centres on the periphery of the moor – Okehampton, Tavistock, Moreton-hampstead – but extremely sketchy for the heart of the moor. The best bets are the #82 "Transmoor Link" (late May to mid-Sept weekends only), between Tavistock and Exeter, taking in Princetown, Two Bridges, Postbridge and Moreton-hampstead en route, and the #98 connecting Tavistock, Princetown, Two Bridges and Postbridge (Mon–Sat only).

INFORMATION

Princetown National Park Visitor Centre Tavistock Road (March & Oct daily 10am–4pm; April–Sept daily 10am–5pm; Nov–Feb Thurs–Sun 10.30am–3.30pm; ☎01822 890414, ⓦdartmoor-npa.gov.uk).

Postbridge National Park Visitor Centre The Postbridge information centre is in the car park off the B3212. (March & Oct Thurs–Sun 10am–4pm; April–Sept

10am–5pm; Nov–Feb Thurs–Sun 10.30am–3.30pm; ☎01822 880272, ⓦdartmoor-npa.gov.uk).

Moretonhampstead tourist office New Street (Easter–Oct daily 9.30am–5pm; Nov–Easter Thurs–Sat 10am–4.30pm, Sun 11am–3pm; ☎01647 440043, ⓦmoretonhampstead.com)

ACCOMMODATION AND EATING

Scattered **accommodation** options include several **camping barns**, which it's always wise to book ahead, particularly at weekends: call the numbers given in our reviews, or else the YHA, which administers them (☎0800 019 1700, ⓦyha.org.uk).

22 Mill Street Chagford ☎01647 432244, ⓦ22millst .com. This smart country restaurant offers top-quality modern European cuisine: two- and three-course menus cost £19/£24 for lunch, £36/£42 for dinner. They also have two luxury guestrooms. Wed–Sat noon–2.30pm & 7–10pm. **£129**

Castle Inn Next to Lydford Castle ☎01822 820241, ⓦcastleinndartmoor.co.uk. Sixteenth-century inn where one of the en-suite rooms has its own roof terrace looking onto the castle (£95); there are also little cottage rooms and one with a four-poster. Free wi-fi. The oak-beamed, fire-lit bar provides good drinks and there's a beer garden and a restaurant. Daily noon–11pm; food served noon–9pm. **£70**

Cyprian's Cot 47 New St Chagford ☎01647 432256, ⓦcyprianscot.co.uk. Comfy, sixteenth-century cottage where you can warm your bones by an inglenook fireplace and in fine weather breakfast and take tea in the garden. Worth booking ahead during summer. **£70**

★**Dartmoor Inn** A386, opposite Lydford turning ☎01822 820221, ⓦdartmoorinn.com. Three spacious guest rooms available above a popular gastropub, each furnished with antiques from France and England. The restaurant menu features tasty options like beetroot risotto and slow-roasted pork belly (mains £11–23) and there's a set

menu for Sun lunch (£24 for three courses). Booking advised. Tues–Sat noon–3pm & 6–9pm; Sun noon–3pm. **£100**

Duchy House Tavistock Rd, Princetown ☎01822 890552, ⓦduchyhouse.co.uk. Some 300yd from the centre of Princetown, this Victorian B&B offers staid but reliable accommodation in traditionally furnished rooms – one with its own bathroom – and a guests' lounge. **£70**

Great Houndtor camping barn Near Manaton ☎08000 191700, ⓦyha.org.uk. This YHA-managed former farmhouse on the eastern edge of Dartmoor offers a cooking area and hot water for showers, and there's a wood burner – but be sure to bring your sleeping bag and other useful camping gear. Per person **£7**

Higher Venton Farm Half a mile south of Widecombe ☎01364 621235, ⓦventonfarm.com. A peaceful sixteenth-century thatched longhouse that was once home to the Dartmoor writer Beatrice Chase. The bedrooms are fine (the cheapest double shares a bathroom), and it's close to a couple of good pubs. **£66**

Kestor Inn Manaton ☎01647 221626, ⓦwww .kestorinn.com. A popular pub with walkers, serving hot food as well as local ales and ciders, and selling maps, provisions and walking guides. There are en-suite rooms available here too, some with good views. Daily 11am–11pm; food served noon–2pm (Sun till 4pm) & 6.30–9pm. **£85**

6

Meadowlea 65 Station Rd, Okehampton ☎ 01837 53200, ⓦ meadowleaguesthouse.co.uk. A short walk south of the centre, below the train station and within 550yd of the Granite Way cycling route, this bike-friendly B&B has seven rooms (four en suite), wi-fi access and cycle storage. **£65**

★ **Mount Tavy Cottage** Half a mile east of Tavistock on the B3357 (Princetown road) ☎ 01822 614253, ⓦ mounttavy.co.uk. Set on a beautiful plot with its own lake, this B&B in a former gardener's cottage has comfortable rooms, organic breakfasts, evening meals and a few self-catering options. **£75**

Plume of Feathers The Square, Princetown ☎ 01822 890240 ⓦ theplumeoffeathersdartmoor.co.uk. B&B, bunkhouse dorms and a campsite right in the centre of Princetown. Reasonably priced meals are available here, with most mains going for around a tenner. Dorms **£18**; doubles **£75**; camping per person **£7**

Sparrowhawk Backpackers 45 Ford St, Moretonhampstead ☎ 01647 440318, ⓦ sparrowhawkbackpackers.co.uk. Excellent, eco-minded hostel with fourteen beds in a light and spacious bunkroom and a private room sleeping up to four. Good kitchen for self-

catering. Dorms **£17**; double **£38**

Warren House Inn 2 miles northeast of Postbridge ☎ 01822 880208, ⓦ warrenhouseinn.co.uk. Set in a bleak tract of moorland, this solitary pub offers fire-lit comfort and very basic meals, including a steak and ale pie with chips and veg (£12). Easter–Nov Mon–Sat 11am–11pm, Sun 11am–10.30pm; Nov–Easter Mon & Tues 11am–3pm, Wed & Thurs 11am–10pm, Fri & Sat 10am–11pm, Sun noon–10pm.

YHA Dartmoor Bellever, near Postbridge ☎ 0845 371 9622, ⓦ yha.org.uk. One of Dartmoor's two YHA hostels lies a mile or so south of Postbridge on the edge of the forest and on the banks of the East Dart River. By bus, take the daily #98 from Tavistock or Princetown (not Sun) or #82 from Princetown or Exeter (summer Sat & Sun only) to Postbridge and walk a mile. Dorms **£21.50**

YHA Okehampton Klondyke Rd, Okehampton ☎ 01837 53916, ⓦ yha.org.uk. Housed in a converted goods shed at the station, this well-run hostel offers a range of outdoor activities as well as bike rental. Camping also available. Dorms **£25**; doubles **£63**; camping per person **£6**

Barnstaple

BARNSTAPLE, at the head of the Taw estuary, makes an excellent North Devon base, well connected to the resorts of Bideford Bay, Ilfracombe and Woolacombe, as well as to the western fringes of Exmoor. The town's centuries-old role as a marketplace is perpetuated in the daily bustle around the huge timber-framed **Pannier Market** off the High Street, alongside which runs **Butchers Row**, its 33 archways now converted to a variety of uses. At the end of Boutport Street, the **Museum of Barnstaple and North Devon** (Nov to mid-March Mon–Sat 10am–4pm, mid-March to Oct Mon–Sat 10am–5pm; free; ☎ 01271 346747) holds a lively miscellany that includes a collection of the eighteenth-century pottery for which the region was famous. The museum lies alongside the Taw, where footpaths make for a pleasant riverside stroll, with the colonnaded eighteenth-century **Queen Anne's Walk** – built as a merchants' exchange – providing some architectural interest. It houses the **Barnstaple Heritage Centre** (April–Oct Tues–Sat 9.30am–4.30pm; Nov–March Tues–Fri 9.30am–4pm, Sat 10am–3.30pm; £3.50; ☎ 01271 373003), which traces the town's social history by means of reconstructions and touch-screen computers.

ARRIVAL AND INFORMATION   BARNSTAPLE

By train Barnstaple's train station is on the south side of the Taw, a 5min walk from the centre. There are good connections with Exeter on the Tarka Line (Mon–Sat hourly, Sun 7 daily; 1hr 10min).

By bus The bus station is centrally located between Silver Street and Belle Meadow Road.

Destinations Bideford (every 10–20min; 30min); Croyde (every 30min; 30min); Exeter (up to 8 daily; 2hr); Ilfracombe (every 20min; 40min).

Tourist office The local tourist office is inside the Museum of North Devon on The Square (Mon–Sat 10am–5pm; ☎ 01271 375000, ⓦ staynorthdevon.co.uk)

ACCOMMODATION

Broomhill Art Hotel Muddiford, 2 miles north of Barnstaple off the A39 ☎ 01271 850262, ⓦ broomhillart.co.uk. Striking combination of gallery, restaurant and hotel where the rooms look onto a sculpture garden. Half-board only at

weekends. **£75**

The Old Vicarage Barbican Terrace ☎ 01271 328504, ⓦ oldvicaragebarnstaple.co.uk. This well-kept Victorian house has modern double and twin rooms, some with freestanding bathtubs and all with good-sized beds.

THE TARKA LINE AND THE TARKA TRAIL

North Devon is closely associated with Henry Williamson's **Tarka the Otter** (1927), which relates the travels and travails of a young otter, and is one of the finest pieces of nature writing in the English language. With parts of the book set in the Taw valley, it was perhaps inevitable that the Exeter to Barnstaple rail route – which follows the Taw for half of its length – should be dubbed the **Tarka Line**. Barnstaple itself forms the centre of the figure-of-eight traced by the **Tarka Trail**, which tracks the otter's wanderings for a distance of more than 180 miles. To the north, the trail penetrates Exmoor (see p.284) then follows the coast back, passing through Williamson's home village of **Georgeham** on its return to Barnstaple. South, the path takes in Bideford (see p.315), and continues as far as Okehampton (see p.310).

Twenty-three miles of the trail follow a former rail line that's ideally suited to **bicycles**, and there are bike rental shops at Barnstaple and Bideford. You can pick up a *Tarka Trail* booklet and free leaflets on individual sections of the trail from tourist offices.

6

Handily, there's on-site parking too. **£82**

Yeo Dale Hotel Pilton Bridge ☎01271 342954, ⓦyeodalehotel.co.uk. Clean rooms in a converted Georgian merchant's house, just a short walk from the centre. The best ones (£125) are on the first floor, and there are cheaper doubles higher up – though taller visitors should beware the steeply sloping ceilings in these rooms. **£05**

EATING AND DRINKING

Old School Coffee House 6 Church Lane ☎01271 372793. This well-preserved building from 1659 now houses a no-frills café/restaurant – nothing fancy, but brimming with atmosphere. The meals are a bit hit and miss but the coffee and cakes are good value (try a slice of the chocolate and raisin cake for 85p). Mon–Sat 9.15am–3pm.

Terra Madre Broomhill Art Hotel, Muddiford ☎01271 850262, ⓦbroomhillart.co.uk. Bar meals, delicious, Mediterranean-style fixed-price lunches (Wed–Sun; £16) and dinners (usually Wed–Sat; £25) and high teas are served at this restaurant attached to a hotel and gallery (see opposite). Lunch Wed–Sun 12.30–1.30pm; dinner Wed–Sat 7.30–8.30pm; high tea Wed–Fri 2–4pm.

Ilfracombe and around

The most popular resort on Devon's northern coast, **ILFRACOMBE** is essentially little changed since its evolution into a Victorian and Edwardian tourist centre. In summer, if the crowds of holiday-makers become oppressive, you can escape on a coastal tour, a fishing trip or the fifteen-mile cruise to Lundy Island (see box, p.316), all available at the small harbour. On foot, you can explore the attractive stretch of coast running east out of Ilfracombe and beyond the grassy cliffs of Hillsborough, where a succession of undeveloped coves and inlets is surrounded by jagged slanting rocks and heather-covered hills.

There are sandy **beaches** here, though many prefer those beyond **Morte Point**, five miles west of Ilfracombe, from where the view takes in Lundy. Below the promontory, the pocket-sized **Barricane Beach**, famous for the tropical shells washed up by Atlantic currents from the Caribbean, is a popular swimming spot.

ARRIVAL AND INFORMATION — ILFRACOMBE AND AROUND

By bus Stagecoach bus #21 runs every 20–30min from/to Barnstaple (40min), Bideford (1hr 30min) and Braunton (30min) stopping at the St James Place Gardens in Ilfracombe, a short walk west of The Quay.

Tourist office The tourist office is at the Landmark Theatre, on the seafront (April–Sept Mon–Thurs 9am–5pm, Fri 10am–5pm, Sat & Sun 10.30am–4.30pm; Oct–March Mon–Fri 9.30am–4.30pm, Sat 10.30am–4.30pm; ☎01271 863001, ⓦvisitilfracombe .co.uk).

ACCOMMODATION

Collingdale 29 St James Place ☎01271 867835, ⓦoceanbackpackers.co.uk. Attractive Victorian house with friendly owners, where six of the nine rooms look out over the harbour. There's also a small bar and a lounge to relax in. **£82**

Ocean Backpackers 29 St James Place ☎01271 867835, ⓦoceanbackpackers.co.uk. Excellent, central hostel that's

6

popular with surfers. Dorms are mostly five- or six-bed, there are doubles available, and there's a well-equipped kitchen and free wi-fi. Dorms **£17.50**; doubles **£45**

★**Westwood** Torrs Park ☎01271 867443, ⓦwest

-wood.co.uk. In a quiet area a 10min walk from the centre (and just 5min from the coast path), this B&B is more like a boutique hotel, with original floors and ceilings, boldly decorated rooms and terrific views. **£95**

EATING AND DRINKING

Combe Cottage 63 High St ☎01271 862605, ⓦcombecottage.co.uk. Along a busy part of the High Street, this dimly lit restaurant is a good choice for lunch during the day (cottage pie £7.85), or a tasty dinner in the evening, with bistro-style mains for around £13. There are only eight tables, so booking is advised. Tues–Thurs 9.30am–2.30pm, Fri & Sat 9.30am–2.30pm & 6pm to around 11pm, Sun 6pm to around 11pm.

The Quay 11 The Quay ☎01271 868090,

ⓦ11thequay.co.uk. By the harbour and with great sea views, Ilfracombe's most famous restaurant (co-owned by artist Damien Hirst, whose works are displayed) offers European-inspired dishes using local ingredients – deep-fried feta cheese fingers, for example, or roasted fillet of cod with pancetta. Most mains are around £16–22. Drinks and snacks are available daily in the relaxed ground-floor bar. Daily noon–2.30pm & 6–9.30pm; reduced hours in winter.

Woolacombe and around

Woolacombe Sands is a broad, west-facing beach much favoured by surfers and families alike. At the more crowded northern end of the beach, a cluster of hotels, villas and retirement homes makes up the summer resort of **WOOLACOMBE**. At the quieter southern end lies the choice swimming and surfing spot of **Putsborough Sands**, whose flat, golden sands are often washed by sets of powerful waves, and the promontory of **Baggy Point**, where gannets, shags, cormorants and shearwaters gather from September to November.

South of here is **Croyde Bay**, another surfers' delight, more compact than Woolacombe, with stalls on the sand renting surfboards and wet suits. South again around the headland is **Saunton Sands**, a magnificent long stretch of wind-blown coast pummelled by seemingly endless ranks of classic breakers.

ARRIVAL AND INFORMATION

WOOLACOMBE AND AROUND

By bus Bus #303 runs between Barnstaple and Woolacombe Sands, half a mile east of town (Mon–Sat 4–6 daily; 45min), whie bus #31 makes the 40min run between Woolacombe and Ilfracombe (Mon–Sat roughly hourly).

Tourist office The Esplanade, Woolacombe (April–Oct Mon–Sat 10am–5pm, Sun 10am–3pm; Nov–March Mon–Sat 10am–1pm; ☎01271 870553, ⓦwoolacombetourism.co.uk).

ACCOMMODATION

North Morte Farm Mortehoe, a mile north of Woolacombe ☎01271 870381, ⓦnorthmortefarm .co.uk. More peaceful than many of the campsites around here, this has panoramic sea views and access to Rockham Beach, though not much shelter. Mortehoe's pubs are a short walk away. Closed Nov–March. Per person **£9.25**

Rocks Hotel Beach Rd, Woolacombe ☎01271 870361, ⓦtherockshotel.co.uk. Woolacombe's best-value accommodation choice is this surfer-friendly place close to

the beach, with smallish but smart, high-spec bedrooms and bathrooms, and a breakfast room styled like a 1950s American diner. Sea-view rooms cost an extra £10. **£79**

Woolacombe Bay Hotel South St, Woolacombe ☎01271 870388, ⓦwoolacombe-bay-hotel.co.uk. This grand building just up from the beach once housed American troops training for the Normandy landings, and is now a tidy hotel with comfortable rooms, good leisure facilities (including an indoor pool) and a restaurant overlooking the water. **£97**

EATING AND DRINKING

Bar Electric Beach Rd, Woolacombe ☎01271 870429. Friendly hangout that stays buzzing until late, with themed food nights and a long list of drinks and meals, including pizzas and pastas (all £10–12). Wed–Fri 5pm–midnight, Sat noon–midnight, Sun noon–3pm; food served Wed–Fri 5–9pm, Sat noon–3pm & 5–9pm, Sun noon–3pm.

Blue Groove Hobbs Hill, Croyde ☎01271 890111, ⓦblue-groove.co.uk. As well as burgers, steaks and seafood, this modern village restaurant/bar offers a good range of international food, from Thai mussels to Greek sharing plates (most mains £10–13). Easter–Nov daily 9am–late, Dec Fri & Sat 9am–late.

★**The Thatch** Hobbs Hill, Croyde ☎01271 890349,

6

SURFING IN NORTH DEVON

Devon's premier **surfing** sites are on the west-facing coast between Morte Point and the Taw estuary. The two extensive fine-sand beaches of **Woolacombe Sands**, to the north, and **Saunton Sands**, south, are long enough to accommodate masses of surfers (and they often do), but smaller **Croyde Bay**, sandwiched between them, does get congested in summer. **Equipment** is available to rent from numerous places in the villages of Woolacombe and Croyde or from stalls on the beach (around £8–12 for 4hr or £10–15/day for a board, £8 for 4hr or £10/day for a wet suit). You can see local surf reports and live webcams at ⓦ magicseaweed .com. If you find yourself without any waves, you can while away half an hour at the tiny **Museum of British Surfing** in Braunton, four miles east of Croyde (Mon & Wed–Sat 10am–4pm, Sun 10am–3pm; £4; ☎01271 815155, ⓦ museumofbritishsurfing.org.uk), which uses interactive exhibits and old boards to tell the story of British board riding – from the early "surf bathers" of the 1920s to today's fearless big-wave surfers.

ⓦ thethatchcroyde.com. Perennially popular thatched pub in the centre of Croyde, worth visiting for its ice-cold local cider and enormous stacks of nachos (from £8.95).

There's often live music on Fri nights, when the pub and its two big beer gardens get especially busy. Mon–Thurs 8.30am–11pm, Fri–Sun 8.30am–midnight.

Bideford and around

Like Barnstaple, nine miles to the east, the handsome estuary town of **BIDEFORD** formed an important link in north Devon's trade network in the Middle Ages, mainly due to its **bridge**, which still straddles the River Torridge. Just northwest is the seafront village of Westward Ho!, which faces a broad, sandy beach blessed with fairly consistent swell. A couple of miles downstream from Bideford, the old shipbuilding port of **APPLEDORE**, lined with pastel-coloured Georgian houses, is worth visiting for a wander and a drink in one of its cosy **pubs**.

ARRIVAL AND INFORMATION   BIDEFORD AND AROUND

By bus One of the handiest bus routes here is #5B (Mon–Sat roughly every 2hr) which links Bideford with Barnstaple (30min) and Exeter (2hr 10min). Buses #21 and #21A (Mon–Sat roughly every 20min; hourly on Sun) make trips to

Westward Ho! (20min) and Appledore (15min) respectively. **Tourist office** In the Burton Art Gallery and Museum, Kingsley Road (Mon–Sat 10am–4pm, Sun 11am–4pm; ☎01237 477676, ⓦ burtonartgallery.co.uk).

ACCOMMODATION AND EATING

Hoops Inn 5 miles west of Bideford along the A39 ☎01237 451222, ⓦ hoopsinn.co.uk. The building dates back to the thirteenth century, but the food at this well-run pub is modern, with inventive dishes like sea bass with saffron potatoes and cockle sauce (£13.95). Mon–Sat 10am–11pm, Sun noon–10.30pm; food served all day.

Westward Living Cornborough Road, Westward Ho! ☎01237 238967, ⓦ themountbideford.co.uk. Ten top-notch self-catering properties set amid serene farmland, each sleeping two to six people. Several of the rentals come with their own private hot tub and one – a single-storey cottage – is specially adapted for wheelchair users. **£140**

Clovelly

West along Bideford Bay, picturesque **CLOVELLY** was put on the map in the second half of the nineteenth century by two books: Charles Dickens' *A Message From the Sea* and *Westward Ho!* by Charles Kingsley, whose father was rector here for six years. The picture-postcard tone of the village has been preserved by strict regulations, but its excessive quaintness and the streams of visitors on summer days can make it hard to see beyond the artifice.

Beyond the **visitor centre**, where an entrance fee to the village is charged, the cobbled, traffic-free main street plunges down past neat, flower-smothered cottages. The tethered sledges here are used for transporting goods, the only way to carry supplies up and

6

LUNDY

There are fewer than thirty full-time residents on **Lundy**, a tiny windswept island twelve miles north of Hartland Point. Now a refuge for thousands of marine birds, Lundy has no cars, just one pub and one shop – indeed little has changed since the Marisco family established itself here in the twelfth century, making use of the shingle beaches and coves to terrorize shipping along the Bristol Channel. The family's fortunes only fell in 1242 when one of their number, William de Marisco, was found to be plotting against the king, whereupon he was hung, drawn and quartered at Tower Hill in London. The castle erected by Henry III on Lundy's southern end dates from this time.

Today the island is managed by the Landmark Trust. Unless you're on a specially arranged diving or climbing expedition, **walking** along the interweaving tracks and footpaths is really the only thing to do here. The shores – mainly cliffy on the west, softer and undulating on the east – shelter a rich variety of **birdlife**, including kittiwakes, fulmars, shags and Manx shearwaters, which often nest in rabbit burrows. The most famous birds, though, are the **puffins** after which Lundy is named – from the Norse *Lunde* (puffin) and *ey* (island). They can only be sighted in April and May, when they come ashore to mate. Offshore, **grey seals** can be seen all the year round.

ARRIVAL AND INFORMATION

By boat Between April and Oct, the *MS Oldenburg* sails to Lundy up to four times a week from Ilfracombe, less frequently from Bideford (around 2hr from both places; day returns £35, child £18, open returns £62). To reserve a place, call ☎ 01271 863636 or visit ⓦ lundyisland.co.uk (day returns are also booked from local tourist offices).

ACCOMMODATION

Self-catering A number of idiosyncratic Landmark Trust properties are available for self-catering by the week. These range from eighteenth-century hideaways for two in a castle keep to weathered fishermen's cottages. They're hugely popular, so book well in advance through the Landmark Trust (☎ 01628 825925, ⓦ landmarktrust.org.uk).

B&B The Landmark Trust can occasionally organise accommodation on a bed and breakfast basis, with meals at the island's pub. **£95**

Camping Lundy has a small campsite (closed Nov– March; book two weeks ahead). Per person **£12**

down the hill since they stopped using donkeys. At the bottom, Clovelly's stony beach and tiny harbour snuggle under a cleft in the cliff wall.

ARRIVAL AND GETTING AROUND   CLOVELLY

By bus Bus #319 from Bideford Quay (Mon–Sat at least 2 daily; 35min) stops outside the visitor centre. The same buses then continue on to Hartland (15min).

Land Rover service If you can't face the return climb to the top of the village, make use of the Land Rover service that leaves from behind the *Red Lion* on the quayside (Easter–Oct 10am–5.30pm, roughly every 15min; £2.50).

INFORMATION

Tourist office There's a visitor centre at the top of the village (daily 10am–4pm, summer school hols 9am–6pm; ⓦ clovelly.co.uk); an entrance fee to the village is payable here (£6.75).

ACCOMMODATION AND EATING

East Dyke Farmhouse Higher Clovelly, near the A39 junction ☎ 01237 431216, ⓦ bedbreakfastclovelly .co.uk. Away from the old village, this 200-year-old building with a beamed and flagstoned dining room has guest rooms with fridges and private bathrooms. No credit cards. **£70**

Red Lion The Quay ☎ 01237 431237, ⓦ clovelly.co.uk. Of the village's two luxurious and pricey hotels, this one enjoys the best position, right on the harbourside. It's got a congenial bar and a formal restaurant specializing in super-fresh seafood. **£150**

Hartland and around

Three miles west of Clovelly, the inland village of **HARTLAND** holds little appeal, but the surrounding coastline is spectacular. You could arrive at **Hartland Point** along minor roads, but the best approach is on foot along the coast path. The jagged black rocks of the dramatic headland are battered by the sea and overlooked by a solitary lighthouse

350ft up. South of Hartland Point, the saw-toothed rocks and near-vertical escarpments defiantly confront the waves, with spectacular waterfalls tumbling over the cliffs.

Hartland Abbey

1.5 miles west of Hartland • **Mansion** Easter to early Oct Sun–Thurs 2–5pm • £11 (includes grounds) • **Grounds** Easter–early Oct Sun–Thurs 11.30am–5pm • £7 • ☎ 01237 441496, ⊕ hartlandabbey.com

Surrounded by gardens and lush woodland, **Hartland Abbey** is an eighteenth-century mansion incorporating the ruins of an abbey dissolved in 1539. The Regency library has portraits by Gainsborough and Reynolds, George Gilbert Scott designed the vaulted Alhambra Corridor and outer hall, and fine furniture, old photographs and frescoes are everywhere. A path leads a mile from the house to cliffs and a small, sandy bay.

6

ARRIVAL AND DEPARTURE	HARTLAND AND AROUND

By bus Stagecoach service #319 (Mon–Sat at least two daily) links Hartland with Clovelly (15min), Bideford (55min) and Barnstaple (1hr 25min).

ACCOMMODATION AND EATING

2 Harton Manor The Square, off Fore St ☎ 01237 441670, ⊕ twohartonmanor.co.uk. Small, friendly B&B offering two rooms above an artist's studio – one en suite with a four poster. Organic, locally sourced and Aga-cooked breakfasts are eaten in the flagstoned kitchen. **£80**

Stoke Barton Farm Stoke, half a mile west of Hartland Abbey ☎ 01237 441238, ⊕ westcountry-camping .co.uk. Right by the fourteenth-century church of St Nectan's, this working farm offers basic camping during the summer. Closed Nov–Feb. Per person **£6.50**

Woodview Campsite 8 miles south of Hartland at Little Youlstone ☎ 01288 331492, ⊕ woodview campsite.co.uk. Although it's tough to reach along skinny single-track roads, this very tidy campsite rewards with great countryside views and a chance for some proper peace and quiet. The toilets and showers are immaculately clean, and there's free wi-fi onsite. Per person **£6**

Cornwall

When D.H. Lawrence wrote that being in **Cornwall** was "like being at a window and looking out of England", he wasn't just thinking of its geographical extremity. Virtually unaffected by the Roman conquest, Cornwall was for centuries the last haven for a **Celtic culture** elsewhere eradicated by the Saxons. Primitive granite crosses and a crop of Celtic saints remain as traces of this formative period, and the Cornish language is present in place names that in many cases have grown more exotic as they have mutated over time.

Cornwall's formerly thriving **industrial economy** is far more conspicuous than in neighbouring Devon. Its more westerly stretches in particular are littered with the derelict stacks and castle-like ruins of the engine houses that once powered the region's **copper** and **tin mines**, while deposits of **china clay** continue to be mined in the area around St Austell, as witnessed by the conical spoil heaps thereabouts. Also prominent throughout the county are the grey nonconformist chapels that reflect the impact of Methodism on Cornwall's mining communities. Nowadays, of course, Cornwall's most flourishing industry is tourism. The impact of the holiday business has been uneven, for instance cluttering **Land's End** with a tacky leisure complex but leaving Cornwall's other great headland, **Lizard Point**, undeveloped. The thronged resorts of **Falmouth**, site of the National Maritime Museum, and **Newquay**, the West's chief surfing and partying centre, have adapted to the demands of mass tourism, but its effects have been more destructive in smaller, quainter places, such as **Mevagissey**, **Polperro** and **Padstow**, whose genuine charms can be hard to make out in full season. Other villages, such as **Fowey** and **Boscastle**, still preserve an authentic feel, however, while you couldn't wish for anything more remote than **Bodmin Moor**, a tract of wilderness in the heart of Cornwall, or the **Isles of Scilly**, idyllically free of development. It would be hard to compromise the sense of desolation surrounding **Tintagel**, site of what is fondly known as King Arthur's Castle, or the appeal of the seaside resorts of **St Ives** and **Bude** – both with great surfing beaches – while, near **St Austell**, the spectacular **Eden Project** celebrates environmental diversity with visionary style.

Looe

The southeast strip of the Cornish coast holds a string of compact harbour towns interspersed with long stretches of magnificent coastline. The first of these towns, **LOOE**, was drawing crowds as early as 1800, when the first "bathing-machines" were wheeled out; it was the arrival of the railway in 1879, though, that really packed its beaches. Though the river-divided town now touts itself as something of a shark-fishing centre, most people come here for the sand, the handiest stretch being the beach in front of East Looe. Away from the river mouth, you'll find cleaner water a mile eastwards at **Millendreath**.

ARRIVAL AND INFORMATION
LOOE

By train Looe's train station is on the east bank of the river, on Station Road. There's a rail link from Liskeard to Looe (roughly hourly, not Sun in winter; 30min).

By bus Most buses to and from Looe stop on the eastern side of the bridge joining East Looe with West Looe. Destinations Liskeard (Mon–Sat hourly, Sun every 2hr;

30min); Plymouth (Mon–Sat hourly, Sun 2 daily; 1hr 10min–1hr 35min); Polperro (Mon–Sat every 20min–1hr, Sun hourly; 30min).

Tourist office New Guildhall, Fore Street (April–Oct daily 10am–5pm; Nov–March daily 10am–3pm; ☎01503 262072, ⓦvisit-southeastcornwall.co.uk).

ACCOMMODATION AND EATING

Old Sail Loft The Quay ☎01503 262131, ⓦtheoldsailloftrestaurant.com. This oak-beamed former warehouse offers the freshest seafood as well as meat-based dishes, such as lemon sole with crab and shellfish butter (£19) or a lamb shank with red wine and shallot sauce (£17). Mon & Wed–Sat noon–2pm & 6–8.45pm (last orders), Tues & Sun 6–8.45pm.

Schooner Point 1 Trelawney Terrace, West Looe ☎01503 262670, ⓦschoonerpoint.co.uk. Just 100yd from Looe Bridge, this family-run guesthouse has great river views from most of its good-value rooms, which include a single with a private shower. **£80**

Shutta House Shutta Rd ☎01503 264233, ⓦshutta house.co.uk. A short walk outside the centre and just across from the station, this neo-Gothic ex-vicarage has clean, airy en-suite rooms, some with garden views, and free wi-fi. **£68**

Polperro

Linked to Looe by frequent buses, **POLPERRO** is smaller and quainter than its neighbour, but has a similar feel. From the bus stop and car park at the top of the village, it's a five- or ten-minute walk alongside the River Pol to the pretty harbour. The surrounding cliffs and the tightly packed houses rising on each side of the stream have an undeniable charm, and the tangle of lanes is little changed since the village's heyday of pilchard fishing and smuggling. However, the influx of tourists has inevitably taken its toll, and the straggling main street – the Coombes – is now an unbroken row of tacky shops and food outlets.

ARRIVAL AND DEPARTURE
POLPERRO

By bus Polperro is served by frequent buses from Looe (Mon–Sat every 20min–1hr, Sun hourly; 30min) and

Plymouth (Mon–Sat hourly; Sun 2 daily; 2hr).

ACCOMMODATION, EATING AND DRINKING

The House on the Props Talland St ☎01503 272310, ⓦhouseontheprops.co.uk. Staying at this quirky B&B right on the harbour is a bit like being on a boat, with snug rooms, wonky floors and awesome views; there's also a tearoom and restaurant on board. **£80**

Penryn House The Coombes ☎01503 272157, ⓦpenrynhouse.co.uk. Relaxed and friendly B&B with a country-house feel. The immaculately clean rooms are small but cosy – those at the back are quietest, but have no view. Parking available. **£75**

EATING AND DRINKING

Blue Peter The Quay ☎ 01503 272743, ⓦ thebluepeter .co.uk. Welcoming harbourside pub serving real ales and local scrumpy. The bar food is good (around £10 for fish and chips) and there's live music at weekends. Daily 11am–11pm; food served noon–3pm & 6–9pm.

Fowey

The ten miles from Polperro west to Polruan are among south Cornwall's finest stretches of the coastal path, giving access to some beautiful secluded **sand beaches**. There are frequent ferries across the River Fowey from Polruan, affording a fine prospect of **FOWEY** (pronounced "Foy"), a cascade of neat, pale terraces at the mouth of one of the peninsula's greatest rivers. The major port on the county's south coast in the fourteenth century, Fowey finally became so ambitious that it provoked Edward IV to strip the town of its military capability, though it continued to thrive commercially, becoming the leading port for china-clay shipments in the nineteenth century.

Fowey's steep layout centres on the distinctive fifteenth-century church of **St Fimbarrus**. Below the church, the **Ship Inn**, which sports some fine Elizabethan panelling and plaster ceilings, held the local Roundhead HQ during the Civil War. From here, Fore Street, Lostwithiel Street and the Esplanade fan out, the **Esplanade** leading to a footpath that gives access to some splendid **coastal walks**. One of these passes Menabilly House, where **Daphne Du Maurier** lived for 24 years – it was the model for the "Manderley" of her novel *Rebecca*. The house is not open to the public, but the path takes you down to the twin coves of **Polridmouth**, where Rebecca met her watery end. The tourist office (see below) houses a small exhibition of Du Maurier's life and work, and can provide information on the eight-day **Fowey Festival** (☎ 01726 879500, ⓦ foweyfestival.com), which takes place each May, with literary workshops, comedy shows and concerts.

ARRIVAL AND INFORMATION FOWEY

By bus Fowey is easily accessible from the west, with buses #524 and #525 running from Par (Mon–Sat every 20–30min, Sun 5 daily; 20min) and St Austell (Mon–Sat every 20–30min, Sun 8 daily; 45min).

By ferry Fowey can be reached by ferry across the river every 10–15min daily from Bodinnick (foot passengers and vehicles) and Polruan (foot passengers only); tickets cost £1.70 for a foot passenger, £3.60–4.60 for a car and passengers (☎ 01726 870232, ⓦ ctomsandson.co.uk).

Tourist office 5 South Street (Mon–Sat 9.30am–5pm, Sun 10am–4pm; ☎ 01726 833616, ⓦ fowey.co.uk).

ACCOMMODATION AND EATING

Coombe Farm A mile southwest of town, off the B3269 ☎ 01726 833123, ⓦ coombefarmbb.co.uk. A 20min walk from town, this place provides perfect rural isolation – and there's a bathing area just 300yd away. Free parking. **£70**

Old Quay House 28 Fore St ☎ 01726 833302, ⓦ theoldquayhouse.com. Pricey harbourside hotel with eleven compact yet fresh-feeling rooms, some of which have balconies. The restaurant here, *Q*, serves plenty of fresh seafood. Daily 12.30–2.30pm & 7–9pm; **£180**

Sam's 20 Fore St ☎ 01726 832273, ⓦ samsfowey.co.uk. With a menu ranging from burgers (£8–14) to seafood (£11–15), this place has 1960s rock'n'roll decor and friendly service. It doesn't take bookings, so arrive early or be prepared to wait. There's a late-closing lounge bar upstairs. Daily noon–9pm (last orders).

St Austell Bay

It was the discovery of china clay, or kaolin, in the downs to the north of **St Austell Bay** that spurred the area's growth in the eighteenth century. An essential ingredient in the production of porcelain, kaolin had until then only been produced in northern China. Still a vital part of Cornwall's economy, the clay is now mostly exported for use in the manufacture of paper, as well as paint and medicines. The conical spoil heaps left by

6

the mines are a feature of the local landscape, the great green and white mounds making an eerie sight.

The town of **ST AUSTELL** itself is fairly unexciting, but makes a useful stop for trips in the surrounding area. Its nearest link to the sea is at **CHARLESTOWN**, an easy downhill walk from the centre of town. This unspoilt port is still used for china clay shipments, and provides a backdrop for the location filming that frequently takes place here. Behind the harbour, the **Shipwreck & Heritage Centre** (March–Oct daily 10am–5pm; £5.95; ☎01726 69897, ⓦshipwreckcharlestown.com) is entered through tunnels once used to convey the clay to the docks, and shows a good collection of photos and relics as well as tableaux of historical scenes.

On either side of the dock, the coarse sand and stone **beaches** have small rock pools, above which cliff walks lead around the bay.

ARRIVAL AND DEPARTURE   ST AUSTELL BAY

By train St Austell is the main rail stop in southeast Cornwall, with regular services from/to Bodmin (every 30min–1hr; 20min) and Truro (every 30min–1hr; 20min); the station is off High Cross Street.

By bus Buses pull in next to St Austell's train station, off High Cross Street.

Destinations Bodmin (Mon–Sat hourly, Sun 4 daily; 50min); Charlestown (Mon–Sat roughly every 15min, Sun every 30min–1hr; 15–30min); Falmouth (2 daily; 1hr); Newquay (hourly; 50min); Plymouth (4 daily; 1hr 20min); Truro (Mon–Sat every 30min–1hr, Sun every 1–2hr; 1hr).

ACCOMMODATION

T'Gallants Harbour Front, Charlestown ☎01726 70203, ⓦt-gallants.co.uk. Elegantly furnished Georgian B&B at the back of the harbour with a variety of en-suite rooms. Those at the front, including one with a four-poster, have sea views and cost more than the others. **£75**

The Eden Project

4 miles northeast of St Austell • Daily: April–Oct 9.30am–6pm; Nov–March 9.30am–3pm; last entry 1hr 30min before closing • £23.50, or £19.95 online, £19.50 if arriving by bus, by bike or on foot; tickets are valid for a year when registered as a donation • ☎01726 811911, ⓦedenproject.com • Arriving by bus, the most useful services are #101 from St Austell train station (20min) and the #527 from Newquay (1hr 15min) and St Austell (25min)

Occupying a 160ft-deep crater whose awesome scale only reveals itself once you have passed the entrance at its lip, the **Eden Project** showcases the diversity of the planet's plant life in an imaginative style. Centre stage are the geodesic "**biomes**" – vast conservatories made up of eco-friendly Teflon-coated, hexagonal panels. One holds groves of olive and citrus trees, cacti and other plants usually found in the warm, temperate zones of the Mediterranean, southern Africa and southwestern USA, while the larger one contains plants from the tropics, including teak and mahogany trees, with a waterfall and river gushing through. Equally impressive are the **grounds**, where plantations of bamboo, tea, hops, hemp and tobacco are interspersed with brilliant displays of flowers. In summer, the grassy arena sees **performances** of a range of music – from Peter Gabriel to Ellie Goulding – and in winter they set up a skating rink.

Mevagissey and around

MEVAGISSEY was once known for the construction of fast vessels, used for carrying contraband as well as pilchards. Today the tiny port might display a few stacks of lobster pots, but the real business is tourism, and in summer the maze of backstreets is saturated with day-trippers, converging on the inner harbour and overflowing onto the large sand beach at **Pentewan** a mile to the north.

Four miles south of Mevagissey juts the striking headland of **Dodman Point**, cause of many a wreck and topped by a stark granite cross built by a local parson as a seamark in 1896. The promontory holds the substantial remains of an Iron Age fort, with an earthwork bulwark cutting right across the point. Curving away to the west, elegant **Veryan Bay** holds a string of exquisite inlets and coves, such as **Hemmick Beach**, a fine place for a dip with rocky outcrops affording a measure of privacy, and **Porthluney Cove**, a crescent of sand whose centrepiece is the battlemented **Caerhays Castle** (mid-March to mid-June Mon–Fri noon–4pm, tours at 11am, 12.30pm and 2pm; gardens mid-Feb to mid-June daily 10am–5pm; last entry 1hr before closing; house £8, garden £8, combined ticket £13; ☎01872 501310, ⓦwww.caerhays.co.uk), built in 1808 by John Nash and surrounded by beautiful gardens. A little further on is the minuscule and whitewashed village of **Portloe**, fronted by jagged black rocks that throw up fountains of seaspray, giving it a good, end-of-the-road feel.

6

Lost Gardens of Heligan

2 miles northwest of Mevagissey, near Pentewan • April–Sept daily 10am–6pm; Oct–March Mon–Fri 10am–5pm, Sun 11am–5pm; last entry 1hr 30min before closing • £11 • ☎01726 845100, ⓦheligan.com • Served by regular buses (#525 and #524) from Mevagissey (20min) and St Austell (35min)

A couple of miles north of Mevagissey lie the **Lost Gardens of Heligan**, a fascinating Victorian garden which had fallen into neglect and was resurrected by Tim Smit, the visionary instigator of the Eden Project (see opposite). A boardwalk takes you through a jungle and under a canopy of bamboo and ferns down to the Lost Valley, where there are lakes, woods and wild-flower meadows.

ARRIVAL AND DEPARTURE

MEVAGISSEY AND AROUND

By bus From St Austell's bus and train station, the #525 and #524 services leave for Mevagissey (Mon–Sat every 30min, Sun hourly; 25min), continuing to the Lost Gardens of Heligan (20min).

ACCOMMODATION AND EATING

Alvorada 17 Church St ☎01726 842055. Small, family-run Portuguese restaurant with dishes such as *caldeirada* (fish stew) and *rojoes* (pork stew) costing around £16.50. Choose a fish dish and there's a chance it'll have been caught by the chef. Usually open from around 6.30pm until late: July & Aug daily; March–June & Sept Tues–Sat; Oct–Feb Thurs–Sat.

Wild Air Polkirt Hill, Mevagissey ☎01726 843302, ⓦwildair.co.uk. Away from the harbour crowds, this wi-fi-enabled B&B has three tastefully furnished rooms, all with en-suite or private bathrooms, and all enjoying lofty views over the harbour and coast. No children. **£80**

YHA Boswinger Boswinger, half a mile from Hemmick Beach and 3.5 miles southwest of Mevagissey ☎0845 371 9107, ⓦyha.org.uk. Set in a former farmhouse, this is a remote spot a mile from the bus stop at Gorran Churchtown (#G1 from St Austell and Mevagissey; Mon–Fri only). Kitchen and meals available. Groups only Nov–March. Dorms **£20.50**; doubles **£58**

Truro

Cornwall's capital, **TRURO**, presents a mixture of different styles, from the graceful Georgian architecture that came with the tin-mining boom of the 1800s to its neo-Gothic cathedral and its modern shopping centre. It's an attractive place, not overwhelmed by tourism and with a range of good-value facilities.

Truro Cathedral

St Mary's St • Mon–Sat 7.30am–6pm, Sun 9am–5pm • Free (£5 suggested donation) • Tours take place April–Oct Mon–Thurs 11am, Fri 11.30am; free • ☎01872 276702, ⓦtrurocathedral.org.uk

Truro's dominant feature is its faux-medieval **cathedral**, completed in 1910 and incorporating part of the fabric of the old parish church that previously occupied the site. In the airy interior, the neo-Gothic baptistry commands attention, complete with emphatically pointed arches and elaborate roof vaulting.

Royal Cornwall Museum

River St • Mon–Sat 10am–4.45pm, last admission 45min before closing • £4.50 • ☎ 01872 272205, ⓦ www.royalcornwallmuseum.org.uk

Truro's **Royal Cornwall Museum** offers a rich and wide-ranging hoard that takes in everything from the region's natural history to Celtic inscriptions. If time is tight you could confine yourself to the renowned collection of minerals on the ground floor and the upstairs galleries holding works by Cornish artists including members of the Newlyn School.

6

ARRIVAL AND INFORMATION

TRURO

By train The train station is just off Richmond Hill, a 10min walk west of the centre.

Destinations Exeter (at least hourly; 2hr 20min); Falmouth (every 30min; 20min); Liskeard (every 30min–1hr; 50min); Penzance (every 30min–1hr; 45min); Plymouth (every 30min–1hr; 1hr 20min).

By bus Buses stop centrally at Lemon Quay or near the train station.

Destinations Falmouth (Mon–Sat every 30min, Sun hourly; 35–50min); Newquay (Mon–Sat every 15min, Sun every 30min; 55min–1hr 25min); Penzance (Mon–Sat every 30min–1hr, Sun 9 daily; 1hr 45min); Plymouth (4–5 daily; 2hr 15min); St Austell (Mon–Sat every 30min–1hr, Sun every 1–2hr; 50min–1hr 15min); St Ives (Mon–Sat every 30min, Sun 1 daily; 1hr–1hr 35min); St Mawes (Mon–Sat 7 daily, Sun 3 daily; 1hr).

Tourist office Municipal Buildings, Boscawen Street (Mon–Sat 9am–5pm ☎ 01872 274555, ⓦ tourism.truro.gov.uk).

ACCOMMODATION

Bay Tree 28 Ferris Town ☎ 01872 240274, ⓦ baytree -guesthouse.co.uk. Homely, restored Georgian house halfway between the train station and the town centre, with a friendly owner and shared bathrooms (one room has its own shower). Singles available. Advance booking recommended. No credit cards. **£60**

Truro Lodge 10 The Parade ☎ 07813 755210, ⓦ trurobackpackers.co.uk. Relaxed hostel in a large Georgian terrace house near the centre. There's a self-catering kitchen, a lounge and a nice veranda, plus free wi-fi. Dorms **£18**; singles **£30**; doubles **£45**

EATING AND DRINKING

One Eyed Cat 116 Kenwyn St ☎ 01872 222122, ⓦ oneeyedcat.co.uk. In a converted chapel, this bar and brasserie has an incongruous setting, but the food, either tapas or more substantial meat and seafood dishes (*moules frites* £12.95), is good. Reservations essential at weekends. Mon–Fri noon–late, Sat & Sun 11.30am–late.

Secret Garden Café 15 Kenwyn St ☎ 01872 271540. Veggie, vegan and gluten-free delights await at this chilled daytime-only café. Super-healthy snacks include salads (from £4.95), and burgers made from beetroot and beans

(£9.75). Cornish ciders and beers are available too. Mon–Sat 10.30am–4.30pm.

Wig & Pen 1 Frances St ☎ 01872 273208, ⓦ stauste llbrewery.co.uk. The pick of Truro's pubs serves St Austell ales and bar food, as well as brunches and cream teas, with some tables outside. Simple bar meals such as stuffed red peppers and seafood pancakes cost around £10. Smarter food is served at *Quills*, in the basement, with mains for £11–20. Mon–Thurs 11am–11pm, Fri & Sat 11am–midnight, Sun 11am–8pm; restaurant Tues–Sat 7–9pm.

Falmouth

Amid the lush tranquillity of the **Carrick Roads** estuary basin, the major resort of **FALMOUTH** is the site of one of Cornwall's mightiest castles, **Pendennis Castle**, and of one of the country's foremost collections of boats in the **National Maritime Museum Cornwall**. The town sits at the mouth of the Fal estuary, at the end of a rail branch line from Truro and connected by ferry to Truro and St Mawes. Round Pendennis Point, south of the centre, a long sandy bay holds a succession of sheltered **beaches**: from the popular **Gyllyngvase Beach**, you can reach the more attractive **Swanpool Beach** by cliff path, or walk a couple of miles further on to **Maenporth**, from where there are some fine cliff-top walks.

National Maritime Museum Cornwall

Discovery Quay • Daily 10am–5pm • £11.50 • ☎ 01326 313388, ⓦ nmmc.co.uk

Vessels from all around the world are exhibited in Falmouth's **National Maritime Museum Cornwall**. Of every size and shape, the craft are arranged on three levels, many of them suspended in mid-air in the cavernous Flotilla Gallery. Smaller galleries examine specific aspects of boat-building, seafaring history and Falmouth's packet ships, and a lighthouse-like lookout tower offers excellent views over the harbour and estuary.

Pendennis Castle

Pendennis Head • April–Sept daily 10am–6pm; Oct daily 10am–5pm; Nov–Feb Sat & Sun 10am–4pm • £7; EH • ☎ 01326 316594, ⓦ english-heritage.org.uk

A few minutes' walk west of the National Maritime Museum, **Pendennis Castle** stands sentinel at the tip of the promontory that separates the Carrick Roads estuary from Falmouth Bay. The extensive fortification shows little evidence of its five-month siege by the Parliamentarians during the Civil War, which ended only when half its defenders had died and the rest had been starved into submission. Though this is a less-refined contemporary of the castle at St Mawes (see below), its site wins hands down, the stout ramparts offering the best all-round views of Carrick Roads and Falmouth Bay.

6

ARRIVAL AND INFORMATION
FALMOUTH

By train The branch rail line from Truro (Mon–Sat every 30min, Sun 10 daily; 30min) stops at Falmouth Town, best for the centre, and Falmouth Docks, 2min away, near Pendennis Castle.

By bus Most buses stop on The Moor, close to the Prince of Wales Pier and just east of the High Street.

Destinations Helston (Mon–Sat hourly, Sun 2–4 daily; 50min); Penzance (Mon–Sat hourly, Sun 1 daily; 1–2hr); St Austell (2 daily; 1hr 10min); Truro (Mon–Sat every 30min, Sun hourly; 40–50min).

Tourist office Prince of Wales Pier (April–Oct Mon–Sat 9.30am–6pm, Sun 9.30am–5pm; Nov–March Mon, Tues & Thurs–Sat 10am–3pm; ☎ 01326 741194, ⓦ discoverfalmouth.co.uk).

ACCOMMODATION

Falmouth Lodge 9 Gyllyngvase Terrace ☎ 01326 319996, ⓦ falmouthbackpackers.co.uk. Clean and friendly backpackers' hostel located a couple of mins' walk from the beach, with a sociable lounge and kitchen and free wi-fi. Dorms **£19**; doubles **£56**

Falmouth Townhouse Grove Place ☎ 01326 312009, ⓦ falmouthtownhouse.co.uk. Chic boutique hotel in a Georgian building just across from the Maritime Museum.

It's all highly designed, with a buzzing bar, spacious guestrooms and quirky bathrooms, though some rooms suffer from street noise at night. **£75**

Royal Duchy Hotel Cliff Rd ☎ 01326 313042, ⓦ royalduchy.co.uk. Big, seafront hotel with everything from fairly plain doubles and singles to a suite with sea views and its own luxurious lounge area. There are two bars here, along with a restaurant and a spa. **£194**

EATING AND DRINKING

Café Cinnamon Old Brewery Yard ☎ 01326 211457. Wholefood, vegetarian and vegan café that offers lunchtime snacks and organic wines. Try the special salads and burgers, which change regularly, and leave room for tasty cakes (£3 a slice). Tues–Sat 10am–4pm.

Chain Locker Quay St ☎ 01326 311085. This harbourside drinker festooned with nautical bits and pieces offers real ales and standard bar meals (£7–10), but its main asset is the outdoor seating – the perfect spot to while away an evening. Mon–Thurs & Sun 11am–11pm, Fri & Sat 11am–midnight; food served noon–9pm.

★**Espressini** 39 Killigrew St ☎ 07580 590248, ⓦ espressini.co.uk. Deliciously fresh croissants and

sourdough sandwiches (£3.60) are available at this little independent café, but it's really the coffee that makes it worth a visit: tasty, single-origin stuff from countries as diverse as Ethiopia, Nicaragua and Papua New Guinea. Mon–Sat 8am–6pm, Sun 10am–4pm.

Gylly Beach Café Gyllyngvase Beach ☎ 01326 312884, ⓦ gyllybeach.com. Cool beachside hangout serving everything from fish finger sandwiches to slow-braised lamb. Breakfast is served until 11.30am, lunch dishes cost £5–10, evening mains upwards of £13. Check the website for events and special meal deals. Daily 9am–late, reduced hours in winter.

St Mawes and around

Situated on the east side of the Carrick Roads estuary, the two-pronged **Roseland peninsula** is a luxuriant backwater of woods and sheltered creeks. The main settlement is **ST MAWES**, a tranquil old fishing port easily reached on ferries from Falmouth.

6

Moving east from St Mawes, you could spend a pleasant afternoon poking around the southern arm of the peninsula, which holds the twelfth- to thirteenth-century church of **ST ANTHONY-IN-ROSELAND** and the **lighthouse** on St Anthony's Head, marking the entry into Carrick Roads. Two and a half miles north of St Mawes, the scattered hamlet of **ST JUST-IN-ROSELAND** holds the strikingly picturesque church of St Just, right next to the creek and surrounded by palms and subtropical shrubbery, its gravestones tumbling down to the water's edge.

St Mawes Castle

Half a mile west of the quay • April–Sept daily 10am–6pm; Oct daily 10am–5pm; Nov–March Sat & Sun 10am–4pm • £4.60; EH • ☎ 01326 270526, ⓦ english-heritage.org.uk

At the end of the walled seafront of St Mawes stands the sister fort of Pendennis Castle, the small and pristine **St Mawes Castle**, built during the reign of Henry VIII to a clover-leaf design. The castle owes its excellent condition to its early surrender to Parliamentary forces during the Civil War in 1646. The dungeons and gun installations contain various artillery exhibits as well as some background on local social history.

ARRIVAL AND GETTING AROUND · ST MAWES AND AROUND

By bus There are regular buses (#550 and #551) between Truro and St Mawes (Mon–Sat 7 daily, Sun 3 daily; 1hr 10min), stopping off at St Just-in-Roseland (7min from St Mawes) en route.

By ferry St Mawes can be reached on frequent ferries from Falmouth's Prince of Wales Pier and Custom House Quay (£8.10 return). Between March and Nov, passenger ferries from St Mawes also cross to the southern arm of the peninsula (daily 9am–5.30pm every 30min; £5.85 return).

By car By road, the fastest route from Truro, Falmouth and west Cornwall involves crossing the River Fal on the chain-driven King Harry Ferry (every 20min: April–Sept Mon–Sat 7.20am–9.20pm, Sun 9am–9.20pm; Oct–March Mon–Sat 7.20am–7.20pm, Sun 9am–7.20pm; £8 return per car; foot passengers and bicycles are transported free in exchange for a charity donation; ☎ 01872 862312 ⓦ falriver.co.uk).

ACCOMMODATION AND EATING

Nearwater Polvarth Road, St Mawes ☎ 01326 279278. There's a subtle nautical theme running through this elegantly furnished B&B, which has three good-sized rooms. The shared lounge has an open fireplace, and when it's warmer, guests can relax in the garden. **£110**

★**Tresanton Hotel** St Mawes ☎ 01326 270055, ⓦ tresanton.com. Cornwall doesn't get much ritzier than this, a slice of Mediterranean-style luxury with bright, sunny colours and a yacht and speedboat available to guests in summer. There's a fabulous restaurant too, where you can have a snack lunch or full meal (mains £20–£35). Daily 12.30–2.30pm & 7.30–9.30pm. **£260**

The Lizard peninsula

The **Lizard peninsula** – from the Celtic *lys ardh*, or "high point" – is mercifully undeveloped. If this flat and treeless expanse can be said to have a centre, it's **Helston**, a junction for **buses** running from Falmouth and Truro and for services to the spartan villages of the peninsula's interior and coast.

Helston

HELSTON is best known for its **Furry Dance** (or Flora Dance), which dates from the seventeenth century. Held on May 8 (unless this falls on Sun or Mon, when the procession takes place on the preceding Sat), it's a stately procession of top-hatted men and summer-frocked women performing a solemn dance through the town's streets and gardens. You can learn something about it and absorb plenty of other local history in the eclectic **Helston Folk Museum** (Mon–Sat 10am–4pm; free; ☎ 1326 564027), housed in former market buildings behind the Guildhall on Church Street.

Porthleven and around

Two and a half miles southwest of Helston, tin ore from inland mines was once shipped from **PORTHLEVEN**. Good **beaches** lie to either side: the best for swimming are around

Rinsey Head, three miles north along the coast, including the sheltered **Praa Sands**. One and a quarter miles south of Porthleven, strong currents make it unsafe to swim at **Loe Bar**, a strip of shingle which separates the freshwater **Loe Pool** from the sea. The elongated Pool is one of two sites which claim to be the place where the sword Excalibur was restored to its watery source (the other is on Bodmin Moor). The path running along the western edge of Loe Pool makes a fine walking route between here and Helston.

Mullion and around

The inland village of **MULLION**, five miles south of Porthleven, has a fifteenth- to sixteenth-century church dedicated to the Breton **St Mellane** (or Malo), with a dog-door for canine churchgoers. A lane leads a mile and a quarter west to **Mullion Cove**, where a tiny beach is sheltered behind harbour walls and rock stacks, though the neighbouring sands at **Polurrian** and **Poldhu**, to the north, are better and attract surfers.

Lizard Point and around

Four miles south of Mullion, the peninsula's best-known beach, **Kynance Cove**, has sheer 100ft cliffs, stacks and arches of serpentine rock and offshore outcrops. The water quality here is excellent – but take care not to be stranded by the tide. A little more than a mile southeast, **Lizard Point**, the southern tip of the promontory and mainland Britain's southernmost point, is marked by a plain lighthouse above a tiny cove and a restless, churning sea. If you're not following the coast path, you can reach the point via the road and footpath leading a mile south from the nondescript village called simply **THE LIZARD**, where you'll find several places to stay and eat.

The east coast

In the north of the peninsula, the snug hamlets dotted around the **River Helford** are a complete contrast to the rugged character of most of the Lizard. On the river's south side, **Frenchman's Creek**, one of a splay of serene inlets, was the inspiration for Daphne Du Maurier's novel of the same name. From Helford Passage you can take a ferry (April–Oct, on demand; £6 return) to reach **Helford**, an agreeable old smugglers' haunt on the south bank.

South of here, on the B3293, the broad, windswept plateau of Goonhilly Downs is interrupted by the futuristic saucers of Goonhilly Satellite Station and the nearby ranks of wind turbines. Heading east, the road splits: left to **ST KEVERNE**, an inland village whose tidy square is flanked by two inns and a church, right to **COVERACK**, a fishing port in a sheltered bay. Following the coast path or negotiating minor roads south will bring you to the safe and clean swimming spot of **Kennack Sands**.

GETTING AROUND	THE LIZARD PENINSULA

By bus From Helston, buses #2, #251 and #504 go to Porthleven (10–15min), #37 goes to Mullion (30min) and The Lizard (45–55min), and #36 goes to Coverack (25min) and St Keverne (30min).

ACCOMMODATION AND EATING

Blue Anchor 50 Coinagehall St, Helston ☎ 01326 562821, ⓦ spingoales.com. Deeply traditional West Country pub, once a fifteenth-century monastery rest house, now brewing its own Spingo beer on the premises. Four B&B rooms are available in an adjacent building. Mon–Thurs & Sun 10am–midnight, Fri & Sat 10am–1am. £65

Mounts Bay Inn On the B3296 in Mullion ☎ 01326 240221, ⓦ mountsbaymullion.co.uk. Mullion's best place for Cornish ales and pub meals (£10–15) with views over Mounts Bay and steps down to a beer garden. Live

bands every fortnight and Cornish songs on the last Sun of the month. Mon–Thurs 11am–11pm, Fri & Sat 11am–midnight, Sun noon–11pm.

Old Vicarage Nansmellyon Rd, Mullion ☎ 01326 240898, ⓔ bandbmullion@hotmail.com. Facing an enclosed garden, this charming guesthouse once provided accommodation to Arthur Conan Doyle. The elegant rooms come with period furnishings and en-suite or private facilities. £86

Poldhu Beach Café Poldhu Cove, near Mullion ☎ 01326 240530, ⓦ poldhu.net. The perfect beach café, with energizing breakfasts, burgers (from £3.50), good coffee and hot chocolate, and locally produced ice cream. Daily 9.30am–4.30/5.30pm, with occasional late opening until 8pm during the summer.

YHA Lizard Lizard Point ☎ 0845 371 9550, ⓦ yha.org .uk. This hostel occupies a former Victorian hotel right on the coast, with majestic views. It gets booked up quickly. Groups only Nov–March. Dorms £22.50; doubles £52

The Penwith peninsula

Though more densely populated than the Lizard, the **Penwith peninsula** is a more rugged landscape, with a raw appeal that is still encapsulated by **Land's End**, despite the commercialization of that headland. The seascapes, the quality of the light and the slow tempo of the local fishing communities made this area a hotbed of artistic activity from the late nineteenth century onwards, when the painters of Newlyn, near **Penzance**, established a distinctive school of painting. More innovative figures – among them Ben Nicholson, Barbara Hepworth and Naum Gabo – were soon afterwards to make **St Ives** one of England's liveliest cultural communities, and their enduring influence is illustrated in the St Ives branch of the **Tate Gallery**, which showcases the modern artists associated with the locality.

Penzance

Occupying a sheltered position at the northwest corner of Mount's Bay, **PENZANCE** has always been a major port, but most traces of the medieval town were obliterated at the end of the sixteenth century by a Spanish raiding party. From the top of **Market Jew Street** (from *Marghas Jew*, meaning "Thursday Market"), which climbs from the harbour and the train and bus stations, turn left into **Chapel Street** to see some of the town's finest buildings, including the flamboyant **Egyptian House**, built in 1835 to contain a geological museum but subsequently abandoned until its restoration thirty years ago. Across the street, the seventeenth-century **Union Hotel** originally held the town's assembly rooms, where news of Admiral Nelson's victory at Trafalgar and the death of Nelson himself was first announced in 1805.

Penlee House Gallery and Museum

Morrab Rd, west of Chapel St • Mon–Sat: Easter–Sept 10am–5pm; Oct–April 10.30am–4.30pm; last admission 30min before closing • £4.50, free on Sat • ☎ 01736 363625, ⓦ penleehouse.org.uk

Long a centre of the local art movements, **Penlee House Gallery and Museum** holds an important collection of **Cornish art**, notably works of the Newlyn School – impressionistic harbour scenes, frequently sentimentalized but often bathed in an evocatively luminous light. There are also displays on local archeology and history, and frequent exhibitions.

ARRIVAL AND DEPARTURE
PENZANCE

By train Penzance's train station lies on the seafront, on Station Road.
Destinations Bodmin (at least hourly; 1hr 10min); Exeter (at least hourly; 3hr); Plymouth (at least hourly; 2hr); St Ives (most via St Erth; hourly; 25–45min); Truro (at least hourly; 40min).
By bus The bus station is next to the train station on the seafront.
Destinations Falmouth (every 1–2hr; 1hr–1hr 45min);

Helston (Mon–Sat hourly, Sun 7 daily; 1hr); Plymouth (7 daily; 2hr 50min–4hr); St Austell (2–3 daily; 1hr 50min–2hr 20min); St Ives (Mon–Sat every 15–20min, Sun every 30min–1hr; 35–50min); Truro (Mon–Fri every 30min–1hr; Sun 8 daily; 40min).
By boat From Easter to Oct boats depart from Penzance Quay for St Mary's on the Isles of Scilly (Mon–Sat 4–6 weekly; 2hr 40min; ☎ 01736 334220, ⓦ islesofscilly -travel.co.uk).

ACCOMMODATION

Abbey Hotel Abbey St, off Chapel St ☎ 01736 366906, ⓦ theabbeyonline.co.uk. Pamper yourself at this homely, seventeenth-century hotel owned by 1960s model Jean

Shrimpton and now run by her son. Lashings of old-fashioned comfort, books and antiques everywhere, and great views. £130

Penzance Backpackers Alexandra Rd, parallel to Morrab Rd ☎01736 363836, ⓦpzbackpack.com. One of the region's tidiest and most welcoming hostels, with en-suite dorms, a kitchen, lounge and laundry, and wi-fi. Dorms £16; doubles £36

Warwick House 17 Regent Terrace ☎01736 363881, ⓦwarwickhousepenzance.co.uk. Handily located near the centre of town and a short stroll up from the promenade, this popular B&B has clean rooms decorated in blue and white – the best ones have views of the water. £92

EATING AND DRINKING

Admiral Benbow 46 Chapel St ☎01736 363448. Characterful pub crammed with gaudy ships' figureheads and other nautical items. The bar meals are pretty standard, but this is a drinking pub, and the atmosphere more than compensates. Daily 11am–11pm; food served noon–3pm & 6–9.30pm.

Archie Browns Bread St ☎01736 362828, ⓦarchie browns.co.uk Vegans, vegetarians and wholefoodies will be happy in this café above a health shop, with its relaxed, friendly vibe and local art on the walls. Dishes include quiches, curries, stews and homity pie (£5–8). Mon–Sat 9am–5pm.

★**Lost and Found** 16 Chapel St ☎07792 358110. Part antique shop, part café, *Lost and Found* is spread across several rooms, each brightened by old maps, instruments and other assorted curios. Sweet-toothed shoppers will love the cupcakes and tray bakes, which go for around £2.75 a pop. Tues–Fri 9.30am–5.30pm, Sat 10am–5.30pm.

Harris's 46 New St ☎01736 364408, ⓦharriss restaurant.co.uk Traditional fine dining at this formal restaurant, with the accent on seafood. Mains such as roast monkfish and grilled sole cost around £20. Be sure to leave room for one of the memorably good desserts. Mon 6.30–8.30pm, Tues–Sat noon–8.30pm.

St Michael's Mount

Off Marazion, 5 miles east of Penzance • **House** April–June & Sept–Oct Mon–Fri & Sun 10.30am–5pm; July & Aug Mon–Fri & Sun 10.30am–5.30pm • £8, £10.50 with garden; NT • **Garden** Mid-April to June Mon–Fri 10.30am–5pm; July to late Aug Thurs & Fri 10.30am–5.30pm; Sept Thurs & Fri 10.30am–5pm • £5, £10.50 with house • At low tide the promontory can be approached on foot via a cobbled causeway (daily tide times on the website); at high tide there are boats from Marazion (£2) • ☎01736 710507, ⓦstmichaelsmount.co.uk

Frequent buses from Penzance leave for Marazion, five miles east, the access point to **St Michael's Mount**, a couple of hundred yards offshore. A vision of the archangel Michael led to the building of a church on this granite pile around the fifth century, and within three centuries a Celtic monastery had been founded here. The present building derives from a **chapel** raised in the eleventh century by Edward the Confessor, who handed it over to the Benedictine monks of Brittany's Mont St Michel, whose island abbey was the model for this one. Following the Civil War, it became the residence of the St Aubyn family, who still inhabit the castle. Some of the buildings date from the twelfth century, but the later additions are more interesting, such as the battlemented **chapel** and the seventeenth-century decorations of the **Chevy Chase Room**, the former refectory.

Mousehole

Accounts vary as to the derivation of the name of **MOUSEHOLE** (pronounced "Mowzle"), though it may be from a smugglers' cave just to the south. In any case, the name evokes perfectly this minuscule fishing port cradled in the arms of a granite breakwater, three miles south of Penzance. The village attracts more visitors than it can handle, so hang around until the crowds have departed before exploring its tight tangle of lanes, where you'll come across Mousehole's oldest house, the fourteenth-century **Keigwin House**, a survivor of the sacking of the village by Spaniards in 1595.

ARRIVAL AND DEPARTURE   MOUSEHOLE

By bus The #6 bus (Mon–Sat every 30min; hourly on Sun) connects Mousehole's harbour with Newlyn (10min) and Penzance (15min).

ACCOMMODATION AND EATING

Ship Inn Harbourside ☎01736 731234, ⓦship mousehole.co.uk. Overlooking the boats, this is a perfect spot for a pint or a Ploughman's Lunch (£7.95) or Cornish fish pie (£12). Accommodation is available in surprisingly modern en-suite rooms, some in an annexe (those with a view cost extra). Mon–Sat 11am–11pm, Sun 11am–10.30pm; food served noon–2.30pm & 6–8.30pm. £95

6

Porthcurno

Eight miles west of Mousehole, one of Penwith's best **beaches** lies at **PORTHCURNO**, sandwiched between cliffs. On the shore to the east, a white pyramid marks the spot where the first transatlantic cables were laid in 1880. On the headland beyond lies an Iron Age fort, **Treryn Dinas**, close to the famous rocking stone called **Logan Rock**, a seventy-ton monster that was knocked off its perch in 1824 by a gang of sailors, among them a nephew of writer and poet Oliver Goldsmith. Somehow they replaced the stone, but it never rocked again.

Minack Theatre

South end of village • Exhibition Centre daily: April–Sept generally 9.30am–5.30pm, but may close at noon on Tues and Thurs when performances take place; Oct–March 10am–4pm; last entry 30min before closing • £4.50 • Theatre performances cost £9–11.50 • ☎ 01736 810181, ⓦ minack.com

Steep steps lead up from the beach of tiny white shells to the **Minack Theatre**, hewn out of the cliff in the 1930s and since enlarged to hold 750 seats, though retaining the basic Greek-inspired design. The spectacular backdrop of Porthcurno Bay makes this one of the country's most inspiring theatres (providing the weather holds) from mid-April to September, when a range of plays, operas and musicals are presented – bring a cushion and a rug. The attached **Exhibition Centre** gives access to the theatre during the day and explains the story of its creation.

ARRIVAL AND DEPARTURE   PORTHCURNO

By bus Only one bus service – #1A – runs to and from Porthcurno, making up to three trips per day to Land's End   (15min), Newlyn (25min) and Penzance (35min).

Land's End

The extreme western tip of England, **Land's End**, lies four miles west of Porthcurno. Best approached on foot along the coastal path, the 60ft turf-covered cliffs provide a platform to view the Irish Lady, the Armed Knight, Dr Syntax Head and the rest of the Land's End outcrops. Beyond, look out for the Longships lighthouse, a mile and a half out to sea, and you can sometimes spot the Wolf Rock lighthouse, nine miles southwest, or even the Isles of Scilly, 28 miles away (see p.331).

ARRIVAL AND DEPARTURE   LAND'S END

By bus Hourly buses run to and from the car park at Land's End, providing easy connections to Newlyn (40min) and Penzance (50min).

Whitesand Bay

To the north of Land's End the rounded granite cliffs fall away at **Whitesand Bay** to reveal a glistening mile-long shelf of beach that offers the best swimming on the Penwith peninsula. The rollers make for good surfing and boards can be rented at **Sennen Cove**, the more popular southern end of the beach.

ARRIVAL AND DEPARTURE   WHITESAND BAY

By bus Bus #1, which connects Penzance with Land's End, stops at Sennen Cove (3 daily Mon–Sat, 2 on Sun).

ACCOMMODATION AND EATING

Pengelly House Sennen Cove ☎01736 871866, ⓦpengellyhouse.com. Guesthouse near the beach, offering three rooms (including a single) with mini-fridges, a large shared bathroom and wi-fi access, but no breakfast (nearby breakfast places are plentiful). **£70**

Trevedra Farm 2 miles northeast of Sennen, off the A30 ☎01736 871818, ⓦtrevedrafarm.co.uk. Popular but spacious campsite with sea views stretching off into the distance. There's a modern block within easy walking distance of the pitches providing good facilities, including a shop and a restaurant serving buffet breakfasts. Per person **£5.50**

St Just-in-Penwith and around

Three miles north of Sennen Cove, the highly scenic headland of **Cape Cornwall** is dominated by the chimney of the Cape Cornwall Mine, which closed in 1870. Half a mile inland is the grimly grey village of **ST JUST-IN-PENWITH**, formerly a centre of the tin and copper industry, with rows of cottages radiating out from Bank Square. The tone is somewhat lightened by **Plen-an-Gwary**, a grassy open-air theatre where miracle plays were once staged, later used by Methodist preachers and Cornish wrestlers.

ARRIVAL AND DEPARTURE

By bus From the bus station in Penzance, bus #10 runs to the centre of St Just (hourly; 25min).

By plane Land's End Airport, around 1.5 miles south of St Just, handles flights to and from St Mary's on the Isles of Scilly (April–Oct Mon–Sat 4–11 daily; 15–20min). For exact times call ☎ 01736 334220 or see ⓦ islesofscilly-travel.co.uk.

ACCOMMODATION AND EATING

Dog & Rabbit North Row, just off Market Square ☎ 01736 449811. Tucked away on a narrow alley, this quirky café does good soups to eat in or take away (£4) plus a good selection of teas and coffees. The walls are covered in art, and there's a noticeboard giving details of local exhibitions, concerts and yoga classes. Thurs–Sat 9am–5pm.

Kegen Teg 12 Market Square ☎ 01736 788562. Organic, local and mainly vegetarian food – try the home-made falafel or Welsh rarebit (both £8.20) – with tasty breakfasts, cakes, smoothies and organic ice cream. Daily 10am–5pm.

Kelynack Caravan and Camping Park Kelynack ☎ 01736 787633, ⓦ kelynackcaravans.co.uk. Secluded campsite, one of the few sheltered ones on Penwith, about a mile south of St Just. There are also B&B rooms and self-catering options. Camping per person **£7.50**; doubles **£80**

Old Fire Station Nancherrow Terrace, near Market Square ☎ 01736 788485, ⓦ oldfirestationstjust.co.uk. Central, modern B&B with an open-plan lounge and breakfast room, and three smallish but airy en-suite bedrooms, the top two with distant sea views. **£70**

YHA Land's End ☎ 0845 371 9643, ⓦ yha.org.uk. Less than a mile south of St Just and a convenient half-mile from the coast path, this hostel has camping facilities and a kitchen, and also sells cooked meals. Take the left fork past the post office to find it. Dorms **£21**; doubles **£50**

Zennor and around

Eight miles northeast of St Just, set in a landscape of rolling granite moorland, **ZENNOR** is where D.H. Lawrence came to live with his wife Frieda in 1916. "It is a most beautiful place," he wrote, "lovelier even than the Mediterranean". The Lawrences stayed a year and a half in the village – long enough for him to write *Women in Love* – before being given notice to quit by the local constabulary, who suspected them of unpatriotic sympathies (their Cornish experiences were later described in *Kangaroo*). Zennor's fascinating **Wayside Museum** is dedicated to Cornish life from prehistoric times (daily: April & Oct 10.30am–4.30pm; May–Sept 10am–5.30pm; £3.95; ☎ 01736 796945). At the top of the lane, the church of **St Sennen** displays a sixteenth-century bench-carving of a mermaid who, according to local legend, was so entranced by the singing of a chorister that she lured him down to the sea, from where he never returned – though his song can still occasionally be heard.

Chysauster

2 miles inland from Zennor • Daily: April–June & Sept 10am–5pm; July & Aug 10am–6pm; Oct 10am–4pm • £3.70; EH • ☎ 07831 757934, ⓦ english-heritage.org.uk

On a windy hillside a couple of miles inland from Zennor, the Iron Age village of **Chysauster** is the best-preserved ancient settlement in the Southwest. Dating from about the first century BC, it contains two rows of four buildings, each consisting of a courtyard with small chambers leading off it, and a garden that was presumably used for growing vegetables.

ARRIVAL AND DEPARTURE

ZENNOR AND AROUND

By bus The #16 and #16A buses from St Ives to Penzance (hourly Mon–Sat) stop near the turn-off for Zennor. From here it's a short stroll into the village.

ACCOMMODATION AND EATING

Gurnard's Head Treen, a mile or so west of Zennor ☎ 01736 796928, ⊛ gurnardshead.co.uk. This relaxed gastropub serves delicious Mediterranean-inspired meals (mains around £16–17; booking advised). Smallish B&B rooms are also available. Daily noon/12.30–11pm; food served noon/12.30–2.30pm & 6/6.30–9pm. **£105**

Zennor Chapel ☎ 01736 798307, ⊛ zennorchapel guesthouse.com. Newly refreshed, this guesthouse in a former Wesleyan chapel has five rooms, each with space for two to four people, and all with en-suite bathrooms. The café downstairs turns out breakfasts 8–10am (not included in rate), and sells coffee and cakes throughout the day. Doubles **£80**; family room **£90**

St Ives

East of Zennor, the road runs four hilly miles on to the steeply built town of **ST IVES**. By the time the pilchard reserves dried up around the early 1900s, the town was beginning to attract a vibrant **artists' colony**, precursors of the wave later headed by Ben Nicholson, Barbara Hepworth, Naum Gabo and the potter Bernard Leach, who in the 1960s were followed by a third wave including Peter Lanyon and Patrick Heron.

Tate St Ives

Porthmeor Beach • March–Oct daily 10am–5.20pm; Nov–Feb Tues–Sun 10am–4.20pm; closes two or three times a year for about ten days, so check ahead • £7, £11 with Hepworth Museum • ☎ 01736 796226, ⊛ tate.org.uk

The place to view the best work created in St Ives is the **Tate St Ives**, overlooking Porthmeor Beach on the north side of town. Most of the paintings, sculptures and ceramics displayed within the airy, gleaming-white building date from 1925 to 1975, with specially commissioned contemporary works also on view as well as exhibitions. The gallery's rooftop **café** is a splendid spot for a coffee.

Barbara Hepworth Museum

Barnoon Hill • March–Oct daily 10am–5.20pm; Nov–Feb Tues–Sun 10am–4.20pm • £6.60 or £11 with the Tate • ☎ 01924 247360, ⊛ tate.org.uk

Not far from the Tate St Ives, the **Barbara Hepworth Museum** provides further insight into the local arts scene. One of the foremost nonfigurative sculptors of her time, Hepworth lived in the building from 1949 until her death in a studio fire in 1975. Apart from the sculptures, which are arranged in positions chosen by Hepworth in the house and garden, the museum has background on her art, from photos and letters to catalogues and reviews.

The beaches

Porthmeor Beach dominates the northern side of St Ives, its excellent water quality and surfer-friendly rollers drawing a regular crowd, while the broader **Porthminster Beach**, south of the station, is usually less busy. A third town beach, the small and sheltered **Porthgwidden**, lies in the lee of the prong of land separating Porthmeor and Porthminster, while east of town a string of magnificent golden beaches lines **St Ives Bay** on either side of the Hayle estuary.

ARRIVAL AND INFORMATION

ST IVES

By train Trains from Penzance (most via St Erth; every 30min–1hr; 30–50min) arrive at the train station on Trelyon Ave, off Porthminster Beach.

By bus The bus station is on Station Hill, just off The Terrace.

Destinations Penzance (Mon–Sat 3–5 hourly, Sun hourly; 50min); Plymouth (3 daily; 3hr 20min–3hr 45min); Truro (Mon–Sat every 30min, Sun 1 daily; 1hr 10min–1hr 40min).

Tourist office Inside the Guildhall on Street-an-Pol, a 5min walk northwest from the bus station (April Mon–Sat 10am–3pm, May Mon–Sat 10am–4pm, Sun 10am–3pm, June daily 10am–4pm, July–Sept daily 9.30am–5pm, Oct–March Mon–Fri 10am–3pm; ☎ 09052 522250, ⊛ stivestic.co.uk).

ACCOMMODATION

Cornerways 1 Bethesda Place ☎ 01736 796706, ⓦ corner ways stives.com. Daphne du Maurier once stayed here; it's now a modern cottage conversion with friendly management and small, bright rooms. Ask about complimentary tickets for the Tate and Hepworth galleries. **£80**

★ **Little Leaf** 16 Park Ave ☎ 01736 795427, ⓦ littleleafguesthouse.co.uk. With friendly young hosts and local art on the walls, this guesthouse has six en-suite rooms, two with fantastic views. Breakfasts are fresh and use locally sourced ingredients. Free wi-fi and use of iPad in

the communal lounge. **£70**

Atlantic Heights 11 Ocean View Terrace ☎ 01872 858 726, ⓦ atlanticheights.net. It's a steep hike away from the centre, but this guesthouse rewards with cracking views from two of its en-suite rooms. Friendly staff. **£70**

St Ives Backpackers The Gallery ☎ 01736 799444, ⓦ backpackers.co.uk/st-ives. Centrally located hostel in an old Wesleyan chapel school from 1845. Dorms have 4–8 beds, and guests can make use of a kitchen, games and free wi-fi. Dorms **£17.95**; double **£40**

EATING

Alba Wharf Rd ☎ 01736 797222, ⓦ thealbarestaurant .com. Sleekly modern harbourfront restaurant with top-class seafood, including a superb fish soup (£7.25). Set-price menus (£16.95 & £19.95) are available 6–7.30pm, otherwise mains are £12–23. Sit upstairs for the best view. Daily noon–2pm & 5.30–10pm.

Blas Burgerworks The Warren ☎ 01736 797272, ⓦ blasburgerworks.co.uk. This "alternative burger bar" doles out extremely good burgers (£9–11), using local ingredients. There's just one small room with four communal tables made from found or reclaimed wood. No reservations. Daily 5–10pm.

The Cornish Deli 3 Chapel St ☎ 01736 795100 ⓦ cornishdeli.com. The tables fill up quickly at this cosy

deli-cum-café, which sells excellent sandwiches (using meat from the local butcher's shop), as well as wine, Cornish chocolate, West Country cheeses and the like. In summer, proper bistro-style meals (£16.95 for two courses) are served in the evenings from 6pm. No credit cards. July–Sept daily 9.30am–9.30pm, Oct–June Mon–Sat 9.30am–4pm.

★ **Porthminster Café** Porthminster Beach ☎ 01736 795352, ⓦ porthminstercafe.co.uk. With its sun deck and beach location, this is an appealing venue for coffees, snack lunches and sophisticated seafood dinners (mains around £20; book ahead). April–Sept daily 9.30am–9.30pm; Nov–March Tues, Wed & Sun 9.30am–4pm, Thurs–Sat 9.30am–9.30pm.

The Isles of Scilly

The **Isles of Scilly** are a compact archipelago of about a hundred islands, 28 miles southwest of Land's End. None is bigger than three miles across, and only five of them are inhabited – **St Mary's**, **Tresco**, **Bryher**, **St Martin's** and **St Agnes**. In the annals of folklore, the Scillies are the peaks of the submerged land of Lyonnesse, a fertile plain that extended west from Penwith before the ocean broke in, drowning the land and leaving only one survivor to tell the tale. In fact they form part of the same granite mass as Land's End, Bodmin Moor and Dartmoor, and despite rarely rising above 100ft, they possess a remarkable variety of landscape. Points of interest include irresistible **beaches**, such as Par Beach on St Martin's; the Southwest's greatest concentration of **prehistoric remains**; some fabulous **rock formations**, and the impressive **Tresco Abbey Gardens**. Along with tourism, the main source of income is flower-growing, for which the equable climate and the long hours of sunshine – their name means "Sun Isles" – make the islands ideal. The profusion of **wild flowers** is even more noticeable than the fields of narcissi and daffodils, and the heaths and pathways are often dense with marigolds, gorse, sea thrift, trefoil and poppies, not to mention a host of more exotic varieties introduced by visiting foreign vessels. The waters hereabouts are held to be among the country's best for **diving**, while between May and September, on a Wednesday or Friday evening, islanders gather for **gig races**, performed by six-oared vessels – some of them more than a hundred years old and 30ft long.

Free of traffic, theme parks and amusement arcades, the islands are a welcome respite from the tourist trail, the main drawbacks being the high cost of reaching them and the shortage of **accommodation**, most of which is on the main isle of St Mary's.

6

St Mary's

The majority of the resident population of just over two thousand is concentrated on the biggest island, **St Mary's**, which has the lion's share of facilities in its capital, **Hugh Town**, and the richest trove of prehistoric sites. The cove-fringed island is also home to **Star Castle**, a huge eight-pointed fortress that was originally built to deter Spanish invasions, and is now a four-star hotel.

Tresco

The second-largest island, **Tresco**, presents an appealing contrast between the orderly landscape around the remains of its ancient abbey and the bleak, untended northern half. The exuberant **Tresco Abbey Gardens** (daily 10am–4pm; £12; ☎01720 424108, ⍟tresco.co.uk), hosting an impressive collection of subtropical plants in the southern part of the island, is the archipelago's most popular visitor attraction.

Bryher

West of Tresco, **Bryher** has the smallest population, the slow routines of island life quickening only in the tourist season. The bracing, back-to-nature feel here is nowhere more evident than on the exposed western shore, where **Hell Bay** sees some formidable Atlantic storms.

St Martin's

East of Tresco, **St Martin's** has a reputation as the least striking of the Scillies with the most introverted population, but its white-sand beaches are as majestically wild as any. **Par Beach** deserves a special mention – there are stunning views from its cliffy northeastern end, and the surrounding waters are much favoured by scuba enthusiasts.

St Agnes

On the southwest rim of the main group, the tidy lanes and picturesque cottages of **St Agnes** are nicely complemented by the weathered boulders and craggy headlands of its indented shoreline. The year-round population here is small (many of the islanders still make their living by farming flowers) and even in summer there are plenty of tranquil spots.

The uninhabited islands

A visit to the isles would be incomplete without a sortie to the **uninhabited islands**, sanctuaries for seals, puffins and other marine birdlife. On the largest, **Samson**, you can poke around prehistoric and more recent remains that testify to former settlement. Some of the smaller islets are worth visiting for their delightfully deserted beaches, though the majority amount to no more than bare rocks. This chaotic profusion of rocks of all shapes and sizes, each bearing a name, is densest at the archipelago's extremities – the **Western Rocks**, lashed by ferocious seas and the cause of innumerable wrecks over the years, and the milder **Eastern Isles**.

ARRIVAL AND DEPARTURE　　　　　　　　　　　　　　　　**THE ISLES OF SCILLY**

Transport to the Isles of Scilly – by plane and by boat – is operated by **Isles of Scilly Travel** (☎01736 334220, ⍟islesofscilly-travel.co.uk).

By plane For most of the year, the main departure points for flights are Land's End Airport, near St Just; Newquay; Exeter; Bristol and Southampton. In winter there are departures only from Land's End and Newquay. For a one-

way flight from Land's End, expect to pay around £70.
By boat Boats to St Mary's depart from Penzance's South Pier between Easter and Oct (2hr 45min). A one-way fare from Penzance will cost in the region of £42.

GETTING AROUND AND INFORMATION

By boat Boats link each of the inhabited islands, though services are sporadic in winter. The St Mary's Boatmen's

Association (☎1720 423999, ⍟scillyboating.co.uk) publishes up-to-date timetables and fares online.

By bike Cycling is the ideal way to get around (bikes can be taken on ferries from the mainland for £13 each way). Alternatively, you can rent bikes from St Mary's Bike Hire on The Strand, Hugh Town (☎ 07796 638506; £10/day).

Tourist office Schiller Shelter, Porthcressa beachfront, St Mary's (mid-March to mid-April Mon–Sat 9am–4pm;

mid-April to mid-May Mon–Sat 9am–5pm, Sun 9am–2pm; mid-May to mid-Sept Mon–Sat 9am–6.30pm, Sun 9am–2pm; mid-Sept to mid-Oct Mon–Sat 9am–5pm; mid-Oct to mid-March Mon–Fri 10am–2pm; ☎ 01720 424031, ⊛ simplyscilly.co.uk).

ACCOMMODATION AND EATING

St Mary's has the great majority of the **accommodation** on the islands; the smaller isles (excepting Tresco) each have two or three B&Bs only, and these are booked up early. Two of the islands – Tresco and St Martin's – have luxury hotels, and all the islands except Tresco have **campsites**, which usually close in winter (camping rough is not allowed). See ⊛ simplyscilly. co.uk for complete accommodation lists. St Mary's also has most of the **restaurants** and **pubs**. Each of the other inhabited islands has a pub serving food and one or two cafés, while all hotels and some B&Bs also provide meals.

Cornwall's Atlantic coast

The north Cornish coast is punctuated by some of the finest beaches in England, the most popular of which are to be found around **Newquay**, the surfers' capital, and **Padstow**, also renowned for its gourmet seafood restaurants. North of the Camel estuary, the coast features an almost unbroken line of cliffs as far as the Devon border; this gaunt, exposed terrain makes a melodramatic setting for **Tintagel Castle**. There are more good beaches at **Bude**, **St Agnes** and **Polzeath**.

Newquay

In a superb position on a knuckle of cliffs overlooking fine golden sands and Atlantic rollers, its glorious natural advantages have made **NEWQUAY** the premier resort of north Cornwall. The "new quay" in question was built in the fifteenth century in what was already a long-established fishing port, up to then more colourfully known as Towan Blistra. The town was given a boost in the nineteenth century when a railway was constructed across the peninsula for china clay shipments; with the trains came a swelling stream of seasonal visitors.

Today, the town centre is a tacky parade of shops, bars and restaurants from which lanes lead to ornamental gardens and cliff-top lawns. The main attraction is the **beaches**. A number of **surfing competitions** and festivals run through the summer, when Newquay can get very crowded – it's also popular with stag and hen parties.

■ ACCOMMODATION		● RESTAURANTS	
Base Surf Lodge	3	The Boat House	2
Harbour Hotel	2	Butcher's Bistro	4
Headland Hotel	1	Fifteen Cornwall	1
Trevella Park	5	Little Kahuna	3
Trewinda Lodge	4		
		■ BAR	
		The Chy	1

NEWQUAY

The beaches

All Newquay's beaches can be reached fairly easily on foot from the centre, otherwise take bus #556 for Porth Beach and Watergate Bay, #585 and #587 for Crantock and #587 for Holywell Bay

In the crook of Towan Head, **Towan Beach** is the most central of the seven miles of firm sandy beaches that line the coast around Newquay. Town beaches such as this and **Porth Beach**, with its grassy headland, can get very busy with families in high season, and are popular with surfers all year, though the latter are more partial to **Watergate Bay** to the north, and **Fistral Bay**, west of Towan Head.

On the other side of East Pentire Head from Fistral, **Crantock Beach** – reachable over the Gannel River by ferry or upstream footbridge – is usually less crowded, and has a lovely backdrop of dunes and undulating grassland. South of Crantock, **Holywell Bay** and the three-mile expanse of **Perran Beach**, enhanced by caves and natural rock arches, are also very popular with surfers.

ARRIVAL AND DEPARTURE   NEWQUAY

By plane Newquay's airport is at St Mawgan, 5 miles northeast of town, with connections to major British and Irish cities, and linked to town by local buses.

Destinations St Mary's, Isles of Scilly (Mon–Sat 2–4 daily, 1 on Sat in winter; 30min); London Gatwick (2–3 daily; 1hr); Manchester (1 daily; 1hr 20min).

By train Newquay is served by trains from Par (3–8 daily, not Sun in winter; 50min); the train station is off Cliff Road, a short walk east of the centre.

By bus The bus station is on Manor Road, near the tourist office.

Destinations Bodmin (hourly; 55min); Padstow (Mon–Sat hourly, Sun 5 daily; 1hr 20min); Plymouth (every 30min–1hr; 1hr 50min–2hr 20min); St Austell (Mon–Sat every 30min–1hr, Sun 3 daily; 50min); Truro (every 20–30min; 50min–1hr 25min).

INFORMATION

Tourist office Marcus Hill (April–Oct Mon–Fri 9am–5.30pm, Sat & Sun 10am–4pm; Nov–March Mon–Fri 10am–4pm, Sat & Sun 10am–3pm; ☎ 01637 854020, ⓦ visitnewquay.org).

ACCOMMODATION

Base Surf Lodge 20 Tower Rd ☎ 07766 132124, ⓦ basesurflodge.co.uk. A good central option for small groups, with fresh, private bunk rooms sleeping 2–6 people. The whole place is geared up for surfers, with board storage facilities and free hot drinks to warm you up post-surf. Beginners should ask about their surf and stay packages, which include lessons. Dorms **£25**.

Harbour Hotel North Quay Hill ☎ 01637 873040, ⓦ theharbour.uk.com. Small, luxurious hotel with stunning views from its stylish rooms, all of which have balconies. Some rooms are tiny, so check first. **£80**

Headland Hotel Fistral Beach ☎ 01637 872211, ⓦ headlandhotel.co.uk. Opened atop a craggy headland in 1900 and still going strong, the hotel that starred in *The*

Witches has nearly a hundred rooms and suites to choose from – many with ocean views – plus self-catering cottages. **£165**

Trevella Park Near Crantock, 1.5 miles southwest of town ☎ 01637 830308, ⓦ trevella.co.uk. It can feel crowded at peak times, but this remains one of the better holiday parks near Newquay, with good, clean facilities for campers and a heated outdoor pool. Per person **£9.35**

Trewinda Lodge 17 Eliot Gardens ☎ 01637 877533, ⓦ trewinda-lodge.co.uk. The owners of this B&B, close to Tolcarne Beach, can give informed advice to surfers (they also run Dolphin Surf School). Rooms are on the small side, but clean and comfortable, and there's wi-fi. **£60**

EATING AND DRINKING

The Boat House Newquay Harbour ☎ 01637 874062, ⓦ theboathousenewquay.co.uk. The most atmospheric place in town, this restaurant sits right by the old harbour. Inevitably, seafood is the main event: locally caught monkfish, plaice and crab (£11–17), and whatever else appears on the daily specials board. March–Dec daily 10am–11pm; food served noon–3pm & 6.30–9.30pm.

★**Butcher's Bistro** 26 Cliff Rd ☎ 01637 874470. Tucked away beside a fast food joint, this small,

maritime-themed bistro does very good steaks and seafood, including fish line-caught by the chef. For a real treat try the seafood feast – a big, steaming bowl of prawns, crab claws, mussels and boneless fish (£19.95) Mon, Tues & Thurs–Sat 6–9.30pm.

The Chy 12 Beach Rd ☎ 01637 873415, ⓦ thekoola .com. Contemporary bar/restaurant with a spacious terrace and upper deck where you can order everything from breakfasts and sandwiches to burgers and seafood dishes (around £10). In the evening, you can sip cocktails and listen to DJs. Mon, Fri & Sat 10am–4am, Tues–Thurs 10.30am–2am, Sun 11am–midnight; food served all day.

★ **Fifteen Cornwall** Watergate Bay ☎ 01637 861000, ⊛ fifteencornwall.co.uk. Overlooking the beach, this contemporary restaurant set up by TV chef Jamie Oliver showcases the culinary talents of trainee chefs. The Italian-inspired but locally sourced dishes are inventive and

delicious; set menus are £28 at lunchtime, £60 in the evening, and breakfasts are also worth tucking into. Daily 8.30–10am, noon–2.30pm & 6.15–9.15pm.

Little Kahuna 4–6 Crantock St ☎ 01637 850440, ⊛ littlekahuna.co.uk. Mouthwatering Asian dishes from Goan fish curries to spicy *som tam* salads are presented beautifully at this intimate (and extremely popular) little restaurant. Mains are around £15, and you'd be wise to book ahead. Daily 5.30pm–late.

6

Padstow and around

PADSTOW attracts nearly as many holiday-makers as Newquay, but has a very different feel. Enclosed within the estuary of the Camel – the only river outlet of any size on Cornwall's north coast – the town has long retained its position as North Cornwall's principal fishing port, and can boast some of the county's best seafood **restaurants**. The **harbour** is jammed with launches and boats offering cruises in the bay, while a **ferry** (see p.336) carries people across the river to **ROCK** – close to the isolated church of **St Enodoc** (John Betjeman's burial place) and to the good beaches around Polzeath. Padstow is also known for its annual **Obby Oss** festival, a May Day romp when a local in horse costume prances through the town preceded by a masked and club-wielding "teaser", in a spirited re-enactment of an old fertility rite.

Church of St Petroc

Church Lane • Usually open for visitors 9am–5pm

On the hill overlooking Padstow, the **Church of St Petroc** is dedicated to Cornwall's most important saint, a Welsh or Irish monk who landed here in the sixth century, died in the area and gave his name to the town – "Petrock's Stow". The building has a fine fifteenth-century font, an Elizabethan pulpit and some amusing carved bench ends – seek out the one to the right of the altar depicting a fox preaching to a congregation of geese.

Prideaux Place

Half a mile west of the quay • Easter–Sept Mon–Thurs & Sun 1.30–4pm; grounds open from 12.30pm • £8.50, grounds only £4 • ☎ 01841 532411, ⊛ prideauxplace.co.uk

Padstow's ancient Prideaux family – whose Cornish origins date back to the Normans – still occupy **Prideaux Place**, an Elizabethan manor house with grand staircases, richly furnished rooms full of portraits, fantastically ornate ceilings and formal gardens. You might recognize some parts of the house, which is used extensively for location filming and has appeared in a plethora of films, including *Oscar and Lucinda* (1997).

The beaches

The area immediately west of Padstow has some fine **beaches** – all within a short walk or drive of the town. On the **west side** of the estuary, round **Stepper Point**, you can reach the sandy and secluded **Harlyn Bay** and, turning the corner southwards, **Constantine Bay**, the best surfing beach hereabouts. The dunes backing the beach and the rock pools skirting it make this one of the most appealing bays on this coast, though the tides can be treacherous and bathing hazardous near the rocks. Three or four miles further south, the slate outcrops of **Bedruthan Steps** were traditionally held to be the stepping-stones of a giant; they can be readily viewed from the cliff-top path and the B3276, with steps descending to the broad beach below (not safe for swimming).

ARRIVAL AND DEPARTURE   **PADSTOW AND AROUND**

By bus Buses #556 from Newquay (Mon–Sat hourly, Sun 4 daily; 1hr 15min) and #555 from Bodmin (Mon–Sat hourly, Sun 6 daily; 55min) pull in on Station Road, above the harbour.

GETTING AROUND AND INFORMATION

By ferry The ferry across the river to Rock operates daily year-round, roughly every 20min during the day (£3 return).

By bus Bus #556 (hourly) connects Padstow with Harlyn Bay (5min) and Constantine Bay (10min). Every 2hr, the same bus calls at Bedruthan (30min).

Tourist office North Quay, by the harbour (Easter–Oct Mon–Fri 9am–5.30pm, Sat & Sun 10am–5pm; Nov–Easter Mon–Fri 10am–4pm, Sat 10am–3pm, Sun 11am–2pm;

> ### TOP 5 DEVON AND CORNWALL SURF SPOTS
> **Croyde Bay** See p.314
> **Fistral** See p.334
> **Saunton Sands** See p.314
> **Watergate Bay** See p.334
> **Whitesand Bay** See p.328

☎ 01841 533449, ⓦ padstowlive.com).

ACCOMMODATION

St Petroc's Hotel Treverbyn Rd ☎ 01841 532700, ⓦ rickstein.com. Restaurateur Rick Stein has extended his Padstow empire to include classy accommodation, including this chic little lodging away from the harbour, with modernist decor and outstanding breakfasts. But even the very small rooms (described as snug in marketing materials) are pricey. **£160**

Treverbyn House Treverbyn Rd ☎ 01841 532855, ⓦ treverbynhouse.com. A short walk up from the harbour, this elegant Edwardian B&B has large, beautifully furnished rooms with wi-fi. Breakfast is served in the dining room or on a terrace in the garden with views over the river. **£120**

YHA Treyarnon Treyarnon Bay, 4.5 miles west of Padstow ☎ 0845 371 9664, ⓦ yha.org.uk. Perfectly sited hostel in a 1930s summer villa right by the beach. Take bus #556 from Padstow or Newquay to Constantine, then walk half a mile. Surf packages available. Camping pitches **£13**; dorms **£21**; doubles **£63**

EATING AND DRINKING

Foodies know Padstow for its high-class **restaurants**, particularly those associated with star chef **Rick Stein**; the waiting list for a table at one of his establishments can be months long, though a weekday reservation out of season can mean booking only a day or two ahead. For something a little cheaper, try Stein's fish and chip shop or his deli, both on South Quay.

★**Margot's Bistro** 11 Duke St ☎ 01841 533441, ⓦ margotsbistro.co.uk. The tables at this small, unassuming restaurant are booked up for weeks in advance, which is testament to the quality of the food: think Cornish rib-eye steaks, fillets of grey mullet and pan-fried sardines. Most mains are £13.50, which makes this place better value than the town's other top restaurants.

Tues 7–8.30pm, Wed–Sat noon–1.30pm & 7–8.30pm.

★**The Seafood Restaurant** Riverside ☎ 01841 532700, ⓦ rickstein.com. The core of Rick Stein's culinary empire, this is one of Britain's top places for fish, with most mains – Singapore chilli crab, Padstow lobster, Newlyn fish pie – costing £25–35. Daily noon–2.30pm & 6.30–10pm.

Tintagel

Despite its romantic name and its famous **castle** standing aloof on a promontory to the north, the village of **TINTAGEL** is for the most part a dreary collection of cafés and B&Bs. Apart from the castle, Tintagel has one other item of genuine interest: the **Old Post Office** on Fore Street (daily: mid-Feb to early April & Oct 11am–4pm; early April to late May 10.30am–5pm; late May to Sept 10.30am–5.30pm; £3.70; NT; ☎ 01840 770024, ⓦ nationaltrust.org.uk/tintagel-old-post-office), a slate-built, rickety-roofed construction dating from the fourteenth century, now restored to its appearance in the Victorian era.

Tintagel Castle

Half a mile northwest of the village • April–Sept daily 10am–6pm; Oct daily 10am–5pm; Nov–March Sat & Sun 10am–4pm • £6.10; EH • ☎ 01840 770328, ⓦ tintagelcastle.co.uk

The wild and unspoiled coast around Tintagel provides an appropriate backdrop for the forsaken ruins of **Tintagel Castle**. It was the twelfth-century chronicler Geoffrey of Monmouth who first popularized the notion that this was the **birthplace of King Arthur**, son of Uther Pendragon and Ygrayne, though the visible ruins in fact belong to a Norman stronghold occupied by the earls of Cornwall. After sporadic spurts of rebuilding, the castle was allowed to decay, and most of it had been washed into the sea by the sixteenth century. The remains of a sixth-century **Celtic monastery** on the headland have provided important insights into how the country's earliest monastic houses were organized.

ARRIVAL AND INFORMATION   TINTAGEL

By bus Buses pull in on Bossiney Road, opposite the tourist office.
Destinations Boscastle (Mon–Sat 6 daily; 10min); Bude (Mon–Sat 5–6 daily; 40min); Camelford (Mon–Sat every 1–2hr; 15min).

Tourist office The tourist office is in the car park off Bossiney Road (daily: April–Oct 10am–4pm; Nov–March 10am–12.30pm; ☎01840 779084, ⓦvisitboscastleandtintagel.com), and has a small exhibition about the region's cultural heritage.

ACCOMMODATION AND EATING

The Avalon Atlantic Road ☎01840 770116, ⓦtint agelbedbreakfast.co.uk. The rooms are nothing special but if you just want a clean and central place to lay your head, you could do worse than this welcoming B&B. The most expensive bedrooms have views of the sea and castle, while the cheaper ones look out over the village and countryside. **£84**

Bosayne Atlantic Rd ☎01840 770514, ⓦbosayne .co.uk. In a quiet spot a few mins' walk from Tintagel's centre, this good-value B&B has en-suite doubles and singles with shared bathrooms, all with an iPod dock and access to free wi-fi. Some rooms have sea views. **£67**

★Charlie's Fore St ☎01840 779500, ⓦonline-deli .co.uk. There's a lot to like about this family-friendly deli-restaurant, not least the excellent home-made cakes and Cornish cream teas (gluten-free scones are available). The staff are friendly, and there's a good selection of pickles and relishes to take home. Mon–Sat 10am–5pm.

YHA Tintagel Dunderhole Point ☎0845 371 9145, ⓦyha.org.uk. Three-quarters of a mile south of Tintagel, the offices of a former slate quarry now house this hostel with great coastal views. There's a kitchen and BBQ area but no restaurant. Dorms **£21.50**

Boscastle

Three miles east of Tintagel, the port of **BOSCASTLE** lies compressed within a narrow ravine drilled by the rivers Jordan and Valency, and ending in a twisty harbour. The tidy riverfront bordered by thatched and lime-washed cottages was the scene of a devastating flash flood in 2004, but the damage has now been repaired. Above and behind, you can see more seventeenth- and eighteenth-century cottages on a circular walk that traces the valley of the Valency for about a mile to reach Boscastle's graceful parish church of **St Juliot**, tucked away in a peaceful glen, where Thomas Hardy once worked as a young architect.

ARRIVAL AND INFORMATION   BOSCASTLE

By bus There are bus stops at the car park and Boscastle Bridge, at the top of the village.
Destinations Bude (Mon–Sat 6 daily; 40min); Camelford (Mon–Sat 6 daily, 25min); Tintagel (Mon–Sat

6 daily; 10min).
Tourist office The Harbour (Mon–Sat: April–Sept 10am–5pm; Oct–March 10.30am–4pm; ☎01840 250010, ⓦvisitboscastleandtintagel.com).

ACCOMMODATION

Boscastle House Doctors Hill ☎01840 250654, ⓦboscastlehouse.co.uk. Six spacious rooms with high ceilings in a tranquil nineteenth-century house that was built for a local doctor. The interiors are fresh and modern, and a couple of the rooms have decent views. **£80**

Old Rectory St Juliot, 1.5 miles east of Boscastle ☎01840 250225, ⓦstjuliot.com. For a real Thomas Hardy experience, head for this luxurious Victorian B&B,

where you can stay in the author's bedroom and roam the extensive grounds. **£110**

★YHA Boscastle Palace Stables, Harbourside ☎0845 371 9006, ⓦyha.org.uk. Fine old hostel in a former stables right by the river. Rooms have two to six beds and there's a self-catering kitchen and a comfy lounge. Groups only Dec–March. Dorms **£22.50**; doubles **£75**

EATING AND DRINKING

Boscastle Farm Shop Hillsborough Farm, a mile east of Boscastle along the B3263 ☎01840 250827, ⓦboscastlefarmshop.co.uk. Busy farm shop just a short

stroll off the coastal path, selling fresh fruit and veg, cuts of local meat and locally made biscuits. The café at the back does good breakfast baps (£3.75) and has views over the sea and countryside. Daily 9am–5pm.

Napoleon Inn High St ☎01840 250204, ⓦnapoleoninn .co.uk. Among Boscastle's excellent pubs, this one in the upper town has tankards hanging off the ceiling, real ale, great food (mains around £12) and live music evenings every Fri. Daily noon–11pm; food served 12.30–8.30pm.

Bude and around

Just four miles from the Devon border, Cornwall's northernmost town of **BUDE** is built around an estuary surrounded by a fine expanse of sands. The town has sprouted a crop of hotels and holiday homes, though these have not unduly spoilt the place nor the magnificent cliffy coast surrounding it.

Of the excellent beaches hereabouts, the central **Summerleaze** is clean and spacious, but the mile-long **Widemouth Bay**, south of town, is the main focus of the holiday crowds (though bathing can be dangerous near the rocks at low tide). Surfers also congregate five miles down the coast at **Crackington Haven**, wonderfully situated between 430ft crags at the mouth of a lush valley. To the **north** of Bude, acres-wide **Crooklets** is the scene of **surfing** and life-saving demonstrations and competitions. A couple of miles further on, **Sandy Mouth** holds a pristine expanse of sand with rock pools beneath the encircling cliffs. It's a short walk from here to another surfers' delight, **Duckpool**, a tiny sandy cove flanked by jagged reefs at low tide, and dominated by the three-hundred-foot **Steeple Point**.

ARRIVAL AND INFORMATION   BUDE AND AROUND

By bus Buses stop on The Strand.
Destinations Boscastle (Mon–Sat 6 daily; 40min); Exeter (Mon–Sat 8 daily, Sun 2 daily; 2hr); Hartland (Mon–Sat 5 daily; 45min).

Tourist office In the car park off the Crescent (April–Sept Mon–Sat 10am–5/6pm, Sun 10am–4pm; Oct–March daily 10am–4pm; ☎01288 354240, ⓦvisitbude.info).

ACCOMMODATION AND EATING

Brendon Arms Falcon Terrace ☎01288 354542, ⓦbrendonarms.co.uk. Large, agreeable old inn with tables on the front lawn, good for a pint of real ale and a snack or bar meal for around £10. Accommodation available. Daily 11am/ noon–midnight; food served noon–2pm & 6–9pm. **£80**

★**Cerenety** A mile south of Bude on Lynstone Lane ☎01288 356778 or ☎07429 016962, ⓦcerenety campsite.co.uk. Back-to-basics, eco-friendly camping just outside Bude, with handsome grassy areas to pitch up on, plus solar-powered showers and composting toilets. In the mornings, hot drinks and breakfast baps can be bought from a little caravan on the site. Pitches **£14**

Life's a Beach Summerleaze Beach ☎01288 355222, ⓦlifesabeach.info. Right on the beach, this is a café by

day, offering baguettes, burgers and drinks, and a romantic bistro strong on seafood in the evening (mains £16.50– 20). Mon–Sat 10.30am–3.30pm & 7–8.45pm, Sun 10.30am–3.30pm.

North Shore 57 Killerton Rd ☎01288 354256, ⓦnorthshorebude.com. Friendly backpackers' hostel 5min from the centre of town, with clean and spacious rooms – including en-suite doubles – a large garden, a kitchen and internet access. Dorms **£20**; doubles **£48**

Upper Lynstone Lynstone ☎01288 352017, ⓦupper lynstone.co.uk. This clean, basic campsite lies some three- quarters of a mile south of town, linked by a panoramic cliff-top walk. There's a shop on site, and electric hook-ups. Closed Oct–Easter. Pitches **£21**

Bodmin Moor

Bodmin Moor, the smallest of the West Country's great moors, has some beautiful tors, torrents and rock formations, but much of its fascination lies in the strong human imprint, particularly the wealth of relics left behind by its **Bronze Age** population. Separated from these by some three millennia, the churches in the villages of **St Neot**, **Blisland** and **Altarnun** are among the region's finest examples of fifteenth-century art and architecture.

Bodmin

BODMIN's position on the western edge of Bodmin Moor, equidistant from the north and south Cornish coasts and the Fowey and Camel rivers, encouraged its growth as a trading town. It was also an important ecclesiastical centre after the establishment of a priory by St Petroc, who moved here from Padstow in the sixth century.

Church of St Petroc

Priory Rd • Open for services April–Sept Mon–Sat 11am–3pm; at other times call to check • Free • ☎ 01208 73867

After Bodmin's priory had disappeared, the town retained its prestige through its **church of St Petroc**, built in the fifteenth century and still Cornwall's largest parish church. Inside, there's an extravagantly carved twelfth-century font and an ivory casket that once held the bones of the saint. The southwest corner of the churchyard holds a sacred well.

Bodmin Jail

Berrycoombe Rd • Daily 10am–5pm • £7.50 ; entry to grounds and café is free • ☎ 01208 76292, ⓦ bodminjail.org

The notorious **Bodmin Jail** is redolent of the public executions that were guaranteed crowd-pullers until 1862, though it didn't finally close until 1927. You can visit part of the original eighteenth-century structure, including the condemned cell and "execution pit", and some grisly exhibits chronicling the lives of the inmates. *The Warder's Room*, a café/restaurant, stays open until late.

Lanhydrock

3 miles southeast of Bodmin; less than 2 miles from Bodmin Parkway station • **House** Tues–Sun: March & Oct 11am–5pm; April–Sept 11am–5.30pm; also open Mon in school hols • £11.30 (includes grounds and gardens); NT • **Gardens** Feb–Nov 10am–6pm • £7 • ☎ 01208 265950, ⓦ nationaltrust.org.uk/lanhydrock

One of Cornwall's most celebrated country houses, **Lanhydrock** originally dates from the seventeenth century but was totally rebuilt after a fire in 1881. Much remains of its Jacobean past within the granite exterior, however; the fifty rooms include a long picture gallery with a plaster ceiling depicting scenes from the Old Testament, while the servants' quarters fascinatingly reveal the daily workings of a Victorian manor house. The grounds have magnificent **gardens** with lush beds of magnolias, azaleas and rhododendrons, and a huge area of wooded parkland bordering onto the River Fowey.

Blisland

BLISLAND stands in the Camel valley on the western slopes of Bodmin Moor, three miles northeast of Bodmin. Georgian and Victorian houses cluster around a village green and a church whose well-restored interior has an Italianate altar and a startlingly painted screen.

The western moor

On **Pendrift Common** above Blisland, the gigantic **Jubilee Rock** is inscribed with various patriotic insignia commemorating the jubilee of George III's coronation in 1809. From this 700ft vantage point you look eastward over the De Lank gorge and the boulder-crowned knoll of **Hawk's Tor**, three miles away. On the shoulder of the tor stand the Neolithic **Stripple Stones**, a circular platform once holding 28 standing stones, of which just four are still upright.

The northern tors

The northern half of Bodmin Moor is dominated by its two highest tors, both of them easily accessible from **CAMELFORD**, an unassuming local centre known for its slate industry. Four miles southeast, **Rough Tor** is the second highest peak on Bodmin Moor at 1311ft. A short distance to the east stand **Little Rough Tor**, where there are the remains of an Iron Age camp, and **Showery Tor**, capped by a prominent formation of piled rocks. Easily visible to the southeast, **Brown Willy** is, at 1378ft, the highest peak in Cornwall, as its original name signified – Bronewhella, or "highest hill". Like Rough Tor, Brown Willy shows various faces, its sugarloaf appearance from the north sharpening into a long multi-peaked crest as you approach. The tor is accessible by continuing from the summit of Rough Tor across the valley of the De Lank or, from the south, by footpath from Bolventor.

6

KING ARTHUR IN CORNWALL

Did **King Arthur** really exist? If he did, it's likely that he was an amalgam of two people: a sixth-century Celtic warlord who united the local tribes in a series of successful battles against the invading Anglo-Saxons, and a local Cornish saint. Whatever his origins, his role was recounted and inflated by poets and troubadours in later centuries. The Arthurian legends were elaborated by the medieval chroniclers Geoffrey of Monmouth and William of Malmesbury and in Thomas Malory's epic, *Morte d'Arthur* (1485), further romanticized in Tennyson's *Idylls of the King* (1859) and resurrected in T.H. White's saga, *The Once and Future King* (1958).

Although there are places throughout Britain and Europe that claim some association with Arthur, it's England's West Country, and **Cornwall** in particular, that has the greatest concentration of places boasting a link. Here, the myths, enriched by fellow Celts from Brittany and Wales, have established deep roots, so that, for example, the spirit of Arthur is said to be embodied in the Cornish chough – a bird now almost extinct. Cornwall's most famous Arthurian site is his supposed birthplace, **Tintagel**, where Merlin apparently lived in a cave under the castle (he also resided on a rock near Mousehole, south of Penzance, according to some sources). Nearby **Bodmin Moor** is littered with places with names such as "King Arthur's Bed" and "King Arthur's Downs", while Camlan, the battlefield where Arthur was mortally wounded fighting against his nephew Mordred, is associated with Slaughterbridge, on the northern reaches of the moor near **Camelford** (which is also sometimes identified as Camelot itself). At **Dozmary Pool**, the knight Bedivere was dispatched by the dying Arthur to return the sword Excalibur to the mysterious hand emerging from the water – though Loe Pool in Mount's Bay also claims this honour. Arthur's body, it is claimed, was carried after the battle to **Boscastle**, on Cornwall's northern coast, from where a funeral barge transported it to Avalon, identified with Glastonbury in Somerset (see p.278).

Bolventor and around

The village of **BOLVENTOR**, lying at the centre of the moor midway between Bodmin and Launceston, is an uninspiring place close to one of the moor's chief focuses for walkers and literary sightseers alike – **Jamaica Inn**.

Jamaica Inn

10 miles northeast of Bodmin along the A30 • Museum open daily: mid-March to Oct 10am–5pm (until 6pm during school summer hols) • £3.95 • ☎ 01566 86250, ⓦ jamaicainn.co.uk

A staging post even before the precursor of the A30 road was laid here in 1769, the inn was described as being "alone in glory, four square to the winds" by **Daphne Du Maurier**, who stayed here in 1930, soaking up inspiration for her smugglers' yarn, *Jamaica Inn*. There's a room inside devoted to the author, and the hotel also has an attached **Smugglers Museum**, illustrating the diverse ruses used for concealing contraband.

Dozmary Pool

A mile south of Bolventor

The car park at *Jamaica Inn* makes a useful place to leave your vehicle and venture forth on foot. Just a mile south, **Dozmary Pool** is another link in the West Country's Arthurian mythologies – after Arthur's death Sir Bedivere hurled Excalibur, the king's sword, into the pool, where it was seized by an arm raised from the depths. Despite its proximity to the A30, the diamond-shaped lake usually preserves an ethereal air, though it's been known to run dry in summer, dealing a bit of a blow to the legend that it is bottomless.

Altarnun

Four miles northeast of Bolventor, **ALTARNUN** is a pleasant, granite-grey village snugly sheltered beneath the eastern heights of the moor. Its prominent **church**, St Nonna's, contains a fine Norman font and 79 bench ends carved at the beginning of the sixteenth century, depicting saints, musicians and clowns.

St Neot and the southeastern moor

Approached through a lush wooded valley, **ST NEOT** is one of the moor's prettiest villages. Its fifteenth-century **church** contains some of the most impressive stained glass windows of any parish church in the country, the oldest glass being the fifteenth-century **Creation Window**, at the east end of the south aisle.

Golitha Falls

One of the moor's most attractive spots lies a couple of miles east of St Neot, below Draynes Bridge, where the Fowey tumbles through the **Golitha Falls**, less a waterfall than a series of rapids. Dippers and wagtails flit through the trees, and there's a pleasant woodland walk to Siblyback Lake reservoir just over a mile away.

Kilmar and Stowe's Hill

North and east of Siblyback Lake are some of Bodmin Moor's grandest landscapes. The quite modest elevations of Hawk's Tor (1079ft) and the lower Trewartha Tor appear enormous from the north, though they are overtopped by **Kilmar**, highest of the hills on the moor's eastern flank at 1280ft. **Stowe's Hill** is the site of the moor's most famous stone pile, **The Cheesewring**, a precarious pillar of balancing granite slabs, marvellously eroded by the wind. A mile or so south down Stowe's Hill stands an artificial rock phenomenon, **The Hurlers**, a wide complex of three circles dating from about 1500 BC. The purpose of these stark upright stones is not known, though they owe their name to the legend that they were men turned to stone for playing the Celtic game of hurling on the Sabbath.

Minions and Trethevy

The Hurlers are easily accessible just outside **MINIONS**, Cornwall's highest village, three miles south of which stands another Stone Age survival, **Trethevy Quoit**, a chamber tomb nearly nine feet high, surmounted by a massive capstone. Originally enclosed in earth, the stones have been stripped by centuries of weathering to create Cornwall's most impressive megalithic monument.

6

ARRIVAL AND INFORMATION

BODMIN MOOR

By train 3 miles outside Bodmin itself, Bodmin Parkway train station has a regular bus connection (hourly; 15min) to the centre of Bodmin.

Destinations Exeter (every 30min–1hr; 1hr 40min); Penzance (every 30min–1hr; 1hr 20min); Plymouth (every 30min–1hr; 45min).

By bus Most buses to and from Bodmin stop on Mount Folly, near the tourist office.

Destinations Newquay (hourly; 50min); Padstow (Mon–Sat hourly, Sun 6 daily; 50min); Plymouth (9 daily; 1hr 10min–1hr 30min); St Austell (Mon–Sat hourly, Sun 5 daily; 50min).

Tourist office Mount Folly, Bodmin (March–May & Oct Mon–Fri 8.45am–4pm plus some Sats 10am–5pm; June–Sept Mon–Fri 8.45am–5pm, Sat 10am–5pm; Nov–Feb Mon–Fri 8.45am–2pm; ☎01208 76616, ⓦbodminlive.com).

ACCOMMODATION AND EATING

★**Bedknobs** Polgwyn, Castle St, Bodmin ☎01208 77553, ⓦbedknobs.co.uk. Victorian villa in an acre of wooded garden, with three spacious and luxurious rooms, the priciest with its own en-suite Airbath and the cheapest with a separate bathroom that includes a spa bath. Friendly, eco-aware hosts and lots of extras. No under-12s. **£85**

Jamaica Inn Bolventor ☎01566 86250, ⓦjamaicainn .co.uk. Despite its fame, this inn immortalized by Daphne du Maurier has lost any trace of romance since its development into a bland hotel and restaurant complex. It occupies a grand site, though, ideal for excursions onto the moor. Mon–Sat 7.30am–midnight, Sun

7.30am–10.30pm; food served 7.30am–11am, noon–3.30pm & 5–9.30pm. **£79**

Mason's Arms Fore St, Camelford ☎01840 213309, ⓦmasonsarmscamelford.co.uk. Traditional, rather poky pub with St Austell ales and some of the best nosh around (mains around £10). Daily 11am–11pm; food served noon 2.30pm & 6–9pm.

Roscrea 18 St Nicholas Rd, Bodmin ☎01208 74400, ⓦroscrea.co.uk. Central, friendly B&B with tasteful Victorian rooms. Breakfasts include eggs laid in the garden, and you can request a great two-course dinner for £18.50 – a good option. **£85**

East Anglia

CLEY WINDMILL, NORFOLK

East Anglia

Strictly speaking, East Anglia is made up of just three counties – Suffolk, Norfolk and Cambridgeshire, which were settled in the fifth century by Angles from today's Schleswig-Holstein – but it has come to be loosely applied to parts of Essex too. As a region it's renowned for its wide skies and flat landscapes – if you're looking for mountains, you've come to the wrong place. East Anglia can surprise, nonetheless: parts of Suffolk and Norfolk are decidedly hilly, with steep coastal cliffs; broad rivers cut through the fenlands; and Norfolk also boasts some wonderful sandy beaches. Fine medieval churches abound, built in the days when this was England's most progressive and prosperous region.

7

Heading into East Anglia from the south takes you through **Essex**, whose proximity to London has turned much of the county into an unappetizing commuter strip. Amid the suburban gloom, there are, however, several worthwhile destinations, most notably **Colchester**, once a major Roman town and now a busy place with an imposing castle, and the handsome hamlets of the bucolic **Stour River Valley** on the Essex–Suffolk border. Essex's **Dedham** is one of the prettiest of these villages, but the prime attraction hereabouts is Suffolk's **Flatford Mill**, famous for its associations with the painter John Constable.

Suffolk boasts a string of pretty little towns – **Lavenham** is the prime example – that enjoyed immense prosperity from the thirteenth to the sixteenth century, the heyday of the wool trade. The county town of **Ipswich** has more to offer than it's given credit for, but really it's the Suffolk coast that holds the main appeal, especially the delightful seaside resort of **Southwold** and neighbouring **Aldeburgh** with its prestigious music festival.

Norfolk, as everyone knows thanks to Noël Coward, is very flat. It's also one of the most sparsely populated and tranquil counties in England, a remarkable turnaround from the days when it was an economic and political powerhouse – until, that is, the Industrial Revolution simply passed it by. Its capital, **Norwich**, is East Anglia's largest city, renowned for its Norman cathedral and castle; nearby are the **Broads**, a unique landscape of reed-ridden waterways that have been intensively mined by boat-rental companies. Similarly popular, the **Norfolk coast** holds a string of busy, very English seaside resorts – **Cromer** and **Sheringham** to name but two – but for the most part it's charmingly unspoilt, its marshes, creeks and tidal flats studded with tiny flintstone villages, most enjoyably **Blakeney** and **Cley**.

Cambridge is much visited, principally because of its world-renowned university, whose ancient colleges boast some of the finest medieval and early-modern architecture in the country. The rest of Cambridgeshire is pancake-flat **fenland**, for centuries an inhospitable marshland, but now rich alluvial farming land. The cathedral town of **Ely**, settled on one of the few areas of raised ground in the fens, is an easy and popular day-trip from Cambridge.

BEACH HUTS, SOUTHWOLD

Highlights

❶ Orford Solitary hamlet with a splendid coastal setting that makes for a wonderful weekend away. **See p.353**

❷ The Aldeburgh Festival The region's prime classical music festival takes place every summer. **See p.354**

❸ Southwold Handsome and genteel seaside town, which is perfect for walking and bathing – with the added incentive of the most inventive Under the Pier Show in the country. **See p.356**

❹ Norwich Market This open-air market is the region's biggest and best for everything from whelks to wellies. **See p.360**

❺ Holkham Bay and beach Wide bay holding Norfolk's finest beach – acres of golden sand set against pine-dusted dunes. **See p.368**

❻ Ely Isolated Cambridgeshire town, with a true fenland flavour and a magnificent cathedral. **See p.370**

❼ Cambridge With some of the finest late medieval architecture in Europe, Cambridge is a must-see, its compact centre graced by dignified old colleges and their neatly manicured quadrangles. **See p.372**

HIGHLIGHTS ARE MARKED ON THE MAP ON P.346

GETTING AROUND

By train Trains from London are fast and frequent: one main line links Colchester, Ipswich and Norwich, another Cambridge and Ely. Among several cross-country services, there are trains between Peterborough, Ely, Norwich and Ipswich.

EAST ANGLIA

By bus Beyond the major towns you'll have to rely on local buses. Services are patchy, except on the north Norfolk coast, which is well served by the Norfolk Coasthopper bus (Ⓦ coasthopper.co.uk).

Colchester

If you visit only one place in Essex, it should be **COLCHESTER**, a lively, medium-sized town with a **castle**, a university and an army base, just fifty miles or so northeast of London. Colchester prides itself on being England's oldest town, and there is indeed documentary evidence of a settlement here as early as the fifth century BC. Today, Colchester makes a potential base for explorations of the surrounding countryside – particularly the **Stour valley** towns of Constable country, within easy reach a few miles to the north.

HIGHLIGHTS

1. Orford
2. The Aldeburgh Festival
3. Southwold
4. Norwich Market
5. Holkham Bay and beach
6. Ely
7. Cambridge

EAST ANGLIA

TOP 5 GREAT PLACES TO STAY

Cley Mill B&B Cley. See p.366
Crown & Castle Orford. See p.357
Gothic House Norwich. See p.362

The Great House Lavenham. See p.351
Ocean House B&B Aldeburgh. See p.355

Brief history

By the first century AD, the town was the region's capital under **King Cunobelin** – better known as Shakespeare's Cymbeline – and when the **Romans** invaded Britain in 43 AD they chose Colchester (Camulodunum) as their new capital, though it was soon eclipsed by London. Later, the conquering Normans built one of their mightiest strongholds here, but the conflict that most marked the town was the **Civil War**. In 1648, Colchester was subjected to a gruelling siege by the Parliamentarian army; after three months, during which the population ate every living creature within the walls and then some, the town finally surrendered and the Royalist leaders were promptly executed for their pains.

Colchester castle

Castle Park • Mon–Sat 10am–5pm, Sun 11–5pm • £7.50 • Guided tours 45min; £2.80 • ☎ 01206 282939, ⓦ www.cimuseums.org.uk/castle

At the heart of Colchester are the remains of its **castle**, a ruggedly imposing, honey-coloured keep, set in attractive parkland stretching down to the River Colne. Begun less than ten years after the Battle of Hastings, the keep was the largest in Europe at the time, built on the site of the Temple of Claudius. Inside the keep, a **museum** holds an excellent collection of Romano-British archeological finds, notably a miscellany of coins and tombstones. The museum also runs regular **guided tours**, giving access to the Roman vaults and the castle roof, which are otherwise out of bounds. Outside, down towards the river in Castle Park, is a section of the old **Roman walls**, whose battered remains are still visible around much of the town centre. They were erected after Boudica had sacked the city and, as such, are a case of too little too late.

Firstsite Contemporary Visual Arts Centre

Lewis Gardens, High St • Daily 10am–5pm • Free • ☎ 01206 577067, ⓦ firstsite.uk.net

In a new and stunningly handsome modern building near the castle, the **Firstsite Contemporary Visual Arts Centre** offers a varied and often challenging programme of temporary exhibitions. Recent exhibitors have included Roger Hiorns and Bruce McLean. The building itself has a lustrous metallic gold sheen and was designed by the Uruguayan architect Rafael Viñoly.

The Town Hall

High St

Colchester's wide and largely pedestrianized **High Street** follows pretty much the same route as it did in Roman times. The most arresting building here is the flamboyant **Town Hall**, built in 1902 and topped by a statue of St Helena, mother of Constantine the Great and daughter of "Old King Cole" of nursery-rhyme fame – after whom, some say, the town was named.

Balkerne Gate

High St

Looming above the western end of the High Street is the town landmark, "**Jumbo**", a disused nineteenth-century water tower, considerably more imposing than the nearby

Balkerne Gate, which marked the western entrance to Roman Colchester. Built in 50 AD, this is the largest surviving Roman gateway in the country, though with the remains at only a touch over 6ft high, it's far from spectacular.

ARRIVAL AND INFORMATION   COLCHESTER

By train Colchester has two train stations, Colchester North for mainline services and Colchester Town for local services to the Tendring peninsula. From Colchester North, it's a 15min walk south into town – follow the signs – whilst Colchester Town station is on the southeast corner of the town centre, about 500yds from the High Street.
Colchester North to: Ipswich (every 30min; 20min); London Liverpool Street (every 20min; 1hr); Norwich (every 30min; 1hr); Sudbury (change at Marks Tey; hourly; 40min).
Colchester Town to: Walton-on-the-Naze (hourly; 50min).
By bus The bus station is on Osborne St, a short walk south

of the castle and the High St, with some services leaving from neighbouring Standwell and Queen streets.
Destinations Chambers bus #753 (ⓦchambersbus .co.uk) links Colchester with Bury St Edmunds (Mon–Sat hourly; 2hr); Lavenham (Mon–Sat hourly; 1hr 30min) and Sudbury (Mon–Sat hourly; 50min). There is also a reasonably frequent bus to Dedham (Mon–Sat 3–4 daily; 40min). Timetable details on ⓦsuffolkonboard.com.
Tourist office On the ground floor of the Hollytrees Museum, on the High Street near the castle (Mon–Sat 10am–5pm; ☏01206 282920, ⓦvisitcolchester.com).

ACCOMMODATION

Four Sevens Guesthouse 28 Inglis Road ☏01206 546093, ⓦfoursevens.co.uk. One of the best of the town's B&Bs, in an attractively remodelled Victorian house with six bright and breezy guest rooms decorated in an uncluttered modern style. Two of the rooms are en suite, which cost an extra £10. On a leafy residential street, a brief walk southwest from the centre. **£65**

North Hill Hotel 51 North Hill ☏01206 574001, ⓦnorthhillhotel.com. In an intelligently revamped older building, this appealing, mid-range hotel has seventeen guest rooms with lots of original features – especially the exposed half-timbered walls and beams. Handy central location too, just north of the High St, but North Hill can be noisy, so you may prefer a room at the back. **£70**

EATING

Colchester's **oysters** have been highly prized since Roman times and today are at their best among the oyster fisheries of **Mersea Island**, about 6 miles south of Colchester; the season runs from September to May.

The Company Shed 129 Coast Rd, West Mersea ☏01206 382700, ⓦthe-company-shed.co.uk. The freshest of oysters served simply at rickety tables in, to quote their own PR, a "romantically weatherbeaten shed". Romantic or not, the oysters are indeed delicious. Tues–Sat 9am–5pm, Sun 10am–5pm. Last orders for eating-in 4pm.
Il Padrino 11 Church St ☏01206 366699, ⓦilpadrinocolchester.co.uk. Opened in 2013, this

excellent Italian café-cum-restaurant serves all the classics for lunch and dinner and even offers breakfast too. The daily specials, chalked up on a blackboard, are a real feature and prices are very reasonable with mains averaging £13 (£9 for pasta dishes). Cosy premises and attentive service. Narrow Church Street is a few yards from the west end of the High Street. Mon 9am–2pm, Tues–Sat 9am–2pm & 6–10pm.

The Stour Valley

Six miles or so north of Colchester, the **Stour River Valley** forms the border between Essex and Suffolk, and signals the beginning of East Anglia proper. The valley is dotted with lovely little villages, where rickety, half-timbered Tudor houses and elegant Georgian dwellings cluster around medieval churches, proud buildings with square, self-confident towers. The Stour's prettiest villages are concentrated along its lower reaches – to the east of the A134 – in Dedham Vale, with **Dedham** the most appealing of them all. The vale is also known as "**Constable Country**", as it was the home of John Constable, one of England's greatest artists, and the subject of his most famous paintings. Inevitably, there's a Constable shrine – the much-visited complex of old buildings down by the river at **Flatford Mill**. Elsewhere, the best-preserved of the old south Suffolk wool towns is **Lavenham**, whilst neighbouring **Sudbury** has a fine museum, devoted to the work of another outstanding English artist, Thomas Gainsborough.

Brief history

The villages along the River Stour and its tributaries were once busy little places at the heart of East Anglia's medieval **weaving trade**. By the 1480s, the region produced more cloth than any other part of the country, but in Tudor times production shifted to Colchester, Ipswich and Norwich and, although most of the smaller settlements continued spinning cloth for the next three hundred years or so, their importance slowly dwindled. Bypassed by the Industrial Revolution, **south Suffolk** had, by the late nineteenth century, become a remote rural backwater, an impoverished area whose decline had one unforeseen consequence: with few exceptions, the towns and villages were never prosperous enough to modernize, so the architectural legacy of medieval and Tudor times survived and now pulls in second-home owners and tourists alike.

GETTING AROUND	THE STOUR VALLEY

By public transport Seeing the Stour Valley by public transport can be problematic – distances are small (Dedham Vale is only about ten miles long), but buses between the villages are patchy, especially on the weekend. The only local rail service is the short branch line between Sudbury and Marks Tey on the London Liverpool Street to Colchester line.

7

Flatford Mill

"I associate my careless boyhood with all that lies on the banks of the Stour," wrote **John Constable**, who was born in **East Bergholt**, nine miles northeast of Colchester, in 1776. The house in which he was born has long since disappeared, so it has been left to **FLATFORD MILL**, a mile or so to the south, to take up the painter's cause. The mill was owned by his father and was where Constable painted his most celebrated canvas, *The Hay Wain* (now in London's National Gallery), which created a sensation when it was exhibited in Paris in 1824. To the chagrin of many of his contemporaries, Constable turned away from the landscape painting conventions of the day, rendering his scenery with a realistic directness that harked back to the Dutch landscape painters of the seventeenth century.

The mill itself – not the one he painted, but a Victorian replacement – is not open to the public and neither is neighbouring **Willy Lott's Cottage**, which does actually feature in *The Hay Wain*, but the National Trust has colonized several local buildings, principally **Bridge Cottage**.

Bridge Cottage

Flatford Mill · Jan & Feb Sat & Sun 10.30am–3.30pm; March Wed–Sun 11am–4pm; April daily 10.30am–5pm; May–Sept daily 10.30am–5.30pm; Oct daily 10.30am–5pm; Nov & Dec Wed–Sun 10.30am–3.30pm · NT · Free, except for parking · ☎01206 298260 · The nearest train station is at Manningtree, 2 miles away

Neat and trim and tidily thatched, **Bridge Cottage** was familiar to Constable and, although none of the artist's paintings is displayed here, it is packed with Constabilia alongside a small exhibition on the artist's life and times. The cottage also has a very pleasant riverside tearoom where you can take in the view.

ACCOMMODATION	FLATFORD MILL

The Granary B&B Flatford Mill ☎01206 298111, ⓦgranaryflatford.co.uk. In the annexe of the old granary that was once owned by Constable's father, this appealing B&B has a real cottage feel with its beamed ceilings and antique furniture. There are two ground-floor guest rooms, both en suite. **£62**

> ### GUIDED WALKS AROUND FLATFORD MILL
>
> Many visitors to Flatford Mill are keen to see the sites associated with Constable's paintings and, although there is something a tad futile about this – so much has changed – the National Trust does organize volunteer-led **guided walks** to several key locations; the nearest are the remains of the Dry Dock next to Bridge Cottage and the *Hay Wain* view itself. For more details, call ☎01206 298260 or consult ⓦnationaltrust.org.uk.

Dedham

Constable went to school just upriver from Flatford Mill in **DEDHAM**, a pretty little village whose wide and lazy main street is graced by a handsome medley of old timber-framed houses and Georgian villas. The main sight as such is the **Church of St Mary** (daily 9am–dusk; free; ⓦ dedham-parishchurch.org.uk), a large, well-proportioned structure with a sweeping, sixteenth-century nave that is adorned by some attractive Victorian stained glass. Constable painted the church on several occasions, and today it holds one of the artist's rare religious paintings, *The Ascension* – though frankly, it's a good job Constable concentrated on landscapes. Be aware that day-trippers arrive here by the coachload throughout the summer.

ARRIVAL AND DEPARTURE
DEDHAM

By bus There is a reasonably frequent bus service to Dedham from Colchester (Mon–Sat 3–4 daily; 40min), but there are no buses between Dedham and Stoke-by-Nayland. See ⓦ suffolkonboard.com.

ACCOMMODATION AND EATING

The Sun Inn High St ☎ 01206 323351, ⓦ thesuninndedham.com. Among Dedham's several pubs, the pick is *The Sun*, an ancient place that has been sympathetically modernized. The menu is strong on local ingredients and offers tasty Italian and British dishes, all washed down with real ales; mains average around £13. They also have several attractive en-suite rooms; rates increase £30 or so on the weekend. Daily: 11am–11pm; food served noon–2.30pm & 6.30–9.30pm. <u>**£120**</u>

Sudbury

By far the most important town in this part of the Stour Valley, **SUDBURY** holds a handful of timber-framed houses that recall its days of wool-trade prosperity, though in fact its salad days were underwritten by another local industry, **silk weaving**. The town's most famous export, however, is **Thomas Gainsborough** (1727–88), the leading English portraitist of the eighteenth century. Although he left Sudbury when he was just 13, moving to London where he was apprenticed to an engraver, the artist is still very much identified with the town: his statue, with brush and palette, stands on Market Hill, the predominantly Victorian marketplace, while a superb collection of his work is on display a few yards away inside the house where he was born, now **Gainsborough's House**.

Gainsborough's House

46 Gainsborough St • Mon–Sat 10am–5pm & Sun 11am–5pm • £6.50 • ☎ 01787 372958, ⓦ gainsborough.org.

On display in **Gainsborough's House** is the earliest of the artist's surviving portrait paintings, *Boy and Girl*, a remarkably self-assured work dated to 1744, though it comes in two pieces as someone, somewhere chopped up the original. Later, during stints in Ipswich, Bath and London, Gainsborough developed a fluid, flatteringly easy style that was ideal for his well-heeled subjects, who posed in becoming postures painted in soft, evanescent colours. Examples of Gainsborough's later work include the particularly striking *Portrait of Abel Moysey, MP* (1771). Look out also for one of Gainsborough's specialities, his wonderful "**conversation pieces**", so called because the sitters engage in polite chitchat – or genteel activity – with a landscape as the backdrop.

ARRIVAL AND INFORMATION
SUDBURY

By train Sudbury train station is a 5–10min walk from the centre via Station Road.
Destinations Marks Tey, on the London to Colchester line (hourly; 20min).
By bus Sudbury bus station is on Hamilton Rd, just south of Market Hill. The main local bus company is H.C. Chambers (☎ 01787 375360, ⓦ chambersbus.co.uk).
Destinations Bury St Edmunds (Mon–Sat hourly; 1hr 10min); Colchester (Mon–Sat hourly; 50min); Lavenham (Mon–Sat hourly; 35min); Stoke-by-Nayland (Mon–Sat hourly; 30min).

Tourist office Inside the library, on Market Hill (April–Sept Mon–Fri 9am–5pm, Sat 10am–4.45pm; Oct–March Mon–Fri 9am–5pm, Sat 10am–2.45pm; ☎ 01787 881320, ⓦ sudburytowncouncil.co.uk).

EATING AND DRINKING

Black Adder Brewery Tap 21 East St ☎ 01787 370876, ⓦ blackaddertap.co.uk. Enjoyable neighbourhood pub where the big deal is the beer – a rotating selection of real ales on draught, but always including something from Mauldons, a local brewer. There's a courtyard patio and pub grub. Mon–Thurs 11am–11pm, Fri & Sat 11am–midnight, Sun noon–10.30pm.

The Secret Garden 21 Friars St ☎ 01787 372030, ⓦ tsg.uk.net. Cosy local tearoom in a very old building, where the sophisticated menu has lots of French flourishes and they do their best to source locally. For lunch, try their ham, spinach and cheddar cheese on focaccia for around £10; dinner might include a seared sea bass fillet or grilled duck breast. Mon–Sat 9am–5pm, plus Fri & Sat 7–9.30pm.

Lavenham

LAVENHAM, eight miles northeast of Sudbury, was once a centre of the region's wool trade and is now one of the most visited villages in Suffolk, thanks to its unrivalled ensemble of perfectly preserved half-timbered houses. In outward appearance at least, the whole place has changed little since the demise of the wool industry, owing in part to a zealous local preservation society, which has carefully maintained the village's antique appearance. Lavenham is at its most beguiling in the triangular **Market Place**, an airy spot flanked by pastel-painted, medieval dwellings whose beams have been warped into all sorts of wonky angles by the passing of the years.

Guildhall of Corpus Christi

Market Place • Jan to early March Sat & Sun 11am–4pm; mid- to late March Wed–Sun 11am–4pm; April–Oct daily 11am–5pm; Nov & Dec Thurs–Sun 11am–4pm • NT • £5.35 • ☎ 01787 247646, ⓦ nationaltrust.org.uk/lavenham-guildhall

On the Market Place you'll find the village's most celebrated building, the lime-washed, timber-framed **Guildhall of Corpus Christi**, erected in the sixteenth century as the headquarters of one of Lavenham's four guilds. In the much-altered interior (used successively as a prison and workhouse), there are modest exhibitions on timber framed buildings, medieval guilds, village life and the wool industry, though most visitors soon end up in the walled garden or the teashop next door.

ARRIVAL AND INFORMATION   LAVENHAM

By bus Buses pull in at the corner of Water and Church streets, a 5min walk from Market Place. Among several services, perhaps the most useful is Chambers bus #753 (ⓦ chambersbus.co.uk), which links Lavenham with Sudbury, Bury St Edmunds and Colchester.
Destinations Bury St Edmunds (Mon–Sat hourly; 40min);

Colchester (Mon–Sat hourly; 1hr 30min); Sudbury (Mon–Sat hourly, 35min).
Tourist office Lady St, just south of Market Place (mid-March to Oct daily 10am–4.45pm; Nov to mid-Dec daily 11am–3pm; Jan to mid-March Sat & Sun 11am–3pm; ☎ 01787 248207, ⓦ heartofsuffolk.co.uk).

ACCOMMODATION AND EATING

★The Great House Market Place ☎ 01787 247431, ⓦ greathouse.co.uk. Delightful, family-run hotel bang in the centre of the village. Each of the five guest rooms is decorated in a thoughtful and tasteful manner, amalgamating the original features of the old – very old – house with the new. Deeply comfortable beds and a great breakfast round it all off. The hotel restaurant specializes in classic French cuisine, with both set meals and à la carte. Main courses start at £20. Food served Wed–Sun noon–2.30pm, Tues–Sat 7–10.30pm. **£125**

★Swan Hotel High St ☎ 01787 247477,

ⓦ theswanatlavenham.co.uk. This excellent hotel is a veritable rabbit warren of a place, its nooks and crannies dating back several hundred years. There's a lovely, very traditional, lounge to snooze in, a courtyard garden, an authentic Elizabethan Wool Hall and a wood-panelled bar. Just as appealing, most of the comfy guest rooms abound in original features and the restaurant is first-rate too, serving imaginative British-based cuisine – roasted wood pigeon and puy lentils for example – with mains starting at around £16. Restaurant daily 7–9pm; brasserie daily noon–2.30pm & 5.30–9pm. **£180**

Ipswich

IPSWICH, situated at the head of the Orwell estuary, was a rich trading port in the Middle Ages, but its appearance today is mainly the result of a revival of fortunes in the Victorian era – give or take some clumsy postwar development. The two surviving reminders of old Ipswich – **Christchurch Mansion** and the splendid **Ancient House** – plus the recently renovated **quayside** are all reason enough to spend at least an afternoon here, and there's also the **Cornhill**, the ancient Saxon marketplace and still the town's focal point, an agreeable urban space flanked by a bevy of imposing Victorian edifices – the Italianate town hall, the old Neoclassical Post Office and the grandiose pseudo-Jacobean Lloyds building.

Ancient House

30 Buttermarket, at corner of St Stephen's Lane • Lakeland store: Mon–Sat 9am–5.30pm

From Cornhill, it's just a couple of minutes' walk southeast to Ipswich's most famous building, the **Ancient House**, whose exterior was decorated around 1670 in extravagant style, a riot of pargeting and stucco work that together make it one of the finest examples of Restoration artistry in the country. The house is now a branch of the Lakeland housewares chain, and as such you're free to take a peek inside to view yet more of the decor, including its hammerbeam roof.

Christchurch Mansion

Soane St • Tues–Sun 10am–5pm • Free • ☎ 01473 433554, ⓦ www.cimuseums.org.uk

Christchurch Mansion is a handsome, if much-restored Tudor building, sporting seventeenth-century Dutch-style gables and set in 65 acres of parkland – an area larger than the town centre itself. The labyrinthine interior is worth exploring, with period furnishings and a good assortment of paintings by Constable and Gainsborough, both inside the main building and in the attached **Wolsey Art Gallery**.

The Wet Dock

Neptune Quay, half a mile south of Cornhill

The **Wet Dock** was the largest dock in Europe when it opened in 1845. Today, after an imaginative refurbishment, it's flanked by apartments and offices, pubs, hotels and restaurants, many converted from the old marine warehouses. Walking around the Wet Dock is a pleasant way to pass an hour or so – look out, in particular, for the proud Neoclassical **Customs House**.

ARRIVAL AND INFORMATION   IPSWICH

By train Ipswich train station is on the south bank of the River Orwell, about 10min walk from Cornhill along Princes Street.
Destinations Bury St Edmunds (hourly; 35min); Cambridge (hourly; 1hr 20min); Colchester (every 30min; 20min); Ely (every 2hr; 1hr); London Liverpool Street (every 30min; 1hr); Norwich (every 30min; 40min).
By bus There are two bus stations: the Cattle Market bus

station, a 5min walk south of Cornhill on Turret Lane, has long-distance and regional services (ⓦ suffolkonboard .com) and the second, Tower Ramparts, immediately north of Cornhill, has local services.
Destinations Aldeburgh (Mon–Sat hourly; 1hr 30min); Orford (Mon–Sat every 1–2hr; 1hr 50min; change at Rendlesham).
Tourist office St Stephen's Church, St Stephens Lane (Mon–Sat 9am–5pm; ☎ 01473 258070, ⓦ allaboutipswich.com).

ACCOMMODATION

Salthouse Harbour Hotel Neptune Quay ☎ 01473 226789, ⓦ salthouseharbour.co.uk. Housed in an imaginatively converted old warehouse down on the quayside, this is the city's best choice, with 70 large,

modern and minimalist-style rooms whose floor-to-ceiling windows look out over Ipswich's harbour. Depending on demand, rates can go up to more than £200. **£140**

EATING AND DRINKING

Aqua Eight 8 Lion St ☎01473 218989, ⓦaquaeight.com. Cool Asian fusion restaurant right in the heart of town. Most mains go for £10–12, but you can't go wrong with the superb steamed silver cod with ginger and scallions in soya sauce for £18.50. It also has a great bar serving good oriental-style meze and finger food. Tues–Thurs noon–2.30pm & 7–10pm, Fri & Sat noon–2.30pm & 5.30–11pm, Sun 5.30–10pm.

The Eaterie Salthouse Harbour Hotel ☎01473 226789, ⓦsalthouseharbour.co.uk. The restaurant lives up to the hotel's high standards (see opposite), with curvy banquettes and a low-lit, warehousey feel. The food is hearty rather than healthy, but served with a flourish and a good eye to detail. There are usually a few specials on the board too; generally starters are £5.95–8.95, mains £12.95–16.95. Daily noon–10pm.

The Suffolk coast

The **Suffolk coast** feels detached from the rest of the county: the main road and rail lines from Ipswich to the seaport of Lowestoft funnel traffic a few miles inland for most of the way, and patches of marsh and woodland make the separation still more complete. The coast has long been plagued by erosion and this has contributed to the virtual extinction of the local fishing industry, and, in the case of **Dunwich**, almost destroyed the whole town. What is left, however, is undoubtedly one of the most unspoilt shorelines in the country – if, that is, you set aside the Sizewell nuclear power station. Highlights include the sleepy isolation of minuscule **Orford** and several genteel resorts, most notably **Southwold** and **Aldeburgh**, which have both evaded the lurid fate of so many English seaside towns. There are scores of delightful **walks** around here too, easy routes along the coast that are best followed with either the appropriate *OS Explorer Map* or the simplified footpath maps available at most tourist offices. The Suffolk coast is also host to East Anglia's most compelling cultural gathering, the three-week-long **Aldeburgh Festival**, which takes place every June.

7

GETTING AROUND   THE SUFFOLK COAST

By public transport Getting around the Suffolk coast requires planning; work out your route in advance on ⓦtravelineeastanglia.org.uk or ⓦsuffolkonboard.com. Some journeys are straightforward – there is, for example, a regular bus from Ipswich to Aldeburgh – but some are more complicated: to get from Southwold to Aldeburgh, for instance, you catch the bus to Halesworth, the train from Halesworth to Saxmundham and then another bus to Aldeburgh, which all in all takes at least a couple of hours.

Sutton Hoo

Tranmer House • Beside the B1083, to the southeast of Woodbridge: follow the signs from the A12 • Exhibition Hall: Jan to early March, Nov & Dec Sat & Sun 11am–4pm, plus additional opening during school holidays; mid-March to Oct daily 10.30am–5pm • £7.50; NT • ☎01394 389700, ⓦnationaltrust.org.uk/Sutton-hoo • No public transport

In 1939, a local farmer-cum-archeologist by the name of Basil Brown investigated one of a group of burial mounds on a sandy ridge at **Sutton Hoo**, on a remote part of the Suffolk coast between Ipswich and Orford. Much to everyone's amazement, including his own, he unearthed the forty-oar burial ship of an Anglo-Saxon warrior king, packed with his most valuable possessions, from a splendid iron and tinted-bronze helmet through to his intricately worked gold and jewelled ornaments. Much of the Sutton Hoo treasure is now in London's British Museum (see p.74), but a scattering of artefacts can be seen in the **Sutton Hoo exhibition hall**, which explains the history and significance of the finds. Afterwards, you can wander out onto the burial site itself, about 500 yards away.

Orford

On the far side of the Tunstall Forest, some twenty miles from Ipswich, two medieval buildings dominate the tiny, eminently appealing village of **ORFORD**. The more impressive is the twelfth-century **castle** (April–Oct daily 10am–5pm; Nov–March Sat & Sun 10am–4pm; £6; EH; ⓦenglish-heritage.org.uk), built on high ground by Henry II, and under siege within months of its completion from Henry's rebellious sons. Most of the castle disappeared centuries ago, but the lofty keep remains, its striking stature hinting at the scale of the original fortifications. Orford's other medieval edifice is **St Bartholomew's church**, where Benjamin Britten premiered his most successful children's work, *Noye's Fludde*, as part of the 1958 Aldeburgh Festival.

Orford Ness National Nature Reserve

Boat trips Mid-April to late June & Oct Sat only; July to Sept Tues–Sat; outward boats 10am–2pm, last boat back 5pm • £9; NT • ☎01728 648024, ⓦ nationaltrust.org.uk/orford-ness

From the top of the castle keep, there's a great view across **Orford Ness National Nature Reserve**, a six-mile-long shingle spit that has all but blocked Orford from the sea since Tudor times. The National Trust offers **boat trips** across to the Ness from Orford Quay, 400yds down the road from the church – and a five-mile hiking trail threads its way along the spit. En route, the trail passes a string of abandoned military buildings, where some of the pioneer research on radar and atomic weapons testing was carried out.

ARRIVAL AND DEPARTURE   ORFORD

By bus There's a long-winded bus service between Orford and Ipswich (Mon–Sat every 1–2hr; 1hr 50min; change at Rendlesham) and a speedier bus service to Aldeburgh (Mon–Sat hourly; 1hr; change at Rendlesham).

ACCOMMODATION AND EATING

Butley Orford Oysterage Market Hill ☎01394 450277, ⓦpinneysoforford.co.uk. A local institution, dishing up great fish and seafood, much of it caught and smoked locally and served in this simple café/restaurant. Hours vary, but usually Mon–Fri 10am–4.30pm, Sat 9am–4.30pm & Sun 10am–4pm.

★**Crown & Castle** Market Hill ☎01394 450205, ⓦ crownandcastle.co.uk. Orford's gentle, unhurried air is best experienced by staying overnight at this outstanding hotel, with eighteen stylish guest rooms (breakfast included), and an excellent restaurant. Local, seasonal ingredients are the focus – rump of Suffolk lamb with broad-bean cream sauce for example – with mains around £20. Food served 12.15–2pm & 6.45–9pm. £205

Aldeburgh

Well-heeled **ALDEBURGH**, a small seaside town just along the coast from Orford, is best known for its annual **arts festival**, the brainchild of composer **Benjamin Britten** (1913–76), who is buried in the village churchyard alongside the tenor Peter Pears, his lover and musical collaborator. They lived by the seafront in Crag House on Crabbe Street – named after the poet, George Crabbe, who provided Britten with his greatest inspiration (see box opposite) – before moving to a large house a few miles away.

Outside of June, Aldeburgh is a relaxed and low-key coastal resort, with a small fishing fleet selling its daily catch from wooden shacks along the pebbled shore. Aldeburgh's slightly old-fashioned/local shop appearance is fiercely defended by its citizens, who caused an almighty rumpus – Barbours at dawn – when Maggi Hambling's 13ft-high *Scallop* sculpture appeared on the beach in 2003. Hambling described the sculpture as a conversation with the sea and a suitable memorial to Britten; many disgruntled locals compare it to a mantelpiece ornament gone wrong.

Aldeburgh's wide **High Street** and its narrow side streets run close to the beach, but this was not always the case – hence their quixotic appearance. The sea swallowed much of what was once an extensive medieval town long ago and today Aldeburgh's oldest remaining building, the sixteenth-century, red-brick, flint and timber **Moot Hall**, which began its days in the centre of town, now finds itself on the seashore. Several **footpaths** radiate out from Aldeburgh, with the most obvious trail leading north along the coast to Thorpeness, and others going southwest to the winding estuary of the **River Alde**.

BENJAMIN BRITTEN AND THE ALDEBURGH FESTIVAL

Born in Lowestoft in 1913, **Benjamin Britten** was closely associated with Suffolk for most of his life. The main break was during World War II when, as a conscientious objector, Britten exiled himself to the USA. Ironically enough, it was here that Britten first read the work of the nineteenth-century Suffolk poet, George Crabbe, whose *The Borough*, a grisly portrait of the life of the fishermen of Aldeburgh, was the basis of the libretto of Britten's best-known opera, *Peter Grimes*, which was premiered in London in 1945 to great acclaim. In 1948, Britten launched the **Aldeburgh Festival** as a showpiece for his own works and those of his contemporaries. He lived in the village for the next ten years, during which time he completed much of his finest work as a conductor and pianist. For the rest of his life he composed many works specifically for the festival, including his masterpiece for children, *Noye's Fludde*, and the last of his fifteen operas, *Death in Venice*.

By the mid-1960s, the festival had outgrown the parish churches in which it began, and moved into a collection of disused malthouses, five miles west of Aldeburgh on the River Alde, just south of the small village of **Snape**. The complex, the **Snape Maltings** (wsnapemaltings .co.uk), was subsequently converted into one of the finest concert venues in the country and, in addition to the concert hall, there are now recording studios, galleries, a tearoom, and a pub, the *Plough & Sail*. The Aldeburgh Festival takes place every June for two and a half weeks. Core performances are still held at the Maltings, but a string of other local venues are pressed into service as well. Throughout the rest of the year, the Maltings hosts a wide-ranging programme of musical and theatrical events. For more information, contact **Aldeburgh Music** (☎01728 687110, waldeburgh.co.uk), which operates two box offices, one at Snape Maltings, the other in Aldeburgh, at 152 High Street. **Tickets** for the Aldeburgh Festival usually go on sale to the public towards the end of March, and sell out fast for the big name recitals.

ARRIVAL AND INFORMATION
ALDEBURGH

By bus Buses to Aldeburgh pull in along the High Street. Destinations Ipswich (Mon–Sat hourly; 1hr 30min); Saxmundham train station (Mon–Sat hourly; 30min).

Tourist office 48 High Street (April–Oct Mon–Sat 10am–5pm & Sun noon–4pm; Nov–March Mon–Sat 10am–3pm; ☎01728 453637, wsuffolkcoastal.gov.uk/tourism).

ACCOMMODATION

Brudenell The Parade ☎01728 452071, wbrudenellhotel.co.uk. This bright and smart seafront hotel has something of a New England feel that sits very comfortably here in Aldeburgh. There's a pleasant sitting room downstairs with sea views and the bedrooms are thoughtfully furnished in a contemporary style. **£190**

★**Ocean House B&B** 25 Crag Path ☎01728 452094, woceanhousealdeburgh.co.uk. In an immaculately maintained Victorian dwelling right on the seafront in the centre of town, *Ocean House* has just three traditional, en-suite guest rooms including a top-floor suite. The English breakfasts, with home-made bread, are delicious. **£100**

EATING AND DRINKING

★**Aldeburgh Fish & Chip Shop** 226 High St ☎01728 454685, waldeburghfishandchips.co.uk. One of Aldeburgh's two outstanding chippies – this is the original, doing takeaway only; most people wander down to the seafront to nibble away there. Tues & Wed noon–2pm, Thurs noon–2pm & 5–8pm, Fri & Sat noon–2pm & 5–9pm, Sun noon–2.30pm.

The Golden Galleon 137 High St ☎01728 454685, waldeburghfishandchips.co.uk. Sit-down fish-and-chip restaurant, sister to the *Fish & Chip Shop* down the road.

Mon–Wed & Fri noon–2pm & 5–8pm; Thurs noon–2pm; Sat noon–2.30pm & 5.30–8pm; Sun noon–7pm.

★**The Lighthouse** 77 High St ☎01728 453377, wlighthouserestaurant.co.uk. Aldeburgh's best restaurant, a relaxed, informal and always busy place in cosy premises. The menu favours locally sourced ingredients, featuring everything from burgers and fish and chips to the likes of venison tagine with couscous. Mains average around £12 at lunchtimes, more in the evening. Daily: coffee: 10am–noon; lunch: noon–2pm; dinner: 6.30–10pm.

Dunwich

Tiny **DUNWICH**, about twelve miles up the coast from Aldeburgh, is probably the strangest and certainly the eeriest place on the Suffolk coast. The one-time seat of the kings of East Anglia, a bishopric and formerly a large port, Dunwich peaked in the twelfth century since when it's all been downhill: over the last millennium something like a mile of land has been lost to the sea, a process that continues at the rate of about a yard a year. As a result, the whole of the medieval city now lies under water, including all twelve churches, the last of which toppled over the cliffs in 1919. All that survives today are fragments of the Greyfriars monastery, which originally lay to the west of the city and now dangles near the sea's edge. For a potted history of the lost city, head for the **museum** (daily: April–Sept 11.30am–4.30pm; Oct noon–4pm; donation; ☎01728 648796, ⑩dunwichmuseum.org.uk) in what's left of Dunwich – little more than one small street of terraced houses built by the local landowner in the nineteenth century.

Dunwich Heath & Beach

Heath: daily 9am–9pm or dusk **NT shop & tearoom** April–Sept daily 10am–5pm; March & Oct Wed–Sun 10am–4pm; Nov–Feb Sat & Sun 10am–4pm • £4.50 for parking; NT • ☎01728 648501, ⑩nationaltrust.org.uk/dunwich-heath-and-beach

From Dunwich's seashore car park, it's possible to walk south along the coast and then cut inland up and over the dunes to **Dunwich Heath**, where heather and gorse spread over a slab of upland that is now owned by the National Trust. You can also drive here – the turning is clearly signed on the more southerly of the two byroads to Dunwich. The parcel of heath at the end of this byroad offers wonderful views over the coast and here also are a set of old coastguard cottages, which now accommodate a National Trust shop and tearoom.

Minsmere RSPB Nature Reserve

Reserve Daily 9am–9pm or dusk **Visitor centre** Daily 9am–5pm, 4pm in the depths of winter • £8 • ☎01728 648281, ⑩rspb.org.uk

From the coastguard cottages at Dunwich Heath, it's a twenty-minute walk south along the dunes and then inland to the **Minsmere RSPB Nature Reserve visitor centre**, though there's a road here too – just watch for the sign on the more southerly of the two byroads into Dunwich. The reserve covers a varied terrain of marsh, scrub and beach, and in the autumn it's a gathering place for wading birds and waterfowl, which arrive here by the hundred. The reserve is also home to a small population of bitterns, one of England's rarest birds. You can rent binoculars from the visitor centre and strike out on the trails to the birdwatching hides.

ARRIVAL AND DEPARTURE   DUNWICH

By bus Buses to Dunwich pull in beside the *Ship Inn*, just back from the coast.

Destination Aldeburgh (Mon–Sat every 1–2hr; 40min).

ACCOMMODATION

Dunwich Coastguard Cottages IP17 3DJ ☎0844 3351287, ⑩nationaltrustcottages.co.uk. The former coastguard cottages at Dunwich Heath now hold several very comfortable one- and two-bedroom apartments. These are available for rent, with a minimum two-night stay. Average weekly cost £650

EATING AND DRINKING

Flora Tea Rooms Dunwich beach ☎01728 648433. Right on the beach, this extremely popular café is a large hut-like affair, where they serve steaming cups of tea and piping hot fish and chips to an assortment of birdwatchers, hikers and anglers. Daily 11am–4pm.

Southwold

Perched on robust cliffs just to the north of the River Blyth, by the sixteenth century **SOUTHWOLD** had become Suffolk's busiest fishing port. Eventually, however, it lost most of its fishery to neighbouring Lowestoft and today, although a small fleet still brings in herring, sprats and cod, the town is primarily a seaside resort, a genteel and eminently appealing little place with none of the crassness of many of its competitors. There are fine

Georgian buildings, a long sandy beach, open heathland, a dinky harbour and even a little industry – in the shape of the Adnams brewery – but no burger bars and certainly no amusement arcades. This gentility was not to the liking of **George Orwell**, who lived for a time at his parents' house at 36 High Street (a plaque marks the spot), but he might well have taken a liking to Southwold's major music festival, **Latitude** (ⓦ latitudefestival .co.uk), which spreads over four days in the middle of July with happy campers grubbing down in Henham Park beside the A12 about five miles west of town.

Market Place and around

The centre of Southwold is its triangular, pocket-sized **Market Place**, sitting at one end of the town's busy High Street and framed by attractive, mostly Georgian buildings. From here, it's a couple of hundred yards north along Church Street to **East Green**, one of the several greens that were left as firebreaks after the town was gutted by fire in 1659. On one side of East Green is **Adnams Brewery**, on the other a stumpy old lighthouse. Close by is Southwold's architectural pride and joy, the **Church of St Edmund**, a handsome fifteenth-century structure whose solid symmetries are balanced by its long and elegantly carved windows.

The Sailors' Reading Room

East Cliff • Daily 9am–dusk • Free • No phone, ⓦ southwoldsailorsreadingroom.co.uk

From Market Place, it's a short stroll along East Street to a cliff-top vantage point, which offers a grand view over the beach. Also on the cliff is the curious **Sailors' Reading Room**, where pensioners gather to shoot the breeze in the mornings amid a room full of model ships, seafaring texts and vintage photos of local tars, all beards and sea boots.

Under the Pier Show

Southwold pier • Daily 9am–7pm, 5pm in winter• Free • ☏ 01502 7221055, ⓦ underthepier.com & ⓦ southwoldpier.co.uk

Jutting out from the beach, **Southwold pier** is the latest incarnation of a structure that dates back to 1899. Revamped and renovated a decade ago, the pier houses the usual – if rather more polite than usual – cafés and souvenir shops, but its star turn is the **Under the Pier Show**, where a series of knowingly playful machines, handmade by Tim Hunkin, provide all sorts of arcade-style sensory surprises, from the "Autofrisk" to the "Rent-a-Dog" and the mischievous (and emotionally rewarding) "Whack-a-banker".

The harbour

The **harbour**, at the mouth of the River Blyth, is an idyllic spot, where fishing smacks rest against old wooden jetties and nets are spread out along the banks to dry. From the mouth of the river, a footpath leads west to a tiny passenger **ferry** (April–Oct Mon–Fri 10am–12.30pm & 2–5pm, Sat & Sun 10am–5pm, but weekends only in early May & early Oct; 90p; ⓦ explorewalberswick.co.uk), which shuffles across the river to Walberswick. If you're heading back towards Southwold, however, keep going along the river until you pass the *Harbour Inn* and then take the path that leads back into town across **Southwold Common**. The whole circular walk takes about thirty minutes.

ARRIVAL AND INFORMATION   SOUTHWOLD

By bus Buses to Southwold pull in on the High Street just to the west of the town centre.

Destinations Halesworth train station, on the Ipswich to Lowestoft line (Mon–Sat hourly; 30min); Norwich (Mon–Fri 1 daily; 1hr).

Tourist office 7 Child's Yard, off High Street (April–Oct Mon–Fri 10am–5pm, Sat 10am–5.30pm, Sun 11am–4pm; Nov–March Mon–Fri 10.30am–3pm, Sat 10am–4.30pm; ☏ 01502 724729, ⓦ visit-sunrisecoast.co.uk).

ACCOMMODATION

The Crown 90 High St ☏ 01502 722275, ⓦ adnams .co.uk. The less upmarket (and less expensive) of Adnams'

two hotels in Southwold, with a dozen or so rooms above a bar/restaurant. Most of the rooms are large and have been recently refurbished with each decorated in a pleasant, contemporary style. **£150**

★**Home@21** 21 North Parade ☎01502 722573, ⓦhomeat21.co.uk. Near the pier, this seafront guesthouse occupies a well-maintained Victorian terrace house. There are three sympathetically updated guest rooms, two of which are en suite and two sea-facing. **£90**

The Swan Market Place ☎01502 722186, ⓦadnams .co.uk. Delightful if pricey hotel occupying a splendid Georgian building right at the heart of Southwold. The main building is a real period piece, its nooks and crannies holding all manner of Georgian details. Some of the guest rooms are here, others (the "Lighthouse Rooms") are in the more modern garden annexe at the back. **£185**

EATING AND DRINKING

★**The Crown** 90 High St ☎01502 722275, ⓦhotels .adnams.co.uk. Deluxe bar food featuring local, seasonal ingredients, all washed down with Adnams ales. Mains average around £16 and tables are allocated on a first-come, first-served basis. Food daily noon–2pm & 6–9pm, drinks till 11pm.

Lord Nelson East St ☎01502 722079, ⓦthelordnelson southwold.co.uk. This lively neighbourhood pub, with its low, beamed ceilings, has a first-rate locally inspired menu. Try, for example, the herring, Nelson smokes (smoked haddock and cod in sauce) or the dressed crab. Food daily noon–2pm & 7–9pm.

★**Tilly's** 51 High St ☎01502 725677. The pick of Southwold's several teashops, serving a great line in sandwiches and home-made cakes both inside and outside in the walled garden. Daily 9am–7pm.

Norwich

One of the five largest cities in Norman England, **NORWICH** once served a vast hinterland of East Anglian **cloth producers**, whose work was brought here by river and then exported to the Continent. Its isolated position beyond the Fens meant that it enjoyed closer links with the Low Countries than with the rest of England and, by 1700, Norwich was the second-richest city in the country after London. With the onset of the Industrial Revolution, however, Norwich lost ground to the northern manufacturing towns – the city's famous mustard company, Colman's, is one of its few industrial success stories – and this has helped preserve much of the ancient street plan and many of the city's older buildings. Pride of place goes to the beautiful **cathedral** and the sterling **castle**, but the city's hallmark is its medieval **churches**, thirty or so squat flintstone structures with sturdy towers and sinuous stone tracery round the windows. Many are no longer in regular use and are now in the care of the **Norwich Historic Churches Trust** (ⓦnorwich-churches.org), whose website describes each church in precise detail.

Norwich's relative isolation has also meant that the population has never swelled to any great extent and today, with just 230,000 inhabitants, it remains an easy and enjoyable city to negotiate. Yet Norwich is no provincial backwater. In the 1960s, the foundation of the **University of East Anglia** (UEA) made it much more cosmopolitan and bolstered its arts scene, while in the 1980s it attracted new high-tech companies, who created something of a mini-boom, making the city one of England's wealthiest. As East Anglia's unofficial capital, Norwich also lies at the hub of the region's **transport** network, serving as a useful base for visiting the Broads and as a springboard for the north Norfolk coast.

Cathedral

Tombland • Daily 7.30am–6pm • Free, but donation requested • ☎ 01603 218300, ⓦ cathedral.org.uk

Of all the medieval buildings in Norwich, it's the **Cathedral** that fires the imagination: a mighty, sand-coloured structure finessed by its prickly octagonal spire, it rises to a height of 315ft, second only to Salisbury Cathedral in Wiltshire. Entered via the Hostry, a glassy, well-proportioned visitor centre, the **interior** is pleasantly light thanks to a creamy tint in the stone and the clear glass windows of much of the **nave**, where the thick pillars are a powerful legacy of the Norman builders who began the cathedral in 1096. The nave's architectural highlight is the ceiling, a finely crafted affair whose delicate and geometrically precise fan vaulting is adorned by several dozen roof **bosses**.

PUBS, BARS & LIVE MUSIC
Fat Cat Freehouse	2
Kings Head	1
Micawbers Tavern	4
Ten Bells	3
Waterfront	5

CAFÉS & RESTAURANTS
The Last Wine Bar	2
Nazma	1
Tatlers	4
Window Coffee	3

ACCOMMODATION
38 St Giles	4
Gothic House	1
Maid's Head Hotel	3
Number 17	2

7

Pushing on down the south (right) side of the ambulatory, you soon reach **St Luke's Chapel** and the cathedral's finest work of art, the *Despenser Reredos*, a superb painted panel commissioned to celebrate the crushing of the Peasants' Revolt of 1381. Accessible from the south aisle of the nave are the cathedral's unique **cloisters**. Built between 1297 and 1450, and the only two-storey cloisters left standing in England, they contain a remarkable set of sculpted **bosses**, similar to the ones in the main nave, but here they are close enough to be scrutinized without binoculars. The dominant theme of the fabulously intricate carving is the **Apocalypse**, but look out also for the bosses depicting green men, originally pagan fertility symbols.

Cathedral precincts

Outside, in front of the main entrance, stands the medieval **Canary Chapel**. This is the original building of Norwich School, whose blue-blazered pupils are often visible during term time – the rambling school buildings are adjacent. A statue of the school's most famous boy, **Horatio Nelson**, faces the chapel, standing on the green of the **Upper Close**, which is guarded by two ornate and imposing medieval gates, **Erpingham** and, a few yards to the south, **Ethelbert**. Beside the Erpingham gate is a memorial to **Edith Cavell**, a local woman who was a nurse in occupied Brussels during World War I. She was shot by the Germans in 1915 for helping Allied prisoners to escape, a fate that made her an instant folk hero; her grave is outside the cathedral ambulatory. Both gates lead onto the old Saxon marketplace, **Tombland**, a wide and busy thoroughfare whose name derives from the Saxon word for an open space.

Elm Hill

Near the north end of Tombland is Elm Hill, a dinky cobbled street – more a gentle slope than a hill – where the quirky half-timbered houses still appeal despite the tourist crowds; **Wright's Court**, down a passageway at no. 43, is one of the few remaining enclosed courtyards that were once a feature of the city.

Market Place

The city's **Market Place** is the site of one of the country's largest open-air **markets** (closed Sun), with stalls selling everything from bargain-basement clothes to local mussels and whelks. Four very different but equally distinctive buildings oversee the market's stripy awnings, the oldest of them being the fifteenth-century **Guildhall**, a capacious flint and stone structure begun in 1407. Opposite, commanding the heights of the marketplace, are the austere **City Hall**, a lumbering brick pile with a landmark clocktower that was built in the 1930s in a Scandinavian style, and **The Forum**, a large and flashy, glassy structure completed in 2001. The latter is home to the city's main library and tourist office (see p.362). On the south side of Market Place is the finest of the four buildings, **St Peter Mancroft** (Mon–Sat 10am–3pm), whose long and graceful nave leads to a mighty stone tower, an intricately carved affair surmounted by a spiky little spire, whilst inside slender columns reach up to the delicate groining of the roof.

Back outside and just below the church is **Gentlemen's Walk**, the town's main promenade, which runs along the bottom of the marketplace and abuts the **Royal Arcade**, an Art Nouveau extravagance from 1899. The arcade has been beautifully restored to reveal the swirling tiling, ironwork and stained glass.

Castle Museum and Art Gallery

Castle Hill • Oct–June Mon–Sat 10am–4.30pm, Sun 1–4.30pm; July–Sept Mon–Sat 10am–5pm, Sun 1–5pm • £7.95 • ☎ 01603 493625, ⓦ museums.norfolk.gov.uk

Perched high on a grassy mound in the centre of town – and with a modern shopping mall drilled into its side – stern **Norwich Castle** dates from the twelfth century. Formerly a reminder of Norman power and then a prison, the castle now holds the **Castle Museum and Art Gallery**, where pride of place goes to the art galleries with their temporary displays and an outstanding selection of work by the **Norwich School**. Founded in 1803, and in existence for just thirty years, this school of landscape painters produced – for the most part – richly coloured, formally composed land- and seascapes in oil and watercolour, paintings whose realism harked back to the Dutch landscape painters of the seventeenth century. The leading figures were **John Crome** (1768–1821) – aka "Old Crome" – and **John Sell Cotman** (1782–1842), each of whom has a gallery devoted to their work.

The **castle keep** itself is no more than a shell, its gloomy walls towering above a scattering of local archeological finds and some gory examples of traditional forms of punishment. More unusual is a bloated model **dragon**, known as Snap, which was paraded round town on the annual guilds' day procession – a folkloric hand-me-down from the dragon St George had so much trouble finishing off. To see more of the keep, join one of the regular **guided tours** that explore the battlements and the dungeons.

University of East Anglia

UEA Campus Earlham Rd • Open access • Free • ☎ 01603 456161, ⓦ uea.ac.uk **Sainsbury Centre for Visual Arts** Tues–Fri 10am–6pm, Sat & Sun 10am–5pm • Free, but admission charged for some exhibitions • ☎ 01603 593199, ⓦ scva.org.uk • To get to the UEA campus by bus from the city centre, take #25 or #35 from Castle Meadow, or #25 from the train station

The **University of East Anglia** (UEA) occupies a sprawling campus on the western outskirts of the city beside the B1108. Its buildings are resolutely modern, an assortment of

concrete-and-glass blocks of varying designs, some quite ordinary, others like the prize-winning "ziggurat" halls of residence, designed by Denys Lasdun, eminently memorable. The main reason to visit is the **Sainsbury Centre for Visual Arts**, which occupies a large, shed-like building designed by Norman Foster. Well-lit and beautifully presented, the body of the permanent collection spreads out over the main floor, beginning with a substantial selection of non-European – particularly Asian and African – artefacts positioned close to some of the European paintings and sculptures they influenced and/or inspired.

ARRIVAL AND INFORMATION

By plane Norwich Airport (ⓦnorwichairport.co.uk) serves national and international destinations and is about 4 miles northwest of the city centre along the A140. There are regular buses to the city centre (20min) from the airport's Park and Ride.

By train Norwich train station is on the east bank of the River Wensum, a 10min walk from the city centre along Prince of Wales Road.

Destinations Cambridge (hourly; 1hr 20min); Cromer (hourly; 45min); Colchester (every 30min; 1hr); Ely (every 30min; 1hr); Ipswich (every 30min; 40min); London Liverpool Street (every 30min; 1hr 50min).

By bus Long-distance buses mostly terminate at the Surrey Street Station, from where it's around 10min walk north to the town centre. Some services also stop in the centre on Castle Meadow.

Destinations: Blakeney (hourly; 2hr); Cromer (2–3 hourly; 1hr 10min); Holt (hourly; 1hr 20min); London Victoria (every 2hr; 3hr 30min–4hr 15min).

Tourist office In the glassy Forum building overlooking Market Place (April–Oct Mon–Sat 9.30am–5.30pm, plus mid-July to mid-Sept Sun 10.30am–3.30pm; Nov–March Mon–Sat 9.30am–5.30pm; ☎01603 213999, ⓦvisitnorwich.co.uk).

ACCOMMODATION

38 St Giles 38 St Giles St ☎01603 662944, ⓦ38stgiles.co.uk. Billing itself as a cross between a B&B and a hotel, this deluxe establishment has five en-suite guest rooms of varying size and description, but all top quality. Great home-made breakfasts too. It's in a handy location, just a few yards from the Market Place. **£130**

★**Gothic House** King's Head Yard, Magdalen St ☎01603 631879, ⓦgothic-house-norwich.com. This particularly charming B&B occupies a slender, three-storey Georgian house down a little courtyard off Magdalen Street. The interior has been meticulously renovated in a period style and the two salon-style bedrooms are reached via the most charming of spiral staircases. The guest rooms are not attached to their bathrooms, but this really is no inconvenience. **£95**

Maid's Head Hotel Tombland ☎01603 209955, ⓦmaidsheadhotel.co.uk. Not everyone's cup of tea perhaps, but this chain hotel is delightfully idiosyncratic – a rabbit warren of a place with all sorts of architectural bits and pieces, from the mock-Tudor facade to the ancient, wood-panelled bar, though there is also a clumpy modern extension. The rooms are mostly large and very comfortable in a standard-issue sort of way, and the location, bang in the centre opposite the cathedral, can't be beat. If you are a light sleeper, you should avoid those rooms that overlook the street especially on the weekend. **£90**

Number 17 17 Colegate ☎01603 764486, ⓦnumber17norwich.co.uk. Family-run guesthouse with eight en-suite guest rooms decorated in a brisk, modern style with solid oak flooring; there are two larger family rooms as well. Good location, in one of the nicest parts of the centre. **£85**

EATING

The Last Wine Bar 76 St George's St ☎01603 626626, ⓦlastwinebar.co.uk. Imaginatively converted old shoe factory, a couple of minutes' walk north of the river, holding an unpretentious wine bar in one section and an excellent restaurant in the other. The food is firmly Modern British, with the likes of braised lamb shank with carrots and parsnips in a rosemary jus (around £15). Mon–Fri noon–2.30pm & 5pm–12.30am, Sat noon–2.30pm & 6pm–12.30am; kitchen closes 10.30pm.

Nazma 15 Magdalen St ☎01603 618701, ⓦnazmabrasseries.co.uk. The menu at this splendid and modern Indian restaurant covers all the classics, each prepared from scratch with the freshest of ingredients. Particularly strong on Bangladeshi cuisine. Eat in or takeaway. Mains around £9. Daily noon–2.30pm & 6pm–midnight.

Tatlers 21 Tombland ☎01603 766670, ⓦtatlersrestaurant.co.uk. Enticing contemporary restaurant, where they stick to local, seasonal ingredients when they can. The portions are a tad nouvelle, but there's a good wine cellar to compensate. Try the wood pigeon. Mains around £16. Tues–Sat noon–2pm & 6-9pm.

Window Coffee 25 Wensum St ☎07913 672491, ⓦthewindowcoffee.com. Odd little place – "little" being the operative word as it's billed as the smallest coffee shop in the world. It occupies the window of what was once a shop, and sells excellent coffee and cakes with a smile. Tues–Fri 8am–3pm & Sat 9am–3pm.

DRINKING

Fat Cat Freehouse 49 West End St ☎01603 624364, ⓦfatcatpub.co.uk. Award-winning pub with a friendly atmosphere and a fantastic range of well-kept, top-quality draught ales. Also a great range of bottled beers, ciders and perries. It's northwest of the city centre off the Dereham Road. Mon–Wed & Sun noon–11pm, Thurs–Sat noon–midnight.

★**Kings Head** 42 Magdalen St ⓦkingsheadnorwich .com. The perfect drinkers' pub with precious little in the way of distraction – there are certainly no one-armed bandits here. The outstanding selection of real ales is supplemented by an equally impressive range of bottled beers, most notably Belgian. The pub has just two smallish rooms, so you may need to be assertive to get served. Daily 11am–11pm.

Micawbers Tavern 92 Pottergate ☎01603 626627. Lodged in an old beamed building on one of the city's prettiest streets, this friendly, busy pub is a local par excellence, featuring an outstanding range of guest ales on draught. There's home-cooked food and Sports TV too. Daily 4pm till late.

Ten Bells 74 St Benedict's St at Ten Bells Lane ☎01603 920292, ⓦtenbellsnorwich.co.uk. Weird and wonderful place that attracts a weird and wonderful clientele, who hunker down among the old sofas and the rickety chairs with barely a light to illuminate proceedings. Lots of students and great cocktails. Mon–Thurs noon–midnight, Fri & Sat noon–1am & Sun noon–11.30pm.

NIGHTLIFE AND ENTERTAINMENT

Cinema City Suckling House, St Andrew's St ☎0871 902 5724, ⓦpicturehouses.co.uk. Easily the best cinema in town, featuring prime new releases plus themed evenings and cult and classic films. Also live feeds, a Kids' Club and regular late-night horror films.

Norwich Arts Centre 51 St Benedict's St ☎01603 660352, ⓦnorwichartscentre.co.uk. Popular rendezvous featuring everything from kids' theatre to world music.

Norwich Puppet Theatre Church of St James, Whitefriars ☎01603 629921, ⓦpuppettheatre.co.uk. Housed in a deconsecrated medieval church beside the busy Whitefriars roundabout, this long-established puppet theatre company has an outstanding reputation for the quality of its puppets and the excellence of its shows. Some performances are aimed at young children – who are simply enraptured – others are for adults.

Theatre Royal Theatre St ☎01603 630000, ⓦtheatreroyalnorwich.co.uk. This is the city's major performance venue, located in a clunky modern building with a capacious auditorium. It casts its artistic net wide, from World Music to opera.

Waterfront 139–141 King St ☎01603 508050,

7

THE NORFOLK BROADS

Three **rivers** – the Yare, Waveney and Bure – meander across the flatlands to the east of Norwich, converging on Breydon Water before flowing into the sea at Great Yarmouth. In places these rivers swell into wide expanses of water known as **"broads"**, which for years were thought to be natural lakes. In fact they're the result of extensive peat cutting – several centuries of accumulated diggings made in a region where wood was scarce and peat a valuable source of energy. The pits flooded when sea levels rose in the thirteenth and fourteenth centuries to create these **Norfolk Broads** (ⓦenjoythebroads.com), now one of the most important wetlands in Europe – a haven for many birds such as kingfishers, grebes and warblers – and one of the county's major tourist attractions. Looking after the Broads, the **Broads Authority** (ⓦbroads-authority.gov.uk) maintains a series of information centres throughout the region.

The Norfolk Broads are crisscrossed by roads and rail lines, but the best – really the only – way to see them is **by boat**, and you could happily spend a week or so exploring the 125 miles of lock-free navigable waterways, visiting the various churches, pubs and windmills en route. Of the many **boat rental** companies, Blakes (☎0844 8567060, ⓦblakes.co.uk) and Norfolk Broads Boating Holidays (☎01603 782207, ⓦbroads.co.uk), are both well established and have rental outlets at **Wroxham**, seven miles northeast of Norwich – and easy to reach by train, bus and car. Prices for cruisers start at around £700 a week for four people in peak season, but less expensive, short-term rentals are widely available too. **Houseboats** are much cheaper than cruisers, but they are, of course, static, or you can opt for a short **boat trip** at a string of Broads locations.

Trying to explore the Broads by car is pretty much a waste of time, but cyclists and walkers can take advantage of the region's network of footpaths and cycle trails. There are **bike rental** points dotted around the region and **walkers** might consider the 62-mile Weavers' Way, a long-distance footpath that winds through the best parts of the Broads on its way from Cromer to Great Yarmouth.

ⓦwaterfrontnorwich.com. This happening club and alternative music venue, which occupies what was once an old beer bottling plant, showcases some great bands, both big names and local talent, and offers club and DJ nights too. Schedule as per website.

North Norfolk coast

About forty miles from one end to the other, the **north Norfolk coast** is one of the UK's top tourist destinations, attracting a wide cross-section of the population to its long sandy beaches and seaside resorts. This stretch of coast begins (or ends) at **Cromer**, perhaps the most appealing of the larger resorts on account of its handsome setting, perched on the edge of blustery cliffs. A few miles to the west is another well-established resort, **Sheringham**, but thereafter the shoreline becomes a ragged patchwork of salt marshes, dunes and shingle spits trimmed by a string of charming villages, principally **Cley**, **Blakeney**, **Burnham Market** and **Wells-next-the-Sea**, all of which are prime targets for an overnight stay.

GETTING AROUND   NORTH NORFOLK COAST

Public transport along the north Norfolk coast is reasonable – no more. Without a car you'll be reliant on local buses to fill in the gaps between train stations.

By train There are hourly trains on the Bittern Line (ⓣ08457 484950, ⓦbitternline.com) from Norwich to Cromer and Sheringham.

By bus Easily the most useful bus is the Norfolk Coasthopper (ⓣ01553 776980 or ⓣ0871 200 2233, ⓦcoasthopper. co.uk), which runs along the coast between Cromer and King's Lynn via a whole gaggle of coastal towns and villages, including Blakeney, Sheringham, Wells and Burnham

Market. Frequencies vary on different stretches of the route and there are more services in the summer than in the winter, but on the more popular stretches buses appear every 30min or hourly, less frequently on Sundays. There are lots of different tickets and discounts; perhaps the most useful is the Coasthopper Rover, which provides unlimited travel on the whole of the route for either one-day (£9), three days (£18) or seven days (£32); tickets can be bought from the driver.

Cromer

Dramatically poised on a high bluff, **CROMER** should be the most memorable of the Norfolk coastal resorts, but its fine aspect has long been undermined by a certain shabbiness in its narrow streets and alleys. Things are at last on the mend, with new businesses arriving to add a touch of flair, and the town council keeps a string of cliff-top mini-parks and gardens in immaculate condition.

It's no more than the place deserves: Cromer has a long history, first as a prosperous medieval port – witness the tower of **St Peter and St Paul**, at 160ft the tallest in Norfolk – and then as a fashionable watering hole after the advent of the railway in the 1880s. There are three things you must do here: take a walk on the beach, stroll out onto the **pier**, and, of course, grab a **crab**: Cromer crabs are famous right across England and several places sell them, reliably fresh, and cooked and stuffed every which way.

ARRIVAL AND INFORMATION   CROMER

By train Cromer has managed to retain its rail link with Norwich; from Cromer station, it's a 5min walk into the centre. Destinations Norwich (hourly; 45min); Sheringham (hourly; 10min).

By bus Buses to Cromer, including the Norfolk Coasthopper (see above), stop on Cadogan Rd, on the western side of the

town centre.
Tourist office North Norfolk Information Centre is on the south side of the town centre on Louden Road (Jan to late May & Sept–Dec daily 10am–4pm; late May to Aug Mon–Sat 10am–5pm, Sun 10am–4pm; ⓣ01263 512497, ⓦvisitnorfolk.co.uk).

ACCOMMODATION

Cliftonville Hotel 29 Runton Rd ⓣ01263 512543,   ⓦcliftonvillehotel.co.uk. Among the big old mansions that line Runton Road just west of the town centre facing out to sea, this is the smartest, its grand Edwardian foyer equipped with an impressive double staircase and oodles of wood panelling. After the foyer, the rooms beyond can't help but seem a tad mundane, but they are large and most have sea views. **£120**

Virginia Court Hotel Cliff Ave ☎01263 512398, ⓦ virginiacourt.co.uk. The new owners of this medium-sized hotel are in the process of a major upgrade – and have started with what's most important: the beds are super comfy, the towels super thick, the duvets super warm and there's free wi-fi. The hotel dates back to Edwardian times, hence the capacious foyer with its wide, sweeping staircase, and the atmosphere is very much that of a traditional seaside hotel, friendly and relaxed. **£140**

EATING AND DRINKING

Mary Jane's Fish & Chip Shop 27 Garden St ☎01263 511208. Many Norfolk tourists are fastidious about their fish and chips, with allegiances strongly argued and felt. This basic, family-owned place is especially popular, for the lightness of the batter and the freshness of the fish. Eat in or take away. Daily from 11am.

Rocket House Café RNLI building, The Gangway ☎01263 519126, ⓦ rockethousecafe.co.uk. Offering sparkling views over the beach, pier and ocean from its giant windows – and from its blustery terrace – this café has the best location in town, though the food lacks subtlety – stick to the crabs and the salads (which start at just £4.50). Mon–Fri 9am–5pm, Sat & Sun 10am–5pm.

Virginia Court Hotel Cliff Ave ☎01263 512398, ⓦ virginiacourt.co.uk. Excellent hotel restaurant, where the emphasis is on local, seasonal ingredients – try, for example, the roast duckling with an orange and redcurrant jus. Mains average £14. Accommodation and dinner deals available. Daily: afternoon teas 2–5pm & dinner 6–8.30pm.

Salthouse

The tiny hamlet of **SALTHOUSE** may look inconsequential today, but the flocks of sheep that once grazed here provided a rich living for the lord of the manor. Today, the main evidence of this past wealth is the **church of St Nicholas**, an imposing and strikingly beautiful edifice stuck on top of a grassy knoll, its prominent position both a reminder to the faithful and a landmark for those at sea.

ARRIVAL AND DEPARTURE   SALTHOUSE

By bus The Norfolk Coasthopper bus (see opposite) pulls in beside The Green, a small triangular piece of grass beside the A149.

EATING AND DRINKING

Cookie's Crab Shack The Green ☎01263 740352, ⓦ salthouse.org.uk. Cookie's has something of a cult following, not for the decor, which is simple in the extreme, but for the freshness and variety of the seafood. Crabs, prawns and smoked fish lead the maritime way, but there's lots more to choose from including samphire, a local delicacy harvested from the surrounding mud flats and salt marshes from late June to mid-September. Daily. Oct–March 10am–4pm; April–Sept 9am–7pm.

Cley Marshes Nature Reserve

A149 • **Reserve** dawn to dusk • **Visitor Centre** daily: April–Oct 10am–5pm; Nov–March 10am–4pm • £4 • ☎01263 740008, ⓦ norfolkwildlifetrust.org.uk

Beside the A149, between Salthouse and Cley (see p.366), **Cley Marshes Nature Reserve**, with its conspicuous, roadside visitor centre, attracts birdwatchers like bees to a honey-pot. Owned and operated by the Norfolk Wildlife Trust (NWT), the visitor centre issues permits for entering the reserve, whose saltwater and freshwater marshes, reed beds and coastal shingle ridge are accessed on several footpaths and overseen by half a dozen hides.

Cley beach and Blakeney Point

Blakeney Point National Trust information centre April–Sept dawn to dusk • Free; NT • No phone, ⓦ nationaltrust.org.uk/blakeney

On the west side of the Cley Marshes Nature Reserve – and about 400 yards east of Cley village – is the mile-long byroad that leads to the shingle mounds of **Cley beach**. This is the starting point for the four-mile hike west out along the spit to **Blakeney**

Point, a nature reserve famed for its colonies of terns and seals. The seal colony is made up of several hundred common and grey seals, and the old lifeboat house, at the end of the spit, is now a National Trust **information centre**. The shifting shingle can make walking difficult, so keep to the low-water mark. The easier alternative is to take one of the **boat trips** to the point from Blakeney or Morston (see box opposite).

Cley

Once a busy wool port, **CLEY** (more formally **Cley-next-the-Sea** and pronounced "cly") is today little more than a row of flint cottages and Georgian mansions set beside a narrow, marshy inlet that (just) gives access to the sea. The sea once dipped further inland, which explains why Cley's fine medieval **church of St Margaret** is located half a mile to the south, at the very edge of the current village, overlooking the green. You're near a couple of splendid **nature reserves** here, both excellent destinations for birdwatchers – and don't miss the **Cley Smokehouse** for superb locally smoked fish.

ARRIVAL AND DEPARTURE CLEY

By bus The Norfolk Coasthopper bus (see p.364) stops outside the Picnic Fayre deli on Cley's main street (which is also the A149).

ACCOMMODATION AND EATING

★**Cley Mill B&B** Cley ☎01263 740209, ⓦcley windmill.co.uk. This outstanding B&B occupies a converted windmill that offers wonderful views over the surrounding marshes. The guest rooms, both in the windmill and the adjoining outhouses, are decorated in attractive period style and the best have splendid beamed ceilings; self-catering arrangements are possible as well. At peak times, there's a minimum two-night stay. The *Mill's* smart and very agreeable restaurant specializes in

traditional, home-made English cooking. Dinner is served at 7.30pm and a three-course set meal costs £32.50 per person. Advance reservations – by 10am of the same day – are required. **£159**

Cley Smokehouse High St, Cley ☎01263 740282, ⓦcleysmokehouse.com. Excellent, famed little place in an old forge on the main street, where they prepare delicious local oak-smoked fish – among other delicacies – to take away. Mon–Sat 9am–5pm, Sun 9.30am–4.30pm.

Blakeney and around

Delightful **BLAKENEY**, a mile or so west of Cley, was once a bustling port, but that was long before its harbour silted up and nowadays it's a lovely little place of pebble-covered cottages with a laidback nautical air. Crab sandwiches are sold from stalls at the quayside, the meandering high street is flanked by family-run shops, and footpaths stretch out along the sea wall to east and west, allowing long, lingering views over the salt marshes.

Blakeney **harbour** is linked to the sea by a narrow channel that wriggles its way through the salt marshes and is only navigable for a few hours at high tide. At low tide the harbour is no more than a muddy creek (ideal for a bit of quayside crabbing and mud sliding). Blakeney is also close to the charming ruins of **Binham Priory**.

ARRIVAL AND DEPARTURE   BLAKENEY

By bus Buses to Blakeney, including the Norfolk Coasthopper (see p.364) pull in at the Westgate bus shelter, a couple of minutes' walk from the harbour.

ACCOMMODATION AND EATING

Blakeney White Horse 4 High St ☎01263 740574, ⓦblakeneywhitehorse.co.uk. This well–regarded inn holds nine guest rooms kitted out in a bright and cheerful version of country-house style. The *White Horse* is also noted for its food. Great play is made of local ingredients, the bread is baked here daily, and they offer lunchtime snacks and à la carte suppers. Mains average £15. Food

served daily noon–2pm & 6–9.30pm. **£80**

King's Arms Westgate St ☎01263 740341, ⓦblakeneykingsarms.co.uk. The best pub in Blakeney by far, this traditional boozer, with its low, beamed ceilings and rabbit-warren rooms, offers top-ranking bar food (mains average £12), largely English but with an international zip. They also have seven, modest en-suite

---

BOAT TRIPS TO BLAKENEY POINT

Depending on the tides, there are **boat trips** to **Blakeney Point** (see p.365) from either Blakeney or **Morston quay**, a mile or so to the west. Passengers have a couple of hours at the point before being ferried back and also get the chance to have a close-up look at the seal colony just off the point. Some boat trips just offer the seal colony. The main **operators** advertise departure times on blackboards by Blakeney quayside; you can reserve in advance with Beans Boats (☎01263 740505, ⊛beansboattrips.co.uk) or Bishop's Boats (☎01263 740753, ⊛bishopsboats.co.uk). All boat trips cost £10.

---

bedrooms. Food served daily, lunch and dinner. **£80**
The Moorings High St ☎01263 740054, ⊛blakeney-moorings.co.uk. Informal, cheerful little bistro where the creative menu is particularly strong on Norfolk meat, fish

and shellfish. A typical main course might be sautéed lamb kidneys with pancetta and rosemary with a white bean ragout (£16.50). Tues–Sat 10.30am–9.30pm, Sun 10.30am–4.30pm.

Wells-next-the-Sea

Despite its name, **WELLS-NEXT-THE-SEA**, some eight miles west of Blakeney, is actually a good mile or so from open water. In Tudor times, before the harbour silted up, this was one of the great ports of eastern England, a major player in the trade with the Netherlands. Today, the port is a shadow of itself, but Wells is a popular coastal resort.

The town divides into three areas, starting with the **Buttlands**, a broad rectangular green on the south side of town, lined with oak and beech trees and framed by a string of fine Georgian houses. North from here, across Station Road, lie the narrow lanes of the town centre with **Staithe Street**, the minuscule main drag. Staithe Street leads down to the **quay**, a somewhat forlorn affair inhabited by a couple of amusement arcades and fish-and-chip shops, and the mile-long byroad that scuttles north to the **beach**, a handsome sandy tract backed by pine-clad dunes. The beach road is shadowed by a high flood defence and a tiny narrow-gauge **railway** that scoots down to the beach (Easter to October every twenty minutes or so from 10.30am; £1.30 each way).

ARRIVAL AND INFORMATION   WELLS-NEXT-THE-SEA

By bus Buses stop on Station Road, in between Staithe Street and the Buttlands; some also travel towards the quay. The town is on route of the Norfolk Coasthopper bus (see p.364).

Tourist office The volunteer-run tourist office is a few yards from the quay on Staithe Street (☎01328 710885, ⊛visitnorthnorfolk.com).

ACCOMMODATION

★**The Crown** The Buttlands ☎01328 710209, ⊛crownhotelnorfolk.co.uk. This enjoyable hotel occupies an especially attractive, three-storey former coaching inn with a handsome Georgian facade. Inside, the first batch of public rooms is cosy and quaint, all low ceilings and stone-flagged floors, and upstairs the dozen guest rooms are decorated in an imaginative and especially soothing style. **£140**
The Merchant's House 47 Freeman St ☎01328 711877, ⊛the-merchants-house.co.uk. Occupying one of the oldest houses in Wells, parts of which date back to the fifteenth century, this deluxe B&B has just two cosy, en-suite guest rooms. It's handily located, just

a couple of minutes' walk from the quayside. **£85**
Pinewoods Holiday Park Beach Rd; ☎01328 710439, ⊛pinewoods.co.uk. Behind a long line of pine-clad sand dunes that abut a splendid sandy beach, *Pinewoods* has been welcoming holiday-makers for over sixty years. It's a sprawling complex that holds touring and static caravans, beach huts, camping pitches and cosy wooden lodges. It is located about 15min walk from the quay and accessible via the narrow-gauge railway (see above). The camp and caravan pitches are open from mid-March to late October, the lodges from mid-March to December. Tariffs vary widely, but in high season a three-bed (six berth) lodge for a week costs around **£750**

EATING

The Crown The Buttlands ☎01328 710209, ⊛crownhotelnorfolk.co.uk. *The Crown* hotel (see above) prides itself on its food, with splendid takes on traditional

British dishes. Mains average around £16. Mon–Sat noon–2.30pm & 6.30–9.30pm, Sun noon–9pm.

7

7

Holkham Hall

Three miles west of Wells on the A149 • **Hall** April–Oct Sun, Mon & Thurs noon–4pm • **Park** April–Oct daily 9am–5pm; Nov–March pedestrians & cyclists only daily 9am–5pm or dusk • Hall £13, plus £2.50 parking (April–Sept) for hall & park • ☎ 01328 713111, ⓦ holkham.co.uk

One of the most popular outings from Wells is to neighbouring **Holkham Hall**, a grand and self-assured (or vainglorious) stately home designed by the eighteenth-century architect William Kent for the first earl of Leicester – and still owned by the family. The severe sandy-coloured Palladian exterior belies the warmth and richness of the interior, which retains much of its original decoration, notably the much-admired marble hall, with its fluted columns and intricate reliefs. The rich colours of the state rooms are an appropriate backdrop for a fabulous selection of **paintings**, including canvases by Van Dyck, Rubens, Gainsborough and Gaspar Poussin.

The **grounds** are laid out on sandy, saline land, much of it originally salt marsh. The focal point is an 80ft-high **obelisk**, atop a grassy knoll, from where you can view both the hall to the north and the triumphal arch to the south. In common with the rest of the north Norfolk coast, there's plenty of **birdlife** – Holkham's lake attracts Canada geese, herons and grebes, and several hundred deer graze the open pastures.

Holkham Bay

The **footpaths** latticing the Holkham estate stretch as far as the A149, from where a half-mile byroad – **Lady Anne's Drive** – leads north across the marshes from opposite the *Victoria Hotel* to **Holkham Bay**, which boasts one of the finest beaches on this stretch of coast, with golden sand and pine-studded sand dunes flanking a tidal lagoon. Warblers, flycatchers and redstarts inhabit the drier coastal reaches, while waders paddle about the mud and salt flats.

ARRIVAL AND DEPARTURE HOLKHAM HALL AND BAY

By bus The Norfolk Coasthopper (see p.364) stops beside the *Victoria Hotel* at the north entrance of the Holkham estate (about a mile from the house) and at the south end of Lady Anne's Drive, which leads (in about 5min) to Holkham Bay.

EATING

Old Bakehouse Tea Room 33 High St ☎ 01328 820454, ⓦ oldbakehousewalsingham.co.uk. In the centre of the village, this long-established tearoom offers a tasty range of home-made cakes, scones and soups plus top-ranking cream teas. Wed–Sun 10.30am–4.30pm.

Burnham Market and around

As you head west from Wells, it's about five miles along the coast to the pretty little village of **BURNHAM MARKET**, where a medley of Georgian and Victorian houses surrounds a dinky little green. The village attracts a well-heeled, north London crowd, most of them here to enjoy the assorted comforts of the *Hoste Arms* (see below) and/or hunker down in their second homes.

Straggling **BURNHAM THORPE**, a mile or so to the southeast of Burnham Market, was the birthplace of **Horatio Nelson**, who was born in the village parsonage on September 29, 1758.

ARRIVAL AND DEPARTURE BURNHAM MARKET AND AROUND

By bus The Norfolk Coasthopper bus (see p.364) stops beside the green on the Market Place in Burnham Market, but it does not pass through Burnham Thorpe.

ACCOMMODATION, EATING AND DRINKING

Hoste Arms Market Place, Burnham Market ☎ 01328 738777, ⓦ thehoste.com. One of the most fashionable spots on the Norfolk coast, this former coaching inn has been sympathetically modernized. The hotel's guest rooms are round the back and range from the small (verging on the cramped) to the much more expansive (and expensive). At the front, the *Hoste's* antique bar, complete with its wooden beams and stone-flagged floor, is merely a foretaste of the several, chi-chi dining areas beyond. Throughout, the menu is a well-balanced mixture of "land and sea", anything from wood pigeon with strawberries to cod in beer batter. Main courses average around £16 in the evening, slightly less at lunch. Daily noon–9.15pm. **£120**

Lord Nelson Walsingham Road, Burnham Thorpe ☎ 01328 738241, ⓦ nelsonslocal.co.uk. They have

kept modernity at bay here at this ancient village pub, from the old wooden benches through to the serving hatch and tiled floor. There's a good range of real ales plus above-average bar food – try, for instance, the Norfolk chicken breast wrapped in ham with a green-herb filling (£14). Mon–Sat noon–3pm & 6–11pm, Sun noon–10.30pm; food served: daily noon–2.30pm & 6–9pm.

Brancaster and around

From Burnham Market, it's a couple of miles west to **BURNHAM DEEPDALE**, which leads seamlessly into **BRANCASTER STAITHE** and then **BRANCASTER**, all three of which spread along the main coastal road, the A149. Behind them, to the north, lies pristine coastline, a tract of lagoon, sandspit and creek that pokes its head out into the ocean, attracting an extravagant range of wildfowl. This is prime **walking** territory and it's best explored along the Norfolk Coast Path as it nudges its way through the marshes which back up towards the ocean. Pushing on west from Brancaster, it's a mile or so more to minuscule **TITCHWELL**, with its handful of flint-walled houses, old stone cross and bird reserve.

Titchwell Marsh RSPB Nature Reserve

Titchwell · Daily dawn to dusk · Free, but £5 parking · **Information centre** Daily: March–Oct 9.30am–5pm; Nov–Feb 9.30am–4pm · ☎ 01485 210779, ⓦ rspb.org.uk

The old sea approaches to Titchwell harbour have now become the RSPB's **Titchwell Marsh Nature Reserve**, whose mix of marsh, reed-bed, mud-flat, lagoon and sandy beach attracts a wide variety of birds, including marsh harriers, bearded tits, avocets, gulls and terns. A series of footpaths explore this varied terrain, there are several well-positioned bird hides, including a super-duper Parrinder hide, and a very helpful shop-cum-information centre.

ARRIVAL AND DEPARTURE	BRANCASTER AND AROUND
By bus The Norfolk Coasthopper bus (see p.364) sticks to the main coastal road, the A149, as it travels through	Burnham Deepdale, Brancaster Staithe, Brancaster and Titchwell.

ACCOMMODATION, EATING AND DRINKING

★ **Titchwell Manor Hotel** Titchwell (A149) ☎ 01485 210221, ⓦ titchwellmanor.com. Facing out towards the salt marshes that roll down towards the sea, this large Victorian hotel is one of the most enjoyable on the Norfolk coast. There are nine guest rooms in the main building with more in the contemporary-style, courtyard complex round the back. Everything is high spec, from the top-quality duvets to the bespoke furniture. The menu is very British with traditional dishes superbly prepared – anything from fish and chips with mushy peas (£13) through to lobster thermidor with new potatoes. Food served daily noon–2.30pm & 6.30-9.30pm, plus snacks and light meals in-between times. **£180**

White Horse Brancaster Staithe ☎ 01485 210262, ⓦ whitehorsebrancaster.co.uk. This combined hotel, pub and restaurant backs straight onto the marshes, lagoons and creeks of the coast – and, even better, the North Norfolk Coast Path runs along the bottom of the car park. The hotel divides into two sections: there are seven en-suite rooms in the main building and eight more at the back with grass roofs. Brancaster is famous for its mussels and oysters, which you can try in the restaurant, or choose the local duck or beef (main courses average £16). Food served: daily noon–2pm & 6.30–9pm; also bar menu daily 11am–9pm. **£140**

King's Lynn

Straddling the canalized River Great Ouse just before it slides into The Wash, **King's Lynn** is an ancient port whose merchants grew rich importing fish from Scandinavia, timber from the Baltic and wine from France, while exporting wool, salt and corn. The good times came to an end when the focus of maritime trade moved to the Atlantic seaboard, but its port struggled on until it was reinvigorated in the 1970s by the burgeoning trade between the UK and the EU. Much of the old centre was demolished during the 1960s and as a result most of Lynn – as it's known locally – is not especially enticing, but it does have a cluster of especially handsome old **riverside buildings**, and its lively, open-air **markets** attract large fenland crowds.

Saturday Market Place and around

Behind the King's Lynn waterfront, the **Saturday Market Place**, the older and smaller of the town's two marketplaces, is a focal point of the old town. In addition to the Saturday market, it's home to Lynn's main parish church, **St Margaret's**, and the striking **Trinity Guildhall**, which has a wonderful, chequered flint-and-stone facade dating to 1421. Just across from the church is the former **Hanseatic Warehouse**, the most evocative of the medieval warehouses that survive along the quayside. Built around 1475, its half-timbered upper floor juts unevenly over the cobbles of St Margaret's Lane. A couple of minutes' walk north of the Saturday Market Place along Georgian Queen Street stands Lynn's finest building, the **Custom House**, which was erected beside Purfleet Quay in 1683.

King Street and around

Beyond the Custom House, **King Street** continues where Queen Street leaves off, and is perhaps the town's most elegant thoroughfare, lined with beautifully proportioned Georgian buildings. On the left, just after Ferry Lane, **St George's Guildhall** is one of the oldest surviving guildhalls in England. It was a theatre in Elizabethan times and is now part of the popular **King's Lynn Arts Centre** (29 King St; ⓦkingslynnarts.co.uk). At the end of King Street, the **Tuesday Market Place** is a handsome square surrounded by Georgian buildings and the plodding Neoclassical **Corn Exchange** (now a theatre); it hosts King's Lynn's main market on Fridays and, yes, Tuesdays.

ARRIVAL AND INFORMATION   **KING'S LYNN**

By train King's Lynn train station is about 500yds east of the town centre.
Destinations Ely (hourly; 30min); London King's Cross (hourly; 1hr 40min); Cambridge (hourly; 45min).
By bus The bus station is right in the centre just to the west of Railway Road. The Norfolk Coasthopper (see p.364)

begins (and ends) its journey at King's Lynn, putting a string of Norfolk destinations within easy reach.
Tourist office In the centre, down by the river at Custom House, Purfleet Quay (Mon–Sat 10am–5pm, Sun noon–5pm; Oct–March closes 4pm; ☎01553 763044, ⓦvisitwestnorfolk.com).

Ely

Perched on a mound of clay above the River Great Ouse about thirty miles south of King's Lynn, the attractive little town of **ELY** – literally "eel island" – was to all intents and purposes a true island until the draining of the fens in the seventeenth century. Until then, the town was encircled by treacherous marshland, which could only be crossed with the help of the local "fen-slodgers" who knew the firm tussock paths. In 1070, **Hereward the Wake** turned this inaccessibility to military advantage, holding out against the Normans and forcing William the Conqueror to undertake a prolonged siege – and finally to build an improvised road floated on bundles of sticks. Centuries later, the Victorian writer Charles Kingsley resurrected this obscure conflict in his novel *Hereward the Wake*. He presented the protagonist as the Last of the English who "never really bent their necks to the Norman yoke and … kept alive those free institutions which were the germs of our British liberty" – a heady mixture of nationalism and historical poppycock that went down a storm.

Since then, Ely has been associated with Hereward, which is more than a little ridiculous as Ely is, above all else, a Norman town: it was the Normans who built the **cathedral**, a towering structure visible for miles across the flat fenland landscape and Ely's principal sight. The rest of Ely is at its busiest to the immediate north of the cathedral on the **High Street**, a slender thoroughfare lined with old-fashioned shops, and at its prettiest down by the **river**, a relaxing spot with a riverside footpath and a tearoom or two. Ely is also within easy driving distance of an undrained and unmolested chunk of fenland, the National Trust's **Wicken Fen**.

Ely Cathedral

June–Sept daily 7am–7pm; Oct–May Mon–Sat 7am–6.30pm, Sun 7am–5pm • Mon–Sat £6.50, Sun free; Mon–Sat fee includes a ground-floor tour, but octagon tours cost an extra £7.50, £9 on Sun (reserve ahead) • ☎ 01353 667735, ⓦ elycathedral.org

Ely Cathedral is one of the most impressive churches in England, but the west facade, where visitors enter, has been an oddly lopsided affair ever since one of the transepts collapsed in a storm in 1701. Nonetheless, the remaining transept, which was completed in the 1180s, is an imposing structure, its dog-tooth windows, castellated towers and blind arcading possessing all the rough, almost brutal charm of the Normans.

The first things to strike you as you enter the **nave** are the sheer length of the building and the lively nineteenth-century painted ceiling, largely the work of amateur volunteers. The nave's procession of plain late Norman arches leads to the architectural feature that makes Ely so special, the **octagon** – the only one of its kind in England – built in 1322 to replace the collapsed central tower. Its construction, employing the largest oaks available in England to support some four hundred tons of glass and lead, remains one of the wonders of the medieval world, and the effect, as you look up into this Gothic dome, is simply breathtaking. When the central tower collapsed, it fell eastwards onto the **choir**, the first three bays of which were rebuilt at the same time as the octagon in the Decorated style – in contrast to the plainer Early English of the choir bays beyond. The other marvel is the **Lady Chapel**, a separate building accessible via the north transept. It lost its sculpture and its stained glass during the Reformation, but its fan vaulting remains, an exquisite example of English Gothic. The south triforium near the main entrance holds the **Stained Glass Museum** (Mon–Sat 10.30am–5pm, Sun noon–4.30pm; £4.50; ⓦ stainedglassmuseum.com), an Anglican money-spinner that exhibits examples of this applied art from 1200 to the 1970s.

Oliver Cromwell's House

29 St Mary's St • April–Oct daily 10am–5pm; Nov–March Mon–Fri & Sun 11am–4pm, Sat 10am–5pm • £4.90 • ☎ 01353 662062, ⓦ visitely.org.uk

Near the cathedral is **Oliver Cromwell's House**, a timber-framed former vicarage that holds a small exhibition on the Protector's ten-year sojourn in Ely, when he was employed as a tithe collector. The tourist office (see p.372) is here as well.

THE FENS

One of the strangest of all English landscapes, **the Fens** cover a vast area of eastern England from just north of Cambridge right up to Boston in Lincolnshire. For centuries, they were an inhospitable wilderness of quaking bogs and marshland, punctuated by clay islands on which small communities eked out a livelihood cutting peat for fuel, using reeds for thatching and living on a diet of fish and wildfowl. Piecemeal land reclamation took place throughout the Middle Ages, but it wasn't until the seventeenth century that the systematic draining of the Fens was undertaken – amid fierce local opposition – by the Dutch engineer **Cornelius Vermuyden**. Drained, the Fens now comprise some of the most fertile agricultural land in Europe – though at least **Wicken Fen** (see p.372) gives the flavour of what went before.

By train Ely lies on a major rail intersection, receiving direct trains from as far afield as Liverpool, Norwich and London, as well as from Cambridge. From the train station, it's a 10min walk to the cathedral, straight up Station Road and then Back Hill before veering right along The Gallery. Destinations Cambridge (every 30min; 20min); Ipswich (every 2hr; 1hr); King's Lynn (hourly; 30min); London King's Cross (every 30min; 1hr); Norwich (every 30min; 1hr).

By bus Buses stop on Market Street immediately north of the cathedral.

Destinations Cambridge (hourly; 1hr)

Tourist office In Oliver Cromwell's House, 29 St Mary's Street (April–Oct daily 10am–5pm; Nov–March Mon–Fri&Sun 11am–4pm, Sat 10am–5pm; ☎ 01353 662062, ⓦ visitely.org.uk).

ACCOMMODATION

Peacocks Tearoom 65 Waterside ☎ 01353 661100, ⓦ peacockstearoom.co.uk. After the success of their tearoom (see below), the owners of *Peacocks* have ventured into B&B, offering two comfortably furnished suites in the same riverside premises. The suites are kitted out in antique style – and very pleasant they are too. **£125**

29 Waterside B&B 29 Waterside ☎ 01353 614329, ⓔ info@29waterside.org.uk. Ely is short of places to stay, but this cosy B&B, in a pair of pretty little brick cottages dating back to the 1750s, helps remedy things. Several original features have been preserved, including the beamed ceilings, and the remainder has been sympathetically modernized. If the sun is out, breakfast can be taken in the garden. **£70**

EATING AND DRINKING

Peacocks Tearoom 65 Waterside ☎ 01353 661100, ⓦ peacockstearoom.co.uk. Down by the river, this popular tearoom serves a delicious range of cream teas, salads, sandwiches, soups and lunches with the odd surprise: try, for example, the chocolate zucchini cake. Also an enormous choice of teas from around the world. Wed–Sun 10.30am–5pm.

Wicken Fen National Nature Reserve

Lode Lane, Wicken • **Nature Reserve** Daily 10am–5pm or dusk **Dragonfly Centre** End May to end Sept Sat & Sun 11am–4pm • £6.15; NT • ☎ 01353 7202734 • ⓦ nationaltrust.org.uk/wicken-fen • No public transport

Wicken Fen National Nature Reserve, nine miles south of Ely, is one of the few remaining areas of undrained fenland and as such is an important wetland habitat. It owes its survival to a group of Victorian entomologists who donated the land to the National Trust in 1899. The seven hundred acres are undrained but not uncultivated – sedge and reed cutting are still carried out to preserve the landscape as it is – and the reserve is easily explored by means of several clearly marked **footpaths**. The reserve holds about ten birdwatching hides and is also one of the best places in the UK to see dragonflies.

Cambridge

On the whole, **CAMBRIDGE** is a much quieter and more secluded place than Oxford, though for the visitor what really sets it apart from its scholarly rival is "**The Backs**" – the green sward of land that straddles the languid River Cam, providing exquisite views over the backs of the old colleges. At the front, the handsome facades of these same colleges dominate the layout of the town centre, lining up along the main streets. Most of the older colleges date back to the late thirteenth and early fourteenth centuries and are designed to a **similar plan**, with the main gate leading through to a series of "courts," typically a carefully manicured slab of lawn surrounded on all four sides by college residences or offices. Many of the buildings are extraordinarily beautiful, but the most famous is **King's College**, whose magnificent **King's College Chapel** is one of the great statements of late Gothic architecture. There are 31 university colleges in total, each an independent, self-governing body, proud of its achievements and attracting – for the most part at least – a close loyalty from its students.

Note that most colleges have restricted **opening times** and some impose admission charges; during the exam period (late April to early June) most of them close their doors to the public at least some of the time.

CAMBRIDGE: TAKING A PUNT

Punting is the quintessential Cambridge activity, though it is, in fact, a good deal harder than it looks. First-timers find themselves zigzagging across the water and "punt jams" are very common on the stretch of the River Cam beside The Backs in summer. **Punt rental** is available at several points, including the boatyard at Mill Lane (beside the Silver Street bridge), at Magdalene Bridge, and at the Garret Hostel Lane bridge at the back of Trinity College. It costs around £25/hr to hire a punt (and most places charge a deposit), with up to six people in each punt. Alternatively, you can embark on a **chauffeured punt** from any of the rental places for about £18/hr per person.

King's College

King's Parade • Term time: Mon–Fri 9.30am–3.30pm, Sat 9.30am–3.15pm, Sun 1.15–2.30pm; rest of year: daily 9.30am–4.30pm • £7.50 including chapel • ☎ 01223 331100, ⓦ www.kings.cam.ac.uk

Henry VI founded **King's College** in 1441, but he was disappointed with his initial efforts. So, four years later, he cleared away half of the town to make room for a much grander foundation. His plans were ambitious, but the Wars of the Roses – and bouts of royal insanity – intervened and by the time of his death in 1471 very little had been finished and work on what was intended to be Henry's **Great Court** hadn't even started. This part of the site remained empty for no less than three hundred years and the Great Court complex of today – facing King's Parade from behind a long stone screen – is largely neo-Gothic, built in the 1820s to a design by William Wilkins. Henry's workmen did, however, start on the college's finest building, the much celebrated **King's College Chapel**, on the north side of today's Great Court.

King's College once enjoyed an exclusive supply of students from Eton and until 1851 claimed the right to award its students degrees without taking any examinations. The first non-Etonians were only accepted in 1873. Times have changed, however, and, if anything, King's is now one of the more progressive colleges, having been one of the first to admit women in 1972.

King's College Chapel

Opening times as for King's College • Entrance either via the main gatehouse on King's Parade or the North Gate, at the end of Senate House Passage

Committed to canvas by Turner and Canaletto, and eulogized in no fewer than three sonnets by Wordsworth, **King's College Chapel** is now internationally famous for its **boys' choir**, whose members process across the college grounds during term time in their antiquated garb to sing **evensong** (Mon–Sat at 5.30pm & Sun 3.30pm) and carols on Christmas Eve. The setting for the choristers is supreme, the chapel impossibly slender, its streamlined buttresses channelling up to a dainty balustrade and four spiky turrets, though the exterior was, in a sense at least, a happy accident – its design predicated by the carefully composed interior. Here, the high and handsome **nave** has an exquisite ceiling, whose fantail tracery is a complex geometry of extraordinary complexity and delicacy. The nave is flooded with kaleidoscopic patterns of light that filter in through copious stained-glass windows. Paid for by Henry VIII, the **stained glass** was largely the work of Flemish glaziers, with the lower windows portraying scenes from the New Testament and the Apocrypha, and the upper windows the Old Testament. Above the **altar** hangs Rubens' tender *Adoration of the Magi* and an exhibition in the side **chantries** puts more historical flesh on Henry's grand plans.

King's Parade

King's College dominates **King's Parade**, the town's medieval High Street, but the higgledy-piggledy shops and cafés opposite are an attractive foil to Wilkins' architectural screen. At the northern end of King's Parade is **Great St Mary's** (May–Aug

CAMBRIDGE

Mon–Sat 9am–5pm, Sun 12.30–5pm; Sept–April closes 4pm; free; ☎01223 462914, ⓦwww.gsm.cam.ac.uk), the university's pet church, a sturdy Gothic structure whose **tower** (£3.50) offers a good view of the surrounding colleges. Opposite the church stands **Senate House**, an exercise in Palladian classicism by James Gibbs, and the scene of graduation ceremonies on the last Saturday in June, when champagne corks fly around the rabbit-fur collars and black gowns.

Gonville and Caius College

Trinity St • No set opening hours • Free • ☎ 01223 332400, ⓦ cai.cam.ac.uk

The northern continuation of King's Parade is Trinity Street, a short way along which, on the left, is the cramped main entrance to **Gonville and Caius College**, known simply as Caius (pronounced "keys"), after the sixteenth-century co-founder John Keys, who latinized his name as was then the custom with men of learning. The design of the college owes much to Keys, who placed three gates on two adjoining courts, each representing a different stage on the path to academic enlightenment: at the main entrance is the **Gate of Humility**, through which the student entered the college; the **Gate of Virtue**, sporting the female figures of Fame and Wealth, marks the entrance to Caius Court; and the exquisite **Gate of Honour**, capped with sundials and decorated with classical motifs, leads onto Senate House Passage.

Clare College

Trinity Lane • Daily 10.45am–4.30pm • Summer £2; winter free • ☎ 01223 333200, ⓦ www.clare.cam.ac.uk

Senate House Passage continues west beyond Caius College's Gate of Honour en route to **Clare College**. Clare's plain period-piece courtyards, completed in the early eighteenth century, lead to one of the most picturesque of all the bridges over the Cam, **Clare Bridge**. Beyond lies the **Fellows' Garden**, one of the loveliest college gardens open to the public (times as college). Back at the entrance to Clare, it's a few steps more to the North Gate of King's College, beside King's College Chapel (see p.373).

7

Trinity College

Trinity St • **College** Daily 10am–4.30pm • £1 • ☎ 01223 338400, ⓦ trin.cam.ac.uk **Wren Library** Mon–Fri noon–2pm, plus Sat during term 10.30am–12.30pm • Free

Trinity College is the largest of the Cambridge colleges and its very long list of famous alumni includes John Dryden and Vladimir Nabokov; the Cambridge spies Blunt, Burgess and Philby; Aleister Crowley and Enoch Powell; Pandit Nehru, Bertrand Russell and Prince Charles.

A statue of Henry VIII, who founded the college in 1546, sits in majesty over Trinity's **Great Gate**, his sceptre replaced long ago with a chair leg by a student wag. Beyond lies the vast asymmetrical expanse of **Great Court**, which displays a superb range of Tudor buildings, the oldest of which is the fifteenth-century clocktower. The centrepiece of the court is a delicate fountain, in which, legend has it, Lord Byron used to bathe naked with his pet bear – the college forbade students from keeping dogs.

On the far side of the Great Court, walk through "the screens" – the narrow passage separating the Hall from the kitchens – to reach **Nevile's Court**, where Newton first calculated the speed of sound. The west end of Nevile's Court is enclosed by one of the university's most famous buildings, the **Wren Library**. Viewed from the outside, it's impossible to appreciate the scale of the interior thanks to Wren's clever device of concealing the internal floor level by means of two rows of stone columns. Natural light pours into the white stuccoed interior, which contrasts wonderfully with the dark lime-wood bookcases, also Wren-designed.

St John's College

St John's St • Daily: March–Oct 10am–5.30pm; Nov–Feb 10am–3.30pm • £5 • ☎ 01223 338600, ⓦ www.joh.cam.ac.uk

Next door to Trinity, **St John's College** sports a grandiloquent Tudor gatehouse, which is distinguished by the coat of arms of the founder, Lady Margaret Beaufort, the mother of Henry VII. Beyond, three successive courts lead to the river, but there's an excess of dull reddish brickwork here – enough for Wordsworth, who lived above the kitchens on F staircase, to describe the place as "gloomy". The arcade on the far side of Third Court leads through to the **Bridge of Sighs**, a chunky, covered bridge built in 1831 but in most respects very unlike its Venetian namesake. The bridge is best viewed from the much older – and much more stylish – Wren-designed bridge a few yards to the south. The Bridge of Sighs links the old college with the fanciful nineteenth-century **New Court**, a crenellated neo-Gothic extravaganza topped by a feast of dinky stone chimneys and pinnacles.

Magdalene College

Magdalene St • **College** Daily 10am–6pm • Free • ☎ 01223 332100, ⓦ www.magd.cam.ac.uk **Pepys Library** Jan to late March, Oct to mid-Dec Mon–Sat 2–4pm; late April to mid-Sept Mon–Fri 2–4pm & 11.30am–12.30pm & 1.30–2.30pm • Free

Founded as a hostel by the Benedictines, **Magdalene College** – pronounced "maudlin" – became a university college in 1542; it was also the last of the colleges to admit women, finally surrendering in 1988. The main focus of attention here is the **Pepys Library**, in the second of the college's ancient courtyards. Samuel Pepys, a Magdalene student, bequeathed his entire library to the college, where it has been displayed ever since in its original red-oak bookshelves. His famous diary is also parked here.

7

Jesus College

Jesus Lane • Daily 10am–5pm • Free • ☎ 01223 339339, ⓦ www.jesus.cam.ac.uk

The intimate cloisters of **Jesus College** are reminiscent of a monastery – appropriately, as the Bishop of Ely founded the college on the grounds of a suppressed Benedictine nunnery in 1496. Beyond the main red-brick gateway, much of the ground plan of the nunnery has been preserved, especially around **Cloister Court**, the first court on the right after the entrance and the prettiest part of the college, dripping with ivy and, in summer, overflowing with hanging baskets. Entered from the Cloister Court, the college **chapel** occupies the former priory chancel and looks like a medieval parish church, though in fact it was imaginatively restored in the nineteenth century, using ceiling designs by William Morris and Pre-Raphaelite stained glass. The poet Samuel Taylor Coleridge was the college's most famously bad student, absconding in his first year to join the Light Dragoons, and returning only to be kicked out for a combination of bad debts and unconventional opinions.

Sidney Sussex College

Sidney St • No set opening times • Free • ☎ 01223 338800, ⓦ www.sid.cam.ac.uk

The sombre, mostly mock-Gothic facade of **Sidney Sussex College** glowers over Sidney Street. The interior is fairly unexciting too, though the long, slender **chapel** is noteworthy for its fancy marble floor, hooped roof and Baroque wood panelling, as well as for being the last resting place of the skull of its most famous alumnus, Oliver Cromwell – though the exact location remains a closely guarded secret. Incidentally, neighbouring **Hobson Street** is named after the owner of a Cambridge livery stable, who would only allow customers to take the horse nearest the door, hence "Hobson's choice".

Christ's College

St Andrew's St • Daily 9.30am–4.30pm • Free • ☎ 01223 334900, ⓦ www.christs.cam.ac.uk

Close to Cambridge's central shopping area, the turreted gateway of **Christ's College** features the coat of arms of the founder, Lady Margaret Beaufort, who also founded St John's. Passing through First Court you come to the Fellows' Building, attributed to Inigo Jones, whose central arch gives access to the **Fellows' Garden**. The poet John Milton is said to have either painted or composed here, though there's no definite proof that he did either; another of Christ's famous undergraduates was Charles Darwin, who showed little academic promise and spent most of his time hunting.

Queens' College

Silver St, but visitors' gate on Queens' Lane • Mid-March to mid-May & late June to Sept daily 10am–4.30pm; Oct Mon–Fri 2–4pm, Sat & Sun 10am–4.30pm; Nov to mid-March daily 10am–4pm • £3 in summer, otherwise free • ☎ 01223 335511, ⓦ www.queens.cam.ac.uk

Queens' College is particularly beautiful, boasting, in the **Old Court** and the **Cloister Court**, two dream-like, fairytale Tudor courtyards: the first of the two is a perfect illustration of the original collegiate ideal, with kitchens, library, chapel, hall and rooms all set around a tiny green. Flanking Cloister Court is the Long Gallery of the President's Lodge, the last remaining half-timbered building in the university, and the tower where Erasmus is thought to have beavered away during his four years here, probably from 1510 to 1514. Equally eye-catching is the wooden **Mathematical Bridge** over the River Cam (visible for free from the Silver Street Bridge), a copy of the mid-eighteenth-century original, which – so it was claimed – would stay in place even if the nuts and bolts were removed.

The Fitzwilliam Museum

Trumpington St • Tues–Sat 10am–5pm, Sun noon–5pm • Free • ☎ 01223 332900, ⓦ www.fitzmuseum.cam.ac.uk

The **Fitzwilliam Museum** displays the city's premier fine and applied art collection in an imposing Neoclassical edifice, which was built to house the vast hoard bequeathed by Viscount Fitzwilliam in 1816. Since then, the museum has been gifted a string of private collections, most of which follow a particular specialism. The **Lower Galleries**, on the ground floor, contain a wealth of antiquities including Egyptian sarcophagi and mummies, fifth-century BC Greek vases, plus a bewildering display of early European and Asian ceramics and sections dedicated to armour, glass and pewterware. Temporary exhibitions are held on the ground floor too. The **Upper Galleries** contain an eclectic assortment of mostly eighteenth, nineteenth- and early twentieth-century European paintings and sculptures, with more modern pieces by Lucian Freud, David Hockney, Henry Moore, Ben Nicholson, Jacob Epstein and Barbara Hepworth.

Scott Polar Museum

Lensfield Rd • Tues–Sat 10am–4pm • Free • ☎ 01223 336540, ⓦ www.spri.cam.ac.uk

The pocket-sized **Scott Polar Museum** begins with a section devoted to the native peoples of the Arctic with an especially enjoyable collection of Inuit soapstone sculptures. It continues with pen sketches of the European explorers who ventured to both poles with varying degrees of success and it's here you'll find a substantial set of documents – original letters and incidental artefacts, etc – relating to the fateful expedition to the South Pole led by Captain Robert Falcon Scott (1868–1912), after whom the museum is named.

Cambridge University Botanic Garden

Main entrance: the Brookside Gate, corner of Trumpington Rd and Bateman St • Daily: Feb, March & Oct 10am–5pm; April–Sept 10am–6pm; Nov–Jan 10am–4pm • £4.50 • ☎ 01223 336265, ⓦ www.botanic.cam.ac.uk

Opened in 1846 and covering forty acres, the **Cambridge University Botanic Garden** has several glasshouses as well as bountiful outdoor displays. The outdoor beds are mostly arranged by natural order, but there's also a particularly interesting series of chronological beds, showing when different plants were introduced into Britain.

ARRIVAL AND INFORMATION	CAMBRIDGE

By plane Cambridge is just 30 miles north of London Stansted Airport; there are hourly trains between the two (30min).

By train Cambridge train station, in the middle of a redevelopment zone with tower blocks sprouting up all around it, is a mile or so southeast of the city centre, off Hills Road. From here, it's an easy if tedious 20min walk into the centre or take any one of several local (Citi) buses to Emmanuel Street.

Destinations Bury St Edmunds (hourly; 40min); Ely (every

30min; 15min); Ipswich (hourly; 1hr 20min); King's Lynn (hourly; 45min); London King's Cross (every 30min; 50min); London Stansted Airport (hourly; 30min); Norwich (hourly; 1hr 20min).

By bus The long-distance bus station is on the east side of the city centre on Drummer Street.

Destinations London Victoria (every 2hr; 2hr).

By car Arriving by car, you'll find much of the city centre closed to traffic and on-street parking well-nigh impossible to find, so most visitors plump for a park-and-ride car park; these are signposted on all major approaches.

Tourist office Handily located on Peas Hill, just off King's Parade (April–Oct Mon–Sat 10am–5pm, Sun 11am–3pm; Nov–March Mon–Sat 10am–5pm; ☎0871 226 8006, ⓦ visitcambridge.org).

GETTING AROUND

By bike Popular with locals and students alike, cycling is an enjoyable way to get around the city. Among a small army of bike rental outlets, one of the biggest is Station Cycles (ⓦ stationcycles.co.uk), which has three local stores including one in the city centre beneath the Grand Arcade shopping centre on Corn Exchange Street (☎01223 307655). Wherever you leave your bike, padlock it securely as bike theft is not infrequent.

7 ACCOMMODATION

Cambridge is light on central accommodation and those few **hotels** and **guesthouses** that do occupy prime locations tend to be expensive. That said, there is a cluster of less pricey places, including a YHA hostel, near the train station and another on Chesterton Lane and its continuation, Chesterton Rd, the busy street running east from the top of Magdalene St. In high season, when vacant rooms are often thin on the ground, the **accommodation-booking service** run by the tourist office can be very useful.

Best Western Plus Gonville Hotel Gonville Place ☎01223 366611, ⓦ gonvillehotel.co.uk. One of the better mid-range hotel choices in Cambridge, this recently refurbished 84-room establishment occupies a long and somewhat undistinguished building just set back off a busy main road. Proficient and efficient lodgings. **£180**

★**Doubletree by Hilton Cambridge** Granta Place, Mill Lane ☎01223 259988, ⓦ doubletree3.hilton.com. This is the city's most appealing hotel by a long chalk, occupying a stylishly designed 1960s building a couple of minutes' walk from the centre. The best rooms have balconies overlooking the river (though the views are hardly riveting); breakfasts are first-rate as you would expect at this price. The hotel is also home to a Marco Pierre White steakhouse. **£250**

Warkworth House Warkworth Terrace ☎01223 363682, ⓦ warkworthhouse.co.uk. Welcoming, family-run B&B with a handful of straightforward, bright and unfussy en suite rooms. In a substantial Victorian property a shortish walk southeast of the bus station off Parkside. **£85**

Worth House 152 Chesterton Rd ☎01223 316074, ⓦ worth-house.co.uk. Very recommendable B&B in a pleasantly upgraded Victorian house a 20min walk from the centre. All the bedrooms are decorated in a bright modern style and have generous en-suite bathrooms. Great breakfasts too. **£70**

YHA Cambridge 97 Tenison Rd ☎0845 3719728, ⓦ yha.org.uk/hostel/cambridge. This long-established but recently revamped hostel occupies a rambling Victorian house near the train station – Tenison Road is a right turn a couple of hundred yards down Station Road. Facilities include a laundry and self-catering, a cycle store, a games room and a small courtyard garden. There are just over one hundred beds in two- to six-bedded rooms and advance reservations are advised. Dorms **£16**, doubles **£45**

EATING

★**Aromi** 1 Bene't St ☎01223 300117, ⓦ aromi.co.uk. The furnishings and fittings may be standard–issue modern, but, oh my word, the food here at this little café is absolutely superb: they offer authentic Sicilian food – pizza slices, focaccia and cannolis, plus a hatful of other delights. Eat in or takeaway. Expect queues at peak times. Mon–Thurs 9am–5pm, Fri–Sun 9am–8pm.

Côte 21 Bridge St ☎01223 311053, ⓦ cote-restaurants.co.uk. One of a medium-sized but burgeoning chain, this informal, bistro–style restaurant has a justified reputation for the excellence of its French-based cuisine, featuring the likes of beef bourguignon and fish parmentier. Breakfast, lunch and dinner, where main courses average a very reasonable £14. Mon–Fri 8am–11pm, Sat 9am–11pm & Sun 9am–10.30pm.

Efe's 78 King St ☎01223 500005, ⓦ efesrestaurant-cambridge.co.uk. Long-established Turkish restaurant, where the decor may be uninspiring, but the chargrilled meats – the house speciality – are extremely tasty. Mains around £10. Mon–Fri noon–2.30pm & 6–11pm; Sat & Sun noon–11pm.

Michaelhouse Café Trinity St ☎01223 309147 ⓦ michaelhouse.org.uk. Good-quality café food – snacks, salads and so forth – in an attractively renovated medieval

church. Great, central location too. Mon–Sat 8am–5pm.
Rainbow Café 9a King's Parade ☎01223 321551, ⓦrainbowcafe.co.uk. Cramped but agreeable vegetarian restaurant with main courses – ranging from Jamaican roti cups to North African tagine – for around £10. Specializes in vegan and gluten-free food plus organic wines. Handy location, down an alley opposite King's College. Tues–Sat 10am–10pm, Sun 10am–4pm.

DRINKING

Champion of the Thames 68 King St ☎01223 351464. Gratifyingly old-fashioned central pub with decent beer and a student/academic crowd. Sun–Thurs noon–11pm, Fri & Sat 11am–11pm.
Eagle 8 Bene't St ☎01223 505020, ⓦgkpubs.co.uk. Owned and operated by Greene King, this ancient city-centre inn, with its antique appearance and cobbled courtyard, is associated with Crick and Watson who discovered DNA in 1953. It gets horribly crowded, but is still worth a pint of anyone's time – Greene King ales are reliably good. Mon–Sat 10am–11pm, Sun 11am–10.30pm.
★**Free Press** 7 Prospect Row ☎01223 368337,

ⓦfreepresspub.com. Classic, traditional and superbly maintained backstreet local with a great selection of real ales and single malts. Walled garden too. Just off Parkside. Mon–Thurs noon–2pm & 6–11pm; Fri & Sat noon–11pm; Sun noon–2.30pm & 7–10.30pm.
Live and Let Live 40 Mawson Rd ☎01223 460261. This smashing pub, in an old corner building among a battery of terrace houses, is the epitome of the traditional local – from the pot-pourri furnishings and fittings through to the wood-panelled alcoves. Mawson Road leads off Mill Road in between Parker's Piece and the train station. Mon–Fri 11.30am–2.30pm & 5.30–11pm; Sat 11.30am–2.30pm & 6–11pm; Sun noon–2pm & 7–10.30pm.

NIGHTLIFE AND ENTERTAINMENT

The **performing arts** scene is at its busiest and best during term time with numerous student drama productions, classical concerts and gigs culminating in the traditional whizzerama of excess following the exam season. The most celebrated concerts are those given by **King's College choir** (see p.373), though the choral scholars who perform at the chapels of St John's College and Trinity are also exceptionally good. The four-day **Cambridge Folk Festival** (ⓦcambridgefolkfestival .co.uk), one of the longest-running folk festivals in the world, takes place in neighbouring Cherry Hinton at the back end of July to early August. For upcoming events, the tourist office (see opposite) issues various free **listings** leaflets and brochures.

Arts Picturehouse 38–39 St Andrew's St ☎0871 902 5720, ⓦpicturehouses.co.uk. Art-house cinema with an excellent, wide-ranging programme.
Cambridge Arts Theatre 6 St Edward's Passage, off King's Parade ☎01223 503333, ⓦcambridge artstheatre.com. The city's main rep theatre, founded by John Maynard Keynes, and launch pad of a thousand-and-one famous careers; offers a top-notch range of cutting-edge and classic productions.

Cambridge Corn Exchange Wheeler St ☎01223 357851, ⓦwww.cornex.co.uk. Revamped nineteenth-century trading hall, now the main city-centre venue for opera, ballet, musicals and comedy as well as regular rock and folk gigs.
Cambridge Junction Clifton Way ☎01223 511511, ⓦjunction.co.uk. Rock, indie, jazz, reggae or soul gigs, plus theatre, comedy and dance at this popular arts venue. Out near the train station.

Duxford Imperial War Museum

Duxford, Jct 10 off the M11 • Daily: mid-March to late Oct 10am–6pm; late Oct to mid-March 10am–4pm • £17.50 • ☎01223 835000, ⓦiwm.org.uk

Eight miles south of Cambridge, the giant hangars of the **Duxford Imperial War Museum** dominate the eponymous airfield. Throughout World War II, East Anglia was a centre of operations for the RAF and the USAF, with the region's flat, unobstructed landscape dotted by dozens of airfields, among which Duxford was one of the more important. In total, the museum holds more than 150 historic aircraft, a wide-ranging collection of civil and military planes from the Sunderland flying boat to Concorde and the Vulcan B2 bombers, which were used for the first and last time in the 1982 Falklands conflict; the Spitfires, however, remain the most enduringly popular. Most of the planes are kept in full working order and are taken out for a spin several times a year at **Duxford Air Shows**, which attract thousands of visitors. There are usually half a dozen air shows a year (as well as temporary exhibitions) and advance bookings are strongly recommended – call ahead or consult the museum website.

The West Midlands and the Peak District

ANNE HATHAWAY'S COTTAGE

The West Midlands and the Peak District

Birmingham, the urban epicentre of the West Midlands, is Britain's second city and was once the world's greatest industrial metropolis, its slew of factories powering the Industrial Revolution. Long saddled with a reputation as an ugly, unappealing city, Birmingham has broken free, redeveloping its central core with vim and architectural verve, its prestige buildings – especially Selfridges and the Symphony hall – helping to redefine and reshape its image. Within easy striking distance is Stratford-upon-Avon, famous as the birthplace of William Shakespeare and for the exemplary Royal Shakespeare Company, the RSC. Beyond are the rural shires that stretch out towards Wales, with the bumpy Malvern Hills, one of the region's scenic highlights in between; you could also drift north to the rugged scenery of the Peak District, whose surly, stirring landscapes enclose the attractive little spa town of Buxton.

8

Change was forced on Birmingham by the drastic decline in its manufacturing base during the 1970s; things were even worse in the **Black Country**, that knot of industrial towns clinging to the western side of the city, where de-industrialization has proved particularly painful. The counties to the south and west of Birmingham and beyond the Black Country – **Warwickshire**, **Worcestershire**, **Herefordshire** and **Shropshire** – comprise a rural stronghold that maintains an emotional and political distance from the conurbation. Of the four counties, **Warwickshire** is the least obviously scenic, but draws by far the largest number of visitors, for – as the road signs declare at every entry point – this is "Shakespeare Country". The prime target is, of course, **Stratford-upon-Avon**, with its handful of Shakespeare-related sites and world-class theatre, but spare time also for the town of **Warwick**, which has a superb church and a whopping castle.

Neighbouring **Worcestershire**, which stretches southwest from the urban fringes of the West Midlands, holds two principal places of interest: **Worcester**, which is graced by a mighty cathedral, and **Great Malvern**, a mannered inland resort spread along the rolling contours of the **Malvern Hills** – prime walking territory. From here, it's west again for **Herefordshire**, a large and sparsely populated county that's home to several amenable market towns, most notably **Hereford**, where the remarkable medieval Mappa Mundi map is displayed in the cathedral, and pocket-sized **Ross-on-Wye**, which is within easy striking distance of an especially scenic stretch of the **Wye River Valley**. Next door, to the north, is rural **Shropshire** which has one of the region's prettiest towns, **Ludlow**, awash with antique half-timbered buildings, and the slow-paced county town of **Shrewsbury**, which is also close to the hiking trails of the **Long Mynd**. Shropshire has a fascinating industrial history, too, for it was here in the **Ironbridge Gorge** that British industrialists built the world's first iron bridge and pioneered the use of coal as a smelting fuel.

IRONBRIDGE, SHROPSHIRE

Highlights

❶ RSC theatres, Stratford-upon-Avon
Shakespeare's birthplace is quite simply the best place in the world to see the great man's plays, performed by the pre-eminent Royal Shakespeare Company. **See p.387 & p.389**

❷ Mappa Mundi, Hereford Cathedral This glorious antique map, dating to around 1000 AD, provides a riveting insight into the medieval mind with all its quirks and superstitions. **See p.395**

❸ Ironbridge Gorge The first iron bridge ever constructed arches high above the River Severn – industrial poetry in motion. **See p.398**

❹ Ludlow A postcard-pretty country town with a collection of half-timbered houses and a

sprawling castle – and some wonderful restaurants, too. **See p.404**

❺ Staying Cool, Birmingham Stay Cool and be cool by renting an apartment at the top of the Rotunda, one of Birmingham's landmark buildings. Enjoy the views – they are simply fabulous. **See p.410**

❻ Buxton Good-looking and relaxed former spa town with good hotels and restaurants – an ideal base for exploring the Peak District. **See p.416**

❼ Hiking in the Peak District The wonderful wilds of the Peak District are crisscrossed by hiking trails – start with an amiable stroll or two near Bakewell. **See p.421**

HIGHLIGHTS ARE MARKED ON THE MAP ON P.384

To the north of the sprawling Birmingham conurbation is **Derbyshire**, whose northern reaches incorporate the region's finest scenery in the rough landscapes of the **Peak District National Park**. The park's many hiking trails attract visitors by the thousand and one of the best bases is the appealing former spa town of **Buxton**. The Peak District is also home to the limestone caverns of **Castleton**, the so-called "Plague Village" of **Eyam** and the grandiose stately pile of **Chatsworth House**, a real favourite hereabouts.

HIGHLIGHTS

1. RSC theatres, Stratford-upon-Avon
2. Mappa Mundi, Hereford Cathedral
3. Ironbridge Gorge
4. Ludlow
5. Staying Cool, Birmingham
6. Buxton
7. Hiking in the Peak District

THE WEST MIDLANDS AND THE PEAK DISTRICT

Birmingham has a major international **airport** and is readily accessible by **train** from London, Liverpool, Manchester, Leeds, York and a score of other towns. It is also well served by the National Express **bus** network, with dozens of buses leaving every hour for destinations all over Britain. Furthermore, Birmingham acts as a public transport hub for the whole of the West Midlands with trains fanning out into the surrounding counties. However, once you leave the rail network behind you'll find local buses thin on the ground, especially in the quieter parts of Worcestershire, Herefordshire and Shropshire. In the Peak District, local buses rule the roost with a dense (if occasionally complicated) network of services that will take you most places on most days.

Stratford-upon-Avon

Despite its worldwide fame, **STRATFORD-UPON-AVON** is at heart an unassuming market town with an unexceptional pedigree. A charter for Stratford's weekly market was granted in the twelfth century and the town later became an important stopping-off point for stagecoaches between London, Oxford and the north. Like all such places, Stratford had its clearly defined class system and within this typical milieu John and Mary **Shakespeare** occupied the middle rank, and would have been forgotten long ago had their first son, William, not turned out to be the greatest writer ever to use the English language. A consequence of their good fortune is that this pleasant little town is all but smothered by package tourist hype and, in the summer at least, its central streets groan under the weight of thousands of visitors. Don't let that deter you: the **Royal Shakespeare Company** offers superb theatre and if you are willing to forgo the busiest attractions – principally

8

SHAKESPEARE: WHAT'S IN A NAME?

Over the past hundred years or so, the deification of **William Shakespeare** (1564–1616) has been dogged by a backlash among a fringe of revisionist scholars and literary figures sometimes known as **"Anti-Stratfordians"**. According to these revisionists, the famous plays and sonnets were not written by a glover's son from Stratford, but by someone else, and William Shakespeare was merely a nom de plume. A variety of candidates has been proposed for the authorship of Shakespeare's works, and they range from the faintly plausible (Christopher Marlowe, Francis Bacon, Ben Jonson, and the Earls of Rutland, Southampton and Oxford) to the manifestly whacko (Queen Elizabeth I, King James I and Daniel Defoe, author of *Robinson Crusoe*, who was born six years after publication of the first Folio).

Lying at the root of the authorship debate are several **unresolved questions** that have puzzled scholars for years. How could a man of modest background have such an intimate knowledge of royal protocol? How could he know so much about Italy without ever having travelled there? Why did he not leave a library in his will, when the author of the plays clearly possessed an intimate knowledge of classical literature? And why, given that Shakespeare was supposedly a well-known dramatist, did no death notice or obituary appear in publications of the day?

The speculation surrounding Shakespeare's work stems from the lack of **definite information** about his life. The few details that have been preserved come mostly from official archives – birth, marriage and death certificates and court records. However, we do know that in around 1587 the young Shakespeare was forced to flee Stratford after being caught poaching. Five companies of players passed through Stratford on tour that year, and it is believed he **absconded** with one of them to London, where a theatre boom was in full swing. *Henry VI*, Shakespeare's first play, appeared soon after, followed by the hugely successful *Richard III*. Over the next decade, Shakespeare's output was prodigious. Thirty-eight plays appeared and most were performed by his own theatre troupes based in London's **Globe** theatre (see p.89).

Success secured Shakespeare the **patronage** of London's fashionable set and the ageing Queen Elizabeth I regularly attended the Globe, as did her successor, James I, whose Scottish ancestry and fascination with the occult partly explain the subject matter of *Macbeth* – Shakespeare knew the commercial value of appealing to the rich and powerful. This, as much as his extraordinary talent, ensured his plays were the most acclaimed of the day, earning him enough money **to retire** comfortably to Stratford, where he abandoned literature in the last years of his life to concentrate on business and family affairs.

STRATFORD-UPON-AVON

CAFÉS, RESTAURANTS & PUBS

Church Street Townhouse	4
Dirty Duck	6
Kingfisher Fish Bar	2
Lambs Restaurant	3
Old Thatch Tavern	1
Windmill Inn	5

ACCOMMODATION

Adelphi Guest House	2
Best Western Grosvenor	1
Church Street Townhouse	5
Falcon	4
Woodstock Guest House	3
YHA Stratford-upon-Avon	6

Shakespeare's Birthplace – you can avoid the crush. All of Stratford's key attractions – many of them owned and run by the **Shakespeare Birthplace Trust** (see p.388) – are dotted around the centre, a flat and compact slice of land spreading back from the River Avon.

Shakespeare's Birthplace

Henley St • Daily: April–June & Sept–Oct 9am–5pm; July–Aug 9am–5.30pm; Nov–March 10am–4pm • Shakespeare Birthplace Trust combination ticket £15.90/£23.90 (see p.388) • ☎ 01789 204016, ⓦ shakespeare.org.uk

Top of everyone's bardic itinerary is **Shakespeare's Birthplace**, comprising a modern visitor centre – the Shakespeare Centre – and the heavily restored, half-timbered building where the great man was born, or rather, where it is generally believed he was born. The visitor centre pokes into every corner of Shakespeare's life and times, making the most of what little hard evidence there is. Next door, the half-timbered birthplace dwelling is actually two buildings knocked into one. The northern, much smaller and later part was the house of Joan, Shakespeare's sister; adjoining it is the main family home, bought by John Shakespeare in 1556 and now returned to something like its original appearance. It includes a glover's workshop, where Shakespeare's father beavered away, though some argue that he was a wool merchant or a butcher. Despite the many historical uncertainties, the house has been attracting visitors for centuries and upstairs one of the old mullioned windows, now displayed in a glass cabinet, bears the scratch-mark signatures of some of them, including Thomas Carlyle and Walter Scott.

Nash's House and New Place

Chapel St • Daily: mid-March to Oct 10am–5pm, Nov to mid-March 11am–4pm, but closed till 2015/16 & exhibits temporarily moved to Harvard House, 26 High St (same hours) • Shakespeare Birthplace Trust combination ticket £15.90/£23.90 (see p.388) • ☎ 01789 204016, ⓦ shakespeare.org.uk

An attractive Tudor building – and also a Birthplace Trust property – **Nash's House** was once owned by Thomas Nash, the first husband of Shakespeare's granddaughter,

Elizabeth Hall. The house is kitted out with a pleasant assortment of period furnishings and has a cabinet of woodcarvings made from the **mulberry tree** that once stood outside and was reputedly planted by Shakespeare himself. It also has displays featuring the archeological bits and pieces retrieved during a recent excavation of the adjacent garden, which contains the foundations of **New Place**, Shakespeare's last residence, though this was demolished long ago. Note, however, that Nash's House will be closed for refurbishment until around 2015/16, its exhibits temporarily relocated to **Harvard House**.

Hall's Croft

Old Town • Daily: mid-March to Oct 10am–5pm, Nov to mid-March 11am–4pm • Shakespeare Birthplace Trust combination ticket £15.90/£23.90 (see p.388) • ☎ 01789 204016, ⓦ shakespeare.org.uk

Stratford's most impressive medieval house is **Hall's Croft**, the former home of Shakespeare's elder daughter, Susanna, and her doctor husband, John Hall. This immaculately maintained house, with its beamed ceilings and rickety rooms, holds a good-looking medley of period furniture and – mostly upstairs – a fascinating display on **Elizabethan medicine**. Hall established something of a reputation for his medical know-how and after his death some of his case notes were published in a volume entitled *Select Observations on English Bodies*.

Holy Trinity Church

Old Town • March & Oct Mon–Sat 9am–5pm, Sun 12.30–5pm, April–Sept Mon–Sat 8.30am–6pm & Sun 12.30–5pm, Nov–Feb Mon–Sat 9am–4pm & Sun 12.30–5pm • Free, but chancel £2 • ☎ 01789 266316, ⓦ stratford-upon-avon.org

The mellow, honey-coloured stonework of **Holy Trinity Church** dates from the thirteenth century. Enhanced by its riverside setting, the dignified proportions of this quintessentially English church are the result, however, of several centuries of chopping and changing, culminating in the replacement of the original wooden spire with today's stone version in 1763. Inside, the nave is flanked by a fine set of stained-glass windows, some of which are medieval, and bathed in light from the clerestory windows up above. Quite unusually, you'll see that the nave is built on a slight skew from the line of the chancel – supposedly to represent Christ's inclined head on the cross. William Shakespeare lies buried in the **chancel**, his remains overseen by a sedate and studious memorial plaque and effigy added just seven years after his death.

Bancroft Basin

In front of the recently remodelled **Royal Shakespeare Theatre**, the manicured lawns of a

---

STRATFORD'S THEATRES

Sitting pretty beside the River Avon are the **Royal Shakespeare Company**'s two main **theatres**, the Swan and the Royal Shakespeare. There was no theatre in Stratford in Shakespeare's day and indeed the first hometown festival in his honour was only held in 1769 at the behest of London-based David Garrick. Thereafter, the idea of building a permanent home in which to perform Shakespeare's works slowly gained momentum, and finally, in 1879, the first Memorial Theatre was opened on land donated by local beer baron Charles Flower. A fire in 1926 necessitated the construction of a new theatre, and the ensuing architectural competition, won by Elisabeth Scott, produced the **Royal Shakespeare Theatre**, a red-brick edifice that has recently been remodelled and extended, its proscenium stage replaced by a thrust stage – to the horror of many and the delight of some. Attached to the main theatre is the **Swan Theatre**, a replica "in-the-round" Elizabethan stage that has also been refurbished, whilst close by is the RSC's third theatre, formerly the Courtyard Theatre and now closed pending its conversion into a more modern auditorium and its renaming as **The Other Place**.

small riverside park stretch north as far as **Bancroft Basin**, where the Stratford Canal meets the river. This is one of the prettiest parts of Stratford with brightly-painted narrowboats bobbing in the water and a fancy pedestrian bridge leading over to the finely sculpted **Gower Memorial** of 1888, where Shakespeare sits surrounded by characters from his plays.

Anne Hathaway's Cottage

Cottage Lane, Shottery • Daily: mid-March to Oct 9am–5pm; Nov to mid–March 10am–4pm • £9.50, or Shakespeare Birthplace Trust combination ticket £23.90 (see below) • ☎ 01789 204016, Ⓦ shakespeare.org.uk

Anne Hathaway's Cottage, a Birthplace Trust property, is just over a mile west of the centre in the well-heeled suburb of **Shottery**. The cottage – actually an old farmhouse – is an immaculately maintained, half-timbered affair with a thatched roof and dinky little chimneys. This was the home of Anne Hathaway before she married Shakespeare in 1582, and the interior holds a comely combination of period furniture, including a superb, finely carved four-poster bed. The garden is splendid too, bursting with blooms in the summertime. The adjacent orchard features more than forty types of tree, shrub and rose mentioned in the plays, with each bearing the appropriate quotation inscribed on a plaque. The nicest way to get to the cottage from the centre is on the signposted **footpath** from Evesham Place, at the south end of Rother Street.

Mary Arden's Farm

Station Rd, Wilmcote CV37 9UN, 3 miles northwest of Stratford, • Mid–March to Oct daily 9am–5pm • £12.50, or Shakespeare Birthplace Trust combination ticket £23.90 (see below) • ☎ 01789 204016, Ⓦ shakespeare.org.uk

Mary Arden's Farm, a further Birthplace Trust property, takes its name from Shakespeare's mother, the only unmarried daughter of her father, Robert, at the time of his death in 1556. Unusually for the period, Mary inherited the house and land, thus becoming one of the neighbourhood's most eligible women – John Shakespeare, eager for self-improvement, married her within a year. The house is a well-furnished example of an Elizabethan farmhouse and a platoon of guides fills in the details of family life and traditions with assorted farmyard activities too.

ARRIVAL AND DEPARTURE   STRATFORD-UPON-AVON

By train Stratford's main train station is on the northwest edge of town, a 10min walk from the centre.
Destinations Birmingham Moor Street & Snow Hill stations (hourly; 1hr 10min/55min); London Marylebone (direct every 3hr; 2hr; with one change, hourly 2hr 20min).

By bus Local buses arrive and depart from Bridge/Wood streets; National Express services and most other long-distance buses pull into the Riverside bus station on the east side of the town centre, off Bridgeway.

INFORMATION

Tourist office Handily located by the bridge at the junction of Bridgeway and Bridgefoot (March–Oct Mon–Sat 9am–5.30pm & Sun 10am–4pm; Nov–Feb Mon–Sat 9am–5.30pm but may close Sun; ☎01789 264293, Ⓦ discover-stratford.com). Among many other useful things, they offer a last-minute accommodation booking service that can be especially handy at the height of the summer.
Shakespeare Birthplace Trust (☎01789 204016,

Ⓦ shakespeare.org.uk) owns five properties – three in the town centre (Shakespeare's Birthplace, Nash's House and Hall's Croft) and two on the outskirts (Anne Hathaway's Cottage and Mary Arden's Farm). Tickets are not available for the three individual properties in the town centre – instead you have to buy a combined ticket for £15.90 or a ticket for all five at £23.90; you can also purchase an individual ticket at the two outlying attractions. Tickets are on sale at all five and online.

ACCOMMODATION

In peak months and during the **Shakespeare birthday celebrations** around April 23, it's pretty much essential to book accommodation well ahead. The town has a dozen or so **hotels**, the pick of which occupy old half-timbered buildings right in the centre, but most visitors choose to stay in a **B&B**; there's a particular concentration to the west of the centre around Grove Road and Evesham Place.

Adelphi Guest House 39 Grove Rd ☎01789 204469, ⓦadelphi-guesthouse.com. Extremely cosy B&B in a good-looking Victorian townhouse a short walk from the centre. The owners have accumulated all sorts of interesting curios – from vintage theatrical posters to ornate chandeliers – and the five double guest rooms are all en suite. The best room, which has a four-poster, is in the attic and offers pleasing views. Top-ranking, home-cooked breakfasts too. **£70**

Best Western Grosvenor Warwick Rd ☎01789 269213, ⓦbwgh.co.uk. Close to the canal, just a couple of minutes' walk from the town centre, the *Grosvenor* occupies a row of pleasant, two-storey Georgian houses. The interior is humdrum-modern but perfectly adequate and there's ample parking at the back. **£80**

Church Street Townhouse 16 Church St ☎01789 262222, ⓦchurchstreettownhouse.com. Twelve deluxe guest rooms decorated in a smart and neat modern manner and equipped with king-size beds. Two nights' minimum stay on the weekend. Convenient, central location and first-rate breakfasts. It's a popular spot, so advance reservations are recommended. **£110**

Falcon Chapel St ☎0844 411 9005, ⓦlegacy-hotels .co.uk. Handily situated in the middle of town, this chain hotel is a rambling affair whose front section, with its half-timbered facade and stone-flagged bar, dates from the sixteenth century. A corridor connects this part of the hotel to the modern block behind, where the rooms are neat, trim and really rather well designed; the rooms in other parts of the hotel, however, are not nearly as appealing. **£95**

Woodstock Guest House 30 Grove Rd ☎01789 299881, ⓦwoodstock-house.co.uk. A smart, neatly kept B&B just a 5min walk from the centre, by the start of the path to Anne Hathaway's Cottage (see opposite). The five extremely comfortable bedrooms are all en suite, decorated in a fetching modern style. **£78**

YHA Stratford-upon-Avon Hemmingford House, Wellesbourne Road, Alveston, 2 miles east on the B4086 ☎0845 371 9661, ⓦyha.org.uk. Occupying a rambling Georgian mansion on the edge of the village of Alveston, this medium sized hostel has dorms, double and family rooms, some of which are en suite, plus wi-fi, car parking and self catering facilities. Breakfasts and evening meals are on offer, too. Advance reservations advised. Local bus from Wood Street in Stratford. Dorms **£18**, doubles **£34**

EATING AND DRINKING

Church Street Townhouse 16 Church St ☎01789 262222, ⓦchurchstreettownhouse.com. Smart, appealing bar and restaurant in one of the town's oldest premises. The menu is creative with due emphasis on local ingredients – try, for example, the vegetable risotto (£11.50) or the pan-roasted turbot with braised oxtail (£20). Daily 8am–10pm.

Dirty Duck 53 Waterside ☎01789 297312, ⓦold englishinns.co.uk. The archetypal actors' pub, stuffed to the gunwales every night with a vocal entourage of RSC thesps and admirers. Traditional beers in somewhat spartan premises plus a terrace for hot-weather drinking. Now one of a large pub chain. Daily 11am–11pm.

Kingfisher Fish Bar 13 Ely St ☎01789 292513. The best fish-and-chip shop in town, a 5min walk from the theatres. Takeaway and sit-down. Mon–Sat 11.30am–1.45pm & 5–9.30pm.

★**Lambs Restaurant** 12 Sheep St ☎01789 292554, ⓦlambsrestaurant.co.uk. A mouthwatering range of stylish English and continental dishes – slow-roasted lamb shank, for example – dished up in a smart restaurant with lots of period features including beamed ceilings and modern art on the walls. Daily specials around £11, other main courses £13–18. Mon & Tues 5–9pm. Wed–Sat noon–2pm & 5–9pm, Sun noon–2pm & 6–9pm.

Old Thatch Tavern Market Place ☎01789 295216. Ancient pub with a convivial atmosphere and a good range of beers attracting a mixed bag of tourists and locals. Daily 11am–11pm.

Windmill Inn Church St ☎01789 297687. Popular pub with a rabbit-warren of rooms and low-beamed ceilings. Flowers beers too. Daily 11am–11pm.

NIGHTLIFE AND ENTERTAINMENT: THE RSC

The Royal Shakespeare Company ☎0844 800 1110, ⓦrsc.org.uk. The RSC works on a repertory system, which means you could stay in Stratford for a few days and see three or four different plays, and not necessarily by Shakespeare: though the RSC does indeed focus on the Bard's plays, it offers other productions too, from new modern writing through to works by Shakespeare's contemporaries. With the Courtyard Theatre/The Other Place closed for a revamp, the RSC is currently confined to two venues – the Royal Shakespeare and the Swan. Tickets start from as little as £14 and can be bought online, by phone (Mon–Sat 10am–6pm), and in person at the Royal Shakespeare box office. Note that some performances are sold out months in advance and although there's always the off-chance of a last-minute return or stand-by ticket (for unsold seats), don't bet on it.

8

Warwick

Pocket-sized **WARWICK**, just eight miles northeast of Stratford, is famous for its massive **castle**, but it also possesses several charming streetscapes erected in the aftermath of a great fire in 1694. An hour or two is quite enough time to nose around the town centre, though you'll need the whole day if, braving the crowds and the medieval musicians, you're also set on exploring the castle and its extensive grounds: either way, Warwick is the perfect day-trip from Stratford.

Warwick Castle

Daily: Core hours April–Sept 10am–6pm; Oct–March 10am–5pm • Various ticketing options from £18 in advance (£24 on the day); parking £6–10 • ☎ 01926 495421; recorded info ☎ 0871 265 2000, ⓦ warwick-castle.com

Towering above the River Avon at the foot of the town centre, **Warwick Castle** is often proclaimed the "greatest medieval castle in Britain". This claim is valid enough if bulk equals greatness, but actually much of the existing structure is the result of extensive nineteenth-century tinkering. It's likely that the Saxons raised the first fortress on this site, though things really took off with the Normans, who built a large motte and bailey here towards the end of the eleventh century. Almost three hundred years later, the eleventh Earl of Warwick turned the stronghold into a formidable stone castle, complete with elaborate gatehouses, multiple turrets and a keep.

The **entrance** to the castle is through the old stable block at the foot of Castle Street. Beyond, a footpath leads round to the imposing moated and mounded **East Gate**. Over the footbridge – and beyond the protective towers – is the main **courtyard**. You can stroll along the ramparts and climb the towers, but most visitors head straight for one or other of the special, very touristy displays installed inside the castle's many chambers and towers. The **grounds** are perhaps much more enjoyable, acres of woodland and lawn inhabited by peacocks and including a large glass **conservatory**. A footbridge leads over the River Avon to **River Island**, the site of jousting tournaments and other such medieval hoopla.

Lord Leycester Hospital

60 High St • Tues–Sun plus Bank Holiday Mon: April–Oct 10am–5pm; Nov–March 10am–4.30pm • £5.90 • ☎ 01926 491422, ⓦ lordleycester.com

The remarkable **Lord Leycester Hospital**, a tangle of half-timbered buildings leaning at fairy-tale angles against the old West Gate, represents one of Britain's best-preserved examples of domestic Elizabethan architecture. It was established as a hostel for old soldiers by Robert Dudley, Earl of Leicester – a favourite of Queen Elizabeth I – and incorporates several beamed buildings, principally the Great Hall and the Guildhall, as well as a wonderful galleried courtyard and an intimate chantry chapel. There's a tearoom too, plus a modest regimental museum (Tue–Sat only) – appropriately enough as retired servicemen (and their wives) still live here.

St Mary's Church

Old Square • Daily: April–Sept 10am–6pm; Oct–March 10am–4.30pm • £2 donation suggested • ☎ 01926 403940, ⓦ stmaryswarwick.org.uk

Rebuilt in a weird Gothic-Renaissance amalgam after the fire of 1694, **St Mary's Church** may not look too exciting from the outside, but inside the chancel, which survived the fire untouched, is a simply glorious illustration of the Perpendicular style with a splendid vaulted ceiling of flying and fronded ribs. On the right-hand side of the chancel is the **Beauchamp Chantry Chapel**, which contains the equally beautiful tomb of Richard Beauchamp, Earl of Warwick, who is depicted in an elaborate, gilded-bronze suit of armour of Italian design from the tip of his swan helmet down to his mailed feet. A griffin and a bear guard Richard, who lies with his hands half-joined in

COVENTRY CATHEDRAL

At the outbreak of World War II, **COVENTRY**, eleven miles north of Warwick, was a major engineering centre and its factories attracted the attentions of the Luftwaffe, who well-nigh levelled the town in a huge bombing raid on November 14, 1940. Out of the ashes arose what is now Coventry's one sight of note, Basil Spence's **St Michael's Cathedral** (Mon–Sat 10am–5pm, Sun noon–4pm; £8; ☎024 7652 1210, ⓦcoventrycathedral.org.uk), raised alongside the burnt-out shell of the old cathedral right in the centre of town and dedicated with a performance of Benjamin Britten's specially written *War Requiem* in 1962. One of the country's most successful postwar buildings, the cathedral's pink sandstone is light and graceful, the main entrance adorned by a stunningly forceful *St Michael Defeating the Devil* by Jacob Epstein. Inside, Spence's high and slender nave is bathed in light from the soaring stained-glass windows, a perfect setting for the magnificent and immense **tapestry** of *Christ in Glory* by **Graham Sutherland**. The choice of artist could not have been more appropriate. A painter, graphic artist and designer, Sutherland (1903–80) had been one of Britain's official war artists, his particular job being to record the effects of German bombing. A canopied walkway links the new cathedral with the old, whose shattered nave flanks the church tower and spire that somehow eluded the bombs.

prayer so that, on the Resurrection, his first sight would be of Christ Triumphant at the Second Coming. The adjacent tomb of Ambrose Dudley is of finely carved and painted alabaster, as is that of Robert Dudley and his wife – the same Dudley who founded the Lord Leycester Hospital (see opposite).

ARRIVAL AND INFORMATION   WARWICK   8

By train Warwick train station is at the northern edge of town, a 15min walk from the centre via Station and Coventry roads.
Destinations Birmingham Snow Hill (every 30min to 1hr; 30min); Stratford-upon-Avon (every 2hr; 30min).

By bus Buses stop on Market St, in the town centre close to Market Place.
Tourist office The old Courthouse, on the corner of Castle and Jury streets (Mon–Fri 9.30am–4.30pm, Sat 10am–4.30pm; ☎01926 492212, ⓦvisitwarwick.co.uk).

ACCOMMODATION AND EATING

Catalan 6 Jury St ☎01926 498930, ⓦcatalantapas .co.uk. This rustic-looking, café/restaurant has a wide-ranging, Mediterranean-inspired menu, but the tasty tapas are its speciality – try, for example, the sardines or the white beans, shallots and leeks in a tomato sauce. Tapas average around £4.50, à la carte mains £15, less at lunch times. Mon–Fri noon–3pm & 6–9.30pm.
Rose and Crown 30 Market Place ☎01926 411117, ⓦroseandcrownwarwick.co.uk. Self-proclaimed as one of

a "group of enthusiasts" rather than a chain, this centrally located pub offers thirteen attractive, competitively priced guest rooms, all en suite, five above the pub and eight just across the street. Each is decorated in a bright and breezy contemporary style. The first rate pub-cum-restaurant offers a lively, creative menu from breakfast through to dinner. Try, for example, the Cornish lamb with green bean and caper beurre noisette. A prime selection of guest beers and house wines, too. Mains average £16. Daily 8am–11pm. **£85**

Worcester and around

In geographical terms, **Worcestershire** can be compared to a huge saucer, with the low-lying plains of the Severn Valley and the Vale of Evesham, Britain's foremost fruit-growing area, rising to a lip of hills, principally the Malverns in the west and the Cotswolds (see p.243) to the south. In character, the county divides into two broad belts. To the north lie the industrial and overspill towns – Droitwich and Redditch for instance – that have much in common with the Birmingham conurbation, while the south is predominantly rural. Bang at the geographical heart of the county is **WORCESTER**, an amenable county town where a liberal helping of half-timbered Tudor and handsome Georgian buildings stand cheek by jowl with some fairly charmless modern developments. The biggest single influence on the city has always been the

River Severn, which flows along Worcester's west flank. It was the river that made the city an important settlement as early as Saxon times, though its propensity to breach its banks has prompted the construction of a battery of defences which tumble down the slope from the mighty bulk of the **cathedral**, easily the town's star turn. Worcester's centre is small and compact, and handily, all the key sights plus the best restaurants are clustered within the immediate vicinity of the cathedral.

Worcester Cathedral

Daily 7.30am–6pm • Free • ☎ 01905 732900, ⓦ worcestercathedral.co.uk

Towering above the River Severn, the soaring sandstone of **Worcester Cathedral** comprises a rich stew of architectural styles dating from 1084. The bulk of the church is firmly medieval, from the Norman transepts through to the late Gothic cloister, though the Victorians did have a good old hack at the exterior. Inside, the highlight is the thirteenth-century **choir**, a beautiful illustration of the Early English style, with a forest of slender pillars rising above the intricately worked choir stalls. Here also, in front of the high altar, is the **table tomb** of England's most reviled monarch, **King John** (1167–1216), who certainly would not have appreciated the lion that lies at his feet biting the end of his sword – a reference to the curbing of his power by the barons when they obliged him to sign the Magna Carta. Just beyond the tomb – on the right – is **Prince Arthur's Chantry**, a delicate lacy confection of carved stonework erected in 1504 to commemorate Arthur, King Henry VII's son, who died at the age of 15. He was on his honeymoon with Catherine of Aragon, who was soon passed on – with such momentous consequences – to his younger brother, the future Henry VIII. A doorway on the south side of the nave leads to the **cloisters**, with their delightful roof bosses, and the circular, largely Norman **chapter house**, which has the distinction of being the first such building constructed with the use of a central supporting pillar.

Worcester Porcelain Museum

Severn St • Easter to Oct Mon–Sat 10am–5pm; Oct–Easter Tues–Sat 10.30am–4pm • £6 • ☎ 01905 21247, ⓦ worcesterporcelainmuseum.org

There was a time when Severn Street, tucked away just to the south of the cathedral, hummed with the activity of one of England's largest porcelain factories, **Royal Worcester**. Those days ended, however, when the company hit the skids and was finally rolled up in 2008 after more than one hundred and fifty years in production. The old factory complex is currently being turned into apartments, but the **Worcester Porcelain Museum** has survived, exhibiting a comprehensive collection of the ornate, indeed fancifully ornate, porcelain for which Royal Worcester was famous.

The Commandery

Sidbury • Easter–Oct Mon–Sat 10am–5pm, Sun 1.30–5pm; Nov to Easter reduced hours – call for details • £5.50 • ☎ 01905 361 821, ⓦ www.whub.org.uk/cms/

Occupying Worcester's oldest building, a rambling, half-timbered structure dating from the early sixteenth century, the **Commandery**, on the far side of the busy Sidbury dual carriageway, holds six different displays tracking through the history of the Commandery and its assorted occupants. The building itself is historically important: **King Charles II** used it as his headquarters during the battle-cum-siege of Worcester in 1651, the end game of his unsuccessful attempt to regain the throne from Cromwell and the Parliamentarians, who had executed his father – King Charles I – in 1649. The high point inside is the medieval **painted chamber**, whose walls are covered with intriguing cameos recalling the building's original use as a monastery hospital. Each relates to a saint with healing powers – for example St Thomas à Becket is shown being stabbed in the head by a group of knights, which was enough to make him the patron saint for headaches.

Greyfriars

Friar St • Late Feb to late Dec Tues–Sat 1–5pm• £4.70; NT • ☎ 01905 23571, ⓦ nationaltrust.org.uk/greyfriars

From the Commandery, it's a short step northwest along Sidbury to narrow **Friar Street**, whose hotchpotch of half-timbered houses and small, independent shops make it Worcester's prettiest thoroughfare. Among the buildings is **Greyfriars**, a largely fifteenth-century townhouse whose wonky timbers and dark-stained panelling shelter a charming collection of antiques. There's an attractive walled garden here too. From Greyfriars, it's a couple of minutes' walk west to the High Street, a couple more back to the cathedral.

ARRIVAL AND INFORMATION

WORCESTER

By train Worcester has two main train stations. The handiest for the city centre is Foregate Street, from where it's about 800yds south to the cathedral along Foregate Street and its continuation The Cross and then High Street. The other train station, Shrub Hill, is further out, about a mile to the northeast of the cathedral.
Destinations Worcester Foregate to: Birmingham Moor Street (every 30min; 1hr); Hereford (hourly; 50min).

By bus The bus station is at the back of the sprawling Crowngate shopping about 600yds northwest of the cathedral.
Destinations Great Malvern (2 hourly; 50min); Hereford (Mon–Sat 2 daily; 1hr 20min)
Tourist office Guildhall, towards the cathedral end of the High Street (Mon–Sat 9.30am–5pm; ☎ 01905 726311, ⓦ visitworcestershire.org).

ACCOMMODATION

Barrington House B&B 201 Henwick Rd ☎ 01905 422965, ⓦ barringtonhouse.eu. Occupying an immaculately restored Georgian property right by the river about a mile north of the centre along the A443 – and across the river from Worcester Racecourse – this is the best B&B in town. It comes with a large garden and has three en-suite guest rooms decorated in a broadly period style. Tasty breakfasts too. **£80**

Diglis House Hotel Severn St ☎ 01905 353510, ⓦ diglishousehotel.co.uk. Medium-sized hotel in an attractive Georgian villa beside the river, about 5min walk south of the cathedral at the end of Severn Street. Some of the guest rooms are in the main building, others in the modern annexe, and all are decorated in a pleasant if somewhat staid version of country-house style. The hotel's prime feature is the large conservatory overlooking the river. **£110**

EATING AND DRINKING

Mac & Jac's Café 44 Friar St ☎ 01905 731331, ⓦ macandjacs.co.uk. With a sister café in Great Malvern (see p.394), this attractive little place occupies an old, half-timbered building near the Cathedral. Offers a delicious range of home-made snacks and meals – try, for example, the pollack and salmon fishcake with green beans, anchovy and caper mayonnaise (£11). Mon–Sat 9am–5pm, plus occasional supper evenings.
Saffrons Bistro 15 New St (a northerly continuation of

Friar St) ☎ 01905 610505, ⓦ saffronsbistro.co.uk. Undoubtedly one of Worcester's best restaurants, this cheerfully decorated little place is strong on locally sourced ingredients – and the proof is in the eating. Try, for example, the delicious slow braised blade of beef with green beans, mushrooms and shallots in a red wine sauce. Reservations advised in the evening. Mains hover around £15. Mon–Fri noon–2.15pm & 5.30–9.30pm, Sat noon–2.15pm & 5.30–10.30pm.

8

The Malvern Hills

One of the more prosperous parts of the West Midlands, **The Malverns** is the generic name for a string of towns and villages stretched along the eastern lower slopes of the

> #### HIKING THE MALVERN HILLS
> Great Malvern tourist office (see p.394) sells hiking maps and issues half a dozen free **Trail Guide leaflets**, which describe circular routes up to and along the hills that rise behind the town. The shortest trail is just one and a half miles, the longest four. One of the most appealing is the 2.5-mile hoof up to the top – and back – of **North Hill** (1307ft), from where there are panoramic views over the surrounding countryside; this hike also takes in *St Ann's Well Café*, where you can taste the local spring water (see box, p.394).

MALVERN HILLS, which rise spectacularly out of the flatlands a few miles to the southwest of Worcester. About nine miles from north to south – between the A44 and the M50 – and never more than five miles wide, the hills straddle the Worcestershire–Herefordshire boundary. Of ancient granite rock, they are punctuated by over twenty summits, mostly around 1000ft high, and in between lie innumerable dips and hollows. It's easy, if energetic, walking country, with great views, and there's an excellent network of **hiking trails**, most of which can be completed in a day or half-day with **Great Malvern** being the obvious base.

Great Malvern

Of all the towns in the Malverns, it's **GREAT MALVERN** that grabs the attention, its pocket-sized centre clambering up the hillside with the crags of North Hill beckoning beyond. The grand old houses, which congregate on and around the top of the main drag, **Church Street**, mostly date from Great Malvern's nineteenth-century heyday as a spa town when the local **spring waters** drew the Victorians here by the train load. You can still sample the waters today (see box below), but the town's principal sight is its splendid **Priory Church**, close to the top of Church Street (daily 9am–5pm; free; ⓦgreatmalvernpriory.org.uk). The Benedictines built one of their abbeys here at Great Malvern and, although Henry VIII closed the place down in 1538, the church's elaborate decoration and fabulous late medieval **stained-glass windows** proclaim the priory's former wealth.

8

ARRIVAL AND INFORMATION
GREAT MALVERN

By train From Great Malvern's rustic train station, with its dainty ironwork and quaint chimneys, it's about 800yd to the town centre – take Avenue Road, which leads to Church St, the steeply sloping main drag.

Destinations Birmingham (hourly; 1hr); Hereford (hourly;

35min); Ledbury (hourly; 15min); Worcester Foregate (hourly; 15min).

Tourist office At the top of Church St, just up and across from the Priory Church (daily 10am–5pm; ☏01684 892289, ⓦvisitthemalverns.org).

ACCOMMODATION

Abbey Hotel Abbey Rd ☏01684 892332, ⓦsarova-abbeyhotel.com. Easily the most conspicuous hotel in Great Malvern, a few yards from the tourist office, much of it occupying a rambling, creeper-clad Victorian building executed in a sort of neo-Baronial style. It's part of a small chain, and the guest rooms, especially in the hotel's lumpy modern wing, can be a little characterless – but they are comfortable enough and some have attractive views back over town. **£90**

Amazing View in The Malverns 8 Hanley Terrace, Malvern Wells, a short drive south along (and just off) the A449 (Wells Rd). ☏01684 565808, ⓦamazingview.info. Deluxe B&B with three, commodious, en-suite guest

rooms in a tastefully modernised Victorian house. Has a superb location perched on the hill with panoramic views across the plain below. Tasty breakfasts, too. **£75**

The Cottage in the Wood Holywell Rd, Malvern Wells, WR14 4LG ☏01684 588860, ⓦcottageinthewood.co.uk. Family-run hotel with a dozen or so cheery, comfortable guest rooms in the main house and a brace of small annexes. The main house is not so much a cottage as a spacious villa built as a dower house to a neigbhbouring estate in the late 1700s. Wooded grounds surround the hotel and there are fine views. The rooms vary considerably in size and comfort, but start at **£99**

TAKING THE GREAT MALVERN WATERS

The gushing **Malvhina spring** in the mini-park at the top of Church Street is the obvious and certainly the most convenient way to taste Great Malvern's waters. There's also a spring at **St Ann's Well Café**, a sweet little café in an attractive Georgian building a stiff 25-minute walk up the wooded hillside from town (normally Easter to June & Sept Tues–Sun 11am–3.30pm; July & Aug daily 10am–4pm; Oct to Easter Fri 11.30am–3.30pm, Sat & Sun 10am–4pm; but check times on ☏01684 560285 or ⓦstannswell.co.uk); the signposted path begins beside the *Mount Pleasant Hotel*, on Belle Vue Terrace, just to the left (south) of the top of Church Street.

EATING AND DRINKING

Mac & Jac's Café 23 Abbey Rd ☏01684 573300, ⓦ macandjacs.co.uk. This bright and cheery café does its level best to source things locally (with the exception of its teas, the house speciality). Offers a particularly good range of salads with a typical dish being crispy duck salad with soy and sesame (£7). Takeaway, too. Next door to the Malvern Museum. Tues–Sat 9am–6pm, Sun 10am–4pm.

The Morgan 52 Clarence Rd ☏01684 578575, ⓦ wyevalleybrewery.co.uk. Near the train station, this is the best pub in town, where you can sample the assorted brews of Herefordshire's much-praised Wye Valley Brewery. Drink outside on the terrace if the sun is out, or inside in the wood-panelled bar. Mon–Thurs noon–3pm & 5–11pm, Fri & Sat noon–11pm & Sun noon–10.30pm.

Herefordshire

Over the Malvern Hills from Worcestershire, the rolling agricultural landscapes of **HEREFORDSHIRE** have an easy-going charm, but the finest scenery hereabouts is along the banks of the **River Wye**, which wriggles and worms its way across the county. Plonked in the middle of Herefordshire on the Wye is the county town, **Hereford**, a sleepy, rather old-fashioned place whose proudest possession, the cathedral's remarkable **Mappa Mundi** map, was almost flogged off in a round of ecclesiastical budget cuts back in the 1980s. Beyond Hereford, the southeast corner of the county has one especially attractive town, **Ross-on-Wye**, a genial little place with a picturesque setting that also serves as a convenient gateway to one of the wilder portions of the **Wye River Valley**, around **Symonds Yat**, where canoeists gather in their droves.

GETTING AROUND   HEREFORDSHIRE

By train Herefordshire possesses one rail line, linking Ledbury and Hereford with points north to Shrewsbury and east to Great Malvern and Worcester.
By bus Local buses provide a reasonable service between

the county's villages and towns, except on Sundays when there's very little at all. For timetable details, consult ⓦ travelinemidlands.co.uk or pop into the nearest tourist office.

Hereford

A low-key county town with a spacious feel, **HEREFORD** was long a border garrison held against the Welsh, its military importance guaranteed by its strategic position beside the River Wye. It also became a religious centre after the Welsh murdered the Saxon king Ethelbert near here in 794. Today, with the fortifications that once girdled the city all but vanished, it's the **cathedral** – and its extraordinary medieval **Mappa Mundi** – which forms the focus of interest. The cathedral lies just to the north of the river at the heart of the city centre, whose compact tangle of narrow streets and squares is clumsily boxed in by the ring road. Taken as a whole, Hereford makes for a pleasant overnight stay, especially as it possesses a particularly fine hotel; also don't leave town without sampling the favourite local tipple, **cider**.

Hereford Cathedral

Daily 9.15am–5.30pm • Free • ☏01432 374202, ⓦ herefordcathedral.org

Hereford Cathedral is a curious building, an uncomfortable amalgamation of styles, with bits and pieces added to the eleventh-century church by a string of bishops and culminating in an extensive – and not especially sympathetic – Victorian refit. From the outside, the sandstone **tower** is the dominant feature, constructed in the early fourteenth century to eclipse the Norman western tower, which collapsed under its own weight in 1786. The crashing masonry mauled the **nave** and its replacement lacks some of the grandeur of most other English cathedrals, though the forceful symmetries of the long rank of surviving Norman arches and piers more than hint at what went before. The **north transept** is, however, a flawless exercise in thirteenth-century taste, its soaring windows a classic example of Early English architecture.

8

The Mappa Mundi

April–Oct Mon–Sat 10am–5pm; Nov–Easter Mon–Sat 10am–4pm, but some closures for maintenance in Jan • £6 • ⓦ themappamundi.co.uk

In the 1980s, the cathedral's finances were so parlous that a plan was drawn up to sell its most treasured possession, the **Mappa Mundi**. Luckily, the government and John Paul Getty Jr. rode to the rescue, with the oil tycoon stumping up a million pounds to keep the map here and install it in a new building, the New Library, which blends in seamlessly with the older buildings it adjoins at the west end of the cloisters.

The Mappa Mundi exhibit begins with a series of interpretative panels explaining the historical background to – and the composition of – the Mappa. Included is a copy of the Mappa in English, which is particularly helpful as the original, which is displayed in a dimly lit room just beyond, is in Latin. Measuring 64 by 52 inches and dating to about 1300, the Mappa provides an extraordinary insight into medieval society. It is indeed a map (as we know it) in so far as it suggests the general geography of the world – with Asia at the top and Europe and Africa below, to left and right respectively – but it also squeezes in history, mythology and theology.

In the same building as the Mappa Mundi is the **Chained Library**, a remarkably extensive collection of books and manuscripts dating from the eighth to the eighteenth century. A selection is always open on display.

Hereford Museum and Art Gallery

Broad St • Wed–Sat 11am–4pm • Free • ☎ 01432 260692, ⓦ herefordshire.gov.uk

After the Mappa, Hereford's other attractions can't help but seem rather pedestrian. Nonetheless, the **Hereford Museum and Art Gallery**, in a flamboyant Victorian building opposite the cathedral, does hold a mildly diverting collection of geological remains and local memorabilia spruced up by temporary art exhibitions.

ARRIVAL AND INFORMATION   HEREFORD

By train Hereford train station is about 800yd northeast of the main square, High Town, via Station Approach, Commercial Road and its continuation Commercial Street.
Destinations Birmingham (hourly; 1hr 30min); Great Malvern (hourly; 30min); Ledbury (every 30min; 20min); Ludlow (every 30min; 30min); Shrewsbury (every 30min; 1hr); Worcester (hourly; 40min).
By bus The long-distance bus station is on the northeast

side of the town centre, just off Commercial Rd; local and regional buses stop in the centre on High Town.
Destinations Ledbury (4 daily; 40min); Ross-on-Wye (Mon–Sat hourly, Sun 5 every 2hr; 1hr); Worcester (Mon–Sat 2 daily; 1hr 20min).
Tourist office 1 King St, opposite the cathedral (April–Sept daily 10am–4pm, Oct–March Mon–Fri 10am–4pm; ☎ 01432 268430, ⓦ visitherefordshire.co.uk).

ACCOMMODATION, EATING AND DRINKING

The Barrels 69 St Owen's St ☎ 01432 274968, ⓦ wyevalleybrewery.co.uk. A popular local just five minutes' walk southeast of High Town, *The Barrels* is the home pub of the local Wye Valley Brewery, whose trademark bitters are much acclaimed. Mon–Thurs 11am–11.30pm, Fri & Sat 11am–midnight, Sun noon–11.30pm.

Cafe@allsaints All Saints Church, Broad St ☎ 01432 370415, ⓦ cafeatallsaints.co.uk. Near the cathedral, in the old church at the top of Broad Street, this excellent café has become something of a local institution since it was founded by a local foodie in the late 1990s. Serves a range of well-conceived and tasty dishes – ricotta pie with salad leaves for instance – at around £6. Mon–Sat 8am–5pm.

★**Castle House** Castle St ☎ 01432 356321, ⓦ castlehse.co.uk. Occupying an immaculately refurbished Georgian mansion and a neighbouring

townhouse not far from the cathedral, it's hard to praise this 24-room hotel too highly: the staff are obliging; the better/bigger rooms are simply delightful, with all sorts of period details; and the breakfast room has a lovely outside terrace. There are two first-rate restaurants – one formal, the other casual – and both emphasise local ingredients with Hereford beef and Gloucestershire pork being prime examples. Main courses start at £10. Food served daily noon–2pm & 6.30–9.30pm (9pm on Sun). **£150**

No. 21 21 Aylestone Hill, HR1 1HR ☎ 01432 279897, ⓦ 21aylestonehill.co.uk. In a substantial, half-timbered Edwardian house just northeast of the centre on the Malvern Road (A4103), this comfortable B&B has four, en-suite guest rooms decorated in soothing shades and complete with period flourishes. It's located within easy walking distance of the centre, near the train station and beside the A465 (Aylestone Hill). **£70**

Ross-on-Wye

Nestling above a loop in the river sixteen miles southeast of Hereford, **ROSS-ON-WYE** is a relaxed and easy-going market town with an artsy/New Age undertow. Ross's jumble of narrow streets converges on **Market Place**, which is shadowed by the seventeenth-century **Market House**, a sturdy two-storey sandstone structure that sports a medallion bust of a bewigged Charles II. Veer right at the top of Market Place, then turn left up Church Street to reach Ross's other noteworthy building, the mostly thirteenth-century **St Mary's Church**, whose sturdy stonework culminates in a slender, tapering spire. In front of the church, at the foot of the graveyard, is a plain but rare **Plague Cross**, commemorating the three hundred or so townsfolk who were buried here by night without coffins during a savage outbreak of the plague in 1637.

ARRIVAL AND INFORMATION ROSS-ON-WYE

By bus Ross bus station is on Cantilupe Rd, a 4min-walk from Market Place; there are no trains.
Destinations Goodrich (Mon–Sat every 2hrs, Sun 5 daily; 20min); Hereford (Mon–Sat hourly, Sun every 2hr; 50min); Ledbury (1 weekly; 40min).

ACCOMMODATION

★ **Linden House** 14 Church St ☏ 01989 565373, ⊛ lindenguesthouse.com. In a fetching Georgian building opposite St Mary's Church, this B&B has three en-suite guest rooms, each of which is cosily decorated, and a self-catering holiday apartment on the top floor. The breakfasts are delicious too – both traditional and vegetarian. **£70**

Old Court House B&B 53 High St ☏ 01989 762275, ⊛ theoldcourthouseandb.co.uk. An unusual B&B in so far as it occupies a rabbit warren of an old stone building, complete with open fires and exposed wooden beams. Has four en-suite guest rooms of varying size, two with four posters. Handily located in the centre of the town. **£80**

EATING AND DRINKING

Pots and Pieces Teashop 40 High St ☏ 01989 566123, ⊛ potsandpieces.com. This appealing little café and giftshop immediately behind the Market House sells a tasty range of snacks and light meals. The toasted tea-cakes are the best for miles around – and don't avoid the home-made cakes. Mon–Fri 9am–5pm & Sat 10am–5pm, plus June–Aug Sun 11am–4pm.

Yaks N Yetis 1 Brookend St ☏ 01989 564963. Not the prettiest of restaurants perhaps, but this is genuine Nepalese (Gurkha) cuisine – and the staff are more than willing to help explain its intricacies. It's delicious and, with mains from around £7, economically priced too. Brookend is a continuation of Broad Street, which runs north from Market Place. Tues–Sun noon–2.30pm & 6–11pm.

The Wye River Valley

Travelling south from Ross along the B4234, it's just five miles to the sullen sandstone mass of **Goodrich Castle** (April–June, Sept & Oct daily 10am–5pm; July & Aug daily 10am–6pm; Nov–March Sat & Sun 10am–4pm; £6.20; EH; ⊛ english-heritage.org. uk), which commands wide views over the hills and woods of the **Wye River Valley**. The castle's strategic location guaranteed its importance as a border stronghold from the twelfth century onwards and today the substantial ruins incorporate a Norman keep, a maze of later rooms and passageways and walkable ramparts. The castle stands next to the tiny village of **GOODRICH**, from where it's around a mile and half southeast along narrow country lanes to the solitary *YHA Wye Valley Hostel* (see p.398), which, with the **Wye Valley Walk** running past the front door, makes a great base (in a no-frills sort of way) for **hikers**.

From Goodrich, it's a couple of miles south along narrow country lanes to a fork in the road – veer right for Symonds Yat East, or keep straight for the wriggly road up to the top of **Symonds Yat Rock**, one of the region's most celebrated viewpoints, rising high above a wooded loop in the River Wye. Down below is **SYMONDS YAT EAST**, a pretty little hamlet that straggles along the east bank of the river. It's a popular spot and one that offers canoe rental and regular **river trips** (40min) – and there's a good hotel here too (see p.398). The road to the village is a dead end, so you have to double back to regain Goodrich

8

(or Symonds Yat Rock), though you can cross the river to **Symonds Yat West** by means of a hand-pulled rope **ferry**, which leaves from outside the *Saracens Head Inn* (see below).

ACCOMMODATION AND EATING   WYE RIVER VALLEY AT SYMONDS YAT

Doward Park Campsite Great Doward, Symonds Yat West ☎01600 890438, ⓦdowardpark.co.uk. Pleasant, partly wooded campsite in a remote location a couple of miles west of Symonds Yat West. Pitches £16

Saracens Head Inn Symonds Yat East ☎01600 890345, ⓦsaracensheadinn.co.uk. There are ten en-suite guest rooms in this village hotel beside the River Wye, each decorated in pleasant modern style with wooden floors and pastel-painted walls. You can eat well both in the restaurant and in the bar, with the menu featuring mostly English favourites – though there are

international dishes as well - with mains averaging £12. Food served daily noon–2.30pm & 6.30–9pm. **£89**

YHA Wye Valley Hostel Near Goodrich HR9 6JJ ☎0845 371 9666, ⓦyha.org.uk. If you're after a remote location, this is the hostel to head for – in a Victorian rectory in its own grounds above the River Wye. There are 78 beds, in anything from two- to ten-bed dorms, as well as camping and self-catering facilities; evening meals are also provided on request. Formerly the *Welsh Bicknor YHA Hostel*. Dorms **£19**, doubles **£39**

Shropshire

One of England's largest and least populated counties, **SHROPSHIRE** (ⓦshropshiretourism .co.uk) stretches from its long and winding border with Wales to the very edge of the urban Black Country. The Industrial Revolution made a huge stride forward here, with the spanning of the River Severn by the very first **iron bridge** and, although the assorted industries that subsequently squeezed into the **Ironbridge Gorge** are long gone, a series of **museums** celebrates their craftsmanship – from tiles through to iron. The River Severn also flows through the county town of **Shrewsbury**, whose antique centre holds dozens of old half-timbered buildings, though **Ludlow**, further south, has the edge when it comes to handsome Tudor and Jacobean architecture. In between the two lie some of the most beautiful parts of Shropshire, primarily the **Long Mynd**, a prime hiking area that is readily explored from the attractive little town of **Church Stretton**.

GETTING AROUND   SHROPSHIRE

By train There are frequent trains from Birmingham to Telford and Shrewsbury, which is also linked to Church Stretton and Ludlow on the Hereford line.

By bus Bus services are patchy, but one small step forward has been the creation of the Shropshire Hills Shuttle bus service (mid-April to Sept Sat & Sun only; every 1–2hr;

ⓦshropshirehillsaonb.co.uk) aimed at the tourist market. The shuttle noses round the Long Mynd as well as the Stiperstones and drops by Church Stretton. An adult Day Rover ticket, valid on the whole route, costs just £7. Timetables are available at most Shropshire tourist offices and on the website.

Ironbridge Gorge

IRONBRIDGE GORGE, the collective title for a cluster of small villages huddled in the Severn Valley to the south of new-town Telford, was the crucible of the Industrial Revolution, a process encapsulated by its famous span across the Severn – the world's first **iron bridge**, engineered by **Abraham Darby** and opened on New Year's Day, 1781. Darby was the third innovative industrialist of that name – the first Abraham Darby started iron-smelting here back in 1709 and the second invented the forging process that made it possible to produce massive single beams in iron. Under the guidance of such creative figures as the Darbys and Thomas Telford, the area's factories once churned out engines, rails, wheels and other heavy-duty iron pieces in quantities unmatched anywhere else in the world. Manufacturing has now all but vanished, but the surviving monuments make the Gorge the most extensive **industrial heritage site** in England – and one that has been granted World Heritage Site status by UNESCO.

The Gorge contains several museums and an assortment of other industrial attractions spread along a five-mile stretch of the Severn Valley. A thorough exploration takes a couple of days, but the highlights – the **Iron Bridge** itself, the **Museum of Iron** and the **Jackfield Tile Museum** – are easily manageable on a day-trip.

Ironbridge village

There must have been an awful lot of nail-biting during the construction of the **Iron Bridge** over the River Severn in the late 1770s. No one was quite sure how the new material would wear and although the single-span design looked sound, many feared the bridge would simply tumble into the river. To compensate, Abraham Darby used more iron than was strictly necessary, but the end result still manages to appear stunningly graceful, arching between the steep banks with the river far below. The settlement at the north end of the span was promptly renamed **IRONBRIDGE**, and today its brown-brick houses climb prettily up the hill from the bridge.

Museum of the Gorge

Wharfage · Daily 10am–5pm · £4.15, but covered by Passport Ticket (see p.401) · ☎ 01952 433424, ⓦ ironbridge.org.uk

Ironbridge village is also home to the **Museum of the Gorge**, in a church-like, neo-Gothic old riverside warehouse about seven hundred yards west of the bridge along the main road. This provides an introduction to the Gorge's industrial history and gives a few environmental pointers too; it also houses the main visitor centre (see p.401).

Coalbrookdale Museum of Iron

Wellington Rd, Coalbrookdale · Daily 10am–5pm · £9.25, but covered by Passport Ticket (see p.401) · ☎ 01952 433424, ⓦ ironbridge.org.uk

At the roundabout just to the west of the Museum of the Gorge, turn right for the half-mile trip up to what was once the Gorge's big industrial deal, the **Coalbrookdale iron foundry**, which boomed throughout the eighteenth and early nineteenth century, employing up to four thousand men and boys. The foundry has been imaginatively converted into the **Museum of Iron**, with a wide range of displays on iron-making in general and the history of the company in particular. There are superb examples of Victorian and Edwardian ironwork here, including the intricate castings – stags, dogs and even camels – that became the house speciality. Also in the complex, across from

IRONBRIDGE GORGE

Darby Houses

Museum of Iron

Coalbrookdale

ACCOMMODATION
Buckatree Hall Hotel	2
Coalbrookdale Villa	1
Coalport YHA Coalport	4
The Library House	3

COACH ROAD · DALE ROAD · PARADISE · LINCOLN HILL · CHURCH HILL · BEECH RD · MADELEY RD

Museum of the Gorge ⓘ

Ironbridge village

Iron Bridge

Bedlam Furnace

Jackfield Bridge · COALFORD

River Severn

COALPORT RD

Blists Hill

N

BALLS LANE

IRONBRIDGE RD

Jackfield Tile Museum

Jackfield

Maws Craft Centre

Footbridge · Tar Tunnel

Coalport

Coalport China Works & Museum

M54 & Telford

Buildwas, Little Wenlock, Much Wenlock & 2

● **RESTAURANTS & PUBS**
Coalbrookdale Inn	1
Restaurant Severn	2

0 ————— 500
yards

8

the foundry beneath a protective canopy, are the ruins of the **furnace** where Abraham Darby pioneered the use of coke as a smelting fuel in place of charcoal.

Bedlam Furnace
B4373, about 600 yards east of Ironbridge Village • Open access • Free

Heading **east** from the Iron Bridge along the north bank of the river, you soon pass the battered brick-and-stone remains of the **Bedlam furnace** (open access; free), one of the first furnaces to use coke rather than charcoal. It was kept alight around the clock, and at night its fiery silhouette was said to have scared passers-by out of their wits – hence the name.

Blists Hill Victorian Town
Coalport Rd • About 1m north of the River Severn – take the signed turning between the Bedlam Furnace and Coalport • Daily 10am–5pm • £16.50, but covered by Passport Ticket (see opposite) • ☎ 01952 433424, ⓦ ironbridge.org.uk

The rambling **Blists Hill Victorian Town** is the Gorge's most popular attraction, enclosing a substantial number of reconstructed Victorian buildings, most notably a school, a candle-maker's, a doctor's surgery, a pub and wrought-iron works. Jam-packed on most summer days, it's especially popular with school parties, who keep the period-dressed employees busy.

Tar Tunnel
Coalport High St, Coalport • On the north bank of the river, 500 yards east of the turning to Blists Hill & on the west edge of Coalport • April–Oct daily 10.30am–4pm • £3.25, but covered by Passport Ticket (see opposite) • ☎ 01952 433424, ⓦ ironbridge.org.uk

Built to transport coal from one part of the Gorge to another, but named for the bitumen that oozes naturally from its walls, the **Tar Tunnel** may not be long, but it's certainly more than a tad spooky and you'll be issued with a hard hat for reassurance.

Coalport China Museum
Coalport • Daily 10am–5pm • £8.50, but covered by Passport Ticket (see opposite) • ☎ 01952 433424, ⓦ ironbridge.org.uk

The most easterly of the industrial sites on the north bank of the River Severn (and yards from the Tar Tunnel), the former **Coalport China works** occupies a sprawling brick complex, which incorporates the **Coalport China Museum**, packed with gaudy Coalport wares. There's also a workshop, where potters demonstrate their skills, and two **bottle-kilns**, those distinctive conical structures that were long the hallmark of the pottery industry.

Jackfield
There are two ways to reach Jackfield from the north bank of the Severn: the Jackfield Bridge just east of Bedlam Furnace and the footbridge beside the Tar Tunnel.

Now a sleepy little village of pretty brown-brick cottages that string along the south bank of the River Severn, **JACKFIELD** was once a sooty, grimy place that hummed to the tune of two large tile factories, Maws and Craven Dunnill. Both were built in the middle of the nineteenth century to the latest industrial design, a fully integrated manufacturing system that produced literally thousands of tiles at breakneck speed. The more easterly of the two has been turned into the **Maws Craft Centre** (ⓦmawscraftcentre.co.uk), which holds more than twenty arts, craft and specialist shops, while the other, about half a mile away, boasts the Jackfield Tile Museum.

Jackfield Tile Museum
Jackfield • Daily 10am–5pm • £8.50, but covered by Passport Ticket (see opposite) • ☎ 01952 433424, ⓦ ironbridge.org.uk

A small part of the expansive Craven Dunnill factory still produces Craven Dunnill tiles (ⓦcravendunnill-jackfield.co.uk), but mostly it's home to the outstanding **Jackfield Tile Museum**. The exhibits here include the superb "Style Gallery" and "Tiles Everywhere Galleries", where room after room illustrates many different types of tile, by style – Art Deco and Art Nouveau through to Arts and Crafts and the Aesthetic Movement – and location, from a London underground station to a butcher's shop.

ARRIVAL AND DEPARTURE

By bus Arriva bus #96 (@arrivabus.co.uk) connects both Shrewsbury (35min) and Telford (30min) bus stations with

IRONBRIDGE GORGE

Ironbridge village (Mon–Sat every 2hr). There's also an Arriva service to Much Wenlock (Mon–Sat every 2hr; 30min).

GETTING AROUND

By bus Bus services along the Gorge are limited to the Gorge Connect (late July to late Aug daily 9am–5pm; every 30min; @arrivabus.co.uk), which links Coalbrookdale in the west with Coalport in the east, taking in Ironbridge village and Blists Hill on the way. A day ticket costs £7; Passport Ticket holders (see below) travel free.

INFORMATION

Tourist information Ironbridge Gorge tourist information (Mon–Fri 9am–5pm, Sat & Sun 10am–5pm; ☎ 01952 433424, @ironbridge.org.uk) is in the Museum of the Gorge, approximately 700 yards west of Ironbridge village along the main road. In addition to local maps and information, they sell attraction passes.

Admissions and passes Each museum and attraction charges its own admission fee, but if you're intending to visit several, then buy a Passport Ticket (£27.50), which allows access to all ten of them once in any calendar year. Passport Tickets are available at all the main sights and at tourist information. An extra £1.50 covers parking at all the sites, except in Ironbridge village, where metered charges apply.

ACCOMMODATION

Buckatree Hall Hotel The Wrekin, Telford, just south of the M54 and Wellington ☎ 01952 641821, @buckatree hallhotel.co.uk. In a pleasant rural setting near the wooded slopes of The Wrekin, the distinctive 1334ft peak that rises high above its surroundings, the *Buckatree* comprises the original Edwardian house and a modern annexe-wing. Most of the rooms have balconies. **£70**

Coalbrookdale Villa 17 Paradise, Coalbrookdale ☎ 01952 433450, @coalbrookdalevilla.co.uk. This B&B occupies an attractive Victorian ironmaster's house set in its own grounds about half a mile up the hill from Ironbridge village in the tiny hamlet of Paradise. Sedately decorated, country-house-style, en-suite bedrooms. **£75**

The Library House 11 Severn Bank, Ironbridge village ☎ 01952 432299, @libraryhouse.com. Enjoyable B&B, the best in the village, in a charming Georgian villa just yards from the Iron Bridge. Four doubles, decorated in a modern rendition of period style. **£90**

YHA Coalport Coalport ☎ 0845 371 9325, @yha.org .uk. At the east end of the Gorge in the former Coalport China factory, this YHA hostel has 80 beds in two- to ten-bedded rooms, self-catering facilities, laundry, a shop and a café. Popular with school groups and for activity breaks. Dorms **£18**, doubles **£27.50**

8

EATING AND DRINKING

Coalbrookdale Inn 12 Wellington Rd, Coalbrookdale ☎ 01952 432166, @thecoalbrookdaleinn.co.uk. On the main road across from the Coalbrookdale iron foundry, this traditional pub offers a top-notch selection of real ales plus filling pub grub, including locally made pork pies. Live music too. Mon–Thurs noon–2pm & 5–11.30pm, Fri–Sun noon–11.30pm.

Restaurant Severn 33 High St, Ironbridge village ☎ 01952 432233, @restaurantseven.co.uk. This smart little place, just a few yards from the bridge, offers an inventive menu with main courses such as venison in a cognac and cranberry sauce. In the evening, a two-course set meal costs around £26. Wed–Sat 6.30–8.30pm, plus occasional Sun noon–1.30pm.

Shrewsbury

SHREWSBURY, the county town of Shropshire, sits in a tight and narrow loop of the River Severn. It would be difficult to design a better defensive site and predictably the Normans built a stone castle here, one which Edward I decided to strengthen and expand in the thirteenth century, though by then the local economy owed as much to the Welsh wool trade as it did to the town's military importance. In Georgian times, Shrewsbury became a fashionable staging post on the busy London to Holyhead/Ireland route and has since evolved into a laidback, middling market town. It's the overall feel of the place that is its main appeal, rather than any specific sight, though to celebrate its associations with **Charles Darwin**, the town is now the possessor of a 40ft-high sculpture entitled **Quantum Leap**: it cost nigh-on half a million pounds, so many locals are rueing the cost rather than celebrating the artistic vision.

The obvious place to start an exploration of Shrewsbury is the **train station** (see below), built in a fetching combination of styles, neo-Baronial meets country house, in the 1840s. Poking up above the train station are the battered ramparts of the **castle**, a pale reminder of the mighty medieval fortress that once dominated the town – the illustrious Thomas Telford turned the castle into the private home of a local bigwig in the 1780s. **Castle Gates** and its continuation **Castle Street/Pride Hill** cuts up from the station into the heart of the river loop where the medieval town took root. Turn left off Castle Street onto St Mary's Street and you soon reach Shrewsbury's most interesting church, **St Mary's**, whose architecturally jumbled interior is redeemed by a magnificent east window. From St Mary's, it's a couple of minutes' walk to **St Alkmund's Church**, from where there's a charming view of the fine old buildings of **Fish Street**, which cuts its way down to the High Street. Turn right here to get to **The Square** which is at the very heart of the town; its narrow confines are inhabited by the **Old Market Hall**, a heavy-duty stone structure dating from 1596.

ARRIVAL AND INFORMATION
SHREWSBURY

By train Shrewsbury train station stands at the northeast tip of the town centre.
Destinations Birmingham (every 30min; 1hr); Church Stretton (hourly; 15min); Hereford (every 30min; 1hr); Ludlow (hourly; 30min); Telford (every 30min; 20min).
By bus Most buses pull into the Raven Meadows bus station, off Smithfield Rd, a 5min walk north of The Square.

Destinations Ironbridge village (Mon–Sat every 2hr; 35min; ⓦ arrivabus.co.uk); Much Wenlock (Mon–Sat hourly; 30min).
Tourist office In The Square (Easter–Sept daily 10am–5pm; Oct–Easter Tues–Sun 10am–5pm; ☎ 01743 258888, ⓦ shropshiretourism.co.uk); shares premises with the Shrewsbury Museum & Art Gallery.

ACCOMMODATION

★ Lion and Pheasant 50 Wyle Cop ☎ 01743 770345, ⓦ lionandpheasant.co.uk. Excellent, medium-sized, town-centre hotel in the shell of a former coaching inn; rooms are in pastel shades with lots of period details. Delicious breakfasts too. **£100**
Old House Suites The Old House, 20 Dogpole ☎ 0781 3610904, ⓦ theoldhousesuites.com. Cannily restored ancient merchant's house offering three suites kitted out in immaculate period style – down to the heavy drapes and

wood panelling. An up-market B&B, whose owner will give you the low-down on the house's history. **£85**
Prince Rupert Hotel Butcher Row, off Pride Hill ☎ 01743 499955, ⓦ princeruperthotel.co.uk. A smart and popular hotel, the *Rupert* occupies a cannily converted old building in the middle of the town centre. There are seventy comfortable guest rooms – including twelve suites – and the pick have a platoon of period details, from wood panelling through to exposed wooden beams. **£100**

EATING AND DRINKING

Admiral Benbow 24 Swan Hill ☎ 01743 244423, ⓦ theadmiralbenbowpub.co.uk/wp. Popular and enterprising, town-centre pub with a beer garden and a fine selection of real ales and Hereford farmhouse ciders and perry. Mon–Fri 5–11pm, Sat noon–11pm & Sun 7–10.30pm.
Golden Cross 14 Princess St ☎ 01743 362507, ⓦ goldencrosshotel.co.uk. This must be the best restaurant in Shrewsbury, a cosy, intimate kind of place (don't be deterred by the mullion windows) that offers a

select international menu – try, for example, the pan-roasted, oriental crusted fillet of sea bass. In the city centre, a 2min walk from The Square. Mains average a very reasonable £13. Daily noon–2.30pm & 5.30–9.30pm.
Good Life Coffee Shop & Restaurant Barracks Passage, just off 73 Wyle Cop ☎ 01743 350455, ⓦ goodlife-shrewsbury.co.uk. Something of a local institution, this excellent café specializes in salads and vegetarian dishes from a daily menu. Locals swear by the quiches. Mains around £7. Mon–Sat 9am–4pm.

Long Mynd

Beginning about nine miles south of Shrewsbury, the upland heaths of the **Long Mynd**, some ten miles long and between two and four miles wide, run parallel to and just to the west of the A49. This is prime **walking** territory and the heathlands are latticed with footpaths, the pick of which offer sweeping views over the border to the Black

FROM TOP AS YOU LIKE IT, THE ROYAL SHAKESPEARE THEATRE, STRATFORD-UPON-AVON (P.385); MOORLANDS AROUND DERWENT, THE PEAK DISTRICT (P.413) >

Mountains of Wales. Also popular with hikers, if even more remote, are the **Stiperstones**, a clot of boggy heather dotted with ancient cairns and earthworks that lies to the west of the Long Mynd.

Church Stretton

Nestled at the foot of the Mynd is **CHURCH STRETTON**, a tidy little village that makes an ideal base for hiking the area. The village also possesses the dinky parish **church of St Laurence**, parts of which – especially the nave and transepts – are Norman. Look out also for the (badly weathered) fertility symbol over the side door, just to the left of the entrance – it's a genital-splaying **sheela-na-gig**, whose sheer explicitness is eye-watering.

ARRIVAL AND INFORMATION

By train The train station is beside the A49 about 600 yards east of High St, which forms the heart of the village. Destinations Hereford (every 1hr–1hr 30min; 40min); Ludlow (every 1hr–1hr 30min; 15min); Shrewsbury (hourly; 15min). **By bus** Most buses pull in beside the train station, but some also continue on to High Street. There's a useful Shropshire Hills Shuttle bus service (see p.398).

Tourist office The library, Church Street (Mon–Sat 9.30am–1pm & 2–5pm; ☎01694 723133, ⓦchurchstretton .co.uk).

ACCOMMODATION

Victoria House 48 High St ☎01694 723823, ⓦvictoriahouse-shropshire.co.uk. The most central of several excellent B&Bs in the area, this extraordinarily cosy little place has six guest rooms above the owner's teashop (see below). The rooms are kitted out with heavy drapes, thick carpets and iron beds; breakfast is delicious. **£55**

YHA Bridges 5 miles west of Church Stretton on the edge of Ratlinghope SY5 0SP ☎01588 650656, ⓦyha.org.uk. On the edge of a tiny village, this hostel occupies a converted village school, has 38 beds in four- to twelve-bedded rooms, a café, camping and a self-catering kitchen. It's an ideal base for hiking to the Long Mynd or the Stiperstones. Dorms **£16**

EATING

Berry's Coffee House 17 High St ☎01694 7224452, ⓦberryscoffeehouse.co.uk. This is the dinkiest of (licensed) cafés, squeezed into antique premises in the centre of the village. They serve delicious snacks and light meals, but their salads are especially tasty – locally-smoked salmon with Berry's dill sauce salad gives the flavour. Reckon on £8 per salad. Daily 9am–5pm.

Jemima's Kitchen 48 High St ☎01694 723823, ⓦvictoriahouse-shropshire.co.uk. Delicious home-made and home-baked snacks and light meals here at this cosy café. Specialist teas and mouth-watering scones, too. Thurs–Sun 9.30am–4pm.

Ludlow

Perched on a hill in a loop of the River Teme, **LUDLOW**, thirty miles from Shrewsbury, is one of the most picturesque towns in the West Midlands, if not in England – a gaggle of beautifully preserved Georgian and black-and-white half-timbered buildings packed around a craggy stone castle, with rural Shropshire forming a drowsy backdrop. These are strong recommendations in themselves, but Ludlow earns bonus points by being something of a gastronomic hidey-hole with a clutch of outstanding **restaurants**, whose chefs and sous-chefs gather at the much-vaunted **Ludlow Food & Drink Festival** (ⓦfoodfestival.co.uk), held over three days every September. The other notable knees-up is the Ludlow Arts & Shakespeare Festival (ⓦludlowartsfestival.co.uk), ten days of musical and theatrical fun held in June or July.

Ludlow Castle

Castle Square • April–July & Sept daily 10am–5pm; Aug daily 10am–6pm; Oct–Dec & mid-Feb to March daily 10am–4pm; Jan to mid-Feb Sat & Sun 10am–4pm • £5 • ☎01584 873355, ⓦludlowcastle.com

Ludlow's large and imposing **castle** dates mostly from Norman times, its rambling ruins incorporating towers and turrets, gatehouses and concentric walls as well as the remains of the 110ft Norman **keep** and an unusual **Round Chapel** built in 1120. With its spectacular setting high above the river, the castle also offers grand views over the surrounding countryside.

Castle Square and around

The castle entrance abuts **Castle Square**, an airy rectangle whose eastern side breaks into several short and narrow lanes, with the one on the left leading through to the gracefully proportioned **Church of St Laurence**, whose interior is distinguished by its stained-glass windows and exquisite misericords in the choir. From the church, it's a few paces to the **Butter Cross**, a Neoclassical extravagance from 1744, and a few more to the **Bull Ring**, home of the **Feathers Hotel**, a fine Jacobean building with the fanciest wooden facade imaginable.

Broad Street

To the south of Castle Square, the gridiron of streets laid out by the Normans has survived intact, though most of the buildings date from the eighteenth century. Steeply sloping **Broad Street** is particularly attractive, flanked by many of Ludlow's five hundred half-timbered Tudor and red-brick Georgian listed buildings. At the foot of Broad Street is Ludlow's only surviving **medieval gate**, which was turned into a house in the eighteenth century.

ARRIVAL AND INFORMATION
LUDLOW

By train Ludlow train station is a 15min walk from the castle – just follow the signs
Destinations Church Stretton (every 1hr–1hr 30min; 15min); Hereford (every 30min; 30min); Shrewsbury (hourly; 30min).
By bus Most buses stop at the top of Mill Street, just off Castle Square.
Destinations Church Stretton (every 2hr; 30min); Hereford (every 2hr; 1hr 20min); Shrewsbury (every 2hr; 1hr 15min).
Tourist office Castle Square (Mon–Sat 10am–4.45pm, plus April–Oct Sun 10.30am–5pm; ☏ 01584 875053, ⓦ ludlow.org.uk).

ACCOMMODATION

Dinham Hall Hotel Dinham ☏ 01584 876464, ⓦ dinhamhall.co.uk. Handily located close to the castle, this deluxe, medium-sized hotel, with its thirteen appealing guest rooms, occupies a rambling, bow-windowed eighteenth-century stone mansion, which has previously seen service as a boarding house for Ludlow School. **£145**

Ludlow Bed & Breakfast 35 Lower Broad St ☏ 01584 876912, ⓦ ludlowbedandbreakfast.blogspot.co.uk. Near the bridge, a 5–10min walk from the castle, this cosy B&B has just two doubles in a pair of Georgian terrace cottages, which have been carefully knocked into one. Great breakfasts. **£75**

EATING

★ La Bécasse 17 Corve St ☏ 01584 872325, ⓦ labecasse.co.uk. Top-ranking restaurant with a strong French influence, where a two-course lunch menu du jour costs a reasonable £32. Try, for example, the boned and rolled local rabbit saddle with smoked bacon and caramelized celery. Reservations essential. Tues–Sat noon–2.30pm & 7–10pm.

The Fish House 51 Bullring ☏ 01584 879790, ⓦ thefishhouseludlow.co.uk. First-class fishmongers with a few tables where they serve sparkling wine and fresh seafood – anything from a plate of smoked mackerel (£4.50) through to dressed crabs, oysters and prawns. Wed–Sat 9am–4pm.

Mr Underhill's Dinham Weir ☏ 01584 874431, ⓦ mr-underhills.co.uk. One of the very best of Ludlow's top-flight restaurants, with a menu skilfully crafted from local ingredients, and some superb, creative vegetarian options (try the asparagus, cep-scented pasta and garden herbs). The eight-course daily market menu costs £70 per person. Reservations essential. Wed–Sun evenings only.

Birmingham

If anywhere can be described as the first purely industrial conurbation, it has to be **BIRMINGHAM**. Unlike the more specialist industrial towns that grew up across the north and the Midlands, "Brum" – and its "Brummies" – turned its hand to every kind of manufacturing, gaining the epithet "the city of 1001 trades". It was here also that the pioneers of the Industrial Revolution – James Watt, Matthew Boulton, Josiah Wedgwood, Joseph Priestley and Erasmus Darwin (grandfather of Charles) – formed

BIRMINGHAM

■ ACCOMMODATION	
Back to Backs Houses	5
Birmingham Central	4
Backpackers	3
Radisson Blu	1
Staybridge Suites	2
Staying Cool	

■ CLUBS & LIVE MUSIC	
The Jam House	1
The Nightingale	2

■ PUBS & BARS	
Old Joint Stock	2
Sunflower Lounge	1
The Wellington	3

● CAFÉS & RESTAURANTS	
Celebrity Indian Restaurant	5
Edmunds	4
Edwardian Tea Room	2
Fumo	2
MPW Steakhouse Bar & Grill	3
Purnells Bistro	1

the **Lunar Society**, an extraordinary melting-pot of scientific and industrial ideas. They conceived the world's first purpose-built factory, invented gas lighting and pioneered both the distillation of oxygen and the mass production of the steam engine. Thus, a modest Midlands market town mushroomed into the nation's economic dynamo with the population to match: in 1841 there were 180,000 inhabitants; just fifty years later that number had trebled.

Now Britain's second-largest city, with a population of over one million, Birmingham has long outgrown the squalor and misery of its boom years and today its industrial supremacy is recalled – but only recalled – by a crop of **recycled buildings**, from warehouses to an old custard factory, and an extensive network of **canals**. This recent (and enforced) shift to a post-manufacturing economy has also been trumped by an intelligent and far-reaching revamp of the city centre that has included the construction of a glitzy **Convention Centre**, a talented reconstruction of the **Bull Ring**, the reinvigoration of the excellent **Birmingham Museum & Art Gallery**, and, at a time when other councils are nervously biting their nails, the building of a lavish, state-of-the-art **Library**. Birmingham has also launched a whole range of cultural initiatives – including the provision of a fabulous new concert hall for the **City of Birmingham Symphony Orchestra** – and boasts both a first-rate restaurant scene and a boisterous nightlife. While Birmingham doesn't have the density of attractions of a capital city, it's well worth at least a couple of days of anyone's time.

The Bull Ring

A few steps from New Street Station, Rotunda Square, at the intersection of New and High streets, takes its name from the soaring **Rotunda**, a handsome and distinctive cylindrical tower that is the sole survivor of the notorious **Bull Ring** shopping centre, which fulfilled every miserable cliché of 1960s town planning until its demolition in 2001. The new Bull Ring shopping centre, which replaced it, has two strokes of real invention. Firstly, the architects split the shops into two separate sections, providing an uninterrupted view of the medieval spire of St Martin's in between – an obvious contrast between the old and the new perhaps, but still extraordinarily effective. The second coup was the design of **Selfridges**' store.

Selfridges

Bull Ring • Core hours: Mon–Fri 10am–8pm, Sat 9am–8pm, Sun 11am–5.30pm • ☎ 0800 123400, ⓦ style.selfridges.com/store/birmingham

Birmingham's **Selfridges** is an extraordinary sight – a billowing organic swell protruding from the Bull Ring's east side, and seen to best advantage from the wide stone stairway that descends from Rotunda Square to St Martin's. Reminiscent of an inside-out octopus, Selfridges shimmers with an architectural chain mail of thousands of spun aluminium discs, an altogether bold and hugely successful attempt to create a popular city landmark.

Victoria Square

Busy **New Street** stretches west from the Bull Ring en route to the handsomely refurbished **Victoria Square**, whose centrepiece is a large and particularly engaging **water fountain** designed by Dhruva Mistry. The waterfall outdoes poor old Queen Victoria, whose statue is glum and uninspired, though the thrusting self-confidence of her bourgeoisie is very apparent in the flamboyant **Council House** behind her, its gables and cupolas, columns and towers completed in 1879. Across the square, and very different, is the **Town Hall** of 1834, whose classical design – by Joseph Hansom, who went on to design Hansom cabs – was based on the Roman temple in Nîmes. The building's simple, flowing lines contrast with much of its surroundings, but it's an appealing structure all the same, and now houses a performing arts venue.

The Birmingham Museum and Art Gallery

Chamberlain Square • Daily 10am–5pm, Fri from 10.30am • Free • ☎ 0121 348 8007, ⓦ bmag.org.uk

The **Birmingham Museum and Art Gallery** (BM&AG), which occupies a grand Edwardian building and one of its neighbours, possesses a multifaceted collection running from fine and applied art through to archeological finds. The key paintings, including the BM&AG's prime collection of Pre-Raphaelites, are spread over one long floor – Floor 2 – which is where you'll also find the **Staffordshire Hoard**, the largest collection of Anglo-Saxon gold ever discovered, with more than 1500 pieces. The museum's collection is too large for it all to be exhibited at any one time, and artworks are regularly rotated, so be sure to pick up a **plan** at reception. There's also a good **café** here (see p.411).

The Pre-Raphaelites

The BM&AG holds a significant sample of **European** paintings and an excellent collection of eighteenth- and nineteenth-century British art, most notably a supreme muster of **Pre-Raphaelite** work. Founded in 1848, the Pre-Raphaelite Brotherhood consisted of seven young artists, of whom Rossetti, Holman Hunt, Millais and Madox Brown are the best known. The name of the group was selected to express their commitment to honest observation, which they thought had been lost with the Renaissance. Two seminal Pre-Raphaelite paintings on display are **Dante Gabriel Rossetti**'s stirring *Beata Beatrix* (1870) and **Ford Madox Brown**'s powerful image of emigration, *The Last of England* (1855). The Brotherhood disbanded in the 1850s, but a second wave of artists carried on in its footsteps, most notably **Edward Burne-Jones**, whose *Star of Bethlehem* – in Room 14 – is one of the largest watercolours ever painted, a mysterious, almost magical piece with earnest Magi and a film-star-like Virgin Mary.

The Industrial Gallery, Gas Hall and the Waterhall Gallery

Sharing Floor 2 is the **Industrial Gallery**, which is set around an expansive atrium whose wrought-iron columns and balconies clamber up towards fancy skylights. The gallery holds a choice selection of ceramics, jewellery and stained glass retrieved from defunct churches all over Birmingham. Here also is the *Edwardian Tea Room*, one of the city's more pleasant places for a cuppa (see p.411). Elsewhere, the cavernous **Gas Hall** is an impressive venue for touring art exhibitions, while the **Waterhall Gallery**, inside the Council House, just across Edmund Street from the main museum building, showcases temporary exhibitions of modern and contemporary art.

Hall of Memory and around

Centenary Square • Mon–Sat 10am–4pm • Free • ⓦ hallofmemory.co.uk

Erected in the 1920s to commemorate the thirteen thousand from Birmingham who died in World War I, the distinctive **Hall of Memory** is an architectural hybrid, a delightful mix of Art Deco and Neoclassical features, whose centrepiece is a domed Remembrance chamber. From the memorial, it's a brief walk to the newly constructed Library and the showpiece **International Convention Centre** (ICC) and **Symphony Hall** with the **Birmingham Repertory Theatre** on the right.

Birmingham Library

Centenary Square • Mon–Fri 8am–8pm, Sat 9am–5pm & Sun 11am–4pm • Free • ☎ 0121 242 4242, ⓦ libraryofbirmingham.com

At a time when many British libraries were under threat, it was a brave move for the City Council to fund the construction of a new **Library**, a prestige structure that was completed in 2013 to a striking design, its cubic superstructure clad with a shimmering filigree of overlapping metal rings. Local opinion seems to be divided as to whether it was a sound investment, but it's certainly a city landmark and the interior has all mod cons plus outside terraces with views over the city centre.

Gas Street Basin

Gas Street Basin is the hub of Birmingham's intricate canal system. There are eight canals within the city's boundaries, comprising 32 miles of canal, with most dug in the late eighteenth century before the railways made them uneconomic. Much of the surviving canal network slices through the city's grimy, industrial bowels, but certain sections have been immaculately restored with Gas Street Basin leading the way. The Basin, which is edged by a delightful medley of old brick buildings, lies at the junction of the Worcester and Birmingham and Birmingham Main Line canals and its dark waters almost invariably bob with a fleet of brightly painted narrowboats.

The Mailbox

Following the towpath along the canal southeast from Gas Street Basin soon brings you to **The Mailbox**, a striking reinvention of Birmingham's old postal sorting office complete with restaurants, hotels, and some of the snazziest shops in the city – including Harvey Nichols – and recently emerging from a thorough refit.

Brindleyplace

Also near Gas Street Basin is the waterside **Brindleyplace**, which is named after James Brindley, the eighteenth-century engineer responsible for many of Britain's early canals. It's an aesthetically pleasing development, even though many of its cafés, restaurants and shops are multinational chains, with an attractive central plaza popular with office staff at lunch times. Just off the central square is the city's much-lauded Ikon Gallery.

Ikon Gallery

1 Oozells Square • Tues–Sun 11am–6pm • Free • ☎ 0121 248 0708, ⓦ ikon-gallery.org

Housed in a substantial Victorian building in the Brindleyplace complex, the splendid **Ikon Gallery** is one of the country's most imaginative venues for touring exhibitions of contemporary art, with recent exhibitions by the likes of Cornelia Parker and Pakistan's Imran Qureshi. Perhaps even better, the gallery organises all sorts of workshops, family days and special events – from 'Art Explorer' days for children to 'Plastic Fantastic' and guided tours of the gallery itself.

Birmingham & Fazeley Canal

Just beyond Brindleyplace, in front of the massive dome of the National Indoor Arena (NIA), the canal forks: the Birmingham Main Line Canal cuts west (to the left) and the more interesting **Birmingham & Fazeley Canal** leads northeast (to the right), running past a sequence of antique brick buildings en route to the quaint **Scotland Street Locks**. Further on, the canal slices past a string of new apartment blocks as well as the (signed) flight of steps that clambers up to Newhall Street, about half a mile beyond the main canal junction – and a few minutes' walk from **St Paul's Square**, where an attractive ensemble of old houses flank the charming Neoclassical **St Paul's church** (ⓦ saintpaulbrum.org).

St Philip's Cathedral

Colmore Row • Mon–Fri 7.30am–6.30pm, 5pm in August; Sat & Sun 8.30am–5pm • Free • ☎ 0121 262 1840, ⓦ birminghamcathedral.com

The string of fancily carved, High Victorian stone buildings on Colmore Row provides a suitable backdrop for **St Philip's Anglican Cathedral**, a bijou example of English Baroque. Consecrated in 1715, the church is a handsome affair, its graceful, galleried interior all balance and poise, its harmonies unruffled by the Victorians, who enlarged the original church in the 1880s, when four stained-glass windows were commissioned from local boy **Edward Burne-Jones**, a leading light of the Pre-Raphaelite movement. The windows are typical of his style – intensely coloured, fastidiously detailed and distinctly sentimental. Three – the *Nativity*, *Crucifixion* and *Ascension* – are at the east end of the church beyond the high altar, the fourth – the *Last Judgement* – is directly opposite.

ARRIVAL AND DEPARTURE
BIRMINGHAM

By plane Birmingham's International Airport is 8 miles east of the city centre off the A45 – and near the M42 (Junction 6); the terminal is beside Birmingham International train station, from where there are regular services into New Street train station (every 10–15min; 12min).

By train Most inter-city trains and many local services use New Street train station, which is right in the heart of the city – and is currently undergoing a long-term (and long overdue) refurbishment. There are, however, two other mainline stations in the city centre. These are Snow Hill and Moor Street, respectively a (signed) 10min-walk north and a 5-minute walk east of New Street station. Moor Street, the prettiest of the three – with much of its Edwardian fabric intact – is used primarily by Chiltern Railways.

Destinations (New St) Birmingham International (every 10–15min; 12min); Coventry (3–5 hourly; 25min); Derby (every 30min; 45min); Great Malvern (hourly; 1hr); Hereford (hourly; 1hr 30min); Ledbury (hourly; 1hr 15min); London Euston (every 30min; 1hr 25min); Shrewsbury (every 30min; 1hr); Telford (Mon–Sat every 30min, Sun hourly; 40min).

Destinations (Moor St) London Marylebone (every 30min; 1hr 50min); Stratford-upon-Avon (hourly; 1hr 10min); Worcester Foregate (every 30min; 1hr).

Destinations (Snow Hill Station) Stratford-upon-Avon (hourly; 1hr); Warwick (every 30min to 1hr; 30min).

By bus National Express long-distance buses arrive at the Birmingham bus station, in Digbeth, from where it's a 10min walk northwest to the Bull Ring.

Destinations London (every 45min; 2hr 45min); Manchester (4–5 daily; 2hr 20min).

GETTING AROUND

Birmingham has an excellent public transport system, whose trains, metro and buses delve into almost every urban nook and cranny. Various companies provide these services, but they are all co-ordinated by Centro (☏ 0121 200 2787, ⊛ centro.org.uk).

INFORMATION

Tourist office In the Library, on Centenary Square (Mon–Fri 10am–6pm, Sat 9am–5pm; ☏ 0844 888 3883, ⊛ visitbirmingham.com). There's also a tourist information kiosk in front of New Street station, at the junction of New Street and Corporation Street (Mon–Sat 9am–5pm, Sun 10am–4pm; same details).

ACCOMMODATION

To see Birmingham at its best, you really need to stay in the centre, preferably in the vicinity of **Centenary Square**, though chain hotels do monopolize the downtown core. Visit Birmingham (⊛ visitbirmingham.com) operates a free **room-booking** service.

Back to Backs Houses 52 Inge St ☏ 0344 335 1287, ⊛ nationaltrustcottages.co.uk. The most distinctive place to stay in town: the National Trust has refurbished a small block of nineteenth-century back-to-back workers' houses conveniently located just to the south of the city centre along Hurst Street. Part of the complex now holds two small "cottages" – really terraced houses – kitted out in Victorian period style, but with the addition of en-suite and self-catering facilities. Each accommodates two guests. **£100**

Birmingham Central Backpackers 58 Coventry St, Digbeth ☏ 0121 643 0033, ⊛ birminghambackpackers .com. Welcoming hostel with self-catering facilities, free wi-fi, a large sociable lounge, a small garden and a café-bar. Dorms have four to twelve bunks per room. A short walk from Digbeth bus station. Dorms from **£16**, Doubles **£40**

Radisson Blu 12 Holloway Circus ☏ 0121 654 6000, ⊛ radissonblu.co.uk. Smart hotel in a tall, sleek skyrise within a few minutes' walk of the centre. The interior is designed in routine modern-minimalist style, but the floor-to-ceiling windows of many of the bedrooms add more than a dash of élan. **£80**

Staybridge Suites One Martineau Place, Corporation St ☏ 0871 423 4948, ⊛ staybridgesuites .com/Birmingham. Classic, 1960s, city-centre office block that has been skilfully converted into a hotel, holding 179 smart, modern suites with fitted kitchenettes. Capacious breakfast area, too. Double rooms from as little as **£50**

★ Staying Cool The Rotunda, New St ☏ 0121 285 1290, ⊛ stayingcool.com. The top three floors of the Rotunda, right at the heart of the city, have been converted into fully furnished, serviced apartments. All the apartments are modern and spotless, and those on the top floor – Floor 20 – come with a balcony from where there are panoramic views over the city. The apartments can be rented for one night – no problem. **£140**

EATING

Central Birmingham has a bevy of first-rate restaurants with a string of smart new venues springing up in the slipstream of the burgeoning conference and trade-fair business. Birmingham's gastronomic speciality is the **balti**, a delicious Kashmiri stew cooked and served in a small wok-like dish called a *karahi*, with naan bread instead of cutlery. The original balti houses are concentrated out in the suburbs of Balsall Heath, Moseley and Sparkhill to the south of the centre, but there are now prime balti houses in the centre too.

Celebrity Indian Restaurant 44 Broad St ☎0121 643 8969, ⓦcelebrityrestaurant.co.uk. Locals swear that the best baltis are served out in the city's suburbs, but this smart, city-centre restaurant runs them close – and saves the journey out. A wide-ranging menu covers all the classics and a 'traditional Brummy balti' will rush you about £10. Daily 5.30pm–midnight.

Edmunds 6 Central Square, Brindleyplace ☎0121 633 4944, ⓦedmundsrestaurant.co.uk. High-style dining in smart, contemporary premises. An inventive menu features seasonal ingredients – venison with dauphine potato, duck liver, parsnip mousseline and hazelnut crumble is typical. A two-course, lunchtime set meal is £15, but will set you back more than twice that in the evenings. Reservations well-nigh essential. Tues–Fri noon–2pm & 5.30–10.30pm, plus Sat 5.30–10pm.

Edwardian Tea Room (BM&AG), Chamberlain Square ☎0121 348 8007, ⓦbmag.org.uk. Recently upgraded, this relaxing café has a great setting in one of the large and fancily decorated halls of the museum's industrial section – check out all those handsome cast-iron columns. The food doesn't quite match up to the surroundings – but stick to the simpler dishes and you won't go wrong. Mon–Sat 11am–4.30pm & Sun 12.30–4.30pm.

★**Fumo** 1 Waterloo St ☎0121 643 8979, ⓦsancarlofumo.co.uk. In smart modern premises, this fast-paced Italian restaurant serves up excellent and authentic Italian cuisine – from the basics (pizzas and pastas) through to more elaborate concoctions like monkfish and prawns marinated in garlic, parsley and lemon. Mains are a snip at around £9. Daily 11.30am–11.30pm.

MPW Steakhouse Bar & Grill The Cube, 200 Wharfside St ☎0121 634 3433, ⓦmpwsteakhouse birmingham.co.uk. Amazingly popular cocktail bar and restaurant, the inspiration of Marco Pierre White. A no-nonsense menu features steaks (as you would expect), but there are other offerings too – for example pork belly, bramley apple with bubble and squeak and mustard sauce (£16.65). One of the reasons for its popularity is the location – on the top-floor of The Cube, a high-rise office block that has been creatively reconfigured, including the addition of a sculpture-like external casing/screen. Mon–Fri noon–2.30pm & 5–10pm; Sat & Sun noon–10pm.

★**Purnells Bistro** 11 Newhall St ☎0121 200 1588, ⓦpurnellsbistro-gingers.com. A new venture by Michelin-starred chef Glynn Purnell, who already operates one of the city's best restaurants – *Purnell's* – this combined cocktail bar and up-market bistro offers "honest portions of food, inspired by rustic home cooking". Quite. À la carte mains average £14 and include such delights as mackerel pastilla with a tomato and olive salsa. Reservations recommended. Food served daily noon–2.30pm & 5–10pm, closed Sun eve.

DRINKING

★**Old Joint Stock** 4 Temple Row West ☎0121 200 1892, ⓦoldjointstocktheatre.co.uk. This charming pub has the fanciest decor in town – with busts and a balustrade, a balcony and chandeliers, all dating from its days as a bank. There's a medium-sized theatre studio upstairs mostly featuring improv comedy and musical theatre. Daily 11am–11pm.

Sunflower Lounge 76 Smallbrook Queensway ☎0121 632 6756, ⓦthesunflowerlounge.com. Quirky pub-cum-bar in modern premises on the inner ring road near New Street station. Attracts an indie/student crowd and covers many bases, with quizzes and big-screen TV plus resident DJs and live gigs. It really is cool without being pretentious – just as they say on their website. Daily hours vary depending on event.

The Wellington 37 Bennetts Hill ☎0121 200 3115, ⓦthewellingtonrealale.co.uk. Specialist real ale pub with a top-notch range of local brews, including those of the much-proclaimed Black Country Brewery, and a good selection of ciders, too. Daily 10am–midnight.

NIGHTLIFE AND ENTERTAINMENT

Birmingham's **club scene** is one of Britain's best, spanning everything from word-of-mouth underground parties to meat-market mainstream clubs. **Live music** is strong, too, with big-name concerts at several major venues and other (often local) bands appearing at some clubs and pubs. Birmingham's showpiece **Symphony Orchestra** and **Royal Ballet** are the spearheads of the city's **classical scene**. The city also lines up a string of top-ranking **festivals** - including the **Jazz Festival** (ⓦbirminghamjazzfestival.com) held for two weeks in July. For details of all upcoming events, performances and exhibitions, ask at the tourist office (see opposite) or consult either ⓦbirminghammail.co.uk or ⓦlivebrum.co.uk.

LIVE MUSIC AND CLUBS

★ **The Jam House** 3 St Paul's Square ☎ 0121 200 3030, ⓦ thejamhouse.com. Jazz, funk, blues and swing club/pub pulling in artists from every corner of the globe. Great vibe; great gigs. Tues–Sat from 6pm.

The Nightingale 18 Kent St ☎ 0121 622 1718, ⓦ nightingaleclub.co.uk. The king/queen of Brum's gay clubs, popular with straights as well. Five bars, three levels, two discos, a café-bar and even a garden. Just south of the Hippodrome (see below). Thurs–Sat from 9pm.

O2 Academy 16–18 Horsefair, Bristol St Ticket line: ☎ 0844 477 2000, ⓦ o2academybirmingham.co.uk. State-of-the-art venue with three rooms hosting either gigs or club nights, though the big deal are the top-ranking artists – Katey P, Paloma Faith, The Kooks and so forth.

CLASSICAL MUSIC, THEATRE, DANCE AND CINEMA

Birmingham Hippodrome Hurst St ☎ 0844 338 5000, ⓦ birminghamhippodrome.com. Lavishly refurbished, the Hippodrome is home to the Birmingham Royal Ballet. Also features touring plays and big pre- and post-West End productions, plus a splendiferous Christmas pantomime.

Birmingham Repertory Theatre Centenary Square, Broad St ☎ 0121 236 4455, ⓦ birmingham-rep.co.uk. Mixed diet of classics and new work featuring local and experimental writing.

Electric Cinema 47 Station St ☎ 0121 643 7879, ⓦ the electric.co.uk. Britain's oldest working cinema, housed in a handsome Art Deco building, with an inventive programme of mainstream and art-house films. Sofas and waiter service also.

Symphony Hall International Convention Centre, Broad St ☎ 0121 345 0600, ⓦ thsh.co.uk. Acoustically one of the most advanced concert halls in Europe, home of the acclaimed City of Birmingham Symphony Orchestra (CBSO; ⓦ cbso.co.uk), as well as a venue for touring music and opera.

Town Hall Broad St ☎ 0121 345 0600, ⓦ thsh.co.uk. Recently refitted and refurbished, the old Town Hall offers a varied programme of pop, classical and jazz music through to modern dance and ballet.

8 Derby

Resurgent **DERBY** may be close to the wilds of the Peak District (see opposite), but it has more in common with its big-city neighbours, Nottingham and Leicester, except that here the industrial base is thriving with **Rolls-Royce** leading the way. Furthermore, recent attempts to spruce up the town have proved particularly successful and there's one prime attraction in the centre too, the **Derby Museum and Art Gallery**. The gallery is located just west of the central **Market Place** and southwest of the city's most impressive building, the **cathedral**, whose ponderous medieval tower rises high above its modest Victorian surroundings. An hour or two will do to see the sights before you hightail it off to the Peak District.

Derby Museum and Art Gallery

The Strand • Tues–Sun 10am–5pm • Free • ☎ 01332 641901, ⓦ derbymuseums.org

Among much else, **Derby Museum and Art Gallery** exhibits a splendid collection of Derby **porcelain**, several hundred pieces tracking through its different phases and styles from the mid-eighteenth century until today. The museum's star turn, however, is its prime collection of the work of **Joseph Wright** (1734–97), a local artist generally regarded as one of the most talented English painters of his generation. Wright's depictions of the scientific world were hugely influential – as in his *The Alchemist Discovering Phosphorus* and *A Philosopher Lecturing on the Orrery*.

ARRIVAL AND INFORMATION   DERBY

By train Derby train station is a mile to the southeast of the city centre – just follow the signs – but it's a dreary walk, so you might as well take a taxi.

Destinations Birmingham New Street (every 20min; 40min); Leicester (every 20min; 30min); London St Pancras (every 30min; 1hr 30min); Nottingham (every 20min; 25min).

By bus The bus station is on Morledge on the southeast side of the city centre. One useful service beginning here is High Peak Buses' (ⓦ highpeakbuses.com) TransPeak service across the Peak District to Manchester.

Destinations Ashbourne (hourly; 40min); Bakewell (hourly; 1hr); Buxton (hourly; 1hr 35min); Manchester (5 daily; 3hr).

Tourist office For the moment at least, Derby tourist information centre remains in a part of the Assembly Rooms, on Market Place, that escaped the recent fire (Mon–Sat 9.30am–4.30pm; ☎ 01332 643411, ⓦ visitderby.co.uk).

EATING AND DRINKING

Brunswick Inn 1 Railway Terrace ☎01332 290677, ⓦbrunswickderby.co.uk. In a good-looking Georgian terrace building just a couple of minutes' walk from the train station, this traditional pub, with its leather banquettes and garden, offers an impressive range of ciders and real ales, some of which are brewed on the premises. Daily 11am–11pm, Sun from noon.

The European 22 Irongate ☎01332 368732, ⓦtheeuropeanrestaurant.co.uk. Friendly, family-run restaurant cum bistro offering a tasty range of Italian dishes – all the classics and then some. Above a shop in an attractive old building, just across the street from the cathedral. Mains average £10, a tad less at lunch times. Mon 6–10pm, Tues–Sat noon–2pm & 6–10pm.

The Kitchen 47 Sadler Gate ☎01332 608619, ⓦthekitchenderby.com. Bright and breezy, independent café with an imaginative range of sandwiches, salads and light bites – and featuring their own home-grown produce. A few yards from Derby Museum. Mon–Sat 8am 5pm.

The Peak District

In 1951, the hills and dales of the **PEAK DISTRICT**, at the southern tip of the Pennine range, became Britain's first National Park. Wedged between Derby, Manchester and Sheffield, it is effectively the back garden for the fifteen million people who live within an hour's drive of its boundaries, though somehow it accommodates the huge influx with minimum fuss.

Landscapes in the Peak District come in two forms. The brooding high moorland tops of **Dark Peak**, to the east of Manchester, take their name from the underlying gritstone, known as millstone grit for its former use – a function commemorated in the millstones demarcating the park boundary. Windswept, mist-shrouded and inhospitable, the flat tops of these peaks are nevertheless a firm favourite with walkers on the **Pennine Way**, which meanders north from the tiny village of **Edale** to the Scottish border. Altogether more forgiving, the southern limestone hills of the **White Peak** have been eroded into deep forested dales populated by small stone villages and often threaded by walking trails, some of which follow former rail routes. The limestone is riddled with complex cave systems around **Castleton** and on the periphery of **Buxton**, a pleasant former spa town lying just outside the park's boundaries and at the end of an industrialized corridor that reaches out from Manchester. Elsewhere, one of the country's most distinctive manorial piles, **Chatsworth House**, stands near **Bakewell**, a town famed locally not just for its cakes but also for its **well-dressing**, a possibly pagan ritual of thanksgiving for fresh water that takes place in about thirty local villages each summer. The well-dressing season starts in May and continues through to mid-September; get exact dates and details on ⓦwelldressing.com.

As for a **base**, Buxton is your best bet by a (fairly) long chalk, though if you're after hiking and cycling you'll probably prefer one of the area's villages – Edale or Castleton will do very nicely.

ARRIVAL AND DEPARTURE
THE PEAK DISTRICT

By train Frequent trains run south from Manchester to end-of-the-line Buxton, and Manchester/Sheffield trains stop at Edale.

By bus The main bus access is on High Peak Buses' (ⓦhighpeakbuses.com) TransPeak service from Derby to Manchester via Bakewell and Buxton (5 daily; 3hr). Otherwise, First (ⓦfirstgroup.com) bus #272 runs from Sheffield to Castleton, via Hathersage and Hope, and TM Travel (ⓦtmtravel.co.uk) bus #65 connects Sheffield to Buxton. See ⓦtravelineeastmidlands.co.uk. for detailed route planning.

GETTING AROUND

By bus Within the Peak District, you'll find local bus services are reasonably frequent, though less so on Sundays and in winter. Local tourist offices almost always have bus and train timetables or see ⓦ travelineeastmidlands.co.uk.

By bike The Peak District has a good network of dedicated cycle lanes and trails, sometimes along former railway lines, and the Peak District National Park Authority (see p.415) operates three cycle rental outlets: at Ashbourne (☎01335 343156); Derwent, Bamford (☎01433 651261); and Parsley Hay, Buxton (☎01298 84493).

THE PEAK DISTRICT

INFORMATION

Visitor centres The Peak District National Park Authority (☎ 01629 816200) operates four visitor centres, including those at Bakewell and Castleton; these supplement a host of town and village tourist information offices.

Maps and guides A variety of Peaks maps and trail guides are widely available, but for the non-specialist it's hard to beat the *Grate Little Guides* (☜ walksaboutthepeakdistrict.co.uk), a series of leaflets that provide hiking suggestions and trail descriptions for a dozen or so localities in a clear and straightforward style. They cost £3 each and are on sale at most tourist information centres. Note that the maps printed on the leaflets are best used in conjunction with an OS map.

Useful websites ☜ visitpeakdistrict.com; ☜ peakdistrict .gov.uk

ACCOMMODATION

There's a plethora of accommodation in and around the Peak District National Park, mostly in **B&Bs**. The Peak District also holds numerous **campsites** and half a dozen or so **YHA hostels** as well as a network of YHA-operated **camping barns**. These are located in converted farm buildings and provide simple and inexpensive self-catering facilities. For further details, consult ☜ yha.org.uk.

Ashbourne and around

Sitting pretty on the edge of the Peaks twelve miles northwest of Derby, **ASHBOURNE** is an amiable little town, whose stubby, cobbled **Market Place** is flanked by a happy ensemble of old red-brick buildings. Hikers tramp in and out of town en route to and from the neighbouring dales with many wandering the popular **Tissington Trail**, which runs north from near Ashbourne for thirteen miles along the route of an old railway line. Cafés and pubs loiter around Ashbourne's **Market Place** and nearby, just down the hill, a suspended wooden beam spans St John's Street. Once a common feature of English towns, but now a rarity, these **gallows** were not warnings to malcontents, but advertising hoardings.

Dovedale

Head north from Ashbourne along the A515 and then follow the signs to the car park, which is on a narrow country road just beyond the hamlet of Thorpe

The **River Dove**, which wriggles its way across the Peak District, is at its scenic best four miles north of Ashbourne in the stirring two-mile gorge that comprises **Dovedale** – confusingly, other parts of the river are situated in different dales. The **hike** along the gorge is a real pleasure and easy to boot, the only problem being the bogginess of the valley after rain, but be warned that the place heaves with visitors on summer weekends and bank holidays.

ARRIVAL AND INFORMATION   ASHBOURNE

By bus The bus station is conveniently located on King Edward St, off Dig Street, a 2min walk from Market Place. Destinations Buxton (every 1–2hr; 1hr 15min); Derby (hourly; 40min); Hartington (every 1–2hr; 35min).

Tourist office Market Place (March–Oct daily 10am–5pm; Nov–Feb Mon–Sat 10.30am–4pm; ☎ 01335 343666, ☜ visitpeakdistrict.com).

EATING AND DRINKING

Bennetts 19 St John St ☎ 01335 342982. Independent department store in the centre of Ashbourne with a wide range of goods plus a particularly cosy café, where they do a good line in home-made cakes, scones and sandwiches. Mon–Sat 9am–4pm.

Bramhalls Deli & Café 22 Market Place ☎ 01335 342631, ☜ bramhallsdeli.co.uk. Pop into this first-rate deli to stock up on local cheeses and hams, terrines, etc. There's a small café here too – tuck into local sausages and Derbyshire oatcakes. Mon–Sat 8am–5pm & Sun 9am–5pm.

Hartington

Best approached from the east, through the boisterous scenery of Hand Dale, **HARTINGTON**, 11 miles north of Ashbourne, is one of the prettiest villages in the Peaks, with an easy ramble of stone houses zeroing in on a tiny duck pond. The village is also within easy walking distance of the River Dove as well as a sequence of handsome limestone dales – **Biggin Dale** is perhaps the pick. The other excitement is cheese – the village has its own specialist **cheese shop** (ⓦhartingtoncheeseshop.co.uk) with a raft of local and international cheeses and a selection of chutneys to lighten the gastronomic load.

ARRIVAL AND DEPARTURE	HARTINGTON
By bus Buses stop on Mill Lane in the centre of the village, a few yards from the duck pond.	Destinations Ashbourne (every 1–2hr; 35min); Buxton (every 1–2hr; 45min).

ACCOMMODATION

The Hayloft Church St ☎01298 84358, ⓦhartingtonhayloft.co.uk. Perhaps the best of Hartington's several B&Bs, in a sympathetically converted barn a few yards from the duck pond and part of a working farm. There are just four guest rooms – each of which is decorated in a straightforward modern style. **£60**

YHA Hartington Hall Bank ☎0845 371 9740, ⓦyha.org .uk. Well-equipped hostel whose 130 beds – in one- to eight-bed dorms – are squeezed into a seventeenth-century manor house, Hartington Hall, about 300 yards from the centre of the village. Facilities include a self-catering kitchen, a café and internet access. Dorms **£19**, doubles **£39**

Buxton

BUXTON, twelve miles north of Hartington, has had more than its fair share of ups and downs, but with its centre revamped and reconfigured, it is without doubt the most agreeable town in the Peak District and its string of excellent B&Bs make it a perfect base for further explorations. Buxton has a long history as a **spa**, beginning with the Romans, who happened upon a spring from which 1500 gallons of pure water gushed every hour at a constant 28°C. Impressed by the recuperative qualities of the water, the Romans came here by the chariot load, setting a trend that was to last hundreds of years. The spa's heyday came at the end of the eighteenth century with the **fifth Duke of Devonshire**'s grand design to create a northern answer to Bath or Cheltenham, a plan ultimately thwarted by the climate, but not before some distinguished buildings had been erected. Victorian Buxton may not have had quite the élan of its more southerly rivals but it still flourished, creating the rows of handsome stone houses that inhabit the town centre today. The town's **thermal baths** were closed for lack of custom in 1972, but Buxton has hung on not least because of its splendid **festival** (see box, p.418).

The Crescent

The centrepiece of Buxton's hilly, compact centre is **The Crescent**, a broad sweep of Georgian stonework commissioned by the fifth Duke of Devonshire in 1780 and modelled on the Royal Crescent in Bath. It was cleaned and scrubbed a few years ago, but has lain idle ever since and plans to turn it into a five-star hotel complete with thermal baths have yet to materialise. Facing The Crescent, and also currently empty, is the old **Pump Room**, an attractive Victorian building where visitors once sampled the local waters; next to it is a **water fountain**, supplied by St Ann's Well and still used to fill many a local water bottle. For a better view of The Crescent and the town centre, clamber up **The Slopes**, a narrow slice of park that rises behind the Pump Room dotted with decorative urns. From here, it's impossible to miss the enormous **dome** of what was originally the Duke of Devonshire's stables and riding school, erected in 1789 and now part of Derby University.

Pavilion Gardens and around

Next to The Crescent, the appealing old stone buildings of **The Square** – though square it isn't – nudge up to the grandly refurbished **Buxton Opera House**, an Edwardian extravagance whose twin towers date from 1903. Stretching back from the Opera House are the **Pavilion Gardens**, a slender string of connected buildings distinguished by their wrought-iron work and culminating in a large and glassy dome, the **Octagon**, which was originally a music hall, and the **Pavilion Arts Centre**. The adjoining **park**, also known as the Pavilion Gardens and cut across by the River Wye, is especially pleasant, its immaculate lawns and neat borders graced by a bandstand, ponds, dinky little footbridges and fountains.

Poole's Cavern

Green Lane • March–Oct daily 9.30am–5pm; Nov–Feb Sat & Sun 10am–4pm, plus weekday tours at fixed times • £9 • ☎ 01298 26978, ⓦ poolescavern.co.uk • 1 mile southwest of central Buxton: take the A53 towards Macclesfield/Leek and watch for the sign

The Peaks are riddled with cave systems and half a dozen have become popular tourist attractions rigged up with underground lighting. One of the best is **Poole's Cavern**, whose network of caves culminates in a vast chamber dripping with stalactites and stalagmites. Visitors have been popping in for centuries – apparently, Mary, Queen of Scots, dropped by and was suitably impressed.

ARRIVAL AND INFORMATION
BUXTON

By train Buxton train station is on Station Road, a 3min walk from the town centre.
Destinations Manchester Piccadilly or Manchester Oxford Road Station (hourly; 1hr).
By bus Buses stop on Market Place, a 4min walk from the Opera House.
Destinations Ashbourne (every 1–2hr; 1hr 15min);

Bakewell (hourly; 30min); Derby (hourly; 1hr 35min); Hartington (every 1–2hr; 45min).
Tourist office Pavilion Gardens, behind the Opera House (daily. April–Oct 9.30am–5pm; Nov–March 10am–4pm; ☎ 01298 25106, ⓦ visitbuxton.co.uk).

ACCOMMODATION

Buxton town centre is liberally sprinkled with **B&Bs** and finding somewhere to stay is rarely a problem, except during the Buxton Festival (see box, p.418), when advance reservations are essential.

Buxton's Victorian Guest House 3a Broad Walk ☎ 01298 78759, ⓦ buxtonvictorian.co.uk. Cosy B&B in a grand Victorian house with a handful of well-appointed, frilly rooms featuring four-posters and Indian-print cushions. Local produce is served up at breakfast whenever feasible. **£94**
★**Grosvenor House** 1 Broad Walk ☎ 01298 72439, ⓦ grosvenorbuxton.co.uk. There are eight unfussy, en-suite guest rooms – seven doubles and one single – in this

attractive B&B, which is located in a handsome Victorian townhouse. The best rooms offer gentle views over the gardens. Delicious home-made breakfasts, too. **£70**
Roseleigh 19 Broad Walk ☎ 01298 24904, ⓦ roseleigh hotel.co.uk. This classic, three-storey gritstone Victorian townhouse, overlooking Pavilion Gardens, is an excellent place to stay. The trim public rooms are decorated in attractive Victorian style, and the en-suite bedrooms are well appointed. Family-run and competitively priced. **£80**

EATING AND DRINKING

Columbine 7 Hall Bank ☎ 01298 78752, ⓦ columbine restaurant.co.uk. The menu at this small and intimate restaurant, right in the centre of Buxton, is short but imaginative, with main courses – such as saddle of monkfish

with crab risotto – averaging £17. Pre-theatre dinners, from about 5pm, can be reserved in advance. May–Oct Mon–Sat 7–10pm; Nov–April Mon & Wed–Sat 7–10pm.
Old Hall Hotel The Square ☎ 01298 22841,

> ## BUXTON FESTIVAL
>
> Buxton boasts the outstanding **Buxton Festival** (box office ☎0845 127 2190, ⓦbuxtonfestival
> .co.uk), which runs for two and a half weeks in July and features a full programme of classical
> music, opera and literary readings. This has spawned the first-rate **Buxton Festival Fringe**
> (ⓦbuxtonfringe.org.uk), also in July, which focuses on contemporary music, theatre and film.

ⓦoldhallhotelbuxton.co.uk. A few steps from the Opera House and occupying a building that dates back to the 1570s, the *Old Hall* offers good quality food in both its (fairly formal) restaurant and in the bar. The menu is Modern British with due prominence given to local/seasonal ingredients. Mains average £16, less at lunch times. Daily noon–2pm & 6–9.30pm.

Old Sun Inn 33 High St ☎01298 23452, ⓦtheoldsuninnbuxton.com. This fine old pub, with its maze of antique beamed rooms, is just south of Market Place. It's a good spot for a fine range of real ales and above-average bar food. Daily noon–11pm.

Castleton and around

A hikers' heaven and haven, pocket-sized **CASTLETON**, a scenic ten miles northeast of Buxton via Sparrowpit and the dramatic **Winnats Pass**, lies on the northern edge of the White Peak, its huddle of old stone cottages ringed by hills and set beside a babbling brook. It's s distinctly unpretentious place – and none the worse for that – and the hikers are joined by platoons of cyclists and cavers, with all gathering together to prepare for the off on **Market Place**, yards from the main drag, just behind the church.

Peveril Castle

Off Market Place • April–Oct daily 10am–5pm; Nov–March Sat & Sun 10am–4pm • EH • £4.60 • ☎01433 620613, ⓦenglish-heritage.org.uk

Overseeing Castleton is **Peveril Castle**, from which the village takes its name. William the Conqueror's illegitimate son William Peveril raised the first fortifications here to protect the king's rights to the forest that then covered the district, but most of the remains – principally the ruinous square keep – date to the 1170s. After a stiff climb up to the keep, you can trace much of the surviving curtain wall, which commands great views over the Hope Valley down below.

Caves around Castleton

The limestone hills pressing in on Castleton are riddled with water-worn **cave systems**, four of which have been developed as tourist attractions complete with subterranean lighting. Each can be reached by car or on foot, though most visitors settle for just one set of caves – the Peak Cavern and the Treak Cliff Cavern are particularly recommended.

Peak Cavern

Off Goosehill • April–Oct daily 10am–5pm; Nov–March Sat & Sun 10am–5pm, plus additional weekday tours (see website for times) • £9.25; joint ticket with Speedwell Cavern £15.50 • ☎01433 620285, ⓦpeakcavern.co.uk

Peak Cavern is the handiest of Castleton's four cave systems, tucked into a gully at the back of the village, its gaping mouth once providing shelter for a rope factory and a small village. Daniel Defoe, visiting in the eighteenth century, noted the cavern's colourful local name, the **Devil's Arse**, a reference to the fiendish fashion in which its interior contours twisted and turned.

Treak Cliff Cavern

Buxton Rd • Daily 10am–5pm • £8.95 • ☎01433 620571, ⓦbluejohnstone.com • About 800 yards west of Castleton up off a minor road (and signed from the A6187)

Treak Cliff Cavern is a major source of a rare sparkling fluorspar known as **Blue John**. Highly prized for ornaments and jewellery since Georgian times, this semi-precious stone comes in a multitude of hues from blue through deep red to yellow, depending on its hydrocarbon impurities. The Treak Cliff contains the best examples of the stone *in situ* and is also the best cave to visit in its own right, dripping – literally – with ancient stalactites, flowstone and bizarre rock formations, all visible on an entertaining forty-minute walking tour through the main cave system.

ARRIVAL AND INFORMATION   CASTLETON

By train There are no trains to Castleton – the nearest you'll get is Hope, a couple of miles or so to the east along the valley on the Manchester–Sheffield line. Regular buses run from near Hope train station to Castleton (every 1–2hr; 10min).

Destinations (from Hope) Edale (hourly; 6min); Hathersage (hourly; 10min); Manchester Piccadilly (hourly; 50min); Sheffield (hourly; 30min).

By bus Castleton's main bus stop is yards from the centre of the village on How Lane (the A6187). The principal bus service is the South Yorkshire First bus #272.

Destinations Bakewell (3 daily; 50min); Hathersage (hourly; 20min); Hope (hourly; 10min); Sheffield (hourly; 1hr).

Tourist office A combined museum, community centre and tourist office on Buxton Road (daily: April–Oct 10am–5pm; Nov–March 10.30am–4.30pm; ☎01629 816572, ⓦ peakdistrict.gov.uk) stands beside the car park on the west side of the village, just off the main street (the A6187).

Maps The tourist office sells hiking leaflets and maps, which are invaluable for a string of walking routes that take you up to the bulging hilltops that rise in every direction.

ACCOMMODATION AND EATING

You should book accommodation in advance at holiday times when Castleton heaves with visitors. The restaurant scene is a tad patchy, but at least things are beginning to improve.

1530 The Restaurant Cruck Barn, Cross St ☎01433 621870, ⓦ1530therestaurant.co.uk. In an old stone building near the centre of the village, this bright and breezy restaurant specialises in Italian cuisine – from pizzas and pastas through to more ambitious dishes, like the sea bass with artichokes and sun-dried tomatoes. Mains average £12, less at lunch times. Daily except Tues noon–2pm & 6–10pm.

Bargate Cottage Market Place ☎01433 620201, ⓦbargatecottage.co.uk. In an old cottage at the heart of the village, this friendly B&B has a handful of en-suite rooms decorated in a cosy, traditional style. The home-made breakfasts are delicious. **£70**

Causeway House Back St ☎01433 623291,

ⓦcausewayhouse.co.uk. The cream of the crop, this B&B occupies an old and well-tended stone cottage just north of Market Place. There are five guest rooms, three en suite, all tastefully kitted out to make the most of the cottage's original features. **£75**

YHA Castleton Losehill Hall Castleton Road, signed off the A6187 ☎0845 371 9628, ⓦyha.org.uk. The YHA has spent a bucket refurbishing this Victorian Neo-Gothic mansion set in its own grounds to the north of the village. It's a well-equipped hostel with a self-catering kitchen, a café, laundry, wi-fi, cycle store and drying room, and its 144 beds are parcelled up into two- to six-bedded rooms, most of which are en suite. Dorms **£18**, doubles **£30**

Edale village

There's almost nothing to **EDALE VILLAGE**, about five miles northwest of Castleton, except for a slender, half-mile trail of stone houses, which march up the main street from the train station with a couple of pubs, an old stone church and a scattering of B&Bs on the way – and it's this somnambulant air that is its immediate appeal. The village is also extremely popular with walkers, who arrive in droves throughout the year to set off on the **Pennine Way** (see box, p.420) – the route's starting point is signposted from outside the *Old Nag's Head* at the head of the village. If that sounds too daunting, note that there are lots of more manageable alternatives, including an excellent **circular walk** (9 miles; 5hr) that takes in the first part of the Pennine Way, leading up onto the bleak gritstone, table-top of **Kinder Scout** (2088ft), below which Edale cowers.

ARRIVAL AND INFORMATION   EDALE VILLAGE

By train At the southern end of the village, Edale train station is on the Sheffield–Manchester line.

Destinations Hope – for Castleton (hourly; 6min); Hathersage (hourly; 15min); Manchester Piccadilly (hourly; 45min); Sheffield (hourly; 35min).

Moorland Centre From Edale train station, it's 400 yards

or so up the road to the Moorland Centre (April–Sept daily 9.30am–5pm; Oct & March Mon–Fri 10am–3.30pm, Sat & Sun 9.30am–4.30pm; Nov & Jan–Feb Sat & Sun 9.30am–3.30pm; closed Dec; ☎01433 670207, ⓦ peakdistrict.gov.uk), who sell all manner of trail leaflets and hiking guides and can advise on local accommodation.

ACCOMMODATION AND EATING

Cheshire Cheese Inn Edale Rd, Hope S33 6ZF between Castleton and Hope ☎01433 623313, ⓦthecheshire cheeseinn.co.uk. Two attractively renovated old stone cottages with a cosy/folksy bar downstairs and four extremely pleasant en-suite guest rooms up above. The good-quality bar food features local, seasonal ingredients. Food served: Tues–Fri noon–2pm & 6–9pm; Sat noon–9pm & Sun noon–7.30pm. Bar: Tues–Fri noon–3pm & 6–10pm; Sat noon–11.30pm & Sun noon–10pm. **£80**

Stonecroft Edale ☎01433 670262, ⓦstonecroft guesthouse.co.uk. The pick of several B&Bs in Edale village, this detached Edwardian house offers two comfortable guest rooms decorated in an unfussy traditional style. **£80**

Upper Booth Camping West of Edale village on the way to Kinder Scout ☎01433 670250, ⓦupper boothcamping.co.uk. This conveniently located campsite and camping barn is a popular spot for walkers on the Pennine Way. Car parking extra. Camping barn per person **£8**, camping per person **£6**

YHA Edale Rowland Cote, Nether Booth, 2 miles east of Edale train station ☎0845 371 9514, ⓦyha.org.uk. With 157 beds in two- to ten-bedded rooms, plus good facilities including a laundry, café and self-catering kitchen, this YHA also offers an extensive range of outdoor activities. These must be booked in advance – as must accommodation. The hostel is signed from the road into Edale, or you can hike across the fields from the nearby Moorland Centre (see p.419). Dorms **£18**, doubles **£40**

Bakewell

BAKEWELL, flanking the banks of the River Wye about thirty miles north of Derby, is famous for both its **Bakewell Pudding** and its **Bakewell Tart**. The former is much more distinctive (and less commonplace), being a sweet and slippery, almond-flavoured confection – now with a dab of jam – invented here around 1860 when a cook botched a recipe for strawberry tart. Almost a century before this fortuitous mishap, the Duke of Rutland set out to turn what was then a remote village into a prestigious spa, thereby trumping the work of his rival, the Duke of Devonshire, in Buxton. The frigidity of the water made failure inevitable, leaving only the prettiness of **Bath Gardens** at the heart of the town centre as a reminder of the venture. Bakewell is within easy striking distance of the big tourist attraction hereabouts, **Chatsworth House** (see opposite).

ARRIVAL AND INFORMATION
BAKEWELL

By bus Buses to Bakewell stop on – or very close to – central Rutland Square; there are no trains.
Destinations Baslow (hourly; 15min); Buxton (hourly; 30min); Chesterfield (hourly; 1hr); Derby (hourly; 1hr 20min); Hathersage (3 daily; 45min); Sheffield (hourly;

1hr 30min).
Tourist office Old Market Hall, Bridge St, right in the centre of town (daily: April–Oct 9.30am–5pm; Nov–Easter 10.30am–4.30pm; ☎01629 816558, ⓦpeakdistrict .gov.uk).

ACCOMMODATION AND EATING

★**Hassop Hall** Hassop, 3 miles north of Bakewell on the B6001 ☎01629 640488, ⓦhassophall.co.uk. Hidden away in the heart of the Peaks, the rugged, solitary hamlet of Hassop is home to the wonderful *Hassop Hall*, a handsome stone manor house. The interior has kept faith with the Georgian architecture – modernization has been

---

THE PENNINE WAY

The 268-mile-long **Pennine Way** (ⓦnationaltrail.co.uk) was the country's first official long-distance footpath, opened in 1965. It stretches north from the boggy plateau of the Peak District's Kinder Scout near **Edale village**, proceeds through the Yorkshire Dales and Teesdale, and then crosses Hadrian's Wall and the Northumberland National Park, before entering Scotland to fizzle out at the village of Kirk Yetholm. One of the most popular walks in the country, either taken in sections or completed in two to three weeks, the Pennine Way is a challenge in the best of weather, since it passes through some of the wildest countryside in Britain. You must certainly be properly equipped and able to use a map and compass. The **National Trail Guides** *Pennine Way: South* and *Pennine Way: North*, are essential, though some still prefer to stick to Wainwright's *Pennine Way Companion*. Information centres along the route – like the one at Edale village (see p.419) – stock a selection of guides and associated trail leaflets and can offer advice.

HIKING AROUND BAKEWELL

Bakewell is a popular starting point for short hikes out into the easy landscapes that make up the town's surroundings, with one of the most relaxing excursions being a four-mile loop along the banks of the **River Wye** to the south of the centre. Chatsworth (see below) is within easy hiking distance, too – about seven miles there and back – or you could venture out onto one of the best known hikes in the National Park – the **Monsal Trail**, which cuts eight miles north and then west through some of Derbyshire's finest limestone dales using part of the old Midland Railway line. The trail begins at Coombs viaduct, one mile southeast of Bakewell, and ends at Blackwell Mill Junction, three miles east of Buxton.

kept to a subtle minimum – and the views out over the surrounding parkland are delightful. The hotel restaurant (reservations required) is also first-class with a two-course set meal costing £28. **£100**

Old Original Bakewell Pudding Shop The Square ☏ 01629 812193, ⓦ bakewellpuddingshop.co.uk. Bakeries all over town claim to make Bakewell Pudding to the original recipe, but the most authentic are served up here. They sell the pudding in several sizes, from the small and handy to the gargantuan, enough to keep the average

family going for a whole day. Mon–Sat 8.30am–6pm, Sun 9am–6pm.

Riverside House Hotel Fennel St, Ashford in the Water ☏ 01629 814275, ⓦ riversidehousehotel.co.uk. The plush and lush *Riverside House* occupies a handsome Georgian building by the banks of the Wye. There are a dozen or so extremely well-appointed rooms here, each decorated in a full-blown country-house style, and the hotel takes justifiable pride in both its gardens and its restaurant (reservations required). **£115**

Chatsworth House

8

4 miles east of Bakewell • Mid-March to late Dec daily 11am–5.30pm, last admission 4.30pm; gardens till 6pm, last admission 5pm • House & gardens £18, gardens only £12 • ☏ 01246 565300, ⓦ chatsworth.org

Fantastically popular, and certainly one of the finest stately homes in Britain, **Chatsworth House** was built in the seventeenth century by the first Duke of Devonshire. It has been owned by the family ever since and although several of them have done a fair bit of tinkering – the sixth duke, for instance, added the north wing in the 1820s – the end result is remarkably harmonious. The property is seen to best advantage from the B6012, which meanders across the estate to the west of the house, giving a full view of its vast Palladian frontage, whose clean lines are perfectly balanced by the undulating partly wooded **parkland**, which rolls in from the south and west.

Many visitors forgo the **house** altogether, concentrating on the gardens – an understandable decision given the predictability of the assorted baubles accumulated by the family over the centuries. Nonetheless, among the maze of grandiose rooms and staircases, there are several noteworthy highlights, including the ornate ceilings of the **State Apartments** and, in the State Bedroom, the four-poster bed in which George II breathed his last. And then there are the **paintings**. Among many, Frans Hals, Tintoretto, Veronese and Van Dyck all have a showing, and there's even a Rembrandt.

Back outside, the **gardens** are a real treat and owe much to the combined efforts of Capability Brown, who designed them in the 1750s, and Joseph Paxton (designer of London's Crystal Palace), who had a bash seventy years later. Among all sorts of fripperies, there are water fountains, a rock garden, an artificial waterfall, a grotto and a folly as well as a nursery and greenhouses. Afterwards, you can wend your way to the **café** in the handsomely converted former stables.

ARRIVAL AND DEPARTURE

CHATSWORTH HOUSE

By bus Buses pull into the bus stop a short walk from Chatsworth House – and at the end of a byroad leading off the B6012.

Destinations Bakewell (hourly; 17min); Baslow (hourly; 12min); Sheffield (hourly; 1hr 10min).

On foot The best way to get to Chatsworth is by walking one of the footpaths that network the estate with the most obvious departure point being Baslow. *The Grate Little Guide to Chatsworth* (see p.415) describes a pleasant 4-mile loop from the village, that takes in the house on the way.

The East Midlands

BURGHLEY HOUSE

9

The East Midlands

Many tourists bypass the four major counties of the East Midlands – Nottinghamshire, Leicestershire, Northamptonshire and Lincolnshire – on their way to more obvious destinations, an understandable mistake given that the region seems, at first sight, to be short on star attractions. Nevertheless, the county towns of Nottingham and Leicester, though undeniably bruised by postwar town planning and industrial development, do have enough sights and character to give them appeal, and Lincoln, with its fine cathedral, is in parts at least a dignified old city. What's more, the countryside hereabouts is sprinkled with prestigious country homes, pretty villages and historic market towns.

In **Nottinghamshire**, Byron's **Newstead Abbey** is intriguing; the Elizabethan **Hardwick Hall** (just over the border in Derbyshire but covered in this chapter) is even better. **Leicestershire** offers Market Bosworth, an amiable country town famous as the site of the battle of Bosworth Field, and a particularly intriguing church at Breedon-on-the-Hill. The county also lies adjacent to the easy countryside of **Rutland**, the region's smallest county, where you'll find another pleasant country town, **Oakham**. Rutland and **Northamptonshire** benefit from the use of limestone as the traditional building material and rural Northamptonshire is studded with handsome stone villages and towns – most notably **Fotheringhay** – as well as a battery of country estates.

Lincolnshire is very different in character from the rest of the region, an agricultural hidey-hole that remains surprisingly remote – locals sometimes call it the "forgotten county". This was not always the case: throughout medieval times the county flourished as a centre of the wool trade with Flanders, its merchants and landowners becoming some of the wealthiest in England. Reminders of the high times are legion, beginning with the majestic cathedral that graces the county town of **Lincoln**. Equally enticing is the splendidly intact stone town of **Stamford**, while out in the sticks, Lincolnshire's most distinctive feature is **The Fens**, whose pancake-flat fields, filling out much of the south of the county and extending deep into Cambridgeshire, have been reclaimed from the marshes and the sea. Fenland villages are generally short of charm, but their **parish churches**, whose spires regularly interrupt the wide-skied landscape, are simply stunning; two of the finest – at Gedney and Long Sutton – are set beside the A17 as it slices across the fens on its way to Norfolk. Very different again is the Lincolnshire **coast**, whose long sandy beach extends, with a few marshy interruptions, from Mablethorpe to **Skegness**, the region's main resort. The coast has long attracted thousands of holiday-makers from the big cities of the East Midlands and Yorkshire, hence its trail of bungalows, campsites and caravan parks, though significant chunks of the seashore are now protected as **nature reserves**, with the Gibraltar Point National Nature Reserve being the pick.

Leicester festivals p.434
Outdoors at Rutland Water p.439
The Nene Way p.441

Guided tours of Lincoln Cathedral p.443
The Lincoln Imp p.444
Shakespeare in the park p.448

LINCOLN CATHEDRAL

Highlights

❶ Newstead Abbey One-time lair of Lord Byron, this intriguing old mansion has superb period rooms, with lots of Byron memorabilia, and lovely gardens. **See p.432**

❷ Hardwick Hall A beautifully preserved Elizabethan mansion that was home to the formidable Bess of Hardwick, one of the leading figures of her age. The gardens and surrounding parkland are wonderful, too. **See p.433**

❸ Lincoln Cathedral One of the finest medieval cathedrals in the land, dominating this

fine old city and seen to best advantage on a guided tour. **See p.443**

❹ Gibraltar Point National Nature Reserve Escape the crowds and enjoy the wonderful birdlife at this first-class nature reserve on the coast. **See p.446**

❺ Stamford Lincolnshire's prettiest town, with its cobbled lanes, lovely old churches, and ancient limestone buildings, well deserves an overnight stay – and you can eat in style here too. **See p.447**

HIGHLIGHTS ARE MARKED ON THE MAP ON P.426

THE EAST MIDLANDS

By train and bus Travelling between the cities of the East Midlands by train or bus is simple and most of the larger towns have good regional links, too. Things are very different in the country, however, where bus services are distinctly patchy.

By plane The region has one international airport, East Midlands (⟡eastmidlandsairport.com), just off the M1 between Derby, Nottingham and Leicester.

Nottingham

With a population of around 305,000, **NOTTINGHAM** is one of England's big cities. A one-time lace manufacturing and pharmaceutical centre (the Boots chain is from here), today it is still famous for its association with **Robin Hood**, the legendary thirteenth-century outlaw. Hood's bitter enemy was, of course, the **Sheriff of Nottingham**, but unfortunately his home and lair – the city's imposing medieval castle – is long gone, replaced by a handsome Palladian mansion that is still called, somewhat confusingly, Nottingham Castle. Nowadays, Nottingham is at its most diverting in and around both the castle and the handsome **Market Square**, which is also the centre of a heaving, teeming weekend nightlife. Within easy striking distance of the city is the former coal mining village of **Eastwood**, home of the **D.H. Lawrence Birthplace Museum** (8a Victoria St, Eastwood, off Nottingham Rd; guided tours by advance booking only; £5; ☎01773 717353, ⟡nottingham.ac.uk/dhlheritage).

Brief history

Controlling a strategic crossing point over the River Trent, the Saxon town of **Nottingham** was built on one of a pair of sandstone hills whose 130ft cliffs looked out over the river valley. In 1068, William the Conqueror built a castle on the other hill, and the Saxons and Normans traded on the low ground in between, the Market Square. The castle was a military stronghold and royal palace, the equal of the great castles of Windsor and Dover, and every medieval king of England paid regular visits. In August 1642, Charles I stayed here too, riding out of the castle to raise his standard and start the Civil War – not that the locals were overly sympathetic. Hardly anyone joined up, even though the king had the ceremony repeated on the next three days.

After the Civil War, the Parliamentarians slighted the castle and, in the 1670s, the ruins were cleared by the Duke of Newcastle to make way for a palace, whose continental – and, in English terms, novel – design he chose from a pattern book, probably by Rubens. Beneath the castle lay a handsome, well-kept market town until the second half of the eighteenth century, when the city was transformed by the expansion of the lace and hosiery industries. Within the space of fifty years, Nottingham's population increased from ten thousand to fifty thousand, the resulting slum becoming a hotbed of radicalism.

The worst of Nottingham's slums were cleared in the early twentieth century, when the city centre assumed its present structure, with the main commercial area ringed by alternating industrial and residential districts. Thereafter, crass postwar development, adding tower blocks, shopping centres and a ring road, ensconced and embalmed the remnants of the city's past.

The Market Square

One of the best-looking central squares in England, Nottingham's **Market Square** is still the heart of the city, an airy open plaza whose shops, offices and fountains are overseen and overlooked by the grand neo-Baroque **Council House**, completed as part of a make-work scheme in 1928. Just off the square there's also a statue honouring one of the city's heroes, the former manager of Nottingham Forest FC, **Brian Clough** (1935–2004), shown in his characteristic trainers and tracksuit. Clough won two European cups with Forest, a remarkable achievement by any standards, but his popularity came as much

9

NOTTINGHAM

Tram Stop
Tram Line

CAFÉS & RESTAURANTS
Annie's Burger Shack 6
Edin's 4
French Living 1
Harts Restaurant 3
Memsaab 2
World Service 5

PUBS & BARS
Broadway Cinema Bar 5
Cast 3
Lincolnshire Poacher 1
Ye Olde Trip to Jerusalem Inn 6

CLUBS & LIVE MUSIC
Cookie Club 4
Stealth 2

ACCOMMODATION
Harts Hotel 2
The Walton Hotel 1

from his forthright personality and idiosyncratic utterances. Two quotes suffice to show the mettle of the man: "I wouldn't say I was the best manager in the business, but I was in the top one", and, on the subject of hoofing the football into the air, "If God had wanted us to play football in the sky, He'd have put grass up there."

Nottingham Castle

Friar Lane • Mid-Feb to Oct daily 10am–5pm; Nov to mid-Feb Wed–Sun 10am–4pm • £5.50 • ⓦ nottinghamcity.gov.uk/castle
Caves 4 daily 1hr guided tours except Mon & Tues in winter • £3 • ⓣ 0115 876 1400

From the Market Square, it's a five-minute walk west up Friar Lane to **Nottingham Castle**, whose heavily restored medieval gateway leads into the immaculately maintained gardens, which slope up to the squat, seventeenth-century ducal **palace**.

Inside, in the **Castle Museum and Art Gallery**, a particular highlight is the "Story of Nottingham", a lively, well-presented account of the city's development, which is currently undergoing a revamp. Here you will find a small but exquisite collection of late medieval **alabaster carvings**, an art form for which Nottingham once had an international reputation. It's worth walking up to the top floor for a turn around the main **picture gallery**, a handsome and spacious room, which displays a curious assortment of mostly English nineteenth-century Romantic paintings.

Just outside the main entrance to the palace, two sets of steps lead down into the maze of ancient **caves** that honeycomb the cliff beneath. Both are open for guided tours with one set leading into **Mortimer's Hole**, a 300ft shaft along which, so the story goes, the young Edward III and his accomplices crept in October 1330 to capture his mother, Isabella, and her lover, Roger Mortimer. The couple had already murdered Edward III's father, the hapless Edward II, and were intent on usurping the crown, but the young Edward proved too shrewd for them and Mortimer came to a grisly end.

The Lace Market

The narrow lanes and alleys of the **Lace Market**, beginning a couple of minutes' walk east of the Market Square, are flanked by large and imposing Victorian factories and warehouses. **Stoney Street** is the Lace Market at its most striking, its star turn being the **Adams Building**, whose handsome stone-and-brick facade combines both neo-Georgian and neo-Renaissance features. Neighbouring **Broadway** doesn't lag far behind, with a line of neat red-brick and sandstone-trimmed buildings performing a neat swerve halfway along the street. At the heart of the Lace Market is the **church of St Mary's** (W stmarysnottingham.org), a good-looking mostly fifteenth-century Gothic structure with a cavernous nave. Sitting ugly on the edge of the Lace Market, there's also the spaceship-like **National Ice Centre** skating rink (W national-ice-centre.com).

Galleries of Justice

High Pavement • Mon–Fri 9am–5pm, tours 10am–4pm, Sat & Sun 10am–5pm, tours 10.30am–4pm • £9.50 • T 0115 952 0555, W galleriesofjustice.org.uk

The Lace Market abuts **High Pavement**, the administrative centre of Nottingham in Georgian times, and it's here you'll find **Shire Hall**, whose Neoclassical columns, pilasters and dome date from 1770. The facade also bears the marks of a real Georgian cock-up: to the left of the entrance, just below street level, the mason carved the word "Goal" onto an arch and then had to have a second bash, turning it into "Gaol"; both versions are clearly visible. The hall now houses the **Galleries of Justice**, whose child-friendly "Crime and Punishment" tour involves lots of role play. The building is actually much more interesting than the hoopla, incorporating two superbly preserved Victorian courtrooms, an Edwardian police station, some spectacularly unpleasant old cells, a women's prison with bath house and a prisoners' exercise yard.

Nottingham Contemporary

Weekday Cross • Tues–Fri 10am–7pm, Sat 10am–6pm, Sun 11am–5pm • Free • T 0115 948 9750, W nottinghamcontemporary.org

Just along the street from the Galleries of Justice is the city's premier art gallery, **Nottingham Contemporary**, which – despite the grand assurances of the architects – looks like something assembled from a giant IKEA flat pack. That said, the gallery's temporary exhibitions are consistently strong; hit shows have included the early paintings of David Hockney and a wonderful, all-encompassing display on Haitian voodoo.

Paul Smith

10 Byard Lane Mon–Sat 10am–6pm, Sun 11am–5pm • T 0115 950 6712 • **20 Low Pavement** Mon–Sat 10am–6pm, Sun 11am–5pm • T 0115 968 5990, W paulsmith.co.uk

Local lad Paul Smith (b.1946) worked in a clothing factory as a young man and only developed a passion for art and design after a bike accident left him incapacitated for six months. He opened his first small shop here on Byard Lane in 1970, since when he has gone on to become one of the major success stories of contemporary British fashion, his trademark multicoloured stripes proving popular on every continent. He also has a much larger, flagship store just around the corner at 20 Low Pavement, though it's his first shop that has become something of a fashion shrine.

9

ARRIVAL AND INFORMATION

By plane East Midlands Airport is 18 miles southwest of the city; Skylink buses (ⓦeastmidlandsairport.com) take a circuitous route into the city centre – allow an hour; buses pull in at the Broad Marsh bus station and terminate at the bus stop on Friar Lane.

By train Nottingham train station is on the south side of the city centre, a 5- to 10min walk (just follow the signs), or a tram ride, from Market Square.

Destinations Birmingham (every 20–30min; 1hr 20min); Leicester (every 30min; 20min); Lincoln (hourly; 1hr 10min); London (hourly; 1hr 45min); Newark (hourly;

30min); Oakham (hourly; 1hr, change at Leicester).

By bus Most long-distance buses arrive at the Broad Marsh bus station, down the street from the train station on the way to the centre, but some – including services to north Nottinghamshire (see opposite) – pull in at the Victoria bus station, a 5min walk north of Market Square.

Tourist office Market Square, on the ground floor of Council House, 1 Smithy Row (Mon–Sat 9am–5.30pm, plus selected Sun 11am–5pm; ☏0844 477 5678, ⓦexperiencenottinghamshire.com).

ACCOMMODATION

★**Harts Hotel** Standard Hill, Park Row ☏0115 988 1900, ⓦhartsnottingham.co.uk. Nottingham may be short of good places to stay, but this chic, privately-owned, hotel does much to fill the gap. The 30 stylish guest rooms have ultramodern fixtures and fittings, Egyptian cotton bed linen and modern paintings on the wall. Completed in 2002, the hotel is the work of the city's leading architect, Julian Marsh, whose inventive use of space is his special hallmark. Handy central location too, plus a delightful bar and a smashing

restaurant next door (see below). **£125**

The Walton Hotel 2 North Road, The Park ☏0115 947 5215, ⓦthewaltonhotel.com. Tends to garner mixed reviews, but this privately owned, small hotel does occupy a good-looking, nineteenth-century building on the edge of the city centre – a 15min walk from Market Square and overlooking busy Derby Road. There are 16 guest rooms here and they do vary considerably, though all have more than a smattering of period furnishings and fittings. **£110**

EATING

Annie's Burger Shack 5 Broadway, Lace Market ⓦanniesburgershack.com. This large and extremely busy burger joint has been a real hit in Nottingham, attracting a groovy crowd, who chomp away at a wide range of top-ranking burgers from "The German" (with grilled sauerkraut) to the "Deathray" (with jalapeños, peppers and chilli paste). There is a first-rate range of craft ales, stouts and ciders too – but come early or expect to queue. Burgers average £10. Daily 8am–10.30am & noon–9.30pm, Fri & Sat till 10.30pm.

Edin's 15 Broad St ☏0115 924 1112, ⓦedinsnotting ham.co.uk. This city centre café-bar has an engaging laidback vibe with its pocket-sized open kitchen, boho furniture and jazzy, bluesy soundtrack. The menu is short, unpretentious and inexpensive or you can settle for a snack, for example the bread and cheese board. Look out for the specials chalked up on the blackboard. Mains cost as little as £6. Daily 9.30am–11.30pm, Sun till 10.30pm.

French Living 27 King St ☏0115 958 5885, ⓦfrenchliving.co.uk. Authentic and extremely tasty French cuisine served in an intimate, candlelit basement. Daytime snacks and baguettes in the ground-floor café too. Evening main courses from £12. Tues–Fri noon–2.30pm & 5–10.30pm, Sat noon–10.30pm.

Harts Restaurant Standard Hill, Park Row ☏0115 988 1900, ⓦhartsnottingham.co.uk. One of the city's most acclaimed restaurants, occupying part of the old general hospital and serving an international menu of carefully

presented meals. Attractive modernist decor and attentive service; reservations are recommended. Mains from about £15. For something rather less expensive, go next door to the bar of *Harts Hotel* (see above), where – among much else – they serve great fish and chips with mushy peas. Restaurant daily noon–2pm & 7–10.30pm, Sun till 9pm.

★**MemSaab** 12 Maid Marian Way ☏0115 957 0009, ⓦmem-saab.co.uk. Arguably the best Indian restaurant in Nottingham with crisp modern decor and bags of space. The food – canny amalgamations of different Indian cooking styles from different regions – is exquisite. The large and imaginative menu has main courses starting from as little as £11. Try the fried cod, Goan fish curry or the slow-cooked lamb flavoured with cardamom. Mon–Thurs 5.30–10.30pm, Fri & Sat 5.30–11pm & Sun 5–10pm.

★**World Service** Newdigate House, Castle Gate ☏0115 847 5587, ⓦworldservicerestaurant.com. Chic restaurant with bags of decorative flair in charming premises up near the castle. A Modern British menu, featuring such offerings as pork cutlets with onion marmalade and rack of lamb with butternut squash *tarte tatin*, is prepared with imagination and close attention to detail. In the evenings, main courses start at around £17, but there are great deals at lunchtimes with two-course set meals costing £15, or £20 for three courses. Daily noon–2pm & 7–10pm, Sun noon–3.30pm.

DRINKING

Central Nottingham's **pubs** literally heave on the weekend and are not for the faint-hearted – and indeed anyone over thirty years old (or even twenty) may well feel marooned. That said, there are one or two more relaxing places among the hullabaloo.

Broadway Cinema Bar Broadway Cinema, 14 Broad St in the Lace Market ☏ 0115 952 6611, ⓦ broadway.org .uk. Informal, fashionable (in an arty sort of way) bar serving an eclectic assortment of bottled beers to a cinema-keen clientele. Filling, inexpensive bar food too. Mon–Wed 9am–11pm, Thurs 9am–midnight, Fri & Sat 9am–1am & Sun 10am–11pm; food served daily 10am–9pm.

Cast Nottingham Playhouse, Wellington Circus ☏ 0115 941 9419, ⓦ nottinghamplayhouse.co.uk. The bar of the Nottingham Playhouse is a popular, easy-going spot with courtyard seating on summer nights. Patrons have the advantage of being able to gaze at a piece of modern art too – Anish Kapoor's whopping, reflective *Sky Mirror*. Daily noon–late.

★ **Lincolnshire Poacher** 161 Mansfield Rd ☏ 0115 941 1584, ⓦ castlerockbrewery.co.uk. Very popular and relaxed pub, where the decor is pleasantly traditional and the customers take their (real) ales fairly seriously. Attracts an older clientele. About half a mile from the Market Square. Mon–Wed 11am–11pm, Thurs–Fri 11am–midnight, Sat 10am–midnight & Sun noon–11pm.

★ **Ye Olde Trip to Jerusalem** Brewhouse Yard, below the castle ☏ 0115 947 3171, ⓦ triptojerusalem.com. Carved into the castle rock, this ancient inn – said to be the oldest in England – may well have been a meeting point for soldiers gathering for the Third Crusade. Its cave-like bars, with their rough sandstone ceilings, are delightfully secretive and there's a good range of ales too. Sun–Thurs 11am–11pm, Fri & Sat 11am–midnight.

NIGHTLIFE

Cookie Club 22 St James St ☏ 0115 950 5892, ⓦ cookieclub.co.uk. Central nightspot casting a wide musical net, from indie/student favourites to goth and retro. Mon, Wed, Fri & Sat 10.30pm–3am.

Stealth Masonic Place, Goldsmith St ☏ 0115 828 3173, ⓦ stealthattack.co.uk. The biggest club in Nottingham hosts live music, wild club nights and a battery of leading DJs.

ENTERTAINMENT

Broadway 14 Broad St in the Lace Market ☏ 0115 9526611, ⓦ broadway.org.uk. The best cinema in the city, featuring a mixed bag of mainstream and avant-garde films.
Nottingham Playhouse Wellington Circus ☏ 0115 941 9419, ⓦ nottinghamplayhouse.co.uk. Long-established theatre offering a wide-ranging programme of plays – Shakespeare through to Ayckbourn – plus dance,

music and comedy, often with a local twist or theme.
Theatre Royal & Royal Concert Hall Theatre Square ☏ 0115 989 5555, ⓦ trch.co.uk. Two venues with one set of contact details: the Theatre Royal is an attractive, well-maintained Victorian theatre and the nearby Concert Hall dates from the 1980s. All the big names in live music, both popular and classical, play at one or the other.

Northern Nottinghamshire

Rural **northern Nottinghamshire**, with its gentle rolling landscapes and large ducal estates, was transformed in the nineteenth century by **coal** – deep, wide seams of the stuff that spawned dozens of collieries, and colliery towns, stretching north across the county and on into Yorkshire. Almost without exception, the mines have closed, their passing marked only by the occasional pithead winding wheel, left, bleak and solitary, to commemorate the thousands of men who laboured here. The suddenness of the pit closure programme imposed by Thatcher and her Conservative cronies in the 1980s knocked the stuffing out of the area, but one prop of its slow revival has been the tourist industry: the countryside in between these former mining communities holds several enjoyable attractions, the best-known of which is **Sherwood Forest** – or at least the patchy remains of it – with one chunk of woodland preserved in the Sherwood Forest National Nature Reserve, supposedly where Robin Hood did his canoodling with Maid Marian. Byron is a pipsqueak in the celebrity stakes by comparison, but his family home – **Newstead Abbey** – is here too, as is **Hardwick Hall**, a handsome Elizabethan mansion built at the behest of one of the most powerful women of her day, Bess of Hardwick (1521–1608).

9

With the exception of Hardwick Hall, all these attractions are easy to reach by **bus** from Nottingham.

Newstead Abbey

10 miles north of Nottingham on the A60 • **Gardens & Grounds** Daily 9am–5pm or dusk; Vehicles with driver & passengers £6; pedestrians & cyclists £1 • **House** Sat & Sun noon–4pm; £5.• ☎ 01623 455900, ⓦ newsteadabbey.org.uk • A fast and frequent Pronto bus (every 20min; 25min; ☎ 01773 712265, ⓦ trentbarton.co.uk) leaves Nottingham's Victoria bus station bound for Mansfield; it stops at the gates of Newstead Abbey, a mile from the house

In 1539, **Newstead Abbey** was granted by Henry VIII to Sir John Byron, who demolished most of the church and converted the monastic buildings into a family home. **Lord Byron** (1788–1824) inherited the estate, which was by then little more than a ruin, in 1798; he restored part of the complex during his six-year residence (1808–14), but most of the present structure actually dates from later renovations, which maintained much of the shape and feel of the medieval original while creating the warren-like mansion that exists today. Inside, a string of intriguing period rooms begins with the neo-Gothic Great Hall and Byron's bedroom, one of the few rooms to look pretty much like it did when he lived here, and then continues on into the Library, which holds a collection of the poet's possessions, from letters and an inkstand through to his pistols and boxing gloves. A further room contains a set of satirical, cartoon-like watercolours entitled *The Wonderful History of Lord Byron & His Dog* by his friend Elizabeth Pigot – there's a portrait of the self-same dog, Boatswain, in the south gallery, and a conspicuous memorial bearing an absurdly extravagant inscription to the mutt in the delightful walled garden at the back of the house. Beyond lie the main **gardens**, a secretive and subtle combination of lake, Gothic waterfalls, yew tunnels and Japanese-style rockeries, complete with idiosyncratic pagodas.

Sherwood Forest

Edwinstowe • Daily dawn–dusk • Free, but parking fee of £3 during school holidays & on weekends (April–Dec) • ☎ 01623 823202, ⓦ nottinghamshire.gov.uk

Most of **Sherwood Forest**, once a vast royal woodland of oak, birch and bracken covering all of northern Nottinghamshire, was cleared in the eighteenth century. It's difficult today to imagine the protection all the greenery provided for generations of outlaws, the most famous of whom was of course **Robin Hood**. There's no "true story" of Robin's life – the earliest reference to him, in Langland's *Piers Plowman* of 1377, treats him as a fiction – but to the balladeers of fifteenth-century England, who invented most of Hood's folklore, this was hardly the point. For them, Robin was a symbol of yeoman decency, a semi-mythological opponent of corrupt clergymen and evil officers of the law; in the early tales, Robin may show sympathy for the peasant, but he has rather more respect for the decent nobleman, and he's never credited with robbing the rich to give to the poor. This and other parts of the legend, such as Maid Marian and Friar Tuck, were added later. Robin Hood may lack historical authenticity, but it hasn't discouraged the county council from spending thousands of pounds sustaining the **Major Oak**, the creaky tree where Maid Marian and Robin are supposed to have plighted their troth. The Major Oak is on a pleasant one-mile woodland walk that begins beside the visitor centre at the main entrance to **Sherwood Forest National Nature Reserve**, which comprises 450 acres of oak and silver birch crisscrossed with footpaths.

ARRIVAL AND INFORMATION   SHERWOOD FOREST

Tourist information The Sherwood Forest National Nature Reserve visitor centre is half a mile north of the village of Edwinstowe, which is itself about 20 miles north of Nottingham via the A614.

By bus Stagecoach's Sherwood Arrow bus (ⓦ stage coachbus.com) links Nottingham's Victoria bus station with Worksop via the visitor centre (hourly; 1hr).

Hardwick Hall

Doe Lea, Chesterfield, Derbyshire • **Hardwick Hall & gardens** Mid-Feb to Oct Wed–Sun noon–4.30pm, early Dec Wed–Sun 11am–3pm • Hall & gardens £12; gardens only £6; NT **Parkland** Daily 9am–6pm or dusk • Free • Parking per vehicle £3 for non-NT members • ☎ 01246 850430 , ⊕ nationaltrust.org • **Hardwick Old Hall** April–Oct Wed–Sun 10am–5pm • £5.40; EH • Discounted combined tickets with Hardwick Hall available • ☎ 01246 850431 • No public transport; by car via the M1: come off at Junction 29 and follow the signs from the roundabout at the top of the slip road ; it's a 3-mile trip.

Born the daughter of a minor Derbyshire squire, Elizabeth, Countess of Shrewsbury (1527–1608) – aka **Bess of Hardwick** – became one of the leading figures of Elizabethan England, renowned for her political and business acumen. She also had a penchant for building and her major achievement, **Hardwick Hall**, begun when she was 62, has survived in amazingly good condition. The house was the epitome of fashionable taste, a balance of symmetry and ingenious detail in which the rectangular lines of the building are offset by line upon line of windows – there's actually more glass than stone – while up above, her giant-sized initials (E.S.) hog every roof line. Inside on the top floor, the **High Great Chamber**, where Bess received her most distinguished guests, boasts an extraordinary plaster frieze, a brightly painted, finely worked affair celebrating the goddess Diana, the virgin huntress – it was, of course, designed to please the Virgin Queen herself. Next door, the breathtaking **Long Gallery** features exquisite furnishings and fittings from splendid chimneypieces and tapestries through to a set of portraits, including one each of the queen and Bess. Bess could exercise here while keeping out of the sun – at a time when any hint of a tan was considered decidedly plebeian.

Outside, the **garden** makes for a pleasant wander and, beyond the ha-ha (the animal-excluding low wall and ditch), rare breeds of cattle and sheep graze the surrounding **parkland**. Finally – and rather confusingly – Hardwick Hall is next to **Hardwick Old Hall**, Bess's previous home, but now little more than a broken-down if substantial ruin.

Leicester

At first glance, **LEICESTER**, some 25 miles south of Nottingham, seems a resolutely modern city, but further inspection reveals traces of its medieval and Roman past, situated immediately to the west of the downtown shopping area near the River Soar. In 2012, its national profile was boosted by the discovery of the remains of **Richard III** beneath a council car park in the centre – the body was originally brought here after the Battle of Bosworth Field (see p.436). There followed a prolonged legal battle with York as to who should keep the king's skeleton, but Leicester won and the body will be ceremonially reinterred in Leicester Cathedral in 2015.

It's probably fair to say that Leicester has a longstanding reputation for looking rather glum, but the centre is very much on the move, with the addition of Highcross, a brand-new shopping centre, and the creation of a Cultural Quarter equipped with a flashy performance venue, **Curve Theatre**. The star turns, however, are the **New Walk Museum and Art Gallery**, which includes an exemplary collection of German Expressionist paintings, and the brand-new **King Richard III Visitor Centre**. More than a third of Leicester's population is **Asian** – the city elected England's first Asian MP, Keith Vaz, in 1987. The focus of the Asian community is the **Belgrave Road** and its environs, an area of terraced houses about a mile to the northeast of the city centre beyond the flyover, where people come from miles around to eat at the splendid **Indian restaurants**.

Brief history

The **Romans** chose this site to keep an eye on the rebellious Corieltauvi, constructing a fortified town beside the Fosse Way (now the A46), the military road running from Lincoln to Cirencester. Later, the Emperor Hadrian kitted the place out with huge public buildings, though the Danes, who overran the area in the eighth century, were not overly impressed and didn't even bother to pilfer much of the stone. Later still, the

9

town's medieval castle became the base of the earls of Leicester, the most distinguished of whom was **Simon de Montfort**, who forced Henry III to convene the first English Parliament in 1265. Since the late seventeenth century, Leicester has been a centre of the **hosiery trade** and it was this industry that attracted a stream of Asian immigrants to settle here from the 1950s onwards.

The city centre

The most conspicuous buildings in Leicester's crowded centre are two large shopping centres, the ultramodern Highcross and the clumpy **Haymarket**, but the proper landmark is the Victorian **clocktower** of 1868, standing in front of the Haymarket and marking the spot where seven streets meet. One of the seven is Cheapside, which leads to Leicester's open-air **market** (Mon–Sat), one of the best of its type in the country and the place where the young **Gary Lineker**, now the UK's best-known football pundit, worked on the family stall. Good-hearted Gary remains a popular figure hereabouts and has been made a freeman of the city, which, among other things, gives him the right to graze his sheep in front of the town hall. East of the clocktower is Leicester's nascent **Cultural Quarter**, whose two main attractions are the **Curve Theatre** (see p.436) and the **Phoenix cinema** (see p.436). One of the seven streets beginning at Leicester's clocktower is Silver Street (subsequently Guildhall Lane), which passes through **The Lanes**, where a medley of small, independent shops gives this part of the centre real character.

Leicester Cathedral

St Martin's • Mon–Sat 8am–6pm, Sun 7am–4pm • Free • ⓦ leicestercathedral.org

Abutting Guildhall Lane is **Leicester Cathedral**, a much-modified eleventh-century structure incorporating two finely carved porches – a stone one at the front and an earlier timber version at the rear. The interior, with its clutch of Gothic arches, holds a whopping big organ and several interesting side chapels, in one of which is a splendid wooden tabernacle.

King Richard III Visitor Centre

St Martin's • Mon–Fri 10am–4pm, Sat & Sun 10am–5pm • £7.95 • ⓣ 0300 300 0900, ⓦ kriii.com

Across the street from the Cathedral, Leicester's old Grammar School is a substantial Victorian red-brick that has been turned into the lavish **King Richard III Visitor Centre** after the royal body was discovered beneath the adjoining car park where the greyfriars friary church had once stood. The Centre has three distinct sections. The first examines Richard's reign and the battle of Bosworth Field that ended it; a second gives visitors the chance to peer down into the makeshift grave where the body was found; and the third relates the story of how the body was discovered – a remarkable tale in itself. This third section also reveals what detailed analysis has discovered about Richard: he suffered from curvature of the spine, enjoyed a high-protein diet and was killed by several blows to the head. It really is intriguing stuff – and it's all immaculately presented.

LEICESTER FESTIVALS

The crowded terraced streets of the Belgrave district, on the northeastern periphery of the centre, are the hub for two major Hindu festivals – **Diwali** (ⓦ whatson.leicester.gov.uk), the Festival of Light, held in October or November, when six thousand lamps are strung out along Belgrave Road, and **Navratri** (ⓦ whatson.leicester.gov.uk), a nine-day celebration in October held in honour of the goddess Durga. In addition, the city's sizeable Afro Caribbean community holds England's second biggest street festival after the Notting Hill Carnival (see box, p.124). It's called the **Leicester Caribbean Carnival** (ⓦ leicestercarnival.com) and it's held on the first weekend in August. ⓦ leicester.gov.uk

The Jewry Wall

Near the Guildhall, beside the large St Nicholas Circle roundabout, you'll spot the conspicuous **church of St Nicholas**; beside that, in a little dell, lie the foundations of the Emperor Hadrian's public baths, which culminate in the **Jewry Wall**, a substantial chunk of Roman masonry some 18ft high and 73ft long. The baths were a real irritation to the emperor: the grand scheme was spoilt by the engineers, who miscalculated the line of the aqueduct that was to pipe in the water, and so bathers had to rely on a hand-filled cistern replenished from the river – which wasn't what he had in mind at all.

Castle Gardens and St Mary de Castro

Castle Gardens, a narrow strip of a park that runs alongside a canalized portion of the River Soar, is a pleasant spot, incorporating the overgrown mound where Leicester's Norman castle motte once stood. At the far end of Castle Gardens, you emerge on The Newarke; turn left and follow the road round, and in a jiffy you'll reach **Castle View**, a narrow lane spanned by the Turret Gateway, a rare survivor of the city's medieval castle. Just beyond the gateway is **St Mary de Castro**, a dignified old church with a dainty crocketed spire where Chaucer may well have got married.

New Walk Museum and Art Gallery

55 New Walk • Mon–Sat 10am–5pm, Sun 11am–5pm • Free • ☎ 0116 225 4900, ⓦ leicester.gov.uk

The **New Walk** is a long and pleasant pedestrianized promenade that's home to the city's best museum, the **New Walk Museum and Art Gallery**. The museum covers a lot of ground, from the natural world to geology and beyond, but one highlight is its extensive collection of Ancient Egyptian artefacts, featuring mummies and hieroglyphic tablets brought back to Leicester in the 1880s. The museum also holds an enjoyable collection of paintings and, although these are rotated regularly, you're likely to see a good range of works by British artists as well as an outstanding collection of German Expressionist works, mostly sketches, woodcuts and lithographs by artists such as Otto Dix and George Grosz.

ARRIVAL AND INFORMATION

LEICESTER

By train Leicester train station is on London Rd, from where it's a 10min walk northwest to the city centre.
Destinations Birmingham (every 30min; 1hr); Lincoln (hourly; 1hr 40min); London (every 30min, 1hr 15min); Nottingham (every 30min; 30min); Oakham (hourly; 30min); Stamford (hourly; 50min).
By bus St Margaret's bus station is on the north side of the centre, just off Gravel Street – to get to the Haymarket, just

follow the signs.
Destinations Ashby-de-la-Zouch (hourly; 1hr 20min); Market Bosworth (hourly; 1hr). Both services provided by Arriva (ⓦ arrivabus.co.uk).
Tourist office In the centre, a short walk south of the Haymarket at 51 Gallowtree Gate (Mon–Sat 9.30am–5.30pm, Sun 11am–5pm; ☎ 0116 299 4444, ⓦ visitleicester.info).

ACCOMMODATION

Belmont Hotel De Montfort St ☎ 0116 254 4773, ⓦ belmonthotel.co.uk. A pleasant and proficient hotel in an attractively modernized and extended Victorian property about 300 yards south of the train station via London Road. It's popular with business folk and tourists alike. **£100**

★ **Maiyango** 13–21 St Nicholas Place ☎ 0116 251 8898, ⓦ maiyango.com. This small, independent hotel – the best

in town – has fourteen slick modern rooms, each with bespoke art work and handmade furniture. Their "superior" rooms have rain showers and king-size beds, whereas the larger deluxe rooms have walk-in wet rooms and bath tubs. The hotel also has a handy location, a brief walk from the principal sights and Leicester's main shopping centres. There's a first-rate restaurant on site too (see p.436). **£80**

EATING AND DRINKING

Visitors come from miles around to eat at the excellent **Indian restaurants** that line-up along **Belgrave Road**, which begins a mile or so northeast of the centre. There are top-notch restaurants in the city centre too and a battery of **bars**, though most of these are chains.

9

★**Chaat House** 108 Belgrave Rd ☎0116 266 0513. In operation for more than thirty years, *Chaat House* is something of a local institution, its simple decor entirely appropriate for an unpretentious, family-run place, where they serve satisfying mounds of vegetarian food in capacious aluminium dishes. Try, for example, the *matar paneer* (peas and cheese in a tomato sauce), with *gulab jamin* for dessert. £20 will cover a meal for two. Near the junction with Roberts Road. Daily noon–10pm.

Globe 43 Silver St ☎0116 253 9492, ⌨www .eversosensible.com/globe/. Traditional pub in an attractive old building at the heart of the city. Smashing range of real ales and good quality bar food too. Sun–Thurs 11am–11pm, Fri & Sat 11am–1am; food served Mon–Sat noon–7pm, Sun noon–5pm.

★**Maiyango** 13–21 St Nicholas Place ☎0116 251 8898, ⌨maiyango.com. Chi-chi lounge-bar and restaurant beneath the hotel of the same name (see p.435). The restaurant mostly uses local, seasonal ingredients and the menu is wide-ranging – try the soy-scented guinea fowl breast in a sweet and sour plum jus, for example, or the courgette flowers with crab and lobster. Afterwards, you can relax in the charming rooftop terrace bar. Set menus and à la carte with mains averaging £16. Mon & Tues 6.30–11pm, Wed & Thurs 12.30–4pm & 6.30–11.30pm, Fri 12.30–4pm & 5–11.30pm, Sat 12.30pm–1am, Sun 6–10.30pm.

Sayonara Thali 49 Belgrave Road ☎0116 266 5888. Flamboyantly decorated vegetarian restaurant that specializes in set thali meals, with several different dishes, breads and pickles served together on large steel plates. Full thalis from £5. Daily noon–9.30pm.

Taps 10 Guildhall Lane ☎0116 253 0904, ⌨taps -leicester.com. Inventive bar and restaurant, whose claim to fame is the beer taps at many of the tables – help yourself and pay later (yes, the taps are monitored as they dispense). Excellent range of bottled beers too, plus vaulted cellars that date back yonks, and an above-average menu – chicken breast stuffed with apples and stilton in a creamy leek sauce, for example, for just £15. Mon–Sat noon–11.30pm.

ENTERTAINMENT

Curve 60 Rutland St ☎0116 242 3595, ⌨curveonline .co.uk. At the heart of the Cultural Quarter, Curve is Leicester's leading performing arts venue, offering a varied programme from within its startlingly dramatic glass facade.

Phoenix 4 Midland St ☎0116 242 2800, ⌨phoenix .org.uk. Just a couple of minutes' walk from Curve, the Phoenix is an outstanding art-house cinema, one of the best in the Midlands.

Western Leicestershire

Leicestershire is arguably one of the more anonymous of the English shires, its undulating landscapes comprising an apparently haphazard mix of the industrial, post-industrial and the rural. The county's highlights are dotted across **western Leicestershire**, beginning with the well-manicured charms of **Market Bosworth**, near **Bosworth Field**, where Richard III met a sticky end in 1485. Here too is the amenable little town of **Ashby-de-la-Zouch**, home to the substantial remains of a medieval castle, **Breedon-on-the-Hill** and its fine hilltop church.

Market Bosworth and around

The thatched cottages and Georgian houses of tiny **MARKET BOSWORTH**, some eleven miles west of Leicester, fan out from a dinky **Market Place**, which was an important trading centre throughout the Middle Ages. From the sixteenth to the nineteenth century, the dominant family hereabouts were the Dixies, merchant-landlords who mostly ended up at the **church of St Peter**. The Dixies were not universally admired, however, and the young Samuel Johnson, who taught at the **Dixie Grammar School** – its elongated facade still abuts the Market Place – disliked the founder, Sir Wolstan Dixie, so much that he recalled his time there "with the strongest aversion and even a sense of horror".

Bosworth Field

Sutton Cheney, a couple of miles south of Market Bosworth • **Heritage Centre** Daily: April–Oct 10am–5pm; Nov–March 10am–4pm • £7.95, plus £2.50 parking • ☎01455 290429, ⌨bosworthbattlefield.com • No public transport

Market Bosworth is best known for the **Battle of Bosworth Field**, which was fought on hilly countryside near the village in 1485. This was the last and most decisive battle of the Wars of the Roses, an interminably long-winded and bitterly violent conflict among the nobility for control of the English Crown. The victor was Henry Tudor, subsequently Henry VII; he defeated Richard III, who famously died on the battlefield. In desperation, Shakespeare's villainous Richard cried out "A horse, a horse, my kingdom for a horse," but in fact the defeated king seems to have been a much more phlegmatic character. Taking a glass of water before the fighting started, he actually said, "I live a king: if I die, I die a king". What happened to Richard's body after the battle was long a matter of conjecture, but in 2012 his skeleton was unearthed in the centre of Leicester beneath a council car park (see p.434).

Bosworth Battlefield Heritage Centre

The **Bosworth Battlefield Heritage Centre** features a workmanlike description of the battle and explains its historical context, though the less said about the ersatz medieval village that has taken shape next door the better. The Heritage Centre also has a section on recent archeological efforts to find the actual site of the battle: unfortunately, it turns out that the battlefield was a couple of miles further west on what is now private land, which leaves the centre, never mind the adjoining circular two-mile **Battle Trail**, which identifies where tradition had the protagonists meet, somewhat marooned. Nevertheless, the ramble along the trail is pleasant enough and on the way you'll pass **King Richard's Well**, a rough cairn where the king was supposed to have had his final drink, and there are views over to the actual battlefield too. Pick up a map at the Heritage Centre before you set out.

ARRIVAL AND DEPARTURE
MARKET BOSWORTH

By bus There are regular Arriva (ⓦarrivabus.co.uk) buses from Leicester to Market Bosworth's Market Place (hourly; 1hr).

ACCOMMODATION AND EATING

Softleys 2 Market Place ⓣ 01455 290464, ⓦsoftleys .com. Right in the centre of the village, this first-rate, family-run hotel has three well-appointed bedrooms decorated in a homely version of country-house style. The rooms are really run as an adjunct to a smart restaurant, where the menu is lively, creative and locally sourced wherever possible – the lamb is especially good. Mains average around £17. Lunch: Tues–Sat noon–2pm, last orders 1.45pm, & Sun noon–3.30pm, last orders 3pm; Dinner: Tues–Thurs 6.30–9.30pm, last orders 9pm, Fri & Sat 6.30–10pm, last orders 9.30pm. **£90**

Ashby-de-la-Zouch and around

ASHBY-DE-LA-ZOUCH, fifteen miles northwest of Leicester, takes its fanciful name from two sources – the town's first Norman overlord was Alain de Parrhoet la Souche and the rest means "place by the ash trees". Nowadays, Ashby is far from rustic, but it's still an amiable little place with one main attraction, its **castle**. It's also within easy striking distance of an especially interesting country house, **Calke Abbey**, and two fascinating churches – **Staunton Harold** and the hilltop Church of St Mary and St Hardulph, at **Breedon-on-the-Hill**, which is noted for its stunning Anglo-Saxon carvings. Note, however, that there is no public transport to these three surrounding attractions.

Ashby Castle

South St, just off the town's main St, Market St • April–June & Sept–Oct Wed–Sun 10am–5pm; July–Aug daily 10am–5pm; Nov–March Sat & Sun 10am–4pm • £4.60; EH

Originally a Norman manor house, Ashby's **castle** was the work of Edward IV's chancellor, Lord Hastings, who received his "licence to crenellate" in 1474. The rambling ruins include substantial leftovers from the old fortifications, as well as the shattered remains of the great hall, solar and chapel, but the star turn is the 100ft-high **Hastings Tower**, a self-contained four-storey stronghold which has survived in good nick. This tower house represented the latest thinking in castle design. It provided much better accommodation than was previously available; living quarters that

9

reflected the power and pride of a burgeoning landowning class. By all accounts, Hastings was very proud of his tower, but he didn't enjoy it for long: in 1483, he was dragged from a Privy Council meeting to have his head hacked off on a log by the order of Richard III, his crime being his lacklustre support for the Yorkist cause.

ARRIVAL AND DEPARTURE
ASHBY-DE-LA-ZOUCH

By bus Arriva (ⓦ arrivabus.co.uk) operates the main bus service from Leicester bus station to Ashby's Market Street (every 30min to 1hr; 1hr 10min).

Breedon-on-the-Hill

It's five miles northeast from Ashby to the unassuming village of **BREEDON-ON-THE-HILL**, which sits in the shadow of the large, partly quarried hill from which it takes its name. A steep footpath and a winding, half-mile by-road lead up from the village to the summit, from where there are smashing views over the surrounding countryside.

Church of St Mary and St Hardulph

Breedon-on-the-Hill • Daily 9.30am–4pm, sometimes later in summer • Free • ⓦ benefice.org.uk/breedon_church • There are no buses to the church and the village is poorly served by bus too.

The fascinating **church of St Mary and St Hardulph** occupies the site of an Iron Age hillfort and an eighth-century Anglo-Saxon monastery. Mostly dating from the thirteenth century, the church is kitted out with a Georgian pulpit and pews as well as a large and distinctly rickety box pew. Much more rare are a number of **Anglo-Saxon carvings** that include individual saints and prophets and wall friezes, where a dense foliage of vines is inhabited by a tangle of animals and humans. The friezes are quite extraordinary, and the fact that the figures look Byzantine rather than Anglo-Saxon has fuelled much academic debate.

Rutland

To the east of Leicestershire lies England's smallest county, **Rutland**, reinstated in its own right in 1997 following 23 unpopular years of merger with its larger neighbour. Rutland has three places of note: **Oakham**, the pocket-sized county town, and **Uppingham** – both rural centres with some elegant Georgian architecture – and the prettier, much smaller stone hamlet of **Lyddington**.

Oakham

The prosperity of well-heeled **OAKHAM**, 24 miles east of Leicester, is bolstered by Oakham School, one of the region's more exclusive private schools, and by its proximity to **Rutland Water**, a large reservoir whose assorted facilities attract cyclists, ramblers, sailors and birdwatchers by the hundred. Oakham's stone terraces and Georgian villas are too often interrupted to assume much grace, but the town does have its architectural moments, particularly in the L-shaped **Market Place**, where a brace of sturdy awnings shelter the old water pump and town stocks, and where **Oakham School** is housed in a series of impressive ironstone buildings.

Oakham Castle

Market Place • Mon 10am–4pm, Wed–Sat 10am–4pm • Free • ☏ 01572 758440, ⓦ rutland.gov.uk

A few steps from the north side of the Market Place stands **Oakham Castle**, a large banqueting hall that was once part of a twelfth-century fortified house. The hall is a good example of Norman domestic architecture and surrounding the building are the grassy banks that once served to protect it. Inside, the whitewashed walls are

---

OUTDOORS AT RUTLAND WATER

The gentle waters and easy, green hills of **Rutland Water** (ⓦ rutlandwater.org.uk) have made it a major centre for outdoor pursuits. There's sailing at Rutland Sailing Club (ⓦ rutlandsc.co.uk), cycle hire with Rutland Water Cycling (ⓦ rutlandcycling.com); and a Watersports Centre at Whitwell on the north shore (ⓦ anglianwater.co.uk/leisure). Rutland Water also attracts a wide range of waterfowl, which prompted the establishment of a **nature reserve** with no fewer than 31 hides and two visitor centres at its west end. The reserve is home to a successful Osprey breeding project (ⓦ ospreys.org.uk).

---

covered with **horseshoes**, the result of an ancient custom by which every lord or lady, king or queen, is obliged to present an ornamental horseshoe when they first set foot in the town.

All Saints' Church

Church St • Daily dawn to dusk • Free • ☎ 01572 724007, ⓦ oakham.oakhamteam.org.uk

From Oakham Market Place, a narrow lane leads along the right-hand side of Oakham School to **All Saints' Church**, whose heavy tower and spire rise high above the town. Dating from the thirteenth century, the church is an architectural hybrid, but the airy interior is distinguished by the intense medieval carvings along the columns of the nave and choir, with Christian scenes and symbols set alongside dragons, grotesques, devils and demons.

ARRIVAL AND DEPARTURE | OAKHAM

By train The only place in Rutland to have a rail connection is Oakham, where the train station is on Station Road, on the northwest side of town, a 10min walk from Market Place.
Destinations Birmingham (hourly; 1hr 30min); Leicester (hourly; 30min); Melton Mowbray (hourly; 10min); Peterborough (hourly; 30min); Stamford (hourly; 15min)).

By bus Monday through Saturday, there is a good bus service between Oakham, Uppingham and Lyddington. In Oakham, the main bus stops are in John St, a 5min walk west of Market Place.
Destinations Lyddington (Mon–Sat hourly; 30min); Nottingham (Mon–Sat hourly; 1hr 20min); Uppingham (Mon–Sat hourly; 15min).

ACCOMMODATION AND EATING

Castle Cottage Café Church Passage, Market Place ☎ 01572 757952, ⓦ castlecottagecafe.co.uk. Cosy little café featuring a tempting range of moderately-priced home-made dishes with a particularly good line in cakes and salads – try, for example, the salmon and prawn tian. Mon–Sat 8.30am–4.30pm & Sun 10am–4pm.

Hambleton Hall Hambleton ☎ 01572 756991, ⓦ hambletonhall.com. Just a couple of miles southeast of Oakham, overlooking Rutland Water in the tiny hamlet of Hambleton, this opulent hotel occupies an imposing Baronial-Gothic mansion set in its own immaculate grounds. It's seriously expensive – and seriously luxurious. **£285**

Northampton

Spreading north from the banks of the River Nene, **NORTHAMPTON** is a workaday town whose modern appearance largely belies its ancient past. Throughout the Middle Ages, this was one of central England's most important towns, a flourishing commercial hub whose now demolished castle was a popular stopping-off point for travelling royalty. A fire in 1675 burnt most of the medieval city to a cinder, and the Georgian town that grew up in its stead was itself swamped by the Industrial Revolution, when Northampton swarmed with **boot- and shoemakers**, whose products shod almost everyone in the British Empire. Errol Flynn kitted himself out with several pairs of Northampton shoes and boots when he was in repertory here in 1933, but he annoyed his suppliers no end by hightailing it out of town after a year,

9

leaving a whopping debt behind him – thereby partly justifying David Niven's cryptic comment "You can count on Errol Flynn, he will always let you down".

Church of All Saints

George Row • Mon–Sat 10am–5pm • Free • ☎ 01604 632845, ⓦ allsaintsnorthampton.co.uk

From Northampton's expansive Market Square, it's just a short walk through to the town's ecclesiastical pride and joy, the **Church of All Saints**, whose unusually secular appearance stems from its finely proportioned, pillared portico and towered cupola. A statue of a bewigged Charles II in Roman attire surmounts the portico, a (flattering) thank you for his donation of a thousand tonnes of timber after the Great Fire of 1675 had incinerated the earlier church. Inside, the handsome interior holds a sweeping timber gallery and a batch of Neoclassical pillars, which lead the eye up to the fancy plasterwork that decorates the ceiling.

Northampton Museum and Art Gallery

4–6 Guildhall Rd • Tues–Sat 10am–5pm, Sun 2–5pm • Free • ☎ 01604 838111, ⓦ northampton.gov.uk

The **Northampton Museum and Art Gallery**, just a couple of minutes' walk from the church of All Saints, celebrates the town's industrial heritage with a wonderful collection of **shoes and boots**. Along with silk slippers, clogs and high-heeled nineteenth-century court shoes, there's one of the four boots worn by an elephant during the British Expedition of 1959, which retraced Hannibal's putative route over the Alps into Italy. There's celebrity footwear too, such as the giant DMs Elton John wore in *Tommy*, plus whole cabinets of heavy-duty riding boots, pearl-inlaid raised wooden sandals from Ottoman Turkey, and a couple of cabinets showing just how long high heels have been in fashion.

Charles Rennie Mackintosh House

78 Derngate • Feb to mid-Dec Tues–Sun 10am–5pm, last entry 4pm • £6.70 • ☎ 01604 603407, ⓦ 78derngate.org.uk • The house is a 5–10min walk southeast of All Saints' church

In 1916–17, the Scottish architect **Charles Rennie Mackintosh** (1868–1928), the most celebrated proponent of Art Nouveau in the UK, played a key role in the remodelling of this Northampton house on behalf of two, well-heeled newly-weds, Florence and Wenman Bassett-Lowke. Since the Mackintosh redesign, **78 Derngate** has had a chequered history, but in recent years it has been painstakingly restored and now shows to fine effect many of Mackintosh's stylistic hallmarks, most notably the strong, almost stern, right angles that are set against the flowing lines of floral-influenced decorative motifs. The adjacent building, number 80, has been turned into a combined visitor centre, restaurant and exhibition space.

ARRIVAL AND INFORMATION   NORTHAMPTON

By train Northampton train station is on the western edge of the city centre, a 10min walk from Market Square.
Destinations Birmingham (every 30min; 1hr); London Euston (every 30min; 1hr).
By bus Buses pull into the new North Gate bus station in between Greyfriars and Bradshaw Street, a couple of minutes' walk from the Market Square.

Destinations Stoke Bruerne (every 2hr; 30min); Leicester (hourly; 2hr).
Tourist office In the former county courthouse across from All Saints on George Row (Mon–Fri 8am–5.30pm, plus April–Sept Sat 10am–2pm; ☎ 01604 367997, ⓦ lovenorthampton.co.uk or ⓦ visitnorthamptonshire .co.uk).

EATING

Sophia's 54 Bridge St ☎ 01604 250654, ⓦ sophias -restaurant.co.uk. This pleasantly turned-out restaurant, a short walk south of All Saints, has an excellent

Mediterranean menu with Italian dishes to the fore. Mains from as little as £12. Mon–Sat 5.30–10.30pm.

Around Northampton

Within easy striking distance of Northampton are several pleasant attractions, including **Stoke Bruerne**, with its splendid set of canal locks, the postcard-pretty hamlet of **Ashby St Ledgers**, and the delightful village of **Fotheringhay**, where Mary, Queen of Scots was imprisoned and executed.

Stoke Bruerne

Heading south out of Northampton on the A508, it's about eight miles to the village of **STOKE BRUERNE**, which sits beside a flight of seven locks on the Grand Union Canal. By water at least, the village is very close to England's second longest navigable tunnel, the one-and-three-quarter-miles-long **Blisworth Tunnel**, constructed at the beginning of the nineteenth century. Before the advent of steam tugs in the 1870s, boats were pushed through the tunnel by "legging" – two or more men would push with their legs against the tunnel walls until they emerged to hand over to waiting teams of horses.

To get out on the water, stroll over the canal bridge to the *Boat Inn* **pub**, jam-packed with narrowboat trinkets, where they operate **narrowboat cruises** to the tunnel (Easter–Sept most days; 30min; £3) as well as longer canal trips (call to book, as sailings don't take place every day; ☎01604 862428, ⬡boatinn.co.uk).

Fotheringhay

Hard to believe today, but **FOTHERINGHAY**, a delightful hamlet nestling by the River Nene about thirty miles northeast of Northampton, was once an important centre of feudal power with both a weekly market and a castle. The castle was demolished long ago, but the magnificent **church of St Mary and All Saints**, rising mirage-like above the green riverine meadows, recalls Fotheringhay's medieval heyday.

Fotheringhay Castle ruins

Signposted down a short and narrow lane on the bend of the road as you come into the village from Oundle • Open access • Free

Precious little remains of **Fotheringhay Castle**, but the fortress witnessed two key events – the birth of Richard III in 1452 and the beheading of Mary, Queen of Scots, in 1587. On the orders of Elizabeth I, Mary – who had been imprisoned for nearly twenty years – was beheaded in the castle's Great Hall with no one to stand in her support, apart, that is, from her dog, which is said to have rushed from beneath her skirts as her head hit the deck. Thereafter, the castle fell into disrepair and nowadays only a grassy mound and ditch remain to mark where it once stood.

Church of St Mary and All Saints

Fotheringhay • Daily 9am–5pm, 4pm in winter • Free • ⬡ friends-of-fotheringhay-church.co.uk/

Begun in 1411 and 150 years in the making, Fotheringay's **church of St Mary and All Saints** is a paradigm of the Perpendicular, its exterior sporting wonderful arching buttresses, its nave lit by soaring windows and the whole caboodle topped by a splendid

---

THE NENE WAY

Northamptonshire has one notable long-distance footpath, **The Nene Way**, which follows the looping course of the river right across the county from Badby in the west to Wansford in the east, passing through Oundle and Fotheringhay on the way; beyond Wansford it continues east, following the river to its mouth at Sutton Bridge (see p.447) on the Lincolnshire coast, a total distance of 110 miles. For the most part it's easy, if sometimes muddy, going. Brochures are available from Northampton's tourist office or consult the Long Distance Walkers Association ⬡ldwa.org.uk.

9

octagonal lantern tower. The interior is a tad bare, but there are two fancily carved medieval pieces to inspect – a painted pulpit and a sturdy stone font.

EATING AND DRINKING   FOTHERINGHAY

The Falcon ☎01832 226254, ⓦthefalcon-inn.co.uk. This excellent pub-restaurant, which occupies a neat stone building with a modern patio, offers an imaginative menu – lamb shank and artichoke for example – with delicious main courses costing around £14. Food served: Mon–Sat noon–2pm & 6–9pm, Sun noon–3pm & 6–8.30pm.

Lincoln

Reaching high into the sky from the top of a steep hill, the triple towers of **LINCOLN**'s mighty **cathedral** are visible for miles across the surrounding flatlands. The cathedral, along with the neighbouring **castle**, are the city's main tourist draws – although, for a smallish place, Lincoln also packs in several good places to eat and one outstanding hotel.

Almost everything of interest is confined to the **Uphill** part of town, within easy walking distance of both castle and cathedral. In addition to the two major sights, this part of town also features a number of historic remains, notably several chunks of Roman wall, the most prominent of which is the second-century **Newport Arch** straddling Bailgate and once the main north gate into the city. There are also several

LINCOLN

RESTAURANTS, CAFÉS & PUBS
Cheese Society Café 4
Morning Star 2
Old Bakery 1
Stokes Café at The Collection 3

ACCOMMODATION
Hillcrest 4
Old Palace Hotel 3
St Clements Lodge 1
White Hart 2

GUIDED TOURS OF LINCOLN CATHEDRAL

The cathedral offers two **guided tours**, both free with the price of admission. The first – the **Floor Tour** (Mon–Sat 2–3 daily) – is a quick trot around the cathedral's defining features, while the second, the **Roof Tour** (Mon–Sat 1–2 daily; 90min), takes in parts of the church otherwise out of bounds. Both are very popular, so it's a good idea to book in advance on ☎ 01522 561600.

well-preserved medieval stone houses, notably on and around the aptly named **Steep Hill** as it cuts down from the cathedral to the city centre.

The key sights can be seen in about half a day, though Lincoln does make for a pleasant overnight stop, particularly in December during its lively open-air **Christmas market**.

Brief history

High ground is in short supply in Lincolnshire, so it's no surprise that the steep hill which is today surmounted by Lincoln Cathedral was fortified early, firstly by the **Celts**, who called their settlement Lindon, "hillfort by the lake", a reference to the pools formed by the River Witham in the marshy ground below. In 47 AD the **Romans** occupied Lindon and built a fortified town, which subsequently became **Lindum Colonia**, one of the four regional capitals of Roman Britain. During the reign of William the Conqueror the construction of the **castle** and **cathedral** initiated Lincoln's medieval heyday – the town boomed, first as a Norman power base and then as a centre of the wool trade with Flanders, until 1369 when the wool market was transferred to neighbouring Boston. It was almost five hundred years before Lincoln could revive, its recovery based upon the manufacture of agricultural machinery and drainage equipment for the neighbouring fenlands. As the nineteenth-century town spread south down the hill and out along the old Roman road – the Fosse Way – so Lincoln became a place of precise class distinctions: the **Uphill** area, spreading north from the cathedral, became synonymous with middle class respectability, **Downhill** with the proletariat.

Lincoln Cathedral

Minster Yard • July & Aug Mon–Fri 7.15am–8pm, Sat & Sun 7.15am–6pm; Sept–June Mon–Sat 7.15am–6pm, Sun 7.15am–5pm; access restricted during services • £6 including guided tour (see box above), free Sunday • ☎ 01522 561600, ⓦ lincolncathedral.com

Not a hill at all, **Castle Hill** is in fact a wide, short and level cobbled street that links Lincoln's castle and cathedral. It's a charming spot and its east end is marked by the arches of the medieval **Exchequergate**, beyond which soars the glorious west front of **Lincoln Cathedral**, a veritable cliff-face of blind arcading mobbed by decorative carving. The west front's apparent homogeneity is, however, deceptive, and further inspection reveals two phases of construction – the small stones and thick mortar of much of the facade belong to the original church, completed in 1092, whereas the longer stones and finer courses date from the early thirteenth century. These were enforced works: in 1185, an earthquake shattered much of the Norman church, which was then rebuilt under the auspices of **Bishop Hugh of Avalon**, the man responsible for most of the present cathedral, with the notable exception of the (largely) fourteenth-century central tower.

The cavernous **interior** is a fine example of Early English architecture, with the nave's pillars conforming to the same general design yet differing slightly, their varied columns and bands of dark Purbeck marble contrasting with the oolitic limestone that is the building's main material. Looking back up the nave from beneath the **central tower**, you can also observe a major medieval miscalculation: Bishop Hugh's roof is out of alignment with the earlier west front, and the point where they meet has all the wrong angles. It's possible to pick out other irregularities, too – the pillars have bases of different heights, and there are ten windows in the nave's north wall and nine in the south – but these are deliberate features, reflecting a medieval aversion to the vanity of symmetry.

9

Beyond the nave lies **St Hugh's Choir**, whose fourteenth-century misericords carry an eccentric range of carvings, with scenes from the life of Alexander the Great and King Arthur mixed up with biblical characters and folkloric parables. Further on is the open and airy **Angel Choir**, completed in 1280 and famous for the tiny, finely carved **Lincoln Imp** (see box below), which embellishes one of its columns. Finally, a corridor off the choir's north aisle leads to the wooden-roofed **cloisters** and the polygonal **chapter house**, where Edward I and Edward II convened gatherings that pre-figured the creation of the English Parliament.

Lincoln Castle

Castle Hill • Daily: April & Sept 10am–5pm; May–Aug 10am–6pm; Oct–March 10am–4pm • £2 • ☎ 01522 782040, Ⓦ lincolnshire.gov.uk

From the west front of the cathedral, it's a quick stroll across Castle Hill to **Lincoln Castle**. Intact and forbidding, the castle walls incorporate bits and pieces from the twelfth to the nineteenth centuries with the wall walkway offering great views over town. The wall encloses a large central courtyard dotted around which are law courts, a new heritage skills centre and two former Victorian prisons, dour red-brick structures with one for debtors, the other, adjoining it to the rear, for felons. The former debtors' prison is currently being revamped to exhibit several rare documents, most notably one of the four surviving copies of the **Magna Carta**, all in time for the eight-hundred-year-anniversary of its signing – in 2015. Meanwhile, the old felons' prison contains a truly remarkable **prison chapel**. Here, the prisoners were locked in high-sided cubicles, where they could see the preacher and his pulpit but not their fellow inmates. This approach was not just applied to chapel visits: the prisoners were kept in perpetual solitary confinement, and were compelled to wear masks when they took to the exercise yard. This system was founded on the pseudo-scientific theory that defined crime as a contagious disease, but unfortunately for the theorists, their so-called Pentonville System of "Separation and Silence", which was introduced here in 1846, drove so many prisoners crazy that it had to be abandoned thirty years later; nobody ever bothered to dismantle the chapel.

The Collection

Danes Terrace • Daily 10am–4pm • Free • ☎ 01522 782040, Ⓦ thecollectionmuseum.com

Occupying two contrasting buildings – a striking modern structure and a really rather grand 1920s edifice close by – **The Collection** is Lincoln's prime museum. Pride of place in the more modern building is the city's extensive collection of archeological artefacts, from prehistoric times onwards; the older building, aka the **Usher Gallery**, focuses on temporary displays of fine art. The Usher's permanent collection includes an eclectic collection of coins, porcelain, watches and clocks. The timepieces were given to the gallery by its benefactor, James Ward Usher, a local jeweller and watchmaker who made a fortune on the back of the **Lincoln Imp** (see box below).

THE LINCOLN IMP

The **Lincoln imp**, carved high on a column in Lincoln cathedral, had long been a source of legend, but it was the entrepreneurial James Ward Usher who turned the wee beastie into a tidy profit in the 1880s, selling Lincoln imp tie-pins, cuff-links, spoons, brooches and beads. Usher also popularized the traditional legend of the imp, a tall tale in which a couple of imps are blown to Lincoln by a playful wind. They then proceed to hop around the cathedral, until one of them is turned to stone for trying to talk to the angels carved into the roof of the Angel Choir. His chum makes a hasty exit on the back of a witch, but the wind is still supposed to haunt the cathedral, awaiting its opportunity to be mischievous again.

9

ARRIVAL AND INFORMATION

LINCOLN

From both the train and bus stations, it's a steep, 15min walk up to the cathedral, or you can take the Walk & Ride minibus (see below).

By train Lincoln train station is on St Mary's Street, right in the city centre.

Destinations Leicester (hourly; 2hr); Newark (hourly; 25min); Nottingham (hourly; 1hr); Peterborough (every 2hr; 1hr); Stamford (hourly; 2hr–2hr 30min, min of 1 change).

By bus The bus station is just north of the train station on Melville Street.

Tourist office 9 Castle Hill, between the cathedral and the castle (Mon–Sat April–Sept 10am–5pm & Sun 10.30am–4pm; Oct–March 11am–3pm; ☎ 01522 545458, ⓦ visitlincoln.com). They have lots of local information and can book accommodation.

GETTING AROUND

By Walk & Ride minibus Alights from St Mary's Street, near the train & bus stations, as well as from the designated bus stop on Silver Street, just off High Street, and from outside The Collection (Mon–Sat 9am–5pm; every 20min; £1.50 single fare, £3 all-day ticket).

ACCOMMODATION

Hillcrest 15 Lindum Terrace ☎ 01522 510182, ⓦ hillcrest -hotel.com. Traditional, very English hotel in a large red-brick house that was originally a Victorian rectory. Sixteen comfortable rooms with all mod cons plus a large, sloping garden. About a 10min walk from the cathedral. **£95**

★**The Old Palace** Minster Yard ☎ 01522 580000, ⓦ theoldpalace.org. Easily the best place to stay in Lincoln, this excellent hotel occupies the one-time bishop's palace, a rambling largely nineteenth-century mansion within earshot of the cathedral. The hotel has 32 rooms, half in the main building, including a tower suite, and the remainder in an immaculately reconfigured 1920s chapel. The hotel's grand drawing room is in the former library and much of the furniture has been made by local carpenters. Smashing views too. **£90**

St Clements Lodge 21 Langworthgate ☎ 01522 521532, ⓦ stclementslodge.co.uk. In a smart, modern house a short walk from the cathedral, this comfortable, very friendly B&B has three cosy, en-suite rooms. Home-made breakfasts too – try the haddock or the kippers. **£75**

White Hart Bailgate ☎ 01522 526222, ⓦ whitehart -lincoln.co.uk. Antique former coaching inn, whose public rooms still have all sorts of hidden nooks and crannies despite a fairly humdrum modern revamp. The bedrooms are in a more traditional, country-house style and the pick overlook the cathedral. Curiously, it was here in an upstairs room during World War I that a local engineering firm set about designing the first 'tanks' at the behest of the government. To camouflage their intentions, the new behemoths were called water carriers – hence "tanks" – and the name stuck. **£95**

EATING AND DRINKING

Cheese Society Café 1 St Martin's Lane ☎ 01522 511003, ⓦ thecheesesociety.co.uk. This bright and breezy little café has become something of a gastronomic landmark hereabouts, its tasty creations featuring all things cheesy, from rarebits, raclettes and baked halloumi dishes through to an especially delicious stilton, red wine and walnut pâté. There are non-cheesy options, too, including a good steak-frites, plus an excellent range of local beers and ciders. The owners run a specialist cheese shop nearby as well at 28 The Strait. Mon–Sat 10am–4.30pm.

Morning Star 11 Greetwellgate ☎ 01522 527079, ⓦ morningstarlincoln.co.uk. Traditional and friendly locals' pub with a good range of ales. Bar food too. Located a couple of minutes' walk from the cathedral – if you want something livelier, head for the bars on Bailgate. Daily noon–2.30pm & 6–11pm.

Old Bakery 26 Burton Rd ☎ 01522 576057, ⓦ theold -bakery.co.uk. Cosy, rural-chic, award-winning restaurant, where the menu is both well considered and inventive – try, for example, the grilled corn polenta and cherry tomatoes with Gorgonzola and green olive purée. Has an excellent cellar and prides itself on the quality of its cheeseboards too. Reservations recommended. Mains average £19. Tues–Sat noon–1.30pm & 6.30–9pm, Sun noon–1.30pm.

Stokes Café at The Collection Danesgate ☎ 01522 523548, ⓦ stokes-coffee.co.uk. Attached to Lincoln's principal museum, this cheerful modern café is a self–service affair where they do a tasty line in crepes, sandwiches and salads. They also have a line-up of special musical events, mainly jazz and classical. The owners, the Stokes family, have been roasting coffee and blending tea in Lincoln for several generations. Daily 10am–4pm.

ENTERTAINMENT

Lincoln Drill Hall Free School Lane ☎ 01522 873891, ⓦ lincolndrillhall.com. Lincoln's prime arts and entertainment venue, featuring everything from stand-up and theatre to classical concerts, rock and pop.

9

The Lincolnshire Wolds and the coast

Northeast and east of Lincoln, the Lincolnshire Wolds are a narrow band of chalky land whose rolling hills and gentle valleys are particularly appealing in the vicinity of **Louth**, a trim little place where conscientious objectors were sent to dig potatoes during World War II. South of Louth, the Wolds dip down to both **Woodhall Spa**, a one-time Victorian spa that served as the HQ of the Dambusters as they prepared for their celebrated Ruhr raid in 1943, and then the imposing remains of **Tattershall Castle**. East of the Wolds lies the coast, with its bungalows, campsites and caravans parked behind a sandy beach that extends, with a few marshy interruptions, north from **Skegness**, the main resort, to Mablethorpe and ultimately Cleethorpes. All this bucket-and-spade and amusement-arcade commercialism is not to everyone's taste, but small portions of the coast have been preserved and protected, most notably in the **Gibraltar Point Natural Nature Reserve** south of Skegness.

Skegness and around

SKEGNESS has been a busy resort ever since the railways reached the Lincolnshire coast in 1875. Its heyday was pre-1960s, before the Brits began to take themselves off to sunnier climes, but it still attracts tens of thousands of city-dwellers who come for the wide, sandy beaches and for a host of attractions ranging from nightclubs to bowling greens. Every inch the traditional English seaside town, Skegness outdoes its rivals by keeping its beaches sparklingly clean and its parks spick-and-span. That said, the seafront, with its rows of souvenir shops and amusement arcades, can be dismal, especially on a rainy day, and you may well decide to sidestep the whole caboodle by heading south along the coastal road to the **Gibraltar Point National Nature Reserve**.

Gibraltar Point National Nature Reserve

Gibraltar Rd, 3 miles south of Skegness • **Reserve** Daily dawn–dusk • Free, but parking from £1; Refreshments available April–Oct daily 10am–4pm; Nov–March Mon–Fri 11am–3pm, Sat & Sun 11am–4pm • ☏ 01754 898057, ⒲ lincstrust.org.uk/gibraltar-point

At the **Gibraltar Point National Nature Reserve**, a network of clearly signed footpaths patterns a narrow strip of salt- and freshwater marsh, sand dune and beach that attracts an inordinate number of birds, both resident and migratory. There are numerous hides dotted about, but at the time of writing the reserve's **Visitor Centre** is being repaired after extensive flood damage in late 2013; for now, refreshments are available in the car park.

ARRIVAL AND INFORMATION
SKEGNESS

By bus and train Skegness bus and train stations are next door to each other, about 10min walk from the seashore – cut across Lumley Square and head straight up the main street to the landmark clocktower.
Destinations by bus Lincoln (Express bus Mon–Sat 4 daily; 1hr 20min).

Destinations by train Boston (hourly; 30min); Grantham (hourly; 1hr 30min); Nottingham (hourly; 2hr).
Tourist office By the seashore, a few yards from the clocktower on Grand Parade and in the Embassy Theatre (core hours Mon–Fri 9.30am–4pm; ☏ 0845 674 0505, ⒲ visitlincolnshire.com).

ACCOMMODATION

Best Western Vine Hotel Vine Rd, Seacroft ☏ 01754 610611, ⒲ bw-vinehotel.co.uk. Skegness has scores of bargain-basement hotels, B&Bs and guesthouses, but this pleasant hotel is a cut above its rivals and has benefited from a recent upgrade. It occupies a rambling old house and the decor is resolutely modern. On a quiet residential street about three-quarters of a mile from the resort's main landmark, the clocktower, and on the road to Gibraltar Point. **£75**

The Lincolnshire Fens

The Fens, that great chunk of eastern England extending from Boston in Lincolnshire right down to Cambridge, encompass some of the most productive farmland in

Europe. Give or take the occasional hillock, this pancake-flat, treeless terrain has been painstakingly reclaimed from the marshes and swamps which once drained into the intrusive stump of **The Wash**, a process that has taken almost two thousand years. In earlier times, outsiders were often amazed by the dreadful conditions hereabouts, but they did spawn the distinctive culture of the so-called **fen-slodgers**, who embanked small portions of marsh to create pastureland and fields, supplementing their diets by catching fish and fowl and gathering reed and sedge for thatching and fuel. This local economy was threatened by the large-scale land reclamation schemes of the late fifteenth and sixteenth centuries, and time and again the fenlanders sabotaged progress by breaking down new banks and dams. But the odds were stacked against the saboteurs, and a succession of great landowners eventually drained huge tracts of the fenland – and by the 1790s the fen slodgers' way of life had all but disappeared. Nonetheless, the **Lincolnshire Fens** remain a distinctive area, with a scattering of introverted little villages spread across the flatlands within easy striking distance of the A17. Several of these villages are distinguished by their imposing **medieval churches** – St Mary Magdalene's in **Gedney** and St Mary's in **Long Sutton** for example – and their soaring spires are seen to best advantage in the pale, watery sunlight and wide skies of the fenland evening. The most impressive church of all, however, looms above the area's largest town, the rough-edged old port of **Boston**, which, with a population of around sixty thousand, is Lincolnshire's second largest settlement.

Gedney

The A17 runs east across the Lincolnshire Fens from Sleaford to King's Lynn (see p.369). En route, it slips past the scattered hamlet of **GEDNEY**, where the massive tower of **St Mary Magdalene** (daily dawn–dusk; free) intercepts the fenland landscape. Seen from a distance, the church seems almost magical, or at least mystical, its imposing lines so much in contrast with its fen-flat surroundings. Close up, the three-aisled nave is beautiful, its battery of windows lighting the exquisite Renaissance alabaster effigies of Adlard and Cassandra Welby, who, in death, face each other on the south wall near the chancel.

Long Sutton

There's more ecclesiastical excitement just a mile or two to the east of Gedney in **LONG SUTTON**, a modest farming centre that limps along the road until it reaches its trim Market Place. Here, the **church of St Mary** (daily dawn–dusk; free) has preserved many of its Norman features, with its arcaded tower supporting the oldest lead spire in the country, dating from around 1200. Look out also for the striking stained-glass windows. Long Sutton once lay on the edge of the five-mile-wide mouth of the **River Nene**, where it emptied into The Wash. This was the most treacherous part of the road from Lincoln to Norfolk, and locals had to guide travellers across the mud flats and marshes on horseback. In 1831, the River Nene was embanked and then spanned with a wooden bridge at **Sutton Bridge**, a hamlet just two miles east of Long Sutton – and a few miles from King's Lynn (see p.369). The present swing bridge, with its nifty central tower, was completed in 1894.

Stamford

STAMFORD, in the southwest corner of Lincolnshire, is delightful, a handsome little limestone town of yellow-grey seventeenth- and eighteenth-century buildings edging narrow streets that slope up from the River Welland. The town's salad days were as a centre of the medieval wool and cloth trade, when wealthy merchants built its medley

9

of stone churches and houses. Stamford was also the home of **William Cecil**, Elizabeth I's chief minister, who built his splendid mansion, **Burghley House**, close by.

The town survived the collapse of the wool trade, prospering as an inland port after the Welland was made navigable to the sea in 1570, and, in the eighteenth century, as a staging point on the Great North Road from London. More recently, Stamford escaped the three main threats to old English towns – the Industrial Revolution, wartime bombing and postwar development – and was designated the country's first Conservation Area in 1967. Thanks to this, its unspoilt streets readily lend themselves to period drama and filmmaking, and although it's the harmony of Stamford's architecture that pleases, rather than any specific sight, there are still a handful of buildings of some special interest as well as an especially charming **High Street**.

Church of St Mary

St Mary's St • No regular opening hours • Free

A convenient place to start an exploration of Stamford is the **Church of St Mary**, sitting pretty just above the main bridge on St Mary's Street. The church has a splendid spire and a small but airy interior, which incorporates the **Corpus Christi** (or north) chapel whose intricately embossed, painted and panelled ceiling dates from the 1480s.

Browne's Hospital

Broad St • Late May–Sept Mon–Sat 11am–4pm, Sun 2–4.30pm • £3 • ⓦ stamfordcivicsociety.org.uk

A short stroll north of St Mary's, wide and handsome Broad Street is home to **Browne's Hospital**, the most extensive of the town's almshouses, dating from the late fifteenth century. Not all of the complex is open to the public, but it's still worth visiting with the first room – the old dormitory – capped by a splendid wood-panelled ceiling. The adjacent chapel holds some delightfully folksy misericords and then it's upstairs for the audit room, which is illuminated by a handsome set of stained-glass windows.

Church of All Saints

All Saints' Place • Daily dawn–dusk • Free • ⓣ 01780 756942, ⓦ stamfordallsaints.org.uk

Entry to the **Church of All Saints**, a stone's throw from Browne's Hospital, is via the south porch, an ornate structure with a fine – if badly weathered – crocketted gable. Inside, much of the interior is routinely Victorian, but the carved capitals are of great delicacy and there's also an engaging folkloric carving of the Last Supper behind the high altar.

High Street St Martin's

Down the slope from St Mary's, across the reedy River Welland on **High Street St Martin's**, is *The George Hotel* (see opposite), a splendid old coaching inn whose Georgian facade supports one end of the gallows that span the street – not a warning to criminals, but a traditional advertising hoarding.

SHAKESPEARE IN THE PARK

One of the most enjoyable of Stamford's several festivals is the **Stamford Shakespeare Company**'s (ⓣ 01780 756133, ⓦ stamfordshakespeare.co.uk) open-air performances of the great man's works set in the grounds of **Tolethorpe Hall**, an Elizabethan mansion just outside Stamford. The season lasts from June to August with the audience protected from the elements by a vast canopy.

Church of St Martin

23 High St St Martin's • Daily 9.30am–4pm • Free

The sombre, late fifteenth-century **Church of St Martin** shelters the magnificent tombs of the lords Burghley, beginning with a recumbent William Cecil (1520–1598) carved beneath twin canopies, holding his rod of office and with a lion at his feet. Immediately behind are the early eighteenth-century effigies of John Cecil and his wife, with the couple depicted as Roman aristocrats, propped up on their elbows, she to gaze at him, John to stare across the nave commandingly.

Burghley House

Barnack Rd • House & gardens: mid-March to late Oct Sat–Thurs 11am–5pm • £13 • ☎ 01780 752451, ⓦ burghley.co.uk. The main entrance is located about mile and a half southeast of Stamford – just follow the signs

Now famous for the prestigious Burghley Horse Trials (ⓦ burghley-horse.co.uk), held over four days in late August and/or early September, Stamford's **Burghley House** is an extravagant Elizabethan mansion standing in parkland landscaped by Capability Brown. Completed in 1587 after 22 years' work, the house sports a mellow yellow ragstone exterior, embellished by dainty cupolas, a pyramidal clocktower and skeletal balustrading, all to a plan by **William Cecil**, the long-serving adviser to Elizabeth I. However, with the notable exception of the Tudor kitchen, little remains of Burghley's Elizabethan interior and, instead, the house bears the heavy hand of John, fifth Lord Burghley, who toured France and Italy in the late seventeenth century, buying paintings and commissioning furniture, statuary and tapestries. To provide a suitable setting for his old masters, John brought in Antonio Verrio and his assistant Louis Laguerre, who between them covered many of Burghley's walls and ceilings with frolicking gods and goddesses. These gaudy and gargantuan murals are at their most engulfing in the **Heaven Room**, an artfully painted classical temple that adjoins the **Hell Staircase**, where the entrance to the inferno is through the gaping mouth of a cat.

ARRIVAL AND INFORMATION
STAMFORD

By train Stamford train station is on the south side of the River Welland, a 5- to 10min walk from the town centre. Destinations Cambridge (hourly; 1hr 10min); Leicester (hourly; 40min); Oakham (hourly; 15min).

By bus The bus station is in the town centre, on Sheepmarket, off All Saints' Street.

Tourist office Right in the centre of town, in the Stamford Arts Centre, 27 St Mary's Street (Mon–Sat 9.30am–5pm; Nov–March Mon–Sat 9.30am–5pm; ☎ 01780 755611, ⓦ southwestlincs.com).

ACCOMMODATION

★ **The George Hotel** 71 High St St Martin's ☎ 01780 750750, ⓦ georgehotelofstamford.com. Stamford's most celebrated hotel by a mile, *The George* is a sympathetically renovated old coaching inn, which comes complete with flagstone floors and antique furnishings; the most appealing of the plush rooms overlook a cobbled courtyard. There's a good restaurant, too (see below). **£165**

Stamford Lodge Guest House 66 Scotgate ☎ 01780 482932, ⓦ stamfordlodge.co.uk. In an attractive, Georgian stone house on the north side of the town centre, this smartly turned-out establishment has five, en-suite guest rooms decorated in a warm and cosy version of period style. **£85**

EATING

The George Hotel 71 High St St Martin's ☎ 01780 750750, ⓦ georgehotelofstamford.com. The food at this excellent hotel (see above) is as classy as the rooms. There are several eating areas, but perhaps the best is the moderately priced and informal *Garden Room* where the emphasis is on British ingredients served in imaginative ways. Main courses here average around £18; you'll pay less if you eat in the hotel's delightfully antiquated *York Bar*. Garden Room daily noon–10.30pm.

Hambleton Bakery 1 Ironmonger St ☎ 01780 754327, ⓦ hambletonbakery.co.uk. If you're after a sandwich, this is the best spot in town, selling a wide range of freshly baked breads with a suitably wide selection of fillings. Mon–Sat 8.30am–5pm.

The Northwest

THE LOWRY, SALFORD QUAYS

The Northwest

Ask most Brits about northwest England and they'll probably mention football and rain. Beyond the stereotypes, however, this is one of the most exciting corners of the country, its dynamic urban centres, pretty countryside, iconic seaside resorts and historic towns offering considerable appeal. One of the world's great industrial cities, Manchester has transformed its cityscape in recent decades to place itself firmly in the vanguard of modern British urban design, and complements its top-class visitor attractions with lively cafés and an exciting music scene. Just thirty miles west, revitalized Liverpool has kept apace of the "northern renaissance", too, and is a city of great energy and charm.

The southern suburbs of Manchester bump into the steep hills of the **Pennine range**, and to the southwest the city slides into pastoral **Cheshire**, a county of rolling green countryside whose dairy farms churn out the famed crumbly white cheese. The county town, **Chester**, with its complete circuit of town walls and partly Tudor centre, is as alluring as any of the country's northern towns, capturing the essence of one of England's wealthiest counties.

The historical county of **Lancashire** reached industrial prominence in the nineteenth century primarily due to the cotton-mill towns around Manchester and the thriving port of Liverpool. Today, neither city is part of the county, but along the coast to the west and north of the major cities stretches a line of **resorts** – from Southport to **Morecambe** – which once formed the mainstay of the northern British holiday. Only **Blackpool** is really worth visiting for its own sake, a rip-roaring resort which has stayed at the top of its game by supplying undemanding entertainment with more panache than its neighbours. For anything more culturally invigorating you'll have to continue north to the historically important city of **Lancaster**, with its Tudor castle. Finally, the Crown Dependency of the **Isle of Man**, just 25 miles off the coast, provides a rugged terrain almost as rewarding as that of the Lake District, but without the seasonal overcrowding.

GETTING AROUND — THE NORTHWEST

By train Both Manchester and Liverpool are well served by trains, with regular high-speed connections to the Midlands and London, and up the west coast to Scotland. The major east–west rail lines in the region are the direct routes between Manchester, Leeds and York, and between Blackpool, Bradford, Leeds and York. The Lancaster–Leeds line slips through the Yorkshire Dales and further south, the Manchester–Sheffield line provides a rail approach to the Peak District.

By bus The major cities, as well as Chester, are connected by frequent bus services.

CROSBY BEACH

Highlights

❶ People's History Museum Manchester's national museum tells the story behind the forces that have shaped human history and the modern world. **See p.458**

❷ Manchester's Northern Quarter Lose yourself in chic shops, café-bars and happening music venues in this vibrant warehouse district. **See p.460**

❸ City walls, Chester The handsome old town of Chester is best surveyed from the heights of its Roman walls. **See p.469**

❹ Culture in Liverpool From the artistic hub of the Baltic Triangle to Antony Gormley's Crosby Beach statues, this dynamic city pulses with creative energy. **See p.471**

❺ Blackpool Pleasure Beach Bright, bawdy and brash, Britain's cheekiest resort is constantly reinventing itself. **See p.481**

❻ Lancaster Castle From the dungeons to the ornate courtrooms, the castle is a historical tour-de-force. **See p.484**

❼ Sunset across Morecambe Bay Drink in one of the country's finest sunsets at the bar in the Art Deco *Midland Hotel*. **See p.485**

❽ Sea-kayaking, the Calf of Man Taking to the water in a kayak allows you to view local seal colonies, seabirds, and the Isle of Man's stunning rugged coast from a unique perspective. **See p.491**

HIGHLIGHTS ARE MARKED ON THE MAP ON P.454

Manchester

MANCHESTER has had a global profile for more than 150 years, since the dawn of the industrial revolution. But today's elegant core of converted warehouses and glass skyscrapers is a far cry from the smoke-covered sprawl George Orwell once described as "the belly and guts of the nation". Its renewed pre-eminence expresses itself in various ways, most swaggeringly in its **football**, as home to the world's most famous and

HIGHLIGHTS

1. People's History Museum
2. Manchester's Northern Quarter
3. City walls, Chester
4. Culture in Liverpool
5. Blackpool Pleasure Beach
6. Lancaster Castle
7. Sunset across Morecambe Bay
8. Sea-kayaking, the Calf of Man

THE NORTHWEST

10

MANCHESTER ORIENTATION

If Manchester can be said to have a centre, it's **Albert Square** and the cluster of buildings surrounding it – the Town Hall, the Central Library and the *Midland Hotel*, originally built in the railway age to host visitors to Britain's greatest industrial city. South of here, the former Central Station now functions as the **Manchester Central** convention centre, with the Hallé Orchestra's home, **Bridgewater Hall**, just opposite. **Chinatown** and the **Gay Village** are just a short walk to the east, while to the northeast, the revamped **Piccadilly Gardens** provides access to the hip **Northern Quarter**. To the southwest is the **Castlefield** district, site of the **Museum of Science and Industry**, and flashy **Spinningfields**, incongruous home of the People's History Museum. The central spine of the city is **Deansgate**, which runs from Castlefield to the cathedral and, in its northern environs, displays the most dramatic core of urban regeneration in the country, centred on the unalloyed modernity of **Exchange Square**.

wealthiest clubs – Manchester United and Manchester City, respectively – but also in a thriving **music scene** that has given birth to world-beaters as diverse as the Hallé Orchestra and Oasis. Moreover, the city's celebrated concert halls, theatres, clubs and cafés feed off the cosmopolitan drive provided by the country's largest **student** population outside London and a high-profile **gay** community.

There are plenty of sights, too: the centre possesses the **Manchester Art Gallery**, the **National Football Museum** and the fantastic **People's History Museum** as well as the **Museum of Science and Industry**, while further out, to the west, the revamped **Salford Quays** are home to the prestigious **Lowry arts centre**, complete with a handsome selection of L.S. Lowry paintings, the stirring and stunning **Imperial War Museum North**, and **MediaCityUK**, the new northern base of the BBC.

Brief history

Despite a **history** stretching back to Roman times, and pockets of surviving medieval and Georgian architecture, Manchester is first and foremost a **Victorian manufacturing city**. Its rapid growth set the pace for the flowering of the Industrial Revolution elsewhere – transforming itself in just a hundred years from little more than a village to the world's major cotton centre. The spectacular rise of **Cottonopolis**, as it became known, arose from the manufacture of vast quantities of competitively priced imitations of expensive Indian calicoes, using water and then steam-driven machines developed in the late eighteenth and nineteenth centuries. This rapid industrialization brought immense wealth for a few but a life of misery for the majority. The discontent came to a head in 1819 when eleven people were killed at **Peterloo**, in what began as a peaceful demonstration against the oppressive **Corn Laws**. Things were, however, even worse when the 23-year-old Friedrich Engels came here in 1842 to work in his father's cotton plant: the grinding poverty he recorded in his *Condition of the Working Class in England* was a seminal influence on his later collaboration with **Karl Marx** in the *Communist Manifesto*.

The **Manchester Ship Canal**, constructed in 1894 to entice ocean-going vessels into Manchester and away from burgeoning Liverpool, played a crucial part in sustaining Manchester's competitiveness. From the late 1950s, however, the docks, mills, warehouses and canals were in dangerous decline. The main engine of change turned out to be the devastating **IRA bomb**, which exploded outside the Arndale shopping centre in June 1996, wiping out a fair slice of the city's commercial infrastructure. Rather than simply patching things up, the city council embarked on an ambitious rebuilding scheme, which transformed the face of the city forever.

Albert Square

Most of Manchester's panoply of **neo-Gothic** buildings and monuments date from the city's heyday in the second half of the nineteenth century. One of the more fanciful is the

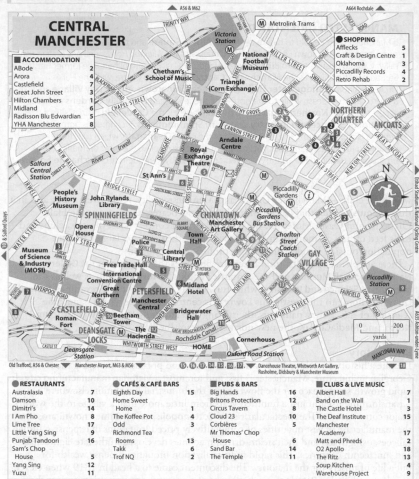

CENTRAL MANCHESTER

A56 & M62 | A664 Rochdale

TRINITY WAY

Ⓜ Metrolink Trams

■ **ACCOMMODATION**

ABode	2
Arora	4
Castlefield	7
Great John Street	3
Hilton Chambers	1
Midland	6
Radisson Blu Edwardian	5
YHA Manchester	8

● **SHOPPING**

Afflecks	5
Craft & Design Centre	1
Oklahoma	3
Piccadilly Records	4
Retro Rehab	2

Victoria Station

National Football Museum

Chetham's School of Music

Triangle (Corn Exchange)

NORTHERN QUARTER

ANCOATS

Cathedral

Arndale Centre

Royal Exchange Theatre

St Ann's

Salford Central Station

People's History Museum

John Rylands Library

SPINNINGFIELDS

Piccadilly Gardens

Opera House

CHINATOWN

Manchester Art Gallery

Piccadilly Bus Station

Chorlton Street Coach Station

GAY VILLAGE

Piccadilly Station

Museum of Science & Industry (MOSI)

Police

Town Hall

Central Library

Free Trade Hall

International Convention Centre

Great Northern

Manchester Central

PETERSFIELD

Midland Hotel

Bridgewater Hall

Cornerhouse

CASTLEFIELD

Roman Fort

DEANSGATE LOCKS

Beetham Tower

The Hacienda

HOME

Deansgate Station

Oxford Road Station

0 — 200 yards

Old Trafford, A56 & Chester | Manchester Airport, M63 & M56 | Dancehouse Theatre, Whitworth Art Gallery, Rusholme, Didsbury & Manchester Museum

● **RESTAURANTS**

Australasia	7
Damson	10
Dimitri's	14
I Am Pho	8
Lime Tree	17
Little Yang Sing	9
Punjab Tandoori	16
Sam's Chop House	5
Yang Sing	12
Yuzu	11

● **CAFÉS & CAFÉ BARS**

Eighth Day	15
Home Sweet Home	1
The Koffee Pot	4
Odd	3
Richmond Tea Rooms	13
Takk	6
Trof NQ	2

■ **PUBS & BARS**

Big Hands	16
Britons Protection	12
Circus Tavern	8
Cloud 23	10
Corbières	5
Mr Thomas' Chop House	6
Sand Bar	14
The Temple	11

■ **CLUBS & LIVE MUSIC**

Albert Hall	7
Band on the Wall	1
The Castle Hotel	3
The Deaf Institute	15
Manchester Academy	17
Matt and Phreds	2
O2 Apollo	18
The Ritz	13
Soup Kitchen	4
Warehouse Project	9

shrine-like, canopied **monument** to Prince Albert, Queen Victoria's husband, perched prettily in the middle of the trim little square that bears his name – **Albert Square**. The monument was erected in 1867, six years after Albert's death, supposedly because the prince had always shown an interest in industry, but perhaps more to curry favour with the grieving queen. Overlooking the prince is Alfred Waterhouse's magnificent, neo-Gothic **Town Hall** (Mon–Fri 9am–5pm; free), whose mighty clocktower, completed in 1877, pokes a sturdy finger into the sky, soaring high above its gables, columns and arcaded windows.

St Peter's Square and around

Just south of the Town Hall is **St Peter's Square**, home to the newly reopened **Central Library** and undergoing further redevelopment. Footsteps away, over on Peter Street, the **Free Trade Hall** was the home of the city's Hallé Orchestra for more than a century – until Bridgewater Hall was completed in 1996. The Italianate facade survived intense wartime bombing and is now a protected part of the *Radisson Blu Edwardian Hotel*, whose modern tower block rises up behind at a (fairly) discreet distance.

Central Library

St Peter's Square • Mon–Thurs 9am–8pm, Fri & Sat 9am–5pm • Free • ☎ 0161 234 1983, ⓦ manchester.gov.uk/centrallibrary • St Peter's Square Metrolink

The circular **Central Library** was built in 1934 as the world's largest municipal library, a self-consciously elegant, classical construction. After a four-year closure, it reopened, beautifully refurbished and extended, in 2014, with its showpiece domed **reading room** restored; check out the display case of sweet wrappers, found stuffed down the desks here over the last eighty years. The **children's library** is modelled on *The Secret Garden* by local author Frances Hodgson Burnett.

Manchester Art Gallery

Mosley St • Daily 10am–5pm, till 9pm Thurs • Free • ☎ 0161 235 8888, ⓦ manchestergalleries.org • St Peter's Square Metrolink

Manchester Art Gallery, as well as attracting big name exhibitions by contemporary artists, holds an invigorating collection of eighteenth- and nineteenth-century art. Spread across **Floor 1**, these works are divided by theme – Face and Place, Expressing Passions and so on – rather than by artist (or indeed school of artists), which makes it difficult to appreciate the strength of the collection, especially when it comes to its forte, the Pre-Raphaelites. There's much else – views of Victorian Manchester, a Turner or two, a pair of Gainsboroughs, and Stubbs' famous *Cheetah and Stag with Two Indians* to name but a few. **Floor 2** features temporary exhibitions and crafts, while the **Ground Floor**'s Manchester Gallery is devoted to a visual history of the city. The **Clore Art Studio** is fun for kids.

Deansgate Locks and around

South of St Peter's Square, on **Lower Mosley Street**, stands Britain's finest concert hall, **Bridgewater Hall**, balanced on shock-absorbing springs to guarantee the clarity of the sound. The apartment block at the corner of Lower Mosley Street and Whitworth Street West bears the name of the site's previous occupant, the infamous **Hacienda Club**, the spiritual home of Factory Records, an independent label that defined a generation of music through such bands as Joy Division, New Order and the Happy Mondays before closing down in 1997.

Turn right along Whitworth Street West and you'll spot the string of café-bars and restaurants that have been shoehorned along the Rochdale canal's **Deansgate Locks**, a pattern repeated along and across the street in the old railway arches abutting Deansgate Station. Look up and you'll see the striking **Beetham Tower**, easily the tallest skyscraper in Manchester and home to a glitzy hotel.

Castlefield

Just west of Deansgate Station, the tangle of railway viaducts and canals that lie sandwiched between Water Street, Liverpool Road and Deansgate make up pocket-sized **Castlefield**. It was here that the country's first man-made canal, the Bridgewater Canal, brought coal and other raw materials to the city's warehouses throughout the eighteenth century. By the early 1960s, the district was an eyesore, but an influx of money cleaned it up, and it now boasts cobbled canalside walks, attractive café-bars and the **Castlefield Urban Heritage Park** (always open; free), centred on an excavated and partially reconstructed Roman fort.

MOSI: The Museum of Science and Industry

Liverpool Rd • Daily 10am–5pm • Free, but admission charge for special exhibitions • ☎ 0161 832 2244, ⓦ mosi.org.uk • Deansgate Metrolink

One of the most impressive museums of its type in the country, the **Museum of Science and Industry** mixes technological displays and blockbuster exhibitions with trenchant analysis of the social impact of industrialization. Key points of interest include the

10

10

Power Hall, which trumpets the region's remarkable technological contribution to the Industrial Revolution by means of a hall full of steam engines, some of which are fired up daily. There's more steam in the shape of a working replica of Robert Stephenson's *Planet*, whose original design was based on the *Rocket*, the work of Robert's father George. Built in 1830, the *Planet* reliably attained a scorching 30mph but had no brakes; the museum's version does, however, and it's used at weekends (noon–4pm; £2, children £1), dropping passengers a couple of hundred yards away at the **Station Building**, the world's oldest passenger railway station. On a rainy September 15, 1830, this was the final stop of the *Rocket*'s infamous inaugural passenger journey from Liverpool, when Liverpool MP William Huskisson was struck and fatally injured.

The **1830 Warehouse** features a sound-and-light show that delves into the history of the city's immense warehouses, and the **Air and Space Hall**, which barely touches on Manchester at all, features vintage planes, cutaway engines and space exploration displays.

Spinningfields

From the old to the über-new, Castlefield blends into **Spinningfields**, a glitzy, corporate district that's home to law courts, financial HQs, designer shops and a crop of see-and-be-seen bars and restaurants, with one standout attraction incongruously perched on its edge.

People's History Museum

Left Bank • Daily 10am–5pm • Free • ☎ 0161 838 9190, ⓦ phm.org.uk • Deansgate Metrolink

The superb **People's History Museum** explores Britain's rich history of radicalism and the struggles of marginalized people to acquire rights and extend suffrage – ideas that developed out of the workers' associations and religious movements of the industrial city and which helped to shape the modern world. Housed in a former pump house and an ultramodern, four-storey extension, the galleries use interactive displays – including coffins and top hats – to trace a compelling narrative from the Peterloo Massacre of 1819 onwards. As the gallery shows, this moment became the catalyst for agitation that led to the 1832 Reform Act, and subsequent rise of the egalitarian Chartist movement. The galleries go on to explore the struggle for female suffrage, the Communist party in Britain, Oswald Mosley's fascists, and the working-class origins of football and pop music, and include the finest collection of trade union banners in the country.

Deansgate and around

Deansgate cuts through the city centre from the Rochdale canal to the cathedral, its architectural reference points ranging from Victorian industrialism to post-millennium posturing. One landmark is the **Great Northern** mall, flanking Deansgate between Great Bridgewater and Peter streets. This was once the **Great Northern Railway Company's Goods Warehouse**, a great sweep of brickwork dating back to the 1890s, originally an integral part of a large and ambitious trading depot with road and rail links on street level and subterranean canals down below.

John Rylands Library

Deansgate • **Library** Mon & Sun noon–5pm, Tues–Sat 10am–5pm **Tour and treasures** Rare books can be seen close up every third Thurs of month 3–4pm (booking required) • Free • ☎ 0161 306 0555, ⓦ library.manchester.ac.uk/rylands • Deansgate Metrolink

Nestling between Spinningfields and the north end of Deansgate, **John Rylands Library** is the city's supreme example of Victorian Gothic – notwithstanding the presence of an unbecoming modern entrance wing. The architect who won the original commission, Basil Champneys, opted for a cloistered neo-Gothicism of narrow stone corridors, delicately crafted stonework, stained-glass windows and burnished wooden panelling. The library, which has survived in superb condition, now houses specialist collections of rare books and manuscripts.

St Ann's Square

Slender **St Ann's Square** is tucked away off the eastern side of Deansgate, a couple of blocks up from the Rylands Library. Flanking the square's southern side is **St Ann's Church** (Tues–Sat 10am–5pm; free), a trim sandstone structure whose Neoclassical symmetries date from 1709, though the stained-glass windows are firmly Victorian. At the other end of the square is the **Royal Exchange**, which houses the much-lauded **Royal Exchange Theatre**. Formerly the Cotton Exchange, this building employed seven thousand people until trading finished on December 31, 1968 – the old trading board still shows the last day's prices for American and Egyptian cotton.

10

Exchange Square

A pedestrian high street – **New Cathedral Street** – runs north from St Ann's Square to **Exchange Square**, with its water features, public sculptures and massive department stores (primarily Selfridges and Harvey Nichols). On the southeast side of the square stands the whopping **Arndale Centre**, once a real Sixties eyesore, but now a modern shopping precinct, clad in glass.

Manchester Cathedral and around

Exchange Station Approach, Victoria St • Mon–Sat 8.30am–6.30pm, Sun 8.30am–7pm • Guided tours Mon–Fri 11am & 2.30pm, Sat 1pm, Sun 2.30pm • Free • ⓦ manchestercathedral.org • Victoria Metrolink

Manchester's **Cathedral** dates back to the fifteenth century, though its Gothic lines have been hacked about too much to have any real architectural coherence. Actually, it's surprising it's still here at all: in 1940, a 1000lb bomb all but destroyed the interior, knocking out most of the stained glass, which is why it's so light inside today.

Chetham's School of Music

Long Millgate • Library Mon–Fri 9am–12.30pm & 1.30–4.30pm • Free • ⓣ 0161 834 7961, ⓦ chethams.org.uk • Victoria Metrolink

The choristers in Manchester cathedral are trained at **Chetham's School of Music**. This fifteenth-century manor house became a school and a free public library in 1653 and was turned into a music school in 1969. There are free recitals during term time and, although there's no public access to most of the complex, you can visit the oak-panelled **Library** with its handsome carved eighteenth-century bookcases. Along the side corridor is the main **Reading Room**, where Marx and Engels beavered away on the square table that still stands in the windowed alcove.

National Football Museum

Urbis Building, Cathedral Gardens • Mon–Sat 10am–5pm, Sun 11am–5pm • Free except for special exhibitions • ⓣ 0161 605 8200, ⓦ nationalfootballmuseum.com • Victoria Metrolink

Manchester's **National Football Museum**, housed in a suitably spectacular structure – the sloping, six-storey glass Urbis building near Victoria train station – houses some true treasures of the world's most popular game. Here you can see the 1966 World Cup Final ball, Maradona's "Hand of God" shirt, and the only surviving version of the Jules Rimet world cup trophy. They also display the personal collection of Sir Stanley Matthews (1915–2000), considered one of the greatest English footballers of all time.

Piccadilly Gardens

Off Portland St and Oldham St • Piccadilly Gardens Metrolink

Piccadilly Gardens, historically the largest green space in the city, was relandscaped in 2002 as a family-friendly space with shady trees, a fountain and water jets, and a pavilion at one end to screen off the traffic. The 200ft **Wheel of Manchester** (Mon–Thurs 10am–9pm, Fri 10am–11pm, Sat 9am–11pm, Sun 9am–8pm; £7) offers far-reaching views. Regular events, including weekend food **markets**, keep the gardens lively.

The Northern Quarter

Oldham Street, which shoots off northeast from Piccadilly Gardens, is the shabby gateway to the hip **Northern Quarter**. Traditionally, this is Manchester's garment district and you'll still find old-fashioned shops and wholesalers selling clothes, shop fittings, mannequins and hosiery alongside the more recent designer shops, music stores and trendy café-bars. The side wall of iconic indie emporium Afflecks (see p.467) sports a colourful series of **mosaics** depicting Manchester legends – from Morrissey to Danger Mouse.

10

Chinatown

From Piccadilly Gardens, it's a short walk south to **Chinatown**, whose grid of narrow streets stretch north–south from Charlotte to Princess Street between Portland and Mosley streets, with the inevitable **Dragon Arch**, at Faulkner and Nicolas, providing the focus for the annual Chinese New Year celebrations.

Along Oxford Road

A couple of blocks out of the Gay Village, you'll come to the junction of Whitworth Street and **Oxford Road**, the latter cutting a direct route south through a string of impressive Manchester University buildings and served by an endless stream of **buses**.

Cornerhouse

Junction of Oxford Rd and Whitworth St • ☎ 0161 200 1500, ⓦ cornerhouse.org • St Peter's Square Metrolink

One block west of the Gay Village, **Cornerhouse** is the dynamo of the Manchester arts scene. In addition to screening art-house films, it has three floors of gallery space, along with a popular café and bar (see p.466). It's due to close in spring 2015, when it will become incorporated into the major new HOME arts centre (see box opposite).

The Manchester Museum

Oxford Rd • Daily 10am–5pm • Free • ☎ 0161 275 2648, ⓦ museum.manchester.ac.uk

The university's Gothic Revival **Manchester Museum** boasts a diverse collection spread over five floors, with displays on rocks, minerals and prehistoric life, meteorites, animal life, the human body and biomedical research. It also boasts one of the country's finest collections on **Ancient Egypt** outside of the British Museum. The redeveloped **Vivarium** is dedicated to the conservation of reptiles and amphibians, with plenty of frogs, snakes and lizards to handle.

The Whitworth Art Gallery

Corner of Oxford Rd and Denmark Rd • See website for new opening times • Free • ☎ 0161 275 7450, ⓦ whitworth.manchester.ac.uk

The university's **Whitworth Art Gallery** was, at time of writing, closed for a £15 million renovation to double and extend its public space into the surrounding Whitworth Park. Alongside its fine collection of pre-1880s and modern art, the gallery contains

---

MANCHESTER'S GAY VILLAGE AND GAY PRIDE

The side roads off Portland Street lead down to the Rochdale canal, where **Canal Street** forms the heart of Manchester's thriving **Gay Village**: the pink pound has filled this area of the city with canalside cafés, clubs, bars and businesses, though these days it's as busy with hooting hen-nighters as with lesbian and gay punters. Always lively, the village is packed to bursting point during Manchester's huge **Gay Pride** festival (ⓦ manchesterpride.com), which usually occurs on the last weekend of August. The village is closed off as thousands of revellers descend for music – big-name performers have included Beth Ditto and Boy George – comedy, theatre and exhibitions, all celebrating lesbian, gay, bi and transgendered sexuality (weekend tickets £22, day tickets £12.50; book online).

A PLACE TO CALL HOME

Due to open in 2015 on the First Street North site, just behind Whitworth Street West and roughly opposite the old Hacienda apartments (see p.457), **HOME** will be Manchester's new cultural hub, a merger between Manchester heavyweights Cornerhouse (see opposite) and the former Library Theatre Company. It will comprise two theatres, five cinema screens, gallery space, production and broadcast facilities, a kitchen and more. Keep up to date on ⓦ homemcr.org.

10

the country's widest range of textiles outside London's Victoria and Albert Museum. It's due to reopen in October 2015.

Salford Quays

After the Manchester Ship Canal opened in 1894, **Salford docks** played a pivotal role in turning the city into one of Britain's busiest seaports. Following their closure in 1982, which left a post-industrial mess just a couple of miles to the west of the city centre, an extraordinarily ambitious redevelopment transformed **Salford Quays**, as it was rebranded, into a hugely popular waterfront complex with its own gleaming apartment blocks, shopping mall and arts centre, **The Lowry**. Also here is the splendid **Imperial War Museum North** and the glitzy new **MediaCityUK** site.

The Lowry

Pier 8, Salford Quays · **Galleries** Mon–Fri & Sun 11am–5pm, Sat 10am–5pm · Free · ☎ 0843 208 6000, ⓦ thelowry.com · Harbour City Metrolink

Perched on the water's edge, **The Lowry** is the quays' shiny steel arts centre. The **Galleries**, which host sixteen different exhibitions each year, are largely devoted to the paintings of **Lawrence Stephen Lowry** (1887–1976), the artist most closely associated with Salford. The earlier paintings – those somewhat desolate, melancholic portrayals of Manchester mill workers – are the most familiar, while later works, repeating earlier paintings but changing the greys and sullen browns for lively reds and pinks, can come as a surprise.

Imperial War Museum North

The Quays, Trafford Wharf North · Daily 10am–5pm · Free · ☎ 0161 836 4000, ⓦ iwm.org.uk · Harbour City Metrolink

A footbridge across the Manchester Ship Canal links The Lowry with the startling **Imperial War Museum North**, which raises a giant steel fin into the air, in a building designed by the architect Daniel Libeskind. The interior is just as striking, its angular lines serving as a dramatic backdrop to the displays, which kick off with the Big Picture, when the walls of the main hall are transformed into giant screens to show regularly rotated, fifteen-minute, surround-sound films. Superb themed displays fill six separate exhibition areas – the "Silos" – focusing on everything from women's work in the World Wars to the 9/11 attacks (with a 23ft section of crumpled steel recovered from the World Trade Center wreckage).

MediaCityUK

BBC Tours · 90min tours Mon, Tues & Wed 10.30am, 12.30pm & 3pm (also Thurs & Fri in school holidays), Sat & Sun times vary · £10, children £6.50 · Book in advance on ⓦ bbc.co.uk/showsandtours · MediaCityUK Metrolink

In 2011, the BBC moved 26 of its London-based departments up north to **MediaCityUK**, a vast, purpose-built workspace for creative and digital businesses. ITV followed suit in 2013, the *Coronation Street* set arrived in 2014, and the whole place has a certain pizzazz, with telly types buzzing about on Segway scooters and the BBC offering insanely popular though mildly underwhelming **tours** (the highpoint of which is the sound studio and its semi-anechoic chamber). You don't have to join a tour, though, to wander around the piazza and visit the **Blue Peter garden**, transplanted here from London complete with Shep's paw print. The site is gradually finding its feet as an after-hours destination too.

The National Cycling Centre

Stuart St, 2 miles east of the city centre ☎ 0161 223 2244 option 3, ⓦ nationalcyclingcentre.com • Daily 7.30am–10pm • Track taster sessions £12 (£9 concessions); BMX starter sessions from £7 (£5 concessions) • From Piccadilly Gardens (Stop D) take bus #216 to Sport City; or Velopark Metrolink

Opposite Man City's football ground (see box opposite), the **National Cycling Centre** is the home of British Cycling and one of the fastest and busiest velodromes in the world. Its stunning, Olympic-standard loop of Siberian pine track, angled at 42.5°, is in constant use, with hour-long taster sessions (bikes and coach provided) available to anyone aged 9 and over; arrive early and you might well catch the end of a Team GB training session. Also on site is a thrilling, international-standard indoor **BMX track** and the start of 7.5miles of **mountain bike** trails. Elsewhere in the city, the centre's facilities include an outdoor BMX track and a mountain-bike skills zone.

ARRIVAL AND DEPARTURE
MANCHESTER

By plane Manchester Airport (☎ 0161 489 3000, ⓦ manchesterairport.co.uk) is 10 miles south of the city centre. There's an excellent train service to Manchester Piccadilly (£4.10 single); the taxi fare is around £25; by the time you read this, there should be a Metrolink service (ⓦ metrolink.co.uk) into the city.

By train Of Manchester's three stations, Piccadilly, on the east side of the centre, sees the largest number of long-distance services, some of which continue on to Oxford Road, just south of the centre. On the city's north side, Victoria Station mainly sees services to Lancashire and Yorkshire. All three stations are connected to the centre via the free Metroshuttle bus service (see below); Piccadilly and Victoria are also on the Metrolink tram line (see below).

Destinations from Manchester Piccadilly Barrow-in-Furness (Mon–Sat 7 daily, Sun 3 daily; 2hr 15min); Birmingham (hourly; 1hr 30min); Blackpool (hourly; 1hr 10min); Buxton (hourly; 1hr); Carlisle (8 daily; 1hr 50min); Chester (every 30min; 1hr–1hr 20min); Lancaster (hourly; 1hr); Leeds (hourly; 1hr); Liverpool (every 30min; 50min); London (hourly; 2hr 20min); Newcastle (10 daily; 3hr); Oxenholme (4–6 daily; 40min–1hr 10min); Sheffield (hourly;

1hr); York (every 30min; 1hr 30min).

Destinations from Manchester Oxford Road Blackpool (hourly; 1hr 15min); Carlisle (8 daily; 1hr 50min); Chester (hourly; 1hr); Lancaster (8 daily; 1hr); Leeds (10 daily; 1hr); Liverpool (every 30min; 50min); Oxenholme (8 daily; 1hr 10min); Penrith (8 daily; 1hr 40min); Sheffield (hourly; 1hr); York (hourly; 1hr 30min).

Destinations from Manchester Victoria Blackpool (6 daily; 1hr 30min); Leeds (every 30min; 1hr 20min); Liverpool (10 daily; 1hr).

By bus Most long-distance buses use Chorlton Street Coach Station, about half-way between Piccadilly train station and Albert Square, though some regional buses also leave from Shudehill Interchange, between the Arndale Centre and the Northern Quarter.

Destinations Birmingham (6 daily; 3hr); Blackpool (5 daily; 1hr 40min); Chester (3 daily; 1hr); Leeds (6 daily; 2hr); Liverpool (hourly; 40min); London (every 1–2hr; 4hr 30min–6hr 45min); Newcastle (6 daily; 5hr); Sheffield (4 daily; 2hr 40min).

Travel information For information on train and bus services, contact TFGM (☎ 0871 200 2233, ⓦ tfgm.com).

GETTING AROUND

On foot About a 30min walk from top to bottom, central Manchester is compact enough to cover on foot.

By bus Three free Metroshuttle bus services (ⓦ tfgm.com) weave across the centre of town, linking the city's train stations and NCP car parks with all the major points of interest; Metroshuttle #1 runs Mon–Fri every 6min 7am–6pm then every 10min until 7pm, Sat every 6min 8am–7pm, Sun & public hols every 10min 10am–6pm; Metroshuttle #2 runs every 10min Mon–Fri 7am–7pm, Sat 8am–7pm, Sun & public hols 10am–6pm; Metroshuttle #3 runs every 10min Mon–Fri 7am–7pm, Sat 8am–7pm, no

service Sun & public hols.

By taxi Mantax (☎ 0161 230 3333) and Streetcars (☎ 0161 228 7878) are two reliable taxi firms.

By tram Metrolink trams (ⓦ metrolink.co.uk) whisk through the city centre bound for the suburbs, along an ever-expanding network of routes. Services run from approximately 6am–12.30am (Mon–Thurs), with last trams running later on Fridays and Saturdays, and Sunday services between around 7am–10.30pm. Ticket machines are on the platform; single journeys cost from £1.20, while day and weekend Travelcards (from £5 off-peak) are good value.

INFORMATION AND TOURS

Tourist information Manchester Visitor Centre, 45–50 Piccadilly Plaza, on the corner of Portland Street (Mon–Sat 9.30am–5.30pm, Sun 10.30am–4.30pm; ☎ 0871 222 8223,

ⓦ visitmanchester.com); it does a useful blog on Fridays.

Listings information In print, Thursday's *City Life* supplement in the *Manchester Evening News*

MANCHESTER FOOTBALL TOURS

Manchester is, of course, home to two mega Premier League football teams. It's tough to get tickets for matches if you're not a season-ticket holder, but **guided tours** placate out-of-town fans who want to gawp at the silverware and sit in the dug-out. You'll need to book in advance.

Old Trafford Sir Matt Busby Way, off Warwick Rd ☎0161 868 8000, ⊚manutd.com; Old Trafford Metrolink. The self-styled "Theatre of Dreams" is the home of Manchester United, arguably the most famous football team in the world. Stadium tours include a visit to the club museum. Tours daily (except match days) 9.40am–6pm; £18, children £12.

Etihad Stadium Sport City, off Alan Turing Way ☎0161 444 1894, ⊚mcfc.co.uk; Etihad Campus Metrolink. United's formerly long-suffering local rivals, Manchester City, became the world's richest club in 2008 after being bought by the royal family of Abu Dhabi. They play at the Etihad Stadium, east of the city centre. Tours daily 9am–5pm; £15, children £10.

10

(⊚manchestereveningnews.co.uk) covers popular events, while *The Skinny*, widely available in the Northern Quarter, is a hip and independent monthly freebie. Online, there's intelligent and incisive guidance on ⊚creativetourist.com,

while ⊚manchesterconfidential.com has informative restaurant reviews.

Walking tours The visitor centre has details of the city's many walking tours (from £7).

ACCOMMODATION

There are many city-centre **hotels**, especially budget chains, which means you have a good chance of finding a smart, albeit formulaic, en-suite room in central Manchester for around £60–70 at almost any time of the year – except when City or United are playing at home. Less expensive **guesthouses** and **B&Bs** are concentrated some way out of the centre, mainly on the southern routes into the city. Prices often halve midweek.

HOTELS

ABode 107 Piccadilly ☎0161 247 7744, ⊚abode manchester.co.uk; Piccadilly Gardens Metrolink. Part of a small chain of boutique hotels, this gem occupies a former cotton warehouse a stone's throw from Piccadilly Station. Rooms are light and elegant, with high ceilings and polished wooden floors. **£210**

Arora 18–24 Princess St ☎0161 236 8999, ⊚manchester.arorahotels.com; Piccadilly Gardens/St Peter's Square Metrolink. Four-star with more than 100 neat, modern rooms in a listed building in a great central location opposite the Manchester Art Gallery. The convivial, obliging staff pride themselves on offering a "real Manchester welcome". Good online discounts. **£99**

Castlefield Liverpool Rd ☎0161 832 7073, ⊚castle field-hotel.co.uk; Deansgate-Castlefield Metrolink. Large, modern, red-brick, warehouse-style hotel handily located opposite MOSI, with nicely appointed rooms, a gym and a pool (free to guests). **£110**

★ **Great John Street** Great John St ☎0161 831 3211, ⊚eclectichotels.co.uk/great-john-street; Deansgate-Castlefield Metrolink. Deluxe hotel in an imaginatively refurbished old school building not far from Deansgate, with thirty individual, spacious and comfortable suites, some split-level. The on-site bar-cum-restaurant has an open fire and deep sofas, with a gallery breakfast room up above. Nice rooftop garden, too. **£240**

Midland Peter St ☎0161 236 3333, ⊚qhotels.co.uk; St Peter's Square Metrolink. Once the terminus hotel for

the old Central Station – and where Mr Rolls first met Mr Royce – this building was the apotheosis of Edwardian style and is still arguably Manchester's most iconic hotel. The public areas today are returned to their former glory, with bedrooms in immaculate chain style. *Mr Cooper's House and Garden*, attached to the hotel, is wonderful for pre-theatre cocktails. Discounted rates if booked online. **£250**

Radisson Blu Edwardian Peter St ☎0161 835 9929, ⊚radissonblu-edwardian.com; St Peter's Square Metro-link. The Neoclassical facade is all that's left of the Free Trade Hall; inside, this five-star hotel has a sleek modern interior full of natural light, tasteful rooms, and all the extras you'd expect – spa, gym and the trendy *Opus One* bar. **£120**

HOSTELS

Hilton Chambers 15 Hilton St ☎0161 236 4414 ⊚hattersgroup.com/Hilton; Piccadilly Gardens Metrolink. Part of a small chain operating in the northwest, this newish hostel is right in the heart of the Northern Quarter, and a great location for exploring the city's nightlife. A range of different rooms (room rates reduce considerably midweek) and some great communal spaces, including an outdoor deck. Dorms **£21**, doubles **£82**

YHA Manchester Potato Wharf, Castlefield ☎0845 371 9647, ⊚yha.org.uk; Deansgate-Castlefield Metrolink. Excellent hostel overlooking the canal that runs close to the Museum of Science and Industry, with 35 rooms (thirty four-bunk, two five-bunk and three doubles). Facilities include laundry, self-catering and a café. Dorms **£20**, doubles **£40**

EATING

Rivalling London in the breadth and scope of its **cafés** and **restaurants**, Manchester has something to suit everyone. Most options are in the city centre, but the **Rusholme** district, a couple of miles south, boasts the widest and best selection of Asian restaurants along its "Curry Mile". From Rusholme it's another couple of miles along Wilmslow Road to **Didsbury**, a leafy suburb with several excellent places to eat.

CAFÉS AND CAFÉ-BARS

Eighth Day 107–111 Oxford Rd ☎0161 273 1850, ⓦ8thday.coop; Metroshuttle #2. Manchester's oldest organic vegetarian café has a shop, takeaway and juice bar upstairs, with a great-value café/restaurant downstairs. Mon–Fri 9am–7pm, Sat 10am–5pm.

Home Sweet Home 49–51 Edge St, Northern Quarter ☎0161 224 9424, ⓦhomesweethomenq.com; Shudehill Metrolink. Queues snake round the block for this gem, with huge portions of American/Tex Mex-influenced mains (from £8), luscious milkshakes and generous slices of the most extravagantly decorated cakes you will ever have seen. Mon–Thurs 9am–10pm, Fri & Sat 9am–11pm, Sun 9am–9pm.

The Koffee Pot 21 Hilton St, Northern Quarter ⓦthekoffeepot.co.uk; Shudehill Metrolink. Beloved by hungover hipsters, this is *the* place for a Full English (£5.80) or Veggie (£5.60) brekkie (served until 2pm) amid much Formica and red leatherette. Often packed. Mon–Fri 7.30am-onwards, Sat 9am–onwards, Sun 10am–onwards.

Odd 30–32 Thomas St, Northern Quarter ☎0161 833 0070, ⓦoddbar.co.uk; Shudehill Metrolink. Oozes Manchester's cosmopolitan pride in kitsch surroundings. Menus in LP sleeves list great food following the quirky theme – the NYPD (New York Pastrami Doorstep; £6.95), for instance – and there's a fab vegan breakfast (£6.75). DJ nights most weekends, and a three-page drinks menu. Mon–Wed & Sun 11am–midnight, Thurs 11am–1am, Fri & Sat 11am–1.30am.

★Richmond Tea Rooms Richmond St, Gay Village ☎0161 237 9667, ⓦrichmondtearooms.com; Metroshuttle #1. Without question the most brilliantly conceived tearoom in Manchester, with an amazing Tim Burton-esque *Alice in Wonderland* theme. The sumptuous afternoon teas (£6.50–23.50) are the stuff of local legend, while the adjoining cocktail lounge is a super-stylish place to kick off an evening. Mon–Thurs 11am–10pm, Fri 11am–11pm, Sat 10am–11pm, Sun 10am–10pm.

Takk 6 Tariff St, Northern Quarter ⓦtakkmcr.com; Shudehill Metrolink. Cool yet cosy Icelandic coffee bar with a living-room feel, home-made cakes, a changing roster of sandwiches (£4), Nordic art and, of course, superior coffee – try the Red Eye (£2.60) if you never want to sleep again. Mon–Fri 8.30am–5pm, Sat 10am–6pm, Sun 11am–5pm.

Trof NQ 8 Thomas St, Northern Quarter ☎0161 833 3197, ⓦtrofnq.co.uk; Shudehill Metrolink. Three storeys of cool, relaxed café-bar populated by trendy young things. It's ideal for a late breakfast or early afternoon drink, and

hosts open-mic nights, poetry readings and DJ sets. Mon & Tues 10am–midnight, Wed & Thurs 10am–1am, Fri 10am–3am, Sat 9am–3am, Sun 9am–midnight.

RESTAURANTS

Australasia 1 The Ave, Spinningfields ☎0161 831 0288, ⓦaustralasia.uk.com; Metroshuttle #1 or #2. A remarkable glass pyramid on street level leads down under (get it?) to Australasia, a buzzing, white-tiled restaurant that's arguably the star of the Spinningfield dining scene. Food is Modern Oz meets Pacific Rim and pricey but well regarded (mains from £15, with the Australian Wagyu steak fillet a whopping £60). Daily noon–midnight.

Damson Orange Building, MediaCityUK ☎0161 751 7020, ⓦdamsonrestaurant.co.uk; MediaCityUK Metrolink. The first independent restaurant in TV Land, with well-cooked dishes such as roasted loin of cod and lamb rump served in an elegant dining room with great views over the piazza. Mains average £20, but there's a well-priced set menu at lunchtime and early evening (two courses £16.95, three £19.95). Mon–Thurs noon–2.45pm & 5–9.30pm, Fri & Sat noon–2.45pm & 5–10pm, Sun noon–5.30pm.

★Dimitri's 1 Campfield Arcade, Deansgate ☎0161 839 3319, ⓦdimitris.co.uk; Metroshuttle #1 or #2. Long-established Manchester favourite: pick and mix from the Greek/Spanish/Italian menu (particularly good for vegetarians) and enjoy it at a semi-alfresco arcade table with a Greek coffee or Lebanese wine; you'll think you're in the Med. Mon–Thurs & Sun 11am–midnight, Fri & Sat 11am–2am.

I Am Pho 44 George St ☎0161 236 1230; St Peter's Square Metrolink. Very cheap, very good Vietnamese in Chinatown serving big bowls of *pho* (noodle soup); try the raw beef one, in which the meat cooks in the broth. Mon–Thurs noon–10pm, Fri & Sat noon–11pm.

★Lime Tree 8 Lapwing Lane, West Didsbury ☎0161 445 1217, ⓦthelimetreerestaurant.co.uk; West Didsbury Metrolink. The finest local food, with a menu that chargrills and oven-roasts as if its life depended on it, using produce from its own smallholding. Main courses cost £14 and up, less at lunchtime. Reservations recommended. Mon & Sat 5.30–10pm, Tues–Fri noon–2.30pm & 5.30–10pm, Sun noon–8pm.

Punjab Tandoori 177 Wilmslow Rd, Rusholme ☎0161 225 2960. Despite the name, this is the only distinctively southern Indian – as opposed to Pakistani – restaurant on Rusholme's "Curry Mile" strip. The special *dosa* starters are great, and prices very reasonable – a full meal should cost no more than £15. A local favourite without pretensions. Daily 3pm–late.

★**Sam's Chop House** Chapel Walks, off Cross St ☎0161 834 3210, ☺samschophouse.co.uk; Market St Metrolink. The restaurant attached to this wonderful old-world pub is a hidden gem. It has a Victorian gas-lit feel and a delightful menu of English food (mains £14–16) – and they really know their wine, too. Mon–Sat noon–3pm & 5.30–11pm, Sun noon–8pm.

★**Yang Sing** 34 Princess St ☎0161 236 2200, ☺yang-sing.com; St Peter's Square Metrolink. One of the best Cantonese restaurants in the country, with authentic dishes ranging from a quick fried noodle plate to the full works. For the most interesting food, stray from the printed menu; ask the friendly staff for advice. Sister restaurant, the *little Yang Sing* on George St, slightly cheaper, is also worth stopping by. Mains from £12. Mon–Sat noon–11.30pm, Sun noon–10.30pm.

★**Yuzu** 39 Faulkner St, Chinatown ☎0161 236 4159, ☺yuzumanchester.co.uk; St Peter's Square Metrolink. Outstanding Japanese in Chinatown with a shortish menu of exceptionally executed sashimi (from £10.50), tempura (from £5.90) dishes and more, plus a tempting range of sake. Tues–Sat noon–2pm & 5.30–10pm.

10

DRINKING, NIGHTLIFE AND ENTERTAINMENT

From Victorian boozers to designer cocktail bars, Manchester does **drinking** in style, while its musical heritage and whopping student population keep things lively and interesting. There's an excellent **live music** scene, of course, and a mercurial roster of **clubs**; note too that many of the city's hip **café-bars** (see opposite) host regular club nights. See print and online listings (see p.462) for information. The bi-annual artist-led **Manchester International Festival** (☺mif.co.uk; next taking place in 2015) has included upwards of twenty world premieres of shows by names such as Damon Albarn and Björk, while the city hosted the inaugural **6 Music Festival** in 2014. As for **classical music**, the city is blessed with the North's most highly prized **orchestra**, the Hallé, which is resident at Bridgewater Hall. Other acclaimed names include the **BBC Philharmonic** and the **Manchester Camerata** chamber orchestra (☺manchestercamerata.com), who perform at a variety of venues. A range of mainstream and fringe **theatres** produce a lively, year-round programme.

PUBS AND BARS

★**Big Hands** 296 Oxford Rd ☎0161 272 7779. Right by the Academy venues, this intimate, über-cool bar is popular with students, usually post-gig as it has a late licence. Mon–Fri 10am–2am, Sat noon–3am, Sun 6pm–1am.

Britons Protection 50 Great Bridgewater St ☎0161 236 5895, ☺britons-protection.com. Cosy old pub with a couple of small rooms, a backyard beer garden and all sorts of Victorian detail – most splendidly the tiles and the open fires in winter. Boasts over 300 whiskies and a large mural depicting the Peterloo Massacre. Mon–Thurs 11am–11.30pm, Fri noon–12.30am, Sat 11am–midnight, Sun noon–11pm.

Circus Tavern 86 Portland St ☎0161 236 5818. Manchester's smallest pub, this Victorian drinking hole is a favourite city-centre pit-stop. You may have to knock to get in; when you do, you're confronted by the landlord in the corridor pulling pints. Daily 11am–11pm.

Cloud 23 Beetham Tower, 301 Deansgate ☎0161 870 1670, ☺cloud23bar.com. Manchester's highest and most popular cocktail bar, with a 23rd-floor glass overhang. Expensive, but worth it for the view of the city and Pennines beyond. Mon–Thurs & Sun 11am–1am, Fri & Sat 11am–2am.

Corbières 2 Half Moon St, just off St Ann's Square ☎0161 834 3381. Look for the Gaudí-esque wall art flanking the door of this longstanding subterranean, slightly dank drinking cellar with arguably the best jukebox in Manchester. Mon–Thurs 11am–11pm, Fri & Sat 11am–midnight, Sun 2–10.30pm.

★**Mr Thomas' Chop House** 52 Cross St ☎0161 832 2245, ☺tomschophouse.com. Victorian classic with Dickensian nooks and crannies. Office workers, daytime drinkers, old goats and students all call it home, and there's good-value, traditional food too. Mon–Thurs 11am–11pm, Fri & Sat 11am–midnight, Sun noon–10.30pm.

Sand Bar 120 Grosvenor St ☎0161 273 1552, ☺www.sandbarmanchester.co.uk. Between the university and the city centre, this is a brilliant modern take on the traditional pub, where students, lecturers and workers shoot the breeze. There's a great selection of beers and wines. Mon–Wed & Sun noon–midnight, Thurs noon 1am, Fri & Sat noon–2am.

The Temple 100 Great Bridgewater St ☎0161 228 9834. Teeny-tiny subterranean boozer in an old public toilet, with an amazing jukebox and bags of atmosphere, if not much elbow room. It's run by the same people as *Big Hands* (see above) and shares its nonchalant, fun-time vibe. Mon–Thurs & Sun noon–midnight, Fri & Sat noon–1am.

TOP 5 FOR MUSIC

Cavern Club Liverpool. See p.480
The Deaf Institute Manchester. See p.466
Liverpool Philharmonic Liverpool. See p.480
Matt and Phreds Manchester. See p.466
Warehouse Project Manchester. See p.466

10

CLUBS AND LIVE MUSIC

Albert Hall 27 Peter St ☎0844 858 8521, ⓦalberthall manchester.com. Former Wesleyan chapel that's now an atmospheric live-music venue hosting a select programme of high-quality, slightly leftfield artists. Hours vary.

★**Band on the Wall** 25 Swan St, Northern Quarter ☎0161 834 1786, ⓦbandonthewall.org. This legendary Northern Quarter joint remains true to its commitment to "real music": it's one of the city's best venues to see live bands – from world and folk to jazz and reggae – and it hosts club nights to boot. Box office Mon–Sat 5–9pm. Mon–Thurs 9am–1am, Fri & Sat 9am–3am, Sun noon–5pm.

★**The Castle Hotel** 66 Oldham St, Northern Quarter ☎0161 237 9485, ⓦthecastlehotel.info. Genuinely good 200-year-old pub with cask and craft ales and an extremely intimate backroom gig space. Jake Bugg played to just seventy-odd people here months before hitting the big time. Hosts regular spoken word nights too. Mon–Thurs noon–1am, Fri noon–2am, Sun noon–midnight.

★**The Deaf Institute** 135 Grosvenor St ☎0161 276 9350 ⓦthedeafinstitute.co.uk. A mile down Oxford Rd, this bar and music hall sits in a funky makeover of the elegant Victorian former deaf institute. Mostly folk, indie and r'n'b, with lots of up-and-coming talent, and a raft of great club nights. Sister venue *Gorilla* (ⓦthisisgorilla.com) on Whitworth Street is also excellent. Mon–Thurs & Sun 10am–midnight, Fri & Sat 10am–3am.

Manchester Academy Oxford Rd ☎0161 275 2930, ⓦmanchesteracademy.net. All three locations – Academy 1 is on the university campus, opposite the medical school; Academy 2 & 3 are inside the Students' Union building on Oxford Road – are popular student venues featuring new and established bands. Hours vary.

Matt and Phreds 64 Tib St, Northern Quarter ☎0161 831 7002, ⓦmattandphreds.com. The city's finest jazz bar, offering everything from swing to gritty New Orleans blues. Mon–Thurs & Sat 6pm–late, Fri 5pm–late.

O2 Apollo Manchester Stockport Rd, Ardwick Green ☎0844 477 7667, ⓦalive.co.uk/O2apollomanchester .co.uk. Medium-sized theatre auditorium for all kinds of concerts; a brilliant place to see big names up close, with bags of atmosphere. Hours vary.

★**The Ritz** Whitworth St West ☎0161 236 3234, ⓦmamacolive.com/theritz. This legendary dancehall has been around for decades (it's where The Smiths first played) and has a sprung dancefloor that really boings when things get going. Jumping live music and plenty of fun club nights, including a roller disco. Hours vary.

Soup Kitchen 31–33 Spear St, Northern Quarter ☎0161 236 5100, ⓦsoup-kitchen.co.uk. Soup-specializing canteen

with a basement club/live-music venue that's among Manchester's finest. Mon–Wed & Sun noon–11pm, Thurs noon–1am, Fri & Sat noon–4pm.

★**Warehouse Project** Underneath Piccadilly Station ⓦthewarehouseproject.com. An internationally acclaimed three-month season of the country's best dance and house acts – 2manydjs, Annie Mac, La Roux – smashing out sessions in a warehouse below the station. Tickets (£25) are like gold dust, so book well in advance. Oct–Dec Fri & Sat.

CLASSICAL MUSIC

Bridgewater Hall Lower Mosley St ☎0844 907 9000, ⓦbridgewater-hall.co.uk. Home of the Hallé Orchestra, the BBC Philharmonic and the Manchester Camerata; also a full programme of chamber, pop, classical and jazz concerts.

Royal Northern College of Music (RNCM) 124 Oxford Rd ☎0161 907 5200, ⓦrncm.ac.uk; Metroshuttle #2. Top-quality classical and modern jazz concerts.

THEATRE, CINEMA AND DANCE

★**Cornerhouse** 70 Oxford St ☎0161 200 1500, ⓦcornerhouse.org; St Peter's Square Metrolink. Engaging centre for contemporary arts, with three cinema screens, changing art exhibitions, recitals and talks, plus a bookshop, café and bar. Will close and be incorporated into HOME (see box, p.461) in Spring 2015.

Dancehouse Theatre 10 Oxford Rd ☎0161 237 9753, ⓦthedancehouse.co.uk; Metroshuttle #2. Home to the Northern Ballet School and the eponymous theatre troupe; venue for dance, drama and comedy.

The Lowry Pier 8, Salford Quays ☎0843 208 6000, ⓦthelowry.com; Harbour City Metrolink. This quayside venue hosts many of the biggest shows, including major National Theatre touring productions, most recently *War Horse*.

Opera House 3 Quay St ☎0844 871 3018, ⓦmanchesteroperahouse.org.uk; Deansgate-Castlefield Metrolink. Major venue for touring West End musicals, drama, comedy and concerts.

Royal Exchange Theatre St Ann's Square ☎0161 833 9833, ⓦroyalexchange.co.uk; Market St Metrolink. The theatre-in-the-round in the Royal Exchange is the most famous stage in the city, with a Studio Theatre (for works by new writers) alongside.

Screenfields The Lawns, Spinningfields ⓦspinning fieldsonline.com/events/screenfields. Seasonal screenings (most Thursdays May–Sept; 7pm) of feel-good summer movies for £3, with deckchairs to rent for a little extra. Enjoyable alfresco viewing and you can bring a picnic (no booze or glass bottles).

SHOPPING

Aside from the high-end boutiques on **King Street**, and the **department stores** around Market Street and Exchange Square, the Northern Quarter has a plethora of smaller independent stores catering for all tastes. If you're around between mid-November and the week before Christmas, make for the **German Christmas Market**, which sees Albert Square transformed into a Bavarian picture postcard.

Afflecks 52 Church St, Northern Quarter ☎ 0161 839 0718, ⓦ afflecks.com; Piccadilly Gardens Metrolink. A Manchester institution, more than fifty independent stalls are spread over four floors mixing everything from goth outfits to retro cocktail dresses and quirky footwear. Mon–Fri 10.30am–6pm, Sat 10am–6pm, Sun 11am–5pm (ground and first floors only).

Craft & Design Centre 17 Oak St, Northern Quarter ☎ 0161 832 4274, ⓦ craftanddesign.com; Shudehill Metrolink. The city's best place to pick up ceramics, fabrics, earthenware, jewellery and decorative art – there's also a good little café. Mon–Sat 10am–5.30pm.

Oklahoma 74–76 High St, Northern Quarter ☎ 0161 834 1136, ⓦ oklahomacafe.co.uk; Shudehill Metrolink. Hidden behind large wooden doors, this charming giftshop cum veggie-café is packed with fun knick-knacks and fripperies, with some pretty jewellery too. Mon–Sat 10am–7pm, Sun 10am–6pm.

Piccadilly Records 53 Oldham St, Northern Quarter ☎ 0161 839 8008, ⓦ piccadillyrecords.com; Piccadilly Gardens Metrolink. The enthusiastic staff, many of them DJs themselves, are more than willing to navigate you through the shelves of collectibles and vinyl towards some special gem, whatever your taste. Mon–Sat 10am–6pm, Sun 11am–5pm.

Retro Rehab 91 Oldham St, Northern Quarter ☎ 0161 839 2050, ⓦ retro-rehab.co.uk; Piccadilly Gardens Metrolink. Gorgeously feminine dresses abound, be they reworked vintage styles or genuine 1950s pieces, in this wonderful little boutique that prides itself on the range of its fashions from across several decades. Mon–Sat 10am–6pm, Sun noon–4pm.

10

DIRECTORY

Hospital Manchester Royal Infirmary, Oxford Road ☎ 0161 276 1234.

Internet Free at the Central Library, St Peter's Square (see p.456) and the Visitor Centre (see p.462), plus 30min free wi-fi in the city centre (accessed on _FreeBeeMcr Wi Fi).

Left luggage Facilities at Piccadilly train station (Mon–Sat 7am–11pm, Sun 8am–11pm; £4 per item for 24hr; ☎ 0161 236 8667).

Police 31 Bootle Street ☎ 0161 872 5050.

Post office 26 Spring Gardens

Chester

CHESTER, forty miles southwest of Manchester across the Cheshire Plain, is home to a glorious two-mile ring of medieval and Roman **walls** that encircles a kernel of Tudor and Victorian buildings, all overhanging eaves, mini-courtyards, and narrow cobbled lanes, which culminate in the raised arcades called the "**Rows**". The centre of the city is full of easy charms that can be explored on foot, and taken altogether Chester has enough in the way of sights, restaurants and atmosphere to make it an enjoyable base for a day or two. Though traditionally viewed as rather staid compared to near neighbours Manchester and Liverpool, it's gradually acquiring a bit of an edge, and with a new arts centre due to open in 2015, it's one to watch.

The Rows

Intersecting at **The Cross**, the four main thoroughfares of central Chester are lined by **The Rows**, galleried shopping arcades that run along the first floor of a wonderful set of half-timbered buildings with another set of shops down below at street level. This engaging tableau, which extends for the first 200 or 300 yards of each of the four main streets, is a blend of genuine Tudor houses and Victorian imitations. There's no clear explanation of the origin of The Rows – they were first recorded shortly after a fire wrecked Chester in 1278 – but it seems likely that the hard bedrock that lies underneath the town centre prevented its shopkeepers and merchants from constructing the cellars they required, so they built upwards instead. The finest Tudor buildings are on **Watergate Street**, though **Bridge Street** is perhaps more picturesque. From The Cross, it's also a brief walk along **Eastgate Street** to one of the old town gates, above which is perched the filigree **Eastgate Clock**, raised in honour of Queen Victoria's Diamond Jubilee.

The Cathedral

St Werburgh St, off Northgate St • Mon–Sat 9am–5pm, Sun 12.30–4pm • Free; £3 donation suggested • Cathedral at Height tours Mon–Sat 10am, 11am, 12.30pm, 1.30pm, 3pm & 4pm; 1hr; £8, children (over 8s only) £6 • ☎ 01244 324756, ⓦ chestercathedral.com

North of The Cross, along **Northgate Street**, rises the neo-Gothic **Town Hall**, whose acres of red and grey sandstone look over to the **Cathedral**, a much modified red sandstone structure dating back to the Normans. The **nave**, with its massive medieval pillars, is suitably imposing, and on one side it sports a splendid sequence of Victorian Pre-Raphaelite mosaic panels that illustrate Old Testament stories in melodramatic style. Close by, the **north transept** is the oldest and most Norman part of the church – hence the round-headed arch and arcade – and the adjoining **choir** holds an intricately carved set of fourteenth-century choir stalls with some especially beastly misericords. The atmospheric East Cloister leads to a gorgeously tranquil **garden**.

The new **Cathedral at Height** tour, an enjoyable hour-long rootle around the building's previously hidden spaces, takes you up onto the roof for panoramic views over five counties – you'll even spot Liverpool's cathedrals.

Around the city walls

East of the cathedral, steps provide access to the top of the **city walls** – a two-mile girdle of medieval and Roman handiwork that's the most complete in Britain, though in places the wall is barely above street level. You can walk past all its towers, turrets and gateways in an hour or so, and most have a tale or two to tell. The fifteenth-century **King Charles Tower** in the northeast corner is so named because Charles I stood here in 1645 watching his troops being beaten on Rowton Moor, two miles to the southeast, while the earlier **Water Tower** at the northwest corner once stood in the river – evidence of the changes brought about by the gradual silting of the River Dee. South from the Water Tower you'll see the **Roodee**, England's oldest racecourse, laid out on a silted tidal pool where Roman ships once unloaded wine, figs and olive oil from the Mediterranean and slate, lead and silver from their mines in North Wales. Races are still held here throughout the year.

The Grosvenor Museum

27 Grosvenor St • Mon–Sat 10.30am–5pm, Sun 1–4pm • Free • ☎ 01244 972197, ⊕ grosvenormuseum.co.uk

Scores of sculpted tomb panels and engraved headstones once propped up the wall to either side of the Water Tower, evidence of some nervous repair work undertaken when the Roman Empire was in retreat. Much of this stonework was retrieved by the Victorians and is now on display at the **Grosvenor Museum**, which also has interesting background displays on the Roman Empire in general and Roman Chester in particular. At the rear of the museum is **20 Castle Street**, a period house with nine rooms tricked out to represent domestic scenes from 1680 to 1925.

The Roman Gardens and around

Immediately to the east of one of the old city gates, **Newgate**, a footpath leads into the **Roman Gardens** (open access), where a miscellany of Roman stonework – odd bits of pillar, coping stones and incidental statuary – is on display. Footsteps away, along Little St John Street, is the shallow, partly excavated bowl that marks the site of the **Roman Amphitheatre** (open access); it is estimated to have held seven thousand spectators, making it the largest amphitheatre in Britain, but frankly it's not much to look at today.

Chester Zoo

Signposted off the A41 2 miles north of Chester • Daily: April–Sept 10am–5/6pm; Oct–March 10am–4/4.30pm; last admission 1hr before closing • £20, £16 in winter; children aged 3–15 £16/£13 • ⊕ chesterzoo.org • Bus #1 (daily every 20min) from the Bus Exchange

Chester's most popular attraction is **Chester Zoo**, one of the best in Europe. It is also the second largest in Britain (after London's), with over eleven thousand animals spread over a hundred landscaped acres. The zoo is well known for its **conservation projects** and has had notable success with its Asiatic lions and giant Komodo dragons. Animals are grouped by region in large paddocks viewed from a maze of pathways, from the monorail or the waterbus, with main attractions including the baby animals, the Tropical Realm and the Chimpanzee Forest with the biggest climbing frame in the country.

ARRIVAL AND INFORMATION	CHESTER

By train The train station is a 10min walk northeast of the centre, down City Road and Foregate Street from the central Eastgate Clock. A shuttle bus (Mon–Sat 8am–6pm, free with rail ticket; every 15min) links the station with the Bus Exchange.

Destinations Birmingham (5 daily; 2hr); Liverpool (every

10

30min; 45min); London (every 20min; 3hr 30min); Manchester (every 30min; 1hr–1hr 20min).

By bus Long-distance buses pull in on Vicar's Lane, opposite one of the town's two tourist offices (see below) and a 5min walk from the city centre, while local buses use the Bus Exchange right in the centre of town, between Princess and Hunter streets, off Northgate Street.

Destinations Liverpool (every 20min; 1hr 20min); Manchester (3 daily; 1hr).

Tourist information Chester has two information offices: one bang in the centre, in the Town Hall, Northgate Street (April–Sept Mon–Sat 9.30am–5.30pm, Sun 10am–4pm; Oct–March Mon–Fri 10am–4pm, Sat 10am–5pm) and the other on Vicar's Lane (same hours, plus Oct–March Sun 10am–4pm). They share the same telephone number and website (☎01244 351609, ⓦvisitchester.com).

ACCOMMODATION

Chester is a popular tourist destination and although most of its visitors are day-trippers, enough of them stay overnight to sustain dozens of **B&Bs** and a slew of **hotels**. At the height of the summer and on high days and holidays – like Chester Races – advance booking is strongly recommended, either direct or via the tourist office.

Chester Backpackers 67 Boughton ☎01244 400185, ⓦchesterbackpackers.co.uk. Close to the city walls and a 5min walk from the train station, in a typically Chester mock-Tudor building. En-suite doubles and two dorms (8- and 18-bed). Dorms £25, doubles £38

The Chester Grosvenor Eastgate St ☎01244 324024, ⓦchestergrosvenor.co.uk. Superb luxury hotel in an immaculately maintained Victorian building in the centre of town. Extremely comfortable bedrooms and a whole host of facilities, not least a full-blown spa (charges apply) and posh chocolatier Rococo onsite. Continental breakfast is included, but it's an extra £7.50 for a cooked breakfast. Rack rates are vertiginous, but look for special offers online. £300

Chester Town House B&B 23 King St ☎01244 350021, ⓦchestertownhouse.co.uk. Old-fashioned B&B in a comfortable seventeenth-century townhouse on a cobbled central street off Northgate Street. Five en-suite rooms and private parking. £75

★**Oddfellows** 20 Lower Bridge St ☎01244 895700, ⓦoddfellowschester.com. Quirky boutique hotel packed with look-at-me touches – from the typewriters climbing the reception walls, to the set table-for-two affixed to the ceiling, to the neon "Good Night" sign en route to the eighteen comfortable, individually styled bedrooms. There's a buzzy bar scene – including the *Secret Garden* – and popular restaurant on site too. £162

EATING

★**Chez Jules** 71 Northgate St ☎01244 400014, ⓦchezjules.com. There's a classic brasserie menu – salade nicoise to rib-eye steak – at this popular spot in an attractive half-timbered building. In the evenings, main courses begin at around £10, with a terrific-value, two-course prix fixe menu (Mon–Sat 5–7pm, Sun all day) for £11.95 and a two-course lunch for £9.95. Mon–Sat noon–3pm & 5–10.30pm, Sun noon–4.30pm.

★**La Brasserie** Chester Grosvenor, Eastgate St ☎01244 324024, ⓦchestergrosvenor.com/chester -brasserie. In the same hotel as the Michelin-starred

Simon Radley's, where the à la carte menu sits at a cool £75, this is a much more affordable yet smart brasserie that serves inventive French and fusion cooking. Main courses average £20, and it's also a great place for a coffee and pastry. Mon–Fri 7am–9.30pm, Sat 11am–10pm, Sun 11am–9pm.

Three Kings Tearoom 90–92 Lower Bridge St ☎01244 317717, ⓦthreekingstearooms.com. An amenable little tearoom with pleasantly fuddy-duddy decor and tasty food – a filling salad and sandwich combo costs about £5. Afternoon tea (£12.50) is popular. Daily 10am–5pm.

DRINKING

Albion Inn Corner of Albion and Park streets ☎01244 340345, ⓦalbioninnchester.co.uk. A Victorian terraced pub in the shadow of the city wall – no fruit machines, no muzak, just good old-fashioned decor (and a World War I theme), tasty bar food and a great range of ales. Hilariously unwelcoming signs outside – basically, if you're on a hen or stag do, or have a child in tow, forget it. Mon–Thurs & Sat noon–3pm & 5–11pm, Fri noon–11pm, Sun noon– 2.30pm & 7–10.30pm.

Brewery Tap House 52–54 Lower Bridge St ☎01244 340999, ⓦthe-tap.co.uk. Up the cobbled ramp, this

converted medieval hall, once owned by the royalist Gamul family and confiscated by Parliament after the English Civil War, serves a good selection of ales from local brewery Spitting Feathers in a tall barn-like room with whitewashed walls. Mon–Sat noon–11pm, Sun noon–10.30pm.

★**Old Harkers Arms** 1 Russell St, below the City Rd bridge ☎01244 344525, ⓦbrunningandprice.co.uk /harkers. Canalside real-ale pub imaginatively sited in a former warehouse about 500 yards northeast of Foregate Street. Quality bar food too. Mon–Sat 11.30am–11pm, Sun noon–10.30pm.

Liverpool

Standing proud in the 1700s as the empire's second city, **LIVERPOOL** faced a dramatic change in fortune in the twentieth century, suffering a series of harsh economic blows and ongoing urban deprivation. The postwar years were particularly tough, but the outlook changed again at the turn of the millennium, as economic and social regeneration brightened the centre and old docks, and the city's stint as European Capital of Culture in 2008 transformed the view from outside. Today Liverpool is a dynamic, exciting place with a Tate Gallery of its own, a series of innovative museums and a fascinating social history. And of course it also makes great play of its musical heritage – as well it should, considering that this is the place that gave the world The Beatles.

10

The main sights are scattered throughout the centre of town, but you can easily walk between most of them. The **River Mersey** provides one focus, whether crossing on the famous ferry to the **Wirral** peninsula or taking a tour of the Albert Dock. **Beatles** sights could easily occupy another day. If you want a cathedral, they've "got one to spare" as the song goes; plus there's a fine showing of British art in the celebrated **Walker Art Gallery** and **Tate Liverpool**, a multitude of exhibits in the terrific **World Museum Liverpool**, a revitalized arts and nightlife urban quarter centred on **FACT**, Liverpool's showcase for film and the media arts, and a whole new cutting-edge creative district known as the **Baltic Triangle**.

Brief history

Liverpool gained its charter from King John in 1207, but remained a humble fishing village for half a millennium until the booming slave trade prompted the building of the first dock in 1715. From then until the abolition of slavery in Britain in 1807, Liverpool was the apex of the **slaving triangle** in which firearms, alcohol and textiles were traded for African slaves, who were then shipped to the Caribbean and America where they were in turn exchanged for tobacco, raw cotton and sugar. After the abolition of the trade, the port continued to grow into a seven-mile chain of docks, not only for freight but also to cope with wholesale European emigration, which saw nine million people leave for the Americas and Australasia between 1830 and 1930. During the 1970s and 1980s Liverpool became a byword for British economic malaise, but the waterfront area of the city was granted **UNESCO World Heritage** status in 2004, spurring major refurbishment of the city's magnificent municipal and industrial buildings.

St George's Hall

St George's Place, off Lime St • Daily 10am–5pm• Free • ☎ 0151 233 3020, ⓦ liverpoolcityhalls.co.uk

Emerging from Lime Street Station, you can't miss **St George's Hall**, one of Britain's finest Greek Revival buildings and a testament to the wealth generated from transatlantic trade. Now primarily an exhibition venue, but once Liverpool's premier concert hall and crown court, its vaulted Great Hall features a floor tiled with thirty thousand precious Minton tiles (usually covered over, but open for a week or two in Aug), while the Willis organ is the third largest in Europe. You can take a self-guided tour, or call for details of the guided tours.

Walker Art Gallery

William Brown St • Daily10am–5pm • Free; audio tour £1.95 • ⓦ liverpoolmuseums.org.uk/Walker

Liverpool's **Walker Art Gallery** houses one of the country's best provincial art collections. The paintings are up on the first floor, but don't miss the ground-floor Sculpture Gallery, nor the Craft and Design Gallery, which displays changing exhibits from a

10

LIVERPOOL

● SHOPPING
Alison Appleton 4
Delfonseca 3
News from Nowhere 1
Utility 2

● CAFÉS & RESTAURANTS
60 Hope Street 6
Egg 3
Fonseca's 1
Italian Club Fish 5
Lunya 2
Side Door 4
Yuet Ben 7

■ ACCOMMODATION
2 Blackburne Terrace 8
Aachen 3
Hard Day's Night 2
Hatters 4
Hope Street 7
International Inn 6
The Nadler 5
Raquet Club 1

■ CLUBS & LIVE MUSIC
Cavern Club 1
Heebie Jeebies 7
The Kazimier 2
Parr Street Studios 8

■ PUBS & BARS
Alma de Cuba 5
Baltic Fleet 11
Berry & Rye 9
Camp and Furnace 12
Philharmonic 6
Salt Dog Slim's 4
Some Place 3
Ye Cracke 10

Anfield

Royal Liverpool
University Hospital

Liverpool
University

Metropolitan
Cathedral

Everyman
Theatre

Philharmonic
Hall

Liverpool
Cathedral

Central Library
Walker Art Gallery
World Museum Liverpool
National Express Buses

St George's Hall
St John's Garden
Empire
Lime Street Station

Royal Court Theatre
Queen Square Bus Station
St John's Shopping Centre
Clayton Square Shopping Centre
NHS Walk-in Centre

Met Quarter
Bluecoat Chambers
Cavern Walks Shopping Centre
FACT

Moorfields
Town Hall
Western Approaches Museum

ROPEWALKS

CHINA TOWN

Liverpool One
Liverpool One Bus Station
Police

Royal Liver Building
Cunard Building
Port of Liverpool Building
Open Eye Gallery

Tate Liverpool
Museum of Liverpool
Maritime Museum

Albert Dock
The Beatles Story
O2 Arena Liverpool

Pier Head

River Mersey

Mersey Railway Tunnel

Goodison Park & A59 Preston
Crosby Beach
Princes Dock
NEW QUAY
Douglas (Isle of Man)
Wallasey
Birkenhead
Baltic Triangle
Queen's Dock
Sefton Park, John Lennon Airport & Speke Hall
A562 Widnes

Ⓜ Merseyrail

0   200
yards

large applied arts collection – glassware, ceramics, fabrics, precious metals and furniture, largely retrieved from the homes of the city's early industrial businessmen. Liverpool's explosive economic growth in the eighteenth and nineteenth centuries is reflected in much of the Walker's collection, as British painting begins to occupy centre stage – notably works by native Liverpudlian George Stubbs, England's greatest animal painter. Impressionists and Post-Impressionists, including Degas, Sickert, Cézanne and Monet, take the collection into more modern times and tastes, before the final round of galleries of contemporary British art. Paul Nash, Lucian Freud, Ben Nicholson, David Hockney and John Hoyland all have work here, much of it first displayed in the Walker's biennial John Moores Exhibition.

10

Children up to 8 years old will love the excellent **Big Art for Little Artists** gallery on the ground floor.

Central Library

William Brown St • Mon–Fri 9am–8pm, Sat 9am–5pm, Sun 10am–5pm • Free • ☎ 0151 233 3069

Next to the Walker Gallery, the city's spectacular **Central Library** was reopened in May 2013 after a three-year, £50 million facelift. Approached via a "Literary Pavement" celebrating the city's considerable contribution to the written word, it centres on a stunning atrium crowned by an elliptical dome made of around 150 pieces of glass. Don't miss the beautiful circular **Picton Reading Room** and, in the **Oak Room**, a copy of John James Audubon's huge *Birds of America*.

World Museum Liverpool

William Brown St • Daily 10am–5pm • Free • ☎ 0151 478 4393, ⓦ liverpoolmuseums.org.uk/WML

The **World Museum Liverpool** is a great family attraction. The dramatic six-storey atrium provides access to an eclectic series of themed exhibits of broad appeal – from natural history to ethnography, insects to antiquities, dinosaurs to space rockets. Excellent sections for children include the Bug House (no explanation required), plus excellent hands-on natural history and archeology discovery centres. The planetarium and theatre have free daily shows, with times posted at the information desk.

Metropolitan Cathedral

On the hill behind Lime St, off Mount Pleasant • Daily 7.30am–6pm • Free; £3 admission to crypt • ⓦ liverpoolmetrocathedral.org.uk

The idiosyncratically shaped Catholic **Metropolitan Cathedral** of Christ the King is denigratingly known as "Paddy's Wigwam" or the "Mersey Funnel". Built in the wake of the revitalizing Second Vatican Council, it was raised on top of the tentative beginnings of Sir Edwin Lutyens' grandiose project to outdo St Peter's in Rome. The present building, to Sir Frederick Gibberd's spectacular Modernist design, is anchored by sixteen concrete ribs supporting the landmark stained-glass lantern, and was consecrated in 1967. Ceremonial steps mark the approach from Mount Pleasant/Hope Street, with a café-bar at the bottom and four huge bells at the top.

Everyman Theatre

Hope St • Tours April–Aug Tues, Thurs & Sat 11.30am (subject to the stage programme) • Free • ☎ 0151 709 4776, ⓦ everymanplayhouse .com

At the foot of the Metropolitan Cathedral is Liverpool's iconic **Everyman Theatre**, reopened in March 2014 to citywide jubilation after a two-year rebuilding programme. Explore it on a tour or just admire its stunning **Portrait Wall** – 105 aluminium shutters featuring life-size photographs of everyday people: a celebration of the theatre's inclusive ethos.

Liverpool Cathedral

Hope St • Daily 8am–6pm • Donation requested • Tower and audio tour Mon–Wed, Fri & Sat 10am–4.30pm, Thurs 10.30am–7.30pm, Sun 11.45am–3.30pm • £5 • ⦿ liverpoolcathedral.org.uk

The Anglican **Liverpool Cathedral** looks much more ancient than the Metropolitan Cathedral, but was actually completed eleven years later, in 1978, after 74 years in construction. The last of the great British neo-Gothic structures, Sir Giles Gilbert Scott's masterwork claims a smattering of superlatives: Britain's largest and the world's fifth-largest cathedral, the world's tallest Gothic arches and the highest and heaviest bells. On a clear day, a trip up the 330ft tower is rewarded by views to the Welsh hills.

10

Ropewalks and around

At the heart of Liverpool's regenerating city centre, **Ropewalks**, the former warehouse and factory district between Bold Street and Duke Street, is anchored by **FACT**, 88 Wood Street (⦿ fact.co.uk) – that's Film, Art and Creative Technology – with its galleries for art, video and new media exhibitions (Tues–Sun 11am–6pm; free), community projects, cinema screens, café and bar. The beautifully proportioned Bluecoat Chambers, built in 1717 as an Anglican boarding school for orphans, is in nearby School Lane. An integral part of Liverpool's cultural life for years, **The Bluecoat** (⦿ thebluecoat.org.uk) includes artists' studios, exhibitions, courses and performances, as well as a fantastic **Display Centre** (⦿ www.bluecoatdisplaycentre.com) where contemporary crafts are for sale. Further southwest is the massive new development of the **Liverpool One** shopping precinct.

In Wolstenholme Square, in the middle of Ropewalks, is *Penelope*, a huge modern sculpture of coloured plexiglass spheres on giant interwoven stalks, created by sculptor Jorge Pardo for the 2006 Biennial; it's especially striking when illuminated at night.

Western Approaches Museum

1–3 Rumford St, off Chapel St • Mon–Thurs & Sat 10.30am–4.30pm • £6 • ⦿ www.liverpoolwarmuseum.co.uk

En route to Pier Head, the **Western Approaches Museum** reveals an underground labyrinth of rooms, formerly headquarters for the Battle of the Atlantic during World War II. The massive Operations Room vividly displays all the technology of a 1940s nerve centre – wooden pushers and model boats, chalkboards and ladders.

The waterfront

Dominating the waterfront are the so-called **Three Graces** – namely the Port of Liverpool Building (1907), Cunard Building (1913) and, most prominently, the 322ft-high Royal Liver Building (1910), topped by the "Liver Birds", a couple of cormorants that have become the symbol of the city. As the waterfront has developed in the last decade or so, it has sprouted a number of attractions, including **Tate Liverpool**, the excellent **Maritime Museum**, the **Beatles Story**, the impressive **Museum of Liverpool** and the marvellous **Open Eye** gallery.

Museum of Liverpool

Pier Head • Daily 10am–5pm • Free • ⦿ 0151 478 4545, ⦿ liverpoolmuseums.org.uk/mol

Huge and flashy, in a show-stopping Danish-designed building, the brilliant **Museum of Liverpool** opened in 2011. Spread over three floors, the galleries play on Liverpool's historic status as the "second city of Empire", exploring the complex political and life histories that have unfolded in a community whose wealth and social fabric were built on international trade. Children will enjoy "Little Liverpool", a gallery where they can design and build their own city, while anyone with any interest in popular culture will

10

FERRY ACROSS THE MERSEY

Though the tumult of shipping which once fought the current in Liverpool has gone, the **Pier Head** landing stage remains the embarkation point for the Mersey Ferry (☎0151 330 1444, ⓦmerseyferries.co.uk) to Woodside (for Birkenhead) and Seacombe (Wallasey). Straightforward ferry-shuttles (£2.80 return) operate during the morning and evening rush hours. At other times the boats run circular fifty-minute "river explorer" **cruises** (hourly: Mon–Fri 10am–4pm, Sat & Sun 10am–6pm; £8.50), which you can combine with a visit to the **Spaceport** space exploration visitor attraction at Seacombe (Mon–Fri 10am–3pm, Sat & Sun & Bank Hols 10am–5pm ; £9, with ferry £13; ☎0151 330 1444, ⓦspaceport.org.uk).

---

have an absolute ball at "Wondrous Place", a memorabilia-rich celebration of sports and music.

Open Eye Gallery

19 Mann Island • Tues–Sun 10.30am–5.30pm; closed during exhibition takeovers, which take place four times a year and last approximately 12 days • Free • ☎ 0151 236 6768, ⓦ openeye.org.uk

On the new Mann Island development just by the Museum of Liverpool sits the **Open Eye Gallery**, the Northwest's only gallery dedicated to photography and related media. As well as presenting an impressive programme of international exhibitions, it contains a permanent archive of around 1600 prints from the 1930s onwards.

Albert Dock

Five minutes' walk south of Pier Head is **Albert Dock**, built in 1846 when Liverpool's port was a world leader. Its decline began at the beginning of the twentieth century, as the new deep-draught ships were unable to berth here, and the dock last saw service in 1972. A decade later the site was given a refit, and it is now one of the city's most popular areas, full of **attractions** – including the **Beatles Story** (see box opposite) – and bars and restaurants.

Merseyside Maritime Museum

Albert Dock • Daily 10am–5pm • Free • ⓦ liverpoolmuseums.org.uk

The **Merseyside Maritime Museum** fills one wing of the Dock; allow at least two hours to see it all. The basement houses **Seized!**, giving the lowdown on smuggling and revenue collection, along with **Emigrants to a New World**, an illuminating display detailing Liverpool's pivotal role as a springboard for more than nine million emigrants. Other galleries tell the story of the Battle of the Atlantic and of the three ill-fated liners – the *Titanic*, *Lusitania* and *Empress of Ireland*. Finally, the unmissable **International Slavery Museum** on the third floor manages to be both challenging and chilling, as it tells dehumanizing stories of slavery while examining contemporary issues of equality, freedom and racial injustice.

Tate Liverpool

Albert Dock • June–Aug daily 10am–5.50pm; Sept–May Tues–Sun 10am–5.50pm • Free, except for special exhibitions • ⓦ tate.org.uk/liverpool

The country's national collection of modern art from the north, **Tate Liverpool** holds popular retrospectives of artists such as Mondrian, Dalí, Magritte and Calder, along with an ever-changing display from its vast collection, and temporary exhibitions of artists of international standing. There's also a full programme of events, talks and tours.

Crosby Beach

Cambridge Rd or Mariners Rd/Hall Rd West, Crosby • Trains from Lime St to Hall Road Station; every 30min; 20min

Seven miles north of Liverpool city centre, **Crosby Beach** was an innocuous, if picturesque, spot until the arrival in 2005 of Antony Gormley's haunting **Another Place**

THE BEATLES TRAIL

Mathew Street, ten minutes' walk west of Lime Street Station, is now a little enclave of Beatles nostalgia, most of it bogus and typified by the **Cavern Walks Shopping Centre**, with a bronze statue of the boys in the atrium. **The Cavern** club where the band was first spotted by Brian Epstein, saw 275 Beatles' gigs between 1961 and 1963; it closed in 1966 and was partly demolished in 1973, though a latter-day successor, the *Cavern Club* at 10 Mathew St, complete with souvenir shop, was rebuilt on the original site. The *Cavern Pub*, across the way, boasts a coiffed Lennon mannequin lounging against the wall and an exterior "Wall of Fame" highlighting the names of all the bands who appeared at the club between 1957 and 1973 as well as brass discs commemorating every Liverpool chart-topper since 1952 – the city has produced more UK No. 1 singles than any other. There's more Beatlemania at **The Beatles Shop**, 31 Mathew Street (ⓦthebeatleshop.co.uk), which claims to have the largest range of Beatles gear in the world.

For a personal and social history, head to the Albert Dock for **The Beatles Story** (daily: April–Oct 9am–5pm, Nov–March 10am–5pm; £12.95; ⓦbeatlesstory.com), which traces the band's rise from the early days to their disparate solo careers. Then it's on to the two houses where John Lennon and Paul McCartney grew up. Both **20 Forthlin Rd**, home to the McCartney family from 1955 to 1964, and the rather more genteel **Mendips**, where Lennon lived with his Aunt Mimi and Uncle George between 1945 and 1963, are only accessible on pre-booked **National Trust** minibus tours (£20, NT members £8.30; ☎0151 427 7231 or ☎0844 800 4791), which run from both the city centre (mid-March to Oct Wed–Sun 10am & 10.50am; Feb to mid-March & Nov 10am, 12.30pm & 3pm) and Speke Hall, seven miles south (mid-March to Oct 2.30pm & 3.20pm). The experience is disarmingly intimate, whether you're sitting in John Lennon's bedroom – which has its original wallpaper – on a replica bed looking out, as he would have done, onto his front lawn, or simply entering Paul's tiny room and gazing at pictures of his childhood.

BEATLES TOURS

Phil Hughes ☎0151 228 4565 or ☎07961 511223, ⓦtourliverpool.co.uk. Small (8-seater) minibus tours run daily on demand with a Blue Badge guide well versed in The Beatles and Liverpool life (4hr; 1–4 people pay £100 in total, 5–8 £20 each). Includes city-centre pick-ups/drop-offs and refreshments.

Magical Mystery Tour ☎0151 236 9091; ⓦcavernclub.org; or book at tourist offices. Tours on the multicoloured Mystery Bus (daily; 2hr; £16.95) leave from Albert Dock.

installation, spread along more than 1000 yards of the shore. An eerie set of a hundred life-size cast-iron statues, each cast from Gormley's own body, are buried at different levels in the sand, all gazing out to sea and slowly becoming submerged as high tide rolls in.

ARRIVAL AND DEPARTURE LIVERPOOL

By plane Liverpool John Lennon Airport (☎0870 129 8484, ⓦliverpoolairport.com) is 8 miles southeast of the city centre; it has an information desk (daily 8am–6pm). The Airlink #500 bus (5.45am–11.45pm; every 30min; £3) runs from the entrance into the city. A taxi to Lime Street costs around £15.

By train Mainline trains pull in to Lime Street Station, northeast of the city centre.
Destinations from Lime St Birmingham (hourly; 1hr 40min); Chester (every 30min; 45min); Leeds (hourly; 1hr 40min); London Euston (hourly; 2hr 20min); Manchester (hourly; 50min); Sheffield (hourly; 1hr 45min); York (11 daily; 2hr 15min).

By bus National Express buses use the station on Norton St, just northeast of Lime Street train station.
Destinations Chester (12 daily; 1hr); London (9 daily; 5hr 10min–6hr 40min); Manchester (hourly; 1hr).

By ferry Ferries to and from the Isle of Man, run by the Isle of Man Steam Packet Company (☎0872 299 2992, ⓦsteam -packet.com), dock at the terminals just north of Pier Head, not far from James Street Merseyrail station. From Belfast, Lagan Seaways and Mersey Seaways (☎0870 609 9299, ⓦdfdsseaways.com) dock over the water on the Wirral at Twelve Quays, near Woodside ferry terminal (ferry or Merseyrail to Liverpool).

GETTING AROUND

By bus Local buses depart from Queen Square and Liverpool One bus station. The circular CityLink service is a perfect way to see the sights (every 12min; day tickets from £3)

By train The suburban Merseyrail system (trains from Chester) calls at four underground stations, including Lime Street and James Street (for Pier Head and the Albert Dock).

10

By bike The largest public bicycle scheme outside of London, Citybike (☎ 0151 374 2034, ⓦ citybikeliverpool .co.uk) has bikes from £3 a day, with stations citywide. You can also rent from Liverpool Bicycle Ltd, 29 Parliament Street (☎ 0151 707 6116, ⓦ liverpool-bicycle.co.uk; £10/ half-day, £15/day).

INFORMATION AND TOURS

Tourist information The best online source of information is ⓦ visitliverpool.com. There are visitor centres at Albert Dock, Anchor Courtyard (daily: April–Sept 10am–5.30pm, Oct–March 10am–5pm; ☎ 0151 233 2008, ⓦ albertdock.com) and Platform 7, Liverpool Lime Street station (daily 9.30am–5pm). Merseytravel (☎ 0151 236 7676, ⓦ merseytravel.gov.uk) has travel centres at Queen Square and the Liverpool One Interchange.

Listings The *Liverpool Echo's* website (ⓦ liverpoolecho .co.uk/whats-on) is always current; while the hip ⓦ the doublenegative.co.uk and ⓦ creativetourist.com will see you right. *The Skinny* is a useful, widely available monthly freebie.

Beatles tours Among the most popular jaunts in the city are those around the Fab Four's former haunts (see box, p.477).

Football tours You're unlikely to get a ticket for a Liverpool game, but there are daily tours around the museum, trophy room and dressing rooms (£16.50; museum only £8.50; ⓦ liverpoolfc.com). Everton, the city's other Premiership side, also offers tours (Mon, Wed, Fri & Sun 11am & 1pm; ☎ 0151 530 5212; £10; ⓦ evertonfc.com).

Walking tours ⓦ visitliverpool.com has details of local guides (most Easter–Sept; from £5).

ACCOMMODATION

Budget chains are well represented in Liverpool, with *Premier, Travel Inn, Ibis, Express by Holiday Inn* and others all with convenient city-centre locations, including down by Albert Dock and near Mount Pleasant.

★**2 Blackburne Terrace** 2 Blackburne Terrace ☎ 0151 702 4840, ⓦ 2blackburneterrace.com. Unspeakably beautiful B&B in a grand Georgian house set back from Blackburne Place, with just four elegant and individually designed rooms boasting high thread-count linens, original artworks and cutting-edge technology. With welcoming hosts and a sumptuous breakfast, this is a hidden, high-end gem. You'll save around £40 by staying midweek. **£180**

Aachen 89–91 Mount Pleasant ☎ 0151 709 3477, ⓦ aachenhotel.co.uk. The best of the Mount Pleasant budget choices, with a range of good-value rooms (with and without en-suite showers), big "eat-as-much-as-you-like" breakfasts, and a bar. **£95**

Hard Day's Night North John St ☎ 0151 236 1964, ⓦ harddaysnighthotel.com. Up-to-the-minute four-star close to Mathew Street. Splashes of vibrant colour and artful lighting enhance the elegant decor. The Lennon and McCartney suites (£950/750 respectively) are the tops. Breakfast not included. **£160**

Hatters 56–60 Mount Pleasant ☎ 0151 709 5570, ⓦ hattersgroup.com/Liverpool. Though it's housed in the former YMCA building – with an institutional feel and gymnasium-size dining hall – *Hatters* has clean rooms, friendly staff and a great location. Standard facilities, including internet. Prices fluctuate wildly according to what's on. Dorms **£30**, doubles **£100**

★**Hope Street** 40 Hope St (entrance on Hope Place) ☎ 0151 709 3000, ⓦ hopestreethotel.co.uk. In an unbeatable location between the cathedrals, this former Victorian warehouse retains its original elegant brickwork and cast-iron columns but now comes with hardwood floors, huge beds and luxurious bathrooms. Fabulous breakfasts, too, served in the highly rated *London Carriage Works* restaurant. Flash sales, held three times a year, offer bargain rooms; register for the email newsletter to snap one up. **£152**

★**International Inn** 4 South Hunter St, off Hardman St ☎ 0151 709 8135, ⓦ internationalinn.co.uk. Converted Victorian warehouse in a great location, with modern en-suite rooms sleeping two to ten people, and 32 new double and twin "Cocoon Pods". Dorms **£20**, doubles **£45**, pods **£55**

The Nadler Formerly Base2Stay, 29 Seel St ☎ 0151 705 2626, ⓦ thenadler.com/liverpool. Smack in the heart of the Ropewalks is this converted warehouse, with more than 100 minimalist rooms that complement the building's original brickwork and well-appointed modern art pieces. Rooms include a "mini-kitchen". Prices are almost halved midweek. **£119**

Racquet Club 5 Chapel St ☎ 0151 236 6676, ⓦ racquetclub.org.uk. Boutique-style townhouse hotel with just eight rooms, each mixing fine linens and traditional furniture with contemporary art and modern fittings. Breakfast is not in the price, but is available courtesy of *Ziba*, the hotel's restaurant. **£110**

EATING AND DRINKING

Many Liverpool venues morph from breakfast hangout to dinner spot to late-night live music space, making categorization increasingly futile. Most **eating** choices are in three distinct areas – at Albert Dock, around Hardman and Hope streets, and along Berry and Nelson streets, the heart of Liverpool's Chinatown. You'll enjoy a perfect evening's **bar-hopping** along Seel Street, while the blossoming **Baltic Triangle**, the old industrial warehouse district south of Chinatown, has become the city's most creative and cutting-edge quarter. Alternatively, take a short taxi ride out to Lark Lane in Aigburth, close to Sefton Park, where a dozen eating and drinking spots pack into one short street.

CAFÉS AND RESTAURANTS

★**60 Hope Street** 60 Hope St ☎0151 707 6060, ⦿60hopestreet.com. The star of the Liverpool gastronomic scene, set in a Georgian terrace, serves British cuisine (mains around £22) with creative flourishes – roast rump of Cumbrian lamb with broccoli purée, for example – and an extensive wine list. It takes some nerve to offer, as a dessert, deep-fried jam sandwich with Carnation milk Ice cream (£8.50), but the confidence is justified. Mon–Fri noon–2.30pm & 5–10.30pm, Sat noon–3pm & 5–10.30pm, Sun noon–8pm.

Egg 16 Newington ☎0151 707 2755, ⦿eggcafe.co.uk. Up on the third floor, this plant-strewn bohemian café serves excellent vegan and vegetarian food with good set-meal deals. Also a nice place for a chai. Mon–Fri 9am–10.30pm, Sat & Sun 10am–10.30pm.

★**Fonseca's** 12 Stanley St ☎0151 255 0808, ⦿delifonseca.co.uk. Bistro with a changing blackboard menu of Italian and British delights, including Welsh black beef braised in local Wapping ale, and crayfish and chicken pie (mains around £13). The small deli counter downstairs offers a sample of the wares at the newer *Delifonseca*, 30min away on the dockside (see p.480). Mon–Thurs noon–2.30 & 5–9pm, Fri & Sat noon–10pm.

Italian Club Fish 128 Bold St ☎0151 707 2110, ⦿theitalianclubfish.co.uk. Proper Italian seafood place with a menu that adapts to what's fresh – try the *Sauté Di Maurizio* (£16.95) There are also a few token meat and vegetarian dishes, all around £13. Mon–Sat 10am–10pm, Sun noon–9pm.

Lunya 18–20 College Lane ☎0151 706 9770, ⦿lunya .co.uk. Gorgeous Catalan and Spanish deli-restaurant in the heart of Liverpool ONE, with a vast tapas selection (from around £5) and menus running the gamut from suckling pig banquet to vegan. Mon & Tues 10am–9pm, Wed & Thurs 10am–9.30pm, Fri 10am–10pm, Sat 9am–10pm, Sun 10am–8.30pm.

Side Door 29a Hope St ☎0151 707 7888, ⦿the sidedoor.co.uk. The intimate Georgian townhouse bistro has a winning combination of Mediterranean food and reasonable prices – with bargain pre-theatre menus from £16.95. Does a great £5 lunch, too. Mon–Wed noon–2pm & 5–9.30pm, Thurs–Sat noon–2pm & 5–10pm.

Yuet Ben 1 Upper Duke St ☎0151 709 5772. In business since 1968, *Yuet Ben* is widely held to be the best Chinese restaurant in Liverpool, with dishes from around £8, great set menus and a fantastic vegetarian choice. Tues–Thurs & Sun 5–11pm, Fri & Sat 5pm–midnight.

PUBS AND BARS

Alma de Cuba St Peter's Church, Seel St ☎0151 702 7394, ⦿alma-de-cuba.com. It may have far more candles now than when it was a church – and even more in the mezzanine restaurant – but the mirrored altar is still the focus of this bar's rich, dark Cuban-themed interior. Daily 11am–2am.

Baltic Fleet 33a Wapping ☎0151 709 3116, ⦿balticfleet publiverpool.com. Restored, no-nonsense, quiet pub with age-old shipping connections and an open fire, just south of the Albert Dock. Beer brewed on site and good pub grub on offer. Mon–Fri & Sun noon–midnight, Sat 11am–midnight.

★**Berry & Rye** 48 Berry St ✉berryandwye@gmail .com. You'll have to hunt hard – or ask a likely local – to find this unmarked bar, but once you're in it's a delight. An intimate, bare-brick gin and whiskey joint with knowledgeable bartenders, turn-of-the-twentieth-century music – often live – and well-crafted cocktails (from £6.50). Highly recommended. Mon–Sat 5pm–2am, Sun 7pm–1am.

★**Camp and Furnace** 67 Greenland St, Baltic Triangle ☎0151 708 2890, ⦿campandfurnace.com. The most creative and exhilarating venue in a city not short on contenders, its huge warehouses spaces – one boasting the city's biggest public screen, one with a mighty furnace at one end, a cosier bar area – host festival-style food slams (Fri), massive, communal Sunday roasts, all sorts of parties and pop-ups, art installations, live performances, the lot. Do not miss it. Mon–Thurs 9am–10pm, Fri & Sat 10am–2am, Sun 10am–midnight/1am.

★**Philharmonic** 36 Hope St ☎0151 707 2837 ⦿nicholsonspubs.co.uk. Liverpool's finest traditional watering hole where the main attractions – beer aside – are the mosaic floors, tiling, gilded wrought-iron gates and the marble decor in the gents. Daily 11am–midnight.

Salt Dog Slim's 79 Seel St ☎0151 709 7172. American-style bar that's a lot of fun, with a young, friendly crowd wolfing delicious hot dogs (from £3.50) washed down with plenty of beers, backed by a solidly indie soundtrack. Upstairs is the supposedly secret *81 Ltd*, which rocks a Prohibition-era speakeasy vibe, though perhaps a tad self-consciously. Daily 5pm–2am.

★**Some Place** 43 Seel St. A green light above an unmarked doorway hints at what lies up the incense-heavy staircase – an utterly gorgeous absinthe bar that is every inch a bohemian fantasy. Savour an absinthe cocktail (from £4.50), drink in the meticulous decor and channel your inner Oscar Wilde. Wed & Thurs 9pm–late, Fri & Sat 8pm–late.

★**Ye Cracke** 13 Rice St ☎0151 709 4171. Crusty backstreet pub off Hope St, much loved by the young Lennon, and with a great jukebox, and cheap-as-chips food (daytime only). Mon–Thurs & Sun noon–11.30pm, Fri & Sat noon–midnight.

10

NIGHTLIFE AND ENTERTAINMENT

Liverpool's **club scene** is famously unpretentious, with posing playing second fiddle to drinking and dancing, while particularly rich in home-grown live music. Popular annual **festivals** include Beatles Week (last week of Aug; ⓦcavernclub.org/beatleweek) and the Liverpool International Music Festival (Aug Bank Hol; ⓦlimfestival.co.uk), with big-name acts playing across the city; while there are plenty of one-off cultural events, such as the jaw-dropping Giants Spectacular (2012 & 2014; ⓦgiantspectacular.com). As for the classical music scene, the **Royal Liverpool Philharmonic Orchestra**, ranked with Manchester's Hallé as the Northwest's best, dominates.

CLUBS AND LIVE MUSIC

Cavern Club 10 Mathew St ☎0151 236 1965, ⓦcavernclub.org. The self-styled "most famous club in the world" has live bands, from Beatles tribute acts to indie pop and rock, at the weekends, along with occasional backstage tours and special events. The atmosphere is always high-spirited, and even though this is not the very same *Cavern* club of the Beatles' days (see box, p.477), there's a certain thrill to it all. Open daily from 10am.

Heebie Jeebies 80–82 Seel St ☎0151 708 7001. Student favourite in a huge brick-vaulted room. Mainly indie and soul, with some live bands. Thurs–Sat 10pm–2am.

★**The Kazimier** 4–5 Wolstenholme Square ☎0151 324 1723, ⓦthekazimier.co.uk. A super-creative, split-level place with a magical garden space (entrance at 32 Seel St); *the* place to come for cabaret-style club nights, gigs and eclectic events. Hours vary but generally noon–midnight.

Parr Street Studios Parr St ☎0151 707 1050, ⓦparrstreet.co.uk. Dynamic working recording studios – the UK's biggest outside London – hosting a long list of big names and home to bars/performance spaces Studio 2 and The Attic. Check website for details of what's on when.

CLASSICAL MUSIC, THEATRE AND CINEMA

Everyman Theatre Hope St ☎0151 709 4776, ⓦeverymanplayhouse.com. Iconic, newly reopened theatre (see p.473), staging a mix of classics with a twist, blockbusters and new writing.

Liverpool Empire Lime St ☎0870 606 3536, ⓦliverpooltheatres.com/empire.htm. The city's largest theatre, a venue for touring West End shows and large-scale opera and ballet productions.

Philharmonic Hall Hope St ☎0151 709 3789, ⓦliverpoolphil.com. Home to the Royal Liverpool Philharmonic Orchestra, and with a full programme of other concerts.

Picturehouse at FACT Wood St ☎0871 704 2063, ⓦpicturehouses.co.uk. The city's only independent cinema screens new films, re-runs, cult classics and festivals.

Playhouse Williamson Square ☎0151 709 4776, ⓦeverymanplayhouse.com. Sister theatre to the Everyman, staging bold productions of great plays in the three-tier main house and new plays in the 70-seat Studio.

Royal Court Theatre Roe St ☎0870 787 1866, ⓦroyalcourtliverpool.co.uk. Art Deco theatre and concert hall, which sees regular plays, music and comedy acts.

SHOPPING

Liverpool is fabulous for shopping, with the brilliantly designed Liverpool ONE shopping complex holding pretty much all the names, a stretch of independent stores on Bold Street and arty originals in the Baltic Triangle.

Alison Appleton 46B Jamaica St, Baltic Triangle ☎0151 709 1188, ⓦalisonappleton.com. Delicate, beautiful handmade teapots, cups and more in a tiny outlet in the heart of Liverpool's most dynamic quarter. Mon–Fri 9am–5pm, Sat 11am–4pm.

Delifonseca Brunswick Dock ⓦdelifonseca.co.uk /delis/dockside. The new food hall of this acclaimed, two-site bistro offers a vast array of fine deli foods and wines. Daily 8am–9pm.

News From Nowhere 96 Bold St ☎0151 708 7270, ⓦnewsfromnowhere.co.uk. Proper radical bookshop in

the heart of Bold Street, packed to the rafters with left-leaning literature, music and more, and with an informative noticeboard. Mon–Sat 10am–5.45pm, Sun (Dec only) 11am–5pm.

Utility 8 Paradise Place ☎0151 702 9116, ⓦutilitydesign.co.uk. Stylish, design-led Liverpool store with three outlets across the city, two of them on Bold Street. This one, in Liverpool ONE, has the longest hours. Make a beeline for the quality Scouse souvenirs, particularly the brilliant wheelie bin desk tidy. Mon–Fri 9.30am–8pm, Sat 9am–7pm, Sun 11am–5pm.

Blackpool

Shamelessly brash **BLACKPOOL** is the archetypal British seaside resort, its "Golden Mile" of piers, amusement arcades, tram and donkey rides, fish-and-chip shops, candyfloss stalls, fun pubs and bingo halls making no concessions to anything but lowbrow fun of the finest kind. It was the coming of the railway in 1846 that made Blackpool what it is today:

Blackpool's own "Eiffel Tower" on the seafront and other refined diversions were built to cater to the tastes of the first influx of visitors, but it was the Central Pier's "open-air dancing for the working classes" that heralded the crucial change of accent. Suddenly Blackpool was favoured destination for the "Wakes Weeks", when whole Lancashire mill towns descended for their annual holiday.

With seven miles of beach – the tide ebb is half a mile, leaving plenty of sand at low tide – a revamped **prom** and an increasingly attractive, gentrified centre, there is more to Blackpool than just amusements. Where other British holiday resorts have suffered from the rivalry of cheap foreign packages, Blackpool has gone from strength to strength. Underneath the populist veneer there's a sophisticated marketing approach, which balances ever more elaborate rides and public art installations with well-grounded traditional entertainment. And when other resorts begin to close up for the winter, Blackpool's main season is just beginning, as more than half a million light bulbs create the **Illuminations** that decorate the prom from late August to early November.

10

Blackpool Tower

Tower Mon–Fri 10am–4.45pm, Sat & Sun 10am–6.15pm • Free entry to tower, but charges for attractions; for multi-attraction all-day tickets from £20 book online 24hr in advance **Circus** 1–3 shows daily; 2hr • £16.95, or included in package • ☎01253 622242, ⑩theblackpooltower.com

Between Central and North piers stands the 518ft-high **Blackpool Tower**, erected in 1894 when it was thought that the northwest really ought not to be outdone by Paris. Ride up to the top for the stunning view and an unnerving walk on the see-through glass floor. The all-day ticket covers all the other tower attractions, including the gilt Edwardian ballroom (otherwise £2.95), with its Wurlitzer organ tea dances and big band evenings, plus dungeon, children's entertainers, adventure playground, cafés and amusements. From the earliest days, there's also been a Moorish-inspired **circus** held between the tower's legs.

The Comedy Carpet

Right outside Blackpool Tower, **The Comedy Carpet** is one of the country's most engaging pieces of public art – a 2200m-square, cross-shaped pavement comprising jokes and catchphrases from around a thousand comedians and writers, both old-school and new, in a dazzling typographic display that recalls a music hall playbill. Opened in 2011 by end-of-the-pier stalwart Ken Dodd, it's a unique celebration of British comedy and a marvellous way to spend an hour.

Blackpool Pleasure Beach

March–Oct daily from 10am • Free, though rides cost; wristband £29.99, cheaper if booked online • ⑩blackpoolpleasurebeach.com

The major draw in town is **Blackpool Pleasure Beach** on the South Promenade, just south of South Pier. Entrance to the

BLACKPOOL

▼ **3**, **4**, Blackpool Pleasure Beach, Sandcastle Waterpark, St Annes & Airport

● CAFÉS & RESTAURANTS		■ ACCOMMODATION		■ CABARET	
AJ's	2	The Big Blue	3	Funny Girls	1
Kwizeen	4	FourRooms	2		
The Lounge	3	Number One	4		
Yorkshire Fisheries	1	Raffles	1		

10

BLACKPOOL – BEHIND THE SCENES

There is, after all, an alternative Blackpool – one of history, heritage and even a spot of culture. Scene of party political conferences over the decades, the **Winter Gardens** (Coronation Street) opened to fanfares in 1878. Among the motley array of cafés, bars and amusements, seek out the extraordinary **Spanish Hall Suite** (in the form of a carved galleon), and the **Opera House** honours board – Lillie Langtry, George Formby and Vera Lynn are all present. From in front of the Opera House, follow Abingdon Street to Queen Street and the porticoed Central Library, next to which the **Grundy Art Gallery** (Mon–Sat 10am–5pm; free) might tempt you in to see its Victorian oils and watercolours, contemporary art and special exhibitions. **North Pier**, the first pier to be opened (1863) on the Blackpool seafront, is now a listed building. Head northbound from here on the tram to the **Imperial Hotel**, whose wood-panelled No. 10 Bar is covered with photographs and mementos of every British prime minister since Lloyd George.

amusement park is free, but you'll have to fork out for the superb array of white-knuckle rides including the 235ft-high "Big One". The wonderful antique wooden roller coasters ("woodies" to aficionados) may seem like kids' stuff, but each is unique – the original "Big Dipper" was invented at Blackpool in 1923 and still thrills, as does the "Grand National" (1935). Caution: do not disregard the warning at the thrilling "Valhalla" ride – you will indeed get (very) wet, so maybe save this one until the end of the day. Recuperate in the park's champagne and oyster bar, which adds a bit of class to the otherwise relentless barrage of fairground noise, shrieking, jangling and fast food.

Great Promenade Show

South from the Pleasure Beach, from the Sandcastle Waterpark down to Squire's Gate • Free

Perhaps nowhere sums up the "new" Blackpool better than the **Great Promenade Show**, a set of ambitious outdoor sculptures, installations and soundscapes set along a mile or so of the new promenade. All relating to some aspect of Blackpool's history or its natural environment, these include the mighty **High Tide Organ**, which gives off haunting music when "played" by the swell of the waves, a set of sculptures of circus characters by **Sir Peter Blake**, and the world's largest **disco ball**, named "They Shoot Horses, Don't They?"

ARRIVAL AND INFORMATION   BLACKPOOL

By plane Blackpool's airport (@blackpoolinternational .com) lies 2.5 miles south of the centre; however it hit financial difficulties in 2014 and was closed at the time of writing.

By train The town's main train station, Blackpool North, is a few minutes' walk west of the town centre on Talbot Road, with a smaller terminus, Blackpool South, just north of the Pleasure Beach on Waterloo Road.

Destinations Manchester (hourly; 1hr 10min).

By bus Buses pull in at the new Blackpool Central Coach Station, behind the Coral Island arcade at the junction of Central Drive and New Bonny Street.

Tourist office Festival House, on the Promenade (Mon & Tues 9am–6pm, Wed–Sat 9am–5pm, Sun 10am–4pm; @01253 478222, @visitblackpool.com). Brand-new, purpose-built information centre; it sells discounted admission tickets for all major Blackpool attractions (except the Pleasure Beach), and travel passes.

GETTING AROUND

By tram Electric trams (@blackpooltransport.com) cover the length of the promenade, from Fleetwood, north of Blackpool, to Starr Gate, south of the Pleasure Beach. Prices vary, but the cheapest option is to buy a Blackpool1 travel card online or from the tourist office (see above) valid for local buses and trams (1/3/7-day, £3.50/10.50/13.50); you'll pay more if you buy on board.

ACCOMMODATION

Bed-and-breakfast **prices** are generally low (from £25/person, even less on a room-only basis or out of season), but rise at weekends and during the Illuminations. To avoid the noisy crowds in peak season, make for the North Shore, beyond North Pier (the grid west of Warbreck Hill Road has hundreds of options).

The Big Blue Ocean Blvd, Pleasure Beach ☎ 0871 222 4000, ⓦ bigbluehotel.com. Spacious family rooms with games consoles and separate children's area, plus boutique-style, dark-wood executive rooms. There's a bar and brasserie, parking and a gym. It's next to the Pleasure Beach (and Blackpool South train station), and most rooms look out on the rides. Parking available. **£135**

★ **FouRooms** 60 Reads Ave ☎ 01253 752171, ⓦ fourroomsblackpool.co.uk. One of Blackpool's best boutique hotels, a tastefully converted Victorian townhouse with airy rooms and original dark wood fittings. The four suites are individually furnished, and staff are keen to help. **£120**

★ **Number One** 1 St Luke's Rd ☎ 01253 343901, ⓦ numberoneblackpool.com. There's no other B&B quite like this – an extraordinarily lavish boutique experience hosted by the ultra-amiable Mark and Claire. There are just three extravagantly appointed rooms here, with more at *Number One South Beach* nearby. Single occupancy starts at £70. Parking available. **£100**

Raffles 73–77 Hornby Rd ☎ 01253 294713, ⓦ raffleshotelblackpool.co.uk. Nice place back from Central Pier and away from the bustle, with well-kept rooms, a bar, and traditional tearooms attached. Winter rates are a good deal. **£78**

EATING

AJ's 65 Topping St ☎ 01253 626111, ⓦ ajs-bistro.co.uk. A festival of meat, this unpretentious restaurant is at its best with steaks and grills, though there's a good range of seafood and poultry. Non-steak mains around £14. Tues–Fri & Sun 5.30pm–late, Sat 5pm–late.

★ **Kwizeen** 49 King St ☎ 01253 290045, ⓦ kwizeenrestaurant.co.uk. This friendly, contemporary bistro is the best restaurant in town, with a seasonally changing menu that emphasizes local produce, from Blackpool tomatoes and Lancashire cheese to Fylde farm ostriches. Mains around £15, though there's a bargain two- or three-course weekday lunch. Mon–Fri 11.45am–1.45pm & 6–9pm,

Sat 6–9pm; occasionally open on Sun.

The Lounge 10a Cedar Square ☎ 01253 291112. Tapas restaurant-cum-café on cobbled Cedar Square, with friendly staff serving a selection of light lunches. Mon–Wed 11am–5pm, Thurs–Sat 11am–11pm, Sun noon–5pm.

Yorkshire Fisheries 14–16 Topping St ☎ 01253 627739, ⓦ yorkshirefisheries.co.uk. Behind the Winter Gardens, this sit-down and takeaway fish and chip shop is commonly agreed to be the best in the centre of town. Mon–Sat 11.30am–7pm, Sun noon–6pm.

NIGHTLIFE AND ENTERTAINMENT

Blackpool has a plethora of **theme bars** and any number of places for **karaoke** or **dancing**. Family-oriented fun revolves around musicals, veteran TV comedians, magicians, ice dance, tribute bands, crooners and stage spectaculars put on at a variety of end-of-pier and historic venues.

Funny Girls 5 Dickson Rd, off Talbot Rd ☎ 01253 649194, ⓦ funnygirlsonline.co.uk. A Blackpool institution – a transvestite-run bar with nightly cabaret shows that attract long (gay and straight) queues. It's a hen party favourite and not to everyone's tastes, but the best place in town if you fancy some unabashedly bawdy Blackpool fun.

The Grand Theatre Church St ☎ 01253 290190, ⓦ blackpoolgrand.co.uk. Built in 1894 for the town's more refined audiences, the Grand has a tradition of distinguishing itself from other amusements, putting on performances of Shakespeare as well as more popular variety shows.

Opera House Winter Gardens, Church St ☎ 01253 625252, ⓦ blackpoollive.com. Set in the Winter Gardens, the Opera House has a star-studded history that includes such populist greats as Charlie Chaplin, George Formby and Vera Lynn. These days you'll find a variety of shows on offer, including West End hits. Also in the Winter Gardens, the Empress Ballroom is a majestic gig venue (same contact details).

Pleasure Beach Theatre Pleasure Beach ☎ 0871 222 9090, ⓦ blackpoolpleasurebeach.com. Spectacular stuff: huge choreographed dance shows, dramatic stunts and blood-pumping musical accompaniment.

Lancaster

LANCASTER, Lancashire's county town, dates back at least as long ago as the Roman occupation, though only scant remains survive from that period. A Saxon church was later built within the ruined Roman walls as Lancaster became a strategic trading centre, and by medieval times a **castle** had been built on the heights above the river. Lancaster became an important port on the slave trade triangle, and it's the **Georgian buildings** from that time – especially those around the castle – that give the town much of its character. Many people choose to stay here on the way to the Lakes or Dales to the north; and it's an easy side-trip the few miles west to the resort of **Morecambe** and to neighbouring **Heysham village**, with its ancient churches, or east through the **Forest of Bowland**.

Lancaster Castle

Daily: tours every 30min 10am–4pm • £8 • ⓦ lancastercastle.com

The site of **Lancaster Castle** has been the city's focal point since Roman times. The Normans built the first defences here, at the end of the eleventh century – two hundred years later it became a **crown court**, a role it maintains today, and until 2011 it was a working prison. Currently, about a third of the battlemented building can be visited on an entertaining hour-and-a quarter-long tour, though court sittings sometimes affect the schedules.

Judges' Lodgings

15 Castle Hill • Easter–June & Oct Mon–Fri 1–4pm, Sat & Sun noon–4pm; July–Sept Mon–Fri 10am–4pm, Sat & Sun noon–4pm • £3 • ⓣ 01524 32808

A two-minute walk down the steps between the castle and the neighbouring **Priory Church of St Mary** brings you to the seventeenth-century **Judges' Lodgings**, once used by visiting magistrates. The top floor is given over to a Museum of Childhood, with memory-jogging displays of toys and games, and a period (1900) schoolroom.

Maritime Museum

Custom House, St George's Quay • Daily: April–Oct 11am–5pm; Nov–March 12.30–4pm • £3 • ⓣ 01524 382264

Down on the banks of the River Lune – which lent Lancaster its name – one of the eighteenth-century quayside warehouses is taken up by part of the **Maritime Museum**. The museum amply covers life on the sea and inland waterways of Lancashire, including the role of Lancaster's residents in the highly profitable slave trade.

Williamson Park

Daily: April–Sept 10am–5pm; Oct–March 10am–4pm • Free

For a panorama of the town, Morecambe Bay and the Cumbrian fells, take a steep 25-minute walk up Moor Lane (or a taxi from the bus station) to **Williamson Park**, Lancaster's highest point. Funded by local statesman and lino magnate Lord Ashton, the park's centrepiece is the 220ft-high Ashton Memorial, a Baroque folly raised by his son in memory of his second wife.

ARRIVAL AND DEPARTURE   LANCASTER

By train Trains pull in at Meeting House Lane, a 5min walk from the town centre.

Destinations Carlisle (every 30min–1hr; 50min); Manchester (every 30min–1hr; 1hr); Morecambe (every 30min–1hr; 10min).

By bus The bus station is on Cable St, a 5min walk from the tourist office.

Destinations Carlisle (4–5 daily; 1hr 20min); Kendal (hourly; 1hr); Manchester (2 daily; 2hr); Windermere (hourly; 1hr 45min).

ON YOUR BIKE

Lancaster promotes itself as a **cycling centre**, and miles of canal towpaths, old railway tracks and riverside paths provide excellent traffic-free routes around the Lune estuary, Lancaster Canal and Ribble Valley, southeast of Lancaster. Typical is the easy riverside path to the **Crook O'Lune** beauty spot, where you can reward yourself with a bacon buttie and an Eccles cake at *Woodie's* famous snack bar.

INFORMATION AND TOURS

Tourist office The Storey, Meeting House Lane, off Castle Hill (Mon–Sat 10am–5pm; ☎01524 582394, ⓦcitycoast countryside.co.uk).

Canal cruises For canal cruises, contact Lancaster Canal Boats (☎01524 389410, ⓦbudgietransport.co.uk).

ACCOMMODATION

Penny Street Bridge Penny St ☎01524 599900, ⓦpennystreetbridge.co.uk. This elegantly restored listed townhouse has 28 oddly shaped rooms, all with airy high ceilings and flat screen TVs. It's worth popping in the bar for a pint of good local ale too. **£79**

★Sun 63 Church St ☎01524 66006, ⓦthesunhotelandbar.co.uk. The city centre's only four-star hotel has sixteen handsome rooms (some with king-sized beds, all with fine bathrooms) above a contemporary bar fashioned from a 300-year-old building. **£88**

EATING AND DRINKING

★The Borough 3 Dalton Square ☎01524 64170, ⓦtheboroughlancaster.co.uk. Great for informal dining, this roomy gastropub – in a refurbished 1824 building – has a rigorously sourced local and organic menu. Moderately priced tapas-style platters offer smoked fish, Lancashire cheese and the like, while mains range from ostrich to salmon. Nine smart new rooms upstairs too (£95). Food served Mon–Thurs & Sun 8–11am & noon–9pm, Fri & Sat 8–11am & noon–9.30pm.

The Music Room Sun St ⓦthemusicroomcafe.com. A quirky, stylish little place with a marvellous glass frontage, serving top-quality coffees (it has its own roaster), teas and melt-in-the-mouth cake. The best place

in town to take a break. Mon–Sat 10am–5pm.

Water Witch Canal towpath, Aldcliffe Lane ☎01524 63828, ⓦthewaterwitch.co.uk. Relaxing canalside pub named after an old canal packet boat. A youthful crowd munches burgers, shoots pool and hogs the canalside tables, and there is an impressive range of real ales and continental lagers. Food served Mon–Fri noon–9pm, Sat noon–9.30pm, Sun noon–8pm.

Whale Tail 78a Penny St ☎01524 845133, ⓦwhaletailcafe.co.uk. Tucked away in a yard and up on the first floor, this cheery veggie and wholefood café serves good breakfasts, quiche, moussaka and baked potatoes. Mon–Fri 10am–4pm, Sat 10am–5pm, Sun 10am–3pm.

NIGHTLIFE AND ENTERTAINMENT

Dukes Moor Lane ☎01524 598500, ⓦdukes -lancaster.org. Lancaster's arts centre is the main cultural destination in town, with cinemas and stages for all manner of theatre and dance performances, exhibition space and a café-bar.

Yorkshire House 2 Parliament St ☎01524 64679. Down-to-earth real ale boozer that's also a cracking alternative live-music venue, pulling in a young crowd. Mon–Wed 7pm–midnight, Sat 7pm–1am, Sat 2pm–1am, Sun 2–11.30pm.

Morecambe and around

The seaside resort of **MORECAMBE** lies five miles west of Lancaster – there's a pleasant cycle path between the two, and bus and train services that can whizz you there in ten minutes. The sweep of the bay is the major attraction, with the Lake District fells visible beyond, while the **Stone Jetty** features bird motifs and sculptures – recognizing Morecambe Bay as Britain's most important wintering site for wildfowl and wading birds. A little way along the prom stands the statue of one of Britain's most treasured

---

THE FOREST OF BOWLAND

The remote **Forest of Bowland** (ⓦforestofbowland.com), designated an Area of Outstanding Natural Beauty, is a picturesque drive east from Lancaster. The name forest is used here in its traditional sense of "a royal hunting ground" – it's a captivating landscape of remote fells and farmland with plenty of walks and populated by rare birds like the golden plover, short-eared owl, snipe and merlin. Head east on the A683, turning off towards High Bentham; once at the village turn right at the sign for the station and you begin the fifteen-mile slog down an old drovers' track (now a very minor road) known as the **Trough of Bowland**. This winds through heather- and bracken-clad hills before ending up at the compact village of Slaidburn. If you've got time, it's worth pushing ahead to **Clitheroe**, a tidy little market town overlooked by a Norman keep.

comedians – Eric Bartholomew, who took the stage name **Eric Morecambe** when he met his comedy partner, Ernie Wise.

Heysham Village

Three miles southwest of Morecambe – you can walk here along the promenade – the shoreside **HEYSHAM VILLAGE** is centred on a group of charming seventeenth-century cottages and barns. Proudest relic is the well-preserved Viking hog's-back tombstone in Saxon **St Peter's Church**, set in a romantic churchyard below the headland. Don't miss the local **nettle beer**, dating from Victorian times, and served in the village tearooms.

10

ARRIVAL AND DEPARTURE   MORECAMBE

By bus and train The bus and train stations are close together near Central Drive; both receive regular services from Lancaster (10min).

ACCOMMODATION

Midland Hotel The Promenade, Marine Road West ☎ 0845 850 3502, ⓦ elh.co.uk/hotels/midland. Lovely four-star Art Deco hotel whose comfortable rooms extend the modernist theme. Even if you're not staying it's worth popping into the electric-blue bar, and taking a drink onto the terrace to watch the sunset. **£94**

The Isle of Man

The **Isle of Man**, almost equidistant from Ireland, England, Wales and Scotland, is one of the most beautiful spots in Britain, a mountainous, cliff-fringed island just 33 miles by 13. There's peace and quiet in abundance, walks around the unspoilt hundred-mile coastline, rural villages and steam trains straight out of a 1950s picture book – a yesteryear ensemble if ever there was one.

Many true Manx inhabitants, who comprise a shade under fifty percent of its 84,500 population, insist that the Isle of Man is not part of England, nor even of the UK. Indeed, although a Crown dependency, the island has its own government, **Tynwald**, arguably the world's oldest democratic parliament, which has run continuously since 979 AD. To further complicate matters, the island maintains a unique associate status in the EU, and also has its own sterling currency (worth the same as the mainland currency), its own laws, an independent postal service, and a Gaelic-based language which is taught in schools and seen on dual-language road signs.

All roads lead to the capital, **Douglas**, the only town of any size. From the summit of **Snaefell**, the island's highest peak, you get an idea of the island's varied scenery, the finest parts of which are to be found in the seventeen officially designated National Glens. Most of these are linked by the 95-mile **Raad Ny Foillan** (Road of the Gull) coastal footpath, which passes several of the island's numerous hillforts, Viking ship burials and Celtic crosses. Scenery aside, the main tourist draw is the **TT (Tourist Trophy) motorcycle races** (held in the two weeks around the late May bank holiday), a frenzy of speed and burning rubber that's shattered the island's peace annually since 1907.

ARRIVAL AND DEPARTURE   THE ISLE OF MAN

By plane The cheapest way to get to the Isle is by air, with several budget airlines – among them Stobart Air (ⓦ aerarann.com at the time of writing), Flybe (ⓦ flybe .com); and easyJet (ⓦ easyjet.com) – offering flights from many British and Irish regional airports.

By ferry Ferries or the quicker fastcraft (Manannan), both run by the Isle of Man Steam Packet Company (☎ 0872 299 2992, ⓦ steam-packet.com), leave from Heysham (ferries; 1 or 2 daily; 3hr 30min) and Liverpool (fastcraft; 1 or 2 daily between March–Nov; 2hr 30min).

GETTING AROUND

Travel passes "Island Explorer" tickets – sold at Douglas' Welcome Centre (see opposite) – give 1 (£16), 3 (£32), or 7 (£47) days' unlimited travel on all buses and trains. **Useful website** ⓦ gov.im/publictransport.

INFORMATION

Manx National Heritage (ⓦ manxnationalheritage.im) run thirteen heritage sites and museums around the Isle of Man including the Old House of Keys, the House of Manannan, Castle Rushen and the Laxey Wheel. They also offer money-saving passes including a 10-Day Holiday pass (£20, available from any attraction).

Douglas

Dubbed "the Naples of the North" by John Betjeman, **DOUGLAS** has developed since its 1950s heyday of seaside holiday-making into a major offshore financial centre. The seafront vista has changed little since Victorian times, and is still trodden by heavy-footed carthorses pulling trams (May–Sept, from 9am–5.30pm; £5.70 return). On Harris Promenade the opulent Edwardian **Gaiety Theatre** sports a lush interior that can be seen on fascinating tours (May–Oct, Sat 10am–12.30pm; £7.50, call ahead; ☎01624 600555, ⓦcfvg.gov.im).

Further up Harris Promenade, approaching Broadway, the **Villa Marina gardens** display classic Victorian elegance with their colonnade walk, lawns and bandstand. The main sight, however, is the **Manx Museum**, on the corner of Kingswood Grove and Crellin's Hill (Mon–Sat 10am–5pm; free), which helps the visitor get to grips with Manx culture and heritage. Finally, out on **Douglas Head** the point looming above the southern bay – the town's Victorian camera obscura has been restored for visits (Easter week, plus May–Sept Sat 1–4pm, Sun & bank hols 11am–4pm, weather permitting; £2).

10

ARRIVAL AND DEPARTURE
DOUGLAS

By plane Ronaldsway Airport (☎01624 821600, ⓦiom-airport.com) is 10 miles south of Douglas, close to Castletown. A regular bus runs into town, while a taxi costs around £20.

By ferry The Isle of Man Steam Packet Company (ⓦsteam-packet.com) ferries from Liverpool, Heysham, Dublin, and Belfast arrive at the 1960s Sea Terminal (April–Oct 7am–8pm; Nov–March 8am–6/8pm), close to the centre of town, at the south end of the promenade.

By train The Steam Railway (March–Nov 9.50am–4.50pm; £5.20–13 return) extends for 15 miles and connects Douglas to Port Soderick, Santon, Castletown, Port St Mary and Port Erin. The Douglas station is alongside the river and fishing port, at the top end of the North Quay. Meanwhile, the Manx Electric Railway (April–Oct daily 9.40am–4.40pm; some later departures in summer; £5.40–13 return), which runs for 17.5 miles from Douglas to Snaefell, departs from the northern end of the seafront at Derby Castle Station.

By bus The Lord Street terminal, the hub of the island's dozen or so bus routes, is 50 yards west of the Sea Terminal's forecourt taxi rank.

GETTING AROUND

By bus Buses #1, #1a, #2, #10, #11, #11a, #12 and #12a run along Douglas' promenade from North Quay; you can also take a horse-drawn tram.

Bike rental Eurocycles, 8a Victoria Rd, off Broadway (Mon–Sat; ☎01624 624909, ⓦeurocycles.co.im) rents bikes.

Car rental Most rental outfits have offices at the airport or can deliver cars to the Sea Terminal. Contact Athol (☎01624 820092, ⓦathol.co.im); Mylchreests (☎0800 019 0335, ⓦmylchreests.com); or Ocean Ford (☎01624 820820, ⓦoceanford.com).

INFORMATION AND TOURS

Cruises Seasonal pleasure cruises on the *MV Karina* head out to Port Soderick or Laxey from Villier steps by the Sea Terminal (daily April–Oct, weather permitting; ☎01624 861724 or ☎07624 493592).

Tourist information The Welcome Centre in the Sea Terminal building (Mon–Sat 8am–6pm, plus Sun 10am–2pm May–Sept only); ☎01624 686766, is a great starting point and the best place for island-wide information. **Useful websites** ⓦgov.im, ⓦvisitisleofman.com and ⓜiomguide.com.

ACCOMMODATION

Admiral House Loch Promenade ☎01624 629551, ⓦadmiralhouse.com. At the ferry terminal end of the prom, this retreat features rooms in bold colours and equipped with elegant bathrooms. The restaurant on the ground floor offers modern European cuisine. __£65__

The Claremont Hotel Loch Promenade ☎01624

10

617068, ⓦclaremonthoteldouglas.com. Centrally located and boasting sea views, complimentary wi-fi and gym access for all guests, The Claremont offers 56 well-appointed rooms. **£105**

The Mereside 1 Empire Terrace, just off the Central Promenade ⓣ01624 676355, ⓦhqbar.im. Small, family-owned B&B with elegant modern fittings and very well maintained modern rooms. There's a good bar/restaurant downstairs. **£70**

The Sefton Harris Promenade ⓣ01624 645500, ⓦseftonhotel.co.im. Next to the Gaiety Theatre, this four-star has sleek, spacious rooms offering either a sea view or

a balcony overlooking the impressive internal water garden. Facilities include gym, internet access, free bikes, a bar and restaurant. **£125**

The Town House Loch Promenade ⓣ01624 626125, ⓦthetownhouse.im. This apart-hotel is set over three floors and offers 6 individually designed suites with complimentary wi-fi and telephone calls. **£85**

Welbeck Hotel Mona Drive, off Central Promenade ⓣ01624 675663, ⓦwelbeckhotel.com. A traditional mid-sized family-run seaside hotel, with comfortable rooms and friendly service. It lies 100yd from the seafront, up the hill. **£90**

EATING

★**The Bay Room** Manx Museum, Kingswood Grove ⓣ01624 612211. Enclosed by the Manx National Heritage Sculpture collection with wonderful views across the bay, this café serves a selection of soups, sandwiches and cakes. Mon–Sat 10am–5pm.

★**Café Tanroagan** 9 Ridgeway St ⓣ01624 612355, ⓦtanroagan.co.uk. The best fish and seafood on the island, straight off the boat, served simply or with an assured Mediterranean twist in a relaxed, contemporary setting. Dinner reservations essential. Mains around £20. Mon–Fri noon–2pm & 6.30–9.30pm, Sat 6.30–9.30pm.

L'Experience Queen's Promenade ⓣ01624 623103, ⓦlex.co.im. This seemingly innocuous whitewashed shack is in fact a long-standing French bistro that serves up

meat dishes as well as daily caught fish specials, and good lunchtime dishes. £18 average for a main. Mon & Wed–Sat noon–2pm & 7–11pm.

Little Fish Café 31 North Quay ⓣ01624 622518, ⓦlittlefishcafe.com. This stylish quayside eatery offers freshly brewed coffee and a breakfast, brunch and evening menu featuring locally-sourced ingredients. Tues–Sat 8am–9pm.

The Ticket Hall Douglas Station, North Quay. A very handy and pleasantly traditional café in the former ticket office at Douglas Station. Serving drinks and snacks until 6pm, with hot lunches and daily specials between noon and 2.30pm. Mon–Thurs 8am–6pm, Fri & Sat 8am–10pm.

DRINKING

Bar George Hill St ⓣ01624 617799, ⓦbargeorge.im. A fashionable haunt housed in a converted Sunday School, opposite St George's church. Mon–Sat till late.

Queen's Hotel Queen's Promenade ⓣ01624 674438. This old seafront pub at the top end of the promenade is

the best place for alfresco drinks, with picnic tables looking out over the sweeping bay. Daily noon–1am

Rovers Return 11 Church St ⓣ01624 611101. Cosy old local where you can try the local Manx beers, including "Old Bushy Tail". Daily 11am–11pm.

Laxey

Filling a narrow valley, the straggling village of **LAXEY**, seven miles north of Douglas, spills down from its train station to a small harbour and long, pebbly beach, squeezed between two bulky headlands. The Manx Electric Railway from Douglas drops you at the station used by the Snaefell Mountain Railway (see below). Passengers disembark and then head inland and uphill to Laxey's pride, the **"Lady Isabella" Great Laxey Wheel** (March–Nov daily 9.30am–4pm; £4.50; ⓦlaxeywheel.co.uk), smartly painted in red and white. With a diameter of more than 72ft it's said to be the largest working water wheel in the world. In **Old Laxey**, around the harbour, half a mile below the station, large car parks attest to the popularity of the beach and river.

Snaefell

Every thirty minutes, the tramcars of the **Snaefell Mountain Railway** (April–Oct daily 10.15am–3.45pm; £11 return) begin their thirty-minute climb from Laxey through increasingly denuded moorland to the island's highest point, the top of **Snaefell** (2036ft) – the Vikings' "Snow Mountain" – from where, on a clear day, you can see

England, Wales, Scotland and Ireland. At the summit, most people are content to pop into the café and bar and then soak up the views for the few minutes until the return journey. But with a decent map and good weather, you could walk back instead, following trails down to Laxey (the easiest and most direct route), Sulby Glen or the Peel–Ramsey road.

Maughold

Bus #16 direct from Ramsey (Mon–Fri only)

10

The Manx Electric Railway trains stop within a mile and a half of **MAUGHOLD**, seven miles northeast of Laxey, a tiny hamlet just inland from the cliff-side lighthouse at Maughold Head. The isolation adds to the attraction of its **parish church**, with its outstanding collection of early Christian and Norse carved crosses – 44 pieces, dating from the sixth to the thirteenth century, and ranging from fragments of runic carving to a 6ft-high rectangular slab.

Peel

The main settlement on the west coast, **PEEL** (bus #5 or #6 hourly from Douglas) is one of the most Manx of all the island's towns, with an imposing medieval **castle** rising across the harbour and a popular sandy **beach** running the length of its eastern promenade.

Peel Castle

March–Nov daily 10am–5pm • £5, combined ticket with House of Manannan £9

What probably started out as a flint-working village on a naturally protected spot gained significance with the foundation of a **monastery** in the seventh or eighth century, parts of which remain inside the ramparts of the red sandstone **Peel Castle**. The site became the residence of the Kings of Mann until the mid-thirteenth century, when they moved to Castle Rushen in Castletown. It's a fifteen-minute walk from the town around the river harbour and over the bridge to the castle.

House of Manannan

Daily 10am–5pm • £6, combined ticket with Peel Castle £9

On the way to the castle, you'll pass the excellent harbourside **House of Manannan** heritage centre named after the island's ancient sea god. You should allow at least two hours to get around this splendid participatory museum, where you can listen to Celtic legends in a replica roundhouse, wander through a replica kipper factory and even examine the contents and occupants of a life-sized Viking ship.

TYNWALD DAY

The trans-island A1 (hourly buses #5 or #6 from Douglas) follows a deep twelve-mile-long furrow between the northern and southern ranges from Douglas to Peel. A hill at the crossroads settlement of **ST JOHN'S**, nine miles along, is the original site of **Tynwald**, the ancient Manx government, which derives its name from the Norse *Thing Völlr*, meaning "Assembly Field". Nowadays the word refers to the Douglas-based House of Keys and Legislative Council, but acts passed in the capital only become law once they have been proclaimed here on **July 5** (ancient Midsummer's Day) in an annual open-air parliament that also hears the grievances of the islanders.

Until the nineteenth century the local people arrived with their livestock and stayed a week or more – in true Viking fashion – to thrash out local issues, play sports, make marriages and hold a fair. Now **Tynwald Day** begins with a service in the chapel, followed by a procession, a fair and concerts.

EATING AND DRINKING PEEL

Creek Inn The Quayside ☎01624 842216, ⓦthecreekinn .co.uk. Popular quayside pub opposite the House of Manannan, serving real ale, with monthly guest beers, and a delicious array of specials. Live music at the weekends. Daily from 10am–midnight; food served noon–10pm.

Marine Hotel Shore Rd ☎01624 842337, ⓦmarine hotelpeel.co.uk. Seafront pub, popular with locals, serving Manx ales, guest beers and bar meals. Daily noon– midnight; food served Mon–Sat noon–9pm, Sun noon–6pm.

10 Port Erin

The small, time-warped resort of **PORT ERIN**, at the southwestern tip of the island, a one-hour train ride from Douglas, has a wide, fine sand beach backing a deeply indented bay sitting beneath green hills. To stretch your legs, head up the promenade past the golf club to the entrance of Bradda Glen, where you can follow the path out along the headland to Bradda Head.

ARRIVAL AND DEPARTURE PORT ERIN

By bus Buses #1 and #2 from Douglas/Castletown, and #8 from Peel/St John's, stop on Bridson St, across Station Road and opposite the *Cherry Orchard* aparthotel.

By train Trains pull in on Station Rd, a couple of hundred yards above and back from the beach.

ACCOMMODATION

Rowany Cottier Spaldrick ☎01624 832287, ⓦrowanycottier.com. Port Erin's best B&B, in a detached

house overlooking the bay, opposite the entrance to Bradda Glen. No credit cards. **£80**

Port St Mary and around

Two miles east of Port Erin, the fishing harbour still dominates little **PORT ST MARY**, with its houses strung out in a chain above the busy dockside. The best beach is away to the northeast, reached from the harbour along a well-worked Victorian path that clings to the bay's rocky edge.

From Port St Mary, a minor road runs out along the Meayll peninsula towards **CREGNEASH**, the oldest village on the island. The **Cregneash Village Folk Museum** (March–Nov daily 10am–4pm; £5) is a picturesque cluster of nineteenth-century thatched crofts populated by craftspeople in period costume; there's a tearoom and information centre. Local views are stunning, and it's just a short walk south to **The Chasms**, a headland of gaping rock cliffs swarming with gulls and razorbills.

The footpath continues around Spanish Head to the turf-roofed **Sound Visitor Centre** (daily 10am–4/5pm; free), which also marks the end of the road from Port St Mary. There's an excellent café, with windows looking out across The Sound to the **Calf of Man**.

ARRIVAL AND DEPARTURE PORT ST MARY

By train Regular steam trains run to Port Erin or back to Douglas from Port St Mary. The station is a 10min walk from the harbour along High St, Bay View Road

and Station Road.
By bus Hourly buses from the harbour serve Port Erin and Douglas.

ACCOMMODATION AND EATING

★Aaron House The Promenade ☎01624 835702, ⓦaaronhouse.co.uk. High up on The Promenade, this guesthouse lovingly recreates a Victorian experience and features brass beds and clawfoot baths in some of the rooms, with home-made scones and jam in the parlour and splendid breakfasts. The bay views from the front are superb. **£40**

Harbour Lights 1 Queen St ☎01624 832064, ⓦharbour-lights.net. In a sea-salty old boathouse next to the harbour, this cheery restaurant serves fresh fish and local produce, as well as cream teas, hot toasted crumpets and light snacks. Thurs–Sat 10am–late, Sun 10am–4pm.

THE CALF OF MAN

It is worth making the effort to visit the **Calf of Man**, a craggy, heath-lined nature reserve lying off the southwest tip of the Isle of Man, where resident wardens monitor the seasonal populations of kittiwakes, puffins, choughs, razorbills, shags, guillemots and others, and grey seals can be seen all year round basking on the rocks.

Charter boats leave from Port St Mary, but the most reliable scheduled service (weather permitting) is from Port Erin pier (May–Sept daily; £20; 10am; ☎01624 832339); call in advance as numbers are limited and weather conditions affect schedules. You can also **sea kayak** around this spectacular coast. **Adventurous Experiences** (☎01624 843034, ⓦadventurousexperiences.com) runs trips from evening paddles (£55) to full-day excursions (from £85) – no experience is required.

10

Castletown and around

From the twelfth century until 1869, **CASTLETOWN** was the island's capital, but then the influx of tourists and the increase in trade required a bigger harbour and Douglas took over. Its sleepy harbour and low-roofed cottages are dominated by **Castle Rushen** (March–Nov, daily 10am–4/5pm; £5.80), formerly home to the island's legislature and still the site of the investiture of new lieutenant-governors.

Old House of Keys

Parliament Square · March–Nov daily 11am & 3pm · £5.50 · ☎01624 648017

Across the central Market Square and down Castle Street in tiny Parliament Square you'll find the **Old House of Keys**. Built in 1821, this was the site of the Manx parliament, the Keys, until 1874 when it was moved to Douglas. The frock-coated Secretary of the House meets you at the door and shows you into the restored debating chamber, where visitors are included in a highly entertaining participatory session of the House, guided by a hologram Speaker.

Rushen Abbey

Ballasalla, 2 miles north of Castletown · Daily: March–Nov, 10am–4pm; May–Sept, 10am–4pm · £5 · Buses #1, #1C, #2, #8 or #X2 from Castletown or steam railway

The island's most important medieval religious site, **Rushen Abbey** lies two miles north of Castletown at Ballasalla ("place of the willows"). A Cistercian foundation of 1134, it was abandoned by its "White Monks" in the 1540s and was subsequently used as a school. The excavated remains themselves – low walls, grass-covered banks and a sole church tower from the fifteenth century – would hold only specialist appeal were it not for the excellent interpretation centre, which explains much about daily life in a Cistercian abbey.

ARRIVAL AND DEPARTURE
CASTLETOWN

By bus Buses #8 (from Peel/Port Erin) and #1 (from Douglas) stop in the main square.

By train Castletown Station is a 5min walk from the centre, out along Victoria Road from the harbour.

Destinations include Ballabeg, Colby, Port St Mary and Port Erin to the south and Ballasalla, Santon, Port Soderick and Douglas to the north.

EATING AND DRINKING

The Abbey Restaurant Ballasalla, 2 miles north of Castletown ☎01624 822393 ⓦtheabbeyrestaurant .co.im. Sat next to Rushen Abbey, this restaurant and café serves up modern European cuisine complemented by a predominantly Southern European wine list. The venue is child-friendly and also boasts a spacious outdoor garden and a private dining room. Tues–Sat 10am–late.

Cumbria and the Lakes

GREAT GABLE, SEEN FROM WAST WATER

11

Cumbria and the Lakes

The Lake District is England's most hyped scenic area, and for good reasons. Within an area a mere thirty miles across, sixteen major lakes are squeezed between the country's highest mountains – an almost alpine landscape of glistening water, dramatic valleys and picturesque stone-built villages. Most of what people refer to as the Lake District lies within the Lake District National Park, which, in turn, falls entirely within the county of Cumbria. The county capital is Carlisle, a place that bears traces of a pedigree that stretches back to Roman times, while both the isolated western coast and eastern market towns like Kendal and Penrith counter the notion that Cumbria is all about its lakes.

Given a week you could easily see most of the famous settlements and lakes – a circuit taking in the towns of Ambleside, Windermere and Bowness, all on **Windermere**, the Wordsworth houses in **Grasmere**, and the more dramatic northern scenery near **Keswick** and **Ullswater** would give you a fair sample of the whole. But it's away from the crowds that the Lakes really begin to pay dividends, in the dramatic valleys of **Langdale** and **Eskdale**, for example, while over on the coast are more off-the-beaten-track destinations, like the estuary village of **Ravenglass** – access point for the **Ravenglass and Eskdale Railway** – and the attractive Georgian port of **Whitehaven**.

GETTING AROUND AND INFORMATION　　　　　CUMBRIA AND THE LAKES

By bus National Express coaches connect London and Manchester with Windermere, Ambleside, Grasmere and Keswick. The North West Explorer Ticket (1-day £10.50, family £25; ⓦstagecoachbus.com/northwest) is valid on the entire regional bus network.
By train Trains leave the West Coast main line at Oxenholme, north of Lancaster, for the branch line service to Kendal and Windermere. The only other places directly accessible by train are Penrith, further north on the West Coast line, and the towns along the Cumbrian coast.
Useful websites ⓦgolakes.co.uk and, for the National Park, ⓦwww.lake-district.gov.uk.

Kendal and around

The self-billed "Gateway to the Lakes" (though nearly ten miles from Windermere), **KENDAL** is the largest of the southern Cumbrian towns. It offers rewarding rambles around the "yards" and "ginnels" on both sides of Highgate and Stricklandgate, the main streets, and while the old Market Place long since succumbed to development, traditional stalls still do business outside the Westmorland Shopping Centre every Wednesday and Saturday.

Outside Kendal, the main trips are to the stately homes of **Sizergh Castle** and **Levens Hall**, just a few miles to the south, both of which have beautifully kept gardens.

Windermere cruises p.499　　　　　**Coniston's speed king** p.505
Top 5 Lake District views p.501　　　**Ullswater lake services** p.514
Walks from Ambleside p.502　　　　　**Potty Penrith** p.515

WORDSWORTH HOUSE, COCKERMOUTH

Highlights

❶ Windermere Enjoy the changing seasons and serene views with a cruise on England's largest lake. **See p.500**

❷ Wray Castle Picnic in the grounds of this extraordinary Victorian holiday home on the shores of Windermere. **See p.502**

❸ Old Dungeon Ghyll Hotel, Langdale The hikers' favourite inn – cosy rooms, stone-flagged floors and open fires – has England's most famous mountains on the doorstep. **See p.503**

❹ Brantwood, Coniston Water John Ruskin's elegant home and inspiring garden is beautifully sited on Coniston Water. **See p.506**

❺ Via Ferrata, Honister Pass The Lake District's biggest thrill sees you scrambling, climbing and hanging on for dear life along the old miners' route up Fleetwith Pike. **See p.510**

❻ Ravenglass and Eskdale Railway It's a great day out on the narrow-gauge railway from coast to mountains. **See p.512**

❼ Wordsworth House, Cockermouth Costumed staff and authentic surroundings bring the eighteenth century back to life at the birthplace of William Wordsworth. **See p.513**

❽ Carlisle Castle Cumbria's mightiest castle dominates the county town. **See p.516**

HIGHLIGHTS ARE MARKED ON THE MAP ON P.496

Kendal Museum

Station Rd • Tues–Sat 10.30am–5pm; closed Christmas week • Free • ☎ 01539 815597, ⓦ kendalmuseum.org.uk

The **Kendal Museum** holds the district's natural history and archeological finds, and town history displays. You'll also find collections related to **Alfred Wainwright** (1907–91), Kendal's former borough treasurer (and honorary clerk at the museum). Wainwright moved to Kendal in 1941, and in 1952, dissatisfied with the accuracy of existing maps, he embarked on his series of painstakingly handwritten walking guides, with mapped routes and delicately drawn views. They have been hugely popular guidebooks ever since, which many treat as gospel in their attempts to "bag" ascents of the 214 fells he recorded.

CUMBRIA & THE LAKES

HIGHLIGHTS

1. Windermere
2. Wray Castle
3. Old Dungeon Ghyll Hotel, Langdale
4. Brantwood, Coniston Water
5. Via Ferrata, Honister Pass
6. Ravenglass and Eskdale Railway
7. Wordsworth House, Cockermouth
8. Carlisle Castle

Abbot Hall

Mon–Sat 10.30am–5pm (Nov–March closes at 4pm), plus July & Aug Sun noon–4pm; closed mid-Dec to mid-Jan **Abbot Hall Art Gallery** £7, under 16s free • ☎ 01539 722464, ⓦ abbothall.org.uk **Museum of Lakeland Life and Industry** £5, under 16s free • ☎ 01539 722464, ⓦ lakelandmuseum.org.uk

The town's two main museums are at the Georgian **Abbot Hall**, by the river near the parish church. The principal hall houses the **Art Gallery**, concentrating in particular on the works of the eighteenth-century "Kendal School" of portrait painters, most famously George Romney. Across the way, the former stables contain the **Museum of Lakeland Life and Industry**, where reconstructed house interiors and workshops exhibit rural trades and crafts, from spinning and weaving to shoe-making and tanning.

Sizergh Castle

Off A591, 3 miles south of Kendal • Easter–Oct Mon–Thurs & Sun 1–5pm; guided tours noon–1pm; gardens Easter–Oct daily 10am–5pm, Nov & Dec 11am–4pm • £9.45, gardens only £5.85; NT • ⓦ nationaltrust.org.uk/sizergh, ☎ 01539 560951 • Bus #555 from Kendal

Sizergh Castle owes its "castle" epithet to the fourteenth-century peel tower at its core, one of the best examples of the towers built as safe havens during the region's medieval border raids. There are guided tours of the rooms – largely Elizabethan – between noon and 1pm; thereafter, you can wander around at will.

Levens Hall

Off A6, 6 miles south of Kendal • Easter to mid-Oct Mon–Thurs & Sun noon–4.30pm, last entry at 4pm; gardens Easter to mid-Oct Mon–Thurs & Sun 10am–5pm • £12.50, gardens only £8.50, under 16s free • ☎ 01539 560321, ⓦ levenshall.co.uk • Bus #555 from Kendal

Levens Hall was refurbished in the classic Elizabethan manner between 1570 and 1640. House stewards are on hand to point out the oddities and curios – for example, the dining room is panelled not with oak but with goat's leather, printed with a deep-green floral design. Outside are beautifully trimmed topiary gardens, featuring yews in the shape of pyramids, peacocks and top hats.

ARRIVAL AND DEPARTURE   KENDAL

By train From Oxenholme on the West Coast main line, there's an hourly branch-line service to Kendal (5min). Kendal's train station is a 10min walk from the centre.
Destinations Oxenholme (for Carlisle, Lancaster or Manchester) (hourly; 5min); Windermere (hourly; 20min).
By bus The bus station is on Blackhall Road (off

Stramongate), with main routes including the #599 (to Windermere, Ambleside and Grasmere) or #555 (to Keswick or Lancaster).
Destinations Ambleside (hourly; 40min); Grasmere (hourly; 1hr), Keswick (hourly; 1hr 30min); Lancaster (hourly; 1hr); Windermere/Bowness (hourly; 30min).

ACCOMMODATION

Beech House 40 Greenside ☎ 01539 720385, ⓦ beechhouse-kendal.co.uk. Boutique B&B with a keen sense of decorative design – think swagged curtains, plumped pillows, richly coloured fabrics, and black-and-white bathrooms with gleaming roll-top baths. **£80**
★ **Punch Bowl Inn** Crosthwaite, 5 miles west of Kendal

☎ 015395 68237, ⓦ the-punchbowl.co.uk. A super-stylish country inn – the earth-toned rooms have exposed beams and superb bathrooms, while the restaurant serves locally sourced food (from pot-roast wood-pigeon to local lamb). Rooms are individually priced, up to £235, and are more expensive still at weekends and holidays. **£120**

EATING AND DRINKING

★ **Grainstore** Brewery Arts Centre, 122 Highgate ☎ 01539 725133, ⓦ breweryarts.co.uk. The arts centre bistro has a mix-and-match menu of Mediterranean dishes – anything from local pork-and-chilli bangers to salmon skewers – plus a range of gourmet pizzas (dishes £4.50–9.50, pizzas £6.50–8.50). You can also get pizza, tapas and real ales in the adjacent *Vats Bar*, and there's often a weekday

lunch service in holiday periods. Mon–Thurs 5–9pm, Fri 5–9.30pm, Sat noon–9.30pm, Sun 12.30–8pm.
Waterside Wholefood Gulfs Rd, bottom of Lowther St ☎ 01539 729743, ⓦ watersidewholefood.co.uk. A handy place by the river for veggie and vegan wholefood snacks or meals (£3.50–7), such as a lentil cottage pie or buckwheat burgers. Mon–Sat 8.30am–4.30pm.

NIGHTLIFE AND ENTERTAINMENT

Brewery Arts Centre 122 Highgate ☎ 01539 725133, Ⓦ breweryarts.co.uk. Hub of everything that's happening in town, with cinema, theatre, galleries and concert hall, not to mention all-day café (closed Sun), bistro (see p.497) and the lively *Vats Bar*.

Cartmel

Around eighteen miles southwest of Kendal, the pretty village of **CARTMEL** is something of an upmarket getaway, with its Michelin-starred restaurant-with-rooms, winding country lanes and cobbled market square brimming with inns and antique shops. You're in luck if you're looking to buy a handmade dolls' house or embroidered footstool, while in the **Cartmel Village Shop** on the square they sell the finest sticky-toffee pudding known to humanity. Quite what the original monks of Cartmel would have made of all this is anyone's guess – the village first grew up around its twelfth-century Augustinian priory and is still dominated by the proud **Church of St Mary and St Michael**.

Holker Hall

Cark-in-Cartmel, 2 miles west of Cartmel · Easter–Oct Mon–Fri & Sun, house 11am–4pm, gardens 10.30am–4.30pm, July & Aug until 5.30pm · £12, gardens only £8, under 16s free · ☎ 01539 558328, Ⓦ holker.co.uk

A couple of miles west of Cartmel lies **Holker Hall**, one of Cumbria's most glorious country estates. The impressive 23-acre **gardens**, both formal and woodland, are the highlight for many, and a celebrated annual garden festival (June) is held here, as well as spring and winter markets. You don't have to pay the entrance fee to visit the excellent Food Hall and Courtyard Café, both of which are also open on Saturdays and in winter (when the hall is otherwise closed).

ACCOMMODATION AND EATING   **CARTMEL**

L'Enclume Cavendish St ☎ 01539 536362, Ⓦ lenclume .co.uk/sr. One of England's most critically acclaimed dining experiences, overseen by the masterful Simon Rogan – expect a succession of artfully constructed dishes, accompanied by intensely flavoured jellied cubes, mousses or foams, or suffused with wild herbs, hedgerow flowers and exotic roots. Lunch is £45, dinner £120, while a dozen highly individual rooms and suites (up to £199, depending on location and size) mix French antique furniture and designer fabrics. Closed first two weeks Jan. Meals served Mon & Tues 6.30–9pm, Wed–Sun noon–1.30pm & 6.30–9pm. **£99**

Windermere town

WINDERMERE town was all but non-existent until 1847 when a railway terminal was built here, making England's longest lake (after which the town is named) an easily accessible resort. Windermere remains the transport hub for the southern lakes, but there's precious little else to keep you in the slate-grey streets. All the traffic pours a mile downhill to Windermere's older twin town, Bowness, actually on the lake, but you should stay long enough to make the twenty-minute stroll up through the woods to **Orrest Head** (784ft), from where you get a 360-degree panorama from the Yorkshire fells to Morecambe Bay. The path begins by the *Windermere Hotel* on the A591, across from Windermere train station.

Lake District Visitor Centre at Brockhole

Brockhole, A591, 3 miles northwest of Windermere town · Easter–Oct daily 10am–5pm; Nov–Easter daily 10am–4pm · Free, parking fee charged · ☎ 01539 446601, Ⓦ brockhole.co.uk · Buses between Windermere and Ambleside run past the visitor centre, or you can take the cruise launch from Waterhead, near Ambleside (see box opposite)

WINDERMERE CRUISES

Windermere Lake Cruises (Ⓦwindermere-lakecruises.co.uk) operates services to Lakeside at the southern tip (£10.50 return, family £20) or to Waterhead (for Ambleside) at the northern end (£10 return, family £29). There's also a direct service from Ambleside to the Lake District Visitor Centre at Brockhole (£7.50 return, family £20), and a shuttle service across the lake between Pier 3 at Bowness and Ferry House, Sawrey (£2.70 each way). An enjoyable circular **cruise around the islands** departs several times daily from Bowness (£7.50, family £20; 45min), while a 24-hour **Freedom-of-the-Lake** ticket costs £18.50, family £50. Services on all routes are frequent between Easter and October (every 30min–1hr at peak times), and reduced during the winter – but there are sailings daily except Christmas Day.

The Lake District National Park Authority has its main visitor centre at **Brockhole**, a late Victorian mansion set in lush grounds on the shores of Windermere, northwest of Windermere town. It's the single best place to get to grips with what there is to see and do in the Lakes, with some excellent natural history and geological displays, lovely gardens and a big range of activities, including bike hire, adventure playground, watersports and high-ropes tree-top adventures.

11

ARRIVAL AND INFORMATION

By train Windermere is as far into the Lakes as you can get by train, on the branch line from Oxenholme, via Kendal. Destinations Kendal (hourly; 15min) and Oxenholme (for London, Carlisle, Lancaster Manchester or Penrith hourly; 20min).

By bus All buses (including National Express coaches from London and Manchester) stop outside Windermere train station.

WINDERMERE TOWN

Destinations Ambleside (hourly; 13min), Bowness (every 20–30min; 15min); Brockhole Visitor Centre (every 20–30min; 7min); Carlisle (3 daily; 2hr 20min); Grasmere (every 20–30min; 30min); Kendal (hourly; 25min); Keswick (hourly; 1hr).

Tourist office Victoria Street (Mon–Sat 9am–5pm, Sun 10am–5pm; Ⓣ01539 446499, Ⓦlakelandgateway.info), 100 yards from the train station.

GETTING AROUND

Bike rental Country Lanes at the train station (Ⓣ01539 444544, Ⓦcountrylaneslakedistrict.co.uk) provides bikes (£23–29/day), plus route maps for local rides.

ACCOMMODATION

★**Archway** 13 College Rd Ⓣ01539 445613, Ⓦarchway guesthouse.co.uk. Four trim rooms in a Victorian house known for its breakfasts – either the traditional Full English or American, pancakes, kippers, home made yoghurt and granola, smoked haddock and the like. **£66**

Brendan Chase 1–3 College Rd Ⓣ01539 445638, Ⓦbrendanchase.co.uk. Popular place with overseas travellers, providing a friendly welcome, a good breakfast and eight comfortable rooms (some en suite). **£60**

Holbeck Ghyll Holbeck Lane, off A591, 3 miles north of Windermere town Ⓣ01539 432375, Ⓦholbeckghyll .com. Luxurious rooms either in the main house or in the lodge or suites in the grounds (with room-and-dinner prices up to £490 a night). There's a sherry decanter in every room, seven acres of gardens, and Michelin-starred food (dinner included in the price). **£250**

Lake District Backpackers High St, across from the tourist office Ⓣ01539 446374, Ⓦlakedistrict backpackers.co.uk. Fourteen basic backpackers' beds in three small dorms, with a couple of two-plus-one private rooms available on request. The price includes a tea-and-toast breakfast. No credit cards. **£15**

YHA Windermere High Cross, Bridge Lane, 1 mile north of Troutbeck Bridge Ⓣ0845 371 9352, Ⓦyha.org .uk. The local YHA hostel is a revamped old mansion with magnificent lake views. Dorms **£19**, rooms **£29**

EATING

Francine's 27 Main Rd Ⓣ01539 444088, Ⓦfrancines restaurantwindermere.co.uk. Drop in during the day for anything from a *pain au chocolat* or a sandwich to a big bowl of mussels (lunch dishes mostly £6–10). Dinner sees the lights dimmed for a wide-ranging continental menu, pork belly confit to seafood casserole, with mains from £12 to £16. Tues–Sun 10am–3pm & 6–11pm.

Hooked Ellerthwaite Square Ⓣ01539 448443, Ⓦhookedwindermere.co.uk. Fabulous contemporary seafood place serving fish straight from the Fleetwood boats. Typical dishes include hake with chorizo, fava beans and garlic, or Thai-style sea bass. Starters are £6–7, mains £17–21. Tues–Sun 5.30–10pm; closed Dec & Jan.

Bowness and Windermere

BOWNESS-ON-WINDERMERE spills back from its lakeside piers in a series of terraces lined with guesthouses and hotels. There's been a village here since the fifteenth century and a ferry service across the lake for almost as long – these days, however, you could be forgiven for thinking that Bowness begins and ends with its best-known attraction, the **World of Beatrix Potter**. At ten and a half miles long, a mile wide in parts and a shade over 200ft deep, the **lake** itself – **Windermere**, incidentally, never "Lake" Windermere – is the heavyweight of Lake District waters. On a busy summer's day, crowds swirl around the trinket shops, cafés, ice-cream stalls and lakeside seats, but you can easily escape out on to the water or into the hills, and there are lots of attractions around town to fill a rainy day.

The World of Beatrix Potter

Old Laundry, Crag Brow • Daily: Easter–Sept 10am–5.30pm; Oct–Easter 10am–4.30pm; closed 2 weeks in Jan • £6.95, all-year family Freedom Pass £30 • ☎ 0844 504 1233, ⓦ hop-skip-jump.com

You either like Beatrix Potter or you don't, but it's safe to say that the elaborate 3D story scenes, audiovisual "virtual walks", themed tearoom and giftshop here at the interactive **World of Beatrix Potter** find more favour with children than the more formal Potter attractions at Hill Top and Hawkshead.

Blackwell

1.5 miles south of Bowness, off A5074 • Daily: March–Oct 10.30am–5pm; Nov–Feb 10.30am–4pm; closed 2 weeks Jan • £7.25, under 16s free • ☎ 01539 446139, ⓦ blackwell.org.uk

Mackay Hugh Baillie Scott's **Blackwell** was built in 1900 as a lakeside holiday home, and boasts a superbly restored Arts and Crafts interior. Lakeland motifs – trees, flowers, birds and berries – abound, while temporary exhibits focus on furniture and decorative art. There's an informative introductory talk (usually weekdays at 2.30pm), plus a tearoom, craft shop and gardens. Parking is available; alternatively, you can walk from Bowness in about 25 minutes (although along a busy road).

Lakeside and Haverthwaite Railway

Easter–Oct 6–7 departures daily • £6.50 return, family £18, or £15.20 (family £42.25) including cruise boat from Bowness • ☎ 01539 531594, ⓦ lakesiderailway.co.uk

From Bowness piers, boats head to the southern reaches of Windermere at Lakeside. This is the terminus of the **Lakeside and Haverthwaite Railway**, whose steam-powered engines puff gently over four miles of track along the River Leven and through the woods of Backbarrow Gorge. Boat arrivals from Bowness connect with train departures throughout the day and, as well as the boat-and-train combination, there are also joint tickets for the Lakes Aquarium and the nearby Lakeland Motor Museum.

ARRIVAL AND DEPARTURE
BOWNESS

By bus The open-top #599 bus from Windermere train station stops at the lakeside piers (every 20–30min; 15min). For onward routes to Ambleside and Grasmere you have to return first to Windermere station.

By ferry The traditional ferry service is the chain-guided contraption from Ferry Nab on the Bowness side (10min walk from the cruise piers) to Ferry House, Sawrey (every 20min; Mon–Sat 7am–10pm, Sun 9am–10pm; 50p, bike and cyclist £1, cars £4.30), providing access to Beatrix Potter's former home at Hill Top and to Hawkshead beyond.

There's also a useful pedestrian launch service between Bowness piers and Ferry House, Sawrey (see box, p.499), saving you the walk down to the car ferry.

GETTING AROUND

Cross Lakes Experience A connecting boat-and-minibus shuttle service (service operates Easter–Oct, up to 10 departures daily; ☎01539 448600, ⊛lake-district.gov .uk/crosslakes) runs from Bowness pier 3 to Beatrix Potter's house at Hill Top (£10 return, family £27.85), and then to Hawkshead (£11.50, family £31.35) and Coniston Water (£20.20, family £54.85).

ACCOMMODATION

Angel Inn Helm Rd ☎01539 444080, ⊛theangel innbowness.com. A dozen chic rooms – all burnished wood and black leather – bring a bit of metropolitan style to Bowness. Snacks, wraps and sandwiches and posh pub food are served in the contemporary bar downstairs, back restaurant or terraced garden. **£90**

Linthwaite House Crook Rd, B5284, 1 mile south of Bowness ☎01539 488600, ⊛linthwaite.com. Contemporary boutique style grafted on to an ivy-covered country house set high above Windermere. A conservatory and terrace offer fabulous lake and fell views, and you can work up an appetite for dinner with a walk in the gardens to the hotel's private tarn. Rates run up to £450, suites up to £650, dinner included. **£290**

★ **Number 80** 80 Craig Walk ☎01539 443584, ⊛number80bed.co.uk. Colin and Mandy's quiet townhouse offers quirky, stylish B&B in four rather dramatic, earth-toned double rooms – a grown-up space for couples (no pets, no children). **£90**

EATING AND DRINKING

Bowness has plenty of places offering pizza, fish and chips, a Chinese stir-fry or a budget café meal – a stroll along pedestrianized **Ash Street** and up **Lake Road** shows you most of the possibilities.

★ **Hole in't Wall** Fallbarrow Rd ☎01539 443488. For a drink and a bar meal (£9–12) you can't beat the town's oldest hostelry, with stone-flagged floors, open fires and real ales, plus a terrace-style beer garden that's a popular spot on summer evenings. Mon–Sat 11am–11pm, Sun noon–11pm.

Ambleside and around

Five miles northwest of Windermere, **AMBLESIDE** town centre consists of a cluster of grey-green stone houses, shops, pubs and B&Bs hugging a circular one-way system, which loops round just south of the narrow gully of stony Stock Ghyll. Huge car parks soak up the day-trip trade, but actually Ambleside improves the longer you spend here, with some enjoyable local walks and also the best selection of accommodation and restaurants in the area. The rest of town lies a mile south at **Waterhead**, where the cruise boats dock, overlooked by the grass banks and spreading trees of Borrans Park. Four miles away, Victorian neo-Gothic **Wray Castle** is a great place to visit for the day.

Armitt Collection

Rydal Rd • Mon–Sat 10am–5pm • £3.50 • ☎01539 431212, ⊛armitt.com

For some background on Ambleside's history, stroll a couple of minutes from the centre along Rydal Road to the **Armitt Collection**, which catalogues the very distinct contribution to Lakeland society made by writers and artists from John Ruskin to Beatrix Potter.

TOP 5 LAKE DISTRICT VIEWS

Castlerigg Stone Circle Keswick. See p.508
Cat Bells Derwent Water. See p.503
Hardknott Roman Fort Eskdale. See p.511
Loughrigg Terrace Grasmere. See p.502
Orrest Head Windermere. See p.498

Wray Castle

Low Wray, 4 miles south of Ambleside, signposted off B5286 • Easter–Oct daily 10am–5pm, last admission at 4pm • £7.20, family ticket £18; NT • ⓦ nationaltrust.org.uk/wray-castle • Free parking at the castle, but car park usually very busy; either take bus #505 to Low Wray turn-off and 1 mile walk, or take Windermere Lake Cruises service from Waterhead or Brockhole (see box, p.499)

Take the boat across to Wray and walk up through the grounds to magnificent **Wray Castle**, a castellated, mock-Gothic mansion built in the 1840s by a wealthy couple as their retirement home. Rather appealingly, it's not presented as a period-piece but rather a family-friendly attraction where you are positively begged to walk on the grass and sit on the chairs. House tours (every hour or so) are available to explain the finer points of the architecture and history, but in the end it's the freedom to play and picnic in lovely surroundings that's the real draw.

ARRIVAL AND INFORMATION   AMBLESIDE

By bus All buses in town stop on Kelsick Rd, opposite the library, with regular local services on the #555/599 to Windermere or Grasmere and Keswick, plus #505 services to Hawkshead/Coniston, and the #516 to Elterwater/ Langdale.

Destinations Windermere (every 30–60min, 14min); Grasmere (every 30–60min, 13min); Keswick (hourly; 45min); Hawkshead/Coniston (every 1–2hr;

20min/30min); and Elterwater/Langdale (5–6 daily; 17min/30min).

By ferry There are ferry services from Bowness and Lakeside; it's a 15min walk into Ambleside from the piers at Waterhead.

Tourist office Central Buildings, Market Cross (Mon–Sat 9am–5.30pm, Sun 10am–5pm; ☎01539 432582, ⓦ exploresouthlakeland.co.uk.

GETTING AROUND

Bike rental Ghyllside Cycles, The Slack (Mon–Sat 9.30am–5.30pm; ☎01539 433592, ⓦ ghyllside.co.uk) rents out bikes at £20/day.

ACCOMMODATION

Lake Rd, running between Waterhead and Ambleside, is lined with **B&Bs**, as are Church St and Compston Road. Fancier places lie out of town, especially a mile to the south at Waterhead by the lake, which is also where you'll find Ambleside YHA. The nearest **campsite**, *Low Wray*, is three miles south and also right by the lake.

Compston House Compston Rd ☎01539 432305, ⓦ compstonhouse.co.uk. There's a breezy New York vibe in this traditional Lakeland house, where the American style extends from the rooms to the breakfasts – home-made pancakes and maple syrup, fluffy omelettes and the like. **£80**

Low Wray Campsite Low Wray, off B5286 (Hawkshead road), 3 miles south; bus #505 ☎01539 463862, ⓦ ntlakescampsites.org.uk or ⓦ 4windslakelandtipis .co.uk or ⓦ long-valley-yurts.co.uk. The beautiful

National Trust site on the western shore of the lake is a glampers' haven. As well as tent pitches (prices vary according to location – some sites are bang on the water's edge), there are wooden camping pods for couples and families (£35–55), tipis (part-week rental from £245, full week from £460) and bell tents (part-week from £165, full week from £355). Bike and kayak hire make it great for families too. Closed Nov–Easter. Pitches **£8.50**

★ **Randy Pike** B5286 (Hawkshead road), 3 miles south, just past Low Wray turn-off ☎01539 436088,

---

WALKS FROM AMBLESIDE

A couple of good walks are accessible straight from the town centre. First, from the footbridge across the river in Rothay Park you can strike up across **Loughrigg Fell** (1099ft). Dropping down to Loughrigg Terrace (2hr), overlooking Grasmere, you then cut south at Rydal on the A591 and follow the minor road back along the River Rothay to Ambleside – a total of 6 miles (4hr).

The walk over **Wansfell to Troutbeck** and back (6 miles; around 4hr) is a little tougher. Stock Ghyll Lane runs up the left bank of the tumbling stream to **Stock Ghyll Force** waterfall. The path then rises steeply to **Wansfell Pike** (1581ft) and down into Troutbeck village, where you can have lunch either at the *Mortal Man* or the nearby *Queen's Head*, both just a short walk from the village centre. The return cuts west onto the flanks of Wansfell and back to Ambleside.

Ⓦ randypike.co.uk. Two amazing, boutique B&B suites open out on to the gardens of what was once a Victorian gentleman's hunting lodge. It's a grown-up, romantic retreat, and you can either stay put with the snack larder, terrace and gardens, or be whizzed down to the owners' *Jumble Room* restaurant in Grasmere (see p.504) for dinner. Prices are £25 higher at weekends. **£200**

Riverside Under Loughrigg ☎01539 432395, Ⓦ www .riverside-at-ambleside.co.uk. Charming guesthouse, half a mile (10min walk) from Ambleside across Rothay

Park. Six large, light country-pine-style rooms available, including a river-facing four-poster (£128) with an en-suite spa bath. **£108**

YHA Ambleside Waterhead, A591, 1 mile south ☎0845 371 9620, Ⓦ yha.org.uk. The YHA's flagship regional hostel has an impressive lakeside location (most rooms have a water view), and 260 beds divided among neatly furnished small dorms, twins, doubles and family rooms (including 11 en-suites). Tour- and activity-bookings, and licensed bar and restaurant. Dorms **£20**, rooms **£32**

EATING AND DRINKING

★**Lucy's On A Plate** Church St ☎01539 431191, Ⓦ lucysofambleside.co.uk. Quirky, hugely enjoyable, informal bistro – if they know you're coming, you'll probably find yourself name-checked on the menu. Daytime café dishes (brunch, dips, pastas, salads, soup and sandwiches, £5–10) give way to a dinner menu (mains £14–19) that is "sourced locally, cooked globally". Daily 11am–9pm.

Zeffirelli's Compston Rd ☎01539 433845,

Ⓦ zeffirellis.com. *Zeffirelli's* independent cinema has five screens at three locations in town. The restaurant attached to the Compston Road screens is famous for its wholemeal-base pizzas, plus Italian-with-a-twist pastas and salads, all vegetarian (pizzas and mains £9–11). The menu's available at lunch and dinner, but *Zeff's* is also open from 10am as a café. There's a great music-bar upstairs, plus an associated fine-dining veggie restaurant (*Fellini's*) elsewhere in town. Daily 10am–10pm.

Great Langdale

Three miles west of Ambleside along the A593, Skelwith Bridge marks the start of **Great Langdale**, a U-shaped glacial valley overlooked by the rocky summits of the **Langdale Pikes**, the most popular of the central Lakeland fells. You can get to the pretty village of **Elterwater** – where there's a tiny village green overlooked by the excellent *Britannia Inn* (see below) – by bus, which then continues on to the **Old Dungeon Ghyll Hotel** (see below) at the head of the valley. Three miles from Elterwater, at **Stickle Ghyll** car park, Harrison Stickle (2414ft), Pike of Stickle (2326ft) and Pavey Ark (2297ft) form a dramatic backdrop, though many walkers go no further than the hour-long climb to **Stickle Tarn** from Stickle Ghyll. Another car park, a mile further west up the valley road by the *Old Dungeon Ghyll Hotel*, is the starting point for a series of more hardcore hikes to resonant Lakeland peaks like Crinkle Crags (2816ft) or Bowfell (2960ft).

ARRIVAL AND DEPARTURE   GREAT LANGDALE

By bus The #516 Langdale Rambler bus from Ambleside runs to Elterwater (5–6 daily; 17min) and the *Old Dungeon Ghyll* (5–6 daily; 30min).

ACCOMMODATION AND EATING

Britannia Inn Elterwater ☎01539 437210, Ⓦ the britanniainn.com. The popular pub on Elterwater's green has nine cosy rooms – cosy being the operative word, since there's not a lot of space in a 500-year-old inn. Rates are £30 higher at weekends. A wide range of beers and good-value food – home-made pies and Cumberland sausage to grilled seabass and Hawkshead trout (mains £10–14) – is served either in the dining room (booking advised) or front bar. Food served daily noon–2pm & 6–9pm. **£99**

Great Langdale ☎01539 463862, Ⓦ ntlakescampsites .org.uk or Ⓦ long-valley-yurts.co.uk. The National Trust's stupendously-sited Langdale campsite has gone stellar

since camping pods (£35–55 per night) and yurts (part-week from £285/full week £385, school and bank hols £365/560) were added into the mix. The bar at the *Old Dungeon Ghyll* is a 5min walk away. Pitches **£8.50**

★**Old Dungeon Ghyll** ☎01539 437272, Ⓦ odg .co.uk. The Lakes' most famous inn is decidedly old-school – well-worn oak, floral decor, vintage furniture – but walkers can't resist its unrivalled location. Dinner (£25, reservations essential) is served at 7.30pm in the dining room, though all the action is in the stone-flagged *Hikers' Bar*, which has real ales and hearty meals (from £9). Food served noon–2pm & 6–9pm. **£116**

11

Grasmere and around

Four miles northwest of Ambleside, **GRASMERE** consists of an intimate cluster of grey-stone houses on the old packhorse road that runs beside the babbling River Rothay. Pretty it certainly is, but it loses some of its charm in high summer thanks to the hordes who descend on the trail of the village's most famous former resident, **William Wordsworth** (1770–1850). The poet, his wife Mary, sister Dorothy and other members of his family are buried beneath the yews in **St Oswald's churchyard**, around which the river makes a sinuous curl. There's little else to the village, save its giftshops, galleries, tearooms and hotels, though the **lake** is just a ten-minute walk away; tremendous views unfold from **Loughrigg Terrace**, on its southern reaches. A four-mile circuit of Grasmere and adjacent **Rydal Water** takes around two hours, with the route passing Wordsworth haunts **Rydal Mount** and **Dove Cottage**.

11 Dove Cottage

Town End, just outside Grasmere on A591 • Daily: March–Oct 9.30am–5.30pm; Nov–early Jan & Feb 9.30am–4.30pm • £7.75, family £17.20 • ☎ 01539 435544, ⓦ wordsworth.org.uk • Buses #555 and #599

Dove Cottage, home to William and Dorothy Wordsworth from 1799 to 1808, was the place where Wordsworth wrote some of his best poetry. Guides, bursting with anecdotes, lead you around the cottage rooms, little changed now but for the addition of electricity and internal plumbing. In the adjacent **museum** are paintings, manuscripts (including that of "Daffodils") and mementos of the so-called "Lake Poets", Robert Southey and Samuel Taylor Coleridge, as well as "opium-eater" Thomas De Quincey who also lived in the cottage for several years.

Rydal Mount

2 miles southeast of Grasmere, A591 • March–Oct daily 9.30am–5pm; Nov–Feb Wed–Sun 11am–4pm; closed for 3 weeks in Jan • £7, gardens only £4, family ticket £16 • ☎ 01539 433002, ⓦ rydalmount.co.uk • Buses #555 and #599

At Dove Cottage Wordsworth had been a largely unknown poet of straitened means, but by 1813 he'd written several of his greatest works (though not all had yet been published) and had been appointed Westmorland's Distributor of Stamps, a salaried position which allowed him to take up the rent of a comfortable family house. **Rydal Mount** remained Wordsworth's home from 1813 until his death in 1850, and the house is still owned by descendants of the poet. You're free to wander around what is essentially still a family home, as well as explore Wordsworth's cherished garden.

ARRIVAL AND DEPARTURE

GRASMERE

By bus The #555 (between Kendal and Keswick) and the #599 (from Kendal, Bowness, Windermere and Ambleside) stop on the village green.

ACCOMMODATION AND EATING

★**Cote How Organic** Rydal, 3 miles southeast, off A591, ☎ 01539 432765, ⓦ cotehow.co.uk. The three characterful rooms at this exclusive, romantic retreat, retain their original fireplaces and antique beds. Eco-credentials are unimpeachable, from rare-breed bacon and organic bread at breakfast to home-made candles and wind-up torches. Lovely organic café too, for great home-made scones. **£150**

★**Grasmere Independent Hostel** Broadrayne Farm, A591, 0.5 miles north ☎ 01539 435055, ⓦ grasmere hostel.co.uk. A stylish gem of a backpackers' hostel, with 24 beds in carpeted en-suite rooms – the price goes up a quid at weekends and two on bank holidays. There's an impressively equipped kitchen, and even a sauna, with the local pub just a few hundred yards away. Dorms **£21**

How Foot Lodge Town End, 0.5 miles southeast ☎ 01539 435366, ⓦ howfootlodge.co.uk. You won't get a better deal on good-quality B&B accommodation than in this light-filled Victorian villa just a few yards from Dove Cottage. **£75**

★**Jumble Room** Langdale Rd ☎ 01539 435188, ⓦ the jumbleroom.co.uk. Funky, relaxed dining spot, where the menu roams the world – blue swimmer crab risotto, Thai salmon salad, or fish in organic beer batter – and, once ensconced, no one's in any hurry to leave. Most mains £14–21. Wed–Sun 5.30–10pm, plus Mon nights & weekend lunches in summer; closed 2 weeks in Dec.

Moss Grove Organic Grasmere ☎ 01539 435251, ⓦ mossgrove.com. Stunning, revamped Victorian-era hotel that's been designed along organic, low-impact lines – thus, handmade beds of reclaimed timber, wallpaper coloured with natural inks, and windows screened by natural wood blinds. **£129**

Thorney How Independent Hostel Off Easedale Rd, 0.75 miles north ☎ 01539 435597, ⓦ thorneyhow .co.uk. The first-ever hostel bought by the YHA (back in 1931) now trades as an indie backpackers, overseen by friendly owners. Facilities are being upgraded, but a café-bar, film nights and electric bike hire already make it a great night's stay. Dorms **£25**

Coniston and around

Coniston Water is not one of the most immediately imposing of the lakes, yet it has a quiet beauty that sets it apart from the more popular destinations. The nineteenth-century art critic and social reformer John Ruskin made the lake his home, and today his isolated house, **Brantwood**, on the northeastern shore, provides the most obvious target for a day-trip. **Arthur Ransome** was also a frequent visitor, his local memories and experiences providing much of the detail in his *Swallows and Amazons* children's books.

Coniston village

The small, slate-grey village of **CONISTON** hunkers below the craggy and coppermine-riddled bulk of **The Old Man of Coniston** (2628ft), which most fit walkers can climb in under two hours. In the village itself, **John Ruskin's grave** lies in St Andrew's original churchyard beneath a beautifully worked Celtic cross.

Ruskin Museum

Yewdale Rd • Easter to mid-Nov daily 10am–5.30pm; mid-Nov to Easter Wed–Sun 10.30am–3.30pm • £6, family £16 • ☎ 01539 441164, ⓦ ruskinmuseum.com

The highly entertaining local museum is named after Coniston's most famous resident but is devoted to all aspects of local life and work, from pre-history to the exploits of Donald Campbell (see box below). Ruskin's fascinating ideas and theories are also given an airing – not to mention his socks, matriculation certificate from Oxford, and letters, manuscripts, sketchbooks and watercolours.

Coniston Water

Steam Yacht Gondola Easter–Oct, 4–5 times daily from 11am, weather permitting • £11, family £27.50; NT • ☎ 01539 432733, ⓦ nationaltrust.org.uk/gondola **Coniston Launch** Easter–Oct hourly 10.45am–5pm; Nov–Easter up to 5 daily • £10.50/family £24 (north route) or £17.15/family £37.30 (south) • ☎ 01768 775753, ⓦ conistonlaunch.co.uk

Coniston Water is hidden out of sight, half a mile southeast of the village. As well as boat and kayak rental from the pier, there are two lake cruise services, which both call at Ruskin's Brantwood as well as various other points around the lake. The National

---

CONISTON'S SPEED KING

On January 4, 1967, **Donald Campbell** set out to better his own world water-speed record (276mph, set three years earlier in Australia) on the glass-like surface of Coniston Water. Just as his jet-powered *Bluebird* hit an estimated 320mph, however, a patch of turbulence sent it into a somersault. Campbell was killed immediately and his body and boat lay undisturbed at the bottom of the lake until both were retrieved in 2001. Campbell's grave is in the small village cemetery behind the *Crown Hotel*, while the *Bluebird* tailfin is displayed in a purpose-built gallery at the local museum, where you can find out more about Campbell and that fateful day.

11

Trust's restored **Steam Yacht Gondola** is the historic choice, while the **Coniston Launch** runs the solar-powered wooden vessels "Ruskin" and "Ransome" on two routes around the lake, north and south. You can stop off at any pier en route, and local walking leaflets are available, as well as special cruises throughout the year.

Brantwood

2.5 miles southeast of Coniston, off B5285 • Mid-March to Nov daily 10.30am–5pm; Dec to mid-March Wed–Sun 10.30am–4pm • £7.20, gardens only £4.95, under 16s free • ☎ 01539 441396, ⊛ brantwood.org.uk

Sited on a hillside above the eastern shore of Coniston Water, **Brantwood** was home to John Ruskin from 1872 until his death in 1900. Ruskin was the champion of J.M.W. Turner and the Pre-Raphaelites and foremost Victorian proponent of the supremacy of Gothic architecture. His **study** and **dining room** boast superlative lake views, bettered only by those from the **Turret Room** where he used to sit in later life in his bathchair. Exhibition rooms and galleries display Ruskin-related arts and crafts, while the excellent *Jumping Jenny Tearooms* has an outdoor terrace with lake views.

ARRIVAL AND GETTING AROUND
CONISTON

By bus The #505 "Coniston Rambler" bus (from Kendal, Windermere, Ambleside or Hawkshead) stops on the main road through Coniston village. The "Ruskin Explorer" ticket (available on the bus) includes return travel on the #505 from Windermere, a return trip on the Coniston Launch to Brantwood and entry to Brantwood itself (from £17.90).

Cross Lakes Experience The boat-and-minibus service from Bowness (Easter–Oct daily; ☎ 01539 448600, ⊛ lake-district.gov.uk/crosslakes) runs as far as the *Waterhead Hotel* pier (for Brantwood and lake services), at the head of Coniston Water, half a mile out of the village.

ACCOMMODATION AND EATING

Bank Ground Farm Coniston Water, east side, north of Brantwood ☎ 01539 441264, ⊛ bankground.com. The lakeside farmhouse was the original model for Holly Howe Farm in *Swallows and Amazons* and later used in the 1970s film. Seven traditionally furnished rooms have oak beams and carved beds, and there's also a farmhouse tearoom. Tearoom Easter–Oct Thurs–Sun noon–5pm, or Thurs–Tues in school summer holidays. **£90**

Black Bull Inn Coppermines Rd, by the bridge ☎ 01539 441335, ⊛ blackbullconiston.co.uk. The village's best

pub has a variety of reasonable B&B rooms (£10 more expensive at the weekends). It also brews its own beer, while local lamb, sausage and trout are menu mainstays (bar meals £9–16). Food served daily noon–9pm. **£100**

Meadowdore Café Hawkshead Old Road, ☎ 01539 441638, ⊛ meadowdore.com. The café B&B is of a high quality and excellent value. There are two en-suite rooms and one with a private bathroom, all tastefully furnished. The café downstairs has a conservatory and slate patio, so summer mornings start with an alfresco brekkie. **£60**

Hawkshead and around

HAWKSHEAD, midway between Coniston and Ambleside, wears its beauty well, its patchwork of cottages and cobbles backed by woods and fells and barely affected by modern intrusions. Huge car parks at the village edge take the strain, and when the crowds of day-trippers leave, Hawkshead regains its natural tranquillity. It's a major stop on both the **Beatrix Potter** and **Wordsworth** trails (Potter's house, Hill Top, is nearby, while William and his brother went to school here), and makes a handy base for days out in **Grizedale Forest**.

Beatrix Potter Gallery

Main St • Feb half-term to Easter Sat–Thurs 11am–3.30pm; Easter–May Sat–Thurs 10.30am–5pm, June–Aug daily 10.30am 5pm, Oct Sat–Thurs 10.30am–5pm • £5, family £12.50, discount available for Hill Top visitors; NT • ☎ 01539 436355, ⊛ nationaltrust.org.uk /beatrix-potter-gallery

Hawkshead's **Beatrix Potter Gallery** occupies rooms once used by Potter's solicitor husband, William Heelis, and contains an annually changing selection of her original sketchbooks, drawings, watercolours, letters and manuscripts. Those less devoted to the "Tales" will find displays on Potter's life as a keen naturalist, conservationist and early supporter of the National Trust more diverting.

Hill Top

Near Sawrey, 2 miles southeast of Hawkshead • Sat–Thurs: Feb half-term to Easter 10.30am–3.30pm; Easter–May & Sept–Oct 10.30am–4.30pm, June–Aug 10am–5.30pm • £9, family £22.50; garden free during opening hours; NT • ☎ 01539 436269, ⓦ nationaltrust.org.uk/hill-top

Beatrix Potter's beloved house, **Hill Top**, lies close to Hawkshead in the gorgeous hamlet of Near Sawrey. A Londoner by birth, Potter bought the farmhouse here with the proceeds from her first book, *The Tale of Peter Rabbit*, and retained it as her study long after she moved out following her marriage in 1913. Bear in mind that entry is by timed ticket, you'll probably have to wait in line to enter the small house, and sell-outs are possible, especially in school holidays (and you can't book in advance).

11

Grizedale Forest

2.5 miles southwest of Hawkshead • Free, parking fee charged • Cross Lakes Experience bus from Hawkshead **Grizedale Forest Centre** Daily; Easter–Oct 10am–5pm, Nov–Easter 10am 4pm • ☎ 01229 860010, ⓦ forestry.gov.uk/grizedale

Grizedale Forest extends over the fells separating Coniston Water and Hawkshead from Windermere, and the picnic spots, open-air sculptures, children's activities, cycle trails and tree-top adventure course make for a great day out away from the main lakes. The best starting point is the **Grizedale Forest Centre**, where there's a café and information point.

Go Ape

Sessions daily at Feb half-term and Easter–Oct, otherwise weekends only and closed certain other days in season • Adults £30, kids £24, advance booking essential, online or by phone • ☎ 0843 770 4785, ⓦ goape.co.uk

Go Ape, a high-ropes adventure course in the thick of Grizedale Forest, has you frolicking in the tree canopy for a couple of hours. You get a quick safety briefing and then make your own way around the fixed-ropes course – fantastic fun involving zip-wires, Tarzan-swings and aerial walkways.

ARRIVAL   HAWKSHEAD

By bus The main bus service to Hawkshead is the #505 Coniston Rambler between Windermere, Ambleside and Coniston.

GETTING AROUND

Cross Lakes Experience The bus shuttle service (Easter–Oct daily; ☎ 01539 448600, ⓦ lake-district.gov.uk /crosslakes) runs from Hawkshead to Grizedale and to the Beatrix Potter house at Hill Top, and on to Sawrey for boat connections back to Bowness.

By bike 4hr rental from £18, full day £25, based at Grizedale Forest Centre (ⓦ grizedalemountainbikes.co.uk, ☎ 01229 860369).

ACCOMMODATION AND EATING

Ann Tyson's Cottage Wordsworth St ☎ 01539 436405, ⓦ anntysons.co.uk. Wordsworth briefly boarded here, on this quaint cobbled street, and now you can too. There are three B&B rooms in the main house (one with an antique carved bed from Ruskin's house at Brantwood), and three slightly more spacious ones to the side. **£74**

★ **Drunken Duck Inn** Barngates crossroads, 2 miles north, off B5285 ☎ 01539 436347, ⓦ drunkenduckinn .co.uk. Stylish restaurant-with-rooms in a beautifully located 400-year-old inn. Smallish standard rooms in the inn itself are cheapest and there's more deluxe

accommodation too (up to £325 a night). Bar meals at lunch (sandwiches, or dishes from belly pork to roast cod, £5–16) give way to more modish dining in the evening, with local sourcing a priority (mains £14–25; reservations essential). Daily noon–4pm & 6–9pm. **£95**

Yewfield Hawkshead Hill, 2 miles northwest off B5285 ☎ 01539 436765, ⓦ yewfield.co.uk. Splendid vegetarian guesthouse set among organic vegetable gardens and wild-flower meadows. The house is a Victorian Gothic beauty, filled with Oriental artefacts and art from the owners' travels. Closed Dec & Jan. **£98**

Keswick and around

Standing on the shores of **Derwent Water**, the market town of **KESWICK** makes a good base for exploring the northern Lake District, particularly delightful **Borrowdale** to the south of town or the heights of Skiddaw (3053ft) and Blencathra (2847ft), which loom over Keswick to the north. Granted its market charter by Edward I in 1276 – **market day** is Saturday, held in the main Market Place – Keswick was an important wool and leather centre until around 1500, when these trades were supplanted by the discovery of local graphite. Keswick went on to become an important pencil-making town; the entertaining **Cumberland Pencil Museum**, across the river (daily 9.30am–5pm; £4.25; ⓦ pencilmuseum.co.uk) tells the whole story.

Don't miss Keswick's most mysterious landmark, **Castlerigg Stone Circle**, where 38 hunks of volcanic stone, the largest almost 8ft tall, form a circle 100ft in diameter, set against a magnificent mountain backdrop. Take the Threlkeld rail line path (signposted by the *Keswick Country House Hotel*) and follow the signs for around a mile and a half all told.

11

Derwent Water

Keswick Launch departures: Easter–Oct daily, Nov–Easter Sat & Sun only • £9.75 return, £2.10 per stage; 1hr summer evening cruise £9.95, family ticket £23.50 • ☏ 01768 772263, ⓦ keswick-launch.co.uk

The shores of **Derwent Water** lie five minutes' walk south of the town centre. It's ringed by crags and studded with islets, and is most easily seen by hopping on the **Keswick Launch**, which runs around the lake calling at several points en route. You can jump off the launch at any of the half a dozen piers on Derwent Water for a stroll, but if you've only got time for one hike, make it up **Cat Bells** (take the launch to Hawes End), a superb vantage point (1481ft) above the lake's western shore – allow two and a half hours for the scramble to the top and a return to the pier along the wooded shore.

Borrowdale

It is difficult to overstate the beauty of **Borrowdale**, with its river flats and yew trees, lying at the head of Derwent Water and overshadowed by Scafell Pike, the highest mountain in England, and Great Gable, reckoned as one of the finest looking. At the straggling hamlet of **Rosthwaite**, seven miles south of Keswick, there are a couple of hotels with public bars, while another mile up the valley, eight from Keswick, there's a café and a car park at Seatoller. From here, it's twenty minutes' walk down the minor road to the hamlet of **Seathwaite**, the base for walks up **Scafell Pike** (3205ft). The classic ascent is up the thrilling Corridor Route, then descending via Esk Hause, a tough, eight-mile (6hr) loop walk in all from Seathwaite.

11

ARRIVAL AND DEPARTURE

KESWICK

By bus Buses (including National Express services from Manchester and London) use the terminal in front of the large Booths supermarket, off Main Street.
Destinations Ambleside (hourly; 45min); Buttermere (2 daily; 30min); Carlisle (3 daily; 1hr 10min); Cockermouth (every 30min–1hr; 30min); Grasmere (hourly; 40min); Honister (Easter–Oct 4 daily; 40min); Kendal (hourly; 1hr 30min); Rosthwaite (every 30min–1hr; 25min); Seatoller (every 30min–1hr; 30min); Windermere (hourly; 1hr).

GETTING AROUND

By bus Local services include the #77A (down the west side of Derwent Water, via the access point for Cat Bells) and the scenic #78 "Borrowdale Rambler", which runs south down the B5289 to Seatoller. You can use either service all day with the "Honister Rambler" ticket (from £8).
Bike rental Keswick Bikes, 133 Main Street (daily 9am–5pm; ☎01768 775202, ⍈keswickbikes.co.uk), rents out bikes from £25/day.

INFORMATION AND TOURS

Tourist office National Park Information Centre, Moot Hall, Market Square (daily: April–Oct 9.30am–5.30pm; Nov–March 9.30am–4.30pm; ☎01768 772645, ⍈lakedistrict.gov.uk).

Guided walks For a good walk in good company – lakeside rambles to mountain climbs – contact Keswick Rambles (regular, sometimes daily, walks from Easter–Oct; £20; ⍈keswickrambles.org.uk).

ACCOMMODATION

B&Bs and **guesthouses** cluster around Southey, Blencathra, Church and Eskin streets, in the grid off the A591 (Penrith road). Smarter guesthouses and **hotels** line The Heads, overlooking Hope Park, a couple of minutes south of the centre on the way to the lake, while nearby **Borrowdale** has several fine old inns and country-house hotels.

Café-Bar 26 26 Lake Rd ☎01768 780863, ⍈cafebar26 .co.uk. Four stylishly decorated rooms on the first floor offer a chintz-free base right in the town centre, while downstairs is a funky café-bar. It's £80 at the weekend. **£64**
★**Ellergill** 22 Stanger St ☎01768 773347, ⍈ellergill .co.uk. Owners Robin and Clare have grafted a chic European feel onto their restored Victorian house, and offer classy B&B with five rooms. **£65**
★**Howe Keld** 5–7 The Heads ☎01768 772417, ⍈howekeld.co.uk. The Fishers' boutique guesthouse puts local crafts and materials centre stage, with furniture and floors handcrafted from Lake District trees, plus green-slate bathrooms and carpets of Herdwick wool. Breakfast is terrific, from the daily home-baked organic bread to veggie

rissoles and other specialities. **£110**
Royal Oak Rosthwaite, on the B5289, 7 miles south ☎01768 777214, ⍈royaloakhotel.co.uk. The Borrowdale hikers' favourite – B&B rooms in a traditional inn with stone-flagged bar, where a hearty lakeland dinner (you get no choice, but a vegetarian alternative is always available) is served promptly at 7pm, and a bacon-and-eggs breakfast at 8.30am. Rates include dinner. **£124**
YHA Keswick Station Rd ☎0845 371 9746, ⍈yha.org .uk. Once a riverside woollen mill, Keswick's YHA is more budget hotel than hostel these days, but still good value. It's big (84 beds in 21 rooms) but you're still advised to book, especially for a twin-bedded or family room. Dorms **£13**, rooms **£25**

EATING AND DRINKING

Abraham's Tea Room George Fisher's, 2 Borrowdale Rd ☎01768 772178, ⓦgeorgefisher.co.uk. Keswick's celebrated outdoors store has a top-floor tearoom for home-made soups, big breakfasts, open sandwiches and other daily specials (£5–7.50). Mon–Fri 10am–5pm, Sat 9.30am–5pm, Sun 10.30am–4.30pm.

★**Dog and Gun** 2 Lake Rd ☎01768 773463. The most welcoming pub in town is a real ale, open fire, dog-friendly kind of place. Local beers aside, the food is a big draw – hearty honest stuff (nothing deep-fried, no chips, dishes £8–10), with house special, Hungarian goulash, made every day to a recipe handed down over the years. Daily noon–11pm.

George St John St ☎017687 72076, ⓦgeorgehotel

keswick.co.uk. Keswick's oldest inn has bags of character. There's a good bistro menu (mains £11–16), available in the restaurant or bar – slow-roast lamb to venison casserole, local trout to fish and chips. Daily 11am–11pm (Fri & Sat until midnight); food served Mon–Thurs noon–2.30pm & 5.30–9pm, Fri–Sun noon–4.30pm & 5.30–9.30pm.

Salsa 1 New St ☎01768 775222, ⓦsalsabistro.co.uk. On the right night *Salsa* can be a real buzz (it's best to book at weekends in summer) – have a drink in the downstairs bar, munch a few nachos and then move upstairs for hearty portions of fajitas, tacos, ribs, wraps, grilled fish or steak (mains £10–17). Mon–Thurs & Sun 5.30–9.30pm, Fri & Sat 5.30–10pm.

ENTERTAINMENT

There's a fair amount going on in Keswick throughout the year, including the **jazz festival** (ⓦkeswick.org) and **mountain festival** (ⓦkeswickmountainfestival.co.uk), both in May, a **beer festival** in June (ⓦkeswickbeerfestival .co.uk), and the **Keswick Agricultural Show** (Aug bank holiday, ⓦkeswickshow.co.uk).

Theatre by the Lake Lake Rd ☎017687 74411, ⓦtheatrebythelake.com. England's loveliest theatre hosts a full programme of drama, concerts, exhibitions, readings and talks. "Words By The Water", a literature festival, takes place here in the spring.

Honister Pass

Near the head of Borrowdale at Seatoller, the B5289 road cuts west, snaking up and over the dramatic **Honister Pass**, en route to Buttermere. At the top lie the unassuming buildings of **Honister Slate Mine** – an unexpectedly great place for daredevil adventurers with its deep mine tours and mountain activities. Come suitably clothed – it's wet or windy up here at the best of times.

Honister Slate Mine

Honister Pass • **Visitor centre, shop and café** Daily 9am–5pm • Free **Tours** Daily 10.30am, 12.30pm & 3.30pm • £12.50, reservations essential • ☎01768 777230, ⓦhonister-slate-mine.co.uk • Bus #77A from Keswick

Slate has been quarried on Honister since the eighteenth century. **Honister Slate Mine**, the last remaining working slate mine in England, was rescued by local entrepreneurs in 1996 and is now operating again as a sustainable, commercial enterprise. To get an idea of what traditional mining entailed, you can don a hard hat and lamp to join one of the hugely informative guided tours, which lead you through narrow tunnels into illuminated, dripping caverns.

Via Ferrata

Daily departures from Honister Slate Mine, reservations essential • Classic £35, family £115, Extreme £39.50, family £135 • ☎01768 777714, ⓦhonister-slate-mine.co.uk • Bus #77A from Keswick

Honister features England's first **Via Ferrata** – a dramatic Alpine-style three-hour mountain climb using a fixed cableway and harness, which allows visitors to follow the old miners' route up the exposed face of Fleetwith Pike (2126ft), the peak that's right above the mines. There are two options, labelled 'Classic' and 'Extreme', and both are terrifying and exhilarating in equal measure. Although you don't need climbing experience, you should check out the photos and videos on the website first to see what you're in for.

Buttermere

Ringed by peaks and crags, the tranquil waters and lakeside paths of **Buttermere** make a popular day-trip from Keswick, with the best approach being the sweeping descent into the valley from Honister Pass. There's no real village here – just a few houses and farms, a couple of hotels and a youth hostel, a café and large car park. The four-mile, round-lake stroll circling Buttermere shouldn't take more than a couple of hours. You can always detour up Scarth Gap to the peak known as **Haystacks** (1900ft) if you want more of a climb and views.

ARRIVAL AND DEPARTURE
BUTTERMERE

By bus The direct bus is the #77 from Keswick via Whinlatter Pass; the #77A comes the long way around through Borrowdale via Honister Pass.

Eskdale

11

Eskdale is perhaps the prettiest of the unsung Lake District valleys, reached on a long and twisting drive from Ambleside, over the dramatic Hardknott Pass. It can also be accessed from the Cumbrian coast by the Ravenglass and Eskdale Railway (see p.512) – either route ends up in the heart of superb walking country around the hamlet of **BOOT**. Here, there's an old mill to explore and several local hikes, not to mention the three-mile walk or drive back out of the valley to the superbly sited **Hardknott Roman Fort** (always open; free), which commands a strategic and panoramic position.

ARRIVAL AND DEPARTURE
ESKDALE

By car There's parking at Dalegarth station and at a couple of other designated areas in Eskdale, but the valley road is very narrow and side-of-the-road parking is well-nigh impossible. Come by train if you can for a hassle-free day out.

By train There are year-round services on the Ravenglass and Eskdale Railway (see p.512), with stops at Eskdale Green (for Stanley House) and Dalegarth station, the latter a short walk from Boot and around 1.5 miles from the *Woolpack Inn* (see below).

ACCOMMODATION AND EATING

Eskdale Campsite Eskdale, Hardknott Pass road, 200 yards east of Boot ☎01946 723253, ⍟hollinsfarmcampsite.co.uk. Small, beautifully sited campsite, just a short walk from the railway and the valley's pubs. For camping without canvas they also have ten heated "pods" per night (£44). Closed 2 weeks Jan, & Feb. Pitches £11.30
★**Stanley House** Eskdale Green ☎01946 723327, ⍟stanleyghyll-eskdale.co.uk. B&B with a home-from-home feel and contemporary air. Accommodation is in a dozen spacious rooms, while downstairs is a huge open-plan kitchen-diner, plus lounge with woodburner. The genial owners – who also run the *Woolpack Inn* up the valley – can arrange a lift to the pub for the night. £110
★**Woolpack Inn** Eskdale, Hardknott Pass road, 1 mile east of Boot ☎01946 723230, ⍟woolpack.co.uk. Friendly country inn that's had a real facelift – eight assorted B&B rooms are slowly being freshened up, while downstairs the bar has a classy urban feel, complete with leather sofas and wood-fired pizza oven. It's also strong on Cumbrian real ales, and the beer garden has spectacular fell views. £90

Ravenglass and around

A sleepy coastal village at the estuary of three rivers, the Esk, Mite and Irt, **RAVENGLASS** is the starting point for the wonderful narrow-gauge **Ravenglass and Eskdale Railway**. It's worth taking some time to look around, though, before hopping on the train or heading out to **Muncaster Castle**, the other main local attraction. The single main street preserves a row of characterful nineteenth-century cottages facing out across the estuarine mud flats and dunes – the northern section, across the Esk, is a **nature reserve** where black-headed gulls and terns are often seen (get there by crossing over the mainline railway footbridge).

Ravenglass and Eskdale Railway

March–Oct, at least 5 trains daily (up to 15 daily in school summer hols); trains also most winter weekends, plus Christmas, New Year and Feb half-term hols • £13 return, family ticket £35 • ☎ 01229 717171, ⦿ ravenglass-railway.co.uk

Opened in 1875 to carry ore from the Eskdale mines to the coastal railway, the 15-inch-gauge track of the **Ravenglass and Eskdale Railway** winds seven miles up through the Eskdale Valley to Dalegarth Station near Boot. The ticket lets you break your journey and get off and take a walk from one of the half-dozen stations en route; the full return journey, without a break, takes an hour and forty minutes. Alternatively, take your bike up on the train (pre-booking essential, £3.50 per bike) and cycle back from Dalegarth down the traffic-free **Eskdale Trail** (8.5 miles, 2hr; route guide available from Ravenglass and Dalegarth stations).

Muncaster Castle

A595, 1 mile east of Ravenglass • Feb half-term hols to first week of Nov; castle Mon–Fri & Sun noon–4.30pm; gardens and owl centre daily 10.30am–5pm or dusk; bird displays daily 2.30pm • £13, £10 without castle entrance • ☎ 01229 717614, ⦿ muncaster.co.uk • There's a footpath (30min) from Ravenglass and free parking at the castle

The **Muncaster Castle** estate, a mile east of Ravenglass, provides one of the region's best days out. Apart from the ghost-ridden rooms of the castle itself, there are also seventy acres of well-kept **grounds and gardens**, at their best in spring and autumn, as well as an entertaining **owl centre** where they breed endangered species (including England's own barn owl).

Whitehaven

Around twenty miles up the coast from Ravenglass, some fine Georgian houses mark out the centre of **WHITEHAVEN** – one of the few grid-planned towns in England and easily the most interesting destination on Cumbria's west coast. Whitehaven had long had a trade in coal, but its rapid economic expansion was largely due to the booming slave trade – the town spent a brief period during the eighteenth century as one of Britain's busiest ports, importing sugar, rum, spices, tea, timber and tobacco.

The Beacon Museum

West Strand, on the harbour • Tues–Sun 10am–4.30pm, plus school and bank hol Mons, last admission 3.45pm • £5.50, family ticket £10 • ☎ 01946 592302, ⦿ thebeacon-whitehaven.co.uk

The best place to swot up on Whitehaven's local history is the enterprising museum on the harbour with interactive exhibitions covering a variety of themes from slaving and smuggling to the history of the nuclear industry at nearby Sellafield. You could easily spend a couple of hours here, teaching yourself how to build a ship, tie a sailor's knot or dress like a Roman centurion.

Rum Story

Lowther St • Daily 10am–4.30pm; closed 3rd week in Jan • £5.45, family ticket £16.45 • ☎ 01946 592933, ⦿ rumstory.co.uk

Housed in the eighteenth-century shop, courtyard and warehouses of the Jefferson family, the **Rum Story** museum is where you can learn about rum, the Navy, temperance and the hideousness of the slaves' Middle Passage, among other matters.

ARRIVAL AND DEPARTURE
WHITEHAVEN

By train From Whitehaven's train station (services to St Bees and Ravenglass, or north to Carlisle) you can walk around the harbour to The Beacon in less than 10min.

By bike Whitehaven is the start of the 140-mile C2C cycle route to Sunderland/Newcastle – a metal cut-out at the harbour marks the spot.

ACCOMMODATION

★**Lowther House** 13 Inkerman Terrace ☎01946 63169, ⌨lowtherhouse-whitehaven.com. A highly personal, period restoration of an old Whitehaven house – there are three charming rooms (one with harbour and sea views); you're welcomed with tea and cake, and breakfast is a chatty affair around your host's kitchen table. **£90**

St Bees

Five miles south of Whitehaven (and easily reached by train or bus), long sands lie a few hundred yards west of the coastal village of **St Bees**. The steep, sandstone cliffs of **St Bees Head** to the north are good for windy walks and birdwatching, while the headland's lighthouse marks the start of Alfred Wainwright's 190-mile **Coast-to-Coast Walk** to Robin Hood's Bay.

Cockermouth

11

There's a lot to admire about the attractive small town and market centre of **COCKERMOUTH** – impressive Georgian facades, tree-lined streets and riverside setting – and there's no shortage of local attractions, not least the logical first stop on the **Wordsworth** trail, namely the house where the future poet was born. In the smartened-up Market Place (with monthly farmers' markets) there are more reminders of bygone days, including a pavement plaque teaching you the basics of talking Cumbrian.

Wordsworth House

Main St • Easter–Oct Sat–Thurs 11am–5pm • £6.70, family ticket £16.75, admission by timed ticket on busy days; NT • ☎01900 824805, ⌨nationaltrust.org.uk/wordsworthhouse

The **Wordsworth House**, where William and sister Dorothy spent their first few years, is presented as a functioning eighteenth-century home – with a costumed cook sharing recipes in the kitchen and a clerk completing the ledger with quill and ink.

Jennings Brewery

Brewery Lane • Tours, March, Nov & Dec Mon–Sat 1–2 daily, April–Oct Mon–Sat 2 daily • £8, children over 12 only £4.50 • ☎0845 129 7190, ⌨www.jenningsbrewery.co.uk

Follow your nose in town, after the heady smell of hops, and you're likely to stumble upon **Jennings Brewery**, near the river. Jennings have been brewers in Cockermouth since 1874 and you don't have to step far to sample their product, available in any local pub. Or you can take the ninety-minute brewery tour, which ends with a free tasting in the bar.

ARRIVAL AND DEPARTURE
COCKERMOUTH

By bus All buses stop on Main Street, with the most useful service the #X4/X5 (hourly, Sun every 2hr) from Penrith (1hr 30min) and Keswick (35min).

ACCOMMODATION AND EATING

★**Bitter End** 15 Kirkgate ☎01900 828993, ⌨bitterend.co.uk. The cosiest pub in town also contains Cumbria's smallest brewery, producing ales like "Farmers'", "Cockersnoot" and "Cuddy Lugs". Food ranges from bangers and mash to peppered tuna (most dishes £10–13, steaks up to £19). Mon–Fri 4–11pm, Sat & Sun 11am–11pm; food served Mon–Fri 4–9pm, Sat & Sun 11am–9pm.

Merienda 7a Station St ☎01900 822790, ⌨merienda .co.uk. Bright and breezy café-bar offering breakfasts, soups, sandwiches, meze plates and cheese platters (£2–7.50). Also open Friday nights for tapas and music. Mon–Thurs & Sat 8am–5pm, Fri 8am–midnight, Sun 10am–4pm.

★**Six Castlegate** 6 Castlegate ☎01900 826786, ⌨sixcastlegate.co.uk. Period-piece house that retains its lofty Georgian proportions, impressive carved staircase and oak panelling, though the half-dozen B&B rooms are contemporary country in style. **£70**

Ullswater

Wordsworth declared **Ullswater** "the happiest combination of beauty and grandeur, which any of the Lakes affords", a judgement that still holds good. At almost eight miles, it's the second longest lake in the National Park, with a dramatic serpentine shape that's overlooked by soaring fells, none higher than **Helvellyn** (3114ft), the most popular of the four 3000ft mountains in Cumbria. Cruises depart from the tiny village of **Glenridding**, at the southern foot of the lake, and also call at lovely **Pooley Bridge**, the hamlet at the head of the lake. Meanwhile, at **Gowbarrow Park**, three miles north of Glenridding, the hillside still blazes green and gold in spring, as it was doing when the Wordsworths visited in April 1802; it's thought that Dorothy's recollections of the visit in her diary inspired William to write his famous "Daffodils" poem. The car park and tearooms here mark the start of a walk up to the seventy-foot falls of **Aira Force** (40min return).

ARRIVAL AND INFORMATION   ULLSWATER

11

By bus Buses from Penrith, Keswick and Bowness/Windermere) stop on the main road in Glenridding.

By boat The Glenridding steamer pier is a 5min walk from the centre, on the lakeside. There's pay-and-display parking by the pier.

By car Parking along the lake is difficult, especially in summer, but it's easy to park in Glenridding and use the bus

or boat to visit local attractions. Use the large pay-and-display car park by the visitor centre.

Tourist office National Park Information Centre, in the main car park at Glenridding (Easter–Oct daily 9.30am–5.30pm; Nov–Easter Sat & Sun only 9.30am–3.30pm, weather dependent; ☎01768 482414, ⊛lakedistrict.gov.uk).

ACCOMMODATION AND EATING

★**The Quiet Site** Watermillock ☎07768 727016, ⊛thequietsite.co.uk. The eco-friendly choice for cool campers is this hilltop site with sweeping views. Grassy camping pitches, a dozen camping pods (from £35) and a bar-in-a-barn (open most summer evenings) offer a bit of glamping comfort. Pitches £16

Sharrow Bay 2 miles south of Pooley Bridge, on the Howtown road ☎01768 486301, ⊛sharrowbay.co.uk. *Sharrow Bay* offers a breathtaking setting and highly refined Michelin-starred food. Needless to say, it's London prices in the country (rooms up to £400 a night, suites up to £700) but there are few places anywhere in England that compare. The dining room is open to nonresidents

(reservations essential); afternoon tea here (£25) is famous, while lunch (from £30) and dinner (£75) are classy, formal affairs – desserts are renowned, notably the "icky sticky toffee pudding", which the hotel claims as its own invention. Lunch at 12.30pm for 1pm, afternoon tea at 4pm, dinner 7.30pm for 8pm. £200

YHA Helvellyn Greenside ☎0845 371 9742, ⊛yha .org.uk. Walkers wanting an early start on Helvellyn stay at this dramatically sited hostel, 900ft and a mile and a half up the valley road from Glenridding. There are lots of beds and private rooms available for families, while the nearest pub, the *Travellers Rest*, is only a mile away. Dorms £13

Penrith and around

The nearest town to Ullswater – just four miles from the head of the lake – is **PENRITH,** whose deep-red buildings are constructed from the same rust-red sandstone used to build

---

ULLSWATER LAKE SERVICES

Ullswater steamer services started in 1859, and the lake still has a year-round ferry and cruise service. The **Ullswater Navigation & Transit Company** (☎01768 482229, ⊛ullswater -steamers.co.uk) runs boats from Glenridding to Howtown on the eastern shore (40min) and on to Pooley Bridge (20min) at the northern tip, and back again. Any one stage costs £6.30 one-way, £10 return, though there's also a one-day, hop-on-hop-off "Round the Lake Pass" (£13.40). In school and summer holidays there are up to nine **daily departures** from Glenridding (basically an hourly service), down to between three and six a day at other times of the year – only Christmas Eve and Christmas Day have no sailings.

> **POTTY PENRITH**
>
> **Potfest** (⟨W⟩potfest.co.uk), Europe's biggest ceramics show, takes place in Penrith over two consecutive weekends (late July/early Aug). The first is **Potfest in the Park**, with ceramics on display in marquees in front of Hutton-in-the-Forest country house, as well as larger sculptural works laid out in the grounds. This is followed by the highly unusual **Potfest in the Pens**, which sees potters displaying their creations in the unlikely setting of the covered pens at Penrith's cattle market, just outside town on the A66. Here, the public can talk to the artists, learn about what inspires them and sign up for free classes.

Penrith Castle in the fourteenth century; this is now a romantic, crumbling ruin, opposite the train station. The town itself is at its best in the narrow streets, arcades and alleys off **Market Square**, and around **St Andrew's churchyard**, where the so-called "Giant's Grave" is actually a collection of pre-Norman crosses and "hogback" tombstones.

11

Dalemain

A592, 2 miles north of Pooley Bridge, or 3 miles southwest of Penrith • Mon–Thurs & Sun: Easter–Oct 11.15am–4pm, gardens & tearoom 10.30am–5pm; Nov to mid Dec & Feb Easter gardens & tearoom only 11am–3pm • £10.50, gardens only £7.50, children free • ☎ 01768 486450, ⟨W⟩dalemain.com • No public transport

Residence to the same family since 1679, the country house of **Dalemain** started life in the twelfth century as a fortified tower, but has been added to by successive generations, culminating with a Georgian facade grafted on to a largely Elizabethan house. Its grounds are gorgeous and, while there's a guided tour of the house in the morning at 11.15am, for the rest of the time (from 11.45am, though house closed for lunch 1–1.30pm), rather remarkably, you're given the run of the public rooms, which the Hasell family still use.

Rheged

Redhills, A66, 1.5 miles southwest of Penrith, and half a mile west of the M6 (junction 40) • Daily 10am–5.30pm • General admission and parking free; admission to one film £6.50, family £19, each extra film £5, family £14.50 • ☎ 01768 868000, ⟨W⟩rheged.com • Bus #X4/X5 from Penrith or Keswick/Cockermouth

Rheged – a Cumbrian "visitor experience", just outside Penrith is billed as Europe's largest earth-covered building, and blends in admirably with the surrounding fells – from the main road you wouldn't know it was there. An impressive atrium-lit underground visitor centre fills you in on the region's history, and you'll also find souvenir shops, food outlets, galleries, workshops, demonstrations and play areas. The staple visit, though, is for the big-screen 3D cinema, showing family-friendly movies.

ARRIVAL AND DEPARTURE   PENRITH

By train Penrith train station is 5min walk south of Market Square and the main street, Middlegate.
Destinations Carlisle (and onward services to Glasgow/ Edinburgh, every 30min; 20min); Lancaster (and onward services to London, every 30min; 40min); Manchester (hourly; 1hr 40min).
By bus The bus station is on Albert St, behind Middlegate, and has regular services to Ullswater, Keswick, Cockermouth and Carlisle.

ACCOMMODATION

Askham Hall Askham, 5 miles south of Penrith ☎ 01931 712350, ⟨W⟩askhamhall.co.uk. Country-house living at its most gracious – the Lowther family's *Askham Hall* boasts stunning rooms (up to £320), a heated outdoor pool and gorgeous gardens to provide a touch of luxury in the Cumbrian countryside. There's both elegant restaurant dining and the *Kitchen Garden Café*, which has an outdoor wood-fired oven for pizzas. __£170__

Brooklands 2 Portland Place ☎ 01768 863395, ⟨W⟩brooklandsguesthouse.com. Handsome 1870s town-house whose colour-coordinated B&B rooms have country pine furniture and small but snazzy bathrooms. __£80__

Crake Trees Manor Crosby Ravensworth, 15 miles southeast of Penrith, A6 via Shap or M6 junction 39 ☎ 01931 715205, ⓦ craketreesmanor.co.uk. A gorgeous barn conversion B&B in the nearby Eden Valley. Rooms boast slate floors, antique beds, serious showers and fluffy wrap-me-up towels; or consider a night in the cosy Shepherds' Hut (£75–90, depending on season) in the grounds. **£95**

★ **George and Dragon Clifton** A6, 3 miles south of Penrith ☎ 01768 865381, ⓦ georgeanddragonclifton .co.uk. This revamped eighteenth-century inn is a class act – country-chic rooms (some up to £155) feature big beds with brocade headboards and slate-floor bathrooms, while the informal downstairs bar and restaurant (around £30 for 3 courses) sources pretty much everything from the adjacent Lowther Estate. Food served daily noon–2.30pm & 6–9pm. **£95**

Carlisle

The county capital of Cumbria, **CARLISLE** has been fought over for more than 2000 years, ever since the construction of Hadrian's Wall – part of which survives at nearby **Birdoswald Fort**. The later struggle with the Scots defined the very nature of Carlisle as a border city: William Wallace was repelled in 1297 and Robert the Bruce eighteen years later, but Bonnie Prince Charlie's troops took Carlisle in 1745 after a six-day siege, holding it for six weeks before surrendering to the Duke of Cumberland. It's not surprising, then, that the city trumpets itself as "historic Carlisle", and is well worth a night's stop.

Carlisle Cathedral

Castle St • Mon–Sat 7.30am–6.15pm, Sun 7.30am–5pm • Free, donation requested • ☎ 01228 548151, ⓦ carlislecathedral.org.uk

Carlisle Cathedral was founded in 1122 but embraces a considerably older heritage. Christianity was established in sixth-century Carlisle by St Kentigern (often known as St Mungo), who became the first bishop and patron saint of Glasgow. Parliamentarian troops during the Civil War caused much destruction, but there's still much to admire in the ornate fifteenth-century choir stalls and the glorious **East Window**, which features some of the finest pieces of fourteenth-century stained glass in the country.

Tullie House Museum and Art Gallery

Castle St • Mon–Sat 10am–5pm, Sun 11am–5pm (Nov–March Sun noon–5pm) • £7, under 18s free • ☎ 01228 618718, ⓦ tulliehouse.co.uk

Among other wide-ranging attractions, the wonderful **Tullie House Museum and Art Gallery** takes an imaginative approach to Carlisle's turbulent past, with special emphasis put on life on the edge of the Roman Empire. Climbing a reconstruction of part of Hadrian's Wall, you learn about catapults and stone-throwers, while other sections elaborate on domestic life, work and burial practices.

Carlisle Castle

Bridge St • April–Sept daily 10am–6pm; Oct daily 10am–5pm; Nov–March Sat & Sun 10am–4pm • £5.90; EH • Guided tours Easter–Oct daily; ask at the entrance • ☎ 01228 591922, ⓦ english-heritage.org.uk

With a thousand years of military occupation of the site, **Carlisle Castle** is loaded with significance – not least as the place where, in 1568, Elizabeth I kept Mary Queen of Scots as her "guest". Guided tours help bring the history to life; don't leave without climbing to the battlements for a view of the Carlisle rooftops.

ARRIVAL AND INFORMATION   CARLISLE

By train Carlisle is on the West Coast mainline (for London–Manchester–Scotland services). There are also Cumbrian coastal services to Whitehaven, and cross-country trains to Newcastle. The Settle to Carlisle Railway, the magnificent scenic railway through the Yorkshire Dales

(ⓦ settle-carlisle.co.uk), also ends its run at Carlisle (see box, p.541).

Destinations Lancaster (every 30min–1hr; 1hr); Newcastle (hourly; 1hr 20min–1hr 40min); Whitehaven (hourly; 1hr 10min).

Birdoswald Roman Fort (15miles) & Scotland

CARLISLE

● **RESTAURANTS & BARS**
The Andalusian	2
Gilded Lily	1

■ **ACCOMMODATION**
Carlisle City Hostel	1
Hallmark	3
Langleigh House	2

A6, M6, Penrith & Lancaster

Hadrian's Wall Bus The seasonal Hadrian's Wall Bus, #AD122 (see p.597) connects Carlisle with Birdoswald Fort (40min), the rest of the Hadrian's Wall sights.

Tourist office Old Town Hall, Green Market (March, April, Sept & Oct Mon–Sat 9.30am–5pm; May–Aug Mon–Sat 9.30am–5pm, Sun 10.30am–4pm; Nov–Feb Mon–Sat 10am–4pm; ☎ 01228 598596, ⓦ discovercarlisle.co.uk).

ACCOMMODATION AND EATING

The Andalusian Warwick Rd ☎ 01228 539665, ⓦ theandalusianbar.co.uk. The gorgeous tile work, carved oak bar, squishy sofas and big fireplaces make for a relaxed meet and greet bar, with tapas (£3–8) to share over drinks. Daily noon–midnight.

Carlisle City Hostel 36 Abbey St ☎ 01228 545637, ⓦ carlislecityhostel.com. Carlisle's indie hostel makes a great townhouse budget base, with four bright bunk rooms offering flexible accommodation for friends, groups, families or solo travellers. One of the rooms is available as a private double/triple – there's also a kitchen, free tea and coffee, bike storage and secure lockers, and the location is excellent. Dorms **£15**

Gilded Lily 6 Lowther St ☎ 01228 593600, ⓦ gildedlily .info. Fabulous-looking restaurant and lounge bar serving cosmopolitan food at lunch and dinner, noodles to local lamb, burgers to piri-piri prawns (mains £10–22). Mon–Thurs 9am–midnight, Fri & Sat 9am–1am, Sun noon–midnight.

Hallmark Court Square ☎ 01228 531951, ⓦ hallmark hotels.co.uk. Right outside the train station, the boutique-style *Hallmark* has a chic look, sleek rooms with big beds, and a contemporary bar and brasserie. **£89**

Langleigh House 6 Howard Place ☎ 01228 530440, ⓦ langleighhouse.co.uk. Nicely presented Victorian townhouse B&B – furnishings reflect the period, and original features abound. **£75**

Birdoswald Roman Fort

Gilsland, Brampton, 15 miles northeast of Carlisle, signposted from A69 • April–Sept daily 10am–6pm; Oct daily 10am–5pm; Nov–March Sat & Sun 10am–4pm • £5.60; EH • ☎ 01697 747602, ⓦ english-heritage.org.uk

One of sixteen major fortifications along Hadrian's Wall, **Birdoswald Fort** has all tiers of the Roman structure intact, while a drill hall and other buildings have been excavated. There's a tearoom and picnic area at the fort.

Yorkshire

MOUNTAIN BIKING IN THE YORKSHIRE DALES

Yorkshire

It's easy to be glib about Yorkshire – to outsiders it's the archetypal "up North" with all the clichés that implies, from flat caps to grim factories. For their part, many Yorkshire locals are happy to play up to these prejudices, while nursing a secret conviction that there really is no better place in the world to live. In some respects, it's a world apart, its most distinctive characteristics – from the broad dialect to the breathtaking landscapes – deriving from a long history of settlement, invention and independence. It's hard to argue with Yorkshire's boasts that the beer's better, the air's cleaner and the people are friendlier.

The number-one destination is undoubtedly **York**, for centuries England's second city, until the Industrial Revolution created new centres of power and influence. York's mixture of medieval, Georgian and Victorian architecture is repeated in towns such as **Beverley**, **Ripon** and **Richmond**, while the Yorkshire coast, too, retains something of its erstwhile grandeur – **Bridlington** and **Scarborough** boomed in the nineteenth century and again in the postwar period, though it's in smaller resorts like **Whitby** and **Robin Hood's Bay** that the best of the coast is to be found today.

The engine of growth during the Industrial Revolution was not in the north of the county, but in the south and west, where Leeds, Bradford, Sheffield and their satellites were once the world's mightiest producers of textiles and steel. A renewed vigour has infused South and West Yorkshire during the last decade; the city-centre transformations of **Leeds** and **Sheffield** in particular have been remarkable, while **Bradford** is a fine diversion on the way to **Haworth**, home of the Brontë sisters.

The **Yorkshire Dales**, to the northwest, form a patchwork of stone-built villages, limestone hills, serene valleys and majestic heights. The county's other National Park, the **North York Moors**, is divided into bleak upland moors and a tremendous rugged coastline between Robin Hood's Bay and Staithes.

GETTING AROUND   **YORKSHIRE**

By train Fast trains on the East Coast main line link York to London, Newcastle and Edinburgh. Leeds is served by trains from London, and is at the centre of the integrated Metro bus and train system that covers most of West and South Yorkshire. There are services to Scarborough (from York) and Whitby (from Middlesbrough), while the Settle to Carlisle line, to the southern and western Dales, can be accessed from Leeds. **Transport passes** The North Country Rover ticket (£84 for four days in eight) covers train travel north of Leeds, Bradford and Hull and south of Newcastle and Carlisle.

Sheffield and around

Yorkshire's second city, **SHEFFIELD** remains linked with its steel industry, in particular the production of high-quality cutlery. As early as the fourteenth century the carefully fashioned, hard-wearing knives of hardworking Sheffield enjoyed national repute, while technological advances later turned the city into one of the country's foremost centres

12

HARROGATE TURKISH BATHS

Highlights

❶ National Coal Mining Museum A working coal mine until the mid-1980s, now a museum; you can even head underground, if you're brave enough. **See p.530**

❷ Bradford curry houses Bradford's Indian restaurants provide wonderful opportunities for gastronomic exploration. **See p.534**

❸ Haworth Visiting the moorland home of the talented and ultimately tragic Brontë sisters is an affecting experience, despite the crowds. See p.535

❹ Malham It's a breathtaking hike from Malham village to the glorious natural amphitheatre of Malham Cove. **See p.539**

❺ Fountains Abbey Enjoy views of the atmospheric ruins of Fountains Abbey set in spectacular Studley Water Gardens. **See p.545**

❻ Harrogate Turkish Baths The late Victorian opulence of Harrogate's magnificently restored Turkish baths is a great place to get pampered. See p.546

❼ Jorvik/Dig!, York Travel through time to Viking York, then seek out new discoveries at Dig! **See p.550 & p.552**

❽ Whitby Follow in the footsteps of Count Dracula and Captain James Cook in this spectacularly pretty former whaling port. See p.566

HIGHLIGHTS ARE MARKED ON THE MAP ON PP.522–523

of heavy and specialist engineering. Unsurprisingly, it was bombed heavily during World War II, and by the 1980s the steel industry's subsequent downturn had tipped parts of Sheffield into dispiriting decline. The subsequent revival has been rapid, however, with the centre utterly transformed by flagship architectural projects. Steel, of course, still underpins much of what Sheffield is about: museum collections tend to focus on the region's industrial heritage, complemented by the startling science-and-adventure exhibits at **Magna**, built in a disused steel works at **Rotherham**, the former coal and iron town a few miles northeast of the city.

Sheffield's **city centre** is very compact and easily explored on foot. Southeast of the **Winter Garden/Peace Gardens** hub, clubs and galleries exist alongside the arts and media businesses of the **Cultural Industries Quarter**. To the northeast, spruced-up warehouses and cobbled towpaths line the canal basin, **Victoria Quays**. The **Devonshire Quarter**, east of the gardens and centred on Division Street, is the trendiest shopping area. A little further out, to the northeast of the city centre and easily accessible by bus or tram, lies the huge **Meadowhall Shopping Complex**, built on the site of one of Sheffield's most famous steelworks.

Peace Gardens

Pinstone St • Open access • Free

In a small natural amphitheatre next to the Town Hall, the splendid, recently remodelled **Peace Gardens** (named in hope immediately after World War II) centre on huge bronze water features inspired by Bessemer converters. It's a lively spot, especially on sunny days, when delighted kids dash in and out of the pavement-level fountains, or float paper boats down the converging ceramic-lined rills representing the rivers that gave Sheffield steel mills their power.

Winter Garden

Surrey St • Mon–Sat 8am–8pm, Sun 8am–6pm • Free • ☎ 0114 273 6895, ⓦ sheffield.gov.uk

A minute's walk east of the Peace Gardens, the stunning **Winter Garden** is a potent symbol of the city's regeneration. A twenty-first-century version of a Victorian conservatory on a huge scale (230ft long, and around 70ft high and wide), it's created from unvarnished, slowly weathering wood and polished glass, and filled with more than two thousand seasonally changing plants and towering trees.

Millennium Gallery

Arundel Gate • Mon–Sat 10am–5pm, Sun 11am–4pm • Free • ☎ 0114 278 2600, ⓦ sheffieldgalleries.org.uk

Backing onto the Winter Garden, the **Millennium Galleries** consist of the **Metalwork Gallery**, devoted to the city's world-famous cutlery industry, including an introduction to the processes involved and a collection of fine silver and stainless steel cutlery, and the diverting **Ruskin Gallery**. Based on the cultural collection founded by John Ruskin in 1875 to "improve" the working people of Sheffield, this includes manuscripts, minerals, watercolours and drawings all relating in some way to the natural world.

Sheffield Cathedral

Church St • Visitor Centre open Mon 8.30am–5pm, Tues–Fri 8.30am–6.30pm, Sat 9.30am–3.30pm, Sun 7.45am–7.30pm, except during school hols when open Mon–Fri 8.30am–5pm, Sat 9.30am–4pm, Sun 7.45am–7.30pm • Details of recitals and tours available on ☎ 0114 279 7412, ⓦ sheffield-cathedral.co.uk

The **Cathedral Church of St Peter and St Paul**, to give **Sheffield Cathedral** its full title, was a simple parish church before 1914, and subsequent attempts to give it a more dignified bearing have frankly failed. It's a mishmash of styles and changes of direction, and you'd need a PhD in ecclesiastical architecture to make any sense of it. That said,

SHEFFIELD

■ ACCOMMODATION

Houseboat Hotels	1
Leopold Hotel	3
Mercure St Paul's Hotel	4
University of Sheffield	2

● RESTAURANTS

The Forum	1
Nonna's	3
Silversmiths	2

■ PUBS, CLUBS & LIVE MUSIC

Crucible, Lyceum and Studio theatres	2
Crystal	3
Devonshire Cat	1
Fat Cat	4
Leadmill	6
Plug	5

the magnificent **Shrewsbury Chapel**, at the east end of the south aisle, is worth a look. Built around 1520, it contains the tombs of the fourth and sixth Earls of Shrewsbury, whose alabaster effigies adorn their tombs.

Kelham Island Museum

Alma St • Mon–Thurs 10am–4pm, Sun 11am–4.45pm • £5 • ☎ 0114 272 2106, ⓦ simt.co.uk

Fifteen minutes' walk north of the cathedral, the **Kelham Island Museum** reveals the breadth of the city's **industrial output** – cutlery, of course, but also Barnes Wallis's 22ft-long Grand Slam bomb, the Sheffield Simplex roadster, and the gigantic River Don steam engine. Many of the old machines are still working, arranged in period workshops where craftspeople show how they were used.

Weston Park Museum

Weston Bank • Mon–Fri 10am–4pm, Sat 11am–5pm, Sun 11pm–4pm • Free • ☎ 0114 278 2600, ⓦ museums-sheffield.org.uk • Bus #51 or #52 from city centre, or Sheffield University tram

You can put the city's life and times into perspective a mile or so west of the centre at the **Weston Park Museum**. Here the imaginatively themed and family-friendly galleries draw together the city's extensive archeology, natural history, art and social history collections.

Magna

Sheffield Rd (A6178), Templeborough, Rotherham, just off the M1 a mile from the Meadowhall Shopping Complex · Daily 10am–5pm · £9.85, family ticket from £25.15 · ☎ 01709 720002, ⓦ visitmagna.co.uk · Bus #69 from either Sheffield or Rotherham Interchanges, or a 15min taxi ride from Sheffield

Housed in a former steelworks building in **ROTHERHAM**, about six miles northeast of Sheffield, **Magna** is the UK's best science adventure centre. The vast internal space comfortably holds four gadget-packed **pavilions**, themed on the elements of earth, air, fire and water. You're encouraged to get your hands on a huge variety of interactive exhibits, games and machines – operating a real JCB, filling diggers and barrows, blasting a rock face or investigating a twister, for example. On the hour, everyone decamps to the main hall for the **Big Melt**, when the original arc furnace is used in a bone-shaking light and sound show that has visitors gripping the railings.

ARRIVAL AND DEPARTURE

By train Sheffield's train station is on the eastern edge of the city centre.

Destinations Leeds (every 12min; 40min–1hr 19min); London (hourly; 2hr 30min); York (every 30min; 53min).

By bus Sheffield Interchange bus and coach station lies about 200yd north of the train station. Buses run to and from most regional and national centres – including all the main South Yorkshire towns; London (every 30 min; 2hr); Birmingham (every 20min; 1hr 10min); Liverpool (hourly; 2hr) and Manchester (every 30min; 1hr).

SHEFFIELD AND AROUND

GETTING AROUND AND INFORMATION

By bus Local buses depart from High Street or Arundel Gate.

By tram The Supertram system (ⓦ supertram.com) connects the city centre with the Meadowhall shopping centre (see box opposite), Halfway, Herdings Park, Malin Bridge and Middlewood, with the stations in between giving comprehensive access to most of the city and connections to the Park and Ride scheme.

Transport info For fare and timetable information, visit the Mini Interchange travel centre on Arundel Gate, behind the Crucible Theatre (Mon–Fri 7am–6pm, Sat 9am–5pm; ☎ 01709 515151 or 0114 201 2675, ⓦ sypte.co.uk).

Tourist office Unit 1, Surrey Street (Mon–Fri 9.30am–1pm & 1.30–5pm, Sat 9.30am–1pm & 1.30–4pm; ☎ 0114 221 1900, ⓦ welcometosheffield.co.uk).

ACCOMMODATION

Houseboat Hotels Victoria Quays ☎ 0114 232 6556 or ☎ 07974 590264, ⓦ houseboathotels.com. Something different – three moored houseboats, available by the night, with en-suite bathrooms and kitchens. You get exclusive use of your own boat, for one to four people. Single occupancy **£79**; families **£99**; boats for four adults **£159**

Leopold Hotel 2 Leopold St ☎ 0114 252 4000, ⓦ leopold hotel.co.uk. Once a boys' grammar school, this place is immaculately modernized but retains some original features. Centrally located, the hotel backs onto remodelled Leopold Square, which has an appealing array of places to eat. **£99**

Mercure St Paul's Hotel 119 Norfolk St ☎ 0114 278 2000, ⓦ mercure.com. Sandwiched between the Peace Gardens and Tudor Square, this modern hotel couldn't be more central. Comfortable rather than innovative, with understated (if a little anodyne) decor and fine views over the city the higher you go. **£94**

University of Sheffield ☎ 0114 289 3500. Self-catering student rooms in the Endcliffe student village (mid-July to late Sept) can be booked through the university. Within walking distance of the city centre. **£44**

EATING

★**The Forum** 127–129 Devonshire St ☎ 0114 272 0569, ⓦ forumsheffield.co.uk. A vibrant mixture of bar, café, music venue and boutique mall, with a lively clientele who use it as a breakfast stop, lunch spot, after-work bar, dinner venue, comedy club and night club. Mon–Thurs & Sun 9am–1am, Fri & Sat 9am–3am.

★**Nonna's** 535–541 Ecclesall Rd ☎ 0114 268 6166, ⓦ nonnas.co.uk. Italian bar/restaurant with a great reputation and a family feel. Authentic Italian cuisine (menus have English descriptions). Mains £14–19. Mon–Sun 8.30am–11pm.

Silversmiths 111 Arundel St ☎ 0114 270 6160, ⓦ silversmiths-restaurant.com. A "kitchen nightmare" turned around in 2008 by Gordon Ramsay in his TV show, city-centre *Silversmiths* supplies top-notch Yorkshire food from local ingredients – venison sausages and pies, spinach tart with Yorkshire Blue cheese – in a 200-year-old silversmith's workshop. Tues is pie night (£8.95) and there's a three-course set menu on Wed and Thurs (£17.90), and a similar early bird (4.45–6.45pm) and dinner menu (mains £12.50–15.50) at weekends. Reservations recommended. Tues–Thurs 5.30–11.30pm, Fri & Sat 4.45pm–midnight.

THE MEADOWHALL CENTRE

Since it opened in 1990 on the site of a derelict steelworks, the **Meadowhall Centre** (☎0845 600 6800, ⓦmeadowhall.co.uk) has dominated Sheffield shopping like a colossus, pulling in thirty million shoppers a year from all over the north of England. Blamed from the start for urban decay as far away as Scunthorpe, it was expected to decimate city-centre shopping in the rest of South Yorkshire. Twenty-five years later, the jury's still out. With hundreds of shops under one roof, it's either Meadowheaven or Meadowhell, depending on your point of view. But even those who hate it find its weatherproof nature and free parking hard to resist.

DRINKING, NIGHTLIFE AND ENTERTAINMENT

For the best insight into what makes Sheffield tick as a party destination take a night-time walk along **Division St** and **West St** where competing theme and retro bars go in and out of fashion. Locals and students also frequent the bars and pubs of **Ecclesall Rd** (the so-called "golden mile"), out of the centre to the southwest.

Crucible, Lyceum and Studio Tudor Square ☎0114 249 6000, ⓦsheffieldtheatres.co.uk. Sheffield's theatres put on a full programme of theatre, dance, comedy and concerts. The *Crucible*, of course, has hosted the World Snooker Championships for thirty years. It also presents the annual Music in the Round festival of chamber music (May), and the Sheffield Children's Festival (late June or July).

Crystal 23–32 Carver St ☎0114 272 5926, ⓦcrystalbar .uk.com. A former scissor factory provides stunning premises for this airy bar/nightclub, good for drinks and great for a night out. Thurs–Sat 10pm–3am.

★**Devonshire Cat** 49 Wellington St, Devonshire Green ☎0114 279 6700, ⓦdevonshirecat.co.uk. Renowned ale house with wide variety of domestic and imported beers, plus good pub food (£7.75–14.25) with drinks matched to every selection. Mon–Thurs 11.30am–11pm, Fri & Sat 11.30am–1am, Sun noon–10.30pm; food served Mon–Sat 11.30am–8pm, Sun noon–6pm.

★**Fat Cat** Alma St ☎0114 249 4801, ⓦthefatcat .co.uk. Bought by real ale enthusiasts in 1981 after a brewery sell-off, the *Fat Cat* is now a Sheffield institution offering a wide range of bottled and draft beers, ciders and country wines, and a hearty pub-grub menu (meals around £4.50). With its open fires, polished mahogany bar and etched mirrors, and its total absence of flashing gaming machines and piped music, this is pub-going as it used to be. Daily noon–11.30pm; food served Mon–Fri noon–3pm & 6–8pm, Sat noon–7pm, Sun noon–2pm.

Leadmill 6–7 Leadmill Rd ☎0114 221 2828, ⓦleadmill.co.uk. In the Cultural Industries Quarter, this place hosts live bands and DJs most nights of the week, with a comedy club on Wed.

Plug 14 Matilda St ☎0114 241 3040, ⓦthe-plug.com. Mid-sized music venue featuring everything from live acoustic folk to diverse club nights, including the award-winning "Jump Around".

Sheffield City Hall Barker's Pool ☎0114 278 9789, ⓦsheffieldcityhall.com. Year-round programme of classical music, opera, mainstream concerts, comedy and club nights, in a magnificent, renovated concert hall.

The Showroom 7 Paternoster Row ☎0114 275 7727, ⓦshowroom.org.uk. The biggest independent cinema outside London, and also a popular meeting place, in its relaxed café bar.

SHOPPING

Sheffield has all the national chain stores and other shops you'd expect in the city centre, with top-end shops concentrated particularly along **Fargate** and **High St** on one side of the Peace Gardens and budget alternatives along **The Moor** on the other. The trendiest shopping is to be found in the **Devonshire Quarter**, based on Division St, while due south there's a new **indoor market** at 77 The Moor (Mon–Sat 8.30am–5.30pm), replacing the old Castlegate Market. Out-of-town shopping is dominated by the **Meadowhall Centre** (see box above), an easy tram ride three miles east of the centre.

Leeds and around

Yorkshire's commercial capital, and one of the fastest-growing cities in the country, **LEEDS** has undergone a radical transformation in recent years. There's still a true northern grit to its character, and in many of its dilapidated suburbs, but the grime has been removed from the impressive Victorian buildings and the city is revelling in its new persona as a booming financial, commercial and cultural centre. The renowned **shops**, **restaurants**, **bars** and **clubs** provide one focus of a visit to contemporary Leeds – it's certainly Yorkshire's top destination for a day or two of conspicuous consumption and indulgence. Museums include the impressive **Royal Armouries**, which hold the national arms and armour collection, while the **City Art Gallery** has one of the best collections of British twentieth-century art outside London. Beyond the city, a number of major attractions are accessible by bus or train: north of town lies the stately home **Harewood House**, while south of Leeds, the neighbouring town of **Wakefield** is home to the stunning **Hepworth Gallery** and not far from the gritty **National Coal Mining Museum** and the **Yorkshire Sculpture Park**.

City Art Gallery

The Headrow • Mon & Tues 10am–5pm, Wed noon–5pm, Thurs–Sat 10am–5pm, Sun 1–5pm • Free • ☎ 0113 247 8256, ⓦ leeds.gov.uk

Sharing a building with the Central Library, the **City Art Gallery** has an important collection of largely nineteenth- and twentieth-century paintings, prints, drawings and sculptures, some on permanent display, others rotated. There's an understandable bias towards pieces by **Henry Moore** and **Barbara Hepworth**, both former students at the Leeds School of Art; Moore's *Reclining Woman* lounges at the top of the steps outside the gallery.

LEEDS

■ **ACCOMMODATION**
42 The Calls	5
Butlers	1
Quebecs	3
Roomzzz	2/4
Student apartments	6

● **SHOPS**
Harvey Nichols	4
Kirkgate Market	5
The Light	2
Trinity Leeds	6
Merrion Centre	1
Victoria Quarter	3

■ **PUBS & BARS**
Bar Fibre	10
Milo	8
Mojo	2
Mr Foley's Cask Ale House	4
North Bar	5
Whitelocks	7

■ **CLUBS & LIVE MUSIC**
Cockpit	11
Hifi	9
Mint Club	3
Oceana	1
The Warehouse	6
Wire	8

● **RESTAURANTS & CAFÉS**
Art's Café	3
Brasserie Blanc	4
Norman Bar	2
Salvo's	1

Henry Moore Institute

The Headrow • Tues–Sun 11am–5.30pm • Free • ☎ 0113 246 7467, ✆ henry-moore.org.co.uk

The City Art Gallery connects with the adjacent **Henry Moore Institute**, which, despite its misleading name, is devoted not to Moore himself but to temporary exhibitions of sculpture from all periods and nationalities.

Royal Armouries

Armouries Drive • Daily 10am–5pm • Free • ☎ 0113 220 1999, ✆ armouries.org.uk • Bus #28 from city centre

On the south side of the riverbank beckons the spectacular glass turret and gunmetal grey bulk of the **Royal Armouries**, purpose-built to house the **arms** and **armour** collection from the Tower of London. One of the best museums of its type in the world, its five enormous galleries hold beautifully displayed weapons for war, tournaments and hunting, armour and other artefacts dating from Roman times onwards. Particularly spectacular are the reconstruction of a tiger hunt; the Indian elephant armour (the heaviest armour in the world) consisting of 8500 iron plates; fabulously decorated ceremonial suits of full plate armour; a Sikh "quoit turban" which carried a blood-curdling array of throwing quoits; garrotting wires and knives; Samurai, Mongol and Indian armour and weapons; and many ornate guns, from a reconstruction of an enormously long Essex punt gun to an exquisite Tiffany-decorated Smith and Wesson .44 Magnum.

Thackray Museum

12

Beckett St • Daily 10am–5pm, last admission 3pm • £7 • ☎ 0113 244 4343, ✆ thackraymuseum.org • Bus #16 #42 #49 #50 #50A or #61 from the city centre (all around 15min, all stop outside the museum)

Essentially a medical history museum, and a hugely entertaining one, the **Thackray Museum**, next to St James' Hospital, has displays on subjects as diverse as the history of the hearing aid and the workings of the human intestine. It's gruesome, too, with a film of a Victorian limb amputation in a gallery called "Pain, pus and blood".

Leeds Industrial Museum

Off Canal Rd, between Armley and Kirkstall Rd, 2 miles west of the centre • Tues–Sat 10am–5pm, Sun 1–5pm • £3.10 • ☎ 0113 263 7861 • Bus #5 or #67

For Leeds' industrial past, visit the vast **Leeds Industrial Museum**. There's been a mill on the site since at least the seventeenth century, and the present building was one of the world's largest woollen mills until its closure in 1969. Although most of its displays naturally centre on the **woollen industry**, and famous offshoots like Hepworths and Burtons, the cinema and printing in the local area are also covered.

Kirkstall Abbey

Abbey Rd, about 3 miles northwest of the city centre • **Abbey** Tues–Sun: April–Sept 10am–4.30pm; Oct–March 10m–4pm • Free • ✆ leeds.gov.uk/kirkstallabbey • **Museum** Tues–Fri & Sun 10am–5pm, Sat noon–5pm • £3.60 • ☎ 0113 230 5492 ✆ www.leeds.gov.uk /abbeyhouse • Buses #33, #33A or #757 from city centre

The bucolic ruins and cloisters of **Kirkstall Abbey**, which was built between 1152 and 1182 by Cistercian monks from Fountains Abbey, are well worth a visit. The former gatehouse now provides the setting for the family-friendly **Abbey House Museum**, which takes a look at Victorian Leeds.

Temple Newsam

Off Selby Rd, 4 miles east of Leeds **House** Tues–Sun: April–Sept 10.30am–5pm; Oct–March 10.30am–4pm • £3.70 • **Rare breeds farm** Tues–Sun: April–Sept 10am–5pm; Oct–March 10am–4pm • £3.30 • ☎ 0113 264 7321, ✆ leeds.gov.uk/templenewsam • On Sun bus

#63a runs to the house from central Leeds and during the rest of the week #19 and #19a run to Colton, from where it is less than a mile's walk; during summer hols, #10 bus runs directly to the house

The Tudor-Jacobean house of **Temple Newsam** shows many of the paintings and much of the decorative art owned by Leeds City Art Gallery. There are paintings from the sixteenth to the nineteenth centuries, furniture (including a number of Chippendale pieces), textiles and tapestries, silver, porcelain and pottery. The estate is over fifteen thousand acres and also contains Europe's largest **rare breeds farm**, where you can see four breeds of pigs, six of sheep, eight of poultry and no fewer than nine of cattle.

Harewood House

Harewood, 7 miles north of Leeds • Opening hours vary widely according to day and season; check website for full details • Freedom ticket, covering all parts of house and gardens £14 • ☎ 0113 218 1010, ⓦ harewood.org • Frequent buses run to Harewood from Leeds, including the #36 (every 20min, every 30min on Sun)

Harewood House – still the home of the Earl and Countess of Harewood – is one of the UK's greatest country mansions. It was created in the mid-eighteenth century by an all-star team: designed by John Carr of York, with interiors by Robert Adam, furniture by Thomas Chippendale and paintings by Turner, Reynolds, Titian and El Greco, all sitting in beautiful **grounds** landscaped by Capability Brown. Tours take in the below-stairs kitchen and servants' quarters as well as innumerable galleries, halls, reception rooms and staircases, dripping with antiques and priceless art treasures, while added attractions include an adventure playground and gardens – including the famous bird garden. Numerous special events, special-interest tours and talks on things like bee-keeping, photography and food keep things lively. Incidentally, the village is pronounced "Harewood" as it is spelt, while the house is pronounced "Harwood".

Hepworth Gallery

Gallery Walk, Wakefield • Tues–Sun 10am–5pm • Free • ☎ 01924 247360, ⓦ hepworthwakefield.org • From Leeds, take a train to Wakefield Westgate and walk, or a bus to Wakefield city centre, then a local bus to Doncaster Rd (a 5min walk) or Bridge St (next to the gallery); alternatively, Wakefield's freecitybus (ⓦ wymetro.com) links all major parts of town, including the Hepworth Gallery

Opened in May 2011, the £35million **Hepworth Gallery** was the largest new gallery to open outside London for decades. A cuboid concrete riverside building designed by Sir David Chipperfield, it has ten display areas housing a wonderful collection of Dame Barbara Hepworth's work – not only finished sculptures, but also working models in plaster and aluminium, lithographs and screen prints. You can even see her original workbench and tools. Other contemporary artists are represented, too, and a flow of new exhibits is assured by close cooperation with the Tate. There's a café and shop, and a children's playground within its pleasant surroundings.

National Coal Mining Museum

Caphouse Colliery, Overton, about 10 miles south of Leeds, halfway between Wakefield and Huddersfield (on the A642, signposted from M1) • Daily 10am–5pm; last tour 3.15pm • Free • ☎ 01924 848806, ⓦ ncm.org.uk • Train from Leeds to Wakefield Westgate, then from the station the #128 bus goes right past the museum, while #232 passes nearby

While the gentry enjoyed the comforts of life in grand houses like Harewood (see above), just a few miles away generations of Yorkshiremen sweated out a living underground. Mining is now little more than a memory in most parts of Yorkshire, but visitors can get all too vivid an idea of pit life through the ages at the excellent **National Coal Mining Museum**. Based in a former pit, Caphouse Colliery, the highlight is an underground **mine tour** (1hr 30min; warm clothes required; arrive early in school hols; no under-5s) with a former miner as your guide.

Yorkshire Sculpture Park

West Bretton, outside Wakefield, a mile from the M1 (junction 38) • Daily 10am–5pm (galleries, restaurant and café 10am–4pm) • Free, parking £7.50/day, £5 for 1–2hr • ☎ 01924 832631, ☜ ysp.co.uk • Train from Leeds to Wakefield Westgate, then bus #96 (Sun #435/436) – a fair bit of walking is necessary

The Yorkshire country estate at West Bretton now serves as the **Yorkshire Sculpture Park**. Trails and paths run across five hundred acres of eighteenth-century parkland, past open-air "gallery spaces" for some of Britain's most famous sculptors. The two big local names represented here are Henry Moore (1898–1986), born in nearby Castleford, and his contemporary Barbara Hepworth (1903–75), from Wakefield. The **visitor centre** is the place to check on current exhibitions and pick up a map – the restaurant has great views over Moore's monumental pieces.

ARRIVAL AND INFORMATION

By train National and local Metro trains use Leeds Station in the city centre.

Destinations Bradford (every 20min; 20min); Carlisle (every 2hr; 2hr 40min); Harrogate (every 30min; 34min); Hull (hourly; 1hr); Knaresborough (every 30min; 45min); Lancaster (4 daily; 2hr); Liverpool (hourly; 1hr 50min); London (every 30min; 2hr 20min); Manchester (every 15min; 1hr); Scarborough (every 30min–1hr; 1hr 20min); Settle (every 2hr; 1hr); Sheffield (every 10–15min; 40min–1hr 25min); Skipton (every 15–30min; 45min); Wakefield (Westgate & Kirkgate; every 10–15min; 12min); York (every 10–15min; 25min).

By bus The bus station is to the east of the centre behind Kirkgate Market, on St Peter's Street, though many buses stop

LEEDS AND AROUND

outside the train station as well. Buses run from the bus station to all parts of the city, the suburbs, the rest of West Yorkshire and, via National Express, the rest of the country.

Destinations Bradford (10–30min; 25min); Halifax (every 30min; 1hr 16min); London (hourly; 4hr 25min); Manchester (every 30min–1hr; 1hr 5min–1hr 45min); Wakefield (every 10min; 31min); York (hourly; 1hr).

Public transport information The Metro Travel Centres at the bus and train stations have up-to-date service details for local transport; information is also available from Metroline on ☎ 0113 245 7676 or ☜ wymetro.com.

Tourist office The Arcade (Mon 10am–7pm, Tues–Fri 9am–7pm, Sat 9am–5.30pm, Sun 10am–4pm; ☎ 0113 242 5242, ☜ leeds.gov.uk or ☜ leedsliveitloveit.com).

12

ACCOMMODATION

There's a good mix of **accommodation** in Leeds. Cheaper lodgings lie out to the northwest in the student area of Headingley, though these are a bus or taxi ride away. The tourist office offers an accommodation **booking line** on ☎ 0800 808050.

★ **42 The Calls** 42 The Calls ☎ 0113 244 0099, ☜ 42thecalls.co.uk. Converted riverside grain mill, where rooms come with great beds and sharp bathrooms. Being next to the Centenary footbridge, it can sometimes suffer from noisy passers-by. **£85**

★ **Butlers** Cardigan Rd, Headingley, 1.5 miles northwest of the centre ☎ 0113 274 4755, ☜ butlers hotel.co.uk. This hotel offers cosy, smart, traditionally furnished rooms on a suburban street; it is next to and associated with *Boundary*. **£69**

★ **Quebecs** 9 Quebec St ☎ 0113 244 8989, ☜ theeton collection.com. The ultimate city-boutique lodgings, boasting

glorious Victorian oak panelling and stained glass, offset by chic rooms. Online deals can cut costs considerably. **£170**

Roomzzz 12 Swine Gate; also at 2 & 361 Burley Rd; ☎ 0113 233 0400, ☜ roomzzz.co.uk. Self-catering, one- and two-bedroom apartments in contemporary style, at three locations – Swine Gate is the most central. All come with great kitchens and widescreen TVs. Reduced rates if you book more than a week in advance. **£88**

Student apartments Clarence Dock ☎ 0113 343 6100, ☜ universallyleeds.co.uk. Self-catering rooms near the Royal Armouries, available every summer holiday (mid-July to mid-Sept). First night **£48**, then **£21**

EATING

★ **Art's Café Bar and Restaurant** 42 Call Lane ☎ 0113 243 8243, ☜ artscafebar.co.uk. A relaxed hangout for drinks, dinner or a lazy Sunday brunch. Mediterranean flavours dominate the well-priced menu, and the wine list is excellent. Mains £10.95–16.50. Daily noon–11pm (Sat till late).

★ **Brasserie Blanc** Victoria Mill, Sovereign St ☎ 0113 220 6060, ☜ brasserieblanc.com. One of the seventeen restaurants established by French celebrity chef Raymond

Blanc all over the country, the Leeds branch is a 5min walk from the train station. Housed in an old mill, with plain brick walls, vaulted ceilings and iron pillars, it offers good food in smart but unstuffy surroundings at unthreatening prices. Set two-course menus from £11.50 (lunch) and £14 (dinner). Mon–Fri noon–2.45pm & 5.30–10pm, Sat noon–10.30pm, Sun noon–9pm (bar open all day).

Norman Bar 36 Call Lane ☎ 0113 234 3988,

Ⓦnormanbar.co.uk. A boho-chic interior with a juice bar, Asian noodle/stir-fry/dim sum menu, and varied club nights. Attracts mainly a young clientele. Light bites £3.95–4.95 (3 for £10). Wed noon–midnight, Thurs & Fri noon–3am, Sat noon–4am.

Salvo's 115 Otley Rd, Headingley ☎0113 275 5017,

Ⓦsalvos.co.uk. Mention pizza to Leeds locals and they'll think of *Salvo's*, though there's a classy Italian menu as well – mains £15.95–19.50 – and a choice list of daily specials. It really is worth the trek out from the centre. Mon–Thurs noon–2pm & 6–10pm, Fri & Sat noon–2pm, Sun noon–9pm.

DRINKING

Bar Fibre 168 Lower Briggate ☎0870 120 0888, Ⓦbarfibre.com. One of Leeds' finest gay-friendly bars comes with plenty of attitude. There's food during the day at *Café Mafiosa*, and regular alfresco parties in the courtyard outside (summer) and roaring fires inside (winter). Mon–Wed & Sun noon–1am, Thurs & Fri noon–3am, Sat noon–4am.

Milo 10–12 Call Lane ☎0113 245 7101. Unpretentious, intimate and offbeat bar, with DJs most evenings, ringing the changes from old soul and reggae to indie and electronica. Mon–Thurs 5pm–2am, Fri 4pm–3am, Sat noon–3am, Sun noon–2am.

★**Mojo** 18 Merrion St ☎0113 244 6387, Ⓦmojobar .co.uk. A great bar with classic tunes ("music for the people" – an eclectic mix with a swerve towards soul), American food, and a classy drinks menu with lots of cocktails. Mon–Thurs 5pm–3am, Fri–Sun 5pm– 4am.

★**Mr Foley's Cask Ale House** 159 The Headrow ☎0113 242 9674. Super Victorian pub near the Town Hall, with several bars on different levels, draught beers listed on a blackboard with strengths and tasting notes, and bottled beers from around the world. Food is served, too, from around a fiver. Mon–Thurs 11am–11pm, Fri & Sat 11am–midnight; Sun noon–7pm.

★**North Bar** 24 New Briggate ☎0113 242 4540, Ⓦnorthbar.com. The city's beer specialist has a massive selection of guest beers (more Belgian than bitter) plus cold meats and cheeses to nibble on. Mon & Tues 11am–1am, Wed–Sat 11am–2am, Sun noon–midnight.

★**Whitelocks** Turk's Head Yard, off Briggate ☎0113 245 3950, Ⓦwhitelocksleeds.com. Leeds' oldest and most atmospheric pub retains its traditional Victorian decor and a good choice of beers. Mon–Thurs 11am–midnight, Fri & Sat 11am–1am, Sun 11am–11.30pm.

NIGHTLIFE

When the pubs close you can move on to one of the city's DJ bars or **clubs**, many of which have a nationwide reputation – not least because Leeds lets you dance until 5am or 6am most weekends. For information about **what's on**, your best bets are the fortnightly listings magazine *The Leeds Guide* (Ⓦleedsguide.co.uk) or the daily *Yorkshire Evening Post*.

Cockpit Bridge House, Swinegate ☎0113 244 1573, Ⓦthecockpit.co.uk. The city's best live music venue, plus assorted indie/new wave club nights.

Hifi 2 Central Rd ☎0113 242 7353, Ⓦthehificlub.co.uk. Small club playing everything from Stax and Motown to hip-hop or drum 'n' bass. Live comedy from top comics.

Mint Club 8 Harrison St ☎0113 244 3168, Ⓦthe mintclub.com. Up-to-the-minute beats (there's a "no-cheese" policy), and the best chill-out space in the city.

Oceana 16–18 Woodhouse Lane ☎0113 243 8229, Ⓦoceanaclubs.com/leeds. Choose between dance, chart, r'n'b and indie in the Venetian Grand Ballroom; 1970s and

1980s disco on Europe's largest illuminated dancefloor; or bars decked out like a Parisian boudoir or ski lodge. Some comedy nights.

The Warehouse 19–21 Somers St ☎0113 234 3535, Ⓦtheleedswarehouse.com. Refurbished in 2010, with a completely new sound system. House, electro and techno bring in clubbers from all over the country, especially for Saturday's Technique night.

Wire 2–8 Call Lane ☎0113 234 0980, Ⓦwireclub .co.uk. A good indie/alternative dance/rock/electronic club associated with *Hifi* (see above) with weekly club nights and individual events.

ENTERTAINMENT

City Varieties Swan St, Briggate ☎0113 243 0808, Ⓦwww.cityvarieties.co.uk. One of the country's last surviving music halls, it hosts a wide range of acts and was from 1953 to 1983 the venue for the TV series "The Good Old Days".

Grand Theatre and Opera House 46 New Briggate ☎0870 121 4901, Ⓦleedsgrandtheatre.com. The regular base of Opera North (Ⓦoperanorth.co.uk) and Northern Ballet (Ⓦnorthernballet.com) also puts on a full

range of theatrical productions.

Hyde Park Picture House Brudenell Rd, Headingley ☎0113 275 2045, Ⓦhydeparkpicturehouse.co.uk. The place to come for classic cinema with independent and arthouse shows alongside more mainstream films; get there on bus #56.

West Yorkshire Playhouse Quarry Hill ☎0113 213 7700, Ⓦwyp.org.uk. The city's most innovative theatre has two stages, plus a bar, restaurant and café.

LEEDS CONCERTS AND FESTIVALS

Temple Newsam, four miles east of the centre (see p.529) hosts numerous concerts and events, from plays to rock gigs and opera. Roundhay Park is the other large outdoor venue for concerts, while Bramham Park, ten miles east of the city, hosts the annual **Leeds Carling Festival** (ⓦleedsfestival.com) at the end of August with rock/indie music on five stages. August bank holiday weekend heralds the **West Indian Carnival** in the Chapeltown area of Leeds.

SHOPPING

Leeds is one of the best cities outside the capital for **shopping**, with numerous independent shops, a throng of classy emporia in the beautifully restored **Victoria Quarter** (ⓦv-q.co.uk) – the "Knightsbridge of the North" – and other arcades that open off **Briggate**. Other options include the shopping complex **The Light** (ⓦthelightleeds.co.uk), the city-centre malls – such as the **Merrion Centre** (ⓦmerrioncentre.co.uk), off Merrion St and the new **Trinity Leeds complex** (ⓦtrinityleeds.com) in Albion Street, not forgetting the eight hundred traders in the Edwardian **Leeds City Markets** in Kirkgate.

Harvey Nichols 107–11 Briggate ☎0113 204 8888, ⓦharveynichols.com/leeds. Harvey Nicks, who opened their first branch outside London here in the Victoria Quarter in 1996, are the lodestone for this chi-chi shopping district. Mon–Wed 10am–6pm, Thurs 10am–8pm, Fri & Sat 10am–7pm, Sun 10.30am–5pm.

Kirkgate Market ⓦleedsmarket.com. The largest covered market in the north of England, housed in a superb Edwardian building. If you're after tripe, haberdashery or big knickers, this is the place to come. Mon–Sat 8am–5.30pm.

Bradford and around

12

BRADFORD has always been a working town, booming in tandem with the Industrial Revolution, when just a few decades saw it transform from a rural seat of woollen manufacture to a polluted metropolis. In its Victorian heyday it was the world's biggest producer of worsted cloth, its skyline etched black with mill chimneys, and its hills clogged with some of the foulest back-to-back houses of any northern city. A look at the Venetian-Gothic **Wool Exchange** building on Market Street, or a walk through **Little Germany**, northeast of the city centre (named for the German wool merchants who populated the area in the second half of the 1800s) provides ample evidence of the wealth of nineteenth-century Bradford.

Contemporary Bradford, perhaps the most multicultural centre in the UK outside London, is valiantly rinsing away its associations with urban decrepitude, and while it can hardly yet be compared with neighbouring Leeds as a visitor attraction, it has two must-see attractions in the **National Media Museum** and the industrial heritage site of **Saltaire**. The major annual event is the **Bradford Mela** (ⓦbradford-mela.info), a one-day celebration of the arts, culture and food of the Indian subcontinent, held in June or July.

National Media Museum

Pictureville • Tues–Sun 10am–6pm • Free, screenings £7.50 • ☎0870 701 0200, ⓦnationalmediamuseum.org.uk

The main interest in the centre of Bradford is provided by the superb **National Media Museum**, which wraps itself around one of Britain's largest cinema screens showing daily **IMAX** and 3D film screenings. Exhibitions are devoted to every nuance of film and television, including topics like digital imaging, light and optics, and computer animation, with fascinating detours into the mechanics of advertising and news-gathering.

Saltaire

3 miles northwest of Bradford towards Keighley • 1853 Gallery Mon–Fri 10am–5.30pm, Sat & Sun 10am–6pm • Free • ☎01274 531163, ⓦsaltmill.org.uk • Trains run from Bradford Forster Square, or take bus #679 from the Interchange

The city's extraordinary outlying attraction of **Saltaire** was a model industrial village

---

TOP 5 MUSEUMS OF SCIENCE AND INDUSTRY

Kelham Island Museum Sheffield.
See p.525
Magna Rotherham. See p.526
National Coal Mining Museum
Wakefield. See p.530

National Media Museum Bradford.
See p.533
National Railway Museum York.
See p.522

---

built by the industrialist Sir Titus Salt. Still inhabited today, the village was constructed between 1851 and 1876, and centred on **Salt's Mill**, which, larger than London's St Paul's Cathedral, was the biggest factory in the world when it opened in 1853. The mill was surrounded by schools, hospitals, parks, almshouses and some 850 homes, yet for all Salt's philanthropic vigour the scheme was highly paternalistic: of the village's 22 streets, for example, all – bar Victoria and Albert streets – were named after members of his family, and although Salt's workers and their families benefited from far better living conditions than their contemporaries elsewhere, they certainly were expected to toe the management line. Salt's Mill remains the fulcrum of the village, the focus of which is the **1853 Gallery**, three floors given over to the world's largest retrospective collection of the works of Bradford-born **David Hockney**.

ARRIVAL AND DEPARTURE
BRADFORD AND AROUND

By train Bradford has two train stations: Bradford Forster Square, just north of the city centre, offers routes to suburbs, towns and cities to the north and west of the city, while Bradford Interchange, off Bridge St, south of the city centre, serves destinations broadly south and west of the city.
Destinations from Bradford Forster Square Ilkley (every 30min; 31min); Keighley (every 30min; 20min); Leeds (every 30min; 22min); Skipton (every 30min; 39min).
Destinations from Bradford Interchange Halifax (every 15min; 12min); Leeds (every 15min; 23min); Manchester

(every 30min; 1hr); Todmorden (every 30min; 35min).
By bus Bradford Interchange is the departure point for regional buses to the rest of West Yorkshire; there's also a National Express coach station here for long-distance services.
Destinations Halifax (every 10min; 40min); Huddersfield (every 20min; 40min); Leeds (every 30min; 30–45min); Liverpool (every 30min–2hr; 3–4hr); London (every 25–90min; 5–6hr); Manchester (every 10min–2hr; 1–2hr); Newcastle (every 2hr; 3hr 30m–4hr 45min); Wakefield (every 20min; 1hr 10min).

GETTING AROUND AND INFORMATION

By bus Bradford's handy free citybus service (Mon–Fri 7am–7pm, every 10min) links the Interchange with Forster Square, Kirkgate, Centenary Square, the National Media Museum, the University and the West End

(📞 0113 245 7676, 🌐 wymetro.com).
Tourist office Britannia House, Broadway (Mon 10am–5pm, Tues–Sat 9am–5pm; 📞 01274 433678, 🌐 visitbradford.com).

EATING

With nearly a quarter of its population having roots in south Asia, Bradford is renowned for its south Asian food shops and restaurants, and was crowned "Curry Capital of England" in 2011. The city boasts literally hundreds of **Indian restaurants**.

Akbar's 1276 Leeds Rd, Thornbury 📞 01274 773311, 🌐 akbars.co.uk. The original in a chain that now has branches across the north of England (and one in Birmingham). It's famed for the quality of its south Asian cuisine, offering a wide range of chicken, lamb and prawn curries and is hugely popular, so at weekends you may end up waiting even when you've booked. Most dishes well under £10. Mon–Fri 5pm–midnight, Sat 4pm–midnight, Sun 2–11.30pm.
★**Mumtaz** 386–410 Great Horton Rd 📞 01274 522533, 🌐 mumtaz.co.uk. *Mumtaz* is probably even

more highly regarded than *Akbar's* (there's another one at Clarence Dock in Leeds), with plaudits from everyone from Dawn French and Amir Khan, through Shilpa Shetty and Frank Bruno, to Queen Elizabeth II herself (or so its website claims). With its delicious Kashmiri food – a range of *karahi* and biryani dishes, with meat, fish and vegetarian options – and smart decor, it's always busy with locals and visitors from all over the country. Remember, though – no alcohol. Expect to pay around £30/person. Mon–Thurs & Sun 11am–midnight, Fri & Sat 11am–1am.

Haworth

Of English literary shrines, probably only Stratford sees more visitors than the quarter of a million who swarm annually into the village of **HAWORTH**, eight miles north of Bradford, to tramp the cobbles once trodden by the Brontë sisters. In summer the village's steep Main Street is lost under huge crowds, herded by multilingual signs around the various stations on the **Brontë trail**. The most popular local walk runs to **Brontë Falls** and **Bridge**, reached via West Lane (a continuation of Main St) and a track from the village, signposted "Bronte Falls", and to **Top Withens**, a mile beyond, a ruin fancifully (and erroneously) thought to be the model for the manor, Wuthering Heights (allow 3hr for the round trip). The moorland setting beautifully evokes the flavour of the book, and to enjoy it further you could walk on another two and a half miles to **Ponden Hall**, claimed by some to be Thrushcross Grange in *Wuthering Heights*.

Brontë Parsonage Museum

Church St • Daily: summer 10am–5.30pm; winter 10am–5pm • £7.50 • ☎ 01535 642323, ⓦ bronte.org.uk

First stop in Haworth should be the **Brontë Parsonage Museum**, a modest Georgian house bought by Patrick Brontë in 1820 and in which he planned to bring up his family. After the tragic early loss of his wife and two eldest daughters, the surviving four children – Anne, Emily, Charlotte and their dissipated brother, Branwell – spent most of their short lives in the place, which is furnished as it was in their day, and filled with the sisters' pictures, books, manuscripts and personal treasures. The **parish church** in front of the parsonage contains the family vault; Charlotte was married here in 1854.

ARRIVAL AND INFORMATION   HAWORTH

By train The nicest way of getting to Haworth is on the steam trains of the Keighley and Worth Valley Railway (Easter week, school hols, July & Aug daily; rest of the year Sat & Sun; day rover ticket £15; ☎ 01535 645214, ⓦ kwvr .co.uk); regular trains from Leeds or from Bradford's Forster Square station run to Keighley, from where the steam train takes 15min to Haworth.

By bus Bus #662 from Bradford Interchange runs to Keighley (every 10min; 50min); change there for the #663, #664 (not Sun) or #665 (every 20–30min; 16–24min).
Tourist office 2–4 West Lane (daily: April–Sept 10am 5pm; Oct–March 10am–4pm, except Wed from 10.30am); ☎ 01535 642329, ⓦ haworth-village.org.uk).

ACCOMMODATION AND EATING

Apothecary 86 Main St ☎ 01535 643642, ⓦ the apothecaryguesthouse.co.uk. Traditional guesthouse opposite the church, in a seventeenth-century building with oak beams, millstone grit walls and quaint passages. The rear rooms, breakfast room and attached café have moorland views. £55
Wilsons of Haworth 15 West Lane ☎ 01535 643209, ⓦ wilsonsofhaworth.co.uk. Top-end B&B with all the bells and whistles you might expect in a quality boutique

hotel; its five luxurious rooms (four doubles and a single), are in a converted row of weavers' cottages within sight of the Bronte museum. £89
YHA Haworth A mile from the centre at Longlands Hall, Lees Lane, off the Keighley road ☎ 0845 371 9520, ⓦ yha.org.uk. YHA hostel overlooking the village; Bradford buses stop on the main road nearby. Closed Mon–Fri Nov to mid-Feb. Dorms £15; doubles £49

12

The Yorkshire Dales

The **Yorkshire Dales** – "dales" from the Viking word *dalr* (valley) – form a varied upland area of limestone hills and pastoral valleys at the heart of the Pennines. Protected as a National Park (or, in the case of Nidderdale, as an Area of Outstanding Natural Beauty), there are more than twenty main dales covering 680 square miles, crammed with opportunities for outdoor activities. Most approaches are from the south, via the superbly engineered **Settle to Carlisle Railway**, or along the main A65 road from towns such as **Skipton**, **Settle** and **Ingleton**. Southern dales like **Wharfedale** are the most visited, while neighbouring **Malhamdale** is also immensely popular due to the fascinating scenery squeezed into its narrow confines around **Malham** village. **Ribblesdale** is more sombre, its villages popular with hikers intent on tackling the famous **Three Peaks** – the mountains of Pen-y-ghent, Ingleborough and Whernside. To the northwest lies the more remote **Dentdale**, one of the least known but most beautiful of the valleys, and further north still **Wensleydale** and **Swaledale**, the latter of which rivals Dentdale as the most rewarding overall target. Both flow east, with Swaledale's lower stretches encompassing the appealing historic town of **Richmond**.

GETTING AROUND AND INFORMATION   THE YORKSHIRE DALES

On foot The Pennine Way cuts right through the heart of the Dales, and the region is crossed by the Coast-to-Coast Walk, but the principal local route is the 84-mile Dales Way (ⓦ dalesway.org.uk). Shorter guided walks (5–13 miles; April–Oct Sun & bank hols £3) are organized by the National Park Authority and Dalesbus Ramblers (ⓦ dalesbusramblers.org.uk).

By bike The Dales has a network of over 500 miles of bridleways, byways and other routes for mountain bikers (ⓦ mtbthedales.org.uk). The main touring cycle route is the

circular 130-mile Yorkshire Dales Cycle Way (ⓦ cyclethedales .org.uk), which starts and finishes in Skipton.

By public transport Bus timetables (ⓦ dalesbus.org) are available at tourist offices across the region, as are *Dales Explorer* timetable booklets, or consult ⓦ traveldales.org.uk.

National Park Centres There are useful National Park Centres (ⓦ yorkshiredales.org.uk) at Grassington, Aysgarth Falls, Malham, Reeth and Hawes (April–Oct daily 10am– 5pm; Nov–March Sat & Sun 10am–4pm; closed Jan, except for Hawes which is open all year).

12 Skipton

Skipton (Anglo-Saxon for "sheep town") sits on the Dales' southern edge, at the intersection of the two routes that cradle the National Park and Area of Outstanding Natural Beauty – the A65 to the western and the A59/61 to the eastern dales. A pleasant market town with a long history, it is defined by its **castle** and **church**, by its long, wide and sloping **High Street**, and by a **water system** that includes the Leeds and Liverpool Canal, its spur the Springs Canal and the Eller Beck.

ARRIVAL AND INFORMATION   SKIPTON

By train Trains run from/to Leeds (every 30min–2hr; 54min) and Bradford (every 30min; 49min), and there's a daily service to London (every 30min; 3hr 10min with one change). The train is by far the best way of getting to Dentdale/Ribblesdale: Dent (every 2hr; 46min); Settle (every 30min–1hr 25min; 30min–1hr).

By bus Buses run from Skipton up Wharfedale towards

Buckden (every 2hr; 1hr), to Malham (every 2–3hr; 35min) and Settle (every 2hr; around 40–50min). Links to the rest of the Dales are more difficult, and usually involve using trains and/or changing buses.

Tourist office Town Hall, High Street (Mon–Sat 9.30am–4pm, first Sun in the month 10am–4pm; ☎ 01756 792809, ⓦ cravendc.gov.uk).

ACCOMMODATION AND EATING

Herriot's Hotel Broughton Rd ☎ 01756 792781, ⓦ herriotsforleisure.co.uk. A short walk along the canal towpath from the centre of Skipton, in a Victorian listed building, the boutique-style hotel and its restaurant, *Rhubarb*, both offer cheerful decor and lots of original features. Rooms vary in size and price, and there are frequent packages available. **£125**

The Woolly Sheep Inn 38 Sheep St ☎ 01756 700966,

ⓦ woollysheepinn.co.uk. Pleasant town centre Timothy Taylor tavern which offers a good range of pub food (from £8) along with sandwiches, steaks and pasta dishes. The nine rooms are comfortable and well furnished, though some are small. Convivial, but can be noisy. Mon–Wed 10am–11pm, Thurs 10am–midnight, Fri & Sat 10am–1am, Sun noon–11pm; food served Mon–Fri & Sun 11.30am–9pm, Sat 11.30am–8pm. **£80**

Ilkley

The small town of **ILKLEY** holds a special place in the iconography of Yorkshire out of all proportion to its size, largely because it's the setting of the county's unofficial anthem *On Ilkley Moor baht 'at*. Vibrant and stylish, Ilkley has plenty to see, including an interesting church, a couple of museums and enough top-end shops, bars and restaurants to keep visiting urbanites happy

All Saints Church

Church St • Office hours Mon, Tues & Thurs 9.15am–1.15pm, Wed 10–11.30am, Fri 9.15am–12.30pm; ☎ 01943 431126

Ilkley's parish church, **All Saints**, was established in AD 627 by King Edwin of Northumbria and Bishop Paulinus of York, whose carved heads you can see in the entrance porch. Inside, highlights include three impressive eighth-century Saxon crosses, a family pew dating from 1633 and a Norman font made of Ilkley Moor stone with a seventeenth-century font cover complete with pulley and counterweight for raising and lowering it.

Manor House Museum

Castle Yard, Church St • Tues 1–5pm, Wed–Sat 11am–5pm, Sun 1–4pm • Free • ☎ 01943 600066

Tucked in just behind All Saints Church, the **Manor House Museum** stands on the site of an original Roman fort (you can see a section of the Roman wall at the rear of the building). The museum contains a collection of Roman artefacts from the fort and surrounding area, and exhibits and information about Ilkley's prehistory and its growth as a Victorian spa town.

Ilkley Moor

A 20min walk from the town centre

Dominating Ilkley's southern skyline is its famous **moor**, somehow smaller yet more forbidding than you might expect. Far from being a remote wilderness, it is very much part of the town's fabric: a place where people can walk, climb or ponder the immensities of time reflected in its ancient rock formations and prehistoric markings. Look out for the Swastika Stone, the Twelve Apostles, the famous Cow and Calf, and a host of cup-and-ring marked rocks. Excellent **information** boards adorn the moor's car parks, and there's more information available at the White Wells Spa Cottage Visitor Centre (Sat & Sun 2–5pm, ☎ 01943 608035), on Wells Road, up on the moor.

ARRIVAL AND INFORMATION ILKLEY

By train Ilkley station, in Station Plaza in the town centre, is the terminus of a line which links the town to Leeds and Bradford (every 30min; 31min).

By bus The bus station is next to the train station. Destinations Bolton Abbey (every 2hr; 17min); Leeds (every 30min; 1hr); Malham (6 daily; 1hr 10min); Skipton (6 daily; 30min)

Tourist office Station Road (April–Sept Mon–Sat 9.30am–4.30pm; Oct–March Mon–Sat 10am–4pm, Tues from 10.30am; ☎ 01943 602319, ⓦ visitilkley.com).

EATING AND DRINKING

Bar t'at Ale and Wine Bar 7 Cunliffe Rd ☎ 01943 608888. With an irresistible name, a huge selection of wines and beers and a good atmosphere, this place also offers a decent range of light lunches, sandwiches, and main meals (£9.50–12.50). The toilets need upgrading, though. Daily noon–11pm; food served Mon–Fri noon–2.30pm & 5.30–9pm, Sat noon–9pm, Sun noon–6pm.

★**The Box Tree** 35–37 Church St ☎ 01943 608484, ⓦ theboxtree.co.uk. One of Yorkshire's handful of Michelin-starred restaurants, offering inventive modern French cuisine in mellow surroundings. There are fixed-price menus at £30 (lunch), £40 (dinner), £60 (called À la carte, though it's not) and £75 (Gourmand). Wed 7–9.30pm, Thurs–Sat noon–2pm & 7–9.30pm, Sun noon–3.30pm.

★**The Flying Duck** 16 Church St ☎ 01943 609587. Occupying the town's oldest pub building, this real ale pub sports old stone walls, beamed ceilings and stone-flagged and wooden-floored rooms. Also has its own brewery in a barn at the rear. Mon–Thurs 11am–11pm, Fri & Sat noon–midnight, Sun noon–11pm.

Piccolino 31–33 Brook St ☎ 01943 605827, ⓦ individualrestaurants.com. Large Italian restaurant in the centre of Ilkley, one of a chain across the country. The star attraction is a roof terrace with terrific views across the town and (this is England after all) a retractable roof and space heaters. Good food (mains around £16–23) and staff helpful. Mon–Sat 10am–11pm, Sun 10am–1.30pm.

12

Wharfedale

The River Wharfe runs south from just below Wensleydale, eventually joining the Ouse south of York. The best of **Wharfedale** starts just east of Skipton at **Bolton Abbey**, and then continues north in a broad, pastoral sweep scattered with villages as picture-perfect as any in northern England. The popular walking centre of **Grassington** is the main village.

Bolton Abbey

BOLTON ABBEY, five miles east of Skipton, is the name of a whole village rather than an abbey, a confusion compounded by the fact that the place's main monastic ruin is known as **Bolton Priory** (daily 9am–dusk; free; ☏01756 710238, ⓦboltonpriory.org .uk). The priory is the starting point for several popular riverside **walks**, including a section of the **Dales Way** footpath that follows the river's west bank to take in Bolton Woods and the **Strid** (from "stride"), an extraordinary piece of white water two miles north of the abbey, where softer rock has allowed the river to funnel into a cleft just a few feet wide. Beyond the Strid, the path emerges at **Barden Bridge**, four miles from the priory, where **Barden Tower** shelters a tearoom.

ARRIVAL AND INFORMATION — BOLTON ABBEY

By train For the loveliest approach to Bolton Abbey, take the Embsay and Bolton Abbey Steam Railway – the station is 1.5 miles by footpath from the priory ruins. The trains (late July and Aug 5 daily; rest of year schedule varies, check website; day rover £9; ☏01756 710614 or ☏795189, ⓦembsayboltonabbeyrailway.org.uk) start from Embsay, 2 miles east of Skipton – the trip from Embsay to Bolton Abbey takes 15min.

Tourist information The main source of information is the estate office (Bolton Abbey, ☏01756 718009, ⓦboltonabbey.com) and there's an information point at Cavendish Pavilion, a mile north of Bolton Abbey.

ACCOMMODATION AND EATING

Cavendish Pavilion ☏01756 710245, ⓦcavendish pavilion.co.uk. A riverside restaurant and café, a mile north of Bolton Priory serving roasts, casseroles and the like at good prices. March–Oct daily 10am–5pm; Nov–Feb Mon–Fri 10am–4pm.

Grassington

GRASSINGTON is Wharfedale's main village, nine miles from Bolton Abbey. The cobbled Market Square is home to several inns, a few giftshops and, in a converted lead miner's cottage, a small **Folk Museum** (April–Oct Tues–Sun 2–4.30pm; free; ☏01756 753287, ⓦgrassingtonfolkmuseum.org.uk) filled with domestic equipment and artefacts relating to local crafts and farming.

ARRIVAL AND INFORMATION — GRASSINGTON

By bus #72/72R buses to Grassington run roughly hourly (not Sun in winter) from Skipton (33min) and then, six times a day, on up the B6160 to Kettlewell, Starbotton and Buckden in upper Wharfedale.

National Park Centre Hebden Road, across from the bus stop (April–Oct daily 10am–5pm; for winter hours, check with centre; ☏01756 751690, ⓦyorkshiredales.org.uk).

ACCOMMODATION AND EATING

★**Angel Barn Lodgings/Angel Inn** Hetton, 4 miles southwest of Grassington ☏01756 730263, ⓦangel hetton.co.uk. The Dales' gastropub par excellence has five immaculate rooms and suites. Over the road in the inn, Modern British food is served either in the bar/brasserie or more formal restaurant. Brasserie daily noon–1.45pm & 6–9.30pm; restaurant Mon–Sat 6–9.30pm, Sun noon–1.45pm. £150

Ashfield House Summers Fold ☏01756 752584, ⓦashfieldhouse.co.uk. Lovely seventeenth-century house, off the square, with a walled garden. The owner is very knowledgeable about the area. Special room rate offers are often available. Dinner is served, mainly to guests, for £36/person. £100

★**Grassington Lodge** 8 Wood Lane ☏01756 752518, ⓦgrassingtonlodge.co.uk. A splash of contemporary style – coordinated fabrics, hardwood floors, Dales photographs – together with a pleasant front terrace enhance this comfortable village guesthouse. £90

12

Upper Wharfedale

KETTLEWELL (Norse for "bubbling spring") is the main centre for **upper Wharfedale**, with plenty of local B&B accommodation plus a youth hostel. It was also one of the major locations for *Calendar Girls*, the based-on-a-true-story film of doughty Yorkshire ladies who bared all for a charity calendar.

ARRIVAL AND DEPARTURE   UPPER WHARFEDALE

By bus There's a Sun and bank hol bus service (#800) from Leeds to Hawes, connecting the top end of Wharfedale with Wensleydale, via Ilkley, Grassington and Kettlewell, among other stops. It takes 3hr 10min for the whole trip, and 1hr 5min from Kettlewell to Hawes.

ACCOMMODATION AND EATING

Blue Bell Inn Kettlewell ☎01756 760230, ⓦbluebellkettlewell.co.uk. Pretty seventeenth-century coaching inn that's very much a traditional pub and serves good, no-nonsense pub grub (lasagne, meat and potato pie and the like; main courses £10–15). Mon–Thurs & Sun noon–10.30pm, Fri & Sat noon–11pm; food served noon–5pm & 6–9pm. **£80**

Racehorses Hotel Kettlewell ☎01756 760233, ⓦracehorseshotel.co.uk. Comfortable, recently refurbished hotel in what was once the *Blue Bell Inn*'s stables. The food is a cut above your standard bar food (home-made paté, for example, or rare-breed belly pork); main courses start at £11. Daily noon–2pm & 6–9pm. **£90**

Malhamdale

A few miles west of Wharfedale lies **Malhamdale**, one of the National Park's most heavily visited regions, thanks to its three outstanding natural features of **Malham Cove**, **Malham Tarn** and **Gordale Scar**. All three attractions are within easy hiking distance of **Malham village**.

12

Malham

MALHAM village is home to barely a couple of hundred people who inhabit the huddled stone houses on either side of a bubbling river. Appearing in spectacular fashion a mile to the north, the white-walled limestone amphitheatre of **Malham Cove** rises 300ft above its surroundings. After a breath-sapping haul to the top, you are rewarded with fine views and the famous limestone pavement, an expanse of clints (slabs) and grykes (clefts) created by water seeping through weaker lines in the limestone rock. A simple walk (or summer shuttle-bus ride) over the moors abruptly brings **Malham Tarn** into sight, its waterfowl protected by a nature reserve on the west bank. Meanwhile, at **Gordale Scar** (also easily approached direct from Malham village), the cliffs are if anything more spectacular than at Malham Cove. The classic circuit takes in cove, tarn and scar in a clockwise **walk from Malham** (8 miles; 3hr 30min).

ARRIVAL AND INFORMATION   MALHAM

By bus Malham village is served year-round by bus from Skipton (3 daily; 35min) and the seasonal Malham Tarn shuttle (Easter–Oct Sun & bank hols 4 daily; 25min) which runs between Settle and the National Park Centre.
National Park Centre At the southern edge of the village (April–Oct daily 10am–5pm; for winter hours, check with centre; ☎01729 833200, ⓦyorkshiredales .org.uk).
Website A good online source of tourist information is ⓦmalhamdale.com.

ACCOMMODATION AND EATING

★**Buck Inn** Cove Road ☎01729 830317, ⓦbuckinn malham.co.uk. Pleasant pub popular with walkers. With good, locally sourced food – especially sausages, pies and steaks (main courses £10–22) – comfortable rooms, and a relaxed attitude to muddy boots, this is the ideal base for a walking holiday. Daily noon–3pm & 6–9pm. **£80**

Miresfield Farm Across the river from the Buck Inn and Lister Arms ☎01729 830414, ⓦmiresfield-farm .com. The first house in the village, by the river, with lovely rural views. The country-pine-bedecked rooms vary in size, and there's a small campsite with toilet and shower. Breakfast available. **£64**

YHA Malham Centre of village, next to the Lister Arms pub ☎0845 371 9529, ⓦyha.org.uk. A purpose-built hostel that's a good bet for families and serious walkers. Open all year. Office open 7–10am & 5–10.30pm. Dorms £13; doubles £49

Ribblesdale

The river Ribble runs south along the western edges of the Yorkshire Dales, starting in the bleak uplands near the Ribblehead Viaduct, flowing between two of Yorkshire's highest mountains, **Ingleborough** and **Pen-y-ghent**, and through the village of **Horton in Ribblesdale** and on to **Settle**, the upper dale's principal town.

Settle

Ribblesdale, west of Malhamdale, is entered from **SETTLE**, starting point of the **Settle to Carlisle Railway** (see box opposite). The small town has a typical seventeenth-century market square (market day Tues), still sporting its split-level arcaded shambles, which once housed butchers' shops, and the **Museum of North Craven Life** (April–Oct Tues 10.30am–4.30pm & Thurs–Sun 12.30–4.30pm; £2.50; ☎01524 251388) housed in the eccentric Folly, dating from the 1670s and earning its name from the strange combination of styles, and the curiously upside-down look created by the fact that there are far more windows on the ground floor than on the first and second – it seems surprising that it hasn't fallen down. The museum contains fairly random odds and ends from the history of the town, and that of the construction of the Settle to Carlisle railway.

ARRIVAL AND INFORMATION

SETTLE

By train The train station, less than a 5min walk from Market Place, down Station Road, is served by the famous Settle to Carlisle railway, one of the most scenic lines in Britain (see box opposite).

By bus Regular #58 buses connect Settle with Skipton (2 daily; 46min); #11 buses go north to Horton-in-Ribblesdale (Mon–Sat every 2hr; 21min); while #581

(every 2hr; 31min) runs to the western Dales. The Malham Tarn shuttle (Dalesbus #881; Easter–Oct Sun & bank hols 4 daily) makes a stop at Settle en route to Malham (25min) and Ingleton (25min).

Tourist information In the town hall, just off Market Place (Mon–Sat 9.30am–4pm; ☎01729 825192). They can provide hiking maps and pamphlets.

ACCOMMODATION AND EATING

The Lion Duke St ☎01729 822203, ⓦthelionsettle .co.uk. Offers comfortable rooms (which cost around £27 more at weekends) and a wide range of locally sourced fish, meats, pies and sausages, with a fine choice of cheeses (mains £7.95–17.95). Mon–Thurs 8am–10pm, Fri & Sat 8am–10.30pm, Sun 8am–9pm. £95

Ye Olde Naked Man Café Market Place ☎01729 823230. For non-alcoholic drinks and good plain food this café is the best bet. Don't be put off by the twee name – the building was once an undertaker's, and the name is a reference to the old Yorkshire saying, "you bring now't into't world and you take now't out". Mon, Tues & Thurs–Sun 9am–5pm, Wed 9am–4pm.

Horton in Ribblesdale

The valley's only village of any size is **HORTON IN RIBBLESDALE**, a noted walking centre which is the usual starting point for the famous **Three Peaks Walk** – namely the 25-mile, 12-hour circuit of Pen-y-ghent (2273ft), Whernside (2416ft) – Yorkshire's highest point – and Ingleborough (2373ft).

ARRIVAL AND INFORMATION

HORTON IN RIBBLESDALE

By bus The #11 service from Settle runs every 2hr (20min).

Tourist and hiking information The *Pen-y-ghent Café* (see opposite) doubles as a tourist office and an unofficial headquarters for the Three Peaks walk. They operate a clocking in/clocking out system; walkers who complete the

route within a 12hr period become eligible to join the Three Peaks of Yorkshire Club. They no longer provide automatic back-up should walkers fail to return - this safety service is temporarily suspended. Opening hours are complicated, so phone to check.

12

THE SETTLE TO CARLISLE RAILWAY

The 72-mile **Settle to Carlisle** line – hailed by some as "England's most scenic railway" – is a feat of Victorian railway engineering that has few equals in Britain. In particular, between Horton and Ribblehead, the line climbs 200ft in five miles, before crossing the famous 24-arched **Ribblehead viaduct** and disappearing into the 2629yd Blea Tunnel. Meanwhile, the station at **Dent Head** is the highest, and bleakest, mainline station in England. The journey from Settle to Carlisle takes 1hr 40min, so it's easy to do the full **return trip** in one day (£40.60). If you're short of time, ride the most dramatic section between Settle and Garsdale (30min). There are connections to Settle from Skipton (20min) and Leeds (1hr); full **timetable** details are available from National Rail Enquiries (☎0845 748 4950) or on ⊛ settle-carlisle.co.uk.

EATING

Pen-y-ghent Café ☎01729 860333. A local institution for more than forty years, not only supplying much-needed hot drinks, snacks and meals, but also information and advice to walkers. Roughly Feb half-term hols to mid-Oct

Mon & Wed–Fri 9am–5.30pm, Sat 8am–6pm, Sun 8.30am–5.30pm; closed mid-Oct to Boxing Day; Jan & Feb hours vary.

The western Dales

The western Dales is a term of convenience for a couple of tiny dales running north from **Ingleton**, and for **Dentdale**, one of the loveliest valleys in the National Park. Ingleton has the most accommodation, but **Dent** is by far the best target for a quiet night's retreat, with a cobbled centre barely altered in centuries.

12

Ingleton and around

The straggling slate-grey village of **INGLETON** sits upon a ridge at the confluence of two streams, the Twiss and the Doe, whose beautifully wooded valleys are easily the area's best features. The 4.5-mile **Falls' Walk** (daily 9am–dusk; entrance fee £6; ☎01524 241930, ⊛ ingletonwaterfallstrail.co.uk) is a lovely circular walk (2hr 30min) taking in both valleys, and providing viewing points over its waterfalls.

Just 1.5 miles out of Ingleton on the Ribblehead/Hawes road (B6255) is the entrance to the **White Scar Cave** (Feb–Oct daily 10am–5pm; Nov–Jan Sat & Sun same hours, weather permitting; £9.50; ☎01524 241244, ⊛ whitescarcave.co.uk). It's worth every penny for the tour (1hr 20min) of dank underground chambers, contorted cave formations and glistening stalactites.

ARRIVAL AND INFORMATION INGLETON AND AROUND

By bus Buses stop at the tourist information centre: the #80 runs from/to Lancaster (every 30min; 1hr 10min) and the #581 and #881 from/to Settle (every 30min; 25min).

Tourist office Community Centre car park, Main Street (Easter–Sept daily 10am–4.30pm, Nov–March 11am–3pm; ☎01524 241049, ☎ visitingleton.co.uk).

ACCOMMODATION AND EATING

The Inglesport Café Main St ☎01524 241146. On the first floor of a hiking supplies store, this café dishes up hearty soups, and potatoes with everything. Mon–Fri 9am–5pm, Sat & Sun 8.30am–5.30pm.
Riverside Lodge 24 Main St ☎01524 241359, ⊛ river sideingleton.co.uk. Clean and tidy, with eight bedrooms decorated individually (if a little fussily) and named after

flowers. There's a small sauna and play room, and an optional evening meal at £16.50. **£66**
YHA Ingleton Sammy Lane ☎015242 41444, ⊛ yha .org.uk. This YHA hostel is in an attractively restored Victorian stone house, set in its own gardens, close to the village centre. Reception 7–10am & 5–11pm. Dorms **£21**; doubles **£49**

Dentdale

In the seventeenth and eighteenth centuries, **Dentdale** supported a flourishing hand-knitting industry, later ruined by mechanization. These days, the hill-farming community supplements its income through tourism and craft ventures, and in **DENT** village itself the main road soon gives way to grassy cobbles.

ARRIVAL AND INFORMATION   DENTDALE

By train While the famous Settle to Carlisle railway (see box, p.541) might seem a good alternative to the bus, be warned that Dent station is over 4 miles from the village itself.

By bus Most of Dent's bus connections are with towns outside Yorkshire – Sedbergh (April–Oct 5 daily; 15min),

Kirkby Stephen and Kendal (Sat 1 daily; 50min) – though there is a service to Settle.

Tourist information Dentdale Heritage Centre, Dent (daily 11am–4pm; ☎01539 625800, ⓦ dentvillage heritagecentre.com). A useful website is ⓦ dentdale.com.

ACCOMMODATION, EATING AND DRINKING

★**George & Dragon** Dent centre ☎01539 625256, ⓦ thegeorgeanddragondent.co.uk. Opposite the fountain in the centre of the village, the *George & Dragon* is bigger and more expensive than the nearby *Sun*, with ten comfortable rooms (though some are small), good service

and a convivial bar. There's an extensive menu of traditional pub food with a twist (try, for example, the "steak and t'owd tup pie") – mains cost between £10.95 and £17.25. Daily 11am–11pm; food served June–Oct 6–9.30pm, Nov–May 6–8.30pm. **£90**

Wensleydale

The best known of the Dales, if only for its cheese, **Wensleydale** is also the largest. With numerous towns and villages, the biggest and busiest being **Hawes**, it has plenty of appeal to non-walkers, too; many of its rural attractions will be familiar to devotees of the **James Herriott** books and TV series.

Hawes

HAWES is Wensleydale's chief town, main hiking centre, and home to its tourism, cheese and rope-making industries. It also claims to be Yorkshire's highest market town; it received its market charter in 1699, and the weekly Tuesday market is still going strong. In the same building as the National Park Centre (see opposite), the recently revamped **Dales Countryside Museum** (April–Oct daily 10am–5pm; closed Jan; for winter hours phone ahead; £4; ☎01969 666210, ⓦ dalescountrysidemuseum.org.uk) focuses on local trades and handicrafts. Another attraction is the **Wensleydale Creamery** on Gayle Lane, a little way south of the town centre (Mon–Fri 9.30am–4pm, Sat & Sun 9.30am–4.30pm; winter hours vary, phone to check; £2.50; ☎01969 667664, ⓦ wensleydale.co.uk). The first cheese in Wensleydale was made by medieval Cistercian monks from ewes' milk; after the Dissolution local farmers made a version from cows' milk which, by the 1840s, was being marketed as "Wensleydale" cheese. The Creamery doesn't make cheese every day, so call first.

Askrigg

The mantle of "Herriot country" lies heavy on **ASKRIGG**, six miles east of Hawes, as the TV series *All Creatures Great and Small* was filmed in and around the village. Nip into the *King's Arms* on Main Street, where you can see stills from the TV series.

HERE FOR THE BEER

If you're a beer fan, the handsome Wensleydale market town of **Masham** (pronounced Mass'm) is an essential point of pilgrimage. At **Theakston brewery** (tours daily July & Aug 11am–4pm; Jan–June & Sept–Dec 11am–3pm; £6.95, reservations advised; ☎01765 680000, ⓦ theakstons.co.uk), sited here since 1827, you can learn the arcane intricacies of the brewer's art and become familiar with the legendary Old Peculier ale. The **Black Sheep Brewery**, set up in the early 1990s by one of the Theakston family brewing team, also offers tours (daily 11am–4pm, evening tours Thurs & Fri, but call for availability; £6.95; ☎01765 680100, ⓦ blacksheepbrewery.com). Both are just a few minutes' signposted walk out of the centre.

Aysgarth

The ribbon-village of **AYSGARTH**, straggling along and off the A684, sucks in Wensleydale's largest number of visitors due to its proximity to the **Aysgarth Falls**, half a mile below. A marked nature trail runs through the surrounding woodlands and there's a big car park and excellent **National Park Centre** on the north bank of the River Ure (see below).

Bolton Castle

Castle Bolton village • Feb–March daily 10am–4pm; April–Oct 10am–5pm (restricted winter opening, call for details) • £8.50, gardens only £3 • ☎ 01969 623981, ⓦ boltoncastle.co.uk

The foursquare battlements of **Bolton Castle** are visible from miles away. Completed in 1399, its Great Chamber, a few adjacent rooms and the castle gardens have been restored, and there's also a café that's a welcome spot if you've hiked here – a superb circular **walk** (6 miles; 4hr) heads northeast from Aysgarth via Castle Bolton village, starting at Aysgarth Falls and climbing up through Thoresby.

ARRIVAL AND GETTING AROUND   WENSLEYDALE

By bus The #156 route runs along Wensleydale from Leyburn to Hawes (every 2hr; 50 min), calling at Aysgarth and Bolton Castle. Less frequently, the #59 runs once a day along a similar route (1 daily; 4/min). The Little White Bus runs from Hawes to Garsdale (2–4 daily; 23min). A post bus service runs between Hawes and Northallerton (Mon–Fri 3 daily; 1hr 45min). There's also a summer Sun and bank hol service (#800) connecting Hawes to Leeds (3hr).

INFORMATION

Tourist information There are National Park Centres at Hawes Dales Countryside Museum, Station Yard (daily 10am–5pm; closed Jan, for winter hours, check with centre; ☎ 01969 666210; ⓦ yorkshiredales.org.uk) and at Aysgarth, by the river (April–Oct daily 10am–5pm; for winter hours check with centre; ☎ 01969 662910). A useful website is ⓦ wensleydale.org.

ACCOMMODATION AND EATING

Herriot's Main St, Hawes ☎ 01969 667536, ⓦ herriotsinhawes.co.uk. Small, friendly guesthouse in an eighteenth-century building off the market square. There are just six rooms – some of which have fell views. Good hearty breakfasts are cooked to order. **£79**
Herriot's Kitchen Main St, Hawes ☎ 01969 667536, ⓦ herriotsinhawes.co.uk. Light lunches, Yorkshire cream teas and a variety of cakes, together with their own preserves made on the premises. Easter–Nov Mon, Tues &

Thurs–Sat 10am–4.30pm, Sun 11am–4.30pm; Nov–March Tues, Sat & Sun same hours.
The Old Dairy Farm Widdale, 3 miles west of Hawes ☎ 01969 667070, ⓦ olddairyfarm.co.uk. Once the home of the original Wensleydale dairy herd, this farm offers luxurious and contemporary accommodation, with fine dining available (main courses around £15). While nonresidents are welcome to dine, there are no fixed opening hours – it is essential to phone first. **£140**

Swaledale

Narrow and steep-sided in its upper reaches beyond the tiny village of Keld, **Swaledale** emerges rocky and rugged in its central tract around Thwaite and Muker before more typically pastoral scenery cuts in at **REETH**, the dale's main village and market centre (market day is Fri). Its desirable cottages sit around a triangular green, where you'll find a couple of pubs, a hotel, a **National Park Centre** (see p.544) and the **Swaledale Museum** (May–Oct daily 10am–5pm; £3; ☎ 01748 884118, ⓦ swaledalemuseum.org), containing an interesting hotchpotch of material on the geology, industry, domestic life and people of the valley. Downriver, the dale opens out into broad countryside and the splendid historic town of **Richmond**.

Richmond

RICHMOND is the Dales' single most tempting destination, thanks mainly to its magnificent **castle**, whose extensive walls and colossal keep cling to a precipice above the River Swale. Indeed, the entire town is an absolute gem, centred on a huge cobbled market square backed by Georgian buildings, hidden alleys and gardens. Market day is Saturday, augmented by a farmers' market on the third Saturday of the month.

Richmond Castle

Riverside Rd • April–Sept daily 10am–6pm; Oct–Nov daily 10am–5pm; Nov–March Sat & Sun 10am–4pm • £4.90; EH • ☎ 01748 822493, ⓦ english-heritage.org.uk

Most of medieval Richmond sprouted around its **castle**, which, dating from around 1071, is one of the oldest Norman stone fortresses in Britain. The star turn is, without doubt, the massive **keep** – which was built between 1150 and 1180 – with its stone staircases, spacious main rooms and fine battlements. From the top, the **views** down into the town, across the turbulent Swale and out across the gentle countryside, are out of this world. For more splendid views, with the river roaring below, take a stroll along Castle Walk, around the outside of the curtain walls.

Richmondshire Museum

Ryder's Wynd, off the Victoria Rd roundabout at the top of King St • April–Oct daily 10.30am–4.30pm • £3 • ☎ 01748 825611, ⓦ richmondshiremuseum.org.uk

For a fascinating chunk of Richmond history, visit the charming **Richmondshire Museum**, off the northern side of the market square. It's full of local treasures, covering subjects as varied as lead mining and toys through the ages, with reconstructed houses and shops recreating village life, and even the set from the TV series *All Creatures Great and Small*.

Theatre Royal

Victoria Rd • Tours mid-Feb to mid-Dec Mon–Sat 10am–4pm, on the hour; suggested £3.50 donation • ☎ 01748 825252, ⓦ georgiantheatreroyal.co.uk

Richmond's tiny Georgian **Theatre Royal** (1788) has the diminutive feel of a toy theatre made from a shoe box. One of England's oldest theatres, it features a sunken pit with boxes on three sides and a gallery above; it is open for both performances and tours.

Easby Abbey

A mile southeast of the town • April–Sept daily 10am–6pm; Oct daily 10am–5pm; Nov–March daily 10am–4pm • Free; EH • ⓦ english-heritage.org.uk

A signposted walk runs along the north bank of the River Swale out to the golden stone walls of **Easby Abbey**. The evocative ruins are extensive, and in places – notably the thirteenth-century refectory – still remarkably intact.

ARRIVAL AND INFORMATION   SWALEDALE

By train There are regular services into Wensleydale and lower Swaledale on the heritage Wensleydale Railway from Leeming to Redmire, and to Darlington, 10 miles to the northeast, on the main east-coast train line.

By bus The main transport hub is Richmond, where buses stop in the market square. Bus #159 runs between Masham, Leyburn and Richmond, while bus #30 (infrequent, not Sun) runs up the valley along the B6270 as far as Keld, 8 miles north of Hawes and at the crossroads of the Pennine Way and the Coast-to-Coast path.

Destinations from Richmond Leyburn (hourly; 25 min); Masham (Mon–Sat hourly; 55min); Ripon (Mon–Sat hourly; 1hr 15min).

Tourist office 2 Queens Road, Richmond (daily 9.30am–5.30pm; ☎ 01748 850549, ⓦ richmond.org.uk).

National Park Centre Hudson House, Reeth (April–Oct daily 10am–5pm; Nov, Dec, Feb & March Sat & Sun 10am–4pm; ☎ 01748 884059).

ACCOMMODATION AND EATING

RICHMOND

Frenchgate Hotel 59–61 Frenchgate ☎ 01748 822087, ⓦ thefrenchgate.co.uk. Georgian townhouse hotel with eight rooms and walled gardens. Its food (set menu £39) has an excellent reputation – spiced loin of Yorkshire rabbit, for example, or Reg's duck breast. Breakfast Mon–Fri 7.30–9.30am, Sat & Sun 8–10am, lunch daily noon–2pm, dinner daily 6–9.30pm. **£118**

Frenchgate House 66 Frenchgate ☎01748 823421, ⓦ66frenchgate.co.uk. Three immaculately presented rooms, plus breakfast with the best – panoramic – view in town. **£85**

★**Millgate House** Millgate ☎01748 823571, ⓦmillgatehouse.com. Shut the big green door of this Georgian house and enter a world of books, antiques, embroidered sheets, handmade toiletries, scrumptious breakfasts and the finest (and least precious) hosts you could wish for. No credit cards. **£110**

Rustique Finkle St ☎01748 821565, ⓦrustiqueyork .co.uk. The clue to *Rustique*'s ambience lies in its name – it concentrates on rustic French food and wine in a bistro setting. The atmosphere is busy and cheerful, and the food's lovely, and very reasonably priced (two courses £13.95, three for £15.95). Daily noon–9pm.

★**Whashton Springs** Near Whashton, 3 miles north of Richmond on Ravensworth Rd ☎01748 822884, ⓦwhashtonsprings.co.uk. This working Dales farm offers a peaceful night in the country in rooms (in the main house or round the courtyard) filled with family furniture. **£76**

REETH

King's Arms High Row ☎01748 884259, ⓦthekingsarms .com. Attractive eighteenth-century inn on the green, offering a range of meals and snacks using locally sourced food, and rooms, all of which are en suite. Daily 11am–11pm; food served daily noon–2.30pm & 6–9pm. **£70**

STONESDALE MOOR

★**Tan Hill Inn** ☎01833 628246, ⓦtanhillinn.com. Reputedly the highest inn in Britain (1732ft above sea level), and claims to be the highest wi-fi hotspot. It's certainly one of the most rural – you might well find sheep in the bar. The seven rooms are comfortable, and the menu covers all the old pub favourites (mains £6.50–14.50). April–Aug daily 10am–9.45pm; Sept–March daily noon–3pm & 7–9pm. Dorms **£25**, doubles **£80**

Ripon and around

The attractive market town of **RIPON**, eleven miles north of Harrogate, is centred upon its small **cathedral** (daily 8.30am–6pm; donation requested; ☎01765 602072, ⓦriponcathedral.org.uk), which can trace its ancestry back to its foundation by St Wilfrid in 672; the original crypt below the central tower can still be reached down a stone passage. The town's other focus is its **Market Place**, linked by narrow Kirkgate to the cathedral (market day is Thurs, with a farmers' market on the third Sun of the month). Meanwhile, three restored buildings – prison, courthouse and workhouse – show a different side of the local heritage, under the banner of the **Yorkshire Law and Order Museums** (all daily: Workhouse 11am–4pm; Prison & Police and Courthouse 1–4pm; combined ticket £9.50; ☎01765 690799, ⓦriponmuseums.co.uk). Just four miles away lies **Fountains Abbey**, the one Yorkshire monastic ruin you must see.

12

Fountains Abbey and Studley Royal

4 miles southwest of Ripon off the B6265 • Feb & March daily 10am–5pm; April–Oct daily 10am–6pm; Oct–Jan Sat–Thurs 10am–5pm; free guided tours of abbey April–Oct daily • £10.50; NT & EH • ☎01765 608888, ⓦfountainsabbey.org.uk • #139 bus from Ripon (Mon, Thurs & Sat 4 daily; 15min)

It's tantalizing to imagine how the English landscape might have appeared had Henry VIII not dissolved the monasteries: **Fountains Abbey** gives a good idea of what might have been. The abbey was founded in 1133 by thirteen dissident Benedictine monks and formally adopted by the Cistercian order two years later. Within a hundred years, Fountains had become the wealthiest Cistercian foundation in England, supporting a magnificent **abbey church**. The **Perpendicular Tower**, almost 180ft high, looms over the whole ensemble, while equally grandiose in scale is the undercroft of the **Lay Brothers' Dormitory** off the cloister, a stunningly vaulted space over 300ft long that was used to store the monastery's annual harvest of fleeces. Its sheer size gives some idea of the abbey's entrepreneurial scope; some thirteen tons of wool a year were turned over, most of it sold to Venetian and Florentine merchants who toured the monasteries.

A riverside walk, marked from the visitor centre car park, takes you through Fountains Abbey to a series of ponds and ornamental gardens, harbingers of **Studley Royal** (same times as the abbey), which can also be entered via the village of Studley Roger, where there's a separate car park. This lush medley of lawns, lake, woodland and **Deer Park** was laid out in 1720 to form a setting for the abbey, and there are some scintillating views from the gardens, though it's the cascades and water gardens that command most attention.

ARRIVAL AND INFORMATION

By bus Ripon is served by #36 buses from/to Harrogate (every 10–25min; 35min) and Leeds (every 20–35min; 1hr 30min); the bus station is just off Market Place.
Tourist information Ripon Town Hall, Market Place

RIPON AND AROUND

(April–Oct Mon–Sat 10am–5pm, Sun 10am–1pm; Nov–March Thurs & Sat 10am–4pm; closes daily 1–1.30pm year round; ☎01765 604625, ⓦripon-internet.com).

ACCOMMODATION AND EATING

The Old Deanery Minster Rd ☎01765 600003, ⓦtheolddeanery.co.uk. Luxurious contemporary hotel opposite the cathedral. The innovative menu (main courses

from £15.95) features dishes such as belly of pork or fried stone bass. Mon–Sat noon–2pm & 7–9pm, Sun 12.30–2.30pm. **£125**

Harrogate

HARROGATE – the very picture of genteel Yorkshire respectability – owes its landscaped appearance and early prosperity to the discovery of Tewit Well in 1571. This was the first of more than eighty ferrous and sulphurous springs that, by the nineteenth century, were to turn the town into one of the country's leading spas. Tours of the town should begin with the **Royal Baths**, facing Crescent Road, first opened in 1897 and now restored to their late Victorian finery. You can experience the beautiful Moorish-style interior during a session at the **Turkish Baths and Health Spa** (separate sessions for men and women; from £15; ☎01423 556746). Just along Crescent Road from the Royal Baths stands the **Royal Pump Room**, built in 1842 over the sulphur well that feeds the baths. The town's earliest surviving spa building, the old Promenade Room of 1806, is just 100yd from the Pump Room on Swan Road – now housing the **Mercer Art Gallery** (Tues–Sat 10am–5pm, Sun 2–5pm; free; ☎01423 556188) and its changing fine art exhibitions.

To the southwest (entrance opposite the Royal Pump Room), the 120-acre **Valley Gardens** are a delight, while many visitors also make for the botanical gardens at **Harlow Carr**, on Crag Lane (daily March–Nov 9.30am–6pm, Nov–Feb 9.30am–4pm; £8.75; ☎01423 565418, ⓦrhs.org.uk), the northern showpiece of the Royal Horticultural Society. These lie 1.5 miles out, on the town's western edge – the nicest approach is to walk (30min) through the Valley Gardens and pine woods, though bus #6 (every 20min) will get you there as well.

ARRIVAL AND INFORMATION

By train The station is on Station Parade, on the eastern edge of the town centre. There are regular services from/to Leeds (every 30min; 37min).
By bus The bus station is next to the train station on Station Parade and is served by #36 buses from/to Leeds (every

HARROGATE

15min–1hr; 40min) and Ripon (every 15min–1hr; 32min).
Tourist office In the Royal Baths on Crescent Road (April–Oct Mon–Sat 9am–5.30pm, Sun 10am–1pm; Nov–March Mon–Sat 9am–5pm; ☎01423 537300, ⓦvisitharrogate .co.uk).

ACCOMMODATION

Acorn Lodge Studley Rd ☎01423 525630, ⓦacornlodgeharrogate.co.uk. A guesthouse with big-hotel aspirations (luxury fittings, individual decor, jacuzzi, in-room massages) but B&B friendliness (and tariffs). Well placed for the town centre (a 5 min walk). **£89**
Balmoral Hotel Franklin Mount ☎01423 508208, ⓦbalmoralhotel.co.uk. Boutique hotel (whose strapline promises "a touch of opulence") occupying a rather grand

terrace of three Edwardian houses a few mins' walk from the town centre. Spacious rooms, luxurious fittings and helpful service make this a winner. **£110**
Studley Hotel Swan Rd ☎01423 560425, ⓦstudleyhotel.co.uk. Mid-sized independent hotel with attached Thai restaurant. The attractive rooms vary in size and cost, and service is good, though the restaurant can get very busy. You can find surprisingly good rates online. **£119**

12

EATING AND DRINKING

★**Betty's** 1 Parliament St ☎01423 502746, ⓦbettys .co.uk. A Yorkshire institution with branches in several North Yorkshire towns (they've refused to open any outside the county), *Betty's* has a uniquely old-fashioned air, with a wrought-iron canopy, large bowed windows, a light airy room, waiting staff in starched linen, and baking that harks back to the past. While they are known for cakes, speciality teas and coffees, they also offer delicious breakfasts and mains – summer vegetable pancakes, for instance, or garlic and thyme chicken. No reservations (except for afternoon tea Fri–Sun), so you may have to wait. Daily 9am–9pm.

Le D2 Bower Rd ☎01423 502700, ⓦled2.co.uk. Quality French food and excellent service in unpretentious surroundings, and at affordable prices – two courses for £12.95 at lunch and £21 in the evening. Tues–Thurs noon–2pm & 6pm–late, Fri & Sat noon–2pm & 5.30pm–late.

The Tannin Level 5 Raglan St ☎01423 560595, ⓦtanninlevel.co.uk. Popular brasserie, smartly understated, with a Michelin-trained cook and super locally sourced food. Earlybird two courses £12.95, à la carte mains around £15–25. Mon–Thurs noon–9pm, Fri & Sat noon–9.30pm, Sun noon–8pm.

Winter Gardens Royal Baths, Parliament St ☎01423 877010. For rock-bottom prices, you can't beat *Wetherspoon's*, a pub chain renowned for revitalizing interesting buildings. This is one of their best – all wrought iron, glass and ornate staircases. Daily 7am–11pm.

York and around

YORK is the North's most compelling city, a place whose history, said George VI, "is the history of England". This is perhaps overstating things a little, but it reflects the significance of a metropolis that stood at the heart of the country's religious and political life for centuries, and until the Industrial Revolution was second only to London in population and importance. These days a more provincial air hangs over the city, except in summer when it comes to feel like a heritage site for the benefit of tourists. That said, no trip to this part of the country is complete without a visit to York, which is also well placed for any number of **day-trips**, the most essential being to **Castle Howard**, the gem among English stately homes.

In town, the **Minster** is the obvious place to start, and you won't want to miss a walk around the old city **walls**. The medieval city is at its most evocative around the streets known as Stonegate and the **Shambles**, while the earlier Viking settlement is entertainingly presented at **Jorvik**, perhaps the city's favourite family attraction. Standout historic buildings include the Minster's Treasurer's House, Georgian Fairfax House, the Merchant Adventurers' Hall, and the stark remnants of York's **Castle**. The two major museum collections are the incomparable **Castle Museum** and the **National Railway Museum** (where the appeal goes way beyond railway memorabilia), while the evocative ruins and gardens of **St Mary's Abbey** house the family-friendly **Yorkshire Museum**.

Brief history

An early **Roman** fortress of 71 AD in time became a city – Eboracum, capital of the empire's northern European territories and the base for Hadrian's northern campaigns. Later, the city became the fulcrum of **Christianity** in northern England: on Easter Day in 627, Bishop Paulinus, on a mission to establish the Roman Church, baptized King Edwin of Northumbria in a small timber chapel. Six years later the church became the first minster and Paulinus the first archbishop of York.

In 867 the city fell to the **Danes**, who renamed it **Jorvik**, and later made it the capital of eastern England (Danelaw). Later Viking raids culminated in the decisive **Battle of Stamford Bridge** (1066) six miles east of the city, where English King Harold defeated Norse King Harald – a pyrrhic victory in the event, for his weakened army was defeated by the Normans just a few days later at the Battle of Hastings, with well-known consequences for all concerned.

The **Normans** devastated much of York's hinterland in their infamous "Harrying of the North". Stone walls were thrown up during the thirteenth century, when the city

12

N

▲ 1 & A19 Thirsk   York District Hospital

PUBS & BARS

Black Swan	2
Blue Bell	5
Swan	8
Three-Legged Mare	1

RESTAURANTS & CAFÉS

Asia Gourmet	1
Ate O Clock	5
Betty's	4
Café Concerto	3
Café No. 8	2
Rustique	6

ACCOMMODATION

Bar Convent	6
Bowman's	1
Cedar Court Grand Hotel	4
The Fort	3
Hedley House Hotel	2
Mount Royale	7
Rowntree Park Caravan Club Site	8
Safestay York	5

CLUBS & LIVE MUSIC

The Basement	4
Fibbers	3
Grand Opera House	7
National Centre for Early Music	6

YORK

0   100   yards

12

became a favoured Plantagenet retreat and commercial capital of the north, its importance reflected in the new title of Duke of York, bestowed ever since on the monarch's second son. Although Henry VIII's Dissolution of the Monasteries took its toll on a city crammed with religious houses, York remained wedded to the Catholic cause, and the most famous of the Gunpowder Plot conspirators, **Guy Fawkes**, was born here. During the **Civil War** Charles I established his court in the city, which was strongly pro-Royalist, inviting a Parliamentarian siege. Royalist troops, however, were routed by Cromwell and Sir Thomas Fairfax at the **Battle of Marston Moor** in 1644, another seminal battle in England's history, which took place six miles west of York.

The city's eighteenth-century history was marked by its emergence as a social centre for Yorkshire's landed elite. While the Industrial Revolution largely passed it by, the arrival of the **railways** brought renewed prosperity, thanks to the enterprise of pioneering "Railway King" George Hudson, lord mayor during the 1830s and 1840s. The railway is gradually losing its role as a major employer, as is the traditional but declining confectionery industry, and incomes are now generated by new service and bioscience industries – not forgetting, of course, the four million annual tourists.

York Minster

Minster Yard • Mon–Sat 9am–5pm, Sun 12.45– 5pm • £10 (including undercroft); combined ticket with tower £15; admission ticket valid for 12 months • Free guided tours of the Minster (1hr) take place Mon–Sat 10am–3pm (subject to availability) and include access to the "Revealing York Minster" and the Orb visitor attractions • ☎ 01904 557200, ⊕ yorkminster.org

York Minster ranks as one of the country's most important sights. Seat of the Archbishop of York, it is Britain's largest Gothic building and home to countless treasures, not least of which is an estimated half of all the medieval stained glass in England. The first significant foundations were laid around 1080 by the first Norman archbishop, Thomas of Bayeux, and it was from the germ of this Norman church that the present structure emerged.

The stained glass windows

Nothing else in the Minster can match the magnificence of the **stained glass** in the nave and transepts. The **West Window** (1338) contains distinctive heart-shaped upper tracery (the "Heart of Yorkshire"), while in the nave's north aisle, the second bay window (1155) contains slivers of the oldest stained glass in the country. The greatest of the church's 128 windows, however, is the majestic **East Window** (1405), at 78ft by 31ft the world's largest area of medieval stained glass in a single window (currently covered with a tarpaulin bearing an image of the window – the renovation is due to be finished by 2016). You can see an ever-changing selection of the window's most famous stained-glass panels in the odd, inverted-cauldron-shape of **"the Orb"**.

The undercroft, treasury and crypt

The Minster's foundations, or **undercroft**, have been turned into a museum, featuring a new interactive gallery "Revealing York Minster". Among precious relics in the adjoining **treasury** is the eleventh-century *Horn of Ulf*, presented to the Minster by a relative of the tide-turning King Canute. There's also access from the undercroft to the **crypt**, the spot that transmits the most powerful sense of antiquity, as it contains sections of the original eleventh-century church, including pillars with fine Romanesque capitals. Access to the undercroft, treasury and crypt is from the south transept, which is also the entrance to the **central tower**, which you can climb for exhilarating rooftop views over the city.

Around the walls

The city's superb **walls** date mainly from the fourteenth century, though fragments of Norman work survive, particularly in the gates (known as "bars"), and the northern sections still follow the line of the Roman ramparts. **Monk Bar** is as good a point of access as any, tallest of the city's four main gates and host to the small **Richard III Museum** (daily: April–Oct 10am–5pm; Nov–March 10am–4pm; £3.50; ☎01904 615505, ⊕ richardiiimuseum.co.uk). For just a taste of the walls' best section – with great views of the Minster and acres of idyllic-looking gardens – take the ten-minute stroll west from Monk Bar to Exhibition Square and **Bootham Bar**, the only gate on the site of a Roman gateway and marking the traditional northern entrance to the city. A stroll round the walls' entire two-and-a-half-mile length will also take you past the southwestern **Micklegate Bar**, long considered the most important of the gates since it marked the start of the road to London; it's now home to the Henry VII Experience (April–Oct 10am–4pm; Nov–March 10am–3pm; £3.50; ☎ 01904 615505).

York Art Gallery

Exhibition Square • Daily 10am–5pm • Free • ☎ 01904 687687, ⓦ yorkartgallery.org.uk

York Art Gallery houses an extensive collection of early Italian, British and northern European paintings. The gallery puts on a year-round series of special exhibitions and events, and is noted for its collections of British studio pottery and twentieth-century British painters. It was closed for redevelopment at the time of writing, but should be open by the time you read this; hours and admission charges are likely to remain the same.

The Yorkshire Museum

Museum Gardens • Daily 10am–5pm • £7.50 • ☎ 01904 687687, ⓦ yorkshiremuseum.org.uk

In the beautiful Museum Gardens between Exhibition Square and the river, next to the romantic ruins of St Mary's Abbey, sits the majestic Grade I listed building of the **Yorkshire Museum**. Five exciting, hands-on galleries comprise the "History of York", a multiscreen, audiovisual display; "Extinct", which covers dinosaurs and more recently extinct creatures; "Meet the People of the Empire" (Roman York); the "Power and the Glory" (Medieval York); and "Enquiry", about how archeology and science can uncover the past.

12 Stonegate

One of York's most picturesque streets, **Stonegate** is as ancient as the city itself. Originally the Via Praetoria of Roman York, it's now paved with thick flags of York stone, which were once carried along here to build the Minster (hence the name). The Tudor buildings that line it retain their considerable charm – **Ye Olde Starre** at no. 40, one of York's original inns, is on every tourist itinerary (you can't miss the sign straddling the street).

Barley Hall

Off Stonegate • Daily 10am–5pm (4pm in winter) • £5.50; combined ticket with Jorvik £14 • ☎ 01904 543400, ⓦ barleyhall.org.uk

Step through an alley known as Coffee Yard (by the *Olde Starre*) to find **Barley Hall**, a fine restoration of a late-medieval townhouse with a lively museum where you can learn about fifteenth-century life by, among other things, playing period games and trying on costumes. Barley Hall is one one of the Jorvik group of attractions.

The Shambles

York's most famous street, and one which appears regularly on its promotional brochures, **The Shambles** could be taken as the epitome of the medieval city. Almost impossibly narrow and lined with perilously leaning timber-framed houses, it was the home of York's butchers (the word "shambles" derives from the Old English for slaughterhouse) – old meat hooks still adorn the odd house.

Jorvik

Coppergate • Daily: April–Oct 10am–5pm; Nov–March 10am–4pm • £9.95, joint ticket with Dig! £14.45, with Barley Hall £14 • ☎ 01904 615505, ⓦ jorvik-viking-centre.co.uk

The city's blockbuster historic exhibit is **Jorvik**, located by the Coppergate shopping centre. Propelling visitors in "time capsules" on a ride through the tenth-century city of York, the museum presents not only the sights but also the sounds and even the smells

CLOCKWISE FROM TOP LEFT LEEDS CORN EXCHANGE (P.527); CASTLE HOWARD (P.553); BEVERLEY MINSTER (P.557); WORLD OF JAMES HERRIOT, THIRSK (P.559) >

of a riverside **Viking city**. Excavations of Coppergate in 1976 uncovered a real Viking settlement, now largely buried beneath the shopping centre outside. But at Jorvik you can see how the unearthed artefacts were used, and watch live-action domestic scenes on actual Viking-age streets, with constipated villagers, axe-fighting and other singular attractions.

Dig!

St Saviourgate • Daily 10am–5pm • £6; joint ticket with Jorvik £14.45; pre-booking advised • ☎ 01904 615505, ⓦ vikingjorvik.com

Where Jorvik shows what was unearthed at Coppergate, the associated attraction that is **Dig!** illustrates the science involved. Housed five minutes' walk away from the museum, in the medieval church of St Saviour, on St Savioursgate, a simulated dig allows you to take part in a range of excavations in the company of archeologists, using authentic tools and methods. Tours (£1) to visit **Dig Hungate**, York's latest major archeological excavation, start from here.

Clifford's Tower

Tower St • Daily: April–Sept 10am–6pm; Oct & Nov 10am–5pm; Nov–March 10am–4pm • £4.30; EH • ☎ 01904 646940, ⓦ cliffordstower.com

There's precious little left of **York Castle**, one of two established by William the Conqueror. Only the perilously leaning **Clifford's Tower** remains, a stark stone keep built between 1245 and 1262 to replace the original wooden keep burned down in 1190 AD when it was being used as a refuge by hundreds of Jews trying to escape anti-Semitic riots in the city. Of a rare quatrefoil (clove-leaf) design, perhaps an experiment to improve sight lines between the top of the keep and the base of the walls, it once had two floors with a supporting central column.

Castle Museum

Eye of York • Daily 10am–5pm • £8.50 • ☎ 01904 687687, ⓦ yorkcastlemuseum.org

Housed in what was once a couple of prisons, displays in the wonderfully inventive **Castle Museum** begin with a series of period rooms from the seventeenth century to the 1980s. There's a large room devoted to Victorian attitudes to birth, marriage and death, followed by a wonderful reconstruction of the sights and sounds of York's Kirkgate during the final years of the nineteenth century, often staffed by people dressed in authentic costume. There are displays, too, of period kitchens (who'd have thought that state-of-the-art equipment from the 1980s could look quite so out of date?), as well as hygiene, costume through the ages, toys and World War II. There's also a superb recreation of the fashion, music and news stories of the 1960s. Finally, the cells in the basement of the prison building contain an affecting series of real-life stories, told by video recordings of actors projected onto cell walls, gleaned from the prison's records.

The National Railway Museum

Leeman Rd, a 10min walk from the train station • Daily 10am–6pm • Free • ☎ 0844 815 3139, ⓦ nrm.org.uk • A "road train" shuttles visitors here from Duncombe Place next to York Minster (April–Oct daily every 30min; £2)

The **National Railway Museum** is a must if you have even the slightest interest in railways, history, engineering or Victoriana. The Great Hall alone features some fifty restored locomotives dating from 1829 onwards, among them *Mallard*, at 126mph the fastest steam engine ever built. The seemingly interminable restoration of one of the museum's greatest engines – the **Flying Scotsman** – continues. The latest estimate is that it will be finished by the summer of 2015 – but don't hold your breath.

Castle Howard

15 miles northeast of York off the A64 • Late March to late Oct & late Nov to mid-Dec house daily 11am–4pm, grounds 10am–5pm; grounds also open Jan to late March & Nov to mid-Dec • £14; grounds only £9.50 • ☎ 01653 648333, ⓦ castlehoward.co.uk • The summer Moorsbus (see p.559) comes out here from Helmsley, while some Yorkshire Coastliner buses run from York, Malton or Pickering; you can also take a bus tour from York

Immersed in the deep countryside of the Howardian Hills, **Castle Howard** is the seat of one of England's leading aristocratic families and among the country's grandest stately homes. The grounds especially are worth visiting, and you could easily spend the best part of a day here. The colossal main house was designed by **Sir John Vanbrugh** in 1699 and was almost forty years in the making – remarkable enough, even were it not for the fact that Vanbrugh was, at the start of the commission at least, best known as a playwright and had no formal architectural training. Shrewdly, Vanbrugh recognized his limitations and called upon **Nicholas Hawksmoor**, who had a major part in the house's structural design – the pair later worked successfully together on Blenheim Palace.

Vanbrugh also turned his attention to the estate's thousand-acre **grounds**, where he could indulge his playful inclinations – the formal gardens, clipped parkland, towers, obelisks and blunt sandstone follies stretch in all directions, sloping gently to two artificial lakes. The whole is a charming artifice of grand, manicured views – an example of what three centuries, skilled gardeners and pots of money can produce.

ARRIVAL AND DEPARTURE
YORK

By train Trains arrive at York Station, just outside the city walls, a 10min walk from the historic core.
Destinations Durham (every 10min; 50min); Harrogate (hourly; 30min); Hull (hourly; 1hr); Leeds (every 10–15min; 25min); London (every 30min; 2hr); Manchester (every 15min; 1hour 25min); Newcastle (every 15min; 1hr); Scarborough (hourly; 50min); Sheffield (every 15–30min; 45min).
By bus National Express buses (☎ 0870 580 8080) and most other regional bus services drop off and pick up on

Rougier St, 200yd north of the train station, just before Lendal Bridge. Companies include East Yorkshire (for Hull, Beverley and Bridlington; ☎ 01482 592929) and Yorkshire Coastliner (for Leeds, Castle Howard, Pickering, Scarborough and Whitby; ☎ 01653 692556).
Destinations Beverley (Mon–Sat hourly, Sun 7 daily; 1hr 10min); Hull (Mon–Sat hourly, Sun 7 daily; 1hr 35min); Leeds (Mon–Fri every 20min; 1hour 20min); Pickering (hourly; 1hr 8min); Scarborough (hourly; 1hr 40min); Whitby (4–6 daily; 2hr 13min).

GETTING AROUND

On foot The historic core is easily explored on foot; from the Minster in the north, for example, to Castle Museum in the south is about a 10min walk. Indeed, one of the best ways to explore the city is to circumnavigate it atop the

splendid city walls.
By taxi There are taxi ranks at Rougier St, Duncombe Place, Exhibition Square and the train station, or call Station Taxis on ☎ 01904 623332.

INFORMATION AND TOURS

Tourist office 1 Museum St, on the corner with Blake Street (Mon–Sat 9am–5pm, July & Aug to 5.30pm, Sun 10am–4pm ☎ 01904 550099, ⓦ visityork.org). There is also a smaller tourist office at the train station.
Listings information *The Evening Press* (ⓦ thisisyork .co.uk), and the monthly *What's On York* (ⓦ whatsonyork .com) provide detailed entertainment, events, festival and exhibition listings for the city.
Bus tours City tours by bus – pick up details at the tourist office – cost around £10. York Pullman (☎ 01904 622992, ⓦ yorkpullmanbus.co.uk) offers day-trips to Castle Howard for £17.50, along with several routes to the Dales.
Walking tours There are various guided walks available (around £6), including evening ghost walks. There's not much to choose between them, though one is free – the

York Association of Voluntary Guides (☎ 01904 550098, ⓦ avgyork.co.uk) offers a guided tour year round (daily 10.15am; 2hr), plus additional tours in summer (April–Oct 2.15pm, and one at 6.45pm June–Aug), from outside the York Art Gallery – just turn up.
River cruises The best river operator is YorkBoat (☎ 01904 628324, ⓦ yorkboat.co.uk), who run a variety of cruises from King's Staith and Lendal Bridge (Feb–Nov; cruises from £7.50, families £20).
York Pass The York Pass (☎ 01904 550099, ⓦ yorkpass.com) gives free entry to over thirty attractions, not only in the city (eg Barley Hall, Clifford's Tower, Dig! and the Fairfax House) but also elsewhere (Castle Howard, Eden Camp, the North York Moors Railway); it costs £36/£48/£58 for one/two/three days respectively, with reductions if you buy it online.

12

12

ACCOMMODATION

The main **B&B** concentration is in the side streets off Bootham (immediately west of Exhibition Square), with nothing much more than a 10min walk from the centre.

★**Bar Convent** 17 Blossom St ☎01904 643238, ⓦbar -convent.org.uk. Unique opportunity to stay in a convent. The grand Georgian building houses a museum and café as well as nine single rooms (£33–37 each), twins, doubles and a family room, self-catering kitchen and guest lounge. **£80**

Bowman's 33 Grosvenor Terrace ☎01904 622204, ⓦbowmansguesthouse.co.uk. Six spotless rooms in a friendly renovated Victorian terrace B&B off Bootham, within easy reach of the city centre. They provide a permit for free on-street parking. **£80**

★**Cedar Court Grand Hotel** Station Rise ☎0845 409 6430, ⓦcedarcourtgrand.co.uk. Splendid five-star hotel a 2min walk from the train station, housed in what was the 1906 headquarters of the North Eastern Railway. Bags of character, with wonderful views of the walls and the Minster, luxurious rooms, a fine-dining restaurant and relaxing bar. **£175**

The Fort Little Stonegate ☎01904 639573, ⓦthefortyork.co.uk. An interesting idea – a "boutique hostel" in the city centre, offering rooms and dorms decorated on themes (log cabin, deep-sea creatures) at a knock-down price. Dorms **£22**; doubles **£78**

Hedley House Hotel 3 Bootham Terrace ☎01904 637404, ⓦhedleyhouse.com. Friendly, comfortable small hotel that is at its best in summer, when the outdoor area with sauna/aqua spa comes into its own. Rooms can be a little chilly in winter – especially in the (separate) annexe. Free car parking on first-come, first-served basis. **£115**

Mount Royale The Mount ☎01904 628856, ⓦmountroyale.co.uk. Lots of antiques, super garden suites (and cheaper rooms), and a heated outdoor pool in summer. Plus a hot tub, sauna and steam room, and a well-regarded restaurant. **£125**

★**Rowntree Park Caravan Club Site** Terry Ave ☎01904 658997, ⓦcaravanclub.co.uk. A wonderful site, the best-located in the city, a 10min walk from the centre, with a back gate that opens onto a street of takeaways, pubs and shops. Open to nonmembers. Mainly for caravans and motorhomes, but with a small tent enclosure – those with tents must arrive on foot. Advance booking essential, especially at weekends. For motorhome plus 2 adults **£26.20**

Safestay York Micklegate House, 88–90 Micklegate ☎01904 627720, ⓦsafestayyork.co.uk. In a handsome 1752 building in the centre of the city, with many impressive features. Beds are in dorms (sleeping 4 to 14) and private rooms, all en suite; prices rise at weekends and drop for multi-night stays. Dorms **£16**; doubles **£80**

EATING

Asia Gourmet 61 Gillygate ☎01904 622728. Small, cheerful restaurant in the city centre with prompt service. Mainly Japanese food (sushi a speciality) though other Asian cuisines are available. Main courses £6.50. Tues & Sun 5–10pm, Wed–Sat 5.30–10pm.

Ate O Clock 13a High Ousegate ☎01904 644080, ⓦateoclock.co.uk. The name is dreadful, but the – largely Mediterranean – food is excellent, and there's attentive service and a relaxed atmosphere. A two-course lunch is £9.50, while main dishes are around £14–£20. Music most Fri evenings. Mon 5.30–9pm, Tues–Fri noon–2pm & 6–9.30pm, Sat noon–2.30pm & 5.30–9.30pm.

Betty's 6–8 St Helen's Square ☎01904 659142, ⓦbettys.co.uk. Famous across Yorkshire, *Betty's* specializes in cakes and pastries like granny used to make (or not) – try the pikelets or the Yorkshire fat rascals – plus hot dishes and puddings to die for. No reservations. In the basement there's a mirror with the signatures of the hundreds of Allied airmen who used *Betty's* as an unofficial mess during World War II. Daily 9am–9pm.

Café Concerto 21 High Petergate ☎01904 610478, ⓦcafeconcerto.biz. Relaxed, Belle Epoque-style bistro facing the Minster, with sheet-music-papered walls and waiting staff in robust aprons. Food is modern European; there are papers to browse. (There's also a two-bedroom apartment available upstairs). Daily 8.30am–10pm.

★**Café No. 8** 8 Gillygate ☎01904 653074, ⓦcafeno8 .co.uk. Limited menu using excellent locally sourced produce (Masham sausages, Yorkshire beef and lamb, Ryedale ice cream, beer from Masham) in unpretentious surroundings. Mains cost around £10 during the day, and £14–17 in the evening, or have two courses midweek for £16.50. Its heated garden is a popular spot. Mon–Fri noon–10pm, Sat & Sun 10am–10pm.

Rustique 28 Castlegate ☎01904 612744, ⓦrustique york.co.uk. French-style bistro serving excellent-value Gallic food and wine. There are a couple of set menus (two courses £13.95, three £15.95); à la carte features all the classics, including steak frites, moules marinière and confit de canard. Mon–Sat noon–10pm, Sun noon–9pm.

DRINKING

Black Swan Peasholme Green ☎01904 679131, ⓦblackswanyork.com. York's oldest pub is an imposing half-timbered, sixteenth-century tavern, with wonderful details – flagstones, period staircase, inglenook – good beer, and occasional jazz and folk nights (ⓦblackswanfolkclub .org.uk). Mon–Sat noon–11pm, Sun noon–10.30pm.

Blue Bell Fossgate ☎ 01904 654904. Built in 1798, the *Blue Bell* is a tiny, friendly local with two rooms, oak-panelling and good real ales. No mobile phones. Recently dropped by the *Good Beer Guide* because of concerns regarding access. Mon–Sat 11am–11pm, Sun noon–10.30pm.

★ **The Swan** 16 Bishopgate ☎ 01904 634968. Lovely local, a Tetley Heritage Inn that offers convivial surroundings, well-kept real ale and a really friendly atmosphere a few minutes from the city centre. Mon–Wed 4–11pm, Thurs 4–11.30pm, Fri 4pm–midnight, Sat noon–midnight, Sun noon–11pm.

Three-Legged Mare 15 High Petergate ☎ 01904 638246. A converted shop provides an airy outlet for York

TOP 5 YORKSHIRE PUBS

Duke of York Whitby. See p.568
Fat Cat Sheffield. See p.527
Star Inn Harome. See p.562
The Swan York. See above
Whitelocks Leeds. See p.532

Brewery's own quality beer. No kids, no juke box, no video games. It's named after a three-legged gallows – it's there on the pub sign, with a replica in the beer garden. Mon–Sat 11am–midnight, Sun noon–11pm.

NIGHTLIFE AND ENTERTAINMENT

York has its fair share of theatres and cinemas, and **classical music concerts** and recitals are often held in the city's churches and York Minster. Major annual events include the **Viking Festival** (⟨w⟩ vikingjorvik.com) every Feb and the **Early Music Festival** (⟨w⟩ ncem.co.uk), perhaps the best of its kind in the country, held in July. The city is also famous for its **Mystery Plays** (⟨w⟩ yorkmysteryplays.co.uk), traditionally held every four years – the next are planned for 2018.

The Basement 13–17 Coney St, below City Screen cinema ☎ 01904 612940, ⟨w⟩ thebasementyork.co.uk. An intimate venue with a variety of nights – from music to comedy to arts events. The first Wed of every month is "Café Scientifique" – a free evening of discussion surrounding current issues in science, while Sun night sees stand-up comedy (7–10pm). Live music events are scattered through the week, along with cabaret, burlesque and club nights. Most nights 8–11pm.

City Screen 13–17 Coney St ☎ 0870 758 3219, ⟨w⟩ picturehouses.co.uk. The city's independent cinema is the art-house choice, with three screens, a Riverside café-

bar, and licensed restaurant.

Fibbers 8 The Stonebow ☎ 01904 651250, ⟨w⟩ fibbers .co.uk. York's primary live music venue, *Fibbers* regularly puts on local and nationally known bands in a lively atmosphere – consult website for details.

Grand Opera House Cumberland St at Clifford St ☎ 0844 871 3024, ⟨w⟩ grandoperahouseyork.org.uk. Musicals, ballet, pop gigs and family entertainment in all its guises.

The National Centre for Early Music St Margaret's Church, Walmgate ☎ 01904 632220, ⟨w⟩ ncem.co.uk. Not just early music, but also folk, world and jazz.

Hull

HULL – officially Kingston upon Hull – dates back to 1299, when it was laid out as a seaport by Edward I. It quickly became England's leading harbour, and was still a vital garrison when the gates were closed against Charles I in 1642, the first serious act of rebellion of what was to become the English Civil War. Fishing and **seafaring** have always been important here, and today's city maintains a firm grip on its heritage with a number of superb visitor attractions.

The Maritime Museum

Queen Victoria Square • Mon–Sat 10am–5pm, Sun 1.30–4.30pm • Free • ☎ 01482 300300, ⟨w⟩ hullcc.gov.uk

The city's maritime legacy is covered in the **Maritime Museum**, housed in the Neoclassical headquarters of the former Town Docks Offices. With displays on fishing, whaling and sailing, this provides a valuable record of centuries of skill and expertise, not to mention courage and fortitude, now fading into the past. Highlights include the whaling gallery, with whale skeletons, fearsome exploding harpoons, the sort of flimsy boats in which whalers of old used to chase the leviathans of the deep, a crow's nest made of a barrel, and oddities such as a whalebone seat, a blubber cauldron and a group of Narwhal tusks. An exhilarating and humbling experience.

The Museums Quarter

Between High St and the River Hull • All attractions Mon–Sat 10am–5pm, Sun 1.30–4.30pm • Free • ☎ 01482 300300, ⓦ hullcc.gov.uk

Over towards the River Hull, you reach the **Museums Quarter** and **High Street**, which has been designated an "Old Town" conservation area thanks to its crop of former merchants' houses and narrow cobbled alleys. At its northern end stands **Wilberforce House**, the former home of William Wilberforce, which contains fascinating exhibits on slavery and its abolition, the cause to which he dedicated much of his life. Next door is **Streetlife**, devoted to the history of transport in the region and centred on a 1930s street scene. The adjoining **Hull and East Riding Museum** is even better, with showpiece attractions including vivid displays of Celtic burials and an impressive full-size model of a woolly mammoth.

The Deep

Tower St • Daily 10am–6pm, last entry 5pm • £11.50 • ☎ 01482 381000 , ⓦ thedeep.co.uk

Protruding from a promontory overlooking the River Humber, Hull's splendid aquarium, **The Deep**, is just ten minutes' walk from the old town. Its educational displays and videos wrap around an immense 30ft-deep, 2.3-million-gallon viewing tank filled with sharks, rays and octopuses. There's an underwater tunnel along the bottom of the tank, together with a magical glass lift in which you can ascend or descend through the water while coming eye to eye with some of the more intriguing denizens of the deep.

ARRIVAL AND INFORMATION   HULL

By train Hull's train station is situated in the Paragon Interchange off Ferensway. There are direct trains between London and Hull, while the city is also linked to the main London–York line via Doncaster as well as to the East Yorkshire coast.
Destinations Bempton (every 30min; 55min); Beverley (Mon–Sat every 25min, Sun 6 daily; 13min); Bridlington (every 30min; 42min); Filey (around 10 daily; 1hr10min); (Leeds (hourly; 1hr); London (6 daily; 2hr 45min);

Scarborough (every 2hr; 1hr 30min); York (hourly; 1hr 10min).
By bus The bus station is near the train station in the Paragon Interchange off Ferensway. Buses run to all parts of the region including York (2hr) and the East Coast (1hr40min to Bridlington; 2hr30min to Scarborough).
Tourist office Carr Lane at Queen Victoria Square (Mon–Sat 10am–5pm, Sun 11am–3pm; ☎ 01482 223559, ⓦ visithull andeastyorkshire.com). Here you can pick up the entertaining "Fish Trail" leaflet, a self-guided trail that kids will love.

ACCOMMODATION

Holiday Inn Hull Marina Castle St ☎ 0871 9422 9043, ⓦ holiday-inn.com. Rooms at the city's best central hotel overlook the marina, and there's a restaurant and bar, plus an indoor pool, gym, sauna and plenty of parking. **£61.50**
Kingston Theatre Hotel 1–2 Kingston Square

☎ 01482 225828, ⓦ kingstontheatrehotel.com. This straightforward, good-value hotel on the city's prettiest square, across from Hull New Theatre, is a 5min walk from the city centre, yet in a quiet neighbourhood. Street parking only (but there's a public car park nearby). **£67.50**

EATING AND DRINKING

Cerutti's 10 Nelson St ☎ 01482 328501, ⓦ ceruttis .co.uk. Facing the old site of the Victoria Pier (now replaced by a wooden deck overlooking the river), this Italian restaurant is especially good for fish dishes. The atmosphere is busy and friendly, and there are frequent special events including live jazz. Main courses are around £13–23, but look out for two- and three-course deals. Mon–Fri noon–2pm, Mon–Sat 6.45–9.30pm.
The George The Land of Green Ginger ☎ 01482 226373. Venerable pub on Hull's most curiously named street – see if you can find England's smallest window. Mon noon–6pm, Tues–Thurs noon–11.00pm, Fri & Sat noon–midnight, Sun noon–10pm.
Pave Café-Bar 16–20 Princes Ave ☎ 01482 333181,

ⓦ pavebar.co.uk. Nice laidback atmosphere with lots going on – live jazz/blues and comedy nights, and readings by the likes of Alexei Sayle, Will Self and Simon Armitage – and a comprehensive menu of home-cooked food served till 7pm (most mains well under £10). Mon–Thurs & Sun 11am–11.00pm, Fri & Sat 11am–11.30pm.
Taman Ria Tropicana 22 Princes Ave ☎ 01482 345640, ⓦ tropicana-hull.co.uk. Specifically Malay (rather than the more generic Malaysian) cuisine. All food is halal, and pork is never used. Check with staff regarding how spicy different dishes are. The "three dishes for £11" option is a good way to try things out. Tues–Sat 5–10.30pm.
Ye Olde White Harte 25 Silver St ☎ 01482 326363, ⓦ yeoldewhiteharte.com. Dating back to the sixteenth

12

century, this place has a pleasant courtyard garden, flagged floors, open brickwork and well-polished furniture, and serves traditional pub grub (mains £5.50–£7.50). Mon–Sat 11am–midnight, Sun noon–midnight.

ENTERTAINMENT

Hull Truck Theatre Company 50 Ferensway ☎01482 323638, ⓦhulltruck.co.uk. Renowned theatre, where, among other high-profile works, many of the plays of award-winning John Godber see the light of day.

Beverley

With its tangle of old streets, cobbled lanes and elegant Georgian and Victorian terraces **BEVERLEY**, nine miles north of Hull, is the very picture of a traditional market town. More than 350 of its buildings are listed, and though you could see its first-rank offerings in a morning, it makes an appealing place to stay.

Beverley Minster

Minster Yard North • March, April, Sept & Oct Mon–Sat 9am–5pm, Sun noon–4.30pm; May–Aug Mon–Sat 9am–5.30pm, Sun noon–5.30pm; Nov–Feb Mon–Sat 9am–4pm, Sun noon–5.30pm • Free, but donations requested • ☎01482 868540, ⓦbeverleyminster.org

The town is dominated by the fine, Gothic twin towers of **Beverley Minster**. The **west front**, which crowned the work in 1420, is widely considered without equal, its survival due in large part to architect Nicholas Hawksmoor, who restored much of the church in the eighteenth century. The carving throughout is magnificent, particularly the 68 misericords of the oak **choir** (1520–24), one of the largest and most accomplished in England. Much of the decorative work here and elsewhere is on a musical theme. Beverley had a renowned guild of itinerant minstrels, which provided funds in the sixteenth century for the carvings on the transept aisle capitals, where you'll be able to pick out players of lutes, bagpipes, horns and tambourines.

St Mary's

Corner of North Bar Within and Hengate • April–Sept Mon–Fri 10am–4.30pm; Oct–March Mon–Fri 10am–4pm, Sun before and after services only • Free • ☎01482 869137, ⓦstmarysbeverley.org

Cobbled Highgate runs from the Minster through town, along the pedestrianized shopping streets and past the main Market Square, to Beverley's other great church, **St Mary's**, which nestles alongside the **North Bar**, sole survivor of the town's five medieval gates. Inside, the chancel's painted panelled ceiling (1445) contains portraits of English kings from Sigebert (623–37) to Henry VI (1421–71), and among the carvings, the favourite novelty is the so-called "Pilgrim's Rabbit", said to have been the inspiration for the White Rabbit in Lewis Carroll's *Alice in Wonderland*.

ARRIVAL AND INFORMATION

BEVERLEY

By train Beverley's train station on Station Square is just a couple of mins' walk from the town centre and the Minster.
Destinations Bridlington (every 30min; 30min); Hull (every 30min; 15min); Sheffield (hourly; 1hr 41min).
By bus The bus station is at the junction of Walkergate and Sow Hill Road, with the main street just a minute's walk away.
Destinations Bridlington (hourly; 1hr) Driffield (hourly; 25min); Hull (every 30min–1hr; hourly; 40min); Scarborough (hourly; 1hr 16min)

Tourist office 34 Butcher Row in the main shopping area (Apr–Sept Mon–Fri 9.30am–5.30pm, Sat 9.30am–4.30pm, Sun 10am–3.30pm; Oct–March Mon–Fri 10am–5pm, Sat 10am–4.30pm; ☎01482 391672, ⓦvisithullandeastyorkshire.com).

ACCOMMODATION AND EATING

★**Cerutti 2** Station Square ☎01482 866700, ⓦceruttis.co.uk. Occupying what was once the station waiting rooms, *Cerutti 2*, run by the same family as *Cerutti's* in Hull, specializes in fish, though there are meat and vegetarian options too (mains around £12–23). Popular with locals, so it's as well to book, especially at weekends.

Tues–Sat noon–2pm & 6.45–9.30pm.
King's Head Hotel 37–38 Saturday Market ☎01482
868103, ⓦkingsheadpubbeverley.co.uk. Tucked into a
corner of busy Saturday Market, this period building has
contemporary decor inside. It's a Marston's pub, with food from
£7, and it can be noisy, especially at weekends, but the rear
rooms are quieter, and ear plugs are provided. Mon–Thurs

9am–11pm, Fri & Sat 9am–1am, Sun 11am–11pm; food
served Mon–Sat 10am–9pm, Sun 10am–8pm. **£79.95**
★**YHA Beverley Friary** Friar's Lane ☎0845 371 9004,
ⓦyha.org.uk. Beautiful medieval monastic house in the
shadow of the Minster. What it lacks in luxury it makes up
for in atmosphere, location and, of course, economy. Dorms
£18; triples **£69**

The East Yorkshire coast

The **East Yorkshire coast** curves south in a gentle arc from the mighty cliffs of
Flamborough Head to Spurn Head, a hook-shaped promontory formed by relentless
erosion and shifting currents. There are few parts of the British coast as dangerous
– indeed, the Humber lifeboat station at **Spurn Point** is the only one in Britain
permanently staffed by a professional crew. Between the two points lie a handful of
tranquil villages and miles of windswept dunes and mud flats. The two main resorts,
Bridlington and **Filey**, couldn't be more different, but each has its own appeal.

Bridlington and around

The southernmost resort on the Yorkshire coast, **BRIDLINGTON** has maintained its
harbour for almost a thousand years. The seafront promenade looks down upon the
town's best asset – its sweeping sandy **beach**. It's an out-and-out family resort, which
means plenty of candyfloss, fish and chips, rides, boat trips and amusement arcades.
The historic core of town is a mile inland, where in the largely Georgian Bridlington
Old Town the **Bayle Museum** (April–Sept Mon–Fri 10am–4pm; £1; ☎01262 674308)
presents local history in a building that once served as the gateway to a fourteenth-
century priory. Every November, Bridlington hosts a highly regarded World Music
Festival, **Musicport** (ⓦmusicportfestival.com), which pulls in some very big names.

Around fourteen miles of precipitous 400ft-high cliffs gird **Flamborough Head**, just to
the northeast of Bridlington. The best of the seascapes are visitable on the peninsula's
north side, accessible by road from Flamborough village.

Bempton

From **BEMPTON**, two miles north of Bridlington, you can follow the cliff-top path all
the way round to Flamborough Head or curtail the journey by cutting up paths to
Flamborough village. The **RSPB sanctuary** at **Bempton Cliffs**, reached along a quiet lane
from Bempton, is the best single place to see the area's thousands of cliff-nesting birds
– it's the only mainland gannetry in England. Bempton also has the second-largest
puffin colony in the country, with several thousand returning to the cliffs each year.
Late March and April is the best time to see the puffins, but the bird sanctuary's
Visitor Centre (daily March–Oct 9.30am–5pm, Nov–Feb 9.30am–4pm; parking £5;
☎01262 851179, ⓦrspb.org.uk) can advise on other breeds' activities.

Filey

FILEY, half a dozen miles north up the coast from Bempton, is at the very edge of the
Yorkshire Wolds (and technically in North Yorkshire). It has a good deal more class as a
resort than Bridlington, retaining many of its Edwardian features, including some
splendid panoramic gardens. It, too, claims miles of wide sandy beach, stretching most
of the way south to Flamborough Head and north the mile or so to the jutting rocks of
Filey Brigg, where a nature trail wends for a couple of miles through the surroundings.

12

ARRIVAL AND GETTING AROUND

By train Bridlington and Filey are linked by the regular service between Hull and Scarborough, and there are regular trains between York and Scarborough, further up the coast.

By bus There are buses from York to Bridlington (every 2hr; 1hr 45min), plus a service from Hull to Scarborough (every

THE EAST YORKSHIRE COAST

2hr; 2hr 50min) via Bridlington and Filey. There's also an hourly service between Bridlington, Filey and Scarborough, while the seasonal Sunday Spurn Ranger service (Easter–Oct; ☎ 01482 222222) gives access to the isolated Spurn Head coastline (though it can no longer go all the way to the point owing to erosion).

The North York Moors

Virtually the whole of the **North York Moors**, from the Hambleton and Cleveland hills in the west to the cliff-edged coastline to the east, is protected by one of the country's finest National Parks. The heather-covered, flat-topped hills are cut by deep, steep-sided valleys, and views here stretch for miles, interrupted only by giant cultivated forests. This is great walking country; footpaths include the superb **Cleveland Way**, one of England's premier long-distance National Trails, which embraces both wild moorland and the cliff scenery of the North Yorkshire coast. Barrows and ancient forts provide memorials of early settlers, mingling on the high moorland with the battered stone crosses of the first Christian inhabitants and the ruins of great monastic houses such as **Rievaulx Abbey**.

GETTING AROUND

By train The steam trains of the North Yorkshire Moors Railway (see box, p.563) run between Pickering and Grosmont and on to Whitby. At Grosmont you can connect with the regular trains on the Esk Valley line, running either 6 miles east to Whitby and the coast, or west through more remote country settlements (and ultimately to Middlesbrough).

By bus The main bus approaches to the moors are from Scarborough and York to the main towns of Helmsley and

THE NORTH YORK MOORS

Pickering pick up the free *Moors Explorer* timetable booklet from tourist offices and park information centres (or consult ☎ 01482 592929 or ⓦ eyms.co.uk). There are also seasonal Moorsbus services (April–Oct; ☎ 01845 597000, ⓦ moors .uk.net/moorsbus) connecting Pickering and Helmsley to everywhere of interest in the National Park. There are several departures daily in the school summer hols, fewer at other times (at least every Sun & bank hol Mon).

12

INFORMATION

National Park Visitor Centres There are two National Park Visitor Centres for the North York Moors, one in Danby (April–Oct daily 10am–5pm, Aug to 5.30pm; for winter hours check with centre; ☎ 01439 772737), and the other in Sutton Bank (April–July & Sept–Oct daily 10am–5pm, Aug daily 9.30am–5.30pm; for winter hours check with centre; ☎ 01845 597426). Both offer exhibitions,

pamphlets and maps, a café and a shop. The National Park's website is ⓦ northyorkmoors.org.uk.

Cleveland Way Project Provides maps and information about the route, including an annual, downloadable accommodation guide (☎ 01439 770657, ⓦ nationaltrail .co.uk/ClevelandWay).

Thirsk

The market town of **THIRSK**, 23 miles north of York, made the most of its strategic crossroads position on the ancient drove road between Scotland and York and on the historic east–west route from dales to coast. Its medieval prosperity is clear from the large, cobbled **Market Place** (markets Mon & Sat), while well-to-do citizens later endowed the town with fine Georgian houses and halls. However, Thirsk's main draw is its attachment to the legacy of local vet Alf Wight, better known as James Herriott. Thirsk was the "Darrowby" of the Herriott books, and the vet's former surgery, at 23 Kirkgate, is now the hugely popular **World of James Herriott** (daily: March–Oct 10am–5pm; Nov–Feb 10am–4pm; £8.50; ☎ 01845 524234, ⓦ worldofjamesherriot.org), crammed with period pieces and Herriott memorabilia.

By train The train station is a mile west of town on the A61 (Ripon road); minibuses connect the station with the town centre.

Destinations Middlesbrough (hourly; 44min); Manchester (hourly; 1hr 50min); London (every 2hr; 2hr 30min).

By bus Buses stop in the Market Place.

Destinations Northallerton (every 2hr; 25–30min); Ripon (every 2hr; 41min); York (every 1–2hr; 1hr).

By car Thirsk is just a 30min drive from York, making it an easy day-trip.

Tourist office 49 Market Place (Jan–March Mon–Sat 10am–3pm; April–June & Sept–Dec Mon–Sat 10am–4pm; July & Aug Mon–Sat 9.30am–4.30pm; ☎ 01845 522755, ⓦ visit-thirsk.org.uk).

ACCOMMODATION AND EATING

Gallery 18 Kirkgate ☎ 01845 523767, ⓦ gallery bedandbreakfast.co.uk. An award-winning B&B with three comfortable rooms and excellent breakfasts in an eighteenth-century Grade II-listed building. It's on a main street, and can get noisy when the pubs close. **£70**

Golden Fleece Market Place ☎ 01845 523108, ⓦ goldenfleecehotel.com. Good rooms and a nice busy atmosphere in this charming old coaching inn nicely

located on Thirsk's large cobbled square. They serve locally sourced food, too. Mon–Sat noon–3pm & 6.30–9.15pm, Sun noon–2pm & 6.30–9pm. **£95**

The Poplars Carlton Miniott ☎ 01845 522712, ⓦ thepoplarsthirsk.com. Near the station and the racecourse, this B&B offers clean rooms and "cottages" (actually cabins; three-night minimum stay). All have their own access. **£65**

Osmotherley and around

Eleven miles north of Thirsk, the little village of **OSMOTHERLEY** huddles around its green. The pretty settlement gets by as a hiking centre, since it's a key stop on the **Cleveland Way** as well as starting point for the brutal 42-mile **Lyke Wake Walk** to Ravenscar, south of Robin Hood's Bay.

Mount Grace Priory

On the A19 • April–Sept daily 10am–6pm; Oct daily 10am–5pm; Nov–March Sat & Sun 10am–4pm • £5.60; NT & EH ☎ 01609 883494, ⓦ nationaltrust.org.uk/mount-grace-priory, ⓦ english-heritage.org.uk • #80/#89 from Northallerton, then a 30min walk

An easy two-mile walk from Osmotherley via Chapel Wood Farm, the fourteenth-century **Mount Grace Priory** is the most important of England's nine Carthusian ruins. The Carthusians took a vow of silence and lived, ate and prayed alone in their two-storey cells, each separated from its neighbour by a privy, small garden and high walls. The foundations of the cells are still clearly visible, and one has been reconstructed to suggest its original layout.

Sutton Bank

The main A170 road enters the National Park from Thirsk as it climbs 500ft in half a mile to **Sutton Bank** (960ft), a phenomenal **viewpoint** from where the panorama extends across the Vale of York to the Pennines on the far horizon. While you're here, call in at the **National Park Visitor Centre** (see p.559) to pick up information on the **walks** and off-road **bike rides** you can make from here.

Kilburn

To the south of the A170, the **White Horse Nature Trail** (2–3 miles; 1hr 30min) skirts the crags of Roulston Scar en route to the **Kilburn White Horse**, northern England's only turf-cut figure, 314ft long and 228ft high. You could make a real walk of it by dropping a couple of miles down to pretty **KILBURN** village (a minor road also runs from the A170, passing the White Horse car park) which has been synonymous with woodcarving since the days of "Mouseman" Robert Thompson (1876–1955), whose woodcarvings are marked by his distinctive mouse motif. The **Mouseman Visitor Centre** (Easter–Oct daily 10am–5pm; Nov & Dec Wed–Sun

11am–4pm; £4.50; ☎01347 869102, ⓦrobertthompsons.co.uk) displays examples
of Thompson's personal furniture.

Coxwold

Most visitors to the attractive village of **COXWOLD** come to pay homage to the novelist
Laurence Sterne, who is buried by the south wall (close to the porch) in the churchyard
of **St Michael's**, where he was vicar from 1760 until his death in 1768. **Shandy Hall**,
further up the road past the church (house May–Sept Wed & Sun 2.30–4.30pm;
gardens May–Sept daily except Sat 11am–4.30pm; also by appointment; house &
gardens £4.50, gardens only £2.50; ☎01347 868465, ⓦlaurencesternetrust.org.uk),
was Sterne's home, now a museum crammed with literary memorabilia. It was here that
he wrote *A Sentimental Journey through France and Italy* and the wonderfully eccentric
The Life and Opinions of Tristram Shandy, Gentleman.

Helmsley and around

One of the moors' most appealing towns, **HELMSLEY** makes a perfect base for visiting
the western moors and Rievaulx Abbey. Local life revolves around a large cobbled
market square (market Fri), dominated by a boastful monument to the second earl of
Feversham, whose family was responsible for rebuilding most of the village in the
nineteenth century. The old **market cross** now marks the start of the 110-mile
Cleveland Way. Signposted from the square, it's easy to find **Helmsley Castle** (daily:
April–Sept 10am–6pm; Oct–Nov 10am–5pm; Nov–March Sat & Sun 10am–4pm;
£5.20; EH; ☎01439 770442, ⓦenglish-heritage.org.uk), its unique twelfth-century
D-shaped keep ringed by massive earthworks.

12

Rievaulx Abbey

Just over 2 miles northwest of Helmsley off the B1257 • April–Sept daily 10am–6pm; Oct to early Nov daily 10am–5pm; mid-Nov to
March Sat & Sun 10am–4pm • £6.20; EH • ☎01439 798228, ⓦ english-heritage.org.uk

From Helmsley you can easily walk across country to **Rievaulx Abbey** on a signposted
path (1hr 30min). Founded in 1132, the abbey became the mother church of the
Cistercians in England, quickly developing into a flourishing community with interests
in fishing, mining, agriculture and the woollen industry. At its height, 140 monks and
up to five hundred lay brothers lived and worked here, though numbers fell
dramatically once the Black Death (1348–49) had done its worst. The end came with
the Dissolution, when many of the walls were razed and the roof lead stripped – the
beautiful ruins, however, still suggest the abbey's former splendour.

Rievaulx Terrace

On the B1257, a couple of miles northwest of Helmsley • Feb–Nov daily 11am–5pm • £5.95; NT • ☎01439 798340 (summer) or
☎01439 748283 (winter), ⓦ nationaltrust.org.uk/rievaulx-terrace

Although they form some sort of ensemble with the abbey, there's no access between
the ruins and **Rievaulx Terrace**. This half-mile stretch of grass-covered terraces and
woodland was laid out as part of Duncombe Park in the 1750s, and was engineered
partly to enhance the views of the abbey. The resulting panorama over the ruins and
the valley below is superb, and this makes a great spot for a picnic.

ARRIVAL AND INFORMATION
HELMSLEY AND AROUND

By bus Buses from Scarborough (every 1hr 15min; 1hr
36min) and Pickering (every 1hr 15min; 35min) stop on or
near the Market Place. In addition, seasonal Moorsbus
services (April–Oct; ☎01845 597000, ⓦmoors.uk.net
/moorsbus), connect Helmsley to most places in the

National Park.
Tourist information There's no tourist office in Helmsley,
but English Heritage are happy to answer queries where
they can on ☎01439 770442. For the Cleveland Way,
contact ☎01439 770173 or check ⓦryedale.gov.uk.

ACCOMMODATION, EATING AND DRINKING

Black Swan Market Place ☎01439 770466, ⓦblack swan-helmsley.co.uk. An interesting Tudor/Georgian ex-coaching inn right on the main square, with a comfortable bar, airy restaurant, award-winning tearoom and charming, attentive staff. The hotel is progressively refurbishing its rooms. Daily 11am–11pm or later at weekends. Restaurant daily 7.30–9.30pm; tearoom daily 10am–5.30pm. **£144**

Feathers Hotel Market Place ☎01439 770275, ⓦfeathershotelhelmsley.co.uk. Pub serving restaurant food – all the staples, from £11.95 – and with a surprisingly large choice of rooms. Mon–Sat 11.30am–midnight, Sun 11.30am–11pm; food served Mon–Fri noon–2.30pm & 5.30–9pm, Sat noon–9pm, Sun noon–8.30pm. **£80**

★Feversham Arms 1 High St ☎01439 770766, ⓦfevershamarmshotel.com. One of Yorkshire's top hotels, multi-award-winning, luxurious yet unpretentious.

It has a pool, underground car park, spa and a terrific fine-dining restaurant. Look out for special deals. Mon–Sat noon–2.30pm & 6.45–9.30pm; Sun 12.30–2.30pm & 6.45–9.30pm. **£196**

★Star Inn Harome, 2 miles southeast of Helmsley ☎01439 770397, ⓦthestatharome.co.uk. The *Star* is not only a spectacularly beautiful thatched inn, but also one of Yorkshire's longest-standing Michelin-starred restaurants. Food is classic British and surprisingly affordable (main courses around £19–24), and the atmosphere is blessedly unpretentious. Accommodation is available in a separate building, and there's an associated shop/deli across the road. Mon 6–11pm, Tues–Sat 11.30–3pm & 6–11pm, Sun noon–11pm; food served Mon 6.15–9.30pm, Tues–Sat 11.30am–2pm & 6.15–9.30pm, Sun noon–6pm. **£150**

Hutton le Hole

Eight miles northeast of Helmsley, one of Yorkshire's quaintest villages, **HUTTON LE HOLE**, has become so great a tourist attraction that you'll have to come off-season to get much pleasure from its stream-crossed village green and the sight of sheep wandering freely through the lanes. Apart from the sheer photogenic quality of the place, the big draw is the family-oriented **Ryedale Folk Museum** (mid-Jan to March & Nov to early Dec daily 10am–4.30pm, April to Oct 10am–5.30pm; £7; ☎01751 417337, ⓦryedalefolkmuseum.co.uk), where local life is explored in a series of reconstructed buildings, notably a sixteenth-century house, a glass furnace, a crofter's cottage and a nineteenth-century blacksmith's shop.

ARRIVAL AND INFORMATION   HUTTON LE HOLE

By bus The #174 travels from/to Pickering once a day (30min).

National Park Information Centre At Ryedale Folk

Museum (mid-Jan to March & Nov to early Dec daily 10am–4.30pm, March to Oct 10am–5.30pm; ☎01751 417367). They have a list of local B&Bs.

ACCOMMODATION AND EATING

The Barn Hotel Hutton-le-Hole ☎01751 417311, ⓦthebarnhotel.info. Comfortable en-suite rooms and tearooms serving home-made cakes, scones, sandwiches and hot specials. Food served March–Oct daily 10.30am–4.30pm. **£79**

The Crown Hutton-le-Hole ☎01751 417343, ⓦcrown huttonlehole.com. Spacious real ale pub where you can

sit outside and enjoy the peace of the village. They serve traditional, freshly cooked food, too; you can eat well for under a tenner. Typically open daily 11am–10pm (later when busy); food served Mon–Thurs 11.45am–2.15pm & 5.30–8.15pm, Fri & Sat 11.45am–2.30pm & 5.30–8.30pm, Sun 11.45am–6pm; the pub is closed Mon & Tues during winter.

Pickering

The biggest centre for miles around, **PICKERING** takes for itself the title "Gateway to the Moors", which is pushing it a bit, though it's certainly a handy halt if you're touring the villages and dales of the **eastern moors**. Its most attractive feature is its motte and bailey **castle** on the hill north of the Market Place (April–Sept daily 10am–6pm; Oct–Nov 10am–5pm; £4.20; EH; ☎01751 474989, ⓦenglish-heritage.org.uk) reputedly used by every English monarch up to 1400 as a base for hunting in nearby Blandsby Park. The other spot worth investigating is the **Beck Isle Museum of Rural Life** on Bridge Street

---

THE NORTH YORKSHIRE MOORS RAILWAY

The **North Yorkshire Moors Railway** (☎01751 472508, ⓦnymr.co.uk) provides a double whammy of nostalgia, with the rolling stock, station furniture and smell of steam conjuring up images of bygone travel (especially to those who remember rail in the mid-twentieth century), while the countryside through which the trains pass is reminiscent of an England which in many places has disappeared. Lately, the railway has been attracting a younger generation, too, as a result of its connection with the **Harry Potter films**: Goathland Station was used in the first of the Harry Potter films as **Hogsmeade**, where Harry and co disembarked from the *Hogwarts Express*.

The line, completed by George Stephenson in 1835 just ten years after the opening of the Stockton and Darlington Railway, connects **Pickering** with the Esk Valley (Middlesbrough–Whitby) line at **Grosmont**, eighteen miles to the north. Scheduled **services** operate year-round (limited to weekends and school hols Nov–March), and a **day-return ticket** costs £19. Daily services also run on the Esk Valley line from Grosmont to the nearby seaside resort of Whitby from April to early November, with a return fare from Pickering of £25.

(Feb–Nov daily 10am–5pm; £6; ☎01751 473653, ⓦbeckislemuseum.org.uk), which has reconstructions of a gents' outfitters and barber's shop, a case full of knickers, and a painting of two giant Welsh guardsmen produced by Rex Whistler for a children's party. **Market** day in town is Monday, and there's a farmers' market on the first Thursday of the month.

ARRIVAL AND INFORMATION   PICKERING

By train The steam trains of the North Yorkshire Moors Railway (see box above) run between Pickering and Grosmont and on to Whitby. The station is a 5min signposted walk from the main street.

By bus Buses stop outside the library and tourist office, opposite the Co-op in the centre of town.

Destinations Helmsley (hourly; 35min); Scarborough (hourly; 53min); Whitby (4–6 daily; 1hr 4min); York (hourly; 1hr 10min).

Tourist office The Ropery, Pickering (March–Oct Mon–Sat 9.30am–5pm, Sun 9.30am–4pm; Nov–Feb Mon–Sat 9.30am–4pm; ☎01751 473791, ⓦryedale.gov.uk).

ACCOMMODATION AND EATING

The tourist office can help with **B&Bs**, though Whitby, just a 20min drive away on the coast, is the better overnight destination (see p.566).

★**The White Swan** Market Place ☎01751 472288, ⓦwhite-swan.co.uk. Delightful traditional coaching inn, fully refurbished and updated, with contemporary and

traditional bedrooms, and fine Modern British food (mains from £13.95). Daily 7.30am–11pm, food served noon–2pm & 6.45–9pm. **£149**

The North Yorkshire coast

The **North Yorkshire coast** is the southernmost stretch of a cliff-edged shore that stretches almost unbroken to the Scottish border. **Scarborough** is the biggest resort, with a full set of attractions and a terrific beach. Cute **Robin Hood's Bay** is the most popular of the coastal villages, with fishing and smuggling traditions, while bluff **Staithes** – a fishing harbour on the far edge of North Yorkshire – has yet to tip over into a full-blown tourist trap. **Whitby**, between the two, is the best stopover, with its fine sands, good facilities, abbey ruins, Georgian buildings and maritime heritage – more than any other local place Whitby celebrates Captain Cook as one of its own. Two of the best sections of the **Cleveland Way** start from Whitby: southeast to Robin Hood's Bay (six miles) and northwest to Staithes (eleven miles), both along thrilling high-cliff paths.

INFORMATION   THE NORTH YORKSHIRE COAST

Tourist information ⓦdiscoveryorkshirecoast.com is a useful source of online information, and there are

tourist offices at Scarborough (see p.565) and Whitby (see p.568).

12

Scarborough

The oldest resort in the country, **SCARBOROUGH** first attracted early seventeenth-century visitors to its newly discovered mineral springs. To the Victorians it was "the Queen of the Watering Places", but Scarborough saw its biggest transformation after World War II, when it became a holiday haven for workers from the industrial heartlands. All the traditional ingredients of a beach resort are still here in force, from superb, clean sands and kitsch amusement arcades to the more refined pleasures of its tight-knit old-town streets and a genteel round of quiet parks and gardens. In addition to the sights detailed below, make sure to drop into the **Church of St Mary** (1180), below the castle on Castle Road, whose graveyard contains the tomb of Anne Brontë (see p.535), who died here in 1849.

Rotunda Museum

Vernon Rd • Tues–Sun 10am–5pm • £3 • ☎ 01723 353665, ⓦ rotundamuseum.co.uk

The second-oldest purpose-built museum in the country (the oldest is in Oxford), the **Rotunda Museum** was constructed to the plans of William Smith, the founder of English geology, and opened in 1829. A fascinating building in its own right, it has recently been updated to include in its venerable shell some high-tech displays on geology and local history. The Dinosaur Coast Gallery is particularly child-friendly.

Art Gallery

The Crescent • Tues–Sun 10am–5pm • £3 • ☎ 01723 384503 ⓦ scarboroughartgallery.co.uk

Scarborough's **Art Gallery**, housed in an Italianate villa, contains the town's permanent collection – largely the work of local artists, and including paintings, posters and photography – which gives an insight into the way the town has been depicted over the centuries.

Scarborough Castle

Castle Rd • April–Sept daily 10am–6pm; Oct daily 10am–5pm; Nov to mid-Feb Sat & Sun 10am–4pm • £5; EH • ☎ 01765 608888, ⓦ english-heritage.org.uk

There's no better place to acquaint yourself with the local layout than **Scarborough Castle**, mounted on a jutting headland between two golden-sanded bays. Bronze and Iron Age relics have been found on the wooded castle crag, together with fragments of a fourth-century Roman signalling station, Saxon and Norman chapels and a Viking camp, reputedly built by a Viking with the nickname of Scardi (or "harelip"), from which the town's name derives.

The bays

The miniature **North Bay Railway** (Easter–Sept daily 10am–4pm; ☎ 01723 368791, ⓦ nbr.org.uk) runs up to the **Sea Life Centre and Marine Sanctuary** on the North Bay at Scalby Mills (daily 10am–5pm; £16.20, £8.10 if ordered online; ☎ 01723 373414, ⓦ visitsealife.com/scarborough), distinguished by its white pyramids. From the harbourside, short **cruises** and **speedboat trips** shoot off throughout the day in the summer. For unique entertainment, head for Peasholm Park, where **naval warfare**, in the shape of miniature man-powered naval vessels, battle it out on the lake (July & Aug Mon, Thurs & Sat; £3.90; details from the tourist office).

The **South Bay** is more refined, backed by the Valley Gardens and the Italianate meanderings of the South Cliff Gardens, and topped by an esplanade from which a **hydraulic lift** (April–Sept daily 10am–5pm) chugs down to the beach.

ARRIVAL AND DEPARTURE   SCARBOROUGH

By train The train station is at the top of town facing Westborough.
Destinations Hull (every 2hr; 1hr 30min); Leeds (hourly; 1hr 16min); York (hourly; 50min).

By bus Buses pull up outside the train station or in the surrounding streets. National Express services (direct from London) stop in the car park behind the station.
Destinations Bridlington (hourly; 1hr 18min); Filey

(hourly; 30min); Helmsley (hourly; 1hr 30min); Hull (hourly; 1hr 30min); Leeds (hourly; 2hr 40min); Pickering (hourly; 1hr); Robin Hood's Bay (hourly; 38min); Whitby (hourly; 1hr); York (hourly; 1hr 35min).

GETTING AROUND AND INFORMATION

By bus Open-top seafront buses (Feb–Nov daily from 9.30am, every 12–20min; £2 return) run between North Bay to the Spa Complex in South Bay.

Tourist offices Scarborough has two sources of tourist information; one inside the Brunswick Shopping Centre on Westborough (April–June & Sept Mon, Tues & Thurs–Sat 9.30am–5.30pm, Wed 10am–5.30pm, Sun 11am–4.30pm; July & Aug same hours except Sun 10.30am–4.30pm; check for winter hours; ☎01723 383636), and the other on Sandside by the harbour (daily: April–June, Sept & Oct 10am–5.30pm; July & Aug 9.30am–7pm, ☎01723 383636).

ACCOMMODATION

Beiderbecke's 1–3 The Crescent ☎01723 365733, ⓦbeiderbeckes.com. Boutique hotel in a sedate terrace (dating from 1832) on the South Cliff, with free parking. Rooms are comfortable and the bar is old-fashioned (in a good way), with live jazz on Sats. They have a stylish, reasonably priced brasserie, too. **£130**

Crescent Hotel The Crescent ☎01723 360929. A spacious, slightly old-fashioned hotel catering for both holiday-makers and business folk, with friendly, helpful staff, comprehensive facilities and a fine restaurant, all housed in mid-nineteenth century splendour. **£107**

YHA Scarborough Burniston Rd, 2 miles north of town ☎01723 361176, ⓦyha.org.uk. In an early seventeenth-century watermill a 15min walk from the sea, this is a good hostel for families with kids. Dorms **£13**; private rooms (for four) **£60**

EATING AND DRINKING

Café Fish 19 York Place, at the intersection with Somerset Terrace ☎01723 500301. More of a top-end fish restaurant than a fish-and-chip shop, where a two-course dinner with wine could feature fish curry, steamed mussels or Thai fishcakes, and will cost from about £30. Gets very busy at weekends. Daily 5.30–10pm.

Café Italia 36 St Nicholas Cliff ☎01723 501973. Enchanting, tiny, authentic Italian coffee bar. They stick to what they're good at: excellent coffee, ice cream and cakes. Daily 9am–9pm.

Golden Grid 4 Sandside ☎01723 360922, ⓦgolden grid.co.uk. The harbourside's choicest fish-and-chip establishment, "catering for the promenader since 1883". Offers grilled fish, crab and lobster, a fruits-de-mer platter and a wine list alongside the standard crispy-battered fry-up. Decent portions of fish from £7.80. Easter–Oct Mon–Thurs 10am–8.30pm, Fri 10am–9pm, Sat 10am–9.30pm, Sun 11am–6.30pm; Nov–Easter opens 11am, closing varies.

ENTERTAINMENT

Scarborough Open Air Theatre Burniston Rd ☎01723 818111, ⓦscarboroughopenairtheatre.com. Europe's largest open air theatre, built in 1932, hosts a range of top-end concerts and gigs by the likes of Jessie J, Boyzone, Status Quo.

Stephen Joseph Theatre Westborough ☎01723 370541, ⓦsjt.uk.com. Housed in a former Art Deco cinema, this premieres every new play of local playwright Alan Ayckbourn and promotes strong seasons of theatre and film. There's a good, moderately priced café/restaurant and a bar open daily except Sun.

Robin Hood's Bay

The most heavily visited spot on this stretch of coast, **ROBIN HOOD'S BAY** is made up of gorgeous narrow streets and pink-tiled cottages toppling down the cliff-edge site, evoking the romance of a time when this was both a hard-bitten fishing community and smugglers' den par excellence. From the upper village, lined with Victorian villas, now mostly B&Bs, it's a very steep walk down the hill to the harbour. The **Old Coastguard Station** (Jan, March, Nov & Dec Sat & Sun 10am–4pm, Feb daily 10am–4pm, April–Oct daily 10am–5pm, late Dec Mon–Wed, Sat & Sun 10am–4pm; free; NT; ☎01947 885900; ⓦnationaltrust.org.uk/yorkshire-coast) has been turned into a visitor centre with displays relating to the area's geology and sealife. When the tide is out, the massive rock beds below are exposed, split by a geological fault line and studded with fossil remains. There's an easy circular walk (2.5 miles) to **Boggle Hole** and its youth hostel, a mile south, returning inland via the path along the old Scarborough–Whitby railway line.

ARRIVAL AND GETTING AROUND   ROBIN HOOD'S BAY

By bus Robin Hood's Bay is connected to Whitby by Arriva #93 buses (hourly; 20min) and to Scarborough by Arriva #93 buses (hourly; 40min).

By bike A couple of miles northwest of Robin Hood's Bay

at Hawsker, on the A171, Trailways (☎01947 820207, ⓦtrailways.info) is a bike rental outfit based in the old Hawsker train station, perfectly placed for day-trips in either direction along the disused railway line.

INFORMATION

Tourist information Though you can pick up a lot of information at the Old Coastguard Station (Jan, March, Nov & Dec Sat & Sun 10am–4pm, Feb daily 10am–4pm, April–Oct daily 10am–5pm, late Dec Mon–Wed, Sat &

Sun 10am–4pm, ☎01947 885900), the nearest official tourist offices are in Whitby (see p.568) and Scarborough (see p.565).

ACCOMMODATION AND EATING

Many people visit Robin Hood's Bay as a day-trip from Whitby. You can ask about accommodation in Whitby's tourist office (see p.568), or simply stroll the streets of the old part of the village to see if any of the small cottage **B&Bs** has vacancies. There are three good **pubs** in the lower village, two of which offer rooms – food at the *Bay Hotel* is the best.

Bay Hotel On the harbour ☎01947 880278, ⓦbayhotel.info. At the traditional start or end of the Coast-to-Coast Walk, this inn offers rooms and bar meals, with main courses at around £9–£11. Mon–Sat 11am–11pm, Sun noon–11pm; food served noon–2pm & 6.30–9pm. **£70**

Swell Café Old Chapel, Chapel St ☎01947 880180, ⓦswell.org.uk. A giftshop and café in an old Wesleyan Chapel, built in 1779, where John Wesley himself once

preached. They serve a good range of snacks, sandwiches, cakes, teas and coffees, and alcoholic drinks, and there are great coastal views from its terrace tables. Daily 10am–4.15pm or later if busy.

YHA Boggle Hole Boggle Hole, Fylingthorpe ☎0845 371 9504, ⓦyha.org.uk. In a former mill in a wooded ravine about a mile south of Robin Hood's Bay at Mill Beck, this hostel has a great location near the beach. Dorms **£18**; doubles **£59**

Whitby

If there's one essential stop on the North Yorkshire coast it's **WHITBY**, with its historical associations, atmospheric ruins, fishing harbour, lively music scene and intrinsic charm. The seventh-century cliff-top **abbey** here made Whitby one of the key foundations of the early Christian period, and a centre of great learning. Below, on the harbour banks of the River Esk, for a thousand years the local herring boats landed their catch until the great **whaling** boom of the eighteenth century transformed the fortunes of the town. Melville's *Moby Dick* makes much of Whitby

---

BRAM STOKER AND DRACULA

The story of **Dracula** is well known, but it's the exact attention to the geographical detail of Whitby – little changed since Bram Stoker first wrote the words – which has proved a huge attraction to visitors. Using first-hand observation of a town he knew well – he stayed at a house on the West Cliff, now marked by a plaque – Stoker built a story which mixed real locations, legend and historical fact: the grounding of Count Dracula's ship on Tate Hill Sands was based on an actual event reported in the local papers.

It's hardly surprising that the town has cashed in on its **Dracula Trail**. The various sites – Tate Hill Sands, the abbey, church and steps, the graveyard, Stoker's house – can all be visited, while down on the harbourside the Dracula Experience attempts to pull in punters to its rather lame horror-show antics. Keen interest has also been sparked among the **Goth** fraternity, who now come to town en masse a couple of times a year (in late spring and around Halloween) for a vampire's ball, concerts and readings.

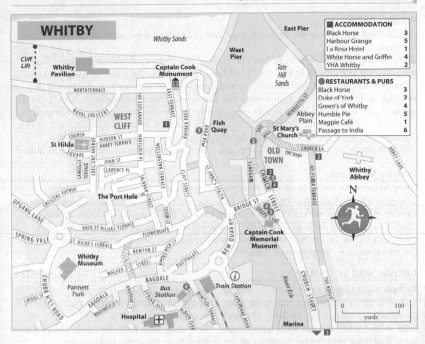

whalers such as William Scoresby, and James Cook took his first seafaring steps from the town in 1746, on his way to becoming a national hero. All four of Captain Cook's ships of discovery – the *Endeavour*, *Resolution*, *Adventure* and *Discovery* – were built in this town.

Walking around Whitby is one of its great pleasures. Divided by the River Esk, the town splits into two halves joined by a swing bridge: the cobbled **old town** to the east, and the newer (mostly eighteenth- and nineteenth-century) town across the bridge, generally known as **West Cliff**. **Church Street** is the old town's main thoroughfare, barely changed in aspect since the eighteenth century, though now lined with tearooms and giftshops. Parallel **Sandgate** has more of the same, the two streets meeting at the small **marketplace** where souvenirs and trinkets are sold, and which hosts a farmers' market every Thursday.

Captain Cook Memorial Museum

Grape Lane • Daily: Feb–March 11am–3pm; April–Oct 9.45am–5pm • £4.80 • ☎ 01947 601900, ⓦ cookmuseumwhitby.co.uk

Whitby, understandably, likes to make a fuss of Captain Cook, who served an apprenticeship here from 1746–49 under John Walker, a Quaker ship owner. The **Captain Cook Memorial Museum**, housed in Walker's rickety old house, contains an impressive amount of memorabilia, including ships' models, letters, and paintings by artists seconded to Cook's voyages.

Church of St Mary

At the north end of Church Street, you climb the famous **199 steps** of the Church Stairs – now paved, but originally a wide wooden staircase built for pall-bearers carrying coffins to the **Church of St Mary** above. This is an architectural amalgam dating back to 1110, boasting a Norman chancel arch, a profusion of eighteenth-century panelling, box pews unequalled in England and a triple-decker pulpit – note the built-in ear trumpets, added for the benefit of a nineteenth-century rector's deaf wife.

Whitby Abbey

Abbey Lane • April–Sept daily 10am–6pm; Oct 10am–5pm; Nov–March Sat & Sun 10am–4pm • £6.60; EH • ☎01947 603568, Ⓦ english-heritage.org.uk

The cliff-top ruins of **Whitby Abbey** are some of the most evocative in England. Its monastery was founded in 657 by St Hilda of Hartlepool, daughter of King Oswy of Northumberland, and by 664 had become important enough to host the **Synod of Whitby**, an event of seminal importance in the development of English Christianity. It settled once and for all the question of determining the date of Easter, and adopted the rites and authority of the Roman rather than the Celtic Church. You'll discover all this and more in the **Visitor Centre** (same hours), which is housed in the shell of the adjacent mansion, built after the Dissolution using material from the plundered abbey.

Whitby Museum

Pannett Park • Tues–Sun 9.30am–4.30pm • £5 • ☎01947 602908, Ⓦ whitbymuseum.org.uk

The gloriously eclectic **Whitby Museum** features more Cook memorabilia, including various objects and stuffed animals brought back as souvenirs by his crew, as well as casefuls of exhibits devoted to Whitby's seafaring tradition, its whaling industry in particular. Some of the best and largest fossils of Jurassic period reptiles unearthed on the east coast are also preserved here.

ARRIVAL AND INFORMATION   WHITBY

By train Whitby's train station is right in the centre of town on Station Square, just south of the swing bridge, conveniently over the road from the Tourist Information Centre and next to the bus station. Whitby is the terminus of the Esk Valley line, which runs here from Middlesbrough, and which connects with the steam trains of the North Yorkshire Moors Railway at Grosmont, which run south to Pickering (see box, p.563).
Destinations Danby (4–5 daily; 40min); Great Ayton (4–5 daily; 1hr 5min); Grosmont (4–5 daily; 16min);

Middlesbrough (4–5 daily; 1hr 30min).
By bus The bus station is next to the train station in the centre of town.
Destinations Robin Hood's Bay (hourly; 19min); Staithes (every 30min; 30min); York (4–6 daily; 2hr).
Tourist office On the corner of Langborne Road and New Quay Road, across the road from the train station (daily: April–June & Sept–Oct daily 9.30am–6pm; July & Aug 9.30am–7pm; Nov–March 9.30am–4.30pm; ☎01723 383636, Ⓦ discoveryorkshirecoast.com or Ⓦ visitwhitby.com).

ACCOMMODATION

Black Horse 91 Church St ☎01947 602906, Ⓦ the -black-horse.com. Four simple en-suite guest rooms above this fine old pub (see below), each named after one of Captain Cook's ships. £60
Harbour Grange Spital Bridge, Church St ☎01947 600817, Ⓦ whitbybackpackers.co.uk. Backpackers' hostel right on the river (eastern side) with 24 beds in five small dorms. Self-catering kitchen and lounge; 11.30pm curfew. £18
★**La Rosa Hotel** 5 East Terrace ☎01947 606981, Ⓦ larosa.co.uk. Eccentric B&B with themed rooms done out in extravagantly individual style courtesy of auctions, eBay and car boot sales. Great fun, with terrific views of the

harbour and the abbey. Breakfast picnic delivered in a basket to your door. Street parking. £110
White Horse and Griffin 87 Church St ☎01947 604857, Ⓦ whitehorseandgriffin.co.uk. In the centre of Whitby's old town, with wonderful views of the harbour. Nicely renovated rooms (and several cottages) with many original features. It's full of character, but can be noisy. £70
★**YHA Whitby** Abbey House, East Cliff ☎0845 371 9049, Ⓦ yha.org.uk. Flagship hostel in a Grade 1 listed building next to the Abbey Visitor Centre. Stunning views, good facilities and a Victorian conservatory, tearoom and restaurant. Rates include breakfast and entry to the abbey. Dorms £15; doubles £59

EATING AND DRINKING

Black Horse 91 Church St ☎01947 602906, Ⓦ the -black-horse.com. Lovely old pub (parts date from the seventeenth century) in the heart of the old town, with real ales and food served all day, including tapas, Yorkshire cheeses and local seafood. Easter–Nov Mon–Sat 11am–11pm, Sun noon–11pm; Dec–Easter noon–4pm & 7–11pm.

★**Duke of York** 124 Church St ☎01947 600324, Ⓦ dukeofyork.co.uk. In a great position at the bottom of the 199 steps, this is a warm and inviting pub, with beams, nautical memorabilia, church pews and views across the harbour and West Cliff. Come for good real ales, modern pub food and music. Daily Mon–Thurs & Sun

12

WHITBY FOLK WEEK

Whitby has a strong **local music** scene, with an emphasis on folk and world music. During the annual **Whitby Folk Week** (ⓦwhitbyfolk.co.uk), held the week preceding the August bank holiday, the town is filled day and night with singers, bands, traditional dancers, storytellers and music workshops. The best place to find out more **information** is at *The Port Hole*, 16 Skinner Street (☏01947 603475), a Fair Trade craft shop that's also the HQ of local collective Musicport (ⓦmusicportfestival.com), who put on gigs from big names in the world/folk scene and hold a renowned annual World Music Festival in Bridlington in November.

11am–11pm, Fri 11am–11.30pm, Sat 11am– midnight; food served noon–9pm.

Green's of Whitby 13 Bridge St ☏01947 600284, ⓦgreensofwhitby.com. A few yards from the swing bridge, and reckoned by many to be the best restaurant in Whitby, friendly and unpretentious *Green's* has a lively bistro downstairs and a more formal dining room on the first floor, with the same menu and prices available in both (mains around £11–£20). Ingredients are locally sourced, with lots of good fish and meat dishes. Mon–Fri noon–2pm & 6.30–9.30pm, Sat & Sun noon–10pm.

★**Humble Pie** 163 Church St ☏07919 074954, ⓦhumblepiemash.com. Tiny sixteenth-century building serving a range of pies, cooked fresh to order – steak, stout and leek, Romany, Homity, haggis and neep, and many more – with mash and peas. The decor is 1940s, with World War II background music. All pies £5.99; soft drinks only. Mon–Sat noon–8pm, Sun noon–4pm.

Magpie Café 14 Pier Rd ☏01947 602058, ⓦmagpiecafe.co.uk. Said by Rick Stein to be one of the best fish-and-chip shops in the country, the *Magpie* has served food from its 1750-built premises since the start of World War II. To call it a fish-and-chip shop is a bit disingenuous – although it provides the normal takeaway service, it also serves lesser-known fish like Woof and John Dory in its restaurant (prices from £10.95, depending on fish) and has an extensive wine list. Usually daily 11.30am–9pm, but check before coming.

Passage to India 30–31 Windsor Terrace ☏01947 606500, ⓦpassagetoindia.eu. Stylish tandoori restaurant near the station, with bright red-and-black decor, great food, and friendly, efficient service. Main courses around £8–12; look out for the Tandoori king prawn *karahi*, or the Lam Kam. Mon–Thurs 5.30pm–midnight, Fri 5.30pm–1am, Sat noon–1am, Sun noon–midnight.

Staithes

Beyond Whitby Sands, a fine coastal walk starts at Sandsend, leads through pretty Runswick Bay, and reaches, in around four hours, the fishing village of **STAITHES**. An improbably beautiful grouping of huddled stone houses around a small harbour, the village is backed by the severe outcrop of Cowbar Nab, a sheer cliff face that protects the northern flank of the village. James Cook worked here in a draper's shop before moving to Whitby, and he's remembered in the **Captain Cook and Staithes Heritage Centre**, on the High Street (Feb–Nov daily 10am–5pm; Dec & Jan Sat & Sun 10am–5pm; £3; ☏01947 841454, ⓦcaptaincookatstaithes.co.uk), which recreates an eighteenth-century street among other interesting exhibits. Other than this, you'll have to content yourself with pottering about the rocks near the harbour – there's no beach to speak of – or clambering the nearby cliffs for spectacular views. At **Boulby**, a mile and a half's trudge up the coastal path (45min), you're walking on the highest cliff (670ft) on England's east coast.

ACCOMMODATION

STAITHES

Endeavour House 1 High St ☏01947 841029 (rooms), ☏07969 054556 (restaurant), ⓦendeavour-restaurant .co.uk. Three lovely doubles in this restaurant-B&B located in a two-centuries-old house by the harbour. Parking available in municipal (£6/day) and private (Glen Vale, £5/day) car parks. There's also a restaurant, run separately from the B&B, with a bistro-type menu (mains from £11.95). Opening times vary – phone for details. **£85**

12

The Northeast

BAMBURGH CASTLE

13

The Northeast

Remote and breathtakingly beautiful, the county of Northumberland forms the bulk of the northeast of England. An enticing medley of delightful market towns, glorious golden beaches, wooded dells, wild uplands and an unsurpassed collection of historical monuments, it's undoubtedly the main draw in the Northeast, and where you should focus the majority of your time. South of Northumberland lies the county of Durham, famous for its lovely university town and magnificent twelfth-century cathedral, while to the southeast and edged by the North Sea is industrial Tyne and Wear. It's home to the busy and burgeoning metropolis of Newcastle upon Tyne, a dynamic and distinctive city crammed with cultural attractions, great shops and an exceptionally energetic nightlife.

While its most recent past is defined by industry and in particular post-industrial hardship, the Northeast has an eventful early history: Romans, Vikings and Normans have all left dramatic evidence of their colonization, none more cherished than the 84-mile-long **Hadrian's Wall**, built by the Romans in 122 AD to contain the troublesome tribes of the far north. Thousands come each year to walk along parts, or all, of the Wall, or to cycle the nearby National Route 72. Neighbouring Northumberland National Park also has plenty for outdoors enthusiasts, with the huge **Kielder Water** reservoir, and surrounding footpaths and cycleways.

As well as Roman ruins, medieval **castles** scatter the region, the best-preserved being Alnwick, with its wonderful gardens, and stocky Bamburgh, on the coast. The shoreline round here, from Amble past Bamburgh to the Scottish border town of Berwick-upon-Tweed – and officially the end of Northumberland – is simply stunning, boasting miles of pancake-flat, dune-backed beach and a handful of off-shore islands. Reached by a tidal causeway, the lonely little islet of **Lindisfarne** – Holy Island – where early Christian monks created the Lindisfarne Gospels, is the most famous, while not far away to the south, near Seahouses, the **Farne Islands** are the perfect habitat for large colonies of seabirds including puffins, guillemots and kittiwakes.

South of Northumberland, the counties of **Durham** and **Tyne and Wear** better illustrate the Northeast's industrial heritage. It was here in 1825 that the world's first railway opened – the Darlington and Stockton line – with local coal and ore fuelling the shipbuilding and heavy-engineering companies of Tyneside. Abandoned coalfields, train lines, quaysides and factories throughout the area have been transformed into superb, child-friendly tourist attractions.

GETTING AROUND   **THE NORTHEAST**

By public transport The main East Coast train line runs along the coast from London King's Cross to Edinburgh, calling at Darlington, Durham, Newcastle and Berwick-upon-Tweed, while cross-country trains and buses serve smaller towns and villages inland. In the more remote areas public transport is spotty, so it's best to have your own car or bike.

LINDISFARNE CASTLE, HOLY ISLAND

Highlights

❶ Durham Cathedral Said to be the finest Norman building in Europe, this awe-inspiring cathedral soars above the River Wear. **See p.577**

❷ Beamish Museum Exceptional open-air museum that recreates the Northeast's industrial past. **See p.580**

❸ Killhope Lead Mining Museum Put on a hard hat and get down the pit to see what life was really like for the Weardale coal miners. **See p.584**

❹ Newcastle nightlife From raucous clubs and chic wine bars to cosy boozers and chilled-out indie gigs, there's something for everybody. **See p.592**

❺ Hadrian's Wall Walk the length of the greatest Roman monument in England. See p.595

❻ Northumberland castles The Northumberland coast is littered with beautiful castles, telling of a violent past ridden with ferocious battles and embittered family feuds. See p.603

❼ Holy Island A brooding lump of rock reached by a tidal causeway, this is a cradle of Christianity, where the splendid, illuminated Lindisfarne Gospels were created. **See p.607**

HIGHLIGHTS ARE MARKED ON THE MAP ON PP.574–575

N

0   miles   10

NORTH SEA

SCOTLAND

Edinburgh

Tweed

A697

A698

Coldstream

Kirk Yetholm

Norham Castle

Cornhill-on-Tweed

Heatherslaw Light Railway

Etal Castle

Etal

Ford

Branxton

Crookham

A697

The Cheviot (2674ft)

B6525

THE CHEVIOT HILLS

REDESDALE

KIELDER FOREST PARK

Kielder

Kielder Water

Leaplish

Belvedere

Falstone

Tower Knowe

Stannersburn

Greenhaugh

Tarset

Byrness

Otterburn

NORTHUMBERLAND NATIONAL PARK

A68

Berwick-upon-Tweed

Scremerston

Beal

Holy Island 7

Waren Mill

Farne Islands

Bamburgh 6

Seahouses

Beadnell

Belford

Wooler

Chillingham Castle 6

Eglingham

A697

Newton-by-the-Sea

Embleton

Dunstanburgh Castle 6

Craster

Alnmouth

Alnwick

A1

B1340

Newton-on-the-Moor

Warkworth 6

Amble

Cragside

Rothbury

A697

Wallington

Cambo

Morpeth

A189

Ashington

Bedlington

Edinburgh

13 Durham

The handsome city of **DURHAM** is best known for its beautiful Norman **cathedral** – there's a tremendous view of it as you approach the city by train from the south – and its flourishing university, founded in 1832. Together, these form a little island of privilege in what's otherwise a moderately sized, working-class city. It's worth visiting for a couple of days – there are plenty of attractions, but it's more the overall atmosphere that captivates, enhanced by the omnipresent golden stone, slender bridges and glint of the river. The heart of the city is the **marketplace**, flanked by the Guildhall and St Nicholas Church. The cathedral and church sit on a wooded peninsula to the west, while southwards stretch narrow streets lined with shops and cafés.

Brief history

Durham's history revolves around its cathedral. Completed in just forty years, the cathedral was founded in 1093 to house the shrine of **St Cuthbert**, arguably the Northeast's most important and venerated saint (see box opposite). Soon after Cuthbert was laid to rest here, the bishops of Durham were granted extensive powers to control the troublesome northern marches of the Kingdom – a rabble of invading Picts from Scotland and revolting Norman earls – ruling as semi-independent **Prince Bishops**, with their own army, mint and courts of law. At the peak of their power in the fourteenth century, the office went into decline – especially in the wake of the Reformation – yet clung to the vestiges of their authority until 1836, when they ceded

ST CUTHBERT

Born in North Northumbria in 653, **Cuthbert** spent most of his youth in Melrose Abbey in Scotland, from where he moved briefly to Lindisfarne Island, which was at that time a well-known centre of religious endeavour. Preferring the peace and rugged solitude of the Farne Islands, he lived on Inner Farne for thirty years. News of his piety spread, however, and he was head-hunted to become Bishop of Lindisfarne, a position he accepted reluctantly. Uncomfortable in the limelight, he soon returned to Inner Farne, and when he died his remains were moved to Lindisfarne before being carted off to Durham Cathedral.

them to the Crown. They abandoned Durham Castle for their palace in Bishop Auckland (see p.580) and transferred their old home to the fledgling Durham University, England's third-oldest seat of learning after Oxford and Cambridge.

Durham Cathedral

July & Aug Mon–Sat 9.30am–8pm, Sun 12.30–8pm; Sept–June Mon–Sat 9.30am–6pm, Sun 12.30–5.30pm • Donation requested; Cathedral Highlights Pass (£5) covers entry to the Monks' Dormitory, the Treasures of St Cuthbert and the audiovisual displays • Guided tours April–Oct 2–3 daily • **Tower** Mon–Sat 10am–4pm, Sun 1–2.30pm; access sometimes restricted, call to check **Monks' Dormitory** April–Oct Mon–Sat 10am–4pm, Sun 2–4.30pm **Treasures of St Cuthbert** Mon–Sat 10am–4.30pm, Sun 2–4.30pm • £5 • ☎ 0191 306 4266, ⓦ durhamcathedral.co.uk

From the marketplace, it's a five-minute walk up Saddler Street to **Durham Cathedral**, considered a supreme example of the Norman-Romanesque style. The awe-inspiring **nave** used pointed arches for the first time in England, raising the vaulted ceiling to new and dizzying heights. The weight of the stone is borne by massive pillars, their heaviness relieved by striking Moorish-influenced geometric patterns. A door on the western side gives access to the **tower**, from where there are beautiful views. Separated from the nave by a Victorian marble screen is the **choir**, where the dark Restoration stalls are overshadowed by the 13ft-high **bishop's throne**. Beyond, the **Chapel of the Nine Altars** dates from the thirteenth century. Here, and around the **Shrine of St Cuthbert**, much of the stonework is of local Weardale marble, each dark shaft bearing its own pattern of fossils. Cuthbert himself lies beneath a plain marble slab, his shrine having gained a reputation over the centuries for its curative powers. The legend was given credence in 1104, when the saint's body was exhumed in Chester-le-Street for reburial here, and was found to be completely uncorrupted, more than four hundred years after his death on Lindisfarne. Almost certainly, this was the result of his fellow monks having (unintentionally) preserved the body by laying it in sand containing salt crystals.

Back near the entrance, at the west end of the church is the **Galilee Chapel**; begun in the 1170s, its light and exotic decoration is in imitation of the Great Mosque of Córdoba. The chapel contains the simple tombstone of the **Venerable Bede** (see p.594), the Northumbrian monk credited with being England's first historian. Bede died at the monastery of Jarrow in 735, and his remains were first transferred to the cathedral in 1020.

The Monks' Dormitory and Treasures of St Cuthbert

A large wooden doorway opposite the cathedral's main entrance leads into the spacious **cloisters**, flanked by what remains of the monastic buildings. On the right of the passage lies the **Monks' Dormitory** with its original twelfth-century oak roof – it now houses the cathedral library. At the end of the passage, in the undercroft, the **Treasures of St Cuthbert** exhibition displays some striking relics, including the cathedral's original twelfth-century lion-head Sanctuary Knocker (the one on the main door is a replica), and a splendid facsimile copy of the Lindisfarne Gospels (the originals are in the British Library in London). A couple of interesting **audiovisual displays** detail the history of the cathedral, too.

13

Palace Green Library

Palace Green • Tues–Fri 10am–4.45pm, Sat & Sun noon–4.45pm • £4.50 • ☎ 0191 334 2972, ⓦ dur.ac.uk/palace.green/whatson

Palace Green Library, between the cathedral and the castle, shows off a wonderful collection of the university's treasures, including medieval manuscripts and incunabula – early printed books. The library is divided into four separate galleries, including one devoted to the History of the Book. Exhibitions change but could feature anything from Japanese enamel pots to Chinese imperial textiles and ancient Egyptian relics.

Durham Castle

Easter & July–Sept daily tours 10am, 11am, noon & hourly 2–5pm; rest of the year daily 2pm, 3pm & 4pm • free, tours £5 • ☎ 0191 334 3800, ⓦ durhamworldheritagesite.com

Durham Castle lost its medieval appearance long ago, and the university subsequently renovated the old keep as a hall of residence. It's only possible to visit the castle on a 45-minute guided tour, highlights of which include the fifteenth-century kitchen, a climb up the enormous hanging staircase and the Norman chapel, one of the few surviving interiors from the period. It's notable for its lively Romanesque carved capitals, including a green man, and what may be the earliest surviving depiction anywhere of a mermaid. Note that out of term-time you can stay here (see opposite).

Crook Hall

Frankland Lane, Sidegate • Easter weekend–Sept Sun–Wed 11am–5pm, Sept–Easter weekend Sun, Mon & Tues 11am–3pm • £7 • ☎ 0191 384 8028, ⓦ crookhallgardens.co.uk

Crook Hall is a hidden gem in Durham, and well worth making the effort to find. A rare mix of medieval, Jacobean and Georgian architecture, with origins dating from the twelfth century, it's said to be one of the oldest inhabited houses in the area. You can explore its rambling rooms, complete with period furniture and rickety staircases, as well as a series of beautifully tended, themed gardens, including the ethereal Silver and White garden, the Shakespeare Garden, planted with herbs used in Elizabethan times, and the delightful Secret Walled Garden. The flower-swathed **coffeeshop** serves delicious cream teas (£3.90 per person).

Durham Light Infantry Museum and Art Gallery

Aykley Heads • Wed–Sun 10.30am–4pm • £3.50 • ☎ 0300 026 6590, ⓦ www.dlidurham.org.uk

Just north of the city centre and set in pleasant open parkland, the **Durham Light Infantry Museum and Art Gallery** tells the story of the DLI, one of the most famous county regiments in the British Army, from their beginnings in 1181, via World War I (when it lost twelve thousand soldiers) to its last parade in 1968. Exhibits include splendid uniforms, a huge collection of more than three thousand medals and weapons, and personal items including letters and photographs. Upstairs, the art gallery features temporary exhibitions showcasing work from emerging and established artists.

ARRIVAL AND INFORMATION   DURHAM

By train Durham's train station is on North Road, a 10min walk from the centre of the city.

Destinations Berwick-upon-Tweed (every 30min; 1hr 10min), Darlington (frequent; 20min); London (every 30–60min; 3hr); Newcastle (frequent; 15min); York (frequent; 50min).

By bus It's a 5min walk to the city centre from the bus station on North Road.

Destinations Bishop Auckland (frequent; 30min); Chester-le-Street (frequent; 20min); Darlington (every 20min; 1hr 10min); Middlesbrough (every 30min; 55min); Newcastle (Mon–Sat every 30min, Sun 4–6 daily; 50min); Stanhope (Mon–Fri 4 daily; 45min).

Tourist information 2 Millennium Place, off Claypath (Mon–Sat 9.30am–5.30pm, Sun 11am–4pm; ☎ 0191 384 3720, ⓦ durhamtourism.co.uk).

GETTING AROUND

Cathedral Bus A minibus runs two routes around Durham serving the train station, the bus station, the marketplace and the cathedral. Tickets cost £1 and are valid all day.

ACCOMMODATION

Durham Castle B&B ☎ 0191 334 4106, ⓦ dur.ac.uk. Out of term-time you can have the unique experience of staying in Durham Castle. Accommodation ranges from standard rooms with shared bathrooms to two grand "state rooms", one with a four-poster and seventeenth-century tapestries. Breakfast is served in the thirteenth-century Great Hall. **£75–195**

Farnley Tower The Ave ☎ 0191 375 0011, ⓦ farnley -tower.co.uk. A 10min walk up a steep hill west from the centre, this fine stone Victorian house has thirteen comfortable rooms with bright, co-ordinated fabrics. The best rooms have sweeping city views. They also run a smart restaurant, *Gourmet Spot*. **£95**

Marriott Hotel Royal County Old Elvet ☎ 0191 386 6821, ⓦ marriotthotels.com. Elegant and luxurious, the *Marriott* has long been regarded as Durham's top hotel. Rooms have huge beds, marble-trimmed bathrooms and comfortable sitting areas. There's a fitness centre and a swimming pool, as well as a selection of restaurants and bars. **£99**

Seaham Hall Lord Byron's Walk, Seaham, 10 miles northeast of Durham ☎ 0191 516 1400, ⓦ seaham -hall.co.uk. Perched on a clifftop overlooking the sea, this hip, exclusive hotel makes a great coastal base for city sightseeing – Durham is only a 20min drive away. It's known for its luxurious spa and pampering treatments and has a wonderful restaurant; spa, dinner, bed and breakfast packages are available. **£195**

The Victorian Town House 2 Victoria Terrace ☎ 0191 370 9963, ⓦ durhambedandbreakfast.com. This friendly and tranquil B&B features three en-suite rooms: one twin, one double and one family room. It's located on a quiet and attractive backstreet backed by gardens and is a 5min walk from the station. **£90**

EATING

Bistro 21 Aykley Heads ☎ 0191 384 4354, ⓦ bistrotwentyone.co.uk. Housed in a lemon-yellow building a 10min walk from the DLI Museum and Art Gallery, *Bistro 21* serves excellent, seasonal cuisine; mains start at £16.50 and could include fishcakes with a parsley cream and buttered spinach or a juicy sirloin steak with triple-cooked chips. The interior is fresh and pretty, with wooden tables, wicker chairs and whitewashed walls. Mon–Sat noon–2pm & 6–10pm, Sun noon–3.30pm.

Finbarrs Waddington St, Flass Vale ☎ 0191 370 9999, ⓦ finbarrsrestaurant.co.uk. This chic restaurant in leafy surroundings serves up anything from full English breakfasts and banana pancakes to dinners of Moroccan lamb with golden raisins; the sweet cherry and pistachio sundaes are delicious. Mains from £15. Mon–Sat 7–9.30am, noon–2.30pm & 6–9.30pm, Sun 7.30–10.30am & noon–9pm.

Flat White 21a Elvet Bridge ☎ 07789 951149, ⓦ flatwhitedurham.co.uk. Durham's hippest café, serving barista-standard coffee and hearty sandwiches served on wooden boards (£5). Sit outside in the sun, or inside at tables made from old sewing machines. Mon–Sat 9.30am–5pm, Sun 10am–4pm.

Vennel's Saddler's Yard, Saddler St ☎ 0191 375 0571. Named after the skinny alley or "vennel" where it stands – near the junction with Elvet Bridge – this café serves up generous sandwiches, salads, quiche (£5–6) and tasty cakes in its sixteenth-century courtyard. Daily 10am–5pm.

DRINKING

Walkergate is the area to head for if you're after loud, lively bars and mainstream nightclubs pumping out cheesy music, but there are also plenty of quieter establishments and more traditional, laidback pubs.

Fabios 66 Sadler St ☎ 0191 383 9290, ⓦ fabiosdurham .com. Just above *La Spaghettata* pizzeria, *Fabios* occupies a series of rooms filled with comfy, rug-draped sofas and chalked-up blackboards offering drinks from around £3. The atmosphere is cool and relaxed, with music a melange of rap, r'n'b and dance. Jazz nights every Wednesday. Daily 6pm–2am.

Swan & Three Cygnets Elvet Bridge ☎ 0191 384 0242. Sitting proudly at the end of Elvet Bridge overlooking the River Wear, this loud and cheery pub serves cheap drinks and is filled with a mixed crowd of locals and students. Mon–Sat 11am–11pm, Sun noon–10.30pm.

Victoria Inn 86 Hallgarth St ☎ 0191 386 5269, ⓦ victoriainn-durhamcity.co.uk. With its three open fires and rickety wooden stools, this cosy, traditional pub specializes in local ales – try the creamy Tyneside Blonde or the hoppy Centurion Bitter – and stocks more than thirty Irish whiskies. Mon–Sat noon–3pm & 6–11pm, Sun noon–3pm & 7–11pm.

13

NIGHTLIFE AND ENTERTAINMENT

Durham's **clubs**, frequented by students during the week and locals at the weekends, are scattered through the city centre and in Walkergate. There's generally no dress code, but the locals tend to make an effort. In addition to shows at the Gala Theatre, you can catch regular **classical concerts** at venues around the city, including the cathedral. Ask the tourist office for more details.

Gala Theatre Millennium Place ☏0191 332 4041, ⓦgaladurham.co.uk. A modern venue staging music of all kinds, plus theatre, cinema, dance and comedy.
Love Shack Walkergate ☏0191 384 5757, ⓦloveshackdurham.com. Large, popular club with two bars, snug booths and a sleek dancefloor. Music is an energetic mix of contemporary club tunes and cheesy classics. Wed & Thurs 10pm–2am, Fri & Sat 8pm–2am.

SHOPPING

★ **Ding Dong Vintage** 45 The Gates ☏07887 536409, ⓦdingdongvintage.com. A hectic jumble of wonderful vintage clothes, hats, bags, shoes and jewellery. The men's section includes an assortment of watches, medals and regimental uniforms. Mon–Sat 10am–5.30pm.
Durham Market Market Place ⓦdurhammarkets .co.uk. Durham's Indoor Market holds a variety of stalls including a haberdashers, sweet shop and fishmongers. Mon–Sat from 9am–5pm.

Farmers' Market Market Place ⓦdurhammarkets .co.uk. Fresh local produce sold on the third Thursday of every month. 9am–3.30pm.
Fowlers Yard Silver St, behind the marketplace ⓦfowlersyarddurham.co.uk. A series of workshops showcasing local trades and crafts. Drop by to watch the craftspeople at work, commission a piece or buy off-the-cuff. Opening hours vary.

Around Durham

The county of Durham has shaken off its grimy reputation in recent years and recast itself as a thriving tourist area. The well-to-do market towns of **Bishop Auckland** and **Barnard Castle** make great day-trips from Durham, and there's plenty of excellent walking and cycling in the wilds of the two Pennine valleys, **Teesdale** and **Weardale**. You'll find some top-class museums in the area, too, including **Beamish**, **Locomotion** and the **Bowes Museum**.

Beamish Museum

10 miles north of Durham, off the A693 • April–Oct daily 10am–5pm; Nov–March Tues–Thurs, Sat & Sun 10am–4pm; in winter, only the town, pit colliery and tramway are open • April–Oct £18; Nov–March Tues–Thurs £9, Sat & Sun £18; 20 percent discount if you get here by bus • ☏0191 370 4000, ⓦbeamish.org.uk • Waggonway #28/28A runs from Newcastle (April–Oct daily, Nov–March Sat & Sun; every 30min; day returns from £2.60); bus #128 runs hourly from Durham (April–Oct Sat only)

The open-air **Beamish Museum** spreads out over three hundred acres, with buildings taken from all over the region painstakingly reassembled in six main sections linked by restored trams and buses. Complete with costumed shopkeepers, workers and householders, four of the sections show life in 1913, before the upheavals of World War I, including a **colliery village** complete with drift mine (regular tours throughout the day) and a large-scale recreation of the High Street in a **market town**. Two areas date to 1825, at the beginning of the northeast's industrial development, including a **manor house**, with horse yard, formal gardens, vegetable plots and orchards. You can ride on the beautifully restored steam-powered carousel, the **Steam Galloper** – dating from the 1890s – and the **Pockerley Waggonway**, which is pulled along by a replica of George Stephenson's *Locomotion* (see opposite), the first passenger-carrying steam train in the world.

Bishop Auckland

BISHOP AUCKLAND, a busy little market town eleven miles southwest of Durham, grew up slowly around its showpiece building, **Auckland Castle**, and became famous

13

TRAILS AND CYCLEWAYS

Coast to Coast (C2C) ⓦ c2c-guide.co.uk. This demanding cycle route runs 140 miles from Whitehaven to Sunderland.

Hadrian's Wall Path ⓦ visithadrianswall.co.uk. An 84-mile waymarked trail allowing you to walk the length of this atmospheric Roman monument.

National Route 72 ⓦ cycle-routes.org

/hadrianscycleway. Cycle path that runs the length of Hadrian's Wall.

Pennine Way ⓦ thepennineway.co.uk. This 270-mile-long footpath starts in the Peak District National Park, runs along the Pennine ridge through the Yorkshire Dales, up into Northumberland, across the Cheviots, and finishes in the Scottish Borders.

throughout England as the homeland of the mighty Prince Bishops. Today the town has paled into lesser significance but still offers enough for a pleasant hour or two's wander.

Auckland Castle

Castle Easter–June & Sept Sun & Mon 2–5pm; July & Aug Sun 2–5pm, Mon & Wed 11am–5pm • £8 **Deer park** Daily 7am–dusk • Free • ☎ 01388 602576, ⓦ aucklandcastle.org

Looking more like a Gothic mansion than a traditional castellated castle, **Auckland Castle** has been the official residence of the Bishop of Durham since 1832, although its origins are in fact much older. Founded in 1183, the palace was established as a hunting lodge for the Prince Bishops and is set within acres of lush parkland. Most of the rooms are today rather sparsely furnished, save the splendid seventeenth-century marble-and-limestone chapel and the long dining room, with its thirteen paintings of Jacob and his sons by Francisco de Zurbarán, commissioned in the 1640s for a monastery in South America. After you've seen the castle, stroll around the parkland and into the adjacent **Bishop's Deer Park**, with its Deer House dating from 1760.

Binchester Roman Fort

Daily: Easter–June & Sept 11am–5pm; July & Aug 10am–5pm • £2.55 • ☎ 0191 370 8712, ⓦ durham.gov.uk

From the town's marketplace, it's a pleasant twenty-minute walk along the banks of the River Wear to the remains of **Binchester Roman Fort**. While most of the stone fort and a civilian settlement that occupied the area remain hidden beneath surrounding fields, the bathhouse with its sophisticated underground heating system (hypocaust) is visible. Excavations are ongoing.

ARRIVAL AND INFORMATION   BISHOP AUCKLAND

By train Bishop Auckland is the end of the line for trains from Darlington (26min); the station is on Newgate Street.

By bus Buses terminate at Saddler Street.

Destinations Durham (frequent; 40min), Newcastle (frequent; 1hr 25min).

Locomotion (National Railway Museum Shildon)

Shildon, 12 miles south of Durham • Daily: April–Sept daily 10am–5pm; Oct–March 10am–4pm • Free • ☎ 01388 777999, ⓦ nrm.org .uk • Trains from Durham and Darlington to Bishop Auckland stop at Shildon station, a 2min walk from the museum. Buses #1 and 1B (to Crook and Tow Law) run from Darlington (Mon–Sat every 30min), stopping at Dale Rd, a 15min walk from the museum

The first passenger train in the world left from the station at Shildon in 1825 – making this the world's oldest railway town. It's a heritage explored in the magnificently realized **Locomotion** (also known as National Railway Museum Shildon), the regional outpost of York's National Railway Museum. It's less a museum and more an experience, spread out around a 1.5mile-long site, with the attractions linked by free bus from the reception building. Depots, sidings, junctions and coal drops lead ultimately to the heart of the museum, **Collection** – a gargantuan steel hangar containing an extraordinary array of seventy locomotives, dating from the very earliest days of steam. With interactive children's exhibits, summer steam rides, rallies and shows, it makes an excellent family day out.

13

Barnard Castle

Affectionately known as "Barney", the honey-coloured market town of **BARNARD CASTLE** lies fifteen miles southwest of Bishop Auckland. The middle of the town is dominated by the splendid octagonal **Market Cross**; built in 1747 and formerly functioning as a market for dairy and butter, it now serves a more mundane purpose as a roundabout.

The castle

Galgate • Daily: April–Sept 10am–6pm; Oct 10am–5pm; Nov–March Sat & Sun 10am–4pm • £4.60; EH • ☎ 01833 638212, ⓦ english-heritage.org.uk

The skeletal remains of the town's **castle** sit high on a rock overlooking the River Tees. It was founded in 1125 by the powerful Norman baron Bernard de Balliol – thus the town's name – and later ended up in the hands of Richard III. Richard's crest, in the shape of a boar, is still visible carved above a window in the inner ward.

Bowes Museum

Half a mile east of the town centre • Daily 10am–5pm • £9.50 • ☎ 01833 690606, ⓦ bowesmuseum.org.uk

Castle aside, the prime attraction in town is the grand French-style chateau that constitutes the **Bowes Museum**. Begun in 1869, the chateau was commissioned by John and Josephine Bowes, a local businessman and MP and his French actress wife, who spent much of their time in Paris collecting ostentatious treasures and antiques. Don't miss the beautiful Silver Swan, a life-size musical automaton dating from 1773 – every afternoon at 2pm he puts on an enchanting show, preening his shiny feathers while swimming along a river filled with jumping fish.

Egglestone Abbey

A mile southeast of Barnard Castle, off the B6277 • April–Oct 10am–6.30pm; rest of the year limited opening hours • Free; EH • ⓦ english -heritage.org.uk

It's a fine mile-long walk from the castle, southeast (downriver) through the fields above the banks of the Tees, to the lovely shattered ruins of **Egglestone Abbey,** a minor foundation dating from 1195. A succession of wars and the Dissolution destroyed most of it, but you can still see the remnants of a thirteenth-century church and the remains of the monks' living quarters, including an ingenious latrine system.

ARRIVAL AND INFORMATION   BARNARD CASTLE

By bus Buses stop either side of Galgate.
Destinations Bishop Auckland (Mon–Sat 6 daily; 50min); Darlington (Mon–Sat every 30min; Sun hourly; 45min); Middleton-in-Teesdale (Mon–Sat hourly; 35min); Raby Castle (Mon–Sat hourly; 15min).

Tourist office Flatts Road, at the end of Galgate by the castle (April–Oct Mon–Thurs & Sat 9.30am–5pm, Fri 9.30am–4.30pm, Sun 10am–4pm; Nov–March Mon–Sat 10am–3pm; ☎ 01833 696356).

ACCOMMODATION

Homelands 85 Galgate ☎ 01833 638757, ⓦ homelandsguesthouse.co.uk. An assortment of pretty rooms with lots of floral soft furnishings and comfortable beds. The owners are very knowledgeable about the area and can recommend plenty of good walks. Breakfast is great, featuring delicious fruit salads and generous cooked options. **£70**

EATING AND DRINKING

Blagraves House 30–32 The Bank ☎ 01833 637668, ⓦ blagraves.com. Supposed to be the oldest house in Barnard Castle, dating back 500 years, this refined restaurant – oozing atmosphere, with its low oak wooden beams, open log fires and plush furnishings – specializes in traditional British cuisine. Dishes such as pan-fried fillet of beef cost from £23. Tues–Sun 7–10pm.

The Bridge Inn Whorlton, 4 miles east ☎ 01833 627341, ⓦ thebridgeinn-whorlton.co.uk. Cosy country pub, with open fires and flagstone floors, in the picturesque village of Whorlton. The food is traditional pub grub – sausages and mash, chicken pie and the like for around £10. Mon–Thurs & Sun noon–11pm, Fri & Sat noon–midnight

Teesdale

13

TEESDALE extends twenty-odd miles northwest from Barnard Castle, its pastoral landscapes on the lower reaches beginning calmly enough but soon replaced by wilder Pennine scenery. Picturesque little villages like **Middleton-in-Teesdale** and Romaldkirk pepper the valley, while natural attractions include the stunning **Cow Green Reservoir** in Upper Teesdale, home to the indigenous Teesdale Violet and the blue Spring Gentian.

Raby Castle

Staindrop, 8 miles northeast of Barnard Castle • Easter week, May, June & Sept Sun–Wed 1–4.30pm; July & Aug Sun–Fri 1–4.30pm • Gardens same days 11am–5pm • £10, park & gardens only £6 • ☎ 01833 660202, ⓦ rabycastle.com

Eight miles from Barnard Castle, up the A688, beckon the splendid, sprawling battlements of **Raby Castle**, reflecting the power of the Neville family, who ruled the local roost until 1569. The Neville estates were confiscated after the "Rising of the North", the abortive attempt to replace Elizabeth I with Mary Queen of Scots, with Raby subsequently passing to the Vane family in 1626, who still own it today. You can explore the interior, with its lavish bedrooms, dining room, kitchen and drawing rooms filled with furniture and artwork dating from the sixteenth and seventeenth centuries.

Middleton-in-Teesdale

Surrounded by magnificent, wild countryside laced with a myriad of public footpaths and cycling trails, the attractive town of **MIDDLETON-IN-TEESDALE** is a popular base for walkers and cyclists. A relaxed little place, it was once the archetypal "company town", owned lock, stock and barrel by the London Lead Company, which began mining here in 1753. Just a few miles out of town is a famous set of waterfalls, **Low Force** and **High Force**.

High Force

Daily 10am–5pm • £1.50, car park £2 • Minibuses from the town centre on Wed only (2 daily; 15min)

Heading on the B6277 northwest out of Middleton-in-Teesdale, you'll first pass the turning off to the rapids of **Low Force**. Another mile up the road is the altogether more spectacular **High Force** waterfall, a 70ft cascade that tumbles over an outcrop of the Whin Sill ridge and into a deep pool. The waterfall is on private Raby land (see above) and is reached by a short woodland walk.

ARRIVAL AND INFORMATION

MIDDLETON-IN-TEESDALE

By bus There are hourly bus services to Middleton-in-Teesdale from Barnard Castle (35min).

Tourist office Market Place (restricted hours, though usually daily 10am–1pm; ☎ 01833 641001).

ACCOMMODATION AND EATING

★ **The Old Barn** 12 Market Place ☎ 01833 640258, ⓦ theoldbarn-teesdale.co.uk. In a very central location next to the tourist office, this sympathetically converted barn has three attractive B&B rooms with rustic furniture, elegant iron beds and Egyptian cotton sheets. There's a little patio garden to chill out in after a hard day's walking. **£68**

Rose & Crown Romaldkirk, 4 miles southwest ☎ 01833

650213, ⓦ rose-and-crown.co.uk. Beautiful ivy-clad eighteenth-century coaching inn set on the village green and next to a pretty Saxon church. Beneath the tastefully decorated rooms is a refined restaurant (mains from £16), serving accomplished dishes such as pan-fried woodpigeon with juniperberry sauce and grilled pancetta, a more relaxed brasserie (mains from £10), and a cosy bar with a wood fire. **£67.50**

Weardale

Sitting to the north of Teesdale, the valley of **WEARDALE** was once hunting ground reserved for the Prince Bishops, but was later transformed into a major centre for lead-mining and limestone quarrying; this industrial heritage is celebrated at the excellent **Killhope Lead Mining musueum** and the **Weardale Museum** near Irehopesburn. The main settlement is **Stanhope**, a small market town with a pleasant open-air heated swimming

13

pool (£3.65; woaspa.co.uk), perfect for cooling off after a long walk in the hills. Just to the east, the village of Wolsingham was a renowned pilgrimage centre in the Middle Ages, while neighbouring Frosterley features the remnants of an eleventh-century chapel.

Weardale Museum

Ireshopeburn, 9 miles west of Stanhope • Easter, May–July & Sept Wed–Sun 2–5pm; Aug daily 2–5pm • £3 • 01388 517433, www.weardalemuseum.co.uk

At Ireshopeburn, west of Stanhope, the **Weardale Museum** tells the story of the dale, in particular its lead mining and the importance of Methodism (the faith of most of the county of Durham's lead miners). There's a reconstructed miner's house as well as the "Wesley Room", dedicated to the founder of Methodism, John Wesley, and filled with his writings, books and belongings.

Killhope Lead Mining Museum

5 miles west of Ireshopeburn and 12 miles east of Stanhope • April–Oct daily 10.30am–5pm • £8.20 including mine visit • 01388 537505, www.killhope.org.uk • Request bus stop on bus #101 (see below)

If you're keen to learn about Weardale's mining past, a visit to **Killhope Lead Mining Museum**, five miles west of Ireshopeburn, is an absolute must. After many successful years as one of the richest mines in Britain, Killhope shut for good in 1910, and now houses a terrific, child-friendly museum that brings to life the difficulties and dangers of a mining life. The site is littered with preserved machinery and nineteenth-century buildings, including the Mine Shop where workers would spend the night after finishing a late shift. The highlight of the visit comes when you descend Park Level Mine – you'll be given wellies, a hard hat and a torch – in the company of a guide who expounds entertainingly about the realities of life underground, notably the perils of the "Black Spit", a lung disease which killed many men by their mid-forties.

ARRIVAL AND INFORMATION
WEARDALE

By bus Bus #101 runs roughly hourly between Bishop Auckland and Stanhope, calling at Wolsingham and Frosterley.
Durham Dales Centre On Stanhope's main road, the Dales Centre houses the tourist office (daily: April–Oct 10am–5pm; Nov–March 10am–4pm; 01388 527650, durhamdalescentre.co.uk) and a café.

GETTING AROUND

By bus Apart from #101, buses are relatively irregular and spotty round these parts. It's best to use the minibuses run by the Weardale Bus Company (01388 528235, weardale-travel.co.uk).

Weardale Railway This volunteer-run steam railway chugs along from Bishop Auckland (see p.580) to Stanhope, stopping at Wolsingham and Frosterley on request; for up-to-date timetables and fares see weardale-railway.org.uk.

ACCOMMODATION

AP Dowfold House Crook, 6 miles east of Wolsingham 01388 762473, dowfoldhouse.co.uk. Wonderful, relaxed B&B in a Victorian house surrounded by lush gardens and with splendid views out over Weardale. Breakfast is the highlight, with lashings of free-range eggs, locally sourced sausages and bacon, home-made bread and jams. **£76**

EATING AND DRINKING

★**Black Bull** Frosterley 01388 527784, blackbullfrosterley.com. Hop off the Weardale Railway (see above) and into this traditional pub with beams, ranges, oak tables and flagstone floors. The ales are excellent, as is the food, which is hearty and delicious; mains, like herb-crusted lamb shoulder with apricot and walnut stuffing, start at £10. Thurs–Sat 11am–11pm, Sun 11am–5pm; food served till 2.30pm on Sun.

Tees Valley

Admittedly not much of a tourist hotspot in comparison to Northumberland or Durham, the **TEES VALLEY** – once an industrial powerhouse and birthplace of one of the greatest developments in Britain, the public steam railway – nevertheless has some enjoyable attractions. **Darlington**, with its strong railway heritage, is a pleasant place to spend a day, while Middlesbrough's **MIMA** and Hartlepool's **Maritime Experience** (Daily: April–Oct 10am–5pm; Nov–March 11am–4pm; £10; ☎01429 860077, ⓦhartlepoolsmaritimeexperience .com) are extremely worthwhile, the latter particularly if you have children to entertain.

Darlington

Abbreviated to "Darlo" by the locals, the busy market town of **DARLINGTON** hit the big time in 1825, when George Stephenson's "Number 1 Engine", later called *Locomotion*, hurtled from here to nearby Stockton-on-Tees at the terrifying speed of fifteen miles per hour. The town subsequently grew into a rail-engineering centre, and didn't look back till the closure of the works in 1966. The origins of the rest of Darlington lie deep in Saxon times. The monks carrying St Cuthbert's body from Ripon to Durham (see p.576) stopped here, the saint lending his name to the graceful riverside church of **St Cuthbert**. The market square, one of England's largest, spreads beyond the church up to the restored and lively **Victorian covered market** (Mon–Sat 8am–5pm).

Head of Steam

North Rd Station, a 20min walk up Northgate from the marketplace • April–Sept Tues–Sun 10am–4pm, Oct–March Wed–Sun 11am–3.30pm • £4.95 • ☎01325 460532, ⓦ www.darlington.gov.uk

Darlington's railway history is celebrated at the wonderful little **Head of Steam** museum, which is actually the restored 1842 passenger station on the original Stockton and Darlington railway route. The highlight is Stephenson's *Locomotion No. 1*, a tiny wood-panelled steam engine, the first-ever steam train to carry fare-paying passengers. Other locomotives jostle for space alongside, including the shiny, racing-green *Derwent*, the oldest surviving Darlington-built steam train. These, along with a collection of station and lineside signs, uniforms, luggage, a reconstructed ticket office and carriages, successfully bring to life the most important era in Darlington's existence.

ARRIVAL AND INFORMATION

DARLINGTON

By train The train station is on Bank Top, a 10min walk from the central marketplace: from the train station walk up Victoria Road to the roundabout and turn right down Feethams.

Destinations Bishop Auckland (frequent; 25min); Durham (frequent; 20min); Newcastle (frequent; 35min).

By bus Most buses stop outside the Town Hall on Feethams.

Destinations Barnard Castle (Mon–Sat every 30min, Sun hourly; 45min); Bishop Auckland (Mon–Sat every 30min, Sun hourly; 1hr); Durham (every 20min; 1hr 10 min).

Tourist office Leaflets about the town and surroundings are available at the library on Crown Street (Mon & Tues 9am–6pm, Thurs 10am–6pm, Wed & Fri 9am–5pm, Sat 9am–4pm; ☎01325 462034).

ACCOMMODATION

Clow Beck B&B Croft-on-Tees, 2 miles south ☎01325 721075, ⓦclowbeckhouse.co.uk. Very welcoming B&B with thirteen individually decorated rooms named after flowers and set round a pretty landscaped garden. The owner is also an accomplished chef, creating delicious breakfasts – the Skipton sausage is very tasty – and evening meals (mains from £17). **£135**

Rockliffe Hall Hurworth-on-Tees, 5 miles south ☎01325 729999, ⓦrockliffehall.com. Swanky hotel in a redbrick Victorian Gothic pile between the villages of Croft-on-Tees and Hurworth, which lays claim to having the UK's longest golf course. The rooms are cool and luxurious, and there's a spa and three restaurants. **£175**

EATING AND DRINKING

★ **Bay Horse** 45 The Green, Hurworth, 5 miles south ☎01325 720663, ⓦthebayhorsehurworth.com. This exquisite pub has a roaring fire, exposed wooden beams, comfy bar stools and chalked-up menus. Tuck into delicious meals such as venison sausage with fondant potatoes and

Yorkshire gravy (£13.95) and make sure you leave room for their puds; the sticky toffee pudding with green apple ice cream (£6.50) is fabulous. Mon–Sat 11am–11pm, Sun noon–10.30pm; no food served Sun evening.

13

Middlesbrough Institute of Modern Art

Middlesbrough, 15 miles east of Darlington, on Centre Square, a 10min walk from the train station • Tues, Wed, Fri & Sat 10am–4.30pm, Thurs 10am–7pm, Sun noon–4pm • Free • ☎ 01642 726720, ⓦ visitmima.com

The stunning **Middlesbrough Institute of Modern Art (MIMA)** is one of the few tourist draws in the industrial town of Middlesbrough. Bringing together its municipal art collections for the first time, changing exhibitions concentrate on fine arts and crafts from the early twentieth century to the present day, with a heavy emphasis on ceramics and jewellery. The collection features work by David Hockney, L.S. Lowry and Tracey Emin, among others.

Newcastle upon Tyne

Vibrant and handsome, **NEWCASTLE UPON TYNE** has emerged from its industrial heyday and its post-industrial difficulties with barely a smut on its face. Its reputation for lively nightlife is just the tip of the iceberg; with its collection of top-class art galleries, museums and flourishing theatre scene – not to mention the shopping – the city is up there with the most exciting in Britain.

The de facto capital of the area between Yorkshire and Scotland, the city was named for its "new castle" founded in 1080 and hit the limelight during the Industrial Revolution – Grainger Town in the city's centre is lined with elegant, listed classical buildings, indicating its past wealth and importance as one of Britain's biggest and most important exporters of coal, iron and machinery. The decline of industry damaged Newcastle badly, signalling decades of poverty and hardship – a period recalled by Antony Gormley's mighty statue the **Angel of the North**, which, since its appearance in 1998, has become both a poignant eulogy for the days of industry and a symbol of resurgence and regeneration.

Castle Keep

Castle Garth • Mon–Sat 10am–5pm, Sun noon–5pm • £4 • ☎ 0191 233 1221, ⓦ www.castlekeep-newcastle.org.uk

Anyone arriving by train from the north will get a sneak preview of the **Castle Keep**, as the rail line splits the keep from its gatehouse, the **Black Gate**, on St Nicholas Street. A wooden fort was built here over an Anglo-Saxon cemetery by Robert Curthose, illegitimate eldest son of William the Conqueror, but the present keep dates from the twelfth century. There's a great view from the rooftop over the river and city.

St Nicolas Cathedral

At the junction of St Nicholas St and Mosley St • Sun–Fri 7.30am–6.30pm, Sat 8am–4pm • Free • ☎ 0191 232 1939, ⓦ stnicholascathedral.co.uk

The **St Nicolas Cathedral**, dating mainly from the fourteenth and fifteenth centuries, is remarkable chiefly for its tower; erected in 1470, it is topped with a crown-like structure of turrets and arches supporting a lantern. Inside, behind the high altar, is one of the largest funerary brasses in England; it was commissioned by Roger Thornton, the Dick Whittington of Newcastle, who arrived in the city penniless and died its richest merchant in 1429.

Quayside

From between the castle and the cathedral a road known simply as The Side – formerly the main road out of the city, and home to the excellent **Side Gallery** – descends to Newcastle's **Quayside**. The river is spanned by seven bridges in close proximity, the most prominent being the looming **Tyne Bridge** of 1928, symbol of the city. Immediately west is the hydraulic **Swing Bridge**, erected in 1876 by Lord Armstrong so

NEWCASTLE UPON TYNE

■ ACCOMMODATION

Jesmond Dene House	2
Kensington House Aparthotel	3
New Northumbria	1
Sleeperz	4

● SHOPS

Attica	2
Biscuit Factory	3
Grainger Market	1
Quayside Market	4

■ LIVE MUSIC

The Cluny	4
Jazz Café	7
Metro Radio Arena	11
O2 Academy	5

● RESTAURANTS

Blackfriars	5
Café 21	7
El Coto	1
Scrumpy Willow and the Singing Kettle	6
Vujon	8

● CAFÉS

Café Royal	2
Pani Café	3
Paradiso	4
Pink Lane Coffee	9

■ PUBS & BARS

As You Like It	1
Baby Lynch	6
Crown Posada	9
Free Trade	3
Tokyo	8

■ CLUBS

| Digital | 10 |
| World Headquarters | 2 |

Ⓜ Metro Stops

that larger vessels could reach his shipyards upriver, while modern road and rail lines cross the river on the adjacent **High Level Bridge**, built by Robert Stephenson in 1849 – Queen Victoria was one of the first passengers to cross, promoting the railway revolution. Beyond the Tyne Bridge is an area of riverside apartments, landscaped promenades, public sculpture and pedestrianized squares, along with a series of fashionable bars and restaurants centred on the graceful **Gateshead Millennium Bridge**, the world's first tilting span, designed to pivot to allow ships to pass.

13

NEWCASTLE ORIENTATION

Visitors are encouraged to think of the city as **Newcastle Gateshead**, an amalgamation of the two conurbations straddling the Tyne. On Gateshead Quays are the **BALTIC** contemporary arts centre and Norman Foster's **Sage** music centre, and on the opposite side, Newcastle's **Quayside** is where you'll find much of the city's nightlife. The city splits into several distinct areas, though it's only a matter of minutes to walk between them. The **castle** and **cathedral** occupy the heights immediately above the River Tyne, while north of here lies the city centre, **Grainger Town**. Chinatown and the two big draws of the **Discovery Museum** and the **Life Science Centre** are west of the centre, while east is the renowned **Laing Gallery**. In the north of the city, on the university campus, is the **Great North Museum: Hancock** and even further north, through the landscaped Exhibition Park, is the **Town Moor**, 1200 acres of common land where freemen of the city – including Jimmy Carter and Bob Geldof – are entitled to graze their cattle. The old industrial **Ouseburn Valley**, home to an alternative cultural scene, interesting galleries, the excellent **Seven Stories** children's museum and some popular bars, is a short walk east along the river from the city centre.

BALTIC

By the Millennium Bridge • Daily except Tues 10am–6pm, Tues 10.30am–6pm • Free • ☎ 0191 478 1810, �🌐 balticmill.com

Fashioned from an old brick flour mill, **BALTIC** sits on the Gateshead riverbank, by the Millennium Bridge. Designed to be a huge visual "art factory", it's second only in scale to London's Tate Modern. There's no permanent collection here – instead there's an ever-changing calendar of exhibitions and local community projects, as well as artists' studios, education workshops, an art performance space and cinema, plus a rooftop restaurant with uninterrupted views of the Newcastle skyline.

The Sage Gateshead

St Mary's Square, Gateshead Quays • Daily 9am–11pm • ☎ 0191 443 4661, 🌐 sagegateshead.com

Sitting on the riverbank, the **Sage Gateshead** is an extraordinary billowing steel, aluminium and glass concert hall complex, best seen at night when it glows with many colours. It's home to the Royal Northern Sinfonia orchestra and Folkworks, an organization promoting British and international traditional music, and there's something on most nights – from music concerts to workshops and lectures, as well as the Gateshead International Jazz Festival every April. The public concourse provides marvellous river and city views, and there are bars, a café and a brasserie.

Ouseburn Valley

The **Ouseburn Valley**, fifteen minutes' walk up the River Tyne from Millennium Bridge, was once at the heart of Newcastle's industrial activities but became a derelict backwater in the mid-twentieth century. A jumble of old Victorian mills and warehouses, the area has seen a remarkable rejuvenation, as artists, musicians, businesses and even residents move in. Lime Street, home to the quirky **Cluny** music bar (see p.593), artists' workshops and the nationally renowned **Seven Stories**, is the hub, but there are plenty of attractions nearby including Europe's biggest commercial art space – the **Biscuit Factory** – an art-house cinema, riding stables and a small working farm.

Seven Stories

30 Lime St • Mon–Sat 10am–5pm, Sun 10am–4pm • £7 • ☎ 0845 271 0777, 🌐 sevenstories.org.uk

Housed in a beautifully converted Victorian riverside mill and spread over seven floors, **Seven Stories** celebrates the art of children's books through displays of original artwork, manuscripts and related documents. The bright, interactive exhibitions change regularly but highlights include original sketches taken from Noel Streatfield's *Ballet Shoes*, material from *Charlie and the Chocolate Factory* by Roald Dahl, Philip Pullman's early drafts, and the unpublished novel by Enid Blyton, *Mr Tumpy's Caravan*. Kids get the opportunity to dress up and create their own art works; there is also a simple café.

Grainger Town

The heart of the city is known as **Grainger Town**, one of the best-looking city centres in Britain. Thrown up in a few short mid-nineteenth-century years by businessmen-builders and architects such as Richard Grainger, Thomas Oliver and John Dobson, the area is known for its classical facades of stone lining splendid, wide streets, and in particular, **Grey Street**, named for the second Earl Grey (he of the tea), prime minister from 1830 to 1834. In 1832, Grey carried the Reform Act – which granted seats in the House of Commons to large cities that had developed during the Industrial Revolution, like Newcastle – through parliament, an act commemorated by **Grey's Monument** at the top of the street. The restored **Grainger Market** (Mon–Sat 9am–5pm), nearby, was Europe's largest covered market when built in the 1830s, and is today home to the smallest branch of Marks & Spencer, known as the Original Penny Bazaar.

Centre for Life

Times Square, off Westmorland Rd and Scotswood Rd • Mon–Wed & Fri–Sat 10am–6pm, Thurs 10am–8pm, Sun 11am–6pm; last admission 3.30pm • £12 • ☎ 0191 243 8210, ⦿ life.org.uk

A five-minute walk west of Central Station, the sleek buildings of the **Centre for Life** reach around the sweeping expanse of Times Square. This ambitious "science village" project combines bioscience and genetics research with a science visitor centre that aims to convey the secrets of life using the latest entertainment technology. Children find the whole thing enormously rewarding – from the sparkling Planetarium to the motion simulator – so expect to spend a good three hours here, if not more.

Discovery Museum

Blandford Square • Mon–Fri 10am–4pm, Sat & Sun 11am–4pm • Free • ☎ 0191 232 6789, ⦿ twmuseums.org.uk

The **Discovery Museum** concentrates on the maritime history of Newcastle and Tyneside, as well as their role in Britain's scientific and technological developments. Highlights include the Tyneside-invented *Turbinia* – which dominates the entrance to the museum – the first ship to be powered by a steam turbine, as well as the Newcastle Story, a walk through the city's past with tales from animatronic characters along the way.

Literary and Philosophical Society

23 Westgate Rd • Mon, Wed & Thurs 9.30am–7pm, Tues 9.30am–8pm, Fri 9.30am–5pm, Sat 9.30am–1pm • Free • ☎ 0191 232 0192, ⦿ litandphil.org.uk

Known as the **Lit and Phil**, this temple-like public library and learned society occupies one of the city's finest Georgian buildings: the domed roof, stucco ceilings and wrought-iron galleries are well worth a look. Established in 1825, it now runs a programme of recitals, jazz concerts, talks and exhibitions.

Laing Art Gallery

New Bridge St • Tues–Sat 10am–5pm, Sun 2–5pm • Free • ⦿ twmuseums.org.uk

The **Laing Art Gallery**, in the east of the city, is home to the northeast's premier art collection: the permanent display is a sweep through British art from the seventeenth century to today, featuring sculpture from Henry Moore and a large collection of John Martin's fiery landscapes, along with a smattering of Pre-Raphaelites, so admired by English industrial barons. Another permanent display highlights a superb collection of

13

Newcastle silver dating from the seventeenth century and some colourful 1930s glassware by George Davidson.

Great North Museum: Hancock

Barras Bridge · **Hancock Museum** Mon–Fri 10am–5pm, Sat 10am–4pm, Sun 11am–4pm · Free; planetarium £2.50 · ☎ 0191 222 6765, ⓦ twmuseums.org.uk **Hatton Gallery** Mon–Sat 10am–5pm · Free · ☎ 0191 222 6059, ⓦ twmuseums.org.uk

A five-minute walk north from Haymarket Metro stop, the **Great North Museum: Hancock** is a clunkily named amalgamation of four museums, the best of which are the Great North Museum, housed in the Hancock building, and the nearby Hatton Gallery. The **Great North Museum** has an engaging mishmash of natural history exhibits – there's a knobbly T-Rex skeleton, some stuffed animals and an aquarium – historical artefacts such as the large-scale replica Hadrian's Wall, and a planetarium. The little **Hatton Gallery**, a two-minute walk away on the university's campus, is famous for housing the only surviving example of German Dadaist Kurt Schwitters' *Merzbau* (a sort of architectural collage); it also hosts a variety of temporary exhibitions.

ARRIVAL AND DEPARTURE

NEWCASTLE UPON TYNE

By plane Newcastle International Airport is 6 miles north of the city (☎ 0871 882 1121, ⓦ newcastleairport.com). It is linked by the Metro to Central Station (every 7–15min 5.45am–midnight; 22min; £3.30) and beyond. You can also take a taxi into the centre (around £17).

By train Central Station is a 5min walk from the city centre or Quayside, and has a Metro station.

Destinations Alnmouth (hourly; 30min); Berwick-upon-Tweed (hourly; 45min); Carlisle (hourly; 1hr 30min); Darlington (frequent; 35min); Durham (frequent; 15min); Hexham (every 30min; 40min); London (frequent; 2hr 45min–3hr 15min); York (frequent; 1hr).

By bus National Express coaches stop on St James's Boulevard, not far from Central Station, while regional

buses stop at Haymarket bus station (Haymarket Metro). Gateshead Interchange is a big bus station served by local and national buses, linked by Metro to the city centre.

Destinations Alnmouth (every 30min; 1hr 30min); Alnwick (every 30min; 1hr 20min); Bamburgh (Mon–Sat 3 daily; Sun 2 daily; 2hr 30min); Beamish (April–Oct daily, Nov–March Sat & Sun; every 30min; 1hr); Berwick-upon-Tweed (Mon–Sat 8 daily; 2hr 30min); Carlisle (Mon–Sat hourly; 2hr 10min); Chester-le-Street (frequent; 45min); Craster (Mon–Sat 7 daily, Sun 4 daily; 1hr 50min); Durham (Mon–Sat every 30min, Sun 4–6 daily; 50min); Hexham (hourly; 50min); Middlesbrough (Mon–Sat every 30min; 1hr); Rothbury (Mon–Sat hourly, Sun 2 daily; 1hr 30min); Seahouses (Mon–Sat 3 daily, Sun 2 daily; 2hr 10min); Warkworth (daily every 30min; 1hr 20min).

GETTING AROUND

By Metro The convenient, easy-to-use Tyne and Wear Metro (daily 5.30am–midnight, every 5–10min or 10–20min in the evening) connects the city centre with the airport and runs out to the suburbs. You can buy a Metro Day Saver ticket for unlimited rides (from £2.60).

By bus All city and local buses stop at Eldon Square shopping centre. Quaylink buses connect major attractions in Newcastle and Gateshead Quays with Newcastle Central Station, Haymarket Bus Station and Gateshead

Interchange. Buses run frequently daily (day ticket £2).

By bike Rent bikes at Saddle Skedaddle, Ouseburn Building, Albion Row (daily 9am–6pm; from £25/day; ☎ 0191 265 1110, ⓦ www.skedaddle.co.uk).

By taxi There are taxi ranks at Haymarket, Bigg Market (in the city centre between Grey Street and Grainger Street) and outside Central Station. To book, contact Noda Taxis (☎ 0191 222 888 or 232 7777, ⓦ noda-taxis.co.uk) at Central Station.

INFORMATION AND TOURS

Public transport information Nexus Traveline has shops at the Central Station, Haymarket, Monument and Gateshead Metro stations (☎ 0871 200 2233, ⓦ nexus.org.uk).

Tourist office The main tourist office is at 8–9 Central Arcade, Market Street (Mon–Fri 9.30am–5.30pm, Sat 9am–5pm, Sun 10am–4pm; ☎ 0191 277 8000, ⓦ newcastlegateshead.com).

Tours City tours and various tours to Hadrian's Wall, Northumberland and Durham are run by Castle City Tours

(from £40 per group of seven people max; ☎ 07780 958679, ⓦ newcastlecitytours.co.uk) while River Escapes Cruises' sightseeing boats (£6/10/12; ☎ 01670 785666, ⓦ rivere scapes.co.uk) depart most weekends throughout the year, and other days in summer, from the Quayside. A hop-on hop-off, open-top sightseeing bus departs from Central Station (April–Oct daily, Nov & Dec Sat & Sun; every 30min–1hr; £8; ☎ 01789 299123, ⓦ city-sightseeing.com). Saddle Skedaddle (see above) also organizes C2C tours and trips to Hadrian's Wall.

13

NEWCASTLE ART GALLERIES

Biscuit Factory 16 Stoddart St, Ouseburn ☎0191 261 1103, ⓦthebiscuitfactory.com. Britain's largest commercial art gallery, displaying and selling anything from pendulum clocks and carved wooden tables to ceramic teapots and quirky necklaces. Free. Mon–Fri 10am–4pm, Sat 10am–6pm, Sun 11am–6pm.

Globe Gallery 53–57 Blanford Sq ☎0191 597 9377, ⓦglobegallery.org. Contemporary arts space that supports local, up-and-coming artists; there's a variety of exhibitions and one-off events. Free. Wed–Sat 11.30am–5pm.

Northern Print Stepney Bank, Ouseburn ☎0191 261 7000, ⓦnorthernprint.org.uk. Little gallery that sells affordable prints by local artists. You can also learn how to make prints at the studio's workshop. Free. Wed–Sat noon–4pm.

Side Gallery 5–9 Side ☎0191 232 2208, ⓦamber -online.com. A long-established, collectively run space with a strong specialism in social documentary photography. Free. Tues–Sat 11am–5pm, Thurs till 7pm, Sun noon–4pm.

ACCOMMODATION

Budget **hotel chains** offer plenty of good-value rooms in the city centre and down by the Quayside, while the biggest concentration of small hotels and guesthouses lies a mile north of the centre in popular, student-filled Jesmond, along and off Osborne Road: take bus #33 from Central Station or Haymarket.

★**Jesmond Dene House** Jesmond Dene Rd, Jesmond ☎0191 212 3000, ⓦjesmonddenehouse.co.uk. An imposing Arts and Crafts house in a very peaceful wooded valley. The sleek, boldly decorated rooms are decked out in decadent velvet and silk furnishings and have enormous bathrooms with underfloor heating. There's fine dining in the garden-room restaurant and breakfasts are particularly luxurious, with smoked salmon, a range of cooked meats and champagne on offer. Rates vary; book well in advance. **£110**

Kensington House Aparthotel 5 Osborne Rd ☎0191 201 0175, ⓦkensingtonaparthotel.com. Twenty-three upmarket apartments of varying sizes, conveniently situated near Jesmond Metro. The decor is modern and sleek, with wood floors, cream carpets and marble kitchen surfaces. Beds are kitted out with luxurious Egyptian cotton sheets and feather down duvets. Six apartments have disabled access. **£115**

New Northumbria 61–69 Osborne Rd, Jesmond ☎0191 281 4961, ⓦthenewnorthumbriahotel.co.uk. In a prime position along Osborne Road among the popular, student-filled restaurants and bars, New Northumbria has 55 rooms, all with large beds and unfussy decor. There's a bar downstairs and an Italian restaurant attached. **£70**

Sleeperz 15 Westgate Rd ☎0191 261 6171, ⓦsleeperz .com/newcastle. A great-value option in the heart of town, part of a little chain that marries functionality with good design. Despite the city-centre location, the 98 compact but comfortable rooms provide a quiet respite from Saturday-night mayhem, and there's a funky breakfast bar/café downstairs. **£52**

EATING

Newcastle has a great variety of places to eat, from expensive, top-quality restaurants showcasing the talents of young and creative chefs, to fun, relaxed cafés and budget-friendly Chinese restaurants (mostly around Stowell Street in Chinatown). The popular chain restaurants are down by the Quayside.

★**Blackfriars** Friars St ☎0191 615945, ⓦblack friarsrestaurant.co.uk. Housed in a beautiful stone building dating back to 1239, Blackfriars offers superb traditional British dishes using local ingredients. Mains could include pork loin with a bacon and cheese Gateshead floddie (potato cakes, originating from Gateshead, and traditionally eaten for breakfast) or a Doddington cheese and onion Wellington with chive cream sauce, and, for afters, dig into sticky toffee pudding with green grape ice cream and Brown Ale caramel (mains from £12, puddings from £6). Booking recommended. Mon–Sat noon–2.30pm & 5.30–late, Sun noon–4pm.

Café 21 Trinity Gardens ☎0191 222 0755,

ⓦcafetwentyone.co.uk. Stylish Parisian-style bistro with crisp white tablecloths, leather banquettes, a classic French menu and slick service. Expect dishes like confit of duck with Lyonnaise potatoes (£19) or wild mushrooms on toasted brioche and a poached egg (£12), and delicious desserts – the Florentine doughnut with strawberry jam & crème chantilly (£7.20) is particularly good. Mon–Sat noon–2.30pm & 5.30–10.30pm, Sun 12.30–3.30pm & 6.30–10pm.

Café Royal 8 Nelson St. Bright and buzzy café with great smoothies, coffees and delectable home-made breads and cakes – try the raspberry scones with clotted cream (£3.50) or hazelnut twists (£2). Mon–Sat 8am–6pm.

13

El Coto 21 Leazes Park Rd ☎0191 261 0555, ⓦelcoto .co.uk. Cute and cosy, this great tapas place has an extensive, good-value menu featuring all the usuals, such as *patatas bravas* and marinated sardines – dishes cost around £5, though paella goes for £10 per person. Daily noon–11pm.

Pani Café 61–65 High Bridge St, off Grey St ☎0191 232 4366, ⓦpaniscafe.co.uk. On a side street below the Theatre Royal, this lively Sardinian café has won a loyal clientele for its good-value sandwiches, pasta and salads (mains around £8). Mon–Sat 10am–10pm.

Paradiso 1 Market Lane ☎0191 221 1240, ⓦparadiso .co.uk. Mellow café-bar hidden down an alley off Pilgrim Street – the snack food in the daytime becomes more substantial at night, with truffle risotto, salmon steaks and the like. There are set menus throughout the day (two courses from £9.95, three courses from £12.95) as well as à la carte. You can dine outdoors in good weather. Mon–Thurs 11am–2.30pm & 5–10.30pm, Fri & Sat 11am–10.45pm.

Pink Lane Coffee 1 Pink Lane ☎07841 383085, ⓦpinklanecoffee.co.uk. The best coffee in town: their beans are slow roasted and the milk is Northumbrian Pedigree. Exposed light bulbs, reclaimed furniture and brickwork tiling makes for a stylish interior. Mon–Fri 7.30am–6pm, Sat 9am–5pm, Sun 10am–4pm.

Scrumpy Willow and the Singing Kettle 89 Clayton St ☎0191 221 2323. Wonderful little organic café/ restaurant with a relaxed atmosphere and pretty, shabby-chic decor – think candles, mirrors and rickety wood furniture. It's great for vegetarians and vegans: pop in for a tasty brunch of eggs Benedict, porridge or pancakes. The evening menu features locally sourced meat and fish including a delicious Kielder lamb with farm vegetables and pearl barley. Mains from £6.95. Mon–Sat 10am–8pm, Sun 11am–4pm.

Vujon 29 Queen St ☎0191 221 0601, ⓦvujon.com. The city's classiest Indian restaurant, housed in an elegant building by the Quayside, serving dishes a cut above the ordinary, from venison Jaipur-style with chilli jam (£15.90) to the spicy duck *salan* (£14.90). Mon–Sat 11.30am–2pm & 5.30–11.30pm, Sun 5.30–11.30pm.

DRINKING

Newcastle's boisterous pubs, bars and clubs are concentrated in several areas: in the **Bigg Market** (between Grey St and Grainger St), around the **Quayside** and in the developing **Ouseburn** area, where bars tend to be quirkier and more sophisticated; in **Jesmond**, with its thriving student-filled strip of café-bars; and in the mainstream leisure-and-cinema complex known as **The Gate** (Newgate St). The **gay** area, known as the "Pink Triangle", focuses on the Centre for Life, spreading out to Waterloo Street and Westmorland and Scotswood roads. Top drinking brew is Newcastle Brown – an ale known locally as "Dog" – produced in this city since 1927.

As You Like It Archbold Terrace ☎0191 281 2277, ⓦasyoulikeitjesmond.com. The top bar in the Jesmond area, and part of the *Mr Lynch* chain (see below). Incongruously sitting beneath an ugly tower block, this funky bar/restaurant has a relaxed vibe, exposed brick walls and a mishmash of furniture. The Supper Club (ⓦthesupperclubjesmond.com), a late-night club night on Fri–Sun (10pm–2am) features jazz, blues and soul. Sun–Thurs noon–midnight, Fri & Sat noon–2am.

Baby Lynch 26 Collingwood St ☎0191 261 8271, ⓦbabylynch.com. Part of a Newcastle-based chain (includes *As You Like It*, *Nancy Bordellos*, *Floritas*, *Madame Koo* and *Mr Lynch*), but still cool for it, *Baby Lynch* oozes 1970s chic with its retro wooden floorboards, cosy booths and bamboo loungers. The cocktail menu is extensive and very tempting (cocktails from £4.95). It gets busy later on, with the overspill from next-door *Floritas*. Fri–Sun 7pm–3am.

Crown Posada 31 Side ☎0191 232 1269, ⓦcrown posadanewcastle.co.uk. A proper old man's boozer: local beers and guest ales in this small wood-and-glass-panelled Victorian pub. You might fancy the dark, malty Hadrian's Gladiator (£3.80) or opt for the golden, hoppy Tyneside Blonde (£3.80). Mon–Wed noon–11pm, Thurs 11am–11pm, Fri 11am–midnight, Sat noon–midnight, Sun noon–10.30pm.

★**Free Trade** St Lawrence Rd ☎0191 265 5764. Walk along the Newcastle Quayside past the Millennium Bridge and look for the shabby pub on the hill, where you are invited to "drink beer, smoke tabs" with the city's pub cognoscenti. Cask beer from local microbreweries, a great free juke box and superb river views from the beer garden. Mon–Thurs 11am–11pm, Fri & Sat 11am–midnight, Sun noon–11pm.

Tokyo 17 Westgate Rd ☎0191 232 1122, ⓦtokyonew castle.co.uk. The dark, sleek main bar's handsome enough, but follow the tealights up the stairs to the outdoor "garden" bar lined by plants and trees, giving the area a secret, exclusive feel. A pre-club favourite for Shindig (see below). Sun–Thurs 5pm–midnight & Fri & Sat 4pm–1am.

NIGHTLIFE

Newcastle's biggest club night is **Shindig**, taking place on Saturdays and switching locations around the city. See ⓦshindiguk.com for the latest. Gigs, club nights and the gay scene are reviewed exhaustively in *The Crack* (monthly; free; ⓦthecrackmagazine.com), available in shops, pubs and bars.

CLUBS

Digital Times Sq ☎0191 261 9755, ⓦyourfutureis digital.com/newcastle. The city's top club, with an amazing sound system pumping out a variety of musical genres. If you like cheesy classics, look out for Born in the Sixties nights, while house, funk and disco fans will get their fix on Saturday's Love nights. Mon & Thurs 10.30pm–2.30am, Fri & Sat 10.30pm–3.30am.

World Headquarters Carliol Square, East Pilgrim St ☎0191 281 3445, ⓦwelovewhq.com. Smallish and down-to-earth club that's always packed. Music is a medley of house, hip-hop, soul and r'n'b and reggae. Downstairs there's a comfy lounge area with squashy sofas and a pool table. Entry fee around £10. Fri & Sat 10.30pm–3am.

LIVE MUSIC VENUES

★**The Cluny** 36 Lime St, Ouseburn Valley ☎0191 230 4474, ⓦtheheadofsteam.co.uk. Based in an old whisky bottling plant, this is the best small music venue in the city, with something going on most nights, from quirky indie bands to contemporary punk-pop. *Cluny 2*, around the corner at 34 Lime Street (same hours), is its spacious sister venue, with less frequent gigs. Sun–Thurs noon–11pm, Fri & Sat noon–1am.

Jazz Café 23–25 Pink Lane ☎0191 232 6505, ⓦjazzcafe-newcastle.co.uk. Slick and intimate jazz club in inauspicious surroundings, hosting top-quality jazz from 9.30pm on Friday and Saturday nights. Tues–Sat 11am–2am.

Metro Radio Arena Arena Way ☎0844 493 4567, ⓦmetroradioarena.co.uk. The biggest concert and exhibition venue in the Northeast; star appearances have included Lady Gaga, Dolly Parton and Tom Jones. Book popular gigs well in advance.

O2 Academy Westgate Rd ☎0844 477 2000, ⓦo2academynewcastle.co.uk. Housed in the former bingo hall, this mainstream venue hosts a variety of big names and local talent.

ENTERTAINMENT

Live Theatre 27 Broad Chare ☎0191 232 1232, ⓦlive.org.uk. Enterprising theatre company that aims to find and develop local, and particularly young, talent – the attached *Caffe Vivo* is good for coffee by day and pre-theatre meal deals by night.

Mill Volvo Tyne Theatre 111 Westgate Rd ☎0844 493999, ⓦmillvolvotynetheatre.co.uk. Beautifully restored Victorian theatre with a wide range of plays, comedy shows and gigs.

Side Cinema 5–9 Side ☎0191 232 2000, ⓦamber-online.com. A quaintly dishevelled fifty-seat cinema: they run an imaginative programme combining art-house movies with live music.

Theatre Royal 100 Grey St ☎0844 811 2121, ⓦtheatreroyal.co.uk. Drama, opera, dance, musicals and comedy; also hosts the annual RSC season in Nov.

Tyneside Cinema 10 Pilgrim St ☎0845 217 9909, ⓦtynesidecinema.co.uk. The city's premier art-house cinema, with coffee, light meals and movie talk in the Art Deco cinema café. The gorgeous restored decor includes Persian-inspired gilded stucco, stained glass and mosaic floors.

SHOPPING

Attica 2 Old George Yard, off Highbridge ☎0191 261 4062, ⓦatticavintage.co.uk. Excellent vintage shop selling all sorts of clothing for men and women – there's a great selection of glamorous evening wear, jewellery and hats as well as some quirky furniture dating from the 1950s, 1960s and 1970s. Mon–Sat 10.30am–5.30pm.

Biscuit Factory 16 Stoddart St, Ouseburn ☎0191 261 1103, ⓦthebiscuitfactory.com. Airy art gallery (see box, p.591) packed with paintings, ceramics, sculptures, jewellery and furniture – all for sale. Prices range from £10 to over £2000. Mon–Fri 10am–5pm, Sat 10am–6pm, Sun 11am–5pm.

Farmers' Market Grey's Monument. Central market selling wonderful locally sourced fruit and veg, jams, meats and fish. First Fri of each month 9.30am–2.30pm.

Grainger Market Grainger Town. One of the city's oldest and best shopping experiences: a centrally located Georgian market painted in pastel colours and featuring old fashioned fishmongers, butchers and a hardware store, alongside delis, giftshops and a French café. Mon & Wed 9am–5pm, Tues & Thur–Sat 9am–5.30pm.

Quayside Market Busy, popular market down on the quayside selling locally produced food, clothes and art and crafts including jewellery. Sun 9.30am–4pm.

DIRECTORY

Hospital Royal Victoria Infirmary, Queen Victoria Road (☎0191 233 6161, ⓦnewcastle-hospitals.org.uk) has 24hr A&E services and a Minor Injuries Unit (daily 8am–9pm). The Westgate Walk-in Centre at Newcastle General Hospital, Westgate Road, is open daily (8am–8pm).

Police Corner of Market and Pilgrim Streets ☎0191 214 6555.

13

Around Newcastle

There are a number of attractions near Newcastle, all accessible by Metro. The train runs east towards **Wallsend**, where **Segedunum** fort marks the beginning of Hadrian's Wall, while further east **Bede's World** pays homage to Christianity's most important historian. Further out, near Sunderland, is the splendid **Washington Wildfowl Centre**, while the Angel and the Goddess of the North are two striking pieces of public art.

Segedunum

Budle St, Wallsend, 4 miles east of Newcastle • April–May & Sept–Nov daily 10am–4.30pm; June–Aug 10am–5pm; Nov–March Mon–Fri 10am–2.30pm • £5.50 • ☎ 0191 236 9347, ⓦ twmuseums.org.uk/segedunum • Newcastle Metro to Wallsend

Wallsend was the last outpost of Hadrian's great border defence and **Segedunum**, the "strong fort" a couple of minutes' signposted walk from the Metro station, has been admirably developed as one of the prime attractions along the Wall. The grounds contain a fully reconstructed bathhouse, complete with heated pools and colourful frescoes, while the "wall's end" itself is visible at the edge of the site, close to the river and Swan Hunter shipyard. From here, the **Hadrian's Wall Path** (see box, p.597) runs for 84 miles to Bowness-on-Solway in Cumbria; you can get your walk "passport" stamped inside the museum.

Bede's World

On the edge of Jarrow, 5 miles east of Newcastle • Daily Feb–March 10am–4.30pm; April–Sept 10am–5.30pm • £5.50 • ☎ 0191 489 2106, ⓦ bedesworld.co.uk • Newcastle Metro to Jarrow, from where it's a 20min walk through the industrial estate

Bede's World sits at the edge of the town of **JARROW** — ingrained on the national consciousness since the 1936 **Jarrow Crusade**, when 201 people marched three hundred miles down to London to protest against the government's refusal to ease unemployment and poverty in the Northeast. The complex explores the life of Venerable Bede (673–735 AD), who lived here as a boy, growing to become one of Europe's greatest scholars and England's first historian – his *History of the English Church and People*, describing the struggles of the island's early Christians, was completed at Jarrow in 731. Exhibits include extracts from Bede's writings and various archeological finds, and outside there's a reconstructed monastic village; children will enjoy the small farmyard complete with pigs, goats and sheep.

Angel of the North

6 miles south of Newcastle upon Tyne, off the A167 (signposted Gateshead South) • Bus #21 or #22 from Eldon Shopping Centre; there's car parking at the site

Since 1998, Antony Gormley's 66ft-high **Angel of the North** has stood sentinel over the A1 at Gateshead. A startling steel colossus that greets anyone travelling up from the south by rail or road, it's sited on top of a former coal-mining site, acknowledging the area's most emotive industry.

Goddess of the North

Cramlington, 9 miles north of Newcastle upon Tyne • Daily dawn–dusk, café & visitor centre 9.30am–4.30pm • ⓦ northumberlandia.com • There's a train station at Cramlington located 2.5 miles from the site, or take bus #X13 from Newcastle

The Angel of the North (see above) has a rival in Charles Jencks' **Goddess of the North** (or *Northumberlandia*) nine miles north in Cramlington. Made out of 1.5 million tonnes of earth from Shotton mine and an epic 34m-high and 400m-long, the recumbent naked Goddess was unveiled in 2013.

13

THE GEORDIE NATION

Tyneside and Newcastle's native inhabitants are known as **Geordies**, the word probably derived from a diminutive of the name "George". There are various explanations of who George was (King George II, railwayman George Stephenson), all plausible, none now verifiable. Geordies speak a highly distinctive dialect and accent, heavily derived from Old English. Phrases you're likely to come across include: haway man! (come on!), scran (food), a'reet (hello) and propa belta (really good) – and you can also expect to be widely addressed to as "pet" or "flower".

Washington Wildfowl and Wetlands Centre

Pattinson, 10 miles east of Newcastle • Daily: April–Oct 9.30am–5.30pm; Nov–March 9.30am–4.30pm • £9.50 • ☎ 0191 416 5454, ⓦ wwt.org.uk • Bus #8 from Sunderland stops at the Waterview Park, a short walk from the wildfowl centre; from Newcastle, take the metro to Washington

Taking up one hundred acres of the north bank of the River Wear in Pattinson (formerly District 15), the popular **Washington Wildfowl and Wetlands Centre** is a lush conservation area of meadows, woods and wetlands that acts as a winter habitat for migratory birds, including geese, ducks, herons and flamingos. In summer, you can watch fluffy ducklings hatch in the Waterfowl Nursery.

Sunderland

SUNDERLAND is fifteen miles east of Newcastle and shares that city's long history, river setting and industrial heritage – but cannot match its architectural splendour. However, it's worth a trip to visit the Sunderland Museum, easily accessible by Metro from Newcastle.

Sunderland Museum

Burdon Road • Mon–Sat 10am–5pm, Sun 2–5pm • Free • ⓦ twmuseums.org.uk/sunderland

The **Sunderland Museum** does a very good job of telling the city's history, relating how Sunderland ships were once sent around the world, and also has much to say about the city's other major trades, notably its production of lustreware and glass. The **Winter Gardens**, housed in a steel-and-glass hothouse, invite a treetop walk to view the impressive polished-steel column of a water sculpture.

ARRIVAL AND INFORMATION   SUNDERLAND

By Metro The main stop for Metros from Newcastle (30–35min) is in the central train station opposite The Bridges shopping centre.

Tourist information The tourist office (Mon–Sat 9am–5pm, bank hols 10am–4pm; ☎ 0191 553 2000, ⓦ sunderland.gov.uk) is behind the central station on the main shopping drag at 50 Fawcett Street.

Hadrian's Wall

Hadrian's Wall (ⓦ visithadrianswall.co.uk) was constructed in 122 AD at the behest of the Roman Emperor Hadrian. Keen for peace and safety within his empire, fearing attacks from Pictish Scotland, Hadrian commissioned a long wall to act as a border, snaking its way from the Tyne to the Solway Firth. It was built up to a height of 15ft in places and was interspersed by milecastles, which functioned as gates, depots and mini-barracks. The best-preserved portions of the Wall are concentrated between **Chesters Roman Fort**, four miles north of Hexham, and Haltwhistle, sixteen miles to the west, which passes **Housesteads Roman Fort**, **Vindolanda** and the **Roman Army Museum**. Most people come to walk or cycle the length of the Wall, but if you're only planning to walk a short stretch, start off at Housesteads and head west for sweeping views. There are plenty of interesting places to stay and eat around and along the Wall, including the handsome market town of **Hexham** (see p.598).

13

Chesters Roman Fort

Four miles north of Hexham • Daily: April–Sept 10am–6pm; Oct–Nov 10am–5pm; Nov–April Sat & Sun 10am–4pm • £5.60; EH • ☎ 01434 681379, ⓦ english-heritage.org.uk

Beautifully sited next to the gurgling River Tyne, **Chesters Roman Fort**, otherwise known as Cilurnum, was built to guard the Roman bridge over the river. Enough remains of the original structure to pick out the design of the fort, but the highlight is down by the river where the vestibule, changing room and steam range of the garrison's **bathhouse** are still visible, along with the furnace and the latrines.

Housesteads Roman Fort

Around 8 miles west of Chesters • Daily: April–Sept 10am–6pm; Oct–March 10am–4pm • £6.40; EH & NT • ☎ 01434 344525

Housesteads Roman Fort is one of the most popular sites on the Wall. The fort is of standard design but for one enforced modification – forts were supposed to straddle the line of the Wall, but here the original stonework follows the edge of the cliff, so Housesteads was built on the steeply sloping ridge to the south. Enter via the tiny **museum**, and walk across to the south gate; next to this lies the ruins of a garrison of up to one thousand infantrymen. It's not necessary to pay for entrance to the fort if you're simply walking along the Wall west from here; the three-mile hike takes in wonderful views as it meanders past **Crag Lough** and over to **Steel Rigg** (which has a car park).

Vindolanda

Access from behind Once Brewed Visitor Centre • Daily: mid- to end March & Oct 10am–5pm; April–Sept 10am–6pm; reduced hours in winter, call in advance • £6.25, joint admission with Roman Army Museum £10 • ☎ 01434 344277, ⓦ vindolanda.com

The garrison fort of **Vindolanda** is believed to have been built and occupied before the construction of the Wall itself. Guarding the important central section of the east–west supply route across Britain, a series of early forts in this location were built of timber, eventually replaced with a stone construction during Hadrian's reign. Preserved beneath the remains of the stone fortress, these early forts are now being excavated – around three to four hundred volunteers take part every day. The museum contains the largest collection of Roman leather items ever discovered on a single site – sandals, purses, an archer's thumb guard – and a fascinating series of **writing tablets** dating to 90 AD. The earliest written records found in Britain, they feature shopping lists, duty rotas and even a birthday party invitation from one Claudia Severa to Sulpicia Lepidina.

Roman Army Museum

7 miles west of Vindolanda • Daily: mid- to end March & Oct 10am–5pm; April–Sept 10am–6pm; reduced hours in winter, call in advance • £5.25, joint admission with Vindolanda £10 • ☎ 01434 344277, ⓦ vindolanda.com

The **Roman Army Museum** aims to illustrate how the Roman soldiers stationed here lived. There's everything from armour and weapons – including javelins, shields and

13

ALONG HADRIAN'S WALL

The best way to visit the Wall is to walk or cycle the length of it. The **Hadrian's Wall Path** (ⓦnationaltrail.co.uk/hadrians-wall-path) runs for 84 miles alongside the Wall itself from Wallsend (see p.594) to Bowness-on-Solway. It takes on average seven days to complete and there's an optional Passport system (May–Oct) involving collecting a series of stamps to prove you've done it. The **National Route 72** (signposted NCN 72; ⓦcycle-routes.org/hadrians cycleway), shares some of the same route as the Footpath, and runs from South Shields to Ravenglass in Cumbria. There's bike hire in Newcastle (see p.590).

swords – to a full-size chariot and a wagon. It's all very entertaining, and successfully brings to life the ruins you may just have seen at Vindolanda.

ARRIVAL AND INFORMATION

HADRIAN'S WALL

By train The nearest train stations are on the Newcastle–Carlisle line at Corbridge, Hexham, Bardon Mill and Haltwhistle.

Tourist office Once Brewed Visitor Centre (April–Oct daily 9.30am–5pm, Sat & Sun 10am–3pm; ☎01434 344396) is

just off the B6318. It has exhibitions about the Wall and Northumberland National Park, access to Vindolanda (see opposite), a tearoom, toilets and a hostel next door (see below). The #AD122 bus (see below) stops here.

GETTING AROUND

By car The B3618 (aka Military Road) runs alongside the Wall. All museums and forts are accessible by car and there's parking at all major sights, Once Brewed Visitor Centre and Steel Rigg.

By bus The little #AD122 (known as the "Hadrian's Wall bus"; Easter–Oct up to 5 times daily in each direction) runs from Newcastle to Corbridge, Hexham, and all the Wall

sites and villages, before heading on to Carlisle and Bowness-on-Solway (the end of the Hadrian's Wall Path). There's also a year-round hourly service on the #685 bus between Newcastle and Carlisle, and other local services from Carlisle and Hexham, which provide access to various points along the Wall.

ACCOMMODATION

In addition to the B&Bs in the countryside around the Wall, Hexham (see p.598), Haltwhistle and Corbridge have a good selection of accommodation.

★**Carraw B&B** Military Rd, Humshaugh ☎01434 689857, ⓦcarraw.co.uk. It's not often you can say "I've slept on Hadrian's Wall", but here you can – this beautiful B&B, run by a friendly couple, is built right next to Hadrian's masterpiece and boasts stunning views. Lovely homely touches, like home-made shortbread and cake on arrival, hot-water bottles and luxurious toiletries make this place really special. Delicious breakfasts – the nutty granola is a winner. Supper £12.50. **£98**

Hadrian's Wall Camping and Caravan Site Melkridge Tilery, 2 miles north of Melkridge, just south of B6318 ☎01434 320495, ⓦhadrianswallcampsite.co.uk. Friendly, family-run site half a mile from the Wall, with showers, café, washing machine and dryer, and bike storage; breakfast and evening meals available. There's also a heated bunk barn sleeping 10 people (£15 per person). Open all year. Pitches **£12**, camper van **£15**

Langley Castle A686, Langley-on-Tyne, 2 miles south of Haydon Bridge ☎01434 688888, ⓦwww.langley castle.com. Suitably regal rooms – four-poster beds, sumptuous furnishings and beautiful bathrooms with

saunas and spa baths – in this turreted medieval castle. The cheaper rooms are in the grounds, looking onto the castle. There's also an atmospheric restaurant, cocktail bar, lounge and gardens. **£195**, castle rooms **£245**

Twice Brewed Inn Military Rd ☎01434 344534, ⓦtwicebrewedinn.co.uk. Just 50 yards up from Once Brewed Visitor Centre and hostel, this friendly community pub has simple rooms, a beer garden, local beers on tap and perhaps the Northeast's largest selection of rums (54 of them). En-suites are slightly pricier. **£59**

★**Willowford Farm** Gilsland ☎01697 747962, ⓦwww.willowford.co.uk. Strictly speaking just over the Northumbrian border in Cumbria, but this farmhouse B&B still makes a lovely, tranquil base to explore the Wall. Rooms are in converted farm buildings and decked out with pretty wooden beams and large beds. Packed lunch £6. **£80**

YHA Once Brewed Military Rd, Once Brewed ☎0845 371 9753, ⓦyha.org.uk. Basic and welcoming youth hostel next to the visitor centre. They have plenty of walking leaflets, a restaurant and self-catering facilities. Dorms **£19.50**, family rooms **£37.50**

13

EATING AND DRINKING

★**Barrasford Arms** Barrasford, 9 miles north of Hexham ☎01434 681237, ⓦbarrasfordarms.co.uk. Endearingly ramshackle, welcoming and homely, this country pub serves great traditional British food with a French twist; dishes could include Cumbrian outdoor-reared chicken with haricot bean and tomato stew (£12) and for pudding sticky pistachio meringue with orange mascarpone (£5). Booking advisable. Mon 6.30–11pm, Tues–Thur noon–2pm & 6.30–11pm, Fri noon–2pm & 6.30–midnight, Sat noon–midnight, Sun noon–11pm; food served Mon 6.30–9pm, Tues–Sat noon–2pm & 6.30–9pm, Sun noon–3pm.

Battlesteads Country Inn and Restaurant Wark-on-Tyne, 12 miles north of Hexham ☎01434 230209, ⓦbattlesteads.com. In a charming little village by a trickling stream, this locally renowned restaurant with a lovely beer garden uses fresh produce sourced from within a 30-mile radius. Leave room for their famed whisky and marmalade bread and butter pudding (£5.75). Best to book. Food served daily noon–3pm & 6.30–9.30pm.

General Havelock Inn Haydon Bridge ☎01434 684376. Eighteenth-century inn that specializes in tasty Modern British food, from crab cakes and Cumberland sausages to chocolate brûlée and ice-cream sundaes. Great locally brewed ales on offer, too. Main meals average around £17. Food served daily noon–3pm & 6–11pm.

Hexham

HEXHAM is the only significant stop between Newcastle and Carlisle, and however keen you are on seeing the Wall, you'd do well to give this handsome market town a night.

The focal point is the **abbey**, whose foundations were originally part of a fine Benedictine monastery founded by St Wilfrid in 671. Claimed, according to contemporaneous accounts, to be the finest this side of the Alps, the church – or rather its gold and silver – proved irresistible to the Vikings, who savaged the place in 876. It was rebuilt in the eleventh century as part of an Augustinian priory, and the town grew up in its shadow.

Hexham Abbey

Daily 9.30am–5pm • ⓦ www.hexhamabbey.org.uk

The stately exterior of **Hexham Abbey** dominates the west side of the central marketplace. Entry is through the south transept, where there's a bruised but impressive first-century tombstone honouring Flavinus, a standard-bearer in the Roman cavalry. The memorial lies at the foot of the broad, well-worn steps of the canons' **night stair**, one of the few such staircases – providing access from the monastery to the church – to have survived the Dissolution. The chancel, meanwhile, displays the inconsequential-looking **frith-stool**, an eighth-century stone chair that was once believed to have been used by St Wilfrid, rendering it holy enough to serve as the medieval sanctuary stool.

The Old Gaol

Hallgate • April–Sept Tues–Sat 11am–4.30pm; Oct–Nov & Feb–March Tues & Sat 11am–4.30pm • £3.95 • ☎01434 652349, ⓦ www.tynedaleheritage.org

Britain's first purpose-built prison, **Hexham Old Gaol** occupies a solid sandstone building to the east of the abbey. It was commissioned by the powerful Archbishop of York in 1330, and constructed using stone plundered from the Roman ruins at Corbridge. Inside there's an entertaining museum extolling the virtues and pitfalls of medieval crime and punishment.

ARRIVAL AND INFORMATION   HEXHAM

By train The train station sits on the northeastern edge of the town centre, a 10min walk from the abbey.

Destinations Carlisle (hourly; 50min); Haltwhistle (hourly; 20min); Newcastle (hourly; 50min).

By bus The bus station is off Priestpopple, a few minutes' stroll east of the abbey.

Destinations Bellingham (Mon–Sat hourly; 45min); Newcastle (hourly; 50min).

Tourist office In the main Wentworth car park, near the supermarket (April–Oct Mon–Sat 9.30am–5pm, Sun 11am–4pm; Nov–March Mon–Sat 9.30am–4.30pm; ☎01434 652220, ⓦ visithadrianswall.co.uk).

FROM TOP HADRIAN'S WALL (P.595); GATESHEAD MILLENNIUM BRIDGE (P.587) >

13

ACCOMMODATION

Hallbank Hallgate, behind the Old Gaol ☎01434 605567, ⓦhallbankguesthouse.com. A restored house in a quiet town-centre location, with eight very comfortable rooms and an associated coffee shop/restaurant. Evening meals available on request. **£90**

Matfen Hall Matfen, 10 miles northeast of Hexham ☎01661 886500, ⓦmatfenhall.com. Large, ritzy country hotel surrounded by acres of green parkland harbouring a golf course and driving range. There's a spa and a good, fine dining restaurant. It's a popular spot for weddings. **£185**

EATING AND DRINKING

★**Bouchon Bistrot** 4 Gilesgate ☎01434 609943, ⓦbouchonbistrot.co.uk. Very stylish restaurant in a handsome terraced townhouse, serving sophisticated French dishes such as lamb shank "de 5 heures" with sautéed potatoes (£15.50) and crème caramel with *langues du chat* (£4.95). Tues–Sat noon–2pm & 6–9.30pm.

Dipton Mill Inn Dipton Mill Rd, 2 miles south of Hexham ☎01434 606577, ⓦdiptonmill.co.uk. A lovely, traditional country pub covered in ivy. While the food is excellent – good pub grub like steak and kidney pie and vegetable casserole – it's most famous for the home-brewed ales, made at Hexhamshire Brewery. Try Old

Humbug, named after the landlord. Mon–Sat noon–2.30pm & 6–11pm, Sun noon–3pm.

★**Rat Inn** Anick, 2 miles northeast of Hexham ☎01434 602814, ⓦtheratinn.com. In a glorious hillside location overlooking Hexham, this quaint pub has a roaring fire in winter and a pretty summer garden. The food is all locally sourced – try the braised local beef in Allendale beer (£10.50). Booking essential for Sunday lunch. On Mondays in summer there are fresh sandwiches available for lunch (from £3.95). April–Sept daily noon–11pm; Oct–March Mon–Fri noon–3pm & 6–11pm.

Northumberland National Park

Northwest Northumberland, the great triangular chunk of land between Hadrian's Wall and the coastal plain, is dominated by the wide-skied landscapes of **Northumberland National Park** (ⓦnorthumberlandnationalpark.org.uk), whose four hundred windswept square miles rise to the Cheviot Hills on the Scottish border. The bulk of the Park is taken up by **Kielder Water and Forest nature reserve**, a superb destination for watersports and outdoor activities; the small town of **Bellingham** on the eastern edge of the park makes a good base for the reserve, as do **Rothbury** and **Wooler**, both of which also provide easy access to some superb walking in the craggy **Cheviot Hills**.

Kielder Water and Forest

Surrounded by 250 acres of dense pine forest **Kielder Water** is the largest reservoir in England. The road from Bellingham follows the North Tyne River west and skirts the forested edge of the lake, passing an assortment of visitor centres, waterside parks, picnic areas and anchorages that fringe its southern shore. Mountain biking, hiking, horseriding and fishing are some of the land-based activities on offer, and of course watersports (waterskiing, sailing, kayaking and windsurfing) are hugely popular, too. The mass of woodlands and wetlands means that **wildlife** is abundant – you might spot badgers, deer, otters, ospreys and red squirrels. **Leaplish Waterside Park** (Birds of Prey Centre daily 10.30am–4pm; Flying demonstrations summer 1.30pm & 3pm, Oct–March 2pm; £7; ☎01434 250400, ⓦkwbopc.com), on the western flank of the reservoir, is the best place to head if you're visiting for the first time and need to get your bearings. There's a purpose-built hub of lodges (see opposite) with cafés and a restaurant, a visitor centre (see below) and a Birds of Prey Centre where you can see a variety of handsome, sharp-taloned beasts, from owls and falcons to vultures and some inscrutable ospreys.

ARRIVAL AND INFORMATION

KIELDER WATER AND FOREST

By bus The #880 from Hexham serves the visitor centres of Tower Knowe, Leaplish (by request) and Kielder Castle via Bellingham (2 daily Tues & Sat). The #714 from Newcastle

upon Tyne runs on Sundays (1 daily) to Tower Knowe, Leaplish (by request) and Kielder Castle.

Visitor centres Tower Knowe: from Bellingham, the first

visitor centre you come to as you head anti-clockwise round the reservoir (daily: April–June & Sept 10am–5pm; July & Aug 10am–6pm; Oct 10am–4pm; ☎ 0845 155 0236); Leaplish: western flank of the reservoir (Feb–Oct daily 9am–5pm; ☎ 01434 251000); Kielder Castle: at the northernmost point of the reservoir (daily 10am–5pm; ☎ 01434 250209).

GETTING AROUND

By bike Purple Mountain (April–Oct 9am–5pm; Nov–March Sat & Sun 9am–5pm; ☎ 01434 250532, ⓦ purplemountain .co.uk) and the Bike Place (Mon–Sat 10am–6pm; ☎ 0845 634 1895, ⓦ thebikeplace.co.uk) are both near Kielder Castle Visitor Centre, and both offer day rental from £20.
By car The nearest petrol station is in Bellingham (14 miles away; closed Sun). For parking, you can buy one ticket at

your first stop (£4) that's valid for all other car parks throughout the day.
By ferry The 74-seater Osprey Ferry (☎ 01434 251000) sails round the reservoir, with stops at Leaplish, Tower Knowe and Belvedere. Tickets (day pass £6.75, short journeys from £4.40) are available at Tower Knowe or Leaplish; prior booking is necessary.

ACCOMMODATION AND EATING

Hollybush Inn Greenhaugh, 12 miles east of Kielder Water ☎ 01434 240391, ⓦ hollybushinn.net. Super little pub in a remote village serving great ales and food, and with four simple and attractive bedrooms upstairs. **£65**
Kielder Lodges Leaplish Waterside Park ☎ 0870 240 3549, or Hoseasons ☎ 01502 502588, ⓦ hoseasons .co.uk. Scandinavian-style self-catering lodges, all with access to the park's pool, sauna, bar and restaurant. Bring plenty of midge repellent. Weekly rates from **£335**
★**Pheasant Inn** Stannersburn ☎ 01434 240382, ⓦ thepheasantinn.com. A traditional country pub on the

road from Bellingham, the *Pheasant Inn* has eight very comfortable bedrooms (including one family room). The highlight is the food, though, served downstairs in the cosy restaurant; expect game pies, Northumbrian cheeses and plenty of fish (mains around £12 in the evening). Booking recommended. Restaurant daily 8–9am & 7–9pm; bar meals noon–2pm & 7–9pm. **£85**
YHA Kielder Butteryhaugh, Kielder village ☎ 0845 371 9126, ⓦ yha.org.uk. Well equipped activity based hostel, with some two- and three-bedded rooms plus small dorms. Dorms **£16.40**, family rooms **£34.95**

Rothbury and around

ROTHBURY, straddling the River Coquet thirty miles northeast of Hexham, prospered as a late Victorian resort because it gave ready access to the forests, burns and ridges of the **Simonside Hills**. The small town remains a popular spot for walkers, with several of the best local trails beginning from the **Simonside Hills** car park, a couple of miles southwest of Rothbury. Nearby, the estates of **Cragside** and **Wallington** are good options if you want to take a break from hiking.

Cragside

1 mile east of Rothbury • House: March–Oct Sat & Sun 11am–5pm, Tues & Fri 1–5pm; gardens: March–Oct 10am–7pm • £15.85, gardens only £9.25; NT • ☎ 01669 620333, ⓦ nationaltrust.org.uk/cragside

Victorian Rothbury was dominated by Sir William, later the first Lord Armstrong, the wealthy nineteenth-century arms manufacturer, shipbuilder and engineer who built his country home at **Cragside**, a mile to the east of the village. He hired Richard Norman Shaw, one of the period's top architects, who produced a grandiose Tudor-style mansion entirely out of place in the Northumbrian countryside. Armstrong was an avid innovator, and in 1880 Cragside became the first house in the world to be lit by hydroelectric power. The surrounding **gardens**, complete with the remains of the original pumping system, are beautiful and there's a pleasant tearoom for a light snack.

Wallington

13 miles south of Rothbury • House: March–Oct Mon & Wed–Fri 1–5pm, Sat & Sun 11am–5pm; gardens: daily 10am–7pm • £9.70, gardens only £6.70; NT • ☎ 01670 773967, ⓦ nationaltrust.org.uk/wallington

South of Rothbury, down the B6342, stands **Wallington**, an ostentatious mansion rebuilt in the 1740s by Sir Walter Blackett, the coal- and lead-mine owner. The house is known for its Rococo plasterwork and William Bell Scott's Pre-Raphaelite murals of scenes from Northumbrian history. Children will love the collection of dolls' houses,

13

one of which has thirty-six rooms and was originally fitted with running water and a working lift. However, it's the magnificent **gardens and grounds** that are the real delight, with lawns, woods and lakes laced with footpaths. There are events, concerts and activities throughout the year, as well as a café and farm shop on site.

ARRIVAL AND INFORMATION

ROTHBURY AND AROUND

By bus Buses from Newcastle stop outside the *Queen's Head* pub in the centre (hourly; 1hr 20min).

National Park Visitor Centre Near the cross on Church Street (April–Oct daily 10am–5pm; Nov–March Sat & Sun 10am–3pm; ☎01669 620887, ⓦtheheartof northumberland.co.uk).

ACCOMMODATION

★Hillcrest 200yd from Rothbury centre ☎01669 621944, ⓦhillcrestbandb.co.uk. Superb B&B in a pretty Georgian house, with two beautifully decorated bedrooms – wooden floorboards, antique furniture, exposed walls and the like – with an intriguing past (the owner will explain). Wonderful breakfasts, too. **£75**

Thistleyhaugh Longframlington, 5 miles east of Rothbury ☎01665 570629, ⓦthistleyhaugh.co.uk.

Gorgeous, ivy-smothered Georgian farmhouse with five luxurious chintzy bedrooms. They serve delicious three-course dinners (7pm; £20) and hearty breakfasts. **£80**

★Tosson Tower Great Tosson, 2 miles southwest of Rothbury ☎01669 620228, ⓦtossontowerfarm.com. Eight lovely rooms on this little working farm in a quiet hamlet with spectacular views out over the Cheviot Hills. Plus some charming self-catering cottages. **£80**

Wooler and around

Stone-terraced **WOOLER** – rebuilt after a terrible fire in the 1860s – is a one-street market town twenty miles north of Rothbury. It's the best base for climbs up **the Cheviot** (2674ft), seven miles to the southwest and the highest point in the Cheviot Hills. From *Wooler Youth Hostel* at 30 Cheviot St, it's four hours there and back; from Hawsen Burn, the nearest navigable point, it's two hours walking there and back. Wooler is also a staging-post on the Pennine Way and the lovely **St Cuthbert's Way** (from Melrose in Scotland to Lindisfarne).

Chillingham Castle

6 miles southeast of Wooler • April–Oct Sun–Fri noon–5pm • £9 • ☎01668 215359, ⓦchillingham-castle.com

Chillingham Castle started life as an eleventh-century tower. The castle was augmented at regular intervals until the nineteenth century, but from 1933 was largely left to the elements for fifty years, until the present owner set about restoring it in his own individualistic way: bedrooms, living rooms and even a grisly torture chamber (designed to "cause maximum shock") are decorated with historical paraphernalia.

Chillingham Wild Cattle

Off the A697 between Alnwick and Belford, signposted The Wild White Cattle • April–Oct Mon–Fri tours hourly 10am–noon, 2pm–4pm, Sun 2pm, 3pm & 4pm; winter by appointment • £15 • ⓦchillinghamwildcattle.com

In 1220, Chillingham Castle's adjoining 365 acres of parkland were enclosed to protect the local wild cattle for hunting and food. And so the **Chillingham Wild Cattle** – a fierce, primeval herd with white coats, black muzzles and black tips to their horns – have remained to this day, cut off from mixing with domesticated breeds. It's possible to visit these unique relics, who number around ninety, but only in the company of a warden, as the animals are potentially dangerous and need to be protected from outside infection. The visit takes about two hours and involves a short country walk before viewing the cattle at a safe

> ### TOP 5 NORTHUMBRIAN CASTLES
> **Alnwick Castle** See p.604
> **Bamburgh Castle** See p.607
> **Chillingham Castle** See above
> **Dunstanburgh Castle** See p.605
> **Warkworth Castle** See oppsite

distance – the closest you're likely to get to big game viewing in England. Bring strong shoes or walking boots if it's wet.

ARRIVAL AND INFORMATION

By bus The bus station is set back off High Street. Destinations Alnwick (Mon–Sat 9 daily; 45min); Berwick-upon-Tweed (Mon–Sat 9 daily; 50min).

Tourist office Cheviot Centre, Padgepool Place (leaflets

and accommodation information available Mon–Fri 9am–5pm; staffed desk Easter–Oct daily 10am–4.30pm; Nov–March Sat & Sun 10am–2pm; ☎01668 282123).

ACCOMMODATION AND EATING

Milan 2 High St, through the arch of the Black Bull hotel ☎01668 283692, ⓦmilan-restaurant.co.uk. Good-value Italian restaurant with exposed brick walls and a jolly ambience, serving large pizzas (from £6.75), pasta dishes (from £7.95) and plenty of meat and fish options. It's a very popular place, so book ahead. Daily 5–10pm.

Tilldale House 34 High St ☎01668 281450, ⓦtilldalehouse.co.uk. Snug seventeenth-century stone cottage in the middle of town with three en-suite bedrooms. With enormous, soft beds, deep-pile carpets, an open fire and great breakfasts, it makes a very cosy and enticing base after a long day hiking in the hills. **£58**

The Northumberland coast

Stretching 64 miles north of Newcastle up to the Scottish border, the low-lying **Northumberland coast** is the region's shining star, stunningly beautiful and packed with impressive sights. Here you'll find the mighty fortresses at **Warkworth**, **Alnwick** and **Bamburgh** and the magnificent Elizabethan ramparts surrounding **Berwick-upon-Tweed**, while in between there are glorious sandy beaches as well as the site of the Lindisfarne monastery on **Holy Island** and the seabird and nature reserve of the **Farne Islands**, reached by boat from Seahouses.

Warkworth

WARKWORTH, a peaceful coastal hamlet set in a loop of the River Coquet a couple of miles from Amble, is best seen from the north, from where the grey stone terraces of the long main street slope up towards the commanding remains of **Warkworth Castle**. From the castle, the main street sweeps down into the village, flattening out at Dial Place and the Church of St Lawrence before curving right to cross the River Coquet; just over the bridge, a signposted quarter-mile lane leads to the **beach**, which stretches for five miles from Amble to Alnmouth.

Warkworth Castle

April–Oct daily 10am–5pm; rest of the year limited opening hours, call before visiting; Duke's Rooms Wed, Sun & bank hols • £5.20; EH • ☎01665 711423, ⓦenglish-heritage.org.uk

Ruined but well-preserved, **Warkworth Castle** has Norman origins, but was constructed using sandstone during the fourteenth and fifteenth centuries. Home to generations of the Percy family, the powerful earls of Northumberland, it appears as a backdrop in several scenes of Shakespeare's *Henry IV, Part II*. The cross-shaped keep contains a great hall, a chapel, kitchens, storerooms and the Duke's Rooms, which are kitted out in period furniture and furnishings.

Warkworth Hermitage

Weather permitting April–Sept Wed & Sun 11am–5pm; rest of the year limited opening hours, call before visiting • Combined ticket with castle; EH • ☎01665 711423, ⓦenglish-heritage.org.uk

A path from the churchyard heads along the right bank of the Coquet to the boat that shuttles visitors across to **Warkworth Hermitage**, a series of simple rooms and a claustrophobic chapel that were hewn out of the cliff above the river some time in the

13

fourteenth century, but abandoned by 1567. The last resident hermit, one George Lancaster, was charged by the sixth earl of Northumberland to pray for his noble family, for which lonesome duty he received around £15 a year and a barrel of fish every Sunday.

ARRIVAL   WARKWORTH

By bus The easiest way to get here by public transport is by train to Alnmouth, followed by the bus (hourly; 30min).

Alnmouth

It's three miles north from Warkworth to the seaside resort of **ALNMOUTH**, whose narrow centre is strikingly situated on a steep spur of land between the sea and the estuary of the Aln. It's a lovely setting and has been a low-key holiday spot since Victorian times, and is particularly popular with golfers: the village's nine-hole course, right on the coast, was built in 1869 (it's claimed to be the second oldest in the country) and dune-strollers really do have to heed the "Danger – Flying Golf Balls" signs which adorn Marine Road.

ARRIVAL AND DEPARTURE   ALNMOUTH

By train Trains pass through from Berwick to the north (every 2hr; 20min) and Newcastle to the south (hourly; 30min).

By bus There are local bus services from Alnwick and Warkworth, and the regular #X18 Newcastle–Alnwick bus also passes through Alnmouth and calls at its train station, 1.5 miles west of the centre.

ACCOMMODATION AND EATING

Red Lion 22 Northumberland St ☎ 01668 30584, ⓦ redlionalnmouth.com. Six spacious and modern rooms, with pine furniture, cream walls and fresh bathrooms, above a popular, traditional pub. The beer garden is perfect for sunny days, and the menu has everything from big open sandwiches (from £4.95) to sirloin steak (£17.50). **£85**

Alnwick

The appealing market town of **ALNWICK** (pronounced "Annick"), thirty miles north of Newcastle and four miles inland from Alnmouth, is renowned for its **castle** and gardens – seat of the dukes of Northumberland – which overlook the River Aln. It's worth spending a couple of days here, exploring the medieval maze of streets, the elegant gatehouses on Pottergate and Bondgate and the best **bookshop** in the north.

Alnwick Castle

April–Oct daily 10am–6pm • £14.50; castle and garden £22 • ☎ 01665 511100, ⓦ alnwickcastle.com

The Percys – who were raised to the dukedom of Northumberland in 1750 – have owned **Alnwick Castle** since 1309. In the eighteenth century, the first duke had the interior refurbished by Robert Adam in an extravagant Gothic style – which in turn was supplanted by the gaudy Italianate decoration preferred by the fourth duke in the 1850s. There's plenty to see inside, including remains from Pompeii, though the **interior** can be crowded at times – not least with families on the *Harry Potter* trail, since the castle doubled as Hogwarts School in the first two films.

Alnwick Garden

Daily 10am–6pm; Grand Cascade and Poison Garden closed in winter • £13.75; garden and castle £26.25 • ☎ 01665 511350, ⓦ alnwickgarden.com

The grounds of the castle are taken up by the huge and beautiful **Alnwick Garden**, designed by an innovative Belgian team and full of quirky features such as a bamboo labyrinth maze, a serpent garden involving topiary snakes, and the popular **Poison Garden**, filled with the world's deadliest plants. The heart of the garden is the computerized Grand Cascade, which shoots water jets in a regular synchronized display, while to the west is

Europe's largest treehouse with a restaurant within (see below). The walled Roots and Shoots community veg garden (no ticket required) is a delight.

Barter Books

Wagonway Rd • April–Sept daily 9am–7pm; Oct–March Mon–Wed & Fri–Sun 9am–5pm, Thurs 9am–7pm • ☎ 01665 604888, ⓦ barterbooks.co.uk

Housed in the Victorian train station on Wagonway Road, and containing visible remnants of the ticket office, passenger waiting rooms and the outbound platform, the enchanting **Barter Books** is one of the largest secondhand bookshops in England. With its sofas, murals, open fire, coffee and biscuits – and, best of all, a model train that runs on top of the stacks – it is definitely worth a visit.

ARRIVAL AND INFORMATION · ALNWICK

By bus The station is on Clayport St, a couple of minutes' walk west of the marketplace.

Destinations Bamburgh (Mon–Sat 7 daily, Sun 4 daily; 1hr 15min); Berwick-upon-Tweed (Mon–Sat 6 daily, Sun 3 daily; 1hr); Craster (Mon–Fri 7 daily, Sat 4 daily; 35min); Wooler (Mon–Sat 9 daily; 45min).

Tourist office 2 The Shambles, off the marketplace (April–June & Sept–Oct Mon–Sat 9.30am–5pm, Sun 10am–4pm; July & Aug daily 9am–5pm; Nov–March Mon–Fri 9.30am–4.30pm, Sat 10am–4pm; ☎ 01665 511 333, ⓦ visitalnwick.org.uk).

ACCOMMODATION

Tate House 11 Bondgate Without ☎ 01665 660800, ⓦ stayinalnwick.co.uk. In a pretty Victorian house opposite Alnwick Gardens, this B&B has three comfortable bedrooms with spotless bathrooms and nice little touches such as hot-water bottles, iPod docks and DVD players. **£75**

YHA Alnwick 4–38 Green Batt ☎ 01665 604661, ⓦ yha .org.uk. A handsome Victorian courthouse nicely converted into a hostel with some private rooms. You're a stroll away form the gardens and castle, and there's a bus stop right outside the front door. Dorms **£18.50**, doubles **£39**

EATING

Alnwick Garden Treehouse Alnwick Gardens ☎ 01665 511852, ⓦ alnwickgarden.com. Glorious restaurant in the enormous treehouse in Alnwick Gardens (you don't have to pay the garden entry fee to visit). There's an open fire in the middle of the room and even tree trunks growing through the floor. Simple meals (sandwiches, quiche and soup) for lunch and in the evening, expensive but tasty mains – honey-glazed duck with braised red cabbage (£18.50) for example, and a refreshing kirsch and blackcurrant sorbet

(£4.95) for pudding. Mon–Wed 11.30am–2.45pm, Thurs–Sun 11.30am–2.45pm & 6.30pm–late.

Station Buffet Barter Books Wagonway Road ☎ 01665 604888, ⓦ barterbooks.co.uk. Set in the old station waiting room at Barter Books this unique café serves home-made food including hamburgers, sandwiches, salads and cakes (meals around £7). April–Sept daily 9am–7pm; Oct–March Mon–Wed & Fri–Sun 9am–5pm, Thurs 9am–7pm.

Craster and around

The tiny fishing village of **CRASTER** – known for its kippers – lies six miles northeast of Alnwick, right on the coast. It's a delightful little place, with its circular, barnacle-encrusted harbour walls fronting a cluster of tough, weather-battered little houses and the cheery *Jolly Fisherman* pub. Other villages worth visiting round here include **Newton-on-Sea** and **Beadnell**, both exuding wind-swept, salty charm. The **coastline** between Dunstanburgh and Beadnell is made up of the long sandy beaches Northumberland is famous for.

Dunstanburgh Castle

April–Sept daily 10am–5pm; Oct daily 10am–4pm; Nov–March Mon & Thurs–Sun 10am–4pm • £4.30; NT & EH • ☎ 01665 576231, ⓦ nationaltrust.org.uk/dunstanburgh-castle/

Looming in the distance, about a thirty-minute walk northwards up the coast from Craster, is stunning **Dunstanburgh Castle**. Built in the fourteenth century, in the wake of civil war, its shattered remains occupy a magnificent promontory, bordered by sheer cliffs and crashing waves.

13

By bus Bus #18 runs from Alnwick to Craster every 2hr (30min).

ACCOMMODATION

Old Rectory Howick, 2 miles south ☎01665 577590, ⓦoldrectoryhowick.co.uk. Just 400yds from the wind-whipped North Sea, this fantastic B&B sits in its own peaceful grounds and has extremely pretty bedrooms and comfortable sitting areas. Superb breakfasts feature plenty of cooked options, including Craster kippers. **£90**

EATING AND DRINKING

There's not much in the way of fine dining round these parts; most villages simply have a traditional pub serving decent meals. Craster's beloved **kippers** are smoked at L. Robson & Sons (☎01665 576223, ⓦkipper.co.uk) in the centre of the village; they also sell salty oak-smoked salmon.

Jolly Fisherman 9 Haven Hill ☎01665 576461. Just above the harbour, this pub has sea views from its back window and a lovely summer beer garden. Not surprisingly for a pub opposite L. Robson & Sons, it serves plenty of fish – crab sandwiches, kipper pâté and a famously good crabmeat, whisky and cream soup. Mon–Fri 11am–3pm & 7–11pm, Sat & Sun 11am–11pm.

Ship Inn Low Newton-by-the-Sea, 5 miles north ☎01665 576262, ⓦshipinnnewton.co.uk. Great, rustic pub in a coastal hamlet serving dishes using ingredients from local suppliers – there's plenty of L. Robson smoked fish on the menu. Mains from £7. Ales are supplied by their own brewery next door. Dinner reservations advised. Mon–Sat 11.30am–11pm, Sun 11am–11pm.

Seahouses and the Farne Islands

Around ten miles north from Craster, beyond the small village of Beadnell, lies the fishing port of **SEAHOUSES**, the only place on the local coast that could remotely be described as a resort. It's the embarkation point for boat trips out to the wind-swept **Farne Islands**, a rocky archipelago lying a few miles offshore.

The Farne Islands

Owned by the National Trust and maintained as a nature reserve, the **Farne Islands** (ⓦfarne-islands.com) are the summer home of hundreds of thousands of migrating seabirds, notably puffins, guillemots, terns, eider ducks and kittiwakes, and home to the only grey seal colony on the English coastline. A number of boat trips potter around the islands – the largest of which is Inner Farne – offering birdwatching tours, grey seal-watching tours and the Grace Darling tour, which takes visitors to the lighthouse on Longstone Island, where the famed local heroine (see opposite) lived.

ARRIVAL AND INFORMATION   SEAHOUSES AND THE FARNE ISLANDS

By bus Buses run from Alnwick to Craster every 2hr (1hr).

By boat Weather permitting, several operators in Seahouses run daily boat trips (2–3hr; from £13) starting at around 10am. Wander down to the quayside, or contact either the National Trust Shop or the tourist office (see below). During the breeding season (May–July) landings are restricted to morning trips to Staple Island and afternoons to Inner Farne. Landing fees for the islands are payable to the National Trust (£5–6).

Tourist information National Trust Shop, 16 Main Street (☎01665 721099), by the Seahouses traffic roundabout. The tourist office is located in the main car park.

ACCOMMODATION

★**St Cuthberts** Seahouses ☎01665 720456, ⓦstcuthbertshouse.com. Award-winning B&B in a beautifully converted 200-year-old chapel. Rooms cleverly incorporate period features like the original arched windows with lovely modern touches such as wet rooms, flatscreen TVs, comfy dressing gowns and slippers. Breakfast is all locally sourced, from the sausages and the eggs to the kippers and the honey. **£105**

13

Bamburgh

One-time capital of Northumbria, the little village of **BAMBURGH** (ⓦbamburgh.org
.uk), just three miles from Seahouses, lies in the lee of its magnificent **castle**. Attractive
stone cottages – holding the village shop, a café, pubs and B&Bs – flank each side of
the triangular green, and at the top of the village on Radcliffe Road is the diminutive
Grace Darling Museum. From behind the castle it's a brisk, five-minute walk to two
splendid sandy **beaches**, backed by rolling, tufted dunes.

Bamburgh Castle

April–Oct daily 11am–5pm • £9.95 • ☏ 01668 214515, ⓦ bamburghcastle.com

Solid and chunky, **Bamburgh Castle** is a spectacular sight, its elongated battlements
crowning a formidable basalt crag high above the beach. Its origins lie in Anglo-Saxon
times, but it suffered a centuries-long decline – rotted by sea spray and buffeted by winter
storms, the castle was bought by Lord Armstrong (of Rothbury's Cragside; see p.601) in
1894, who demolished most of the structure to replace it with a hybrid castle-mansion.
Inside there's plenty to explore, including the sturdy keep that houses an unnerving
armoury packed with vicious-looking pikes, halberds, helmets and muskets; the King's
Hall, with its marvellous teak ceiling that was imported from Siam (Thailand) and carved
in Victorian times; and a medieval kitchen complete with original jugs, pots and pans.

Grace Darling Museum

Radcliffe Rd • Easter–Oct daily 10am–5pm; Oct–Easter Tues–Sun 10am–4pm • Free • ☏ 01668 214910, ⓦ rnli.org.uk

The Grace Darling Museum celebrates the life of famed local heroine Grace Darling. In
September 1838, a gale dashed the steamship *Forfarshire* against the rocks of the Farne
Islands. Nine passengers struggled onto a reef where they were subsequently saved by Grace
and her lighthouseman father, William, who left the safety of the Longstone lighthouse to
row out to them. *The Times* trumpeted Grace's bravery, offers of marriage and requests for
locks of her hair streamed into the Darlings' lighthouse home, and for the rest of her brief
life Grace was plagued by unwanted visitors – she died of tuberculosis aged 26 in 1842,
and was buried in Bamburgh, in the churchyard of the thirteenth-century St Aidan's.

ARRIVAL AND DEPARTURE
BAMBURGH

By bus A regular bus service links Alnwick and Berwick-upon-Tweed with Bamburgh, stopping on Front Street by the green. Destinations Alnwick (Mon–Sat 7 daily, Sun 5 daily, 1hr 15min); Berwick-upon-Tweed (Mon–Sat 3 daily, Sun 2 daily; 40min); Craster (Mon–Sat 7 daily, Sun 5 daily; 30–40min); Seahouses (Mon–Sat 7 daily, Sun 5 daily, 10min).

ACCOMMODATION AND EATING

Copper Kettle 21 Front St ☏ 01668 14315, ⓦ copperkettletearooms.com. Sweet little tearoom, with a sunny sitting area out the back, serving tasty cakes, teas and coffees – try the fruit loaf or the tempting carrot cake with icing. Also light meals such as sandwiches (£5), jacket potatoes (£6.50) and pies (£6). Daily 10am–6pm.

Victoria Hotel Front St ☏ 01668 214431, ⓦ victoriahotel.net. This smart boutique hotel has elegant rooms in a variety of sizes – one with lovely castle views – a couple of relaxing bars and a more expensive brasserie (dinner only). Rates include breakfast. **£80**

Holy Island

It's a dramatic approach to **HOLY ISLAND** (ⓦwww.lindisfarne.org.uk), past the barnacle-
encrusted marker poles that line the three-mile-long causeway. Topped with a stumpy
castle, the island is small (just 1.5 miles by one), sandy and bare, and in winter it can
be bleak, but come summer day-trippers clog the car parks as soon as the causeway is
open. Even then, though, Lindisfarne has a distinctive and isolated atmosphere. Give
the place time and, if you can, stay overnight, when you'll be able to see the historic
remains without hundreds of others cluttering the views. The island's surrounding tidal
mud flats, salt marshes and dunes have been designated a **nature reserve**.

13

Brief history

It was on **Lindisfarne** (as the island was once known) that St Aidan of Iona founded a monastery at the invitation of King Oswald of Northumbria in 634. The monks quickly established a reputation for scholarship and artistry, the latter exemplified by the **Lindisfarne Gospels**, the apotheosis of Celtic religious art, now kept in the British Library. The monastery had sixteen bishops in all, the most celebrated being the reluctant **St Cuthbert**, who never settled here – within two years, he was back in his hermit's cell on the Farne Islands, where he died in 687. His colleagues rowed the body back to Lindisfarne, which became a place of pilgrimage until 875, when the monks abandoned the island in fear of marauding Vikings, taking Cuthbert's remains with them.

Lindisfarne Priory

Priory & museum April–Sept daily 10am–6pm; Oct daily 10am–5pm; Nov–Jan & March Sat & Sun 10am–4pm; Feb daily 10am–4pm • £5.40; EH • ☎ 01289 389200, ⓦ english-heritage.org.uk

Just off the village green, the tranquil, pinkish sandstone ruins of **Lindisfarne Priory** date from the Benedictine foundation. The **museum** next door displays a collection of incised stones that constitute all that remains of the first monastery.

Lindisfarne Castle

March–Oct Tues–Sun, hours vary according to tide but always include noon–3pm; Jan & Feb Sat & Sun 10am–3pm • £7.40; NT • ☎ 01289 389244, ⓦ nationaltrust.org.uk/lindisfarne-castle

Stuck on a small pyramid of rock half a mile away from the village, **Lindisfarne Castle** was built in the middle of the sixteenth century to protect the island's harbour from the Scots. It was, however, merely a decaying shell when Edward Hudson, the founder of *Country Life* magazine, stumbled across it in 1901. He promptly commissioned Edwin Lutyens (1869–1944) to turn it into an Edwardian country house, and installed a charming walled garden in the castle's former vegetable gardens, to designs by Gertrude Jekyll.

ARRIVAL AND INFORMATION   **HOLY ISLAND**

By bus The #477 bus from Berwick-upon-Tweed to Holy Island (35min) is something of a law unto itself given the interfering tides, but basically service is daily in August and twice-weekly the rest of the year.
Crossing the causeway The island is cut off for about

5hr a day. Consult tide timetables at a tourist office, in the local paper or at ⓦ lindisfarne.org.uk
Castle shuttle A minibus trundles the half a mile to the castle from the main car park, The Chare (every 20min 10.20am–4.20pm; £1).

ACCOMMODATION AND EATING

Due to the size of the island and the small number of B&Bs, it's imperative to **book in advance** if you're staying overnight.

★**Bamburgh View** Fenkle St ☎ 01289 389212, ⊜ bamburghview@btinternet.com. Sweet, friendly B&B very near the priory, with three airy, wood-floored rooms, good showers and generous breakfasts. **£85**
Café Beangoose Selby House ☎ 01289 389083, ⓦ cafebeangoose.co.uk. Overlooking the green, this excellent restaurant is in a family home, its small rooms complete with knick-knacks and snoozing cats. Meals are hearty and locally sourced: braised beef, sea trout and the like for around £11. Holiday cottages available (£885/ week). May–Oct daily dinner; hours depend on tides.

St Aidan's Winery In the modern building behind the green ☎ 01289 389230 ⓦ lindisfarne-mead.co.uk. If you're keen to sample some of the world-famous Lindisfarne mead, this is the place to come. They also sell home-made chutneys, biscuits and jams. Hours depend on tides.
The Ship Marygate ☎ 01289 389311. The best pub on the island; friendly and traditional, with open fires and wood-panelled walls. The ales are good, as is the inexpensive pub grub. They have four cosy, en-suite rooms upstairs. **£104**

Berwick-upon-Tweed

Before the union of the English and Scottish crowns in 1603, **BERWICK-UPON-TWEED**, twelve miles north of Holy Island, was the quintessential frontier town, changing hands no fewer than fourteen times between 1174 and 1482, when the Scots finally ceded the stronghold to the English. Interminable cross-border warfare ruined Berwick's economy, turning the prosperous Scottish port of the thirteenth century into an impoverished English garrison town. By the late sixteenth century, Berwick's fortifications were in a dreadful state and Elizabeth I, fearing the resurgent alliance between France and Scotland, had the place rebuilt in line with the latest principles of military architecture. Berwick was reborn as an important seaport between 1750 and 1820, and is still peppered with elegant **Georgian mansions** dating from that period.

Berwick's **walls** – one and a half miles long and still in pristine condition – are no more than 20ft high but incredibly thick. They are now the town's major attraction; it's possible to walk the mile-long circuit (1hr) round them, allowing for wonderful views out to sea, across the Tweed and over the orange-tiled rooftops of the town. Protected by ditches on three sides and the Tweed on the fourth, the walls are strengthened by immense bastions.

Barracks

April–Sept Mon–Fri 10am–6pm; Oct–March limited opening hours • £4.20; EH • ☎ 01289 304493, ⓦ english-heritage.org.uk

The town's finely proportioned **Barracks**, designed by Nicholas Hawksmoor (1717) functioned as a garrison until 1964, when the King's Own Scottish Borderers regiment decamped. Inside there's the rather specialist **By the Beat of the Drum** exhibition, tracing the lives of British infantrymen from the Civil War to World War I, as well as the King's Own Scottish Borderers Museum, the Berwick Borough Museum and the **Gymnasium Gallery** of contemporary art.

ARRIVAL AND INFORMATION
BERWICK-UPON-TWEED

By train From the train station it's a 10min walk down Castlegate and Marygate to the town centre.
Destinations Durham (every 30min; 1hr 10min); Edinburgh (hourly; 45min); Newcastle (hourly; 45min).
By bus Most regional buses stop on Golden Square (where Castlegate meets Marygate), though some may also stop in front of the train station.
Destinations Bamburgh (Mon–Sat 6 daily, Sun 2 daily; 40min); Holy Island (Aug 2 daily, rest of the year 2 weekly; 35min); Newcastle (Mon–Sat 7 daily; 2hr 15min); Wooler

(Mon–Sat 9 daily; 50min).
Tourist office 106 Marygate (April, May & Oct Mon–Sat 10am–5pm; June–Sept Mon–Sat 10am–5pm & Sun 11am–3pm; Nov–March Mon–Sat 10am–4pm; ☎ 01289 330733).
Tours The tourist office can book you onto a walking tour of town (Easter–Oct Mon–Fri 2 daily; £4.50, ⓦ explore-northumberland.co.uk) or onto the Hidden Berwick tour (April–Sept Sun–Fri, 1 daily; £6), which includes entry into an eighteenth-century gun bastion not usually open to the public.

ACCOMMODATION

No.1 Sallyport Bridge St ☎ 01289 308827, ⓦ sallyport.co.uk. Berwick's most luxurious B&B, with six sensational rooms in a seventeenth-century house. The two spacious doubles and four lavish suites (£40 more) are elegantly furnished. They also have a little café full of delicious goodies, and serve simple dinners in the evenings. __£110__
Queen's Head 6 Sandgate ☎ 01289 307852, ⓦ queensheadberwick.co.uk. One of the best pubs in town has six

snug rooms, including a family room. Great evening meals and breakfasts, too (mains around £15). __£90__
YHA Berwick Dewars Lane ☎ 0845 371 9676, ⓦ yha.org.uk. Set in a remarkable eighteenth-century granary building which, thanks to a fire in 1815, has a lean greater than the Leaning Tower of Pisa. Thirteen en-suite rooms, some private and family, plus a bistro and gallery. Dorms __£18__ , doubles __£78__

EATING, DRINKING AND ENTERTAINMENT

Barrel's Ale 59 Bridge St ☎ 01289 308013, ⓦ the barrels.co.uk. Atmospheric pub specializing in (frequently changing) cask ales, lagers and stouts. It's also a great music venue, hosting an eclectic mix of jazz, blues, rock and indie bands. Mon–Thurs noon–11.30pm, Fri–Sat

noon–1am, Sun noon–midnight.
The Maltings Eastern Lane ☎ 01289 330999. ⓦ maltingsberwick.co.uk. Berwick's arts centre has a year-round programme of music, theatre, comedy, film and dance and a licensed café.

South Wales

ST GOVAN'S HEADLAND, PEMBROKESHIRE

South Wales

The most heavily populated part of Wales, and by far the most anglicized, is the south. This is a region of distinct character, whether in the resurgent seaport cities of Cardiff and Swansea, the mining-scarred Valleys or the dramatically beautiful Glamorgan and Pembrokeshire coasts. Monmouthshire, Wales's easternmost county, abuts the English border and contains the bucolic charms of the River Wye and Tintern Abbey. To the west and north, although the coal mines no longer operate, the world-famous Valleys retain their tight-knit towns and a rich working-class heritage, and some excellent museums and colliery tours, including Big Pit at Blaenafon and the Rhondda Heritage Park in Trehafod.

14

The Valleys course down to the great ports of the coast, which once shipped Wales's products all over the world. The greatest of them all was **Cardiff**, now Wales's upbeat capital and an essential stop. Further west is Wales's second city, **Swansea** – rougher, tougher and less anglicized than Cardiff, it sits on an impressive arc of coast that shelves round to the delightful **Gower peninsula**, replete with grand beaches, rocky headlands, bracken heaths and ruined castles.

Carmarthenshire, often missed out, is well worth visiting: of all the routes radiating from the county town of Carmarthen, the most glorious is the winding road to **Llandeilo** along the **Tywi Valley**, past ruined hilltop forts and two of the country's finest gardens. Immediately east sits Wales's most impressively sited castle at **Carreg Cennen**, high on a dizzy rock-plug on the edge of the Black Mountain. The wide sands fringing Carmarthen Bay stretch towards the popular seaside resort of **Tenby**, a major stop on the 186-mile **Pembrokeshire Coast Path**. The rutted coastline of **St Bride's Bay** is the most glorious part of the coastal walk, which leads north to brush past the impeccable mini-city of **St Davids**, whose exquisite cathedral shelters in a protective hollow. Nearby are plenty of opportunities for spectacular coast and hill walks, boat crossings to nearby islands, wildlife-watching and numerous outdoor activities.

GETTING AROUND   SOUTH WALES

By train Southeast Wales is by far the easiest part of the country to travel around, with the **M4** connecting to swift dual carriageways. South Wales is also the only part of the country with a half-decent train network, and most suburban and rural services interconnect with Cardiff, Newport or Swansea.

By bus Bus services fill in virtually all of the gaps left by trains, though often rather slowly.

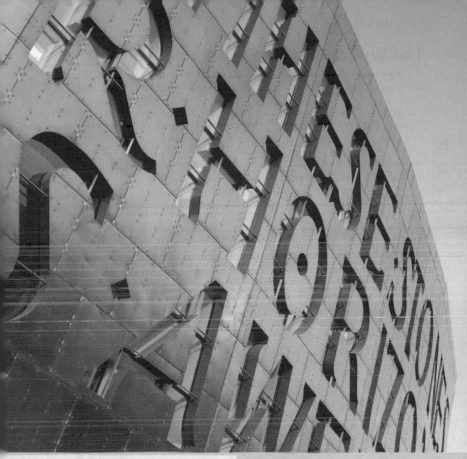

WALES MILLENNIUM CENTRE

Highlights

❶ Blaenafon Industrial heritage at its finest, thanks to a thrilling deep-mine museum and the fascinating ironworks town. **See p.619**

❷ Wales Millennium Centre, Cardiff Bay
A symphony of opposites – industry and art, grandeur and intimacy – the WMC is a bold and brilliant asset to the capital. **See p.627**

❸ National Waterfront Museum, Swansea
A celebration of Welsh innovation and industry – one of the best museums in Wales. **See p.636**

❹ The Gower Holding some of the country's most inspirational coastal and rural scenery, culminating in the stunning Rhossili Bay. **See p.637**

❺ Carreg Cennen The most magnificently sited castle in Wales, this fantasy fortress offers splendid views and endless possibilities for exploration. **See p.642**

❻ The Pembrokeshire Coast Path A narrow ribbon of mainly cliff-top footpath that winds its way through some magnificent coastal scenery. **See p.646**

❼ St Davids Inspirational city (little more than a village, in fact) with a splendid cathedral and heart-racing boat trips out to offshore islands. **See p.651**

HIGHLIGHTS ARE MARKED ON THE MAP ON P.614

14

The Wye Valley

The **Wye Valley** (Ⓦvisitwyevalley.com), along with the rest of Monmouthshire, was finally recognized as part of Wales in the local government reorganization of 1974. Before then, the county was officially included as part of neither England nor Wales, so that maps were frequently headlined "Wales and Monmouthshire". Most of the rest of Monmouthshire is undoubtedly Welsh, but the woodlands and hills by the meandering River Wye have more in common with the landscape over the border. The two main centres are **Chepstow**, with its massive castle, and the spruce, old-fashioned town of **Monmouth**, sixteen miles upstream. Six miles north of Chepstow lie the atmospheric ruins of the Cistercian **Tintern Abbey**.

INFORMATION   THE WYE VALLEY

Tourist information The excellent Old Station Visitor Centre (April–Oct daily 10.30am–5.30pm; ☎01291 689566) is a mile or so along the road from Tintern Abbey to Monmouth in the former Tintern station; two refurbished carriages house an exhibition on the Wye Valley, and you can pick up leaflets on walks, including the surrounding wildflower meadows and cliff rambles above the meandering river. Bus #69 between Chepstow and Monmouth stops outside.

HIGHLIGHTS

1. Blaenafon
2. Wales Millennium Centre, Cardiff Bay
3. National Waterfront Museum, Swansea
4. The Gower
5. Carreg Cennen
6. The Pembrokeshire Coast Path
7. St Davids

SOUTH WALES

Chepstow

Of all the places that call themselves "the gateway to Wales", **CHEPSTOW** (Cas-Gwent), sitting on the western bank of the River Wye, has probably the best claim. Although lacking the immediate charm of many other Welsh market towns, there is, nonetheless, an identifiably medieval street-plan hemmed in by the thirteenth-century **Port Wall**.

Chepstow Castle

Bridge St • March–June, Sept & Oct daily 9.30am–5pm; July & Aug daily 9.30am–6pm; Nov–Feb Mon–Sat 10am–4pm, Sun 11am–4pm • £4.50; CADW • ☎ 01291 624065

14

Strategically sited within a tight loop of the River Wye, **Chepstow Castle** was the first stone castle to be built in Britain. The Lower Ward, dating mainly from the thirteenth century, was the largest of the three enclosures. Here you'll find the **Great Hall**, now colourfully re-created as the Earl's chamber. Twelfth-century defences separate the Lower Ward from the Middle Ward, dominated by the still-imposing ruins of the **Great Tower**, built in 1067. Beyond this, the far narrower Upper Ward leads up to the Barbican **watchtower** from where there are superb views down to the estuary.

14

WALKS FROM CHEPSTOW

Chepstow is the starting point for three of Wales's most popular long-distance walks: the famous Offa's Dyke Path, the Wye Valley Walk, and the newly inaugurated **Wales Coast Path**; this path begins in Riverside Gardens, near the Old Wye Bridge, before cutting inland across fields and then meeting up with the Severn Estuary. Guides and maps for all three paths can be obtained from the tourist office (see below).

Chepstow Museum

Bridge St • July–Sept Mon–Sat 10.30am–5pm, Sun 2–5pm; Oct & March–June Mon–Sat 11am–5pm, Sun 2–5pm; Nov–Feb Mon–Sat 11am–4pm, Sun 2–4pm • Free • ☎ 01291 625981

Housed in a handsome Georgian townhouse, **Chepstow Museum** contains a wealth of nostalgic photographs and paintings of the trades once supported by the River Wye, as well as records of the town's brief life as a shipbuilding centre in the early twentieth century. Take a look, too, upstairs at the rather fine eighteenth-century topographical prints of Chepstow Castle.

ARRIVAL AND INFORMATION
CHEPSTOW

By train The train station is a 5min walk south of High St. Destinations Cardiff (every 30–60min; 35min); Gloucester (every 30–60min; 30min); Newport (every 30–60min; 25min).
By bus The bus station is on Thomas St, a 5min walk west of the High St, just beyond the West Gate.

Destinations Bristol (hourly; 50min); Monmouth (hourly; 50min); Newport (every 30min; 25min–1hr); Tintern (4–8 daily; 20min).
Tourist information Castle car park, off Bridge St (Mon–Fri 10am–1pm & 2–4pm, Sat & Sun 9.30am–1pm & 2–5pm; ☎ 01291 623772, ☜ chepstowtowncrier.org.uk).

ACCOMMODATION

Castle View Hotel 16 Bridge St ☎ 01291 620349, ☜ castleviewhotel.com. This seventeenth-century building has bags of charm, with thirteen cosy rooms featuring crooked floors, thick oak beams and exposed stone walls; some have castle views. **£72**

George Hotel Moor St ☎ 01291 625363. A hostelry of sorts for several centuries, the *George's* large, simply furnished, and occasionally careworn rooms sit above a ground-floor bar and restaurant, though they are reasonably well insulated. Breakfast is extra. **£50**

EATING AND DRINKING

Boat Inn The Back ☎ 01291 628192. Convivial waterside pub, with black timber beams, bare brick walls, maritime paraphernalia and a warm, welcoming atmosphere; there's a decent selection of ales too. Mon–Thurs & Sun 9.30am–11pm, Fri & Sat 9.30am–midnight.
Lime Tree 24 St Mary's St ☎ 01291 620959. Two-storey café-bar with leather sofas and softly lit corners that's a lovely spot for breakfast (pancakes, smoothies) or lunch (burgers £8.75); there's also regular nightly fun (jazz,

acoustic and quizzes). Daily 8.30am–11pm.
Riverside Wine Bar 18a The Back ☎ 01291 628300, ☜ theriversidewinebar.co.uk. Cracking location aside, this handsome riverside restaurant offers super tapas and modern Mediterranean cuisine, such as paella, and chicken and bacon skewers; there's a good selection of gluten-free dishes too. Tapas £3.95, mains £10–15. Mon–Thurs & Sun 10.30am–11pm, Fri & Sat 10.30am–midnight.

Tintern Abbey

Six miles north of Chepstow, off the A466 • March–June, Sept & Oct daily 9.30am–5pm; July & Aug daily 9.30am–6pm; Nov–Feb Mon–Sat 10am–4pm, Sun 11am–4pm • £5.50; CADW• ☎ 01291 689251 • Bus #69 (4–8 daily) between Chepstow and Monmouth stops by the abbey

Tintern Abbey has inspired writers and painters for more than two centuries – Wordsworth and Turner among them. Such is its popularity, however, that it's best to go out of season or at either end of the day to avoid the crowds. The abbey was

TOP 5 CASTLES
Caerphilly Castle See p.629
Carreg Cennen See p.642
Chepstow Castle See p.615
Pembroke Castle See p.647
Raglan Castle See p.618

founded in 1131 by Cistercian monks from Normandy, though most of the remaining buildings date from the massive rebuilding and expansion of the fourteenth century, when Tintern was at its mightiest. Its survival after the Dissolution is largely due to its remoteness, as there were no nearby villages ready to use the abbey stone for rebuilding.

The centrepiece of the complex is the magnificent Gothic **church**, whose remarkable tracery and intricate stonework remain intact. Around the church are the less substantial ruins of the monks' domestic quarters and cloister, mostly reduced to one-storey rubble. The course of the abbey's waste-disposal system can be seen in the Great Drain, an irregular channel that once linked kitchens, toilets and the infirmary with the nearby Wye. The **Novices' Hall** lies handily close to the Warming House, which together with the kitchen and infirmary would have been the abbey's only heated areas, suggesting that novices might have gained a falsely favourable impression of monastic life before taking their final vows.

14

Monmouth

Enclosed on three sides by the rivers Wye and Monnow, **MONMOUTH** (Trefynwy), fifteen miles north of Chepstow, retains some of its quiet charm as an important border post and county town, and makes a good base for a drive – or a long hike – around the Three Castles of the pastoral border country to the north. The centre of the town is **Agincourt Square**, a handsome open space at the top of the wide, shop-lined Monnow Street. The street narrows to squeeze through the seven-hundred-year-old **Monnow Bridge**, crowned with its hulking stone gate of 1262.

Shire Hall
Agincourt Square • April–Sept daily 10am–4pm; Oct–March Mon–Sat 10am–4pm • £2, including audiovisual guide • ☎ 01600 775257, ⓦ shirehallmonmouth.org.uk

The arched, Georgian **Shire Hall**, built in 1724 as a law court, was where, in 1839, the three ringleaders of the Chartists – Frost, Williams and Jones – were sentenced to death (though this was later commuted to transportation). The Chartists were responsible for drafting the 1838 People's Charter, which called for widespread political and social reform throughout the UK, and demanded, among other things, a vote for every man aged over 21 and secret ballots. The hall continued to function as a court until 1992, and you can still see the original courtrooms and the holding cells. Embedded in the facade is an eighteenth-century statue of the Monmouth-born King Henry V, victor of the Battle of Agincourt in 1415, and just in front is the pompous statue of another local, the Honourable Charles Stewart Rolls, co-founder of Rolls-Royce and, in 1910, the first man to pilot a double flight over the English Channel.

Castle Hill
Regimental Museum Castle Hill • April–Oct daily 2–5pm; Nov–March Sat & Sun 2–4pm • Free • ☎ 01600 772175, ⓦ monmouthcastlemuseum.org.uk

Almost opposite Shire Hall is **Castle Hill**, which you can walk up to glimpse some of the scant ruins of the **castle**, founded in 1068. The neighbouring **Great Castle House** is the headquarters of the Royal Monmouthshire Royal Engineers, whose distinguished history is relayed in the small **Regimental Museum.** Formed in 1539, the regiment is the most senior in the British Army Reserve (Territorial Army), and unique for having the word "Royal" in its title twice.

ARRIVAL AND INFORMATION **MONMOUTH**

By bus The bus station is at the bottom of Monnow St. Destinations Abergavenny (6 daily; 45min); Chepstow (hourly; 50min); Raglan (hourly; 20min); Tintern (4–8 daily; 35min).

Tourist information In the foyer of the Shire Hall (April–Sept daily 10am–4pm; Oct–March Mon–Sat 10am–4pm; ☎ 01600 775257, ⓔ monmouth.tic @monmouthshire.gov.uk).

14

ACCOMMODATION AND EATING

Bistro Prego 7 Church St ☎01600 712600, Ⓦpregomonmouth.co.uk. Eight tightly packed en-suite rooms in a cosy B&B located above the town's finest restaurant. There's also a comfortable lounge with widescreen TV. The restaurant offers imaginative Italian-influenced dishes like tagliatelle with venison ragu, and hake with aubergine caponata (£13); there's Peroni on tap. Restaurant daily 11am–10pm. **£65**

Gate House Old Monnow Bridge ☎01600 713890. Occupying an enviable spot by the medieval bridge, and with a veranda perched over the water, the *Gate House* is one of the best spots in town for a pint on a sunny day. Daily 11am–11pm.

Monnow Bridge Campsite Drybridge St ☎01600 714004. Simple, clean and convenient town-centre site with no facilities save for toilets and showers; cross Monnow Bridge, turn right and it's behind the *Three Horseshoes Pub*. Pitches **£10**

Punch House 4 Agincourt Square ☎01600 713855, Ⓦsabrain.com/punchhouse. The generously-sized rooms above this popular tavern have been snappily refurbished, with their grey-painted timber beams, contemporary furnishings and mirrored walls, while the uneven floors and doors lend further character. Good spot too, for morning coffee or an afternoon beer. Daily 8.30am–11pm, Fri & Sat till midnight. **£70**

Raglan Castle

March–June, Sept & Oct daily 9.30am–5pm; July & Aug 9.30am–6pm; Nov–Feb Mon–Sat 10am–4pm, Sun 11am–4pm • £4.50; CADW • ☎01291 690228 • Bus #60 (every 30min) from Monmouth, as well as hourly buses from Usk

Unassuming **RAGLAN** (Rhaglan), seven miles west of Monmouth, is known for its glorious **castle**, whose fussy and comparatively intact style distinguishes it from so many other crumbling Welsh fortresses. The last medieval fortification built in Britain, designed to combine practical strength with ostentatious style, Raglan was begun by Sir William ap Thomas in 1435 on the site of a Norman motte. The **gatehouse**, still the main entrance, houses fantastic examples of the castle's decoration in its heraldic shields, intricate stonework edging and gargoyles. In the mid-fifteenth century, ap Thomas's grandson, William Herbert II, built two courts around the original gatehouse, hall and keep: the cobbled **Pitched Stone Court** – designed to house functional rooms like the kitchen, with its two vast, double-flued chimneys, and the servants' quarters – and to the left, **Fountain Court**, a well-proportioned grassy space surrounded by opulent state rooms and grand apartments. Separating the two are the original hall, from 1435, the buttery, the remains of the chapel and the dank, cold cellars below.

White Castle

Eight miles northwest of Monmouth and 6 miles east of Abergavenny • **Castle** April–Oct daily 10am–5pm • £3 • Grounds daily, free; CADW • ☎01600 780380

So named after the white rendering on its exterior, **White Castle** (Castell Gwyn), is the most awesome of the Three Castles (see box below), set in rolling countryside with superb views over to the hills surrounding the River Monnow. The grassy Outer Ward

---

THE THREE CASTLES

The fertile, low-lying land between the Monnow and Usk rivers was important for easy access into the agricultural lands of South Wales, and in the eleventh century the Norman invaders built a trio of strongholds here to protect their interests. In 1201, **Skenfrith**, **Grosmont** and **White** castles were presented by King John to Hubert de Burgh, who employed sophisticated new ideas on castle design to replace the earlier, square-keeped structures. In 1260, the advancing army of Llywelyn ap Gruffydd began to threaten the king's supremacy in South Wales, and the three castles were refortified in readiness. Gradually, the castles were adapted as living quarters and royal administration centres, and the only return to military usage came in 1404–05, when Owain Glyndŵr's army pressed down to Grosmont, only to be defeated by the future King Henry V. The castles slipped into disrepair and were finally sold separately in 1902, the first time since 1138 that the three had fallen out of single ownership.

is enclosed by a curtain wall with four towers, divided by a moat from the brooding mass of the Inner Ward. A bridge leads to the dual-towered Inner Gatehouse, where you can climb the western tower for its sublime vantage point. At the back of the Inner Ward are the massive foundations of the Norman keep, demolished in about 1260.

Skenfrith Castle

Skenfrith (Ynysgynwraidd), 7 miles northeast of White Castle • Open access • Free; NT • ☎ 01874 625515

The thirteenth-century **Skenfrith Castle**, in the attractive border village of Skenfrith (Ynysgynwraidd), has an irregular rectangle of sturdy red sandstone walls. Dominating the site, atop a large earth mound, is a roofless circular keep that replaced an earlier Norman structure. Below are the vestiges of the great hall and private apartments; the domestic buildings alongside feature a thirteenth-century window with intact iron bars.

Grosmont Castle

Grosmont, five miles upstream of Skenfrith • Open access • Free; CADW • ☎ 01600 780380

Right on the English border, the dilapidated **Grosmont Castle** sits on a small hill above its village. A wooden bridge above the dry moat brings you into the small central courtyard, dominated on the right hand side by the ruins of a large Great Hall dating from the early thirteenth century.

The Valleys

No other part of Wales is as instantly recognizable as the **Valleys**, a generic name for the strings of settlements packed into the narrow gashes in the mountainous terrain to the north of Newport and Cardiff. Each of the Valleys depended almost solely on coal mining which, although nearly defunct as an industry, has left its mark on the staunchly working-class towns: row upon row of brightly painted terraced housing, tipped along the slopes at incredible angles, are broken only by austere chapels, the occasional remaining pithead and the dignified memorials to those who died underground.

This may not be traditional tourist country, but it's one of the most interesting and distinctive corners of Wales, with a rich social history. Some former mines have reopened as gutsy museums – **Big Pit** at Blaenafon and the **Rhondda Heritage Park** at Trehafod are the best – while other excellent civic museums include those at **Pontypridd** and **Aberdare**. There's also a more traditional visitor attraction in the form of **Llancaiach Fawr Manor**.

Blaenafon

Fourteen miles north of Newport, the valley of the Llwyd opens out at the airy iron and coal town of **BLAENAFON** (sometimes Blaenavon), a UNESCO World Heritage Site. A spirited and evocative place, its population today stands at around five thousand, a third of its size in the nineteenth century.

Blaenafon ironworks

North St • April–Oct daily 10am–5pm; Nov–March Fri & Sat 9.30am–4.30pm, Sun 11am–4.30pm • Free; CADW • ☎ 01495 792615

The town's boom kicked off at the **Blaenafon ironworks**, just off the Brynmawr road, founded in 1789. Limestone, coal and iron ore – ingredients for successful iron-smelting – were abundant locally, and the Blaenafon works was one of the largest in Britain until it closed in 1900. This remarkable site contains three of the five original Georgian blast furnaces, one with its cast house still attached, and the immense water-balance lift. Also here are the workers' cottages, some unchanged and others converted into a museum offering a thorough picture of the process and the lifestyle that went with it.

14

WORKING THE BLACK SEAM

The land beneath the inhospitable South Wales Valleys had some of the most abundant and accessible natural seams of **coal and iron ore** to be found, and were readily milked in the boom years of the nineteenth and early twentieth centuries. Wealthy, predominantly English capitalists came to Wales and ruthlessly stripped the land of its natural assets, while simultaneously exploiting those who risked life and limb underground. The mine owners were in a formidably strong position as thousands flocked to the Valleys in search of work and some sort of sustainable life.

In 1920, there were 256,000 men working in the 620 mines of the South Wales coalfields, providing a third of the world's coal. Vast Miners' Institutes jostled for position with the Nonconformist chapels, whose muscular brand of Christianity was matched by the zeal of the region's politics – trade-union-led and avowedly left-wing. Great socialist orators rose to national prominence, cementing the Valleys' reputation as a world apart from the rest of Britain, let alone Wales. Even Britain's pioneering National Health Service, founded by a radical Labour government in the years following World War II, was based on a Valleys' community scheme devised by local politician Aneurin Bevan. More than half of the original pits closed in the harsh economic climate of the 1930s, as coal seams became exhausted and the political climate changed. In the 1980s, further closures threatened to bring the number of men employed in the South Wales coalfields down to four figures, and the miners went on strike from 1984–85. The last of the deep pits closed in 2008.

Big Pit National Mining Museum

A mile west of town off the B4246 • Feb–Nov daily 9.30am–5pm, hourly tours between 10am–3.30pm; Dec & Jan call for tour times and availability • Free, car park £3 • ☎ 029 2057 3650, ⓦ museumwales.ac.uk • #30 bus (hourly) from Newport stops outside the entrance

Guided tours at the evocative **Big Pit National Mining Museum** involve being kitted out with a lamp, helmet and very heavy battery pack, and then lowered 300ft into the labyrinth of shafts and coalfaces. The guides – mostly ex-miners – lead you through explanations and examples of the different types of coal mining, while all the while streams of rust-coloured water flow by. The dank and chilly atmosphere must have terrified the small children who were once paid twopence for a six-day week pulling the coal wagons along the tracks. Back on the surface, the old pithead baths – one of the last remaining in the country – now holds a compelling, and very moving, museum documenting the lives and times of the miners and their families.

ARRIVAL AND INFORMATION   BLAENAFON

By bus The town's main bus stop is at the top of High St, which runs parallel to Broad Street, the main focus of activity in town; buses run every ten minutes to Newport (1hr).

Tourist information The Blaenavon Heritage Centre is on Church Rd (Tues–Sun: April–Sept 9am–5pm; Oct–March 9am–4pm; ☎01495 742333, ⓦvisitblaenavon .co.uk). Also here is an enlightening exhibition on the history of the town's coal-mining and ironworking industries, as well as a café.

ACCOMMODATION AND EATING

Coffi 1860 76 Broad St ☎01495 790127. Park yourself down at one of the stripped wooden tables under the original green-and-cream-coloured tiling and tuck into a home-made pastry washed down with a steaming cup of coffee. Mon–Sat 7.30am–4pm, Sun 9am–3pm.

Lion Hotel 41 Broad St ☎01495 792516, ⓦthelionhotelblaenavon.co.uk. The town's one hotel is a bright affair, its twelve deep-burgundy-coloured rooms comprising warm fluffy carpets, cool fabrics, and sparkling, marble-tiled bathrooms; somewhat surprisingly, there's a sauna and steam room here too. £85

The Taff and Cynon valleys

The River Taff flows into the Bristol Channel at Cardiff, after passing through a couple of dozen miles of industry and population. The first town in the Taff vale is **Pontypridd**, one of the cheeriest in the Valleys, and probably the best base. Continuing north, valleys meet at **Abercynon**, where the River Cynon flows in from **Aberdare**, site of the excellent **Cynon Valley Museum**. Just outside Abercynon is the enjoyable sixteenth-century **Llancaiach Fawr** manor house.

Pontypridd

PONTYPRIDD, twelve miles north of Cardiff, is built up around its quirky arched **bridge** that was once the largest single-span stone bridge in Europe, built in 1775 by local amateur stonemason William Edwards. Across the river is **Ynysangharad Park**, the focal point of which is the recently restored lido, a Grade-II listed building originally constructed in 1927 but which closed in 1991. Here too you'll find Sir W. Goscombe John's statue honouring Pontypridd weaver Evan James, who composed the stirringly nationalistic song *Hen Wlad fy Nhadau* (*Land of My Fathers*), now the Welsh national anthem.

14

Pontypridd Museum

Taff St • Mon–Sat 10am–5pm • Free • ☎ 01443 490/48

A lovingly restored church by the bridge houses the illuminating **Pontypridd Museum**, a treasure-trove of photographs, videos, models and exhibits that paints a warm picture of the town and its outlying valleys, as well as paying homage to the town's famous sons, singer Tom Jones and opera star Sir Geraint Evans.

ARRIVAL AND INFORMATION   PONTYPRIDD

By train The train station is a 10min walk south of the old bridge on High Street.

Destinations Abercynon (every 15min; 10min); Aberdare (every 30min; 35min); Cardiff (every 20–30min; 30min).

By bus Pontypridd bus station is north of the arched bridge on Morgan St, on the western bank of the river.

Destinations Abercynon (every 15min; 10min); Aberdare (every 15min; 50min); Cardiff (every 15min; 35min).

Tourist information The TIC is inside the Pontypridd Museum on Taff St (Mon–Sat 10am–5pm; ☎ 01443 490748).

ACCOMMODATION AND EATING

Blueberry Hotel Market St ☎ 01443 485331, ⓦ blueberryhotel.com. Appropriately appealing name for this sparkling little hotel, whose nine rooms are fashioned in one of two styles, cool, crisp white-on-white, or classic French furnished. Breakfast is extra. **£69**

★**Bunch of Grapes** Ynysangharad Rd ☎ 01443 402934, ⓦ bunchofgrapes.org.uk. A terrific combination of restaurant/pub, whose imaginative menu (pan-fried guinea fowl with home-smoked new potato and caramelized pumpkin; £15) is the best for miles around. The beer's great too, with typically more than half a dozen real ales on at any one time. It's on a residential street beyond the park and A470 flyover. Daily 11am–11pm.

THE ABERFAN DISASTER

North of Abercynon, the Taff Valley contains one sight that's hard to forget. Two neat lines of distant arches mark the graves of 144 people killed in October 1966 by an unsecured slag heap collapsing on Pantglas primary school in the village of **Aberfan**. Among the dead were 116 children, who died huddled in panic at the beginning of their school day. A humbling and beautiful valediction can be seen on one of the gravestones, that of a 10-year-old boy, who, it simply records, "loved light, freedom and animals". Official enquiries all told the sorry tale that this disaster was almost inevitable, given the cavalier approach to safety so often displayed by the coal bosses. Gwynfor Evans, then newly elected as the first Plaid Cymru (Welsh Nationalist) MP in Westminster, spoke with well-founded bitterness when he said: "Let us suppose that such a monstrous mountain had been built above Hampstead or Eton, where the children of the men of power and wealth are at school". But that, of course, would never have happened.

Llancaiach Fawr Manor

Near Nelson • Tues–Sun 10am–5pm (last admission one hour before closing) • £7.50 • ☎ 01443 412248, ⓦ llancaiachfawr.co.uk • Mon–Sat hourly bus #X38 from Pontypridd

Five miles north of Pontypridd at **Abercynon**, the Cynon River flows into the Taff from Aberdare in the northwest. Two miles east, just north of the village of **NELSON**, is **Llancaiach Fawr Manor**. A Tudor house, built around 1530, the manor has been transformed into a living history museum set in 1645, during the Civil War, with guides dressed as house servants and speaking the language of seventeenth-century Britain. It's is all very deftly done, with authentic period colour and numerous fascinating anecdotes. Special tours include seventeenth-century evenings, and, between October and March, candlelit and ghost tours, befitting the manor's status as, allegedly, one of the country's most haunted residences.

The Cynon Valley Museum & Gallery

Depot Rd, Aberdare • Mon–Sat 9am–4.30pm • Free • ☎ 01685 886729, ⓦ cvmg.co.uk

Eight miles northwest of Abercynon, towards the top of the Cynon Valley, is the spacious town of **ABERDARE** (Aberdâr), built on the local iron, brick and brewing industries. The main reason to come here is for the **Cynon Valley Museum & Gallery**, in an old tram depot next to the Tesco superstore. Exhibits portray the valley's social history, from the appalling conditions of the mid-nineteenth century, when nearly half of all children born here died by the age of 5, to stirring memories of the 1926 General Strike and the 1984–85 Miners' Strike. Alongside are some fun videos and exhibits on Victorian lantern slides, teenage life through the ages, the miners' jazz bands and Aberdare's role as a centre of early Welsh-language publishing. There's also a bright art gallery and decent café here.

Rhondda Fawr

Pointing northwest from Pontypridd, the **Rhondda Fawr** – sixteen miles long and never as much as a mile wide – is undoubtedly the most famous of all the Welsh Valleys, as well as being the heart of the massive South Wales coal industry. For many it immediately conjures up Richard Llewellyn's 1939 book – and subsequent Oscar-winning weepie – *How Green Was My Valley*, although this was, strictly speaking, based on the author's early life in nearby Gilfach Goch, outside the valley. Between 1841 and 1924 the Rhondda's population grew from under a thousand to 167,000, squeezed into ranks of houses grouped around sixty or so pitheads. The Rhondda, more than any other of the Valleys, became a self-reliant, hard-living, chapel-going, poor and terrifically spirited breeding ground for radical religion and firebrand politics – for decades, the Communist Party ran the town of Maerdy (nicknamed "Little Moscow" by Fleet Street in the 1930s). The last pit in the Rhondda closed in 1990, but what was left behind was not some dispiriting ragbag of depressing towns, but a range of new attractions, cleaned-up hillsides and some of the friendliest pubs and communities to be found anywhere in Britain.

MALE VOICE CHOIRS

Fiercely protective of its reputation as a land of song, Wales demonstrates its fine voice most affectingly in its ranks of **male voice choirs**. Although found all over the country, it is in the southern, industrial heartland that they are loudest and strongest. Their roots lie in the Nonconformist religious traditions of the seventeenth and eighteenth centuries, when Methodism in particular swept the country, and singing was a free and potent way of cherishing the often persecuted faith. Classic hymns like *Cwm Rhondda* and the Welsh national anthem, *Hen Wlad Fy Nhadau* (*Land of My Fathers*), are synonymous with the choirs. Each Valleys town still has its own choir, most of whom welcome visitors to sit in on rehearsals. Ask at the local tourist office or library, and take the chance to hear one of the world's most distinctive choral traditions in full, roof-raising splendour.

Rhondda Heritage Park

Coed Cae Rd, Trehafod • April–Sept daily 9am–4.30pm; Oct–March Tues–Sun 9am–4.30pm• Guided tours 10am, noon & 2pm • £5.60 •
☎ 01443 682036, ⓦ rhonddaheritagepark.com • The park is a few minutes' walk from Trehafod train station

The best attraction hereabouts is the **Rhondda Heritage Park** at **TREHAFOD**. The site was opened in 1880 by William Lewis (later Lord Merthyr), and by 1900 some five thousand men were employed here, producing more than a million tonnes of coal a year. Wandering around the yard, you can see the 140ft-high chimney stack, which fronts two iconic latticed shafts, named Bertie and Trefor after Lewis's sons. **Guided tours** take you through the engine-winding houses, lamp room and fan house, and give you a simulated "trip underground", with stunning visuals and sound effects re-creating 1950s' life through the eyes of colliers.

Cardiff and around

Official capital of Wales since only 1955, buoyant **CARDIFF** (Caerdydd) grew swiftly into its new role. A number of massive developments, not least the shiny Welsh National Assembly and Millennium Centre on the rejuvenated Cardiff Bay waterfront, and a fabulous city-centre sports stadium, give the city the feel of an international capital, if not always with a very Welsh flavour.

Cardiff's sights are clustered in fairly small, distinct districts. The compact commercial centre is bounded by the **River Taff**, which flows past the tremendous **Millennium Stadium**; in this rugby-mad city, the atmosphere in the pubs and streets when Wales have a home match – particularly against the old enemy, England – is charged with good-natured, beery fervour. Just upstream, the Taff is flanked by the wall of Cardiff's extraordinary **castle**, an amalgam of Roman remains, Norman keep and Victorian fantasy. North of the castle is a series of white Edwardian buildings grouped around **Cathays Park**: the City Hall, Cardiff University and the superb **National Museum**. A mile south of the centre, **Cardiff Bay**, once a bustling port, now a classy waterside development, houses the stunning Welsh National Assembly and Millennium buildings, and a stack of bars and restaurants. North of the city, a number of sights warrant a visit: **Llandaff Cathedral**, with its strange clash of Norman and modern styles; the thirteenth-century fairy-tale castle of **Castell Coch**, on a hillside in the woods; and the massive **Caerphilly Castle**. To the west, there's the hugely popular **National History Museum** at St Fagans.

Brief history

The second Marquess of Bute built Cardiff's first dock in 1839, opening others in swift succession. The Butes owned massive swathes of the rapidly industrializing South Wales Valleys and insisted that all coal and iron exports use the family docks in Cardiff, which became one of the world's busiest ports. The twentieth century saw varying fortunes: the dock trade slumped in the 1930s and the city suffered heavy bombing in World War II, but with the creation of Cardiff as capital in 1955, optimism and confidence in the city blossomed. Many government and media institutions have since moved here from London, and the development of the dock areas around the modern Assembly building in Cardiff Bay has given a largely positive boost to the cityscape.

Central Cardiff

Cardiff **centre** forms a rough square bounded by the castle, Queen Street and Central stations and the Motorpoint Arena. Dominating the skyline is the magnificent **Millennium Stadium**.

14

CENTRAL CARDIFF

ACCOMMODATION
The Big Sleep	5
Jolyon's at No `0	1
NosDa	2
Riverhouse Backpackers	4
Sandringham Hotel	3
Sleeperz	6

PUBS & BARS
Cayo Arms	2
City Arms	8
Cricketers	3
Pen and Wig	1
Queen's Vaults	10
Y Mochyn Du	4

CLUBS & LIVE MUSIC
10 Feet Tall	6
Café Jazz	11
Clwb Ifor Bach	5
Gwdihw	9
Moon Club	7

CAFÉS & RESTAURANTS
Café Citta	4
Fish at 85	2
Madame Fromage	5
The Plan	6
Potted Pig	3
The Smoke House	1

University

NEWPORT ROAD

FITZALAN PLACE

FITZALAN ROAD

Queen St Station

STATION TERRACE

DUMFRIES PLACE

Capitol Shopping Centre

GUILDFORD STREET

GUILDFORD CRESCENT

CHURCHILL WAY

CHURCHILL WAY

WINDSOR PLACE

PARK LANE

CHARLES STREET

STUTTGARTER STRASSE

PARK PLACE

EDWARD STREET

QUEEN STREET

DAVID STREET

DAVID ST

MARY ANN STREET

Cardiff Arena

Cineworld Multiplex

ADAM STREET

TREDEGAR ST

BUTE TERRACE

SANDON STREET

John Lewis

Cardiff Library

St David's Centre

Bute Dock East

HERBERT STREET

TYNDALL STREET

BUTE STREET

CUSTOM HOUSE ST

New Theatre

BOULEVARD DE NANTES

GREYFRIARS ROAD

GREYFRIARS PLACE

CROCKHERBTOWN LANE

St David's Centre

THE HAYES

BAKERS ROW

BREWERY QUARTER

CAROLINE STREET

CANAL ST

MILL LANE

PENARTH RD

THE FRIARY

KINGSWAY

DUKE ST

St John's Church

Cardiff Market

Old Library

WORKING STREET

TRINITY ST

ST JOHN STREET

CHURCH ST

HIGH STREET

ST MARY STREET

WHARTON ST

MORGAN ARCADE

Cardiff Bus Information

Bus and Coach Station

Central Station

Cardiff Castle

CASTLE ARCADE

QUAY STREET

WOMANBY ST

WESTGATE STREET

CASTLE STREET

WOOD STREET

PARK STREET

Millennium Stadium

Bute Park

Waterbus Stop

CARDIFF BRIDGE

COLDSTREAM TERRACE

River Taff

FITZHAMON EMBANKMENT

PLANTAGENET STREET

DESPENSER STREET

BAGOT STREET

MARK STREET

GREEN STREET

CLARE ROAD

TUDOR STREET

Waterbus Stop

Cardiff Bay

▲ 1 Cathays Park, Civic Centre & Sherman Theatre

▼ Cathedral Road, Llandaf 1, 2, 3, 4 & 5

N

0   200
0   yards   200

Millennium Stadium

Westgate St · Daily tours, subject to events, hourly Mon–Sat 10am–5pm, Sun 10am–4pm · £9.50 · ☎ 029 2082 2228,
ⓦ millenniumstadium.com

Since opening in 1999, the **Millennium Stadium** has become an iconic symbol not only
of Cardiff but also of Wales as a whole. With its trademark retractable roof, and seating
for 74,500 people, it has hosted sporting matches of every description, as well as an
array of huge rock gigs and other spectaculars. **Stadium tours** start from the **Cardiff
Arms Store** by Gate 3 on Westgate Street and take you into the press centre, dressing
rooms, VIP areas, players' tunnel and pitchside.

Cardiff Arcades

Secreted away between The Hayes and St Mary Street and High Street are some half a
dozen renovated arcades, a series of Victorian and Edwardian galleries where you'll find
many alluring little independent shops and cafés. Particularly impressive are the **High
Street and Castle arcades**, packed with great clothes shops, quirky giftshops,
independent little coffee houses and a range of esoteric emporia where you can pick up
fliers for clubs and events. A few yards further down towards Central Station is the
elegant Edwardian **indoor market** and further still the **Royal and Morgan arcades**,
linking St Mary Street with the lower end of The Hayes.

The Cardiff Story

Old Library, The Hayes · Mon–Sat 10am–4pm · Free · ☎ 029 2078 8334, ⓦ cardiffstory.com

On The Hayes, the beautifully colonnaded frontage of the **Old Library** houses both the
city's tourist office and the eminently enjoyable **Cardiff Story**. Using old artefacts,
hands-on gizmos and audiovisual displays, it's an enlightening romp through the city's
colourful history, with particular emphasis on how it was shaped by the docks and the
local coal industry. Don't miss the stunning **tiled corridor**; something of a hidden gem,
this was the original library entrance, its ornate floor-to-ceiling tiles produced by Maw
& Co in 1882.

Cardiff Castle

Daily: March–Oct 9am–6pm; Nov–Feb 9am–5pm · £12; House Tour £3 extra; Clocktower Tour £4 extra (weekends only) ·
☎ 029 2087 8100, ⓦ cardiffcastle.com

The political, geographical and historical heart of the city is **Cardiff Castle**. An
intriguing hotchpotch, the fortress hides inside a vast walled yard corresponding
roughly to the outline of the original fort built by the Romans. The neat Norman
motte and **keep** look down onto the turrets and towers of the **Castle Apartments**,
which date in part from the fourteenth and fifteenth centuries, but were much
extended in Tudor times, when residential needs began to overtake military
priorities. In the late nineteenth century, the third Marquess of Bute lavished a
fortune on upgrading his pile, commissioning architect and decorator William
Burges to aid him. With their passion for the religious art and symbolism of the
Middle Ages, they transformed the crumbling interiors into palaces of vivid colour
and intricate design.

Among the most impressive rooms are the **Drawing Room**, the **Arab Room**, decorated
by imported craftsmen, the grand **Banqueting Hall**, which dates originally from 1428,
but was transformed by Bute and Burges with the installation of a riotously kitsch
fireplace, and the **library**, possessed of a similarly fanciful chimneypiece. Two guided
tours are available for an additional charge: the House Tour includes all of the above,
plus access to the fabulous **Winter Smoking Room** and the **Nursery**, with hand-painted
tiles and silhouette lanterns depicting contemporary nursery rhymes; the Clocktower
Tour also takes in the **Clock Chamber**, **Bachelor's Bedroom** and, above that, the **Summer
Smoking Room**, both decorated in rich patterns of gold, maroon and cobalt, with many
of the images inspired from medieval myths and beliefs.

14

14

Cathays Park and around

On the northern edge of the city centre is **Cathays Park**, a large rectangle of lawns and flowerbeds that forms the focus for the impressive buildings of the **civic centre**. Dating from the early twentieth century, the gleaming white buildings are arranged with pompous Edwardian precision, and speak volumes about Cardiff's self-confidence, a full half-century before it was officially declared capital of Wales. The dragon-topped, domed **City Hall** is the magnificent centrepiece, an exercise in every cliché of ostentatious civic self-glory, with a roll call of statues of male Welsh heroes including Llywelyn ap Gruffydd, St David, Giraldus Cambrensis and Owain Glyndŵr.

National Museum and Gallery

Cathays Park • Tues–Sun 10am–5pm • Free • ☎ 029 2039 7951, ⓦ museumwales.ac.uk

The fine **National Museum and Gallery** starts with the epic **Evolution of Wales** exhibition, with hugely detailed displays on the country's natural history. Next door, the even better **Origins archeology gallery** holds a dazzling assortment of mostly Bronze and Iron-age treasures. Pride of place goes to the **Red Lady of Paviland Cave**, a red-stained skeleton discovered in 1823 on the Gower which was later revealed to be that of a young man. It's around 26,000 years old, making it the earliest known burial in Britain.

The first floor is given over to the museum's extraordinary **art collection**. The great eighteenth-century Welsh artists, and in particular Richard Wilson, William Parry and Thomas Jones, are well represented; of the fine landscapes, look out for Wilson's *Caernarfon Castle* and *Dolbadarn Castle*, and Jones's *A View from Radnorshire*, and the memorable *The Bard*.

Galleries Eleven to Sixteen begin with nineteenth-century French Art and include Millet (the haunting, unfinished *Peasant Family* and lovely, pastoral *Goose Girl at Gruchy*), Boudin and Manet. Gallery Twelve concentrates on **modern art from the 1930s**, with some terrific pieces by Welsh supremo Ceri Richards, and Surrealists such as Magritte.

Best of all, though, is Gallery Sixteen, which has a fabulous collection of **Impressionists** and **Post-Impressionists**. Dominating the room are several pieces by Monet, including an uncharacteristically grey *Thames at London*, in addition to Cézanne, Sisley (with his views of Penarth and Langland Bay), Pissarro and Renoir (a chirpy portrait of *La Parisienne*). The centrepiece here, though, is Van Gogh's magnificent *Rain at Auvers*, painted just weeks before his suicide. Look out, too, for the wonderful **sculpture collection** in the Rotunda, including many by the one-man Victorian Welsh statue industry, Goscombe John.

Cardiff Bay

A thirty-minute stroll from the city centre, **Cardiff Bay** has become one of the world's biggest regeneration projects, the downbeat dereliction of the old docks having been almost completely transformed into a designer heaven. In years gone by, when the docks were some of the busiest in the world, the area was better known by its evocative name of **Tiger Bay**, immortalized by local lass Shirley Bassey.

The Bay area now comprises three distinct parts, situated either side of **Roald Dahls Plass**, the main square named after the Cardiff-born children's author (1916–90): on the eastern side the civic precincts around the glorious **Wales Millennium Centre**, to the west the shiny **millennium waterfront**, including the **Mermaid Quay** retail and leisure complex, and, set back from the water's edge, the suburb of **Butetown**.

ARRIVAL   **CARDIFF BAY**

Trains run every 20min from Queen Street station to Cardiff Bay station and Baycar **bus** #6 leaves from Central station. You can also take an hourly **waterbus** from Bute Park and Taff's Mead Embankment to Mermaid Quay.

Wales Millennium Centre

Guided tours daily 11am & 2.30pm • £6 • ☎ 029 2063 6464, ⊛ wmc.org.uk

The mesmerizing **Wales Millennium Centre** is a vibrant performance space built in 2004 for theatre and music. Likened by critics to a copper-plated armadillo or a great snail, the WMC soars gracefully over the Bay rooftops, its exterior swathed in Welsh building materials, topped with a stainless-steel shell tinted with a bronze oxide to resist salty air.

Guided tours of the building allow complete backstage access, as well as intimate views of the main auditorium, the acoustically sensational Donald Gordon Theatre. The ground floor houses a visitor centre, the main box office, a music shop, souvenir shop, bar and brasserie. Daily **free performances**, of anything from poetry to hip-hop, take place in the foyer, usually at lunchtime and 6pm.

Pierhead Building

Daily 10.30am–4.30pm • Free • ☎ 0845 0105500, ⊛ pierhead.org

Down by the water's edge is the magnificent red-brick **Pierhead Building**, a typically ornate neo-Gothic terracotta pile that was built for the Cardiff Railway Company, formerly the Bute Dock Company. It now houses an enjoyable **exhibition** documenting the rise and fall of the local coal-exporting industry, as well as the genesis of the neighbouring National Assembly for Wales, a striking building designed by Richard Rogers for its opening in 2006.

Norwegian church

Harbour Drive • Mon–Fri 11am–4pm, Sat & Sat 10am–4pm; opening hours can vary depending on special events • ☎ 029 2087 7959, ⊛ norwegianchurchcardiff.com

The lovely white, stumpy-spired **Norwegian church** is an old seamen's chapel that once served the needs of thousands of Scandinavian sailors, though it's better known as the place where Roald Dahl was christened (his parents were Norwegian). It's now a convivial café and performance and exhibition space.

The Doctor Who Experience

Discovery Quay • Daily 10am–5pm • £15 • ☎ 0844 801 3663, ⊛ doctorwhoexperience.com

A large, humpbacked-shaped hangar houses the **Doctor Who Experience**, devoted to the cult BBC programme that was first aired in 1963 and which has largely been filmed in Cardiff since its relaunch in 2005. The visit begins with a cleverly conceived, multi-sensory "journey through time", in which you join the Doctor in confronting various adversaries; thereafter, you're free to wander around the two floors of original props and artefacts.

Cardiff Bay Barrage

Daily 7am–10pm • Free • ☎ 029 2087 7900, ⊛ cardiffharbour.com • Waterbuses shuttle between the waterfront and the southern end of the barrage at Penarth (daily 10.30am–4.30pm; £4 return)

Central to the whole Bay project is the **Cardiff Bay Barrage**, built right across the Ely and Taff estuaries, transforming a vast mud flat into a freshwater lake and creating eight miles of useful waterfront. It's a fine bit of engineering, and it's well worth a wander along the embankment to see the lock gates and sluices; there's a great kids' play area and skate park here too. For something more strenuous, you could tackle the 6.2-mile **Bay Trail**, a circular path for both walkers and cyclists that wends its way around the bay and across to Penarth.

14

Butetown

The area immediately inland from the Bay is the salty old district of **Butetown**, whose inner-city dereliction still peeps through the rampant gentrification. James Street is the main commercial focus, while to its north are the old buildings around the **Exchange Building**, built in the 1880s as Britain's central **Coal Exchange**.

Butetown History & Arts Centre

4/5 Dock Chambers, Bute St • Tues–Fri 10am–5pm, Sat & Sun 11am–4.30pm • Free • ☎ 029 2025 6757, ⓦ bhac.org

The **Butetown History & Arts Centre** records and celebrates the multicultural pedigree of the district, which is home, for example, to one of Britain's oldest black communities, many of whom settled here following the outbreak of World War I. Pop in to view the excellent archives or one of their consistently fine temporary exhibitions.

Craft in the Bay

The Flourish • Daily 10.30am–5.30pm • Free • ☎ 029 2048 4611, ⓦ makersguildinwales.org.uk

Craft in the Bay, housed in a jazzily revamped old warehouse on Lloyd George Avenue, showcases a wide range of contemporary applied art and craft from practitioners all over Wales, as well as overseas. In addition to exhibitions, they also have crafts for sale and run workshops.

Llandaff Cathedral

Llandaff, 2 miles northwest of the city centre along Cathedral Rd • Daily 8am–7pm • Free • ☎ 029 2056 4554, ⓦ llandaffcathedral.org.uk • Bus #33 or #33A

The small, quiet suburb of **Llandaff** is home to a church that has now grown up into the city's **cathedral**. It's believed to have been founded in the sixth century by St Teilo, but was rebuilt in Norman style in around 1120, and worked on well into the thirteenth century. From the late fourteenth century on it fell into an advanced state of disrepair, and one of the twin towers and the nave roof eventually collapsed. Restoration only began in earnest in the 1840s, when **Pre-Raphaelite** artists such as Edward Burne-Jones, Dante Gabriel Rossetti and William Morris were commissioned to make colourful new windows and decorative panels. Their work is best seen in the south aisle.

The fusion of different styles and ages is evident from outside, especially in the mismatched western towers. Inside, the nave is dominated by Jacob Epstein's overwhelming *Christ in Majesty*, a concrete parabola topped with a soaring Christ figure. At the west end of the north aisle, the **St Illtyd Chapel** features Rossetti's cloying triptych *The Seed of David*. In the south presbytery is a tenth-century Celtic cross, the only survivor of the pre-Norman cathedral.

Castell Coch

Five miles north of Cardiff • March–June, Sept & Oct daily 9.30am–5pm; July & Aug daily 9.30am–6pm; Nov–Feb Mon–Sat 10am–4pm, Sun 11am–4pm • £5.50; CADW • ☎ 029 2081 0101 • Bus #26A from Cardiff bus station

The turreted **Castell Coch** was once a ruined thirteenth-century fortress. Like Cardiff Castle, it was rebuilt and transformed into a fantasy structure in the late 1870s by William Burges for the third Marquess of Bute. With its working portcullis and drawbridge, Castell Coch is pure medieval fantasy, isolated on its almost alpine hillside, yet only a few hundred yards from the motorway and Cardiff suburbs. There are many similarities with Cardiff Castle, notably the lavish decor, culled from religious and moral fables.

> **CAERPHILLY: THE BIG CHEESE**
>
> In addition to its castle, Caerphilly is also known for its crumbly white cheese, which has inspired the vibrant **Big Cheese Festival** (w caerphilly.gov.uk/bigcheese), held over three days in late July in the shadow of the castle. It's a hoot, with concerts, street theatre, historical re-enactments, a funfair, falconry and, naturally, a cheese race.

Caerphilly Castle

Caerphilly, 7 miles north of Cardiff • April–June, Sept & Oct daily 9.30am–5pm; July & Aug daily 9.30am–6pm; Nov–March Mon–Sat 10am–4pm, Sun 11am–4pm • £5.50; CADW • ☎ 029 2088 3143 • Both trains and buses depart from Cardiff every 15–20min

Caerphilly (Caerffili), seven miles north of Cardiff, has a particularly staggering town-centre **castle**, the first in Britain built concentrically, with an inner system of defences overlooking the outer ring. Looming out of its vast surrounding moat, the medieval fortress with its cock-eyed tower occupies more than thirty acres, presenting an awesome promise not entirely fulfilled inside. The castle was begun in 1268 by Gilbert de Clare as a defence against Llywelyn the Last. For the next few centuries Caerphilly was little more than a decaying toy, given at whim by kings to their favourites. By the turn of the twentieth century, it was in a sorry state, sitting amid a growing industrial town that saw fit to build in the then-dry moat and castle precincts. Houses and shops were demolished in order to allow the moat to be reflooded in 1958. The most interesting section of the castle is the massive eastern gatehouse, which includes an impressive upper hall and oratory and, to its left, the wholly restored and re-roofed **Great Hall**.

St Fagans National History Museum

St Fagans, 4 miles west of Cardiff • Daily 10am–5pm • Free • ☎ 029 2057 3500, w museumwales.ac.uk • Buses #32 and #320 from Cardiff bus station

St Fagans (Sain Ffagan) has a rural feel that is only partly disturbed by the busloads of tourists rolling in to visit the excellent **National History Museum**, built around **St Fagans Castle**, a country house erected in 1580 and now furnished in early nineteenth-century style.

Beyond the castle lies the **open-air museum**, an outstanding assemblage of buildings from all corners of Wales that have been carefully dismantled and rebuilt on this site. Highlights include the diminutive, whitewashed Pen-Rhiw Chapel, built in Dyfed in 1777; the pristine and evocative St Mary's Board School, built in Lampeter in Victorian times; and the stern mini-fortress of a toll house that once guarded the southern approach to Aberystwyth, from 1772. The superb Rhyd-y-car **ironworkers' cottages**, from Merthyr Tydfil, were originally built in around 1800; each of the six houses are furnished in the style of a different period, stretching from 1805 to 1985.

ARRIVAL AND DEPARTURE   CARDIFF

By plane Cardiff international airport (☎ 01446 711111, w cardiff-airport.com) is ten miles southwest of the city in Rhoose, near Barry. The most direct way to reach the city centre is by Express bus #T9, which runs every twenty minutes (£5) and takes you from the main terminal into the city in thirty minutes. Alternatively, you can take a shuttle bus from the main terminal to Rhoose Cardiff International Airport train station and then a connecting train (Mon–Sat hourly, Sun every 2hr; £3.70 combined ticket). A taxi from the airport to Cardiff Central will cost around £30.

By train Cardiff Central train station is served by all intercity services as well as many suburban and Valley Line services. Queen Street station, at the eastern edge of the centre, is for local trains only.

Destinations from Cardiff Central Abergavenny (every 45min; 40min); Bristol (every 30min; 50min); Caerphilly (every 15min; 20min); Carmarthen (hourly; 1hr 45min); Chepstow (every 30–60min; 35min); Haverfordwest (9 daily; 2hr 30min); London (hourly; 2hr); Newport (every 15–30min; 10min); Swansea (every 30min; 1hr).

By bus The main bus station is off Wood St, on the southwestern side of the city centre near Cardiff Central.

14

Destinations Abergavenny (hourly; 2hr 20min); Blaenafon (hourly, 1 change; 1hr 30min); Brecon (8 daily; 1hr 35min); Caerphilly (every 20min; 40min); Chepstow (every 30min–1hr, 1 change; 1hr 20min); London (6 daily; 3hr 20min); Newport (every 20min; 40min); Swansea (every 20min; 1hr).

GETTING AROUND

Cardiff is compact enough to walk around, and even the bay area is just a 30min stroll from Central station. Once you're out of the centre, however, it's best to rely on local buses.

By bus Information and passes are available from inside the library on The Hayes (Mon, Tues, Thurs–Sat 11am–5pm; ☏ 029 2066 6444; ⓦ cardiffbus.com). A one-way trip anywhere in the city costs £1.80 (payable on the bus). Useful passes, which can also be bought on buses, include the "Day to Go" ticket (£3.60), giving a day's unlimited travel around Cardiff and Penarth, which can be extended to Barry and the Vale of Glamorgan with the "Day to Go Plus" ticket (£4.90). The Network Dayrider ticket (£8) covers all the above plus much of the rest of southeast Wales. A

"Weekly to Go" ticket (£15) is good for seven days' unlimited travel around Cardiff and Penarth, while the "Weekly to Go Plus" ticket (£19) covers the entire Cardiff area network.

By waterbus A scenic waterbus service (hourly 10.30am–4.30pm; £4 single; ☏ 029 2034 5163, ⓦ cardiffaquabus.co.uk) operates between Bute Park, near Cardiff Castle, to Mermaid Quay in the bay, though occasionally (depending on the river flow), the service will only run as far as Taff's Mead Embankment, diagonally across from the Millennium Stadium.

INFORMATION

Tourist office In the Old Library on The Hayes (Mon–Sat 9.30am–5pm, Sun 10am–4pm; ☏ 029 2087 3573, ⓦ visitcardiff.com). Tickets for various events can be

purchased here, and the staff can also book accommodation. Pick up a copy of *Buzz*, a free monthly guide to events in the city.

ACCOMMODATION

The Big Sleep Bute Terrace ☏ 029 2063 6363, ⓦ thebigsleephotel.com; map p.624. Snazzy budget option occupying a former 1960s office block turned retro-designer hotel; the vivid, blue-shaded rooms are available in doubles, triples and family rooms. **£70**

★**Jolyon's at No. 10** 10 Cathedral Rd ☏ 029 2009 1900, ⓦ jolyons10.com; map p.624. There's no scrimping on style at this gorgeous boutique hotel, which accommodates 21 handsomely presented rooms (eight of which are larger suites) manifesting Italian/French-inspired furnishings. **£99**

NosDa 53–59 Despenser St ☏ 029 2037 8866, ⓦ nosda.co.uk; map p.624. Hip hostel/budget hotel on the riverbank opposite the Millennium Stadium. Accommodation is in singles, doubles (some en-suite) and four- to ten-bed dorms, with quirky touches including fold-down beds disguised as modern art. Dorms **£21.50**, doubles **£44**

★**Riverhouse Backpackers** 59 Fitzhamon Embankment ☏ 029 2039 9810, ⓦ riverhousebackpackers .com; map p.624. Cosy, contemporary backpackers' hostel in a Victorian villa with mixed and female-only dorms, twin rooms, and a self-catering kitchen, welcoming dining/lounge area and a sunny wraparound garden-terrace. Dorms **£18**, doubles **£44**

Sandringham Hotel 21 St Mary St ☏ 029 2023 2161, ⓦ sandringham-hotel.com; map p.624. Pleasantly old-fashioned, family-run hotel offering plain but clean decor, good service and a friendly atmosphere. One of the better-value options. **£40**

Sleeperz Station Approach ☏ 029 2047 8747, ⓦ sleeperz .com; map p.624. Cleverly utilizing the architectural space in between the rail line and two roads, this vibrant, funkily designed hotel has cool, light-filled rooms in breezy white/orange and black/grey colour schemes; the corner cabin bunk rooms are particularly neat. Breakfast costs extra. **£55**

EATING

The city has a great mix of places serving innovative **Welsh cuisine** and ethnic food, though the best restaurants are located just outside the centre up in Pontcanna; you'll also find a plethora of places down on Mermaid Quay in Cardiff Bay.

Café Citta 4 Church St ☏ 029 2022 4040; map p.624. A friendly, laidback pizzeria straight out of Italy, with a fine little log-burning oven knocking up freshly cooked pizzas (£7–8) using dough and sauces made on the premises, and locally sourced ingredients. Tues–Sat 11am–11pm, Sun noon–6pm.

★**Fish at 85** 85 Pontcanna St ☏ 029 2023 5666, ⓦ fishat85.co.uk; map p.624. Wholesalers, fishmongers and restaurant all in one, and quite brilliant it is too. The "Catch menu" allows customers to pick something from the counter, which could be, for example, brill, snapper or red mullet, along with an accompanying sauce, and then have it cooked just the way you like it. Alternatively, just select something from the menu, like whole roasted Sand sole and brown shrimp *beurre noisette* (£18.50). Tues–Sat noon–3pm & 6–10pm.

★**Madame Fromage** 21–25 Castle Arcade ☎029 2064 4888, ⊚madamefromage.co.uk; map p.624. A small slice of Paris at this delightful corner café cum deli where cheese is king – the menu offers a lot more, however, from quiche to lamb cawl and charcuterie platters. Afterwards, check out the shop's tempting stock of jams, pickles and chutneys. Mon–Fri 10am–5.30pm, Sat 9.30am–5.30pm, Sun noon–5pm.

★**The Plan** 28–29 Morgan Arcade ☎029 2039 8764; map p.624. Without question, the place in Cardiff to come for coffee, a great-looking two-storey café with floor-to-ceiling windows, offering a super range of drinks as well as light meals derived from locally sourced organic produce. Mon–Sat 8.45am–5pm, Sun 10.30am–4pm.

Potted Pig 27 High St ☎029 2022 4817, ⊚the pottedpig.com; map p.624. This venue – in the reconditioned vaults of a former bank – is a terrific spot to tuck into all things piggy, like potted pig with toast and pickles, or roast belly of pork (£12). The wine card complements the food brilliantly. Just the place for a romantic liaison. Tues–Sat noon–2.30pm & 7–10pm, Sun noon–2pm.

The Smoke House 77 Pontcanna St ☎029 2034 4628, ⊚the-smoke-house.com; map p.624. Lunchtime deli foods are laid out in crates on the counter (check out the pig pie), then, in the evening, the American barbecue – dry rubbed using naturally smoked spices and seasoning – takes over, rustling up a sizzling array of meats (ribs, patties, steaks) served on heavy wooden boards. Wash it all down with a Honker's craft beer. Deli: Mon–Fri 11am–2.30pm; restaurant: Tues–Fri 6.30–10.30pm, Sat noon–2.30pm & 6.30–10.30pm, Sun noon–2.30pm.

14

DRINKING

The **pub** scene is lively, with some wonderful Edwardian palaces of etched, smoky glass and deep red wood, where you'll find Cardiff's very own Brains bitter. Some of the city's most enjoyable pubs are located up on Cathedral Road.

Cayo Arms Cathedral Rd, Pontcanna ☎029 2039 1910; map p.624. In the shadow of the cricket ground, two conjoined Victorian townhouses have formed this large, busy and proudly Welsh pub, with Tomos Watkin beers, decent food and a lively crowd. Mon–Sat noon–11pm, Sun noon–10.30pm.

City Arms 10 Quay St ☎029 2064 1913; map p.624. Opposite the Millennium Stadium, this no-nonsense boozer is always popular, especially on international match days and before gigs at *Clwb Ifor Bach* just around the corner. Brains beers as well as some choice guest ales. Mon–Thurs 11am–11pm, Fri & Sat 11am–2.30am, Sun noon–10.30pm.

Cricketers 66 Cathedral Rd ☎029 2034 5102, ⊚cricketerscardiff.co.uk; map p.624. Set in a gorgeous Victorian townhouse, the beautiful-looking *Cricketers* combines a sunny interior with lively beer gardens both front and back. The cask-conditioned Welsh beers are some

of Cardiff's best and the food is very creditable too. Daily noon–11pm.

Pen and Wig 1 Park Grove ☎029 2064 9090; map p.624. Large boozer in a quiet residential street, popular with both local professionals and students for the fine selection of very reasonably priced guest ales. Unspoilt flagstone-floored interior and decent beer garden. Mon–Fri 10am–midnight, Sat 10am–1am, Sun noon–11.30pm.

Queen's Vaults 29 Westgate St ☎029 2022 7966; map p.624. Cavernous rugby-memorabilia pub across from the Millennium Stadium, with antique fittings, large TV screens and pool tables, hence its enormous popularity with local sports fans. Mon–Thurs & Sun 10am–11pm, Fri & Sat till midnight.

★**Y Mochyn Du** Sophia Close, off Cathedral Rd ☎029 2037 1599, ⊚ymochyndu.com; map p.624. This old gatekeeper's lodge is a fine place to sup a pint of

---

CARDIFF ROCKS

Welsh music has a fantastically strong pedigree, and Cardiff has spawned its fair share of great **bands**, not least the wonderful Super Furry Animals whose lead singer, Gruff Rhys, has also made several Welsh-language albums. Hailing from the nearby mining town of Blackwood, pop/rock champions the Manic Street Preachers have been making thrilling records for the best part of twenty years, while bands such as Los Campesinos! have more recently taken up the baton. Great places to catch live music include the *Moon Club* (see p.632) and the inimitable *Clwb Ifor Bach* (see p.632), which has long been a bastion of Welsh-language bands. Cardiff is also home to the world's oldest record shop, **Spillers** (Morgan's Arcade; Mon–Sat 9.30am–5.45pm), founded in 1894; you could easily spend a couple of hours leafing through its hard-to-find records of all genres.

14

Welsh-brewed beer, either in the conservatory or outside among the greenery. Popular with Welsh-speakers.

Mon–Fri noon–11pm, Sat noon–midnight, Sun noon–10.30pm.

NIGHTLIFE AND ENTERTAINMENT

Cardiff is renowned for its rumbustious nightlife, not to mention one of the best live music scenes in the UK (see box, p.631). Moreover, you'll find high-class classical music, opera and dance, as well as superb theatre, with many performances in Welsh.

10 Feet Tall 11a Church St ☏ 029 2022 8883, ⓦ 10feettall.co.uk; map p.624. Perenially popular tapas-cum-cocktail bar that rocks hard most nights of the week, but the vibe is ramped up a notch when the basement *Undertone* club – hosting gigs and various themed nights – clicks into gear. Daily noon–3am.

Café Jazz 21 St Mary St ☏ 029 2038 7026, ⓦ cafe jazzcardiff.com; map p.624. Unassuming but popular venue, below the *Sandringham Hotel*, hosting a diverse range of jazz concerts Monday through Friday; electric blues, funk, swing, gypsy jazz and the like. Entrance typically £3–6.

Chapter Arts Centre Market Rd, Canton ☏ 029 2030 4400, ⓦ chapter.org. Although best known for its art-house movies, this superb multifunctional arts complex also hosts comedy, local and touring theatre and dance companies, and art exhibitions; there's invariably a strong Welsh theme to events here.

Clwb Ifor Bach Womanby St ☏ 029 2023 2199, ⓦ clwb .net; map p.624. Cardiff's premier venue for Welsh-language bands (hence the "Welsh Club" moniker), this is a sweaty and enjoyable live music venue and club with nightly gigs and sessions. Tues–Sat 10pm–3am.

★ **Gwdihw** 6 Guildford Crescent ☏ 029 2039 7933, ⓦ gwdihw.co.uk; map p.624. Pronounced "goody-hoo", and meaning Owl, this is a wonderful little corner café/bar, its exterior painted bright orange and the interior decked out with stripped wood flooring, odd bits of furniture and

retro bits and bobs. Daily happenings include showings of alternative films, poetry recitals, micro-festivals and regular bouts of live music on the dinky little stage. Sun–Wed 3pm–midnight, Thurs noon–midnight, Fri & Sat noon–2.30am.

Moon Club Womanby St ☏ 029 2037 3022, ⓦ the moonclub.net; map p.624. This superb club has really come to the fore recently for its prolific roster of gigs (typically three or four a week) by both domestic and foreign bands, with affordably priced tickets (£5–6).

St David's Hall The Hayes ☏ 029 2087 8444, ⓦ stdavidshallcardiff.co.uk. Part of the massive St David's shopping centre, this large venue is home to visiting orchestras and musicians from jazz to opera to folk, and is frequently used by the excellent BBC National Orchestra of Wales.

Sherman Theatre Senghennydd Rd, Cathays ☏ 029 2064 6900, ⓦ shermancymru.co.uk. Excellent two-auditorium rep theatre hosting a mixed bag of new and translated classic Welsh-language pieces, stand-up comedy, children's entertainment, drama, music and dance.

Wales Millennium Centre Roald Dahls Plass, Cardiff Bay ☏ 029 2063 6464, ⓦ wmc.org.uk. Permanent home of the Welsh National Opera (ⓦ wno.org.uk), together with a collection of other music and dance companies. Also the place to see West End spectaculars and other big touring shows.

DIRECTORY

Hospital The city's main hospital is the University Hospital of Wales, Heath Park (☏ 029 2074 7747).

Left luggage There are left-luggage lockers inside the tourist information office (see p.630).

Police Cardiff Central Police Station, King Edward VII Ave, Cathays Park (☏ 029 2022 2111); Cardiff Bay Police Station, James St (☏ 029 2022 2111).

Swansea

Dylan Thomas called **SWANSEA** (Abertawe) – his birthplace – an "ugly, lovely town", which fellow poet Paul Durcan updated to "pretty, shitty city". Both ring true. Sprawling and boisterous, with around 200,000 people, Swansea may be only the second city of Wales, but it's the undoubted Welsh capital of attitude, coated in a layer of chunky bling. The city centre was massively rebuilt after devastating bomb attacks in World War II, and a jumble of tower blocks now dot the horizon. But closer inspection reveals Swansea's multifarious charms: some intact old corners of the city centre, the spacious and graceful suburb of **Uplands**, a wide **seafront** overlooking Swansea Bay and a bold marina

CLOCKWISE FROM TOP THREE CLIFFS BAY, GOWER (P.637); CASTELL COCH (P.628); CELTIC CROSS, CAREW (P.649) >

development around the old docks. Spread throughout are some of the best-funded **museums** in the country, including the stunning National Waterfront Museum.

Brief history

Swansea's Welsh name, Abertawe, refers to the mouth of the **River Tawe**, a grimy ditch that is slowly recovering after centuries of abuse by heavy industry. The city itself dates back to 1099 when William the Conqueror's troops built a castle here. A settlement grew around this, later exploiting its location between the coalfields and the sea to become a shipbuilding centre, and then, by 1700, the largest coal port in Wales. Copper smelting took over as the area's dominant industry in the eighteenth century, and this attracted other metal trades, developing the region into one of the world's most prolific metal-bashing centres.

14

The city centre

The train station faces out onto the High Street, which runs south into Castle Street and past the remains of the Norman **castle**, facing the revamped Castle Square. Continuing south from here, Wind Street (pronounced as in "whined") is nocturnal Swansea's main drag, chock-full of theme and chain bars, pubs and restaurants, with a few more unusual establishments sprinkled into the mix.

CAFÉS & RESTAURANTS	
Gallini's	5
Joe's	4
Mosaic	1
Rose Indienne	3
Slice	2

PUBS & BARS	
Cross Keys	4
Noah's Yard	1
No Sign Bar	5

CLUBS & LIVE MUSIC	
The Garage	6
Monkey Café	1
Uplands Tavern	2

ACCOMMODATION	
Dragon	2
Grand Hotel	1
Mirador	3
Morgans	4

Glynn Vivian Art Gallery

Alexandra Rd • Tues–Sun 10am–5pm • Free • ☎ 01792 516900, ⓦ glynnviviangallery.org

The **Glynn Vivian Art Gallery** is a delightful Edwardian showcase of inspiring Welsh art including the huge, frantic canvases of Ceri Richards, Wales's most respected postwar painter, and works by Gwen John and her brother Augustus, whose mesmerizing portrait of Caitlin Thomas, Dylan's wife, is a real highlight. The gallery also houses a large collection of fine porcelain – of which Swansea was a noted centre in the early nineteenth century.

14

Swansea Market

Oxford St • Mon–Fri 8am–5.30pm, Sat 7.30am–5.30pm • ☎ 01792 654296, ⓦ swanseaindoormarket.co.uk

The main shopping streets lie to the south of town, notably below the Quadrant Centre where the curving-roofed indoor **market** makes a lively sight. Long-established stalls sell local delicacies such as laver bread (a delicious savoury made from seaweed), as well as cockles trawled from the nearby Loughor Estuary, typical Welsh cakes, fish and cheeses.

Cwmdonkin Park and Dylan Thomas's Birthplace

Dylan Thomas's Birthplace 5 Cwmdonkin Drive • Daily 10.30am–4.30pm • £8 • ☎ 01792 472555, ⓦ 5cwmdonkindrive.com

A thirty-minute walk from the city centre, leafy avenues rise past the sharp terraces of **Cwmdonkin Park**, at the centre of which is a memorial to Dylan Thomas inscribed with lines from *Fern Hill*, one of his best-known poems. On the eastern side of the park, a blue plaque at **5 Cwmdonkin Drive** denotes this solid Victorian semi as the poet's **birthplace** in 1914. Thomas lived here until he was twenty, and while nothing remains from his time, the house has been sympathetically restored to re-create the atmosphere of early twentieth-century Swansea. **Guided tours** of the surprisingly spacious interior include the grand lounge, his father's study, the kitchen and Thomas's boxy bedroom. There isn't always someone present at the house, so it's best to call in advance.

Maritime Quarter

The spit of land between Oystermouth Road, the sea and the Tawe Estuary has been christened the **Maritime Quarter**, with its vast centrepiece marina surrounded by contemporary apartments, cafés, shops, museums and a leisure centre.

Swansea Museum

Victoria Rd • Tues–Sun 10am–5pm • Free • ☎ 01792 653763 • ⓦ swanseamuseum.co.uk

The city's old South Dock features the enticingly old-fashioned **Swansea Museum**, whose highlight is the Cabinet of Curiosities, a roomful of glass cases stuffed with everything from offbeat household items and memento mori – miniature shrines containing photos and models of the deceased – to intriguing local photos, including several of Winston Churchill during his visit here in World War II. There's also a marble bust of a Gower boy, Edgar Evans, who perished with Scott in Antarctica in 1912.

Dylan Thomas Centre

Somerset Place • Daily 10am–4.30pm • Free • ☎ 01792 463980, ⓦ dylanthomas.com

Wales's national literature centre, the airy **Dylan Thomas Centre** offers a superb exhibition on the life and times of the poet. There is some unique archive material on display here; original worksheets, bar tabs, the writer's only known painting, and the last photos of Thomas before his death, taken, appropriately enough, in a New York bar. Also on display are the doors of the shed in which Thomas wrote at Laugharne. In the meantime, a fascinating video on his life and work plays continuously.

14

National Waterfront Museum

Oystermouth Rd • Daily 10am–5pm • Free • ☏ 01792 638950, ⓦ museumwales.ac.uk

Swansea's sublime **National Waterfront Museum** was carved out of the shell of the old Industrial and Maritime Museum, which has been stunningly extended to house a breathtakingly varied set of exhibitions dealing with Wales's history of innovation and industry. The museum is divided into fifteen zones, looking at topics such as energy, landscape, coal, genealogy, networks and money, and each section is bursting with interactive technology. Look out too for the many superb heritage pieces, such as the 1907 Robin Goch (Redbreast) monoplane, one of the very few pre-World War I planes still in existence.

ARRIVAL AND INFORMATION   SWANSEA

By train Swansea is the main interchange for trains out to the west of Wales, and for the slow line across to Shrewsbury in England. The station is at the top end of High St.
Destinations Cardiff (every 30min; 55min); Carmarthen (hourly; 50min); Haverfordwest (9 daily; 1hr 30min); Llandrindod Wells (3 daily; 2hr 20min); London (hourly; 3hr); Newport (every 30min; 1hr 20min); Pembroke (5 daily; 2hr 5min); Tenby (6 daily; 1hr 40min).
By bus The large bus station is sandwiched between the Quadrant shopping centre and the Grand Theatre.
Destinations Cardiff (every 30min; 1hr); Carmarthen (every 30min; 1hr 35min); Mumbles (every 10min; 15min); Oxwich (9 daily, 1 change; 1hr); Port Eynon (9 daily, 1 change; 1hr 15min); Rhossili (10 daily; 1hr).
Tourist information Plymouth St, next to the bus station (June–Sept Mon–Sat 9.30am–5.30pm, Sun 10am–4pm; Oct–May Mon–Sat 9.30am–5.30pm; ☏ 01792 468321, ⓦ visitswanseabay.com).

ACCOMMODATION

For a reasonably large city, Swansea is not exactly endowed with a surfeit of great **accommodation**. That said, there are some inexpensive hotels and B&Bs lining the seafront Oystermouth Rd, while it's just a stone's throw to the Gower, where there are further, albeit slightly pricier, options. There are no hostels in Swansea, and the nearest campsite is west of the city towards Mumbles.

Dragon Kingsway Circle ☏ 01792 657100, ⓦ dragon -hotel.co.uk. Despite its officious-looking facade, this landmark central hotel is an elegant and modern establishment with plush, a/c rooms coloured vivid red; the luxury amenities include a gym, indoor pool and beauty salon, plus a lounge and piano bar. Breakfast is extra. £75
Grand Hotel Ivey Place, High St ☏ 01792 645898, ⓦ the grandhotelswansea.co.uk. Accomplished yet pleasingly informal hotel opposite the train station with softly coloured, a/c rooms with flat-screen TV/DVD player, and sparkling bathrooms with fantastic showers. Convivial café/ sports bar downstairs. Breakfast is extra. £75

Mirador 14 Mirador Crescent ☏ 01792 466976, ⓦ themirador.co.uk. Swansea's most inspirational accommodation, a family-run townhouse in the Uplands area with seven fun rooms, each themed on a particular country and furnished accordingly (African, Oriental, Egyptian, Roman and so on). £69
Morgans Somerset Place ☏ 01792 484848, ⓦ morgans hotel.co.uk. Swansea's showpiece boutique hotel, split between the sumptuously converted old Port Authority HQ and the beautiful Regency terrace townhouse opposite. The superbly appointed rooms boast hardwood flooring, polished wood fittings, Egyptian-cotton bed linen and goosedown duvets. £65

EATING

Gallini's 3 Fishmarket Quay ☏ 01792 456285, ⓦ gallinisrestaurant.co.uk. This somewhat ordinary-looking but cheery Italian restaurant offers some terrific flavour combinations such as prawns in chilli and lime jam. The downstairs coffee shop is a relaxing spot to kick back with a fresh cup of coffee and take in the view across the marina. Restaurant daily noon–2.30pm & 6pm–midnight; coffee shop daily 10am–5pm.
Joe's 85 St Helen's Rd ☏ 01792 653880. This perennially popular outlet has been doling out some of the country's finest ice cream since 1922. All the classic flavours are here, as well as many specialist creations, such as raspberry crumble, hazelnut fudge and lemon meringue. Daily 11am–9pm.
★**Mosaic** 218 High St ☏ 01792 655225, ⓦ mosaics wansea.com. Modern industrial design and understated cool mark this café-cum-restaurant out as something a little different to most places in Swansea. The daytime menu comprises scrummy light bites like king prawn chowder, and flatbread with grilled bacon, peanut butter and sweet chilli, while, on Friday and Saturday evenings, tapas and meze dishes are served – a great accompaniment to the live music. Tues–Thurs noon–4pm, Fri & Sat

noon–4pm & 6.30pm–late.

★**Rose Indienne** 73–74 St Helen's Rd ☎01792 467000, ⓦrose-indienne.co.uk. Comfortably the best of Swansea's many Indian restaurants, the beautifully appointed *Rose Indienne* offers some genuinely exciting and unusual dishes, for example Goan duck curry, and salmon marinated in masala with mint chutney (£11.95). Mon–Sat noon–2.30pm & 5.30–midnight, Sun noon–midnight.

Slice 73–75 Everley Rd ☎01792 290929, ⓦslice swansea.co.uk. Located out in the Sketty area, the diminutive *Slice* – so named because of the quirkily shaped building – offers a level of cuisine unmatched anywhere in the city, with confident contemporary dishes such as roast cod, potato and chorizo terrine (three courses £35). Booking is essential. Wed & Thurs 6.30–10pm, Fri–Sun noon–2pm & 6.30–10pm.

14

DRINKING

Swansea has a proliferation of **pubs** and **bars**; most of the action centres on Wind Street – not a place for the faint-hearted on a Friday or Saturday evening – though the Uplands area, to the west of the city centre, has its fair share of good-time party places.

Cross Keys Inn 12 St Mary St ☎01792 630921. Dating from the 1700s, Swansea's oldest hostelry is a deceptively large affair, offering good ales, a sunny beer garden (BBQs in summer), and a loyal band of rugby followers. Mon–Sat 11am–11pm, Sun noon–10.30pm.

Noah's Yard 38 Uplands Crescent ☎01792 447360. Classy wine bar with big bay windows, bare brick walls and Art Deco lighting, Chesterfield sofas and trunks for tables, as well as lots of postmodern artwork including a piece by Banksy, the infamous street artist. Live jazz every Monday at 8.30pm (£3). Daily 2pm–midnight.

No Sign Bar 56 Wind St ☎01792 465300. If you deign/dare to visit one place on Wind St, make it *No Sign*, one of

the oldest hostelries in town. A narrow frontage leads into a long, warm pub interior with bare brick walls, pale wood flooring and squishy sofas, while down in the vaulted cellar, you'll catch live music most weekends. Mon–Sat 11am–1am, Sun noon–11pm.

Uplands Tavern 42 Uplands Crescent ☎01792 458242. Next to *Noah's Yard*, this former haunt of Dylan Thomas the walls of the Dylan snug corner are plastered with some fabulous photos – is today a bastion of local live music, especially rock and blues, usually Thursdays through to Saturdays. Sun–Thurs 11am–11pm, Fri & Sat 11am–midnight.

NIGHTLIFE AND ENTERTAINMENT

The **club** scene is extremely diverse, and many places double up as live music venues, showcasing a varied and exciting range of bands and other entertainment. There's plenty of high-end culture too, including great theatre, largely courtesy of the city's Thomas connections.

Brangwyn Hall The Guildhall, Guildhall Rd South ☎01792 635432. Vastly impressive music hall in the Art Deco civic centre which hosts regular concerts by the BBC National Orchestra of Wales and others.

Dylan Thomas Theatre Dylan Thomas Square, Maritime Quarter ☎01792 473238, ⓦdylanthomas theatre.org.uk. Thriving community operation staging reruns of Thomas's classics, intertwined with other modern works in the Little Theatre.

★**The Garage** 47 Uplands Crescent ☎01792 475147, ⓦwhitez.co.uk. The city's premier live music venue, by virtue of its quality (and wonderfully varied) acts and understatedly cool atmosphere; rock and roll is to the fore,

but there's much else besides. Tricky to find, the entrance is through Whitez pool club. Sun–Tues 8.30am–8pm, Wed–Sat 8.30am–11pm.

Monkey Café 13 Castle St ☎01792 480822, ⓦmonkey cafe.co.uk. Groovy, inexpensive, mosaic-floored café with a relaxed atmosphere that draws a pretty diverse crowd. Daily happenings include live music, DJs, burlesque, and tango and salsa classes. On a good night, it's the best place in town. Sun–Thurs 11am–2am, Fri & Sat 11am–4.30am.

Taliesin Arts Centre Swansea University ☎01792 602060, ⓦtaliesinartscentre.co.uk. Welsh, English and international visiting theatre, film, dance and music (jazz, world), including offbeat and alternative fare.

The Gower peninsula

A fifteen-mile-long finger of undulating sandstone and limestone, **Gower** (Gŵyr) is a world of its own, pointing into the Bristol Channel to the west of Swansea. The area is fringed by sweeping yellow bays and precipitous cliffs, with caves and blowholes to the south, and wide, flat marshes and cockle beds to the north. Bracken heaths dotted with prehistoric remains and tiny villages lie between, and there are numerous castle ruins and curious churches lurking about. Out of season, the winding lanes afford wonderful opportunities for exploration, but in high summer – July and August especially – they can be horribly congested. Frequent buses from Swansea serve the whole peninsula.

Gower starts in Swansea's western suburbs, following the curve of Swansea Bay to the pleasantly old-fashioned resort of **Mumbles** and finishing at **Rhossili Bay**. West of Port Eynon, the coast becomes a wild, frilly series of inlets and cliffs, topped by a five-mile path that stretches all the way to the peninsula's glorious westernmost point, **Worms Head**. The northern coast merges into the tidal flats of the Loughor Estuary.

14

Mumbles

At the far westernmost end of Swansea Bay and on the cusp of Gower, **MUMBLES** (Mwmbwls) is a lively and enjoyable alternative base to Swansea. Derived from the French word *mamelles*, or "breasts" (a reference to the twin islets off the end of Mumbles Head), the town's seafront is an unbroken curve of stylish B&Bs, cafés and restaurants, leading down to the refurbished pier and the rocky plug of Mumbles Head. Around the headland, reached either by the longer coast road or by a short walk over the hill, is the district of **Langland Bay**, whose sandy beach is popular with surfers.

Oystermouth Castle

April–Sept daily 11am–5pm • £2.50

The hilltop above town is crowned by the ruins of **Oystermouth Castle**, founded as a Norman watchtower and strengthened to withstand attacks by the Welsh, before being converted for residential purposes during the fourteenth century. A sensitive long-term restoration project has now restored the castle to something like its former glory. The keep, hall and Great Chamber form the earliest part of the castle (roughly late twelfth and early thirteenth centuries), with the remainder (including the chapel block) later additions. Inside the chapel, stairs lead up to a glass bridge platform, from where you can see the superb traceried east window, which frames magnificent views of the bay. The ramparts, too, afford lush vistas over the Mumbles headland, Swansea and its sweeping bay.

ARRIVAL AND INFORMATION   MUMBLES

By bus Regular buses from Swansea (10min) stop right in the centre at Oystermouth Square.
Tourist information In the Methodist church on

Mumbles Rd, just beyond the Newton Rd junction (Easter–Sept Mon–Sat 10am–5pm; Oct–Easter 10am–4pm; ☎01792 361302, ⓦmumblesinfo.org.uk).

ACCOMMODATION

Coast House 708 Mumbles Rd ☎01792 368702, ⓦthecoasthouse.co.uk. Welcoming and very affordable seafront guesthouse with four fresh-looking rooms, two of which have glorious sea views. Feb–Nov. **£70**
Langland Road B&B 17 Langland Rd ☎01792 361170, ⓦlanglandroad.co.uk. Gay-friendly bed and breakfast providing five smartly turned out rooms with DVD players and iPod docking stations. To get there, head

to the top of Newton Road and turn left by the church. **£75**
Tides Reach 388 Mumbles Rd ☎01792 404877, ⓦtidesreachguesthouse.com. Seven spacious and immaculate rooms in this elegant, cheerfully run guesthouse, where you can also enjoy the homely lounge and delightful courtyard garden bursting with roses and honeysuckle. **£75**

EATING AND DRINKING

Café 93 93 Newton Rd ☎01792 368793, ⓦcafe93 .com. Cheery, two-floored pink-and-white café at the top of the road, with tea, coffee and cakes, alongside crisp pizzas and juicy burgers, including veggie burgers. Mon 9am–5pm, Tues 9am–8pm, Wed–Sat 9am–11pm.
The Kitchen Table 626 Mumbles Rd ☎01792 367616,

ⓦthekitchentablecafe.co.uk. Comforting café-cum-restaurant, sporting formica-covered kitchen-style tables and mix and match chairs, and serving organic, home-made burgers and tasty veggie dishes. Sun–Tues 9.30am–4.30pm, Wed–Sat 9.30am–4.30pm & 6–11pm.

★**P.A.'s Wine Bar** 95 Newton Rd ☎01792 367723, ⓦpaswinebar.co.uk. Mumbles' most rewarding restaurant, whose myriad seafood possibilities (chargrilled fillet of sea bass with spring onion and ginger, £18) perfectly complement its outstanding repertoire of wines. The vine-covered terrace is a fine spot to eat in warmer weather. Mon–Sat noon–

2.30pm & 6–11pm, Sun noon–2.30pm.

Verdi's Knab Rock ☎01792 369135. Overlooking the sea near the pier, this Welsh–Italian institution is well regarded for its superb pizzas and ice creams, sorbets and sundaes; the coffee's not half bad either. April–Oct daily 10am–9pm; Oct–March Fri–Sun 10am–6pm.

Rhossili and around

The spectacularly sited village of **RHOSSILI** (Rhosili), at the western end of Gower, is a centre for walkers and beach loungers alike. Dylan Thomas wrote of the "rubbery, gull-limed grass, the sheep-pilled stones, the pieces of bones and feathers" to the west of the village, and you can follow his footsteps to **Worms Head**, an isolated string of rocks, accessible for only five hours at low tide.

Rhossili Bay

Below Rhossili, a great curve of white sand stretches into the distance, a dazzling coastline vast enough to absorb the crowds, especially if you are prepared to head north towards **Burry Holms**, an islet that is cut off at high tide. The northern end of the beach can also be reached by the small lane from Reynoldston, in the middle of the peninsula, to **Llangennith**, on the other side of the towering, 633ft Rhossili Down.

ARRIVAL AND INFORMATION

RHOSSILI AND AROUND

By bus Buses drop off in Rhossili by the car park near the *Worm's Head Hotel*.

Tourist information The National Trust Centre (Jan & Feb Tues–Sun 10.30am–4pm; March–Dec daily 10.30am–4.30pm; June–Aug daily 10.30am–5pm; ☎01792 390707), at the head of the road beyond the village, stocks some excellent local walking maps and a tide timetable.

ACCOMMODATION

Hillend Head through Llangennith and it's just beyond the hamlet of Hillend itself ☎01792 386204, ⓦhillendcamping.com. Large, fabulously sited campsite behind the dunes and with direct access to the glorious beach. Two of the four fields are set aside for families and couples. Shop and on-site café/bar. April–Oct. Pitches **£20**

King Arthur Hotel Reynoldston ☎01792 390775, ⓦkingarthurhotel.co.uk. The village's convivial pub has half a dozen comfortable en-suite rooms upstairs, though the annexe offers larger, more attractive rooms, with French windows and cast-iron beds and tables. **£75**

King's Head Llangennith ☎01792 386212, ⓦkings headgower.co.uk. The most prominent accommodation in the village is in this sixteenth-century pub, offering rooms of a fairly high standard (some with sea views), both in the pub annexe and, better still, in the newer stone building across the car park. **£85**

★**Western House** Llangennith, on the lane towards the beach ☎01792 386620, ⓦwesternhousebandb .co.uk. Three wildly colourful and wonderfully oddball rooms in this red limewashed B&B, whose remarkably chilled-out proprietors will ensure nothing less than a totally relaxing stay. **£65**

YHA Port Eynon ☎0845 371 9135, ⓦyha.org.uk. In a tremendous beachside location, this Victorian-era lifeboat station has been converted into a super hostel, with four- to eight-bed dorms as well as double rooms. Shared shower facilities, self-catering kitchen and lounge. Groups only Nov–March. Dorms **£18**, doubles **£42**

SURFING ON THE GOWER

The Gower has some of Britain's finest **surf**, with the bays and beaches of Langland, Caswell, Oxwich, Rhossili and Llangennith offering the best and most consistent waves. Check ⓦgowerlive.com for live webcams and tide times. For **equipment rental**, the best place is PJ's Surfshop in Llangennith (☎01792 386669, ⓦpjsurfshop.co.uk), which has a wide range of surfboards (£11/day), boogie boards (£6/day) and wet suits (£11/day). At the *Hillend* campsite, the Welsh Surfing Federation's Surf School (☎01792 386426, ⓦwsfsurfschool.co.uk) runs half-day **surfing courses** (£25 for the first lesson; £20 for subsequent lessons).

14

14

EATING AND DRINKING

Bay Bistro Rhossili ☎ 01792 390519. Easy-going café serving light meals, including terrific burgers (mango and carrot black-eyed bean burger), home-made cakes, coffee and tea; park yourself inside on one of the sunken armchairs or out on the windy terrace, although the coastal views are not as good as those from the *Worm's Head* next door. Daily: June–Sept 10am–5.30pm & 7–9pm; Oct–May 10am–5.30pm.

King Arthur Hotel Reynoldston ☎ 01792 390775, ⓦ kingarthurhotel.co.uk. The hotel's restaurant is fine, but better is the lovely woody bar, where you can chomp on some succulent Welsh rump washed down with one of the superb guest ales; in fine weather, though, most locals head out to the green and drink amongst the sheep. Restaurant daily noon–2.30pm & 6–9pm; bar daily 10am–11pm.

Carmarthenshire

Frequently overlooked in the stampede towards the resorts of Pembrokeshire, **Carmarthenshire** is a quiet part of the world. **Kidwelly**, with its dramatically set castle, is the only reason to stop before **Carmarthen**, which sadly fails to live up to its status as regional capital. Better to press on up the bucolic Tywi Valley, visiting the **National Botanic Garden** and the more intimate grounds of **Aberglasney** on the way to **Llandeilo**. The wonderfully sited **Carreg Cennen** castle is well worth a stop-off, while the coastal village of **Laugharne** has become a place of pilgrimage for Dylan Thomas devotees.

Kidwelly

The sleepy little town of **KIDWELLY** (Cydweli) is dominated by its imposing **castle**, established around 1106 by Henry I's minister Roger, Bishop of Salisbury.

Kidwelly Castle

Just north of the town centre • March–June, Sept & Oct daily 9.30am–5pm; July & Aug daily 9.30am–6pm; Nov–Feb Mon–Sat 10am–4pm, Sun 11am–4pm • £4; CADW • ☎ 01554 890104, ⓦ cadw.wales.gov.uk

Kidwelly Castle is strategically sited overlooking the River Gwendraeth and vast tracts of coast. Entering through the massive gatehouse, completed in 1422, you can still see portcullis slats and the murder holes through which noxious substances could be tipped onto intruders. This forms the centrepiece of the impressively intact outer ward walls, which give great views over the grassy courtyard and rectangular inner ward to the river.

ARRIVAL AND DEPARTURE   KIDWELLY

By train Kidwelly train station, half a mile west of the town centre down Station Rd, is on the main line between Swansea (15 daily; 30min) and Carmarthen (15 daily; 15min).

ACCOMMODATION AND EATING

Carmarthen Bay Touring & Campsite Tanylan Farm ☎ 01267 267306, ⓦ tanylanfarmholidays.co.uk. A caravan-oriented campsite perched beside the estuary north of Kidwelly. March–Sept. Pitches **£16–24**

Penlan Isaf Farm ☎ 01554 890266; ⓦ kidwelly farmcottages.co.uk. Superb B&B in barn conversions with great views over the town and coast. You'll receive a warm welcome and excellent food. **£60**

Time for Tea 7 Bridge St ☎ 01554 892908. Family-run place offering daytime meals, snacks, shakes and coffees, much of it using local produce. Mon–Sat 9am–4pm, Sun 10am–noon.

Carmarthen

In the early eighteenth century **CARMARTHEN** (Caerfyrddin) was Wales's largest town and it remains the regional hub, a solid, if hardly thrilling, commercial centre best known as the supposed birthplace of the wizard Merlin.

The most picturesque part of town is around Nott Square, where the handsome eighteenth-century **Guildhall** sits at the base of Edward I's uninspiring **castle**. From the top of Nott Square, King Street heads northeast towards the **St Peter's Church** and the Victorian School of Art, which has metamorphosed into **Oriel Myrddin** (Mon–Sat 10am–5pm; free), a craft centre and excellent gallery that acts as an imaginative showcase for local artists.

Carmarthenshire County Museum

Abergwili, 2 miles east of Carmarthen • Tues–Sat 10am–4.30pm • Free • ☎ 01267 228696, ⓦ carmarthenmuseum.org.uk • 6 buses daily; 12min

The severe grey Bishop's Palace in Abergwili, the seat of the Bishop of St Davids between 1542 and 1974, now houses the **Carmarthenshire County Museum**. The interesting exhibitions include the history of Welsh translations of the New Testament and Book of Common Prayer – both first translated here, in 1567.

14

ARRIVAL AND INFORMATION — CARMARTHEN

By train Trains between Swansea and Pembrokeshire stop at the station on the south side of the River Tywi.
Destinations Cardiff (20 daily; 1hr 45min–2hr); Fishguard (4 daily; 1hr); Haverfordwest (11 daily; 40min); Pembroke (9 daily; 1hr 10min); Swansea (26 daily; 50min); Tenby (9 daily, 50min).

By bus The bus station is on Blue St, north of the river.
Destinations Aberystwyth (hourly; 2hr 20min); Haverfordwest (3 daily, 1hr); Kidwelly (every 30min; 25min); Laugharne (6 daily; 30min); Llandeilo (10 daily; 40min); Swansea (every 30min; 1hr 20min); Tenby (1 daily; 1hr 10min).

Tourist information Castle House, between the castle's ring walls (9.30am–4.30pm: April–Nov Mon–Sat, Dec–March Mon & Wed–Sat; ☎ 01267 231557). There's an authentic re-creation of the police station and cells that were here from 1860.

ACCOMMODATION AND EATING

Caban y Dderwen 11 Mansel St ☎ 01267 238989. The best spot in town for snacks and light lunches, including pan-fried laverbread with cockles (£6). Mon–Wed, Fri & Sat 9am–5pm, Thurs 9am–3.30pm, Sun noon–2.30pm.

Diablo's on the Quay Coracle Way ☎ 01267 223000, ⓦ diablos.co. Cosy restaurant by the river that's ideal for the express lunch (£8.50) or full meals (mains such as the vegetarian pie of the week, ham hock or pan-roasted trout; £10–14). There's also an outside deck for cocktails. Daily noon–late; food served daily noon–3pm (Sun to 4pm) & 6–9pm.

Rose and Crown Lammas St ☎ 01267 232050, ⓦ roseandcrowncarmarthen.co.uk. Ancient coaching inn well-refurbished with chic rooms, DVD players and full Welsh breakfasts in the bar downstairs. **£65**

Y Dderwen Fach 98 Priory St ☎ 01267 234193, ⓦ ydderwenfach.co.uk. The best of the central budget B&Bs, in a simple seventeenth-century house. Some rooms have bathtubs; others have shared showers. **£50**

The Tywi Valley

The **River Tywi** curves and darts its way east from Carmarthen through some of the most magical scenery in South Wales as well as passing a couple of budding gardens: one, the **National Botanic Garden of Wales**, and the other a faithful reconstruction of walled gardens around the long-abandoned house of **Aberglasney**. The twenty-mile trip to Llandeilo is punctuated by gentle, impossibly green hills topped with ruined castles, notably the wonderful **Carreg Cennen**: it's not hard to see why the Merlin legend has taken such a hold in these parts.

The National Botanic Garden of Wales

Seven miles east of Carmarthen • Daily: April–Sept 10am–6pm; Oct–March 10am–4.30pm • £8.50, Nov–Feb £5, half price for those arriving by bike or public transport • ☎ 01558 668768, ⓦ gardenofwales.org.uk • Bus #279 runs once daily from Carmarthen train station, 25min

Opened in 2000, the great glass "eye" of the **National Botanic Garden of Wales** quickly became the centrepiece of the Tywi Valley. Its central walkway leads past lakes, sculpture and geological outcrops from all over Wales, with walks down towards slate-bed plantings and wood and wetland habitats. A double-walled garden has been teased back to life (providing vegetables for the restaurant), and enhanced with the addition of a small, exquisite Japanese garden, a tropical house and a bee garden that's home to a million bees. At the top of the hill is Norman Foster's stunning oval **glasshouse**, packed with endangered plants from South Africa, Chile, California and the Mediterranean. The whole centre, including the excellent café, is sustainably managed, and the surrounding land has been turned over to either organic farming or the restoration of some typical Welsh habitat.

Aberglasney

5 miles northeast of the Botanic Garden, half a mile south of the A40 near Broad Oak • Daily: April–Sept 10am–6pm; Oct–March 10.30am–4pm • £8 • ☎ 01558 668998, ⓦ aberglasney.org

Five miles northeast of the National Botanic Garden, a much older garden can be found at **Aberglasney**. While a partly ruined manor house is the estate's centrepiece, interest is focused on the stunning **gardens** where archeologists have peeled back half a century's neglect to reveal interlinking walled gardens mostly constructed between the sixteenth and eighteenth centuries. A walkway leads around the top of what is thought to be Britain's only secular cloister garden, giving access to a set of six Victorian aviaries from where there are great views over the Jacobean pool garden. One oddity is the **yew tunnel**, planted around three hundred years ago and trained over to root on the far side. The house's glassed-in atrium now shelters subtropical plants.

Llandeilo

Newton House: April–Oct daily 11am–6pm; Nov–March Fri–Sun • £4.40; NT • ⓦ nationaltrust.org.uk

Fifteen miles east of Carmarthen, the handsome market town of **LLANDEILO** is heading upmarket, with a growing group of chichi cafés and shops just off the main Rhosmaen Street.

There's little to see in town, but a mile west is the tumbledown shell of the largely thirteenth-century **Dinefwr Castle**, set on a wooded bluff above the Tywi and reached through gorgeous parkland. However, the Rhys family aspired to something a little more luxurious, and in 1523 built a "new" castle, half a mile away, now named **Newton House**. Today the interiors are arranged just as they were a hundred years ago.

ARRIVAL AND DEPARTURE   LLANDEILO

By train Llandeilo train station, on the scenic Heart of Wales line from Swansea to Shrewsbury, is just east of the centre. Destinations Shrewsbury (4 daily; 2hr 50min); Swansea (5 daily; 1hr 10min).

By bus Buses stop on New Rd. Destinations include Carmarthen (8 daily; 40min) and Swansea (6 daily; 90 min).

ACCOMMODATION AND EATING

The Angel 62 Rhosmaen St ☎ 01558 822765, ⓦ angelbistro.co.uk. Convivial pub serving great food. The back room is a slightly more formal restaurant (mains £11–15); Thurs features an internationally themed buffet. Mon–Sat 11.30am–3pm & 6–11pm.

Cawdor Arms 70 Rhosmaen St ☎ 01558 823500, ⓦ thecawdor.com. Llandeilo's focal point, this former coaching inn has been given a postmodern makeover with delightful, simply decorated rooms (all different) and stunning attic suites. Rates vary, going up to £200. £65

Fronlas 7 Thomas St ☎ 01558 824733, ⓦ fronlas.com. This large terraced house has been creatively transformed into a modern three-room B&B, all bare boards, funky lighting, wild wallpapers and minimalist design. Breakfasts are largely organic and of local ingredients. The lounge has an honesty bar and a good DVD collection. £60

Rosetta 139 Rhosmaen St ☎ 01558 823444. A great deli (for fine Welsh cheeses and organic bread) and health food shop, with seating upstairs to savour the coffee. Mon–Fri 9.30am–5.30pm, Sat 9.45am–5pm.

Carreg Cennen Castle

4 miles southeast of Llandeilo • Daily: April–Oct 9.30am–6.30pm; Nov–March 9.30am–4pm • £4; CADW • ☎ 01558 822291, ⓦ carregcennencastle.com

Isolated in rural hinterland in the far western extremes of the Brecon Beacons National Park (see p.662), **Carreg Cennen Castle** is one of the most magnificently positioned castles in Wales. Urien, one of King Arthur's knights, is said to have built his fortress on the fearsome rocky outcrop, although the first known construction dates from 1248. Carreg Cennen fell to the English King Edward I in 1277, and was largely destroyed in 1462 by the Earl of Pembroke, who believed it to be a rebel base. The most astounding aspect of the castle is its commanding position, 300ft above a sheer drop down into the green valley of the small River Cennen. The highlights of a visit are the views down into the river valley and the long, damp descent into a pitch-black **cave** that is said to have served as a well. Torches are essential (£1 rental from the excellent tearoom near the car park) – continue as far as possible and then turn them off to experience absolute darkness.

Laugharne

The village of **LAUGHARNE** (Talacharn) is a delightful spot, with its ragged castle looming over reeds and tidal flats, and narrow lanes snuggling in behind. Catch it in high season, though, and you're immediately aware that Laugharne is increasingly being taken over by the legend of the poet **Dylan Thomas**. The village plays its Thomas connections with curiously disgruntled aplomb – nowhere more so than his old boozing hole, **Brown's Hotel**, on the main street, where Thomas's cast-iron table still sits in a window alcove in the front bar. The poet is buried in the graveyard of the parish church just north of the centre, his grave marked by a simple white cross.

Dylan Thomas Boathouse

Dylan's Walk • Daily: May–Oct & Easter weekend 10am–5.30pm; Nov–April 10.30am 3.30pm · £4 · ☎ 01994 427420, ⓦ dylanthomasboathouse.com

Down a narrow lane by the estuary is the **Dylan Thomas Boathouse**, the simple home of the Thomas family from 1949 until Dylan's death in 1953. It's an enchanting museum, with views of the peaceful, ever-changing water and light of the estuary and its "heron-priested shore". Along the narrow lane, you can peer into the green garage where he wrote: curled photographs of literary heroes, a pen collection and scrunched-up balls of paper suggest that he could return at any minute.

Laugharne Castle

South end of King St • April–Sept daily 10am–5pm · £3.80; CADW · ☎ 01994 427906, ⓦ cadw.wales.gov.uk

At the bottom of the main street, the gloomy hulk of **Laugharne Castle** broods over the

---

DYLAN THOMAS

Dylan Thomas was the stereotypical Celt – fiery, verbose, richly talented and fond of a drink. Born in 1914 into a middle-class family in Swansea, Dylan's first glimmers of literary greatness came when he joined the *South Wales Evening Post* as a reporter. Some of his most popular tales in the *Portrait of the Artist as a Young Dog* were inspired during this period.

Rejecting what he saw as Swansea's coarse provincialism, Thomas arrived in London as a broke 20-year-old in 1934, weeks before his first volume of poetry was published as the first prize in a competition. Another volume followed shortly afterwards, cementing the engaging young Welshman's reputation in the literary establishment. Marrying in 1937, he returned to Wales and settled in the hushed backwater of Laugharne. Short stories – crackling with rich and melancholy humour – tumbled out as swiftly as poems, further widening his base of admirers, though, like so many other writers, Thomas only gained star status posthumously. Perhaps better than anyone, he wrote with an identifiably Welsh rhythmic wallow in the language.

Thomas, especially in public, liked to adopt the persona of an archetypal stage Welshman, as he saw it: sonorous tones, loquacious, romantic and inclined towards a stiff tipple. This went down particularly well in the United States, where he journeyed on lucrative lecture tours. It was on one of these that he died, in 1953, supposedly from a massive whisky overdose, although it now seems likely he was a victim of pneumonia or diabetes and incompetent doctors. Just one month earlier, he had put the finishing touches to what many see as his masterpiece: *Under Milk Wood*, a "play for voices".

14

estuary. Built in the twelfth and thirteenth centuries, most of the original buildings were obliterated in Tudor times when it was transformed into a splendid mansion, largely destroyed in the Civil War. The Inner Ward is dominated by two original towers, one of which you can climb for sublime views from the domed roof over the huddled town. This is now surrounded by an attractive formal garden with fine mature trees.

ARRIVAL AND DEPARTURE   LAUGHARNE

By bus Buses run from Carmarthen to Pendine via Laugharne (5 services daily Mon–Sat; 30min).

ACCOMMODATION

Tiny Laugharne has no tourist office and only limited **accommodation**, so book ahead in season.

Ants Hill Caravan Park 📞 01994 427293, 🖥 antshill .co.uk. The nearest campsite to Laugharne lies a few hundred yards north. Has an outdoor heated swimming pool (summer only). March–Oct. Pitches **£20**

Boat House Inn 1 Gosport St 📞 01994 427263, 🖥 the boathousebnb.co.uk. Stylish, comfortable four-room B&B

right in the centre. Great breakfasts might include vanilla waffles or smoked salmon. **£80**

Swan Cottage 20 Gosport St 📞 01994 427409. Appealing one-room B&B with good rates for singles and extended stays. Excellent breakfasts, served in the pleasant garden, weather permitting. **£70**

EATING AND DRINKING

Café Culture 6 Grist Square 📞 01994 427422. This lively Mediterranean-style licensed café serves breakfasts till noon, then a range of pastas and other Italian dishes (£10–17) as well as Greek moussaka and Welsh cawl. Mon–Fri 8am–6pm, Sat & Sun 8am–10pm.

The Cors Newbridge Rd 📞 01994 427219, 🖥 thecors .co.uk. Excellent Modern Welsh cuisine served casually by candlelight. The menu might include smoked haddock

crème brûlée or grilled sewin (sea trout), with mains for around £20. Booking essential. Thurs–Sat evenings.

New Three Mariners Victoria St 📞 01994 427426, 🖥 newthreemarinersinn.co.uk. Cheery pub that offers the best drinking in town, coffees and decent bar meals (the *Old Three Mariners* across the road is now a roofless smoking area. Open Mon–Fri 4–11pm, Sat & Sun noon–midnight.

Southern Pembrokeshire

Anyone exploring the far southern reaches of Pembrokeshire will pass through **Tenby**, the quintessential British seaside resort built high on cliffs with views across to monastic **Caldey Island**. The coast zigzagging west from Tenby is a strange mix of caravan parks, Ministry of Defence shooting ranges, spectacularly beautiful bays and gull-covered cliffs. The coastal road passes idyllic coves, the lily ponds at **Bosherston** and the remarkable and ancient **St Govan's Chapel**, squeezed into a rock cleft above the crashing waves. The ancient town of **Pembroke** really only warrants a visit to its impressive castle and the fine Bishop's Palace in neighbouring **Lamphey**. **Buses** to most corners of the peninsula radiate from Tenby, Pembroke and Haverfordwest.

Tenby

On a natural promontory of great strategic importance, beguilingly old-fashioned **TENBY** (Dinbych-y-Pysgod) is everything a seaside resort should be. Narrow streets wind down from the medieval centre past miniature gardens that face the afternoon sun, and steps lead down to dockside arches where fishmongers sell the morning's catch.

First mentioned in a ninth-century bardic poem, Tenby grew under the twelfth-century Normans, who erected a castle on the headland in their attempt to colonize South Pembrokeshire and create a "**Little England beyond Wales**". Three times in the twelfth and thirteenth centuries the town was ransacked by the Welsh. The castle was then strengthened and the stout town walls – largely still intact – were built. Tenby prospered as a port between the fourteenth and sixteenth centuries, and although

CALDEY ISLAND

Celtic monks first settled **Caldey Island** (Ynys Pyr), a couple of miles off Tenby, in the sixth century. This community may have been wiped out in Viking raids, but in 1136 Benedictine monks founded a priory here. After the dissolution of the monasteries in 1536, the island was bought and sold until 1906, when it was again sold to a Benedictine order, and subsequently to Reformed Cistercians, who have run the place since then.

A short woodland walk from the island's jetty leads to its main settlement: a tiny post office, the popular Tea Gardens and a **perfume shop** selling the herbal fragrances distilled by the monks from Caldey's abundant flora. The narrow road to the left leads past the abbey to the heavily restored **chapel of St David**, whose most impressive feature is the round-arched Norman door.

A lane leads south from the village to the old **priory**, and the remarkable, twelfth-century **St Illtud's church**, which houses one of the most significant pre-Norman finds in Wales, the sandstone **Ogham Cross**, under the stained-glass window on the south side of the nave. It is carved with an inscription from the sixth century, which was added to, in Latin, during the ninth. The lane continues south, climbing up to the gleaming white island **lighthouse**, built in 1828, from where there are memorable views.

Caldey Island is accessible by **boat** from Tenby Harbour, or Castle Beach when the tide is out (every 20min, 10am–5pm: Easter–Oct Mon–Fri plus Sat May–Sept; 20min each way; £11 return; ☎01834 844453, ⓦcaldey-island.co.uk). Tickets (not for any specific sailing) are sold at the kiosk at the harbour.

14

decline followed, the arrival of the railway renewed prosperity as the town became a fashionable resort.

Old Town

Today, wandering the medieval streets is one of Tenby's delights. The town is triangle-shaped, with two sides formed by the coast meeting at Castle Hill, and the third by the remains of the 20ft-high town **walls**, built in the late thirteenth century and massively strengthened by Jasper Tudor in 1457. The only town gate still standing is the **Five Arches**, a semicircular barbican that combined day-to-day practicality with hidden lookouts and angles acute enough to surprise invaders.

St Mary's Church

Between St George's St and Tudor Square • ☎01834 845484, ⓦstmaryschurchtenby.com

The centre's focal point is the 152ft-high spire of the largely fifteenth-century **St Mary's church**. Its pleasantly light interior shows the elaborate ceiling bosses in the chancel to good effect, and the tombs of local barons demonstrate Tenby's important mercantile tradition.

Tudor Merchant's House

Quay Hill • 11am–5pm: April–July & Oct daily except Tues; Feb half term & Aug daily; March & Nov Sat & Sun • £3; NT • ☎01834 842279, ⓦnationaltrust.org.uk

Wedged in a corner of Quay Hill is the fifteenth-century **Tudor Merchant's House**. A compact building on three floors, it has been filled with reproduction Tudor furniture that visitors are welcome to sit on. The rear herb garden gives a good view of the huge Flemish chimney.

ARRIVAL AND INFORMATION   TENBY

By train Tenby's station is just west of the town centre, at the foot of Warren St.

Destinations Carmarthen (9 daily; 50min); Pembroke (9 daily; 20min); Swansea (8 daily; 1hr 45min).

By bus Some buses stop at South Parade, at the top of

Trafalgar Rd, although most call at the bus shelter on Upper Park Rd.

Destinations Carmarthen (1 daily; 1hr); Haverfordwest (hourly; 1hr); Manorbier (hourly; 20min); Pembroke (hourly; 45min).

14

Tourist office Upper Park Rd (Easter–Oct Mon–Fri 9.30am–5pm, Sat & Sun 10am–4pm; Nov–Easter Mon– Sat 10am–4pm; ☎ 01834 842402.

ACCOMMODATION

Atlantic The Esplanade ☎ 01834 842881, ⓦ atlantic -hotel.uk.com. The best hotel along the South Beach, with high-standard rooms (some with sea views), a decent restaurant and a pool and spa. Rates include breakfast; watch out for good off-season specials. **£110**

Glenholme Picton Terrace ☎ 01834 843909, ⓦ glenholmetenby.co.uk. Agreeable eight-room B&B near the town centre, with en-suite rooms and cycle storage. **£52**

Langdon Villa Guest House 3 Warren St ☎ 01834 849467, ⓦ langdonguesthousetenby.co.uk. Handy for the station, this four-star B&B has a range of double and twin rooms and puts on a hearty breakfast. **£55**

Meadow Farm Northcliff ☎ 01834 844829, ⓦ meadow farmtenby.co.uk. Under a mile north of town on the coastal path, this campsite in a grassy field has limited facilities but long views over the town towards Caldey Island. April–Oct. Per person **£8**.

YHA Manorbier Skrinkle Haven ☎ 0845 371 9031, ⓦ yha.org.uk. Modern hostel in an old MoD building overlooking the cliffs 5 miles west of Tenby, near the Manorbier bus route. Meals and camping facilities available. March–Oct. Dorms **£19**, doubles **£54**

EATING AND DRINKING

Caffè Vista 3 Crackwell St ☎ 01834 849636. Great little licensed Greek-Australian-run café with excellent panini, espresso and cakes, plus a small selection of dishes such as beef or butterbean stew. Good harbour views from the terrace and free wi-fi. Summer Sun–Wed 9am–5pm, Thurs–Sat 9am–10.30pm; rest of year daily 9am–5pm.

Coach and Horses Upper Frog St ☎ 01834 842704. Animated, wooden-beamed pub (said to be the oldest in Tenby) with good beer, well-prepared bar meals and some tasty Thai dishes. Food served daily noon–3pm & 6–9pm.

Lifeboat Tavern St Julian's St ☎ 01834 844948. Popular and welcoming pub, with a young clientele and live music performances on Tues and Sun. Daily noon–midnight, food served Mon–Fri noon–9pm, Sat & Sun noon–7pm.

★ **The Plantagenet** Quay Hill ☎ 01834 842350. For a splurge, try this cosy and thoroughly enjoyable restaurant in one of Tenby's oldest houses – ask for a table inside the massive tenth-century Flemish chimney. Dinner mains go for £21–27 (£16 for vegetarian), but lunch is cheaper (£8–13). April–Oct & Christmas/New Year daily noon–2.30pm & 5–10pm; Nov, Dec & March Fri 5–10pm, Sat noon–2.30pm & 5–10pm, Sun noon–2.30pm.

West of Tenby

The coastal path south and west of Tenby skirts the gorgeous long beach of **Penally**, then hugs the clifftop for a couple of miles to **Lydstep Haven** (fee charged for the sands). A mile further west is the cove of Skrinkle Haven, and above it the excellent

---

THE PEMBROKESHIRE COAST NATIONAL PARK AND COAST PATH

The **Pembrokeshire Coast** is Britain's only predominantly sea-based national park (ⓦ pcnpa .org.uk), hugging the rippled coast around the entire southwestern section of Wales. Established in 1952, the park is not one easily identifiable mass, rather a series of occasionally unconnected coastal and inland scenic patches.

Crawling around almost every wriggle of the coastline, the **Pembrokeshire Coast Path** winds 186 miles from Amroth, just east of Tenby, to its northern terminus at St Dogmael's near Cardigan. For the vast majority of the way, the path clings precariously to cliff-top routes, overlooking seal-basking rocks, craggy offshore islands, unexpected gashes of sand and shrieking clouds of seabirds. The most popular and ruggedly inspiring segments of the coast path are the stretch along the southern coast from the castle at Manorbier to the tiny cliff chapel at Bosherston; either side of St Bride's Bay, around St David's Head and the Marloes peninsula; and the generally quieter northern coast either side of Fishguard, past undulating contours, massive cliffs, bays and old ports.

Spring is perhaps the finest season for walking: the crowds are yet to arrive and the cliff-top flora is at its most vivid. The best of the numerous publications about the coast path is Brian John's *National Trail Guide* (£13), which includes 1:25,000 maps of the route. The national park publishes an accommodation list on ⓦ pcnpa.org.uk.

Manorbier hostel (see opposite). A couple of miles further on, the quaint village of **MANORBIER** (Maenorbŷr), pronounced "manner-beer", was the birthplace in 1146 of the Welsh-Norman historian, writer and ecclesiastical reformist Giraldus Cambrensis (Gerald of Wales).

Manorbier Castle

Off the B4585, 1.2 miles south of the train station · April–Sept, Feb & Oct half terms daily 10am–5pm · £5 · ☎ 01834 871394, ⓦ manorbiercastle.co.uk · Buses run hourly to Haverfordwest (75min), Lamphey (15min), Pembroke (20min) and Tenby (20min)

Founded in the early twelfth century, the baronial residence of **Manorbier Castle** sits above the village and its beach on a hill of wild gorse. Strong Norman walls surround gardens and a grassy courtyard in which the remains of chapel and staterooms jostle for position with the nineteenth-century domestic residence. Views from the ramparts are wonderful, taking in the corrugated coastline, bushy dunes, deep-green fields and smoking chimneys of the village houses. There's a warren of dark passageways to explore, occasionally opening out into little cells populated by lacklustre wax figures, including Gerald himself.

The Stackpole Estate

Access by 387/388 Coastal Cruiser which makes a loop from Pembroke (30min), calling 3 times daily at Bosherton and Stackpole Village and twice at St Govan's and Stackpole Quay; Thurs and Sat only in winter.

The tiny rocky harbour at **Stackpole Quay**, reached by a small lane from East Trewent and part of the National Trust's Stackpole Estate, is a good starting point for walks along the breathtaking cliffs to the north. Another walk leads half a mile south to one of Wales's finest beaches, **Barafundle Bay**, its soft sands fringed by wooded cliffs at either end. The path continues around the coast, through the dunes of **Stackpole Warren**, to **Broadhaven South**, where a pleasant little beach overlooks several rocky islets. Road access is through the village of **BOSHERSTON** where three beautifully landscaped fingers of water known as **Bosherston Lakes** (NT; free) were created in the late eighteenth century. The westernmost lake is the most scenic, especially in late spring and early summer when the lilies that carpet its surface are in full bloom.

A lane from Bosherston (often closed Mon–Fri, due to military use) dips south across the MoD training grounds to a spot overlooking the cliffs where tiny **St Govan's Chapel** is wedged: it's a remarkable building, at least eight hundred years old. Steps descend straight into the sandy-floored chapel, now empty save for the simple stone altar.

Pembroke

The old county town of **PEMBROKE** (Penfro) sits below its fearsome castle on the southern side of Pembroke River, but is surprisingly restful. There's one long main street of attractive Georgian and Victorian houses and some intact stretches of medieval town wall, but little else to keep you.

Castle

Westgate Hill · Daily: April–Aug 9.30am–5.30pm; March, Sept & Oct 10am–5pm; Nov–Feb 10am–4pm · £5.50 · ☎ 01646 684585, ⓦ pembrokecastle.co.uk

Pembroke's history is inextricably bound up with that of its **castle**, founded by the Normans as the strongest link in their chain of fortresses across South Wales. During the Civil War, Pembroke was a Parliamentarian stronghold until its military governor suddenly switched allegiance to the king, whereupon Cromwell's troops sacked the castle after a 48-day siege. Yet despite this battering, and centuries of subsequent neglect, the castle still inspires awe with its sheer, bloody-minded bulk. The soaring gatehouse, housing some excellent history displays, leads into the large, grassy courtyard around the vast Norman **keep**, 75ft high and with walls 18ft thick. Beyond this, steps lead far down

14

into **Wogan Cavern**, a huge natural cave, dank and slimy, where light beams in through a barred hole in the wall facing out over the waterside path.

ARRIVAL AND INFORMATION PEMBROKE

By train Pembroke's train station lies at the eastern end of Main St.
Destinations Lamphey (9 daily; 3min); Manorbier (9 daily; 12min); Pembroke Dock (9 daily; 10min); Tenby (9 daily; 20min).
By bus Buses stop near the castle on Main St. The Coastal Cruiser is a hikers' bus that takes a loop from Pembroke to Angle via Bosherston and Stackpole; journey times depend on whether you take the #387 (anticlockwise) or #388 (clockwise).
Destinations Bosherston (May–Sept 6 daily; Oct–April Mon,

Thurs & Sat 4 daily; 35min–1hr); Haverfordwest (hourly; 55min); Manorbier (hourly; 20min); Pembroke Dock (3 hourly; 10min); Stackpole (May–Sept 6 daily; Oct–April Mon, Thurs & Sat 4 daily; 30min–1hr 15min); Tenby (hourly; 40min).
By ferry Irish Ferries (☎0870 517 1717, ⬤irishferries .com) operate two daily services from Rosslare in Ireland to Pembroke Dock, 2 miles northwest of Pembroke and starting point of trains to Carmarthen and Swansea.
Tourist office Commons Rd, parallel to Main St (Easter–Oct Mon–Fri 10am–4pm, Sat 10am–1pm; winter Tues–Sat 10am–1pm; ☎01646 776499).

ACCOMMODATION

Penfro 111 Main Street ☎01646 682753, ⬤pembroke -bed-and-breakfast.co.uk. Three large rooms in a fine Georgian townhouse, some without bathroom or TV; there's a lovely spacious garden at the rear. **£70**

Tregenna 7 Upper Lamphey Rd ☎01646 621525, ⬤tregennapembroke.co.uk. If *Penfro* is full, try one of the four en-suite rooms here, about 800m beyond the train station. **£55**

EATING AND DRINKING

Cornstore Café North Quay ☎01646 684290, ⬤thecornstore.com/cafe/. Down by the river, this little café, linked to an interior design shop, is a great spot for espresso, scrumptious home-made cakes and light meals made from local produce. Mon–Sat 10am–5pm.
Old King's Arms 13 Main St ☎01646 683611, ⬤oldkingsarmshotel.co.uk. For something substantial try the traditional dining room at this historic inn. Most food is locally sourced, with meaty mains around £14–20

at dinner (cheaper for Sunday lunch); bar food is cheaper and lighter, and they do real ales, too. Bar 11am–11pm daily; food served daily noon–2.15pm & 6.30–10pm.
Watermans Arms Northgate St, over the bridge ☎01646 682718, ⬤watermansarmspembroke.co.uk. It's hard to beat a summer evening here, whiling away the hours on a veranda overlooking the mill pond. Bar daily noon–11pm; lunch noon–3pm daily, dinner 5.30–9pm Mon–Sat.

Lamphey

The pleasant village of **LAMPHEY** (Llandyfai), two miles east of Pembroke and accessible on **buses** and **trains** between Tenby and Pembroke, is best known for the ruined **Bishop's Palace**, off a quiet lane to the north of the village. There's also a handful of good **places to stay** nearby.

Bishop's Palace

Off the Ridgeway, just north of town • Daily: April–Oct 10am–5pm; Nov–March 10am–4pm • April–Oct £3.50; Nov–March free; CADW • ☎01646 672224, ⬤cadw.wales.gov.uk

Once a country retreat for the bishops of St Davids, Lamphey's **Bishop's Palace** dates from around the thirteenth century, but was abandoned following the Reformation. Stout walls surround the scattered ruins and grassy banks under which other buildings have long been lost. Most impressive are the remains of the Great Hall, at the complex's eastern end, topped by fourteenth-century arcaded parapets.

ARRIVAL AND DEPARTURE LAMPHEY

By bus Buses stop at the church, south of the lane to the Bishop's Palace.
Destinations Haverfordwest (hourly; 1hr); Pembroke (hourly; 8min); Tenby (hourly; 40min).

By train Station is centrally sited, on Station Rd just off A4139.
Destinations Trains leave every 2hr to Carmarthen (70min), Pembroke (5min), Pembroke Dock (15min), Swansea (2hr) and Tenby (20min).

ACCOMMODATION

Lamphey Court Hotel & Spa Opposite Bishop's Palace ☎ 01646 672273, ⊛ lampheycourt.co.uk. Grand if slightly over-the-top accommodation, with spa, opposite the palace ruins. **£99**

Portclew House B&B Two miles south of Lamphey,

Freshwater East ☎ 01646 672800, ⊛ portclewhouse .co.uk. Just half a mile from the superb beach of Freshwater East, this Grade II-listed Georgian house, in two acres of grounds, offers seven spacious rooms, plus self-catering units. **£60**

Carew

Tiny **CAREW**, four miles northeast of Pembroke, is a pretty place beside the River Carew. By the main road just south of the river crossing stands a 13ft **Celtic cross**, the graceful taper of the shaft covered in fine tracery of ancient Welsh designs. To get there take a bus from Pembroke (4 daily; 10min) or Tenby (9 daily; 30min).

Carew Castle and Tidal Mill

Central Carew • April–Oct daily 10am–5pm; Nov–March castle only Mon–Fri 11am–3pm • April–Oct £4.75; Nov–March £4 • ⊛ carewcastle.com

An Elizabethan walled garden houses the ticket office for **Carew Castle and Tidal Mill**. Little remains of the castle, a hybrid of defensive necessity (c.1100) and Elizabethan whimsy, but its large, impressive bare walls give a good sense of scale. A few hundred yards west is the **Tidal Mill**, used commercially until 1937 and now the only tide-powered mill in Wales. The impressive eighteenth-century exterior belies the pedestrian displays inside.

Mid- and northern Pembrokeshire

The most westerly point of Wales is one of the country's most enchanting. The region's chief town, **Haverfordwest** is rather soulless, but it's the jumping-off point for stunning **St Bride's Bay**. The coast here is broken into rocky outcrops, islands and broad, sweeping beaches curving between two headlands that sit like giant crab pincers facing out into the warm Gulf Stream. The southernmost headland winds around every conceivable angle, offering calm, east-facing sands at **Dale** and sunny expanses of south-facing beach at **Marloes**. At **Martin's Haven**, boats depart for the offshore islands of **Skomer**, **Skokholm** and **Grassholm**. To the north, there's spectacularly lacerated coast around **St Davids peninsula**, with towering cliffs interrupted only by occasional strips of sand. The tiny city of **St Davids** is a definite highlight: rooks and crows circle above the impressive ruins of the huge Bishop's Palace and the delicate bulk of the cathedral, the most impressive in Wales.

The wild, rugged coast that forms the very southern tip of Cardigan Bay is breathtakingly beautiful, and noticeably less commercialized and far more Welsh than the shores of south and mid-Pembrokeshire. From the crags and cairns above St David's Head, the coast path perches precariously on the cliffs where only the thousands of seabirds have access. Hidden coves and secluded beaches slice into the rocky headlands, at their most magnificent around **Strumble Head**, where a picturesque lighthouse stands on a tiny islet. From here, there's only wilderness to detain you en route to charming **Newport** – unless you're heading for **Fishguard** and the ferries to Ireland.

Haverfordwest

In the seventeenth and eighteenth centuries, the town of **HAVERFORDWEST** (Hwlffordd), ten miles north of Pembroke, prospered as a port and trading centre. Despite its natural advantages, it is scarcely a place to linger, though as the main transport hub and shopping centre for western Pembrokeshire, you are likely to pass through.

ARRIVAL AND INFORMATION

HAVERFORDWEST

By train Trains stop a 10min walk east of the Old Bridge. Destinations Cardiff (7 daily; 2hr 25min); Carmarthen (10 daily; 40min); Swansea (7 daily; 1hr 30min).

By bus The bus station is at the end of the Old Bridge. Destinations Broad Haven (6 daily; 20min); Cardigan (hourly; 1hr 20min); Carmarthen (3 daily; 1hr); Fishguard (hourly; 40min); Manorbier (hourly; 1hr 10min); Newport, Pembrokeshire (hourly; 1hr); Pembroke (hourly; 55min); St Davids (hourly; 45min); Tenby (hourly; 1hr).

Tourist office Dew St, behind the library (Mon, Wed & Thurs 9.30am–5pm, Tues & Fri 9.30am–7pm, Sat 9.30am–1pm; ☎ 01437 775244).

GETTING AROUND

By bike Mike's Bikes, 17 Prendergast, a quarter of a mile northeast of the bus station (Mon–Sat 9am–5.30pm; ☎ 01437 760068, ⓦ mikes-bikes.co.uk). The region's best bike rental, supplying mountain bikes and hybrid tourers (both £12/day) with panniers, lock and helmet, and tag-alongs for kids.

ACCOMMODATION AND EATING

Casa Maria 2 Castle Square ☎ 01437 779194, ⓦ casa mariadeli.co.uk. At the start of the walk up to the castle ruins, this classy deli sells Spanish, French and Welsh cheeses, meats and olives, with a café upstairs serving tapas with wine. Mon–Sat 9.30am–5.30pm (takeaways to 4pm); also tapas to 8pm Fri.

College Guest House 93 Hill St ☎ 01437 763710, ⓦ collegeguesthouse.com. One of several decent B&Bs near the Leisure Centre (free parking) at the top of Hill St. £78

East Hook Farmhouse Portfield Gate ☎ 01437 762211, ⓦ easthookfarmhouse.co.uk. Delightful Georgian farm-house 3 miles west, serving delicious breakfasts; also a self-catering cottage. £80

The George's 24 Market St ☎ 01437 766683, ⓦ the georges.uk.com. A great option for lunch, taking a wholefood approach to delicious peasant dishes. You can eat in a lovely walled garden if the weather allows, or the cellar bistro if not. Tues–Sat 10am–5.30pm.

Dale

DALE, fourteen miles west of Haverfordwest, has a sheltered east-facing shore making it excellent for bathing and **watersports**, but it can be unbearably crowded in peak season. West Wales Wind, Surf and Sailing (☎ 01646 636642, ⓦ surfdale.co.uk) gives instruction in power-boating, windsurfing, surfing, sailing and kayaking (April–Oct; £35–65 per half-day), and rents gear.

ARRIVAL AND DEPARTURE

DALE

By bus Various bus stops, including the seafront (B4327). Services run three times daily from Haverfordwest (55min) and Milford Haven (30min).

ACCOMMODATION

DALE

Allenbrook Castle Way ☎ 01646 636254, ⓦ allenbrook-dale.co.uk. A luxurious, charming, richly furnished country house hotel close to the beach. All rooms look out over the garden and towards the sea. No children. £80

Richmond House off South St ☎ 07974 925009, ⓦ richmond-house.com. On the waterfront (and next to the local pub), this is a comfortable B&B with nicely decorated, cabin-style rooms, all en suite. £80

Marloes

MARLOES, a mile north of Dale, is an unexciting little place, but the broad, deserted beach is magnificent, offering safe swimming as well as fine views of the island of Skokholm. The coast path and a narrow road continue for two miles to the National Trust-owned **Deer Park**, the grassy far tip of the southern peninsula of St Bride's Bay – and **Martin's Haven**, from where you can take a **boat** out to the islands of Skomer (where you can disembark), Skokholm and Grassholm.

ARRIVAL AND DEPARTURE

MARLOES

By bus Coastal Cruiser runs 3 times daily from St Davids May–Sept (90min); Oct–April Thurs & Sat only.

SKOMER, SKOKHOLM AND GRASSHOLM ISLANDS

Weather permitting, **boats** (April–Oct Tues–Sun & bank hols 10am, 11am & noon; £21; no booking required) cross from Martin's Haven to **Skomer Island**, a 722-acre flat-topped island whose rich birdlife and spectacular carpets of wild flowers make it perfect for birdwatching and walking.

Though no landings are permitted, fast cruises leave from Dale to loop around **Skokholm Island** (daily 9.30am, 3.30pm & 6.30pm; 2hr 30min; £40; booking essential; ☎ 01646 603109, ⓦ dale-sailing.co.uk), a couple of miles south of Skomer and far smaller, more rugged and remote, noted for its cliffs of warm red sandstone. Britain's first bird observatory was founded here in 1933, and there are still huge numbers of petrels, gulls, puffins, oystercatchers and Manx shearwaters.

The same company also offers cruises out to the tiny outpost of **Grassholm Island**, five miles west of Skomer (daily 12.30pm; 2hr 30min; £40). Some 80,000 or so screaming gannets nest here, and though you cannot land, boats stop to watch the wildlife.

14

ACCOMMODATION

YHA Marloes Sands Runwayskiln ☎ 0845 371 9333.   Marloes Sands. 11pm curfew. May–Sept. **£19**
Converted farm buildings overlooking the northern end of

St Davids

ST DAVIDS (Tyddewi) is one of the most enchanting spots in Britain. This miniature city – really just a large village – sits at Wales's very westernmost point in bleak, treeless countryside, above its purple- and gold-flecked **cathedral**, the country's spiritual heart. Supposedly founded by the Welsh patron saint himself in 550 AD, the shrine of St David has drawn pilgrims for a millennium and a half – William the Conqueror included – and by 1120, Pope Calixtus II decreed that two journeys to St Davids were the spiritual equivalent of one to Rome. Today, with so many historical sites, outdoor-pursuit centres, surf beaches, good cafés, superb walks, bathing and climbing, St Davids and its peninsula are a must-visit.

From the central **Celtic cross**, the main street runs under the thirteenth-century **Tower Gate**, forming the entrance to the serene **Cathedral Close**, backed by a windswept landscape of treeless heathland. The cathedral lies down to the right, hidden in a hollow by the River Alun. This apparent modesty is explained by reasons of defence, as a towering cathedral, visible from the sea on all sides, would have been vulnerable to attack. On the other side of the babbling Alun stand the ruins of the **Bishop's Palace**.

St Davids Cathedral

Immediately west of the central Cross Square • Mon–Sat 8.30am–5.30pm, Sun 12.45–5.30pm; evensong Sun 6pm • £3 donation requested • Guided tours (Aug Mon 11.30am & Fri 2.30pm, other times by appointment; £4) arranged at the bookshop in the nave • ☎ 01437 720202, ⓦ stdavidscathedral.org.uk

Entering **St Davids Cathedral**, you at once have a full view of its most striking feature, the intricate, latticed oak **roof** of the low, twelfth-century nave, added to hide emergency restoration work in the sixteenth century. The nave floor still has a

ST DAVIDS

■ ACCOMMODATION		● CAFÉS & RESTAURANTS	
Alandale	3	Cwtch*	2
Crug Glâs	1	The Refectory	1
Glan-y-môr	5		
Ramsey House	4	■ PUB	
St Davids YHA Hostel	2	Farmers Arms	1

14

OUTDOOR ACTIVITIES AROUND ST DAVIDS

Several local companies run **boat trips** to the outlying islands (see box, p.651), and there are all manner of activities from **biking** to **rock climbing**.

Preseli Venture Halfway to Fishguard near Mathry ☎01348 837709, ⓦpreseliventure.co.uk. Coasteering, sea kayaking, surfing, walking and biking.

TYF 1 High St ☎01437 721611, ⓦtyf.com. TYF pioneered coasteering, an exhilarating multi-sport combination that involves scrambling over rocks, jumping off cliffs and swimming across the narrow bays of St Davids peninsula. Coasteering is possible for just about anyone (even non-swimmers) and is available all year, along with surfing, kayaking and rock climbing. Also multi-day sessions and courses.

Ma Simes Surf Hut 28 High St ☎01437 720433, ⓦmasimes.co.uk. The place to rent surfboards (£12/day) or book a lesson (£35/half-day). Next door the **unsunghero surf shop** (28a High St; ☎07799 626779, ⓦunsungherosurf.co.uk) makes its own boards and rents surf and kayak gear.

pronounced slope and the support buttresses inserted in the northern aisle look incongruously new and temporary. The choir stalls include a unique **monarch's stall**, complete with royal crest, for, unlike any other British cathedral, the Queen is an automatic member of the St Davids Cathedral Chapter. Separating choir and presbytery is an unusual **parclose screen** of finely traced woodwork; beyond this is the tomb of Edmund Tudor, father of King Henry VII. The back wall of the **presbytery** was once the eastern end of the cathedral, as can be seen from the two lines of windows. The upper row has been left intact, while the lower three were filled with delicate gold mosaics in the nineteenth century. On the south side are two thirteenth-century bishops' tombs, facing the disappointingly plain tomb of St David, largely destroyed in the Reformation. Behind the filled-in lancets at the back of the presbytery is **Bishop Vaughan's chapel**, with an exquisite fan tracery roof built in 1508–22. A peephole looks back into the presbytery, over a casket reputedly containing some of the intermingled bones of St David and his friend, St Justinian.

The Bishop's Palace

The Close • March–June, Sept & Oct daily 9am–5pm; July & Aug daily 9am–6pm; Nov–March Mon–Sat 10am–4pm, Sun 11am–4pm • £3.50; CADW • ☎01437 720517, ⓦcadw.wales.gov.uk

The splendid fourteenth-century **Bishop's Palace** has a huge central quadrangle fringed by a neat jigsaw of ruined buildings built in extraordinarily richly tinted stone. The **arched parapets** that run along the top of most of the walls were a favourite feature of the Bishop Gower. Two ruined but still impressive halls – the **Bishop's Hall** and the enormous **Great Hall**, with its glorious rose window – lie off the main quadrangle; beneath the Great Hall, dank vaults contain an interesting exhibition on the palace and the indulgent lifestyles of its occupants. The destruction of the palace is largely due to sixteenth-century Bishop Barlow, who supposedly stripped the buildings of their lead roofs to provide dowries for his five daughters' marriages to bishops.

Oriel y Parc Landscape Gallery

National Park tourist office and gallery, High St: Easter–Oct daily 9.30am–5.30pm; Nov–Easter Mon–Sat 10am–4.30pm • Free • ☎01437 720392, ⓦpembrokeshirecoast.org.uk

The **Oriel y Parc Landscape Gallery** features paintings by Graham Sutherland plus rotating loans from the National Museum of Wales. The thoughtfully curated displays aim to interpret the landscape and natural world of the National Park.

ARRIVAL AND INFORMATION   ST DAVIDS

By bus From mid-April to Sept, the Celtic Coaster bus (#403) connects the Grove car park (by the tourist office) and the centre of St Davids with Whitesands Bay, St Justinians and Porth Clais. Buses from Haverfordwest stop on the High St; buses to and from Fishguard and Whitesands Bay stop on New St (when arriving) and Nun St (when leaving).

Destinations Broad Haven (3 daily; 45min); Fishguard (7 daily; 50min); Haverfordwest (hourly; 45min); Marloes (3 daily; 1hr 20min).

Tourist office East end of the High St (Easter–Oct daily 9.30am–5.30pm; Nov–Easter Mon–Sat 10am–4.30pm; ☎01437 720392, ⊛stdavids.co.uk). National Trust visitor centre is in the Captain's House on Cross Square (Mon–Sat 10am–5pm, Sun 10am–4pm; ☎01437 720385).

ACCOMMODATION

Alandale 43 Nun St ☎01437 720404. Small, friendly, central guesthouse (built for coastguard officers in the 1880s) with a bike shed, lounge and five en-suite rooms, some with long views; healthy breakfasts. **£90**

★ **Crug Glâs** Abereiddi, 4 miles northeast ☎01348 831302, ⊛crug-glas.co.uk. Luxurious country house on a working farm. Breakfasts are excellent (great bacon) and delicious four-course evening meals are available (main courses £15–25). **£115**

Glan-y-mor Caerfai Rd, half a mile south ☎01437 721788, ⊛glan-y-mor.co.uk. The nearest campsite to town, with pub and restaurant on site. No bookings.

March–Sept. Pitches **£12**

Ramsey House Lower Moor ☎01437 720321, ⊛ramseyhouse.co.uk. Quality B&B on the road to Porth Clais, with six boutique-style rooms and excellent breakfasts (with their own hen and duck eggs). They also do three-course evening meals for £40 and have a bar. March–Nov. **£100**

YHA St Davids Llaethdy, 2 miles northwest near Whitesands Bay ☎0845 371 9141, ⊛yha.org.uk. Large, renovated hostel in a former farmhouse and outbuildings. Daytime lockout and 11pm curfew. April–Oct. Dorms **£20.50**; doubles **£50**

EATING AND DRINKING

A Cwtch* 22 High St ☎01437 720491, ⊛cwtch restaurant.co.uk. Some of Pembrokeshire's finest dining can be found at the award-winning Cwtch* (pronounced "cutsh"), an intimate and easy-going restaurant that's all slate and wood and blackboard menus, featuring top-quality local ingredients. You'll pay £26/30 for two/three courses; booking recommended. Daily 6–9.30pm Mid-Feb to Easter & Nov–Dec Wed–Sat 6–9.30pm, Sun noon–2.30pm; Feb half term, Easter & Oct Mon–Sat 6–9.30pm, Sun noon–2.30pm; Easter–Sept daily 5–9.30pm.

Farmers Arms Goat St ☎01437 721666, ⊛farmers stdavids.co.uk. Lively and very friendly local, with a terrace overlooking the cathedral – especially enjoyable on a summer's evening. Decent pub grub also available. Easter–Sept daily 11am–midnight; rest of year Mon–Thurs 4pm–midnight, Fri 3pm–midnight, Sat & Sun 11am–midnight.

The Refectory St Davids Cathedral ☎01437 721760. The beautiful St Mary's Hall is a great spot for tea and cakes. Also serves delicious meals at moderate prices. Daily: Nov–Easter 11am–4pm; Easter–Nov 10am–5pm.

St Davids peninsula

Surrounded on three sides by inlets, coves and rocky stacks, St Davids is an easy base for some excellent walking around the headland of the same name. A mile south, the popular **Caerfai Bay** provides a sandy beach in the purple sandstone cliffs – rock which was used in the construction of the cathedral.

St Non's Bay and Porth Clais

Immediately south of St Davids (reached by Goat St), the craggy indentation of **St Non's Bay** is where St Non reputedly gave birth to St David during a tumultuous storm around 500 AD. The bay has received pilgrims for centuries, resulting in the foundation of a tiny, isolated **chapel** in the pre-Norman age; the ruins of the subsequent thirteenth-century chapel now lie in a field near the sadly dingy well and coy shrine marking the birthplace of the nation's patron saint.

Just west of St Non's, **Porth Clais** is supposedly where St David was baptized by a bishop with the unlikely name of St Elvis. This was the city's main harbour from Roman times, its remains still visible at the bottom of the turquoise creek. Today, commercial traffic has long gone, replaced by fishing boats and dinghies.

Whitesands Bay and Ramsey Island

From **St Justinians**, two miles west of St Davids, the coast path leads north over another lowly headland to the magnificent **Whitesands Bay** (Porth-mawr), a narrow arc

14

of dune-backed sand that's popular with both surfers and families alike, and is also accessible by road from St Davids. From here though, there's no further road access to the coast for some distance, giving this section of the coast path a thoroughly untamed feel, and making it perfect for wildlife-watching.

The harbour at St Justinians has a ticket hut for the boats over to **Ramsey Island**. This enchanting dual-humped plateau, less than two miles long, has been under the able stewardship of the RSPB since 1992. Birds of prey circle above the island, but it's better known for the tens of thousands of seabirds that noisily crowd the cliffs on its western side and the seals lazing sloppily about.

ARRIVAL AND DEPARTURE   RAMSEY ISLAND

Thousand Islands Expeditions **boat trips** (April–Oct daily; 📞 01437 721721, 🌐 thousandislands.co.uk; £17) allow up to six hours on Ramsey. During the springtime nesting season you actually see more from boats which circle the island but don't land: try Voyages of Discovery (daily; 📞 01437 721911, 🌐 ramseyisland.co.uk; £25).

Fishguard

From St Davids peninsula the main road runs northeast, parallel to numerous small and less-commercialized bays, to the wild and windswept **Strumble Head**, perhaps the best place in Wales for watching seabirds. This protects **FISHGUARD** (Abergwaun), an attractive, hilltop town mainly of interest as the port for the **ferries** to and from Rosslare in Ireland.

In the centre of town is the **Royal Oak Inn**, where a bizarre Franco-Irish attempt to conquer Britain in 1797 at nearby Carregwastad Point is remembered. Having landed in the wrong place and then got hopelessly drunk, the hapless forces surrendered after two days. This was supposedly triggered by the sight of a hundred local women marching towards them. Due to their stovepipe hats and red flannel shawls they mistook them for British infantry and instantly capitulated. Even if this is not true, it is undisputed that 47-year-old cobbler's wife Jemima Nicholas, the "Welsh Heroine", single-handedly captured fourteen French soldiers with nothing but a pitchfork. Her grave can be seen next to the uninspiring Victorian church, **St Mary's**, behind the pub. The fabulous **Fishguard Tapestry**, telling the story of this ramshackle invasion, hangs in the town hall across the road (Mon–Wed, Fri & Sat 9.30am–5pm, Thurs 9.30am–6.30pm; Oct–March closes 1pm on Sat; Sun school holidays & bank holiday weekends 10am–4pm; free).

ARRIVAL AND INFORMATION   FISHGUARD

By train Trains call at Fishguard & Goodwick station on Station Hill in Goodwick (where occasional buses to Fishguard stop across the road, except Sun) and terminate at Fishguard Harbour on Quay Road in Goodwick.
Destinations Cardiff (6 daily; 2hr 40min); Carmarthen (7 daily; 50min); Swansea (7 daily; 1hr 50min).
By bus Buses stop in the central Market Square, right outside Fishguard's tourist office, and on Station Hill in Goodwick, half a mile from the ferry terminal.
Destinations Cardigan (hourly; 40min); Haverfordwest (hourly; 40min); Newport, Pembrokeshire (hourly; 15min); St Davids (6–8 daily; 45min).

By ferry Stena Line ferries (📞 08705 707070, 🌐 stenaline .com) leave twice daily for Rosslare in Ireland. A taxi (📞 01348 873075, 875129, 872088) into town costs around £4.
Tourist office The main office is in the town hall on the central Market Square (Mon–Fri 9am–5pm, June–Aug also Sat 10am–4pm; 📞 01347 776636). There's a second office (daily: Easter–Oct 9.30am–5/6pm, Nov–Easter 10am–3.45pm; 📞 01348 874737) on The Parrog on the Goodwick foreshore; it's in the Ocean Lab, an education centre with an exhibition on marine life and detailed information on the coastal path.

ACCCOMMODATION

Cefn-y-Dre 📞 01348 875663, 🌐 cefnydre.co.uk. Just a mile south of town along Hamilton St, there's a relaxed and understated elegance to this lovely country house. Just three rooms, attractive grounds, tasty breakfasts, and superb home-cooked meals (£26.50; reserve in advance)

prepared by wonderful hosts. **£79**
Hamilton Lodge 21–23 Hamilton St 📞 01348 874797, 🌐 hamiltonbackpackers.co.uk. Cosy, very central and well-set-up hostel with dorms, doubles and twins, and a free light breakfast. Bedding is provided. Dorms **£17**, doubles **£45**

EATING AND DRINKING

Pepper's aka Café Celf 16 West St ☎ 01348 873867, ⟳ westwalesartscentre.com. Arty café that's great for a restful cake and espresso or a lunch platter with smoked salmon, salami or roast vegetables (£7–11). Mon–Sat 10am–10.30pm.

Royal Oak Market Square ☎ 01348 872514, ⟳ the royaloakfishguard.co.uk. Historic pub with real ales and a separate area for good pub lunches. There's also a long-established folk night on Tues – participants very welcome. Daily noon–11pm, Fri & Sat to 1.30am; food daily noon–4pm.

Ship Inn Lower Town ☎ 01348 874033. Eccentric, unmissable pub with fine ales and lots of interesting clutter all over the walls and ceiling, including black-and-white photos of the filming of *Under Milk Wood* and *Moby Dick*. Daily noon–11pm.

Newport

Newport (Trefdraeth) is an ancient and proud little town set on a gentle slope leading down to the Nevern estuary. There's little to do except stroll around, but you'd be hard pressed to find a better place to do it. The footpath that runs along the river either side of the bridge is marked as the Pilgrims' Way; follow it eastwards for a delightful riverbank stroll to Nevern, a couple of miles away. Another popular local walk is up to the craggy and magical peak of **Carn Ingli**, the Hill of Angels, behind the town.

Newport's nearest beach, the **Parrog**, is complete with sandy stretches at low tide. On the other side of the estuary is the vast dune-backed **Traeth Mawr beach**. Newport also makes a good jumping-off point for **Pentre Ifan**, a couple of miles south, with its massive, four-thousand-year-old capstone.

ARRIVAL AND INFORMATION   NEWPORT

By bus Buses stop on Bridge St in the centre of town. Destinations Cardigan (hourly; 20min); Fishguard (hourly; 15min); Haverfordwest (hourly; 1hr).

Tourist office Long St (April–Oct Mon–Sat 10am–5.30pm; Nov–March Mon, Wed & Fri 10.30am–1pm & 1.30–3.30pm, Sat 10.30am–1.30pm; ☎ 01239 820912).

ACCOMMODATION

The Globe B&B Upper St Mary St ☎ 01239 820296, ⟳ theglobebedandbreakfast.co.uk. About the cheapest around, with shared bathroom and continental breakfast included. **£73**

Morawelon The Parrog ☎ 01239 820565, ⟳ campsite -pembrokeshire.co.uk. Seaside campsite about 300 yards from town, nicely set in pleasant gardens and with its own café overlooking the beach, and coin-op showers. March–Oct. Per person **£6**

YHA Newport hostel Lower St Mary St ☎ 0845 371 9543. This classily converted school has dorms and a couple of private rooms; self-catering only. Dorms **£15**; doubles **£75**

EATING AND DRINKING

★ Cnapan East St ☎ 01239 820575, ⟳ cnapan.co.uk. Classic dinner-only restaurant with comfortable rooms, where spicy mussel chowder might be followed by guinea fowl with gooseberry and elderflower sauce. £26/32 for two/three courses. Booking essential. Wed–Mon 6.15–8.45pm (last orders) mid-March–Dec.

Golden Lion East St ☎ 01239 820321, ⟳ golden lionpembrokeshire.co.uk. Nice old pub with bare stone walls and timber beams; along with real ales, they serve a superb menu of carefully prepared pub food and fancier restaurant-style dishes, either in the bar or more formally out the back. Bar noon–midnight; food served daily noon–2pm & 6–9pm.

★ Llys Meddyg East St ☎ 01239 820008, ⟳ llys meddyg.com. You can eat in the Georgian dining room, cellar bar or partly walled kitchen garden in this lovely restaurant with rooms; exquisitely prepared dinners might include local baby crab cakes with papaya mustard then wild bass with a sweet and sour mushroom broth. Lunches are no less appealing. Cellar bar & restaurant 6.30–9pm Mon–Sat (closed Mon & Tues winter), noon–3pm & 6.30–9pm Sun (lunch only in winter); kitchen garden 10.30am–5pm & 5.30–8.45pm (summer only).

TOP 5 RESTAURANTS

Cnapan Newport. See above
Cwtch* St Davids. See p.653
Fish at 85 Cardiff. See p.630
Llys Meddyg Newport. See above
Slice Swansea. See p.637

Mid-Wales

VIEW OVER THE MARKET TOWN OF BRECON

Mid-Wales

Mid-Wales is a huge, beautiful region, crisscrossed by mountain passes, dotted with characterful little towns and never far from water – whether sparkling rivers, great lakes or the sea of the Cambrian Coast. This is the least-known part of Wales, and it's here that you'll find Welsh culture at its most natural, folded into the contours of the land as it has been for centuries. By far the most popular attraction is the Brecon Beacons National Park, stretching from the dramatic limestone country of the Black Mountain (singular) in the west through to the English border beyond the Black Mountains. The best bases are the tiny city of Brecon or the market towns of Abergavenny and Hay-on-Wye, the former a foodie paradise, the latter a must for bibliophiles.

15

North of the Beacons lie the old spa towns of Radnorshire, the most enjoyable of which are **Llanwrtyd Wells**, known throughout the land for its eccentric events, and twee **Llandrindod Wells**. The quiet countryside to the north, crossed by spectacular mountain roads such as the **Abergwesyn Pass** from Llanwrtyd, is barely populated, dotted with ancient churches and introspective villages. In the east, the border town of **Knighton** is the home of the flourishing **Offa's Dyke Path** industry. Like many country towns in Mid-Wales, beautiful **Llanidloes** has a healthy stock of old hippies among its population, contributing to a thriving arts and crafts community and a relaxed atmosphere. **Montgomeryshire** is the northern portion of Powys, similarly underpopulated and remote. Its largest town, **Welshpool**, is home to Powis Castle, one of the country's finest fortresses.

The enduringly popular **Cambrian Coast** stretches from Cardigan up to Harlech, starting off with cliff-top paths and small sandy coves which give way to wide sandy beaches around higgledy-piggledy **New Quay** and neat Georgian **Aberaeron**. The beguiling "capital" of Mid-Wales, **Aberystwyth**, is a great mix of seaside resort, university city and market town backed by the Vale of Rheidol Railway to **Devil's Bridge**. Further north, **Machynlleth** revels in beaches, mountains and the showpiece **Centre for Alternative Technology**. Beyond the great mountain massif of **Cadair Idris**, the beautiful **Mawddach Estuary** leads to Dolgellau, a base for mountain biking in **Coed-y-Brenin** and the first of the huge North Wales castles at **Harlech**.

GETTING AROUND
MID-WALES

By train Services are restricted to the Heart of Wales line from Shrewsbury to Swansea via Knighton, Llandrindod Wells, Llanwrtyd Wells and smaller stops in between; and the Cambrian line, from Shrewsbury to Machynlleth via Welshpool. At Machynlleth, the line splits, with one heading south to Aberystwyth, the other going north along the coast to Llŷn.

By bus Buses plug virtually all of the gaps not covered by train, though you'll find just a few daily services between some towns, and sometimes none at all on Sundays. One of the most useful long-distance buses is the #T4, which runs from Cardiff up through the heart of Powys, calling in at Brecon and Llandrindod Wells along the way, though there's no service on Sundays. The #X50 and #X32, which jointly cover the coast between Cardigan and Dolgellau, are useful.

BOG SNORKELLING, LLANWRTYD WELLS

Highlights

❶ Brecon Beacons National Park Trek to your heart's content among these wild, rambling moors, with dozens of thundering waterfalls. **See p.662**

❷ Abergavenny food Some of Britain's finest restaurants, along with a lip-smacking food festival. **See p.666**

❸ Llanwrtyd Wells Bizarre events galore, notably the Man versus Horse Marathon, the World Bog Snorkelling Championships and the Real Ale Wobble. **See p.669**

❹ New Quay Follow Dylan Thomas's footsteps through the salty seaside town that inspired *Under Milk Wood*. **See p.679**

❺ Aberaeron Even if you're not in town for Aberaeron's Seafood Festival, stroll around its colourful Georgian harbour lined by great places to sleep and eat. **See p.680**

❻ Aberystwyth A lively, seaside university town, steeped in Welsh culture. **See p.681**

❼ Bwlch Nant yr Arian Visit mid-afternoon to see dozens of red kites squabbling over ten kilos of beef and lamb; it's a remarkable sight. **See p.684**

❽ Harlech Castle The glorious views across to the Llŷn peninsula are as good a reason as any to visit Harlech's hulking castle. **See p.688**

HIGHLIGHTS ARE MARKED ON THE MAP ON PP.660-661

ENGLAND

Ruabon
Chirk
Oswestry

Llangollen
Llangollen Railway

Corwen

Llandrillo

BERWYN MOUNTAINS

Llanarmon Dyffryn Ceiriog

Pistyll Rhaedr

Llanrhaeadr-ym-Mochnant

Pennant Melangell

Llanfyllin

Llanwddyn

Lake Vyrnwy

A495

A483

Welshpool
Powis Castle
Welshpool & Llanfair Railway

Montgomery

Berriew

A483

A458

Llanfair-Caereinion

Gregynog Hall

Newtown

Caersws

A470

A483

Llanidloes

NORTH WALES

Dee

Conwy

Bala

Bala Lake Railway

SNOWDONIA NATIONAL PARK

Coed-y-Brenin

Blaenau Ffestiniog

Trawsfynydd

A470

RHINOG RANGE

Harlech

8

A496

Dolgellau

A470

A487

A493

Barmouth

Fairbourne

Arddudwy Beach

Castell-y-Bere

Cader Idris (2930ft)

Abergynolwyn

Corris Craft Centre

Centre for Alternative Technology

Machynlleth

Tywyn

Tal-y-llyn Railway

Aberdyfi

River Dyfi

Plynlimon (2469ft)

Dylife

Llyn Clywedog

Llangurig

A44

Ponterwyd

Bwlch Nant yr Arian

7

Rheidol

Vale of Rheidol

Borth

6

Aberystwyth

Tremadog Bay

Porthmadog

A487

Pwllheli

Abersoch

Aberdaron

Cardigan Bay

N

The Brecon Beacons National Park

The **Brecon Beacons National Park** has the lowest profile of Wales's three national parks, but it is nonetheless the destination of thousands of walkers. Rounded, spongy hills of grass and rock tumble and climb around river valleys that lie between sandstone and limestone uplands, peppered with glass-like lakes and villages that seem to have been hewn from one rock. The park straddles three Welsh counties: Carmarthenshire, Powys and Monmouthshire, covering 520 square miles. Most remote is the far western side, where the vast, open terrain of the Black Mountain is punctuated by craggy peaks and hidden upland lakes. The southern flanks bare bony limestone ribs, beneath which are the chasms of the **Dan-yr-ogof caves**. East of this wilderness, **Fforest Fawr** forms miles of tufted moorland tumbling down to a rocky terrain of rivers, deep caves and spluttering waterfalls around **Ystradfellte.** The heart of the national park comprises the **Brecon Beacons** themselves, a pair of 2900ft hills and their satellites. East of Brecon, the **Black Mountains** stretch over the English border, and offer the region's most varied scenery, from rolling upland wilderness to the gentler **Vale of Ewyas**. The Monmouthshire and Brecon Canal defines the eastern limit of the Beacons and forges a passage along the Usk Valley between them and the Black Mountains. This is where you're likely to end up staying, in towns such as the county seat of **Brecon**, the charming village of **Crickhowell**, or sprightly **Abergavenny**, nestled below the Black Mountains.

Brecon

BRECON (Aberhonddu) is a handsome county town at the northern edge of the central Beacons. The proliferation of Georgian buildings and its proximity to the hills and lakes of the national park make it a popular stopping-off place and a good base for day-walks in the well-waymarked hills to the south.

Regimental Museum

The Watton • Easter–Sept Mon–Fri 10am–5pm, Sat 10am–4pm, plus certain Sundays; Oct–March Mon–Fri 10am–5pm • £5 • ☏ 01874 613310, ⓦ rrw.org.uk

Midway along the Watton is the foreboding frontage of the South Wales Borderers' **barracks**, which is also home to its **Regimental Museum**, packed with mementos from the regiment's three-hundred-year existence. As well as an extraordinary stash of guns and medals, there's comprehensive coverage of campaigns in Burma, the Napoleonic and Boer wars, both World Wars and the ongoing mission in Afghanistan. There's even a piece of the Berlin Wall.

Brecon Cathedral

Priory Hill • Daily 8.30am–6pm • ☏ 01874 623857, ⓦ breconcathedral.org.uk

From the town centre crossroads, High Street Superior goes north, becoming The Struet, running alongside the rushing waters of the Honddu. Off to the left, a footpath climbs up to the **cathedral**, whose lofty interior, framed by a magnificent timber roof,

---

THE CENTRAL BEACONS NEAR BRECON

Popular for walking and pony trekking, the central **Brecon Beacons**, grouped around the two highest peaks in the national park, are easily accessible from Brecon, which lies just six miles to the north. The panorama fans out from the **Brecon Beacons Mountain Centre** (daily: March–June, Sept & Oct 9.30am–5pm; July & Aug 9.30am 5.30pm; Nov Feb 9.30am–4.30pm; ☏ 01874 623366, ⓦ breconbeacons.org), on a windy ridge just off the A470 turn-off at Libanus, six miles southwest of Brecon. **Pen y Fan** (2907ft) is the highest peak in the Beacons. Together with **Corn Du** (2863ft), half a mile to the west, they form the most popular ascents in the park.

CAFÉS & RESTAURANTS
Bridge Café	2
The Felin Fach Griffin	1
The Hours Café	3
Tipple & Tiffin	4

ACCOMMODATION
Beacons Guesthouse	2
The Coach House	3
Priory Mill Farm	1
YHA Llwyn-y-Celyn	4

BRECON

is graced with a few Norman features from the eleventh century, including a hulking font. More impressive is the **Cresset Stone**, a concrete boulder indented with thirty scoops in which to place oil or wax candles. The mid-sixteenth-century **Games Monument**, in the southern aisle, is made of oak and depicts a woman whose identity remains uncertain with hands clasped in prayer but whose arms and nose appear to have been unceremoniously hacked off.

ARRIVAL AND INFORMATION

By bus Buses stop above the car park on Heol Gouesnou. Destinations Abergavenny (Mon–Sat hourly; 40min–1hr); Cardiff (6 daily; 1hr 40min); Craig-y-nos/Dan-yr-ogof (7 daily; 40min); Crickhowell (Mon–Sat hourly 25–45mins); Hay-on-Wye (6 daily; 45min); Libanus (every 30–60min;

15min); Llandrindod Wells (Mon–Sat 7 daily; 1hr).
Tourist office In the car park off Lion St (Mon–Sat 9.30am–5.30pm, Sat & Sun 10am–4pm; ☎ 01874 622485, ⓦ breconbeacons.org); its vast stock of material includes a good range of walking maps.

ACCOMMODATION

Beacons Guesthouse 16 Bridge St, Llanfaes ☎ 01874 623339, ⓦ thebreconbeacons.co.uk. Converted townhouse concealing a large number of rooms (some with shared showers), all leading off a central spiral staircase. Pleasant guest lounge and a dinky cellar bar with just two tables. **£60**
The Coach House 12/13 Orchard St, Llanfaes ☎ 01874 620043, ⓦ coachhousebrecon.com. High-class and very hospitable guesthouse with rooms furnished with designer accessories. Great Welsh breakfasts, including vegetarian options. **£80**
Priory Mill Farm Hay Rd ☎ 01874 611609,

ⓦ priorymillfarm.co.uk. Lovely, low-key riverside campsite, with wooden cabins for showers and trays for log fires. It's on the northern edge of town, reached by a 10min walk along the riverbank. March–Oct. Pitches **£8**
YHA Llwyn-y-Celyn 7 miles southwest of Brecon, near Libanus ☎ 0845 371 9029, ⓦ yha.org.uk. Traditional farmhouse hostel surrounded by woodland and overlooking the River Tarell, just off the A470 and main bus route to Merthyr. Good facilities, as well as home-cooked food and Brecon Brewing ale on tap. Nov–Feb weekends only. Dorms **£15**; doubles **£48**

15

> **BRECON JAZZ FESTIVAL**
>
> Held over the second or third weekend of August, the **Brecon Jazz Festival** (ⓦbreconjazz
> .com) is one of Britain's most prestigious music gatherings, with more than thirty years under
> its belt. The line-up is invariably outstanding, with artists of the calibre of Burt Bacharach, Femi
> Kuti and Zoe Rahman playing venues as diverse as Brecon Cathedral, Christ College and the
> Market Hall. Running concurrently, the Brecon Fringe Festival (ⓦbreconfringe.co.uk) features
> alternative, predominantly local bands playing cafés, pubs and galleries.

EATING

Bridge Café 7 Bridge St ☎01874 622024, ⓦbridge cafe.co.uk. Good-looking café-bistro, by the bridge, featuring a homespun interior with oak flooring, kitchen-style tables and chairs, and fireside sofas. The menu changes monthly but expect a range of dishes like Greek-style casserole in red wine with new potatoes (£12). The only letdown is its very limited opening hours. March–Oct: Thurs–Sat 6.30–11pm, Sun 9–11am.

The Felin Fach Griffin Felin Fach, A470 3 miles northwest ☎01874 620111, ⓦeatdrinksleep.ltd.uk. High-end restaurant well worth a visit for its superb Modern Welsh cuisine; the meat is sourced locally (Bwlch venison with artichoke), the fish is delivered from Cornwall (monkfish tail with pancetta and parsley butter; £17.95), and veggies and fruit hand-picked from the kitchen garden. Daily 11.30am–11pm.

The Hours Café 15 Ship St ☎01874 622800, ⓦthe -hours.co.uk. Cheerful daytime café-cum-bookshop, with sloping floors and black timber beams, where you can enjoy warm salads and toasted sandwiches, hearty soups, cakes and a good range of Fairtrade coffees. Tues–Sat 10am–5pm.

★**Tipple & Tiffin** Theatr Brycheiniog, Canal Wharf ☎01874 611866, ⓦbrycheiniog.co.uk/tipple.html. A fetching waterside setting and easy-going atmosphere mark this place out as Brecon's most inviting restaurant; tapas-style dishes designed for sharing (deep fried cockles, crispy duck leg; £8), along with a few more substantial options chalked up on a blackboard. Tues–Sat 10am–10pm, Sun noon–4pm.

The Fforest Fawr

Covering a vast expanse west of the central Brecon Beacons, the **Fforest Fawr** (Great Forest) seems something of a misnomer for an area of largely unforested sandstone hills dropping down to a porous limestone belt in the south. The name, however, refers to its former status as a hunting area. The hills rise up to the south of the A40, west of Brecon, with the dramatic A4067 defining the western side of the range and the A470 dividing it from the central Beacons.

Ystradfellte and around

In the heart of the Brecon Beacons, a twisting mountain road crosses a bleak plateau and descends into one of Britain's classic limestone landscapes. The hamlet of **YSTRADFELLTE** is hugely popular for its walks over great pavements of bone-white rock next to cradling potholes, disappearing rivers and crashing **waterfalls**. At **Sgwd Clun Gwyn** (White Meadow Fall), the river crashes 50ft over two large, angular steps of rock before hurtling down the course for a few hundred yards to two more falls – the impressive **Sgwd Isaf Clun Gwyn** (Lower White Meadow Fall) and, around the wooded corner, the **Sgwd y Pannwr** (Fall of the Fuller). A little further along the Hepste is **Sgwd yr Eira** (Fall of Snow), whose rock below the main tumble has eroded, allowing access behind a dramatic 20ft curtain of water.

Dan-yr-ogof Showcaves

April–Oct daily 10am–3.30pm · £13.75 · ☎01639 730284, ⓦshowcaves.co.uk

Six miles of upland forest and grass-covered mountains lie between Ystradfellte and the **Dan-yr-ogof Showcaves** to the west. Discovered in 1912, they are claimed to form the largest system of subterranean caverns in northern Europe. The path leads you into the **Dan-yr-ogof** showcave, framed by stalactites and frothy limestone deposits, from where you'll be steered around a circular route of about a mile and a half. Back outside, you pass a re-created and rather downbeat Iron Age "village" to get to the **Cathedral Cave**, an impressive 150ft-long, 70ft-high cavern. Reached via a precarious path behind the tacky dinosaur park, the final viewable cavern, **Bone Cave** was inhabited by prehistoric tribes.

INFORMATION	THE FFOREST FAWR
The Waterfalls Centre Pontneddfechan, a couple of miles south of Ystradfellte (Easter–Sept daily 9.30am–5pm, closed 1–1.30pm; Oct–Easter Sat & Sun	9.30am–3pm; ☎01639 721795) can provide lots of good information on walks to the many falls.

The Black Mountains

The easternmost section of the national park centres on the **Black Mountains**, far quieter than the central belt of the Brecon Beacons and skirted by the wide valley of the River Usk to the south and the Wye to the north. The only exception to the range's unremitting sandstone is an isolated outcrop of limestone, long divorced from the southern belt, that peaks north of Crickhowell at Pen Cerrig-calch (2302ft). The Black Mountains have the feel of a landscape only partly tamed by human habitation: tiny villages, isolated churches and enchanting lanes are folded into an undulating green landscape that levels out to the south around the village of **Crickhowell**.

15

Crickhowell

Compact **CRICKHOWELL** (Crug Hywel) lies on the northern bank of the wide and shallow Usk. Apart from a grand seventeenth-century **bridge**, with thirteen arches visible from the eastern end and only twelve from the west, spawning many a local myth, there's not much to see in town. That said, it is a hugely popular destination for walkers, especially in March when the annual **Walking Festival** (ⓦcrickhowellfestival .com) takes place here; it's also the setting for the country's premier music gathering, the **Green Man Festival** (ⓦgreenman.net).

Table Mountain (1481ft) provides a spectacular northern backdrop, topped by the remains of the 2500-year-old hillfort (*crug*) of Hywel, accessed on a path past The Wern, off Llanbedr Road. Many walkers follow a route north from Table Mountain, climbing two miles up to the plateau-topped limestone hump of **Pen Cerrig-calch** (2302ft) and on to Pen Allt-mawr from where a circular route can be completed.

ARRIVAL AND INFORMATION	CRICKHOWELL
By bus Buses run from the main square at the top of the High Street. Destinations Abergavenny (Mon–Sat hourly; 20min); Brecon (Mon–Sat hourly; 25–45min).	**Tourist office** The Crickhowell Resource and Information Centre on Beaufort St (daily 10am–5pm; ☎01873 811970, ⓦcrickhowellinfo.org.uk) also has a café, internet access (£1.50/30min) and an upstairs gallery selling quality local art.

ACCOMMODATION AND EATING

Bear Hotel Beaufort St ☎01873 810408, ⓦbearhotel .co.uk. A grand old coaching inn whose architectural quirks have lent themselves to some highly idiosyncratic rooms. Those in the hotel itself possess more character, while those in the old courtyard stables are a touch more polished. **£99**

Bridge End Inn Bridge St ☎01873 810338, ⓦthe bridgeendinn.com. Comprising part of the town's former tollhouse, this is a truly old-fashioned pub with flagstone flooring, a stone fireplace and brass, copper pots hanging from the walls and ceilings, and a sweet riverside garden. Daily 11am–11.30pm.

★**Nantyffin Cider Mill** Brecon Rd ☎01873 810775, ⓦcidermill.co.uk. Housed in a great stone barn a mile or so

along the A40 towards Brecon, the old mill (with the cider press still intact) is now a tip-top restaurant where it'd be remiss not to try one of the delicious steaks (£16) straight out of the Inka (charcoal) oven. There's a serious wine list here too and a choice of ciders, while the Thursday "Pie and Pints" night is good fun. Bar daily 10.30am–11pm; food served Wed–Sun noon–3pm & 6–11pm.

★**Ty Gwyn** Brecon Rd ☎01873 811625, ⓦtyqwyn .com. Impressive eighteenth-century stone gatehouse a 5min walk north of town, offering three warm and sunny rooms, each one on the theme of a Welsh writer (Dylan, Cordell, Vaughan). Breakfast is taken in the delightful conservatory dining room. **£72**

Abergavenny

Flanking the Brecon Beacons National Park, **ABERGAVENNY** (Y Fenni), seven miles southeast of Crickhowell, is a busy and breezy market town which people flock to primarily for its outstanding cuisine – this reaches its zenith during the September **Food Festival**. The town is also a useful base for walkers bound for the local mountains: **Sugar Loaf**, **the Blorenge**, and the legendary **Skirrid Mountain** (Ysgyryd Fawr). Stretching north from town, the **Vale of Ewyas** runs along the foot of the Black Mountains, where the astounding churches at Partrishow and Cwmyoy are lost in rural isolation.

Abergavenny also makes a good base for visiting Monmouthshire's "Three Castles" (see box, p.618), set in the pastoral border country to the east.

The castle and town museum

Castle St • March–Oct Mon–Sat 11am–1pm & 2–5pm, Sun 2–5pm; Nov–Feb Mon–Sat 11am–1pm & 2–4pm • Free • ☎ 01873 854282, ⊚ abergavennymuseum.co.uk

From the train station, Monmouth Road rises gently, eventually becoming High Street, off which you'll find the fragmented remains of the medieval **castle**. Entrance is through the sturdy, though now roofless, gatehouse, to the right of which stands an extensive portion of the curtain wall. The old Victorian keep now houses the **town museum**, which displays ephemera from Abergavenny's history. Glorious views aside, the grounds are a lovely spot for a picnic.

Church of St Mary

Monk St • Daily 11am–3pm • Free • ☎ 01873 858787, ⊚ stmarys-priory.org

Abergavenny's **Church of St Mary** contains some superb detail, not least the **Jesse Tree**, one of the finest late medieval sculptures in Britain. Tombs here span the entire medieval period, including those of Sir William ap Thomas, founder of Raglan Castle, and Dr David Lewis (died 1584), the first Principal of Jesus College, as well as effigies of members of the notorious de Braose family.

Tithe Barn

Monk St • Mon–Sat 10am–4pm • Free • ☎ 01873 858787

Adjacent to the church is the splendidly restored fourteenth-century **Tithe Barn**, which in times past has variously functioned as a coach house, a theatre for travelling actors and even a disco. It's now a heritage centre, with a well-curated exhibition on the history of the town, though this is somewhat overshadowed by the **Abergavenny Tapestry**, a large, vibrant cloth stitched by more than fifty volunteers; it took four years and was completed just in time for the millennium. There's a fine café here, too.

ARRIVAL AND INFORMATION

By train The station is a 5min walk southeast of town on Station Rd.

Destinations Cardiff (every 30–60min; 45min); Hereford (every 45–60min; 25min); Newport (every 30min–60min; 30min).

By bus Buses depart from Swan Meadows bus station, at the bottom of town on Cross St.

Destinations Brecon (hourly; 40min–1hr); Cardiff (hourly; 2hr); Clydach (every 30min; 40min); Crickhowell (Mon–Sat hourly; 15min); Llanfihangel Crucorney (7 daily; 15min);

Monmouth (6 daily; 45min); Raglan (6 daily; 25min).

Tourist office The TIC is inside the Tithe Barn on Monk St (daily: April–Oct 10am–5pm; Nov–March 10am–4pm; ☎ 01873 853254, ⊚ visitabergavenny.co.uk) and nominally functions as the Brecon Beacons National Park office too.

Bike rental Hopyard Cycles in Govilon, a couple of miles west of town (☎ 01873 830219, ⊚ hopyardcycles.co.uk; mountain bikes from £15/day), can deliver bikes (for a small charge) throughout the area.

ACCOMMODATION

Angel Hotel 15 Cross St ☎ 01873 857121, ⊚ angel hotelabergavenny.com. Occupying an old coaching inn, Abergavenny's premier central hotel is a warren of corridors with a range of very classy rooms, fitted out in soft beige tones, with plush carpets, big comfy beds and large bathrooms replete with posh toiletries. **£101**

Black Sheep Backpackers 24 Station Rd ☎ 01873 859125, ⓦ blacksheepbackpackers.com. A few paces down from the station, this converted railway hotel has accommodation in six- to ten-bed dorms (with shared showers), as well as en-suite doubles. There are self-catering facilities and a laundrette across the road. Continental breakfast included. Dorms £16; doubles £60

★**Kings Arms** 29 Neville St ☎ 01873 855074, ⓦ kingsarmsabergavenny.co.uk. Limewash beams, bare, sloping wood floors and low, crooked doorways are all identifiably quirky features of this pleasing, sixteenth-century coaching inn. The pub itself combines old (stone fireplace and wonderful curving beams on the low ceiling) and new (neat modern furnishings) to smart effect. Good local beer from the Wye Valley and very creditable food in the restaurant section; for example, belly of pork with black pudding mash and spiced apple gravy (£13.75). Mon–Thurs & Sun 11am–11pm, Fri & Sat 11am–1am; food served daily noon–3pm & 6–9.30pm. Rooms £85

Pyscodlyn Farm Llanwenarth Citra, 2 miles west of town off A40 ☎ 01873 853271, ⓦ pyscodlyncaravanpark.com. Primarily a caravan site, but there is one sheltered field for campers. Good access as all Brecon or Crickhowell buses pass by. Also sells day fishing licences. Pitches £14

EATING AND DRINKING

★**The Foxhunter** Nantyderry, 7 miles southeast of town ☎ 01873 881101, ⓦ thefoxhunter.com. Modern British cuisine by chef Matt Tebbutt, served in a lovingly restored former stationmaster's house and named after a locally bred, 1952 Olympic Games gold-medal winning horse. In addition to mouthwatering offerings like duck breast with roasted black figs and honey and thyme (£22), there's a fantastic wild-food menu available (£40), or you can partake in a specially tailored foraging trip. Tues–Sat noon–3pm & 7–10pm, Sun noon–3pm.

The Hardwick Old Raglan Rd ☎ 01873 854220, ⓦ thehardwick.co.uk. Headed up by chef Stephen Terry, this fabulous-looking pub, two miles east of town, offers a choice of brilliantly simple but fantastically presented dishes such as free-range chicken breast with chargrilled sweetcorn and barbecued beans (£22). The Sunday three-course set lunch is superb value at £26. Bar daily 11am–11pm; food served daily noon–3pm & 6.30–10pm.

Miserable Cow Cibi Walk Precinct ☎ 07910 460548. There's nothing miserable about this cheery open-air café, complete with formica-covered tables and separate smoking/non smoking sections. Serves fine Fairtrade coffee alongside sweet and savoury treats. Mon–Sat 7.30am–6pm, Sun 9am–4pm.

Trading Post 14 Neville St ☎ 01873 855448, ⓦ tradingpostcatering.co.uk. The former eighteenth-century *Cow Inn* – cast your eyes up to the row of cows' heads on the front of the building – is now a sprightly coffee house and bistro, and an ideal spot for poring over one of the papers while sipping on a cappuccino or tucking into some Welsh rarebit. Mon–Sat 9am–5pm.

15

The Vale of Ewyas

The main A465 Hereford road leads six miles north out of Abergavenny to Llanfihangel Crucorney, where the B4423 diverges off to the north into the enchanting Vale of Ewyas along the banks of the Honddu River. In Llanfihangel Crucorney, the reputedly haunted **Skirrid Inn** was first mentioned in 1110 and is thus thought to be the oldest pub in Wales. It's said that some 180 people were hanged here during the seventeenth century; you can still see the beam that bears the scorch marks of the rope. It's an atmospheric spot for a drink.

Llanthony Priory

Daily 10am–4pm • Free; CADW • ⓦ cadw.wales.gov.uk

Four miles from Llanfihangel Crucorney stand the wide-open ruins of **Llanthony Priory**. The priory was founded in around 1100 by the Norman knight William de Lacy, who, it is said, was so captivated by the spiritual beauty of the site that he renounced worldly living and founded a hermitage, attracting like-minded recluses and forming Wales's first Augustinian priory. The roofless church, with its pointed transitional arches and squat tower, was constructed in the latter half of the twelfth century and retains a real sense of spirituality and peace.

Hay-on-Wye

Straddling the Anglo-Welsh border some twenty miles west of Hereford, the hilly little town of **HAY-ON-WYE** has an attractive riverside **setting** and narrow, winding streets lined with an engaging assortment of old stone houses, but is known to most people for one thing – **books**. Hay saw its first bookshop open in 1961; today it has more than thirty, many of which are highly specialized, focusing on areas like travel, poetry or murder mystery. The prestigious **Hay Festival of literature and the arts** (⊛hayfestival.com), is held over ten days at the end of May, when London's literary world decamps here en masse.

ARRIVAL AND INFORMATION
HAY-ON-WYE

By bus Buses stop on Oxford Rd, just along from the tourist office.
Destinations Brecon (6 daily; 45min); Hereford (5 daily; 1hr).
Tourist office In the craft centre on Oxford Rd (daily:

Easter–Oct 10am–1pm & 2–5pm; Nov–Easter 11am–1pm & 2–4pm; ☎01497 820144, ⊛hay-on-wye.co.uk). The useful free booklet (*Hay-on-Wye Booksellers, Printsellers & Bookbinders*) details the town's bookshops, galleries, restaurants and bars.

ACCOMMODATION

Hay has plenty of accommodation, though prices are a little higher here than in places nearby, and there are no hostels. Everywhere gets booked up months in advance for the festival.

★**Old Black Lion** Lion St ☎01497 820841, ⊛old blacklion.co.uk. Very well regarded thirteenth-century inn which has charming en-suite rooms both above the pub and in the neighbouring annexe, which are slightly more appealing. **£99**
Radnors End A 10min walk from town across the Hay Bridge on the road to Clyro ☎01497 820780, ⊛hay-on -wye.co.uk/radnorsend. Small but neat camping field in a beautiful setting overlooking Hay, with on-site showers and laundry facilities. March–Oct. Pitches **£6**
Seven Stars 11 Broad St ☎01497 820886, ⊛theseven -stars.co.uk. Former town pub near the clocktower, with

eight modestly sized but cosy rooms, some with original oak beams and window frames. There's also an indoor swimming pool and sauna. **£84**
The Start Hay Bridge ☎01497 821391, ⊛the-start .net. Neatly renovated Georgian house on the riverbank, with three rooms boasting antique furnishings and handmade quilts. The vegetable garden provides many of the ingredients for the scrummy breakfast. **£75**
★**Tinto House** 13 Broad St ☎01497 821556, ⊛tinto -house.co.uk. Charming old house with three large, sumptuous rooms, each different, and a self-contained unit in the old stable block which has splendid garden views. **£90**

EATING AND DRINKING

Blue Boar Castle St ☎01497 820884. Tasteful, wood-panelled real-ale pub centred around a gently curving bar and two stone fireplaces, with a separate dining area to one side. Daily 9am–11pm; food served 11.30am–2pm & 6–9.30pm.
The Granary Broad St ☎01497 820790. This unpretentious café-bistro offers a wide range of excellent meals, with good veggie options. Save space for the wonderful desserts and espresso. Mains £10. Daily 9am–5.30pm, school holidays until 9pm.
The Old Stables Tearooms Bear St ☎07796 484766. Barely half a dozen tables are crammed into this delightful place, with chalked-up boards offering superb Welsh produce and a fantastic array of teas and home-made tarts.

On a warm day, eat in the flower-filled yard. Tues–Fri 10.30am–3pm, Sat 10.30am–4.30pm.
Shepherd's Ice Cream 9 High Town ☎01497 821898. Popular Georgian-style café/ice-cream parlour doling out local ice cream made from sheep's milk; flavours include raspberry cheesecake and banana toffee crunch. Mon–Fri 9.30am–5.30pm, Sat 9.30am–6pm, Sun 10.30am–5.30pm.
★**Three Tuns** Broad St ☎01497 821855, ⊛three-tuns .com. Set in Hay's second-oldest building (after the castle), the ancient stonework, outdoor terrace and crackling open fires make for an atmospheric dining spot. Menu includes creations such as seared scallops with truffle cauliflower purée and fennel dressing (£15). Daily 11am–11pm.

SHOPPING

Richard Booth's Bookshop 44 Lion St ☎01497 820322, ⊛boothbooks.co.uk. Just beyond the main square, High Town, this slicked-up, three-storey emporium (despite the name, no longer owned by Booth) offers unlimited browsing potential. Superb stock of first edition, rare and antiquarian books, mostly at a price. Incorporated into the rear of the bookshop is the wonderful little Bookshop Cinema, screening

art-house movies at weekends. Bookshop Mon–Sat 9am–5.30pm, Sun 11am–5pm.
Rose's Books 14 Broad St ☎01497 8200130, ⊛stella books.com. Opposite the clocktower, Rose's Books has a wonderful stock of rare and collectable children's and illustrated books. Mon–Fri 10am–5.30pm, Sat & Sun 9.30am–5.30pm.

15

The Wells towns

The **spa towns** of Mid-Wales, strung out along the Heart of Wales rail line between Swansea and Shrewsbury, were once all obscure villages, but with the arrival of the great craze for spas in the early eighteenth century, anywhere with a decent supply of apparently healing water joined in on the act. Royalty and nobility spearheaded the fashion, but the arrival of the railways opened them to all. Today, the best of the bunch is undoubtedly the westernmost spa of **Llanwrtyd Wells**, hunkered down beneath stunning mountain scenery and renowned for its bizarre events. **Llandrindod Wells**, the most famous spa, attracted the international elite in its Victorian heyday, and has two excellent museums to enjoy. In between, the larger town of **Builth Wells** was very much the spa of the Welsh working classes and there's no real reason to stop, except in mid-July when it hosts the absorbing **Royal Welsh Show**, Britain's biggest rural jamboree.

Llanwrtyd Wells

15

Of the four spa towns, **LLANWRTYD WELLS**, twenty miles northwest of Brecon, is the most appealing. This was where the Welsh – Dyfed farmers along with Nonconformist middle classes from Glamorgan – flocked to the great eisteddfodau (festivals of Welsh music, dance and poetry) in the valley of the River Irfon; today, it's the Welsh capital of eccentric events (see box below).

In town, Dolecoed Road winds for half a mile along the river to the *Dolecoed Hotel*, built near the spa's original sulphurous spring. Although the distinctive aroma had been noted in the area for centuries, it was truly "discovered" in 1732 by the local priest, Theophilus Evans, who drank from an evil-smelling spring after seeing a rudely healthy frog pop out of it. The spring, named **Ffynnon Drewllyd** (Stinking Well), bubbles up among the dilapidated spa buildings a hundred yards behind the hotel.

ARRIVAL AND DEPARTURE   LLANWRTYD WELLS

By train The train station is a 5min walk east of town on Station Rd. Destinations Builth Wells (4 daily; 20min); Knighton (4 daily; 1hr 10min); Llandrindod Wells (4 daily; 30min); Shrewsbury (4 daily; 2hr); Swansea (4 daily; 2hr).

By bus Buses stop on the main square. Destinations include Builth Wells (5 daily; 25min).

ACCOMMODATION

★**Ardwyn House** Station Rd ☎01591 610768, ⓦardwynhouse.co.uk. Stunning turn-of-the-twentieth-century period piece with three, richly detailed en-suite rooms, including roll-top baths, cast-iron fireplaces and antique light fittings. Downstairs, guests can avail themselves of a marvellous book-lined billiards room and

---

WACKY WALES: LLANWRTYD WELLS

Belying its appearance as a sleepy kind of place, Llanwrtyd Wells has its distinctly zany moments. Although a host of events take place here throughout the year, three in particular take precedence. In mid-June, the **Man versus Horse Marathon** is a punishing 22-mile endurance test between man and beast over various types of terrain. Then, at the end of August, it's the turn of the **World Bog-Snorkelling Championships**, in which competitors must complete two lengths of a water-filled trench cut through a peat bog – the current world record, posted in 2014, is one minute twenty-two seconds. Then in November, there's the wonderfully named **Real Ale Wobble**, two days of combined mountain biking and beer drinking, an event for the somewhat less serious-minded cyclist. Visit ⓦgreen-events.co.uk for full event listings

A fourth major event takes place bi-annually (every even-numbered year); in the wake of the 2012 Olympic Games in London, organizers here decided to set up their own **World Alternative Games** (ⓦworldalternativegames.co.uk), two weeks of weird and wonderful competitions (over sixty in total) such as worm charming, belly flopping and wife carrying.

THE ABERGWESYN PASS

A lane from Llanwrtyd meets up with another road from Beulah at the riverside hamlet of **ABERGWESYN**, five miles north. From here, you can drive the quite magnificent winding thread of an ancient cattle-drovers' road – the **Abergwesyn Pass** – up the perilous **Devil's Staircase** and through dense conifer forests to miles of wide, desolate valleys where sheep graze unhurriedly. At the little bridge over the tiny Tywi River, a track heads south past an isolated, gas-lit hostel at **DOLGOCH**. Remote paths lead from the hostel through the forests and hillsides to the exquisitely isolated chapel at **Soar-y-Mynydd** and over the mountains to the next hostel at **TYNCORNEL**, five miles from Dolgoch.

15

honesty bar. **£80**

Lasswade Station Rd ☎ 01591 610515, ⓦ lasswade hotel.co.uk. A few paces down from *Ardwyn House*, this is a lovely Edwardian residence overlooking lush fields with eight tranquil, florally decorated rooms. There's a five percent discount for those arriving by train. **£75**

Stonecroft Lodge Dolecoed Rd ☎ 01591 610332, ⓦ stonecroft.co.uk. This self-catering guesthouse, adjoining the inn of the same name, looks fairly grubby from the outside, but it has a perfectly acceptable selection of triple-, quad- and six-bed rooms, though all are with shared shower facilities. There's also a lounge and fully equipped kitchen for use. Dorms **£16**

EATING AND DRINKING

★ Carlton Riverside Irfon Crescent ☎ 01591 610248, ⓦ carltonriverside.com. The food at this well-regarded place run by Mary Ann Gilchrist is traditional Welsh, prepared with supreme flair and imagination – such as slow-braised beef in Welsh ale with punchnep (root vegetables) and buttered cabbage (£15.95) and with a wine list to match. The restaurant itself has just half a dozen well-spaced, crisply laid tables offering river views. There's also a cool little cellar bar serving home-baked pizza. Mon–Sat 7–11pm; cellar bar Thurs–Sat 7–11pm.

★ Drover's Rest Riverside Restaurant The Square ☎ 01591 610264, ⓦ food-food-food.co.uk. Bric-a-brac and other accoutrements fill this warm, cottage-like restaurant, where wholesome traditional Welsh dishes are the order of the day; Brecon venison in red wine, Celtic pork tenderloin, as well as some delicious cheese-based vegetarian dishes; a three-course set menu is great value at £29.95. Cookery and art classes are also run here. Reservations essential. Tues & Thurs–Sun 10.30am–3.30pm & 7.30–10pm.

Neuadd Arms The Square ☎ 01591 610236. Lively place and home to the Heart of Wales Brewery, which currently produces seven fabulous ales (including Welsh Black, a delicious stout that you can soak up with good bar food, including some great curries). Note the memorial top hat on the exterior wall, in honour of Screaming Lord Sutch, who performed here on several occasions. Daily 11am–midnight; food served noon–2pm & 6–9.30pm.

Llandrindod Wells

Once the most chichi spa resort in Wales, **LLANDRINDOD WELLS** (Llandrindod) is a pale imitation of its former self. That said, many of its fine Victorian buildings still stand, and there are two superb museums. It was the railway that made Llandrindod, arriving in 1864 and bringing carriages full of well-to-do Victorians to the fledgling spa. The town blossomed, new hotels were built, neat parks were laid out and it came to rival many of the more fashionable spas and resorts over the border.

Radnorshire Museum

Temple St • April–Sept Tues–Fri 10am–4pm, Sat 10am–4pm; Oct–March Tues–Fri 10am–4pm, Sat 10am–1pm • £1 • ☎ 01597 824513

The small but entertaining **Radnorshire Museum** evokes the area's history with exhibits ranging from archeological finds to items from Victorian spa days. Among the pick of these is a Sheela-na-gig, a typically explicit and remarkably well-preserved carved relief of a figure displaying its vulva, which was found in the local parish church, and a log-boat dredged up from the Ifor River in 1929 and thought to date from around 1200 AD.

National Cycle Collection

Temple St • May–Oct Mon–Fri 10am–4pm; Nov–April Tues, Thurs & Fri 10am–4pm • £4 • ☎ 01597 825531, ⓦ cyclemuseum.org.uk

The **National Cycle Collection** is a nostalgic exhibition showcasing more than 280 bikes, ranging from a reproduction 1818 hobbyhorse to relatively modern folding bikes and choppers, including some contraptions that look far too uncomfortable to have been a success. The museum holds some notable machinery, not least a bike belonging to the prolific, if little-known, George Nightingale, the first man to ride 25 miles in under an hour (in 1938). There are also bikes belonging to another serial record-breaking time trialist, Eileen Sheridan, and 1992 Olympic gold medallist Chris Boardman.

Rock Park

Quietly tucked away on the southwest side of town, and accessed via several paths, **Rock Park** is a delightful spot for a leisurely ramble. Part Victorian arboretum (including Douglas fir, Japanese red cedar), part native woodland, it's also the site of numerous mineral-rich springs, such as the Chalybeate spring, consisting of an ornate pink marble fountain and drinking basin. At the heart of the park, the once-lavish **spa pump room** is now, somewhat more prosaically, a conference centre, though the iron-and-glass-framed pavilion, connecting the pump room and old treatment centre, still resonates. From here, a path leads to "**Lovers' Leap**", a Victorian fake cliff overlooking the river.

15

ARRIVAL AND INFORMATION — LLANDRINDOD WELLS

By train The station is a 5min walk east of town on Station Rd

Destinations Knighton (4 daily; 40min); Llanwrtyd Wells (4 daily; 30min); Shrewsbury (4 daily; 1hr 40min); Swansea (4 daily; 2hr 30min).

By bus Buses pull in by the train station.

Destinations Aberystwyth (1 daily; 1hr 40min); Brecon (7

daily Mon–Sat; 1hr); Builth Wells (hourly; 20min); Disserth (16 daily; 45min); New Radnor (8 daily Mon–Sat; 30min); Rhayader (7 daily; 25min).

Tourist office In front of the Radnorshire Museum on Temple St (Easter–Oct Mon–Fri 10am–4pm, Sat 10am–1pm; Nov–Easter Mon–Sat 10am–1pm; ☎ 01597 822600, ⊛ llandrindod.co.uk).

ACCOMMODATION AND EATING

The Cottage Spa Rd ☎ 01597 825435, ⊛ thecottage bandb.co.uk. Handsome Edwardian property with seven differently configured rooms, all laden with period-style furnishings. No TVs in the rooms but guests are welcome to use the lounge. **£65**

Greylands High St ☎ 01597 822253, ⊛ greylands questhouse.co.uk. Tall Victorian red-brick house in the town centre, near the station, with seven comfortable, good-value rooms. **£60**

Herb Garden Café 5 Spa Centre ☎ 01597 823082.

Fresh, organic salads and platters, juicy house burgers and a stack of sweet treats at this attractive, friendly diner; the big windows and squashy sofas make it a great place to kick back. Mon–Sat 9.30am–5pm.

Llanerch Inn Llanerch Lane ☎ 01597 822234. Opposite the train station, this sixteenth-century hostelry is central Llandrindod's only pub, and predates most of the surrounding town by quite some time. Enjoy a pint in front of the stone fireplace or a well-cooked, classic pub meal. Daily 7am–11pm.

Elan Valley

From the workaday market town of **RHAYADER**, ten miles west of Llandrindod Wells, the B4518 heads southwest four miles to the gorgeous **Elan Valley**. It was here that the poet Shelley spent his honeymoon in buildings now submerged by the waters of the valley's reservoirs, a nine-mile-long string of four lakes built between 1892 and 1903 to supply water to the rapidly growing industrial city of Birmingham, 75 miles east.

Frequent guided **walks** head off from the valley's visitor centre, and a road tucks in along the first reservoir, Caban Coch, to the **Garreg Ddu** viaduct, where it winds along for four spectacular miles to the vast, rather chilling 1952 dam on **Claerwen Reservoir**. More remote and less popular than the Elan lakes, Claerwen is a good base for a serious **walk** from the far end of the dam across eight or so harsh but beautiful miles to the monastery of Strata Florida. Alternatively, you can follow the path that skirts around the northern shore of Claerwen to the lonely **Teifi Pools**, glacial lakes from which the River Teifi springs.

Back at the Garreg Ddu viaduct, a more popular road continues north along the long, glassy finger of Garreg Ddu reservoir, before doubling back on itself just below the awesome **Pen-y-garreg** dam and reservoir; if the dam is overflowing, the vast wall of foaming water is mesmerizing. At the top of Pen-y-garreg lake, it's possible to drive over the final dam on the system, at **Craig Goch**. Thanks to its gracious curve, elegant Edwardian arches and neat little green cupola, this is the most photographed of all the dams.

Gigrin Farm Red Kite Feeding Station

A quarter-mile south of Rhayader, just off the A470 • Daily: summer 1–5pm; winter 1–4pm • £5 • ☎ 01597 810243, ⓦ gigrin.co.uk

Gigrin Farm is a working sheep farm that's become an official RSPB **red kite feeding station**. Every day at 2pm (3pm in summer), they put out meat scraps to attract hundreds of these beautiful birds that were once close to extinction in the UK. It's a breathtaking spectacle, with the huge animals, swooping down over a well-placed hide, displaying their aerial agility and magnificent wingspan.

15

ARRIVAL AND INFORMATION   ELAN VALLEY

There is no **public transport** to the Elan Valley, so you will require a car or a bike, or you can hike.

Tourist office Just below the dam of the first reservoir, Caban Coch, the Elan Valley visitor centre (daily 10am–4.30pm; ☎ 01597 810898, ⓦ elanvalley.org.uk) has useful leaflets on walks around the valley, a permanent exhibition about the history and ecology of the area, a tearoom and bike hire (£5/1hr, £20/day).

Bike rental Clive Powell Mountain Bikes, West St, Rhayader (daily 9am–5.30pm; £6/hr, £24/day; ☎ 01597 811343, ⓦ clivepowell-mtb.co.uk). They also do servicing and repairs.

ACCOMMODATION AND EATING

Crown Inn North St, Rhayader ☎ 01597 811099. Most agreeable of the town's several boozers, with lots of small, dark wooden tables gathered around a large stone fireplace, and Brains beer. Daily noon–11pm.

Elan Valley Hotel Elan ☎ 01597 810448, ⓦ elan valleyhotel.co.uk. Delightful, privately run country house on the Rhayader side of Elan village, which offers eleven subtly decorated, individually styled rooms, good food in its well-regarded restaurant and a lively bar. **£85**

Ty Morgans East St ☎ 01597 811666, ⓦ tymorgans .com. Superb building housing nine effortlessly cool rooms, most of which still feature their original red or grey bare brick walls and oak-beamed ceilings. The buzzy bar/bistro offers a mouthwatering burger menu in addition to more sophisticated dishes (pan-seared duck breast with braised red cabbage; £12.99). The bistro leads through to the bustling *Strand* coffee house and deli. Bistro daily 8am–10pm; coffee house daily 8am–5pm. **£80**

Wyeside Immediately north of town off the A470 ☎ 01597 810183, ⓦ wyesidecamping.co.uk. On the banks of the Wye, this is a smart site with separate camping and caravan areas and clean, modern amenities. March–Oct. Pitches **£17**

Montgomeryshire

The northern part of Powys is made up of the old county of **Montgomeryshire** (Maldwyn), an area of enormously varying landscapes and few inhabitants. The solid little town of **Llanidloes** is a base for ageing hippies on the banks of the infant River Severn (Afon Hafren). To the east, the muted old county town of **Montgomery**, with its fine Georgian architecture, perches amid gentle, green hills above the border and Offa's Dyke. Further north, **Welshpool**, the only major settlement, is packed in above the wide flood plain of the Severn; with its good pubs and hotels it's a fair base for Montgomeryshire's one unmissable sight, the sumptuous **Powis Castle** and its exquisite terraced gardens.

CLOCKWISE FROM TOP HARLECH CASTLE (P.688); ABERAERON (P.680); SHEEP IN THE BRECON BEACONS (P.662) >

Llanidloes

The small market town of **LLANIDLOES**, twelve miles north of Rhayader, has developed from a rural village to a weaving town, and is now an arty, alternative-lifestyle kind of place. One of Mid-Wales's prettiest towns, it centres on four main streets, which all meet at the market hall – the main thoroughfare is Great Oak Street, a wide, handsome road framed by well-proportioned, two- and three-storey buildings variously accommodating shops, restaurants and tenements.

The Old Market Hall and exhibition centre

Great Oak St • Late May–Sept Tues–Sun 11am–4pm • Free • ☎ 01686 412388

At the junction of the town's four main streets is the superb black-and-white **Old Market Hall**, built on timber stilts around 1600, allowing the market – now long since moved – to take place on the cobbles underneath. The only surviving timber-framed market hall in Wales, it's also known as the Booth Hall, and remained a popular trading place until the early twentieth century. At one time or another it has also functioned as a law court, a meeting place for the Quakers, a flannel store, and the local Working Men's Institute. Today it houses an **exhibition centre** with a fascinating display on other similarly timbered buildings in Llanidloes and further afield; you can pick up a free trail leaflet outlining the finest.

Town hall and museum

Great Oak St • Museum Tues, Thurs & Fri 11am–1pm & 2–4pm, Sat 11am–2pm • £1 • ☎ 01686 413777

From the market hall, the broad Great Oak Street heads west to the **town hall**, originally built as a temperance hotel to challenge the boozy *Trewythen Arms* opposite. A plaque on the closed hotel commemorates Llanidloes as an unlikely place of industrial and political unrest, when, in April 1839, Chartists stormed the hotel, dragging out and beating up special constables who had been despatched to the town in a futile attempt to suppress political activism among the town's flannel-weavers. In the town hall, you'll also find the eclectic **museum**, where the diverting collection of old local prints and mementos pales beside the stuffed two-headed lamb, born locally in 1914.

ARRIVAL AND INFORMATION   LLANIDLOES

By bus China St curves down to the car park where all buses arrive and depart.

Destinations Aberystwyth (3 daily; 1hr); Newtown (7 daily; 30min); Ponterwyd (3 daily; 40min); Shrewsbury (6 daily; 2hr); Welshpool (6 daily; 1hr 10min).

Tourist information There's no tourist office in town, but the Llani Leisure shop, at 16 Long Bridge St (daily 9am–5.30pm, closed Sun Oct–March; ☎ 01686 414893, ⓦ llanidloes.com), stocks lots of literature on the town and surrounds.

ACCOMMODATION AND EATING

Dol-llys Farm Trefeglwys Rd ☎ 01686 412694, ⓦ dolllyscaravancampsite.co.uk. Large site around a 15min walk north of town, where you can choose from a pitch on the level field near the facilities, or a more secluded spot down by the river, where campfires are permitted. Easter–Oct. Per person **£7**

★**Lloyds Hotel** Cambrian Place ☎ 01686 412284, ⓦ lloydshotel.co.uk. Superbly run, idiosyncratic hotel with seven beautifully conceived rooms, each awash with colour and character. The personal touch is evident everywhere, right down to the wall-mounted sepia prints and watercolours. *Lloyds* is also the place to come for a totally unique dining experience; pre-dinner drinks are served at 7.30pm followed by a surprise four-course menu (£35), and ending with teas and coffees – the food could

be absolutely anything so contact the hosts in advance if there is anything you don't eat. Advance booking is essential. Sittings vary from week to week. **£86**

Red Lion 8 Long Bridge St ☎ 01686 412270. The most agreeable of the town's pubs; the main lounge bar has comfy leather seating huddled around an imposing stone fireplace festooned with brass, while the noisier other room is principally for bar games. Daily 11am–midnight.

Unicorn Hotel 4 Long Bridge St ☎ 01686 411171. A small hotel of considerable charm and quality, hosting six crisp, generous and impeccably clean rooms; there's a substantial breakfast to look forward to as well. The fabulous daytime bistro/evening restaurant offers some deliciously sauced dishes, such as pan-fried sea bass with garlic and saffron (£16). Tues–Sat 10.30am–2.30pm & 6.30–10pm. **£70**

Montgomery

Tiny **MONTGOMERY** (Trefaldwyn), around twenty miles northeast of Llanidloes, is Montgomeryshire at its most anglicized. From the mound of its **castle**, situated just on the Welsh side of Offa's Dyke, there are wonderful views over the lofty church tower and the handsome Georgian streets, notably the impressively symmetrical main road – appropriately named Broad Street – which swoops up to the little red-brick **town hall**, crowned by a pert clocktower. Montgomery is within striking distance of one of the best-preserved sections of **Offa's Dyke** (see box below), traced by the long-distance footpath that runs on either side of the B4386.

Old Bell Museum

Arthur St • April–Sept Wed–Fri & Sun 1.30–5pm (daily in Aug), Sat 10.30am–5pm • £1 • ☎ 01686 668313, ⊚ oldbellmuseum.org.uk

The **Old Bell Museum**, formerly a temperance house and butcher's, is now an unusually enjoyable local history collection. Crammed into every nook and cranny of this marvellous little building are artefacts from excavations, scale models of local castles, mementos from Montgomery civic life and displays on the region's various trades, with due prominence given to the likes of clogmakers, clockmakers, carpenters and tanners.

Church of St Nicholas

The Rectory, Lion Bank • Daily 8am–6pm • Free

The rebuilt tower of Montgomery's parish **Church of St Nicholas** dominates the snug proportions of the buildings around it. Largely thirteenth-century, the highlights of its spacious interior include a 1600 monument to local landowner Sir Richard Herbert and his wife. Their eight children – who included prominent Elizabethan poet George Herbert – have been carved in beatific kneeling positions behind them.

ARRIVAL AND DEPARTURE

MONTGOMERY

By bus Buses pick up and drop off in front of the Town Hall at the bottom of Broad St.

Destinations Newtown (8 daily; 30min); Shrewsbury (4 daily; 50min); Welshpool (8 daily; 25min).

Tourist information There's no tourist office in Montgomery, but the grey telephone box, located on a grassy triangle as you enter the town on the Welshpool road, has leaflets and information on local events.

ACCOMMODATION AND EATING

Brynwylfa 4 Bishops Castle St ☎ 01686 668555, ⊚ brynwylfa.co.uk. Off the main square, there are just two rooms in this beautiful townhouse, one with exposed brick walls, the other with a gorgeous roll-top bath. **£70**

Castle Kitchen 8 Broad St ☎ 01686 668795. Sociable café/deli with an open kitchen doling out both savoury (soups, quiches and tarts) and sweet (cakes and pastries) delights. The busy downstairs area extends to a

vine-covered terrace, and upstairs is all wonky flooring and stripey walls. Mon–Sat 9.30am–4.30pm, Sun 11am–4pm.

★**The Checkers** Broad St ☎ 01686 669822, ⊚ the checkersmontgomery.co.uk. The five wonderfully stylish rooms in this erstwhile coaching inn are characterized by higgledy-piggledy beams and low ceilings and doorways. The outstanding, Michelin-starred restaurant is an inviting setting

---

OFFA'S DYKE

Offa's Dyke has provided a potent symbol of Welsh–English antipathy ever since it was created in the eighth century as a demarcation line by King Offa of Mercia, ruler of central England. George Borrow, in his classic book *Wild Wales*, notes that, once, "It was customary for the English to cut off the ears of every Welshman who was found to the east of the dyke, and for the Welsh to hang every Englishman whom they found to the west of it".

The earthwork – up to 20ft high and 60ft wide – made use of natural boundaries like rivers in its run north to south, and is best seen in the sections near **Knighton**. Today's England–Wales border crosses the dyke many times, although the basic boundary has changed little since Offa's day. A glorious, 177-mile **long-distance footpath** runs the length of the dyke from Prestatyn in the north to Chepstow, and is one of the most rewarding walks in Britain.

15

for the classically French seasonal menus featuring the likes of *assiette* of guinea fowl with puy lentils and Monbazillac sauce (£21). Booking essential. Restaurant Tues–Thurs 6–10pm, Fri & Sat noon–2pm & 6–10pm. **£125**

Ivy House Church Bank ☎01686 668746, ⦿ivy housetearooms.com. Sweet, flowery tearoom serving veggie snacks, teas and cakes, as well as food to take away. Daily 9am–5pm.

Welshpool

Eastern Montgomeryshire's chief town of **WELSHPOOL** (Y Trallwng), seven miles north of Montgomery, was formerly known as just Pool, its prefix added in 1835 to distinguish it from the English seaside town of Poole in Dorset. Lying in the valley of the River Severn, just three miles from the English border, it's an attractive place, with fine Tudor, Georgian and Victorian buildings in the centre, and the fabulous **Powis Castle** nearby.

Powysland Museum

Canal Wharf • Mon, Tues, Thurs & Fri 11am–1pm & 2–5pm; June–Aug also Sat & Sun 10am–1pm & 2–5pm; Oct–April also Sat 11am–2pm • Free • ☎ 01938 554656

A humpback bridge over the **Montgomery Canal** hides the canal wharf and a wharfside warehouse that has been carefully restored as the **Powysland Museum**. The impressive local history collection includes archeological nuggets such as those from an old local woodhenge, and displays medieval remains from the now-obliterated local Cistercian abbey of Strata Marcella. There's also a nostalgic look at the Welshpool & Llanfair Light Railway.

Welshpool & Llanfair Light Railway

Raven Square • Generally 2–4 trains on operating days: April to early July & Sept Tues–Thurs, Sat & Sun; mid-July to Aug daily; Oct holidays & weekends only • £13 return • ☎ 01938 810441, ⦿ wllr.org.uk

Broad Street changes name five times as it rises up the hill towards the tiny Raven Square station of the **Welshpool & Llanfair Light Railway**. The eight-mile narrow-gauge rail line was open to passengers for less than thirty years prior to its closure in 1931. Now, scaled-down engines once more chuff their way along to the peaceful little village of **Llanfair Caereinion**, a good base for daytime walks.

Powis Castle

A mile from Welshpool up Park Lane • Daily: March & Oct castle 12.30–4pm, gardens 11am–4pm; April–Sept castle 12.30–5pm, gardens 10am–6pm; Nov & Dec castle noon–4pm, gardens 11am–4pm • Castle and gardens £13, gardens only £9.60; NT • ☎ 01938 551944

In a land of ruined castles, the sheer scale and beauty of **Powis Castle** is quite staggering. On the site of an earlier Norman fort, the castle was started in the reign of Edward I by the Gwenwynwyn family; in 1587, Sir Edward Herbert bought the castle and began to transform it into the Elizabethan palace that survives today.

The sumptuous period rooms are impressive, from the vast and kitsch frescoes by Lanscroon above the balustraded staircase to the mahogany bed, brass and enamel toilets and decorative wall hangings of the state bedroom. Many rooms throughout the castle were remodelled in the Jacobean style in the early 1900s, hence the proliferation of oak panelling and elaborate plasterwork ceilings. The former ballroom houses the **Clive Museum** – named after the diplomat Robert Clive (aka Clive of India on account of his political and military deeds in the country during the mid-eighteenth century), and his son Edward, who married into the family in 1784; it's a remarkable collection of diaries, notes, letters, paintings, tapestries, weapons and jewels.

The **gardens**, designed by Welsh architect William Winde, are spectacular. Dropping down from the castle in four huge, stepped terraces, the design has barely changed since the seventeenth century, with a charming orangery and trim topiary.

By train The station is at the bottom of Severn St, behind the neo-Gothic turrets of the old Victorian station.
Destinations Aberystwyth (8 daily; 1hr 30min); Birmingham (8 daily; 1hr 25min); Machynlleth (8 daily; 1hr); Newtown (8 daily; 15min); Pwllheli (2 daily; 3hr 30min); Shrewsbury (8 daily; 25min).
By bus Buses use the Old Station on Severn Rd.
Destinations Llanidloes (6 daily; 1hr 20min); Llanfyllin (4

daily Mon–Sat; 30min); Llanymynech (5 daily; 30min); Montgomery (7 daily; 25min); Oswestry (4 daily; 45min); Shrewsbury (6 daily; 45min).
Tourist office In the Vicarage Gardens car park (Mon–Sat 9.30am–5pm, Sun 10am–4pm; ☎01938 552043, ⓦwelshpool.org). It's one of the few tourist offices in the region, with stacks of information.

Bistro 7 7 Hall St ☎01938 552879, ⓦbistroseven .co.uk. By some distance the best place to eat in Welshpool. The menu – chalked up above the bar – is noticeable for its strong flavours, like roast loin of cod in a leek cider sauce, and paprika and garlic pork chops with a chorizo hash (£11.50). The fun interior has vintage ads dispersed around the walls. Mon–Sat 11am–10pm.
The Raven Inn Raven Square ☎01938 553070. The perky *Raven* has a great reputation for its menu, featuring carnivorous treats such as steak and pepper grilled kebabs, and home-made burgers (£12). Tues–Sun noon–11pm.

Royal Oak The Cross ☎01938 552217. Traditional Georgian coaching inn with a range of spruce rooms, which come in two categories; the standard rooms are fine, but the "contemporary" options are marginally more polished. **£89**
Trefnant Hall Farm Four miles southwest of Welshpool, beyond Powis Castle ☎01686 640262, ⓦtrefnanthall.co.uk. You'll need your own transport to get to this isolated Georgian farmhouse, whose three florally decorated rooms have delightful views of green sloping fields. Guests are free to use the lounge with its gorgeous fireplace. **£60**

15

The Cambrian Coast

Cardigan Bay (Bae Ceredigion) takes a huge bite out of the west Wales coast, leaving behind the Pembrokeshire peninsula in the south and the Llŷn in the north. Between them lies the **Cambrian Coast**, a loosely defined mountain-backed strip periodically split by tumbling rivers, which stretches from Cardigan up to Harlech. Large sand-fringed sections are peppered with low-key coastal resorts, peopled in the summer by families from the English Midlands.

The southern Ceredigion coast is broken by some spirited little ports, all soaked in a relaxed, upbeat and firmly Welsh culture: the old county town of **Cardigan**; higgledy-piggledy **New Quay**; and pretty Georgian **Aberaeron**. Ceredigion's main town is ebullient **Aberystwyth**, a great base for the waterfalls and woods of the **Vale of Rheidol**.

To the north, the flat river plain and rolling hills of the **Dyfi Valley** lay justifiable claim to being one of the greenest corners of Europe. Their focal point is the genial town of **Machynlleth**, a candidate for the Welsh capital in the 1950s and site of Owain Glyndŵr's embryonic fifteenth-century Welsh parliament. Machynlleth looks up at one of Wales's most inspirational mountains, **Cadair Idris** (2930ft), incised by the Talyllyn Valley (with its toy railway) and the delightful Dysynni Valley. On its northern flank, the beautiful **Mawddach Estuary** snakes its way seaward from grey-stone **Dolgellau**, springboard for the mountain biking and forest pursuits at **Coed-y-Brenin**. The coast begins to feel more like North Wales at hilltop fortress of **Harlech** where the castle overlooks the dunes and the Llŷn.

Cardigan and around

An ancient former port of **CARDIGAN** (Aberteifi) was founded by the Norman lord Roger de Montgomery in 1093 around a castle, which is currently undergoing extensive renovation work. From the castle, Bridge Street sweeps up to the turreted oddity of the **Guildhall**, through which you access the town's **covered market**, a typically eclectic mix of fresh food, local crafts and secondhand stalls. Cardigan sits at the lowest bridging point of the **River Teifi**, one of Wales's most eulogized rivers, for its rich spawn of fresh fish, its meandering rural charm and the coracles that have been a regular feature since pre-Roman times.

Welsh Wildlife Centre

Daily: mid-Feb to March, Nov & Dec 10am–4pm; April–Oct 10am–5pm • Free, parking £3 • ☎ 01239 621600, ⓦ welshwildlife.org • You can drive from Cardigan (a very roundabout route of about 4 miles) but the best approach is to walk (or cycle) the mile from Cardigan's river bridge along the bed of an old railway

An elegant, modern timber-and-glass structure in the centre of the Teifi Marshes, the **Welsh Wildlife Centre** is home to informative displays and an airy café with expansive views over the reserve, plus an adventure playground to keep kids entertained. You can easily spend half a day here exploring the four themed trails, the shortest of which is an easy ten-minute walk around the meadow, and the longest a 45-minute trail through the wetlands. There are also seven observation hides (including an otter hide) dotted around the reserve, with binocular hire available. This area is best explored, however, on **kayak** or **canoe trips** run by Cardigan Bay Active (see below).

Cilgerran Castle

Cilgerran, a couple of miles up the Teifi River from Cardigan • Daily: April–Oct 10am–5pm; Nov–March 10am–4pm • April–Oct £3.20; Nov–March free; NT • ☎ 01239 621339, ⓦ nationaltrust.org.uk

The attractive village of **CILGERRAN** clusters behind the bulk of its **castle**, on a high wooded bluff above the river. This is the site of an attack in 1109 that culminated in the abduction of Nest (the "Welsh Helen of Troy") by a love-struck Prince Owain of Powys. Her husband, Gerald of Pembroke, escaped the attack by slithering down a toilet waste chute through the castle walls. The two massive drum towers still dominate the castle, and the outer walls are traced by vertiginously high walkways. The outer ward is a good example of the keepless castle that evolved in the thirteenth century.

Tresaith

The best destination on the lovely south Ceredigion coast is tiny **TRESAITH**, eight miles northeast of Cardigan, which staggers down impossibly narrow lanes to a delightful beach and the *Ship Inn*. A few yards around the rocks to the right, a refreshing small waterfall cascades right onto the beach.

Llangrannog

Four miles north of Tresaith, **LLANGRANOG** comes wedged between bracken and gorse-beaten hills, the streets winding to the tiny seafront. The beach can become horribly congested in midsummer, when it's better to follow the cliff path to **Cilborth Beach**, and on to the glorious National Trust-owned headland, **Ynys Lochtyn**.

ARRIVAL AND INFORMATION

CARDIGAN AND AROUND

By bus Buses to Cardigan stop on Finch Square. Destinations Aberaeron (hourly; 1hr); Aberystwyth (hourly; 1hr 45min); Cenarth (hourly; 15min); Cilgerran (5 daily; 15min); Llangrannog (2 daily; 15min); New Quay (hourly; 50min); Tresaith (2 daily; 10min).

Tourist office The Cardigan tourist office is in Theatr Mwldan, Bath House Rd (July & Aug Mon–Sat 10am–5pm, Sun noon–5pm; Sept–June Mon–Sat 10am–5pm; ☎ 01239 613230, ⓦ visitcardigan.com).

ACTIVITIES

Canoeing and kayaking Cardigan Bay Active, whose main office is down on the quay (☎ 01239 612133, ⓦ cardiganbayactive.co.uk), but who also have a centre at the Teifi Marshes (☎ 01239 613961), runs gentle, guided canoeing trips along the Teifi (£35), and more adventurous kayaking trips (£40) bumping over a few rapids.

ACCOMMODATION

★**Caemorgan Mansion** Caemorgan Rd, one mile northeast of town just off the A487 ☎ 01239 613297, ⓦ caemorgan.com. An outstanding level of comfort and hospitality awaits at this marvellous guesthouse, whose five rooms have been appointed to the highest order, and include, among other things, luxury Egyptian cotton linen, underfloor heating, and smart drinks stations with fresh milk; and you won't find better cooked Welsh breakfasts anywhere. **£120**

Ffynnon Fendigaid Rhydlewis, 3 miles south of Llangrannog ☎01239 851361, ⊛ffynnonf.co.uk. Eclectically decorated rural B&B in six acres of semi-wild grounds – badgers have been spotted. Walkers are welcome (pick-ups possible) and the owners do a great breakfast. **£75**

Llety Caravan Park Tresaith ☎01239 810354, ⊛lletycaravanpark.co.uk. Amid the static caravans there's a wonderful (if significantly sloping) cliff-top field for tents and tourers with a pretty footpath that descends straight to the beach. Good toilets and showers. Pitches **£16**

Llety Teifi Pendre ☎01239 615566, ⊛lletyteifi -guesthouse.co.uk. A raspberry-pink boutique guesthouse with ten contemporary rooms in a Victorian townhouse with its own restaurant/bar. Breakfast is taken in the conservatory. **£75**

YHA Poppit Sands 4 miles northwest of Cardigan ☎0845 371 9037, ⊛yha.org.uk. Remote hostel on the northern end of the Pembrokeshire Coast Path, with great views. The #407 bus stops within half a mile. March–Oct. Camping per person **£5.50**; dorms **£18**; doubles **£45**

EATING AND DRINKING

Ferry Inn St Dogmaels, just over a mile west of Cardigan ☎01239 615172, ⊛ferry inn.com. A great spot with loads of seating beside the Teifi, great beer and range of tasty meals in hearty portions at moderate prices (mains from £11). Daily noon–11.30pm.

Fforest Café Cambrian Quay ☎01239 615286. The main reason to visit this easy-going waterside café is to sample one of the wood-fired pizzas (£7) under the ingeniously conceived pizza tipi – and there's live music on Saturday evenings too. June–Sept Tues–Sat 10am–9.30pm.

Glasshouse Café Welsh Wildlife Centre ☎01239 621212. With 360-degree views of the Teifi Marshes through its all-glass surrounds, this restful café is a great spot to tuck into a Welsh cheese ploughman's or some Homity Pie (£7.75), perhaps followed by a slice of polenta lemon cake. Daily 10am–5pm.

New Quay and around

NEW QUAY (Cei Newydd) lays claim to being the original Llareggub in Dylan Thomas's *Under Milk Wood*. Certainly, it has the little tumbling streets, prim Victorian terraces, cobbled stone harbour and air of dreamy isolation that Thomas evoked in his play. Although there is a singular lack of excitement in town, it's a pleasant base for good beaches, dolphin-spotting and walks along the rocky promontory of **New Quay Head**, where the invigorating coast path steers along the top of aptly named **Bird Rock**.

Cardigan Bay Marine Wildlife Centre

April–Oct daily 9am–5pm · Donation requested · ☎01545 560032, ⊛cbmwc.org

Tucked away down the slipway above New Quay's beach, the **Cardigan Bay Marine Wildlife Centre** has excellent interactive and interpretative displays on the dolphins, seals and seabirds of Cardigan Bay. They also organize (weather permitting) daily whale-dolphin-watching boat trips (see box below).

ARRIVAL AND INFORMATION

By bus Buses stop at the top of Church St. Destinations Aberaeron (hourly; 20min); Aberystwyth (hourly; 1hr); Cardigan (hourly; 50min).

Tourist office On the corner of Church St and Wellington Place (April–Oct Mon–Sat 10am–5pm; ☎01545 560865, ⊛discoverceredigion.co.uk).

DOLPHIN-SPOTTING

One of only two pods in Britain, the Cambrian Coast's **bottlenose dolphins** are one of New Quay's major attractions, and can often be seen frolicking by the harbour wall, particularly when the tide is full and the weather calm. A mile-wide strip of the coastal waters forms the Ceredigion Marine Heritage Coast, in summer plied by boat trips geared around sightings. The best trips are those run by **Dolphin Survey Boat Trips** (part of the CBMWC; April–Oct daily; ☎01545 560032, ⊛dolphinsurveyboattrips.co.uk; £12 for 1hr, or £18 for 2hr). Your fee goes towards marine mammal research, partly done by the on-board ranger.

ACCOMMODATION AND EATING

The Black Lion Glanmor Terrace ☎01545 561144, ⓦ blacklionnewquay.co.uk. Dylan Thomas's favourite New Quay watering hole has been smartened up considerably, with nine rooms (five with superlative sea views) characterized by high ceilings, sash windows and stripy, boldly coloured curtains. **£70**

Hungry Trout 2 South John St ☎01545 560680, ⓦ thehungrytrout.co.uk. A couple of delightful rooms, both with sea views above New Quay's finest seafood restaurant, where you might try crayfish tails with avocado salad, and poached sea trout in a white wine parsley cream (£15). Outside seating for those summer evenings. Food served daily 8am–10pm. **£85**

The Lime Crab South John St ☎01545 561400. Eye-catching, lime-coloured fish and chip shop that offers a slightly more refined take on your average chippie, with the likes of scallops, salt and pepper squid, and mackerel goujons, all for around £7 each. Daily 11.30am–8pm.

Seahorse Inn Margaret St ☎01545 560736. This fine, traditional local, a world away from the holiday bustle down the street, is little more than one room with exposed stonework, fake beams, pool table and a limited range of good ales. Known to Dylan Thomas as the *Commercial*, it was the model for the *Sailor's Arms* in *Under Milk Wood*. Daily 11am–11.30pm.

15

Aberaeron

ABERAERON, seven miles northeast of New Quay, comes as something of a surprise. This little nugget of Georgian architecture was built by the Reverend Alban Gwynne, who spent his wife's inheritance dredging the Aeron Estuary and constructing a planned town around it as a new port for Mid-Wales. The colourful terraces of quoin-edged buildings around **Alban Square** and along **Quay Parade** are undeniably pretty, though the moneyed weekenders from Cardiff (and even London) are more interested in the excellent array of places to stay as well as the good restaurants. Aberaeron's beach is unappealing, so head out along the coast path or just amble around the streets and waterfront and graze in its cafés and pubs.

Llanerchaeron

Three miles east of Aberaeron along the A482 **House & gardens** April–Oct daily 10.30am–5.30pm; reduced hours in winter • £7.30; NT • ⓦ nationaltrust.org.uk **Parkland** All year dawn–dusk • Free; NT • ☎01545 570200

Aberaeron's one essential sight, **Llanerchaeron**, was once an integrated smallholding typical of this region. Today the estate boasts exquisite kitchen gardens and a pristine, Nash-designed main house. The original, mostly Edwardian set-piece rooms only hint at the fact that this was someone's home little more than two decades ago. This is much more apparent in the servants' quarters and the serviced courtyard which acted as laundry, dairy, salting room and home brewery.

ARRIVAL AND INFORMATION   ABERAERON

By bus The main bus stop is on the north side of Alban Square, from where it's a walk across the road down towards the harbour area.

Destinations Aberystwyth (every 30min; 40min); Cardigan (hourly; 1hr); Carmarthen (hourly; 1hr 30min);

New Quay (hourly; 20min).

Tourist office Down by the harbour at 3 Pen Cei (July–Sept daily 10am–5pm; Oct–June Mon–Sat 10am–5pm; ☎01545 570602, ⓦ discoverceredigion.co.uk).

ACCOMMODATION AND EATING

Cadwgan 10 Market St ☎01545 570149. Unpretentious local that's like walking into someone's living room: someone who serves a rotating roster of real ales and a few bar snacks, that is. Daily 11am–10pm or later.

★ **Harbourmaster Hotel** 1 Pen Cei ☎01545 570755, ⓦ harbour-master.com. Wonderful hotel with ultramodern rooms all with crisp white linen softened by Welsh wool throws. The restaurant (£25 for two courses) serves the likes of Cardigan Bay lobster with Thai butter and

Asian slaw, or you might plump for some salt and pepper squid with chilli jam in the bistro, which also serves breakfast until 11.45am. Bistro daily 8am–10pm; restaurant daily noon–2.30pm & 6.30–9pm. **£135**

The Monachty Market St ☎01545 570389, ⓦ monach tyaberaeron.co.uk. A reasonable budget option in a town full of otherwise pricey establishments, the seven light-filled rooms here come with big dollops of colour, and are well-insulated from the noise of the pub below. **£60**

Naturally Scrumptious 18 Market St ☎01545 574733, ⓦnaturallyscrumptious.co.uk. Excellent deli groaning with Welsh cheese, pies, posh sausages and panini. The cakes are best eaten with a coffee or one of their fine teas in the hot-pink-painted café to the rear. Mon–Sat 10am–4.30pm.

Aberystwyth

The liveliest seaside resort in Wales, **ABERYSTWYTH** is an essential stop. With two long, gentle bays curving around between rocky heads, its position is hard to beat, and being rooted in all aspects of Welsh culture, it is possibly the most enjoyable and relaxed place to gain an insight into the national psyche. As the capital of sparsely populated Mid-Wales, and with one of the most prestigious university colleges in the country, it offers plenty of things to do, and has a nice array of Victorian and Edwardian seaside trappings. Politics here are firmly radical Welsh — in a country that still struggles with its inherent conservatism, Aberystwyth is a blast of fresh air.

Constitution Hill and the Cliff Railway

Cliff Railway April–June, Sept & Oct daily 10am–5pm; July & Aug daily 10am–6pm; Nov–March Wed–Sun 10.30am–4pm • £4 return • ☎ 01970 617642, ⓦ aberystwythcliffrailway.co.uk **Camera obscura** April–Oct daily 11am–5pm • £1

The 430ft-high **Constitution Hill** (Y Graig Glais) rises sharply from the rocky beach at the long Promenade's northern end. It's accessible on foot, though if you don't fancy the invigorating but stiff walk up, you can take the clanking 1896 **Cliff Railway**, which

15

ABERYSTWYTH

■ **ENTERTAINMENT**
Aberystwyth Arts Centre — 2
Côr Meibion — 4
Drwm — 3

■ **PUB**
Ship and Castle — 1

■ **ACCOMMODATION**
Glan-y-mor Leisure Park — 3
Gwesty Cymru — 2
Maes-y-Môr — 1
'Ti Hafod — 4

● **CAFÉS & RESTAURANTS**
Agnelli's — 4
Gwesty Cymru — 1
Treehouse — 3
Ultracomida — 2

CARDIGAN BAY

▼ Tanybwlch & Pen Dinas (0.5 miles)   ▼ Cardigan (40 miles)

creeps up the crooked tracks at scarcely more than walking pace from the grand terminus building at the top of Queen's Road, behind the Promenade. On a clear day, the views of Cardigan Bay are fantastic.

At the top of Constitution Hill you'll find a café, picnic area, telescopes and an octagonal **camera obscura**, a device popular in the pre-TV era using a mirror and hefty lens to project close-up and long-shot views over the town, the surrounding mountains and bays. The existing structure was built in 1985 on the ground plan of the Victorian original, but with its scale expanded to make it the largest of its type in the world.

The seafront

Ceredigion Museum Terrace Rd · Mon–Sat: Easter–Oct 10am–5pm; Nov–Easter noon–4.30pm · Free · ☎ 01970 633088, ⓦ ceredigion.gov.uk

From the bottom of Constitution Hill, the **Promenade** – officially Marine Terrace – arcs away to the south, past ornate benches decorated with snakes, a continuous wall of hotels and guesthouses, a prim bandstand and a shingle beach. The atmospheric **Ceredigion Museum** is housed over three floors in the ornate Edwardian Coliseum music hall, which last functioned as a cinema in 1977. Mementos of the building as a theatre and cinema give a sense of place to an otherwise wonderfully disparate collection, the most fascinating section of which charts the seafaring exploits in the Bay, where, during the course of the eighteenth and nineteenth centuries, over a thousand ships were built.

Marine Terrace continues past the spindly **pier** to the dazzling, John Nash-designed **Old College**, all turrets, friezes and mosaics. Originally a villa, it was converted into a hotel to soak up the anticipated masses arriving on the new railway. When the venture failed, the building was sold to the fledgling university.

National Library of Wales

Penglais Rd · Mon–Fri 9.30am–6pm, Sat 9.30–5pm · Free; 1hr guided tours Mon 11am & Wed 2.15pm · ☎ 01970 632800, ⓦ llgc.org.uk · Bus #03 (every 20min, Sat & Sun hourly) from the bus station

In the lively university area, east of town, the massive white-stone Edwardian **National Library of Wales** possesses fine manuscripts including the oldest extant Welsh text, the twelfth-century *Black Book of Carmarthen*, and the earliest manuscript of *The Mabinogion*. Occasionally these form part of the typically excellent temporary exhibitions. Displays from the library's permanent collection of books, manuscripts and papers include the **World of the Book**, which looks at the history of the written word and publishing in Wales.

Aberystwyth Arts Centre

University campus, off Penglais Rd · ☎ 01970 623232, ⓦ aberystwythartscentre.co.uk

The excellent **Aberystwyth Arts Centre**, a quarter of a mile uphill from the National Library, is a curious mix of 1960s brutalism and postmodern elegance. You can take in the various temporary art and ceramics exhibitions, browse designer crafts and bookshops, catch a movie or simply have a drink in the **café**, which affords sublime views over the town and bay.

ARRIVAL AND INFORMATION   ABERYSTWYTH

By train Vale of Rheidol and mainline trains (to Machynlleth: 10 daily; 30min) use the same station on Alexandra Rd, a 10min walk from the seafront.

By bus The main bus station is adjacent to the train station on Alexandra Rd.

Destinations Aberaeron (every 30min; 40min); Cardigan

(hourly; 1hr 45min); Machynlleth (hourly; 40min); New Quay (hourly; 1hr).

Tourist office Just off the seafront on Terrace Rd (July & Aug daily 10am–5pm; Sept–June Mon–Sat 10am–5pm; ☎ 01970 612125).

ACCOMMODATION

Glan-y-mor Leisure Park Clarach Bay, 3 miles north · ☎ 01970 828900, ⓦ sunbourne.co.uk. On the other side

of Constitution Hill, with on-site caravans and tent pitches, plus a superb range of leisure facilities including (for a fee) a heated indoor pool and gym. Pitches **£20**

★ **Gwesty Cymru** 19 Marine Terrace ☎ 01970 6122252, ⓦ gwestycymru.com. This classy guesthouse offers eight colour-themed, artfully designed rooms (four with sea view), each with handcrafted oak furnishings inlaid with slate, crisp white cotton sheets, and applestone-tiled bathrooms. The hotel's accomplished slate-floored restaurant offers an exciting, thoroughly modern Welsh menu featuring the likes of gingerbread-crusted rack of lamb with buttered leeks in Welsh cider sauce (£18.75), and blueberry and Brecon Gin Bakewell. Mon–Sat noon–

2.30pm & 6–9pm, Sun noon–2.30pm. **£100**

Maes-y-Môr 25 Bath St ☎ 01970 639270, ⓦ maesymor .co.uk. Brightly painted and very central hostel-cum-guesthouse with nine rooms (seven twins, a double and a family room), though bathrooms are shared; there's a kitchen for use by guests, as well as laundry facilities. Breakfast not included. **£50**

Yr Hafod 1 South Marine Terrace ☎ 01970 617579, ⓦ yrhafod.co.uk. Good-value seafront accommodation, with spacious, well-maintained and tastefully decorated rooms (some en-suite and several with sea views). **£70**

EATING AND DRINKING

★ **Agnelli's** 3 Bridge St ☎ 07969 959466. You'll find the best espresso for miles around at this warm and welcoming Italian-run deli/café. Hot drinks go down a treat with a slice of Sicilian cannoli with vanilla; there's more substantial fare too, such as grilled Tuscan sausages with pancetta (£8), and baked aubergines in a parmesan crust. Mon & Tues 10am–7pm, Wed–Fri till 8pm, Sat 9am–6pm.

Ship and Castle Corner of Vulcan and High sts ☎ 01970 612334. Much smarter inside than out, this nicely refurbished pub offers a pool table, a great jukebox and takes considerable pride in having the best selection of real ales in town. Daily 2pm–midnight.

Treehouse 14 Baker St ☎ 01970 615791, ⓦ tree housewales.co.uk. Upbeat café situated above a bustling

little organic shop. While the lunchtime menu is largely of a vegetarian bent, there is usually one meat-based special each day, and there are gluten-free options too (mains £7.50); it's no less enjoyable a spot for coffee and cake, which are all home-made. Mon–Fri 10am–5pm, Sat 9am–5pm.

Ultracomida 31 Pier St ☎ 01970 630686, ⓦ ultra comida.co.uk. Spain comes to Aber in this fabulous deli, its walls lined with Iberian wines, meats and olives, alongside Welsh cheeses and all manner of other goodies. Meanwhile, you can sample tapas, like chorizo in Welsh cider, or salt cod salad (£2.50–3.50 each), in the casual restaurant/bar through to the rear. Deli Mon–Sat 10am–6pm, Sun noon–5pm; restaurant Mon 10am–5pm, Tues–Sat 10am–9pm, Sun noon–4pm.

ENTERTAINMENT

Aberystwyth Arts Centre The University, Penglais ☎ 01970 623232, ⓦ aberystwythartscentre.co.uk. The town's main venue for art-house cinema, touring theatre, classes, events and wide-ranging temporary exhibitions.

Côr Meibion Aberystwyth ☎ 01970 202980, ⓦ aber

choir.co.uk. Visitors are welcome to attend rehearsals of the Male Voice Choir, which take place at the Aberystwyth Rugby Club on Plascrug Avenue (Thurs 7–8.30pm).

Drwm National Library, Penglais ☎ 01970 632800, ⓦ drwm.llgc.org.uk. Hip centre for film, lectures and concerts.

The Vale of Rheidol

Inland from Aberystwyth, the River Rheidol winds its way up to a secluded, wooded valley, where old industrial workings have sometimes moulded themselves into the contours, rising up past waterfalls and hamlets to **Devil's Bridge**. The latter is best accessed by narrow-gauge railway; otherwise you need your own transport.

Vale of Rheidol Railway

April–Oct 2–4 trains most days • £18 return • ☎ 01970 625819, ⓦ rheidolrailway.co.uk

Steam trains on the narrow-gauge **Vale of Rheidol Railway** wheeze their way along steep hillsides from the Aber terminus to Devil's Bridge. It was built in 1902, ostensibly for the valley's lead mines but with a canny eye on its tourist potential as well, and has run ever since. The trip takes one hour each way, and is most enjoyable from the comfortable first-class observation carriage (£2.50 extra each way) or the open-sided "summer car".

Devil's Bridge

Twelve miles east of Aberystwyth, folk legend, picturesque scenery and travellers' lore combine at **DEVIL'S BRIDGE** (Pontarfynach), a tiny settlement built solely for the growing visitor trade of the last few hundred years.

The **bridge** spanning the chasm of the churning River Mynach is actually three stacked bridges – the eleventh-century original, a stone arch from 1753 and the modern road bridge. Enter the turnstile (£1) upstream of the bridge and head down slippery steps to the deep cleft for a remarkable view of the **Punch Bowl**, where the water pounds and hurtles through the gap crowned by the bridges.

Mynach Falls

Easter–Oct daily 9.45am–5.30pm • £3.75; outside these times plus Nov–Easter, pay £2 in the turnstile

Across the road from the Punch Bowl the trails around the crashing **Mynach Falls** offer even more dramatic sights as the path tumbles down into the valley below the bridges. The scenery here is magnificent: sharp, wooded slopes rise away from the frothing river and distant mountain peaks surface on the horizon.

Bwlch Nant yr Arian

A44, 9 miles east of Aberystwyth • Visitor centre daily: Easter–Sept 10am–5pm; Oct–Easter generally 10.30am to dusk • Free; parking £1.50 • ☎ 01970 890453, ⓦ forestry.gov.uk/bwlchnantyrarian • Buses #47 and #525 from Aberystwyth stop right outside the entrance.

Bwlch Nant yr Arian forest centre is famous for its red kites, easy walks and varied mountain biking. From the **visitor centre**, which has a decent café with a lovely deck, three well-marked walking trails (30min, 1hr & 2hr) head out into the evergreen forest and among the abandoned lead-mining detritus. The easiest and shortest trail loops around a lake past the kite hide, a superb spot for watching the daily red kite feeding (3pm, 2pm in winter) when 10kg of beef and lamb lure up to two hundred kites. The woods also offer top-class **mountain biking**, with three dedicated trails: two red (9km and 16km) and one black, the latter some 35km long and taking around four to five hours to complete; pick up a bike trail map from the shop, though there are no rentals here.

Machynlleth and around

Eighteen miles northeast of Aberystwyth is **MACHYNLLETH** (pronounced "ma-hun-cthleth"), a bustling little place with a great vibe, as well as being the undisputed centre of all things "New Age", thanks in large part to the nearby **Centre for Alternative Technology**. The wide main street, **Heol Maengwyn**, is busiest on Wednesdays, when a lively market springs up; **Heol Penrallt** intersects this at the fussy clocktower.

Owain Glyndŵr Centre

Heol Maengwyn • March–Dec daily 11am–3pm (closed Sun & Mon during term-time) • £2.50 • ☎ 01654 702932, ⓦ canolfanglyndwr.org

The **Owain Glyndŵr Centre**, in the partly fifteenth-century **Parliament House**, charts the course of Owain Glyndŵr's life, his military campaigns, his downfall, and the 1404 parliament in the town, when he controlled almost all of what is now known as Wales and even negotiated international recognition of the sovereign state (see box opposite).

Museum of Modern Art Wales

Heol Penrallt, towards the station • Mon–Sat 10am–4pm • Free • ☎ 01654 703355, ⓦ momawales.org.uk

The **Museum of Modern Art Wales**, housed in a beautifully serene old chapel, hosts an ongoing programme of temporary exhibitions. It also has a peaceful, arty **café**, and hosts films, theatre, comedy and concerts, along with the **Gŵyl Machynlleth festival**, held in August, which combines classical and some folk music with theatre and debate.

Centre for Alternative Technology

A487, 3 miles north of Machynlleth • Daily: Easter–Oct 10am–5pm • £8.50 summer, £1 off for walkers, cyclists and bus users, 50 percent off for train arrivals • ☎ 01654 705950, ⓦ cat.org.uk • Bus #34 (Mon–Sat hourly, Sun 4) from Machynlleth

After the oil crisis of 1974, seven acres of a once-derelict slate quarry were turned into the **Centre for Alternative Technology** (**CAT**), an almost entirely sustainable community.

OWAIN GLYNDŴR, WELSH HERO

Owain Glyndŵr has remained a potent figurehead of Welsh nationalism since he rose up against the occupying English in the early fifteenth century. He was born into an aristocratic family, and studied English in London, where he became a distinguished soldier of the English king. When he returned to Wales to take up his claim as Prince of Wales, he became the focus of a rebellion born of discontent with the English rulers.

Glyndŵr garnered four thousand supporters and attacked Ruthin, Denbigh, Rhuddlan, Flint and Oswestry, before finally encountering English resistance at Welshpool. In a vain attempt to break the spirit of the rebellion, England's Henry IV drew up severely punitive laws, even outlawing Welsh-language bards and singers. Even so, by the end of 1403, Glyndŵr controlled most of Wales. In 1404, he was crowned king of a free Wales and assembled a parliament at Machynlleth, where he drew up mutual recognition treaties with France and Spain. Glyndŵr made plans to carve up England and Wales into three as part of an alliance against the English king, but started to lose ground before eventually being forced into hiding (where he died). The anti-Welsh laws remained in place until the coronation of Henry VII, who had Welsh origins, in 1485, and Wales was subsequently subsumed into English custom and law.

At one stage, eighty percent of the power was generated from wind, sun and water, but this is no back to the land hippy commune. Much of the on site technology was developed and built here, though with the rise of eco-consciousness the emphasis has shifted more towards promoting its application in urban situations. CAT's water-balanced **cliff railway** (Easter–Oct) whisks visitors 200ft up from the car park to the beautiful main site, sensitively landscaped using local slate and wood, and you can easily spend half a day sauntering around. There's plenty for kids, a good wholefood restaurant and an excellent shop.

Corris Mine Explorers

Corris Craft Centre, A487, 6 miles north of Machynlleth • Tours all year on demand, book ahead • 1hr Taster £11, 2hr Explorer £22, 4hr Expedition £42 • ☎ 01654 761244, ⱳ corrismineexplorers.co.uk

Corris Mine Explorers take adventure enthusiasts – kitted out in climbing harnesses and helmets – deep into a cool, dark, disused slate mine that has been barely touched since it closed down in 1970. Ancient tallow candles are stuck to the walls, hand drills lie scattered along the passageways and winch flywheels still spin at the slightest touch. Adventurous parties might be clipped into safety wires in order to sidle along the steeply shelving walls of a vast slate cavern, while others might just want to hear fascinating stories about mining life. Wear something warm.

ARRIVAL AND DEPARTURE

MACHYNLLETH

By train The station is a 5min walk up Heol Penrallt from the town's central clocktower.

Destinations Aberdyfi (8 daily; 20min); Aberystwyth (9 daily; 30min); Harlech (8 daily; 1hr 20min); Porthmadog (8 daily; 1hr 50min).

By bus Buses stop close to the town's central clocktower, and many also call at the train station.

Destinations Aberdyfi (8 daily; 20min); Aberystwyth (hourly; 45min); Corris (hourly; 15min); Dolgellau (mostly hourly; 30min).

ACCOMMODATION AND EATING

Mach Indie Hostel Off Heol Powys ☎ 07788 747074, ⱳ machhostel.uk. Easy-going, walker- and cyclist-friendly hostel in the heart of town with a mix of dorms and family rooms, as well as camping in their grassy yard; there's also a self-catering kitchen, drying room, bike storage shed and bike wash facility. Dorms **£17.50**, pitches **£5**

Maenllwyd Newtown Rd ☎ 01654 702928, ⱳ maenllwyd.co.uk. Comfortable eight-room B&B in a former manse, one of which is a good-sized family room; there's also a large garden plus off-street parking **£65**

Quarry Café Heol Maengwyn ☎ 01654 702624. This popular, CAT-run veggie café is like stepping back into the 1980s; it does cheesy vegetable bakes, wholesome salads and the "Big Mach" burger (with lentil patty and soya mayo (£7.95). Mon–Fri 9am–4pm, Sat 10am–3pm.

15

Wynnstay Arms Heol Maengwyn ☎01654 702941, ⓦwynnstay-hotel.com. Some rooms in this former coaching inn have heavy beams, creaky floors and a four-poster, others are relatively modern. While the classic slate-floored restaurant itself is justifiably popular (loin of venison with red cabbage and root vegetable sauce; £16.95), it's the superb pizzeria in an adjoining building to the rear that most people come here for. The bar is a fine place for a beer. Bar daily 11am–11pm; restaurant daily noon–2pm & 6.30–9pm; pizzeria Tues–Sat 4.30–9.30pm. **£90**

★**Ynyshir Hall** A487, 6 miles southwest beside the Ynys-hir Nature Reserve ☎01654 781209, ⓦynyshir hall.co.uk. Sublime country-house hotel in expansive manicured grounds. The ten rooms, each named after a famous artist, are as opulent as they come. Its superb restaurant, meanwhile, serves up Modern British dishes using seafood from the Dyfi Estuary, river fish and local game, as well as ingredients plucked from the kitchen garden and surrounding woods; the five-course à la carte lunch menu (£29.50) is great value, or, alternatively, pop over for the full afternoon tea (£19.50). Daily noon–2pm, 3–5pm & 7–10pm. **£205**

Aberdyfi and around

The proud maritime heritage of **ABERDYFI** (Aberdovey) has largely been replaced by its reincarnation as a well-heeled resort. With its south-facing aspect across the Dyfi estuary, it's a lovely base for exploring the Talyllyn and Dysynni valleys to the north. There's not much in the way of activities – though you can swim at Cemetery Beach, about a mile and a half north.

ARRIVAL AND INFORMATION

ABERDYFI

By train Aberdyfi is served by two train stations: the request-only Penhelig, half a mile east (the most convenient for the centre of town); and Aberdyfi, half a mile west of the tourist office.
Destinations Machynlleth (9 daily; 20min); Porthmadog (8 daily; 1hr 30min); Tywyn (8 daily; 15min).

By bus The #28 & #X29 stop close to the TIC.
Destinations Machynlleth (8 daily; 20min); Tywyn (8 daily; 10min).
Tourist office Wharf Gardens (Easter–Oct daily 9.30am–5pm; ☎01654 767321, ⓦaberdovey.org.uk.

ACCOMMODATION AND EATING

Britannia Inn 13 Seaview Terrace ☎01654 767426, ⓦbritannia-aberdovey.co.uk. There is usually a lively atmosphere at this town centre pub, especially when the sun comes out and everyone piles onto the deck for the sunset with a pint of real ale. Meals are a significant cut above the usual pub standard and might include Aberdyfi crab (£12.95). Mon–Wed 11am–midnight, Thurs–Sat 11am–1am, Sun noon–midnight.

Llety Bodfor 1 Bodfor Terrace ☎01654 767475, ⓦlletybodfor.co.uk. The fairly typical frontage of this Aberdyfi townhouse does little to suggest that within lies the town's swankiest accommodation; three stylish rooms, each on its own floor and all with sea views. The guest lounge, meanwhile, is equipped with a piano, games, DVDs and a stack of old vinyl. Breakfast not included. **£125**

Talyllyn Railway

Station Rd, Tywyn, 4 miles north of Aberdyfi • April–Oct 2–7 trains daily, plus some winter weekends • £14.50 unlimited one-day travel • ☎01654 710472, ⓦtalyllyn.co.uk

Experience the lower Talyllyn Valley aboard the cute 27-inch gauge **Talyllyn Railway**, the inspiration for Thomas the Tank Engine. The railway tootles seven miles inland from Tywyn through the delightful wooded valley to the old slate quarries at Nant Gwernol. From 1866 to 1946, the rail line hauled slate to Tywyn Wharf station. Five years after the quarry's closure, rail enthusiasts took over the running of services, making this the world's first volunteer-run railway. The round trip takes just over two hours, but you can get on and off as frequently as the schedule allows, taking in some fine broadleaf forest walks (best at Dolgoch Falls station), or the small village of **Abergynolwyn**.

The Dysynni Valley

The **Dysynni Valley** has more sights than the Talyllyn Valley, but limited public transport. A mile and a half northwest of Abergynolwyn, a side road cuts northeast to the hamlet of **Llanfihangel-y-Pennant** where the church contains a fabulous three-dimensional patchwork map of the Dysynni Valley. Nearby, visit the scant, moody ruins of **Castell-y-Bere** (free access; CADW), a fortress built by Llywelyn the Great in 1221 to protect the mountain passes. Three miles seaward stands the impressive **Craig y Deryn** (Birds' Rock), a 760ft-high cliff where breeding cormorants have remained loyal to the spot despite being left landlocked by the receding sea.

Dolgellau and around

The handsome former county town of **DOLGELLAU** still maintains an air of unhurried importance, never more so than when all the area's farmers pile into town for market. With the lofty crags of **Cadair Idris** framing the grey squares and streets, Dolgellau feels as Welsh as it is possible to be.

Coed-y-Brenin

A470, 7 miles north of Dolgellau • **Visitor Centre** April–Oct daily 9.30am–5pm; Nov–March Mon–Fri 9.30am–4.30pm, Sat & Sun 9am–5pm • Parking £5 all day • ☎ 01341 440747, ⓦ forestry.gov.uk/coedybrenin

For years, mountain bikers from around Britain and beyond have been flocking to Coed-y-Brenin for some of Wales's finest downhill runs. With the addition of dedicated forest running and walking trails, orienteering and Geocaching courses and a kids' play area, it has developed into one of the most popular spots in southern Snowdonia. At the visitor centre you can rent bikes (from £25 a day), buy a pack of trail maps (£2.50; or download free from the website), take a shower (£1) and recover in the very decent café.

15

ARRIVAL AND INFORMATION

DOLGELLAU

By bus Buses pull into Eldon Square. Most northbound services head inland past Coed-y-Brenin.
Destinations Bala (8 daily; 35min); Machynlleth (mostly hourly; 30min); Porthmadog (6 daily; 50min).
Tourist office Eldon Square (daily 9.30am–12.30pm &

1–5pm; ☎ 01341 422888, ⓦ discoverdolgellau.com).
Bike rental Dolgellau Cycles, Smithfield St (Easter–Oct daily 9.30am–5pm; ☎ 01341 423332, ⓦ dolgellaucycles .co.uk); rent bikes suitable for the Mawddach Trail (£13 half-day, £20 full day) and also does repairs and servicing.

ACCOMMODATION

Ffynnon Love Lane ☎ 01341 421 774, ⓦ ffynnon townhouse.com. Six impeccable rooms in this large house, variously furnished with mahogany beds, slipper baths and French chandeliers, but all with separate sitting areas and great views. Rates include afternoon tea on arrival and daily newspapers, and there's an honesty bar in the lounge. Two-night minimum stay at weekends. **£150**
George III Hotel A493, Penmaenpool, 2 miles west of Dolgellau ☎ 01341 422525, ⓦ georgethethird.co.uk.

Handsome seventeenth-century hotel at the head of the Mawddach Estuary (bus #28), with six rooms in the main hotel building itself, and five smartly updated ground-level rooms in the Lodge, the former train station buildings. This is also a superb spot for a pub meal overlooking the Mawddach Estuary or a sunset drink in the dark-wood bar. Daily 11am–10.30pm. **£100**
★**Graig Wen** A493, 5 miles west of Dolgellau near Arthog ☎ 01341 250482, ⓦ graigwen.co.uk. Access is steep but the Mawddach Estuary views make it all

---

WALKS AROUND DOLGELLAU

There are some great **walks** and beautiful cycle trails around Dolgellau. Here are a couple of the best; the Dolgellau tourist office (see above) has details of many more.

Precipice Walk (3–4 miles; 2hr; negligible ascent). Easy-going loop with great views to the 1000ft ramparts of Cadair Idris and along the Mawddach Estuary – best in late afternoon or early morning sun.
Cadair Idris: Pony Path (9 miles; 4–5hr; 2800ft ascent). If the weather is fine, don't miss this classic and

enjoyable ascent of Cadair Idris. Early views to the craggy flanks of the massif are tremendous, but they disappear as you climb steeply to the col, where you turn left on a rocky path to the summit shelter on Penygadair (2930ft).

worthwhile at this wonderfully tranquil campsite with B&B. There's camping in both the upper and lower (car-free) fields, the latter offering a wilder camping experience with compost toilets and campfires. Per person **£7**

★**Y Meirionnydd** Smithfield Square ☎01341 422554,

⊛themeirionnydd.com. This solid stone Georgian townhouse has been refashioned as a chic five-roomed hotel with light tones and blond woods offset by feature cushions and curtains; the retro Roberts radios are a great addition too. **£85**

EATING AND DRINKING

Dylanwad Da 2 Smithfield St ☎01341 422870, ⊛dylanwad.co.uk. Part wine bar, part café, this charmingly run establishment is a great place to visit any time of day, be it for a glass of Rioja with some cheese, or a cup of coffee and a slice of cake. Tues–Sat 10am–4pm plus Fri & Sat eve 7–9pm.

Mawddach A496, 2 miles northwest ☎01341 421752, ⊛mawddach.com. Dark and slate-floored downstairs, airy with bare boards and exposed beams upstairs, this contemporary restaurant occupies a converted barn with views of Cadair Idris. The menu, meanwhile, comprises

simply prepared and beautifully cooked dishes such as Welsh black beef and red wine with leek and potato pie and star anise-glazed carrots (£15.50). Wed–Sat noon–2.30pm & 6.30–9.30pm; Sun noon–2.30pm.

★**Siop Coffi T.H.** Glyndŵr St. This large, perennially busy café was once the town's ironmongers, as the old fixtures and fittings testify: a long, raised wooden table where folk tap away on laptops (free wi-fi), and the former glassed-in office, which is now a snug. Freshly made baguettes and panini, sumptuous cakes and freshly roasted coffee. Mon–Sat 9am–5pm, Sun 10am–4pm.

Harlech

Charming **HARLECH**, twenty miles northwest of Dolgellau, is one of the highlights of the Cambrian Coast, with its time-worn castle dramatically clinging to its rocky outcrop and the town cloaking the ridge behind, commanding one of Wales's finest views over Cardigan Bay to the Llŷn.

Harlech Castle

March–June, Sept & Oct daily 9.30am–5pm; July & Aug daily 9.30am–6pm; Nov–Feb Mon–Sat 10am–4pm, Sun 11am–4pm • £4.25; CADW • ☎01766 780552, ⊛cadw.wales.gov.uk

Harlech's substantially complete **castle** sits on its 200ft-high bluff, a site chosen by Edward I for one more link in his magnificent chain of fortresses. Begun in 1285, it was built of a hard Cambrian rock, known as Harlech grit, hewn from the moat. Harlech withstood a siege in 1295, but was taken by Owain Glyndŵr in 1404. The young Henry VII withstood a seven-year siege at the hands of the Yorkists until 1468, when the castle was again taken. It fell into ruin, but was put back into service for Charles I during the Civil War; in March 1647, it was the last Royalist castle to fall. The first defensive line comprised the three successive pairs of gates and portcullises built between the two massive half-round towers of the **gatehouse**, where an **exhibition** now outlines the castle's history. Much of the castle's outermost ring has been destroyed, leaving only the 12ft-thick curtain walls rising up 40ft to the exposed **battlements**. Only the towering gatehouse prevents you from walking the full circuit.

ARRIVAL AND INFORMATION HARLECH

By train The train station is on the A496 below the castle. Destinations Barmouth (8 daily; 25min); Machynlleth (8 daily; 1hr 20min); Porthmadog (8 daily; 20min).

By bus Buses generally call both at the train station and at the southern end of High St.

Destinations Barmouth (hourly; 30min); Blaenau Ffestiniog (3 daily; 35min).

Tourist office The TIC (Easter–Oct daily 9.30am–12.30pm & 1–5.30pm; ☎01766 780658) is on the High St.

ACCOMMODATION AND EATING

★**Castle Cottage** Pen Llech ☎01766 780479, ⊛castlecottageharlech.co.uk. Established "restaurant with rooms" with a contemporary yet cosily informal feel. The seven rooms are natural-toned and very well

appointed, many with massive weathered beams and slate floors. In the gorgeous restaurant, meanwhile, you can choose from either a two- (£35) or three-course (£40) menu, for which you get canapés followed by the likes of

15

lobster and prawn soup with Cognac, and roasted porchetta with Dauphinoise potatoes and Calvados jus. Daily 7–10pm. **£130**

Cemlyn Tea Shop Stryd Fawr ☎01766 780425, ⊛cemlynteashop.co.uk. Upmarket café serving the best loose-leaf teas and espresso coffees around, plus home-made gluten- and dairy-free cakes, and afternoon tea (£6). If you can, grab a table on the sunny terrace where you can soak up the marvellous coastal views. Mid-March to Dec Wed–Sun 10am–5pm.

Pen-y-Garth Old Llanfair Rd ☎01766 781352, ⊛pen-y-garth.co.uk. High-standard B&B in a former YHA with three, mostly all-white rooms, each with a view of either the castle or coast. Cyclists, walkers and vegetarians are particularly welcome – they can also do packed lunches. **£70**

Shell Island ☎01341 241453, ⊛shellisland.co.uk. Massive 300-acre campsite with heaps of beachside sites. Campers must pitch tents at least 60ft from each other (unless agreed otherwise), guaranteeing relative solitude amid spectacular scenery, with simply stunning sunsets. No walk-ins; you must have a vehicle. March–Oct. Per person **£7.50**

15

North Wales

CAERNARFON

North Wales

The A55 motorway may mean the North Wales coast is very accessible, but this hasn't tamed the wilder aspects of this stunningly beautiful area. Without doubt, Snowdonia is the crowning glory of the region. A tightly packed bundle of soaring cliff-faces, jagged peaks and plunging waterfalls, the area measures little more than ten miles by ten, but has enough mountain paths to keep even the most experienced hiker occupied for weeks. The folds of the mountains may reveal some atmospheric Welsh castle ruin or decaying piece of quarrying equipment while the lowlands are perfect for lakeside rambles and rides on antiquated steam trains.

Snowdonia is the heart of the massive **Snowdonia National Park** (Parc Cenedlaethol Eryri), which extends north and south, beyond the bounds of Snowdonia itself (and this chapter), to encompass the Rhinogs, Cadair Idris (see p.687) and 23 miles of superb coastal scenery. One of the best approaches to Snowdonia is along the **Dee Valley**, a fertile landscape much fought over by the Welsh and the English. There's a tangibly Welsh feel to fabulous **Llangollen**, a great base for a variety of ruins, rides and rambles, as well as the venue for the colourful **International Musical Eisteddfod** festival. Pressing on along the A5 – the region's second main road – you hit the fringes of Snowdonia at **Betws-y-Coed**, which is slightly twee but great for gentle walks and mountain biking. As you head deeper into the park, old mining and quarry towns such as **Beddgelert** or **Llanberis** make good bases for walks or adrenaline activities in former slate capital **Blaenau Ffestiniog**, while on the eastern fringes of Snowdonia, **Bala** tempts with whitewater rafting down the Tryweryn.

To the west of Snowdonia, the former slate port of **Porthmadog** is home to the quirky "village" of **Portmeirion** and two superb narrow-gauge steam railways: the **Ffestiniog Railway** and **Welsh Highland Railway**. Beyond lies the gentle rockiness of the **Llŷn peninsula**, a wellspring of Welsh language where Wales ends in a flourish of small coves and former fishing villages. Roads loop back along the **Llŷn** to **Caernarfon**, which is overshadowed by its stupendous castle.

Two historic bridges span the picturesque Menai Strait between the mainland and the island of **Anglesey**, a gentle patchwork of beautiful beaches, ancient sites and Edward's final castle in the handsome town of **Beaumaris**. Back on the mainland, the university and cathedral city of **Bangor** is the area's most cosmopolitan haunt, while **Conwy**'s gritty castle and narrow streets huddle around a scenic quay. Victorian **Llandudno** is easily the best of the north coast's seaside resorts, with the cultural sights of **Bodelwyddan Castle** and the cathedral of **St Asaph** within day-trip distance.

GETTING AROUND
NORTH WALES

By train Getting around North Wales by train is a pleasure. Fast services along the north coast run all the way to the Irish ferries at Holyhead on Anglesey, while the delightful Conwy Valley line threads inland to link up with the narrow-gauge Ffestiniog Railway at Blaenau Ffestiniog. This in turn meets the Porthmadog–Caernarfon Welsh Highland Railway through Beddgelert and across the southern flanks of Snowdon.

The Llangollen International Music Eisteddfod p.696
Whitewater rafting at Bala p.697
Betws-y-coed biking p.699

Top 5 outdoor activities p.700
Walks from the Ogwen Valley p.701
Ascending Snowdon p.704
Watersports in Abersoch p.708

VIEW FROM SNOWDON

Highlights

❶ Llangollen Small but substantial, this enjoyable riverside town features a romantic house, an impressive aqueduct and lovely castle ruins. **See p.695**

❷ Snowdon Scale Wales's highest mountain, with six hiking paths and a cog railway converging on the summit-top café and bar. **See p.697**

❸ Llŷn peninsula Not just a pastoral drop off the radar with a gorgeous coastline, especially around Aberdaron, but a heartland of the Welsh language. **See p.706**

❹ Portmeirion Spend the day at this surreal seaside "village" made from bits of rescued architecture, the setting for the cult TV series *The Prisoner*. **See p.707**

❺ Caernarfon Castle One of the greatest of Edward I's "Iron Ring" of thirteenth-century castles, with other superb examples at Beaumaris and Conwy. **See p.710**

❻ Beaumaris A fine castle and Georgian townscape make this a splendid base for exploring Anglesey's beaches and Neolithic remains. **See p.712**

❼ Conwy The pick of North Wales's towns, with its imposing castle and intact ring of medieval walls enclosing a fascinating centre. **See p.716**

❽ Llandudno The town's gentility is nicely offset by the ruggedness of the neighbouring limestone hummock of the Great Orme, which is reached by cable car. **See p.719**

HIGHLIGHTS ARE MARKED ON THE MAP ON P.694

NORTH WALES

N

Dublin & Dun Laoghaire

HIGHLIGHTS
1. Llangollen
2. Snowdon
3. Llŷn Peninsula
4. Portmeirion
5. Caernarfon castle
6. Beaumaris
7. Conwy
8. Llandudno

ENGLAND

Liverpool
Birkenhead
Shotton
Flint
Holywell
Prestatyn
Point of Ayr
Rhuddlan
St Asaph
Rhyl
Abergele
Bodelwyddan
Denbigh
Llanrhaeadr
Ruthin
Mold
Moel Famau
CLWYDIAN RANGE
Fort Fenni
Llangollen Railway
Wrexham
Erddig
Chirk Castle
Chirk
Oswestry
Llangollen
Llanarmon Dyffryn Ceiriog
BERWYN MOUNTAINS
Corwen
Llandrillo
Dee
Lake Vyrnwy
MID WALES
Bala Lake Railway
Bala
Alwen Reservoir
Llyn Brenig
Clwyd
Liverpool Bay
Colwyn Bay
Llandudno
Great Orme Head
Bodnant
Llanrwst
Betws-y-Coed
River Conwy
Conwy
Conwy Bay
Penmaenmawr
Puffin Island
Penmachno
Penrhyn Castle
Beaumaris
Penmon Priory
Bangor
Menai Bridge
Llanfairpwll
Betheda
CARNEDD RANGE
Llyn Cowlyd
Capel Curig
Moel Siabod
Blaenau Ffestiniog
Ffestiniog
SNOWDONIA NATIONAL PARK
Trawsfynydd
Llyn Trawsfynydd
Harlech
Anglesey
Moelfre
Amlwch
Cemaes
Llyn Alaw
Llanerchymedd
Llangefni
Newborough Warren
Holyhead
Holy Island
Llyn Ogwen
Llyn Padarn
Llanberis
Llyn Peris
GLYDER RANGE
Tryfan
Snowdon
Beddgelert
Moel Hebog
Porthmadog
Portmeirion
Tremadog Bay
Criccieth
Caernarfon
Dinas
Waunfawr
Welsh Highland Railway
Penygroes
Clynnog-fawr
Caernarfon Bay
Yr Eifl
THE LLŶN
Llanaelhaearn
Nefyn
Morfa Nefyn
Porth Dinllaen
Porth Colmon
Llangwnnadl
Aberdaron
Porth Oer (Whistling Sands)
Bardsey Sound
Llangybi
Llanystumdwy
Pwllheli
Llanbedrog
Abersoch
Sarn Meyllteyrn
Tudweiliog
St Tudwal's Islands
Porth Neigwl (Hell's Mouth)
Cardigan Bay

miles
0   10

Plas Newydd

By bus Buses plug the gaps, especially the Snowdon Sherpa services, which provide hiker access all around Snowdon and the Ogwen Valley. There is no useful bus or train service linking Llangollen with Snowdonia along the A5: instead head along the north coast to either Llandudno Junction or Bangor then inland from there.

Llangollen

LLANGOLLEN, just six miles from the English border, is the embodiment of a Welsh town, clasped tightly in the narrow Dee Valley where a weighty Gothic bridge straddles the river. This was an important town long before the early Romantics arrived at the end of the eighteenth century. Turner came to paint the swollen river and the Cistercian ruin of **Valle Crucis**; John Ruskin found the town "entirely lovely in its gentle wildness"; and writer George Borrow made Llangollen his base for the early part of his 1854 tour detailed in *Wild Wales*. The rich and famous also came to visit the "Ladies of Llangollen" at **Plas Newydd**. But by this stage some of the town's rural charm had been eaten up by the works of one of the century's finest engineers, Thomas Telford, who squeezed both his London–Holyhead trunk road and the **Llangollen Canal** alongside the river.

Plas Newydd

Half a mile up Hill St from the southern end of Castle St • April–Oct Wed–Mon 10am–5pm • £5.50; grounds free; NT • ☎ 019/8 862834, ⓦ nationaltrust.org.uk

Standing in twelve acres of formal gardens, the two-storey mock-Tudor **Plas Newydd** was, for almost fifty years, home to the **Ladies of Llangollen**. Lady Eleanor Butler and Sarah Ponsonby were a lesbian couple from Anglo-Irish aristocratic backgrounds, who tried to elope at the end of the eighteenth century. After two botched attempts dressed in men's clothes, they were grudgingly allowed to leave their respective ancestral homes in Ireland in 1778 with enough allowance to settle in Llangollen, where they became celebrated hosts. Despite their desire for a "life of sweet and delicious retirement", they didn't seem to mind the constant stream of gentry who called on them. Walter Scott was well received, though he found them "a couple of hazy or crazy old sailors" in manner, and like "two respectable superannuated clergymen" in their mode of dress. Visitors' gifts of sculpted **wood panelling** formed the basis of the riotous friezes of woodwork that cover the walls of their modest house; this is set off by a mixed bag of furniture in a style similar to that owned by the ladies.

Llangollen Railway

Llangollen station, Abbey Rd • April–Sept Mon–Fri 3 services (usually steam), plus up to 7 steam and diesel services almost every weekend year-round • £12 return • ☎ 01978 860979, ⓦ llangollen-railway.co.uk

The hills around Llangollen echo to the shrill cry of steam engines easing along the **Llangollen Railway**, shoehorned into the north side of the valley. From Llangollen's time-warped station ancient carriages proudly sporting the liveries of their erstwhile owners are hauled along ten miles of the old Ruabon–Barmouth line to Corwen.

Castell Dinas Brân

Follow signs from Llangollen Wharf • Open access • Free

The panoramic view, especially at sunset, justifies the 45-minute slog up to **Castell Dinas Brân** (Crow's Fortress Castle), a few evocative stumps of masonry perched on a hill 800ft above town. This was once the district's largest and most important Welsh fortress, built in the 1230s by the ruler of northern Powys, Prince Madog ap Gruffydd Maelor. Edward I captured it as part of his first campaign against Llywelyn ap Gruffydd, but the castle was left to decay.

16

THE LLANGOLLEN INTERNATIONAL MUSIC EISTEDDFOD

Llangollen is heaving all summer, and never more so than in early July, when for six days the town explodes in a frenzy of music, dance, poetry and colour. Unlike the National Eisteddfod, which is a purely Welsh affair, the **International Music Eisteddfod** (☎01978 862001, ⓦinternational-eisteddfod.co.uk) draws amateur performers from fifty countries, all competing for prizes inside the 6000-seat Royal International Pavilion, and at several other venues. The eisteddfod has been held in its present form since 1947 when forty choirs from fourteen countries performed. Today, more than 4000 participants lure up to 150,000 visitors, and there is an irresistible *joie de vivre* as brightly costumed dancers stroll the streets and fill the restaurants.

The eisteddfod is followed by the less frenetic **Llangollen Fringe** (☎0800 145 5779, ⓦllangollenfringe.co.uk), with a number of more "alternative" acts – music, dance, comedy and so on – performing over the third week in July.

Valle Crucis Abbey

A542, 1.5 miles northwest of Llangollen • April–Oct daily 10am–5pm; Nov–March open access • April–Oct £3.50; Nov–March free; CADW • ☎01978 860326, ⓦcadw.wales.gov.uk

The gaunt ruin of **Valle Crucis Abbey** greets you with its largely intact west wall, pierced by the frame of a rose window. Though one of the last Cistercian foundations in Wales, and Britain's first Gothic abbey, it is no match for Tintern Abbey (see p.616), but nevertheless stands majestically in a pastoral – and much-less-visited – setting. After the Dissolution in 1535, the church fell into disrepair and the monastic buildings were used as farm buildings. Now they hold displays on monastic life, reached by a detour through the mostly ruined cloister and past the weighty vaulting of the chapter house.

Llangollen Canal

When it was built in 1806, the **Llangollen Canal** was one of Britain's finest feats of canal engineering. Its architect, Thomas Telford, succeeded in building a canal without locks through fourteen miles of hilly terrain, most spectacularly by means of the 100ft-long **Pontcysyllte Aqueduct**, passing 127ft over the River Dee at Froncysyllte, four miles east of Llangollen. Both canal and aqueduct are now a UNESCO World Heritage Site. **Canal trips** (Easter–Oct daily; £13.50; ☎01978 860702, ⓦhorsedrawnboats.co.uk) across the aqueduct leave from Llangollen Wharf, almost opposite the train station.

Erddig Hall

Off the A483, 10 miles northeast of Llangollen • Daily: mid-March to Oct 12.30–4.30pm; Nov & Dec 11am–3.30pm • £9.90, outbuildings & gardens only £6.30; NT • ☎01978 355314, ⓦnationaltrust.org.uk

The ancestral home of the Yorke family, the seventeenth-century **Erddig Hall** has now been restored to its 1922 appearance: the family's State Rooms upstairs have their share of fine furniture and portraits, but the real interest lies in the quarters of the servants, whose lives were fully documented by their unusually benevolent masters. Eighteenth- and early nineteenth-century portraits of staff are still on display in the Servants' Hall, each of which has a verse written by one of the Yorkes. You can also see the blacksmith's shop, lime yard, stables, laundry, kitchen, still-used bakehouse and the lovely walled garden.

ARRIVAL AND INFORMATION
LLANGOLLEN

By train The nearest station is 5 miles away at Ruabon, reached by frequent buses on the Llangollen–Wrexham run.

By bus Buses from Bala (8 daily; 1hr) and Dolgellau (8 daily; 1hr 45min) stop on Parade St (as do daily National Express coaches on the Wrexham–Llangollen–Birmingham–London run: tickets are sold at the tourist office).

Tourist office Y Capel, Castle St (Easter–Oct daily 9.30am–5.30pm; Nov–Easter Mon–Sat 9.30am–5pm, Sun 9.30am–4pm; ☎01978 860828, ⓦllangollen.org.uk).

ACCOMMODATION

Cornerstones 15–19 Bridge St ☎01978 861569, ⓦcornerstones-guesthouse.co.uk. River views from three of the five rooms and over-the-top exuberance in this luxury sixteenth-century B&B. Amenities include DVD library, well-appointed guest lounges and an extensive breakfast. Midweek deals are available. **£80**

★**Glasgwm** Abbey Rd ☎01978 861975, ⓦglasgwm -llangollen.co.uk. Relaxed B&B with plenty of books, a piano and engaging hosts whose good taste is reflected in the decor of the doubles, twin and single (which has its own deep bath). They'll do Offa's Dyke pick-ups and drop-offs, as well as packed lunches and dinners. **£55**

Llangollen Hostel Berwyn St ☎01978 861773, ⓦllangollenhostel.co.uk. Neat bunks in modernized rooms (mostly en suite with 4–6 bunks) in a Victorian townhouse plus well-equipped kitchen, comfy lounge and free wi-fi. Bunks **£18**, en-suite room **£45**

★**Tyddyn Llan Country House** Llandrillo, 15 miles southwest ☎01490 440264, ⓦtyddynllan.co.uk. Elegant Georgian "restaurant with rooms", where the emphasis is on Bryan Webb's Modern British food (two courses £45, three for £55). The restaurant is open to nonguests for dinner and for lunch Fri–Sun (£21.50/£29). **£195**

Wern Isaf Farm ☎01978 860632, ⓦwernisaf.co.uk. Simple but lovely farmhouse campsite almost a mile up the steep Wern Road (turn right over the canal on Wharf Hill). April–Oct. Pitches **£14**

EATING, DRINKING AND ENTERTAINMENT

Côr Meibion Froncysyllte Acrefair School Hall, just off the A539, 5 miles east ⓦfronchoir.com. Visitors are welcome to attend the rehearsals of Côr Meibion Froncysyllte, one of Wales's most exalted male voice choirs. Directions are on their website. Mon & Thurs 7–9pm.

★**The Corn Mill** Dee Lane ☎01978 869555, ⓦbrunningandprice.co.uk/cornmill. Superb conversion of a town centre mill, with a sunny riverside deck. Good all day for coffee and well-prepared café-bar food such as beef and horseradish sandwiches (£6) and bistro mains (£11–19). The real ales are well kept. Mon–Sat 11am–11pm, Sun 11am–10.30pm; food daily noon–9.30pm (Sun to 9pm).

★**Gales Wine Bar** 18 Bridge St ☎01978 860089, ⓦgalesofllangollen.co.uk. Old church pews, wooden floors, a blackboard menu of delicious, bistro-style food (mains £11–18) and a good selection of wines from around the world make this long-standing, chilled-out place a Llangollen favourite. Mon–Sat noon–2pm & 6–9.30pm.

Sun Inn Regent St ☎01978 860079, ⓦsunllan.com. Convivial, slate-floored locals' pub with basic meals for a fiver, a wide range of beers and live bands (of just about any stripe) most nights. Daily 5pm–1am or later.

Snowdonia

The mountains of **Snowdonia** provide the most dramatic and alluring of all Welsh scenery, a compact, barren land of tortured ridges dividing glacial valleys, whose sheer faces belie the fact that the tallest peaks only just top 3000ft. It was to this mountain fastness that Llywelyn ap Gruffydd, the last true prince of Wales, retreated in 1277 after his first war with Edward I; it was also here that Owain Glyndŵr held on most tenaciously to his dream of regaining for the Welsh the title of Prince of Wales. Centuries later, the English came to remove the mountains: slate barons built huge fortunes from Welsh toil and reshaped the patterns of Snowdonian life forever, as men looking for steady work in the quarries left the hills and became town dwellers.

WHITEWATER RAFTING AT BALA

The little town of **BALA** (Y Bala), on the border of the park, twenty miles southwest of Llangollen, sits at the northern end of Wales's largest natural lake, **Llŷn Tegid**. Nearby, waters crash down the Tryweryn River, perfect for **whitewater rafting**. Water is released around 200 days a year at the National White Water Centre (March to mid-Oct Mon–Fri 11am–2pm, Sat & Sun 8.30am–4.30pm; ☎01678 521083, ⓦukrafting.co.uk), crashing down a mile and a half of Grade III rapids where numerous rafting options include the Taster (40–60min; £32) involving two runs down the course. The two-hour session (£66) typically gives you four runs, or you can step up a notch to the Orca Adventure (half-day; £88) involving two runs down in a normal raft followed by a chance to tackle the rapids in a more challenging two-person inflatable.

Thousands of hikers arrive every weekend to walk up **Snowdon** massif (Eryri) over steep, exacting and constantly varying terrain. Several of the ascent routes are superb, and you can always take the cog railway up to the summit café from **Llanberis**. But the other mountains are as good, and far less busy, and give unsurpassed views of Snowdon. The **Glyderau** and **Tryfan** – best tackled from the **Ogwen Valley** – are particular favourites for more experienced walkers.

But Snowdonia isn't all about walking. Small settlements are dotted in the valleys, usually coinciding with some enormous mine or quarry. Foremost among these are **Blaenau Ffestiniog**, the former slate capital of Wales turned activities town, and **Beddgelert**. Both have mines that are open to the public. The only place of any size not associated with slate mining is **Betws-y-Coed**, a largely Victorian resort away from the higher peaks.

Betws-y-Coed and around

BETWS-Y-COED (pronounced "betoos-er-coyd"), sprawled out around the confluence of the Conwy, Llugwy and Lledr valleys, overlooked by the conifer-clad slopes of the **Gwydyr Forest Park**, and centred on the low cataract of **Pont-y-Pair Falls**, is almost totally devoted to the needs of visitors, particularly walkers – there are seven outdoor gear retailers but no decent grocery shop. The town has the best choice of accommodation in the region, but after an hour mooching around you'll soon want to head out into the hinterland. Serious mountain walkers should continue west, but for everyone else there are some delightful, easy strolls to the local beauty spots of the **Conwy** and **Swallow** falls.

16

■ ACCOMMODATION						● CAFÉS & RESTAURANTS			
Bryn Elltyd	16	Llyn Gwynant		Rynys Farm	12	Bryn Tyrch Inn	3	Sygun Fawr	7
Bryn Tyrch Inn	6	Campsite	13	St Curig's Church	6	Caffi Caban	1	Tŷ Gwyn	5
Cae Gwyn	5	Pen-y-Gwryd		Sygun Fawr	15	Conwy Falls Café	6		
Cae'r Blaidd	17	Hotel	8	The Vagabond	9	Glaslyn Ices/Café Glyndŵr	9	■ PUBS & BARS	
Gwern Gôf Uchaf	2	Pengwern	11	YHA Idwal Cottage		Hebog	8	CeLL B	3
Gwydir Castle	1	Plas Coch	4	YHA Pen-y-Pass	7	Pen-y-Gwryd Hotel	4	The Stables	2
Hafod y Llan	14	Plas Curig		YHA Snowdon Ranger	10	Pete's Eats	2	Vaynol Arms	1

BETWS-Y-COED BIKING

Gwydir Forest Park, just outside town, is one of the top trail-riding locales in Wales. The classic route is the **Marin Trail** (15-mile loop; 2–4hr) with mostly forest track ascents and numerous singletrack descents of varying difficulty. The scenery is great, with mountain views along the higher sections. For **rental**, contact Beics Betws (☎01690 710766, ⊕bikewales.co.uk) behind the post office (from £28 a day).

Conwy Falls

On A5, 3 miles south of Betws-y-Coed • £1.50 • Access all hours via turnstile

South of Betws-y-Coed the river plunges 50ft over the **Conwy Falls** into a deep pool. After paying the fee, you can view the falls on the right and a series of rock steps to the left; these were cut in 1863 as a kind of primitive fish ladder so spawning fish could swim up the waterfall, but are now superseded by a tunnel through the rock on the far side.

Fairy Glen

Signposted off A470 towards Blaenau Ffestiniog • Car park £1, turnstile 50p • Access all hours

A mile or so southeast of the village, after negotiating a series of rapids, the waters of the Conwy River follow a staircase of drops and enter **Fairy Glen**, a lovely cleft in a small wood; it is named after the Welsh fairies, the Tylwyth Teg, once believed to live hereabouts.

Swallow Falls

Two miles west of Betws-y-Coed along the A5 towards Capel Curig • £1.50 • Access all hours via turnstile

Swallow Falls is the region's most visited sight. You can pay to view this pretty cascade, or better still, catch a glimpse from the **Llugwy Valley Walk** (3 miles; 400ft ascent; 1hr 30min), a forested path from the north side of Pont-y-Pair Falls which follows the twisting and plunging river upstream towards Capel Curig. Along the way you pass the steeply sloping **Miners' Bridge**, below which are a series of idyllic plunge pools, perfect for swimming.

Gwydir Castle

B5106, 2.5 miles north of Betws-y-Coed • April–Oct Tues–Fri & Sun 10am–4pm • £3 • ☎01492 641687, ⊕ gwydir-castle.co.uk

Former home of the powerful Wynn family, **Gwydir Castle** is actually a low-slung manor house begun around 1490 with later additions. Its core is a three-storey solar tower, whose windows relieve the gloom of the great halls, each with enormous fireplaces and stone-flagged or heavy timber floors. Most of the original fittings and Tudor furniture were sold in 1921, and much of the rest of the house was ruined in a fire a few months later. The subsequent restoration was kept simple – tapestries cover the solid stone walls, a few tables and chairs are scattered about and you'll see some fine painted glass. Some of the original furnishings have been tracked down, including the magnificent **Dining Room** once shipped to America but now reinstalled. Outside, the **Dutch Garden** has peacocks and a fine Cedar of Lebanon dating back to 1625.

Go Below

Meet at Conwy Falls Café, 2 miles southeast of Betws-y-Coed • £49, book a day or two in advance • ☎01690 710108, ⊕ www.go-below.co.uk

Go Below allows you to head underground, exploring magical old **mine workings** with harness, helmet and headlamp. You'll get a nice balance between learning about the mine and getting active on zip-lines, abseiling and even paddling across a small subterranean lake.

Plas-y-Brenin: the National Mountaineering Centre

A4086, 400yd south of the centre • **Climbing wall** daily 10am–9pm • £6 • ☎01690 720214, ⊕ pyb.co.uk

As well as its internationally renowned residential courses, **Plas-y-Brenin** runs two-hour indoor-climbing and lake-canoeing taster sessions during August and other school holidays

TOP 5 OUTDOOR ACTIVITIES

Mine exploring with Go Below See p.699
Mountain biking Gwydir Forest See p.699
Rafting the Tryweryn See p.697

Rock climbing from Plas-y-Brenin
See p.699
Summitting Snowdon See p.704

(£25). Kids who want a full-day taster of canoeing, skiing and abseiling can be left on the "3 in a Day" adventure session (£40), where adults are welcome too. There's also a good bar and talks on recent international expeditions (usually Mon, Wed & Sat 8pm; free).

ARRIVAL AND INFORMATION

By train The train station serves the Conwy Valley Railway (ⓦ conwy.gov.uk/cvr).
Destinations Blaenau Ffestiniog (6 daily; 30min); Llandudno Junction (6 daily; 30min).
By bus Buses (including the Snowdon Sherpa) fan out from near the train station.
Destinations Blaenau Ffestiniog (Mon–Sat 8 daily; 20min); Capel Curig (5 daily; 10min); Idwal Cottage (3

BETWS-Y-COED

daily; 20min); Llanberis (4 daily; 30min); Llandudno (6 daily; 50min); Llanrwst (every 2hr; 10min); Penmachno (6 daily; 10min); Pen-y-Pass (6 daily; 15min).
Tourist office In Royal Oak Stables (daily; Easter to mid-Oct 9.30am–5pm; mid-Oct to Easter 9.30am–4pm; ⓣ01690 710426), and has displays and a film giving a quick overview of Snowdonia.

ACCOMMODATION

★Bryn Tyrch Inn A5 at Capel Curig, 6 miles west of Betws-y-Coed ⓣ01690 720223, ⓦbryntyrchinn.co.uk. Modernized twelve-room inn offering simple, tasteful rooms with TVs and well-appointed bathrooms. Also four-bunk B&B dorm rooms (minimum 3 people). The warm and lively restaurant and bar has real ales, good meals (mains mostly £12–17) and a wonderful view of Snowdon. Two nights minimum at weekends. Mid-Jan to mid-Dec. Food mid-Jan–Easter & Oct–mid-Dec Fri–Sun noon–9pm; Easter–Sept noon–9pm. Dorms **£25**, doubles **£79**
★Gwydir Castle Llanrwst, 3 miles north ⓣ01492 641687, ⓦgwydir-castle.co.uk. A rare opportunity to stay in an authentic Tudor manor that still maintains the air of a family home. Two splendid bedrooms have been fitted out in baronial style with four-poster beds, deep baths and eclectic decor. TVs are anathema – amen to that. No children under 12. **£95**
★Plas Curig A5 at Capel Curig ⓣ01690 720225, ⓦsnowdoniahostel.co.uk. Wales's only five-star hostel features beautiful slate floors and reclaimed wood in public areas and splendid bunk rooms – custom-built pannelled

bunks have privacy curtains, bed lights and lockable storage. It has four- and eight-bed dorms, doubles, twins and family rooms (no en suites). Check-in 5–10pm. Feb–Nov. Dorms **£25**, doubles **£55**
★Rynys Farm A5, 2 miles southeast near the Conwy Falls ⓣ01690 710218, ⓦrynys-camping.co.uk. Pure rural bliss on a beautiful National Trust-listed farm campsite with plenty of flat sites tucked behind trees or against dry-stone walls, great valley views, good facilities and eco-ethics. Charming owners, too. Also has a wonderful yurt and shepherd's hut plus a static caravan that sleeps four. Camping per person **£7.50**, caravan **£40**, hut **£45**, yurt **£50**
The Vagabond Craiglan Rd ⓣ01690 710850, ⓦthevagabond.co.uk. Central independent hostel with 36 bunks (with sheets) in 4- to 8-bunk dorms and good facilities including free wi-fi, secure bike lock-up and off-street parking. There's a self-catering kitchen but they also serve breakfasts (£5) and evening meals (£7) and have an inexpensive bar with patio seating. Bookings recommended at weekends when B&B is obligatory. Dorms **£15**

EATING AND DRINKING

★Conwy Falls Café A5, 2 miles southeast of Betws-y-Coed ⓣ01690 710696, ⓦconwyfalls.com. Quality and provenance are watchwords at this friendly, relaxed café; meals from spinach and mushroom burgers to stone-baked pizzas are always fresh, wholesome and home-made. There's free wi-fi and they occasionally host music events. Easter to mid-Oct Mon–Thurs & Sun 9am–4pm, Fri & Sat 9am–9pm; mid-Oct–Easter Fri & Sat 9am–9pm, Sun 9am–4pm.

The Stables Royal Oak Hotel, High St ⓣ01690 710219. Recently refurbished, the village's liveliest bar provides good beer, outdoor seating, sports on the TV, and occasional live jazz. Passable pub-grub such as home-made lasagne, local beef burgers, pies, and fish and chips (mains average £9). Daily 11am–11pm.
★Tŷ Gwyn A5, 0.5 mile southeast ⓣ01690 710383, ⓦtygwynhotel.co.uk. First choice for historic atmosphere is this beamed, former coaching inn – traditional British

16

dishes such as local trout with prawns and crème fraiche (£15) or shepherd's pie made with 24-hour-roast lamb (£18) are served in the intimate bar or slightly more formal restaurant. Reservations essential. Jan noon–2pm & 6.30–9pm; Feb–Dec daily noon–2pm & 6.30–9pm.

The Ogwen Valley

Northwest of Capel Curig, the A5 forges through the **Ogwen Valley**, which separates the imposing Carneddau massif from the rock-peppered summits of the **Glyderau** range and distinctive triple-peaked **Tryfan**, perhaps Snowdonia's most demanding mountain. West of Tryfan, the road follows the shores of **Llyn Ogwen**, to the YHA hostel, the start of some of the UK's finest walks (see below).

Zip World Velocity

Signposted off A5 south of Bethesda · Booking centre 9am–6pm · £50 · ☎ 01248 601444, ⓦ zipworld.co.uk

Who would've imagined a disused quarry could be so much fun? Europe's longest zip wire was strung across a former slate quarry in 2013 to provide a one-mile ride at speeds of up to 70mph. Reservations are essential and there are restrictions on weight, height and age. Note too that the weather can affect your ride and that Zip World offers rescheduling, not refunds.

ARRIVAL AND DEPARTURE   THE OGWEN VALLEY

By bus Five buses a day run along the valley between Bethesda and Capel Curig, with connections to Betws-y-Coed and Bangor.

ACCOMMODATION

★ **Gwern Gôf Uchaf** A5, 3 miles west of Capel Curig ☎ 01690 720294, ⓦ tryfanwales.co.uk. Superbly sited campsite at the base of Tryfan with a modern shower block, 14-berth bunkhouse, kitchen and a drying room: bring a sleeping bag and food. Pitches **£5**, bunkhouse **£10**

YHA Idwal Cottage A5, 5 miles west of Capel Curig ☎ 01629 592700, ⓦ yha.org.uk. Perfectly sited for walkers, this immaculate refurbished YHA in a former quarry manager's house has mostly four-bunk dorms, a double, a single, family rooms and an alcohol licence, but no meals. Opens 5pm. Feb, Nov & Dec weekdays only; March–Oct daily. Pitches **£11**, dorms **£18**, rooms **£48**

Llanberis and around

LLANBERIS, ten miles west of Capel Curig, is the nearest you'll get in Wales to an alpine climbing village, its main street thronged with weather-beaten walkers and mountaineers. At the same time, this is very much a Welsh rural community, albeit a

---

WALKS FROM THE OGWEN VALLEY

Tourists hike up Snowdon (see box, p.704), but mountain connoisseurs prefer the sharply angled peaks of Tryfan and the Glyderau, with their challenging terrain, cantilevered rocks and fantastic views back to Snowdon. If you're going to attempt the walks, arm yourself with either the 1:50,000 OS *Landranger* #115 or the 1:25,000 OS *Outdoor Leisure* #17 map.

Cwm Idwal (1.5 miles return; 1hr; 200ft ascent). An easy hike on a well-graded path leading up to Llŷn Idwal, nestled in the magnificent cirque of Cwm Idwal. The area was designated Wales's first nature reserve in 1954, after botanists discovered rare arctic-alpine plants growing here. Tackling the rough, rocky paths right around the lake can turn this into a half-day outing, partly beneath huge sloping cliffs – the Idwal Slabs.

Tryfan Miners' Track (5 miles; 4–6hr; 2000ft ascent).

The standard route up Tryfan, from the car park at Idwal Cottage. You'll need to use your hands for the final section up the South Ridge of Tryfan, past the Far South Peak to the summit. You can then tackle the 5ft jump between Adam and Eve, the two chunks of rhyolitic lava which crown this regal mountain. Don't underestimate the seriousness of the leap: it's only when you see the mountain dropping away on all sides that it hits home quite how disastrous it would be to overshoot.

depleted one now that slate is no longer being torn from the flanks of Elidir Fawr, the mountain across the town's twin lakes. The town is inextricably linked with **Snowdon**, the highest British mountain outside Scotland.

Dinorwig Power Station Underground Tour

Tours start from the Electric Mountain complex on the A4086 • Easter–Oct daily; Nov–Easter Tues, Thurs & Sat–Sun • £8.50 • ☎ 01286 870636, ⦿ electricmountain.co.uk

Views north from Llanberis are dominated by the entrance to the **Dinorwig Pumped Storage Power Station**, hollowed out of the ground in the mid-1970s and visited on a bus tour. It actually consumes more electricity than it produces, but benefits the national grid by being able to instantly supply electricity to cope with the early evening surge in demand. This is one of Snowdonia's more popular rainy-day activities, so book ahead if the weather turns foul.

Padarn Country Park

Open access • Free • Beside Lake Padarn, 0.5 miles northeast of village centre

At **Padarn Country Park** lakeside oak woods are gradually recolonizing the discarded workings of the defunct **Dinorwig Slate Quarries**, formerly one of the largest slate quarries in the world. Equipment and engines that once hauled materials up inclined tramways have been partly restored and punctuate the paths which link the levels chiselled out of the hillside.

National Slate Museum

Easter–Oct daily 10am–5pm; Nov–Easter daily except Sat 10am–4pm • Free • ☎ 01286 870630, ⦿ museumwales.ac.uk • Beside Lake Padarn, 0.5 miles northeast of village centre

The fort-like former quarry's maintenance workshops now house Wales's **National Slate Museum** where a 50ft-diameter water wheel that once powered cutting machines still turns. Most of the equipment was still in use until the quarries closed in 1969 and is quite familiar to the former quarry workers who demonstrate their skills at turning an inch-thick slab of slate into six, even eight, perfectly smooth slivers. The slate was delivered to the slate-dressing sheds by means of a maze of tramways, cranes and rope lifts, all kept in good order in the fitting and repair shops. Look out for the slate workers' cottages, furnished in the style of 1861, 1901 and 1969.

ARRIVAL AND INFORMATION

LLANBERIS

By bus Buses stop along High Street. Frequent Sherpa #S1 buses travel up daily to Pen-y-Pass, the recommended approach even if you have a car, since the Pen-y-Pass car park is expensive and almost always full. Use the park-and-ride car park at the bottom of the pass, near the *Vaynol Arms*.

Destinations Bangor (hourly; 45min); Betws-y-Coed (6

daily; 30min); Caernarfon (every 30min; 25min); Capel Curig (7 daily; 30min); Pen-y-Pass (at least hourly; 15min).
Tourist office In Electric Mountain (manned Fri–Tues 10am–4pm, open with leaflets June–Aug daily 9.30am–5.30pm; Sept–May daily 10am–4.30pm; ☎ 01286 870765).

ACCOMMODATION

Cae Gwyn Nant Peris, 2 miles southeast of Llanberis ☎ 01286 870718. Climbers and bikers make up the bulk of the clientele in this field campsite and very primitive bunkhouse (bring everything). It's almost opposite the *Vaynol Arms* pub and handy for the Pen-y-Pass park-and-ride. Camping per person £6, bunkhouse £12
Llŷn Gwynant Campsite A498, 2.5 miles south of Pen-y-Pass ☎ 01766 890853, ⦿ gwynant.com. Wonderful lakeside campsite with access to Snowdon's Watkin Path. Can be up to 400 tents here on summer weekends, but

radios are banned and mobile phones won't get a signal. You can rent kayaks and canoes (June–Sept). Mid-March to Oct. Per person £9
★**Pen-y-Gwryd Hotel** A mile east of Pen-y-Pass ☎ 01286 870211, ⦿ pyg.co.uk. Wonderfully rustic hotel where the 1953 Everest expedition stayed while training; there are plenty of mementos. Rooms (some en suite) are priced per person; some share magnificent Edwardian bathrooms. Even if you don't stay or eat – plain mid-priced home-cooking – pop in for a pint. Two-night minimum Sat

& Sun. Jan & Feb weekends only; March–Oct daily. Per person **£43**

★**Plas Coch** High St ☎ 01286 872122, ✆ plas-coch .co.uk. Beautifully refurbished B&B with seven en-suite rooms plus an extra bathroom with a tub for post-hike soaks. The owners are going the extra mile, and offer packed lunches to hikers. **£75**

YHA Pen-y-Pass Pen-y-Pass ☎ 0845 371 9534, ✆ yha .org.uk. The only accommodation at Pen-y-Pass has just had a £1.3m renovation to update what was long a popular walkers' hostel – George Mallory's ill-fated Everest team stayed here – into a modern stay. There's access from 7am till midnight, a few private twins (some en suite), a bar and good meals. Open all year. **£18**

EATING AND DRINKING

★**Caffi Caban** Yr Hen Ysgol, Brynrefail, 2.5 miles northwest of Llanberis ☎ 01286 685500, ✆ caban-cyf .org. Relaxed, bright, licensed café which specializes in healthy organic meals· breakfasts (£4–7), sandwiches, baguettes or blackboard specials such as crab mousse with avocado or field mushrooms stuffed with bulghur and goat's cheese (£7.50). Delicious cakes and free wi-fi, too. Daily 9am–4pm.

Pete's Eats 40 High St ☎ 01286 870117. A Llanberis legend for walkers, climbers and hikers with cheap caff food – full walker's breakfasts (£5), lamb burgers or fish

and chips (£6) – in large portions. There are heaps of magazines and maps to browse and free wi-fi, so it's always busy when the weather turns bad. Summer daily 8am–8pm; winter Mon–Fri 9am–6.30pm, Sat & Sun 8am–4pm

Vaynol Arms Nant Peris, 2 miles east of Llanberis ☎ 01286 872672. Slate-floored pub with good beer, hearty bar meals (£8) and plastered with mountain and slate-mining photos. Always alive with locals midweek, and with climbers and campers at weekends. Mon–Fri 5–11pm, Sat & Sun noon–11pm

Snowdon

Hardened walkers sometimes dismiss **Snowdon** (3560ft) as overcrowded, and it can certainly be busy in summer, when a thousand visitors a day are pressed into the postbox-red carriages of the **Snowdon Mountain Railway**, while another 1500 pound the well-maintained paths. But this fine mountain massif sports some of the finest walking and scrambling in the park: hike early, late or out of season if you want a bit more solitude.

The Snowdon Mountain Railway

A4086, opposite the *Royal Victoria Hotel* • Mid-March to Nov 6, 25 trains daily • Summit return £27, one way £20; phone booking fee £3.50; £6 discount if reserving for 9am train by phone a day in advance • ☎ 0844 493 8120, ✆ snowdonrailway.co.uk

The **Snowdon Mountain Railway** is Britain's only rack-and-pinion railway, completed in 1896. Trains (sometimes pushed by seventy-year-old steam locos) still climb to the summit in just under an hour from the eastern end of Llanberis to the smart summit café (mid-May to Oct). Inside is a bar and a post office where, for a few pennies, you can enchant your friends with a "Summit of Snowdon – Copa'r Wyddfa" postmark. Times, type of locomotive and final destination vary with demand and ice conditions at the top: to avoid disappointment, buy your tickets early on clear summer days.

Beddgelert

A huddle of grey houses around a bridge, **BEDDGELERT** is arguably the prettiest village in the area. A sentimental tale tells how the town got its name: Gelert's Grave (*bedd* means burial place) is supposedly the final resting place of a local prince's faithful dog, Gelert, slain by his master by mistake. In truth, the sentimental yarn is a Victorian fabrication by a publican to lure tourists – the full tale is related by the enclosed "grave" just south of town.

Aberglaslyn Gorge

A few hundred yards downstream from Beddgelert, the river crashes down the picturesque **Aberglaslyn Gorge** towards Porthmadog. You can walk past Gelert's Grave, then cross over the bridge onto a path along the left bank for a mile, affording a closer look at the river's course through chutes and channels. Return the same way; the round trip takes around an hour.

16

ASCENDING SNOWDON

The following are justifiably the most popular of the seven accepted **walking** routes up Snowdon. All are easy to follow in good weather but you should still carry the 1:25,000 OS Explorer #OL17 map.

Llanberis Path (5 miles to summit; 3200ft ascent; 3hr). The easiest and longest route up Snowdon, following the rail line, which gets gradually steeper, to the "Finger Stone" at Bwlch Glas (Green Pass). This marks the arrival of the routes coming up from Pen-y-Pass to join the Llanberis Path for the final ascent to Yr Wyddfa, the summit.

Miners' Track (4 miles to summit; 2400ft ascent; 2hr 30min). The easiest of the three routes up from Pen-y-Pass, a broad track leading south then west to the dilapidated remains of the former copper mines in Cwm

Dyli. Skirting around the right of a lake, the path climbs more steeply to the lake-filled Cwm Glaslyn, then again to Upper Glaslyn, followed by a switchback ascent to the junction with the Llanberis Path.

Pig Track (3.5 miles to summit; 2400ft ascent; 2hr 30min). A steeper and stonier variation on the Miners' Track, leaving from the western end of the Pen-y-Pass car park and climbing up to Bwlch y Moch (the Pass of the Pigs) before meeting the Miners' Track prior to the zigzag up to the Llanberis Path.

GUIDES AND BIKES

If you're not equipped or confident enough to get out on the rock by yourself, there are various companies who will **guide** you. You could also consider **cycling** up the mountain: in addition to many easy rides, the Llanberis Path, Snowdon Ranger Path and Pitt's Head Track to Rhyd-Ddu are open to cyclists, although there's restricted cycle access to and from the summit between 10am and 5pm (May–Sept).

High Trek Snowdonia Tal y Waen, Deiniolen ☎ 01286 871232, ⓦ climbing-wales.co.uk. High Trek guide everything from straightforward hillwalking to scrambling, rock climbing (all abilities), navigation and winter climbing.

Llanberis Bike Hire 34 High St ☎ 01286 872787. Rental (£24/day; £15/half-day) and a good source of information about local rides.

Welsh Highland Railway

Late March to Oct 2, 4 trains daily • Sample return fares: to Caernarfon £35; to Waunfawr £11.50; one child under 16 free with an adult • ☎ 01766 516000, ⓦ festrail.co.uk

Beddgelert is linked to Caernarfon and Porthmadog by the **Welsh Highland Railway** (see p.706). You could just ride through the Aberglaslyn Gorge to Nantmor, then walk back to Beddgelert along the Fisherman's Path (1hr) or walk the new Lon Gwyrfai path and cycle track to Rhyd Ddu (4.5 miles) then catch the train back. Bikes can be rented in Beddgelert from beside the station.

ARRIVAL AND DEPARTURE   BEDDGELERT

By bus Beddgelert is on two bus routes: the #S4 Snowdon Sherpa from Caernarfon and the #S97 between Pen-y-Pass and Porthmadog. Services stop on the main street.
Destinations Caernarfon (Mon–Sat 8 daily; 30min); Pen-y-Pass (4 daily; 20min); Porthmadog (Mon–Sat 8 daily, Sun

3 daily; 30–50min).
Tourist office The tourist office on the A498 in the village centre seems set to close (previously Easter–Oct daily 9.30am–5.30pm; Nov–Easter Fri, Sat & Sun 9.30am–4.30pm; ☎ 01766 890615, ⓦ beddgelerttourism.com).

ACCOMMODATION AND EATING

★**Hafod y Llan** Nantgwynant, A498, 4 miles north ☎ 01766 510129. One for camping purists, this simple tent-only site is on a National Trust farm managed to enhance the landscape for conservation. Highly scenic, campfires are permitted, and has a dryer, located by the start of the Watkin Path up Snowdon. Showers 50p. April–Oct. Per person **£7**
Hebog Caernarfon Road ☎ 01766 890400, ⓦ hebog -eatandsleep.co.uk. Rustic-chic bistro with a good-value menu prepared from local ingredients – superb full Welsh breakfasts, jacket potatoes, Welsh beef ciabattas or larger

mains like home-made meatballs, fishcakes with chilli sauce or duck confit (£9–12) – outside tables beside the river and takeaway fish and chips. Daily 8am–10pm.
Sygun Fawr 1 mile northeast off A498 ☎ 01766 890258, ⓦ sygunfawr.co.uk. The smartest of the local hotels specializes in peace (no TVs) and views. The latter stretch to Snowdon from some country-styled rooms. Its restaurant, open to nonresidents, serves the likes of slow-cooked Welsh lamb shank with red wine jus (mains £13–16). Mid-Feb to Nov. Food served Tues–Sun 6–10pm. **£85**

16

Blaenau Ffestiniog

BLAENAU FFESTINIOG sits at the head of the Vale of Ffestiniog, hemmed in by bare slopes strewn with splintered slate. When clouds hunker low in this great cwm and rain sheets the grey roofs, it can be a terrifically gloomy place. Thousands of tonnes of slate were once hewn from the labyrinth of underground caverns here each year, and for some time the town was only kept alive by its slate-cavern tour and the wonderful, narrow-gauge **Ffestiniog Railway** (see p.706). However, a couple of new attractions in the old slate quarries have seen the town rebrand itself as the adrenaline capital of North Wales.

Llechwedd Slate Caverns

A470, 1 mile north of town • Daily 9.30am–5.30pm, last tour 4.30pm • Tour £14.95 • ☎01766 830306, ⓦ llechwedd-slate-caverns.co.uk

In 1898, as housing demand boomed during the Industrial Revolution, Snowdonia's quarries were producing half a million tonnes of dressed slate a year. For a sense of what slate meant to Blaenau Ffestinog, visit the **Llechwedd Slate Caverns**. The Victorian Mine Tour uses a steeply inclined railway to descend into the deepest part of the mine – a labyrinth of impressive tunnels that angle back into the gloom.

Antur Stiniog mountain-bike park

A470, 1 mile north of town • Thurs–Sun 9am–5.30pm, except daily during school holidays • £27.50 full day, £16 half-day; hire from £30/50 for a half-full day • ☎01766 238007, ⓦ anturstiniog.com

Launched in 2012, the newest mountain-bike centre in Wales is almost as popular as the slate mine next-door. It's an ambitious downhill and freeride park with five trails – a family friendly blue-grade trail for novices plus two red and two black runs – and bike transport back up to the trailheads. While walk-up visitors are accommodated, it's worth booking ahead to guarantee a slot. Bike hire and food in a small café is available at the centre.

Zip World Titan

A470, 1 mile north of town • Booking centre 9am–6pm • £50 • ☎01248 601444, ⓦ zipworld.co.uk

This project in former slate quarries is not just the longest zip-line course in the world – it has three tracks (890m, 630m and 450m) – but the only one which allows you to fly downhill alongside family or friends at speeds up to 70mph. Reservations are essential and there are restrictions on weight, height and age. Note too that the weather can affect your ride and that Zip World offers rescheduling, not refunds.

ARRIVAL AND DEPARTURE
BLAENAU FFESTINIOG

By train The central train station serves both the Ffestiniog Railway and mainline services.
Destinations Betws-y-Coed (6 daily; 30min); Llandudno (6 daily; 1hr 20min); Llandudno Junction (6 daily; 1hr).

By bus Buses stop outside the train station.
Destinations Betws-y-Coed (Mon–Sat 8 daily; 25min); Harlech (Mon–Sat 3 daily; 40min); Llandudno (Mon–Sat 8 daily; 1hr 10min); Porthmadog (Mon–Sat hourly; 30min).

ACCOMMODATION AND EATING

★**Bryn Elltyd** 1 mile from Blaenau in Tanygrisiau ☎01766 831356, ⓦ accommodation-snowdonia.com. The former slate mine manager's house beside the Ffestiniog Railway is now Wales's only carbon-neutral B&B thanks to the efforts of its environmentalist owner. Accommodation is in homely rooms or sweet cabins in the garden. £76
Cae'r Blaidd A470, 3 miles south ☎01766 762765, ⓦ caerblaidd.com. Spacious Victorian country house set in four acres of woodland with just three country-style rooms, two with fabulous views of the Moelwyn mountains.

Sustaining breakfasts and table d'hôte dinners (£19.50 for 3 courses) are excellent and the hosts run guided hiking, climbing and scrambling trips. £85
CeLL B Park Square ☎01766 832001, ⓦ cellb.org. Community arts centre in a former police station with gigs, occasional cinema nights, an informal café-bar with mountain views and free wi-fi. Being a community enterprise, the hours are very flexible. In 2014 it had won planning permission to create a 20-bed bunkhouse, thereby providing accommodation.

16

The Llŷn

The most westerly part of North Wales, **the Llŷn** forms a cliff- and cove-lined finger of land that juts out south and west from Snowdonia, separating Cardigan and Caernarfon bays. Its hills taper along its spine, carrying an ancient route to Aberdaron, where pilgrims once sailed for Ynys Enlli (Bardsey Island). Most come to the Llŷn nowadays for its beaches, especially those of **Abersoch** and **Aberdaron**, and sense of escapism. The peninsula's main town, **Pwllheli**, is really only of interest as the terminus for Cambrian Coast **trains** and as a hub for local **buses**.

Nowhere in Wales is more remote and staunchly Welsh: the term Stryd Fawr is used instead of High Street and in most local shops you'll only hear Welsh spoken. The Llŷn is reached through one of the two gateway towns: **Porthmadog**, home to the private "dream village" of **Portmeirion** and terminus of the **Ffestiniog Railway**; or **Caernarfon**, where a magnificent fortress guards the mouth of the Menai Strait.

Since the Wales Coast Path opened in 2012, the Llŷn has been discovered by walkers on the north and south coasts – a route similar to that in Pembrokeshire but far quieter.

Porthmadog

In a region stuffed with wonderful views, **PORTHMADOG**, at the crook of the Cambrian Coast and the Llŷn, has some of the finest – up the Vale of Ffestiniog and across the estuary of the Glaslyn River to the mountains of Snowdonia. The town itself makes little of its wonderful position, but it's a good base for exploring. Wales's heritage railway obsession reaches its apogee here with two fantastic lines – the **Ffestiniog Railway** and the **Welsh Highland Railway** – and if steam trains don't blow your whistle, you can head for the wonderful Italianate folly of **Portmeirion**.

Ffestiniog Railway

April–Oct 4–8 services daily; Nov–March services several days a week • Sample fares: return day-ticket £21; return to Tan-y-Bwlch £13.50; one under-16 travels free with an adult • ☎ 01766 516024, ⚲ festrail.co.uk

The **Ffestiniog Railway** ranks as Wales's finest narrow-gauge rail line, twisting and looping up 650ft from the wharf at Porthmadog to the slate mines at Blaenau Ffestiniog, thirteen miles away. The gutsy little engines make light of the steep gradients and chug through stunning scenery, from broad estuarine expanses to the deep greens of the Vale of Ffestiniog, only fading to grey on the final approaches to the slate-bound upper terminus at Blaenau Ffestiniog. In the late nineteenth century the rail line was carrying 100,000 tonnes a year of Blaenau Ffestiniog slate, but after the collapse of the slate-roofing industry the line was abandoned (in 1946) and fell into disrepair. Reconstruction of the tracks was complete by 1982.

After Porthmadog, trains stop at **Minffordd**, a mile from Portmeirion.

Welsh Highland Railway

Late March to Oct 2–4 trains daily • Sample return fares: to Beddgelert £19.20; to Caernarfon £35; to Waunfawr £11.50; one under-16 travels free with an adult • ☎ 01766 516000, ⚲ festrail.co.uk

One of the most scenic lines in a land packed with charming railways, the restored narrow-gauge **Welsh Highland Railway** connects Porthmadog with Caernarfon, 25 miles away, rising from sea level to 650ft along the southern flank of Snowdon and passing gorgeous scenery. The full Porthmadog–Caernarfon round trip gives you five hours on the train and an hour in Caernarfon.

16

Portmeirion

Three miles east of Porthmadog near Minffordd • Daily 9.30am–7.30pm • £10; free afternoon entry if you pre-book a meal at the *Portmeirion Hotel* or have lunch at *Castell Deudraeth*; £2 entry Nov–March with downloaded voucher • Guided tours daily 10.30am–5pm (20min; free) • ⓦ portmeirion-village.com • Walk there in an hour from Porthmadog, or catch the #1b bus, which goes right to the gate. By train, take either the main line or Ffestiniog trains to Minffordd, from where it's a signposted 25min walk

Best known as "The Village" in the 1960s cult British TV series *The Prisoner*, the Italianate private village of **PORTMEIRION** in Tremadog Bay was the brainchild of eccentric architect Clough Williams-Ellis. In the 1920s, he devised the site as a "Home for Fallen Buildings" – endangered structures from all over Britain and abroad were dismantled then rebuilt here around a Mediterranean piazza. The idea was to create an ideal village using a "light-opera sort of approach", and the result is certainly theatrical: a stage set with a lucky dip of buildings arranged to distort perspectives and reveal glimpses of the seascape behind.

More than three thousand visitors a day come to ogle in summer, when it can be a delight; fewer in winter, when it seems just bizarre.

Criccieth Castle

Criccieth, 5 miles west of Porthmadog • April–Oct daily 10am–5pm; Nov–March 9.30am–4pm • £3.50, Nov–March Mon–Thurs & Sun 10am–4pm, Free; CADW • ⓣ 01766 522227, ⓦ cadw.wales.gov.uk • Buses every 30min–1hr from Porthmadog, 20min

Battle-worn **Criccieth Castle**, with its distinctive twin-towered gatehouse, was started by Llywelyn ap Iorwerth in 1230, strengthened by Edward I around 1285, and razed by Owain Glyndŵr in 1404. It's a great spot to sit and look over Cardigan Bay to Harlech, but leave time for the ticket office, where there's a wonderful animated cartoon about twelfth-century Wales.

16

ARRIVAL AND INFORMATION   PORTHMADOG

By train Porthmadog's mainline train station is at the north end of the High Street, while the Ffestiniog and Welsh Highland station is by the harbour about half a mile to the south.
Destinations Barmouth (6 daily; 45min); Blaenau Ffestiniog (by Ffestiniog Railway; April–Oct 4–8 daily; Nov–March several weekly; 1hr); Harlech (8 daily; 30min); Machynlleth (8 daily; 2hr); Pwllheli (8 daily; 25min).
By bus National Express buses stop outside Tesco in between Porthmadog's two train stations; local buses stop

near the tourist office.
Destinations Beddgelert (8 daily; 25min); Blaenau Ffestiniog (Mon–Sat hourly; 30min); Caernarfon (Mon–Sat 6 daily; 40min); Criccieth (Mon–Sat every 30min, Sun 7 daily; 15min); Dolgellau (3–4 daily; 50min); Pen-y-Pass (4 daily; 45min); Pwllheli (Mon–Sat every 30min, Sun 7 daily; 40min).
Tourist office By the harbour on Porthmadog High St (Easter–Oct daily 10am–5pm; late Oct–Easter Mon–Sat 10am–3.30pm; ⓣ 01766 512981, ⓦ visitsnowdonia.info).

ACCOMMODATION

★**Castell Deudraeth** Portmeirion ⓣ 01766 772400, ⓦ portmeirion-village.com. Chic designer hotel in a remodelled Victorian "castle" decorated in muted tones and modern streamlined furnishings. Only a 10min walk from Portmeirion village, where you're free to roam and use the outdoor heated pool. They have a sophisticated Modern British bistro on site, too. **£189**
★**Hotel Portmeirion** Portmeirion ⓣ 01766 770000, ⓦ portmeirion-village.com. The spirit of Clough Williams-Ellis remains in styling that's equal parts grand and eccentric, enjoyed by former guests like H.G. Wells, George Bernard Shaw and Noël Coward. Though lacking public areas, rooms are excellent and all different, many with beautiful views. Also lets luxurious self-catering cottages by the week (or half-week from Nov–March) that sleep up

to eight people. **£174**
Tyddyn Llwyn Black Rock Rd ⓣ 01766 512205, ⓦ tyddynllwyn.com. Beyond the caravans is a family campsite on a grassy hillside, with clean facilities and a pub with a restaurant on site. It's a 15min walk along the road to Morfa Bychan following Bank Place southwest off High St. March–Oct. Pitches **£20**
Yr Hen Fecws 16 Lombard St ⓣ 01766 514625, ⓦ henfecws.com. While compact, the en-suite rooms in this B&B are immaculate and comfortable, with fabrics in tasteful shades of dove grey and ruby and exposed stone walls in many. Breakfast is in the owners' café next door, serving fresh home-made bistro dishes. The best-value accommodation in the town centre. Café Mon–Sat 8am–4pm. **£75**

EATING AND DRINKING

Moorings Bistro 4 Ivy Terrace, Borth-y-Gest, 1 mile south of Porthmadog ☎01766 513500, ⓦmoorings bistroborthygest.com. Great little bistro, not least for the estuary views from its terrace. Specializes in local seafood dishes (circa £14), but also serves vegetarian dishes like mushroom, cranberry and brie Wellington. Mon, Tue & Thurs 11am–3pm & 6–9pm, Fri & Sat 9am–3pm & 6–9pm, Sun 9am–4pm, closed Wed.

Y Llong (The Ship) 14 Lombard St ☎01766 512990. The best pub in town is all low ceilings and old photos of the harbour, real ales and above-average pub grub. Mon–Fri noon–2pm & 5–11pm, Sat & Sun noon–11pm.

Y Sgwar The Square, Tremadog ☎01766 515451, ⓦysgwar-restaurant.co.uk. Well-prepared and -presented meals at this casual, stylish restaurant – good for home-made steak-and-ale pies at lunch (average £12) or more elaborate dinners. The three-course early bird special (Mon–Fri 6–7pm; £19) is excellent value. Daily noon–2pm & 6–9pm.

Abersoch

The former fishing village of **ABERSOCH**, pitched in the middle of two golden bays, is a largely anglicized resort, catering to affluent boat-owners and holidaying families. At high tide the harbour is an attractive spot to stroll. It is only five minutes' walk to the closest beach, **Abersoch Bay**, a long, clean strand lined by several dozen colourful beach huts. Surfers make for **Porth Neigwl** (Hell's Mouth), two miles to the southwest, which is one of the finest **surf** beaches in Wales – though beware of the undertow if you're swimming.

ARRIVAL AND INFORMATION

16

ABERSOCH

By bus Buses from Pwllheli (Mon–Sat 10–11 daily, Sun 4 daily; 20–30min) loop through the middle of Abersoch, stopping on Lôn Pen Cei. To continue to Aberdaron by bus, you must take a Pwllheli-bound service as far as Llanbedrog, then change onto the #17.

Tourist office In The Vestry on Lôn Engan (June–Sept daily 10.30am–3.30pm; Oct–May Sat & Sun 11am–2pm; ☎01758 712929, ⓦabersochtouristinfo.co.uk).

ACCOMMODATION AND EATING

Angorfa Lôn Sarn Bach ☎01758 712967, ⓦangorfa .com. Bare boards and white linen characterize this superior budget B&B. The two attic rooms have the best view, and breakfast is served in the daytime café downstairs. Note that the business was for sale at the time of writing. **£85**

Coconut Kitchen Lôn Pont Morgan ☎01758 712250. The best Thai place for miles: go for classics like beef Massaman or green chicken curry (around £12) or dishes that feature local fish and seafood like local prawn and pollock fishcakes. Takeaways available. Daily 5.30–10pm.

The Dining Room Lôn Sarn Bach ☎01758 740709, ⓦthediningroomabersoch.co.uk. Casual, wood-floored dinner-only bistro with a short menu plus daily specials, all cooked from fresh ingredients: expect hake rarebit with crispy Anglesey bacon and plum tomato jellies, or ribeye with black pepper and brandy sauce (£13–18). Fish specials on Friday. Daily 7–10pm; closed Mon–Wed in winter.

★**Venetia** Lôn Sarn Bach ☎01758 713354, ⓦvenetia wales.com. Chic boutique hotel with five individually styled rooms and plush bathrooms. Marco's Italian heritage influences the menu which is usually strong on fish and seafood, such as grilled bream with creamed kale and pancetta or canneloni of butternut squash. Most mains £13–17. Food served Wed–Sun 6.30–10pm. **£128**

WATERSPORTS IN ABERSOCH

Abersoch Sailing School ☎01758 712963, ⓦabersochsailingschool.com. Sailing lessons and rental of Laser dinghies, catamarans, kayaks and pedalos from the town's main beach; dinghies from £45 for 2hr.

Offaxis Town centre ☎01758 713407, ⓦoffaxis.co.uk. This wakeboarding and surfing academy offers lessons (£30) and rents gear (from £10/day). It's located where the through-road turns behind the harbour.

West Coast Surf Lôn Pen Cei ☎01758 713067, ⓦwestcoastsurf.co.uk. On the high street, they rent surfing gear (boards £10, wet suits £8) and offer lessons (£30 for 2hr).

Llŷn Adventures ☎07751 826714, ⓦllynadventures .com. This activities provider runs coasteering trips around the peninsula's superb coastline as well as kayaking and surfing trips (all £30, 3hr). March–Oct.

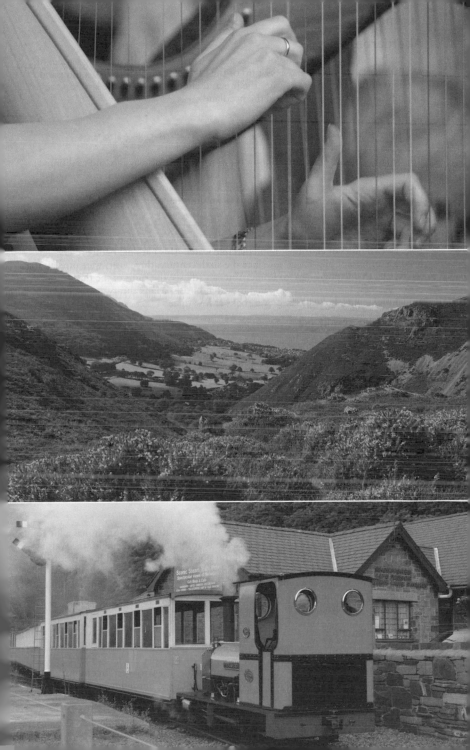

Aberdaron

You really feel you're at the end of Wales at the lovely lime-washed fishing hamlet of **ABERDARON**, two miles short of the tip of the Llŷn. For the best part of a thousand years up until the sixteenth century the inn and church here were the last stops on a pilgrim trail to Ynys Enlli, around the headland.

Porth y Swnt

Daily: March & Oct–Dec 10am–4pm; April–June & Sept 9am–5pm; July & Aug 9am–6pm • £2; NT • ☎ 01758 703814, ⓦ nationaltrust.org.uk

This small National Trust attraction in the village centre displays art and traditional crafts. But the meagre exhibits take second place to audioguides with interviews with local geologists, artists, gardeners, walkers, poets and farmers. The result is an oral history that subtly reveals something of the unique character of the Llŷn peninsula.

Ynys Enlli (Bardsey Island)

Bardsey Island or **Ynys Enlli** (The Island of the Currents) is separated from the tip of the Llŷn by two miles of churning, unpredictable water. This national nature reserve has been an important pilgrimage site since the sixth century: three visits were proclaimed equivalent to one pilgrimage to Rome. You can still see the ruins of the thirteenth-century abbey, but most visitors come to watch **birds** – Manx shearwaters, fulmars and guillemots – plus the **seals** lazed over rocks at low tide.

ARRIVAL AND DEPARTURE

ABERDARON

By bus The only public transport to Aberdaron is the #17 bus from Pwllheli (Mon–Sat 8 daily; 40min).

By boat Bardsey Boat Trips (£30 return; ☎ 07971 769895, ⓦ bardseyboattrips.com) head to Ynys Enlli from Porth Meudwy, a tiny cove a mile south of Aberdaron. Sailings are dependent on sea conditions and a viable load of passengers.

ACCOMMODATION AND EATING

Mynydd Mawr Llanllawen Fawr, 2 miles southwest ☎ 01758 760223. A couple of peaceful grassy fields right by the entrance to Mynydd Mawr and with views across to Ynys Enlli. Hot showers and electricity hook-up available. You'll need your own transport to access it. March–Oct. Pitches **£15**

The Ship ☎ 01758 760204, ⓦ theshiphotelaberdaron .co.uk. The cheaper of the village's two pubs lacks the sea view but has better food – expect the likes of local crab starters (£8) and a range of home-made meat and veggie mains (£10–14). Food served daily noon–2pm & 6.30–9pm. **£89**

Caernarfon

CAERNARFON, superbly set at the southern entrance to the Menai Strait, has a lot going for it. Its distinctive polygonal-towered **castle** is an undoubted highlight, the **Welsh Highland Railway** connects the town with the slopes of Snowdon and Porthmadog (see p.703 & p.706), and the modern marina development adds **Galeri Caernarfon**, a modest but interesting arts centre. The town walls are no match for Conwy's, but there is some great accommodation nearby, making this a good base for exploring both sides of Snowdon, the Llŷn and even Anglesey.

Caernarfon Castle

July & Aug daily 9.30am–6pm; March–June, Sept & Oct daily 9.30am–5pm; Nov–Feb Mon–Sat 10am–4pm, Sun 11am–4pm • £6.75; CADW • ☎ 01286 677617, ⓦ cadw.wales.gov.uk

In 1283, Edward I started work on **Caernarfon Castle**, the strongest link in his Iron Ring, a decisive hammer-blow to any Welsh aspirations to autonomy and the ultimate symbol of Anglo-Norman military might – it withstood two sieges by Owain Glyndŵr with a garrison of only 28 men-at-arms. As you enter through the **King's Gate**, the castle's strength is immediately apparent. Embrasures and murder holes between the

Bangor (9 miles) ▲

CAERNARFON

■ **ACCOMMODATION**
Cadnant Valley	3
Totters	2
Victoria House	1
Y Goeden Eirin	4

■ **PUB**
| Black Boy Inn | 1 |

● **CAFÉS & RESTAURANTS**
| Blas | 1 |
| Oren | 2 |

16

octagonal towers face in on no fewer than five gates and six portcullises, and that's once you have crossed the moat. Inside, the huge lawn gives a misleading impression as the wall dividing the two original wards, and all the buildings that filled them, crumbled away long ago. The towers are in a much better state, linked by an exhausting honeycomb of wall-walks and tunnels. The tallest is the **Eagle Tower**, whose three slender turrets are adorned with eagle sculptures and give the best views of the town.

ARRIVAL AND INFORMATION

CAERNARFON

By train The Welsh Highland Railway (see p.704 & p.706) operates from a small station on St Helen's Rd. Ride to Beddgelert and back, or just as far as Snowdon Ranger, from where you can explore the Snowdon Ranger Path (late March to Oct 2–4 trains daily; £23.60 to Beddgelert, £32 to Porthmadog; ☎01286 677018, ⓦfestrail.co.uk).

By bus National Express and local buses stop on Penllyn, just steps from the central Y Maes (Castle Square).

Destinations Bangor (Mon–Sat hourly, Sun 6 daily; 25min); Beddgelert (Mon–Sat 7 daily; 30min); Llanberis (Mon–Sat hourly, Sun 5 daily; 25min); Porthmadog (Mon–Sat 6 daily; 40min); Pwllheli (Mon–Sat roughly hourly, Sun 3 daily; 45min).

Tourist office Castle St (Easter–Sept daily 9.30am–4.30pm; Oct–Easter Mon–Sat 10am–3.30pm; ☎01286 672232).

ACCOMMODATION

Cadnant Valley Llanberis Rd ☎01286 673196, ⓦcwmcadnantvalley.co.uk. Pleasant wooded campsite arranged over terraces which feels far more rural than its location 10min' walk east of the centre suggests. March–Oct. __£12__

★ **Totters** Plas Porth Yr Aur, 2 High St ☎01286 672963, ⓦtotters.co.uk. Excellent, central hostel with lovely communal spaces, including a fourteenth-century cellar kitchen. There's also a great attic en-suite double with sea views and *Over The Road*, a separate self-contained house sleeping six (£20–25 per person). Dorm £17, double £40 **Victoria House** 13 Church St ☎ 01286 678263, ⓦ thevictoriahouse.co.uk. Very comfortable and good-value B&B within the town walls. Decor is Victorian-styled in rooms that come with flatscreen TV/DVD, free wi-fi and complimentary drinks. £70

Y Goeden Eirin Dolydd, 4 miles south of Caernarfon ☎ 01286 830942, ⓦ ygoedeneirin.co.uk. Stylish and hospitable farmhouse B&B with eco-credentials and an artistic sensibility. Dinner (£28 for 4 courses) is a relaxed affair served on oak tables; try the local red wine. £80

EATING AND DRINKING

Black Boys Inn Northgate St ☎ 01286 673604, ⓦ black-boy-inn.com. Ancient hostelry with two wonderful low-beamed bars and the best pub meals in town. Daily 11am–11pm.

★ **Blas** 23–25 Hole in the Wall St ☎ 01258 677707, ⓦ blascaernarfon.co.uk. Excellent cooking from local ingredients such as *conchiglioni* with mushroom ragu and crushed hazelnuts have seen this sweet modern bistro embraced by Caernarfon locals. Lunches (£7–10) include

home-made lamb burgers or club sandwiches. Daily Tues–Sat 10.30am–3pm & 6–9pm, Sun noon–3pm.

Oren 26 Hole in the Wall St ☎ 01286 674343. This delightful wood-floored restaurant, run by a Welsh-speaking Dutchman, offers a limited set menu that changes weekly, typically with a theme. Casual and eclectic, but there's no faulting the quality of the local produce and the price – £16.50 for three courses. Reservations required. Fri & Sat from 7pm, other evenings on request.

Anglesey

Across the Menai Strait from Caernarfon, the island of **Anglesey** (Ynys Môn) welcomes visitors to "Mam Cymru", the Mother of Wales, attesting to the island's former importance as the national breadbasket. The land remains predominantly pastoral, with small fields, stone walls and white houses reminiscent of parts of Ireland or England. Linguistically and politically, though, Anglesey is intensely Welsh, with seventy percent of the islanders being first-language Welsh-speakers. Many people head straight to **Holyhead** and the Irish ferries, but this would be to miss out on Anglesey's many charms, among them the ancient castle town of **Beaumaris**, the Whistler mural at **Plas Newydd** and superb coastal scenery. The island was the crucible of pre-Roman druidic activity in Britain, and the area is scattered with **Neolithic remains** from a pagan past.

Beaumaris

The original inhabitants of **BEAUMARIS** (Biwmares) were evicted by Edward I to make way for the construction of his new castle and bastide town, dubbed "beautiful marsh" in an attempt to attract English settlers. Today the place can still seem like the small English outpost Edward intended, with its elegant Georgian terrace along the front (designed by Joseph Hansom, of cab fame) and more plummy English accents than you'll have heard for a while.

Beaumaris Castle

Castle St • March–June, Sept & Oct daily 9.30am–5pm; July & Aug daily 9.30am–6pm; Nov–March Mon–Sat 10am–4pm, Sun 11am–4pm • £5.25; CADW • ☎ 01248 810361, ⓦ cadw.wales.gov.uk

Beaumaris Castle might never have been built had Madog ap Llywelyn not captured Caernarfon in 1294. When asked to build the new castle, James of St George abandoned the Caernarfon design in favour of a concentric plan, developing it into a highly evolved symmetrical octagon. Sited on flat land at the edge of town, the castle is denied the domineering majesty of Caernarfon or Harlech, its low outer walls appearing almost welcoming until you begin to appreciate the concentric layout of the defences protected by massive towers, a moat linked to the sea and the Arab-influenced staggered entries through the two gatehouses. Despite more than thirty years' work, the project was never quite finished, leaving the inner ward empty. You can explore a number of inner and outer **wall walks**, and wander through miles of internal passages in the walls.

Beaumaris Old Courthouse

Castle St • April–Sept daily except Fri 10.30am–5pm; Oct & half-terms Sat & Sun 10.30am–5pm • £3.60 • ☎ 01248 811691,
ⓦ visitanglesey.co.uk

Almost opposite the castle stands the Jacobean **Beaumaris Old Courthouse**, built in 1614 and used as an Assizes court until 1971. Take a look at *The Lawsuit*, a plaque in the magistrates' room depicting two farmers pulling the horns and tail of a cow while a lawyer milks it.

Beaumaris Gaol

Steeple Lane • April–Sept daily except Fri 10.30am–5pm; October & half-terms Sat & Sun 10.30am–5pm • £4.50 • ☎ 01248 810921,
ⓦ visitanglesey.co.uk

Some citizens were transported from Beaumaris Courthouse to the colonies for their crimes. Others wound up in the 1829 **Beaumaris Gaol**, which was considered a model prison, with running water and toilets in each cell, and an infirmary. Still, it's a gloomy place: witness the windowless punishment cell, the yard for stone-breaking and the treadmill water-pump operated by the prisoners.

Puffin Island Cruises

Beaumaris Pier • Easter–Sept daily 10am–5pm • £8 • ☎ 01248 810251, ⓦ starida.co.uk

Interesting as Beaumaris is, a fine day might be better spent **cruising to Puffin Island**, five miles northeast. Numbers permitting, you can book an hour-long excursion around, but not onto, the island spotting nesting razorbills, guillemots and puffins, and also go fishing on cruises (from £25/3hr).

ARRIVAL AND DEPARTURE   BEAUMARIS

Regular **buses** (#53, #56, #57 and #58) to Beaumaris include services from Bangor (every 30min; 20–35min).

ACCOMMODATION

★**Cleifiog** Townsend ☎ 01248 811507, ⓦ cleifiogbandb.co.uk. Three beautiful rooms in a Georgian townhouse with great views across Menai Strait to Snowdonia. A welcome tray with jars of biscuits and coffee, plus a great breakfast, round out the welcoming hospitality. **£90**

Victoria Cottage Victoria Terrace ☎ 01248 810807, ⓦ victoriacottage.net. Good boutique B&B with two spacious en-suite rooms and two cheaper loft rooms that share a bathroom with a big bath. **£90**

Ye Olde Bull's Head Inn 18 Castle St ☎ 01248 810329, ⓦ bullsheadinn.co.uk. This ancient coaching inn has accommodation in antique rooms in the main building and chic — more expensive — modern rooms in the adjacent *Townhouse*, all with an excellent breakfast. **£105**

EATING AND DRINKING

The Pier House The Front ☎ 01248 811055. On a sunny day, there is nowhere better for a bite or coffee than this waterfront bistro with picture-postcard views across the Strait. On the menu are breakfasts, sandwiches, fish and chips plus larger mains like local *moules marinière* or steak and ale pie (mains average £8–10). Daily 9am–9pm.

Red Boat Ice Cream Parlour 34 Castle St ⓦ redboatgelato.com. Slip into one of the booths in this retro ice-cream parlour with an ever-changing selection of superb made-on-the-premises gelato and sorbet. Daily 10am–6pm.

★**Ye Olde Bull's Head Inn** 18 Castle St ☎ 01248 810329, ⓦ bullsheadinn.co.uk. Excellent combination: a cosy old-fashioned bar, bare-boards conservatory brasserie (mains around £14) and superb *Loft* restaurant, serving inventive modern dishes (£47.50 for 3 courses). Brasserie noon–2pm (till 3pm Sun) & 6–9pm daily; Loft Tues–Sat 7–9.30pm.

Llanfairpwllgwyngyllgogerychwyrndrobwllllandysiliogogogoch (Llanfairpwll)

In the 1880s a local tailor invented the longest place name in Britain in a successful attempt to draw tourists. It does just that, but most will be utterly disappointed when they arrive at **Llanfairpwllgwyngyllgogerychwyrndrobwllllandysiliogogogoch**, which translates as "St Mary's Church in the hollow of white hazel near a rapid whirlpool and the Church of St Tysilio near the red cave" – commonly shortened to **LLANFAIRPWLL**. There's little here but a train station – the stop for the obligatory sign photo – and Anglesey's main **tourist office**; the nearby house of **Plas Newydd**, however, is worth a visit.

Plas Newydd

A4080, 1.5 miles southwest of Llanfairpwll • **House**: March–mid-March Sat & Sun 11am–3pm; mid-March–early Nov Sat–Wed free guided tours 11–noon, noon–4.30pm free-flow access • **Gardens**: Jan & Feb Sat & Sun 11am–4pm; March–June & Sept–early Nov Sat–Thurs 10.30am–5.30pm; July & Aug daily 10.30am–5.30pm • £9.35, garden only £7.35; NT • ☎ 01248 715272, ⊕ nationaltrust.org.uk

The marquesses of Anglesey still live at **Plas Newydd**, a modest three-storey mansion with incongruous Tudor caps on slender octagonal turrets. Corridors of oil paintings and period rooms lead to the highlight, a 58ft-long wall with a trompe l'oeil painting by **Rex Whistler**, who spent a couple of years here in the 1930s. Walking along his imaginary seascape, your position appears to shift as the mountains of Snowdonia and a whimsical composite of elements, culled from Italy as well as Britain, change perspective. Portmeirion is there, as is the Round Tower from Windsor Castle, and Whistler appears both as a gondolier and as a gardener in one of the two right-angled panels at either end. The prize exhibit in the **Cavalry Museum**, a few rooms further on, is the world's first articulated false leg, all wood, leather and springs, designed for the first marquess, who lost his leg at Waterloo.

ARRIVAL AND INFORMATION LLANFAIRPWLL

16

By train Train station is beside the main road (A5) in central Llanfairpwll.

Destinations Bangor (9 daily; 10min); Holyhead (9 daily; 30min).

By bus Bus #42 (Llagefni–Bangor via Llanfairpwll) stops outside Plas Newydd (Mon–Sat 10 daily, Sun 2 daily).

Destinations Bangor (every 30min; 15min); Holyhead (hourly; 1hr).

Tourist office Holyhead Rd (April–Oct Mon–Sat 9.30am–5.30pm, Sun 9.30am–4.30pm; Nov–March Mon–Sat 9.30am–5pm, Sun 9.30–4.30pm; ☎ 01248 713177, ⊕ visitanglesey.co.uk).

Holyhead

Drab **HOLYHEAD** (Caergybi; pronounced in English "holly-head") is Anglesey's largest town and the terminus for ferry routes to Ireland. It isn't somewhere you'll want to spend much time, though it has some lovely coastline all about and the cliff-top delights of **South Stack** (Ynys Lawd), just over Holyhead Mountain, two miles to the west (no buses).

South Stack Lighthouse

Easter–Sept Sat–Thurs 10.30am–5pm • £5.15

A twisting path with more than four hundred steps leads down from the South Stack car park to a suspension bridge over the surging waves, once the keeper's only access to the now fully automated pepper-pot **lighthouse**, built in 1809. Views on to the cliffs are stupendous as you climb down to the island and, once there, you'll find exhibitions on local wildlife and you can take a tour of the lighthouse itself. Tickets are issued at the RSPB-run *South Stack Kitchen*, a café-cum-interpretative centre a hundred yards back along the lane.

Ellin's Tower Seabird Centre

Easter–Sept daily 10am–5pm; visitor centre daily 10am–5pm • Free • ☎ 01407 762100, ⊕ rspb.org.uk/wales

Views of the cliffs below the *South Stack Kitchen* are best from the RSPB-run **Ellin's Tower Seabird Centre**, where binoculars and closed-circuit TV give an unrivalled opportunity to watch up to three thousand birds – razorbills, guillemots and a few puffins – nesting on the nearby sea cliffs while choughs and peregrines wheel outside the tower's windows.

ARRIVAL AND DEPARTURE

By train Local Arriva trains and long-distance Virgin trains arrive at the train station beside the ferry port.

Destinations Bangor (22 daily; 30–40min); Conwy (11 daily; 1hr); Llandudno (18 daily; 1hr 20min); Llanfairpwll (9 daily; 30min).

By bus Local and National Express buses stop by the passenger ferry terminal.

Destinations Bangor (hourly; 1hr 15min); Llanfairpwll (hourly; 1hr).

By ferry Irish Ferries (ⓦ irishferries.com) and Stena Line (ⓦ stenaline.com) run to Dublin and Dun Laoghaire using ferries (4hr) and fast catamarans (2hr). Between the two operators, around 8 ferries operate 24 hours a day.

ACCOMMODATION AND EATING

Harbourfront Bistro Newry Beach ☎ 01407 763433, ⓦ harbourfrontbistro.co.uk. Sandwiches, toasted baguettes, cakes and good coffee, plus dishes such as pan-seared tiger prawns (£10) and veggie pasta

bake (£8) served in a bistro with good harbour views – a good spot to wait for a ferry. Reservations required for dinner. Wed & Sun noon–2.30pm, Thurs–Sat noon–2.30pm & 6–9pm.

The north coast

Anglesey connects with the mainland at the university town of **Bangor**, a lively enough place that's best used as base for visiting **Penrhyn Castle** or as a springboard for Snowdonia. Heading east you encounter the **north coast** proper, where the castle town of **Conwy** and elegant **Llandudno** are the essential stops.

16

Bangor

BANGOR, across the bridge from Anglesey, is not big, but as the largest town in Gwynedd and home to Bangor University, it passes in these parts for cosmopolitan. For the visitor there's little to see. Yet Bangor is a hotbed of Welsh nationalism, hardly surprising in such a staunchly Welsh-speaking area, and it's a dramatic contrast from the English-speaking north-coast resorts.

Bangor Cathedral

Glanrafon • Daily 9am–5pm • Free

Bangor's thirteenth- to fifteenth-century **cathedral** boasts the longest continuous use of any cathedral in Britain, easily predating the town. A hint of its ancient origins can be gleaned from the blocked-in window dating from the Norman rebuilding of 1071. Pop in if only to see the sixteenth-century wooden **Mostyn Christ**, depicted bound and seated on a rock.

Bangor Pier

Mon–Fri 8.30am–dusk, Sat & Sun 10am–dusk • 50p

For a good look down the Menai Strait to Telford's graceful bridge (the world's first large iron suspension bridge, completed in 1826), walk along Garth Road to Bangor's pristine Victorian pier, which reaches halfway to Anglesey.

Penrhyn Castle

A5 at Llandygai, 2 miles east of Bangor • House March to Oct daily 11am–5pm; Nov–Dec Sat & Sun noon–3pm • **Gardens & railway museum** March–Oct daily 11am–5pm; Nov–Feb daily noon–3pm • £10.35 or £6.75 for grounds & railway museum only; NT • ☎ 01248 363219, ⓦ nationaltrust.org.uk • Buses #5, #6, #67 and #75 run frequently from Bangor to Penrhyn's gates, though it's still a mile to the house

The awkward truth of **Penrhyn Castle** is that it is testament to the Anglo-Welsh gentry's oppression of the rural Welsh. Built on the profits of a Welsh slate mine, this nineteenth-century neo-Norman fancy drips with luxury in its three hundred opulent rooms.

The house was built by Caribbean sugar plantation owner, slave trader and vehement anti-abolitionist Richard Pennant, First Baron Penrhyn, who built a port on the northeastern edge of Bangor in order to ship his Bethesda slate to the world. But it was his self-aggrandizing great-great-nephew, George Dawkins, who inherited the 40,000-acre estate and transformed the neo-Gothic hall. With the aid of architect Thomas Hopper, Dawkins spent thirteen years from 1827 encasing his inheritance in a Norman-style fortress with a five-storey keep.

Three-foot-thick oak doors separate the rooms, ebony is used to dramatic effect, and a slate bed was built for the visit of Queen Victoria. The decoration is glorious, and fairly true to Romanesque style. The family also amassed Wales's largest private painting collection, including a Gainsborough landscape, Canaletto's *The Thames at Westminster* and a Rembrandt portrait. Also open are the Victorian kitchen and servants' quarters.

ARRIVAL AND DEPARTURE
BANGOR

By train Bangor's train station lies at the south end of Holyhead Rd.

Destinations Chester (21 daily; 1hr); Conwy (11 daily; 20min); Holyhead (22 daily; 30–40min); Llandudno (18 daily; 40min).

By bus National Express and local buses stop in the centre of town.

Destinations Beaumaris (every 30min; 20–35min); Caernarfon (every 10min; 25min); Conwy (every 15min; 45min); Holyhead (hourly; 1hr 15min); Llanberis (hourly; 45min); Llandudno (every 15min; 1hr); Llanfairpwll (every 30min; 15min).

ACCOMMODATION

Treborth Hall Farm A487, 1.8 miles southwest of upper Bangor between the two Menai Strait bridges ☎ 01248 364104, ⊛ treborthleisure.co.uk. The nearest campsite to town is a relaxed spot, partly in an old walled garden. There are coin-op showers (£1) and everything is well kept. #5

buses pass the entrance. April–Oct. Pitches **£12**

Y Garth Garth Rd ☎ 01248 362277, ⊛ thegarth guesthouse.co.uk. Probably the best value in the centre, this decent B&B has ten en-suite rooms and full breakfast ("you won't eat till tea-time", they promise). **£60**

EATING AND DRINKING

★ **Blue Sky** Rear of 236 High St ☎ 01248 355444, ⊛ blueskybangor.co.uk. Airy, casual daytime café with mismatched tables, free wi-fi and delicious breakfasts, soups, sandwiches, burgers and platters (often organic; £5–8) plus great coffee. Check the website for evening gigs and movies. Mon–Sat 9.30am–5.30pm and occasional evenings.

Kyffin 129 High St ☎ 01248 355161. A sweet little vegetarian and vegan café with Fairtrade coffee and a warm atmosphere that makes you want to stick around for home-made light lunches such as spicy lentil lasagne or broccoli and apple tart (mostly under £6). Mon–Sat 9.30am–5pm.

Conwy

CONWY, wonderfully set on the Conwy Estuary, twenty miles east of Bangor, is backed by a forested fold of Snowdonia. The town has a fine **castle** and a complete belt of 30ft-high town **walls** encircling a compact core of medieval and Victorian buildings. This makes it extremely easy to potter around, and though you'll see everything you need to in a day, you may well find yourself lingering longer.

Conwy Castle

Entrance Rose Hill St or Llanrwst Rd • Daily: March–June, Sept & Oct 9.30am–5pm; July & Aug 9.30am–6pm; Nov–March 10am–4pm • £6.75; joint ticket with Plas Mawr £8.75; CADW • ☎ 01492 592358, ⊛ cadw.wales.gov.uk

Conwy Castle is the toughest-looking link in Edward I's fortresses around North Wales. With 1500 men, James of St George took just five years to construct eight massive **towers** in a rectangle around the two wards on a strategic knoll near the mouth of the river. In 1401, on Good Friday, when the fifteen-strong castle guard were at church, two cousins of Owain Glyndŵr took the castle and razed the town for Glyndŵr's cause. It was re-fortified for the Civil War then stripped of all its iron, wood and lead, and was left substantially as it is today.

CONWY

The outer ward's 130ft-long **Great Hall** and the **King's Apartments** are both well preserved, but the only part of the castle to have kept its roof is the **Chapel Tower**, named for the small room built into the wall.

Aberconwy House

Castle St • March–June, Sept & Oct daily 11am–5pm; July & Aug daily 10am–5pm; Nov & Dec Sat & Sun noon–3pm • £3.40; NT • ☎ 01492 592246, ⓦ nationaltrust.org.uk

Aberconwy House is the oldest in Conwy, built about 1300 and variously used as a bakery, antique shop, sea captain's house and temperance hotel. Its incarnations are re-created in rooms furnished with a simple yet elegant collection of rural furniture.

Plas Mawr

20 High St • April–Sept daily 9am–5pm; Oct Tues–Sun 9.30am–4pm • £5.75, joint ticket with castle £8.75; CADW • ☎ 01492 580167, ⓦ cadw.wales.gov.uk

The Dutch-style **Plas Mawr** is among the best-preserved Elizabethan townhouses in Britain, built in 1576 for Robert Wynn, one of the first Welsh people to live in the town. Much of the dressed stonework was replaced during renovations in the 1940s and 1950s, but the interior sports more original features, in particular the friezes and superb moulded-plaster ceilings depicting fleurs-de-lis, griffons, owls and rams.

The smallest house in Great Britain

Conwy Quay • Easter to mid-Oct daily 10am–5pm • £1

The two tiny rooms of the **smallest house in Great Britain** are together only 9ft high and 6ft wide. You'll have to duck to get in, a problem that by all accounts vexed the last resident, a 6ft 3in fisherman, until he left in around 1900.

Bodnant Garden

Tal-y-Cafn, off A470, 8 miles south of Conwy • March–Oct daily 10am–5pm (till 8pm Wed May–Aug); late Oct–Feb daily 10am–4pm • £9.50, £4.75 in winter; NT • ☏ 01492 650460, ⓦ nationaltrust.org.uk • #25 bus from Llandudno and Llandudno Junction roughly every hour

During May and June, the 160ft laburnum tunnel flourishes and banks of rhododendrons are in glorious bloom all over **Bodnant Garden**, Wales's finest formal garden. Laid out in 1875 by English industrialist Henry Pochin, the garden spreads over eighty acres, divided into an upper terraced garden and lower Pinetum and Wild Garden. Shrubs and plants provide a blaze of colour throughout the opening season, but autumn is a perfect time to be here, with hydrangeas still in bloom and fruit trees shedding their leaves.

ARRIVAL AND INFORMATION

CONWY

By train Llandudno Junction, less than a mile across the river to the east, serves as the main train station for services from Chester to Holyhead, as well as for trains heading south to Betws-y-Coed and Blaenau Ffestiniog. Only slow, regional services stop in Conwy itself (on request).
Destinations Bangor (Mon–Sat 11 daily; 20min); Holyhead (11 daily; 1hr); Llandudno Junction (11 daily; 4min).

By bus Local buses stop either on Lancaster Square or outside the town walls on Town Ditch Rd. Head to Llandudno to pick up National Express coaches.
Destinations Bangor (every 15min; 45min); Llandudno (every 15min; 20min).
Tourist office In the same building as the castle ticket office (April–Oct daily 9am–5pm; Nov–March Mon–Sat 9.30am–4pm, Sun 11am–4pm; ☏ 01492 592248).

ACCOMMODATION

16

Glan Heulog Llanrwst Rd, half a mile out on the B5106 Trefriw Rd ☏ 01492 593845, ⓦ conwy-bedandbreakfast.co.uk. Toile and modern wallpapers, country charm and friendly owners make this one of Conwy's best small guesthouses. A Victorian house with six en-suites, including one family room. **£72**
★**Gwynfryn** 4 York Place ☏ 01492 576733, ⓦ gwynfrynbandb.co.uk. A modern country ambience makes this central B&B a fine choice; its five tastefully decorated rooms – mostly en suite, one with a private bathroom – have a small fridge and DVD player, and access to a film library and free wi-fi. **£70**
Swan Cottage 18 Berry St ☏ 01492 596840, ⓦ swancottageconwy.con. While some rooms are small and modern decor trends have yet to arrive, this is

nevertheless a friendly and super-central B&B with three en-suite rooms, two with great estuary views, one tucked into the attic. **£60**
★**Tir y Coed** Rowen ☏ 01492 650219, ⓦ tirycoed.com. This has style and luxury to spare, whether in immaculate standard doubles or the large Rowen Suite, yet remains as relaxed as you'd hope of a small country five-star hotel in the lovely village of Rowen. Modern decor is quietly opulent, your hosts utterly charming. Nor will you go hungry – the in-house restaurant is excellent. No children under 14. **£135**
YHA Conwy Lark Hill ☏ 0845 371 9732, ⓦ yha.org.uk. Spacious, modernized hostel a 10min walk from town up the Sychnant Pass Rd, open all day, with good meals and bike rental. Dorms **£21**, twins **£35**

EATING AND DRINKING

★**The Albion** cnr Upper Gate St ☏ 01492 582484, ⓦ albionalehouse.weebly.com. Four local breweries, including the excellent Conwy Brewery, joined forces to run this Grade II-listed pub. There's no muzak, no TVs, just eight ales on tap, bar snacks like local pies, open fires and the charm of a 1920s wooden interior. Mon–Thurs noon–11pm, Fri & Sat noon–midnight.
Archway 12 Bangor Rd ☏ 01492 592 458. Quality eat-in and take-out fish and chip restaurant also doing pizza and pies. On a fine evening take your haul to the quay and wash it down with a pint from the *Liverpool Arms*. Daily 11am–10pm or later.
Dawson's Castle Hotel, High St ☏ 01492 582800, ⓦ castlewales.co.uk. Smart bar and restaurant where the

emphasis is on quality ingredients cooked well and served without too much fuss. Come for a pint or pre-dinner cocktail in the bar then something like local haddock and chorizo risotto (£8) followed by tandoori monkfish with vanilla mash (£16). Mon–Thurs & Sun 7.30am–9.30pm, Fri & Sat 7.30am–10pm.
★**Watson's Bistro** Chapel St ☏ 01492 596326, ⓦ watsonsbistroconwy.co.uk. The best food in town in a relaxed bistro with outside seating beneath the town walls: expect filo of chestnut mushrooms, leeks and puy lentils in brandy cream (£16) or pan-roast hake with prawns and samphire (£18). Early dinner menus are a bargain at £11 for two courses. Mon & Tues 5.30–8pm, Wed–Sun noon–2pm & 5.30–8pm (Fri & Sat till 9pm).

Llandudno

The hummocky limestone hills of the 680ft **Great Orme** and Little Orme frame the gently curving Victorian frontage of **LLANDUDNO**, four miles north of Conwy. Despite the modern holiday-makers to this seaside resort, Llandudno retains an undeniably dignified air from its Victorian heyday, bolstered by its ever-improving selection of chic hotels and quality restaurants.

Llandudno's early history revolves around the **Great Orme** where St Tudno built a monastic cell in the sixth century that gave the town its name. In the mid-nineteenth century, local landowner Edward Mostyn exploited the growing craze for sea-bathing and built a town for the upper-middle classes which quickly became synonymous with the Victorian ideal of a respectable seaside resort. The embodiment of Llandudno's ornate Victoriana is the splendid **pier** – seven hundred feet of kids and candyfloss, strollers and sea views.

The Oriel Mostyn

12 Vaughan St • Tues–Sun 10.30am–5pm • Free • ☎ 01492 879201, ⓦ mostyn.org

The elaborate terracotta brick facade of the **Oriel Mostyn** gives little clue as to the raw interior spaces of this refurbished gallery – all rough-cast bare concrete – named after Lady Mostyn, for whom it was originally built in 1901. The five rooms are almost always showing something of interest, much of it by leading Welsh artists. There's also a good arts shop and the bare *Café Lux*.

The Great Orme

Though low by local standards, the view from the top of the **Great Orme** (Pen y Gogarth) ranks alongside those from loftier summits in Snowdonia, combining the seascapes east towards Rhyl and west over the sands of the Conwy Estuary with the northern limit of the Carneddau range where Snowdonia crashes into the sea. This huge lump of carboniferous limestone was subject to some of the same stresses that folded Snowdonia, producing fissures filled by molten mineral-bearing rock.

16

Great Orme Tramway

Church Walks • Daily: Easter–late Oct 10am–6pm; Oct 10am–5pm • £4 single, £6 return • ☎ 01492 879306, ⓦ greatormetramway.co.uk

The base of the Great Orme is traditionally circumnavigated on **Marine Drive**, a five-mile anticlockwise circuit from just near Llandudno's pier. The best way to get to the copper mines and the grasslands on top of the Orme is by the San Francisco-style **Great Orme Tramway**, which creaks up from the bottom of Old Road, much as it has done since 1902.

Great Orme Aerial Cable Car

Happy Valley • Easter–Sept daily, roughly 10am–5pm, depending on the weather • £8/£8.50 single/return • ☎ 01492 877205

Near the base of the pier and close to the start of Marine Drive, the **cable car** is an alternative aerial route up the Orme – when it isn't too windy, it lifts people to the top in open four-seater cabins, which swing over the formal gardens of **Happy Valley**.

Great Orme Copper Mines

Mid-March to Oct daily 10am–5pm • £6.75 • ☎ 01492 870447, ⓦ greatormemines.info

A Bronze Age settlement developed around what are now the **Great Orme Copper Mines**, accessed via the tramway. Hard hats and miners' lamps are provided for the self-guided **tour** through just a small portion of the tunnels, enough to give you a feel for the cramped working conditions and the dangers of falling rock.

ARRIVAL AND INFORMATION   LLANDUDNO

By train Direct services to Llandudno's forlorn train station arrive from Betws-y-Coed and Chester; for all other services change at Llandudno Junction, near Conwy.

Destinations Bangor (18 daily; 40min); Betws-y-Coed (4 daily; 40min); Blaenau Ffestiniog (6 daily; 1hr 20min); Chester (roughly hourly; 1hr 10min); Holyhead (18 daily;

1hr 20min); Llandudno Junction (every 30min; 10min).

By bus Local buses stop on either Mostyn St or Gloddaeth St, while National Express buses from Chester, Bangor and Pwllheli (bookings at the tourist office) stop at the Coach Park on Mostyn Broadway. Alpine run an open-top double-decker bus looping from Llandudno to Conwy and back (late May to mid-Sept every 30min 10am–4pm; £7.50; ☎01492 879133) – perfect for a

half-day visit to Conwy.

Destinations Bangor (every 15min; 1hr); Betws-y-Coed (4–6 daily daily; 50min); Blaenau Ffestiniog (6–8 daily; 1hr 10min); Conwy (every 15min; 20min).

Tourist office In the Library Building, Mostyn St (Easter–Sept Mon–Sat 9am–4.30pm; ☎01492 577577, ⓦ visit llandudno.org.uk). Stocks a free map of Great Orme footpaths.

ACCOMMODATION

Finding a place to stay is not usually a problem, though booking ahead is wise. Most of the budget places congregate along St David's Rd, just west of the station, and on Deganwy Ave. The nearest **camping** is at Conwy.

★**The Cliffbury** 34 St David's Rd ☎01492 877224, ⓦ thecliffbury.co.uk. Stylish wallpapers, sparkling white bathrooms, free wi-fi and dedicated hosts define this classy B&B on a quiet street with six individually decorated rooms; superiors are bigger and come with DVD player and robes. Breakfast ingredients are locally sourced where possible. Generally two-night minimum. **£65**

★**Escape** 48 Church Walks ☎01492 877776, ⓦ escapebandb.co.uk. One of the most celebrated B&Bs in North Wales, this is effortlessy chic in nine individually designed rooms that combine clean-lined modernism, retro or antique pieces, yet is playful rather than po-faced; book online to select your room. Free wi-fi, great breakfasts, a guest lounge with honesty bar and lovely hosts complete the

package. **£90**

Glenthorne 2 York Rd ☎01492 879591, ⓦ glenthorne -guesthousellandudno.co.uk. Very good Welsh-speaking guesthouse with seven modern rooms and a welcoming atmosphere – a relaxing home from home with evening meals available on request. Minimum two nights. **£64**

Llandudno Hostel 14 Charlton St ☎01492 877430, ⓦ llandudnohostel.co.uk. Family-run, forty-bed hostel in the centre of town with dorm beds, doubles, a family room and a friendly atmosphere. Sheets, towels and a continental breakfast are supplied, but there's no self-catering kitchen. Often full with school groups during term time, so call ahead. Dorms **£18**

EATING AND DRINKING

The Albert 56 Madoc St ☎01492 877188, ⓦ albertllandudno.co.uk. What looks like a standard-issue pub provides one of the finest pub menus in town – blackboard specials like seafood spaghetti or salmon with pea and asparagus risotto (£10–14) plus great Sunday roasts – as well as several fresh local ales. Daily 11.30am–10pm or later; food daily noon–9pm.

★**Bodysgallen Hall** A470, 3 miles south of town ☎01492 584466, ⓦ bodysgallen.com. A manor house with modern British dishes (£29 two courses; smart(ish) dress required) like lamb with pea and chive crème fraiche in the restaurant and the likes of club sandwiches and salads in the *1620* bistro (Mon–Fri 2-course lunches for £14 if booked in advance). Restaurant Tues–Sun 12.30–2.30pm & 5–10pm; bistro Mon–Sat 12.30–

3pm & 5.30–9pm.

Osborne's 17 North Parade ☎01492 860330, ⓦ osbournehouse.co.uk. Opulent café and restaurant lit by chandeliers with modern dishes like herb-crusted salmon and lemon butter (£12.95) or slow-roast lamb. Lunch menus are lighter. Come early for a cocktail or an excellent afternoon tea (£13). Mon–Thurs & Sun 10.30–9.30pm, Fri & Sat till 10pm.

The Seahorse 7 Church Walks ☎01492 875315, ⓦ the -seahorse.co.uk. This two-in-one dinner-only restaurant – intimate and smarter upstairs, a sociable brasserie in the cellar – remains one of the town's best options. The menu is predominantly fish and seafood (£28 for 2 courses): expect the likes of haddock chowder, fresh seafood or Parma-ham-wrapped monkfish. Daily 4.30–10pm.

Bodelwyddan Castle and around

Bodelwyddan, off junction 25 of A55, 2 miles west of St Asaph • Generally open mid-April–Oct Wed–Sun plus Mon & Tues in school holidays 10.30am–5pm; Nov to mid-April Sat & Sun 10.30am–4pm – see website for full opening times • £6.95 including audio tour and grounds, grounds only £4.20 • ☎01745 584060, ⓦ bodelwyddan-castle.co.uk • Bus #13 Llandudno–Prestatyn via Bodelwyddan village (Mon–Sat hourly)

The finest art showcase in North Wales is **Bodelwyddan Castle**, an outpost of the National Portrait Gallery half a mile south of Bodelwyddan village. The opulent Victorian interiors provide a suitable setting for hundreds of paintings by Millais,

16

Rossetti, Browning, John Singer Sargent and Landseer, among others. Look out for two portraits highlighting the Pre-Raphaelite movement's support for social reform: William Holman Hunt's portrayal of the vociferous opponent of slavery and capital punishment, Stephen Lushington; Ford Madox Brown's double portrait of Henry Fawcett, prime mover in the passing of the 1867 Reform Bill, and suffragette Millicent Garrett.

St Asaph Cathedral

St Asaph (Llanelwy), 2 miles east of Bodelwyddan • Daily 9am–6.30pm • Free • ⓦ stasaphcathedral.org.uk

ST ASAPH (Llanelwy) is home to Britain's smallest **cathedral**, founded around 570 by St Kentigern and no bigger than many village churches. From 1601 until his death in 1604, the bishopric was held by **William Morgan**, who was responsible for the translation of the first Welsh-language Bible, without which the language may have died out. A thousand Morgan Bibles were printed, of which only nineteen remain, one of them displayed in the south transept along with notable prayer books and psalters.

16

Edinburgh and the Lothians

THE ROYAL MILE, EDINBURGH

17 Edinburgh and the Lothians

Edinburgh, the showcase capital of Scotland, is a venerable, cosmopolitan and cultured city famed worldwide for its annual festival. The setting is wonderfully striking: perched on a series of extinct volcanoes and rocky crags which rise from the generally flat landscape of the Lothians, with the sheltered shoreline of the Firth of Forth to the north. "My own Romantic town", Sir Walter Scott called it, although it was another native, Robert Louis Stevenson, who perhaps best captured the feel of his "precipitous city", declaring that "No situation could be more commanding for the head of a kingdom; none better chosen for noble prospects". Edinburgh's ability to capture the literary imagination has seen it dubbed a World City of Literature by UNESCO, who have also conferred World Heritage Site status on much of the centre.

The area north of the castle, the dignified, Grecian-style **New Town** was laid out in the eighteenth century after the announcement of a plan to improve conditions in the city. The **Old Town**, on the other hand, with its tortuous alleys and tightly packed closes, is unrelentingly medieval, associated in popular imagination with the city's underworld lore of murderers Burke and Hare and of schizophrenic Deacon Brodie, inspiration for Stevenson's *Strange Case of Dr Jekyll and Mr Hyde*.

Set on the hill which sweeps down from the fairy-tale castle to the royal **Palace of Holyroodhouse**, the Old Town preserves all the key reminders of its role as a historic capital, augmented now by the dramatic and unusual new **Scottish Parliament** building, opposite the palace. A few hundred yards away, a tantalizing glimpse of the wild beauty of Scotland's scenery can be had in **Holyrood Park**, an extensive area of open countryside dominated by **Arthur's Seat**, the largest and most impressive of the volcanoes. Among Edinburgh's many museums, the exciting **National Museum of Scotland** houses ten thousand of Scotland's most precious artefacts, while the **National Gallery of Scotland** and its offshoot, the **Scottish National Gallery of Modern Art**, house two of Britain's finest collections of paintings.

Beyond the centre, Edinburgh's liveliest area is **Leith**, the city's medieval port, whose seedy edge is softened by a series of great bars and restaurants, along with the presence of the former royal yacht **Britannia**. The wider rural surroundings of Edinburgh, known as the **Lothians**, mix rolling countryside and attractive country towns with some impressive historic ruins.

Brief history

It was during the **Dark Ages** that the name Edinburgh – at least in its early forms of Dunedin or Din Eidyn ("fort of Eidyn") – first appeared. Built upon the Castle Rock volcano, at the heart of today's city, the strategic fort served as Scotland's **southernmost border post** until 1018, when King Malcolm I established the River Tweed as the

SCOTTISH PARLIAMENT, EDINBURGH

Highlights

❶ The Old Town The evocative heart of the historic city, with its tenements, closes, courtyards, ghosts and catacombs cheek-by-jowl with many of Scotland's most important buildings. **See p.730**

❷ Edinburgh Castle Perched on an imposing volcanic crag, the castle dominates Scotland's capital, its ancient battlements protecting the Crown Jewels. **See p.730**

❸ Scottish Parliament Enric Miralles' quirky design is a dynamic modern presence in Holyrood's historic royal precinct. **See p.736**

❹ Holyrood Park Wild moors, rocky crags and an 800ft peak (Arthur's Seat), all slap in the middle of the city. **See p.737**

❺ National Museum of Scotland The treasures of Scotland's past housed in a dynamic and superbly conceived building. **See p.737**

❻ The Edinburgh Festival In August and early September, around a million visitors flock to the world's biggest arts festival, which is in fact a series of separate festivals: bewildering, inspiring, exhausting and endlessly entertaining. **See pp.746–747**

❼ Café Royal Circle Bar There are few finer pubs in which to sample a pint of local 80 Shilling beer, accompanied by six oysters (once the city's staple food). **See p.753**

HIGHLIGHTS ARE MARKED ON THE MAP ON P.726

N

Berwick-upon-Tweed

Barns
Ness
Dunbar

EAST
LOTHIAN

LAMMERMUIR HILLS

Tantallon
Castle

North Berwick

North
Berwick
Law

East Linton

National Museum
of Flight

SCOTTISH
BORDERS

Dirleton
Gullane
Drem

Haddington

Gifford

Jedburgh

Aberlady

Pencaitland

Galashiels

Firth of Forth

Prestonpans

Musselburgh

Dalkeith

Newtongrange

MOORFOOT HILLS

Peebles & Innerleithen

Portobello

MID
LOTHIAN

Leith

Craigmillar
Castle

Roslin

Rosslyn
Chapel

Penicuik

Newhaven

EDINBURGH

Corstorphine

Hillend

Flotterstone

Highlights

FIFE

Inchcolm

Cramond

Forth Rail Bridge

North Queensferry

PENTLAND HILLS

Bigger

Perth

Dunfermline

South
Queensferry

Hopetoun
House

EICA:
Ratho

Water of Leith

Rosyth

WEST
LOTHIAN

Livingston

Linlithgow

Bo'ness

Bathgate

Whitburn

Fauldhouse

Stirling & Falkirk

Glasgow

HIGHLIGHTS

1 The Old Town
2 Edinburgh Castle
3 Scottish Parliament
4 Holyrood Park
5 National Museum of Scotland
6 The Edinburgh Festival
7 Café Royal Circle Bar

5 miles

EDINBURGH &
THE LOTHIANS

permanent frontier. In the reign of Malcolm Canmore in the late eleventh century, the castle became one of the main seats of the court, and the town, which was given privileged status as a **royal burgh**, began to grow. Sadly, any structures that existed prior to the twelfth century probably succumbed to frequent Scots and English besiegement.

Turbulent Middle Ages

Under King James IV (1488–1513), the city enjoyed a short but brilliant **Renaissance era**, which saw the construction of a new palace alongside Holyrood Abbey. This period came to an abrupt end in 1513 with the calamitous defeat at the Battle of Flodden leading to several decades of political instability. In the 1540s, English king Henry VIII's attempt to force a royal union with Scotland led to the sack of Edinburgh, prompting the Scots to turn to France: French troops arrived to defend the city, while the young Scottish queen Mary was dispatched to Paris as the promised bride of the Dauphin, later François II. While the French occupiers succeeded in removing the English threat, they themselves antagonized the locals, who had become increasingly sympathetic to the ideals of the **Reformation**. When the radical preacher John Knox returned from exile in 1555, he quickly won over the city to his Calvinist message.

The Scottish Enlightenment

James VI's rule saw the foundation of the University of Edinburgh in 1583, but following the **Union of the Crowns** in 1603, when James assumed the throne of England in addition to that of Scotland, the city was totally upstaged by London. The **Union of the Parliaments** of 1707 dealt a further blow to Edinburgh's political prestige, though the guaranteed preservation of the national church and the legal and educational systems ensured that it was never relegated to a purely provincial role. On the contrary, it was in the second half of the eighteenth century that Edinburgh achieved the height of its intellectual influence, led by natives such as David Hume and Adam Smith. Around the same time, the city began to expand beyond its medieval boundaries, laying out the **New Town**, a masterpiece of the Neoclassical style and grand town planning.

The nineteenth century and beyond

Industrialization affected Edinburgh less than any other major city in the nation, and it never lost its white-collar character. Through the Victorian era Edinburgh cemented its role as a conservative bastion of the establishment, controlling Scotland's legal, ecclesiastical and education systems. Nonetheless, the city underwent an enormous **urban expansion** in the nineteenth century, annexing, among many other small burghs, the large port of **Leith**.

In 1947 Edinburgh was chosen to host the great **International Festival** which served as a symbol of the new peaceful European order; despite some hiccups, it has flourished ever since, in the process helping to make tourism a mainstay of the local economy. During the 1980s Glasgow, previously the poor relation but always a tenacious rival, began to challenge the city's status as a cultural centre, and it took the re-establishment of a devolved **Scottish Parliament** in 1999 for Edinburgh to reassert its status in a meaningful way. There was a notable upturn in the city's standing, augmented by significant achievements in scientific research and the arts.

The financial sector soon burgeoned, with the Royal Bank of Scotland becoming the second largest banking group in the UK in the early years of the new century. Its near collapse and subsequent bail-out by the UK government during the 2009 economic crisis dented not only the city's self-confidence, but also the arguments made by nationalist politicians that Scotland has the stability and economic prowess to prosper as an independent country under the leadership of Alex Salmond, the polls narrowed in the run-up to the 2014 referendum causing panic in Westminster. The Unionists may have ultimately won, but with the 55 percent to 45 percent margin, many believe future independence is still on the table.

CENTRAL EDINBURGH

CLUBS & LIVE MUSIC VENUES		THEATRES & CINEMAS	
The Bongo Club	12	Cameo	25
Cabaret Voltaire	1	Dance Base	16
CC Bloom's	3	Edinburgh Playhouse	4
The Liquid Room	11	Festival Theatre	21
Lulu's	9	Filmhouse	20
Planet	2	King's Theatre	26
Queen's Hall	27	Royal Lyceum	19
Royal Oak	13	The Stand	5
Sandy Bell's	23	Traverse Theatre	14
Usher Hall	18		

Dusit	14	Mother India's Café	21	Spoon	22
The Edinburgh Larder	3	Mussel Inn	16	Urban Angel	8/11
L'Escargot Bleu	5	Ondine	18	Valvona & Crolla	6
Fruitmarket Gallery Café	1	Peter's Yard	24	Valvona & Crolla Vincaffè	10
La Garrigue	2	Timberyard	23	The Witchery by the Castle	20
The Honours	15	The Scottish Café and			
Kalpna	25	Restaurant	17		

17 The Old Town

Edinburgh's **OLD TOWN**, although only about a mile long and 400 yards wide, represented the total extent of the twin burghs of Edinburgh and Canongate for the first 650 years of their existence, and its general appearance and character remain indubitably medieval. Containing the majority of the city's most famous tourist sights, the Old Town is compact enough to explore in a single day, though a thorough visit requires a bit longer. No matter how pressed you are, make sure you spare time for at least a taste of the wonderfully varied scenery and breathtaking vantage points of **Holyrood Park**, an extensive tract of open countryside on the eastern edge of the Old Town that includes **Arthur's Seat**, the peak of which rises so distinctively in the midst of the city.

Edinburgh Castle

Daily: April–Sept 9.30am–6pm; Oct–March 9.30am–5pm; last entry 1hr before closing · £16, audioguides £3.50 · Guided tours every 15min in high season; 20min; free · ☎ 0131 225 9846, ⓦ edinburghcastle.gov.uk

The history of Edinburgh, and indeed of Scotland, is indissolubly bound up with its **castle**, which dominates the city from its lofty seat atop an extinct volcanic rock. The disparate styles of the fortifications reflect the change in its role from defensive citadel to national monument, and today, as well as attracting more visitors than anywhere else in the country, the castle is still a military barracks and home to Scotland's Crown Jewels. The oldest surviving part of the complex is from the twelfth century, while the most recent additions date back to the 1920s.

The Esplanade

The castle is entered via the **Esplanade**, a parade ground laid out in the eighteenth century and enclosed a hundred years later by ornamental walls. For most of the year it acts as a coach park, though huge grandstands are erected for the Edinburgh Military Tattoo (see box, p.747). A shameless and spectacular pageant of swinging kilts and pipe bands, the tattoo makes full use of its dramatic setting.

THE STONE OF DESTINY

Legend has it that the **Stone of Destiny** (also called the Stone of Scone) was "Jacob's Pillow", on which he dreamed of the ladder of angels from earth to heaven. Its real history is obscure, but it's known to have been moved from Ireland to Dunadd by missionaries, and thence to Dunstaffnage, from where Kenneth MacAlpine, king of the Dalriada Scots, brought it to the abbey at Scone, near Perth, in 838. There it remained for almost five hundred years, used as a coronation throne on which all kings of Scotland were crowned.

In 1296, an over-eager Edward I stole what he believed to be the Stone and installed it at Westminster Abbey, where, apart from a brief interlude in 1950 when it was removed by Scottish nationalists and hidden in Arbroath for several months, it remained for seven hundred years. All this changed in December 1996 when, after an elaborate ceremony-laden journey from London, the Stone returned to Scotland, in one of the doomed attempts by the Conservative government to win back Nationalist converts. Much to the annoyance of the people of Perth and the curators of Scone Palace (see p.831), and to the general indifference of the people of Scotland, the Stone was placed in Edinburgh Castle.

However, speculation surrounds the authenticity of the Stone, for the original is said to have been intricately carved, while the one seen today is a plain block of sandstone. Many believe that the canny monks at Scone palmed this off onto the English king (some say that it's nothing more sacred than the cover for a medieval septic tank), and that the real Stone of Destiny lies hidden in an underground chamber, its whereabouts a mystery to all but the chosen few.

The lower defences

Edinburgh Castle has a single entrance, a 10ft-wide opening in the **gatehouse**, one of many Romantic-style additions made in the 1880s. Rearing up behind is the most distinctive and impressive feature of the castle's silhouette, the sixteenth-century **Half Moon Battery**, which marks the outer limit of the actual defences. Once through the gatehouse, you'll find the main ticket office on your right, with an information centre alongside. Continue uphill along Lower Ward, showing your ticket at the **Portcullis Gate**, a handsome Renaissance gateway marred by the addition of a nineteenth-century upper storey with anachronistic arrow slits. Beyond this is the wide main path known as Middle Ward, with the six-gun **Argyle Battery** to the right. Further west on **Mill's Mount Battery**, a well-known Edinburgh ritual takes place – the daily firing of the **one o'clock gun**. Originally designed for the benefit of ships in the Firth of Forth, these days it's an enjoyable ceremony for visitors to watch and a useful time signal for city centre office workers. Both batteries offer wonderful panoramas over Princes Street and the New Town to the coastal towns and hills of Fife across the Forth. There's an interesting little exhibition about the history of the firing of the gun in a room immediately below Mill's Mount Battery.

National War Museum

Located in the old hospital buildings, down a ramp between the restaurant immediately behind the one o'clock gun and the Governor's House, the **National War Museum** covers the last four hundred years of Scottish military history. Scots have been fighting for much longer than that, of course, but the slant of the museum is very definitely towards the soldiers who fought *for* the Union, rather than against it. The various rooms are packed with uniforms, medals and other interesting memorabilia, carefully avoiding favouritism towards any of the Scottish regiments, each of which has strong traditions more forcefully paraded in the various regimental museums found in different parts of Scotland – the Royal Scots and the Scots Dragoon Guards, for instance, both have displays in other parts of Edinburgh Castle.

St Margaret's Chapel

Near the highest point of the castle, **St Margaret's Chapel** is the oldest surviving building within. Built by King David I as a memorial to his mother, and used as a powder magazine for three hundred years, this tiny Norman church was rediscovered in 1845 and eventually re-dedicated in 1934.

The battlements in front of the chapel offer the best of all the castle's extensive views. Here you'll see the famous fifteenth-century siege gun, **Mons Meg**, which could fire a 500-pound stone nearly two miles. Just below the battlements there's a small, immaculately kept **cemetery**, the last resting place of the **soldiers' pets**. Continuing eastwards, you skirt the top of the Forewall and Half Moon batteries, passing the 110ft-deep **Castle Well** en route to **Crown Square**, the highest, most important and secure section of the complex.

Crown Square

The eastern side of Crown Square is occupied by the **Palace**, a surprisingly unassuming edifice begun in the 1430s. The palace owes its Renaissance appearance to King James IV, though it was remodelled for Mary, Queen of Scots, and her consort Henry, Lord Darnley, whose entwined initials (MAH), together with the date 1566, can be seen above one of the doorways.

Another section of the Palace houses the nation's **Crown Jewels**, properly known as the **Honours of Scotland**; you get to see them by joining a slow-moving line that shuffles past a series of historical tableaux before reaching the Crown Room. One of the most potent images of Scotland's nationhood, the jewel-encrusted **crown** made for James V by the Scottish goldsmith James Mosman, incorporates the gold circlet worn by Robert the Bruce and is topped by an enamelled orb and cross. Sitting alongside is the incongruously plain **Stone of Destiny** (see box opposite).

17

On the south side of Crown Square is James IV's hammerbeam-ceilinged **Great Hall**, used for meetings of the Scottish Parliament until 1639; opposite, the serene Hall of Honour houses the **Scottish National War Memorial**, created in 1927 by the architect Sir Robert Lorimer and two hundred Scottish artists and craftsmen.

The Royal Mile

The **Royal Mile**, the name given to the ridge linking the castle with Holyrood, was described by Daniel Defoe in 1724, as "the largest, longest and finest street for Buildings and Number of Inhabitants, not in Bretain only, but in the World". Almost exactly a mile in length, it is divided into four sections – Castlehill, Lawnmarket, High Street and Canongate. From these, branching out in a herringbone pattern, are a series of tightly packed closes and steep lanes entered via archways known as "pends". After the construction of the New Town much of the housing along the Royal Mile degenerated into a slum, but has since shaken off that reputation, with bijou flats, holiday apartments, student residences and offices now inhabiting the tightly packed buildings.

Scotch Whisky Experience

354 Castlehill • Daily: June–Aug 10am–6.30pm; Sept–May Mon–Fri 10am–5pm, Sat & Sun 10am–5.30pm; last tour 1hr before closing • £13.50 • ☏ 0131 220 0441, ⓦ scotchwhiskyexperience.co.uk

A short way downhill from the castle esplanade, the **Scotch Whisky Experience** mimics the kind of tours offered at distilleries in the Highlands, and while it can't match the authenticity of the real thing, the centre does offer a thorough introduction to the "water of life" (*uisge beatha* in Gaelic). On the ground floor, a well-stocked shop gives an idea of the sheer range and diversity of the drink, while downstairs there's a pleasant whisky bar and restaurant, *Amber* (see p.750).

The Hub

348 Castlehill • Mon–Sat 9.30am–5pm, Sun 11am–5pm; extended hours in Festival • ☏ 0131 473 2015, ⓦ thehub-edinburgh.com

The imposing black church at the foot of Castlehill is **The Hub**, also known as "Edinburgh's Festival Centre". It's open year-round, providing performance, rehearsal and exhibition space, a ticket centre and a café. The building itself was constructed in 1845 to designs by James Gillespie Graham and Augustus Pugin, one of the architects of the Houses of Parliament in London. Permanent works of art have been incorporated into parts of the centre, including over two hundred delightful 1ft-high sculptures depicting Festival performers and audiences.

Gladstone's Land

477b Lawnmarket • Daily: April–June, Sept & Oct 10am–5pm; July & Aug 10am–6.30pm • £6.50; NTS (National Trust Scotland) • ☏ 0844 493 2120

Doing its best to maintain its dignity among a sea of cheap tartan gifts and discounted woolly jumpers, **Gladstone's Land** is the Royal Mile's best surviving example of a typical seventeenth-century tenement. The tall, narrow building – not unlike a canal-side house in Amsterdam – would have been home to various families living in cramped conditions. The arcaded and wooden-fronted ground floor is home to a reconstructed cloth shop; pass through this to encounter a warren of tight little staircases, tiny rooms, creaking floorboards and peek-hole windows.

Writers' Museum

Lady Stair's Close • Mon–Sat 10am–5pm, also Sun noon–5pm in Aug • Free • ☏ 0131 529 4901, ⓦ edinburghmuseums.org.uk

The arched entranceway to Lady Stair's Close is one of a number of attractive courtyards just off the Royal Mile. Within the seventeenth-century Lady Stair's House is the **Writers' Museum**, dedicated to Scotland's three greatest literary lions: Sir Walter Scott, Robert Louis Stevenson and Robert Burns. The house itself holds as much

17

ROBERT LOUIS STEVENSON

Born in Edinburgh into a distinguished family of lighthouse engineers, **Robert Louis Stevenson** (1850–94) was a sickly child, with a solitary childhood dominated by his governess, Alison "Cummie" Cunningham, who regaled him with tales drawn from Calvinist folklore. Sent to the university to study engineering, Stevenson rebelled against his upbringing by spending much of his time in the lowlife howffs and brothels of the city.

Stevenson's early successes were two **travelogues**, *An Inland Voyage* and *Travels with a Donkey in the Cevennes*, kaleidoscopic jottings based on his journeys in France, where he went to escape Scotland's weather, which was damaging his health. It was there that he met Fanny Osbourne, an American ten years his senior. Having married the now-divorced Fanny, Stevenson began an elusive search for an agreeable climate that led to Switzerland, the French Riviera and the Scottish Highlands. He belatedly turned to the novel, achieving immediate acclaim in 1881 for **Treasure Island**, a moralistic adventure yarn that began as an entertainment for his stepson and future collaborator, Lloyd Osbourne. In 1886, his most famous short story, **Dr Jekyll and Mr Hyde**, despite its nominal London setting, offered a vivid evocation of Edinburgh's Old Town: an allegory of its dual personality of prosperity and squalor, and an analysis of its Calvinistic preoccupations with guilt and damnation. The same year saw the publication of the historical romance **Kidnapped**, an adventure novel that exemplified Stevenson's view that literature should seek above all to entertain. In 1887 Stevenson left Britain for good, travelling first to the United States. A year later, he set sail for the South Seas, and eventually settled in **Samoa**, where he died suddenly from a brain haemorrhage in 1894.

interest as the slightly lacklustre collection of portraits, manuscripts and knick-knacks, its tight, winding stairs and poky, wood-panelled rooms offering a flavour of the medieval Old Town. The open courtyard outside, known as the Makars' Court after the Scots word for the "maker" of poetry or prose, features a series of paving stones inscribed with quotations from Scotland's most famous writers.

The High Kirk of St Giles

High St • May–Sept Mon–Fri 9am–7pm, Sat 9am–5pm, Sun 1–5pm; Oct–April Mon–Sat 9am–5pm, Sun 1–5pm • Free • ☎ 0131 225 9442, ✉ stgilescathedral.org.uk

The dominant building on the High Street, the central section of the Royal Mile, is the **High Kirk of St Giles**, the original parish church of medieval Edinburgh, from where John Knox launched and directed the Scottish Reformation.

The resplendent **crown spire** of the kirk is formed from eight flying buttresses and dates back to 1485, while **inside**, the four massive piers supporting the tower were part of a Norman church built here around 1120. In the nineteenth century, St Giles was adorned with a whole series of funerary monuments on the model of London's Westminster Abbey; around the same time it acquired several attractive Pre-Raphaelite stained-glass windows designed by Edward Burne-Jones and William Morris.

At the southeastern corner of St Giles, the **Thistle Chapel** was built by Sir Robert Lorimer in 1911 as the private chapel of the sixteen knights of the Most Noble Order of the Thistle, the highest chivalric order in Scotland. Based on St George's Chapel in Windsor, it's an exquisite piece of craftsmanship, with an elaborate ribbed vault, huge drooping bosses and extravagantly ornate stalls showing off Lorimer's bold Arts and Crafts styling.

Mary King's Close

2 Warriston's Close, High St • Tours daily every 15min: April–Oct daily 10am–9pm; Nov–March Sun–Thurs 10am–5pm, Fri & Sat 10am–9pm; 1hr • £12.95 • ☎ 0845 070 6244, ✉ realmarykingsclose.com

Subterranean **Mary King's Close** (also known as **The Real Mary King's Close**) is one of Edinburgh's most unusual attractions. When work on the City Chambers began in 1753, the tops of the existing houses on the site were simply sliced through at the level of the High Street and the new building constructed on top of them. Because the tenements had been built on a steep hillside, this process left parts of the houses,

17

together with the old streets (or closes) that ran alongside them, intact but entirely enclosed among the basement and cellars of the chambers. You can visit this rather spooky "lost city" on **tours** led by costumed actors.

Scottish Storytelling Centre

43–45 High St • Mon–Sat 10am–6pm, also Sun noon–6pm in July & Aug • £5 entry to John Knox House • ☏ 0131 556 9579, ⦿ scottishstorytellingcentre.co.uk

There are two distinct parts to the **Scottish Storytelling Centre**: one half is a stylish contemporary development based around an airy Storytelling Court with a small permanent exhibition about Scottish stories from ancient folk tales to Harry Potter. By contrast, the **John Knox House** is a fifteenth-century stone-and-timber building that, with its distinctive external staircase, overhanging upper storeys and busy pantile roof, is a classic example of the Royal Mile in its medieval heyday. Regular performances and events, often aimed at a younger audience, take place in the centre.

Canongate

For over seven hundred years, the **Canongate** district, through which the eastern section of the Royal Mile runs, was a burgh in its own right, officially separate from the capital. A notorious slum area even into the 1960s, it has been the subject of some of the most ambitious **restoration** programmes in the Old Town, though the lack of harmony between the buildings renovated in different decades is fairly obvious. For such a central district, it's interesting to note that most of the buildings here are residential, and by no means are they all bijou apartments. The eclectic range of **shops** includes a gallery of historic maps and sea charts, a permanent Christmas shop and an old-fashioned whisky bottler.

Canongate Kirk

153 Canongate • Mon–Sat 10.30am–4.30pm, Sun 12.30–4.30pm, depending on volunteer staff and church services • Free • ☏ 0131 556 3515, ⦿ canongatekirk.org.uk

Built to house the congregation expelled from Holyrood Abbey when the latter was commandeered by James VII (James II in England), **Canongate Kirk** is the church used by the Queen when she's at Holyrood and was the location for Britain's "other royal wedding" of 2011, when Prince William's cousin Zara Philips married England rugby player Mike Tindall. The kirk has a modesty rarely seen in churches built in later centuries, with a graceful curved facade and a bow-shaped gable to the rear. The surrounding churchyard provides an attractive and tranquil stretch of green in the heart of the Old Town and affords fine views of Calton Hill; it also happens to be one of the city's most exclusive cemeteries – well-known internees include the political economist Adam Smith, Mrs Agnes McLehose (better known as Robert Burns's "Clarinda") and Robert Fergusson. Fergusson's headstone was donated by Burns, a fervent admirer, and a statue of the young poet can be seen just outside the kirk gates.

Museum of Edinburgh

142 Canongate • Mon–Sat 10am–5pm, also Sun noon–5pm in Aug • Free • ☏ 0131 529 4143, ⦿ edinburghmuseums.org.uk

The **Museum of Edinburgh** is the city's principal collection devoted to local history, and is as interesting for the labyrinthine network of wood-panelled rooms as for its rather quirky array of artefacts. These do, however, include a number of items of real historical significance, in particular the National Convention, the petition for religious freedom drawn up on a deerskin parchment in 1638, and the original plans for the layout of the New Town drawn by James Craig (see p.739).

Scottish Poetry Library

5 Crichton's Close • Tues, Wed & Fri 10am–5pm, Thurs 10am–7pm, Sat 10am–4pm • Free • ☏ 0131 557 2876, ⦿ spl.org.uk

A sweet note of modern architectural eloquence amid a cacophony of large-scale developments, the **Scottish Poetry Library** incorporates a section of an old city wall, and the attractive, contemporary design harmoniously combines brick, oak, glass, Caithness stone and blue ceramic tiles. The library contains Scotland's most comprehensive collection of native poetry, and visitors are free to read the books, periodicals and leaflets found on the shelves, or listen to recordings of poetry in English, Scots and Gaelic.

Holyrood

At the foot of Canongate lies **Holyrood**, with its ruined thirteenth-century **abbey** and the **Palace of Holyroodhouse**, the residence of the Queen and other royals when they're in town. The area has been transformed by Enric Miralles' dazzling but highly controversial **Scottish Parliament**, which was deliberately landscaped to blend in with the cliffs and ridges of Edinburgh's most dramatic natural feature, the nearby **Holyrood Park** and its slumbering peak, Arthur's Seat.

The Palace of Holyroodhouse

Daily: April–Oct 9.30am–6pm; Nov–March 9.30am–4.30pm; last admission 1hr 30min before closing · £11.30, £16 joint ticket with the Queen's Gallery · ☎ 0131 556 5100, ⊚ royalcollection.org.uk

The **Palace of Holyroodhouse** is largely a seventeenth-century creation, planned for Charles II. Tours of the palace move through a series of royal **reception rooms** featuring some outstanding encrusted plasterwork, each more impressive than the last – an idea Charles II had picked up from his cousin Louis XIV's Versailles – while on the northern side of the internal quadrangle, the **Great Gallery** extends almost the full length of the palace and is dominated by portraits of 96 Scottish kings, painted by Jacob de Wet in 1684 to illustrate the lineage of Stewart royalty: the result is unintentionally hilarious, as it's clear that the artist's imagination was taxed to bursting point in his commission to paint so many different facial types without having an inkling as to what the subjects actually looked like. Leading from this into the oldest part of the palace, known as James V's tower, the formal, ceremonial tone gives way to dark medieval history, with a tight spiral staircase leading to the chambers used by Mary, Queen of Scots. These contain various relics, including jewellery, associated with the queen, though the most compelling viewing is a tiny supper room, from where, in 1566, Mary's Italian secretary, David Rizzio, was dragged by conspirators, who included her jealous husband, Lord Darnley, to the outer chamber and stabbed 56 times; a brass plaque on the wall points out what are rather unconvincingly identified as the bloodstains on the wooden floor.

Holyrood Abbey

Immediately adjacent to the palace · Free as part of palace tour

The evocative ruins of **Holyrood Abbey**, some of which date from the thirteenth century, lie next to the palace. The roof tumbled down in 1768, but the melancholy scene has inspired artists down the years, among them Felix Mendelssohn, who in 1829 wrote "Everything is in ruins and mouldering ... I believe I have found the beginning of my Scottish Symphony there today". Next to the abbey are the formal palace gardens, open to visitors in summer and offering some pleasant strolls.

The Queen's Gallery

Daily: April–Oct 9.30am–6pm; Nov–March 9.30am–4.30pm; last admission 1hr before closing · £6.50 or £16 joint ticket with Holyroodhouse · ☎ 0131 556 5100, ⊚ royalcollection.org.uk

17 Essentially an adjunct to Holyrood palace, the **Queen's Gallery** is located in the shell of a former church directly. It's a compact space with just two principal viewing rooms used to display changing exhibitions from the Royal Collection, a vast array of art treasures held by the Queen on behalf of the British nation. Because the pieces are otherwise exhibited only during the limited openings of Buckingham Palace and Windsor Castle, the exhibitions here tend to draw quite a lot of interest.

Scottish Parliament

Horse Wynd • Mon, Fri & Sat 10am–5pm, Tues–Thurs 9am–6.30pm; closed late Dec and early Feb • Free access; guided tours 1hr, free, bookings not essential • ☎ 0131 348 5200, ⓦ scottish.parliament.uk

By far the most controversial public building to be erected in Scotland since World War II, the **Scottish Parliament** houses the country's directly elected assembly. A separate parliament to look after the running of internal Scottish affairs was reintroduced to the British constitution in 1999, nearly two hundred years after the previous Scottish parliament had joined the English assembly at Westminster as part of the Union of the two nations in 1707. The home of the directly elected parliament was eventually opened in 2004, late and dramatically over budget – initial estimates for the building's cost were tentatively put at £40 million; the final bill was over £400 million. Made up of various linked elements rather than one single building, the complex was designed by Catalan architect **Enric Miralles**, whose death in 2000, halfway through the building process, caused ripples of uncertainty as to whether he had in fact set down his final draft. However, the finished product is an impressive – if imperfect – testament to the ambition of Miralles, and it has won over the majority of the architectural community, scooping numerous awards including Britain's prestigious Royal Institute of British Architects (RIBA) Stirling Prize in 2005.

There's free access into the entrance lobby, entered from Horse Wynd, where you'll find a small exhibition providing some historical, political and architectural background. If parliament is in session, it's normally possible to watch proceedings in the debating chamber from the public gallery. To see the rest of the interior properly you'll need to join one of the regular **guided tours**, well worth doing to get a more detailed appreciation of the building's design.

Some of the most memorable features of the building are the fanciful motifs and odd architectural signatures running through the design, including the anvil-shaped cladding, and the extraordinary windows of the offices for MSPs (Members of the Scottish Parliament), said to have been inspired by a monk's contemplative cell. The stark concrete of the interior may not be to all tastes, though several of the staircases and passageways remain evocative of the country's medieval castles.

The main **debating chamber** is grand yet intimate, with light flooding in through high windows and a complex network of thick oak beams, lights and microphone wires. The European-style layout is a deliberate move away from the confrontational Westminster model, though some have been quick to point out that while the traditional inter-party insults still fly, the quality of the parliamentarians' rhetoric rarely matches that of the soaring new arena.

Our Dynamic Earth

Holyrood Rd • April–June, & Sept & Oct daily 10am–5.30pm; July & Aug daily 10am–6pm; Nov–March Wed–Sun 10am–5.30pm; last entry 1hr 30min before closing • Adult £11, child £7.25 • ☎ 0131 550 7800, ⓦ dynamicearth.co.uk

Sitting beneath a miniature version of London's Millennium Dome, **Our Dynamic Earth** is a high-tech attraction aimed at children between 5 and 15. Galleries cover the formation of the Earth and continents with crashing sound effects and a shaking floor, while the calmer grandeur of glaciers and oceans is explored through magnificent large-screen landscape footage; further on, the polar regions – complete with a real iceberg – and tropical jungles are imaginatively re-created.

> **ASCENDING ARTHUR'S SEAT**
>
> The usual starting point for the ascent of **Arthur's Seat**, which at 823ft above sea level towers over Edinburgh's numerous high points, is Dunsapie Loch, reached by following the tarred Queen's Drive in a clockwise direction from the Information Centre in Holyrood Park (30–40min walk). Part of a volcano which last saw action 350 million years ago, its connections to the legendary king are fairly sketchy: the name is likely to be a corruption of the Gaelic **Ard-na-said**, or "height of arrows". From Dunsapie Loch it's a twenty-minute climb up grassy slopes to the rocky summit. On a clear day, the views might just stretch to the English border and the Atlantic Ocean; more realistically, the landmarks which dominate are Fife, a few Highland peaks and, of course, Edinburgh laid out on all sides.

Holyrood Park

Information Centre, Holyrood Lodge, Horse Wynd • Daily: 8.30am–4.30pm • Free • ☎ 0131 652 8150

Holyrood Park – or Queen's Park – a natural wilderness in the heart of the modern city, is one of Edinburgh's greatest assets. Packed into an area no more than five miles in diameter is an amazing variety of landscapes – hills, crags, moorland, marshes, glens, lochs and fields – representing a microcosm of Scotland's scenery. While old photographs of the park show crops growing and sheep grazing, it's now most used by walkers, joggers, cyclists and other outdoor enthusiasts. A single tarred road, **Queen's Drive**, loops through the park, but you need to get out and stroll around to appreciate it fully. You can pick up a map of suggested walks as well as details on the geology and flora, from the Park Information Centre.

The University of Edinburgh and around

Founded as the "Tounis College" in 1583 by James VI (later James I of England), the **University of Edinburgh** is the largest in Scotland, with nearly twenty thousand students. The earliest surviving part is the **Old College** on South Bridge, an imposing quadrangle designed by Robert Adam (1728–1792) and finished in modified form by William Playfair (1789–1857), one of Edinburgh's greatest architects. These days the Old College houses only a few university departments as well as the small **Talbot Rice Art Gallery** (Tues–Fri 10am–5pm, Sat noon–5pm; free; ☎ 0131 650 2210, ⓦ ed.ac.uk) displaying part of the University's art and bronze collection; the main campus colonizes the streets and squares to the south.

Surgeons' Hall Museum

Nicolson St • April–Oct daily 10am–5pm; Nov–March Mon–Fri 10am–4pm • £5 • ☎ 0131 527 1711, ⓦ museum.rcsed.ac.uk

Inside the stately **Surgeons' Hall**, a handsome Ionic temple built by Playfair as the headquarters of the Royal College of Surgeons, is one of the city's most unusual and morbidly compelling **museums**. In the eighteenth and nineteenth centuries Edinburgh developed as a leading centre for medical and anatomical research, nurturing world-famous figures such as James Young Simpson, pioneer of anaesthesia, and Joseph Lister, the father of modern surgery. The intriguing exhibits range from early surgical tools to a pocketbook covered with the leathered skin of serial killer William Burke.

National Museum of Scotland

Chambers St • Daily 10am–5pm • Free • ☎ 0300 123 6789, ⓦ nms.ac.uk

The **National Museum of Scotland** fuses a grand Victorian building with an extension built in the 1990s. The recently refurbished older section is a traditional, grand city museum covering natural history, indigenous cultures, science and crafts from around the world. Alongside it, the clean lines and imaginatively designed interior of the modern section offer a fresh perspective on Scottish history from earliest man to the present day, laid out in broadly chronological order over seven levels.

17

Scotland Galleries

The seven levels of the National Museum's modern extension make up Scotland's premier historical museum. The nation's beginnings and earliest peoples are covered in the basement, with artefacts including the **Cramond Lioness**, a sculpture from a Roman tombstone found recently in the Firth of Forth, along with carved stones and jewellery from Pictish times. Moving up through the museum, look out for the famous **Lewis chessmen**, idiosyncratic twelfth-century pieces carved from walrus ivory, along with pieces relating to the more significant periods of Scotland's past, including the Highland uprisings under Bonnie Prince Charlie (whose silver travelling canteen is on display). **Industry and Empire** covers the era of heavy industry and mass emigration, while **Scotland: A Changing Nation** traces the different experiences of people living and working in contemporary Scotland, through film, objects and personal stories.

From the small **roof garden**, accessed by a lift, sweeping views open out to the Firth of Forth, the Pentland hills and across to the Castle and Royal Mile skyline. Other fine views can be enjoyed from the museum's stylish *Tower* restaurant.

Elsewhere in the Museum

Centred on a soaring, three-storey atrium, the former **Royal Museum of Scotland**, a dignified Venetian-style palace with a cast-iron interior modelled on the Crystal Place in London, reopened in 2011 following a £47 million refurbishment. There's much to appreciate simply from the building itself, with the main **Grand Gallery** flooded by natural light and encircled by two levels of balcony. The main exhibits are found in rooms off the Grand Gallery, the most notable (particularly for younger visitors) being the **natural history** collection with stuffed animals, dinosaur skeletons and numerous sea creatures suspended from the ceiling among giant plasma screens showing wildlife in action. An area dedicated to **science and technology** has everything from robots and space ships to a stuffed model of Dolly the sheep.

The Grassmarket

Tucked in below the castle's high southern edifice is an open, partly cobbled area known as the **Grassmarket**, which was used as the city's cattle market from 1477 to 1911 and was also the location of Edinburgh's public gallows – the spot is marked by a tiny garden. Despite the height of many of the surrounding buildings, Grassmarket offers an unexpected view up to the precipitous walls of the castle and, come springtime, it's sunny enough for cafés to put tables and chairs along the pavement. In the northwest corner is the award-winning modern architecture of **Dance Base** (☎0131 225 5525, ⍟dancebase .co.uk), Scotland's National Centre for Dance, which holds classes, workshops and shows.

GREYFRIARS

The **statue of Greyfriars Bobby** at the southwestern corner of **George IV Bridge**, just across the road from the Museum of Scotland, must rank as Edinburgh's most sentimental tourist attraction. According to the legend – no doubt embellished down the years – Bobby was a Skye terrier acquired as a working dog by a police constable named John Gray. When Gray died in 1858, Bobby was found a few days later sitting on his grave, a vigil he maintained until his death fourteen years later. Bobby's legendary dedication was picked up by Disney, whose 1960 feature film of the story ensured that streams of tourists have paid their respects ever since.

The grave Bobby mourned over is in the **Greyfriars Kirkyard**, which has a fine collection of seventeenth-century gravestones and mausoleums, including one to the Adam family of architects. The kirkyard is visited regularly by ghost tours (see box, p.748) and was known for grave-robbing in the early 1800s, when freshly interred bodies were exhumed and sold to the nearby medical school. Greyfriars Kirk itself was built in 1620 on land that had belonged to a Franciscan convent, though little of the original late Gothic-style building remains.

17

The Grassmarket's pubs and restaurants are busy by night, while by day you can admire the architectural quirks and interesting shops, in particular the string of offbeat boutiques on curving **Victoria Street**, an unusual two-tier thoroughfare, with arcaded shops below and a pedestrian terrace above.

The New Town

The **NEW TOWN**, itself well over two hundred years old, stands in total contrast to the Old Town: the layout is symmetrical, the streets are broad and straight, and most of the buildings are Neoclassical. Originally intended to be residential, today the New Town is the bustling hub of the city's professional, commercial and business life.

The existence of the New Town is chiefly due to the vision of **George Drummond**, who made schemes for the expansion of the city soon after becoming Lord Provost in 1725. Work began on the draining of the Nor' Loch below the castle in 1759, a job that took some sixty years. The North Bridge, linking the Old Town with the main road leading to the port of Leith, was built between 1763 and 1772 and, in 1766, following a public competition, a plan for the New Town by 22-year-old architect **James Craig** was chosen. Its gridiron pattern was perfectly matched to the site: central **George Street**, flanked by showpiece squares, was laid out along the main ridge, with parallel **Princes Street** and **Queen Street** on either side, built up on one side only, so as not to block the spectacular views of the Old Town and Fife.

The layout of the greater New Town is a remarkable grouping of squares, circuses, terraces, crescents and parks along with **Charlotte Square** and the assemblage of curiosities on and around **Calton Hill**. However, it also contains assorted Victorian additions, notably the **Scott Monument** on Princes Street, the **Royal Botanic Garden** on its northern fringe, as well as two of the city's most important public collections – the **National Gallery of Scotland** and, further afield, the **Scottish National Gallery of Modern Art**.

Princes Street

Although only allocated a subsidiary role in the original plan of the New Town, **Princes Street** had developed into Edinburgh's principal thoroughfare by the middle of the nineteenth century, a role it has retained ever since. Its unobstructed views across to the castle and the Old Town are undeniably magnificent. Indeed, without the views, Princes Street would lose much of its appeal; its northern side, dominated by large outlets of the familiar national chains, is almost always crowded with shoppers, and few of the original eighteenth-century buildings remain.

Princes Street Gardens

Dawn to dusk • Free • Ferris wheel Late Nov–early Jan daily 10am–10pm; £7

It's hard to imagine that the **gardens** that flank nearly the entire length of Princes Street were once the stagnant, foul-smelling Nor' Loch, into which the effluent of the Old Town flowed for centuries. The railway has since replaced the water and today a sunken cutting carries the main lines out of Waverley Station. The gardens were originally the private domain of Princes Street residents and their well-placed acquaintances, only becoming a public park in 1876. The larger and more verdant western section has a floral clock and the Ross Bandstand, a popular Festival venue, while at Christmas the eastern section is home to numerous funfair attractions including a towering Ferris wheel.

The Scott Monument

East Princes Street Gardens • Daily: April–Sept 10am–7pm; Oct–March 10am–4pm • £4

Erected in memory of the prolific author and patriot Sir Walter Scott within a few years of his death, this 200ft sandstone structure is closely modelled on Scott's beloved

17

Melrose Abbey (see p.765), while the rich sculptural decoration shows sixteen Scottish writers and 64 characters from Scott's famous *Waverley* novels. On the central plinth at the base of the monument is a **statue** of Scott with his deerhound Maida, carved from a thirty-tonne block of Carrara marble. Inside the memorial a tightly winding spiral staircase climbs 287 steps to a narrow platform near the top: from here, you can enjoy some inspiring vistas of the city below, and hills and firths beyond.

The National Gallery of Scotland

The Mound • Daily 10am–5pm, Thurs till 7pm • Free, charge for some temporary exhibitions • ☎ 0131 624 6200, ⓦ nationalgalleries.org

Built as a "temple to the fine arts" in 1850 by William Henry Playfair (1790–1857) the **National Gallery** houses Scotland's finest array of European and Scottish art from the early 1300s to the late 1800s. Its modest size makes it a manageable place to visit in a couple of hours and affords a pleasantly unrushed atmosphere. The vast collection is one of the finest in the world and shared between the National Portrait Gallery (see opposite) and the National Gallery of Modern Art (see p.743). Consequently many of the great masterpieces are displayed on rotation.

Early works

A gallery highlight is a superb painting by **Botticelli**, *The Virgin Adoring the Sleeping Christ Child* which, along with **Raphael**'s graceful tondo *The Holy Family with a Palm Tree*, has undergone careful restoration to reveal a striking luminosity and depth of colour. Of the four mythological scenes by **Titian**, the sensuous *Three Ages of Man* is one of his most accomplished early compositions. Alongside the Titians, **Bassano**'s *Adoration of the Kings* and a dramatic altarpiece, *The Deposition of Christ*, by **Tintoretto**, as well as several other works by **Veronese**, complete the fine **Venetian** section.

European highlights

Rubens' *The Feast of Herod* is an archetypal example of his sumptuously grand manner. Among the four canvases by **Rembrandt** are a poignant *Self-Portrait Aged 51* and the ripely suggestive *Woman in Bed*. *Christ in the House of Martha and Mary* is the largest and probably the earliest of the thirty or so surviving paintings by **Vermeer**.

Impressionist masters have a strong showing, including a collection of **Degas**' sketches, paintings and bronzes, **Monet**'s *Haystacks* (*Snow*) and **Renoir**'s *Woman Nursing Child*. Representing the Post-Impressionists are three exceptional works by **Gauguin**, including *Vision After the Sermon*, set in Brittany, **Van Gogh**'s *Olive Trees*, and **Cézanne**'s *The Big Trees* – a clear forerunner of modern abstraction.

Scottish and English works

Of **Sir Henry Raeburn**'s large portraits, the swaggering masculinity of *Sir John Sinclair in Highland Dress* shows the artist's technical mastery, though he was equally confident when working on a smaller scale, as seen in one of the gallery's most popular pictures, *The Rev Robert Walker Skating on Duddingston Loch*. The gallery also owns a brilliant array of watercolours by **Turner**, faithfully displayed each January when damaging sunlight is at its weakest; at other times two of his fine Roman views are displayed in a dim gallery.

George Street and around

Parallel to Princes Street, and originally designed as the central thoroughfare of the New Town, **George Street** leads along the crest of the hill that sweeps down to the Forth. At the western end is **Charlotte Square**, designed by Robert Adam in 1791, a year before his death. Generally regarded as the epitome of the New Town's elegant simplicity, the square was once the most exclusive residential address in Edinburgh, and though much of it is now occupied by offices, the imperious dignity of the architecture is still evident. Indeed, the north side is once again the city's premier address, with the official residence of the First Minister of the

17

CONTEMPORARY ART IN EDINBURGH

In addition to the contemporary art collections in the city's national galleries there are a number of smaller, independent galleries around the city.

The Collective Gallery City Observatory & City Dome, 38 Calton Hill ☎ 0131 556 1264, ⓦ collectivegallery.net. Tends to focus on young local artists, and doesn't flinch from showing experimental modern work. Tues–Sun: April–July & Sept 10am–5pm; Aug 10am–6pm; Oct–March 10am–4pm.

Edinburgh Printmakers 23 Union St ☎ 0131 557 2479, ⓦ edinburgh-printmakers.co.uk. A highly respected studio and gallery dedicated to contemporary printmaking. Tues–Sat 10am–6pm.

Fruitmarket Gallery 45 Market St ☎ 0131 225 2383, ⓦ fruitmarket.co.uk. The stylish modern design of this dynamic and much-admired art space is the capital's first port of call for top-grade international artists. Mon–Sat 11am–6pm, Sun noon–5pm.

Ingleby Gallery 15 Carlton Rd ☎ 0131 556 4441, ⓦ inglebygallery.com. Ingleby's reputation for ambitious projects and innovative artists makes it one of the nation's foremost small private art galleries, often featuring Scotland's premier stars such as Alison Watt, Kenny Hunter and Callum Innes. Mon–Sat 10am–6pm, plus Sun noon–5pm in Aug.

Open Eye Gallery 34 Abercromby Place ☎ 0131 557 1020, ⓦ openeyegallery.co.uk. One of the city's best commercial galleries, regularly featuring shows by Scotland's top contemporary artists. Mon–Fri 10am–6pm, Sat 10am–4pm.

Scottish Gallery 16 Dundas St ☎ 0131 558 1200, ⓦ scottish-gallery.co.uk. The longest established of a number of small galleries on this New Town street; some of the most striking works are in the basement area, dedicated to applied art. Mon–Fri 10am–6pm, Sat 10am–4pm.

Scottish Government at no. 6 (Bute House), the Edinburgh equivalent of 10 Downing Street. In August each year, the gardens in the centre of the square are colonized by the temporary tents of the Edinburgh International Book Festival (see box, p.797).

The Georgian House

7 Charlotte Square • Daily: March 11am–4pm; April–June, Sept & Oct 10am–5pm; July & Aug 10am–6pm; Nov 11am–3pm • £6.50; NTS • ☎ 0844 493 2118

The **Georgian House** provides a revealing sense of well-to-do New Town living in the early nineteenth century. The rooms are impressively decked out in period furniture – look for the working barrel organ which plays a selection of Scottish airs – and hung with fine paintings, including portraits by Ramsay and Raeburn. In the basement are the original wine cellar and a kitchen complete with an open fire.

Scottish National Portrait Gallery

1 Queen St • Fri–Wed 10am–5pm (6pm in Aug), Thurs 10am–7pm • Free, entrance charge for some temporary exhibitions • ☎ 0131 624 6200, ⓦ nationalgalleries.org

The recently refurbished **Scottish National Portrait Gallery** occupies a fantastic red-sandstone neo-Gothic palace, an 1889 building designed by Sir Robert Rowand Anderson that makes an extravagant contrast to the New Town's prevailing Neoclassicism. The exterior is encrusted with statues of famous national heroes, a theme reiterated by William Hole's frieze depicting notable figures from Scotland's past in the stunning two-storey entrance hall. Other galleries provide a star-studded romp through Scottish history with a few thematic cultural diversions along the way, all told through portraits – paintings and photographs – and complemented by changing exhibitions.

Calton Hill

Edinburgh's tag as the "Athens of the North" is nowhere better earned than on **Calton Hill**, the volcanic peak that rises up above the eastern end of Princes Street. The hill and its odd collection of grandiose buildings aren't just for looking *at*: this is also one of the best viewpoints from which to appreciate the whole city and the sea beyond.

17

Old Royal High School

Set majestically on the slopes of Calton Hill looking towards Arthur's Seat sits one of Edinburgh's greatest buildings, the **Old Royal High School**. With its bold central portico of Doric columns and graceful symmetrical colonnaded wings, Thomas Hamilton's elegant building of 1829 is regarded by many as the epitome of Edinburgh's Athenian aspirations. Once considered as a possible home for the Scottish Parliament, it's currently used as council offices, with plans to convert it into a hotel.

Nelson Monument

32 Calton Hill • April–Sept Mon–Sat 10am–7pm, Sun noon–5pm; Oct–March Mon–Sat 10am–3pm • £4 • ☎ 0131 556 2716

Robert Louis Stevenson reckoned that Calton Hill was the best place to view Edinburgh, "since you can see the Castle, which you lose from the Castle, and Arthur's Seat, which you cannot see from Arthur's Seat". Though the panoramas from ground level are spectacular enough, those from the top of the **Nelson Monument**, perched near the summit with an appearance like a giant sandstone chess rook, are even better. Prior to the 14-step ascent you'll pass the small ground-level exhibition with details of the structure's maritime connections and a model of Nelson's flagship, *Victory*.

National Monument

The **National Monument** is often referred to as "Edinburgh's Disgrace", yet many locals admire this unfinished and somewhat ungainly attempt to replicate the Parthenon atop Calton Hill. Begun as a memorial to the dead of the Napoleonic Wars, the project's shortage of funds led architect William Playfair to ensure that it would still serve as a striking landmark, despite having only twelve completed columns. With a bit of effort and care you can climb up and around the monument, sit and contemplate from one of the huge steps or meander around the base of the mighty pillars.

Mansfield Place Church

Mansfield Place • Viewing of the murals one Sun afternoon each month, more often during the Festival •
🖂 fmtc@mansfieldtraquair.org.uk, 🌐 mansfieldtraquair.org.uk

The highlight of the Broughton Street area, northeast of the central New Town, is the neo-Norman **Mansfield Place Church**, by the corner of Broughton and East London streets. It contains a cycle of **murals** by the Dublin-born **Phoebe Anna Traquair**, a leading light in the Scottish Arts and Crafts movement. Covering vast areas of the walls and ceilings of the main nave and side chapels, the wonderfully luminous paintings depict biblical parables and texts, with rows of angels, cherubs flecked with gold and worshipping figures painted in delicate pastel colours.

The Royal Botanic Garden

Arboretum Place • Daily: Feb & Oct 10am–5pm; March–Sept 10am–6pm; Nov–Jan 10am–4pm • Free; glasshouses £5; guided tours (April–Sept 11am & 2pm) £5 • ☎ 0131 248 2909, 🌐 rbge.org.uk

Just beyond the northern boundaries of the New Town, the seventy-acre **Royal Botanic Garden**, with origins as far back as the seventeenth century, rivals Kew (see p.105) as a must-see botanical attraction. Filled with mature trees and a huge variety of native and exotic plants and flowers, the "Botanics" (as they're commonly called) are most popular simply as a place to stroll and lounge around on the grass. The main entrance is the West Gate on Arboretum Place, through the contemporary, eco-designed **John Hope Gateway**, where you'll find interpretation areas, a shop and a restaurant. Towards the eastern side of the gardens, a series of ten **glasshouses**, including a soaring 1850s Palm House, shows off a steamy array of palms, ferns, orchids, cycads and aquatic plants. Scattered around are a number of outdoor sculptures, and some parts have fabulous vistas: the lawns near **Inverleith House**, a gallery showing changing exhibits of contemporary art, offer one of the city's best views of the castle and Old Town's steeples and monuments.

The Scottish National Gallery of Modern Art

Belford Rd • Daily 10am–5pm, till 6pm in Aug • Free, entrance charge for some temporary exhibitions • ☎ 0131 624 6200,
Ⓦ nationalgalleries.org

At the far northwestern fringe of the New Town, the **Scottish National Gallery of Modern Art** was Britain's first collection devoted solely to twentieth-century painting and sculpture, and now covers two grand Neoclassical buildings on either side of Belford Road. The extensive wooded grounds serve as a **sculpture park**, featuring works by Jacob Epstein, Henry Moore, Barbara Hepworth and, most strikingly, Charles Jencks, whose *Landform*, a swirling mix of ponds and grassy mounds, dominates the area in front of the gallery.

Modern One

The gallery on the western side of Belford Road, **Modern One**, divides its display spaces between temporary exhibitions and selections from the gallery's own holdings; the latter are arranged thematically, but are almost constantly moved around. The collection starts with early twentieth-century Post-Impressionists, then moves through the Fauvists, German Expressionism, Cubism and Pop Art, with works by **Lichtenstein** and **Warhol** establishing a connection with the extensive holdings of Eduardo Paolozzi's work in the Modern Two. There's a strong section on living **British artists**, from Gilbert & George to **Britart** stars, while modern **Scottish** art ranges from the Colourists to the distinctive styles of contemporary Scots including John Bellany, a portraitist of striking originality, and the poet-artist-gardener Ian Hamilton Finlay.

Modern Two

Modern Two was refurbished to make room for the huge collection of work of Edinburgh-born sculptor **Sir Eduardo Paolozzi**, described by some as the father of Pop Art. There's an awesome introduction to Paolozzi's work in the form of the huge *Vulcan*, a half-man, half-machine that squeezes into the Great Hall immediately opposite the main entrance – view it both from ground level and the head-height balcony to appreciate the sheer scale of the piece. In the rooms to the right of the main entrance Paolozzi's London studio has been expertly re-created, right down to the clutter of half-finished casts, toys and empty pots of glue.

The ground floor holds a world-renowned collection of **Dada** and **Surrealist** art; Marcel Duchamp, Max Ernst and Man Ray are represented. Look out for Dalí's *The Signal of Anguish* and *Magritte's Magic Mirror* along with work by Miró and Giacometti – all hung on crowded walls with an assortment of artefacts and ethnic souvenirs. Elsewhere, look out for 2009 Turner Prize winner Richard Wright's major wall-painting *The Stairwell Project*, his most complex and ambitious work to date in Britain.

Out from the centre

Just over a mile northeast of the city centre is **Leith**, one of the capital's fine-dining hot spots; it's a fascinating mix of cobbled streets and new developments, with the vibrant, picturesque old port at its heart. To the centre's west, Britain's only pandas draw in the crowds at Edinburgh's **zoo**, a perennial favourite with children.

Leith

Although **LEITH** is generally known as the port of Edinburgh, it developed independently of the city up the hill, its history bound up in the hard graft of fishing, shipbuilding and trade. The presence of sailors, merchants and continental traders also gave the place a

17

cosmopolitan – if slightly rough – edge, which is still obvious today. While the stand-alone attractions are few, Leith is an intriguing place, not just for the contrasts to central Edinburgh, but also for its nautical air and its excellent cafés, pubs and restaurants.

Leith's initial revival from down-and-out waterfront began in the 1980s around the area known as the **Shore**, the old harbour at the mouth of the Water of Leith. More recently, the massive dock areas beyond are being transformed at a rate of knots, with landmark developments including a vast building housing civil servants from the Scottish Government, and Ocean Terminal, a shopping and entertainment complex beside which the former royal yacht **Britannia** has settled into her retirement.

The Royal Yacht Britannia

Ocean Terminal, Leith • Daily: April–June & Oct 9.30am–4pm; July–Sept 9.30am–4.30pm; Nov–March 10am–3.30pm • £12.75 • ☎ 0131 555 5566, ⓦ royalyachtbritannia.co.uk • Tour buses leave from Waverley Bridge; otherwise, take buses #11 or #22 from Princes St, or #35 from the Royal Mile

Launched in 1953, **Britannia** was used by the royal family for 44 years for state visits, diplomatic functions and royal holidays. Video clips of the vessel's most famous moments are shown in the **visitor centre** (within Ocean Terminal) along with royal holiday snaps, and you can roam around the yacht itself, which has been largely kept as she was while in service, with a well-preserved 1950s dowdiness – a far cry from the opulent splendour which many expect.

Edinburgh Zoo

134 Corstorphine Rd • Daily: April–Sept 9am–6pm; March & Oct 9am–5pm; Nov–Feb 9am–4.30pm • £16.50 • Penguin parade April–Sept daily 2.15pm, plus sunny days in March & Oct • ☎ 0131 334 9171, ⓦ edinburghzoo.org.uk • Buses #12, #26 & #31 from town

A couple of miles west of the city centre, **Edinburgh Zoo**, established in 1913, has a reputation for preserving rare and endangered species. With its imaginatively designed habitats and viewing areas, the place is permanently packed with kids. Historically, the zoo's most famous attraction was its penguin parade, though a pair of pandas – the only ones in the UK – have nabbed the top spot since their arrival in 2011. If you want to see them, book a time slot on the website before you arrive, even during quieter times.

ARRIVAL AND DEPARTURE

EDINBURGH

By air Edinburgh International Airport (☎ 0844 448 8833, ⓦ edinburghairport.com) is at Turnhouse, 7 miles west of the city centre, close to the start of the M8 motorway to Glasgow. Trams (every 8–15min 6am–11pm; 35min; £5) connect with Murrayfield Stadium and Haymarket train station en-route to the centre, terminating at St Andrews Square. Airlink shuttle buses (#100; every 10–15min 4am–midnight; every 30min midnight–4am; 30min; £4) connect to Waverley Station in the centre of town. Taxis charge £18–22 for the same journey, which takes about 25min.

Destinations Belfast (Sun–Fri 6 daily, Sat 4 daily; 50min); Cardiff (1–2 daily; 1hr 10min); Dublin (9 daily; 1hr 10min); Kirkwall (Mon–Fri 2 daily, Sat & Sun 1 daily; 1hr 55min); London City (Mon–Fri 7 daily, Sun 4 daily; 1hr 20min); London Gatwick (Mon–Fri 12 daily, Sat & Sun 5 daily; 1hr 15min); London Heathrow (Mon–Fri 15 daily, Sat & Sun 11–15 daily; 1hr); London Luton (Mon–Fri 7 daily, Sat & Sun 4 daily; 1hr 20min); London Stansted (Mon–Fri 6 daily, Sat & Sun 4–6 daily; 1hr

10min); Stornoway (Mon–Fri 3 daily, Sat 2, Sun 1; 1hr 10 min); Sumburgh (Shetland) (3 daily; 1hr 25min); Wick (daily; 55min).

By train Waverley Station (☎ 0845 748 4950) is the main arrival point for all mainline trains. The other mainline train stop, Haymarket Station is just under 2 miles west of town on the lines from Waverley to Glasgow, Fife and the Highlands, and is only really of use if you're staying nearby.

Destinations from Waverley Station Aberdeen (hourly; 2hr 20min); Birmingham (hourly; 5hr); Dunbar (8 daily; 30min); Dundee (hourly; 1hr 45min); Falkirk (every 15min; 25min); Fort William (change at Glasgow, 3 daily; 4hr 55min); Glasgow (every 15–30min; 50min); Inverness (6 daily direct; 3hr 50min); London (hourly; 4hr 30min); Manchester (3 daily; 4hr); Newcastle upon Tyne (hourly; 1hr 30min); North Berwick (hourly; 30min); Oban (2–3 daily, change at Glasgow; 4hr 10min); Perth (6 daily; 1hr 15min); Stirling (every 30min; 45min); York (hourly; 2hr 30min).

By bus The terminal for local and intercity services is on

THE EDINBURGH FESTIVAL

For all its appeal as a historic and attractive capital city, Edinburgh is perhaps best known for its incredible annual **Festival**, which takes place every August and transforms the place into an overwhelming mass of cultural activity. To even attempt to get a handle on what's going on, it's worth appreciating that the "Edinburgh Festival" is an umbrella term that encompasses several different festivals. The principal events are the **Edinburgh International Festival** and the much larger **Edinburgh Festival Fringe**, but there are also **Book**, **Jazz and Blues** and **Art** festivals going on, as well as a **Military Tattoo** on the Castle Esplanade.

The sheer volume of the Festival's output can be bewildering: virtually every branch of arts and entertainment is represented, and world-famous stars mix with pub singers in the daily line-up. It can be a struggle to find **accommodation**, get hold of the **tickets** you want, book a table in a **restaurant** or simply get from one side of town to another; you can end up seeing something truly dire, or something mind-blowing; you'll inevitably try to do too much, stay out too late or spend too much – but then again, most Festival veterans will tell you that if you don't experience these things then you haven't really "done" the Festival.

Dates, venues, names, star acts, happening bars and burning issues change from one year to the next. This **unpredictability** is one of the Festival's greatest charms, so be prepared for – indeed, enjoy – the unexpected.

THE EDINBURGH INTERNATIONAL FESTIVAL

The **Edinburgh International Festival**, or the "Official Festival", was the original Edinburgh Festival, conceived in 1947 as a celebration of pan-European culture in the postwar era. Initially dominated by opera, other elements such as top-grade theatre, ballet, dance and classical music now carry as much weight, and it's still a highbrow event, its high production values and serious approach offering an antidote to the Fringe's slapdash vigour.

Performances take place at the city's larger venues such as the Usher Hall and the Festival Theatre and, while ticket prices run to over £60, it is possible to see shows for £10 or less if you're prepared to queue for the handful of tickets kept back until the day. The festival culminates in a **Fireworks Concert** beside the castle, visible from various points in the city.

THE EDINBURGH FESTIVAL FRINGE

Even standing alone from its sister festivals, the **Fringe** is easily the world's largest arts gathering. Each year sees more than 40,000 performances from more than 750 companies, with more than 21,000 participants from all over the world. There are something in the region of 1500 shows every day, round the clock, in 250 venues around the city. Much more than any other part of the Festival, it's the dynamism, spontaneity and sheer exuberance of the Fringe that dominate Edinburgh every August.

These days, the most prominent aspect of the Fringe is **comedy**, but you'll also find a wide range of theatre, musicals, dance, children's shows, exhibitions, lectures and music – and a decent range of free shows.

While the Fringe is famous for its tiny and unexpected auditoriums, five Fringe giants (Assembly, Pleasance, Gilded Balloon, Underbelly and C Venues) colonize clusters of different-sized spaces for the duration of the Festival. These are all safe bets for decent shows and a bit of star-spotting. And while it's nothing like as large as the venues reviewed below, you shouldn't ignore the programme put on at the Traverse Theatre (see p.755). Long a champion of new drama, the "Trav" combines the avant-garde with professional presentation and its plays are generally among the Fringe's most acclaimed.

---

the east side of St Andrew Square, a 2min walk from Waverley Station.
Destinations Aberdeen (hourly; 3hr 50min); Birmingham (2–3 daily; 6hr 50min); Dundee (hourly; 1hr 45min–2hr); Glasgow (every 15min; 1hr 10min); Inverness (hourly; 3hr 30min–4hr 30min); London (10 daily; 7hr 50min); Newcastle upon Tyne (5 daily; 2hr 45min); Perth (hourly; 1hr 20min).

INFORMATION

Main tourist office Princes Mall, 3 Princes St, near the northern entrance to the train station (June Mon–Sat 9am–6pm, Sun 10am–6pm; July & Aug Mon–Sat 9am–7pm, Sun 10am–7pm; Sept–May Mon–Sat 9am–5pm; Sun

INFORMATION

International Festival Box Office The Hub, Castlehill; Mon–Fri 10am–5pm except during the Festival, Mon–Sat 9am–7.30pm, Sun 10am–7.30pm; ☎ 0131 473 2099, ⓦ eif.co.uk.

Festival Fringe Office 180 High St; June–mid-July Mon–Sat noon–3pm; mid-end July daily 10am–6pm; Aug 10am–9pm. Fringe tickets (generally £5–15) available from here, online or at venues; ☎ 0131 226 0000, ⓦ edfringe.com.

Useful website For up-to-date information any time of year, visit ⓦ edinburghfestivals.co.uk, which has links to the home pages of most of the main festivals.

Publications Each festival produces its own programme well in advance and during the Festival various publications are widely available. Local what's-on guide *The List* comes out weekly during the Festival and manages to combine comprehensive coverage with an on-the-pulse sense of what's hot. Of the local newspapers, *The Scotsman* carries a dedicated daily Festival supplement with an events diary and respected reviews, while various freebie newspapers are also available – the best is *Fest*, which mixes news with pithy reviews and yet more listings.

FRINGE VENUES

Assembly Rooms 50 George St ☎ 0844 693 3008, ⓦ arfringe.com. Having gone through a major refurbishment recently, this Neoclassical masterpiece of a building is now back at the forefront of the Fringe with its impressive line-up of top-of-the-range drama and big-name music and comedy acts.

Gilded Balloon Teviot Row House, Bristo Square ☎ 0131 622 6552, ⓦ gildedballoon.co.uk. The comedy-focused Gilded Balloon bases its operations in a students' union, the gothic Teviot Row.

Pleasance Courtyard 60 The Pleasance ☎ 0131 556 6550, ⓦ pleasance.co.uk. A slighty raucous atmosphere, thanks to its busy courtyard bar, with offbeat comedy and whimsical appearances by panellists on Radio 4 game shows.

Underbelly 58 Cowgate & Bristo Square ☎ 0844 545 8252, ⓦ underbelly.co.uk. Underbelly are one of

the "big five" Fringe companies operating fifteen comedy and cabaret spaces, including the giant, inflatable upside-down cow, "the Udderbelly", found in Bristo Square.

THE OTHER FESTIVALS

Edinburgh Art Festival ☎ 0131 226 6558, ⓦ edinburghartfestival.com. A relative newcomer on the scene, held throughout August and including high-profile exhibitions by internationally renowned contemporary artists as well as retrospectives of work by pioneering twentieth-century artists. Virtually every art gallery in the city participates, from small private concerns to blockbuster shows at the National Galleries of Scotland's five venues.

Edinburgh International Book Festival ☎ 0845 373 5888, ⓦ edbookfest.co.uk. Taking place in mid-August, this is the world's largest celebration of the written word. It's held in a tented village in Charlotte Square and offers talks, readings and signings by a star-studded line-up of visiting authors and politicians, as well as panel discussions and workshops.

Edinburgh Jazz and Blues Festival ☎ 0131 473 2000, ⓦ edinburghjazzfestival.com. Immediately prior to the Fringe in the first week in August, easing the city into the festival spirit. Highlights include nightly jam sessions and a colourful New Orleans-style Mardi Gras and street parade.

The Military Tattoo ☎ 0131 225 1188, ⓦ edintattoo.co.uk. Staged in the spectacular stadium of the Edinburgh Castle Esplanade every night during August, the Tattoo is an unashamed display of pomp and military pride. The programme of choreographed drills, massed pipe bands, historical tableaux, energetic battle re-enactments, national dancing and pyrotechnics has been a feature of the Festival for over half a century, its emotional climax provided by a lone piper on the Castle battlements. Followed by a quick fireworks display, it's a successful formula barely tampered with over the years. Tickets (£25–50) should be booked well in advance.

10am–5pm; ☎ 0845 225 5121, ⓦ edinburgh.org).

Airport tourist office Main Concourse opposite gate 5

(daily: April–Oct 6.30am–10.30pm; Nov–March 7am–9pm) ☎ 0131 344 3120.

GETTING AROUND

By bus The city is generally well served by buses; the white-and-maroon Lothian Buses provide the most frequent and comprehensive coverage (timetables and passes from offices on Waverley Bridge, Shandwick Place or

Hanover St; ☎ 0131 555 6363, ⓦ lothianbuses.com); all buses referred to here are run by Lothian unless otherwise stated. Tickets cost £1.50 single or £3.50 for a day-pass payable to the driver (who cannot provide change).

17

By tram One solitary route connects the airport with Murrayfield Stadium, Haymarket, Princes St and St Andrew Square (☏ 0800 328 3934, ⌨ edinburghtrams.com). Tickets can be bought from vending machines at the tram stops and will cost £1.50 single or £7.50 single to the airport. Bus day-tickets are also valid on the tram.

By bike Although hilly, Edinburgh is a reasonably bike-friendly city, with several cycle paths. The local cycling action group, Spokes (☏ 0131 313 2114, ⌨ spokes.org.uk), publishes

an excellent map. For rental, try Biketrax, 13 Lochrin Place (☏ 0131 228 6633, ⌨ biketrax.co.uk), in Tollcross.

By car It is a very bad idea to take a car into central Edinburgh due to the phenomenally high cost of parking. Illegally parked cars are very likely to be fined £30 within minutes by one of the swarms of patrolling inspectors.

By taxi You can hail black cabs on the street, pick them up from a rank or phone for a booking. Try Central Taxis (☏ 0131 229 2468) or City Cabs (☏ 0131 228 1211).

ACCOMMODATION

Edinburgh has a greater choice of accommodation than anywhere else in Britain outside London. **Hotels**, self-catering apartments and large backpacker **hostels** are essentially the only options you'll find right in the heart of the city, but within relatively easy reach of the centre the selection of **guesthouses**, **B&Bs**, **campus accommodation** and even **campsites** broadens considerably. Making **reservations** is worthwhile at any time of year, and is strongly recommended for stays during the Festival and around Hogmanay, when places can get booked out months in advance. VisitScotland operates a booking centre for accommodation all over the country, including Edinburgh (☏ 0845 859 1006, ⌨ visitscotland.com).

HOTELS

Hotel prices are significantly higher than elsewhere in Scotland, with double rooms starting at £85 per night. Budget chains offer the best value if you want basic accommodation right in the centre, with rooms available for £85–95; £95 upwards will get you something more stylish.

OLD TOWN

Ibis Edinburgh Centre 6 Hunter Square ☏ 0131 619 2800, ⌨ ibis.com. Probably the best-located chain hotel cheapie in the Old Town, within sight of the Royal Mile;

rooms are modern and inexpensive, but there are few facilities other than a rather plain bar. **£94**

Ten Hill Place 10 Hill Place ☏ 0131 662 2080, ⌨ tenhillplace.com. A contemporary, efficient hotel linked to the historic Royal College of Surgeons, with 78 sleek and smartly styled bedrooms, all run according to an environmentally conscious policy. **£95**

Travelodge Edinburgh Central 33 St Mary's St ☏ 0871 984 6137, ⌨ travelodge.co.uk. Possibly Edinburgh's least charming hotel and often overrun with stag and hen parties, but you can't argue with its location,

---

CITY TOURS

Despite the compactness of the city centre, open-top **bus tours** are big business, with several companies taking slightly varying routes around the main sights. All cost the same, depart from Waverley Bridge and allow you to get on and off at leisure. There are also several **walking tours**, many of which depart from the central section of the Royal Mile near the High Kirk of St Giles; ghost tours and specialist tours are also available. **Advance booking** is recommended for all the tours below, and for the specialist tours in particular and cost upwards from £10 per person.

City of the Dead Graveyard Tour Tour starts outside St Giles Cathedral, High St ☏ 0131 225 9044, ⌨ cityofthedeadtours.com. Spine-tingling night-time tours around the Old Town.

Edinburgh Literary Pub Tour Tour starts outside The Beehive Inn, Grassmarket ☏ 0800 169 7410, ⌨ edinburghliterarypubtour.co.uk. Good specialist tour that mixes a pub crawl with extracts from local authors acted out along the way.

Geowalks Tour starts by pond outside Scottish Parliament ☏ 0131 555 5488, ⌨ geowalks.co.uk. Guided walks up Arthur's Seat in the company of a qualified geologist.

MacTours Waverley Bridge ☏ 0131 220 0770,

⌨ edinburghtour.com. The most engaging bus tour operator, using a fleet of vintage buses.

Mercat Tours Tours start at the Mercat Cross, High St ☏ 0131 225 5445, ⌨ mercattours.com. Reliable operator for walking tours and Old Town ghost tours.

Rebustours Tour starts in the Royal Oak pub, Infirmary St · Sat only ☏ 0131 553 7473, ⌨ rebustours.com. Trace the footsteps of Inspector Rebus, hero of Ian Rankin's bestselling detective novels.

Trainspotting Tour starts in Port O'Leith pub, Constitution St, Leith ☏ 0131 555 2500, ⌨ leithwalks.co.uk. A tour that takes you to places made famous from Irvine Welsh's novels.

just off the Royal Mile, nor its room prices. **£89**

★ **The Witchery Apartments** Castlehill, Royal Mile ☎0131 225 5613, ⓦthewitchery.com. Nine riotously indulgent suites grouped around this famously spooky restaurant just downhill from the castle; expect antique furniture, big leather armchairs, tapestry-draped beds, oak panelling and huge roll-top baths, as well as ultramodern sound systems and complementary champagne. **£325**

NEW TOWN

Express by Holiday Inn Edinburgh City Centre Picardy Place, Broughton ☎0131 558 2300, ⓦhieedinburgh .co.uk. It's by a busy roundabout, but otherwise in a good location in an elegant old Georgian tenement near the top of Broughton St, with 161 rooms featuring neat but predictable chain hotel decor and facilities. **£109**

★ **Gerald's Place** 21b Abercromby Place ☎0131 558 7017, ⓦgeraldsplace.com. A homely taste of New Town life at an upmarket but wonderfully hospitable and comfy basement B&B. **£139**

The Glasshouse 2 Greenside Place, Broughton ☎0131 525 8200, ⓦtheetoncollection.co.uk. Incorporating the castellated facade of the former Lady Glenorchy's Church, this ultra-hip hotel has 65 chi-chi rooms with push-button curtains and sliding doors opening onto a huge, lush roof garden scattered with Philippe Starck furniture. Perfect if you're in town for a weekend of flash indulgence. **£180**

Ramsay's Bed and Breakfast 25 East London St, Broughton ☎0131 557 5917, ⓦramsaysbedand breakfastedinburgh.com. Well located just around the corner from Broughton St, this terraced townhouse has four simple and neat bedrooms, all with en-suite bathrooms. A full Scottish breakfast is served, and families are welcome. **£85**

LEITH AND NORTH EDINBURGH

The Inverleith Hotel 5 Inverleith Terrace, Inverleith ☎0131 556 2745, ⓦinverleithhotel.co.uk. Pleasant option near the Botanic Gardens, with ten rooms of various sizes in a Victorian terraced house; all are en suite and tastefully decorated with wooden floors, antiques and tapestries. Free parking is available 500m away. **£86**

Malmaison 1 Tower Place ☎0844 693 0652, ⓦmalmaison.com. Chic, modern hotel set in the grand old seamen's hostel just back from the wharf-side. Bright, bold original designs in each room, as well as a stereo and satellite TV. Also has a gym, room service, Parisian brasserie and café-bar serving lighter meals. **£99**

SOUTH OF THE CENTRE

★ **94DR** 94 Dalkeith Rd, Newington ☎0131 662 9265, ⓦ94dr.com. A boutique guesthouse offering three different styles with its couture, bespoke and tailored rooms. Front-facing rooms have a view of Arthur's Seat. **£110**

Cluaran House 47 Leamington Terrace, Viewforth

☎0131 221 0047, ⓦcluaran-house-edinburgh.co.uk. Tasteful and welcoming B&B with original Victorian features and paintings. Serves good wholefood breakfasts. Close to the Meadows with bus links (including #11 & #23) from nearby Bruntsfield Place. **£90**

HOSTELS, SELF-CATERING AND CAMPUS ACCOMMODATION

Edinburgh is one of the UK's most popular backpacker destinations, and there are a large number of hostels in and around the centre, ranging in size, atmosphere and quality. Custom-built self-catering serviced apartments with no minimum let are popular, and make a viable alternative to guesthouses. Campus accommodation is available in summer, and while a good option for solo travellers, you can get better value on doubles elsewhere.

OLD TOWN

Brodies 1 93 High St ☎0131 556 2223, ⓦbrodies hostels.co.uk. Tucked down a typical Old Town close, with four straightforward dorms sleeping up to a dozen and limited communal areas. It's smaller than many hostels, and a little bit more homely as a result. Dorm **£13**; double **£65**

★ **Castle Rock Hostel** 15 Johnston Terrace ☎0131 225 9666, ⓦcastlerockedinburgh.com. Tucked below the Castle ramparts, with 200 or so beds arranged in large, bright dorms, as well as triple and quads and some doubles. The communal areas include a games room with pool and table tennis. Dorm **£15**; double **£45**

Smart City Hostel 50 Blackfriars St ☎0131 524 1989, ⓦsmartcityhostels.com. A five-star hostel just off the Royal Mile, with 622 beds in private rooms or dorms. A reasonable bar-bistro serves good-value food and breakfasts, and there's a late-night bar for residents. Dorm **£18**; double **£59**

NEW TOWN AND AROUND

Canon Court Apartments 20 Canonmills ☎0800 027 1035, ⓦcanoncourt.co.uk. A block of smart, comfortable self-catering one- and two-bedroom apartments not far from Canonmills Bridge over the Water of Leith, at the northern edge of the New Town. A double-bed apartment for two starts from **£93**

Edinburgh Central SYHA 9 Haddington Place, Leith ☎0131 524 2090, ⓦedinburghcentral.org. In a handy location near the top of Leith Walk, this five-star hostel has single, double and eight-bed rooms with en-suite facilities. There is a reasonably priced bistro and self-catering kitchen facilities. Dorm **£20**; double **£72**

SOUTH OF THE CENTRE

Argyle Backpackers 14 Argyle Place, Marchmont ☎0131 667 9991, ⓦargyle-backpackers.co.uk. Quiet, less intense version of the typical backpackers' hostel, pleasantly located in three adjoining townhouses near the

17

Meadows in studenty Marchmont. It's walking distance to town, or you can get bus #41 from the door. The small dorms have single beds, and there are a dozen or so double/twin rooms, as well as a pleasant communal conservatory and garden at the back. Dorm £18; double £56

University of Edinburgh, Pollock Halls of Residence

18 Holyrood Park Rd, Newington ☎0131 651 2007, ☺edinburghfirst.com. Unquestionably the best setting of any of the university accommodation, right beside Holyrood Park, with a range of accommodation from single rooms (£50) and en-suite doubles to self-catering flats (from £450 per week). Mostly available Easter & June to mid-Sept, though some rooms year-round. Double £82

EATING

Edinburgh's dining scene is a feather in the city's cap – with five restaurants holding **Michelin stars**, it can justifiably claim second place behind London in the UK's fine-dining pecking order. Under this level, small diners and bistros predominate, and Edinburgh is an excellent place if you like **fish** and shellfish. Plenty of tourist-oriented restaurants offer **haggis** and other classic clichés, mostly with little culinary merit; a better idea is to seek out the crop of places using locally sourced, quality ingredients available from small and **artisan producers** around Scotland. During the **Festival** the majority of restaurants keep longer hours than are given below, but they are also much busier.

ROYAL MILE AND AROUND

CAFÉS, BISTROS AND CASUAL DINING

★ **David Bann's Vegetarian Restaurant** 56–58 St Mary's St ☎0131 556 5888, ☺davidbann.com. Thoroughly modern vegetarian restaurant, open long hours and offering a wide choice of interesting dishes such as chilli pancake with grilled sweet potato, courgette and chocolate sauce (£11.90) or olive polenta with roasted vegetables and goats curd. Prices are reasonable and the overall design is stylish and classy. Mon–Fri noon–10pm, Sat & Sun 11am–10pm.

The Edinburgh Larder 15 Blackfriars St ☎0131 556 6922, ☺edinburghlarder.co.uk. Just 20yd off the Royal Mile, this popular bistro acts like a neighbourhood café, with friendly staff, food that dares to depart from the norm, and almost all ingredients sourced from the smaller Scottish producers around Edinburgh. The menu changes seasonally, with soups and starters costing around £5 and mains upwards of £12.50. Mon–Sat 8am–5pm, Sun 9am–5pm except Jan & Feb daily 9am–5pm.

Fruitmarket Gallery Café 45 Market St ☎0131 226 1843, ☺fruitmarket.co.uk. This attractive café feels like an extension of the gallery space, its airy, reflective ambience enhanced by the wall of glass onto the street. Stop in for soups, coffees or some haggis and black pudding bonbons (£5.25) – part of the common trend to gentrify the national dish. Mon–Sat 11am–5.30pm, Sun noon–4.30pm.

Mother India's Cafe 3–5 Infirmary St ☎0131 524 9801, ☺motherindia.co.uk. This Glasgow-based operation has a refreshing approach to Indian food, serving freshly prepared tapas-style dishes that allow you to eat well but also lightly, with disarmingly simple combinations such as ginger chicken and spinach leaf (£4.95). Old stone walls and original photos on the walls help maintain an informal but buzzy atmosphere. Mon–Thurs noon–2pm & 5–10.30pm, Fri & Sat noon–11pm, Sun noon–10pm.

★ **Spoon** 6a Nicholson St ☎0131 623 1752, ☺spoonedinburgh.co.uk. A lovely, large, first-floor room opposite the Festival Theatre with quirky retro fittings and a reliable menu. You can just stop off for a coffee or stay to sample their well-made rustic dishes; expect punchy flavours and good ingredients in classics like mushroom and bean stew or slow-cooked lamb flank, available as part of the two-course pre-theatre menu (£12). Mon–Sat 10am–11pm, Sun noon–5pm.

Timberyard 10 Lady Lawson St ☎0131 221 1222, ☺timberyard.co. This swanky yet somehow rustic old workshop makes for a genial atmosphere with its shared, candlelit benches indoors and sunny courtyard garden. The food focuses on high-quality Scottish produce, some of it sourced from the nearby farmers' market. À la carte mains start at £11. Food served Tues–Sat noon–2pm & 5.30–9.30pm; bar stays open until 1am.

FINE DINING

Amber Scotch Whisky Heritage Centre, 354 Castlehill ☎0131 477 8477, ☺amber-restaurant.co.uk. Neat, contemporary place serving light food such as "Scottish tapas" at lunchtime and more substantial dishes in the evenings, when a "whisky sommelier" will suggest the best drams to accompany plates like monkfish shank in spiced bisque (£16.55). Sun–Thurs noon–7.30pm, Fri & Sat noon–9.30pm.

La Garrigue 31 Jeffrey St ☎0131 557 3032, ☺lagarrigue.co.uk. A place of genuine charm and quality, with a menu and wine list dedicated to the produce and traditions of the Languedoc region of France. The care and honesty of the cooking shines through in dishes such as the traditional cassoulet or slow-cooked beef cheeks with winter veg. They offer two courses for the set price of £28. Daily noon–2.30pm & 6.30–9.30pm.

★ **Ondine** 2 George IV Bridge ☎0131 226 1888, ☺ondinerestaurant.co.uk. Tucked in next to the swanky *G & V Hotel*, this seafood restaurant and oyster bar from Edinburgh chef Roy Brett, once Rick Stein's main chef in Padstow, turns out some sublime dishes such as grilled lemon sole with brown shrimps and capers (£25), using native shellfish and fish from sustainable sources. Mon–Sat noon–3pm & 5.30–10pm.

The Witchery by the Castle Castlehill ☎0131 225 5613, ⓦthewitchery.com. An upmarket restaurant set in magnificently over-the-top medieval surroundings full of Gothic panelling, tapestries and heavy stonework, all a mere broomstick-hop from the Castle. The style of the menu matches the decor, with a banquet of hearty game and meat dishes on offer such as lamb Wellington for two (£60). To experience this place on a budget aim for the lunch or pre- or post-theatre set menu for under £16. Daily noon–11.30pm.

NEW TOWN AND AROUND
CAFÉS

★ **Artisan Roast** 57 Broughton St ☎07526 236 615, ⓦartisanroast.co.uk. If you're into the black stuff, this is a must. A narrow, grungy shop lined with hessian, they roast on site, make coffee with skill and care, and delight in taking pops at mainstream coffee culture. Perch on a stool in the main shop or shuffle through to cushioned benches in "the Mooch". Other than pastries and cakes, they don't serve much food. Mon–Thurs 8am–7.30pm, Fri 8am–6.30pm, Sat 9am–6.30pm, Sun 10am–6.30pm.

The Gallery Café Scottish National Gallery of Modern Art One, Belford Rd, Dean Village ☎0131 624 6200, ⓦnationalgalleries.org/visit/café. The cultured setting (which includes a lovely outside eating area) and appealing, mid-priced menu of hearty soups and light lunches such as the mushroom filo parcels with a choice of two excellent salads (£6.50) pull in reassuring numbers of locals. Mon–Fri 9am–4.30pm, Sat & Sun 10am–4.30pm.

The Scottish Café and Restaurant National Gallery of Scotland, The Mound ☎0131 226 6524, ⓦcontini.com/scottish-cafe-and-restaurant. An admirable (and mostly successful) attempt to bring the best of Scottish produce to a busy venue. Choose luxury porridge or a buttery (the local equivalent of a croissant) for a morning snack, or go whole hog with a hearty Scottish breakfast (£13) featuring black pudding, haggis and other artery tightening treats. Mon–Wed, Fri & Sat 9am–5pm, Thurs 9am–7pm, Sun 10am–5pm.

★ **Valvona & Crolla** 19 Elm Row, Leith Walk ☎0131 556 6066, ⓦvalvonacrolla.com. The café at the back of what is arguably Britain's finest Italian deli serves authentic and delicious breakfasts, lunches and daytime snacks including an antipasto plate of cured meats, roast vegetables and bruschetta (£10.50). V&C also has a wine bar and evening restaurant (Vincaffè) at 11 Multrees Walk, just off St Andrew Square. Mon–Thurs 8.30am–5.30pm, Fri & Sat 8am–6pm, Sun 10.30am–3.30pm.

BISTROS AND CASUAL DINING

The Dogs 110 Hanover St ☎0131 220 1208, ⓦthedogsonline.co.uk. British gastropub cooking taken

to a whole new level with confident use of traditional ingredients like offal and lamb chops paired with thoroughly modern flavours – braised ox cheek with dark chocolate sauce and horseradish mash (£12.50) for example. There's a good-value wine list and unconventionally offhand but well-meaning service. Variations on the formula reappear almost next door at sister restaurants Amore Dogs (the Italian version) and Seadogs (the fishy version) at 43 Rose St. Daily noon–4pm & 5–10pm.

Dusit 49a Thistle St, West End ☎0131 220 6846, ⓦdusit.co.uk. The bold but effective blend of Thai flavours and well-sourced Scottish ingredients brings a bit of originality and refinement to the often-predictable Thai dining scene. Specialities include gaeng phet red curry with chicken, bamboo shoots, aubergine, chilli and basil (£11.95). Mon–Sat noon–3pm & 6–11pm, Sun noon–11pm.

L'Escargot Bleu 56 Broughton St ☎0131 557 1600, ⓦlescargotbleu.co.uk. A nice step up from the rustic, no-frills French bistro that's still in evidence across Edinburgh. Here, classic French country cooking is brought to bear on a range of locally sourced produce, from duck leg confit with Scottish wild mushrooms to coq au vin but made with local beer instead of wine (£16.50). Mon–Thurs noon–2.30pm & 5.30–10pm, Fri & Sat noon–3pm & 5.30–10.30pm.

Mussel Inn 61–65 Rose St ☎08432 892 481, ⓦmussel-inn.com. After feasting on a kilo of mussels and a basket of chips for under £15 you'll realize why there's a demand to get in here. They have close ties to west-coast shellfish farmers, which helps ensure that the journey from sea to plate is short and swift. Mon–Thurs noon–3pm & 5.30–10pm, Fri–Sun noon–10pm.

Urban Angel 121 Hanover St ☎0131 225 6215, ⓦurban-angel.co.uk. Right-on and easy-going subterranean bistro with a diverse and adaptable blackboard menu using lots of organic and Fairtrade produce. They'll do you a raw superfood salad for £9 or a gourmet burger and fries for £12.90. There's a second, equally attractive branch at 1 Forth St just off Broughton St. Mon 8am–5pm, Tues–Sat 8am–8pm, Sun 9am–5pm.

FINE DINING

21212 3 Royal Terrace, Calton Hill ☎0845 222 1212, ⓦ21212restaurant.co.uk. The most challenging and polarizing restaurant to arrive in Edinburgh in recent years; some (including the Michelin inspectors) love chef Paul Kitching's shopping-list style of cooking and whimsical concoctions, while others are convinced they've been had. As part of a £69, five-course dinner you might encounter a dish such as baked sea bass fillet with lemon and saffron pancakes, pink radish, shiitake mushrooms and cardamom ginger butter sauce. Tues–Sat lunch & dinner.

★ **The Dining Room, Scotch Malt Whisky Society** 28 Queen St ☎0131 220 2044 ⓦthediningroomedinburgh.co.uk. This stylish, relatively modern club isn't nearly as

17

stuffy as you'd expect, and the classy ground-floor restaurant, open to nonmembers, is excellent, serving three courses à la carte for £35 or £28.50 if you go veggie. Dishes reflect what's in season including interesting foraged foods and bygone ingredients; you might find mead and wild garlic paired with roast lamb or nettle purée and pickled blueberries with pigeon ballotine. Mon noon–2.30pm, Tues–Sat noon–2.30pm & 5–9.30pm.

The Honours 58a Castle St ☎0131 220 2513, ⓦthehonours.co.uk. A brasserie in the grand Parisian style, but with Michelin-starred chef Martin Wishart overseeing proceedings (but not cooking – his talented partner Paul Tamburrini does that here); standards and quality are high. The à la carte offers rabbit in mustard for £18.50 and a good range of seafood and offal dishes – or you can gnaw on oriental pork chops as part of the £18.50 two-course set menu. Tues–Sat noon–2.30pm & 6–10pm.

SOUTHSIDE
CAFÉS, BISTROS AND CASUAL DINING

The Apartment Bistro 7–13 Barclay Place, Bruntsfield ☎0131 228 6456, ⓦapartmentrestaurant.com. A sultry, Parisian-style brasserie with a varied menu to suit all budgets. At the top end you'll find dishes like seabass fillets with porcini and Amontillado sauce for £17 or you can opt for the bargain £15 three-course set menu. Wed–Mon noon–11pm, Tues 4–11pm.

Kalpna 2–3 St Patrick's Square, Newington ☎0131 667 9890, ⓦkalpnarestaurant.com. Longstanding Gujarati–Indian restaurant serving up delightfully light vegetarian and vegan curries. A choice of four thaalis featuring rich curries, sweet chutneys and traditional breads are available in the evening starting from £13, while at lunchtime it's all you can eat for £8. Mon–Sat noon–2pm & 5.30–10.30pm; May–Sept Sun 6–10.30pm.

Peter's Yard 27 Simpson Loan (Quartermile) ☎0131 228 5876, ⓦpetersyard.com. A Swedish outfit with the bread ovens on view and baskets of delicious loaves out front. Set on the edge of The Meadows, it's popular with flush-feeling students and professionals drawn by the excellent sourdough pizzas (£10), coffee and bakery treats. Mon–Fri 7.30am–7pm, Sat & Sun 9am–7pm.

Sweet Melinda's 11 Roseneath St, Marchmont ☎0131 229 9531, ⓦsweetmelindas.co.uk. A pleasant seafood restaurant in a timber-panelled room with a friendly, neighbourhood feel. Two lunchtime taster courses, such as grilled sardines with capers, thyme and garlic butter followed by salmon and trout rillettes with crostini, cost just £7.50. Tues–Sat noon–2pm & 6–10pm.

LEITH AND NEWHAVEN

With some of the city's top restaurants, great seafood places and well-worn, friendly pubs, Leith and its neighbouring harbour district of Newhaven are among the best places to eat and drink in Edinburgh.

CAFÉS, BISTROS AND CASUAL DINING

Chop Chop 76 Commercial Quay, Leith ☎0131 553 1818, ⓦchop-chop.co.uk. Specializes in food from around the northeastern Chinese province of Jilin. Its dumplings – at around £4.50 – are a particular draw, as is the £20.25 unlimited banquet. Success on one of Gordon Ramsay's TV shows has seen it blossom. Mon–Thurs 6–10pm, Fri 6–10.30pm, Sat noon–2pm & 5–10.30pm, Sun 12.30–2.30pm & 5–10pm.

Loch Fyne Restaurant 25 Pier Place, Newhaven Harbour ☎0131 559 3900, ⓦlochfyneseafoodandgrill.co.uk. Fantastic location by the fish market and old stone harbour at Newhaven for this English-based chain with strong connections to Scotland's west coast. Best for simple oysters and fish with a glass of wine, though there are plenty of mains including seafood tagliatelle for £15. Mon–Thurs 11.30am–10pm, Fri 11.30am–10.30pm, Sat 10am–11pm, Sun 10am–10pm.

Porto & Fi 47 Newhaven Main St ☎0131 551 1900, ⓦportofi.com. A bright daytime café not far from Newhaven's old stone harbour, with tempting cakes alongside serious daily specials, including the house fish pie topped with leek mash (£10.25), from an accomplished kitchen. Mon–Sat 8am–8pm, Sun 10am–6pm.

The Shore 3 The Shore, Leith ☎0131 553 5080, ⓦfishersbistros.co.uk. A well-lived-in bar/restaurant with huge mirrors, wood panelling and aproned waiters who'll deliver you smart fish and chips with mushy peas for £12.50. Live jazz, folk and hubbub float through from the adjoining bar. Fri & Sun noon–1am, Mon–Thurs noon–2.30pm & 5pm–1am.

The Water of Leith Café Bistro 52 Coburg St ☎0131 555 2613, ⓦthewaterofleithcafebistro.co.uk. A wee bit out on its own, but this welcoming, family-friendly spot is right beside the Water of Leith walkway. The French chef's wide experience shows in the quality of dishes such as smoked haddock and salmon fishcakes with home-made tartare sauce (£6.95). Tues–Sun 10am–5.30pm.

FINE DINING

★ **The Kitchin** 78 Commercial Quay, Leith ☎0131 555 1755, ⓦthekitchin.com. Opened in 2006 by young Scottish chef Tom Kitchin and the winner – less than six months later – of a Michelin star, this upwardly mobile operation puts itself at the more relaxed end of the fine-dining spectrum and offers some tantalizing à la carte dishes including rolled pig's head with crispy ear salad (£22) and razor clams with chorizo, as well as tasting menus from £75. Tues–Thurs 12.15–2.30pm & 6.30–10pm, Fri & Sat 12.15–2.30pm & 6.30–10.30pm.

Restaurant Martin Wishart 54 The Shore, Leith ☎0131

553 3557, ⓦ martin-wishart.co.uk. The eponymous chef is one of the leading lights of the Scottish culinary scene, and was the first Michelin-star holder in Edinburgh. Though relatively small and demure, his original restaurant (he also runs a brasserie, *The Honours*, in the New Town) wows the gourmets with highly accomplished and exquisitely presented dishes featuring Scottish-sourced fish and meat. A two-course lunch is £28.50, a six-course evening tasting menu £75 or £70 for the vegetarian version. Tues–Fri noon–2pm & 7–10pm, Sat noon–1.30pm & 7–10pm.

DRINKING

Many of Edinburgh's **pubs**, especially in the Old Town, have histories that stretch back centuries, while others, particularly in the New Town, are unaltered Victorian or Edwardian period pieces. Add a plentiful supply of trendy modern bars, and there's enough to cater for all tastes. Note that the **opening hours** quoted below may well be extended during Festival.

THE ROYAL MILE AND AROUND
★**Bow Bar** 80 West Bow, Old Town ⓣ 0131 226 7667. Wonderful old wood-panelled bar and one of the most pleasant, convivial drinking spots in the city centre. Choose from among nearly 150 whiskies or a changing selection of first-rate Scottish and English cask beers. Mon–Sat noon–midnight, Sun noon–11pm.

Jolly Judge 7 James Court ⓦ 0131 225 2669. Atmospheric, low ceilinged bar in a close just down from the Castle which features in the Literary Pub Tour (see box, p.748). Cosy in winter and pleasant outside in summer. Mon–Sat noon–midnight, Sun noon–11pm.

Peartree House 36 West Nicolson St, Newington ⓣ 0131 667 7533. Fine bar in an eighteenth-century house with old sofas and a large courtyard – one of central Edinburgh's very few beer gardens. Mon–Thurs 11am–11.45pm, Fri & Sat 11am–12.45am, Sun 12.30–11.45pm.

Under the Stairs 3a Merchant St, Old Town ⓣ 0131 466 8550, ⓦ underthestairs.org. Comfy, shabby-chic bar with great cocktails, popular with the pre-clubbing crowd. Food served late, with sharing plates available right up till closing time. Mon–Sat noon–1am, Sun noon–midnight.

NEW TOWN AND WEST END
99 Hanover Street 99 Hanover St, New Town ⓣ 0131 225 8200. This plush, boutique bar is a popular pre-clubbing destination at weekends for Edinburgh's "it" crowd. Regular guest DJs, previously including Grandmaster Flash and Eddie Pillar, provide the soundtrack while the bar does a roaring trade with its house cocktail menu. Mon–Thurs 4pm–1am, Fri 3pm–1am, Sat noon–1am & Sun 12.30pm–1am.

Blue Blazer 2 Spittal St, Tollcross ⓣ 0131 229 5030. This traditional Edinburgh howff with an oak-clad bar and church pews serves good real ales and has a great choice of whiskies and rums. Mon–Sat 11am–1am, Sun 12.30pm–1am.

The Bon Vivant 55 Thistle St, New Town ⓣ 0131 225 3275, ⓦ bonvivantedinburgh.co.uk. Classy city-centre bar, with an excellent wine list and good choice of champagne by the glass, as well as interesting food available in tapas-sized portions. Daily noon–1am.

★**Café Royal Circle Bar** 17 West Register St, New Town ⓣ 0131 556 1884, ⓦ caferoyaledinburgh.co.uk. Worth a visit just for its Victorian decor, notably the huge elliptical island bar and tiled portraits of renowned inventors. The beer and food are good, too. The *Café* is a better bet than its equally venerable, but much more staid, neighbouring *Oyster Bar* restaurant. Mon–Wed 11am–11pm, Thurs 11am–midnight, Fri & Sat 11am–1am, Sun 12.30pm–11pm.

Tigerlily 125 George St, New Town ⓣ 0131 225 5005, ⓦ tigerlilyedinburgh.co.uk. The daddy of all George Street's decadent destination bars, where the locals come to see and be seen. Can be lots of fun – but only if you're wearing the right clothes. Daily 8am–1am.

Traverse Bar Café Traverse Theatre, 10 Cambridge St, West End ⓣ 0131 228 5383, ⓦ traverse.co.uk/eating-drinking. Much more than just a theatre bar, attracting a lively, sophisticated crowd who dispel any notion of a quiet interval drink. Good food available. One of the places to be during the Festival. Mon–Wed 11am–midnight, Thurs–Sat 11am–1am, Sun performance dependent.

The Voodoo Rooms 19a West Register St, New Town ⓣ 0131 556 7060, ⓦ thevoodoorooms.com. Glamorous gilt and plush booths attract a dressed-up crowd, especially at the weekend. Frequent live music, performance and club nights, including Edinburgh's legendary retro night, Vegas! (ⓦ vegasscotland.co.uk). Mon–Thurs 4pm–1am, Fri–Sun noon–1am.

LEITH
Kings Wark 36 The Shore ⓣ 0131 554 9260, ⓦ thekingswark.com. Real ale in a restored fifteenth-century pub right in the heart of Leith. There's an attached restaurant, and great bar meals – check in at the bar for a table. Mon–Thurs noon–11pm, Fri & Sat noon–midnight, Sun 11am–11pm.

The Roseleaf 23/24 Sandport Place ⓣ 0131 476 5268, ⓦ roseleaf.co.uk. Chintzy-cool local that's a little off the beaten track but worth the trip for the pot-tails alone – funky cocktails served in vintage teapots. Daily 10am–1am.

★ **The Shore** 3 The Shore ⓣ 0131 553 5080, ⓦ fishersbistros.co.uk. Atmospheric traditional bar with an adjacent restaurant (see p.752). There's regular live jazz or folk music as well as real ales and good bar snacks. Fri & Sun noon–1am, Mon–Thurs noon–2.30pm & 5pm–1am.

17

NIGHTLIFE AND ENTERTAINMENT

Inevitably, Edinburgh's **nightlife** is at its best during the Festival (see box, pp.746–747), which can make the other 49 weeks of the year seem like an anticlimax. However, at any time the city has plenty to offer, especially in the realm of **theatre** and **music**. The best way to find out **what's on** is to pick up a copy of *The List*, a free monthly listings magazine covering both Edinburgh and Glasgow. The entry fee to clubs usually depends on when you're out. Friday and Saturday nights range from £10 to £15 for the main venues while weeknights average around a fiver.

CLUBS

The Bongo Club 66 Cowgate ☎0131 558 8844, ⓦthebongoclub.co.uk. Legendary Edinburgh club and arts venue; its line-up is eclectic but always worth checking out. Look out for the monthly drum'n'bass night Xplicit, or funk, jazz and Latin night Four Corners. Daily 11pm–3am, opens earlier on occasion.

Cabaret Voltaire 36–38 Blair St ☎0131 247 4704, ⓦthecabaretvoltaire.com. Atmospheric nightclub in the Old Town's underground vaults, hosting some of the city's best club nights, including disco and deep house favourite The Gettup. Daily 11pm–3am.

The Liquid Room 9c Victoria St ☎0131 225 2564, ⓦliquidroom.com. Recently refurbished, with a cutting-edge sound and light system. One of the best of the larger venues with nights such as Wednesday's student-oriented Tribe and irregular retro night Rewind, as well as regular live music. Daily 10.30pm–3am.

Lulu's 125b George St ☎0131 225 5005, ⓦlulu edinburgh.co.uk. Sultry, subterranean nightspot beneath OTT bar and restaurant *Tigerlily*. A place to see and be seen, with its well-groomed clientele trying not to spill their mojitos while striding to the latest floorfillers. Daily 9pm–3am.

GAY CLUBS AND BARS

CC Bloom's 23–24 Greenside Place ☎0131 556 9331. Edinburgh's most enduring gay club, with a big dancefloor, stonking rhythms and a young, friendly crowd.

Planet 6 Baxter's Place ☎0131 556 5551. Loud and outrageous bar beside the Playhouse Theatre; a popular meeting point. Daily 11am–3am.

LIVE MUSIC VENUES

Queen's Hall 85–89 Clerk St ☎0131 668 2019, ⓦthequeenshall.net. Converted Georgian church which now operates as a concert hall; it's used principally by the Scottish Chamber Orchestra and Scottish Ensemble, and is much favoured by jazz, blues and folk groups.

Royal Oak 1 Infirmary St ☎0131 557 2976, ⓦroyal -oak-folk.com. Traditional pub hosting regular informal folk sessions and the "Wee Folk Club" on Sun from 8.30pm.

Sandy Bell's 25 Forrest Rd ☎0131 225 2751, ⓦsandybellsedinburgh.co.uk. A friendly bar that's a good bet for folk music most nights of the week.

Usher Hall Cnr Lothian Rd & Grindlay St ☎0131 228 1155, ⓦusherhall.co.uk. Edinburgh's main civic concert hall is excellent for choral and symphony concerts, but less suitable for solo vocalists. The upper circle seats are cheapest and have the best acoustics.

THEATRE AND DANCE

Dance Base 14–16 Grassmarket ☎0131 225 5525, ⓦdancebase.co.uk. Scotland's sparkling new National Centre for Dance is used mostly for modern dance workshops and classes, but also hosts occasional performances.

Edinburgh Playhouse 18–22 Greenside Place ☎0844 871 3014, ⓦedinburgh-playhouse.co.uk. The largest theatre in Britain, formerly a cinema. Used largely for

---

SHOPPING IN EDINBURGH

Princes Street, one of Britain's most famous shopping streets, is all but dominated by standard chain outlets, though no serious shopper should miss out on a visit to Edinburgh's venerable department store, Jenners, opposite the Scott Monument. More fashionable upmarket shops are to be found on and around parallel **George Street**, including a street (Multrees Walk) of exclusive international fashion boutiques on the east side of St Andrew Square. There's nothing compelling about central Edinburgh's two big shopping malls, **Princes Mall** and the **St James Centre**, which are dominated by the big names.

For more original outlets, head for **Victoria Street** and the **Grassmarket** where you'll find an eclectic range of antique, crafts, food and book shops. Along and around the **Royal Mile**, meanwhile, several distinctly offbeat places sit among the tacky souvenir sellers. Edinburgh's only regular **markets** are its farmers' market, on Castle Terrace, immediately west of the Castle, which draws around 35 local produce stalls from south and east Scotland (Sat 9am–1pm), as well as the linked Grassmarket (Sat 10am–5pm) and Stockbridge (Sun 10am–5pm) markets (in the Grassmarket and Kerr St respectively) which are a haven for exciting hot street-food, cakes and local banter.

HOGMANAY

Edinburgh hosts one of the world's landmark **New Year's Eve street parties**, with around 100,000 people on the streets of the city seeing out the old year. For the street party, stages are set up in different parts of the city centre, with big-name rock groups and local ceilidh bands playing to the increasingly inebriated masses. The high point of the evening is, of course, midnight, when hundreds of tonnes of fireworks are let off into the night sky above the Castle, and Edinburgh joins the rest of the world singing **"Auld Lang Syne"**, an old Scottish tune with lyrics by Robert Burns, Scotland's national poet. For information go to ⓦedinburghshogmanay.org.

extended runs of popular musicals and occasional rock concerts and comedy shows.

Festival Theatre Nicolson St ☎0131 529 6000, ⓦfctt.org.uk. The largest stage in Britain, principally used for Scottish Opera and Scottish Ballet's appearances in the capital, but also for everything from the children's show *Singing Kettle* to Engelbert Humperdinck.

King's Theatre 2 Leven St ☎0131 529 6000, ⓦfctt .org.uk. Stately Edwardian civic theatre that majors in pantomime, touring West End plays and the occasional major drama or opera performance.

Royal Lyceum 30 Grindlay St ☎0131 248 4848, ⓦlyceum.org.uk. Fine Victorian civic theatre with a compact auditorium. The leading year-round venue for mainstream drama.

Traverse Theatre 10 Cambridge St ☎0131 228 1404, ⓦtraverse.co.uk. One of Britain's premier venues for new plays and avant-garde drama from around the world.

Going from strength to strength in its custom-built home beside the Usher Hall, with a great bar downstairs.

COMEDY

The Stand 5 York Place ☎0131 558 7272, ⓦthestand .co.uk. The city's top comedy spot, with a different act every night and some of the UK's top comics headlining at the weekends.

ART-HOUSE CINEMAS

Cameo 38 Home St, Tollcross ☎0131 228 2800, ⓦpicturehouses.co.uk. A treasure of an art-house cinema; screens the more challenging mainstream releases and cult late-nighters. Tarantino's been here and thinks it's great.

Filmhouse 88 Lothian Rd ☎0131 228 2688, ⓦfilmhousecinema.com. Three screens showing an eclectic programme of independent, art-house and classic films. The café is a hangout for the city's film buffs.

DIRECTORY

Hospital Royal Infirmary, Little France (☎0131 536 1000), has a 24hr casualty department. There's also a minor injuries clinic at the Western General, Crewe Rd South (daily 8am–9pm; ☎0131 537 1000), and a casualty department for children at Royal Hospital for Sick Children, 9 Sciennes

Rd (☎0131 536 0000).

Left luggage Counter by platform 1 at Waverley Station (from £6/ item; daily 7am–11pm; ☎0131 558 3829).

Police In an emergency call ☎999, otherwise dial ☎101.

East Lothian

East Lothian consists of the coastal strip and hinterland immediately east of Edinburgh, bounded by the Firth of Forth to the north and the Lammermuir Hills to the south. All of it is within easy day-trip range from the capital, though there are places you can stay overnight if you're keen to explore. Often mocked as the "home counties" of Edinburgh, there's no denying its well-ordered feel, with prosperous farms and large estate houses dominating the scenery. The main attractions are on or near the coast, with the trip east from Edinburgh taking you past wide sandy beaches by **Aberlady** and famous golf courses at **Gullane**. The town of **North Berwick** is the main focal point on the coast, with dramatic cliff-top ruins at **Tantallon** and the supersonic draw of **Concorde** at the Museum of Flight both within easy reach.

North Berwick and around

NORTH BERWICK has a great deal of charm and a somewhat faded, old-fashioned air, its guesthouses and hotels extending along the shore in all their Victorian and Edwardian

17

sobriety. The town's small harbour is set on a headland which cleaves two crescents of sand, though it is the two volcanic heaps, the offshore **Bass Rock** – resembling a giant molar – and 613ft-high **North Berwick Law**, which are the town's defining features.

Scottish Seabird Centre

Harbour Lodge, 7 Beach Rd • April–Aug daily 10am–6pm; Nov–Jan Mon–Fri 10am–4pm, Sat & Sun 10am–5pm; Feb, March, Sept & Oct Mon–Fri 10am–5pm, Sat & Sun 10am–5.30pm • £8.95 • ☎01620 890202, ⓦ seabird.org

Housed in an attractively designed new building by the harbour, the **Scottish Seabird Centre** offers access to gannets and puffins that thrive on the rocky outcrops in the sea before North Berwick. There are live links from the centre to cameras mounted on the islands showing close-up pictures of the nesting sites. At the risk of getting wet (and cold) you can also hop aboard one of the thrilling speedboat rides to the islands (weather permitting). Contact the centre to see what trips are available on any given day.

ARRIVAL AND DEPARTURE   NORTH BERWICK

By train North Berwick is served by a regular (usually hourly; 30min) train from Edinburgh Waverley, with discount deals for those heading for the Seabird Centre. From the station it's a 10min walk east to the town centre.

By bus First Group buses #X24 and #X25 depart from Edinburgh's Leith St, just outside the St James Centre (every 30min; 1hr 30min) and run along the coast via Aberlady, Gullane and Dirleton stopping near North Berwick's seafront.

ACCOMMODATION AND EATING

The Glebe House B&B Law Rd ☎01620 892 608, ⓦ glebehouse-nb.co.uk. A grand eighteenth-century manse in secluded grounds 100yd inland but still overlooking the sea. With decor befitting of its period, the rooms are spacious yet homely. Breakfast choices swing from healthy yoghurt and muesli to a hearty Scottish fry-up. **£120**

Lobstershack The Harbour ☎07910 620480, ⓦ lobstershack.co.uk. Get lobster, langoustine and mackerel straight from the boats at this harbourside hut with a handful of outdoor tables and chairs. The menu's more sophisticated than you'd think and it's licensed. A half

lobster and chips comes in at around £13. June–Sept daily noon–8pm; mid–April–May Sat & Sun only noon–8pm; closes in bad weather.

Seabird Centre Café The Harbour ☎01620 890202, ⓦ seabird.org. A great location with outdoor decking and panoramic views over the beach and Bass Rock. Some nice light options including smoked mackerel pâté with salad & oatcakes (£5.75) among a mainstream and kid-friendly menu. Nov–Jan Mon–Fri 10am–4pm, Sat & Sun 10am–5pm; Feb, March, Sept & Oct Mon–Fri 10am–5pm, Sat & Sun 10am–5.35pm; April–Aug daily 10am–6pm.

Tantallon Castle

Three miles east of North Berwick on the A198 • April–Sept daily 9.30am–5.30pm; Oct–March daily 9.30am–4.30pm • £5.50; HS • ☎01620 892 727 • From North Berwick's High St take the Dunbar bus (Eves Coaches #120; Mon–Sat 6 daily, Sun 2 daily; 6min), or walk along the cliffs in around 1hr

With a sheer drop down to the sea on three sides and a sequence of moats and ditches on the fourth, the melodramatic ruins of **Tantallon Castle**'s desolate invincibility is daunting, especially when the wind howls over the remaining battlements and the surf crashes on the rocks far below.

National Museum of Flight

Five miles south of North Berwick on the B1347 • April–Oct daily 10am–5pm; Nov–March Sat & Sun 10am–4pm • £10 • ☎0300 123 678, ⓦ nms.ac.uk/flight • First Bus runs the #121 service from North Berwick to Haddington via the museum (Mon–Sat 5 daily; 25min)

Standing on an old military airfield by East Fortune, the **National Museum of Flight** is home to *Alpha Alpha*, British Airways' first **Concorde**. The supersonic passenger jet, one of only twenty such planes built, has been reassembled to show how she looked when decommissioned in 2003. A visit onboard is restricted to a slightly stooped wander through the forward half of the aircraft, while a display follows the Concorde project as a whole, from the early days of Anglo–French bickering to the tragic Paris crash of

2000. In and around the older hangars on the site, you can see more than fifty vintage aircraft including a Vulcan bomber, a Comet airliner, a Spitfire and a Tigermoth.

17

Midlothian

Immediately south of Edinburgh lies the old county of **MIDLOTHIAN**, once called Edinburghshire. It's one of the hilliest parts of the Central Lowlands, with the Pentland chain running down its western side, and the Moorfoots defining its boundary with the Borders to the south.

Roslin

The tranquil village of **ROSLIN**, seven miles south of the centre of Edinburgh, has two claims to fame: it was near here, at the Roslin Institute, that the world's first cloned animal, Dolly the sheep, was created in 1997, and it's also home to the mysterious, richly decorated, late Gothic **Rosslyn Chapel**.

Rosslyn Chapel

Chapel Loan • April–Sept Mon–Sat 9.30am–6pm, Sun noon–4.45pm, Oct–March Mon–Sat 9.30am–4.30pm, Sun noon–4.15pm • £9 • ☏ 0131 440 2159, ⊕ rosslynchapel.org.uk • Roslin can be reached by bus #15 from Princes Street (every 30min; 50min)

Revered for its sublime stone carvings – some of the finest in the world – and subject of intrigue and mystery for its alleged Crusader connections, fifteenth-century **Rosslyn Chapel** is more like a cathedral than a chapel in its dimensions. Its exterior bristles with pinnacles, gargoyles, flying buttresses and canopies, while inside the stonework is, if anything, even more intricate. Among the carvings are representations of cacti and Indian corn, compounding the legend that the founder's grandfather, the daring sea adventurer Prince Henry of Orkney, did indeed set foot in the New World a century before Columbus. The greatest and most original carving of all is the extraordinary knotted **Apprentice Pillar** at the southeastern corner of the Lady Chapel. According to local legend, the pillar was made by an apprentice during the absence of the master mason, who killed him in a fit of jealousy on seeing the finished work.

West Lothian

To many, West Lothian is a poor relative to the rolling, rich farmland of East and Midlothian, with a landscape dominated by motorways, industrial estates and giant hillocks of ochre-coloured mine waste called "bings". However, in the royal palace at **Linlithgow**, the area boasts one of Scotland's more magnificent ruins. Nearby, the village of **South Queensferry** lies under the considerable shadow of the **Forth rail and road bridges**, though it's an interesting enough place in its own right, with a historic high street and the stately home of **Hopetoun** nearby.

Linlithgow

Fifteen miles west of Edinburgh is the ancient royal burgh of **LINLITHGOW**. The town itself has largely kept its medieval layout, but development since the 1960s has, sadly, stripped it of some fine buildings, notably around the **Town Hall** and **Cross** – the former marketplace – on the long High Street.

Linlithgow Palace

Kirkgate, just off High St • Daily: April–Sept 9.30am–5.30pm; Oct–March 9.30am–4.30pm • £5.50; HS • ☏ 01506 842 896

Hidden from the main road, **Linlithgow Palace** is a splendid fifteenth-century ruin

17

> ## ROSSLYN'S SECRETS
>
> The imagery of certain carvings found in Rosslyn Chapel, together with the history of the family, the St Clairs, which owns the chapel, leave little doubt about its links to the **Knights Templar** and **Freemasonry**. The Masonic connection was said to have saved the chapel from the armies of Oliver Cromwell, himself a Freemason, which destroyed the surrounding area but spared Rosslyn. More intriguing still are claims that, because of such connections, Rosslyn Chapel has been the repository for items such as the lost Scrolls of Solomon's Temple in Jerusalem, the true Stone of Scone and, most famously, the Holy Grail. The chapel is regularly drawn into conspiracy theories on these themes, most famously in recent years through Dan Brown's bestseller *The Da Vinci Code*; the chapel's appearance in the film of the same name precipitated a huge surge in visitor numbers, which detracts a little from the mysterious air of the place.

romantically set on the edge of Linlithgow Loch. The palace's royal connections are strong: from the top of the northwest tower, Queen Margaret looked out in vain for the return of James IV from the field of Flodden in 1513 (the views from her bower, six storeys up from the ground, are exceptional). The ornate octagonal **fountain** in the inner courtyard, with its intricate figures and medallion heads, flowed with wine for the wedding of James V and Mary of Guise; their daughter Mary was born here on 8 December 1542 and just six days later began her reign as the famous Queen of Scots.

ARRIVAL AND INFORMATION   LINLITHGOW

By train Linlithgow is on the main train routes from Edinburgh to both Glasgow Queen Street and Stirling; the station lies at the southern end of town.

Destinations Edinburgh Waverley & Haymarket (4 hourly; 20min); Glasgow (2 hourly; 30min); Stirling (2 hourly; 30min).

ACCOMMODATION AND EATING

Belsyde House Signposted off the A702, just southwest of town ☎ 01506 842 098, ⓦ belsydehouse .co.uk. An upmarket, spacious and well-appointed late eighteenth-century house on a sheep and cattle farm beside the Union Canal on the outskirts of Linlithgow. **£66**

Champany Inn Champany ☎ 01506 834 532, ⓦ champany.com. The old-school restaurant, which until recently held a Michelin star, serves seriously expensive steaks and seafood as well as top-notch South African

wines, though there's also a less formal chop- and ale-house as well as smart rooms. Two-course lunches start at £25.50. Mon–Fri 12.30–2pm & 7–10pm, Sat 7–10pm.

Taste 47 High St ☎ 01506 844445, ⓦ taste-deli-cafe .co.uk. Decent deli with café attached: pick up a picnic to eat in the grounds of the palace or eat in on soup and a half sandwich (£6.50). Mon–Wed 8.30am–4.30pm, Thurs–Fri 8.30am–5.30pm, Sat 9am–5.30pm, Sun 10am–4.30pm.

EICA:Ratho

Five miles west of Edinburgh Airport, signposted just beyond the Newbridge junction of the M8 and M9 • Mon–Fri 9am–10pm, Sat & Sun 9am–6pm • Free, times and charges for activities vary • ☎ 0131 333 6333, ⓦ eica-ratho.co.uk • Take the tram to Hermiston Gate and change for Lothian bus #20 to Ratho (every 30min; 13min), then follow canal path west for 2 minutes from *The Bridge Inn*

Edinburgh International Climbing Arena, or **EICA:Ratho**, is the world's largest indoor climbing facility, incorporating a series of remarkable artificial climbing walls. The spectacular vision of its architect founders was to enclose a disused quarry, creating a giant arena that's now used for international climbing competitions as well as classes (from £48) for climbers of all levels, including beginners and kids. Above the arena, just under the glass roof, is "Aerial Assault" (£11.50), a stomach-churning, suspended obstacle course 100ft off the ground – thankfully, you are safely attached via a sliding harness.

South Queensferry

Eight miles northwest of Edinburgh city centre is the small town of **SOUTH QUEENSFERRY**, located at the southern end of the two mighty Forth bridges. It's an attractive old settlement, with a narrow, cobbled High Street lined with tightly packed buildings, most of which date from the seventeenth and eighteenth centuries.

Queensferry Museum

53 High St • Mon & Thurs–Sat 10am–1pm & 2.15–5pm, Sun noon–5pm • Free • ☏ 0131 331 5545

The tiny **Queensferry Museum** exhibits photos and relics of the town's history, showing its importance as a ferry port. Commercial services embarked here from the eleventh century until 3 September 1964, after which the magnificent – yet soon to be replaced – road bridge was opened. Details about the Forth Road Bridge's construction, and that of the unique Victorian rail bridge a little further east, are also displayed here.

ARRIVAL AND DEPARTURE SOUTH QUEENSFERRY

By train From Edinburgh Waverley take the train to Dalmeny (every 30min; 20min). From there it's a mile to town: head west on Station Rd then turn right on The Loan.

By bus First bus #X38 connects with Edinburgh (3 hourly; 1hr) and Stirling (3 hourly; 1hr 5min).

ACCOMMODATION AND EATING

★ **The Boathouse** 19b High St ☏ 0131 331 5429, ⓦ theboathouse-sq.co.uk. A great location with views out above the water to the two Forth bridges. Excellent seafood options, such as Scottish halibut with an orange, ginger and pink peppercorn reduction (£20) in the main restaurant; the easy-going bistro and small wine bar offer simpler food. Mon–Sat noon–9.30pm, Sun 12.30–9pm.

Orocco Pier 17 High St ☏ 0870 118 1664, ⓦ oroccopier .co.uk. A stylish contemporary drinking spot on South Queensferry's medieval High Street, boasting unbeatable views over the water to the Forth bridges and serving pleasant bistro food such as mussels or smoked haddock with leek mash (£9.95). They also have smart guest rooms and serviced apartments. Daily 7am–10pm. **£120**

Hopetoun House

On the south shore of the Forth, west of South Queensferry • Mid-April–Sept daily 10.30am–5pm • £9.20 house and grounds, £4.25 grounds only • ☏ 0131 331 2451, ⓦ hopetounhouse.com • There's no scheduled public transport to Hopetoun House but it's possible to pre-book a Taxibus for just £2.50 by visiting ⓦ travelinescotland.com

Hopetoun House ranks as one of the most impressive stately homes in Scotland. The original house was built at the turn of the eighteenth century for the first Earl of Hopetoun by Sir William Bruce, the architect of Holyroodhouse. A couple of decades later, William Adam carried out an enormous extension, engulfing the structure with a curvaceous main façade and two projecting wings – superb examples of Roman Baroque pomp and swagger. The **grounds** include a long, regal driveway, lovely walks along woodland trails and the banks of the Forth, and plenty of picnic spots.

Inchcolm

From South Queensferry's Hawes Pier, just west of the rail bridge, ferry services head out to the island of **Inchcolm**, about five miles northeast. The island is home to the best-preserved medieval **abbey** in Scotland, founded in 1235 after King Alexander I was stormbound here. Although the structure as a whole is half-ruined today, the tower, octagonal chapter house and echoing cloisters are intact and well worth exploring. The ninety minutes you're given ashore by the boat timetables also allows time for a picnic on the abbey's lawns or the chance to explore Inchcolm's old military fortifications.

If you're lucky, you might spot **dolphins** or porpoises from the boat crossing to the island.

ARRIVAL AND DEPARTURE INCHCOLM

By ferry Ferries to Inchcolm (April–Oct) are run by *Maid of the Forth* (☏ 0131 331 5000, ⓦ maidoftheforth.co.uk; £17.50 including landing fee) and *Forth Belle* (☏ 0870 118 1866, ⓦ forthtours.com; £13 plus £5.50 landing fee).

Southern
Scotland

GALLOWAY FOREST PARK

Southern Scotland

Dominated by the Southern Uplands, a chain of bulging round-topped hills, southern Scotland divides neatly into three regions: the Borders, Dumfries and Galloway, and Ayrshire. Although none of them has the highest of tourist profiles, those visitors who whizz past on their way north to Edinburgh, Glasgow or the Highlands are missing out on a huge swathe of Scotland that is in many ways the very heart of the country. Over the centuries, its inhabitants, particularly in the Borders, bore the brunt of long, brutal wars with the English; its farms have fed Scotland's cities since industrialization; and two of the country's greatest literary icons, Sir Walter Scott and Robbie Burns, lived and died here.

North of the inhospitable Cheviot Hills, which separate Scotland from England, the **Borders** region is dominated by the meanderings of the **River Tweed**. The towns here have provided inspiration for countless folkloric ballads telling of bloody battles with the English and clashes with the notorious Border Reivers, who conducted raids on border settlements. The delightful small town of **Melrose** is the most obvious base, and has the most impressive of the four **Border abbeys** founded by the medieval Canmore kings, all of which are now reduced to romantic ruins.

Dumfries and Galloway, in the southwestern corner of Scotland, gets even more overlooked than the Borders. If you do make the effort to get off the main north–south highway to Glasgow, you'll find more ruined abbeys, medieval castles, forested hills and dramatic tidal flats and sea cliffs ideal for birdwatching. The key resort is the modest, charming town of **Kirkcudbright**, halfway along the Solway coast, indented by sandy coves.

Ayrshire is rich farming country, with fewer sights than its neighbours; almost everything of interest is confined to the coast. The **golf courses** along its gentle coastline are among the finest links courses in the country, while fans of **Robert Burns** could happily spend several days exploring the author's old haunts, especially at **Ayr**, the county town, and the nearby village of **Alloway**, the poet's birthplace.

GETTING AROUND   SOUTHERN SCOTLAND

By train The Borders have limited train services, with a more comprehensive range in Dumfries and Galloway and a reasonable network in Ayrshire.

By bus Buses will get you practically everywhere mentioned in this chapter, although there is no link between the Borders and the rest of the region.

The Borders

The **Borders** region is sandwiched between the Cheviot Hills on the English border and the Pentland and Moorfoot ranges to the south of Edinburgh. The finest section of the lush **Tweed Valley** lies between **Melrose** and **Peebles**, where you'll find a string of

AILSA CRAIG

Highlights

❶ Melrose Abbey Border abbey with superbly preserved sculptural detail. **See p.765**

❷ Traquair House The oldest continuously inhabited house in Scotland, virtually unchanged since the fifteenth century. **See p.769**

❸ Caerlaverock One of Scotland's most photogenic moated castles, beside a superb site for waterfowl and waders. **See p.773**

❹ Kirkcudbright One-time artists' colony, and the best-looking town on the "Scottish Riviera". **See p.775**

❺ Galloway Forest Park Go mountain biking along remote forest tracks, or hiking on the Southern Upland Way. **See p.776**

❻ Alloway The village where poet Robert Burns was born, and the best of many Burns pilgrimage spots in the region. **See p.779**

❼ Culzean Castle Stately home with a fabulous cliff-edge setting, surrounded by acres of gardens and woods reaching down to the shore. **See p.780**

❽ Dumfries House An eighteenth-century architectural masterpiece, designed by the Adam brothers and decked out by Thomas Chippendale. **See p.780**

❾ Ailsa Craig Take a boat out to this volcanic lump and watch baby gannets learn the art of flying and diving for fish. **See p.781**

HIGHLIGHTS ARE MARKED ON THE MAP ON P.764

attractions, from Sir Walter Scott's eccentric mansion at **Abbotsford** to the ancient seat of **Traquair House**, along with the region's famous **abbeys**, founded in the reign of King David I (1124–53).

Melrose and around

Minuscule **MELROSE**, tucked in between the Tweed and the gorse-backed Eildon Hills, is the most beguiling of towns, its narrow streets trimmed by a harmonious ensemble of styles, from pretty little cottages and tweedy shops to high-standing Georgian and Victorian facades. Its chief draw is its ruined **abbey**, but it's also well positioned for exploring the Tweed Valley, with the Scott-related attractions of **Abbotsford** and **Dryburgh** nearby.

18

Melrose Abbey

Abbey St • Daily: April–Sept 9.30am–5.30pm; Oct–March 9.30am–4.30pm • £5.50; HS • ☎ 01896 822562

The pink- and red-tinted stone ruins of **Melrose Abbey** soar above their riverside surroundings. Founded in 1136, Melrose was the first Cistercian settlement in Scotland and grew rich selling wool and hides to Flanders. The English repeatedly razed the abbey, most viciously in 1385 and 1545, and most of the remains date from the intervening period. The site is dominated by the **Abbey Church**, which has lost its west front, and whose nave is reduced to the elegant window arches and chapels of the south aisle. Amazingly, however, the stone **pulpitum** (screen), separating the choir monks from their lay brothers, is preserved. Beyond, the **presbytery** has its magnificent perpendicular window, lierne vaulting and ceiling bosses intact, with the capitals of the surrounding columns sporting the most intricate of curly kale carving. In the **south transept**, another fine fifteenth-century window sprouts yet more delicate, foliate tracery and the adjacent cornice is enlivened by weathered angels playing musical instruments. Look out, too, for the Coronation of the Virgin on the east end gable, and the numerous mischievous **gargoyles**, such as the pig playing the bagpipes on the roof on the south side of the nave. The sculptural detailing at Melrose is easy to miss if you don't know where to look, so using the free audioguide, or buying yourself a guidebook, is a good idea.

Abbotsford

2 miles west of Melrose • **Visitor centre** Daily: April–Sept 10am–5pm; Oct–March 10am–4pm • Free • **House and gardens** Daily: April–Sept 10am–5pm; Oct & Nov 10am–4pm • £8.75 • ☎ 01896 752043, ⓦ scottsabbotsford.co.uk • The fast, frequent Melrose–Galashiels bus provides easy access to Abbotsford: ask for the Tweedbank island on the A6091, from where the house is a 10min walk

Abbotsford was designed to satisfy the Romantic inclinations of **Sir Walter Scott**, who lived here from 1812 until his death. The building took twelve years to evolve, with the fanciful turrets and castellations of the Scots Baronial exterior incorporating copies of medieval originals. Despite all the exterior pomp, the interior is surprisingly small and poky, with just six rooms open for viewing on the upper floor. Visitors start in the wood-panelled study, with its small writing desk made of salvage from the Spanish Armada, at which Scott banged out the Waverley novels at a furious rate. The wood-panelled library boasts his extraordinary assortment of memorabilia, including Napoleon's pen case and blotting book, Rob Roy's purse and *skene dhu* (knife), and the inlaid pearl crucifix that accompanied Mary, Queen of Scots, to the scaffold. Henry Raeburn's famous portrait of Scott hangs in the drawing room.

Dryburgh Abbey

Around 5 miles southeast of Melrose • Daily: April–Sept 9.30am–5.30pm; Oct–March 9.30am–4.30pm • £5.50; HS • ☎ 01835 822381, ⓦ historic-scotland.gov.uk • There is no public transport to the abbey, though it's just a mile's walk north of St Boswells on the A68, and a pleasant 4 miles from Melrose. Drivers and cyclists should approach via Scott's View

Hidden away in a U-bend in the Tweed, the remains of **Dryburgh Abbey** occupy an idyllic position against a hilly backdrop. Founded in the twelfth century by the

18

> ## SIR WALTER SCOTT
>
> As a child, **Walter Scott** (1771–1832), disabled by polio, was sent to recuperate at his grandfather's farm in Smailholm, where his imagination was fuelled by his relative's tales of the old, violent troubles in the Borders. Throughout the 1790s he transcribed hundreds of old Border ballads, publishing a three-volume collection entitled *Minstrelsy of the Scottish Borders* in 1802. An instant success, *Minstrelsy* was followed by Scott's own *Lay of the Last Minstrel*, a narrative poem whose strong story and rose-tinted regionalism proved very popular. More **poetry** was to come, most successfully *Marmion* (1808) and *The Lady of the Lake* (1810).
>
> However, despite having two paid jobs, his finances remained shaky. He had become a partner in a printing firm, which put him into debt, not helped by the enormous sums he spent on his mansion, Abbotsford. From 1813, writing to pay the bills, Scott thumped out a flood of historical novels, producing his best work within the space of ten years: *Waverley* (1814), *The Antiquary* (1816), *Rob Roy* and *The Heart of Midlothian* (both 1818), as well as two notable novels set in England, *Ivanhoe* (1819) and *Kenilworth* (1821).
>
> In 1825 Scott's money problems reached crisis proportions after an economic crash bankrupted his printing business. Attempting to pay his creditors in full, he found the quality of his writing deteriorating with its increased speed. His last years were plagued by illness; in 1832 he died at Abbotsford and was buried within the ruins of Dryburgh Abbey.

Premonstratensians, virtually nothing survives of the nave of the **Abbey Church**, though the transepts have fared better, their chapels now serving as private burial grounds for, among others, Sir Walter Scott and Field Marshal Haig, the infamous World War I commander. The night stairs, down which the monks stumbled in the early hours of the morning, survive in the south transept, and lead even today to the monks' dormitory. Leaving the church via the east processional door in the south aisle, with its dog-tooth decoration, you enter the cloisters, the highlight of which is the barrel-vaulted **Chapter House**, complete with low stone benches and blind interlaced arcading.

ARRIVAL AND INFORMATION
MELROSE

By bus Buses stop on Buccleuch Street; from there it's a brief walk north to the abbey ruins.
Destinations Edinburgh (1 daily; 1hr 20min); Galashiels (Mon–Sat every 15–30min, Sun at least hourly; 15min); Jedburgh (Mon–Sat every 1–2hr, Sun 3 daily; 30min);

Kelso (Mon–Sat 8–10 daily, Sun 4 daily; 35min); Selkirk (Mon–Sat hourly, Sun 3 daily; 20–30min).
Tourist information Abbey St, just south of the abbey (April–Oct Mon–Sat 10am–5pm, Sun 1–5pm; ☏01896 822283).

ACCOMMODATION

Dunfermline House 3 Buccleuch St ☏01896 822411, ⓦdunfermlinehouse.co.uk. The decor at this pretty townhouse feels a little dated, but the rooms are cosy and clean nonetheless, with views of either the abbey or the Eildon Hills. **£60**
Gibson Caravan Park High St ☏01896 822969, ⓦcaravanclub.co.uk. A level, peaceful and immaculately run Caravan Club site (which welcomes nonmembers and tent campers) conveniently situated right in the centre opposite the Greenyards rugby grounds. Pitches **£24.30**
★**Old Bank House** 27 Buccleuch St ☏01896 823712,

ⓦoldbankhousemelrose.co.uk. Solid Victorian townhouse with charming hosts and three attractive, pristinely maintained en-suite rooms (two twins and a double). Breakfast is served in the old bank manager's office. **£65**
The Townhouse Market Square ☏01896 822645, ⓦthetownhousemelrose.co.uk. Small, smart hotel on the main square, with eleven stylishly renovated en-suite doubles, with contemporary furnishings and TVs. There's also an excellent brasserie, plus a more formal restaurant (mains around £15). **£130**

EATING AND ENTERTAINMENT

Hoebridge Inn Hoebridge Rd East, Gattonside; 500yd past Melrose Abbey and across the old suspension bridge ☏01896 823082, ⓦthehoebridgeinn.com. French and Scottish flavours take up a good chunk of the menu at this family-run restaurant, housed in a converted bobbin mill

from the nineteenth century. Dishes include a toasted goats' cheese salad (£12) and a roasted rump of Scottish lamb (£17.95). Tues–Sat noon–2pm & 6–9pm, Sun 12.30–2.30pm.
Marmion's Brasserie Buccleuch St ☏01896 822245,

@ marmionsbrasserie.co.uk. Pleasant brasserie that serves up everything from breakfast and simple lunches to three-course dinners. The menu is strong on classics such as venison steak and chicken supreme (mains £11–17). Mon–Sat 9am–9pm.

The Wynd Buccleuch Street @ 01896 820028, @ sites .google.com/site/thewyndtheatre. Melrose's very own pint-sized theatre, tucked away down an alleyway north of the main square, hosts films, gigs and dramatic performances, plus special shows suitable for young kids.

Kelso and around

18

KELSO, ten miles or so downstream from Melrose, grew up in the shadow of its now-ruined Benedictine **abbey**, once the richest and most powerful of the Border abbeys. Sadly, very little survives today, although at first sight, it looks pretty impressive, with the heavy Norman west end of the abbey church almost entirely intact at the end of Abbey Row. Beyond, little remains, though it is possible to make out the two transepts and towers that gave the abbey the shape of a double cross, unique in Scotland.

Kelso town is centred on **The Square**, a large cobbled expanse presided over by the honey-hued Ionic columns, pediment and oversized clock bell tower of the elegant Town Hall. Leaving the Square along Roxburgh Street, take the alley down to the **Cobby Riverside Walk**, where a brief stroll leads to Floors Castle. En route, but hidden from view by the Islet in the middle of the river, is the spot where the Teviot meets the Tweed. This bit of river, known as The Junction, has long been famous for its salmon fishing, with permits costing thousands – booked years in advance.

Floors Castle

A mile northwest of Kelso; from the town centre, follow Roxburgh St to its northern end and bear left at the fork • Daily: Easter–Sept 10.30am–5pm; Oct 10.30am–3.30pm • £8.50; grounds & garden only £4.50 • @ 01573 223333, @ roxburghe.net

Stand on Kelso's handsome bridge over the Tweed and you can easily make out the pepper-pot turrets and castellations of Floors Castle, a vast, pompous mansion to the northwest. The bulk of the building was designed by William Adam in the 1720s, and, picking through the Victorian modifications, the interior still demonstrates his uncluttered style. However, you won't see that much of it, as Floors is still privately owned, with just ten rooms and a basement open to the public. Highlights include paintings by Matisse, Augustus John and Odilon Redon, and some fine Brussels and Gobelin tapestries.

Mellerstain House

6 miles northwest of Kelso off the A6089 • May–Sept Fri Mon noon–5pm • £8.50; gardens only £5 • @ 01573 410225, @ mellerstain.com • Bus #66 from Kelso (Mon–Fri at least 1 daily) stops on the B6397, a mile southwest of the property

Mellerstain House represents the very best of the Adam family's work – William designed the wings in 1725, and his son Robert the castellated centre fifty years later. Robert's love of columns, roundels and friezes culminates in a stunning sequence of plaster-moulded, pastel-shaded ceilings: the **library** is the high-point of the tour for admirers of his work, with four unusual, long panels in plaster relief of classical scenes that relegate the books to second place. The art collection, which includes works by Constable, Gainsborough, Ramsay and Veronese, is also noteworthy. After a visit you can wander the formal Edwardian gardens, which slope down to the lake.

ARRIVAL AND INFORMATION

KELSO

By bus Buses arrive and depart from Woodmarket, a brief walk from The Square.
Destinations Edinburgh (4–6 daily; 2hr); Melrose (Mon–Sat 7 daily, Sun 5 daily; 30min).

Tourist information Town House, The Square (Jan–March Mon, Fri & Sat 10am–2pm; April–Nov Mon–Sat 10am–5pm, Sun 10am–2pm; @ 01573 228055).

ACCOMMODATION AND EATING

Cobbles Inn 7 Bowmont St @ 01573 223548, @ thecobbleskelso.co.uk. Restaurant and bar housed in a

former pub just north of The Square – pub grub includes burgers and fish and chips for around £10, while the restaurant offers more elaborate two- and three-course menus featuring pheasant and beef for around £20. Mon–Thurs 11.30am–11pm, Fri & Sat 11am till late, Sun noon–11pm.

★ **The Old Priory** Woodmarket ☏ 01573 223030,

ⓦ theoldpriorykelso.com. A tasteful Georgian townhouse, just off The Square, with a very pretty garden. Rooms are spacious and light, with lovely wooden furniture, and there's a shared sitting room that guests are free to relax in. **£85**

Selkirk and around

The royal burgh of **SELKIRK** lies just five miles southwest of Melrose. The old town sits high up above the river of Ettrick Water; down by the riverside, the imposing grey-stone woollen mills are mostly boarded up now, an eerie reminder of a once prosperous era. Situated on the edge of some lovely countryside, the town serves as the gateway to the picturesque, sparsely populated valleys to the west.

At the centre of Selkirk you'll find the tiny **Market Square**, overlooked by a statue of Sir Walter Scott; the former Town House, now dubbed **Sir Walter Scott's Courtroom** (April–Sept Mon–Fri 10am–4pm, Sat 11am–3pm; Oct Mon–Sat noon–3pm; free), is where he served as sheriff for 33 years. Just off Market Square to the south is **Halliwell's House Museum** (April–Oct Mon–Sat 11am–4pm, Sun noon–3pm; free), an old-style hardware shop with an informative exhibit on the industrialization of the Tweed Valley.

Bowhill House

3 miles west of Selkirk off the A708 · **House** Throughout July (daily) and on selected bank holidays (see website), guided tours run every 30min from 12.30–3pm · £10, including access to grounds **Country Estate** Easter holidays 10am–5pm; April–June & Sept Sat & Sun 10am–5pm, Mon & Wed–Fri 10am–4pm; July & Aug daily 10am–5pm · £4 · ☏ 01750 22204, ⓦ bowhill.org · **Walk** (1hr) from Selkirk along the north bank of Ettrick Water and cross over General's Bridge and into the estate, or take a taxi from Selkirk (£8)

A pleasant three-mile walk from Selkirk, **Bowhill House** is the property of the seriously wealthy Duke of Buccleuch. Beyond the grandiose mid-nineteenth-century mansion's facade of dark whinstone is an outstanding collection of French antiques and European **paintings**: in the dining room, for example, there are portraits by Reynolds and Gainsborough, and a Canaletto cityscape, while the drawing room features Boulle furniture, Meissen tableware, paintings by Ruysdael, Leandro Bassano and Claude Lorraine, as well as two more family portraits by Reynolds. Look out also for the Scott Room, which features a splendid portrait of Sir Walter by Henry Raeburn, and the Duke of Monmouth's execution shirt.

The wooded hills of Bowhill's **Country Estate** are crisscrossed by scenic footpaths and cycle trails. The woods also shelter the 72-seat **Bowhill Theatre**, in the house's former game larder, which hosts the occasional production.

ARRIVAL AND INFORMATION

SELKIRK

By bus Regular buses arrive in the Market Square from Edinburgh (1–2 hourly; 1hr 45min) and Melrose (Mon–Sat hourly, Sun 3 daily; 20min).

Tourist information Halliwell's House, off Market Square (April–Oct Mon–Sat 11am–4pm, Sun noon–3pm; ☏ 01750 20054).

ACCOMMODATION

Glen Hotel Yarrow Terrace ☏ 01750 20259, ⓦ glenhotel.co.uk. An imposing hunting, shooting and fishing Victorian pile near the bridge, with nine clean rooms – including two family rooms and a double with a four-poster bed – and friendly staff. **£90**

Heatherlie House Hotel Heatherlie Park ☏ 01750 721200, ⓦ heatherliehotel.co.uk. A large Victorian mansion set in its own wooded grounds, with six en-suite rooms, plus a separate two-bedroom cottage that's available to rent privately. Double **£80**, cottage **£125**

Peebles and around

Fast, wide, tree-lined and fringed with grassy banks, the Tweed looks at its best at **PEEBLES**, a handsome royal burgh that sits on the north bank, fifteen miles northwest of Selkirk. The town itself has a genteel, relaxed air, its wide, handsome High Street bordered by houses in a medley of architectural styles, mostly dating from Victorian times, and ending in the soaring crown spire of the **Old Parish Church** (daily 10am–4pm; free) at the western end.

Tweedale Museum & Gallery

High St • Mon–Fri 10.30am–12.30pm & 1–4pm, Sat 9.30am–12.30pm • Free • ☎ 01721 724820

Halfway down the High Street is the **Tweedale Museum & Gallery**, stuffed with casts of the world's most famous sculptures. Although most were lost long ago, today's "Secret Room" has two handsome friezes: one a copy of the Elgin marbles taken from the Parthenon; the other of the **Triumph of Alexander**, originally cast in 1812 to honour Napoleon.

Traquair House

6 miles southeast of Peebles, a mile or so south of the A72 • Daily: April–Sept 11am–5pm; Oct 11am–4pm, Nov Sat & Sun 11am–3pm • £8.50, grounds only £4 • ☎ 01896 830323, ☑ traquair.co.uk

The Maxwell Stuarts have lived in **Traquair House** since 1491, making it the oldest continuously inhabited house in Scotland. The whitewashed facade is strikingly handsome, with narrow windows and trim turrets surrounding the tiniest of front doors – in other words it's a welcome change from other grandiose stately homes. Inside, you can see original vaulted cellars, where locals once hid their cattle from raiders; the twisting main staircase as well as the earlier medieval version, later a secret escape route for persecuted Catholics; a carefully camouflaged priest's hole; and even a **priest's room** where a string of resident chaplains lived in hiding. In the **museum room** there is a wealth of treasures, including a fine example of a Jacobite Amen glass, a rosary and crucifix owned by Mary, Queen of Scots, and the cloak worn by the Earl of Nithsdale during his dramatic escape from the Tower of London.

Spare time for the surrounding **gardens**, where you'll find a **hedge maze**, several craft workshops and the **Traquair House Brewery**, which claims to be the only British brewery that still ferments totally in oak. There's a café serving snacks in an estate cottage on the redundant avenue that leads to the locked **Bear Gates**; Bonnie Prince Charlie left the house through these gates, and the then-owner promised to keep them locked till a Stuart should ascend the throne.

ARRIVAL AND INFORMATION

PEEBLES

By bus Buses, including services from Edinburgh (1–2 hourly, 1hr) stop outside Peebles' post office on the High St.
Tourist information 23 High St (Jan–March Mon–Sat 9am–5pm; April–June Mon–Sat 9am–5pm, Sun 11am–4pm, July & Aug Mon–Sat 9am–5.30pm, Sun 11am–4pm; Sept–Dec Mon–Sat 9am–5pm; ☎01721 723159).

ACCOMMODATION AND EATING

Osso Innerleithen Rd ☎01721 724477, ☑osso restaurant.com. Sandwiches, tapas, meze and comfort food for around £10 at lunchtime, and a more imaginative evening menu featuring dishes like lobster and shrimp macaroni. Mon & Tues 10am–4.30pm, Wed–Sat 10am–4.30pm & 6–9pm, Sun 10am–4.30pm.

Rosetta Holiday Park Rosetta Rd, on the north-western edge of town ☎01721 720770, ☑rosetta holidaypark.com. In a quiet spot near Peebles Golf Club, with mature woodland all around, this holiday park is a good choice for campers. There's a bar/restaurant on-site, and playground to keep kids busy. Pitches **£18**

MOUNTAIN BIKING IN GLENTRESS

One of seven forest biking centres in southern Scotland – known collectively as the 7 Stanes (☑/stanesmountainbiking.com) – **Glentress Forest**, two miles east of Peebles on the A72, has some of the best mountain biking in Scotland. There are seven superb, carefully crafted purpose-built trails, colour-coded according to difficulty, and there's a helpful bike hire centre, Alpine Bikes (☎01721 724522, ☑alpinebikes.co.uk; bikes from £22/day).

18

★**The Sunflower** 4 Bridgegate ☎01721 722420, ⓦsunflowerrestaurant.co.uk. A tiny, colourful restaurant, just off Northgate, which does everything from adventurous bruschette and sandwiches to fishcakes and feta cheese tarts (mains £10.50). Mon–Wed 10am–3pm, Thurs–Sat 10am–3pm & 6–9pm.

Traquair House 6 miles east of Peebles, just south of the A72 ☎01896 830323, ⓦtraquair.co.uk. It's possible to spend a night or two at this landmark building, in one of three spacious B&B rooms decked out with antiques and canopied beds. Breakfast is served in a suitably grand manner. **£190**

Winkston Farmhouse Edinburgh Rd ☎01721 721264, ⓦwinkstonholidays.co.uk. This grand Georgian country house is a mile and a half north of Peebles – the rooms are spacious and smart enough, with pine furniture and free wi-fi. **£70**

Jedburgh

JEDBURGH nestles in the lush valley of the Jed Water, ten miles south of Melrose. During the interminable Anglo-Scottish Wars, this was the quintessential frontier town, a heavily garrisoned royal burgh incorporating a mighty castle and abbey. Though the castle was destroyed by the Scots in 1409 to keep it out of the hands of the English, the abbey survived, albeit in ruins. Today, Jedburgh is the first place of any size that you come to on the A68, having crossed over Carter Bar from England, and as such gets quite a bit of passing tourist trade.

Jedburgh Abbey

Daily: April–Sept 9.30am–5.30pm; Oct–March 9.30am–4.30pm • £5.50; HS • ☎01835 863925, ⓦhistoric-scotland.gov.uk

Founded in the twelfth century as an Augustinian priory, **Jedburgh Abbey** is the best preserved of all the Border abbeys, its vast church towering over a sloping site right in the centre of town beside the Jed Water. Entry is through the **visitor centre** at the bottom of the hill, where you can view Jedburgh's most treasured archeological find, the **Jedburgh Comb**, carved around 1100 from walrus ivory and decorated with a griffin and a dragon. Enter the **Abbey Church** itself via the west door to fully appreciate the three-storey nave's perfectly proportioned parade of columns and arches.

Jedburgh Castle Jail

Castlegate • Easter–Oct Mon–Sat 10am–4.30pm, Sun 1–4pm • Free • ☎01835 863254, ⓦmuseumsgalleriesscotland.org.uk

At the top of Castlegate stands **Jedburgh Castle Jail**, an impressive castellated nineteenth-century pile built on the site of the old royal castle. As well as detailed information about Jedburgh's history, there's a fascinating insight into conditions in jail, deportation, crime and punishment. The cells themselves are, for the period, remarkably comfortable, reflecting the influence of reformer John Howard.

Mary, Queen of Scots' House

Queen St • March–Nov Mon–Sat 10am–4.30pm, Sun 11am–4pm • Free • ☎01835 863331

At the Market Place, signs will guide you to **Mary, Queen of Scots' House**. Despite the name, it seems unlikely that Mary ever actually stayed in this particular sixteenth-century home, though she did visit the town in 1566. The highlights are a copy of Mary's death mask and one of the few surviving portraits of the Earl of Bothwell.

ARRIVAL AND INFORMATION

JEDBURGH

By bus Buses pick up and drop off at Canongate just east of the Market Place.

Destinations Edinburgh (Mon–Sat every 1–2hr, Sun 5 daily; 1hr 40min); Kelso (Mon–Sat 8–12 daily, Sun 4 daily; 25min); Melrose (Mon–Sat 8–10 daily, Sun 2 daily; 30min).

Tourist information Murray's Green (April–June, Sept & Oct Mon–Sat 9.15am–5pm, Sun 10am–4pm; July & Aug 9am–5.30pm, Sun 10am–5pm; Nov–March Mon–Sat 10am–4pm; ☎01835 863170, ⓦjedburgh.org.uk).

ACCOMMODATION AND EATING

There's a shortage of good eating places in Jedburgh, but do make sure to try the local speciality, **Jethart Snails**, sticky boiled sweets invented by a French POW in the 1700s and on sale everywhere.

Clock Tower Bistro Abbey Place ☎01835 869788. Smart without being stuffy, this relaxed bistro turns out sandwiches and light meals at lunchtime (from £5.25), and more sophisticated evening meals supported by inventive sides – think haggis bon bons and cumin-scented green beans. Mains £10–15. Tues–Sat 10am–4pm & 6–9pm.

Jedwater Caravan Park 5 miles south of town on the A68 ☎01835 840219, ⓦjedwater.co.uk. The cheaper and more secluded of two campsites near Jedburgh, with a pleasant riverside location. The site has its own shop selling food and drinks. March–Oct. Pitches **£20**

Meadhon House 48 Castlegate ☎01835 862504, ⓦmeadhon.co.uk. Pronounced "mawn", this is the finest of several B&Bs among Castlegate's old houses, with comfortable yet reasonably priced en-suite rooms, free wi-fi, and overnight storage space for bikes. **£65**

Willow Court The Friars ☎01835 863702, ⓦwillow courtjedburgh.co.uk. Attention to detail and small luxuries, such as Egyptian-cotton bed sheets and sweet-smelling toiletries, put this place a cut above most of Jedburgh's B&Bs. **£80**

Dumfries and Galloway

The southwest corner of Scotland, **Dumfries and Galloway** has stately homes, deserted hills and ruined abbeys to compete with the best of the Borders. It also has the **Solway coast**, a long, indented coastline of sheltered sandy coves that's been dubbed the "Scottish Riviera" – it's certainly Scotland's warmest, southernmost stretch of coastline.

Dumfries is the largest town in the region, and only really a must for those on the trail of **Robert Burns**. Further west is enticing **Kirkcudbright**, once a bustling port thronged with sailing ships, later an artists' retreat, and now a tranquil, well-preserved little town. Contrasting with the essentially gentle landscape of the Solway coast is the brooding presence of the **Galloway Hills** to the north, their beautiful moors, mountains, lakes and rivers centred on the **Galloway Forest Park**, a hillwalking and mountain-biking paradise.

Dumfries

On the wide banks of the River Nith a short way inland from the Solway Firth, **DUMFRIES** is the largest town in southwest Scotland. Long known as the "Queen of the South" (as is its football club), the town flourished as a medieval seaport and trading centre. Enough remains of the original, warm red sandstone buildings to distinguish Dumfries from other towns in the southwest, though its main appeal is its associations with **Robert Burns**.

18

Dumfries Museum

Rotchell Rd • April–Sept Mon–Sat 10am–5pm, Sun 2–5pm; Oct–March Tues–Sat 10am–1pm & 2–5pm • Free; camera obscura £2.70 • ⓣ 01387 253374, ⓦ dumfriesmuseum.com

On the hill above the Robert Burns Centre stands the **Dumfries Museum**, from where there are great views over the town. The museum is housed partly in an eighteenth-century windmill, which was converted into the town's observatory in the 1830s, and features the world's oldest working **camera obscura** on its top floor. In April 2014, the museum was broken into, and thieves made off with a haul worth more than £34,000, including an Olympic gold medal won by Scottish curler Rhona Martin in 2002.

Old Bridge House Museum

Mill Rd, a little upstream from the Robert Burns Centre • April–Sept Mon–Sat 10am–5pm, Sun 2–5pm • Free • ⓣ 01387 256904

Devorgilla Bridge, built in 1431, is one of the oldest bridges in Scotland. Attached to its southwestern end is the town's oldest house, built in 1660 and now home to the tiny, quirky **Old Bridge House Museum**, stuffed full of Victorian bric-a-brac, including a teeth-chattering range of dental gear; the house was once an inn, which Burns would undoubtedly have visited.

ARRIVAL AND INFORMATION

DUMFRIES

By train The station is a 5min walk northeast of the town centre on Lovers Walk.
Destinations Carlisle (Mon–Sat 13 daily, Sun 5 daily; 40min); Glasgow Central (Mon–Sat 9 daily, Sun 2 daily; 1hr 50min).
By bus Buses stop at Whitesands beside the River Nith.
Destinations Caerlaverock (Mon–Sat 7 daily, Sun 2 daily;

30min); Carlisle (Mon–Sat 1–2 hourly, Sun 7 daily; 1hr 35min); Castle Douglas (Mon–Sat 1–2 hourly, Sun 8 daily; 45min); Edinburgh (Mon–Sat 6 daily, Sun 2 daily; 2hr 50min); Kirkcudbright (Mon–Sat 5 daily, Sun 3 daily; 1hr 10min); New Abbey (Mon–Sat 11 daily, Sun 3 daily; 15min); Newton Stewart (Mon–Sat 10 daily, Sun 5 daily; 1hr 30min); Stranraer (Mon–Sat 10 daily, Sun 4 daily; 2hr 10min).

ON THE BURNS TRAIL IN DUMFRIES

Burns' House Burns St ⓣ 01387 255297, ⓦ dumgal .gov.uk. Simple sandstone building where the poet died of rheumatic heart disease in 1796, a few days before the birth of his last son, Maxwell. Inside, one of the bedroom windows bears his signature, scratched with his diamond ring. Free. April–Sept Mon–Sat 10am–5pm, Sun 2–5pm; Oct–March Tues–Sat 10am–1pm & 2–5pm.

Burns Statue Northern end of High St. Presiding over a roundabout, this sentimental piece of Victorian frippery in white Carrara marble features the great man holding a posy. His faithful hound, Luath, lies curled around his feet.

Midsteeple High St. Burns' body lay in state here in Dumfries' most singular building, a wonky hotchpotch of a place built in 1707 to fulfil the multiple functions of

prison, clocktower, courthouse and arsenal.

Robert Burns Centre (RBC) Mill Rd ⓣ 01387 264808, ⓦ rbcft.co.uk. A free exhibition on the poet's years in Dumfries plus an optional 20min slide show (£2.35). Feature-length films from Hollywood and beyond are shown here in the evening. April–Sept Mon–Sat 10am–5pm, Sun 2–5pm; Oct–March Tues–Sat 10am–1pm & 2–5pm.

St Michael's Church 39 Cardoness St ⓦ stmichaelschurchdumfries.org. Originally buried in a simple grave near St Michael's Church, in 1815 Burns was dug up and moved across the graveyard to a purpose-built mausoleum, a Neoclassical eyesore which houses a statue of him being accosted by the Poetic Muse. Mon–Fri 10am–4pm.

Tourist information 64 Whitesands (April to mid-July & Oct Mon–Sat 9.30am–5pm; mid-July to Sept Mon–Sat 9.30am–5pm, Sun 11am–4pm; Nov–March Mon–Sat 9.30am–4pm; ☎ 01387 253862).

ACCOMMODATION AND EATING

Glenaldor House 5 Victoria Terrace ☎ 01387 264248, ⓦ glenaldorhouse.co.uk. A light and bright Victorian house near the station with four en-suite bedrooms and bountiful breakfasts, including haggis from the local butcher's shop. **£65**

Globe Inn 56 High St ☎ 01387 252335, ⓦ globe inndumfries.co.uk. This *howff* has a bit more atmosphere than other pubs in town. Its oak-panelled rooms, crammed with Burns memorabilia – he was a regular – have changed little since his time. Live music every Monday night. Mon–Wed 10am–11pm, Thurs–Sun 10am–midnight.

Hullabaloo RBC, Mill Rd ☎ 01387 259679, ⓦ hullabaloorestaurant.co.uk. A cosy restaurant on the top floor of the RBC (see box opposite), with a summer

terrace overlooking the river. Wraps, bagels and ciabatta sandwiches are on offer for lunch, with more adventurous global dishes for dinner (mains £12–18). Easter–Sept Mon 11am–4pm, Tues–Sat 11am–4pm & 6–11pm, Sun noon–3pm; Oct–Easter Mon 11am–4pm, Tues–Sat 11am–4pm & 6–11pm.

Marthrown of Mabie Mabie Forest, 5 miles southwest of town ☎ 01387 247900, ⓦ marthrownofmabie.com. Choose to stay in a simple bunkhouse, a replica Iron Age roundhouse or a stove-warmed yurt (sleeps four) at this tranquil campsite in the heart of a forest known for its excellent mountain biking trails. There's space to pitch tents, too, along with cooking areas, an outdoor shower, and a wood-fired hot tub. Cash only. Pitches **£15**, bunkhouse **£19.50**, tipi **£70**, yurt **£150**

Around Dumfries

Notable sights around Dumfries include grand **Drumlanrig Castle** with its fine paintings, moated **Caerlaverock**, and the picturesque ruins of thirteenth-century **Sweetheart Abbey**; the **Caerlaverock Wetland Centre** is a good destination for twitchers.

Drumlanrig Castle

18 miles north of Dumfries · **House** Easter and May–Aug daily 11am–4pm · £10 · **Country park** April–Sept daily 10am–5pm · £6 · ☎ 01848 331555, ⓦ drumlanrig.co.uk · On Sundays, one bus service (#246) departs Dumfries in the morning, taking 35min to reach the road outside the house; from Mon–Sat the same service (roughly hourly) stops on the A76, a mile or so from the entrance

Drumlanrig Castle is not a castle at all, but the grandiose stately home of the Duke of Buccleuch and Queensberry. The highlights of the richly furnished interior are the **paintings**, in particular Rembrandt's *Old Woman Reading* and Hans Holbein's formal portrait of Sir Nicholas Carew. As well as the house, Drumlanrig has a host of other attractions, including formal **gardens** and a forested **country park**.

Caerlaverock Castle

8 miles southeast of Dumfries · Daily: April–Sept 9.30am–5.30pm; Oct–March 9.30am–4.30pm · £5.50; HS · ☎ 01387 770244 · Bus #6A from Dumfries (Mon–Sat 5 daily, Sun 2 daily; 30min) runs to Caerlaverock along the B725

Caerlaverock Castle is a picture-perfect ruined castle, moated, built from rich local red sandstone, triangular in shape and with a mighty double-towered gatehouse. The most surprising addition, however, lies inside, where you're confronted by the ornate Renaissance facade of the **Nithsdale Lodging**, erected in the 1630s by the first earl of Nithsdale. The decorated tympana above the windows feature lively mythological and heraldic scenes. Sadly, six years later Nithsdale and his garrison were forced to surrender after a thirteen-week siege and bombardment by the Covenanters, who wrecked the place. It was never inhabited again.

Caerlaverock Wildfowl and Wetlands Trust

Eastpark Farm, 8 miles southeast of Dumfries · Daily 10am–5pm · £7.05 · ☎ 01387 770200, ⓦ wwt.org.uk · Bus #6A from Dumfries to Caerlaverock (Mon–Sat 5 daily, Sun 2 daily) runs past the start of the 2-mile lane leading off the B725 to the centre

The **Caerlaverock Wildfowl and Wetlands Trust (WWT) Centre** spreads over 1400 acres of protected salt marsh and mud flat edging the Solway Firth, three miles east of

Caerlaverock Castle. Famous for the 25,000 or so Svalbard barnacle geese that winter here between September and April, it also has wild whooper swans and offers two-day wildlife photography courses; see website for details.

ACCOMMODATION   CAERLAVEROCK

WWT Caerlaverock Wetland Centre Eastpark Farm, Caerlaverock ☎ 01387 770200, �🌐 wwt.org.uk. You can stay in the centre's converted farmhouse, which has its own observation tower, a mix of simple double, twin and family rooms, plus a kitchen and washing machine for guests' use. Staff can arrange to have you picked up from Dumfries (£10 each way, including a stop for supplies at the local supermarket, if you need it). **£60**

Sweetheart Abbey

A ten-minute walk east of New Abbey • April–Sept daily 9.30am–5.30pm; Oct–March Mon–Wed, Sat & Sun 9.30am–4.30pm • £4.50; HS • ☎ 01387 850397 • From Dumfries, bus #372 runs to New Abbey (15min), stopping outside the post office

Sweetheart Abbey, lying romantically ruined to the east of the village of **NEW ABBEY**, takes its name from its founder, Devorgilla de Balliol, who carried the embalmed heart of her husband, John Balliol (of Oxford college fame) for the last 22 years of her life – she is buried with the casket, in the presbytery. The last of the Cistercian abbeys to be founded in Scotland – in 1273 – Sweetheart is dominated by the red sandstone abbey church, which remains intact, albeit minus its roof. Its grassy nave is flanked by giant compound piers supporting early Gothic arches, and above them a triforium. The other great survivor is the precinct wall, a massive structure made from rough granite boulders.

EATING   SWEETHEART ABBEY

Abbey Cottage Tearoom Near the abbey ☎ 01387 850377, �🌐 abbeycottagetearoom.com. This delightful cottage tearoom is renowned for its good coffee, teas, home-made cakes and light lunches (jacket potatoes from £5.40), and enjoys an unrivalled view over the abbey. There's a garden for sunny days. April–Oct 10am–5pm; Nov, Dec, Feb & March Wed–Sun 11am–4pm.

The Colvend coast

The **Colvend coast**, twenty miles or so southwest of Dumfries, is one of the finest stretches of coastline along the so-called "Scottish Riviera". The best approach is via the A710, which heads south through New Abbey, before cutting across a handsome landscape of rolling farmland to **ROCKCLIFFE**, a beguiling little place of comfortable villas around a rocky sand and shell bay, sheltered beneath wooded hills.

For vehicles, Rockcliffe is a dead end, but it's the start of a pleasant half-hour's walk along the Jubilee Path to neighbouring **KIPPFORD**, a tiny, lively yachting centre strung out along the east bank of the Urr estuary. At low tide you can walk over the Rough Firth causeway from the shore below across the mud flats to **Rough Island**, a humpy twenty-acre bird sanctuary owned by the National Trust for Scotland – it's out of bounds in May and June during the nesting season.

GETTING AROUND AND ACCOMMODATION   THE COLVEND COAST

By bus One of the more useful bus services in the area is the frequent #372, which links Dumfries with Sandyhills and New Abbey. The #372A is also handy, running between Sandyhills, Kippford and Rockcliffe.

Anchor Hotel Kippford ☎ 01556 620205, �🌐 anchorkippford.co.uk. Right on Kippford's waterfront, the popular *Anchor Hotel* is a good reward for the gentle stroll required to get here from Rockcliffe. The place serves local fish (mains around £10) and good ale; there's also a real fire in winter. Daily 11am–midnight.

Castle Point Caravan Site Just south of Rockcliffe ☎ 01556 630248, ⌨ castlepointcc.com. Secluded campsite with free wi-fi, just south of Rockcliffe village and a stone's throw from the seashore (there are three sandy beaches within walking distance). Late March to mid-October. Pitches **£23**

Millbrae House Rockcliffe ☎ 01556 630217, ⌨ millbraehouse.co.uk. Excellent B&B in a whitewashed cottage near the bay. Rooms are bright and elegantly furnished and breakfast is served in the conservatory. A couple of self-catering options are also available. **£68**

Castle Douglas and around

Most folk come to **CASTLE DOUGLAS**, eighteen miles southwest of Dumfries, in order to visit the nearby attractions of **Threave Garden** and **Threave Castle**. It's a small, low-rise town with a couple of decent accommodation options to choose from, and painted cottages lining the grid-like streets.

Threave Garden

A mile southwest of Castle Douglas • Late March to Oct daily 10am–5pm; Nov & Dec Fri–Sun 10am–5pm; Feb to late March Fri–Sun 10am–5pm • £7.50 or £12.50 with admission to Threave Castle (see below); NTS • ☎ 08444 932245, ⓦ nts.org.uk

18

Threave Garden is a pleasant mile or so's walk southwest of Castle Douglas along the shores of Loch Carlingwark. The garden features a magnificent spread of flowers and woodland, sixty acres divided into more than a dozen areas from the bright, old-fashioned blooms of the Rose Garden to the brilliant banks of rhododendrons in the Woodland Garden. In springtime, thousands of visitors turn up for the flowering of more than two hundred types of daffodil.

Threave Castle

Around 2 miles west of Castle Douglas • To visit the house you must join a guided tour (April–Sept 9.30am–4.30pm; Oct 9.30am–3.30pm; book ahead) • £4.50, including boat fare; HS • ☎ 07711 223101, ⓦ nts.org.uk/Property/Threave-Estate

Built for Archibald the Grim, the sturdy, rectangular fortress of **Threave Castle** was completed shortly after the War of Independence, in around 1370. The rickety curtain-wall to the south and east is all that remains of the artillery fortifications, hurriedly constructed in the 1450s in a desperate – and unsuccessful – attempt to defend the castle against James II's newfangled cannon. The place was wrecked in 1640 after a siege, but enough remains to make it worth exploring. The best way of reaching the castle from Threave Garden is to walk through the estate. However you decide to get there, follow the signs to the Open Farm, from where it's a lovely fifteen-minute walk down to the River Dee. Here you ring a brass bell for the boat to take you over to the flat and grassy island on which the stern-looking tower house stands.

ARRIVAL AND INFORMATION   CASTLE DOUGLAS

By bus Most services from Dumfries and Kirkcudbright stop on Carlingwark St, towards the southern edge of town. Destinations Dumfries (Mon–Sat 7 daily; Sun 3 daily; 35–50min), Kirkcudbright (Mon–Sat hourly, Sun 6 daily; 20min).
Tourist information King St (April–June Mon–Sat

10am–5pm, Sun 11am–3pm; July & Aug Mon–Sat 9.30am–6pm, Sun 10am–4pm; Sept & Oct Mon–Sat 10am–5pm; ☎ 01556 502611).
Bike rental Bikes, useful for getting out to Threave, are available from the Castle Douglas Cycle Centre, Church St (Mon–Sat 9am–5pm; ☎ 01556 504542, ⓦ cdbikes.co.uk).

ACCOMMODATION AND EATING

Designs 179 King St ☎ 01556 504552, ⓦ designs gallery.co.uk. Nice daytime café at the back of a crafts gallery with a lovely conservatory and garden, serving great ciabattas (£5) and decent coffee. Mon–Sat 9.30am–5pm.

Lochside Caravan and Camping Site Loch Carlingwark ☎ 07824 528467. Trees surround this well-maintained campsite, a short walk from the bottom of King St down Marle St. Campers can also fish on the loch. Easter–Oct. Pitches £19.55

Kirkcudbright

KIRKCUDBRIGHT – pronounced "kir-coo-bree" – hugging the muddy banks of the River Dee ten miles southwest of Castle Douglas, is the only major town along the Solway coast to have retained a working harbour. In addition, it has a ruined **castle** and an attractive town centre, a charming medley of simple two-storey cottages and medieval pends, Georgian villas and Victorian townhouses, all brightly painted.

18

MacLellan's Castle

Castle St • April–Sept daily 9.30am–5.30pm • £4.50; HS • ☎ 01557 331856, ⓦ historic-scotland.org.uk

The most surprising sight in Kirkcudbright is **MacLellan's Castle**, a pink-flecked sixteenth-century tower house sitting at one end of the high street by the harbourside. Part fortified keep and part spacious mansion, the castle was built in the 1570s for the then Provost of Kirkcudbright, Sir Thomas MacLellan of Bombie. Its interior is well preserved, from the kitchen (complete with bread oven) to the spyhole known as the "**laird's lug**", behind the fireplace of the Great Hall.

Broughton House

High St • April–Oct daily noon–5pm; Feb & March garden only daily 11am–4pm • £6.50; NTS • ☎ 0844 493 2246, ⓦ nts.org.uk

Broughton House, a smart Georgian townhouse and former home of the artist **Edward Hornel** (1863–1933), stands on the L-shaped High Street, near the castle. Hornel, an important member of the late nineteenth-century Scottish art scene, spent his childhood a few doors down the street, and returned in 1900 to establish an artists' colony with some of the "Glasgow Boys" (see box, p.795). At the back of the house Hornel added a studio and a vast gallery, now filled with the mannered, vibrant paintings of girls at play, which he churned out in the latter part of his career. Hornel's trip to Japan in 1893 imbued him with a lifelong affection for the country, and his densely packed, rambling **gardens** have a strong Japanese influence.

Tolbooth Art Centre

High St • Mid-April to Sept Mon–Sat 10am–4pm, Sun 1–4pm • Free • ☎ 01557 331556, ⓦ dumgal.gov.uk

For background information on Kirkcudbright, visit the imposing, church-like **Tolbooth**, with its stone-built clocktower and spire. Built in the 1620s, the building now houses the **Tolbooth Art Centre**, which has a small display of paintings including Hornel's striking *Japanese Girl*, and S.J. Peploe's Colourist view of the Tolbooth.

ARRIVAL AND INFORMATION   KIRKCUDBRIGHT

By bus Buses to and from Dumfries (at least 1 daily; 1hr 10min) pull up in the harbour car park, next to the tourist office.

Tourist information Harbour Square (Feb & March

GALLOWAY FOREST PARK

Galloway Forest Park (ⓦ forestry.gov.uk) is Britain's largest forest park, with a spectacularly varied landscape of mountain peaks, lochs, coast and moorland, cut through by the Southern Uplands Way. It has **visitor centres** (generally April–Oct daily 10am–4pm) at Clatteringshaws Loch, Glentrool and Kirroughtree. Each has a tearoom, several waymarked walks and information on activities and events. The only **tarmacked road** to cross the park is the desolate twenty-mile stretch of the A712 between Newton Stewart and New Galloway, known as the **Queen's Way**.

Both Glentrool and Kirroughtree visitor centres have **mountain bike trails**, which form part of southern Scotland's outstanding mountain-biking facilities, known as the 7 Stanes (ⓦ 7stanes.co.uk). Of the two, Kirroughtree, three miles east of the town of Newton Stewart, is by far the most varied and fun, with lots of exciting singletrack trails for all abilities and good bike-rental facilities.

About seven miles east of Newton Stewart, at the **Grey Mare's Tail Bridge**, various **hiking trails** delve into the pine forests beside the tarmacked road, crossing gorges, waterfalls and burns. **Clatteringshaws Loch**, meanwhile, a reservoir surrounded by pine forest at the southeastern edge of the park, has a fourteen-mile footpath running right around it. Serious hikers should head for **Glentrool**, at the western edge of the park, about ten miles north of Newton Stewart, where a narrow lane twists the five miles over to Loch Trool.

The entire park has been designated a "dark sky park", with a couple of panoramic spots reserved for stargazing (ⓦ forestry.gov.uk/darkskygalloway).

Mon–Sat 11am–4pm; April–June Mon–Sat 10am–5pm, Sun 11am–4pm; July & Aug Mon–Sat 9.30am–6pm, Sun 10am–5pm; Sept & Oct Mon–Sat 10am–5pm, Sun 11am–3pm; ☏ 01557 330494).

ACCOMMODATION AND EATING

Baytree House 110 High St ☏ 01557 330824, ⓦ baytreekirkcudbright.co.uk. An imposing Georgian townhouse in the centre, with a friendly welcome and a fine breakfast. A self-contained studio with its own garden is also available to rent on a self-catering basis (min. one-week stay). Double __£82__, studio __£375__

Castle Bistro 5 Castle St ☏ 01557 330569, ⓦ the castlerestaurant.net. Reinvented as a bistro, this smart little place focuses on flavour-packed local ingredients like wild venison and king scallops (mains around £12) and stocks French house wines and whiskies from the Isle of Skye. Mon–Sat 6pm till late, Wed–Sat lunch with prior booking.

18

Wigtown

WIGTOWN, seven miles south of Newton Stewart, is a tiny place with a remarkable main square, a vast, triangular-shaped affair laid out as it was in medieval times. Overlooking and dominating the square and its central bowling green are the gargantuan **County Buildings**, built in French Gothic style. Wigtown styles itself as "Scotland's National Book Town", with a highly rated **literary festival** in late September and more than twenty **bookshops** occupying some of the modest houses that line the square, and more elsewhere in the vicinity (ⓦ wigtownbookfestival.com).

ARRIVAL AND DEPARTURE   WIGTOWN

By bus Buses stop on the main square, running to Newton Stewart (Mon–Sat hourly, Sun 6 daily; 15min) and Stranraer (Mon–Sat 2 daily; 1hr 30min).

Whithorn and around

WHITHORN, fifteen miles south of Wigtown, is a one-street town where, in 397 AD, **St Ninian** is thought to have founded the first Christian church north of Hadrian's Wall. No one can be sure where Ninian's church actually stood, but his tomb at Whithorn soon became a popular place of pilgrimage. These days, it takes a serious leap of the imagination to envisage Whithorn as a medieval pilgrimage centre; start by watching the audiovisual show at the **Whithorn Story Visitor Centre** (Easter–Oct daily 10.30am–5pm; £4.50) on the main street. More compelling are the Christian standing crosses and headstones housed in the nearby **museum** (admission covered by same ticket).

Isle of Whithorn

The pilgrims who crossed the Solway to visit St Ninian's shrine landed at the **ISLE OF WHITHORN**, four miles south of town; it's no longer an island, but an antique and picturesque little seaport. Walk down to the end of the harbour to pick up signs to the minuscule remains of the thirteenth-century **St Ninian's Chapel**, which some believe was the site of the original Candida Casa.

ACCOMMODATION AND EATING   ISLE OF WHITHORN

Steam Packet Inn Harbour Row ☏ 01988 500334, ⓦ thesteampacketinn.biz. Right on the quayside, serving above-average pub grub (pies, curries and burgers are all less than a tenner each), plus some fancier mains. The bar does a good range of guest ales, and caters for the local fishermen as well as visitors. Five of the comfy rooms here have views over the harbour. Daily 11am–11pm. __£80__

The Rhinns of Galloway

The hilly, hammer-shaped peninsula at the western end of the Solway coast is known as the **Rhinns of Galloway**. The main town is **STRANRAER** but unless you're heading to (or coming from) Northern Ireland, there's really no reason to go there. The ferry company Stena Line had a base at the port, but have now moved five miles north to **CAIRNRYAN**.

Portpatrick

The old seafaring port of **PORTPATRICK**, on the Rhinns of Galloway, is the nicest place to stay on the peninsula, with an attractive pastel-painted seafront that wraps itself round a small rocky bay sheltered by equally rocky cliffs.

18

ARRIVAL AND DEPARTURE   PORTPATRICK

By bus Buses leave from South Crescent, next to the sandy bay, for Ayr (Mon–Sat 8 daily, Sun 4 daily; 1hr 30min) and Stranraer (hourly; 25min).

ACCOMMODATION AND EATING

★**Campbell's Restaurant** 1 South Crescent ☎01776 810314, ⓦcampbellsrestaurant.co.uk. This modern, buzzy little place serves great local seafood, from west coast scallops (£16.75) to locally caught lobster; you might even see the owner nipping out in his boat. Tues–Sun noon–2.30pm & 6–9pm.

Rickwood House Hotel Heugh Road ☎01776 810270, ⓦportpatrick.me.uk. Fresh and welcoming four-star B&B, a short stroll up from the harbour. All of the rooms are en-suite (including the family room), and some have views of the water. A three-night minimum applies in summer. **£72**

Mull of Galloway

The **Mull of Galloway**, twenty miles south of Portpatrick, is a precipitous headland. Crowned by a classic whitewashed Stevenson lighthouse, from which you can see the Isle of Man, it really feels like the end of the road. It's the southernmost point in Scotland, and a favourite nesting spot for guillemots, razorbills and kittiwakes. The headland has a **lighthouse** that can be climbed on summer weekends (April–June & Sept Sat & Sun 10am–4pm; July & Aug Sat–Wed 10am–4pm; £2.50).

ARRIVAL AND EATING   MULL OF GALLOWAY

By bus The nearest bus stop is 4 miles north at Drummore, with services to Port Logan (Mon–Sat 5 daily; 10 min) and Stranraer (Mon–Sat 6 daily; 40 min).

★**Gallie Craig Café** Drummore ☎01776 840558, ⓦgalliecraig.co.uk. Just below the car park and perched

on the cliff edge, this excellent coffee house/restaurant serves hot meals and tasty snacks. The terrace is a splendid spot for a bit of armchair birdwatching. Feb & March Sat–Wed 11am–4pm; April–Oct daily 10am–5.30pm; Nov Sat & Sun 11am–4pm.

Ayrshire

The rolling hills and rich soil of **Ayrshire** are not really at the top of most visitors' Scottish itinerary. **Ayr**, the county town and birthplace of Robert Burns, won't distract you for long. Most folk stick to the coastline, attracted by the wide, flat sandy **beaches** and the vast number of **golf** courses. South of Ayr, the most obvious points of interest are **Culzean Castle**, with its Robert Adam interior and extensive wooded grounds, and the offshore islands of **Ailsa Craig**, while to the east is fascinating **Dumfries House**. North of Ayr is **Irvine**, home to the Scottish Maritime Museum.

Ayr and around

AYR is by far the largest town on the Firth of Clyde coast. It was an important seaport and trading centre for many centuries, and rivalled Glasgow in size and significance right up until the late seventeenth century. Nowadays, it pulls in the crowds for the Scottish Grand National and the Scottish Derby (ⓦayr-racecourse.co.uk), and for the fact that Robbie Burns was born in the neighbouring village of **Alloway** (see opposite).

The town centre, wedged between Sandgate and the south bank of the River Ayr, is busy most days with shoppers from all over the county. East of the High Street, the medieval **Auld Brig** is one of the oldest stone bridges in Scotland, built during the reign of James IV (1488–1513). A short stroll upstream brings you to the much-restored **Auld Kirk**, the church funded by Cromwell as recompense for the one he incorporated into the town's fortress. The dark and gloomy interior retains the original pulpit (ask at the tourist office about access; see below). All you can see of Cromwell's zigzag **Citadel**, built to the west of the town centre in the 1650s, is a small section of the old walls.

18

ARRIVAL AND INFORMATION

AYR

By plane Ayr is the nearest large town to Glasgow Prestwick Airport (☎08712 230700, ⓦglasgowprestwick.com), which lies 3 miles north of town and is connected by frequent trains to Ayr and Glasgow.

By train The station is a 10min walk southeast of the town centre.

Destinations Glasgow Central (up to 4 hourly; 50min); Irvine (up to 4 hourly; 15–20min); Prestwick Airport (up to 4 hourly; 7min); Stranraer (Mon–Sat 6 daily, Sun 3 daily;

1hr 20min).

By bus The station is at the foot of Sandgate, near the tourist office.

Destinations Glasgow (every 15min; 1hr 15min); Stranraer (9 daily; 1hr 40min–2hr).

Tourist Information 22 Sandgate (April–Sept daily 9am–5pm; Oct–March Mon–Sat 9am–5pm; ☎01292 290300).

ACCOMMODATION AND EATING

Heads of Ayr Dunure Rd, 5 miles southeast of town ☎01292 442269, ⓦheadsofayr.com. Out of town along the coastal A719, this caravan and campsite is small and quiet. As a bonus, there's a sandy beach within walking distance. March–Oct & winter weekends. **£21**

Savoy Park Hotel 16 Racecourse Rd ☎01292 266112, ⓦsavoypark.com. The rooms inside this impressive Scots Baronial building, notable for its red sandstone walls and turrets, are a cut above others in town. It's worth splashing out on an executive or superior room if possible (up to £115 per night), if only for the antique furnishings and wood panelling. **£95**

Stage Door Café 12 Carrick St ☎01292 280444, ⓦstagedoorcafe.co.uk. Aptly named (it's part of the Gaiety Theatre), this place draws in the crowds with fresh, reasonably priced dishes like North Sea monkfish and slow-braised Scottish ox cheeks. Three courses cost £22.50 after 6.30pm; slightly less before. Daily 10am–11pm.

West Kirk 58a Sandgate ☎01292 880416. For a quiet pint of real ale, head for this music-free *Wetherspoon* church-to-pub conversion, its wooden balconies held up by pistachio-coloured fluted pillars. Basic pub food is also available. Mon–Thurs 8am–midnight, Fri 8am–1am, Sat & Sun 8am–midnight.

Alloway

ALLOWAY, formerly a small village but now on the southern outskirts of Ayr, is the birthplace of Robert Burns (1759–96), Scotland's national poet. The several places associated with him have been linked together as the **Robert Burns Birthplace Museum**.

Robert Burns Birthplace Museum

Murdoch's Lone and around • Daily: April–Sept 10am–5.30pm; Oct–March 10am–5pm • £8.50, including entry to the cottage; NTS • ⓦburnsmuseum.org.uk

The **museum** on Murdoch's Lone shows original manuscripts and some of Burns' personal belongings with a good dash of technology and interactive elements. Burns was born in what is now known as **Burns Cottage**: a low, whitewashed, single-room thatched cottage north of the museum on Alloway (the B7024), where animals and people lived under the same roof.

Other Burns sights

Burns Monument • Daily April–Sept 9am–5pm; Oct–March 10am–4pm • Free

Alloway Kirk is where Robert's father William is buried, and where Burns set much of *Tam o' Shanter*. You can still see its plain, roofless ruins today. Down the road from the church, the **Brig o' Doon**, the picturesque thirteenth-century humpback bridge over which Tam is forced to flee for his life, still stands, curving gracefully over the river.

18

ROBERT BURNS

The eldest of seven, **Robert Burns** was born in Alloway on January 25, 1759. His tenant-farmer father's bankruptcy had a profound effect on the boy, leaving him with an antipathy towards authority. After the death of his father, Robert, now head of the family, moved them to a farm at Mossgiel where he began to write in earnest: his first volume, *Poems Chiefly in the Scottish Dialect*, was published in 1786. The book proved immensely popular with ordinary Scots and Edinburgh literati alike, with *Holy Willie's Prayer* attracting particular attention. The object of Burns' poetic scorn was the kirk, whose ministers had condemned him for fornication.

Burns spent the winter of 1786–87 in the capital, but despite his success he felt financially trapped, unable to leave farming. His radical views also landed him in a political snare, his recourse being to play the unlettered ploughman-poet who might be excused impetuous outbursts and hectic womanizing. He made useful contacts in Edinburgh, however, and was recruited to write songs set to traditional Scottish tunes: works including *Auld Lang Syne* and *Green Grow the Rushes, O*. At this time, too, he produced *Tam o' Shanter* and a republican tract, *A Man's a Man for a' That*.

Burns fathered several illegitimate children, but in 1788 married **Jean Armour**, a stonemason's daughter with whom he already had two children, and moved to Ellisland Farm, near Dumfries. The following year he was appointed excise officer and could leave farming. But his years of labour, allied to a rheumatic fever, damaged his heart, and he died in Dumfries in 1796, aged 37.

Burns' work, inspired by romantic nationalism and tinged with wry wit, has made him a potent symbol of "Scottishness". Today, Burns Clubs all over the world mark the poet's birthday with the Burns' Supper, complete with haggis, piper and whisky – and a ritual recital of *Ode to a Haggis*.

High above the river and bridge towers the **Burns Monument**, a striking Neoclassical temple in a small, carefully manicured garden.

ARRIVAL AND DEPARTURE   ALLOWAY

By bus To reach Alloway from Ayr town centre, take bus #8 or #361 from Sandgate (Mon–Sat hourly). Both services stop on Doonholm Rd, a short walk east of the museum.

Culzean Castle

10 miles south of Ayr • **Castle** Easter–Oct daily 10.30am–5pm • £15.50; NTS • **Park** Daily 9.30am to dusk • £10.50 • ☎ 0844 493 2149, ⓦ culzeanexperience.org • No public transport runs directly to the castle, but the #60 and #360 buses from Ayr should pass the road leading to the entrance

Sitting on the edge of a sheer cliff, looking out over the Firth of Clyde to Arran, **Culzean Castle** (pronounced "Cullane") couldn't want for a more impressive situation. The current castle is actually a grand, late eighteenth-century stately home, designed by Scottish Neoclassical architect **Robert Adam**. Adam's most brilliantly conceived work is the Oval Staircase, where tiers of classical columns lead up to a huge glazed cupola. Other highlights include a portrait of Napoleon by Lefèvre, a superb Chippendale four-poster bed and a boat-shaped cradle. Many folk come here purely to stroll and picnic in the castle's 500-acre **country park**, mess about by the beach, or have tea and cakes.

Dumfries House

Just north of Cumnock, 15 miles east of Ayr • April–Oct 11am–4pm, pre-booked guided tour only • £9 • ☎ 01290 425959, ⓦ dumfries-house.org.uk • From Ayr take the #42 bus to Auchinleck (every 30min; 30min); the house is 1.5 miles to the south

The handsome Palladian villa of **Dumfries House** is an essential stop for anyone with an interest in domestic architecture. Lively tours illuminate the beauty of the furnishings: the house was built and decked out swiftly – between 1756 and 1760 – meaning its Rococo decorative scheme is in perfect harmony with the graceful sandstone exterior. Chief among the treasures is a huge collection of **Chippendale furniture**.

AILSA CRAIG

If the weather's half decent, it's impossible to miss **Ailsa Craig**, ten miles off the south Ayrshire coast in the middle of the Firth of Clyde. The island's name means "Fairy Rock" in Gaelic, though it actually looks more like an enormous muffin. It would certainly have been less than enchanting for the persecuted Catholics who escaped here during the Reformation. The island's granite has long been used for making curling stones, and in the late nineteenth century 29 people lived here, either working in the quarry or at the Stevenson lighthouse. With its volcanic, columnar cliffs and 1114ft summit, Ailsa Craig is now a **bird sanctuary** – home to some forty thousand gannets. The **best time** to make the trip is at the end of May and in June when the fledglings are learning to fly. Several companies in the town of **GIRVAN** offer **cruises** round the island, but only Mark McCrindle, who also organizes sea-angling trips, is licensed to land (May to late Sept 1–2 daily; ☎01465 713219, ⓦailsacraig.org.uk). It takes about an hour to reach the island. Timings and prices depend on the length of trip, tides and weather; booking ahead is essential.

18

Irvine

IRVINE, twelve miles north of Ayr, was once the principal port for trade between Glasgow and Ireland, and later for coal from Kilmarnock. Its halcyon days are recalled in an enjoyable living-history **museum**, spread across several locations around the town's beautifully restored old harbour.

Scottish Maritime Museum

Various locations • March till late Dec daily 10am–5pm • £7 • ☎ 01294 278283, ⓦ scottishmaritimemuseum.org

The best place to start a tour of the **Scottish Maritime Museum** sights is in the late nineteenth-century **Linthouse Engine Shop**, on Harbour Road, housing everything from old sailing dinghies and canoes to giant ship's turbines. Free guided tours set off regularly for the nearby **Shipyard Worker's Tenement Flat**, which has been restored to its appearance in 1910, when a family of six to eight plus a lodger would have occupied its two rooms and scullery. Moored at the **pontoons** on Harbour Street is an assortment of craft that you can board, including the oldest seagoing steam yacht in the country.

ARRIVAL AND DEPARTURE   IRVINE

Arriving at Irvine's adjacent **train** (trains from Glasgow roughly every 15min; 35min) or **bus stations**, you'll find yourself exactly halfway between the harbour, to the west, and the Rivergate shopping complex and old town, to the east.

Glasgow and the Clyde

RIVERSIDE MUSEUM, GLASGOW

Glasgow and the Clyde

19

Set on the banks of the mighty River Clyde, Glasgow, Scotland's largest city, is a former industrial giant. The city changed its image irrevocably in 1990, however – when it energetically embraced its status as European City of Culture – and has continued to transform itself ever since, with the most recent feather in its cap being the hosting of the Commonwealth Games in 2014. The cityscape has been spruced up, and many visitors are knocked out by the buildings, from long rows of sandstone terraces to the fantastical spires of the Kelvingrove Museum. Glasgow is without doubt, in its own idiosyncratic way, a cultured, vibrant and irrepressibly sociable place that's well worth getting to know.

The city has some of the best-financed and most imaginative museums and galleries in Britain – among them the showcase **Burrell Collection** and the palatial **Kelvingrove Art Gallery and Museum** – nearly all of which are free. Glasgow's **architecture** is some of the most striking in the UK, from the restored eighteenth-century warehouses of the **Merchant City** to the hulking Victorian prosperity of George Square. Most distinctive of all is the work of local luminary Charles Rennie Mackintosh, whose elegantly Art-Nouveau designs appear all over the city, reaching their apotheosis in the stunning **School of Art**. Development of the old shipyards of the Clyde, notably in the space-age shapes of the **Glasgow Science Centre** and the dynamic new **Riverside Museum**, hint at yet another string to the city's bow: combining design with innovation. The metropolis boasts thriving live-music venues, distinctive places to eat and drink, busy theatres, concert halls and an opera house. Despite all the upbeat hype, however, Glasgow's gentrification has passed by deprived inner-city areas such as the **East End**, home of the staunchly change-resistant **Barras market** and some forbidding pubs. Indeed, even in the more stylish quarters, there's a gritty edge that reinforces the city's peculiar mix of grime and glitz.

Glasgow makes an excellent base from which to explore the **Clyde valley and coast**, easily accessible by a reliable train service. Chief among the draws is the remarkable eighteenth-century **New Lanark** mills and workers' village, a World Heritage Site, while other day-trips might take you towards the scenic Argyll sea lochs, past the old shipbuilding centres on the Clyde estuary.

Brief history

Glasgow's earliest history, like so much else in this surprisingly romantic city, is obscured in a swirl of myth. Its name is said to derive from the Celtic *Glas-cu*, which loosely translates as "the dear, green place". It is generally agreed that the first settlers arrived in the sixth century to join Christian missionary **Kentigern** – later to become St Mungo – in his newly-founded monastery on the banks of the tiny Molendinar Burn.

Highlights

❶ Necropolis Elegantly crumbling graveyard on a city-centre hill behind the ancient cathedral, with great views giving a different perspective on the city. **See p.794**

❷ Kelvingrove Art Gallery and Museum Splendid civic collection in a magnificent red sandstone building in the West End; a regular Sunday outing for Glaswegians. **See p.794**

❸ Clydeside The river that made Glasgow: walk or cycle along it, take a boat on it, cross a bridge over it, or get a view of it from the absorbing new Riverside Museum. **See p.796**

❹ Burrell Collection An inspired and eclectic art collection displayed in a purpose-built museum in leafy Pollok Park. **See p.798**

❺ Hit the West End Wander the laneways of the West End on a Friday or Saturday night, and see Glasgow at its glammed up, exuberant best. **See p.798**

❻ New Lanark Stay for next to nothing in the hostel at this lovely eighteenth-century planned village where there's fascinating background on mill life, as well as superb woodland walks. **See p.806**

HIGHLIGHTS ARE MARKED ON THE MAP ON P.787

HIGHLIGHTS

1. Necropolis
2. Kelvingrove Art Gallery and Museum
3. Clydeside
4. Burrell Collection
5. Hit the West End
6. New Lanark

GLASGOW & THE CLYDE

The university and the port

William the Lionheart granted the town an official charter in 1175, after which it continued to grow in importance, peaking in the mid-fifteenth century when the **university** was founded on Kentigern's site – the second in Scotland after St Andrews. This led to the establishment of an archbishopric, and hence city status, in 1492, and, due to its situation on a large, navigable river, Glasgow soon expanded into a major industrial **port**. The first cargo of tobacco from Virginia offloaded in Glasgow in 1674, and the 1707 Act of Union between Scotland and England – despite demonstrations against it in Glasgow – led to a boom in trade with the colonies. Following the **Industrial Revolution** and James Watt's innovations in steam power, coal from the abundant seams of Lanarkshire fuelled the ironworks all around the Clyde, worked by the cheap hands of the Highlanders and, later, those fleeing the Irish potato famine of the 1840s.

Shipbuilding and decline

The **Victorian** age transformed Glasgow beyond recognition. The population boomed from 77,000 in 1801 to nearly 800,000 at the end of the century, and new tenement blocks swept into the suburbs in an attempt to cope with the choking influxes of people. By the turn of the twentieth century, Glasgow's industries had been honed into one massive **shipbuilding** culture. Everything from tugboats to transatlantic liners were fashioned out of sheet metal in the yards that straddled the Clyde. In the 1930s, however, unemployment spiralled, and Glasgow could do little to counter its popular image as a city dominated by inebriate violence and (having absorbed vast numbers of Irish emigrants) sectarian tensions. The **Gorbals** area in particular became notorious as one of the worst slums in Europe. The city's image has never been helped by the depth of animosity between its two great rival football teams, Catholic **Celtic** and Protestant **Rangers**.

19

The city reinvented

Shipbuilding, and many associated industries, died away almost completely in the 1960s and 1970s, leaving the city depressed and directionless. Then, in the 1980s, the self-promotion campaign began, snowballing towards the year-long party as European City of Culture in 1990. Glasgow then beat off competition from Edinburgh and Liverpool to become **UK City of Architecture and Design** in 1999, and won the right to host the **Commonwealth Games** of 2014. These various titles have helped Glasgow break the industrial shackles of the past and evolve into a city of stature, confidence and style.

The city centre

Glasgow's large **city centre** is ranged across the north bank of the River Clyde. At its geographical heart is **George Square**, a nineteenth-century municipal showpiece crowned by the enormous **City Chambers** at its eastern end. Behind this lies the **Merchant City**, an area that blends magnificent Victorian architecture with yuppie conversions. The grand buildings and trendy cafés cling to the borders of the run-down **East End**, a strongly working-class district that chooses to ignore its rather showy

---

TOP 5 GLASGOW MUST-DOS

A visit to Sharmanka Kinetic Theatre See p.791
A stroll in the Botanic Gardens See p.796

Oysters at Rogano See p.801
A night out in the West End See p.802
A movie at the GFT See p.804

neighbour. The oldest part of Glasgow, around the **Cathedral**, lies immediately north of the East End.

George Square

Now hemmed in by the city's grinding traffic, the imposing architecture of **George Square** reflects the confidence of Glasgow's Victorian age. The wide-open plaza

SEE 'GLASGOW CITY CENTRE' MAP

almost has a continental airiness about it, although there isn't much subtlety about the 80ft column rising up at its centre. It's topped by a statue of Sir Walter Scott, even though his links with Glasgow are, at best, sketchy. Haphazardly dotted around the great writer's plinth are a number of dignified statues of assorted luminaries, ranging from Queen Victoria to Scots heroes such as James Watt and wee Robbie Burns.

City Chambers

Free guided tours Mon–Fri 10.30am & 2.30pm • ☎ 0141 287 4018 • Buchanan Street underground

The florid splendour of the **City Chambers**, opened by Queen Victoria in 1888, occupies the entire eastern end of the square. Built from wealth gained by colonial trade and heavy industry, it epitomizes the aspirations and optimism of late-Victorian city elders. Inside, you can wander around the ground floor, with its domed mosaic ceilings and two mighty Italian-marble stairwells; free **guided tours** explore the labyrinthine interior.

The Gallery of Modern Art

Royal Exchange Square • Mon–Thurs & Sat 10am–5pm, Fri & Sun 11am–5pm • Free • ☎ 0141 287 3050, ⓦ glasgowlife.org.uk • Buchanan Street underground

Occupying one of Glasgow's grandest eighteenth-century merchant's residences, the **Gallery of Modern Art (GOMA)** has not quite lived up to the potential of the building and location. The spacious ground-floor gallery is principally used for temporary exhibitions of conceptual art, while the smaller galleries on the two upper floors are either linked together for larger exhibitions or used to show smaller themed shows by contemporary artists from around the world.

19

GLASGOW CITY CENTRE

● RESTAURANTS		● CAFÉS		■ PUBS & BARS		■ CLUBS & LIVE MUSIC	
The 13th Note Café	9	Café Gandolfi and		The Arches	10	The Arches	10
Brian Maule at Le Chardon d'Or	2	Bar Gandolfi	6	Babbity Bowster	9	King Tut's Wah	
City Merchant	5	Trans Europe-Café	8	Bar 10	6	Wah Hut	2
Dakhin	5	Where the Monkey		Corinthian	7	Polo Lounge	8
The Dhabba	7	Sleeps	1	Horseshoe Bar	4	Sub Club	11
Gamba	3			Pot Still	1	The Tunnel	5
Rogano	4			Underground	3		

Accommodation (from map):

■ ACCOMMODATION	
Babbity Bowster	5
The Brunswick	4
Euro Hostel	6
Malmaison	2
Mark's Hotel	1
University of Strathclyde	3

The Merchant City

The grid of streets that lies immediately east of the City Chambers is known as the **Merchant City**, an area of eighteenth-century warehouses and homes that was sandblasted and swabbed clean with greater enthusiasm and municipal money than any other part of Glasgow in an attempt to bring residents back into the city centre. The expected flood of yuppies was more of a trickle, but the expensive designer shops, cool bars and bijou cafés continue to flock here, giving the area a pervasive air of sophistication. A *Merchant City Trail* leaflet, which guides you around a dozen of the most interesting buildings in the area, is available at the tourist information (see p.799).

Sharmanka Kinetic Theatre

Trongate 103 • Tues, Wed & Fri 3pm, Thurs & Sun 1pm & 3pm, Sat 3pm & 4.15pm; 45/70min show • £5/8 • ☎ 0141 552 7080, ⓦ sharmanka.com • St Enoch underground

Founded by Russian émigrés Eduard Bersudsky and Tatyana Jakovskaya, the **Sharmanka Kinetic Theatre** is like a mad inventor's magical workshop, with dozens of allegorical contraptions made from old wheels, levers, lights, carved wooden figures and scrap metal which spark into life during performances. A unique art form, Sharmanka (Russian for barrel organ or hurdy-gurdy) is at once hypnotic, playful and deeply poignant, with its mechanical sculptures, or "kinemats" imprisoned in their relentless routine.

Sauchiehall Street

Glasgow's most famous street, **Sauchiehall Street**, runs in a straight line west from the northern end of Buchanan Street, past some unexciting shopping malls to a few of the city's most interesting sights.

Willow Tea Rooms

217 Sauchiehall St • Mon–Sat 9am–5.30pm, Sun 10.30am–5.30pm • ☎ 0141 332 0521, ⓦ willowtearooms.co.uk • Cowcaddens underground

Enthusiasts of the work of **Charles Rennie Mackintosh** should head for the **Willow Tea Rooms**, above Henderson the Jeweller. This is a faithful reconstruction on the site of the 1904 original, which was created for Kate Cranston, one of Mackintosh's few contemporary supporters in the city. Taking inspiration from the word *Sauchiehall*, which means "avenue of willow", he chose the willow leaf as a theme to unify everything from the tables to the mirrors and the ironwork.

Glasgow School of Art

167 Renfrew St • Mackintosh Story tours approx hourly 10am–4pm; 1hr • ☎ 0141 353 4526, ⓦ gsa.ac.uk • Cowcaddens underground

Rising above Sauchiehall Street to the north is one of the city centre's steepest hills, with Dalhousie and Scott streets veering up to Renfrew Street, where you'll find Charles Rennie Mackintosh's **Glasgow School of Art**. In 2014, this much-loved building was severely damaged by fire, and the masterpiece library was destroyed; trustees of the Mackintosh Appeal to restore the building include actors Peter Capaldi (a former GSA student) and Brad Pitt. The programme of restoration is under way, and for the time being there is no public access to the interior, though student-led tours of the exterior and the new **Reid building** opposite are in operation.

Widely considered to be the pinnacle of Mackintosh's work, the school is a characteristically angular building of warm sandstone that, due to financial constraints, had to be constructed in two stretches (1897–99 and 1907–09). There's a clear change in the architect's style from the earlier severity of the mock-Baronial east wing to the softer lines of the western half. All over the school, from the roof to the stairwells, Mackintosh introduced unique touches – Japanese lantern shapes, images of seeds and roses and stylized Celtic illuminations. While the fabric and the contents of the

19

CHARLES RENNIE MACKINTOSH

The work of the architect **Charles Rennie Mackintosh** (1868–1928) is synonymous with the image of Glasgow. Historians may disagree over whether his work was a forerunner of the Modernist movement or merely the sunset of Victorianism, but he undoubtedly created buildings of great beauty, idiosyncratically fusing Scots Baronial with Gothic, Art Nouveau and modern design. Since the postwar years Mackintosh's ideas have become particularly fashionable, giving rise to a certain amount of ersatz **"Mockintosh"** in his home city, with his distinctive lettering and design details used time and again. Fortunately, there are also plenty of examples of the genuine article, making the city a pilgrimage centre for art and design students.

As a young child Mackintosh began to cultivate his interest in drawing from nature during walks in the countryside taken to improve his health. This talent was to flourish when he joined the **Glasgow School of Art** in 1884: here Mackintosh met Herbert MacNair and the sisters Margaret and Frances MacDonald, whose work was in sympathy with his, fusing the organic forms of nature with a linear, symbolic, Art Nouveau style. Nicknamed **"The Spook School"**, the four created a new artistic language, using extended vertical design, stylized abstract organic forms and muted colours, reflecting their interest in Japanese design and the work of Whistler and Beardsley. However, it was **architecture** that truly challenged Mackintosh.

His big break came in 1896, when he won the competition to design a new home for the **Glasgow School of Art** (see p.791). This is his most famous work, but a number of smaller buildings document the development of his style. In the 1890s Glasgow went wild for tearooms, and Miss Cranston, who dominated the Glasgow teashop scene and ran the most elegant establishments, gave Mackintosh great freedom of design. In 1896 he started to plan the interiors for her growing business and, over the next twenty years, designed articles from teaspoons to furniture and, finally, as in the case of the **Willow Tea Rooms** (see p.791), the structure itself.

Despite his success, the spectre of limited budgets was to haunt Mackintosh. These constraints didn't manage to dull his creativity, though his forceful personality and originality did not endear him to construction workers: he would frequently change his mind or add details at the last minute, often over-stretching budgets. This lost him the support of local builders and architects and prompted him to move to Suffolk in 1914 to escape the "philistines" of Glasgow. World War I curtailed building projects and effectively ended Mackintosh's career; from 1923 he lived in the south of France where he gave up architectural work in favour of painting.

MACKINTOSH SIGHTS

The one-day **Mackintosh Trail Ticket** pass (£16) includes entry to twelve principal Mackintosh buildings as well as unlimited Underground and bus travel. It can be bought from the tourist information, from any of the attractions on the trail or from the Charles Rennie Mackintosh Society (Ⓦ crmsociety.com).

House for an Art Lover Bellahouston Park ☏ 0141 353 4770, Ⓦ www.houseforanartlover.co.uk. The building which arguably displays Mackintosh at his most flamboyant was one he never saw built, constructed in Bellahouston Park in 1996, 95 years after plans for it were submitted to a German architectural competition. Opening hours vary; call for details.

The Lighthouse Mitchell Lane, off Argyle St. One of Mackintosh's earliest commissions: a new building to house the Glasgow *Herald* constructed in 1894. A massive tower rises up from the corner, giving the building its popular name.

Queens Cross Church Junction of Garscube and Maryhill roads in the northwest of the city ☏ 0141 946 6600, Ⓦ mackintoshchurch.com. Mackintosh designed few religious buildings: this church of 1896 is the only completed example standing. Hallmarks include a sturdy box-shaped tower and an asymmetrical exterior with complex heart-shaped floral motifs in the large chancel window. April–Sept Mon–Fri 10am–5pm; Oct–Nov Mon–Fri 10am–4pm; Dec Mon, Wed & Fri 10am–4pm; £4.

Scotland Street School Just south of the river opposite Shields Road underground. Dating from 1904, this is Mackintosh's most symmetrical work, with a whimsical nod to history in the Scots Baronial conical tower roofs and sandstone building material. Mon–Thurs & Sat 10am–5pm, Fri & Sun 11am–5pm. Free.

building largely survived the fire, much of the precious detail – and the library – is having to be reconstructed.

Tenement House

145 Buccleuch St • March–Oct daily 1–5pm • £6; NTS • ☎ 0844 493 2197 • Cowcaddens underground

On the first floor of a typical tenement block still inhabited today, the fascinating **Tenement House** holds the perfectly preserved home of one Agnes Toward, who moved here with her mother in 1911, changing nothing and throwing very little out until she was hospitalized in 1965. The flat gives every impression of still being lived in, with a cluttered hearth and range, kitchen utensils, recessed beds, framed religious tracts and sewing machine all untouched.

The East End

East of Glasgow Cross, down Gallowgate beyond the train lines, lies the **East End**, the district that perhaps most closely corresponds to the old perception of Glasgow. Hemmed in by Glasgow Green to the south and the old university to the west, this densely-packed industrial area essentially created the city's wealth. Timely, isolated pubs, tatty shops and cafés sit amid the dereliction, in sharp contrast to the gloss of the Merchant City just a few blocks west. You're definitely off the tourist trail here, though it's not as threatening as it may feel. Between London Road and the River Clyde are the wide and tree-lined spaces of **Glasgow Green**. Reputedly Britain's oldest public park, the Green has been common land since at least 1178, and has been a popular spot for Sunday afternoon strolls for centuries.

People's Palace

Glasgow Green • Mon–Thurs & Sat 10am–5pm, Fri & Sun 11am–5pm • Free • ☎ 0141 276 0788, Ⓦ glasgowlife.org.uk

A squat, red sandstone Victorian structure, built as a museum back in 1898, **People's Palace** offers a wonderfully haphazard evocation of the city's history. Many displays are designed to bring back a warm glow of nostalgia, and it's all refreshingly unpretentious, with visitors almost always outnumbered by Glaswegian families.

Glasgow Cathedral

Castle St • April–Sept Mon–Sat 9.30am–5.30pm, Sun 1–5pm; Oct–March Mon–Sat 9.30am–4.30pm, Sun 1–4.30pm • Free • ☎ 0141 552 8198, Ⓦ glasgowcathedral.org.uk • Buchanan Street underground

Built in 1136, destroyed in 1192 and rebuilt soon after, stumpy-spired **Glasgow Cathedral** was not completed until the late fifteenth century. Dedicated to the city's patron saint and reputed founder, St Mungo, the cathedral is effectively on two levels,

---

GLASGOW TENEMENTS

Originally conceived as a convenient way to house the influx of workers in the late 1800s, the **Glasgow tenement** design became more refined as the wealthy middle classes began to realize its potential. Mainly constructed between 1860 and 1910, these tenements, decked out with bay windows, turrets and domes, were home to the vast majority of Glaswegians for much of the twentieth century, and developed a culture and vocabulary all of their own: the "hurley", for example, was the bed on castors which was kept below the box bed in an alcove of the kitchen; a "single end" tenement comprised just one room; and the "dunny" was the secluded bottom end of the "close" (entrance way), the perfect spot for games of hide and seek as well as romantic and nefarious encounters.

19

the crypt being part of the lower church. On entering, you arrive in the impressively lofty nave of the **upper church**, with the lower church entirely hidden from view. Beyond the nave, the **choir** is concealed by the curtained stone pulpit, making the interior feel a great deal smaller than might be expected from outside. In the choir's northeastern corner, a small door leads into the gloomy **sacristy**, in which Glasgow University was first founded over five hundred years ago. Two sets of steps from the nave lead down into the **lower church**, where you'll find the dark and musty **chapel** surrounding the tomb of St Mungo. The saint's relics were removed in the late Middle Ages, although the tomb still forms the centrepiece. The chapel itself is one of the most glorious examples of medieval architecture in Scotland, best seen in the delicate fan vaulting rising up from the thicket of cool stone columns.

The Necropolis

Behind the Cathedral • ⓦ glasgownecropolis.org • Buchanan Street underground

19

Inspired by the Père Lachaise cemetery in Paris, the atmospheric **Necropolis** is a grassy mound covered in a fantastic assortment of crumbling and tumbling gravestones, ornate urns, gloomy catacombs and Neoclassical temples. Paths lead through the rows of eroding, neglected graves and from the summit, next to the column topped with an indignant John Knox, there are superb **views** of the city and its trademark mix of grit and grace.

The West End

The urbane **West End** seems a world away from Glasgow's industrial image and the bustle of the centre. In the 1800s, wealthy merchants established huge estates here away from the soot and grime of city life, and in 1870 the ancient university was moved from its cramped home near the cathedral to a spacious new site overlooking the River Kelvin. Elegant housing swiftly followed, the Kelvingrove Art Gallery and Museum was built to house the 1888 International Exhibition and, in 1896, the Glasgow District Subway – today's underground – started its circuitous shuffle from here to the city centre.

The hub of life hereabouts is **Byres Road**, running between Great Western Road and Dumbarton Road past Hillhead underground station. Shops, restaurants, cafés, some enticing pubs and hordes of students give the area a sense of style and vitality, while glowing red-sandstone tenements and graceful terraces provide a suitably upmarket backdrop.

The main sights straddle the banks of the cleaned-up River Kelvin, which meanders through the gracious acres of the **Botanic Gardens** and the slopes, trees and statues of **Kelvingrove Park**. Overlooked by the Gothic towers and turrets of **Glasgow University**, Kelvingrove Park is home to the pride of Glasgow's civic collection of art and artefacts, **Kelvingrove Art Gallery and Museum**, off Argyle Street.

Kelvingrove Art Gallery and Museum

Argyle St • Mon–Thurs & Sat 10am–5pm, Fri & Sun 11am–5pm • Free • ⓣ 0141 276 9599, ⓦ glasgowlife.org.uk • Kelvin Hall underground

Founded on donations from the city's Victorian industrialists and opened at an international fair held in 1901, the huge, red sandstone fantasy castle of **Kelvingrove Art Gallery and Museum** is a brash statement of Glasgow's nineteenth-century self-confidence. Intricate and ambitious both in its riotous exterior detailing and within, Kelvingrove offers an impressive and inviting setting for its exhibits. The wide – and sometimes bizarre – range of objects on show, from a World War II Spitfire suspended from the roof of the West Court to suits of armour, ancient Egyptian relics

THE GLASGOW BOYS AND THE COLOURISTS

In the 1870s a group of Glasgow-based painters formed a loose association that was to imbue Scottish art with a contemporary European flavour far ahead of the rest of Britain. Dominated by five men – Guthrie, Lavery, Henry, Hornel and Crawhall – "**The Glasgow Boys**" came from very different backgrounds, but all rejected the eighteenth-century conservatism which spawned little other than sentimental, anecdotal renditions of Scottish history peopled by "poor but happy" families.

Sir James Guthrie, taking inspiration from the *plein air* painting of the Impressionists, spent his summers in the countryside, observing and painting everyday life. Instead of happy peasants, his work shows individuals staring out of the canvas, detached and unrepentant, painted with rich tones but without undue attention to detail or the play of light. Typical of his finest work during the 1880s, *A Highland Funeral* (in the Kelvingrove collection; see opposite) was hugely influential for the rest of the group, who found inspiration in its restrained emotional content, colour and unaffected realism. Seeing it persuaded **Sir John Lavery**, then studying in France, to return to Glasgow. Lavery was eventually to become an internationally popular society portraitist, his subtle use of paint revealing his debt to Whistler, but his earlier work, depicting the middle class at play, is filled with light and motion.

An interest in colour and decoration united the work of friends **George Henry** and **E.A. Hornel**. The predominance of pattern, colour and design in Henry's *Galloway Landscape*, for example, is remarkable, while their joint work *The Druids* (both part of the Kelvingrove collection, see opposite), in thickly-applied impasto, is full of Celtic symbolism. In 1893 both artists set off for Japan, funded by Alexander Reid and later William Burrell, where their work used vibrant tones and texture for expressive effect and took Scottish painting to the forefront of European trends.

Newcastle-born **Joseph Crawhall** was a reserved and quiet individual who combined superb draughtsmanship and simplicity of line with a photographic memory to create watercolours of an outstanding naturalism and originality. Again, William Burrell was an important patron, and a number of Crawhall's works reside at the Burrell Collection (see p.798).

The Glasgow Boys school reached its height by 1900 and did not outlast World War I, but the influence of their work cannot be underestimated, shaking the foundations of the artistic elite and inspiring the next generation of Edinburgh painters, who became known as the "**Colourists**". Samuel John Peploe, John Duncan Fergusson, George Leslie Hunter and Francis Cadell shared an understanding that the manipulation of colour was the heart and soul of a good painting. All experienced and took inspiration from the avant-garde of late nineteenth-century Paris as well as the landscapes of southern France. **J.D. Fergusson**, in particular, immersed himself in the bohemian, progressive Parisian scene, rubbing shoulders with writers and artists such as Picasso. Some of his most dynamic work, which can be seen in the Fergusson Gallery in Perth (see p.831), displays elements of Cubism, yet is still clearly in touch with the Celtic imagery of Henry, Hornel and, indeed, Charles Rennie Mackintosh. The work of the Scottish Colourists has become highly fashionable and valuable, with galleries and civic collections throughout the country featuring their work prominently.

19

and priceless paintings by Rembrandt, Whistler and Raeburn, form the basis of an undeniably rich and deliberately varied civic collection.

Most visitors will be drawn to the **paintings**, most famous of which is Salvador Dalí's stunning *St John of the Cross*. You can also acquaint yourself with significant **Scottish art** including works by the Glasgow Boys and the Scottish Colourists (see box above). There's a special section of paintings, furniture and murals devoted to Charles Rennie Mackintosh and the "**Glasgow Style**" he and his contemporaries inspired.

Glasgow University

University Visitor Centre & Shop Oct–May Mon–Sat 9.30am–5pm, June–Sept Mon–Sat 9.30am–5pm, Sun 11am–3pm **Guided tours** From the Visitor Centre, bookings advised • Thurs–Sun 2pm • £10 • ☎ 0141 330 5360, ⓦ src.gla.ac.uk/tours • Kelvin Hall/Hillhead underground

Dominating the West End skyline, the gloomy turreted tower of **Glasgow University**, designed by Sir George Gilbert Scott in the mid-nineteenth century, overlooks the glades edging the River Kelvin. Access to the main buildings and museums is from University Avenue, running east form Byres Road.

The Hunterian Museum and Art Gallery

University Ave • Tues–Sat 10am–5pm, Sun 11am–4pm • Free • ☎ 0141 330 4221, Ⓦ gla.ac.uk/hunterian

Beside Glasgow University's Visitor Centre is the **Hunterian Museum**, Scotland's oldest public museum, dating back to 1807. The collection was donated to the university by ex-student William Hunter, a pathologist and anatomist whose eclectic tastes form the basis of a diverting zoological and archeological jaunt. Opposite, across University Avenue, is Hunter's more frequently visited bequest, the **Hunterian Art Gallery**, best known for its wonderful works by James Abbott McNeill Whistler: only Washington, DC, has a larger collection. The gallery's other major collection is of nineteenth- and twentieth-century Scottish art, including the quasi-Impressionist Scottish landscapes of William McTaggart, a forerunner of the Glasgow Boys movement, itself represented here by Guthrie and Hornel. Finally, the monumental dancing figures of J.D. Fergusson's *Les Eus* preside over a small collection of work by the Scottish Colourists.

Mackintosh House

Hillhead St • Tues–Sat 10am–5pm, Sun 11am–4pm • Free, £5 for special exhibitions • ☎ 0141 330 4221, Ⓦ gla.ac.uk/hunterian

A side gallery off the Hunterian Art Gallery leads to the **Mackintosh House**, a re-creation of the interior of the now-demolished Glasgow home of Margaret MacDonald and Charles Rennie Mackintosh. Its exquisitely cool interior contains more than sixty pieces of Mackintosh furniture on three floors. In addition, a permanent gallery shows a selection of his two-dimensional work, from watercolours to architectural drawings.

The Botanic Gardens

730 Great Western Rd • **Botanic Gardens** Daily 7am–dusk **Kibble Palace** Daily: summer 10am–6pm; winter 10am–4.15pm • Free • ☎ 0141 276 1614, Ⓦ glasgowbotanicgardens.com • Hillhead underground

At the northern, top end of Byres Road, where it meets the Great Western Road, is the main entrance to the **Botanic Gardens**. The best-known glasshouse here, the hulking, domed **Kibble Palace**, houses lush ferns, exotic blooms and swaying palms from around the world. Nearby, in the **Main Range Glasshouse**, stunning orchids, cacti, ferns and tropical fruit luxuriate in the humidity. In addition to the area around the main glasshouses, there are some beautifully remote paths in the gardens that weave along the closely wooded banks of the deep-set River Kelvin, linking up with the walkway running alongside the river all the way down to Dumbarton Road, near its confluence with the Clyde.

Clydeside

"The **Clyde** made Glasgow and Glasgow made the Clyde" runs an old saying, full of sentimentality for the days when the river was the world's premier shipbuilding centre, and when its industry lent an innovation and confidence that made Glasgow a major city of the British Empire. Despite the hardships heavy industry brought, every Glaswegian would follow the progress of the skeleton ships under construction in the riverside yards, cheering them on their way down the Clyde as they were launched. The last of the great liners to be built on **Clydeside** was the *QE2* in 1967. Such events are hard to visualize today: shipbuilding is restricted to a couple of barely viable yards. However, the river is once again becoming a focus of attention, with striking new buildings including the titanium-clad **Armadillo** concert hall, **Glasgow Science Centre** and the Zaha Hadid-designed **Riverside Museum**.

THE WAVERLEY

One of Glasgow's best-loved treasures is the **Waverley** (☎ 0845 130 4647, ⓦ waverleyexcursions .co.uk), the last seagoing paddle steamer in the world, which spends the summer cruising "doon the watter" to various ports on the Firth of Clyde and the Ayrshire coast from its base at Glasgow Science Centre. Built on Clydeside in 1947, she's an elegant vessel to look at, not least when she's thrashing away at full steam with the hills of Argyll or Arran in the background. Contact for sailing times and itinerary.

The Glasgow Science Centre

50 Pacific Quay • April–Oct daily 10am–6pm; Nov–March Wed–Fri 10am–3pm, Sat & Sun 10am–5pm • £10.50 • ☎ 0141 420 5000, ⓦ glasgowsciencecentre.org • Govan underground

On the south bank of the Clyde, linked to the SECC by pedestrian Bell's Bridge, are the three space-age, titanium-clad constructions which make up the **Glasgow Science Centre**. Of the three buildings, the largest is the curvaceous, wedge-shaped **Science Mall**. Behind the vast glass wall facing the river, four floors of interactive exhibits range from lift-your-own-weight pulleys to thermograms. The centre covers almost every aspect of science, from simple optical illusions to cutting-edge computer technology, including a section on moral and environmental issues – all good fun, although weekends and school holidays are a scrum. Meanwhile, a bubble-like **IMAX theatre** shows science- and nature-based documentaries, while the 416ft-high **Glasgow Tower** has a viewing tower offering panoramic vistas of central Glasgow.

Riverside Museum

100 Pointhouse Place • Mon–Thurs & Sat 10am–5pm, Fri & Sun 11am–5pm • Free; Tall Ship £5 • ☎ 0141 287 2720, ⓦ glasgowlife.org.uk • Govan underground

Just west of the Science Centre, on the other side of the river, the magnificent new **Riverside Museum** – Scotland's Museum of Transport and Travel – houses artefacts from Glasgow's old transport museum, and a lot more besides. The wave-like titanium-clad building by Zaha Hadid is an attraction in its own right, its cathedral-like interior home to a huge, dramatically displayed collection of trains, boats, trams, cars and ship models. Interactive exhibits provide engaging background on the city's social fabric, with walk-through streets incorporating real interiors from Glasgow shops and cafés.

The Southside

The section of Glasgow south of the Clyde is generally described as the **Southside**, though within this area there are a number of recognizable districts, including the notoriously deprived **Gorbals** and Govan, which are sprinkled with new developments but still derelict and tatty in many parts. There's little reason to venture here unless you're making your way to the Clydeside museums (see above) and the famously innovative Citizens' Theatre (see p.803). Further south, inner-city decay fades into altogether gentler and more salubrious suburbs, including Queen's Park, home to Scotland's national football stadium **Hampden Park**, Pollokshaws and the rural landscape of Pollok Park, which contains one of Glasgow's major museums, the **Burrell Collection**.

Scottish Football Museum

Hampden Park • Mon–Sat 10am–5pm, Sun 11am–5pm • £7 • ☎ 0141 616 6139, ⓦ scottishfootballmuseum.org.uk • Trains from Central station to Mount Florida; every 10min; 10min

Two and a half miles south of the city centre, just west of the tree-filled Queen's Park, the floodlights and giant stands of Scotland's national football stadium, **Hampden Park**,

19

THE OLD FIRM

Football, or *fitba'* as it's pronounced locally, is one of Glasgow's great passions – and one of its great blights. While the city can claim to be one of Europe's premier footballing centres, it's known above all for one of the most bitter rivalries in any sport, that between **Celtic** and **Rangers**. Two of the largest clubs in Britain, with weekly crowds regularly topping 60,000, the Old Firm, as they're collectively known, have dominated Scottish football for a century; in the last twenty years they've lavished vast sums of money on foreign talent in an often frantic effort both to outdo each other and to stay in touch with the standards of the top English and European teams.

The roots of Celtic, who play at Celtic Park in the eastern district of Parkhead (☎0871 226 1888, ⓦcelticfc.net), lie in the city's immigrant Irish and **Catholic** population, while Rangers, based at Ibrox Park in Govan on the Southside (☎0871 702 1972, ⓦrangers.co.uk), have traditionally drawn support from local **Protestants**: as a result, sporting rivalries have been enmeshed in a sectarian divide, and although Catholics do play for Rangers, and Protestants for Celtic, sections of supporters of both clubs seem intent on perpetuating the feud. While large-scale violence on the terraces and streets has not been seen for some time – thanks in large measure to canny policing – Old Firm matches often seethe with bitter passions, and sectarian-related assaults do still occur in parts of the city.

However, there is a less intense side to the game, found not just in the fun-loving "Tartan Army" which follows the (often rollercoaster) fortunes of the Scottish national team, but also in Glasgow's smaller clubs, who actively distance themselves from the distasteful aspects of the Old Firm and plod along with home-grown talent in the lower reaches of the Scottish league. All-important reminders that it is, after all, only a game.

---

loom over the surrounding suburban tenements and terraces. It's home to the engaging **Scottish Football Museum**, with memorabilia, video clips and displays covering almost every aspect of the game. On view is the Scottish Cup, the world's oldest football trophy and a re-creation of the old changing room at Hampden, as well as a bizarre life-sized reconstruction of the most famous goal in Scottish footballing history, scored during the 1978 World Cup in Argentina.

The Burrell Collection

Pollok Park, 6 miles southwest of the city centre • Mon–Thurs & Sat 10am–5pm, Fri & Sun 11am–5pm • Free • ☎ 0141 287 2550, ⓦ glasgowlife.org.uk • From the centre take a train to Pollokshaws West station (not to be confused with Pollokshields West), or bus #45, #47, #48 or #57 to Pollokshaws Road; alternatively, a taxi costs around £10. A free minibus (every 30min 10am–4.30pm) runs from the park gates to the collection

The outstanding **Burrell Collection**, the lifetime collection of shipping magnate Sir William Burrell (1861–1958), is, for some, the principal reason for visiting Glasgow. Sir William's only real criterion for buying a piece was whether he liked it or not, enabling him to buy many unfashionable works that cost comparatively little but subsequently proved their worth.

The simplicity and clean lines of the Burrell building are superb, with large picture windows giving sweeping views over woodland and serving as a tranquil backdrop to the objects inside. An airy covered **courtyard** includes the **Warwick Vase**, a huge bowl containing fragments of a second-century AD vase from Emperor Hadrian's villa in Tivoli. On three sides of the courtyard, a trio of dark and sombre panelled rooms have been re-erected in faithful detail from the Burrells' Hutton Castle home, their tapestries, antique furniture and fireplaces displaying the same eclectic taste as the rest of the museum.

Elsewhere on the ground floor, Greek, Roman and earlier artefacts include an exquisite mosaic Roman cockerel from the first century BC and a 4000-year-old Mesopotamian lion's head. Nearby, also illuminated by enormous windows, the excellent **Oriental Art** collection forms nearly a quarter of the whole display, ranging from Neolithic jades through bronze vessels and Tang funerary horses to cloisonné. Burrell considered his **medieval and post-medieval European art**, which encompasses silverware, glass, textiles and sculpture, to be the most valuable part of his collection: these are ranged across a maze of small galleries.

Upstairs, the cramped and comparatively gloomy **mezzanine** is probably the least satisfactory section of the gallery, not the best setting for its sparkling array of paintings by artists that include Degas, Manet, Cézanne and Boudin.

ARRIVAL AND DEPARTURE   GLASGOW

By plane Glasgow International Airport (☎0870 040 0008, ⓦglasgowairport.com) is at Abbotsinch, 8 miles southwest of the city. From here, the 24-hour Glasgow Shuttle (£6) runs from bus stop 1 into the central Buchanan Street bus station (every 10min during the day; 10min). Airport taxis charge around £20. Glasgow's second airport, Prestwick (☎0871 223 0700, ⓦglasgowprestwick.com), lies 30 miles south of Glasgow, near Ayr. The simplest way to get from here to Glasgow is by train to Central station (Mon–Sat every 30min, Sun hourly; 45min): there's a station right by the terminal (alight at the airport, not Prestwick Town).

Destinations from Glasgow International Barra (2 daily; 1hr 10min); Belfast (Mon–Fri 7 daily, Sat & Sun 3 daily; 45min); Benbecula (Mon–Sat 2 daily, Sun 1 daily; 1hr); Campbeltown (Mon–Fri 2 daily; 40min); Dublin (3 daily; 55min); Islay (Mon–Fri 2 daily, Sat 1 daily; 40min); Kirkwall (1 daily; 1hr 20min); London City (Mon–Fri 4 daily, Sun 1 daily; 1hr 35min); London Gatwick (Mon–Fri 11 daily, Sat & Sun 4 daily; 1hr 30min); London Heathrow (Mon–Fri 18 daily, Sat & Sun 10 daily; 1hr 20min); London Luton (Mon–Fri 5 daily, Sat 2 daily, Sun 3 daily; 1hr 15min); London Stansted (Mon–Fri 5 daily, Sat 3 daily, Sun 4 daily; 1hr 20min); Shetland (Mon–Fri 2 daily, Sat & Sun 1 daily; 1hr 30min); Stornoway (Mon–Fri 4 daily, Sat & Sun 2 daily; 1hr 10min); Tiree (Mon–Sat 1 daily; 50min).
Destinations from Glasgow Prestwick London Stansted (4 daily; 1hr 10min).

By train Nearly all trains from England come into Central station, which sits over Argyle St, one of the city's main

shopping thoroughfares. Bus #398 from the front entrance on Gordon St (every 10min) shuttles to Queen Street station, at the corner of George Square, terminus for trains serving Edinburgh and the north. The walk between the two takes about 10min.

Destinations from Glasgow Central Ardrossan for Arran ferry (every 30min; 45min); Ayr (every 30min; 50min); East Kilbride (every 30min; 30min); Gourock (every 30min; 50min); Greenock (every 30min; 40min); Lanark (every 30min; 50min); London (hourly; 5–6hr); Paisley (every 10min; 10min); Queen's Park (every 15min; 6min); Stranraer (4 daily; 2hr 15min); Wemyss Bay (every 30min; 50min).

Destinations from Glasgow Queen Street Aberdeen (hourly; 2hr 30min); Balloch (every 30min; 45min); Dumbarton (every 20min; 30min); Dundee (hourly; 1hr 20min); Edinburgh (every 15min; 50min); Fort William (1–3 daily; 3hr 40min); Helensburgh (every 30min; 45min); Inverness (3 daily; 3hr 25min); Milngavie (every 30min; 25min); Oban (1–3 daily; 3hr); Perth (hourly; 1hr); Stirling (hourly; 30min).

By bus Buchanan Street bus station is the arrival point for regional and intercity coaches.

Destinations Aberdeen (hourly; 3hr 15min); Campbeltown (3 daily; 4–5hr); Dundee (every 30min; 1hr 50min); Edinburgh (every 15min; 1hr 10min); Fort William (4 daily; 3hr); Glen Coe (4 daily; 2hr 30min); Inverness (1 direct daily; 4–5hr); Kyle of Lochalsh (3 daily; 5–6hr); Loch Lomond (hourly; 45min); London (5 daily; 8–9hr); Oban (3 daily; 2hr 50min); Perth (hourly; 1hr 35min); Portree (3 daily; 6–7hr); Stirling (hourly; 45min).

INFORMATION

Tourist information 11 George Square (April & May Mon–Sat 9am–6pm, Sun 10am–6pm; June & Sept Mon–Sat 10am–7pm, Sun 10am–6pm; July & Aug Mon–Sat 9am–8pm, Sun 10am–6pm; Oct–March Mon–Sat 9am–6pm; ☎0141 204 4400, ⓦpeoplemakeglasgow.com); there's another in Glasgow Airport's international arrivals hall

(May–Sept daily 7.30am–5pm; Oct–April Mon–Sat 7.30am–5pm, Sun 8am–5pm; ☎0141 848 4440).
Listings information The best resource for finding out what's on in the city is the comprehensive, lively and informative *The List* magazine (ⓦlist.co.uk), published fortnightly.

GETTING AROUND

Although it can be tough negotiating Glasgow's steep hills, walking is the best way to explore any one part of the city. However, as the main sights are scattered – the West End, for example, is a good 30min walk from the centre – you'll probably need to use the comprehensive public transport system. If you're travelling beyond the city centre or the West End, or to the main sights on the Southside, you may need to use the bus and train networks. The **Travel Centre** on St Enoch's Square (Mon–Sat 6.30am–5.30pm, Sun 10am–6pm) has full details on transport in and around the city.

By underground The best way to get between the city centre and the West End is to use the underground (Mon–Sat 6.30am–11pm, Sun 10am–6.30pm), whose stations are marked with a large orange U.

By bus The array of different bus companies and the routes they take is perplexing even to locals; pick up individual timetables at the Travel Centre.

By train The suburban train network is swift and convenient. Suburbs south of the Clyde are connected to Central station, either at the mainline station or the subterranean low-level station. The trains are an excellent way to link to points west and northwest of Glasgow, including Milngavie (for the start of the West Highland Way), Balloch (for Loch Lomond) and Helensburgh.

By bike West End Cycles, 16 Chancellor St (☎0141 357 1344, ⓦgwcycles.co.uk) has a good selection and is located close to the start of the Glasgow to Loch Lomond route, one of a number of cycle routes that radiate out from the city.

By taxi Glasgow Taxi Ltd (☎0141 429 7070); Glasgow Private Hire (☎0141 774 3000).

ACCOMMODATION

There's a good range of accommodation in Glasgow, from a large, well-run SYHA hostel through to some fashionable (and not overpriced) designer hotels in the centre. In general, **prices** are significantly lower than in Edinburgh, and given that many hotels are business-oriented, you can often negotiate good deals at weekends.

19

CITY CENTRE AND THE MERCHANT CITY

Babbity Bowster 16–18 Blackfriars St, off High St ☎0141 552 5055, ⓦbabbitybowster.com; map p.790. Best known as a pub (see p.802), *Babbity Bowster* also features six plain, serviceable rooms in a great Merchant City location. No breakfast. **£65**

★ **The Brunswick** 106 Brunswick St ☎0141 552 0001, ⓦbrunswickhotel.co.uk; map p.790. Small, independent designer hotel in the heart of the Merchant City; fashionable but good value with minimalist furniture and a smart bar and restaurant. **£60**

Euro Hostel 318 Clyde St ☎08455 399956, ⓦeuro-hostels.co.uk; map p.790. Glasgow isn't short of bed space, thanks to this bright pink, liveried, seven-storey hostel smack in the centre. Its 360 beds are all bunks, but they're in smart en-suite rooms sleeping two, four, six or more – some have great views. Continental breakfast included. **£10**

Malmaison 278 West George St ☎0141 572 1000, ⓦmalmaison.com; map p.790. Glasgow's version of the sleek, chic mini-chain, an austere Grecian-temple frontage masking a superbly comfortable designer hotel. Have a drink at their *Cosmo* bar. **£119**

Mark's Hotel 110 Bath St ☎0141 353 0800, ⓦmarkshotels.com; map p.790. An angular, glass-fronted central hotel, with rooftop views from the upper floors, 103 smartly appointed rooms and a chic bar and restaurant. Double, triple and family rooms available. **£70**

University of Strathclyde ☎0141 553 4148, ⓦstrath.ac.uk/conferencingandevents; map p.790. Various sites, most of which are around the cathedral. B&B in single rooms is available near the main campus on Cathedral St. June to mid-Sept. Singles **£22.50**; flats **£60**

WEST END

★ **Alamo Guesthouse** 46 Gray St ☎0141 339 2395, ⓦalamoguesthouse.com; map pp.788–789. Good-value, family-run boarding house next to Kelvingrove Park. The small but comfortable rooms are decorated in soft colours and have antique furnishings; some even feature chandeliers. **£52**

Amadeus Guesthouse 441 North Woodside Rd ☎0141 339 8257, ⓦamadeusguesthouse.co.uk; map pp.788–789. Handily located near Great Western Rd, but on a quiet street opposite the River Kelvin, this place offers stylish en-suite rooms in a welcoming Victorian townhouse. **£60**

★ **Hotel du Vin at One Devonshire Gardens** 1 Devonshire Gardens, Great Western Rd ☎0141 339 2001, ⓦhotelduvin.com; map pp.788–789. Glasgow's most exclusive and exquisite small hotel, a 10min walk up the Great Western Rd from the Botanic Gardens. Rooms are grandly furnished in rich colours, some with four posters and jacuzzi. **£145**

Kirklee 11 Kensington Gate ☎0141 334 5555, ⓦkirkleehotel.co.uk; map pp.788–789. Characterful West End B&B in an extravagant red-sandstone Edwardian townhouse, with antique furniture and walls crammed with paintings and etchings. A panelled hallway and parquet floors add to the atmosphere. **£85**

★ **Queensgate Apartments** ☎07796 651451, ⓦqueensgateapartments.com; map pp.788–789. A choice of attractive and cosy flats in traditional tenement buildings. Three apartments are within walking distance of the West End's vibrant Byres Road and all have TVs, wi-fi and other mod cons. A good option for families or groups. Per week **£400**

SYHA hostel 7–8 Park Terrace ☎0141 332 3004, ⓦsyha.org.uk; map pp.788–789. This popular, well-equipped hostel occupies a wonderful townhouse in one of the West End's grandest terraces. It's a 10min walk south of Kelvinbridge underground station; bus #44 from the city centre leaves you with a short stroll west up Woodlands Rd. Dorms **£15**; doubles **£58**

University of Glasgow ☎0141 330 4116, ⓦcvso.co.uk; map pp.788–789. Low-priced and very varied self-catering rooms and flats which are mostly in the West End. June to mid-Sept. Per person **£20**

EATING

Glasgow's **restaurant scene** is reasonably dynamic, with new places replacing old (and sometimes not very old) every year. Most places to eat are concentrated in the commercial hub and Merchant City district of the city centre, as well as in the trendy West End. Modern Scottish cuisine, combining excellent fresh local ingredients with Mediterranean-style cooking techniques, is on the menus of the city's best restaurants. Glasgwegians have a particular fondness for Indian and Chinese food, too.

CITY CENTRE AND THE MERCHANT CITY

CAFÉS AND DINERS

★**The 13th Note Café** 50–60 King St ☎0141 553 1638, ⓦ13thnote.co.uk; map p.790. Inexpensive veggie and vegan food (from £6), with Greek and other Mediterranean influences, in a hip bar and experimental music venue on arty King St. Daily noon–midnight.

★**Café Gandolfi and Bar Gandolfi** 64 Albion St ☎0141 552 6813, ⓦcafegandolfi.com; map p.790. Gandolfi was one of the first to test the waters in the revived Merchant City in the 1980s and today it's a landmark. Designed with distinctive wooden furniture, the café serves up Scottish staples (including great black pudding), soups, salads, fish and continental cuisine (mains £11–19). The food's equally good in the contemporary bar upstairs. Daily 9am–11.30pm.

★**Café Source** 1 St Andrew's Square ☎0141 548 6020, ⓦstandrewsinthesquare.com; map pp.788–789. In the basement of St Andrew's, an eighteenth-century church patterned on London's St Martin in the Fields, and now a folk music and Scottish dance centre. The café serves up inexpensive Scottish favourites featuring local produce, with everything from haggis to braised shin of beef (from £8). Frequent live jam sessions and a monthly jazz supper club. Mon–Thurs & Sun 10am–11pm, Fri & Sat 10am–midnight.

★**Trans-Europe Café** 25 Parnie St ☎0141 552 7999, ⓦtranseuropecafe.co.uk; map p.790. A fun, railway-style diner which takes culinary inspiration from various European capitals and dishes up excellent soup and gourmet sandwiches at reasonable prices (from £6). Mon–Thurs & Sun 10am–5pm Fri & Sat 10am–5pm & 6.30–10pm.

Where the Monkey Sleeps 182 West Regent St ☎0141 226 3406, ⓦmonkeysleeps.com; map p.790. Owned by graduates of the nearby Glasgow School of Art who acquired their barista skills between classes, this hip, home-grown café features freshly-prepared sandwiches and salads (£3–5), and the espresso is superb. Mon–Fri 7am–3pm.

RESTAURANTS

Brian Maule at Le Chardon d'Or 176 West Regent St ☎0141 248 3801, ⓦbrianmaule.com; map p.790. Owner-chef Maule, who worked with the Roux brothers at Le Gavroche restaurant in London, turns out fancy yet unpretentious French-influenced food along the lines of grilled sea bass with fennel and broad beans in a Pernod cream. Mains from £25. Mon–Fri noon–2.30pm & 5–10pm, Sat noon–3pm & 5–11pm.

City Merchant 97 Candleriggs ☎0141 553 1577, ⓦcitymerchant.co.uk; map p.790. A popular brasserie that blazed the Merchant City trail. Fresh Scottish produce from Ayrshire lamb to the house speciality: west coast seafood. Mains from £18. Mon–Sat noon–10.30pm, Sun 4.30–9.30pm.

★**Dakhin** 89 Candleriggs ☎0141 553 2585, ⓦdakhin.com; map p.790. Owned by the same people as The Dhabba (see below), this first-floor restaurant specializes in reasonably priced South Indian cuisine (from £10 per main). Be sure to try a rice dosa. Mon–Fri noon–2pm & 5–11pm, Sat & Sun 1–11pm.

The Dhabba 44 Candleriggs ☎0141 553 1249, ⓦthedhabba.com; map p.790. Not your typical Glasgow curry house. Prices are higher and portions are smaller, but the menu has some truly interesting options and fresh ingredients that place it steps above most others (mains £9–27). Mon–Fri noon–2pm & 5–11pm, Sat & Sun 1–11pm.

★**Gamba** 225a West George St ☎0141 572 0899, ⓦgamba.co.uk; map p.790. This modern basement restaurant offers one of the best meals in Glasgow. Contemporary continental sophistication prevails, with dishes such as mussel and oyster stew or grilled halibut with scallop cream (£17–25). If you love fish, come here. Mon–Sat noon–2.30pm & 5–10pm, Sun 5–9pm.

Rogano 11 Exchange Place ☎0141 248 4055, ⓦroganoglasgow.com; map p.790. An Art Deco fish restaurant and Glasgow institution since 1935, decked out in the style of the *Queen Mary* ocean liner. Mains cost around £25; *Café Rogano*, in the basement, is cheaper, or just have some oysters at the bar. Daily noon–10.30pm.

WEST END

CAFÉS AND DINERS

★**Kember & Jones** 134 Byres Rd ☎0141 337 3851, ⓦkemberandjones.co.uk; map pp.788–789. This café and deli is a popular spot in the competitive Byres Rd, serving freshly made salads and sandwiches from around £6 along with irresistible cakes and pastries. Mon–Fri 8am–10pm, Sat 9am–10pm, Sun 9am–6pm.

Tchai Ovna 42 Otago Lane ☎0141 357 4524, ⓦtchaiovna.com; map pp.788–789. A low-key bohemian hangout overlooking the Kelvin River, offering

19

savoury vegetarian options (try the red dahl curry at £5.90), cakes, snacks and a selection of teas from around the world. Mon–Sun 11am–11pm.

★**University Café** 87 Byres Rd ☎0141 339 5217; map p.788–789. This institution dates back to the 1910s and has been adored by at least three generations of students and West End residents, with its formica tables in snug booths, glass counters and original architectural features. The favourites are fish'n'chips or mince'n'tatties rounded off with an ice-cream cone – you won't spend more than a tenner. Mon–Thurs 9am–10pm, Fri & Sat 9am–10.30pm, Sun 10am–10pm.

RESTAURANTS

Ashoka Ashton Lane 19 Ashton Lane ☎0141 337 1115, ⓦashokarestaurants.com; map p.788–789. Lively curry house with franchises across the west of Scotland; all offer consistent quality and reasonable prices (two lunchtime courses from £8). Mon–Thurs noon–midnight, Fri & Sat noon–1am, Sun 5pm–midnight.

Chow 98 Byres Rd ☎0141 334 9818, ⓦchowrestaurant .co.uk; map p.788–789. This bijou diner with extra seating upstairs offers excellent-value meals – hot tossed shredded chicken, for example – in a sleek, modern setting. Mains from £9. Mon–Thurs noon–2.15pm & 5–11.30pm, Fri & Sat noon–2.15pm & 5pm–midnight, Sun 4.30–11.30pm.

Mother India 28 Westminster Terrace, off Sauchiehall St ☎0141 221 1663, ⓦmotherindiaglasgow.co.uk; map p.788–789. One of the best Indian restaurants in Glasgow, serving home-cooking with original specials and affordable favourites in laidback surroundings (mains from £8). Mon–Thurs 5.30–10.30pm, Fri noon–11pm, Sat noon–11pm, Sun 1–10pm.

Number Sixteen 16 Byres Rd ☎0141 339 2544, ⓦnumber16.co.uk; map p.788–789. A local favourite, with daily menus of modern, seasonal Scottish cooking using produce from pigeon to sea bream. Mains from £16. Mon–Sat noon–2.30pm & 5.30–10pm, Sun 1–3pm & 5.30–9pm.

★**Stravaigin** 28–30 Gibson St ☎0141 334 2665, ⓦstravaigin.com; map p.788–789. Scottish meat and fish are given an international makeover using a host of unexpected ingredients, offering unusual combinations such as Thai-spiced Aberdeen Angus beef carpaccio or ham and pistachio terrine. Look out for the occasional "wild food" nights. There's exceptional-value food in the street-level bar-café, and adventurous fine dining in the pricier basement restaurant. Café mains from £10; restaurant mains from £13. Mon–Fri 9am–1am, Sat & Sun 11am–1am.

The Ubiquitous Chip 12 Ashton Lane ☎0141 334 5007, ⓦubiquitouschip.co.uk; map p.788–789. Opened in 1971, *The Chip* led the way in headlining upmarket Modern Scottish cuisine. Some say it's living on its reputation, but it's still up there; come for organic salmon with lime and vanilla mash or wood pigeon in a wild mushroom sauce. Two-course menu with appetizer £35, three courses with appetizer £40; the brasserie upstairs has mains from £10. Mon–Sat noon–2.30pm & 5.30–11pm, Sun 12.30–3pm & 6.30–11pm.

DRINKING

Most drinking dens in the **city centre**, the **Merchant City** and the **West End** are places to experience real Glaswegian bonhomie, with a good selection of characterful pubs featuring folk music, as well as more upscale bar/clubs.

CITY CENTRE AND THE MERCHANT CITY

The Arches 253 Argyle St ☎0141 565 1035, ⓦthearches.co.uk; map p.790. The basement bar is a focal point in this contemporary arts centre beneath Central station. Decent pub grub and an arty clientele. Good club nights, too (see opposite). Mon–Sat 11am–midnight.

★**Babbity Bowster** 16–18 Blackfriars St, off High St ☎0141 552 5055, ⓦbabbitybowster.com; map p.790. Lively place with an unforced and kitsch-free Scottish feel that features spontaneous folk sessions at the weekend. Good beer and wine, tasty food and some outdoor seating. Mon–Sat 11am–midnight, Sun 12.30pm–midnight.

Bar 10 10 Mitchell St ☎0141 572 1448, ⓦnavan taverns.com/bar10; map p.790. Across from the Lighthouse, and considered the granddaddy of stylish Glasgow bars. Still popular and suitably chic. Mon–Sat 10am–midnight, Sun noon–midnight.

Corinthian 191 Ingram St ☎0141 552 1101, ⓦthecorinthianclub.co.uk; map p.790. A remarkable renovation of a florid, early Victorian Italianate bank with three bars, a restaurant and a casino: dress smartly. Daily 11am till late.

Horseshoe Bar 17 Drury St ☎0141 248 6368, ⓦthehorseshoebarglasgow.co.uk; map p.790. An original "Gin Palace" and, with the longest continuous bar in the UK, this is reputedly Glasgow's busiest drinking hole, which features karaoke upstairs. A must for pub aficionados. Mon–Sat 10.30am–midnight, Sun 12.30pm–midnight.

Pot Still 154 Hope St ☎0141 333 0980, ⓦthepotstill .co.uk; map p.790. Whisky galore – at least five hundred different single malts are found in this traditional pub, which offers a decent ale selection as well. Daily 11am–midnight.

WEST END

Firebird 1321 Argyle St ☎0141 334 0594, ⓦfire birdglasgow.com; map p.788–789. An airy, modern

19

drinking spot near the Kelvingrove Art Gallery, with a wood-stoked pizza oven producing tasty snacks, plus DJs to keep the pre-clubbing crowd entertained. Mon–Thurs noon–midnight, Fri & Sat noon–1am, Sun noon–midnight.

Lismore Lounge 206 Dumbarton Rd ☎ 0141 576 0103; map p.788–789. Decorated with specially commissioned stained-glass panels depicting the Highland Clearances, this bar is a meeting point for the local Gaels, who come to

chat, relax and enjoy impromptu music sessions. Daily 11am–midnight.

Òran Mór Byres Rd at corner of Great Western Rd ☎ 0141 357 6200, ⓦ oran-mor.co.uk; map p.788–789. An impressive player on Glasgow's nightlife scene, with a big bar, club and performance space auditorium (plus two different dining rooms) all set within a beautifully – and expensively – restored Kelvinside parish church. Mon–Sat 9am–3am, Sun 12.30pm–3am.

NIGHTLIFE AND ENTERTAINMENT

Glasgow is a great place for **contemporary music**, with loads of new bands emerging every year, many of them making the big time, and the city's **clubs** are excellent, with a range of places for every dance taste as well as a small but thriving gay scene. Glasgow is no slouch when it comes to the **performing arts**, either: it's home to Scottish Opera, Scottish Ballet and the Royal Scottish National Orchestra. Most of the larger theatres, multiplexes and concert halls are in the city centre; the West End is home to just one or two venues, while the Southside can boast two theatres noted for cutting-edge drama, the Citizens' and Tramway. For detailed **listings**, check *The List* (ⓦ list.co.uk), or consult Glasgow's *Herald* or *Evening Times* newspapers.

CLUBS

The Arches 253 Argyle St ☎ 0141 565 1000, ⓦ thearches.co.uk; map p.790. In converted railway arches under Central station, the club portion of this huge arts venue offers an eclectic array of music: hard house, trance, techno and funk. One of *DJ* magazine's top 10 clubs in the world. 11pm–3am on club nights.

Sub Club 22 Jamaica St ☎ 0141 248 4600, ⓦ subclub .co.uk; map p.790. Near-legendary venue, home to quality underground house and techno nights, as well as the brilliantly entertaining bi-monthly night mash-up Optimo (Espacio). Tues–Sun 11pm–3am.

The Tunnel 84 Mitchell St ☎ 0141 204 1000, ⓦ tunnelglasgow.co.uk; map p.790. Contemporary and progressive house club with arty decor (have a look at the gents' cascading waterfall walls) and fairly strict dress codes – leave your trainers at home. Wed, Fri & Sat 11pm–3am.

GAY CLUBS AND BARS

Polo Lounge 84 Wilson St, off Glassford St ☎ 0845 659 5905, ⓦ pologlasgow.co.uk; map p.790. Original Victorian decor – marble tiles and open fires – and gentleman's-club atmosphere upstairs, with dark, pounding nightclub downstairs; attracts a mixed gay and gay-friendly crowd. Mon, Tues, Thurs & Sun 11pm–3am, Wed & Fri 10pm–3am, Sat 9pm–3am.

Underground 6a John St ☎ 0141 553 2456, ⓦ underground-glasgow.com; map p.790. This bar is geared more towards the art of conversation than dance, although the (free) jukebox is fantastic; welcomes men and women. Mon–Sat noon–midnight, Sun 12.30pm–midnight.

LIVE MUSIC VENUES

Barrowland 244 Gallowgate ☎ 0141 552 4601,

ⓦ glasgow-barrowland.com; map pp.788–789. Legendary East End ballroom that hosts some of the sweatiest and best gigs you may ever encounter. With room for a couple of thousand, it mostly books bands securely on the rise but still hosts some big-time acts who return to it as their favourite venue in Scotland.

City Halls Candleriggs ☎ 0141 353 8000, ⓦ glasgowconcerthalls.com. This Merchant City performance space, in a renovated old fruit market, is home to the BBC Scottish Symphony and hosts many of the annual Celtic Connections concerts.

Glasgow Royal Concert Hall 2 Sauchiehall St ☎ 0141 353 8000, ⓦ glasgowconcerthalls.com. One of Glasgow's less memorable modern buildings, this is the venue for big-name touring orchestras and the home of the Royal Scottish National Orchestra. It also hosts major rock and R&B stars, and middle-of-the-road music-hall acts.

King Tut's Wah Wah Hut 272a St Vincent St ☎ 0141 221 5279, ⓦ kingtuts.co.uk; map p.790. Famous as the place where Oasis were discovered, and still presenting one of the city's best live music programmes. It's also a good bar, with an excellent jukebox.

O2 Academy 121 Eglinton St ☎ 0870 771 2000, ⓦ glasgow-academy.co.uk; map pp.788–789. With a capacity of 2500, this is the city's principal mid-sized venue. Less atmosphere than the *Barrowland*, but gets reliably big names.

THEATRE

Arches Theatre 253 Argyle St ☎ 0141 565 1000, ⓦ thearches.co.uk. Home to its own avant-garde theatre company, reviving old classics and introducing new talent in a hip subterranean venue.

Citizens' Theatre 119 Gorbals St ☎ 0141 429 0022, ⓦ citz.co.uk. The "Citz" has evolved from its 1960s working-class roots into one of Britain's most respected

19

SHOPPING IN GLASGOW

The main area for spending in the city centre is formed by the Z-shaped and mostly pedestrianized route of **Argyle**, **Buchanan** and **Sauchiehall** streets. Along the way you'll find **Princes Square**, a stylish and imaginative shopping centre hollowed out of the innards of a soft sandstone building. The interior, all recherché Art Deco and ornate ironwork, holds lots of pricey, fashionable shops. Otherwise, make for the **West End** or the **Merchant City**, which have more eccentric and individual offerings. The latter is the place for secondhand and antiquarian **bookshops** as well as quirky vintage and one-off fashion stores on the lanes off Byres Road.

19

and innovative contemporary theatres. Three stages, concessions for students and free preview nights.

Theatre Royal 282 Hope St ☎0141 332 9000, ⊛atgtickets.com/glasgow. This late nineteenth-century playhouse, recently extended and revamped, was revived in the mid-1970s as the opulent home of Scottish Opera, whose repertoire features large-scale and adventurous productions. It also hosts visiting theatre groups, including the Royal Shakespeare Company, and orchestras.

Tramway 25 Albert Drive, off Pollokshaws Rd ☎0845 330 3501, ⊛tramway.org. Based in a converted tram terminus, whose lofty proportions make it a remarkable venue for experimental productions by directors such as Peter Brook and Robert Lepage. They've also played a significant role in promoting visual art by artists such as David Mach, Douglas Gordon and Christine Borland.

Tron Theatre 63 Trongate ☎0141 552 4267, ⊛tron.co.uk. A varied repertoire of mainstream and challenging productions from itinerant companies including Glasgow's Vanishing Point, and live folk music in the theatre bar.

ART-HOUSE CINEMAS

Glasgow Film Theatre 12 Rose St ☎0141 332 6535, ⊛glasgowfilm.org/theatre. Dedicated art, independent and rep cinema house with a history going back to 1939. The glamorous Art Deco *Café Cosmo* is an excellent place for pre-show drinks.

Grosvenor 24 Ashton Lane ☎0845 166 6002, ⊛grosvenorcinema.co.uk. Two-screen neighbourhood film house with a bar and sofas that you can reserve for screenings of mostly mainstream films.

DIRECTORY

Hospital There is a 24hr casualty department at the Royal Infirmary, 84 Castle St near Glasgow Cathedral (☎0141 211 4000).

Left luggage Buchanan St bus station has left-luggage facilities, and there are lockers at Central and Queen St train stations.

Police Strathclyde Police HQ, Pitt St (☎0141 532 2000).

Post office Main office at 47 St Vincent St (Mon–Fri 8.30am–5.45pm, Sat 9am–5.30pm); city centre branch at 87–91 Bothwell St (Mon–Sat 9am–5.30pm).

The Clyde

The **River Clyde** is the dominant physical feature of Glasgow and its environs, an area that comprises the largest urban concentration in Scotland, with almost two million people living in the city and satellite towns. Little of this hinterland can be described as beautiful, with crisscrossing motorways and grim housing estates dominating much of the landscape. Beyond the sprawl, however, rolling green hills, open expanses of water and attractive countryside eventually begin to dominate, holding promises of wilder country beyond.

West of the city, regular trains and the M8 motorway dip down from the southern bank of the Clyde to **Paisley**, where the distinctive cloth pattern gained its name, before heading back up to the edge of the river again as it broadens into the **Firth of Clyde**. North of Glasgow trains terminate at tiny Milngavie (pronounced "Mill-guy"), which acts as the start of Scotland's best-known long-distance footpath, the **West Highland Way** (see box, p.818).

Southeast of Glasgow, the industrial landscape of the **Clyde valley** eventually gives way to far more attractive scenery of gorges and towering castles. Here lies the stoic town of **Lanark**, where eighteenth-century philanthropists built their model workers' community around the mills of **New Lanark**.

Paisley

Founded in the twelfth century as a monastic settlement around an abbey, **PAISLEY** expanded after the eighteenth century as a linen-manufacturing town, specializing in the production of highly-fashionable imitation Kashmiri shawls. It quickly eclipsed other British centres producing the cloth, eventually lending its name to the swirling pine-cone design. Inside the **Museum and Art Gallery**, opposite the university (Mon–Fri 11am–4pm, Sun 2–5pm; free), the Shawl Gallery deals with the growth and development of the Paisley pattern.

Opposite the town hall is Paisley's **Abbey** (Mon–Sat 10am–3.30pm; free), which was built on the site of the town's original settlement and massively overhauled in the Victorian age. The unattractive, fat grey facade of the church does little justice to its renovated interior, which is tall, spacious and ornately decorated.

ARRIVAL AND INFORMATION   PAISLEY

By plane Glasgow International Airport lies 2 miles north of town; buses connect the airport with the train station (every 10min).

By train Regular trains from Glasgow Central connect with Paisley's Gilmour Street station in the centre of town.

By bus Buses from Glasgow's Buchanan Street station run to Paisley (daily every 30min; 45min).

Tourist information 9a Gilmour St (Mon–Sat 9am–5pm; ☎ 0141 889 0711).

Dumbarton Castle

Dumbarton • April–Sept daily 9.30am–5.30pm; Oct–March Sat–Wed 9.30am–4.30pm • £4.50; HS • ☎ 01389 732167 • Trains from Glasgow Central run to Dumbarton (daily every 20min; 30min), a 15min walk from the castle

Heading west out of Glasgow, the A82 road and the train tracks follow the north bank of the river, passing through Clydebank, another ex-shipbuilding centre, and Bowling, the western entry point of the Forth & Clyde Canal. Three miles beyond Bowling, they reach the town of **DUMBARTON**, founded in the fifth century, but today for the most part a brutal concrete sprawl. Only **Dumbarton Castle**, which sits atop a twin outcrop of volcanic rock surrounded by water on three sides, is worth stopping to see. First founded as a Roman fort, the castle became a royal seat from which Mary, Queen of Scots, sailed for France to marry Henri II's son in 1548. Since the 1600s, the castle has been used as a garrison and artillery fortress to guard the approaches to Glasgow; most of the current buildings date from this period.

Helensburgh

HELENSBURGH, twenty miles or so northwest of Glasgow, is a smart, Georgian grid-plan settlement overlooking the Clyde estuary. The inventor of TV, John Logie Baird, was born here, and in 1902 Charles Rennie Mackintosh was commissioned by the Glaswegian publisher Walter Blackie to design the iconic **Hill House**.

FERRIES: GOUROCK AND WEMYSS BAY

Northwest of Glasgow on the coast lies the dowdy old resort of **GOUROCK**, once a holiday destination for generations of Glaswegians, but today only of real significance as a **ferry terminal**: both CalMac (☎ calmac.co.uk) and the more frequent Western Ferries (☎ www .western-ferries.co.uk) ply the route across the Firth of Clyde to Dunoon on the Cowal peninsula (20min), while a passenger ferry (☎ spt.co.uk) runs year-round to Kilcreggan (15min) and Helensburgh (30min) on the north bank of the Clyde. Immediately south of Gourock, **WEMYSS BAY**, where thousands of Glaswegians used to alight for their steamer trip "doon the watter", is today of note only for its splendid 1903 train station and the CalMac **ferry** connection to Rothesay on Bute (see box, p.844).

Hill House

Upper Colquhoun St • April–Oct daily 1.30–5.30pm • £10.50; NTS • ☎ 0844 493 2208

Without doubt the best surviving example of Mackintosh's domestic architecture, **Hill House** is stamped with his very personal, elegant interpretation of Art Nouveau – right down to the light fittings and fire irons – characterized by his sparing use of colour and stylized floral patterns. Various upstairs rooms are given over to interpretative displays on the architect's use of light, colour, form and texture, while changing exhibitions on contemporary domestic design from around Britain are a testament to Mackintosh's ongoing influence and inspiration. After exploring the house, head for the **tearoom** in the kitchen quarters, or wander round the beautifully laid out **gardens**.

ARRIVAL	HELENSBURGH
By train There are hourly trains from Glasgow Queen Street (50min) and Edinburgh Waverley (1hr 50min) to	Helensburgh Central. It's a half-hour walk up Sinclair Street to Hill House, or take a taxi from the rank outside the station.

19

The Clyde valley

Mostly following the course of the Clyde upstream, the journey southeast of Glasgow into Lanarkshire is dominated by endless suburbs, industrial parks and wide strips of concrete highway. The principal road here is the M74, though you'll have to get off the motorway to find the main points of interest, which tend to lie on or near the banks of the river. The **National Museum of Rural Life**, set on a historic farm, offers an in-depth look at the history of agriculture in Scotland, while further south lies the remarkable eighteenth-century planned village of **New Lanark**.

National Museum of Rural Life

East Kilbride, 7 miles southeast of Glasgow • Daily 10am–5pm • £7; NTS • Transport isn't straightforward if you don't have your own vehicle. Bus #31 from Glasgow's St Enoch Centre to East Kilbride takes you past the museum (Stewartfield Way), or you can get the train from Glasgow Central to East Kilbride, and then take a taxi for the final 3 miles (☎ 01355 241212)

Situated on the edge of **EAST KILBRIDE** new town, the **National Museum of Rural Life** is an unexpected union of historic farm and modern museum. The 170-acre farm, **Kittochside**, avoided the intensive farming that came to dominate agriculture in Britain after World War II, and today showcases traditional methods. On its edge, the custom-built museum uses light and space extremely well to explore the Scots' relationship with the land over centuries. A tractor and trailer shuttles visitors the half-mile up to the eighteenth-century **farmhouse**, which is furnished much as it would have been in the 1950s, the crucial decade just before traditional methods using horses and hand-tools were replaced by tractors and mechanization.

New Lanark

25 miles southeast of Glasgow • Daily 10am–4pm • Passport ticket £8.50 • ☎ 01555 661345, ⓦ newlanark.org

A UNESCO-designated World Heritage Site, the eighteenth-century planned village of **NEW LANARK** lies a mile below the neat little market town of **Lanark**. The first sight of the place, hidden away down in the gorge, is unforgettable: large, broken, curving walls of honeyed warehouses and tenements, built in Palladian style, are lined up along the turbulent river's edge. The community was founded by David Dale and Richard Arkwright in 1785 to harness the power of the Clyde waterfalls in their cotton-spinning industry, but it was Dale's son-in-law, Robert Owen, who revolutionized the social side of the experiment in 1798, creating a "village of unity". Believing the welfare of the workers to be crucial to industrial success, Owen built adult educational facilities, the world's first day-nursery and playground, and schools in which dancing and music were obligatory and there was no punishment or reward.

While you're free to wander around the village, which, rather unexpectedly for such a historic site, is still partially residential, you need to buy a passport ticket to get into any of the **exhibitions**. The Neoclassical building that now houses the visitor reception was opened by Owen in 1816 under the utopian title of **The Institute for the Formation of Character**. These days, it houses the **New Millennium Experience**, which whisks visitors on a chairlift through a social history of the village, conveying Robert Owen's vision not just for the idealized life at New Lanark, but also what he predicted for the year 2000.

Other parts of New Lanark village prove just as fascinating: everything, from the cooperative store to the workers' tenements and workshops, was built in an attempt to prove that industrialism need not be unaesthetic. Situated in the Old Dyeworks, the **Scottish Wildlife Trust Visitor Centre** (daily: 10am–4pm; £3) provides information about the history and wildlife of the area. Beyond the visitor centre, a riverside path leads you the mile or so to the major **Falls of the Clyde**, where, at the stunning tree-fringed Cora Linn, the river plunges 90ft in three tumultuous stages.

ARRIVAL AND INFORMATION

NEW LANARK

By train You can catch a train from Glasgow Central to Lanark (every 30min; 50min); from there either walk (it's 1.5 miles away) or take a local bus (#240X) or taxi from the station.

Tourist information In the Horsemarket, 100 yards west of the station (May–Sept daily 10am–5pm; Oct–April Mon–Sat 10am–5pm; ☎ 01555 661661).

ACCOMMODATION

New Lanark Mill ☎ 01555 667200, ⓦ newlanarkhotel .co.uk A four-star hotel converted from an eighteenth-century mill building, with good views and lots of character; the *Mill* restaurant serves decent food, and there's a swimming pool and sauna. **£79**

SYHA hostel Wee Row, Rosedale St ☎ 01555 666710, ⓦ syha.org.uk. A very appealing hostel, with double, twin, four- and five-bed rooms in a restored millworkers' tenement row. April–Oct. Dorms **£14**; doubles **£65**

19

Central Scotland

CULROSS PALACE

Central Scotland

Central Scotland, the strip of mainland north of the densely populated Glasgow–Edinburgh axis and south of the main swathe of Highlands, has been the main stage for some of the most important events in Scottish history. Stirling, its imposing castle perched high above the town, was historically the most important bridging point across the River Forth. From the castle battlements you can see the peaks of the forested Trossachs region, with its wild and wonderful archetypal Scottish scenery. Popular for walking and, in particular, cycling, much of the Trossachs, together with the attractive islands and "bonnie, bonnie banks" of Loch Lomond, form the core of Scotland's first national park.

To the east, between the firths of Forth and Tay, lies the county of **Fife**, a Pictish kingdom that boasts a fascinating coastline sprinkled with historic fishing villages and sandy beaches, as well as the historic university town of **St Andrews**, famous worldwide for its venerable golf courses. A little to the north, the ancient town of **Perth** has as much claim as anywhere to be the gateway to the Highlands. Spectacular **Highland Perthshire** begins north and west of Perth – an area of glorious wooded mountainsides and inviting walks, particularly around Rannoch Moor.

20

GETTING AROUND   CENTRAL SCOTLAND

While Stirling, Falkirk and Perth are well served by **trains** from all over Scotland, the rest of the region is only accessible on sporadic local **bus** services so you may find it easier to have your own transport. Many people opt to explore the Trossachs by mountain bike.

Stirling and around

Straddling the River Forth a few miles upstream from the estuary at Kincardine, **STIRLING** appears, at first glance, like a smaller version of Edinburgh. With its crag-top castle, steep, cobbled streets and mixed community of locals, students and tourists, it's an appealing though parochial place.

Stirling was the scene of some of the most significant developments in the evolution of the Scottish nation. It was here that the Scots under William Wallace defeated the English at the **Battle of Stirling Bridge** in 1297, only to fight – and win again – under Robert the Bruce just a couple of miles away at the **Battle of Bannockburn** in 1314; this victory is explored in a new visitor centre. The town enjoyed its golden age in the fifteenth to seventeenth centuries, most notably when its castle was the favoured residence of the Stuart monarchy and the setting for the coronation in 1543 of the young Mary, future Queen of Scots. By the early eighteenth century the town was again besieged, its location being of strategic importance during the Jacobite rebellions of 1715 and 1745. Today Stirling is known

THE TROSSACHS

Highlights

❶ **Stirling Castle** Impregnable, impressive and resonant with history. If you see only one castle in Scotland, make it this. **See p.814**

❷ **Falkirk Wheel** The most remarkable piece of modern engineering in Britain, this fascinating contraption lifts boats 100ft between two canals. **See p.816**

❸ **The Trossachs** Pocket Highlands with shining lochs, wooded glens and noble peaks. Great for hiking and mountain biking. **See p.819**

❹ **Himalayas putting green, St Andrews** The world's finest putting course right beside the world's finest golf course; a snip at £1.50 a round. **See p.824**

❺ **The East Neuk** Buy freshly cooked lobster from the wooden shack at Crail's historic stone harbour or dine in style at *The Cellar* restaurant in the fishing town of Anstruther. **See p.826**

❻ **Forth Rail Bridge** An icon of Victorian engineering spanning the Firth of Forth, floodlit to stunning effect at night. **See p.829**

❼ **The Fergusson Gallery, Perth** A touch of Antibes in Perthshire: the gallery celebrates the vibrant work of J.D. Fergusson and his dancer wife Margaret Morris. **See p.831**

❽ **Rannoch Moor** One of the most inaccessible places in Scotland, where hikers can discover a true sense of remoteness. **See p.836**

HIGHLIGHTS ARE MARKED ON THE MAP ON PP.812–813

CENTRAL SCOTLAND

for its **castle** and the lofty **Wallace Monument**, a mammoth Victorian monolith high on Abbey Craig to the northeast.

The historic element of the region is reflected in the cathedral at **Dunblane** and the imposing castle at **Doune** (an icon to Monty Python fans), while the **Falkirk Wheel** is recognized as a marvel of modern engineering.

Stirling Castle

Upper Castle Wynd • Daily: April–Sept 9.30am–6pm; Oct–March 9.30am–5pm • £14; HS • ☎ 0131 668 8831, ⓦ stirlingcastle.gov.uk

Stirling Castle must have presented would-be invaders with a formidable challenge. Its impregnability is most daunting when you approach the town from the west, from where the sheer 250ft drop down the side of the crag is most obvious. The rock was first fortified during the Iron Age, though what you see now dates largely from the fifteenth and sixteenth centuries. Built on many levels, the main buildings are interspersed with delightful gardens and patches of lawn, while endless battlements, cannon ports, hidden staircases and other nooks and crannies make it thoroughly explorable and absorbing. Free **guided tours** begin by the well in the Lower Square.

Central to the castle is the magnificently restored **Great Hall**, which dates from 1501–03 and was used as a barracks by the British army until 1964. The building stands out across Stirling for its controversially bright, creamy yellow cladding, added after the discovery during renovations of a stretch of the original sixteenth-century limewash. Inside, the hall has been restored to its original state as the finest medieval secular building in Scotland, complete with five gaping fireplaces and an impressive hammerbeam ceiling of rough-hewn wood. A major restoration of the **Palace**, with specially commissioned tapestries and furniture, has returned the rooms to their appearance in the mid-sixteenth century.

On the sloping upper courtyard of the castle, the **Chapel Royal** was built in 1594 by James VI for the baptism of his son, to replace an earlier chapel that was deemed insufficiently impressive. The interior is charming, with a seventeenth-century fresco of elaborate scrolls and patterns. Go through a narrow passageway beyond the Chapel Royal to get to the **Douglas Gardens**, reputedly the place where the eighth Earl of Douglas, suspected of treachery, was thrown to his death by James II in 1452. It's a lovely, quiet corner of the castle, with mature trees and battlements over which there are splendid views of the rising Highlands beyond, as well as a bird's-eye view down to the **King's Knot**, a series of grassed octagonal mounds which, in the seventeenth century, were planted with box trees and ornamental hedges.

The Old Town

Stirling evolved from the top down, starting with its castle and gradually spreading south and east onto the low-lying flood plain. In the eighteenth and nineteenth centuries, as the threat of attack decreased, the centre of commercial life crept down towards the River Forth, with the modern town growing on the edge of the plain over which the castle had stood guard.

Leaving the castle, head downhill into the old centre of Stirling, fortified behind the massive, whinstone boulders of the **town walls**, built in the mid-sixteenth century and intended to ward off the advances of Henry VIII, who had set his sights on the young Mary, Queen of Scots, as a wife for his son, Edward. The walls now constitute some of the best-preserved town defences in Scotland, and can be traced by following the path known as **Back Walk**, which leads right under the castle, taut along the edge of the crag. Though a little overgrown in places, it's a great way to take in the castle's setting, and in various places you'll catch panoramic views of the surrounding countryside.

20

The Tolbooth

Jail Wynd • Mon–Sat 10am–6pm • ☎ 01786 274000, ⓦ stirling.gov.uk/tolbooth

Built on the site of Stirling's medieval prison, the **Tolbooth** is now an inspirational music and arts centre, a striking modern redevelopment of a 1705 structure. During renovations a secret staircase was discovered, along with a complete skeleton thought to have been that of the last man publicly hanged in Stirling. Inside, a top-floor viewing platform looks out over the Old Town rooftops. In addition to performances (see p.817) the Tolbooth hosts music workshops, summer ceilidhs and contemporary art shows.

The National Wallace Monument

1.5 miles north of the Old Town • Daily: March–May & Oct 10am–5pm; June 10am–6pm; July & Aug 9am–6pm; Sept 9.30am–5.30pm; Nov–Feb 10.30am–4pm • £9.50 • ☎ 01786 472140, ⓦ nationalwallacemonument.com • Bus #63 from the town centre

The prominent **National Wallace Monument** is a freestanding, five-storey tower built in the 1860s as a tribute to Sir William Wallace, the freedom fighter who led Scottish resistance to Edward I, the "Hammer of the Scots", in the late thirteenth century. The crag on which the monument is set was the scene of Wallace's greatest victory, when he sent his troops charging down the hillside onto the plain to defeat the English at the Battle of Stirling Bridge in 1297. Exhibits inside the tower include Wallace's long steel sword and a life-sized "talking" model of Wallace, who tells visitors about his preparations for the battle. If you can manage the climb – up 246 spiral steps – to the top of the 220ft-high tower, you'll be rewarded with superb views across to Fife and Ben Lomond.

Battle of Bannockburn Visitor Centre

Two miles south of Stirling centre, on the A872 • Daily: March–Oct 10am–5.30pm; Nov–Feb 10am–5pm • £11; NTS • ☎ 0844 493 2139 • Buses #24, #52 or #57 from Stirling bus station or Murray Place

All but surrounded by suburban housing, a new **visitor centre** commemorates the most famous battle in Scottish history, when King Robert the Bruce won his mighty victory over the English at the **Battle of Bannockburn** on June 24, 1314. It was this battle, the climax of the Wars of Independence, which united the Scots under Bruce and led to independence from England; Bruce employed brilliantly innovative tactics in mustering his army to defeat a much larger English force.

The actual site of the main battle is still a matter of debate: most agree that it didn't take place near the present visitor centre, but on a boggy plain a mile or so to the west. The new centre itself, timed for the eight hundredth anniversary of the battle, is largely devoid of the kind of artefacts which bring Culloden (see p.895) so movingly to life, and the 3D video game technology presentation is aimed exclusively at children. That said, it's popular, so be sure to book ahead.

Dunblane Cathedral

The Cross, Dunblane, 5 miles north of Stirling • April–Sept Mon–Sat 9.30am–5pm & Sun 2–5pm; Oct–March Mon–Sat 9.30am–4pm & Sun 2–4pm • Free; HS • ☎ 01786 825388, ⓦ dunblanecathedral.org.uk • Regular trains connect Dunblane with Stirling and points north

The attractive small town of **DUNBLANE** has been an important ecclesiastical centre since the seventh century, when the Celts founded the Church of St Blane here. **Dunblane Cathedral** dates mainly from the thirteenth century, and restoration work carried out a century ago has returned it to its Gothic splendour. Inside, note the delicate blue-purple stained glass, and the exquisitely carved pews, screen and choir stalls, all crafted in the early twentieth century. Memorials within the cathedral include a tenth-century Celtic cross-slab standing stone and a modern, four-sided standing stone by Richard Kindersley commemorating the tragic shooting in 1996 of sixteen Dunblane schoolchildren and their teacher. In 2012, the town erupted in celebrations when local tennis star Andy Murray won both Olympic gold and the Wimbledon championship.

Doune Castle

8 miles west of Stirling • April–Sept daily 9.30am–6.30pm; Oct–March Mon–Wed & Sat 9.30am–4.30pm, Sun 2–4.30pm • £5.50; HS • ☎ 01786 841742 • From Stirling bus station, take bus #1 (Callander) to Doune's main street

Standing on a small hill in a bend of the River Teith in the sleepy village of **DOUNE**, the stern-looking, fourteenth-century **Doune Castle** is a marvellous semi-ruin. The castle's greatest claim to fame is as the setting for the 1970s movie *Monty Python and the Holy Grail*; the shop by the gatehouse keeps a scrapbook of stills from the film, as well as a selection of souvenirs including bottles of Holy Grail Ale.

The Falkirk Wheel

Lime Rd, 2 miles west of Falkirk, which is 10 miles southeast of Stirling on the M9 to Edinburgh • **Wheel** Daily: April–Oct every 30min 9.30am–4.30pm; Nov–March hourly 10am–3pm • £8.95 **Visitor Centre** Daily 9.30am–6pm • Free • ☎ 08700 500208, ⓦ thefalkirkwheel.co.uk • Trains to Falkirk from Edinburgh (every 15–30min; 30min), Glasgow Queen St (every 15–30min; 25min) and Stirling (every 30min; 15min); taxis can take you the 2.5 mile journey from the station to the wheel. There are also buses from Stirling (every 30min; 15min)

The town of **FALKIRK** has a good deal of visible history, going right back to the remains of the Roman Antonine Wall. A massive transformation came in the eighteenth century with the construction of canals connecting Glasgow and Edinburgh; within a few years, however, the trains arrived, and the canals gradually fell into disuse. While Falkirk's canals were a very visible sign of the area's industrial heritage, it was only recently that their leisure potential was realized, thanks to British Waterway's £84.5

million **Millennium Link** project to restore them and re-establish a navigable link between east and west coasts.

The icon of this project is the remarkable **Falkirk Wheel**. The giant grey wheel, the world's first rotating boat-lift, scoops boats in two giant buckets, or caissons, and moves them the 79ft between the levels of the Forth & Clyde and Union canals linked to Glasgow and Edinburgh respectively. Beneath the wheel, the **visitor centre** sells tickets for a one-hour **boat trip** from the lower basin into the wheel, along the Union Canal, and back again. If you want to simply see the wheel in action, walk around the basin and adjoining towpaths.

ARRIVAL AND INFORMATION STIRLING

By train The train station is in the centre of town on Goosecroft Road.
Destinations Aberdeen (hourly; 2hr 5min); Dundee (hourly; 55min); Edinburgh (every 30min; 1hr); Falkirk (every 30min; 15min); Glasgow Queen St (every 20min; 30min); Inverness (3–5 daily; 2hr 55min); Perth (hourly; 30min).
By bus The bus station, on Goosecroft Rd, can be accessed from the Thistle shopping centre.
Destinations Aberfoyle (4 daily; 45min); Bridge of Allan (1–2hr, 13min); Callander (1–2hr; 45min); Dollar (every

2hr; 30min); Doune (1–2hr; 25min); Dunblane (hourly; 20min); Dundee (hourly; 1hr 30min); Edinburgh (hourly; 1hr); Falkirk (hourly; 30min); Glasgow (hourly; 50min); Inverness (every 2hr; 3hr 20min); Perth (hourly; 40min); St Andrews (every 2hr; 1hr 55min).
Tourist information 41 Dumbarton Rd (April & May Mon–Sat 9am–5pm; June & Sept Mon–Sat 9am–6pm, Sun 10am–4pm; July & Aug Mon–Sat 9am–7pm, Sun 9.30am–6pm; Oct Mon–Sat 9.30am–5pm; Nov–March Mon–Fri 10am–5pm, Sat 10am–4pm, ☏01786 475019, ⌨ visitstirling.org).

ACCOMMODATION

Castlecroft Ballengeich Rd ☏01786 474933, ⌨ castlecroft-uk.com. Modern guesthouse with six en-suite rooms on the site of the King's Stables just beneath the castle rock, with terrific views north and west and a very friendly welcome. **£60**
Kilronan House 15 Kenilworth Rd, Bridge of Allan ☏01786 831054, ⌨ kilronan.co.uk. A grand Victorian family house built in 1855 with spacious en suite B&B rooms in the Bridge of Allan, a couple of miles north of Stirling and easily reached by regular buses. **£64**
No. 10 10 Gladstone Place ☏01786 472681, ⌨ cameron10.co.uk. Modernized Victorian home with neat, uncluttered decor providing friendly and pleasant B&B accommodation. It's close to the city centre, but on a

quiet and elegant King's Park street. **£60**
Stirling University ☏01786 467141, ⌨ stir.ac.uk /about/short-breaks-and-vacations. Campus accommodation in halls of residence (singles £35) and self-catering flats a couple of miles north of the town centre. The campus is served by regular buses from Murray Place in the town centre. June to mid-Sept. **£50.50**
SYHA Hostel St John St ☏01786 473442, ⌨ stirling @syha.org.uk. Located at the top of the town (a strenuous trek with a backpack), in a converted church with an impressive 1824 Palladian facade. All rooms have en-suite showers and toilets, and facilities include a games room and internet access. Dorms **£14**; doubles **£28**

20

EATING AND ENTERTAINMENT

Allan Water Café 15 Henderson St, Bridge of Allan ☏01786 833060, ⌨ allanwatercafe.co.uk. Established in 1902, this traditional Italian café serves reasonably-priced fish suppers with mushy peas (£9) and their very own ice cream, made to a secret family recipe. Mon–Sat 8am–8.30pm, Sun 9am–8.30pm.
Darnley Coffee House Bow St ☏01786 474468. A bit old-fashioned but with plenty of Old Town atmosphere and serving reasonably-priced lunches, soups, teas and home-made cakes (lunch from £5) in an impressive barrel-vaulted interior. Daily 9am–9pm.
Hermann's 58 Broad St ☏01786 450632, ⌨ hermanns .co.uk. Stirling's classiest option, set in the historic Mar Place House towards the top of the Old Town. It offers upmarket Austrian-Scottish dining such as *Jagerschnitzel*

(veal) or Scottish lamb with cheese potatoes in the evening (mains from £16). Daily noon–2pm & 6–9pm.
Jam Jar 28 Henderson St, Bridge of Allan ☏01786 831616, ⌨ jamjarcafe.co.uk. A great little neighbourhood bistro with hip bare-brick decor and a futuristic wood-burning stove. Big breakfasts, healthy lunches plus pizzas, burgers and more sophisticated mains including shoulder of lamb bonbons and herb-crusted salmon (mains £8.50–£14.50). Daily 7.30am–11pm.
★**Tolbooth** Jail Wynd ☏01786 274000, ⌨ stirling .gov.uk/tolbooth. By far the best option for a night out, the *Tolbooth* (see p.815) has a glamorous high-ceilinged bar (open only when there's an event on) and eclectic live music programme. Look out for their boisterous ceilidhs in July & Aug. Open daily.

Loch Lomond

The largest stretch of fresh water in Britain (23 miles long and up to five miles wide), **Loch Lomond** is thought of as the epitome of Scottish scenic splendour, thanks in large part to the ballad that fondly recalls its "bonnie, bonnie banks". In reality, however, the peerless scenery of the loch can be tainted by the sheer numbers of tourists and day-trippers.

Designated Scotland's first national park in 2002, the **Loch Lomond and the Trossachs National Park** (ⓦlochlomond-trossachs.org) covers a large stretch of scenic territory from the lochs of the Clyde Estuary to Loch Tay in Perthshire, with the centrepiece being Loch Lomond. The most popular gateway into the park is the town of **Balloch**, nineteen miles from Glasgow city centre. Both Balloch and the western side of the loch around Luss are often packed with day-trippers and tour coaches, though the loch's eastern side, abutting the Trossachs, is very different in tone, with wooden ferryboats puttering out to a scattering of tree-covered islands off the village of **Balmaha**.

Balloch

Little more than a suburb of the much larger factory-town of Alexandria, to the south, **BALLOCH**, the settlement in the southwestern corner of Loch Lomond, has few redeeming features. However, its road and train links with Glasgow ensured that it was chosen as the focal point of the national park: the location for the huge **Loch Lomond Shores** complex.

Loch Lomond Shores

National Park Gateway Centre Daily 9.30am–6pm • ☎ 08707 200631 • **Drumkinnon Tower** Daily 10am–5pm • £13.20 • ☎ 01389 721000, ⓦ visitsealife.com/loch-lomond • **Can You Experience** ☎ 01389 602576, ⓦ canyouexperience.com • ⓦ lochlomondshores.com

---

THE WEST HIGHLAND WAY

Opened in 1980, the spectacular **West Highland Way** was Scotland's first long-distance footpath, stretching some 95 miles from Milngavie (pronounced "mill-guy") six miles north of central Glasgow, to Fort William, where it reaches the foot of Ben Nevis, Britain's highest mountain. Today, it is by far the most popular such footpath in Scotland, and while for many the range of scenery, relative ease of walking and nearby facilities make it a classic route, others find it a little too busy in high season.

The route runs along the eastern shores of Loch Lomond, over the Highland Boundary Fault Line, then round Crianlarich, crossing the open heather wilderness of **Rannoch Moor**. It passes close to **Glen Coe**, notorious for the massacre of the MacDonald clan, before reaching **Fort William**. Apart from one stretch halfway along when the path is within earshot of the main road, this is wild, remote country, and you should be well prepared for sudden and extreme weather changes.

Though this is emphatically not the most strenuous of Britain's long-distance walks, a moderate degree of fitness is required as there are some steep ascents. If you're looking for an added challenge, you could work in a climb of Ben Lomond or Ben Nevis. You might choose to walk individual sections of the Way (the eight-mile climb from Glen Coe up the Devil's Staircase is particularly spectacular), but to tackle the whole thing you need to set aside at least seven days; avoid a Saturday start from Milngavie and you'll be less likely to be walking with hordes of people, and there'll be less pressure on accommodation. Most walkers tackle the route from south to north, and manage between ten and fourteen miles a day, staying at hotels, B&Bs and bunkhouses en route. Camping is permitted at recognized sites.

Although the path is clearly waymarked, you may want to check one of the many maps or guidebooks published: the **official guide**, published by Mercat Press, includes a foldout map as well as descriptions of the route, with detailed cultural, historical, archeological and wildlife information. For further details on the Way, including a comprehensive accommodation list and various tour options, see ⓦ west-highland-way.co.uk.

THE ISLANDS OF LOCH LOMOND

Many of Loch Lomond's 37 **islands** are privately owned, and, rather quaintly, an old wooden mail-boat still delivers post to four of them. It's possible to join the **mail-boat cruise**, which is run by MacFarlane & Son from the jetty at Balmaha (May–Oct Mon, Thurs & Sat 11.30am returns 2pm; July & Aug daily 11.30am returns 2pm; Oct–April Mon & Thurs 10.50am returns 12.50pm; £10; ☎01360 870214, ⓦbalmahaboatyard.co.uk). There's time for a stop on Inchmurrin Island, the largest and most southerly of the islands, inhabited by just ten permanent people; if you're looking for an island to explore, however, a better bet is **Inchailloch**, the closest to Balmaha. Owned by Scottish Natural Heritage, it has a two-mile, signposted nature trail. You can row here yourself using a boat hired from MacFarlane & Son (from £10/hr or £40/day), or use their on-demand ferry service (£5 return).

Signposted from miles around, **Loch Lomond Shores** contains the **National Park Gateway Centre**, which has background, tourist information and a leaflet outlining all transport links within the park, as well as internet access and a "retail crescent". Alongside, **Drumkinnon Tower** is a striking cylindrical building housing an aquarium, and, next to that, Can You Experience organizes a number of **activities**, including nature walks and canoe, bike and pedalo rental.

Balmaha

The tranquil **eastern shore** of Loch Lomond is far better for walking and appreciating the loch's natural beauty than the overcrowded western side. The dead-end B837 from Drymen will take you halfway up the east bank, as far as you can get by car or bus, while the West Highland Way (see box opposite) sticks close to the shores for the entire length of the loch, beginning at the tiny lochside settlement of **BALMAHA**. The village stands on the Highland Boundary Fault, the geological fault that separates the Highlands from the Lowlands; if you stand on the viewpoint above the pier, you can see the fault line clearly marked by a series of woody islands that form giant stepping-stones across the loch.

20

ARRIVAL AND INFORMATION   LOCH LOMOND

BALLOCH

By train Balloch has good train connections with Glasgow (every 30min; 40min).

By bus Buses connect with Balmaha (every 2hr; 25min) and Luss (hourly; 15min).

BALMAHA

By bus The #309 bus from Balloch and Drymen runs to Balmaha every 2hr.

National Park Centre Next to the large car park (April–Sept daily 10am–5.30pm; ☎01360 870470). They have good information on local forest walks.

ACCOMMODATION

Cashel Rowardennan, 2 miles north of Balmaha ☎01360 870234. A lovely, secluded Forestry Commission campsite on the loch shore with a decent loo block. Campers can launch craft from here onto the loch, and Ben Lomond is just four miles away. April–Oct. Pitches **£17.50**

Oak Tree Inn Balmaha ☎01360 870357, ⓦoak-tree -inn.co.uk. This well-run inn is set back from the boatyard,

and offers en-suite doubles and bunk-bed quads. There's also a convivial pub, where food is served all day. **£85**
★**Passfoot Cottage B&B** Balmaha ☎01360 870324, ⓦpassfoot.com. This friendly and appealing little option is housed in a whitewashed toll cottage, enjoying an idyllic location and lochside garden. Great for walks along the shore. **£80**

The Trossachs

Often described as the Highlands in miniature, the **Trossachs** area boasts a magnificent diversity of scenery, with dramatic peaks and mysterious, forest-covered

> **TOP 5 PLACES TO WALK**
> **Ben Lawers** See p.834   **Queen Elizabeth Forest Park** See box
> **Loch Lomond** See p.818   opposite
> **Pass of Killiecrankie** See p.836   **Rannoch Moor** See box, p.836

slopes that live up to all the images ever produced of Scotland's wild land. It is country ripe with stirring tales of brave kilted clansmen, a role fulfilled by **Rob Roy Macgregor**, the seventeenth-century outlaw whose name seems to attach to every second waterfall, cave and barely discernible path. The Trossachs' high tourist profile was largely attributable in the early days to the novels of Sir Walter Scott, which are set in the area. Since then, neither the popularity nor beauty of the region have waned, and in high season the place is jam-packed with coaches full of tourists as well as walkers and mountain-bikers taking advantage of the easily accessed scenery. Autumn is a better time to come, when the hills are blanketed in rich, rusty colours and the crowds are thinner.

Aberfoyle

Each summer the sleepy little town of **ABERFOYLE**, twenty miles west of Stirling, dusts itself down for its annual influx of tourists. Though of little appeal itself, Aberfoyle's position in the heart of the Trossachs is ideal. From here, the A821 road to **Loch Katrine** winds its way into the Queen Elizabeth Forest, snaking up **Duke's Pass** (so called because it once belonged to the Duke of Montrose).

The Lake of Menteith

About 4 miles east of Aberfoyle towards Doune

The **Lake of Menteith** is a superb fly-fishing centre and Scotland's only lake (as opposed to loch), so named due to a historic mix-up with the word *laigh*, Scots for "low-lying ground", which applied to the whole area. From the northern shore, you can take a little ferry out to the **Island of Inchmahome** in order to explore the lovely ruined Augustinian abbey.

Inchmahome Priory

Daily: April–Sept 10am–4.30pm; Oct 9.30am–3.30pm • £5.50 including ferry; HS • ☎ 01877 385294

Founded in 1238, **Inchmahome Priory** is the most beautiful island monastery in Scotland, its remains rising tall and graceful above the trees. The masons employed to build the priory are thought to be those who built Dunblane Cathedral (see p.816); certainly the western entrance there resembles that at Inchmahome.

ARRIVAL AND INFORMATION   ABERFOYLE

By bus Buses connect with Callander (late June to mid-Oct 4 daily Thurs–Tues; 25min) and Port of Menteith (late June to mid-Oct 4 daily Thurs–Tues; 10min).

Tourist information The excellent Queen Elizabeth Forest Park Visitor Centre at the David Marshall Lodge is located a mile north of Aberfoyle on the A821. They have

maps of the walks and cycle routes in the forest, information on the flora and fauna of the area, which includes roe deer and birds of prey, and a nice café with splendid views over the tree tops (Jan & Feb 10am–3pm; March & April & Oct–Dec 10am–4pm; May, June & Sept 10am–5pm; ☎ 01877 382383).

ACCOMMODATION AND EATING

Lake of Menteith Hotel Port of Menteith ☎ 01877 385258, ⓦ www.lake-hotel.com. The *Lake of Menteith* (see above) is a beautiful place to stay with spacious, glamorous rooms: the hotel enjoys a lovely waterfront setting next to

Port of Menteith's Victorian Gothic parish church, and also has a classy restaurant. Ask – of course – for a room with a lake view. **£138**

20

Loch Katrine

Heading down the northern side of the Duke's Pass you come first to **Loch Achray**, tucked under Ben A'an. At the head of the loch, a road leads the short distance to the southern end of **Loch Katrine** at the foot of Ben Venue (2370ft).

Cruises on Loch Katrine

April–Oct daily · £15.50 return; shorter 45min cruises with no stops £12 · ☎ 01877 376315, ⓦ lochkatrine.com

An elegant Victorian passenger **steamer**, the SS *Sir Walter Scott*, has been plying the waters of Loch Katrine since 1900, chugging up to the wild country of Glengyle. It makes various cruises each day, but only the first (departing at 10.30am) stops off at Stronachlachar every day; on Wednesdays and weekends there's a second trip to Stronachlachar departing at 2.30pm. A popular combination is to **rent a bike** from the Katrinewheelz hut by the pier (☎ 01877 376366, ⓦ katrinewheelz.co.uk; £20/day), take the steamer up to Stronachlachar, then cycle back around the north side of the loch.

ARRIVAL   LOCH KATRINE

By bus Buses connect with Callander (late June to mid-Oct 4 daily Thurs–Tues; 25min) and Port of Menteith (late June to mid-Oct 4 daily Thurs–Tues; 10min).

EATING AND DRINKING

★ **Byre Inn** Brig O'Turk ☎ 01877 376292, ⓦ byreinn .co.uk. A tiny country pub and classy restaurant set in an old stone barn with wooden pews and a welcoming open fire; it's the starting point for waymarked walks to lochs Achray, Drunkie and Venachar. There are snacks such as Cullen Skink crumble (£5.50) and larger mains including sausage and mash in an all-in-one Yorkshire pudding (£11.95). Mon–Sat 11am–11pm, Sun noon–11pm.

Callander

CALLANDER, on the eastern edge of the Trossachs, sits on the banks of the River Teith at the southern end of the **Pass of Leny**, one of the key routes into the Highlands. Significantly larger than Aberfoyle, eleven miles west, it is a popular summer holiday base and suffers in high season for being on the main tourist trail from Stirling through to the west Highlands. There are no attractions as such in the town itself.

ARRIVAL AND GETTING AROUND   CALLANDER

By bus Callander has bus connections with Loch Katrine (late June to mid-Oct 4 daily Thurs–Tues; 55min).
Square Wheels 4 Ancaster Square. Handily located in the centre of Callander, offering bike rental, sales, repairs and accessories (☎ 01877 331052, ⓦ cyclehirecallander .co.uk).

HIKING AND BIKING IN THE TROSSACHS

The Trossachs is ideal for exploring **on foot** or on a **mountain bike**. This is partly because the terrain is slightly more benign than the Highlands proper, but much is due to the excellent management of the **Queen Elizabeth Forest Park**, a huge chunk of the national park between Loch Lomond and Loch Lubnaig. The main visitor centre for the area, David Marshall Lodge, is just outside Aberfoyle (see opposite).

For **hill-walkers**, the prize peak is Ben Lomond (3192ft), best accessed from Rowardennan on Loch Lomond's east shore. Other highlights include Ben Venue (2370ft) and Ben A'an (1520ft) on the shores of Loch Katrine, as well as Ben Ledi (2857ft), just northwest of Callander, which all offer relatively straightforward but very rewarding climbs and, on clear days, stunning views. Walkers can also choose from any number of waymarked routes through the forests and along lochsides; pick up a map of these at the visitor centre.

The area is also a popular spot for **mountain biking**, with a number of useful rental shops (see above), a network of forest paths and one of the more impressive stretches of the National Cycle Network cutting through the region from Loch Lomond to Killin.

Wheels Cycling Centre Next to Trossachs Tryst (see below), 1.5 miles southwest of Callander ☎01877 331100, ⓦscottish-cycling.co.uk. The best bike rental place in the area, with front- or full-suspension models available, as well as baby seats and children's cycles.

ACCOMMODATION

Arden House Bracklinn Rd ☎01877 330235, ⓦardenhouse.org.uk. A grand Victorian guesthouse in its own gardens with good views and woodland walks from the back door. There's a putting lawn, and home baking is provided daily. April–Oct. £85

Roman Camp Country House Hotel Main St ☎01877 330003, ⓦromancamphotel.co.uk. The town's most upmarket option is this romantic, turreted seventeenth-century hunting lodge situated in twenty-acre gardens on the River Teith. £160

★Trossachs Tryst Invertrossachs Rd ☎01877 331200, ⓦscottish-hostel.com. A friendly, well-equipped and comfortable 32-bed hostel and activity centre with self-catering dorms and family rooms; they only accept whole-house bookings. It's located a mile southwest of town, down a turn-off from the A81 to Port of Monteith. Bike rental available. Price depends on the number of people staying. Per person £17–50

EATING AND DRINKING

Lade Inn Kilmahog, a mile west of Callander ☎01877 330152, ⓦtheladeinn.com. Pub food can be had at this convivial inn where the owners are particularly keen on real ales; an on-site shop sells bottled beers from all over Scotland. Mon–Fri noon–2.30pm & 5.30pm–9pm, Sat noon–9pm, Sun 12.30–8pm.

★Mhor Fish 75–77 Main St ☎01877 330213, ⓦmhor .net. One of a new breed of fish and chip shops; with a sustainable fish policy, daily specials and everything from snacks to bistro-style seafood dishes – and you can get fish suppers, burgers, pies and haggis to take away. Daily 10am–10pm.

20

Fife

The ancient Kingdom of **Fife** is a small area, barely fifty miles at its widest point, but one which has a definite identity, inextricably linked with the waters that surround it on three sides – the Tay to the north, the Forth to the south, and the cold North Sea to the east. Despite its small size, Fife encompasses several different regions, with a marked difference between the rural north and the semi-industrial south. Fishing still has a role, but ultimately it is to **St Andrews**, the home of the world-famous Royal and Ancient Golf Club, that most visitors are drawn. South of St Andrews, the tiny stone harbours of the **East Neuk** fishing villages are an appealing extension to any visit to this part of Fife.

Inland from St Andrews is the absorbing village of **Falkland** with its impressive ruined palace. To the **south**, the perfectly preserved town of **Culross** is the most obvious draw with its cobbled streets and collection of historic buildings.

St Andrews

Confident, poised and well groomed, if a little snooty, **ST ANDREWS**, Scotland's oldest **university town** and a pilgrimage centre for **golfers** from all over the world, is situated on a wide bay on the northeastern coast of Fife. Of all Scotland's universities, St Andrews is the most often compared to Oxford or Cambridge, both for the dominance of gown over town, and for the intimate, collegiate feel of the place. In fact, the university attracts a significant proportion of English undergraduates, among them Prince William, who spent four years studying here, where he met fellow student and future wife Kate Middleton.

According to legend, the town was founded, pretty much by accident, in the fourth century. **St Rule** – or Regulus – a custodian of the bones of St Andrew in Patras in southern Greece, had a vision in which an angel ordered him to carry five of the saint's bones to the western edge of the world, where he was to build a city in his honour. The conscientious courier set off, but was shipwrecked on the

ST ANDREWS

ACCOMMODATION
Aslar House 1
Kinkell 4
Old Fishergate House 2
St Andrews Tourist Hostel 3

EATING
The Doll's House 3
The Peat Inn 4
The Seafood Restaurant 1
Tailend Fish Bar 2

NIGHTLIFE
The Central 3
Ma Bells 1
The One Under 2

NORTH SEA

West Sands

St Andrews Links
Trust Clubhouse

Himalayas Putting
Course

Ladies Putting
Club Clubhouse

Swilken Burn

The Old Course

British Golf Museum

Royal & Ancient
Golf Club

St Andrews Aquarium

Castle

Cathedral

St Rule's
Tower

Harbour
East Sands

Long Pier

SHOREHEAD

GREGORY PLACE

Preservation
Trust Museum

Queen
Mary's House

St Leonard's
School

PINDS ROAD

Crawford
Arts Centre

St Salvator's
College

EAST SCORES

CASTLE STREET

BUTTS WYND

NORTH STREET

Eyre
Theatre

St Mary's
College

ABBEY STREET

New
Picture
House

Holy
Trinity

CHURCH ST

MARKET STREET

SOUTH STREET

QUEEN'S GARDENS

Ladebraes Lane

MURRAY
PLACE

MURRAY PARK

THE SCORES

GOLF PLACE

GRANNIE CLARK'S WYND

BRUCE EMBANKMENT

THE LINKS

WEST SANDS ROAD

GIBSON PLACE

OLD STATION ROAD

WINDMILL ROAD

GOLFLANDS GARDENS

GILL STREET

PILMOUR TERRACE

HOPE STREET

ST MARY'S PLACE

HOWARD
PLACE

PLAYFAIR
CRESCENT

CITY ROAD

STATION ROAD

Bus Station

West Port

BRIDGE ST

DOUBLEDYKES ROAD

ARGYLE STREET

Ladebraes Walk

GUARDBRIDGE ROAD

KENNEDY GARDENS

WARD GDNS

GDNS

A86

Crail, Kinkell 4

Botanic Gardens & 4 (¾ miles)

Leuchars & Dundee

N

0   200   yards

20

rocks close to the present harbour. Struggling ashore with his precious burden, he built a shrine to the saint on what subsequently became the site of the **cathedral**; St Andrew became Scotland's patron saint and the town its ecclesiastical capital.

On the three main thoroughfares, **North Street**, **Market Street** and **South Street** – which run west to east towards the ruined Gothic cathedral – are several of the original university buildings from the fifteenth century. Narrow alleys connect the cobbled streets, attic windows and gable ends shape the rooftops, and here and there you'll see the old wooden doors with heavy knockers and black iron hinges.

St Andrews Cathedral

The Pends **Visitor centre** Daily: April–Sept 9.30am–5.30pm; Oct–March 9.30am–4.30pm • £4.50, with castle £7.20; HS **Grounds** Daily 9am–5.30pm • Free • ☎ 01334 472563

The ruin of the great **St Andrews Cathedral**, at the east end of town, gives only an idea of the importance of what was once Scotland's largest cathedral. Founded in 1160, the cathedral was plundered and left to ruin during the Reformation by supporters of John Knox, fresh from a rousing meeting.

In front of the cathedral window a slab is all that remains of the high altar, where the relics of St Andrew were once enshrined. Previously, it is believed that they were kept in **St Rule's Tower**, the austere Romanesque monolith next to the cathedral, which was built as part of an abbey in 1130. From the top of the tower (a climb of 157 steps) there's a good view of the town and surroundings, and of the remains of the monastic buildings that made up the priory. Around the entire complex is a sturdy wall dating from the sixteenth century, more than half a mile long and with three gateways.

20

GOLF IN ST ANDREWS

St Andrews **Royal and Ancient Golf Club** (or "R&A") has been the international governing body for golf since 1754, when a meeting of 22 of the local gentry founded the Society of St Andrews Golfers, being "admirers of the ancient and healthful exercise of golf". The game itself has been played here since the fifteenth century. Those early days were instrumental in establishing Scotland as the home of golf, for the rules were distinguished from those of the French game by the fact that participants had to manoeuvre the ball into a hole, rather than hit an above-ground target. It was not without its opponents, however – particularly James II who, in 1457, banned his subjects from playing since it was distracting them from archery practice.

The approach to St Andrews from the west runs adjacent to the famous **Old Course**, the oldest course in the world, and just one of seven in the immediate vicinity of the town. The R&A's strictly private **clubhouse**, a stolid, square building dating from 1854, is at the eastern end of the Old Course overlooking both the 18th green and the long strand of the West Sands. The British Open Championship was first held here in 1873, having been inaugurated in 1860 at Prestwick in Ayrshire, and since then it has been held at St Andrews regularly, pulling in enormous crowds.

PLAYING GOLF

St Andrews Links Trust Alongside the fairway of the first hole of the Old Course ⓦ standrews.org .uk. It is possible to play on St Andrew's courses, including the venerated Old Course itself (for this you'll need a valid handicap certificate and must enter a daily ballot for tee times; the green fees, for those who are successful, are £160 in summer). For full details contact the trust, which looks after all the courses in town.

Himalayas Arguably the best golfing experience in St Andrews, even if you can't tell a birdie from a bogey, this fantastically lumpy eighteen-hole putting course is in an ideal setting next to the Old Course and the sea. Officially the Ladies Putting Club, founded in 1867, with its own clubhouse, it has grass as perfectly manicured as the championship course, and you can have all the thrill of sinking a six-footer in golf's most famous location, at the bargain price of £2. April–Sept Mon–Sat 10.30am–6.30pm, Sun noon–6.30pm.

St Andrews Castle

The Scores • Daily: April–Sept 9.30am–5.30pm; Oct–March 9.30am–4.30pm • £5.50, with cathedral £7.20; HS • ☎ 01334 477196

Not far north of the cathedral, the rocky coastline curves inland to the ruined **castle**, with a drop to the sea on two sides and a moat on its inland side. Founded around 1200 and extended over the centuries, it was built as part of the Palace of the Bishops and Archbishops of St Andrews. There's not a great deal left of the castle, since it fell into ruin in the seventeenth century, and most of what can be seen dates from the sixteenth century, apart from the fourteenth-century Fore Tower.

British Golf Museum

Bruce Embankment • April–Oct Mon–Sat 9.30am–5.30pm, Sun 10am–5pm; Nov–March Mon–Sat 10am–4.30pm • £6 • ☎ 01334 460046, ⓦ britishgolfmuseum.co.uk

Pictures of golfing greats from Tom Morris to Tiger Woods, along with clubs and a variety of memorabilia donated by famous players, are displayed in the admirable **British Golf Museum**, on the waterfront below the Royal and Ancient Golf Club clubhouse, which tells the story of British golf from its beginnings to the present day.

The beaches

St Andrews has two great **beaches**: West Sands, which stretch for two miles from just below the R&A Clubhouse, and the shorter, more compact, East Sands that curve round from the harbour beyond the cathedral. The West Sands are best known from the opening sequences of the Oscar-winning film *Chariots of Fire*. The blustery winds, which are the scourge of golfers and walkers alike, do at least make the beach a great place to **fly kites**.

20

ARRIVAL AND INFORMATION

ST ANDREWS

By train St Andrews' nearest train station (on the Edinburgh–Dundee line) is 5 miles northwest at Leuchars, across the River Eden, from where regular buses make the 15min trip into town. When you buy your rail ticket to Leuchars, ask for a St Andrews rail-bus ticket, which includes the bus fare.
Destinations Aberdeen (1–2 hourly; 1hr 30min); Dundee (1–2 hourly; 15min); Edinburgh (1–2 hourly; 1hr).
By bus The bus station is on Station Road, just off City Road and near the town centre.

Destinations Anstruther (2 hourly; 25min); Crail (hourly; 25min); Dundee (1–2 hourly; 35min); Dunfermline (hourly; 1hr 15min); Edinburgh (1–2 hourly; 1hr 50min); Glasgow (every 30min; 2hr 25min); Glenrothes (hourly; 40min); Kirkcaldy (every 30min; 1hr); Stirling (every 2hr; 1hr 55min).
Tourist information 70 Market St (April–June & Sept daily 10am–5pm; Nov–March Mon–Sat 10am–4pm; July & Aug Mon–Sat 9.15am–6pm, Sun 10am–5pm; ☎ 01334 472021, ⓦ visitstandrews.com).

ACCOMMODATION

There's no shortage of accommodation both in town and around, although average **prices** in all categories vie with Edinburgh's as the highest in Scotland. Rooms often fill up in summer, when you should definitely book in advance.

Aslar House 120 North St ☎ 01334 473460, ⓦ aslar .com. A smart guesthouse in a three-storey townhouse with an unusual round tower at the back. Rooms are traditionally furnished, and there's a good breakfast buffet with Scottish specialities. **£96**

Kinkell 2 miles south of town, off the A917 ☎ 01334 472003, ⓦ kinkell.com. Countryside B&B in a lovely family farmhouse near the beach; the house is furnished with lovely antiques, and breakfast includes eggs from their own hens. **£100**

★**Old Fishergate House** North Castle St ☎ 01334 470874, ⓦ oldfishergatehouse.co.uk. Seventeenth-century townhouse in the oldest part of St Andews, with two spacious

twin rooms brimming with period features. It's characterful without being cluttered; breakfast options inlcude smoked haddock omelette and Scotch pancakes. **£100**

St Andrews Tourist Hostel St Mary's Place ☎ 01334 479911, ⓦ hostelsaccommodation.com /hostels. Superbly-located backpacker hostel in a converted townhouse above *The Grill House* restaurant, with plenty of dorm beds, but no doubles. The cheapest option in town, and not the quietest. **£10**

University of St Andrews Various locations ☎ 01334 462000. Rooms for rent in various student residences between June and Sept, all on a B&B basis. Self-catering houses also available. Per person **£50**

EATING

The Doll's House 3 Church Square ☎01334 477422, ⓦ dolls-house.co.uk. Stylish modern dishes based around top Scottish produce, with a continental feel to the outdoor tables. Mains £10–18 at dinner, with good-value lunch menus. Daily noon–3pm & 5–10.30pm.

★**The Peat Inn** Cupar, 6 miles southwest of town ☎01334 840206, ⓦ thepeatinn.co.uk. Maintaining its reputation as one of Scotland's gourmet hot spots after 25 years, *The Peat Inn* offers fine dining using top local produce – roast loin of lamb in a pistachio crust with roast apricots, for example – in an intimate room. Menus range from a three-course set lunch (£24) to a six-course tasting menu (£65). They also have eight plush, if pricey, suites. Tues–Sat 12.30–1.30pm & 7–9pm.

★**The Seafood Restaurant** The Scores ☎01334 479475, ⓦ theseafoodrestaurant.com. The venue has as much of a wow-factor as the fish-dominated menu (three courses £50; try the sea trout with citrus mash): an amazing location in a custom-built glass building on the beach between the Aquarium and the Old Course. Mon–Sat noon–2.30pm & 6–10pm, Sun 12.30–3pm.

Tailend Fish Bar 130 Market St ☎01334 474070. A terrific and popular takeaway – a modern twist on the traditional chippy, dishing up locally-sourced fresh fish. There are reasonably priced fish suppers with crisp batter and excellent chips, plus specials such as sea bass, swordfish or skate. A simple café adjoins the takeaway. Daily 11.30am–10pm.

DRINKING AND ENTERTAINMENT

Byre Theatre Abbey St ☎01334 475000, ⓦ byretheatre.com. Occupies a stylish modern building, with a pleasant bar and bistro. Productions range from important Scottish drama to populist musicals.

The Central Market St ☎01334 478296. Prominent, popular old pub right in the heart of town serving real ales and pub grub. Mon–Thurs 11am–11.45pm, Fri & Sat 11am–midnight, Sun 12.30–11.45pm.

Ma Bells 40 The Scores ☎01334 472611, ⓦ standrews-golf.co.uk. In the basement of the *Hotel du Vin*, this is a lively pub serving cheap food and often thronged with students. Mon 11am–midnight, Tues–Sat 11am–1am, Sun 12.30pm–midnight.

The One Under 16 Pilmour Links ☎01334 473393, ⓦ theoneunder.com. Stylish hotel bar with views of the Old Course, gastropub food and mean espresso martinis. Daily: May–Sept noon–11pm; Oct–April noon–2.30pm & 6–9pm.

The East Neuk

Extending south of St Andrews as far as Largo Bay, the **East Neuk** is famous for its quaint fishing villages replete with crow-stepped gables and red pan-tiled roofs, the Flemish influence indicating a history of strong trading links with the Low Countries. The area is dotted with blustery **golf courses**, and there are plenty of bracing coastal paths, including the waymarked **Fife Coastal Path**: tracing the shoreline between St Andrews and the Forth Rail Bridge, it's at its most scenic in the East Neuk stretch.

Crail

CRAIL is the archetypally charming East Neuk fishing village, its maze of rough cobbled streets leading steeply down to a tiny stone-built harbour surrounded by piles of lobster creels, and with fishermen's cottages tucked into every nook and cranny in the cliff. Though often populated by artists at their easels and camera-toting tourists, it is still a working harbour, and if the boats have been out you can buy fresh lobster and crab cooked to order from a small wooden shack on the harbour edge (see opposite). You can trace the history of the town at the **Crail Museum and Heritage Centre**, 62 Marketgate (April Sat 10am–5pm, Sun noon–5pm; May–Sept Mon–Sat 10am–5pm, Sun noon–5pm; free), while the **Crail Pottery**, 75 Nethergate (Mon–Fri 9am–5pm, Sat & Sun 10am–5pm), is worth a visit for its wide range of locally made pottery.

ARRIVAL AND INFORMATION   CRAIL

By bus Bus #95 runs hourly to St Andrews (25min) and Leven (for connections to Edinburgh; 1hr) from the High Street.

Tourist information Crail Museum and Heritage Centre, 62 Marketgate (June–Sept Mon–Sat 11am–4pm, Sun 1–4pm; ☎01333 450869).

EATING

Crail Harbour Gallery and Tearoom Shoregate ☎ 01333 451896, ⓦ crailharbourgallery.co.uk. Tucked into a wee seventeenth-century cottage on the way down to the harbour, with a terrace overlooking the Isle of May. They serve Fairtrade coffees, hot chocolate and panini, plus local crab, smoked salmon and herring (snacks from £6).

Daily 11am–5pm.

★**Lobster Hut** The harbour. This tiny lobster and crab shack offers fresh seafood with sea views, and is the best place in town for a snack; a half lobster costs £11. Eat at the nearby picnic tables. Mid-April to early Oct Tues–Sun noon–4pm.

Anstruther

ANSTRUTHER is the largest of the East Neuk fishing harbours, with an attractively old-fashioned air and no shortage of character in its houses and narrow streets, it's also home to the wonderfully unpretentious **Scottish Fisheries Museum**.

Scottish Fisheries Museum

Harbourhead • April–Sept Mon–Sat 10am–5.30pm, Sun 11am–5pm; Oct–March Mon–Sat 10am–4.30pm, Sun noon–4.30pm • £7 • ☎ 01333 310628, ⓦ scotfishmuseum.org

Set in an atmospheric complex of sixteenth- to nineteenth-century buildings with timber ceilings and wooden floors, the **Scottish Fisheries Museum** chronicles the history of the fishing and whaling industries with ingenious displays, including a series of exquisite ships' models built on site by a resident model-maker.

Isle of May

Boats from Anstruther May & June Mon, Wed–Sun 1 daily; July–Sept 1 daily; 4–5hr for a round trip • £24 • ☎ 01333 310103, ⓦ isleofmayferry.com

Located on the rugged **Isle of May**, several miles offshore from Anstruther, is a lighthouse erected in 1816 by Robert Louis Stevenson's grandfather, as well as the remains of Scotland's first lighthouse, built in 1636. The island is now a **nature reserve** and bird sanctuary.

ARRIVAL AND INFORMATION

ANSTRUTHER

By bus Buses stop at the harbour and serve Edinburgh (1–2 hourly; 2hr 15min) and St Andrews (hourly; 25min).
Tourist information Scottish Fisheries Museum,

Harbourhead (April–Sept Mon–Sat 10am–5.30pm, Sun 11am–5pm; Oct Mon–Sat 10am–4.30pm, Sun noon–4.30pm; ☎ 01333 311073).

EATING

★**The Cellar** 24 East Green ☎ 01333 310370, ⓦ thecellaranstruther.co.uk. Tucked in beside the museum in one of the village's oldest buildings, once a cooperage and smokehouse, this fantastic restaurant

serves classy dishes including Scottish crab with rapeseed and Black Isle lamb with couscous. Three courses £42. Wed 6.30–9pm, Thurs–Sun 12.30–1.45pm & 6.30–9pm.

Central Fife

The main A92 road cuts right through **Central Fife**, ultimately connecting the Forth Road Bridge on the southern coast of Fife with the Tay Road Bridge on the northern coast. The main settlement of this inland region is **Glenrothes**, a new town created after World War II in old coal-mining territory. Generally, the scenery in this part of the county is pleasant rather than startling, though it's worth making a detour to **Falkland** and its magnificent ruined palace.

Falkland

The **Howe of Fife**, north of Glenrothes, is a low-lying stretch of ground (or "howe") at the foot of the twin peaks of the heather-swathed **Lomond Hills** – West Lomond (1696ft) and East Lomond (1378ft). Nestling in the lower slopes of East Lomond, the narrow streets of **FALKLAND** are lined with fine and well-preserved seventeenth- and eighteenth-century buildings.

Falkland Palace

March–Oct Mon–Sat 10am–5pm, Sun 1–5pm • £12.50; NTS • ☎ 0844 4932186

The village grew up around **Falkland Palace**, which stands on the site of an earlier castle, home to the Macduffs, the earls of Fife. James IV began the construction of the present palace in 1500; it was completed and embellished by James V, and became a favoured country retreat for the royal court. The palace was completely restored by the third Marquess of Bute, and today it is a stunning piece of architecture, complete with parapets, mullioned windows, round towers and massive walls. Free audioguides lead you round a cross section of public and private rooms in the south and east wings. Outside, the **gardens** are also worth a look, their well-stocked herbaceous borders lining a pristine lawn. Don't miss the high walls of the oldest real (or Royal) tennis court in Britain – built in 1539 for James V and still used.

ARRIVAL AND DEPARTURE   FALKLAND

By bus Buses stop on New Road, just east of the palace. **Destinations** Perth (Mon–Sat hourly, Sun 2 daily; 55min); St Andrews (Mon–Sat hourly, Sun 5 daily; 1hr 30min).

ACCOMMODATION AND EATING

★ **Ladywell House B&B** Half a mile south of Falkland ☎ 01337 858414, ⓦ ladywellhousefife.co.uk. A fine Georgian country house set in walled gardens. Meals are served in the spacious conservatory, and there's a smart drawing room. **£140**

★ **Pillars of Hercules Organic Farm** Just west of Falkland on the A912 ☎ 01337 857749, ⓦ pillars.co.uk. A great little farm shop and café; you can camp here, and there's a bothy available to hire. They also host monthly restaurant nights with live music. Daily 9am–6pm. Pitches **£8**; bothy **£100**

Southern Fife

Although the coast of **southern Fife** is predominantly industrial – with everything from cottage industries to the refitting of nuclear submarines – mercifully, only a small part has been blighted by insensitive development. Thanks to its proximity to the early coal mines, the charming village of **Culross** was once a lively port which enjoyed a thriving trade with Holland, the Dutch influence obvious in its lovely gabled houses. It was from nearby **Dunfermline** that Queen Margaret ousted the Celtic Church from Scotland in the eleventh century; her son, David I, founded an abbey here in the twelfth century. Southern Fife is linked to Edinburgh by the two **Forth bridges**, the red-painted girders of the Rail Bridge representing one of Britain's great engineering spectacles.

Culross

CULROSS (pronounced "Coorus") is one of Scotland's most picturesque settlements, owing to the work of the National Trust for Scotland, which has been renovating its whitewashed, pan-tiled buildings since 1932. For an excellent introduction to the burgh's history, head to the **National Trust Visitor Centre** (April, May & Sept Thurs–Mon noon–5pm; June–Aug daily noon–5pm; Oct Thurs–Mon noon–4pm; NTS; joint ticket for Town House, Palace and Study £10.50; Town House and Study by 1hr guided tour only: 1.30pm, 2.30pm & 3.30pm), located in the **Town House** facing Sandhaven, where goods were once unloaded from ships.

The charm of Culross was revealed simply by wandering through its narrow streets looking for old inscriptions above windows and investigating crooked passageways. Leading uphill from the Town House, a cobbled alleyway known as **Back Causeway** leads up to the **Study** (same hours as visitor centre), a restored house that takes its name from the small room at the top of the corbelled projecting tower, reached by a turnpike stair. Further up the hill from the Study lie the remains of **Culross Abbey**, founded by Cistercian monks on land given to the church in 1217 by the Earl of Fife.

Culross Palace

April, May & Sept Thurs–Mon noon–5pm; June–Aug daily noon–5pm; Oct Thurs–Mon noon–4pm • Joint ticket for Town House, Palace and Study £10.50; NTS • ☎ 0844 4932189

The most impressive building in the village is the ochre-coloured **Culross Palace**, built by wealthy coal merchant George Bruce in the late sixteenth century; it's not a palace at all but a grand and impressive house, with lots of small rooms and connecting passageways. Inside, well-informed staff point out the wonderful painted ceilings, pine panelling, antique furniture and curios; outside, dormer windows and crow-stepped gables dominate the walled court in which the house stands.

ARRIVAL CULROSS

By bus From Dunfermline (where there's a train station), take Stagecoach bus #71, #74 or #78 (1–2 hourly; 30min), all of which stop at Culross Palace; buses also run to Stirling (Mon–Sat hourly; 50min).

Dunfermline

Scotland's capital until the Union of the Crowns in 1603, DUNFERMLINE lies inland seven miles east of Culross, north of the Forth bridges. Ringed by shabby development, the town is not initially charismatic, but the abbey and surrounds make it worth the trip.

Dunfermline Abbey

April–Sept daily 9.30am–5.30pm; Oct–March Mon–Wed & Sat 9.30am–4.30pm, Thurs 9.30am–12.30pm, Sun 2–4.30pm • £4.50; HS • ☎ 01383 724586

The oldest part of **Dunfermline Abbey** is attributable to Queen Margaret, who began building a Benedictine priory in 1072, the remains of which can still be seen beneath the nave of the present church; her son, **David I**, raised the priory to the rank of abbey in the following century. In 1303, during the first of the **Wars of Independence**, the English king Edward I occupied the palace and ordered the destruction of most of the monastery buildings. **Robert the Bruce** helped rebuild the abbey, and when he died of leprosy 25 years later he was buried here, although his body went undiscovered until building began on a new parish church in 1821. Inside, the stained glass is impressive, and the columns are artfully carved into chevrons, spirals and arrowheads.

ARRIVAL AND DEPARTURE DUNFERMLINE

By train The station is on the south side of the centre, with its main entrance off St Margaret's Drive.
Destinations Edinburgh (every 30min; 35min); Kirkcaldy (hourly; 40min).
By bus Buses stop at Queen Anne St, between Carnegie Drive and High St.

Destinations Culross (1–2 hourly; 20min); Edinburgh (every 30min; 40min); Glasgow (every 30min; 1hr 10min); Kirkcaldy (hourly; 30min); North Queensferry (every 30min; 11min); Stirling (every 2hr; 1hr 15min).

North Queensferry

The highlight of Fife's **south coast** is one of Scotland's largest man-made structures, the impressive Forth Rail Bridge, which joins Fife at **NORTH QUEENSFERRY**. Until the opening of the road bridge, this small fishing village was the northern landing point of the ferry from South Queensferry (see p.758), but today everything in the village is quite literally overshadowed by the two great bridges, each about a mile and a half in length, which traverse the Firth of Forth at its narrowest point.

Forth Rail Bridge

The cantilevered **Forth Rail Bridge**, built from 1883 to 1890 by Sir John Fowler and Benjamin Baker, ranks among the supreme achievements of Victorian engineering, with some fifty thousand tonnes of steel used in the construction of a design that manages to express grace as well as might. The only way to cross the rail bridge is on a train heading to or from Edinburgh, though this doesn't allow much of a perspective of

20

the spectacle itself. For the best **panorama**, use the pedestrian and cycle lanes on the east side of the road bridge.

Forth Road Bridge

Derived from American models, the suspension format chosen for the **Forth Road Bridge**, alongside the rail bridge, makes an interesting modern complement to the older structure. Erected between 1958 and 1964, it finally killed off the 900-year-old ferry, and now attracts such a heavy volume of traffic that a second road crossing is being considered.

Deep Sea World

Battery Quarry • Mon–Fri 10am–5pm, Sat & Sun 10am–6pm • £13.50 • ☎ 01383 411880, ⓦ deepseaworld.com

Tucked beneath the mighty rail bridge is **Deep Sea World**, one of Scotland's most popular family attractions. Full of weird and wonderful creatures from sea horses to piranhas, the highlight is a huge aquarium that boasts the world's largest underwater viewing tunnel, through which you glide on a moving walkway while sharks, conger eels and all manner of fish from the deep swim nonchalantly past.

ARRIVAL	NORTH QUEENFERRY
By train Trains connect North Queensferry with Edinburgh every 15min (20min), and there is a similar frequency of services north to Inverkeithing (3min).	**By bus** There are hourly services to Dunfermline (30min) from the main road.

20

Perthshire

Genteel, attractive **Perthshire** is, in many ways, the epitome of well-groomed rural Scotland. An area of gentle glens, mature woodland, rushing rivers and peaceful lochs, it's the long-established domain of Scotland's well-to-do country set. First settled more than eight thousand years ago, it was ruled by the Romans and then the Picts before Celtic missionaries established themselves.

The ancient town of **Perth** occupies a strategic position at the mouth of the River Tay; salmon, wool and, by the sixteenth century, whisky, were exported, while a major import was Bordeaux claret. At nearby **Scone**, Kenneth MacAlpine established the capital of the kingdom of the Scots and the Picts in 846. When this settlement was washed away by floods in 1210, William the Lion founded Perth as a royal burgh.

North and west of Perth, **Highland Perthshire** is made up of gorgeous and mighty woodlands, particularly along the banks of the River Tay. The area is dotted with neat, confident towns and villages like **Dunkeld** and **Birnam**, with its mature trees and lovely ruined cathedral, and **Aberfeldy** set deep among farmland east of Loch Tay. Further north, the countryside becomes more sparsely populated and spectacular, with some

---

OUTDOOR ACTIVITIES IN PERTHSHIRE

In Perthshire, outdoor activities range from gentle strolls through ancient oak forests to white-knuckle rides down frothing waterfalls.

Highland Safaris Aberfeldy ☎ 01887 820071, ⓦ highlandsafaris.net. An inspiring introduction to wild Scotland in which you're taken by 4WD to search for golden eagle eyries, stags and pine martens.

Nae Limits Dunkeld and Ballinluig ☎ 01796 482600, ⓦ naelimits.co.uk. Canyoning, cliff-jumping, bungee jumping and sphere-ing (which involves tumbling down

a hillside inside a giant plastic ball) for adrenalin junkies.

National Kayak School Aberfeldy ☎ 01631 565310, ⓦ nationalkayakschool.com. Everything from whitewater kayaking courses to sea-kayaking holidays.

Splash Aberfeldy ☎ 01887 829706, ⓦ rafting.co.uk. Rafting on larger craft through the best rapids on the Tay at Grandtully.

wonderful walking country, especially around **Pitlochry**, **Blair Atholl** and the wild expanses of **Rannoch Moor** to the west.

Perth and around

Surrounded by fertile agricultural land and beautiful scenery, the bustling market town of **PERTH** was Scotland's capital in the fifteenth century, and expanded in the eighteenth. Today, with the whisky and insurance trades employing significant numbers, it remains an important town.

Two large areas of green parkland, known as the North and South Inch, flank the **centre**; the city's main shopping areas are **High Street** and **South Street**, as well as St John's shopping centre on King Edward Street. Perth is at its most attractive along **Tay Street**, with a succession of grander buildings along one side and the attractively landscaped riverside embankment on the other.

Fergusson Gallery

Corner of Tay St and Marshall Place • May–Aug Mon–Sat 10am–5pm, Sun 1–4.30pm; Sept–April Mon–Sat 10am–5pm • Free • ☎ 01738 783425, ⓦ pkc.gov.uk/museums

Perth's highlight is the **Fergusson Gallery**, occupying a striking, round, Victorian sandstone water tower, and home to an extensive collection of work by J.D. Fergusson, foremost artist of the Scottish Colourist movement (see box, p.795). Greatly influenced by Impressionist and Post-Impressionist artists, he created a distinctive approach that marries both movements' freedom of style with bold use of colour and lighting – shown, for example, in his portrait of Elizabeth Dryden, *The Hat with the Pink Scarf*. As well as oils, the collection includes sketches, notebooks and sculpture: among the latter, look out for *Eastre: Hymn to the Sun*, an exotic and radiant brass head inspired by his dancer wife and collaborator Margaret Morris.

Scone Palace

A couple of miles north of Perth on the A93 • April–Oct daily 9.30am–5.30pm • £10.50, grounds only £6.30 • ☎ 01738 552300, ⓦ scone-palace.co.uk • Bus #3 or #58 from Perth

Scone Palace (pronounced "skoon") is one of Scotland's finest historical country homes. Owned and occupied by the Earl and Countess of Mansfield, the two-storey building on the eastern side of the Tay is stately but not overpowering, more a home than an untouchable monument. The rooms, although full of priceless antiques and lavish furnishings, feel lived-in.

The abbey that stood here in the sixteenth century was where all Scottish kings until James IV were crowned. Long before that, Scone was the capital of Pictavia, and it was here that Kenneth MacAlpine brought the famous Coronation **Stone of Destiny**, or Stone of Scone, now to be found in Edinburgh Castle, and where he ruled as the first king of a united Scotland. A replica of the (surprisingly small) stone can be found on Moot Hill, opposite the palace.

In the **grounds** you'll also find a beech-hedge maze in the pattern of the heraldic family crest and avenues of venerable trees. Scone was the birthplace of botanist and plant collector **David Douglas**, and following the trail named after him brings you to a fragrant pinetum planted in 1848 with many of the exotics he discovered in California and elsewhere.

ARRIVAL AND INFORMATION
PERTH

By train The station is in the southwest of town on Leonard St.

Destinations Aberdeen (hourly; 1hr 40min); Blair Atholl (3–7 daily; 45min); Dundee (hourly; 25min); Dunkeld (3–7 daily; 20min); Edinburgh (every 1–2hr; 1hr 25min);

Glasgow Queen St (hourly; 1hr); Inverness (4–9 daily; 2hr); Pitlochry (4–9 daily; 30min); Stirling (hourly; 30min).

By bus The bus station is opposite the train station on Leonard St.

Destinations Aberfeldy (10 daily; 1hr 15min); Crieff (hourly;

45min); Dundee (hourly; 45min); Dunkeld (hourly; 30min); Edinburgh (hourly; 1hr 20min); Glasgow (hourly; 1hr 35min); Gleneagles (hourly; 25min); Inverness (hourly; 2hr 45min); Pitlochry (hourly; 45min); Stirling (hourly; 50min).

Tourist information West Mill St (April–July, Sept & Oct Mon–Sat 9.30am–5pm, Sun 10.30am–3.30pm; Aug Mon–Sat 9.30am–6pm, Sun 10am–4.30pm; Nov–March Mon–Sat 9.30am–4.30pm).

ACCOMMODATION

Kinnaird House 5 Marshall Place ☎01738 628021, ⓦkinnaird-guesthouse.co.uk. A warm welcome in a lovely townhouse overlooking South Inch Park, with six well-equipped double/twin en-suite rooms and lots of organic options on the breakfast menu. **£70**

Parklands Hotel 2 St Leonards Bank ☎01738 622451, ⓦtheparklandshotel.com. Of the numerous central hotels, aim for the fourteen-bedroom *Parklands* close to the train station, which has a dash of contemporary styling and touches of luxury; there's a good restaurant and bistro on site. **£110**

EATING AND DRINKING

63 Tay Street 63 Tay St ☎01738 441451, ⓦ63taystreet.com. At the top end of the market in Perth – and indeed the country – serving classy and expensive Modern Scottish food with Mediterranean influences. Mains from £14 at lunch; four-course dinner menu £42. Tues–Sat noon–2pm & 6.30–9pm.

Café Tabou 4 St John's Place ☎01738 446698, ⓦcafetabou.co.uk. For moderately priced food try *Café Tabou* with its menu of French classics and outdoor seating. There are lots of seafood options, including oyster,

langoustines and mussels, with set lunch menus (£11–15), pre-theatre menus, and dinner mains from £14. Mon 10am–3pm, Tues–Thurs 10am–9.30pm, Fri & Sat 10am–10pm, Sun noon–3pm.

Kerachers 168 South St ☎01738 449777, ⓦkerachers -restaurant.co.uk. Homely upstairs restaurant, located in a restored Wesleyan chapel, best known for its elegant fish dishes (3 courses £27.50). Tues–Thurs 6–9.30pm, Fri 6–10pm, Sat 6–10.30pm.

Strath Tay

North of Perth, both the railway and main A9 trunk road speed through some of Perthshire's most attractive countryside before heading into the bleaker Highlands. Magnificent woodland spreads around the valley – or "strath" – of the River Tay, as it heads towards the sea from attractive **Loch Tay**. On the eastern side of the loch, the Tay calmly glides past the attractive country town of **Aberfeldy**. The loch itself, meanwhile, is set up among the high Breadalbane mountains, which include the striking peak of **Ben Lawers**, Perthshire's highest, and the hills that enclose the long, enchanting **Glen Lyon**.

Dunkeld

Twelve miles north of Perth, **DUNKELD** was proclaimed Scotland's ecclesiastical capital by Kenneth MacAlpine in 850. The town is one of the area's most pleasant communities, with handsome whitewashed houses, appealing arts and crafts shops, a picturesque cathedral and a vibrant folk music venue.

Dunkeld Cathedral

Daily: May–Sept 9.30am–6.30pm; Oct–April 9.30am–4pm • Free • ⓦ dunkeldcathedral.org.uk

Dunkeld's partly ruined **cathedral** is on the northern side of town, in an idyllic setting amid lawns and trees on the east bank of the Tay. The present structure consists of the fourteenth-century choir and the fifteenth-century nave; the choir, restored in 1600 (and several times since), now serves as the parish church, while the nave remains roofless apart from the clocktower.

Loch of the Lowes

Two miles east of Dunkeld off the A923 • **Visitor centre** April–Sept 10am–5pm • £4 • ☎ 01350 727337, ⓦ scottishwildlifetrust.org.uk

The **Loch of the Lowes** nature reserve, covering 95 hectares, offers a rare chance to see breeding ospreys, as well as other wildfowl, woodland birds and red squirrels; the **visitor centre** has video relay screens and will point you in the direction of the best vantage points.

20

ARRIVAL AND INFORMATION DUNKELD

By train Dunkeld & Birnam station is served by fast and frequent services from Perth (10 daily; 20min); the station is just south of the A9 in Birnam.

Tourist information The Cross, town centre (April–June,

Sept & Oct Mon–Sat 10am–4.30pm, Sun 10.30am–3.30pm; July & Aug Mon–Sat 9.30am–6.30pm, Sun 10am–4pm; ☎01350 727688).

EATING AND DRINKING

Robert Menzies Deli 1 Atholl St, Dunkeld ☎01350 728028, ⓦscottish-deli.com. You can pick up snacks, sandwiches, Scottish beers and fresh fruit here; they also have a tiny café. There's been a deli here for more than fifty years, and the shop retains its original fittings. Mon–Fri 9.30am–5.30pm, Sat 9am–5.30pm, Sun 10am–4.30pm.

★**Taybank Hotel** Tay Terrace ☎01350 727340, ⓦthetaybank.squarespace.com. A characterful beacon for music fans, who come for the regular live sessions in the convivial bar. Decent bar meals, too (the stovies are a speciality). Mon–Fri & Sun 11am–11pm, Sat 11am–11.30pm.

Birnam

Dunkeld is linked to its sister community, **BIRNAM**, just to the south, by Thomas Telford's seven-arched bridge of 1809. This little village has a place in history thanks to Shakespeare, for it was on Dunsinane Hill, to the southeast of the village, that Macbeth declared: "I will not be afraid of death and bane Till Birnam Forest come to Dunsinane", only to be told later by a messenger "I look'd toward Birnam, and anon me thought The Wood began to move…"

The **Birnam Oak**, a gnarly old character propped up by crutches on the waymarked riverside walk, is inevitably claimed to be a survivor of the infamous mobile forest. Several centuries after Shakespeare, another literary personality, Beatrix Potter, drew inspiration from the area: there's a Potter-themed exhibition and garden, aimed at both children and adults, on the main road in the impressive barrel-fronted **Birnam Institute** (daily 10am–5pm; ⓦbirnaminstitute.com; free), a modern theatre, arts and community centre.

A mile and a half west of Birnam is **The Hermitage**, set in a grandly wooded gorge of the plunging River Braan. Here you'll find a pretty eighteenth-century folly, known as Ossian's Hall, which neatly frames a dramatic waterfall. Nearby, you can see a Douglas fir, claimed to be the tallest tree in Britain.

20

ARRIVAL AND INFORMATION BIRNAM

By train Dunkeld & Birnam station is served by fast and frequent services from Perth (10 daily; 20min); the station

is just south of the A9 in Birnam.

ACCOMMODATION

★**Jessie Mac's** Murthly Terrace ☎01350 727324, ⓦjessiemacs.co.uk. Great little hostel/B&B set in a turreted end-of-terrace Victorian villa. Breakfasts are excellent, with meat provided by an award-winning local

butcher and local salmon. You can also self-cater. Dorms and rooms are colourful, with funky details and flatscreen TVs. Dorms £18; doubles £56

Aberfeldy

A prosperous settlement of large stone houses and 4WDs, **ABERFELDY** acts as a service centre for the wider Loch Tay area. The town's main attraction is **Dewar's World of Whisky** at the Aberfeldy Distillery (April–Oct Mon–Sat 10am–6pm, Sun noon–4pm; Nov–March Mon–Sat 10am–4pm; ⓦdewarswow.com; from £7.50), which puts on an impressive show of describing the making of whisky. The rest of the small town centre is a busy mixture of craft and tourist shops, the most interesting being **The Watermill** on Mill Street (Mon–Sat 10am–5pm, Sun 11am–5pm; ⓦaberfeldywatermill.com), an inspiring bookshop and art gallery in a restored, early nineteenth-century mill.

By bus Buses connect Aberfeldy with Perth (6 daily; 1hr 20min), stopping at Chapel Street.

Tourist information The Square (April–June, Sept & Oct

Mon–Sat 9.30am–5pm, Sun 11am–3pm; July & Aug Mon–Sat 9.30am–6.30pm, Sun 10am–4pm; Nov–March Mon–Sat 10am–4pm; ☎01887 820276).

EATING

The Watermill Mill St ☎01887 822896, ⊛aberfeldywatermill.com. Your best bet for a good coffee or a light lunch. There are comfy sofas, and the

excellent soups, sandwiches and cakes are made locally, mainly with organic ingredients. Mon–Sat 10am–5pm, Sun 11am–5pm.

Loch Tay

A fourteen-mile-long stretch of fresh water. **Loch Tay** virtually hooks together the western and eastern Highlands. Guarding the northern end of the loch is **KENMORE**, a cluster of whitewashed estate houses and well-tended gardens. The main draw here is a fantastic heritage museum, the **Scottish Crannog Centre**.

Scottish Crannog Centre

Kenmore • Daily: April–Oct 10am–5.30pm; Nov 10am–4pm • £8.50 • ☎01887 830583, ⊛crannog.co.uk

Crannogs are Iron Age loch dwellings built on stilts over the water. Originally they would have had a gangway to the shore; upon the approach of hostile intruders, whether animal or human, the gangway would quickly be raised. At the **Scottish Crannog Centre** visitors can walk out over the loch to a superbly reconstructed, thatched, wooden crannog. The whole place is set up to look as it would have 2500 years ago, complete with sheepskin rugs and wooden bowls, and is an ideal attraction for curious kids.

Ben Lawers

Dominating the northern side of Loch Tay is moody **Ben Lawers** (3984ft), Perthshire's highest mountain; from the top there are incredible views towards both the Atlantic and the North Sea. The ascent – which should not be tackled unless you're properly equipped for Scottish hillwalking – takes around three hours from the **NTS visitor centre** (April–Sept daily 10am–5pm), located at 1300ft and reached by a winding hill road off the A827.

By bus From June to October, use the hop-on, hop-off Ring of Breadalbane Explorer bus connecting Aberfeldy,

Kenmore, Killin, Comrie and Crieff (4 circuits 9am–9pm).

Glen Lyon

North of Breadalbane, the mountains tumble down into **Glen Lyon** – at 34 miles long, the longest enclosed glen in Scotland. The narrow singletrack road through the glen starts at **Keltneyburn**, near Kenmore at the northern end of the loch; a few miles on, the village of **FORTINGALL** is little more than a handful of pretty thatched cottages, although locals make much of their 5000-year-old yew tree, believed (by them at least) to be the oldest living thing in Europe. The venerable tree can be found in the churchyard, showing its age a little but well looked after, with a timeline nearby listing some of the events the yew has lived through. One of these, bizarrely, is the birth of Pontius Pilate, reputedly the son of a Roman officer stationed near Fortingall in the last years BC.

By bus The #91 bus connects Fortingall with Aberfeldy, but only runs on Mon, Thurs & Fri (2 daily; 30min).

Highland Perthshire

North of the Tay valley, Perthshire doesn't discard its lush richness immediately, but there are clear indications of the more rugged, barren influences of the Highlands proper. The principal settlements of **Pitlochry** and **Blair Atholl**, both just off the A9, are separated by the narrow gorge of Killiecrankie, a crucial strategic spot in times past for anyone seeking to control movement of cattle or armies from the Highlands to the Lowlands. Greater rewards, however, are to be found further from the main drag, most notably in the winding westward road along the shores of **Loch Tummel** and **Loch Rannoch** past the distinctive peak of **Schiehallion**, which eventually leads to the remote wilderness of **Rannoch Moor**.

Pitlochry

PITLOCHRY has, on the face of it, a lot going for it, not least the backdrop of Ben Vrackie and the River Tummel slipping by. However, there's little charm to be found on the main street, filled with crawling traffic and endless shops selling cut-price woollens, knobbly walking sticks and glass baubles; a better stop is the station's excellent charity bookshop.

Edradour Distillery

A couple of miles east of Pitlochry on the A924 • March & April, Nov & Dec Mon–Sat 10am–4pm, Sun noon–4pm; May & Oct Mon–Sat 10am–5pm, Sun noon–5pm; June–Sept 9.30am–5pm, Sun noon–5pm; Jan & Feb Mon–Sat 10am–4pm • £7.50 • ⊕ edradour.co.uk

The one attraction with some distinction in Pitlochry is the **Edradour Distillery**, Scotland's smallest, in an idyllic position tucked into the hills. Although the tour of the distillery itself isn't out of the ordinary, the lack of industrialization and the fact that the whole traditional process is done on site gives Edradour more personality than many of its rivals.

20

ARRIVAL AND INFORMATION   PITLOCHRY

By train Pitlochry is on the main train line to Inverness (hourly; 1hr 40min). The station is on Station Rd, just south of the centre.

By bus Regular buses from Perth (every 1–2hr; 40min) and Inverness (7 daily; 2hr 10min) stop near the train station.

Tourist information 22 Atholl Rd (April–June & Oct

Mon–Sat 9am–5pm, Sun 10am–5pm; July–Sept Mon–Sat 9am–6pm, Sun 10am–6pm; Nov–March Mon–Sat 10am–4pm; ☎ 01796 472215).

Cycling info Escape Route, 3 Atholl Rd (☎ 01796 473859, ⊕ escape-route.biz), can provide advice on local cycling routes, bike rental and general outdoor gear.

ACCOMMODATION

★ **Craigatin House and Courtyard** 165 Atholl Rd ☎ 01796 472478, ⊕ craigatinhouse.co.uk. On the northern section of the main road through town, this attractive, contemporary B&B has large beds, soothing decor and a pleasant garden. **£90**

Pitlochry Backpackers Hotel 134 Atholl Rd ☎ 01796 470044, ⊕ pitlochrybackpackershotel.com. This central hostel is based in a former hotel and offers dorms along with around ten twin and double rooms. Dorms **£18**; doubles **£52**

EATING, DRINKING AND ENTERTAINMENT

Pitlochry is the domain of the tearoom, and you have to hunt to find decent places for a full **meal**.

Moulin Inn Moulin, on the outskirts along the A924 ☎ 01796 472196, ⊕ moulininn.co.uk. The best bet for traditional pub grub (mains from £14), this award-winning inn is handily placed at the foot of Ben Vrackie. The original building dates back to 1695. Daily noon–2pm & 6–11pm.

Pitlochry Festival Theatre Port Na Craig ☎ 01796 484626, ⊕ pitlochry.org.uk. On the western edge of town, just across the river, Scotland's renowned "Theatre in the Hills" stages a variety of productions – mostly

mainstream theatre from the resident repertoire company, along with regular music events – during the summer season (May–Oct) and on ad hoc dates the rest of the year.

Port-na-craig Inn By Pitlochry Theatre ☎ 01796 472777, ⊕ portnacraig.com. This ancient stone-built inn has a beautiful riverside location near Pitlochry's theatre, and a light-filled conservatory. The food uses fresh local ingredients, some of them home-grown, for dishes such as Buckie haddock in beer batter (£12.95). Daily 10am till late.

20

RANNOCH MOOR

Rannoch Moor occupies roughly 150 square miles of uninhabited and uninhabitable peat bogs, lochs, heather hillocks, strewn lumps of granite and a few gnarled Caledonian pine, all of it more than 1000ft above sea level. Perhaps the most striking thing about the moor is its inaccessibility: one road, between Crianlarich and Glen Coe, skirts its western side, while another struggles west from Pitlochry to reach its eastern edge at Rannoch Station. The only regular form of transport is the **West Highland railway**, which stops at Rannoch and, a little to the north, Corrour station, which has no road access at all. From Rannoch station it's possible to catch the train to Corrour and walk the nine miles back; it's a longer slog west to the eastern end of Glen Coe (see p.904), the dramatic peaks of which poke up above the moor's western horizon. Determined hillwalkers will find a clutch of Munros around Corrour, including remote Ben Alder (3765ft), high above the forbidding shores of Loch Ericht.

SYHA Loch Ossian A mile from Corrour train station on the shores of Loch Ossian ☎ 0870 004 1139, ✉ lochossian@syha.org.uk. This comfortable, cosy – and remote – eco-hostel is a great place for hikers seeking somewhere genuinely off the beaten track. Good wildlife-watching opportunities, too. **£18**

Loch Tummel

West of Pitlochry, the B8019/B846 makes a memorably scenic, if tortuous, traverse of the shores of **Loch Tummel** and then **Loch Rannoch**. These two lochs and their adjoining rivers were much changed by massive hydroelectric schemes built in the 1940s and 1950s, yet this is still a spectacular stretch of countryside and one which deserves leisurely exploration. **Queen's View** at the eastern end of Loch Tummel is an obvious vantage point, looking down the loch to the misty peak of **Schiehallion** (3520ft), whose name comes from the Gaelic meaning "Fairy Mountain". One of Scotland's few freestanding hills, it's a popular, fairly easy and inspiring climb, with views on a good day to both sides of the country and north to the massed ranks of Highland peaks. The path up starts at Braes of Foss, just off the B846: allow three to four hours to the top and back.

Loch Rannoch

Beyond Loch Tummel, at the eastern end of Loch Rannoch, the small community of **KINLOCH RANNOCH** doesn't see a lot of passing trade other than fishermen and hillwalkers. Otherwise, the only real destination here is **Rannoch station**, a lonely outpost on the Glasgow–Fort William West Highland train line, sixteen miles further on at the end of the road.

ARRIVAL AND ACCOMMODATION   LOCH RANNOCH

By train Rannoch station sees trains to Corrour (3–4 daily; 12min); Fort William (3–4 daily; 1hr); Glasgow Queen St (3–4 daily; 2hr 45min) and London Euston (sleeper service; Sun–Fri daily; 11hr).

By bus Buses run to Kinloch Rannoch from Pitlochry (3 daily; 50min); local buses from Kinloch Rannoch (Broons Bus #85; 4 daily; 40min) and a postbus from Pitlochry

(#223; Mon–Sat 8am) provide connections to Rannoch station.

Moor of Rannoch Rannoch station ☎ 01882 633238, ✇ moorofrannoch.co.uk. Pleasant, small hotel in a handsome whitewashed building. Despite a friendly welcome, there's still a feeling of isolation in this empty landscape. Mid-Feb to Oct. **£114**

Pass of Killiecrankie

Four miles north of Pitlochry, the A9 cuts through the **Pass of Killiecrankie**, a breathtaking wooded gorge which falls away to the River Garry below. This dramatic setting was the site of the **Battle of Killiecrankie** in 1689, when the Jacobites quashed the forces of General Mackay. Legend has it that one soldier of the Crown, fleeing for his life, made a miraculous jump across the 18-foot **Soldier's Leap**, an impossibly wide chasm halfway up the gorge. Exhibits at the slick **NTS visitor centre** recall the battle and examine the gorge in detail. **Guided walks** from the centre take you through thick, mature forest, full of interesting plants and creatures.

INFORMATION	PASS OF KILLIECRANKIE

Killiecrankie NTS visitor centre East side of the Pass of   ☎ 0844 493 2194).
Killiecrankie (April–Oct daily 10am–5.30pm; parking £2;

Blair Atholl

Three miles north of Killiecrankie, the village of **BLAIR ATHOLL** makes for a much quieter and more idiosyncratic stop than Pitlochry. You can wander round the **Watermill** on Ford Road (April–Oct daily 10.30am–5.30pm; ⓦ blairathollwatermill. co.uk), which dates from 1613, and witness flour being milled. The mill also has a nice tearoom (see below).

Blair Castle

April–Oct daily 9.30am–5.30pm (last admission); Nov–March occasional weekends – see website for details • £9.90, grounds only £5.45 • ☎ 01796 481207, ⓦ blair-castle.co.uk

By far the most important and eye-catching building in these parts is **Blair Castle**, seat of the Atholl dukedom. This whitewashed, turreted castle looks particularly impressive as you sweep along the driveway leading from the centre of Blair Atholl village, especially if a piper is playing. The pipers belong to the Atholl Highlanders, a select group retained by the duke as his private army – a unique privilege afforded to him by Queen Victoria, who stayed here in 1844. Highlights are the soaring **entrance hall**, with every spare inch of wood panelling covered in weapons of some description, and the vast **ballroom**, with its timber roof, antlers, and mixture of portraits.

ARRIVAL AND INFORMATION	BLAIR ATHOLL	**20**

By train Trains from Pitlochry heading north arrive at Blair Atholl station (every 2–3hr; 9min).

By bus There are Citylink bus services from Edinburgh (hourly; 2hr 30min), Glasgow (hourly; 2hr 40min), Perth (hourly; 1hr) and Inverness (hourly; 2hr) to the *Atholl Arms* in Blair Atholl.

Atholl Estates Information Centre Opposite the Blair Castle Caravan Park, just off the A9 (April–Oct daily 9am–4.45pm; ☎ 01796 481646, ⓦ athollestatesranger service.co.uk). They provide details of the extensive network of local walks and bike rides and information on surrounding flora and fauna.

EATING

Blair Atholl Watermill Ford Rd ☎ 01796 481321 ⓦ blairathollwatermill.co.uk. Lovely little working mill where you can enjoy home-baked scones and light lunches in its timber-beamed tearoom. April–Oct daily 9am–5pm.

Argyll

HIGHLAND CATTLE, MULL

21

Argyll

Cut off for centuries from the rest of Scotland by the mountains and sea lochs that characterize the region, Argyll remains remote and sparsely populated, its scatter of offshore islands forming part of the Inner Hebridean archipelago. Geographically and culturally, this is a transitional area between Highland and Lowland, boasting a rich variety of scenery from subtropical gardens warmed by the Gulf Stream to flat, treeless islands on the edge of the Atlantic. It's in the folds and twists of the countryside, the interplay of land and water, and the views out to the islands that the strengths and beauties of mainland Argyll lie – the one area of man-made sights you shouldn't miss, however, is the cluster of Celtic and prehistoric sites near Kilmartin.

The eastern duo of **Bute** and **Arran** are the most popular of Scotland's more southerly islands, the latter – now, strictly, part of Ayrshire – justifiably so, with spectacular scenery ranging from the granite peaks of the north to the Lowland pasture of the south. Of the Hebridean islands covered in this chapter, mountainous **Mull** is the most visited, and is large enough to absorb the crowds, many of whom are only passing through en route to the tiny isle of **Iona**, a place of spiritual pilgrimage for centuries. **Islay**, best known for its malt whiskies, is fairly quiet even in the height of summer, as is neighbouring **Jura**, which offers excellent walking. And, for those seeking further solitude, there are the more remote islands of **Tiree** and **Coll**, which, although swept with fierce winds, have more sunny days than anywhere else in Scotland.

GETTING AROUND   ARGYLL

Argyll's **public transport** options are minimal, though buses do serve most major settlements, and the train line reaches Oban. In the remoter parts and on the islands, you'll have to rely on walking, shared taxis and the postbus. If you're planning to take a **vehicle** across to one of the islands, make sure to reserve both your outward and return journeys as early as possible, as the ferries get very booked up.

Isle of Bute

The island of **BUTE** is in many ways simply an extension of the Cowal peninsula, from which it is separated by the narrow Kyles of Bute. Thanks to its consistently mild climate, extensive sandy beaches and a **ferry link** with Wemyss Bay, Bute (ⓦvisitbute .com) has been a popular holiday and convalescence spot for Clydesiders for over a century.

ARRIVAL AND DEPARTURE   ISLE OF BUTE

By ferry Regular CalMac ferries (ⓦcalmac.co.uk) run from Wemyss Bay, 30 miles west of Glasgow, to Rothesay (every 45min; 30min). There's also a small CalMac ferry crossing from Colintraive, 25 miles south of Inveraray, to Rhubodach, 6 miles north of Rothesay (frequently; 5min).

Hiking up Goat Fell p.856	Geese on Islay p.859
Islay whisky p.858	George Orwell on Jura p.861

TOBERMORY

Highlights

① Mount Stuart, Bute An architecturally overblown aristocratic mansion, set in the most beautiful grounds in the region. **See p.844**

② Tobermory, Mull The archetypal picturesque fishing village, ranged around a sheltered harbour and backed by steep hills. **See p.847**

③ Isle of Iona A centre of Christian culture since the sixth century, Iona is, despite the crowds, a very special place. **See p.849**

④ Golden beaches Argyll abounds in stunning sandy beaches, with lovely stretches at Coll, Tiree and Islay. **See p.850, p.851 & p.857**

⑤ Isle of Gigha The ideal island-scape: sandy beaches, friendly folk and the azaleas of Achamore Gardens – you can even stay at the laird's house. **See p.854**

⑥ Goat Fell, Arran Spectacular views over north Arran's craggy mountain range and the Firth of Clyde. **See p.856**

⑦ Whisky distilleries, Islay With a generous scattering of often beautifully situated distilleries to choose from, Islay is the ultimate whisky-lover's destination. **See p.858**

HIGHLIGHTS ARE MARKED ON THE MAP ON PP.842–843

HIGHLIGHTS
1 Mount Stuart, Bute
2 Tobermory, Mull
3 Isle of Iona
4 Isle of Gigha
5 Goat Fell, Arran
6 Whisky distilleries, Islay

0 miles 10

N

21

Rothesay and around

Bute's only town, **ROTHESAY** is a handsome Victorian resort set in a wide, sweeping bay, backed by green hills, with a classic palm-tree promenade and 1920s pagoda-style Winter Gardens. Even if you're just passing through, you should pay a visit to the ornate **Victorian toilets** (daily: Easter–Sept 8am–7.45pm; Oct–Easter 9am–4.45pm; 30p) on the pier, built by Twyfords in 1899 and now one of the town's most celebrated sights: they're a feast of marble, ceramics and brass. Rothesay also features the militarily useless, but architecturally impressive, moated ruins of **Rothesay Castle** (April–Sept daily 9.30am–5.30pm; Oct daily 9.30am–4.30pm; Nov–March Mon–Wed, Sat & Sun 9.30am–4.30pm; HS; £4.50; ⓦhistoric -scotland.gov.uk), built in the twelfth century and now hidden amid the town's backstreets.

Mount Stuart

3 miles south of Rothesay • **House** March–Oct Mon–Fri & Sun 11am–5pm, Sat 11am–1pm • £11.50 • **Gardens** March–Oct daily 10am–6pm • £6.50 • ☎01700 503877, ⓦmountstuart.com

Bute's highlight is **Mount Stuart**, seat of the fantastically wealthy seventh Marquess of Bute (aka former racing driver Johnny Dumfries). The mansion, built for the third marquess between 1879 and World War II, is an incredible High Gothic fancy, drawing architectural inspiration from all over Europe. The sumptuous interior and lovely gardens – established in the eighteenth century by the third earl of Bute – are extremely impressive.

ARRIVAL AND INFORMATION

By ferry CalMac ferries from Wemyss Bay arrive in the centre of town by the Winter Gardens (every 45min; 30min).

By island bus Buses arrive at and depart from Guildford Square, opposite the ferry terminal.

Destinations Kilchattan Bay (Mon–Sat 4 daily, Sun 3 daily; 30min); Mount Stuart (every 45min; 15min); Rhubodach (Mon–Fri 1–2 daily; 20min).

Tourist information 15 Victoria St, opposite the pier (daily 9.30am–5pm; longer hours in peak season; ☎01700 502151, ⓦvisitbute.com).

ACCOMMODATION

★**Balmory Hall** Balmory Rd, Ascog, halfway between Rothesay and Mount Stuart ☎01700 500669, ⓦbalmoryhall.com. A luxurious Victorian mansion, superbly run, and set in its own grounds. Rooms range from a self-catering gate lodge to a two-bedroom suite. **£170**

★**Boat House** 15 Battery Place ☎01700 502696, ⓦtheboathouse-bute.co.uk. A stylish boutique B&B with classy contemporary furnishings and decor though not all rooms are en suite. The full Scottish breakfasts include haggis, eggs Benedict and smoked haddock. **£65**

Bute Backpackers 36 Argyle St ☎01700 501876, ⓦbutebackpackers.co.uk. The only hostel on Bute is this conveniently located "backpackers' hotel", situated on the seafront and just a 5min walk from the pier with a mix of single, twin, double and family rooms. Twins **£40**

Cannon House 5 Battery Place ☎01700 502819, ⓦcannonhousehotel.co.uk. A fantastically elegant Georgian hotel, with a slightly old-fashioned atmosphere and very comfortable floral rooms: six doubles and one twin (several with sea views), near the pier. **£60**

EATING AND DRINKING

Mount Stuart Café Mount Stuart house ☎01700 505276, ⓦmountstuart.com. Beautiful café-restaurant serving sandwiches, salads and light lunches (from £5) on the first floor of the Mount Stuart visitor centre, giving great views into the trees. Mon & Tues 10am–6pm, Wed–Sun 10am–10pm.

Russian Tavern Port Royal Hotel, 37 Marine Rd, Port Bannatyne, 1 mile north of Rothesay ☎01700 505073, ⓦbutehotel.com. A highly original and engaging Russian-run pub serving fresh smoked sprats and razorfish with blini, washed down with real ales. Mains £12–17. Daily 12.30–10.30pm.

Squat Lobster 29 Gallowgate ☎01700 503603. Cosy little restaurant specializing in local seafood – you get a free bottle of house wine with two mains, or bring your own; mains from £6.95. Takeaway fish and chips and occasional live music. Mon & Tues noon–4pm, Wed–Sun noon–9pm.

Inveraray

The traditional county town of Argyll, and a classic example of eighteenth-century urban planning, **INVERARAY** was built in the 1770s by the Duke of Argyll in order to distance his newly rebuilt castle from the hoi polloi in the town and to establish a commercial and legal centre for the region. Inveraray has changed very little since and remains an absolute set piece of Scottish Georgian architecture, with the brilliant white arches of Front Street reflected in the still waters of Loch Fyne creating a truly memorable setting.

Squeezed onto a promontory some distance from the duke's new castle, Inveraray's "New Town" has a distinctive **Main Street** (set at a right angle to Front Street), flanked by whitewashed terraces whose window casements are picked out in black. At the top of the street the road divides to circumnavigate the town's Neoclassical church, originally built in two parts: the southern half served the Gaelic-speaking community, while the northern half served those who spoke English.

Inveraray Jail

East of the church • Daily: April–Oct 9.30am–6pm; Nov–March 10am–5pm • £9.50 • ☎ 01499 302381, ⦿ inverarayjail.co.uk

Inveraray Jail, whose attractive Georgian courthouse and grim prison blocks ceased to function in the 1930s, is now an enjoyable museum graphically recounting prison conditions from medieval times to the modern day. You can try out the minute "Airing Yards" where the prisoners got to exercise for an hour a day and, in the semicircular courthouse with its great views over the loch, listen to a re-enactment of a trial of the period.

Inveraray Castle

A 10min walk north of Main St • April–Oct daily 10am–5.45pm • £9.20 • ☎ 01499 302203, ⦿ www.inveraray-castle.com

Inveraray Castle remains the family home of the Duke of Argyll. Built in 1745, it was given a touch of the Loire in the nineteenth century with the addition of dormer windows and conical corner spires. Inside, the most startling feature is the armoury hall, where the displays of weaponry – supplied to the Campbells by the British government to put down the Jacobites – rise through several storeys. Otherwise, the interior is pretty unremarkable, though it is worth looking out for Rob Roy's rather sad-looking sporran and dirk handle.

ARRIVAL AND INFORMATION INVERARAY

By bus Buses pick up and drop off on Front St, opposite the tourist office.

Destinations Glasgow (4–6 daily; 1hr 45min); Oban (Mon–Sat 4 daily, Sun 2 daily; 1hr 5min); Tarbert (2–3 daily; 1hr 30min).

Tourist information Front St (April–Oct Mon–Sat 9am–5pm, Sun noon–5pm; Nov–March Mon–Fri 10am–3pm, Sat & Sun 11am–3pm; ☎ 01499 302263).

ACCOMMODATION AND EATING

★**Cairndow Oyster Bar & Restaurant** 6 miles up the A83 towards Glasgow ☎ 01499 600482, ⦿ lochfyne .com. The best place to sample Loch Fyne's delicious fresh fish and seafood. *Cairndow* sells more oysters than anywhere else in the country, plus lots of other fishy treats; you can stock up on provisions and take away, or sit down and eat at the restaurant (mains £11–36). Daily 9am–9pm.

Inverary Hostel Dalmally Rd ☎ 01499 302454, ⦿ inverarayhostel.co.uk. A very simple and plain low-key wooden hut of a hostel, a short way north up the A819 Dalmally road. There's a small lounge and a communal dining area. April–Oct. **£17**

★**Newton Hall** Shore Rd ☎ 01499 302484, ⦿ newton hallguesthouse.co.uk. A former church, built in 1895, and now a guesthouse just a 5min walk from the centre of town. The views over the loch are lovely, and each of the seven rooms is luxurious and individually styled. Feb–Nov. **£80**

★**Rudha-Na-Craige** The Avenue ☎ 01499 302668, ⦿ rudha-na-craige.com. A beautifully restored Scottish Baronial house on the southern edge of town next to the golf course. Free wi-fi, a baby grand piano that guests are welcome to play and elegant light-filled bedrooms. **£95**

21

Oban

The solidly Victorian resort of **OBAN** (Ⓦoban.org.uk) enjoys a superb setting distinguished by a bizarre granite amphitheatre, dramatically lit at night, on the hilltop above the town. Despite a small population it's by far the largest port in northwest Scotland, and the main departure point for ferries to the Hebrides.

McCaig's Tower

Oban's landmark, **McCaig's Tower**, is a stiff ten-minute climb from the quayside. Built in imitation of Rome's Colosseum, it was the brainchild of a local businessman a century ago, who had the twin aims of alleviating off-season unemployment among the local stonemasons and creating a museum, art gallery and chapel. In his will, McCaig gave instructions for the lancet windows to be filled with bronze statues of the family, though no such work was ever undertaken. Instead, the folly has been turned into a sort of walled garden, and provides a wonderful seaward panorama, particularly at sunset.

ARRIVAL AND INFORMATION

OBAN

By ferry The CalMac ferry terminal (Ⓣ01631 566688) for the islands is on Railway Pier, near the train station.
Destinations Achnacroish, Lismore (Mon–Sat 4–5 daily, Sun 2 daily; 50min); Coll (daily except Wed & Fri; 2hr 40min); Colonsay (daily except Tues & Sat; 2hr 15min); Craignure, Mull (daily every 2hr; 45min); Lochboisdale (3–5 weekly; 5hr 20min–7hr); Tiree (1 daily; 3hr 40min).
By train Trains from Glasgow Queen Street (Mon–Sat 3–4 daily, Sun 1–3 daily; 3hr) pull up on Station Square.

By bus Oban's bus station is right next door to the train station.
Destinations Glasgow (Mon–Sat 4 daily, Sun 2 daily; 3hr); Mallaig (1 daily; 2hr 30min).
Tourist information In a converted church on Argyll Square (April–June, Sept & Oct daily 10am–5pm; July & Aug Mon–Sat 9am–7pm, Sun 10am–5pm; Nov–March Mon–Sat 10am–5pm, Sun noon–5pm; Ⓣ01631 563122).

ACCOMMODATION

Alt na Craig House Glenmore Rd Ⓣ01631 564524, Ⓦguesthouseinoban.com. A handsome Victorian house just south of town, with a woodland garden, views of the bay and rooms – some with sea views – decked out in boutique style. **£120**
Kilchrenan House Corran Esplanade Ⓣ01631 562663, Ⓦkilchrenanhouse.co.uk. A tasteful, hospitable place in a grand Victorian villa near the cathedral – the ten rooms

are spacious with antique furnishings and many have sea views. **£70**
Oban Backpackers Breadalbane St Ⓣ01631 562107, Ⓦobanbackpackers.com. The friendliest, cheapest and most central of Oban's three hostels with differently-sized dorms both here and in two buildings nearby; the big, open lounge/dining area has mismatched sofas, a pool table and a real fire. Breakfast included. March–Oct. **£16**

EATING AND DRINKING

Coast 104 George St Ⓣ01631 569900, Ⓦcoastoban.com. A stylish option serving acclaimed and original fish, game and meat dishes (mains from £16). Mon–Sat noon–2pm & 5.30–9pm, Sun 5.30–9pm.
The Lorne Stevenson St Ⓣ01631 570020, Ⓦthelornebar.co.uk. An attractive and popular pub that serves real ales, forty different kinds of malt and local seafood (around £9), as well as light snacks at lunch time.

Mon–Thurs noon–1am, Fri & Sat noon–2am, Sun 12.30pm–2am.
Waterfront On the waterfront, near the station Ⓣ01631 563110, Ⓦwaterfrontoban.co.uk. Upstairs in the old Fishermen's Mission, and enjoying lovely views over the bay, this restaurant uses the best of the daily catch: oysters, scallops, halibut and salmon (from £14 per main). Daily noon–2.15pm & 5.30–9.30pm.

Isle of Mull

Just forty minutes from Oban by ferry, **MULL** (Ⓦholidaymull.co.uk) is by far the most accessible of the Hebrides. As so often, first impressions largely depend on the weather

– it's the wettest of the Hebrides (and that's saying something) – and without the sun the large tracts of moorland, particularly around the island's highest peak, Ben More (3196ft), can appear bleak and unwelcoming. There are, however, areas of more gentle pastoral scenery around **Dervaig** in the north, and the indented west coast varies from the sandy beaches around **Calgary** to the cliffs of Loch na Keal. The most common mistake is to try and "do" the island in a day or two: slogging up the main road to the picturesque capital of Tobermory, then covering the fifty-odd miles between there and Fionnphort, in order to visit **Iona**. Mull is a place that will grow on you only if you have the time and patience to explore.

ARRIVAL AND DEPARTURE
ISLE OF MULL

By ferry There are frequent daily car ferries from Oban to Craigmore (booking ahead advisable), plus a smaller and less-expensive daily car ferry from Lochaline on the Morvern peninsula to Fishnish, 6 miles northwest of

Craignure. Another, even smaller car ferry connects Kilchoan on the Ardnamurchan peninsula (see p.907) with Tobermory, Mull's capital.

Craignure

CRAIGNURE is little more than a scattering of cottages with a small shop, a bar, toilets and a CalMac ticket and **tourist office**, but some visual drama is provided by two castles which lie immediately southeast: private Torosay Castle and Duart.

Duart Castle

Lochdon, immediately southeast of Craignure • April Mon–Thurs & Sun 11am–4pm; May–Oct daily 10.30am–5pm • £5.75 • ☎ 01680 812309, ⓦ duartcastle.com • The Duart Coach meets the 9.50am, 11.55am & 2pm ferries, Mon–Fri & Sun; 10min

On a picturesque spit of rock, **Duart Castle** is clearly visible from the Oban–Craignure ferry. Headquarters of the once-powerful MacLean clan from the thirteenth century, it was burnt down by the Campbells and confiscated after the 1745 rebellion. Finally in 1911, the 26th clan chief, Fitzroy MacLean (1835–1936), managed to buy it back and restore it. You can peek at the dungeons, climb up to the ramparts, study the family photos, and learn about the world scout movement – the 27th clan chief became Chief Scout in 1959.

ARRIVAL AND INFORMATION
CRAIGNURE

By ferry Car ferries travel from Oban to Craignure (April–Oct Mon–Sat 6–7 daily, Sun 4–5 daily; 45min).
By bus Buses run to Craignure (by the main road near the ferry terminal) from Fionnphort (Mon–Sat 3–4 daily, Sun 1 daily; 1hr 10min), Fishnish (3 daily; 10min) and Tobermory

(4–6 daily; 45min).
Tourist information Opposite the pier (April–June, Sept & Oct 9am–5pm; July & Aug 9am–7pm; Nov–March Mon–Sat 9am–5pm, Sun 10am–noon & 2–5pm); ☎ 01680 812 377, ⓦ visitscotland.com.

ACCOMMODATION AND EATING

Craignure Inn 400m up the road towards Fionnphort ☎ 01680 812305, ⓦ craignure-inn.co.uk. A snug pub to hole up in, just a minute's stroll up the road towards Fionnphort. They serve dinner nightly, with an emphasis on local food (mains from £13). **£82**

Shieling campsite 1km up the road towards Fionnphort ☎ 01680 812496, ⓦ shielingholidays .co.uk. Quiet and very appealing family-run campsite on the south side of Craignure Bay, behind the village hall, with views across to Ben Nevis. April–Oct. Pitches **£16.50**

Tobermory

Mull's chief town, **TOBERMORY**, at the northern tip of the island, is easily the most attractive fishing port on the west coast of Scotland, with its clusters of brightly coloured houses and boats sheltering in a bay backed by a steep bluff. Apart from the beauty of the setting, the harbour's shops are good for browsing, and you could pay a visit to the **Mull Museum**, on Main Street (Easter to mid-Oct Mon–Fri 10am–4pm, Sat

21

10am–1pm; free), which packs in a great deal of information as well as artefacts – including a few objects salvaged from the sixteenth-century wreck of the *San Juan*, a Spanish Armada ship that sank in the bay. A stiff climb up Back Brae will bring you to the island's main arts centre, **An Tobar** (March, April & Oct–Dec Mon–Sat 10am–5pm; May–Sept Mon–Sat 10am–5pm, Sun 1–4pm; free; ⓦcomar.co.uk), which hosts exhibitions and live events, and has a café with comfy sofas set before a real fire.

ARRIVAL AND INFORMATION
TOBERMORY

By ferry The CalMac terminal is at the far end of Main Street, in the northernmost part of the bay.

Destiantions Kilchoan (May–Aug daily; Sept–April Mon–Sat; every 90 min; 35min).

By bus The bus station is in the main Ledaig car park, by the distillery.

Destinations Calgary (Mon–Sat 2 daily; 45min), Dervaig (Mon–Fri 3 daily, Sat 2 daily; 30min) and Fishnish (2–4 daily; 40min).

Tourist information Main St (April–Oct Mon–Fri 9am–5pm, Sat & Sun noon–5pm; longer hours in summer; ☎01680 812377, ⓦtobermory.co.uk).

ACCOMMODATION AND EATING

There are several **accommodation** options on **Main Street**, which is also the place to go for places to eat, including a highly rated fish-and-chip van (which also serves scallops) on the old pier.

★**Café Fish** The Pier, Main Street ☎01688 301253, ⓦthecafefish.com. A lively little place with glorious sea views, serving superb seafood such as queen scallops (£8.50) and creel-caught squat lobster (£17). Book in advance. Daily 10am–11pm.

Glassbarn Tearooms Glengorm Rd ⓦglass barntearooms.blogspot.com. The prettiest eating option on Mull: a spacious glasshouse with sofas and wooden furniture serving good coffee, snacks and cakes. They also make and sell Isle of Mull cheese: you can see the cows being milked at 4pm. Tues–Sun 10am–4.30pm.

★**Highland Cottage** Breadalbane St ☎01688 302030, ⓦhighlandcottage.co.uk. A luxurious B&B run by a very welcoming couple in a quiet street high above the harbour; the outstanding four-course Scottish menu in the restaurant costs around £40 a head. Restaurant daily 7–11pm. **£150**

SYHA hostel Main St ☎01688 302 481, ⓦsyha.org.uk. Small, friendly and superbly located hostel on the harbour front, with two- to six-bed rooms, plus shared shower facilities, kitchen, TV lounge and laundry. March–Oct. **£18**

The Water's Edge Tobermory Hotel, Main St ☎01688 302091, ⓦthetobermoryhotel.com. Scottish seafood, venison and cheese are served in this upmarket hotel restaurant: they charge £27 for two courses. Daily 6–9pm.

Isle of Staffa

Seven miles off the west coast of Mull, **Staffa** is the most romantic and dramatic of Scotland's many uninhabited islands. On its south side, the perpendicular rock face features an imposing series of black basalt columns, known as the Colonnade, which have been cut by the sea into cathedralesque caverns, most notably **Fingal's Cave**. The Vikings knew about the island – the name derives from their word for "Island of Pillars" – but it wasn't until 1772 that it was "discovered" by the world. Turner painted it, Wordsworth explored it, but Mendelssohn's *Die Fingalshöhle*, inspired by the sounds of the sea-wracked caves he heard on a visit here in 1829, did most to popularize the place – after which Queen Victoria gave her blessing, too. The geological explanation for these polygonal basalt organ-pipes is that they were created by a massive subterranean explosion some sixty million years ago, when a huge mass of molten basalt burst forth onto land and, as it cooled, solidified into what are essentially crystals.

TOURS
ISLE OF STAFFA

Boat tours From April to October several operators offer boat trips to Staffa: long-established Turus Mara (☎0800 085 8786, ⓦturusmara.com) sets out from Ulva Ferry and charges around £50 return, as does Gordon Grant Marine (☎01681 700338, ⓦstaffatours.com), departing from Fionnphort. Iolaire (☎01681 700358, ⓦstaffatrips.co.uk) charge £30 for passage from Fionnphort.

Ben More and the Ross of Mull

From the southern shores of Loch na Keal, which almost splits the island of Mull in two, rise the terraced slopes of **Ben More** (3169ft) – literally "big mountain" – a mighty extinct volcano. Stretching for twenty miles west of Ben More as far as Iona is Mull's rocky southernmost peninsula, the **Ross of Mull**, which, like much of Scotland, appears blissfully tranquil in good weather, and desolate and bleak in bad.

Fionnphort

The main reason to visit **FIONNPHORT** is for its ferries to Iona (see below). This is probably the least attractive place to stay on the Ross, though it has a nice sandy bay backed by pink, granite rocks. Partly to ease congestion on Iona, and to give their neighbours a slice of the tourist pound, Fionnphort was chosen as the site for the little-visited **St Columba Centre** (Easter–Sept daily 10.30am–1pm & 2–5.30pm; free); inside, a small exhibition outlines Iona's history, tells a little of Columba's life, and has a few facsimiles of the illuminated manuscripts produced by the island's monks.

ARRIVAL AND DEPARTURE   FIONNPHORT

By ferry Passenger-only ferries run from Fionnphort to   winter; 5min; £4.95 return, bicycles free).
Iona (daily, every 30min in summer; less frequent in

Isle of Iona

Less than a mile off the southwest tip of Mull, **IONA** (wisle-of-iona.com), just three miles long and not much more than a mile wide – has been a place of pilgrimage for several centuries, and a site of Christian worship for more than 1400 years. It was to this flat Hebridean island that **St Columba** fled from Ireland in 563 and established a monastery, compiling a vast library of illuminated manuscripts and converting more or less all of pagan Scotland as well as much of northern England. This history and the island's splendid isolation have lent it a peculiar religiosity; in the much-quoted words of Dr Johnson, who visited in 1773, "That man is little to be envied … whose piety would not grow warmer among the ruins of Iona". Today, however, the island can barely cope with the constant flood of day-trippers, so in order to appreciate the special atmosphere and to have time to see the whole island, including the often-overlooked west coast, you should stay at least one night.

Baile Mòr

The passenger ferry from Fionnphort drops you off at the island's main village, **BAILE MÒR** (literally "large village"), which is in fact little more than a single terrace of cottages facing the sea. Just inland lie the extensive pink-granite ruins of the **Augustinian nunnery**, built around 1200 but disused since the Reformation which, if nothing else, gives you an idea of the state of the present-day abbey before it was restored. Just south of the manse and church stands the fifteenth-century **MacLean's Cross**, a fine, late medieval example of the distinctive, flowing, three-leaved foliage of the Iona school.

Across the road to the north of MacLean's Cross is the **Iona Heritage Centre** (Easter–Oct Mon–Sat 10.30am–4.15pm; £3; ☎ 01681 700576, wionaheritage.co.uk), with displays on the social history of the island over the last two hundred years, including the Clearances, which nearly halved the island's population of five hundred in the mid-nineteenth century.

Iona Abbey

A 5min walk from the Heritage Centre • Daily: April–Sept 9.30am–5.30pm; Oct–March 9.30am–4.30pm • £7.10; HS • ☎ 01681 700512

No buildings remain on the island from Columba's time: the present **Iona Abbey** dates

21

from the arrival of the Benedictines in around 1200, was extensively rebuilt in the fifteenth and sixteenth centuries, and restored virtually wholesale early last century. Adjoining the facade is a small steep-roofed chamber, believed to be St Columba's grave; now a small chapel. The three high crosses in front of the abbey date from the eighth to tenth centuries, and are decorated with the Pictish serpent-and-boss and Celtic spirals for which Iona's early Christian masons were renowned. For reasons of sanitation, the cloisters were placed, contrary to the norm, on the north side of the church (where running water was available); entirely reconstructed in the late 1950s, they now shelter a useful historical account of the abbey's development.

Oran's Cemetery
South of Iona Abbey

Iona's oldest building, plain **St Oran's Chapel**, features an eleventh-century arched door; it stands at the centre of Iona's sacred burial ground, **Reilig Òdhrain** (Oran's Cemetery), which is said to contain the graves of sixty kings of Norway, Ireland, France and Scotland, including Duncan and Macbeth. The best of the early Christian gravestones and medieval effigies that lay in the Reilig Òdhrain have been removed to the **Infirmary Museum** behind the abbey (ⓦionahistory.org.uk/infirmary).

ARRIVAL AND DEPARTURE   ISLE OF IONA

By ferry Passenger-only ferries run from Fionnphort to Iona (daily, every 30min in summer; less frequent in winter; 5min; £4.95 return, bicycles free).

ACCOMMODATION AND EATING

As demand far exceeds supply you should book **accommodation** well in advance. If you want to stay with the **Iona Community**, contact the MacLeod Centre (ⓣ01681 700404, ⓦiona.org.uk), popularly known as the "Mac".

Argyll Near the jetty ⓣ01681 700334, ⓦargyll hoteliona.co.uk. The nicer of the island's two hotels, housed in a terrace of stone-built cottages overlooking the Sound of Iona. They grow much of the organic produce used in the restaurant, as well as making use of local fish and meat. Feb–Nov. **£70**

★ **Iona Hostel** Lagandorain; follow the road past the abbey for 1km ⓣ01681 700781, ⓦionahostel.co.uk. In the north of the island, this simple, very attractive hostel sleeps 22 in five bedrooms. There's an open-plan kitchen and a living room with wood-burning stove, windows on three sides and sweeping views out to the Treshnish Isles. To reach the hostel, follow the road past the abbey for half a mile. **£21**

Martyrs' Bay Restaurant By the jetty ⓣ01681 700382, ⓦmartyrsbay.co.uk. Good seafood dishes served in the restaurant and in the convivial pub attached, the only one on the island; the tourist hordes invariably pack this place out for steaks and seafood (from £10.95). Daily 11am–11pm.

Isle of Coll

The fish-shaped rocky island of **Coll** (ⓦvisitcoll.co.uk), with a population of around a hundred, lies less than seven miles off the coast of Mull. The CalMac ferry drops off at Coll's only real village, **ARINAGOUR**, whose whitewashed cottages dot the western shore of Loch Eatharna. Half of Coll's population lives here, where you'll find the island's hotel and pub, post office, churches and a couple of shops.

On the southwest coast there are two edifices, both confusingly known as **Breachacha Castle**. The older is a restored fifteenth-century tower house, and now a training centre for overseas aid volunteers. The less attractive "new castle", to the northwest, is made up of a central block built around 1750 and two side pavilions added a century later, and has been converted into holiday homes. Much of the area around the castles is now owned by the RSPB, with the aim of protecting the island's small corncrake population. A vast area of **giant sand dunes** lies to the west of the castles, with two glorious, golden, sandy bays stretching for more than a mile on either side.

ARRIVAL AND DEPARTURE

By ferry Throughout the summer, the CalMac ferry from Oban calls daily at Coll (2hr 40min) and Tiree (3hr 40min).

Destinations Barra (Thurs 1 daily; 4hr); Oban (daily except Wed & Fri; 2hr 40min).

ACCOMMODATION AND EATING

Coll Hotel Arinagour ✆ 01879 230334, ⊛ collhotel .com. Small, family-run hotel offering decent accommodation in six rooms, four of which overlook the bay. Delicious meals in the *Gannet Restaurant* (from £12); the place also doubles as the island's social centre. **£100**

First Port of Coll In the old harbour stores ✆ 01879 230488. Simple café in the stores overlooking the bay, offering hot meals all day (from £9) and lots of home-made puds, using as much local produce as possible. Takeaway also available. Closed Oct. Mon & Thurs–Sat 11am–2pm & 5–9pm, Sun noon–6pm.

Garden House In the west of the island, near Breachacha beach ✆ 01879 230374. Campsite in the shelter of an old walled garden surrounded by an RSPB reserve and five minutes from Breachacha beach. April–Sept. Per person **£7**

Tigh-na-Mara Arinagour ✆ 01879 230354, ⊛ tighna mara.info. Purpose-built modern guesthouse near the pier with seven bedrooms, two of them family rooms and some en suite. You can seal- and wildlife-spot from the dining room. **£70**

Isle of Tiree

Tiree (⊛ isleoftiree.com) as its Gaelic name *tir-iodh* ("land of corn") suggests, was once known as the breadbasket of the Inner Hebrides, thanks to its acres of rich machair (sandy, grassy, lime-rich land). Nowadays crofting and tourism are the main sources of income for the small resident population. One of the most distinctive features of the island is its architecture, in particular the large numbers of "pudding" or "spotty" houses, where only the mortar is painted white. The sandy beaches attract large numbers of windsurfers for the **Tiree Wave Classic** every October. The **ferry** calls at Gott Bay Pier, now best known for **An Turas** (The Journey), Tiree's award-winning artistic "shelter".

Scarinish

The village of **SCARINISH** is home to a post office, public toilets, a supermarket, a butcher's and a bank, with a petrol pump back at the pier, as well as **An Iodhlann** (July & Aug Mon–Fri 11am–5pm; Sept–June Mon, Wed & Thurs 9am–1pm, Tues & Fri 10.30am–3.30pm; ⊛ aniodhlann.org.uk; £3) – meaning "haystack" in Gaelic – the island's two-roomed archive, which puts on occasional exhibitions about island life.

Hynish

Below the higher of Tiree's two landmark hills is **HYNISH**, with its restored **harbour**, designed by Alan Stevenson in the 1830s to transport building materials for the magnificent 140ft-tall **Skerryvore Lighthouse**, which lies on a sea-swept reef some twelve miles southwest of Tiree. Up on the hill behind the harbour stands a stumpy granite signal tower, whose signals used to be the only contact the lighthouse keepers had with civilization. The tower now houses a **museum** (May–Sept) telling the history of the Herculean effort required to erect the lighthouse, which, weather permitting, you can see from a viewing platform.

ARRIVAL AND GETTING AROUND

By plane Flights connect Tiree with Glasgow (Mon–Sat 1 daily; 45min); the airport lies 3 miles west of Scarinish.

By ferry Car ferries arrive in Scarinish from Barra (summer Wed 1 daily; 3hr 5min) and Oban (summer daily; 3hr 40min).

By minibus Ring'n'Ride is a useful service that will take you anywhere on the island (Mon–Sat 7am–6pm, Tues 7am–10pm; ✆ 01879 220419).

21

ACCOMMODATION AND EATING

Cèabhar Sandaig ☎ 01879 220684, ⊛ ceabhar.com. A very welcoming self-catering place and restaurant with five bedrooms, a communal lounge, and games cupboard. The proximity to the beach makes it popular with surfers. Per week **£850**

Elephant's End Gott Bay ☎ 01879 220694. Local goodies such as crab, lobster and langoustine (all around £12) served in a homely little restaurant. Mon–Sat 10am–4pm & 7pm till late, Sun 12.30–2.30pm & 7pm till late.

Millhouse Drumaglea, Cornaigmore ☎ 01879 220435, ⊛ tireemillhouse.co.uk. Great hostel in a snugly converted barn dating from the early 1900s, near Loch Bhasapol, in the northwest of the island. The open-plan kitchen/lounge opens onto a patio from where you can watch the sunset. Dorms **£18**, twins **£40**

Wild Diamond Watersports Loch Bhasapol ☎ 01879 220399, ⊛ wilddiamond.co.uk. Campsite in the south-west of the island, with watersport activities around the loch. Per person **£12**

Mid-Argyll

Mid-Argyll is a vague term that loosely describes the central wedge of land south of Oban and north of Kintyre. The highlights of this gently undulating scenery lie along the sharply indented west coast, in particular the rich Bronze Age and Neolithic remains in the **Kilmartin** valley. Separating **Kilmartin Glen** from the Knapdale peninsula is the **Crinan Canal**, a shortcut for boats disinclined to round the Mull of Kintyre, which ends in the pint-sized, picturesque port of Crinan.

Kilmartin Glen

The **Kilmartin Glen** is the most important prehistoric site on the Scottish mainland, whose most remarkable relic is the **linear cemetery**, where several cairns are aligned for more than two miles to the south of the village of Kilmartin. These are thought to represent the successive burials of a ruling family or chieftains, but nobody can be sure. The best view of the cemetery's configuration is from the Bronze Age **Mid-Cairn**, but the Neolithic **South Cairn**, dating from around 3000 BC, is by far the oldest and the most impressive, with its large chambered tomb roofed by giant slabs. Close to the Mid-Cairn, the two **Temple Wood stone circles** appear to have been the architectural focus of burials in the area from Neolithic times to the Bronze Age. Visible to the south are the impressively cup-marked **Nether Largie standing stones** (no public access), the largest of which looms over 10ft high.

Kilmartin House Museum

Kilmartin • March–Oct daily 10am–5.30pm • £5 • ☎ 01546 510278, ⊛ kilmartin.org

The **Kilmartin House Museum** in the tiny village of Kilmartin is an enlightening and entertaining exhibition on the area's prehistory, set within the old manse next to the village church. The church is also worth a look, as it shelters the badly damaged and weathered **Kilmartin crosses**, while a separate enclosure in the graveyard houses a large collection of medieval grave slabs of the Malcolms of Poltalloch.

Dunadd

South of Kilmartin, beyond the linear cemetery

The raised peat bog of Moine Mhòr (Great Moss) is best known as home to the Iron Age fort of **Dunadd**, one of Scotland's most important Celtic sites, occupying a distinctive 176ft-high rocky knoll once surrounded by the sea, but currently stranded beside the winding River Add. It was here that Fergus, the first king of Dalriada, established his royal seat, having arrived from Ireland in around 500 AD. Its strategic position, the craggy defences and the view from the top are all impressive, but it's the **stone carvings** (albeit now fibreglass copies) between the twin summits which make Dunadd so remarkable: several lines of Pictish inscription in *ogam* (an ancient alphabet of Irish origin), the faint outline of a boar, a hollowed-out footprint and a small basin. The footprint and basin have been interpreted as being part of the royal coronation rituals of the kings of Dalriada. It's thought that the Stone of Destiny was used at Dunadd before being moved to Scone Palace (see p.831).

ARRIVAL AND DEPARTURE   KILMARTIN GLEN

By bus Bus #423 between Oban and Ardrishaig runs   through the glen (Mon–Fri 4 daily, Sat 2 daily).

ACCOMMODATION AND EATING

★**Dunchraigaig House** A mile or so south of Kilmartin ☎01546 510396, ⓦdunchraigaig.co.uk. A large detached Victorian house opposite the Ballymeanoch standing stones, where you can have home-made clootie dumpling for breakfast; rooms are attractively furnished in cosy country style. **£80**

Kilmartin Museum Café Kilmartin House Museum, Kilmartin ☎01546 510278, ⓦkilmartin.orq. Lovely stone-built licensed café with a green oak conservatory. Home-made soup, lunches (mains around £9) and cake. Daily: March–Oct 10am–5pm; Nov & Dec 11am–4pm.

Crinan Canal

In 1801 the nine-mile-long **Crinan Canal** opened, linking Loch Fyne at Ardrishaig, south of Lochgilphead, with the Sound of Jura, thus cutting out the long and treacherous journey around the Mull of Kintyre. The canal runs parallel to the sea for quite some way before hitting a flight of locks either side of **CAIRNBAAN** (there are fifteen in total); a walk along the towpath is both picturesque and pleasant. There are usually one or two yachts passing through the locks, but the most relaxing place from which to view the canal in action is **CRINAN**, a pretty little fishing port at its western end.

ARRIVAL AND DEPARTURE   CRINAN CANAL

By bus Bus #926 connects Glasgow with the Crinan Canal,   via Lochgilphead (3 daily).

ACCOMMODATION AND EATING

Cairnbaan Hotel Cairnbaan ☎01546 603668, ⓦcairnbaan.com. An eighteenth-century coaching inn overlooking the canal at Lock 5, with twelve cosy, if chintzy, rooms. There's a decent restaurant and bar meals (from £12) featuring locally caught seafood (from £13). Free wi-fi. Food served daily noon–2.30pm & 6–9.30pm. **£85**

Crinan Hotel Crinan ☎01546 830261, ⓦcrinanhotel .com. It's worth having a pint or one of the excellent bar

meals at the hotel's *Crinan Seafood Bar*, which has lovely views out to sea and an outdoor terrace; rooms are done out in floral fabrics, and many have balconies for canal views. Bar daily noon–2.30pm & 6–8.30pm. **£90**

★**Seaview Cottage** Crinan ☎0141 3326936, ⓦcanalsidecottages.co.uk/cottages/seaview-cottage. Beautifully restored and stylishly furnished, this lock keeper's cottage had two bedrooms, a log fire and a garden. Available for short or long lets. **£79**

Kintyre

But for the mile-long isthmus between West Loch Tarbert and the much smaller East Loch Tarbert, the little-visited peninsula of **KINTYRE** (ⓦkintyre.org) – from the Gaelic *Ceann Tire*, "land's end" – would be an island. Despite its relative proximity to Scotland's Central Belt, Kintyre remains quiet and unfashionable; its main towns, Tarbert and Campbeltown, have few obvious attractions, but that's part of their appeal. In many ways, it's a peninsula in a time warp, where you can hole up in perfect solitude.

Tarbert

A distinctive rocket-like church steeple heralds the fishing village of **TARBERT** (in Gaelic *An Tairbeart*, meaning "isthmus"), sheltering an attractive little bay backed by rugged

21

hills. Tarbert's harbourfront is pretty, and is best appreciated from the rubble of Robert the Bruce's fourteenth-century **castle** above the town to the south.

ARRIVAL AND INFORMATION	TARBERT

By ferry Regular ferries connect Tarbert with Portavadie (hourly; 25min). The ferry terminal is on Pier Road, a 10min walk along Harbour Street.

By bus Buses arrive in the centre of town on Campbeltown Road and Barmore Road.

Destinations Campbeltown (Mon–Sat 4 daily, Sun 2 daily;

1hr 15min); Claonaig (Mon–Sat 3 daily; 30min); Glasgow (3 daily; 3hr 15min); Kennacraig (3–6 daily; 15min) and Tayinloan (3–6 daily; 30min).

Tourist information Harbour St (April–Oct Mon–Fri 11am–5pm, Sat & Sun 11am–5pm; ☎ 01880 820429).

ACCOMMODATION AND EATING	

Victoria Hotel Barmore Rd ☎ 01880 821039, ⓦ victoriahotel-tarbert.co.uk. Behind its garish yellow exterior, this is a comfortable old hotel overlooking the

harbour. Seafood is served in the conservatory restaurant, including pan-seared Loch Fyne scallops (£15). Restaurant noon–2pm & 6–9pm. **£70**

Isle of Gigha

Gigha (ⓦ gigha.org.uk) – pronounced "geeya" – is a low-lying, fertile island three miles off the west coast of Kintyre, reputedly occupied for 5000 years. Like many of the smaller Hebrides, Gigha was bought and sold numerous times after its original lairds, the MacNeils, sold up in 1865, and was finally bought by the islanders themselves in 2002. The island is so small – six miles by one – that most visitors come here just for the day. The real draw, apart from the peace and quiet, is the white sandy **beaches**.

The ferry from Tayinloan, 23 miles south of Tarbert, deposits you at Gigha's only village, **ARDMINISH**, where you'll find the post office and shop, and a lovely beach. A mile and a half south, the **Achamore Gardens** (daily 9am–dusk; £4) were established by the first postwar owner, Sir James Horlick (of hot-drink fame). Their spectacularly colourful display of azaleas is best seen in early summer.

ARRIVAL AND GETTING AROUND	ISLE OF GIGHA

By ferry Regular CalMac ferries connect Gigha with Tayinloan (hourly; 20min).

Bike rental The island post office offers bike rental.

ACCOMMODATION AND EATING	

The Boathouse Ardminish ☎ 01583 505123, ⓦ boathousegigha.co.uk. This licensed, converted boathouse by the CalMac pier is the place to go for delicious local food (mains £10–25) and, occasionally, live music and quiz nights. Book ahead for their gorgeously sited camping overlooking the

beach. April–Oct daily 11.30am–10pm. Pitches **£9**

Gigha Hotel Ardminish Bay ☎ 01583 505254, ⓦ gigha .org.uk/accom. The island's only hotel is owned by the community: it has a great bar and serves excellent locally-produced food. The basic rooms have wonderful sea views. **£80**

Campbeltown

CAMPBELTOWN's best feature is its setting, in a deep bay sheltered by Davaar Island and the surrounding hills. With a population of around 5000, it's Kintyre's largest town and its shops are by far the best place to stock up on supplies. Campbeltown's heyday was the Victorian era, when shipbuilding was going strong; coal was shipped by canal from Drumlemble, the fishing fleet was vast and Campbeltown had no fewer than 34 whisky distilleries – today only a few remain.

Whisky tours

If you're interested in visiting distilleries, pop into **Cadenhead's** whisky shop at 7 Bolgam St (☎ 01586 551710), which runs parallel with Longrow. Here you can sign up for a guided tour (ⓦ springbankwhisky.com; Mon–Sat 10am & 2pm; from £6.50) of

Springbank, the deeply traditional, family-owned distillery that does absolutely everything – from malting to bottling – on its own premises.

ARRIVAL AND INFORMATION CAMPBELTOWN

By plane Flights from Glasgow connect with Campbeltown (Mon–Fri 2 daily; 35min); the airport is located 3 miles northwest of town towards Machrihanish.

By bus Campbeltown is served by buses from Glasgow (2–3 daily; 4hr 25min) and Tarbert (Mon–Sat 4 daily, Sun 2 daily; 1hr 15min). The town's main bus terminal is in front of the swimming pool on the Esplanade.

By ferry The ferry terminal is on the south side of the harbour, from where it's a five-minute walk Into the centre. Destinations Ardrossan (Fri & Sun 1 daily; 2hr 40min).

Tourist information Old Quay (April–June & Sept Mon–Sat 10am–5pm, Sun noon–4pm; July & Aug Mon–Sat 9am–6pm, Sun 11am–5pm; Oct–March Mon–Fri 10am–4pm; ☎ 01586 552056).

ACCOMMODATION, EATING & ENTERTAINMENT

Ardshiel Hotel Kilkerran Rd ☎ 01586 552133, ⓦ ardshiel.co.uk. Well-run hotel in a former whisky distiller's Victorian mansion on a lovely leafy square. There's a bar, and meals served in the *Garden Restaurant* are good (from £12). **£70**

★**Oatfield House** Just under 3 miles from the town centre down the A842 to Southend ☎ 01586 551551,

ⓦ oatfield.org. A beautifully renovated, whitewashed laird's house set in its own grounds. Shetland ponies, a walled garden, pond and free wi-fi. **£80**

Wee Pictures Hall St ☎ 01586 553899, ⓦ weepictures .co.uk. On the town's palm-tree-dotted waterfront you'll find this little Art Deco cinema, built in 1913 and still going strong. Mon, Thurs, Sat & Sun.

Mull of Kintyre

The bulbous, hilly end of Kintyre, south of Campbeltown, features some of the most spectacular scenery on the whole peninsula, mixed with large swathes of Lowland-style farmland. Most people venture southwest of Campbeltown to make a pilgrimage to the **Mull of Kintyre**, made famous by the mawkish number-one hit by Paul McCartney, with the help of the Campbeltown Pipe Band. The nearest Britain gets to Ireland – whose coastline, just twelve miles away, appears remarkably close on fine days – this storm-wracked spot offers nothing specifically to see other than the view and a memorial to the 29 military personnel who died in 1994 when an RAF helicopter crashed into the hillside. The roads up to the "**Gap**" (1150ft) – where you must leave your car – and particularly down to the lighthouse, itself 300ft above the ocean waves, are terrifyingly tortuous.

Isle of Arran

Shaped like a kidney bean and occupying centre stage in the Firth of Clyde, **Arran** (ⓦ visitarran.net) is the most southerly (and therefore the most accessible) of all the Scottish islands. The Highland–Lowland dividing line passes right through its centre – hence the cliché about it being like "Scotland in miniature" – leaving the northern half sparsely populated, mountainous and bleak, while the lush southern half enjoys a much milder climate. The population of around five thousand – many of whom are incomers – tend to stick to the southeastern quarter of the island, leaving the west and the north relatively undisturbed.

ARRIVAL AND DEPARTURE ISLE OF ARRAN

By ferry CalMac **ferries** run from Ardrossan, 14 miles north of Ayr, to Brodick (4–6 daily; 55min). A small ferry

runs from Claonaig, 8 miles south of Tarbert, to Lochranza (8–9 daily; 30min).

Brodick

As the island's capital and main communication hub, **BRODICK** (from the Norse *breidr vik*, "broad bay") is the busiest town on Arran. Although the resort is a place of only

21

HIKING UP GOAT FELL

The desolate north half of Arran – effectively the Highland part – features bare granite peaks, the occasional golden eagle and miles of unspoilt scenery, within reach only to those prepared to do some serious hiking. Arran's most accessible peak is also the island's highest, **Goat Fell** (2866ft), which can be ascended in just three hours from Brodick, though it's a strenuous hike. You can also hike up Goat Fell from Corrie, Arran's prettiest little seaside village, six miles north of Brodick, where a procession of pristine cottages lines the road to Lochranza and wraps itself around an exquisite little harbour and pier.

---

moderate charm, it does at least have a grand setting in a wide, sandy bay set against a backdrop of granite mountains.

Brodick Castle

North side of the bay • **Castle** Daily: April–Sept 11am–4pm; Oct 11am–3pm • £12.50; NTS • **Country park** Daily 9.30am to sunset • £7; NTS • ☎ 0844 493 2152, ⓦ nts.org.uk

The local dukes of Hamilton used to rule the town of Brodick from the **castle**, on a steep bank on the north side of the bay. The interior is comfortable if undistinguished, but the **walled garden** and extensive **country park** contain a treasury of exotic plants and trees and command a superb view across the bay. Hidden in the grounds is a bizarre Bavarian-style summerhouse lined entirely with pine cones, one of three built by the eleventh duke to make his wife, Princess Marie of Baden, feel at home.

ARRIVAL AND INFORMATION   BRODICK

By ferry Ferries arrive on the south side of Brodick Bay, a short walk from the town centre, from Ardrossan (4–6 daily; 55min).

Getting around Island buses connect Brodick with Blackwaterfoot (Mon–Sat 8–10 daily, Sun 4 daily; 30min); Corrie (3–5 daily; 20min); Lamlash (Mon–Sat hourly, Sun 4

daily; 10–15min) and Lochranza (3–5 daily; 45min). An Arran Rural Rover day-ticket costs around £5.

Tourist information By the CalMac pier (June–Sept daily 9am–5pm; Oct–May Mon–Sat 9am–5pm; ☎ 01770 303776).

ACCOMMODATION

★**The Barn** Southwest edge of Brodick in Glencloy ☎ 01770 303615, ⓦ arranbarn.co.uk. A charming early nineteenth-century B&B with real style. Breakfast includes eggs from the barn's chickens. Free wi-fi. March–Oct. **£60**

Dunvegan Guest House Shore Rd ☎ 01770 302811, ⓦ dunveganhouse.co.uk. An attractive stone-built Victorian B&B with a traditional feel but tastefully

modernized en-suite rooms. The best choice if you need to stay close to the ferry terminal. **£60**

Glen Rosa Campsite 2 miles from the town centre, off the B880 to Blackwaterfoot ☎ 01770 302380, ⓦ arrancamping.co.uk. A lovely, but very basic, farm site (cold water only and no showers, but campfires permitted). Per person **£4**

Lamlash and around

The southern half of Arran is less spectacular and less forbidding than the north; it's more heavily forested, the land is more fertile and the vast majority of the population lives here. With its distinctive Edwardian architecture and mild climate, **LAMLASH** epitomizes the sedate charm of southeast Arran.

Holy Island

Ferries run more or less hourly from Lamlash • £12 return • ☎ 07970 771960

You can take a boat out from Lamlash to the slug-shaped hump of **Holy Island**, which shelters the bay, and where a group of Tibetan Buddhists have established a retreat. Providing you don't dawdle, it's possible to scramble up to the top of **Mullach Mòr**

(1030ft), the island's highest point, and still catch the last ferry back. Otherwise, consider staying at the Buddhist centre (see below).

ARRIVAL AND DEPARTURE

By bus Irregular buses make the short (10min) journey from Brodick to Lamlash.

ACCOMMODATION AND EATING

★**Glenisle Hotel & Restaurant** Lamlash ☎01770 600559, ⓦglenislehotel.com. A cut above your average Lamlash B&B: every room of this Victorian hotel overlooking the bay has been tastefully refurbished, and the restaurant serves tasty dishes from beetroot gravadlax to home-made burgers with gruyère and onion chutney (from £10 for a

LAMLASH AND AROUND

main). Restaurant daily noon–9.30pm. **£115**

Peace Centre Holy Island ☎01770 601100, ⓦholyisland .org. The Buddhist centre on Holy Island welcomes visitors. Guests can join in the daily meditation sessions. Smoking, alcohol and sex are prohibited. All room rates include veggie full-board. Dorms **£28**, singles **£47**, twins **£72**

Lochranza

The ruined castle which occupies the mud flats of the surrounding bay, and the brooding north-facing slopes of the mountains which frame it, provide **LOCHRANZA** with one of the most spectacular settings on the island. Despite being the only place of any size in this sparsely populated area, Lochranza attracts far fewer visitors than other Arran resorts. The castle is worth a brief look inside, but Lochranza's main tourist attraction is the island's modern **distillery** (mid-March to Oct Mon–Sat 10am–6pm, Sun 11am–6pm; Nov–Feb daily 11am–4pm; ☎01770 830264, ⓦarranwhisky.com; £3.50), distinguished by its pagoda-style roofs.

ARRIVAL AND DEPARTURE

By ferry CalMac ferries arrive and depart from the pier, a 10min walk north of Lochranza distillery. A small ferry runs

LOCHRANZA

from Claonaig, 8 miles south of Tarbert, to Lochranza (8–9 daily; 30min).

ACCOMMODATION

★**Castlekirk** ☎01770 830202, ⓦcastlekirk.co.uk. A converted free church (with an art gallery attached) that retains lots of original features, including a rose window in the breakfast room with views out over the castle. The four rooms all have unusual, pitched ceilings, and only the double is en suite. **£65**

Lochranza Caravan & Camping Site ☎01770 830273, ⓦarran-campsite.com. Beautifully placed by

the golf course on the Brodick road, where red deer come to graze in the early evening. The well-equipped campsite has a friendly tearoom serving all-day breakfasts and light snacks (from £6). March–Oct. Pitches **£20**

SYHA hostel ☎01700 830631, ⓦsyha.org.uk. Popular hostel halfway between the distillery and the castle, surrounded by deer and with views over the bay. Mid-Feb to Oct. Dorms **£16**, doubles **£45**

Isle of Islay

The fertile, largely treeless island of **ISLAY** (ⓦislayinfo.com) is famous for one thing – single malt **whisky**. The smoky, peaty, pungent quality of Islay whisky is unique, recognizable even to the untutored palate, and most of the island's distilleries offer fascinating guided tours, ending with the customary complimentary dram. In medieval times, Islay was the political centre of the Hebrides, with **Finlaggan**, near **Port Askaig**, the seat of the MacDonalds, lords of the Isles. The picturesque, whitewashed villages you see on Islay today, however, date from the planned settlements founded by the Campbells in the late eighteenth and early nineteenth centuries. Apart from whisky and solitude, the other great draw is the **birdlife** – there's a real possibility of spotting a golden eagle, or the rare, crow-like chough, and no possibility at all of missing the scores of white-fronted and barnacle geese who winter here in their thousands.

21

By ferry CalMac ferries from Kennacraig, 12 miles south of Tarbert, go either to Port Ellen or Port Askaig (3–4 daily; 2hr 5min/2hr 20min). On Wednesdays, the ferry also makes a day-trip to Colonsay from Port Askaig (Wed 1 daily; 1hr 10min). There's also a small ferry that runs between Port Askaig and Feolin Ferry on Jura (Mon–Sat hourly, Sun 7–8 daily; 10min).

By plane Islay's airport, 6 miles north of Port Ellen in Glenegedale, has regular flights from Glasgow (Mon–Fri 2 daily, Sat 1 daily; 40min).

Port Ellen and around

Laid out as a planned village in 1821 by Walter Frederick Campbell, and named after his wife, **PORT ELLEN** is the chief port on Islay, with the island's largest fishing fleet and main CalMac ferry terminal. The neat whitewashed terraces that overlook the town's bay of golden sand are pretty enough, but the view is dominated by the village's modern maltings, whose powerful odours waft across the town.

The only reason to pause in this part of the island is to head off east along a dead-end road that passes three **distilleries** in as many miles (see box below). Another six miles down the track and you eventually come to the simple thirteenth-century **Kildalton Chapel**, which has an eighth-century Celtic ringed cross made from the local "bluestone". The exceptional quality of the scenes matches any to be found on the crosses carved by the monks in Iona.

ISLAY WHISKY

Islay has woken up to the fact that its **whisky distilleries** are a major tourist attraction. Nowadays, just about every distillery offers guided tours, traditionally ending with a generous dram, and a refund (or discount) for your entrance fee if you buy a bottle in the shop: here are some of our favourites. Phone ahead to make sure there's a tour running, as times do change.

Ardbeg Port Ellen ☎01496 302244, ⟨w⟩ardbeg.com. Ardbeg is traditionally considered the saltiest, peatiest malt on Islay (and that's saying something). The distillery has been thoroughly restored, yet it still has bags of character inside. The *Old Kiln Café* is excellent (daily 10am–4.30pm). Guided tours regularly 10.30am, noon & 3pm; £5.

Bowmore ☎01496 810441, ⟨w⟩bowmore.co.uk. Bowmore is the most touristy of the Islay distilleries, and by far the most central (with unrivalled disabled access). Guided tours April–Sept Mon–Sat 9am–5pm; Oct–March Mon–Sat 9am–12.30pm, Sat 9am–12.30pm; from £6.

Bruichladdich Bruichladdich ☎01496 850190, ⟨w⟩bruichladdich.com. Rescued in 2001 by a group of whisky fanatics, and then bought by Remy-Cointreau in 2012; they also make The Botanist Gin. Guided tours April–Sept Mon–Fri 10am, 11am, 1pm, 2pm & 4pm, Sat 10am, 11am, 1pm & 2pm, Sun 1pm & 2pm; Oct Mon–Fri 10am, 11am, 1pm & 3pm, Sat 10am, 11am, 1pm & 2pm; Nov–March Mon–Sat 10am & 2pm; £6.

Bunnahabhainn Port Askaig ☎01496 840646, ⟨w⟩bunnahabhain.com. A visit to Bunnahabhain (pronounced "Bunna-have-in") is really only for whisky obsessives. The whisky is the least characteristically Islay and the distillery is only in production for a few months each year. Tours by appointment only Mon–Sat 9.45am–5pm, Sun 11am–4pm.

Kilchoman Rockside Farm, Bruichladdich ☎01496 850011, ⟨w⟩kilchomandistillery.com. Established in 2005, Kilchoman is a very welcoming, tiny, farm-based enterprise that grows its own barley, as well as distilling, maturing and bottling its whisky on site. Mon–Fri 11am & 3pm; £6.

Lagavulin Lagavulin ☎01496 302749, ⟨w⟩discovering-distilleries.com/lagavulin. Lagavulin is the classic, all-round Islay malt, with lots of smoke and peat and the distillery enjoys a fabulous setting. Guided tours March Mon–Fri 11.30am & 1.30pm, Sat & Sun 10.30am & 1.30pm; April–May Mon–Sun 9.30am, 11.30am & 3.30pm; June–Aug Mon–Sun 9.30am, 11.30am, 2.30pm, 3.30pm; Sept–Oct Mon–Sun 9.30am, 11.30am & 3.30pm; Nov–Feb Mon–Fri 11.30am & 1.30pm, Sat 1.30pm; £6.

Laphroaig Port Ellen ☎01496 302418, ⟨w⟩laphroaig.com. Another classic smoky, peaty Islay malt, and another great setting – you also get to see the malting and see and smell the peat kilns. Guided tours March & April daily 10am, 2pm & 3.30pm; May–Sept daily 10am, 2pm, 2.30pm & 3.30pm; Nov & Dec daily 10am & 2pm; Jan & Feb 11.30am & 2pm; £6.

ARRIVAL AND DEPARTURE

By ferry CalMac ferries arrive in the centre of town, on the west side of the bay from Kennacraig (3–4 daily; 2hr 20min).

ACCOMMODATION

★**Glenegedale House Hotel** Glenegedale ☎01496 300400, ⓦglenegedalehouse.co.uk. This whitewashed nineteenth-century guesthouse opposite the airport offers luxurious rooms full of character, plus delicious home-cooking and fantastic breakfasts. **£110**

Kintra Farm Kintra, 3 miles west of Port Ellen

PORT ELLEN AND AROUND

By bus Island buses connect Port Ellen with Bowmore (Mon–Sat 10 daily, Sun 4 daily; 20–30min). The bus stop is on Charlotte Street in the centre of the village.

☎01496 302051, ⓦkintrafarm.co.uk. Lovely set of farm buildings at the southern tip of sandy Laggan Bay. The Victorian farmhouse has three rooms (two en-suite) and offers B&B, or you can camp in the nearby dunes – book ahead for Gaelic lessons. April–Sept. Pitches **£14**, doubles **£70**

Bowmore

BOWMORE, Islay's administrative capital, lies on the north side of the monotonous peat bog of Duich Moss, on the southern shores of the tidal Loch Indaal. It's a striking place, laid out in 1768 on a grid plan rather like Inveraray, with the whitewashed terraces of Main Street climbing up the hill in a straight line from the pier on Loch Indaal to the town's crowning landmark, the **Round Church**. Built in the round so that the devil would have no corners in which to hide, it has a plain, wood-panelled interior, with a lovely tiered balcony and a big central mushroom pillar.

ARRIVAL AND INFORMATION

By bus Island buses connect Bowmore to other destinations on Islay; they stop on the main square.
Destinations Port Askaig (Mon–Sat 6–8 daily, Sun 4 daily; 25min), Port Charlotte (Mon–Sat 5–6 daily, Sun 3 daily; 25min) and Port Ellen (Mon–Sat 10 daily, Sun 4

BOWMORE

daily; 20–30min).
Tourist information Islay's only tourist information is on The Square (April–Oct Mon–Sat 10am–5pm, Sun noon–3pm; Nov–March Mon–Fri 10am–3pm; ☎01496 810254).

ACCOMMODATION AND EATING

Lambeth House Jamieson St ☎01496 810597, ⓔlambethguesthouse@tiscali.co.uk. Newly modernized B&B run by a welcoming couple who offer three-course evening meals as well as breakfast. All rooms are en suite and there's free wi-fi. **£90**

Harbour Inn Main St ☎01496 810330, ⓦharbour

-inn.com. You can warm yourself by a peat fire in the cosy pub, where they also do bar food, or sidle next door to the restaurant (booking advisable) – the seafood specials (from £12) are super-fresh. They also have seven elegant rooms. Daily noon–2.30pm & 6–9.30pm. **£135**

Port Charlotte

PORT CHARLOTTE is Islay's prettiest village with its immaculate whitewashed cottages clustered around a sandy cove overlooking Loch Indaal. On the northern fringe of the village, in a whitewashed former chapel, the imaginative **Museum of Islay Life** (April–Sept Mon–Fri 10.30am–4.30pm; £3) has a children's corner, quizzes, a good library of

---

GEESE ON ISLAY

If you're visiting Islay between mid-September and the third week of April, it's impossible to miss the island's staggeringly large wintering population of **barnacle and white-fronted geese**. During this period, the geese dominate the landscape, feeding incessantly off the rich pasture, strolling by the shores, and flying in formation across the winter skies. You can see the geese just about anywhere on the island – there are an estimated fifteen thousand white-fronted and forty thousand barnacles here (and rising) – though in the evening, they tend to congregate in the tidal mud flats and fields around **Loch Gruinart**.

21

books about the island and tantalizing snippets about eighteenth-century illegal whisky distillers. The **Wildlife Information Centre** (Easter–Oct Sun–Fri 10am–4pm; June–Aug daily 10am–4pm; £2.50), housed in the former distillery warehouse, is also worth a visit for anyone interested in the island's fauna and flora.

ARRIVAL AND DEPARTURE	PORT CHARLOTTE

By bus Island buses run from Bowmore to Port Charlotte (Mon–Sat 5–6 daily, Sun 3 daily; 25min), stopping just outside the *Port Charlotte Hotel*.

ACCOMMODATION AND EATING	

The Monachs Nerabus, 3 miles along the road to Portnahaven ☎01496 850049, ⚲islayguesthouse .co.uk. A spacious, luxury new-build B&B villa with stupendous sea views. Free wi-fi. **£120**

Port Charlotte Hotel ☎01496 850360, ⚲port charlottehotel.co.uk. You'll receive a warm welcome here at one of Islay's most comfortable, relaxing places to stay – the seafood lunches served in the bar are very popular, and there's a good, more expensive restaurant (mains around £15). Noon–2pm & 6pm. **£195**

Port Mòr Campsite Just outside on the village on the road to Portnahaven ☎01496 850441, ⚲islandofislay .co.uk. Community-run campsite, with sea views and tip-top modern facilities, hot showers and a café. Feb–Nov. Per person **£8**

SYHA hostel ☎01496 850 385, ⚲syha.org.uk. Capacious modern hostel in an old bonded warehouse bordering a gorgeous sandy beach and next door to the Wildlife Information Centre. April–Oct. **£18**

Loch Finlaggan

Just beyond Ballygrant, on the road from Bowmore to Port Askaig, a narrow road leads north to **Loch Finlaggan**, site of a number of prehistoric crannogs (artificial islands) and, for 400 years from the twelfth century, headquarters of the Lords of the Isles, semi-autonomous rulers over the Hebrides and Kintyre. Duckboards allow you to walk out across the reed beds of the loch and explore the main crannog, **Eilean Mòr**, where several carved gravestones are displayed under cover in the chapel. These seem to support the theory that the Lords of the Isles buried their wives and children there, while having themselves interred on Iona.

ACCOMMODATION	LOCH FINLAGGAN

★Kilmeny Country House Just southwest of Ballygrant ☎01496 840668, ⚲kilmeny.co.uk. This whitewashed farmhouse has enjoyably plush rooms furnished with antiques; the gourmet dinners (Tues & Thurs only) are worth the extra £35 or so a head, and breakfasts are superb. **£130**

Isle of Jura

The long, whale-shaped island of **Jura** is one of the wildest and most mountainous of the Inner Hebrides, its entire west coast uninhabited and inaccessible except to the dedicated walker. Jura's distinctive Paps – so called because of their smooth breast-like shape, though there are in fact three of them – seem to dominate every view off the west coast of Argyll, their glacial rounded tops covered in a light dusting of quartzite scree. The island's name is commonly thought to derive from the Norse *dyr-oe* (deer island) and, appropriately enough, the current deer population of 6000 far outnumbers the 180 humans. With just one road, which sticks to the more sheltered eastern coast, just one hotel and a smattering of B&Bs, Jura is an ideal place to go for peace, quiet and some great walking.

Anything that happens on Jura happens in the island's only real village, **CRAIGHOUSE**, eight miles up the road from Feolin Ferry. The village enjoys a sheltered setting, overlooking Knapdale on the mainland – so sheltered, in fact, that there are even a few palm trees thriving on the seafront. There's a shop, a post office, the island hotel and a

GEORGE ORWELL ON JURA

In April 1946, Eric Blair (better known by his pen name of **George Orwell**), suffering badly from TB and intending to give himself "six months' quiet" in which to write his new novel *The Last Man in Europe* (later to become *1984*), moved to a remote farmhouse called **Barnhill**, on the northern tip of Jura. He lived out a spartan existence there for two years but due to ill health was forced to return to England shortly before his death. The house, 23 miles north of Craighouse, up an increasingly poor road, is as remote today as it was in Orwell's day, and is now let out as a **self-catering cottage** (☎01786 850274).

tearoom, plus the tiny **Isle of Jura distillery** (☎ 01496 820240, ⓦjurawhisky.com), which is very welcoming to visitors.

ARRIVAL AND DEPARTURE

ISLE OF JURA

By ferry The main car ferry departs from Port Askaig on Islay to Feolin (Mon–Sat hourly, Sun 3 daily; 10min; ☎01496 840681), 8 miles west of Craighouse. There's also a passenger ferry service from Tayvallich, on the Argyll mainland, to Craighouse (Mon, Fri & Sat 2 daily, Sun 1 daily; 1hr; ☎07768 450000, ⓦjurapassengerferry.com).

ACCOMMODATION AND EATING

Jura Hotel Craighouse ☎01496 820243, ⓦjurahotel .co.uk. It's not much to look at from the outside, but it is warm and friendly within, and the centre of the island's social scene. The cheaper rooms are not en suite. The hotel does moderately expensive bar meals (around £12), and has a shower block and laundry facilities round the back for those who wish to camp in the hotel garden. Pitches **£5**, doubles **£94**

Sealladh na Mara Knockrome ☎01496 820349. A modern croft house B&B, 4 miles north of Craighouse, with two pristine all-white first-floor rooms with wooden floors and lovely views over the island. **£80**

Northeast Scotland

DUNNOTTAR CASTLE

Northeast Scotland

A large triangle of land thrusting into the North Sea, northeast Scotland comprises the area east of a line drawn roughly from Perth north to the fringe of the Moray Firth at Forres. The area takes in the county of Angus, the city of Dundee and, beyond the Grampian Mountains, the counties of Aberdeenshire and Moray and the city of Aberdeen. Geographically diverse, the landscape in the south of the region is comprised predominantly of undulating farmland, but as you travel further north of the Firth of Tay this gives way to wooded glens, mountains and increasingly harsh land fringed by a dramatic coast of cliffs and long, sandy beaches.

The long-depressed city of **Dundee** is valiantly trying to shed its postindustrial image with a reinvigorated cultural scene and an impressive waterfront development based around **Discovery**, the ship of Captain Scott ("of the Antarctic"). A little way up the Angus coast lie the historically important towns of **Arbroath** and **Montrose**, which are linked by an especially inviting stretch of coastline, with scarlet cliffs and sweeping bays. Further south towards Dundee, these are replaced by gentler dunes and long, sandy beaches, while inland the long fingers of the **Angus Glens** – heather-covered hills tumbling down to rushing rivers – are overlooked by the southern peaks of the Grampian Mountains. **Glen Clova** is one of the most popular, along with **Glen Shee**, which attracts large numbers of people to its ski slopes. Handsome if uneventful market towns such as **Blairgowrie** are good bases for the area, and extravagant **Glamis Castle** is well worth a visit.

The northeast was the southern kingdom of the **Picts**, reminders of whom are scattered throughout the region in the form of beautifully carved stones found in fields, churchyards and museums, such as the one at **Meigle**. The area never grew particularly prosperous, and a handful of feuding and intermarrying families grew to wield disproportionate influence, building many of the region's **castles** and religious buildings and developing and planning its towns.

Many of the most appealing settlements are along the coast, but while the fishing industry is but a fondly held memory in many parts, a number of the northeast's ports were transformed by the discovery of **oil** in the North Sea in the 1960s – particularly **Aberdeen**, Scotland's third-largest city.

North of the glens and west of Aberdeen is **Deeside**, a fertile, ruggedly attractive area made famous by the Royal Family: **Balmoral** has been a royal residence since Victoria's time. Beyond are the eastern sections of the **Cairngorms National Park** and travelling north into Moray brings you to Scotland's most productive whisky-making area, **Speyside**.

GETTING AROUND NORTHEAST SCOTLAND

By train Trains from Edinburgh and Glasgow connect with Dundee, Aberdeen and other coastal towns, while an inland line from Aberdeen heads northwest to Elgin and on to Inverness.

By bus The region has a reasonably comprehensive scheduled bus service; only in the most remote and mountainous parts does public transport disappear altogether.

By car Northeast Scotland is well-served by an extensive road network, with fast links between Dundee and Aberdeen, while the area north and west of Aberdeen is dissected by a series of efficient routes.

Top 5 castles and abbeys p.871
Skiing at Glen Shee p.873

The Malt Whisky Trail p.882
The Findhorn Foundation p.884

ARBROATH SMOKIES

Highlights

❶ McManus Art Galleries and Museum
Dundee's most impressive Victorian building is
the place to come for ceramics, fine art and
contemporary photography. **See p.868**

❷ Arbroath smokies A true Scottish delicacy:
succulent haddock best eaten when it's still
warm from the oak smoker. **See p.871**

❸ Meigle Pictish stones Fascinating carved
relics of a lost culture, standing alone in fields, or
protected from the elements in museums such
as the one at Meigle. **See p.873**

❹ Dunnottar Castle The moodiest cliff-top
ruin in the country, built in the ninth century
and surrounded by crashing seas. **See p.877**

❺ Speyside's whiskies See the distilleries and
landscapes of places such as Glenfiddich,
Glenlivet and Glen Grant – visits give you a
splendid opportunity to taste their whiskies too.
See p.881

**❻ Museum of Scottish Lighthouses,
Fraserburgh** Lights, lenses and legends at one
of the quirkiest and most intriguing small
museums in the country. **See p.883**

HIGHLIGHTS ARE MARKED ON THE MAP ON PP.866–867

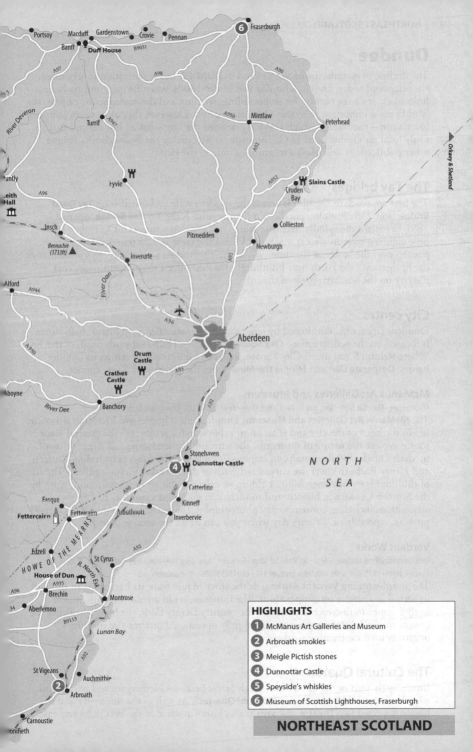

HIGHLIGHTS

1. McManus Art Galleries and Museum
2. Arbroath smokies
3. Meigle Pictish stones
4. Dunnottar Castle
5. Speyside's whiskies
6. Museum of Scottish Lighthouses, Fraserburgh

NORTHEAST SCOTLAND

Dundee

The decline of manufacturing wasn't kind to **DUNDEE**, but regeneration is very much the buzzword today. The city's heyday was in the 1800s, when its train and harbour links made it a major centre for shipbuilding, whaling and the manufacture of **jute**, the world's most important vegetable fibre after cotton. However, this, along with jam and **journalism** – the three Js which famously defined the city – has all but disappeared. Only local publishing giant D.C. Thomson, which makes the *Beano* comic, among other publications, still plays a meaningful role in the city.

22

The Tay bridges

The best approach to Dundee is across the modern mile-and-a-half-long **Tay Road Bridge** from Fife. Running parallel a mile upstream is the **Tay Rail Bridge**, opened in 1887 to replace the spindly structure which collapsed in a storm in December 1879 only eighteen months after it was built, killing the crew and 75 passengers on a train passing over the bridge at the time. While the Tay bridges aren't nearly as spectacular as the bridges over the Forth near Edinburgh, they do offer a magnificent panorama of the city on the northern bank of the firth.

City centre

Dundee's city centre, dominated by large shopping malls filled with bland chain stores, is focused on the pedestrianized **City Square**, a couple of hundred yards north of the Tay. Where Reform Street meets City Square, look out for a couple of statues to Dundee heroes: **Desperate Dan** and **Minnie the Minx**, from the *Dandy* and *Beano* comics.

McManus Art Galleries and Museum

Albert Square • Mon–Sat 10am–5pm, Sun 12.30–4.30pm • Free • ☎ 01382 307200, ⓦ mcmanus.co.uk

The **McManus Art Galleries and Museum**, Dundee's most impressive Victorian structure, lies in the heart of the city and is an unmissable stop for art lovers. The ground-floor rooms explore the nature of museums, the surrounding landscape and the making of modern Dundee, while upstairs an impressive collection by masters including Rossetti and Henry Raeburn cover the curved red walls of the splendid Victoria gallery. The rest of this floor is equally engrossing, holding an eclectic ethnographic collection, work by the Scottish Colourists, historic and modern ceramics, and a number of fine art acquisitions including contemporary photography. The museum's bright **café** is a good pit-stop, especially on a sunny day when you can sit on the terrace outside.

Verdant Works

West Henderson Wynd, Blackness • April–Oct Mon–Sat 10am–6pm, Sun 11am–6pm; Nov–March Wed–Sat 10.30am–4.30pm, Sun 11am–4.30pm • £8.75, joint ticket with Discovery Point £15 • ☎ 01382 309060, ⓦ rrsdiscovery.com

The award-winning **Verdant Works** tells the story of jute from its harvesting in India to its arrival in Dundee on clipper ships. The museum, set in an old jute mill, makes a lively attempt to re-create the turn-of-the-century factory floor, the highlight being the chance to watch jute being processed on fully operational quarter-size machines originally used for training workers.

The Cultural Quarter

Immediately west of the city centre, High Street becomes Nethergate and passes into what has been dubbed Dundee's "**Cultural Quarter**". As well as the university and the highly respected **Rep Theatre**, the area is also home to some of the best pubs and cafés in the city.

CENTRAL DUNDEE

DCA

152 Nethergate • Complex daily 10am–midnight; galleries Mon–Wed & Fri 11am–6pm, Thurs 11am–8pm • Free • ☎ 01382 909900, ⓦ dca.org.uk

The **DCA**, or Dundee Contemporary Arts, is a stunningly designed five-storey complex incorporating galleries, a print studio, a cool design shop and an airy café-bar. It's worth visiting for the stimulating temporary and touring exhibitions of contemporary art, as well as an eclectic programme of art-house films and cult classics.

Discovery Point

Discovery Quay • April–Oct Mon–Sat 10am–6pm, Sun 11am–6pm; Nov–March Mon–Sat 10am–5pm, Sun 11am–5pm • £8.75, joint ticket with Verdant Works £15 • ☎ 01382 309060, ⓦ rrsdiscovery.com

Just south of the city centre in the waterfront area, which is currently undergoing a massive £1bn transformation, the domed **Discovery Point** is an impressive development centring on the Royal Research Ship *Discovery*. Something of an icon for Dundee's renaissance, *Discovery* is a three-mast steam-assisted vessel built in Dundee in 1901 to take Captain Robert Falcon Scott on his polar expeditions. A combination of brute strength and elegance, she has been beautifully restored, with polished wood panels and brass trimmings giving scant indication of the privations suffered by the crew. In the Antarctic, temperatures on board would plummet to -28°C and turns at having a bath came round every 47 days. Before you step aboard there are a series of interactive displays about the construction of the ship and Scott's journeys, including the chill-inducing "Polarama" about life in Antarctica.

Keep your eye out for the site of the **V&A Museum of Design**, just east of the boat, which is due to be completed by 2017.

ARRIVAL AND INFORMATION   DUNDEE

By plane Dundee Airport, just west of the city centre, is served by flights from London Stansted (Mon–Fri 2 daily, Sun 1 daily; 1hr 30min). There are no buses into the centre; a taxi will cost around £6.

By train Trains stop just north of the river, near Riverside Drive.
Destinations Aberdeen (every 30min; 1hr 15min); Arbroath (every 30min; 20min); Edinburgh (every 30min–1hr; 1hr 30min); Glasgow (every 30min–1hr; 1hr 30min); Montrose (every 30min–1hr; 30min).

By bus Most long-distance buses operated by Stagecoach

Strathtay (☎01382 313700) arrive at the Seagate bus station, a couple of hundred yards east of the centre. Local buses leave from High St or nearby Union St (☎01382 201121).
Destinations Aberdeen (hourly; 2hr 20min); Arbroath (every 30min; 30–50min); Blairgowrie (1–2 hourly; 50min–1hr); Glamis (2–5 daily; 35min); Kirriemuir (hourly; 55min); Meigle (hourly; 40min); Montrose (hourly; 1hr).

Tourist information 16 City Square (Mon–Fri 9am–4.30pm, Sat 9.30am–4pm; ☎01382 527527, ⓦangusanddundee.co.uk).

ACCOMMODATION

Dundee isn't bursting with interesting accommodation options, but it's comparatively inexpensive and there's a well-located hostel. You'll find plenty of rooms out in the suburb of **Broughty Ferry**, a 20min bus ride away.

Aberlaw Guest House 230 Broughty Ferry Road ☎01382 456929, ⓦaberlaw.co.uk. Well-run guesthouse 1.5 miles from the city centre, with spotlessly clean rooms (including a large family room) and a welcoming owner who knows the local area inside out. **£80**

Apex City Quay Hotel & Spa West Victoria Dock Rd ☎01314 410440, ⓦapexhotels.co.uk. This large, sleek hotel down by the docks is still one of the city's smartest options, with its own spa, swimming pool and restaurant. **£90**

Dundee Backpackers Hostel 71 High St ☎01382 224646, ⓦhoppo.com. Dundee's only hostel, with dorm beds spread around a warren-like former merchant's house

that dates back to 1560. Private rooms are also available. Dorms **£15**; doubles **£39**

Dundee Student Villages ☎01382 573111, ⓦScotland 2000/seabraes. En-suite single (£30) or double rooms, or exclusive use of self-catered flats sleeping up to eight (min. stay 3 nights) located at Seabraes, just west of the city centre. Bland but cheap. July & Aug only. Doubles **£42.50**, flats **£222**

Fisherman's Tavern 10–16 Fort St, Broughty Ferry ☎01382 775941, ⓦfishermanstavern.co.uk. Neat contemporary rooms, mostly en suite and one with facilities for disabled guests, above a cosy and popular traditional pub with a roaring fire and good real ales. **£74**

EATING

The **west end** of Dundee, around the main university campus and Perth Road, is the best area for eating and drinking. The suburb of **Broughty Ferry** (a 20min bus ride away) is a pleasant alternative, with a good selection of pubs and restaurants that get particularly busy on summer evenings.

The Blue Marlin Camperdown Street, City Quay ☎01382 534001, ⓦthebluemarlin.co.uk. As the name suggests, this attractive seafood restaurant serves lunches and dinners with tempting dishes like mussels (£14) and prawn and monkfish skewers (£24). Tues–Sat noon–2pm & 5–9/9.30pm.

Castlehill Restaurant 22 Exchange St ☎01382 220008, ⓦcastlehillrestaurant.co.uk. Smart, contemporary dining in a very intimate setting, where the focus is on products sourced from local suppliers. Dishes include Scottish crab with fennel and apple purée, and Hebridean salmon with summer vegetables (two courses £28). Tues–Sat noon–2.30pm & 5.30–10pm.

The Playwright 11 South Tay Street ☎01382 223113, ⓦtheplaywright.co.uk. Swanky, well-staffed restaurant right by the Repertory Theatre, serving indulgent à la carte

dishes (think milk-poached veal loin with a mozzarella tempura; £24.95) and cheaper pre-theatre and lunch menus. Mon–Sat noon–2.30pm & 5–9.30pm.

★**Sol y Sombra** 27 Gray St, Broughty Ferry ☎01382 776941, ⓦsolysombratapasbar.co.uk. The super-friendly welcome at this snug tapas bar is followed up with a seemingly endless stream of terracotta pots filled with olives, sweet peppers, potatoes, morcilla (Spanish blood sausage), chorizo and manchego, plus lots of regional specialities. There's no menu, so just ask for the set meal (£19.95). You won't leave hungry. Daily 10am–midnight.

T Ann Cake 27 Exchange St ☎01382 203950. Cute and very popular little café in the city centre doing good coffee, plus tasty bakes and sandwiches. Try the home-made lemonade, which goes for £1.25 a glass. Tues–Fri 10am–5pm, Sat 10am–4pm.

DRINKING

Ship Inn 121 Fisher St, Broughty Ferry ☎01382 779176, ⊛theshipinn-broughtyferry.co.uk. A narrow pub with a warm atmosphere and nautical feel right on the waterfront with good views over the Tay. Good seafood dishes and a fine selection of beers. Mon–Sat 11am–midnight, Sun 12.30pm–midnight.

The Social 10 South Tay St ⊛socialdundee.co.uk. Good pre-club hangout, often packed with students, where you can get a Smirnoff and Coke for £3 (or £1.50 if you download the bar's app). Regular open-mike nights. Sun–Thurs noon–midnight, Fri & Sat noon–2am.

Trades House Bar 40 Nettergate ☎01382 229494. A converted bank fronted with stained-glass windows, which provides a friendly atmosphere for boozing in the heart of the city. Serves simple pub meals for around £7.50. Daily 10/11am–midnight.

ENTERTAINMENT

DCA 152 Nethergate ☎01382 909900, ⊛dca.org.uk. The DCA (see p.869) has cinema screens showing a range of foreign and art-house movies alongside more challenging mainstream releases.

Dundee Repertory Theatre Tay Square ☎01382 223530, ⊛dundeereptheatre.co.uk. Right at the heart of the Cultural Quarter on Tay Square, north of Nethergate, is the prodigious Rep, home to an indigenously-produced contemporary theatre and the only permanent repertory company in Scotland.

The Reading Rooms 57 Blackscroft ⊛reading roomsdundee.com. From rock 'n' roll and disco to soul, blues and punk, you'll find it here. The schedule (available online) is mostly taken up by DJs and club nights, but guitar bands play too. Thurs–Sat, typically 10.30pm–3.30am.

The Angus coast

Two roads link Dundee to Aberdeen and the northeast coast of Scotland. By far the more pleasant option is the slightly longer A92 coast road, which joins the inland A90 at Stonehaven, just south of Aberdeen. Intercity **buses** follow both roads, while the coast-hugging train line from Dundee is one of the most picturesque in Scotland, passing attractive beaches and impressive cliffs, and stopping in the old seaports of **Arbroath** and **Montrose**.

Arbroath

Since it was settled in the twelfth century, local fishermen have been landing their catches at **ARBROATH**, about fifteen miles northeast of Dundee. The town's most famous product is the **Arbroath smokie** – line-caught haddock, smoke-cured over smouldering oak chips and still made here in a number of family-run smokehouses tucked in around the harbour. One of the most approachable and atmospheric is **M&M Spink's** tiny whitewashed premises at 10 Marketgate (☎01241 875287, ⊛arbroathsmokies.co.uk); chef and food writer Rick Stein described the fish here, warm from the smoke, as "a world-class delicacy".

Arbroath Abbey

Abbey St • Daily: April–Sept 9.30am–5.30pm; Oct–March 9.30am–4.30pm • £5.50; HS • ☎01241 878756

The town's real glory days came with the completion in 1233 of **Arbroath Abbey**, whose rose-pink sandstone ruins were described by Dr Johnson as "fragments of magnificence". Founded in 1178 but not granted abbey status until 1285, it was the scene of one of the most significant events in Scotland's history when, on April 6, 1320, a group of Scottish

---

TOP 5 CASTLES AND ABBEYS

Arbroath Abbey See above
Crathes Castle See p.879
Dunnottar Castle See p.877

Glamis Castle See p.874
Balmoral Castle See p.880

22

barons drew up the **Declaration of Arbroath**, asking the pope to reverse his excommunication of Robert the Bruce and recognize him as king of a Scottish nation independent from England. The wonderfully resonant language of the document still makes for a stirring expression of Scottish nationhood: "For so long as one hundred of us remain alive, we will never in any degree be subject to the dominion of the English, since it is not for glory, riches or honour that we do fight, but for freedom alone, which no honest man loses but with his life". It was duly dispatched to Pope John XXII in Avignon, who in 1324 agreed to Robert's claim. The **visitor centre** at the Abbey Street entrance offers in-depth background on these events and other aspects of the history of the building.

ARRIVAL AND DEPARTURE   ARBROATH

By train The train station is on Keptie St in the centre of town.
Destinations Aberdeen (every 30min; 1hr); Dundee (every 30min; 20min); Montrose (roughly every 30min; 15min).

By bus Buses stop on Catherine St, near the train station.
Destinations Aberdeen (hourly; 1hr 45min); Dundee (every 30min; 30min); Forfar (hourly; 45min); Montrose (roughly every 30min; 25min).

ACCOMMODATION

★ **Brucefield Boutique B&B** Cliffburn Road ☎ 01241 875393, ⊛ brucefieldbandb.com. Rooms at this renovated 1920s manor house are as good as those in the region's best hotels, with high-end bathroom amenities and plush beds. Downstairs there's a sitting room with a free minibar, and outside there are seats overlooking a

croquet lawn. **£110**
Old Vicarage 2 Seaton Rd ☎ 01241 430475, ⊛ theoldvicaragebandb.co.uk. Simple and friendly, the *Old Vicarage* has an impressive breakfast table that includes hot Arbroath smokies, a freshly baked loaf and home-made preserves. Min two-night stay in summer. **£85**

Montrose and around

A seaport and market town since the thirteenth century, **MONTROSE** sits on the edge of a virtually landlocked two-mile-square lagoon of mud known as the Basin. It's a great little town to visit, with a pleasant old centre.

Montrose Basin Wildlife Centre

Around a mile west of Montrose along the A92 • March–Oct daily 10.30am–5pm; Nov–Feb Fri–Sun 10.30am–4pm • £4 • ⊛ montrosebasin.org.uk

On the south side of the Basin, the well-run **Montrose Basin Wildlife Centre** has binoculars, high-powered telescopes, bird hides and remote-control video cameras. Arctic terns often make an appearance during the summer, and there's a good chance of seeing wood pigeons and great crested grebes throughout the year. Family-friendly guided walks also depart from the centre (see the website for a schedule).

The House of Dun

4 miles west of Montrose • April–June, Sept & Oct Wed–Sun noon–5pm; July & Aug daily 11am–5pm • £10.50; NTS • Accessible on the Montrose–Brechin bus #30; ask the driver to let you off outside

The Palladian **House of Dun**, crammed full of period furniture and objets d'art, was built in 1730 for David Erskine, Laird of Dun, to designs by William Adam. Inside, the ornate relief plasterwork is the most impressive feature, extravagantly emblazoned with Jacobite symbolism. The buildings in the courtyard – a hen house, gamekeeper's workshop and potting shed – have been renovated, and include a tearoom and a craft shop.

ARRIVAL AND ACCOMMODATION   MONTROSE

By train The train station lies a block back from High St on Western Rd.
Destinations Aberdeen (1–2 hourly; 45min); Arbroath

(every 30min; 15min); Dundee (every 30min; 30min); Stonehaven (1–2 hourly; 20min).
By bus Most buses stop on the High St, or at the

railway station.
Destinations Aberdeen (hourly; 1hr 20min); Brechin (for the House of Dun; every 30min; 20min); Stonehaven (every 30min; 50min).

36 The Mall The Mall, towards the north of town ☎ 01674 673646, ⓦ 36themall.co.uk. Attractive B&B accommodation with en-suite facilities in every room. The breakfast menu includes fish smoked in nearby Arbroath. **£80**

The Angus Glens and around

Immediately north of Dundee, the low-lying Sidlaw Hills divide the city from the rich agricultural region of **Strathmore**, whose string of tidy market towns lies on a fertile strip along the southernmost edge of the heather-covered lower slopes of the Grampian Mountains. These towns act as gateways to the **Angus Glens** (ⓦ angusglens.co.uk), a series of tranquil valleys penetrated by single-track roads and offering some of the most rugged and majestic landscapes in northeast Scotland. It's a rain-swept, wind-blown, sparsely populated area, whose roads become impassable with the first snows, sometimes as early as October, and where the summers see clouds of ferocious midges. The most useful road through the glens is the A93, which cuts through **Glen Shee**, linking Blairgowrie to Braemar on Deeside (see p.880). It's pretty dramatic stuff, threading its way over Britain's highest main road, the **Cairnwell Pass** (2199ft).

22

Blairgowrie

The upper reaches of **Glen Shee**, the most dramatic and best-known of the Angus Glens, are dominated by its **ski fields**, ranged over four mountains above the Cairnwell mountain pass. To get to Glen Shee from the south you'll pass through the well-heeled little town of **BLAIRGOWRIE**, set among raspberry fields on the glen's southernmost tip and a good place to pick up information and plan your activities.

ARRIVAL AND EATING

BLAIRGOWRIE

By bus The #57 bus connects Blairgowrie with Perth (hourly; 50min) and Dundee (hourly; 1hr).
Tourist information 26 Wellmeadow (April–June, Sept & Oct Mon–Sat 9.30am–5.30pm, Sun 10am–4pm; July & Aug Mon–Sat 9am–6pm, Sun 9.30am–5.30pm; Nov–March Mon–Sat 9.30am–4.30pm, Sun 11am–3pm).

Cargills Lower Mill St ☎ 01250 876735, ⓦ cargillsbistro .com. Family-run café serving inexpensive meals plus good coffee and cakes. The menu has a couple of good veggie options, including a mushroom risotto (£12.20). Mon & Tues 10am–5pm, Wed–Sun 10am–9pm.

Meigle Museum

15 miles north of Dundee on the B954 • April–Sept daily 9.30am–5.30pm • HS • £4.50 • ☎ 01828 640612 • Bus #57 from Dundee's Seagate bus station (12–15 daily Mon–Sat, Sun 6 daily; 35min) stops close to the museum on the B954 (Dundee Road)

The tiny settlement of **MEIGLE** is home to Scotland's most important collection of early Christian and **Pictish inscribed stones**. The exact meaning and purpose of the stones

---

SKIING AT GLEN SHEE

Scotland's **ski resorts** make for a fun day out for anyone from beginners to experienced skiers and, given that **Glen Shee** is both the most extensive and the most accessible of Scotland's ski areas, just over two hours from both Glasgow and Edinburgh, it's as good an introduction as any to the sport in Scotland.

For information, contact Glenshee Ski Centre (☎ 01339 741320, ⓦ ski-glenshee.co.uk), which also offers ski rental and can connect you with companies offering lessons. **Ski rental** starts at around £13 a day, and lessons cost around £40/hour. **Lift passes** cost £29/day or £116 for a five-day (Mon–Fri) ticket. For the latest snow and **weather conditions**, phone the centre itself or check out the Ski Scotland website (ⓦ ski.visitscotland.com).

22

and their enigmatic symbols is obscure, as is the reason why so many of them were found here. The most likely theory is that Meigle was once an important ecclesiastical centre that attracted secular burials of prominent Picts. Housed in a modest former schoolhouse, the **Meigle Museum** displays some 26 pieces dating from the seventh to the tenth centuries, all found in and around the nearby churchyard. The majority are either gravestones that would have lain flat, or cross slabs inscribed with the sign of the cross, usually standing. Most impressive is the 7ft-tall great cross slab, said to be the gravestone of Guinevere, wife of King Arthur.

Glen Isla

It was near **ALYTH**, three miles north of Meigle, that – legend has it – King Arthur's wife Guinevere was held captive by Mordred. The sleepy village lies at the south end of **Glen Isla**, which runs parallel to Glen Shee and is linked to it by the A926. Ten miles or so up the glen is the tiny hamlet of **Kirkton of Glenisla**.

ARRIVAL AND ACCOMMODATION · GLEN ISLA

By bus Transport connections into the glen are limited: occasional buses run to Alyth from Blairgowrie and Kirriemuir, while bus #57 from Dundee (hourly) passes through Meigle and continues to Alyth.

Glenisla Hotel Kirkton of Glenisla ☎ 01575 582223, ⊚ glenisla-hotel.com. This cosy country hotel doubles as a great place for home-made bar food (mains around £10.50) and convivial drinking. Rooms are comfy, though a little on the small side. **£77.50**

West Freuchies Just outside Kirkton of Glenisla ☎ 01575 582716, ⊚ glenisla-westfreuchies.co.uk A comfortable bed and breakfast whose first-floor rooms have views over the hills. There's also self-catering accommodation nearby in a converted mill (min 1 week stay). Approaching from Alyth, a right-hand turn leads northeast to the B&B (signposted before you reach Kirkton of Glenisla). Doubles **£77.50**, mill **£600**

Glamis Castle

Dundee Road, about 5 miles south of Kirriemuir · Daily: Mid-April to Nov 10am–6pm (last admission 4.30pm) · £10.90 · ☎ 01307 840393, ⊚ glamis-castle.co.uk · Bus #22 runs from Dundee to Glamis village twice a day (35min), but both departures are late in the afternoon. On Sat & Sun, bus #254 covers the same route earlier in the day (1 daily; 30min). The castle is a mile north of the village

The wondrously over-the-top, five-storey pink-sandstone **Glamis Castle** is set in an extensive landscaped park complete with Highland cattle and pheasants beside the picturesque village of **GLAMIS** (pronounced "glahms"). One of the country's most famous castles, featuring in *Macbeth* and with **royal connections** (as the childhood home of the late Queen Mother and birthplace of the late Princess Margaret), it's an essential stop on every bus tour of Scotland.

Obligatory guided tours take in the fifteenth-century **crypt**, where the 12ft-thick walls enclose a haunted "lost" room, the family **chapel** and **Duncan's Hall**, a fifteenth-century guardroom, the – inaccurate – setting for Duncan's murder by Macbeth. Glamis' **grounds**, including the Italian Gardens, are worth a few hours in their own right, with verdant walks out to Earl John's Bridge and through the woodland.

Glen Clova/Glen Doll

With its stunning cliffs, heather slopes and valley meadows, **Glen Clova** – which in the north becomes **Glen Doll** – is one of the loveliest of the Angus Glens. Although it can get unpleasantly congested in peak season, the area is still remote enough to enable you to lose the crowds with little effort. Wildlife is abundant, with deer on the mountains, wild hare and even grouse and the occasional buzzard. The meadow flowers on the valley floor and arctic plants (including great splashes of white and purple saxifrage) on the rocks also make it something of a botanist's paradise.

There is no public transport to Glen Clova. The nearest town is Kirriemuir, 14 miles south off the B955.

Glen Clova Hotel Along the B955 in Clova ☎01575 550350, ⓦclova.com. The hamlet of Clova consists of little more than this hearty place, which also runs a bunkhouse and a private fishing loch. The restaurant serves up traditional Scottish food, such as venison casserole and haggis. Bunkhouse **£20**, doubles **£90**

Aberdeenshire and Moray

22

Aberdeenshire and Moray cover a large chunk of northern Scotland – some 3500 square miles, much of it open and varied country dotted with historic and archeological sights, from neat NTS properties and eerie prehistoric standing stones to quiet kirkyards and a rash of dramatic castles. Geographically, the counties break down into two distinct areas: the **hinterland**, once barren and now a patchwork of fertile farms, rising towards high mountains, sparkling rivers and gentle valleys; and the **coast**, a classic stretch of rocky cliffs, remote fishing villages and long, sandy beaches.

For visitors, the large city of **Aberdeen** is the obvious focal point of the region, and while it's not a place to keep you engrossed for long, it does have some intriguing architecture, attractive museums and a lively social scene. From here, it's a short hop west to **Deeside**, visited annually by the Royal Family, where the trim villages of **Ballater** and **Braemar** act as a gateway to the spectacular Cairngorms National Park, which covers much of the upland areas in the west of this region. Further north, the "Malt Whisky Country" of **Speyside** has less impressive scenery but numerous whisky distilleries, while the **coast** beyond features dramatic cliffs and long beaches punctuated by picturesque fishing villages.

Aberdeen and around

The third-largest city in Scotland, **ABERDEEN**, commonly known as the "Granite City", lies 120 miles northeast of Edinburgh on the banks of the rivers Dee and Don, smack in the middle of the northeast coast. Based around a working harbour, it's a place that people either love or hate. Certainly, while some extol the many tones and colours of Aberdeen's **granite** buildings, others see only uniform grey and find the city grim and cold. The weather doesn't help: Aberdeen lies on a latitude north of Moscow and the cutting wind and driving rain (even if it does transform the buildings into sparkling silver) can be tiresome.

In the twelfth century, Alexander I noted "Aberdon" as one of his principal towns, and by the thirteenth century it had become a centre for **trade and fishing**. A century or so later Bishop Elphinstone founded the Catholic university in the area north of town known today as **Old Aberdeen**, while the rest of the city developed as a mercantile centre and important port. By the mid-twentieth century, Aberdeen's traditional industries were in decline, but the discovery of **oil** in the North Sea transformed the place from a depressed port into a boom town. Since the 1970s, oil has made Aberdeen a hugely wealthy and self-confident place. Despite (or perhaps because of) this, it can sometimes feel like a soulless city, existing mainly as a departure point for the transient population who live on the oil platforms out to sea.

Castlegate

Any exploration of the **city centre** should begin at the open, cobbled **Castlegate**, where Aberdeen's long-gone castle once stood. At its centre is the late seventeenth-century **Mercat Cross**, carved with a unique gallery of Stewart sovereigns alongside some fierce gargoyles. The view up gently rising Union Street – a jumble of grey spires, turrets and jostling double-decker buses – is quintessential Aberdeen.

22

CENTRAL ABERDEEN

● CAFÉS & RESTAURANTS				■ ACCOMMODATION				■ CLUBS AND LIVE MUSIC	
Books and Beans	1	Musa	4	Aberdeen Youth Hostel	1	Dutch Mill	2	Lemon Tree	2
Food Story Café	5	Shri Beema's	3	Allan Guest House	4	Ferryhill House	6	The Tunnels	6
Fusion	2			Deeside Holiday Park	5	Marcliffe Hotel	3		

■ PUBS & BARS

Brewdog Aberdeen	3
The Illicit Still	4
Ninety-Nine Bar & Kitchen	7
Prince of Wales	5
Slains Castle	8
St Machar Bar	1

The Aberdeen Art Gallery

Schoolhill • Tues–Sat 10am–5pm, Sun 2–5pm • Free • ☎ 01224 523700, ⓦ aagm.co.uk

Aberdeen's engrossing **Art Gallery**, purpose-built in 1884, is entered via the airy **Centre Court**. Barbara Hepworth's central fountain dominates, while nearby are a number of pieces of contemporary art, with British work to the fore. The **Memorial Court**, a white-walled circular room beneath a skylit dome, serves as the city's principal war memorial and houses the Lord Provost's book of condolence for the 167 people who died in the 1988 Piper Alpha oil rig disaster. The **upstairs** rooms house the main body of the gallery's painting collection. This includes a superb collection of Victorian narrative art, some decent twentieth-century British painting and a collection of Impressionist art, including works by Boudin, Courbet, Sisley, Monet, Pissarro and Renoir.

Maritime Museum

Shiprow • Tues–Sat 10am–5pm, Sun noon–3pm • Free • ☎ 01224 337700, ⓦ aagm.co.uk

Just off cobbled Shiprow, peering towards the harbour through a striking glass facade, the engrossing **Maritime Museum** combines a modern, airy museum with the aged, labyrinthine corridors of **Provost Ross's House**. Just inside the entrance you'll see a blackboard updated daily with the price of a barrel of crude oil, and suspended above the foyer, visible from five different levels, is a spectacular 27ft-high model of an oil rig. The older industries of herring fishing, whaling, shipbuilding and lighthouses also have their place, with well-designed displays, many drawing heavily on personal reminiscences.

Old Aberdeen

Take bus #20 from Marischal College (1–2 hourly; 10 min)

An independent burgh until 1891, tranquil **Old Aberdeen** has maintained a village-like identity. Dominated by **King's College** and **St Machar's Cathedral**, its medieval cobbled streets, wynds and little lanes are beautifully preserved.

King's College Chapel

King's Campus, University of Aberdeen • Mon–Fri 9.30am–3.30pm • Free • ☎ 01223 331212

King's College Chapel, the first and finest of the college buildings, was completed in 1495, with a chunky Renaissance spire. The highlights of the interior, which, unusually, has no central aisle, are the ribbed, arched wooden ceiling and the rare and lovely examples of medieval Scottish woodcarving in the screen and the stalls.

St Machar's Cathedral

The Chanonry • Daily 10am–4pm, except during services • Free • ☎ 01224 485988, ⓦ stmachar.com

St Machar's Cathedral sits on the leafy Chanonry, overlooking Seaton Park and the River Don. The site was reputedly founded in 580 AD by Machar, a follower of Columba, when he was sent by the latter to find a grassy platform near the sea, overlooking a river shaped like the crook on a bishop's crozier. This setting fitted the bill perfectly, and the cathedral, a huge fifteenth-century fortified building, became one of the city's first great granite edifices.

The beach

Aberdeen can surely claim to have the best sandy **beach** of all Britain's large cities. Less than a mile east of Union Street is a great two-mile sweep of clean sand, broken by groynes and lined all along with an esplanade, where most of the city's population seems to gather on sunny days. Further north, most of the beach's hinterland is devoted to golf links.

Dunnottar Castle

15 miles south of Aberdeen, 2 miles south of Stonehaven • Daily: April–Sept 9am–6pm; Oct–March 10am–5pm or sunset • £6 • ☎ 01569 762173, ⓦ dunnottarcastle.co.uk

South of Aberdeen, the A92 and the main train line follow the coast to the pretty little harbour town of **STONEHAVEN**. Two miles south, the stunningly capricious **Dunnottar Castle** is one of Scotland's finest ruined castles, a huge ninth-century fortress set on a three-sided sheer cliff jutting into the sea – a setting striking enough to be chosen as the backdrop for Zeffirelli's 1990 film version of *Hamlet*. Once the principal fortress of the northeast, the ruins are worth a good root around, and there are many dramatic views out to the crashing sea. Bloodstained drama splatters the castle's past – not least in 1297, when the entire English Plantagenet garrison was burned alive here by William Wallace.

ARRIVAL AND INFORMATION

By plane Aberdeen's Dyce Airport lies 7 miles northwest of town. Frequent buses (up to six hourly) run from the airport to Union Square.

Destinations Birmingham (up to 1–5 daily; 1hr 30min); Bristol (Mon–Fri 2 daily, Sun 1 daily; 1hr 20min); Durham (1–4 daily; 1hr); East Midlands (2–3 daily Mon–Fri, Sun 1 daily; 1hr 25min); Kirkwall, Orkney (2–5 daily; 50min); Leeds Bradford (2–3 daily Mon–Fri, Sun 1 daily; 1hr 10min); London City (Mon–Fri 2–4 daily, Sun 2 daily; 1hr 45min); London Gatwick (1–2 daily; 1hr 40min); London Heathrow (at least 9 daily; 1hr 40min); London Luton (1–2 daily; 1hr 20min); Manchester (at least 3 daily; 1hr 15min); Newcastle (Mon–Fri 3–4 daily, Sun 1 daily; 55min); Norwich (Mon–Fri 5 daily, Sat & Sun 1–2 daily; 1hr 20min); Southampton (Mon–Fri 1–2 daily, Sun 1 daily; 2hr 40min); Stornoway (Mon–Fri 1 daily; 55min); Wick (Mon–Fri 2–3 daily; 35min).

ABERDEEN AND AROUND

By train The main station is on Guild St, in the centre of the city.

Destinations Arbroath (every 30min; 1hr); Dundee (every 30min; 1hr 15min); Edinburgh (every 30min–1hr; 2hr 35min); Elgin (Mon–Sat 11 daily, Sun 5 daily; 1hr 30min); Glasgow (hourly; 2hr 35min); Inverness (Mon–Sat 11 daily, Sun 5 daily; 2hr 15min); London (1–3 daily; 8–12hr; sleeper service Sun–Fri 1 daily; 10hr); Montrose (every 30min; 40min); Nairn (Mon–Sat 11 daily, Sun 5 daily; 1hr 50min); Stonehaven (every 30min; 15min).

By bus The terminal is beside the train station.

Destinations Ballater (hourly; 1hr 45min); Banff (every 30min; 1hr 55min); Braemar (every 1–2hr; 2hr 15min); Cullen (every 30min; 2hr 30min); Elgin (hourly; 2hr 30min); Fraserburgh (every 30min; 1hr 30min); Macduff (every 30min; 2hr); Stonehaven (every 30min; 50min).

By ferry Aberdeen has links to Lerwick in Shetland and Kirkwall in Orkney, with regular crossings from Jamieson's Quay in the harbour (☎08456 000449, ⊛ northlinkferries.co.uk).

Destinations Kirkwall, Orkney (Thurs, Sat & Sun plus Tues in summer; 6hr); Lerwick, Shetland (daily; 12hr 30min overnight).

Tourist information 23 Union St (July & Aug Mon–Sat 9am–6.30pm, Sun 10am–4pm; Sept–June Mon–Sat 9.30am–5pm, Sun 11am–4pm; ☎01224 269180).

ACCOMMODATION

Aberdeen has a good range of accommodation, but places get booked a long way in advance and prices shoot up during the week, when businesspeople flood into the city.

Aberdeen Youth Hostel 8 Queen's Rd ☎01224 646988, ⊛ syha.org.uk. Clean SYHA hostel in a grand stone mansion a mile from the train station, with dorms and private rooms. To get there take bus #X17 from Union St. Dorms £23, doubles £60

Allan Guest House 56 Polmuir Rd ☎01224 584484, ⊛ theallan.co.uk. Attractive Victorian guesthouse in a peaceful spot near Duthie Park, and just 5min from the city centre on bus #17. Free wi-fi, DVD library and good breakfasts. £70

Deeside Holiday Park Around 8 miles southwest of the city centre, just off the B979 ☎01224 733860. Well-run and exceedingly popular caravan site in a quiet country setting where birdsong fills the air. It's an easy 25-minute drive from the city centre. Pitches £18

Dutch Mill 7 Queen's Rd, opposite the youth hostel ☎01224 322555, ⊛ dutchmill.co.uk. Cosy, business-like rooms a mile west of the centre. They're above a bar and restaurant serving the usual pub staples, from prawn cocktails to gammon steaks. Mon–Sat 10am–midnight, Sun noon–midnight. £65

Ferryhill House 169 Bon Accord St ☎01224 590867, ⊛ ferryhillhousehotel.co.uk. A mansion set in its own grounds within walking distance of Union St. Good-value lunches and a great Malt Room for guests to sample real ales and whisky by a roaring fire. £85

Marcliffe Hotel North Deeside Rd, Pitfodels ☎01224 861000, ⊛ marcliffe.com. 4 miles west of the city centre, this 42-room hotel in its own grounds is by far the most luxurious and tasteful option in the Aberdeen area. There's a spa, and a fine restaurant with a suitably upmarket ambience. £180

EATING

Most of Aberdeen's cafés and restaurants are clustered around **Union** and **Belmont** streets; you'll find them pricier than elsewhere in northeast Scotland.

Books and Beans 22 Belmont St ☎01224 646438. As the name suggests, secondhand books go hand in hand here with decent lattes (£2.59), fresh soups and panini filled with Scottish cheddar, meatballs and the like. Mon–Sat 7.45am–4.30pm, Sun 9.45am–3.45pm.

Food Story Café 15 Thistle Street ⊛ foodstorycafe .co.uk. Bright, pine-clad café with a healthy approach to food: expect organic porridge topped with chia seeds, vegetable-packed salads (from £2.50) and gluten-free cakes. Mon–Wed 7am–5pm, Thus & Fri 7am–6pm, Sat 9am–6pm.

★ Fusion 10 North Silver St ☎01224 652959, ⊛ fusionbarbistro.com. Designed as more of a style-conscious evening hangout, *Fusion* is actually best visited at lunchtime, when tempting mains go for around £11. In the evening, two-course menus featuring tempting fish dishes and home-made pasta cost £24.95. Tues–Sat noon till late.

Musa Exchange St ☎01224 571771, ⊛ musaaberdeen .com/food. Based in an old church and banana warehouse, this good-value café, gallery and music venue has a terrific vibe, with live music and mouthwatering dining: produce for their risottos, fish and meat dishes (from £12.50) is provided by small Scottish suppliers. Tues–Sat noon till late.

Shri Beema's 17 Belmont St ☎01224 645555, ⊛ shribheemas.com. On the first floor and accessed through a dingy stairwell, this popular Indian restaurant does cheap, two-course lunches on weekdays (£9.99 per person) and has a vast menu with plenty of South Indian specialities. Mon–Fri noon–2.30pm & 5–11pm, Sat & Sun noon–3.30pm & 5–11pm.

DRINKING

Brewdog Aberdeen 17 Gallowgate ☎01224 631223, ⊛ brewdog.com. Hipster-friendly bar operated by the Brewdog chain, which sets itself apart from the crowd with exposed brickwork, dangly light bulbs and a cracking selection of Scottish ales (bottles around £4.50).

Mon–Thurs noon–midnight, Fri & Sat noon–1am, Sun 12.30pm–midnight.

The Illicit Still Netherkirkgate, Broad Street ☎01224 623123. Follow the stairs down past sneering gargoyles to this subterranean bar, with cowhide-covered seats and intimate little booths where diners tuck into burgers, salads and pasta dishes (around £10). Daily 11am/noon till late.

Ninety-Nine Bar & Kitchen 1 Back Wynd ☎01224 631640, ⓦ99aberdeen.com. Best known for its cocktails, which take their names from classic films (anyone for a glass of Ron Burgundy?), this lounge-like bar also does decent meals, including pulled lamb kebabs (£10.95). Mon–Thurs 11am–midnight, Fri & Sat 11am–1am, Sun 12.30pm–midnight.

Prince of Wales 7 St Nicholas Lane ☎01224 640597. Opened in 1850, the quintessential Aberdeen pub has a 20ft-long bar and flagstone floor. With fine pub grub, renowned real ales and a Sunday-evening folk session, it's little wonder that it's often crowded. Mon–Thurs 10am–midnight, Fri & Sat 10am–1am, Sun 11am–midnight.

St Machar Bar 97 High St, Old Aberdeen ☎01224 483079, ⓦthemachar.com. The medieval quarter's only pub, a poky, old-fashioned bar attracting an intriguing mix of King's College students and workers. Mon–Sat 11am–11pm, Sun 12.30–6pm.

Slains Castle 14–18 Belmont Street ☎01224 631877, ⓦeerie-pubs.co.uk. An old church is the perfect setting for this gothic-style theme bar, whose cocktail list includes potions named after the seven deadly sins (£4.25). Live bands every Friday. Mon–Thurs 11am–midnight, Fri & Sat 11am–1am, Sun noon–midnight.

22

NIGHTLIFE AND ENTERTAINMENT

Belmont Filmhouse 49 Belmont St ☎01224 343500, ⓦbelmontfilmhouse.com. Classic, cult and foreign-language films are among the offerings at this art-house cinema, which also hosts a weekly film quiz in its café bar.

His Majesty's Theatre Rosemount Viaduct ☎01224 641122, ⓦboxofficeaberdeen.com. The city's main theatre resides in a beautiful Edwardian building, with an extensive programme ranging from serious drama and opera to panto.

Lemon Tree 5 West North St ☎01224 337688, ⓦboxofficeaberdeen.com. The fulcrum of the city's arts scene, with a great buzz and regular live music, club nights and comedy, as well as decent theatre.

The Tunnels Carnegies Brae ☎01224 619930, ⓦthetunnels.co.uk. One of the city's most popular live music venues, established within old tunnels under Union St. Live bands and a different musical genre every evening including reggae, hip-hop, ska and Northern Soul. See website for show times.

Deeside

More commonly known as **Royal Deeside**, the land stretching west from Aberdeen along the River Dee revels in its connections with the Royal Family, who have regularly holidayed here, at **Balmoral**, since Queen Victoria bought the estate. Eighty thousand Scots turned out to welcome her on her first visit in 1848, but some weren't so charmed: one local journalist remarked that the area was about to be "desolated by cockneys and other horrible reptiles". Today, most locals are fiercely protective of the royal connection.

Deeside is undoubtedly handsome in a fierce, craggy way, and the royal presence has helped keep a lid on unattractive mass development. The villages strung along the A93, the main route through the area, are well-heeled, with an old-fashioned air, and visitor facilities are first-class. It's an excellent area for **outdoor activities**, too, with hiking routes into the Grampian and Cairngorm mountains, good mountain-biking, horseriding and skiing.

Crathes Castle

15 miles west of Aberdeen; up to three buses leave hourly from Union St, Aberdeen, stopping opposite the castle (45min) • Daily: April–Oct 10.30am–5pm; Nov–March Sat & Sun 11am–4pm • £12.50; NTS • ⓦnts.org.uk

Crathes Castle is a splendid sixteenth-century granite tower house adorned with flourishes such as overhanging turrets, gargoyles and conical roofs. Its thick walls, narrow windows and tiny rooms loaded with heavy old furniture make it all rather claustrophobic, but well worth visiting for some wonderful painted ceilings, either still in their original form or sensitively restored; the earliest dates from 1602. The grounds include an impressive walled garden complete with yew hedges subjected to a spot of topiary.

22

Aboyne

A dozen or so miles west of Crathes Castle on the A93 • Hourly Stagecoach Bluebird buses run from Union St in Aberdeen (Mon–Sat; 1hr 20min)

ABOYNE is a typically well-mannered Deeside village at the mouth of **Glen Tanar**, which runs southwest from here for around ten miles deep into the Grampian hills. The glen, with few steep gradients and some glorious stands of mature Caledonian pine, is ideal for walking, mountain biking or horseriding; the Glen Tanar Equestrian Centre (☎01339 886448) offers one- and two-hour **horse rides**.

Ballater

Ten miles west of Aboyne, the neat and ordered town of **BALLATER** stands attractively hemmed in by the river and fir-covered mountains. It was here that Queen Victoria first arrived in Deeside by train from Aberdeen back in 1848; she wouldn't allow a station to be built any closer to Balmoral, eight miles further west. Although the line has long been closed, the town's rather self-important royalism is much in evidence with oversized "By Appointment" crests sported above the doorways of most businesses.

Ballater is an excellent base for local **walks** and **outdoor activities**. There are numerous hikes from Loch Muik (pronounced "mick"), including the well-worn but strenuous all-day trek up and around Lochnagar (3789ft), the mountain much-painted and written about by Prince Charles.

Balmoral Estate

8 miles west of Ballater, off the A93 • April–July daily 10am–5pm • £11 • ☎013397 42534, ⊛balmoralcastle.com • Bus #201 from Ballater (around 8 daily; 15min) stops at Crathie – a ten-minute walk east of the castle

Originally a sixteenth-century tower house built for the powerful Gordon family, **Balmoral Castle** has been a royal residence since 1852. The Royal Family traditionally spend their summer holidays here each August, but despite its fame it can be something of a disappointment even for a dedicated royalist – only the ballroom, an exhibition room and the grounds are open to the public.

ARRIVAL AND INFORMATION   BALLATER

By bus Buses stop at the northern end of Golf Road, near the A93.
Destinations: Aboyne (hourly; 20min); Banchory (hourly; 40min); Braemar (roughly hourly; 35min).

Tourist information is in the renovated former train station (daily: July & Aug 9.30am–6pm; Sept–June 10am–5pm; ☎013397 55306).

ACCOMMODATION AND EATING

Auld Kirk Braemar Road ☎01339 755762, ⊛theauldkirk.co.uk. As the name suggests, this pleasingly unorthodox B&B is housed in a renovated church. The place used to operate as a popular restaurant and B&B guests can still eat evening meals here; book ahead. **£100**

Ballater Caravan Park South of Anderson Road, close to the river ☎01339 755727, ⊛ballatercaravanpark .com. Large campsite down by the water which mostly

attracts touring caravans. Tents are welcome though, and there's laundry facilities and showers. April–Oct. Pitches **£20**

Habitat @ Ballater Bridge Square ☎01339 753752, ⊛habitat-at-ballater.com Excellent and well-equipped hostel tucked away off the main road. Choose between a bunk bed with its own locker, or one of the private rooms. Dorms **£20**, doubles **£50**

Braemar

At 1100ft above sea level, the village of **BRAEMAR** is an invigorating, outdoor kind of place, well-patronized by committed hikers, but probably best known for its Highland Games, the annual **Braemar Gathering**, on the first Saturday of September (⊛braemargathering.org). Since Queen Victoria's day, successive generations of royals have attended and the world's most famous Highland Games have become rather an overcrowded, overblown event. You're not guaranteed to get in if you just turn up; the website has details of how to book tickets in advance.

ARRIVAL AND INFORMATION	BRAEMAR

By bus Buses arrive and depart from the Mar Road roundabout, just west of the village centre.
Destinations Ballater (roughly hourly; 30–40min); Spittal of Glenshee (1 daily; 40min).

Tourist information The Mews, in the middle of the village on Mar Road (daily: April–June 9.30am–5pm; July & Aug 9.30am–6pm; Sept & Oct 9.30am–5pm; Nov–March 9.30am–4.30pm; ☎ 01339 741600).

22

ACCOMMODATION AND EATING	

Braemar Lodge A quarter of a mile south of the village on Glenshee Road ☎ 01339 741627, �🅦 braemar lodge.co.uk. The seven, tartan-accented hotel rooms here seem a bit pricey, check out the bunkhouse on the same plot, which has budget beds and laundry facilities. Bunkhouse **£16**, doubles **£120**

The Gathering Place Invercauld Rd, by Braemar Mountain Sports ☎ 01339 741234, �🅦 the-gathering -place.co.uk. Bistro in the heart of the village selling mouthwatering Scottish-based mains (£12–19) including a game pie made with ale and red wine. Food served

Tues–Sat 6–8.30pm.
SYHA Braemar Corrie Feragie, 21 Glenshee Road ☎ 01339 741659, �🅦 syha.org.uk. SYHA hostel in a former shooting lodge, which has bike storage facilities and a big communal kitchen. A short stroll from the centre. Dorms **£18.50**, twins **£44**

Taste Airlie House, beside the Mar Road roundabout ☎ 01339 741425, �🅦 taste-braemar.co.uk. Reliably good coffee shop and moderately-priced contemporary restaurant, serving home-made, gluten-free soups and sandwiches for around £4. Tues–Sat 10am–5pm.

Speyside

Strictly speaking, the term **Speyside** refers to the entire region surrounding the River Spey, but to most people the name is synonymous with the **whisky triangle**, stretching from just north of Craigellachie, down towards Tomintoul in the south and east to Huntly. There are more whisky distilleries and famous brands (including Glenfiddich and Glenlivet) concentrated in this small area than in any other part of the country. Running through the heart of the region is the River Spey, whose clean, clear, fast-flowing waters not only play such a vital part in the whisky industry, but also make it one of Scotland's finest angling locations. At the centre of Speyside, the quiet market town of **Dufftown** and the well-kept nearby villages of **Craigellachie** and **Aberlour** make good bases for a tour of whisky country.

Dufftown and around

The cheery community of **DUFFTOWN**, founded in 1817 by James Duff, the fourth Earl of Fife, proudly proclaims itself "Malt Whisky Capital of the World" with good reason – it produces more of the stuff than any other town in Britain and hosts two annual whisky festivals (one at springtime and another in the autumn). There are seven active distilleries around Dufftown, as well as a cooperage; an extended stroll around the outskirts gives a good idea of the density of whisky distilling going on, with glimpses of giant warehouses filled with barrels of the heady liquid, and whiffs of fermenting barley or peat smoke lingering on the breeze.

On the edge of town along the A941 is the town's largest working distillery, **Glenfiddich** (see box, p.882), as well as the old Dufftown train station, which has been restored by enthusiasts and is now the departure point for the **Keith & Dufftown Railway** (April, May & Sept Sat & Sun 3 daily, June–Aug Fri–Sun 3 daily; 40min; ☎ 01340 821181, ⍟ keith-dufftown-railway.co.uk; £10 return), which uses restored diesel locomotives to chug through whisky country to Keith, home of the Strathisla distillery (see box, p.882).

Craigellachie

Four miles north of Dufftown, the small settlement of **CRAIGELLACHIE** sits above the confluence of the sparkling waters of the Fiddich and the Spey,

22

THE MALT WHISKY TRAIL

There are eight distilleries on the official **Malt Whisky Trail** (ⓦmaltwhiskytrail.com), a clearly signposted seventy-mile meander around Speyside. All offer a guided tour with a tasting to round it off; if you're driving you'll sometimes be offered a miniature to take away. You could cycle or walk parts of the route, using the Speyside Way (see p.884). The following are selected highlights.

Cardhu On the B9102 at Knockando; April Mon–Fri 10am–5pm; May & June Mon–Sat 10am–5pm; July–Sept Mon–Sat 10am–5pm, Sun 11am–4pm; Oct–March Mon–Fri 10am–3pm; tours hourly; £5. Established over a century ago, when the founder's wife would raise a red flag to warn crofters if the authorities were on the lookout for their illegal stills. With attractive, pagoda-topped buildings, it sells rich, full-bodied whisky with distinctive peaty flavours that comes in an attractive bulbous bottle.

Glenfiddich On the A941 just north of Dufftown; daily 9.30am–4.30pm; free. The biggest and slickest of all the Speyside distilleries, despite the fact that it's still owned by the same Grant family who founded it in 1887. It's a light, sweet whisky packaged in triangular bottles – unusually, the bottling is still done on the premises and can be seen as part of the tours, which are offered in various languages.

Glen Grant Rothes; April–Oct daily 9.30am–5.30pm; Nov–March Mon–Sat 9.30am–5pm, Sun noon–5pm; £5. A well-known, floral whisky aggressively marketed to the younger customer. The highlight here is the attractive Victorian gardens, a combination of well-tended lawns and mixed, mature trees, which include a tumbling waterfall and a hidden whisky safe.

Glenlivet On the B9008 to Tomintoul; April–Oct Mon–Sat 9.30am–4pm, Sun noon–4pm; free. A famous name in a lonely hillside setting. This was the first licensed distillery in the Highlands, following the 1823 act that aimed to reduce illicit distilling and smuggling. The Glenlivet 12-year-old malt is a floral, fragrant, medium-bodied whisky.

Speyside Cooperage Craigellachie; Mon–Fri 9.30am–4pm; £3.50. The only stop on the official trail that isn't a distillery, with fascinating glimpses into how coopers make casks – a highly skilled job and a vital part of the industry.

Strathisla Keith; April–Oct Mon–Sat 9.30am–5pm, Sun noon–5pm; £7.50. A small, old-fashioned distillery claiming to be Scotland's oldest (1786); it's certainly one of the most attractive, with the River Isla rushing by. Inside there's an old-fashioned mashtun and brass-bound spirit safes. You can arrive here on one of the restored trains of the Keith & Dufftown Railway (see p.881).

---

spanned by a beautiful iron bridge built by Thomas Telford in 1815. The main sight here is the **Speyside Cooperage**, which is on Speyside's official Malt Whisky Trail (see box above).

ARRIVAL AND DEPARTURE

By bus Buses run from Aberlour (Mon–Sat hourly; 15min) and Elgin (Mon–Sat hourly; 50min), stopping near the clocktower in the middle of Dufftown.

DUFFTOWN AND AROUND

By train Trains plying the Keith & Dufftown Railway (see p.881) stop at the station a mile north of town on the A941.

ACCOMMODATION AND EATING

Dufftown Glassworks 16 Conval Street ⓣ01340 821534, ⓦdufftownglassworks.com. This combined café and gallery is a smart place to sit with a cuppa and plan your trip around whisky country. The tray-bakes here (around £2) are scrumptious. Daily 10.30am–5pm.

Loch Park Adventure Centre 3 miles northeast of Dufftown on the Drummuir Castle Estate ⓣ01542 810334, ⓦlochpark.co.uk. It's possible to camp, rent kayaks (£12) and fish (£18) at this outdoor centre, which also has self-catering bunkhouse accommodation. Unfortunately there's no public transport this far, and groups are given priority – so call ahead. Camping per person £5, tents £2, dorms £15

Morven On the main square ⓣ01340 820507, ⓦmorvendufftown.co.uk. A simple, inexpensive and well-run B&B that's conveniently located in the middle of town. Minimum stay of two nights applies. £50

Taste of Speyside Just off the main square at 10 Balverie St ⓣ01340 820860, ⓦatasteofspeyside.com. Quality Scottish food at the town's most popular restaurant, where mains include a vegetable crumble made with tomato and basil sauce. Expect to pay around £20 for two courses. Tues–Sat noon–2pm and 6–9pm.

The Moray coast

The **coast** of northeast Scotland from Aberdeen to Inverness has a rugged, sometimes bleak, fringe with pleasant if undramatic farmland rolling inland. Still, if the weather is good, it's well worth spending a couple of days meandering through the various little fishing villages and along the miles of deserted, unspoilt beaches.

The largest coastal towns are **Peterhead** and **Fraserburgh**, both dominated by sizeable fishing fleets; the latter's **Museum of Scottish Lighthouses** is one of the most attractive small museums in Scotland. Most visitors, however, are more drawn to the quieter spots along the Moray coast, including the charming villages of **Pennan**, **Gardenstown**, **Portsoy** and nearby **Cullen**. The other main attractions are **Duff House** in Banff, a branch of the National Gallery of Scotland, and the **Findhorn Foundation** near Forres.

22

Museum of Scottish Lighthouses

Kinnaird Head, Stevenson Rd, Fraserburgh • April–Oct daily 10am–5pm; Nov–March Wed–Sun 11am–4pm • £6 • ☏ 01346 511022, ⓦ lighthousemuseum.org.uk • Hourly buses from Peterhead (40min) and less frequent services from Macduff (3 daily; 50min) stop at the bus station on Hanover Street; the museum is a 10min walk to the north

Large and severe-looking **FRASERBURGH** is home to the excellent **Museum of Scottish Lighthouses**. Here you can see a collection of huge lenses and prisms gathered from decommissioned lighthouses, and a display on various members of the famous "Lighthouse" Stevenson family (including the father and grandfather of author Robert Louis Stevenson), who designed many of them. The highlight is the tour of Kinnaird Head lighthouse itself, preserved as it was when the last keeper left in 1991, with its century-old equipment still in perfect working order.

Pennan

PENNAN, twelve miles west of Fraserburgh, is a tiny fishing hamlet consisting of little more than a single row of whitewashed stone cottages tucked between a cliff and the sea. The movie *Local Hero* was filmed here in 1982; one of the landmarks from the film, the *Pennan Inn*, offers rooms and a pub/restaurant.

ARRIVAL AND ACCOMMODATION   PENNAN

At the time of writing there were no scheduled bus services to Pennan, so you'll need to drive; be warned, the road down to Pennan is narrow and steep.

Pennan Inn By the waterfront ☏ 01346 561201, ⓦ thepennaninn.co.uk. The area's most recognisable landmark, the *Pennan Inn* has three en-suite rooms. You can also grab traditional pub food or a Thai curry in the bar (mains around £10). **£80**

Banff

Heading west along the coast from Pennan brings you, after ten miles, to **Macduff** and its neighbour **BANFF**, separated by the beautiful seven-arch bridge over the River Deveron. Banff's mix of characterful old buildings and boarded-up shops give little clue to the extravagance of **Duff House**, the town's main attraction.

Duff House

Just south of the town centre • April–Oct daily 11am–5pm; Nov–March Thurs–Sun 11am–4pm • £7.10; HS • ☏ 01261 818181, ⓦ duffhouse.org.uk

Built to William Adam's design in 1730, this elegant four-storey Georgian Baroque house has been painstakingly restored and reopened as an outpost of the **National Gallery of Scotland**. While the emphasis is on displaying period artwork rather than any broader selection of the gallery's paintings, temporary exhibitions of work from the collections are mounted regularly.

22

By bus Buses run regularly from Fraserburgh to Banff (Mon–Sat 2–4 daily; 55min).

Tourist information Banff's tourist office (April–Sept Mon–Sat 10am–5pm; Oct Mon–Sat 10am–4pm; ☎01261 812419) is at Collie Lodge in the town centre, close to where Carmelite St, Low St and Strait Path meet.

Cullen to Spey Bay

CULLEN, twelve miles west of Banff, is strikingly situated beneath a superb series of arched viaducts. The town is made up of two sections: Seatown, by the harbour, and the new town on the hillside. The local delicacy, **Cullen Skink** – a soup made from milk (or cream), potato and smoked haddock – is available at local hotels and bars.

West of Cullen, the scruffy, working fishing town of **BUCKIE** marks one end of the **Speyside Way** long-distance footpath which follows the coast west for five miles to windy **Spey Bay**, at the mouth of the river of the same name (which can also be reached by a small coastal road from Buckie). It's a remote spot bounded by sea, river and sky; it's here you'll find the **WDC Scottish Dolphin Centre** (April–Oct daily 10.30am–5pm; Nov–March Sat & Sun 10.30am–5pm; ⓦwdcs.org; free), whose main mission is researching the Moray Firth dolphin population (see box, p.895).

Findhorn

Located at one end of a wide sweep of sandy beach, **FINDHORN** is a tidy village with some neat fishermen's cottages and a delightful harbour dotted with moored yachts. Findhorn is best known, however, for the controversial **Findhorn Foundation** (see box below), based beside the town's caravan park about a mile before you reach the village itself.

THE FINDHORN FOUNDATION

In 1962, with little money and no employment, Eileen and Peter Caddy, their three children and friend Dorothy Maclean, settled on a caravan site at Findhorn. Dorothy believed that she had a special relationship with what she called the "devas … the archetypal formative forces of light or energy that underlie all forms in nature – plants, trees, rivers", and from the uncompromising sandy soil they built a remarkable garden filled with plants and vegetables, far larger than had ever been seen in the area.

A few of those who came to see the phenomenon stayed to help out and tune into the spiritual aspect of the daily life of the nascent community. With its emphasis on inner discovery and development, but unattached to any particular doctrine or creed, the **Findhorn Foundation** has today blossomed into a permanent community of a few hundred people, with a well-developed series of courses and retreats on subjects ranging from astroshamanic healing to organic gardening, drawing another eight thousand or so visitors each year. The original caravan still stands, surrounded by a whole host of newer timber buildings and eco-friendly homes employing solar power, earth roofs and other green initiatives.

The foundation is not without controversy: a community leader once declared that "behind the benign and apparently religious front lies a hard core of New Agers experimenting with hallucinatory techniques marketed as spirituality." Whatever the truth, Findhorn can be accused of being overly well-heeled, as betrayed by a glance into the shop or a tally of the smart cars parked outside the well-appointed eco-houses. However, there's little doubt that the community appeals to large numbers of people: it continues to prosper and is well known around the world. The reputation of the place is such that it attracts visitors both sympathetic and sceptical – and both find something to feed their preconceptions.

The Findhorn Foundation's **visitor centre** (May–Sept Mon–Fri 10am–5pm, Sat & Sun 1–4pm; Oct–April Mon–Fri 10am–5pm; ☎01309 690311, ⓦfindhorn.org) has information on staying within the community, either as part of an introductory "Experience Week" (cost based on your income), or simply overnighting; there are a number of eco-houses nearby offering B&B. Guided tours of the park (see website for times) cost £8 per person.

Moray Art Centre

The Park, on the Findhorn Foundation site • Tues–Fri 10am–4pm, Sat noon–5pm • Free • ☎ 01309 692426, ⓦ morayartcentre.orq

It's worth taking a look at the **Moray Art Centre**, on the same plot as the foundation but not officially a part of it. The centre, in a terracotta-hued ecofriendly building, hosts eclectic and imaginative temporary exhibitions (from contemporary photography to hand-drawn illustrations) and also runs regular art classes.

ARRIVAL AND DEPARTURE   FINDHORN

By bus Findhorn is served by the #31 bus from Elgin (every 2hr; 35min) and Forres (every 2hr; 15min). The bus stop is a mile north of the Findhorn Foundation.

22

The Highland region

LOCH MAREE, WESTER ROSS

The Highland region

Scotland's Highland region, covering the northern two-thirds of the country, holds much of the mainland's most spectacular scenery. You may be surprised at just how remote much of it still is: the vast peat bogs in the north, for example, are among the most extensive and unspoilt wilderness areas in Europe, while a handful of the west coast's isolated crofting villages can still be reached only by boat. The only major city, Inverness, is best used as a springboard for more remote areas where you can soak in the Highlands' classic combination of mountains, glens, lochs and rivers, surrounded on three sides by a magnificently pitted and rugged coastline.

23

South of Inverness, the **Strathspey** region, with a string of villages lying along the River Spey, is dominated by the dramatic **Cairngorm mountains**, an area brimming with attractive scenery and opportunities for outdoor activity. The Monadhliath mountains lie between Strathspey and **Loch Ness**, the largest and most famous of the necklace of lochs which make up the **Great Glen**, an ancient geological faultline which cuts southwest across the region from Inverness to the town of **Fort William**. From Fort William, located beneath Scotland's highest peak, Ben Nevis, it's possible to branch out to some fine scenery – most conveniently the beautiful expanses of **Glen Coe**, but also in the direction of the appealing **west coast**, notably the remote and tranquil **Ardnamurchan peninsula**, the "Road to the Isles" to **Mallaig**, and the lochs and glens that lead to **Kyle of Lochalsh** on the most direct route to Skye. Between Kyle of Lochalsh and **Ullapool**, the main settlement in the northwest, lies **Wester Ross**, home to quintessentially west-coast scenes of sparkling sea lochs, rocky headlands and sandy beaches set against some of Scotland's most dramatic mountains, with Skye and the Western Isles on the horizon.

The little-visited **north coast**, stretching from wind-lashed **Cape Wrath**, at the very northwest tip of the mainland, east to **John O'Groats**, is even more rugged, with sheer cliffs and sand-filled bays bearing the brunt of frequently fierce Atlantic storms. The main settlement on this coast is **Thurso**, jumping-off point for the main ferry service to Orkney.

On the fertile **east coast**, stretching north from Inverness to the old herring port of **Wick**, green fields and woodland run down to the sweeping sandy beaches of the **Black Isle** and the **Cromarty and Dornoch firths**. This region is rich with historical sites, including the **Sutherland Monument** by Golspie, **Dornoch**'s fourteenth-century sandstone cathedral, and a number of places linked to the Clearances, a poignantly remembered chapter in the Highland story.

OLD FORGE PUB, KNOYDART

Highlights

❶ West Highland Railway From Glasgow to Mallaig via Fort William: the further north you travel, the more spectacular it gets. **See p.892**

❷ The Cairngorms Scotland's grandest mountain massif, a place of rare plants, wild animals, inspiring vistas and challenging outdoor activities. **See p.896**

❸ Glen Coe Stunning, moody, poignant and full of history – a glorious place for hiking or simple admiration. **See p.904**

❹ Knoydart Only accessible by boat or a two-day hike over the mountains, this peninsula

also boasts mainland Britain's most isolated pub, the welcoming *Old Forge*. **See p.908**

❺ Wester Ross Scotland's finest scenery – a heady mix of high mountains, rugged sea lochs, sweeping bays and scattered islands. **See p.910**

❻ Ceilidh Place, Ullapool The best venue for modern Highland culture, with evenings of music, song and dance. **See p.914**

❼ Cromarty Set on the fertile Black Isle, this charming small town boasts beautiful vernacular architecture and dramatic east-coast scenery. **See p.920**

HIGHLIGHTS ARE MARKED ON THE MAP ON PP.890–891

THE HIGHLAND REGION

N

0 _____ 20

miles

HIGHLIGHTS

1 West Highland Railway
2 The Cairngorms
3 Glen Coe
4 Knoydart
5 Wester Ross
6 Ceilidh Place, Ullapool
7 Cromarty

NORTH MINCH

Lewis

Hoy

Pentland Firth

Stroma

Duncansby Head

John O'Groats

Castle of Mey

Dunnet Head

Dunnet Bay

Scrabster

Thurso

Dounreay

Strathy Pt.

Melvich

Bettyhill

BORGIE FOREST

Tongue

Kyle of Tongue

Ben Loyal (2504ft)

Ben Hope (3040ft)

Altnaharra

Loch Naver

Syre

Strath Naver

Kinbrace

Forsinard

Flow Country

Halkirk

A882

A836

Grey Cairns of Camster

Loch of Yarrows

Hill o' Many Stanes

Wick

Sinclair's Bay

Ness Head

Lybster

Dunbeath

Badbea

Helmsdale

Morven (2316ft)

Kildonan

A897

Brora

Dunrobin Castle

Golspie

BEN BHRAGGIE

Rogart

Loch Fleet

Fearn Peninsula

Dornoch Firth

Tarbat Ness

Portmahomack

Dornoch

Tain

Lairg

Fall of Shin

Bonar Bridge

Ardgay

Carbisdale Castle

Croick

Loch Shin

A836

A837

Ben Wyvis (3432ft)

Cape Wrath

Kyle of Durness

Smoo Cave

Durness

Keoldale

Kinlochbervie

Sandwood L.

Sheigra

Handa Island

Loch Laxford

Tarbet

Scourie

Laxford Bridge

Kylestrome

Kylesku

Drumbeg

Pt. of Stoer

Achmelvich

Lochinver

Eddrachillis Bay

Loch Eriboll

Foinaven (2980ft)

A894

Eas-Coul-Aulin Falls

Inchnadamph

Loch Assynt

Canisp (2779ft)

Ben More Assynt (3273ft)

Suilven (2398ft)

A837

COIGACH

Achiltibuie

Summer Isles

Scoraig

Ullapool

Loch Broom

Corrieshalloch Gorge

Braemore

Little Loch Broom

A835

A832

Gruinard Bay

Gruinard Island

Loch Ewe

Cove

Inverewe

Poolewe

Rua Reidh

THE WEST HIGHLAND RAILWAY

Scotland's most famous railway line is the brilliantly engineered **West Highland Railway**, running from Glasgow to Mallaig via Fort William. The line is in two sections: the southern part travels from **Glasgow** Queen Street station along the Clyde estuary and up Loch Long before switching to the banks of Loch Lomond on its way to **Crianlarich**, where the train divides with one section heading for Oban. After climbing around Beinn Odhar on a unique horseshoe-shaped loop of viaducts, the line traverses desolate **Rannoch Moor**, where the track had to be laid on a mattress of tree roots, brushwood and thousands of tonnes of earth and ashes. The train then swings into Glen Roy, passing through the dramatic **Monessie Gorge** and entering **Fort William** from the northeast.

The second leg of the journey, from Fort William to Mallaig, is arguably even more spectacular, and from mid-May to October one of the scheduled services is pulled by the **Jacobite Steam Train** (Mon–Fri, also Sat & Sun late June to late Sept; departs Fort William 10.15am, also 2.30pm June–Aug, departs Mallaig 2.10pm, also 6.40pm June–Aug; day-return £34; ☎01524 732100, ⓦwestcoastrailways.co.uk). Shortly after leaving Fort William the railway crosses the Caledonian Canal beside Neptune's Staircase (an impressive set of eight canal locks) by way of a swing bridge at **Benavie**, before travelling along the shores of Loch Eil and crossing the magnificent 21-arch viaduct at **Glenfinnan**, where the steam train, in its "Hogwarts Express" livery, was filmed for the *Harry Potter* movies. At Glenfinnan station there's a small **museum** dedicated to the history of the West Highland line, as well as two old railway carriages that have been converted into a restaurant and a bunkhouse (see p.908). Not long afterwards the line reaches the coast, where there are unforgettable views of the Small Isles and Skye as it runs past the famous silver sands of **Morar** and up to **Mallaig**, where there are connections to the ferry that crosses to Armadale on Skye.

If you're planning on travelling the West Highland line, and in particular linking it to other train journeys (such as the similarly attractive route between Inverness and Kyle of Lochalsh), it's worth considering one of ScotRail's multiday **Highland Rover tickets** (ⓦscotrail.co.uk).

GETTING AROUND   **THE HIGHLAND REGION**

Unless you're prepared to spend weeks on the road, the Highlands are too vast to see in a single trip. Most visitors, therefore, base themselves in one or two areas, exploring the coast or hills on foot, and making longer hops across the interior by car or public transport. With a little forward planning you can see a surprising amount using **buses** and **trains**. Bear in mind that on Sundays bus services are sporadic at best, and you may well find most shops and restaurants closed.

Inverness and around

Straddling a nexus of road and rail routes, **INVERNESS** is the hub of the Highlands, and an inevitable port of call if you're exploring the region by public transport: **buses** and **trains** leave for communities right across the far north of Scotland. Though it has few conventional sights, the city has an appealing setting on the banks of the River Ness.

Inverness Museum and Art Gallery

Castle Wynd • April–Oct Tues–Sat 10am–5pm; Nov–March Thurs–Sat 10am–5pm • Free • ☎01463 237114, ⓦinverness.highland.museum

Below **Inverness Castle** (which is closed to the public), the **Inverness Museum and Art Gallery** offers an insight into the social history of the Highlands, with treasures from the times of the Picts and Vikings, taxidermy exhibits such as "Felicity" the puma, caught in Cannich in 1980, and interactive features including an introduction to the Gaelic language.

ARRIVAL AND INFORMATION   **INVERNESS**

By plane Inverness Airport (☎01667 462445, ⓦhial .co.uk/inverness-airport) is at Dalcross, 7 miles east of the city. Taxis to the centre cost £14 (try Inverness Taxis on ☎01463 222222).

Destinations Birmingham (1 daily; 1hr 30min); Bristol (1 daily; 1hr 20min); Kirkwall (1–2 daily; 45min); London (Gatwick 2 daily, 1hr 35min; Luton 1 daily, 1hr 20min); Manchester (1 daily; 1hr 20min); Stornoway (up to 4 daily; 40min).

By train The station lies just off Academy St, northeast of the centre.

Destinations Aberdeen (Mon–Sat 11 daily; Sun 6 daily; 2hr 15min); Aviemore (Mon–Sat 11 daily, Sun 7 daily; 40min); Edinburgh (Mon–Sat 8 daily, Sun 5 daily; 3hr 30min); Glasgow Queen St (Mon–Sat 3 daily; Sun 5 daily; 3hr 20min); Kyle of Lochalsh (Mon–Sat 4 daily, Sun 1 daily; 3hr); London King's Cross (Mon–Fri & Sun 2 daily, Sat 1 daily; 8–11hr); Thurso (Mon–Sat 4 daily, Sun 1 daily; 3hr 45min); Wick (Mon–Sat 4 daily, Sun 1 daily; 4hr 15min).

By bus The main bus hub is near the train station, close to the public library and just northeast of the centre.

Destinations Aberdeen (hourly; 3hr 40min); Aviemore (7 daily Mon–Sat; 45min); Drumnadrochit (1–2 hourly; 25min); Fort Augustus (1–3 daily; 1hr); Fort William (up to 9 daily; 2hr); Glasgow (7 daily; 3hr 35min–4hr); Kyle of Lochalsh (3 daily; 2hr 10min); Nairn (up to 3 hourly; 35–45min); Perth (8 daily; 2hr 45min); Portree (3 daily; 3hr 10min); Thurso (Mon–Sat 5 daily, Sun 3 daily; 3hr 30min); Ullapool (Mon–Sat 4 daily, Sun 2 daily; 2hr 25min); Wick (1 daily; 3hr).

Tourist information Castle Wynd (April & May Mon–Sat 9am–5pm, Sun 10am–5pm; June Mon–Sat 9am–6pm, Sun 9.30am–5pm; July & Aug Mon–Sat 9am–6.30pm, Sun 9.30am–6pm; Sept & Oct Mon–Sat 9am–5pm, Sun 10am–4pm; Nov–March Mon–Sat 9am–5pm, Sun 10am–3pm; ☎ 01463 252401, ⊛ visitscotland.com).

23

ACCOMMODATION

Bught Caravan and Camping Site Bught Park, a mile south of the centre ☎ 01463 236920, ⊛ invernesscaravanpark.com. Inverness's main campsite on the west bank of the river near the sports centre. Has

ACCOMMODATION	
Bught Caravan and Camping Site	5
Furan Guest House	6
Glenmoriston Town House Hotel	3
Inverness Student Hotel	1
Loch Ness Country House Hotel	7
Ness Bank Guesthouse	2
Rocpool Reserve	4

PUBS & BARS	
Blackfriars	2
Hootananny's	3

CLUBS & LIVE MUSIC	
Blackfriars	2
Hootananny's	3
The Ironworks	1

CAFÉS & RESTAURANTS	
Abstract	7
Joy of Taste	4
Leakey's Second-Hand Bookshop & Cafe	1
The Mustard Seed	2
No 27	5
Rocpool Restaurant	6
Velocity	3

BOAT CRUISES FROM INVERNESS

Inverness is the departure point for a range of **day-tours** and **cruises** to nearby attractions, including Loch Ness and the Moray Firth. **Loch Ness cruises** typically incorporate a visit to a monster exhibition at **Drumnadrochit** and **Urquhart Castle** – try Jacobite Cruises (from £13.50; ☎01463 233999, ⓦjacobite.co.uk) or **Cruise Loch Ness** (from £12.15; ☎01320 366277, ⓦcruiselochness.com).

good facilities, but it can get very crowded at the height of the season. Easter to Sept. Per person **£10**

Furan Guest House 100 Old Edinburgh Rd ☎01463 712094, ⓦfuran.co.uk. Good-value B&B a mile south of the centre, run by former hoteliers. A good choice of spotlessly clean rooms and a friendly resident cat. Book direct for the best rates. **£80**

Glenmoriston Town House Hotel 20 Ness Bank ☎01463 223777, ⓦglenmoristontownhouse.com. A smart, contemporary hotel by the riverside just a few minutes' walk from the town centre, with muted decor and a good dining experience on offer at *Abstract* (see below). **£184**

Inverness Student Hotel Castle St ☎01463 236556, ⓦinvernessstudenthotel.com. The better of the two

hostels on this road, a short walk from the main shopping area. Dorms are a little worn out but are clean and bright nonetheless. **£16**

Loch Ness Country House Hotel Off the A82 Fort William Rd ☎01463 230512, ⓦlochnesscountry househotel.co.uk. Luxurious country-house hotel 3 miles southwest of central Inverness offering modern Scottish food, fine wines and more than two hundred malts, as well as very comfortable and spacious rooms. **£179**

Ness Bank Guesthouse 7 Ness Bank ☎01463 232939, ⓦnessbankguesthouse.co.uk. Five comfortable rooms in a lovely Grade II-listed Victorian house on the river; the in-room information packs have handy tips on the local area, and there are plenty of eating options nearby. Min two-night stay applies in summer. **£78**

EATING AND DRINKING

Abstract 20 Ness Bank ☎01463 223777, ⓦabstract restaurant.com. This award-winning French restaurant within *Glenmoriston Town House Hotel* (see above) stylishly serves unexpected combinations of flavours – like pistachio with black olive and artichoke; mains start at £16.50. Tues–Sat 6–10pm.

Joy of Taste 25 Church St ☎01463 241459, ⓦthejoyoftaste.co.uk. Sparkly green cloths cover *Joy of Taste's* tables, which are worked by a team of volunteers, each with a stake in the restaurant's success. The lunch menu, with fish, veggie and meat dishes from £6.95, represents superb value. Refreshingly different. Mon–Sat noon–3pm & 5.30pm till late, Sun 5.30–9.30pm.

★Leakey's Bookshop Church St ☎01463 239947. Prise yourself away from the old books and maps at Scotland's largest used bookshop to enjoy a cup of tea or a warming bowl of soup (£3.30) at the upstairs café. Mon–Sat 10am–5.30pm.

The Mustard Seed 16 Fraser St ☎01463 220220, ⓦmustardseedrestaurant.co.uk. Airy, welcoming restaurant with great-value Mediterranean-style lunches

and tasty, à la carte dining (mains around £16). Daily noon–3pm & 5.30–10pm.

Number 27 27 Castle St ☎01463 241999, ⓦfacebook .com/number27inverness. Skinny bar/restaurant with a wide range of beers (there's a new guest ale every Sunday) and hearty main meals (like haggis, neaps and tatties) for £8.50. Mon–Sat noon till late, Sun 12.30pm till late.

Rocpool Restaurant 1 Ness Walk ☎01463 717274, ⓦrocpoolrestaurant.com. Another of the city's excellent, smartish dining options, with a contemporary setting, attentive staff and deliciously rich food. The Speyside venison roasted with Parma ham and black pudding costs £21.95. Mon–Sat noon–2.30pm & 5.45–10pm.

★Velocity 1 Crown Ave ☎01463 419956, ⓦvelocity love.co.uk. A must for cycling enthusiasts (or anyone with a taste for good coffee and organic cakes), this café-cum-bicycle-workshop sits in a quiet and leafy part of town. Sells big doorstep sandwiches (£4), runs beer-tasting evenings, and has maps covering local cycling routes. Mon, Wed, Fri & Sat 9.30am–5pm, Tues 10am–5pm, Thurs 9.30am–9pm, Sun 11am–5pm.

NIGHTLIFE AND ENTERTAINMENT

Blackfriars 93–95 Academy St ☎01463 233881, ⓦblackfriarshighlandpub.co.uk. Lively pub, dating back to the late eighteenth century, where you can enjoy live folk or ceilidh music while supping a pint of real ale. Daily 11am–11pm.

Eden Court Theatre ☎01463 234234, ⓦeden-court .co.uk. Near the cathedral, the Eden Court Theatre is a major arts venue and a hub for dance and theatrical performances in the Highlands. Hollywood films are also screened here.

Hootananny's 67 Church St ☎01463 233651,

THE DOLPHINS OF THE MORAY FIRTH

The **Moray Firth**, a great wedge-shaped bay forming the eastern coastline of the Highlands, is one of only three areas of UK waters that support a resident population of **dolphins**. More than a hundred of these beautiful, intelligent marine mammals live in the estuary, the most northerly breeding-ground in Europe for this particular species – the bottle-nosed dolphin (*Tursiops truncatus*) – and you stand a good chance of spotting a few, either from the shore or a boat.

One of the best places in Scotland, if not in Europe, to look for them is **Chanonry Point**, on the Black Isle (see p.919) – a spit of sand protruding into a narrow, deep channel, where converging currents bring fish close to the surface, and thus the dolphins close to shore; a rising tide is the most likely time to see them. **Kessock Bridge**, a mile north of Inverness, is another prime dolphin-spotting location. You can go all the way down to the beach at the small village of North Kessock, underneath the road bridge, or stop above the village in a car park just off the A9 at the **Dolphin and Seal Centre** and listening post (June–Sept daily 9.30am–12.30pm & 1–4.30pm; free), run by Whale and Dolphin Conservation (WDC), where hydrophones allow you to eavesdrop on the clicks and whistles of underwater conversations.

Several companies run dolphin-spotting **boat trips** around the Moray Firth. However, researchers claim that the increased traffic is causing the dolphins unnecessary stress. If you decide to go on a cruise to see the dolphins – and perhaps minke whales, porpoises, seals and otters – make sure the operator is a member of the Dolphin Space Programme's **accreditation scheme** (see ⊛dolphinspace.org for a list). Trips (April–Oct, around £14/hr) are very popular, so book well in advance.

23

⊛hootananny.co.uk. A popular pub with excellent, free ceilidhs on Saturday afternoons from 2.30–4.30pm, plus real ale and simple bar meals (fish and chips £8.45). Mon–Thurs noon–1am, Fri & Sat noon–3am, Sun 6.30pm–midnight.

The Ironworks 122b Academy Street ☎08717 894173, ⊛ironworksvenue.com. Large live venue which is the place to come for touring bands, tribute acts, stand-up comedy and the occasional club night (see website for event details).

Culloden

6 miles east of Inverness off the B9006; take Stagecoach bus #2B (hourly; 30min) • **Visitor centre** Daily: April, May, Sept & Oct 9am–5.30pm; June–Aug 9am–6pm; Nov, Dec, Feb & March 10am–4pm • £11; NTS • ⊛nts.org.uk/culloden

The windswept moorland of CULLODEN witnessed the last-ever battle on British soil when, on April 16, 1746, the Jacobite cause was finally subdued – a turning point in the history of the Scottish nation. Your first stop should be the superb **visitor centre**, where costumed actors and state-of-the-art technology tell the tragedy of Culloden through the words, songs and poetic verse of locals and soldiers who experienced it. The *pièce de résistance* is the powerful "battle immersion theatre" where visitors are surrounded on all sides by lifelike cinematography and the sounds of the raging, bloody scenes of the fight. Go up to the rooftop platform to enjoy the elevated view across the actual battlefield before walking around the battle site armed with a nifty audioguide. Flags mark out the positions of the two armies while simple headstones mark the **clan graves**.

Fort George

13 miles northeast of Inverness, near Ardersier • Daily: April–Sept 9.30am–5.30pm; Oct–March 9.30am–4.30pm • £8.90; HS • ☎01667 460232

Fort George, an old Hanoverian bastion with walls a mile long, is considered by military architectural historians to be one of the finest fortifications in Europe. Crowning a sandy spit that juts into the middle of the Moray Firth, it was built between 1747 and 1769 as a base for George II's army, in case the Highlanders should attempt to rekindle the Jacobite flame. By the time of its completion, however, the

23

THE DEFEAT OF THE JACOBITES

The second Jacobite rebellion had begun on August 19, 1745, with the raising of the Stuarts' standard at Glenfinnan on the west coast (see p.908). Shortly after, Edinburgh fell into Jacobite hands, and Bonnie Prince Charlie began his march on London. The ruling Hanoverians had appointed the ambitious young Duke of Cumberland to command their forces, which included troops from the Lowlands and Highlands. The duke's pursuit, together with bad weather and lack of funds, eventually forced the Jacobite forces – mostly comprised of Highlanders – to retreat north. They ended up at Culloden, where, ill fed and exhausted after a pointless night march, they were hopelessly outnumbered by the government forces. The open, flat ground of Culloden Moor was totally unsuitable for the Highlanders' style of courageous but undisciplined fighting, which needed steep hills and lots of cover to provide the element of surprise, and they were routed.

After the battle, in which 1500 Highlanders were slaughtered (many of them as they lay wounded on the battlefield), Bonnie Prince Charlie fled west to the hills and islands, where loyal Highlanders sheltered and protected him. He eventually escaped to France, leaving his supporters to their fate – and, in effect, ushering in the end of the clan system. The clans were disarmed, the wearing of tartan and playing of bagpipes forbidden, and the chiefs became landlords greedy for higher and higher rents. The battle also unleashed an orgy of violent reprisals on Scotland, as unruly government troops raped and pillaged their way across the region; within a century, the Highland way of life had changed out of all recognition.

---

uprising had been firmly quashed and the fort has been used ever since as barracks; note the armed sentries at the main entrance and the periodic crack of live gunfire from the nearby firing ranges.

Walking on the northern, grass-covered casemates, which look out into the estuary, you may be lucky enough to see a school of bottle-nosed **dolphins** (see box, p.895) swimming in with the tide.

The Cairngorms and Strathspey

Rising high in the heather-clad hills above remote Loch Laggan, forty miles south of Inverness, the **River Spey**, Scotland's second longest river, drains northeast towards the Moray Firth through one of the Highlands' most spellbinding valleys. Famous for its ancient forests, salmon fishing and ospreys, the area around the upper section of the river, known as **Strathspey**, is dominated by the sculpted **Cairngorms**, Britain's most extensive mountain massif, unique in supporting subarctic tundra on its high plateau. Outdoor enthusiasts flock to the area to take advantage of the superb hiking, watersports and winter snows, aided by the fact that the area is easily accessible by road and rail from both central Scotland and Inverness. A string of villages along the river provide useful bases for setting out into the wilder country, principal among them **Aviemore**.

Aviemore and around

AVIEMORE was first developed as a ski and tourism resort in the mid-1960s and, over the years, fell victim to profiteering developers with scant regard for the needs of the local community. Although a face-lift has removed some of the architectural eyesores of that era, the settlement remains dominated by a string of soulless shopping centres and sprawling housing estates surrounding a Victorian railway station. That said, Aviemore is well-equipped with visitor facilities, and is the most convenient base for the Cairngorms.

Strathspey Steam Railway

Aviemore Station, Dalfaber Road • July & Aug 3 daily; less frequent service at other times • Return £13.95 • ☎ 01479 810725,
ⓦ strathspeyrailway.co.uk

The main attractions of Aviemore are its **outdoor pursuits**, though train enthusiasts are drawn to the restored **Strathspey Steam Railway**, which chugs the short distance (around ten miles) between Aviemore and Broomhill (return trip 90min), just beyond Boat of Garten village.

ARRIVAL AND INFORMATION

By train The railway station is on Grampian Rd, just south of the tourist office.

Destinations: Edinburgh (Mon–Sat 12 daily, Sun 7 daily; 3hr); Glasgow (11 daily, Sun 7 daily; 2hr 45min); Inverness (Mon–Sat 12 daily, Sun 7 daily; 35min).

By bus Buses arrive and depart outside the train station.

Destinations: Cairngorm ski area (hourly; 30min); Edinburgh (6 daily; 2hr 30min–3–4hr); Glasgow (7 daily;

AVIEMORE AND AROUND

2hr 40min); Grantown-on-Spey (Mon–Sat up to 3 hourly, Sun 4 daily; 35min); Inverness (roughly hourly; 45min).

Tourist information 7 The Parade, Grampian Rd (April & May Mon–Sat 9am–5pm, Sun 10am–5pm; June Mon–Sat 9am–6pm, Sun 9.30am–5pm; July & Aug Mon–Sat 9am–6.30pm, Sun 9.30am–6pm; Sept & Oct Mon–Sat 9am–5pm, Sun 10am–4pm; Nov–March Mon–Sat 9am–5pm; ☎ 01479 810930, ⓦ visitscotland.com).

ACTIVITES

SKIING

Scottish skiing on a commercial level first really took off in Aviemore. February and March are usually the best times to ski, but there's a chance of decent snow at any time between mid-November and April. Lots of places – not just in Aviemore itself – sell or rent equipment; for a rundown of ski schools and rental facilities in the area, visit ⓦ ski .visitscotland.com. The Cairngorm Ski Area (ⓦ cairngorm mountain.org), 9 miles southeast of Aviemore, above Loch Morlich in Glenmore Forest Park, is well served in winter by buses from Aviemore. Facilities include a ski school and a

separate terrain park for skiers and boarders. If there's lots of snow, the area around Loch Morlich and into the Rothiemurchus Estate provides enjoyable cross-country skiing.

G2 Outdoor Plot 10, Dalfaber Industrial Estate, Aviemore ☎ 01479 811008, ⓦ g2outdoor.co.uk. One-to-one tuition in the art of telemarking (£120/2hr) and back-country skiing. In summer, they also run kayaking and canyoning trips.

Mountain Spirit 62 Grampian Rd, Aviemore ☎ 01479 811788, ⓦ mountainspirit.co.uk. This friendly and

---

WALKS AROUND AVIEMORE

Ordnance Survey Explorer Maps nos. 402 & 403

Walking of all grades is a highlight of the Aviemore area, though you should heed the usual safety guidelines. These are particularly important if you want to venture into the subarctic climatic zone of the Cairngorms. However, as well as the high mountain trails, there are some lovely and well-signposted low-level walks in the area.

LOCH AN EILEAN

It takes an hour or so to complete the gentle circular walk around pretty Loch an Eilean (with its ruined castle) in the Rothiemurchus Estate, beginning at the end of the back road that turns east off the B970 a mile south of Inverdruie. The helpful estate visitor centres at the lochside and by the roadside at Inverdruie provide more information on other woodland trails.

RYVOAN PASS

Another good, half-day walk leads along a well-surfaced forestry track from *Glenmore Lodge* up towards the **Ryvoan Pass**, taking in An Lochan Uaine, known as the "Green Loch" and living up to its name, with amazing colours that range from turquoise to slate grey depending on the weather.

MEALL A' BHUACHALLIE

The **Glenmore Forest Park Visitor Centre** (daily 9am–5pm; ☎ 01479 861220, ⓦ scotland .forestry.gov.uk) by the roadside at the turn-off to *Glenmore Lodge* is the starting point for the three-hour round-trip climb of Meall a'Bhuachallie (Me-all ah Bvuh-ka-lee) (2654ft), which offers excellent views and is usually accessible year-round.

well-stocked shop is the place to visit for equipment (to buy or rent), from ski boots and poles to mountaineering gear. Daily 9am–5.30pm.

The Ski School In the Day Lodge, near the funicular railway's base station in the Cairngorm Ski Area ☏08455 191191, ⓦtheskischool.co.uk. A good bet for ski/board rental and lessons, not least because of its proximity to the funicular, which whizzes skiers up to the slopes. Courses run mid-Dec–early April.

MOUNTAIN BIKING

Bothy Bikes 5 Granish Way, Dalfaber, half a mile north of Aviemore's train station ☏01479 810111, ⓦbothybikes.co.uk. Guiding, maps and high-quality (front suspension) bike rental (£20/day), plus great advice. Daily 9am–5.30pm.

OUTDOOR TRAINING

National Outdoor Training Centre Glenmore Lodge, 8 miles east of Aviemore ☏01479 861256, ⓦglenmorelodge.org.uk. For a crash course in surviving Scottish winters, you could do worse than try a week at the National Outdoor Training Centre, at the east end of Loch Morlich. This superbly equipped and organized centre (complete with cosy après-ski bar) offers winter and summer courses in hillwalking, mountaineering, alpine ski-mountaineering, avalanche awareness and much more.

WATERSPORTS

Loch Insh Watersports Centre 6 miles south of Aviemore near Kincraig ☏01540 651272, ⓦlochinsh .com. Offers sailing, windsurfing and canoeing trips and rents mountain bikes (£19/day), as well as boats for fishing.

FISHING

Rothiemurchus Estate Inverdruie ☏01479 810703, ⓦrothiemurchus.com. Has a stocked rainbow trout-fishing loch, where success is virtually guaranteed. A one-hour lesson followed by an hour's fishing costs £45. July & Aug 9.30am–9pm, Sept–June 9.30am–5.30pm.

ACCOMMODATION

Aviemore Bunkhouse Dalfaber Rd, next to the Old Bridge Inn ☏01479 811181, ⓦaviemore-bunkhouse .com. A large modern place beside a cosy pub and within walking distance of the station, with six- and eight-bed dorms, as well as private rooms. Dorms £19, doubles £50

Aviemore SYHA 25 Grampian Rd ☏01479 810345, ⓦsyha.org.uk. Aviemore's large SYHA hostel, with its own bike store and drying room, has rather plain rooms but is within easy walking distance of the town centre. Dorms £20, twins £45

Glenmore Lodge 8 miles east of Aviemore ☏01479 861256, ⓦglenmorelodge.org.uk. Excellent accommo-dation at this popular outdoor centre. There are twin rooms (breakfast included), plus self-catering lodges (two-night min). The superb facilities include a pool, weights room, sauna and indoor climbing wall. Twins £76, lodges £215

Ravenscraig Guest House Grampian Rd ☏01479 810278, ⓦaviemoreonline.com. This welcoming, family-friendly B&B has a handy central location. Single, double and family rooms are available, plus a wide choice of breakfast options, including sausages bought from a local butcher. Singles £48, doubles £78, family rooms £115

Rothiemurchus Caravan Park 2 miles southeast of Aviemore in Coylumbridge ☏01479 812800, ⓦrothiemurchus.net. Relaxed site for tents and caravans, nestled among tall pine trees at Coylumbridge on the way to Loch Morlich. Per person £11

EATING AND DRINKING

★**Mountain Café** 111 Grampian Rd ☏01479 812473, ⓦmountaincafe-aviemore.co.uk. Above Cairngorm Mountain Sports in the centre of town, the Kiwi-run *Mountain Café* is reasonably priced, serving an all-day menu of wholesome snacks (sandwiches and wraps cost £5.75) and freshly prepared meals. Specializes in wheat- and gluten-free food. Mon & Fri–Sun 8.30am–5.30pm, Tues–Thurs 8.30am–5pm.

The Old Bridge Inn Dalfaber Rd, next to Aviemore Bunkhouse ☏01479 811137, ⓦoldbridgeinn.co.uk. Fire-warmed pub that hosts regular live music sessions and serves up decent dinners; the menu includes a whole grilled sea bream with potatoes and dressed leaves for £16. Fri & Sat noon–1am, Sun–Thurs noon–midnight.

Cairngorm Ski Area

9 miles southeast of Aviemore • Ski season generally Dec–April, but varies depending on snowfall • ☏01479 861319, ⓦcairngormmountain.org • Buses (#31; hourly) from Aviemore stop at the *Coire Cas* car park, near the funicular railway's base station • **Cairn Gorm Mountain Railway** Departs from the base station • Daily: May–Oct 10.20am–4.30pm; Nov–April 9am–4.30pm; last train up 4pm • Every 30min • £10.50 for a day-pass • **Ranger office** Daily: April–Oct 8.30am–5pm; Nov–March 8.30am–4.30pm

Though it's on a tiny scale by continental European and North American standards, occasionally snow and sun coincide at the **Cairngorm Ski Area**, high above Loch

CAIRNGORMS NATIONAL PARK

The **Cairngorms National Park** (🌐 cairngorms.co.uk) covers some 1500 square miles and incorporates the **Cairngorms massif**, the UK's largest mountainscape and only sizeable plateau over 2500ft. While Aviemore and the surrounding area is the main point of entry, particularly for those planning outdoor activities, it's also possible to access the eastern side of the park from both Deeside and Donside in Aberdeenshire. There are 52 summits higher than 2953ft in the park, as well as a quarter of Scotland's native woodland, and a quarter of the UK's threatened wildlife species. Vegetation ranges from one of the largest tracts of ancient **Caledonian pine and birch forest** remaining in Scotland at Rothiemurchus to subarctic tundra on the high plateau, where **alpine flora** such as starry saxifrage and the star-shaped pink flowers of moss campion peek out of the pink granite in the few months of summer when the ground is free of snow. **The bird of prey** you're most likely to see is the **osprey**, especially at Loch Garten's osprey observation centre (see below), or fishing on the lochs around Aviemore.

23

Morlich in Glenmore Forest Park, to offer beginner and expert alike a great day on the pistes. The controversial (bitterly opposed by conservationists) **Cairn Gorm Mountain Railway**, a two-car funicular system, runs to the top of the Cairngorm Ski Area (3600ft), not far from the summit of Cairn Gorm mountain (4085ft); it departs from the base station, by the Coire Cas car park, year-round. At the top is an exhibition/interpretation area and a café/restaurant from which spectacular views can be had on clear days. There is no access beyond the confines of the top station unless you're embarking on a winter skiing trip or a guided walk; folks wanting to explore the subarctic Cairngorm plateau have to trudge up from the car park at the bottom. The base station also houses a **ranger office** where you can find out about various trails, check the latest weather report and – on fine days between May and October – join guided walks.

Abernethy Forest RSPB Reserve

Loch Garten, 7 miles northeast of Aviemore and 8 miles south of Grantown-on-Spey • **Observation centre** April–Aug daily 10am–6pm (last admission 5pm) • £5 • ☎ 01479 831476 • From Aviemore, buses run roughly hourly to Boat of Garten; the visitor centre is 2.5 miles east across the bridge

The **Abernethy Forest RSPB Reserve**, on the shore of **Loch Garten**, is famous as the nesting site of the **osprey**. Having completely disappeared from the British Isles, a single pair of these exquisite white-and-brown raptors mysteriously reappeared in 1954 and built a nest in a tree half a mile or so from the loch; the birds are now well established here and elsewhere across the Highlands. The best time to visit is between April and August, when the RSPB opens an **observation centre**, complete with telescopes and CCTV monitoring of the nest.

The Great Glen

The **Great Glen**, a major geological faultline cutting diagonally across the Highlands from Fort William to Inverness, is the defining geographic feature of the north of Scotland. A huge rift valley was formed when the northwestern and southeastern sides of the fault slid in opposite directions for more than sixty miles, while the present landscape was shaped by glaciers that retreated only around 8000 BC. The glen is impressive more for its sheer scale than its beauty, but the imposing barrier of loch and mountain means that no one can travel into the northern Highlands without passing through it. With the two major service centres of the Highlands at either end it makes an obvious and rewarding route between the west and east coasts.

Of the Great Glen's four elongated lochs, the most famous is **Loch Ness**, home to the mythical monster; lochs **Oich**, **Lochy** and **Linnhe** (the last of these a sea loch) are less renowned, though no less attractive. All four are linked by the Caledonian Canal. The southwestern end of the Great Glen is dominated by **Fort William**, the second-largest town in the Highland region. Situated at the heart of the Lochaber area, it's a useful base and an excellent hub for outdoor activities. Dominating the scene to the south is **Ben Nevis**, Britain's highest peak, best approached from scenic Glen Nevis. The most famous glen of all, **Glen Coe**, lies on the main A82, half an hour's drive south of Fort William. Nowadays the whole area is unashamedly given over to tourism, and Fort William is swamped by bus tours throughout the summer, but, as ever in the Highlands, within a thirty-minute drive you can be totally alone.

Loch Ness

23

Twenty-three miles long, unfathomably deep, cold and often moody, **Loch Ness** is bounded by rugged heather-clad mountains rising steeply from a wooded shoreline with attractive glens opening up on either side. Its fame, however, is based overwhelmingly on its legendary inhabitant Nessie, the "Loch Ness monster", who ensures a steady flow of hopeful visitors to the settlements dotted along the loch, in particular **Drumnadrochit**. Nearby, the impressive ruins of **Castle Urquhart** – a favourite monster-spotting location – perch atop a rock on the lochside and attract a deluge of bus parties in summer. Almost as busy in high season is the village of **Fort Augustus**, at the more scenic southwest tip of Loch Ness, where you can watch queues of boats tackling one of the Caledonian Canal's longest flights of locks.

Drumnadrochit

Situated above a verdant, sheltered bay of Loch Ness fifteen miles southwest of Inverness, touristy **DRUMNADROCHIT** is the southern gateway to remote Glen Affric

---

NESSIE

The world-famous **Loch Ness monster**, affectionately known as **Nessie** (and by aficionados as *Nessiteras rhombopteryx*), has been a local celebrity for some time. The first mention of a mystery creature crops up in St Adamnan's seventh-century biography of **St Columba**, who allegedly calmed an aquatic animal that had attacked one of his monks. In 1934, the *Daily Mail* published London surgeon R.K. Wilson's sensational photograph of the head and neck of the monster peering up out of the loch, and the hype has hardly diminished since. Encounters range from glimpses of ripples by anglers to the famous occasion in 1961 when thirty hotel guests saw a pair of humps break the water's surface and cruise for about half a mile before submerging.

Photographic evidence is showcased in the two "Monster Exhibitions" at Drumnadrochit, but the most impressive of these exhibits – including the famous black-and-white movie footage of Nessie's humps moving across the water, and Wilson's original head and shoulders shot – have now been exposed as fakes. Indeed, in few other places on earth has watching a rather lifeless and often grey expanse of water seemed so compelling, or have floating logs, otters and boat wakes been photographed so often and with such excitement. Yet while even high-tech sonar surveys carried out over the past two decades have failed to come up with conclusive evidence, it's hard to dismiss Nessie as pure myth. After all, no one yet knows where the unknown layers of silt and mud at the bottom of the loch begin and end: best estimates say the loch is more than 750ft deep, deeper than much of the North Sea, while others point to the possibilities of underwater caves and undiscovered channels connected to the sea. Technological advances have also expanded the scope for Nessie-watching: the slightly barmy ⓦlochness.co.uk offers round-the-clock **webcams** for views across the loch, while ⓦlochnessinvestigation.org is packed with research information. The local tourist industry's worst fear – dwindling interest – is about as unlikely as an appearance of the mysterious monster herself.

and the epicentre of Nessie-hype, complete with a rash of tacky souvenir shops and two rival monster exhibitions.

Loch Ness Centre & Exhibition

Loch Ness Centre & Exhibition Along the A82 • Daily: Easter–June 9.30am–5pm; July & Aug 9.30am–6pm; Sept & Oct 9.30am–5pm; Nov–Easter 10am–3.30pm • £7.45 • ☎ 01456 450573, ⓦ lochness.com • **Deepscan cruise** Hourly • Easter–Sept 10am–6pm • 1hr • £14 • ☎ 01456 450218 • **Nessie Hunter cruise** Hourly • Easter–Oct 9am–6pm • 1hr • £15 • ☎ 01456 450395, ⓦ loch-ness-cruises.com

The **Loch Ness Centre & Exhibition** is the better bet of the two monster exhibitions, offering an in-depth rundown of eyewitness accounts and information on various research projects that have attempted to shed further light on the mysteries of the loch. **Nessie-spotting cruises** on the loch aboard *Deepscan* run from here; the *Nessie Hunter* can be booked at the nearby Nessieland Monster Centre.

Castle Urquhart

2 miles southeast of Drumnadrochit off the A82 • Daily: April–Sept 9.30am–6pm; Oct 9.30am–5pm; Nov–March 9.30am–4.30pm • £7.90; HS • ☎ 01456 450551

Most photographs allegedly showing the monster have been taken a couple of miles southeast of Drumnadrochit, around the thirteenth-century ruined lochside **Castle Urquhart**. It's one of Scotland's classic picture-postcard ruins, crawling with tourists by day but particularly splendid when floodlit at night after the crowds have gone.

23

ARRIVAL AND INFORMATION

DRUMNADROCHIT

By bus Buses arrive and depart from near the post office, in the middle of town on the A82.

Destinations: Fort Augustus (up to 10 daily; 35min); Fort William (up to 9 daily; 1hr 30min); Inverness (at least hourly; 30min).

Tourist information In the main car park (April, May, Sept & Oct Mon–Sat 9.30am–5pm, Sun 10am–3pm; June Mon–Sat 9am–5pm, Sun 10am–4pm; July & Aug Mon–Sat 9am–6pm, Sun 9.30am–5pm; Nov–March Tues–Sat 9.30am–3.30pm; ☎ 01456 459086).

ACCOMMODATION AND EATING

The Baking Birds 3 Victoria Buildings, near the junction with the A831 ☎ 01456 450332. Tucked away off the main road, this pretty little bakery sells excellent home-made cakes as well as savoury pies and hot drinks, making it a great place to refuel before a long drive. Mon–Sat 9am–4pm.

Benleva Kilmore Rd, Kilmore ☎ 01456 450080, ⓦ benleva.co.uk. Small, basic hotel in nearby Kilmore, a fifteen-minute walk from the monster centres of Drumnadrochit. The six en-suite rooms have tartan bedspreads and free wi-fi. **£80**

Fiddlers' Café Bar Just south of the village green on the A82 ☎ 01456 450678, ⓦ fiddledrum.co.uk. Busy, friendly bar with plenty of outside seating and, it's claimed, more than five hundred single-malt whiskies. The

mostly meaty menu has a couple of veggie options, including a grilled vegetable-and-brie burger (£10.95). Daily 12.30–2.30pm & 6–9.30pm.

Glenkirk B&B 300m west of Nessieland Monster Centre along A831 ☎ 01456 450802, ⓦ lochnessbandb .com. Bright, friendly B&B in a former church located a few minutes' walk from the centre, with simple yet smartly decorated bedrooms. **£90**

Loch Ness Backpackers Lodge Coiltie Farmhouse, Lewiston; follow the signs to the left when coming from Drumnadrochit ☎ 01456 450807, ⓦ lochness -backpackers.com. For a cheap bed, head for this immaculate and friendly hostel, which has dorms, private rooms and good facilities including a bar and a fire-warmed lounge. Dorms **£18**, doubles **£40**

Glen Affric

A vast area of high peaks, remote glens and few roads lies west of Drumnadrochit, including **Glen Affric**, generally held as one of Scotland's most beautiful landscapes and heaven for walkers, climbers and mountain-bikers. The approach is through the small settlement of **CANNICH**, fourteen miles west of Drumnadrochit on the A831.

Hemmed in by a string of Munros, Glen Affric is great for picnics and pottering, particularly on a calm and sunny day, when the still water reflects the islands and surrounding hills. From the car park at the head of the singletrack road along the glen,

23

ten miles southwest of Cannich, there's a selection of **walks**: the trail around Loch Affric will take you a good five hours but captures the glen, its wildlife and Caledonian pine and birch woods in all their remote splendour.

ARRIVAL AND DEPARTURE   GLEN AFFRIC

By bus Ross's Minibuses (☎01463 761250, ⓦross-minibuses.co.uk) runs scheduled services into the glen from July–Sept from Inverness, Cannich and Drumnadrochit; its vehicles will also carry bikes if given

advance notice.
Destinations Cannich (Mon, Wed & Fri 4 daily; 30min); Drumnadrochit (Mon, Wed & Fri 1 daily; 1hr 35min); Inverness (Mon, Wed & Fri 1 daily; 2hr 10min).

ACCOMMODATION AND EATING

Cannich Camping & Caravan Park In the centre of Cannich ☎01456 415364, ⓦhighlandcamping.co.uk. Mountain bikes can be rented (£17/day) at this pretty, well-shaded campsite, which has good facilities, including

wi-fi and a TV room. Wooden camping pods can be rented by the night, and there's a decent café on site. Camping per person **£7.50**, pods **£22**

Fort Augustus

FORT AUGUSTUS, a tiny, busy village at the scenic southwestern tip of Loch Ness, was named after George II's son, the chubby lad who later became the "Butcher" Duke of Cumberland of Culloden fame; today, the village is dominated by comings and goings along the Caledonian Canal, which leaves Loch Ness here. From its berth near the swing bridge, *Cruise Loch Ness* (hourly March–Oct, twice daily Nov–March; 1hr; £13.50; ☎01320 366277, ⓦcruiselochness.com) sails five miles up Loch Ness, using sonar technology to provide impressive, live 3D imagery of the deep.

ARRIVAL AND INFORMATION   FORT AUGUSTUS

By bus Frequent buses ply the A82, linking Fort Augustus' tourist office with Inverness and Drumnadrochit to the north and Fort William, 30 miles south.
Destinations: Drumnadrochit (up to 10 daily; 35min); Fort William (up to 9 daily; 1hr); Inverness (up to 9 daily; 1hr).
Tourist information The Car Park, north of the canal and

river, along the A82 (April & May Mon–Sat 9.30am–5pm, Sun 10am–4pm; June Mon–Sat 9am–5pm, Sun 10am–4pm; July & Aug Mon–Sat, Sun 10am–4pm; Sept & Oct Mon–Sat 9.30am–5pm, Sun 10am–3pm; Nov–March daily 10am–3pm; ☎01320 366779).

ACCOMMODATION

Corrie Liath Market Hill, half a mile south of the centre along the A82 ☎01320 366409, ⓦcorrieliath.co.uk. Small, thoughtfully managed B&B whose comfortable rooms have books and DVDs for guests to enjoy. The garden has a BBQ hut for use in the summertime. **£72**
Morag's Lodge Bunoich Brae, on the northern side of

town ☎01320 366289, ⓦmoragslodge.com. Quality budget accommodation in a bright and colourful hostel; the atmosphere livens up with the daily arrival of backpackers' minibus tours. Family rooms available. Dorms **£22**, doubles **£52**, family rooms **£69**

Fort William

With its stunning position on Loch Linnhe, tucked in below the snow-streaked bulk of Ben Nevis, the important regional centre of **FORT WILLIAM** (often known as "Fort Bill"), should be a gem. Sadly, the same lack of taste that nearly saw the town renamed "Abernevis" in the 1950s is evident in the ribbon bungalow development and dual carriageway – complete with grubby pedestrian underpass – which have wrecked the waterfront. The main street and the little squares off it are more appealing, though occupied by some decidedly tacky tourist giftshops.

ARRIVAL AND INFORMATION   FORT WILLIAM

By train Trains arrive at Station Square near the town centre.

Destinations Arisaig (3–4 daily; 1hr 10min); Crianlarich (3–4 daily; 1hr 50min); Glasgow (2–3 daily; 3hr 45min);

Glenfinnan (3–4 daily; 30min); London (Sun–Fri 1 nightly; 12hr); Mallaig (3–4 daily; 1hr 25min).

By bus Most buses stop near the train station.

Destinations Acharacle (Mon–Sat 1–2 daily; 1hr 30min); Drumnadrochit (8–9 daily; 1hr 30min); Edinburgh (1 daily; 4hr 10min); Fort Augustus (9 daily; 50min); Glasgow (8 daily; 3hr); Inverness (9 daily; 2hr); Kilchoan (2 daily; 2hr 30min–3hr); Kyle of Lochalsh (2 daily; 2hr); Mallaig

(Mon–Fri 3 daily; 1hr 20min); Oban (Mon–Sat 3 daily; 1hr 30min); Portree, Skye (4 daily; 3hr).

Tourist information 15 High St (April & May Mon–Sat 9am–5pm, Sun 10am–5pm; June Mon–Sat 9am–6pm, Sun 9.30am–5pm; July & Aug Mon–Sat 9am–6.30pm, Sun 9am–6pm; Sept & Oct Mon–Sat 9am–5pm, Sun 10am–4pm; Nov–March Mon–Sat 9am–5pm, Sun 10am–3pm; ☎01397 701801, ⓦvisithighlands.com).

ACCOMMODATION

Calluna Heathercroft, Connachie Rd ☎01397 700451, ⓦfortwilliamholiday.co.uk. Well-run self-catering (four-bed apartments) and hostel accommodation just a 10min walk from the centre of town. On-site laundry facilities and a bouldering wall. The owners can also help to organize mountaineering trips. Dorms **£16**, apartments **£340**

Fort William Backpackers Alma Rd ☎01397 700711, ⓦfortwilliambackpackers.com. A rambling, busy, archetypal backpacker hostel a five minute walk uphill from town, with great views and large communal areas. Guests get free tea and coffee. Dorms **£10**, twins **£47**

Great Glen Yurts 3 miles northeast of Fort William off A82 (signposted from Torlundy) ☎01397 700711, ⓦgreatglenyurts.com. Rotund and spacious, these luxury yurts occupy a magnificently peaceful setting with views of Ben Nevis. There's an open-sided kitchen for sociable evening meals. April–Oct. **£90**

Inverlochy Castle Torlundy, 3 miles north of the town centre on the A82 ☎01397 702177, ⓦinverlochycastlehotel.co.uk. Close to the thirteenth-century fortress of the same name, this is one of Scotland's grandest and most luxurious country-house hotels with plush accommodation and Michelin-star food. **£465**

Nevis Bank Inn Belford Rd ☎01397 705721, ⓦnevisbankinn.co.uk. The small, functional hotel rooms here are a little on the plain side (and expensive too), but they're comfortable and quiet – and there's parking right outside. **£138**

St Andrews Guest House Fassifern Rd ☎01397 703038, ⓦstandrewsguesthouse.co.uk. Comfortable and very reasonable B&B in a converted granite choir school five minutes' walk uphill from the High Street, featuring various inscriptions and stained-glass windows. **£60**

EATING AND DRINKING

Crannog Restaurant At the pier, just off the bypass on entering Fort William ☎01397 705589, ⓦcrannog.net. Red-roofed restaurant with lochside views and fresh seafood, such as Mallaig monkfish with rice and salsa (£19.50), plus a decent wine list. Daily noon–2.30pm & 6–9pm.

Grog and Gruel 66 High St ☎01397 705078, ⓦgrogandgruel.co.uk. Loud and friendly, the downstairs alehouse at *Grog and Gruel* is a good bet for Scottish beer. The upstairs restaurant is more relaxed and does a good mix of Mexican dishes, including a wild boar chilli (£11.25). Thurs–Sat 11am–1am, Sun 11am–midnight.

THE NEVIS RANGE

Seven miles northeast of Fort William by the A82, on the slopes of **Aonach Mòr**, one of the high mountains abutting Ben Nevis, the **Nevis Range** (☎01397 705825, ⓦnevis-range.co.uk) is Scotland's highest winter ski area. Bus #41 runs from Fort William (Mon–Sat 4 daily, Sun 2 daily) to the base station of the country's only **gondola** system (daily: Easter–June & Sept–Oct 10am–5pm; July & Aug 9.30am–6pm; early Nov & late Dec–Easter 9am–sunset; £11.50 return). The 1.5-mile gondola trip, rising 2000ft, gives an easy approach to some high-level walking as well as spectacular views from the terrace of the self-service restaurant at the top station. From the top of the gondola station, you can experience Britain's only World-Cup-standard **downhill mountain-bike course** (mid-May to mid-Sept 10.15am–3.45pm; £13 includes gondola one way), a hair-raising 3km route that's not for the faint-hearted. There are also 25 miles of waymarked off-road bike routes, known as the Witch's Trails (open all year), on the mountainside and in the Leanachan Forest, ranging from gentle paths to cross-country scrambles. At the entrance to the lower gondola station, Alpine Bikes (May–Sept daily 9am–5pm ☎01397 705825, ⓦalpinebikes.com) rents general mountain bikes (from £22) as well as full-suspension ones for the downhill course.

Glen Nevis

A ten-minute drive south of Fort William, **GLEN NEVIS** is among the Highlands' most impressive glens: a U-shaped glacial valley hemmed in by steep bracken-covered slopes and swathes of blue-grey scree. Herds of shaggy Highland cattle graze the valley floor, where a sparkling river gushes through glades of trees.

A great **low-level walk** (six miles round-trip) runs from the end of the road at the top of Glen Nevis. The rocky path leads through a dramatic gorge with impressive falls and rapids, then opens out into a secret hanging valley, carpeted with wild flowers and featuring a high waterfall at the far end. Of all the walks in and around Glen Nevis, however, the **ascent of Ben Nevis** (4406ft), Britain's highest summit, inevitably attracts the most attention. Despite the fact that it's quite a slog up to the summit, and it's by no means the most attractive mountain in Scotland, in high summer the trail is teeming with hikers, whatever the weather. It can snow round the summit any day of the year, so take the necessary precautions; in winter, of course, the mountain should be left to the experts. The most obvious **route** to the summit, a Victorian pony path up the whaleback south side of the mountain, built to service the observatory that once stood on the top, starts from the helpful **Glen Nevis Visitor Centre** (see below): allow a full day for the climb (8hr).

ARRIVAL AND INFORMATION
GLEN NEVIS

By bus The #41 service from Fort William (3 daily; 20min) runs via the SYHA hostel to the Lower Falls car park, almost 5 miles up the Glen Nevis road.

Tourist information The Glen Nevis Visitor Centre is 1.5 miles southeast of Fort William along the Glen Nevis road (April–Oct daily 9am–5pm; ☎01397 705922).

ACCOMMODATION AND EATING

★Ben Nevis Inn Achintee, Glen Nevis, 50m east of Achintee Farm Guest House ☎01397 701227, ⓦben-nevis-inn.co.uk. A basic and cosy bunkhouse (booking advised) in the basement of a lively 250-year-old pub. The place has a terrific atmosphere and the menu – with a pan-seared rump steak for £18.50 – is especially tempting after a day on the mountain. March–Oct daily

noon–11pm; Nov–Feb Thurs–Sun noon–11pm. £15.50
Glen Nevis SYHA Hostel 2.5 miles along the Glen Nevis road from Fort William, opposite the start of the path to the summit ☎01397 702336, ⓦsyha.org.uk. Though basic and far from town, this friendly hostel is an excellent base for walkers. Very busy in summer, so book ahead. Dorms £22, doubles £55

Glen Coe

Sixteen miles south of Fort William on the A82, breathtakingly beautiful **Glen Coe** (literally "Valley of Weeping") is the best known of the Highland glens: a spectacular mountain valley between velvety-green conical peaks, their tops often wreathed in cloud, their flanks streaked by cascades of rock and scree. In 1692 it was the site of a notorious massacre, in which the MacDonalds were victims of a long-standing government desire to suppress the clans. When clan chief **Alastair MacDonald** missed the deadline of January 1, 1692, to sign an oath of allegiance to William III, a plot was hatched to make an example of "that damnable sept". **Campbell of Glenlyon** was ordered to billet his soldiers in the homes of the MacDonalds, who for ten days entertained them with traditional Highland hospitality. In the early morning of February 13, the soldiers turned on their hosts, slaying between 38 and 45, and causing more than three hundred to flee.

Beyond the small village of **GLENCOE** at the western end of the glen, the glen itself (a property of the National Trust for Scotland since the 1930s) is virtually uninhabited, and provides outstanding climbing and walking. Enlightening ranger-led **guided walks** (Easter & June–Sept; book ahead) leave from the centre a mile southeast of the village (see p.906), which also has an exhibition with a balanced account of the massacre.

ARRIVAL AND INFORMATION   GLEN COE

By bus To get to the Glen Coe Visitor Centre from Fort William's bus station, hop on one of the Glasgow-bound Scottish Citylink coaches (up to 8 daily; 30–45min).
Tourist information The NTS visitor centre is a mile southeast of Glencoe village (April–Oct daily 9.30am–5.30pm; Nov–March Thurs–Sun 10am–4pm; NTS; £6.50; ☎08444 932222, ⓦnts.org.uk).

ACCOMMODATION AND EATING

★**Clachaig Inn** 2.5 miles south of Glencoe village on the minor road off the A82 ☎01855 811252, ⓦclachaig .com The liveliest, best-known hotel in the area is a great place to reward your exertions with cask-conditioned ales and heaped platefuls of food; it's an easy stroll away from the *Red Squirrel* campsite. Daily 11am–11pm. **£102**
Glencoe hostel Between Glencoe village and the Clachaig Inn ☎01855 811906, ⓦglencoehostel.co.uk.
Occupying rustic whitewashed buildings, this attractive hostel is cheaper than the SYHA alternative, with a drying room, internet access and laundry. **£16.75**
Red Squirrel 150m south of the turn-off to Glencoe Independent Hostel ☎01855 811256, ⓦredsquirrel campsite.co.uk. Sylvan year-round campsite, just south of the SYHA hostel on the road to *Clachaig Inn*. Campfires and pets permitted. No bookings. Pitches **£19**

The west coast

The Highlands' starkly beautiful **west coast** – stretching from the **Morvern peninsula** (opposite Mull) in the south to wind-lashed **Cape Wrath** in the far north – is arguably the finest part of Scotland. Serrated by fjord-like sea lochs, the long coastline is scattered with windswept white-sand beaches, cliff-girt headlands, and rugged mountains sweeping up from the shoreline. When the sun shines, the sparkle of the sea, the richness of colour and the clarity of the views out to the scattered Hebrides are simply irresistible. This is the least populated part of Britain, with just two small towns and yawning tracts of moorland and desolate peat bog between crofting settlements.

Lying within easy reach of Inverness, the popular stretch of the coast between Kyle of Lochalsh and Ullapool features the region's more obvious highlights: the awesome mountainscape of **Torridon**, **Gairloch**'s sandy beaches, the famous botanic gardens at **Inverewe**, and **Ullapool** itself, a picturesque and bustling fishing town from where ferries leave for the Outer Hebrides. However, press on further north, or south, and you'll get a truer sense of the isolation that makes the west coast so special. Traversed by few roads, the remote northwest corner of Scotland is wild and bleak, receiving the full force of the North Atlantic's frequently ferocious weather. The scattered settlements of the far southwest, meanwhile, tend to be more sheltered, but they are separated by some of the most extensive wilderness areas in Britain – lonely peninsulas with evocative Gaelic names like **Ardnamurchan** and **Knoydart**.

GETTING AROUND   THE WEST COAST

Without your own vehicle, transport can be a problem. However, there's a direct **train** service from Inverness to Kyle of Lochalsh and from Fort William to Mallaig, and a useful **summer bus** service (late May to Sept) connects Inverness to Ullapool, Lochinver, Scourie and Durness. **Driving** is a much simpler option: the roads aren't busy, though they are frequently singletrack and scattered with sheep.

The "Rough Bounds"

The remote and sparsely populated southwest corner of the Highlands, from the empty district of **Morvern** to the isolated peninsula of **Knoydart**, is a dramatic, lonely region of mountain and moorland fringed by a rocky, indented coast whose stunning white beaches enjoy wonderful views to Mull, Skye and other islands. Its Gaelic name,

Garbh-chiochan, translates as the "**Rough Bounds**", implying a region geographically and spiritually apart. Even if you have a car, you should spend some time here exploring on foot; there are so few roads that some determined hiking is almost inevitable.

The Ardnamurchan peninsula

A nine-mile drive south of Fort William down Loch Linnhe, the five-minute ferry crossing at **Corran Ferry** (every 20–30min; Mon–Sat 6.30am–9.20pm, Sun 8.45am–9.20pm; car £7.60; foot passengers and bicycles free) provides the most direct point of entry for Morvern and the rugged **Ardnamurchan peninsula**. The most westerly point on the British mainland, the peninsula lost most of its inhabitants during the infamous Clearances and is now sparsely populated, with only a handful of tiny crofting settlements clinging to its jagged coastline. It boasts some beautiful, pristine, empty beaches – especially about three miles north of the Ardnamurchan lighthouse at **Sanna Bay**, a shell-strewn strand and series of dunes that offers truly unforgettable vistas of the Small Isles to the north, circled by gulls, terns and guillemots. The coastal hamlet of **SALEN** marks the turn-off for Ardnamurchan Point: from here it's a further 25 miles of slow, scenic driving along the single track road which follows the northern shore of Loch Sunart.

Nàdurra

Glenborrodale • April–Oct Mon–Sat 10am–5.30pm, Sun 11.30am–5pm; Nov–March Tues Fri 10.30am–3.30pm, Sun 11.30am–3.30pm • £4.50 • ☎ 01972 500209, ⒲ nadurracentre.co.uk

Just west of the hamlet of **GLENBORRODALE**, look out for the engaging **Nàdurra Centre**, which provides an inspiring introduction to the diverse flora, fauna and geology of Ardnamurchan: CCTV cameras relay pictures of the comings and goings of heron, a pine marten's nest, and sea and golden eagles feeding nearby.

Ardnamurchan Point Lighthouse

Ardnamurchan Point • Easter–Oct daily 10am–5pm (tours of the tower run from 11am–4pm) • £6 • ☎ 01972 510210, ⒲ ardnamurchanlighthouse.com • Book ahead at peak times

Rocky and windy, **Ardnamurchan Point** is most famous for its **lighthouse**. The lighthouse buildings house a small café and an absorbing **exhibition**. Best of all is the chance to climb up the inside of the Egyptian-style lighthouse tower; at the top, a guide tells tall tales relating to the lighthouse and shows you around the lighting mechanism.

ARRIVAL AND ACCOMMODATION   THE ARDNAMURCHAN PENINSULA

By ferry A car ferry runs from Kilchoan to Tobermory on Mull (Mon–Sat 7.20am–6pm 7 daily; May–Aug Mon–Sat 7.20am–6pm 7 daily, Sun 9.30am–4pm 5 daily; 35min; ⒲ calmac.co.uk).
Ardnamurchan campsite Ormsaigbeg ☎ 01972

510766, ⒲ ardnamurchanstudycentre.co.uk. This back to basics site with lovely coastal views is located by the Ardnamurchan Study Centre, about half a mile beyond the Ferry Stores. Easter–Sept. Per person £8

The Road to the Isles

The "**Road to the Isles**" (⒲ road-to-the-isles.org.uk) from Fort William to Mallaig, followed by the West Highland Railway and the narrow, winding A830, traverses the mountains and glens of the Rough Bounds before breaking out onto a spectacularly scenic coast of sheltered inlets, white beaches and wonderful views to the islands of Rùm, Eigg, Muck and Skye. This is country associated with **Bonnie Prince Charlie**, whose adventures of 1745–46 began and ended on this stretch of coast, with his first, defiant gathering of the clans at **Glenfinnan**, nineteen miles west of Fort William at the head of lovely **Loch Shiel**.

23

Glenfinnan

Visitor centre Daily: April–June, Sept & Oct 10am–5pm; July & Aug 9.30am–5.30pm • £3.50; NTS • Shiel Buses runs a service from Mallaig's high school to Glenfinnan (June–Oct Mon–Fri 4 daily, Sat 1 daily; 1hr)

GLENFINNAN is a poignant place, a beautiful stage for the opening scene in a brutal drama that was to change the Highlands forever. The **visitor centre** and café opposite the monument, gives an account of the 1745 uprising through to the rout at **Culloden** eight months later (see p.895).

ACCOMMODATION AND EATING   GLENFINNAN

Sleeping Car Station Cottage ☎01397 722295, ⓦ glenfinnanstationmuseum.co.uk. This converted railway carriage by the museum is heaven for train fanatics, with original features and enough space for ten people in bunk beds. Guests can make meals in the onboard kitchen. **£14**

Arisaig and around

ARISAIG, scattered round a sandy bay at the west end of the Morar peninsula, makes a good base for exploring the coast. A **bypass** whizzes cars (and, more importantly, fish lorries) on their way to Mallaig, but you shouldn't miss the slower coast road, which enjoys the best of the scenery.

Stretching north of Arisaig is a string of stunning **beaches** backed by flowery machair, with barren granite hills and moorland rising up behind, and wonderful seaward views of Eigg and Rùm.

Mallaig

A cluttered, noisy port whose pebble-dashed houses struggle for space with great lumps of exposed granite strewn over the hillsides sloping down to the sea, **MALLAIG**, 47 miles west of Fort William, isn't pretty. As the main ferry stop for Skye, the Small Isles and Knoydart, it's always full of visitors, though the continuing source of the village's wealth is its **fishing** industry. When the fleet is in, trawlers encircled by flocks of raucous gulls choke the harbour, and the pubs, among the liveliest on the west coast, host bouts of serious drinking.

ARRIVAL AND DEPARTURE   MALLAIG

By ferry The CalMac ticket office (☎01687 462403), serving passengers for Skye and the Small Isles, is near the tourist office on the harbour. For Knoydart, Western Isles Cruises (☎01687 462233, ⓦ westernislescruises.co.uk) sails to Inverie, on the Knoydart peninsula.
Destinations Armadale, Skye (Mon–Sat 8 daily, Sun at least 4 daily; 30min); Canna (Mon, Wed, Fri & Sun 1 daily, Sat 2 daily; 2hr 45min); Eigg (Mon, Thurs, Sat & Sun 1 daily; 1hr 15min); Inverie (April–Oct Mon–Sat 2 daily; 50 min); Muck (Tues & Thurs–Sun 1 daily; 2hr); Rùm (Mon, Wed, Fri–Sun 1 daily; 1hr 30min).

ACCOMMODATION AND EATING

Cornerstone Main St ☎01687 462306, ⓦ seafood restaurantmallaig.com. Fish and chips – or crab claws with white pepper and citrus mayo if you're feeling decadent – plus langoustines, prawns, haddock, monkfish, sole and mussels (mains from £10–22). Daily 8.15–10.30am, noon–2.30pm & 5–9.30pm.
Seaview Main Street ☎01687 462 059, ⓦ seaviewguesthousemallaig.com. Big stone house with views over the busy harbour. The rooms are bright with decor that feels more hotel than simple B&B. Conveniently, if you've just arrived off the car ferry, there's easy parking too. **£75**
Sheena's Backpackers' Lodge Station Rd ☎01687 462764, ⓦ mallaigbackpackers.co.uk. The dorms above the popular *Tea Garden Restaurant* have simple metal bunks and slightly whiffy bathrooms, but it's the cheapest place to stay around here – and there's a kitchen for cooking your own meals. **£17**

The Knoydart peninsula

Flanked by **Loch Nevis** ("Loch of Heaven") in the south and the fjord-like inlet of **Loch Hourn** ("Loch of Hell") to the north, **Knoydart peninsula**'s knobbly green peaks – three of them Munros – sweep straight out of the sea, shrouded for much of the time in a pall of grey mist. To get to the heart of the peninsula, you must catch a **boat** from Mallaig, or else **hike** for a couple of days across rugged moorland and mountains and sleep rough in old stone bothies (most of which are marked on Ordnance Survey maps).

At the end of the eighteenth century, around a thousand people eked out a living from this inhospitable terrain through crofting and fishing. These days the peninsula supports around seventy, most of whom live in the hamlet of **INVERIE**. Nestled beside a sheltered bay on the south side of the peninsula, it has a pint-sized post office, a shop, and mainland Britain's most remote pub.

ARRIVAL AND DEPARTURE
THE KNOYDART PENINSULA

By ferry Western Isles Cruises (☎01687 462233, ⓦwesternislescruises.co.uk) sails to Inverie from Mallaig

(April–Oct Mon–Sat 2 daily; 50 min).

ACCOMMODATION AND EATING

★**Doune Stone Lodges** Doune ☎01687 462667, ⓦdoune-knoydart.co.uk. Rebuilt from ruined crofts and offering pine-fitted en-suite doubles right on the shore, this place combines isolation with creature comforts. It's not easy to get to by land, but they'll pick you up by boat from Mallaig (£30/person). Minimum stay three nights. Full board. **£80**

Knoydart Foundation Bunkhouse Inverie ☎01687 462163, ⓦknoydart-foundation.com. A simple and straightforward option, with dorm rooms, a kitchen and a

sitting room housed in old steadings a 10min walk from the Old Forge. **£17**

★**Old Forge** Inverie ☎01687 462267, ⓦtheoldforge .co.uk. The Old Forge is one of Scotland's finest pubs, with a convivial atmosphere where visitors and locals mix happily. Generous bar meals (from £10) often feature freshly-caught seafood. There's also real ale, an open fire, and a good chance of live music in the evening. Mon–Thurs & Sun 11am–midnight, Fri & Sat 11am–1am; food served noon 3pm & 6.30 9.30pm.

Kyle of Lochalsh and around

As the main gateway to Skye, **KYLE OF LOCHALSH** used to be an important transit point for tourists and locals. However, with the building of the **Skye Bridge** in 1995, Kyle was left as merely the terminus for the train route from Inverness, with little else to offer. Of more interest is nearby **Eilean Donan Castle**, perched at the end of a stone causeway on the shores of **Loch Duich**. A few miles north of Kyle of Lochalsh is the delightful village of **Plockton**, a refreshing alternative to its utilitarian neighbour, with cottages grouped around a yacht-filled bay and Highland cattle wandering the streets.

ARRIVAL AND DEPARTURE
KYLE OF LOCHALSH

By train The station is at the southern end of town, off Station Road.
Destinations Dingwall (Mon–Sat 4 daily, Sun 2 daily; 2hr), Inverness (Mon–Sat 4 daily, Sun 2 daily; 2hr 40min) and Plockton (Mon–Sat 4 daily, Sun 2 daily; 10min).
By bus Buses run to Kyle of Lochalsh from Glasgow (3

daily; 5hr 15min) via Fort William (1hr 50min) and Invergarry (1hr 15min), and from Inverness (3 daily; 2hr) via Invermoriston, and all continue at least as far as Portree on Skye: book in advance for all of them (☎08712 663333, ⓦcitylink.co.uk). Buses also shuttle across the bridge to Kyleakin on Skye every 30min or so (7min).

Eilean Donan Castle

10 miles north of Shiel Bridge on the A87; take bus #917 from Kyle of Lochalsh (around 7 daily; 15min) • Daily Feb–Dec 10am–6pm (last admission 5pm) • £6.50 • ☎01599 555202, ⓦeileandonancastle.com

Eilean Donan Castle is one of Scotland's most photographed monuments. The forbidding crenellated tower rises from the water's edge, joined to the shore by a narrow stone bridge and with sheer mountains as a backdrop. The original castle was established in 1230 by Alexander II to protect the area from the Vikings. Later, during a Jacobite uprising in 1719, it was occupied by troops dispatched by the king of Spain to help the "**Old Pretender**", James Stuart. However, when King

George heard of their whereabouts, he sent frigates to take the Spaniards out, and the castle was blown up with their stocks of gunpowder. Thereafter, it lay in ruins until John Macrae-Gilstrap had it rebuilt between 1912 and 1932. Eilean Donan has since featured in several major **films**, including *Highlander*, *Entrapment*, and the James Bond adventure *The World is Not Enough*. Three floors, including the banqueting hall, the bedrooms and the troops' quarters, are open to the public, with various Jacobite and clan relics also on display, though like many of the region's most popular castles, the large numbers of people passing through make it hard to appreciate the real charm of the place.

Plockton

At the seaward end of islet-studded Loch Carron lies the unbelievably picturesque village of **PLOCKTON**: a chocolate-box row of neatly painted cottages ranged around the curve of a tiny harbour and backed by a craggy landscape of heather and pine. The unique brilliance of Plockton's light has also made it something of an artists' hangout, and during the summer the waterfront, with its row of shaggy palm trees, even shaggier Highland cattle, flower gardens and pleasure boats, is invariably dotted with painters dabbing at their easels.

ARRIVAL AND ACCOMMODATION
PLOCKTON

By train Trains run from Plockton's station, half a mile south of the village centre, to Kyle of Lochalsh (4 daily; 12min) and Inverness (4 daily; 2hr 20min).

By bus Buses from Kyle of Lochalsh (Mon–Fri 1 daily; 15min) stop on the road outside the station.

Plockton Hotel 41 Harbour St ☏01599 544274, ⓦplocktonhotel.co.uk. This waterfront hotel has comfortable, contemporary rooms (some of which have excellent views of the harbour) and serves fresh local seafood in its restaurant (mains around £15). There are cheaper rooms in an annexe a few doors down. Daily 6–9pm. Annexe **£80**, doubles **£130**

Tigh Arran In Duirinish, 2 miles south of Plockton ☏01599 544307, ⓦplocktonbedandbreakfast.com. In the gorgeous village of Duirinish, where hairy Highland cows come to drink from a gentle stream, this B&B feels a lot like a family home. Its rooms are bright and airy, with nice extras like DVD players and iPod docks. **£60**

Wester Ross

The western seaboard of the old county of Ross-shire, **Wester Ross** blends all the classic elements of Scotland's **coastal scenery** – dramatic mountains, sandy beaches, whitewashed crofting cottages and shimmering island views – in spectacular fashion. Though popular with generations of adventurous Scottish holiday-makers, only one or two places feel blighted by tourist numbers, with places such as **Applecross** and the peninsulas north and south of **Gairloch** maintaining an endearing simplicity and sense of isolation. There's some tough but wonderful **hiking** to be enjoyed in the mountains around **Torridon** and **Coigach**, while **boat trips** out among the islands and the prolific sea- and birdlife of the coast are another draw. The main settlement is the attractive fishing town of **Ullapool**, port for ferry services to Stornoway in the Western Isles, but a pleasant enough place to use as a base, not least for its active social and cultural scene.

The Applecross peninsula

The most dramatic approach to the **Applecross peninsula** (the English-sounding name is a corruption of the Gaelic *Apor Crosan*, meaning "estuary") is from the south, up a glacial U-shaped valley and over the infamous **Bealach na Bà** (literally "Pass of the Cattle"). Crossing the forbidding hills behind Kishorn, and rising to 2053ft, with a gradient and switchback bends worthy of the Alps, this route – a popular cycling piste – is hair-raising in places, and the panoramic views across the Minch to Raasay and Skye augment the experience.

Applecross

The sheltered, fertile coast around **APPLECROSS** village, where the Irish missionary monk Maelrhuba founded a monastery in 673 AD, comes as a surprise after the bleakness of the moorland approach. Maybe it's the journey, but Applecross feels like an idyllic place: you can wander along lanes banked with wild iris and orchids, and explore beaches and rock pools on the shore.

ARRIVAL AND ACCOMMODATION   APPLECROSS

By bus Buses operated by Lochcarron Garage (●01520 722205) make a loop from the post office in Applecross to Inverness and back twice a week (Wed & Sat). Book in advance.
Applecross Inn ●01520 744262, ●applecross .uk.com. This old, family-run inn right beside the sea is the focal point of the community, with rooms upstairs, and a lively bar that serves delicious local produce and seafood (fish pie £10.50). Food served daily noon–9pm. **£130**

Potting Shed Café and Restaurant A mile down the road from the village ●01520 744440, ●apple crossgarden.co.uk. This is a culinary and visual delight, where the walled Victorian garden, woods and sea provide fresh, rich pickings for the chefs, who serve delicious dishes in a laidback atmosphere. Fairly inexpensive in its daytime incarnation as a café, it's pricier in the evening (most mains around £18). Daily 8.30am–8.30pm.

Loch Torridon

Loch Torridon marks the northern boundary of the Applecross peninsula, its awe-inspiring setting enhanced by the appealingly rugged mountains of **Liathach** and **Beinn Eighe**, hulks of reddish 750-million-year-old Torridonian sandstone tipped by streaks of white quartzite. Some 15,000 acres of the massif are under the protection of the National Trust for Scotland, which runs a **Countryside Centre**, by Torridon village at the head of the loch (Easter–Sept Sun–Fri 10am–5pm; free), where you can learn about the local geology, flora and fauna.

ARRIVAL AND ACCOMMODATION   LOCH TORRIDON

By bus Buses operated by Lochcarron Garage (●01520 722205) travel from Applecross to Inverness twice a week (Wed & Sat; full journey 3hr 15min), skirting the southern edge of the loch and stopping off at Achnasheen. Book ahead.
SYHA Torridon At the eastern end of Upper Loch Torridon, in the village ●01445 791284, ●syha.org .uk. The building housing this SYHA might be dated, but the location – right at the foot of the mountains – is

timeless. There are dorms, private rooms, two lounges, plus a drying room and a self-catering kitchen. Dorms **£20**, twins **£48**
Torridon By Achnasheen, just off the A896 ●01445 700300, ●thetorridon.com. On the south side of the loch stands one of the area's grandest hotels, a smart, rambling Victorian building set amid well-tended lochside grounds. **£235**

Loch Maree

About eight miles north of Loch Torridon, **Loch Maree**, dotted with Caledonian pine-covered islands, is one of the west's scenic highlights. It's best visited by car

---

WALKS AROUND TORRIDON

There can be difficult conditions on virtually all hiking routes around Torridon, and the weather can change rapidly. If you're relatively inexperienced but want to do the magnificent ridge walk along the **Liathach** (pronounced "lee-ach") massif, or the strenuous traverse of **Beinn Eighe** (pronounced "ben ay"), join a National Trust Ranger Service guided hike (July & Aug; Torridon Countryside Centre; ●01445 791221).

A rewarding walk, even in rough weather, is the seven-mile hike up the coast from **Lower Diabaig**, ten miles northwest of Torridon village, to **Redpoint**. On a clear day, the views across to Raasay and Applecross from this gentle path are superlative, but you'll have to return along the same trail, or else make your way back via Loch Maree on the A832. The *Ordnance Survey Explorer Map* no. 433 is particularly useful for Torridon.

23

and viewed from the A832 road that skirts the loch's southern shore, passing the **Beinn Eighe Nature Reserve**, the UK's oldest wildlife sanctuary. Parts of the reserve are forested with Caledonian pinewood, which once covered the whole of the country, and it is home to pine marten, wildcat, buzzards and golden eagles. A mile north of Kinlochewe, the well-run **Beinn Eighe Visitor Centre** (April–Oct daily 9am–5pm) on the A832, offers excellent information on the area's rare species.

Gairloch and around

GAIRLOCH spreads itself around the northeastern corner of the wide sheltered bay of Loch Gairloch. During the summer, Gairloch thrives as a low-key holiday resort with several tempting sandy beaches and some excellent coastal walks within easy reach. The main supermarket and **tourist office** (see below) are in Achtercairn, right by the **Gairloch Heritage Museum** (April–Oct Mon–Fri 10am–5pm, Sat 11am–3pm; £4), which has eclectic, appealing displays covering geology, archeology, fishing and farming.

The Gairloch coast

The area's main attraction is its beautiful coastline, easily explored on a wildlife-spotting **cruise**: several operators, including Gairloch Marine Life Centre & Cruises (Easter–Oct 3 daily; ☎01445 712636, ⓦporpoise-gairloch.co.uk; from £20), run informative and enjoyable boat trips across the bay from Gairloch in search of dolphins, seals and even the odd whale. One of the most impressive stretches of **coastline** is around the north side of the bay, along the singletrack B8021, at **BIG SAND**, which has a cleaner and quieter beach than Gairloch. Three miles beyond is the **Rubha Reidh lighthouse** (see opposite).

Three miles south of Gairloch, a narrow singletrack lane winds west to **BADACHRO**, a sleepy former fishing village in a very attractive setting with a wonderful **pub**. Beyond Badachro, the road winds for five more miles along the shore to **REDPOINT**, a straggling hamlet with beautiful beaches of peach-coloured sand and great views to Raasay, Skye and the Western Isles.

Inverewe Garden

Around 6 miles northeast of Gairloch on the A832 • **Visitor centre and gardens** Daily: April & Sept 10am–5pm; May 10am–5.30pm; June–Aug 9.30am–6pm **Gardens only** Nov–March 10am–3pm • £10.50; NTS • ☎08444 932225

Run by the National Trust for Scotland, **Inverewe Garden** is located in the trim little village of **Poolewe**, which sits by a small bay at the sheltered southern end of Loch Ewe. A verdant oasis of foliage and riotously colourful flower collections, the garden forms a vivid contrast to the wild, heathery crags of the adjoining coast. Taking advantage of the area's famously temperate climate (a consequence of the Gulf Stream, which draws a warm sea current from Mexico to within a stone's throw of these shores), plants from all over the world grow here, flourishing on rich soil brought over as ballast on Irish ships to overlay the previously infertile beach gravel and sea grass. The **visitor centre** houses an informative display on the history of the garden and is the starting point for **guided walks**.

ARRIVAL AND INFORMATION

By bus Public transport options are extremely limited, but with careful planning it's possible to get to and from Gairloch. Buses stop near *The Old Inn* on the A832. Destinations Inverness (Mon, Wed & Sat 1 daily; 2hr 40min); Torridon (Mon–Fri 1 daily; 1hr).

GAIRLOCH AND AROUND

Tourist information The tourist office is within the large, wooden-built Gale Centre (☎01445 712071; Mon–Sat 10am–5pm, Sun 11am–5pm), on the road leading south out of town. There's a café onsite, as well as a fridge stocked with local seafood to buy and cook at home.

ACCOMMODATION AND EATING

Gairloch has a good choice of accommodation, but you might prefer to stay out along the road north to **Melvaig** or south to **Redpoint** (see above).

Badachro Inn Badachro ☎01445 741255, ⓦbadachro
inn.com. Right by the water's edge: you can sit in the
beer garden watching the boats come and go and tuck into
fresh seafood (creel-caught local prawns £14.25) with a
pint of real ale. Mon–Sat noon–midnight, Sun
12.30–11.30pm.

Dry Island The island immediately north of
Badachro Inn ☎01445 741263, ⓦdryisland.co.uk. A
rickety footbridge leads across to this tiny private island,
which has two small and simple self-catering cottages,
one with its own deck overlooking the loch. One of the
owners, Ian, is a fisherman and regularly takes visitors
on shellfish safaris. Min stay one week. Cottage **£450**

Kerrysdale House South of the harbour, off the A832
☎01445 712292, ⓦkerrysdalehouse.co.uk. At the
southern edge of Gairloch, just before the turn-off to
Badachro, this atmospheric and tastefully furnished place
is set back in its own lovely gardens. **£68**

★**Mountain Coffee** The harbour ☎01445 712006,
ⓦtheoldinn.net. Long running, eco-minded bookshop
and cafe where acoustic tunes fill the air and bits of old
travel and adventure memorabilia clutter the walls. A cup

of coffee and a slice of their chewy Rocky Road cake
shouldn't cost you more than a fiver. Daily 9am–6pm,
closes earlier in winter.

★**Rua Reidh Lighthouse** Rubha Reidh ☎01445
771263, ⓦwww.ruareidh.co.uk. Marooned 3 miles
beyond Big Sand at Rubha Reidh (pronounced "roo-a-ray"),
this working lighthouse has mesmerizing sea views, plus
recently refreshed doubles and family rooms (£100) offered
on a bed and breakfast basis (min stay 2 nights). **£55**

Sands Caravan and Camping Just south of Big
Sand ☎01445 712152, ⓦsandscaravanandcamping
.co.uk. Camp among the sand dunes and wake up to
stunning sea views at this well-run site. If pitching your
own tent sounds too much like hard work, stay in one of the
heated wooden "wigwams", which sleep three to five
people. April–Sept. Pitches **£15**, wigwam **£32**

The Steading Right by the museum ☎01445
712382. Modern, bistro-style place strung out with
pretty fairy lights. Here you can grab a cheap breakfast
in a tasty lunchtime sharing platter (a selection of
Scottish and continental cheeses costs £12.95). Daily
9.30am–8pm.

Ullapool

ULLAPOOL, northwest Scotland's principal centre of population, was founded at the
height of the herring boom in 1788 by the British Fisheries Society, on a sheltered arm
of land jutting into Loch Broom. The grid-plan town is still an important fishing
centre, though the **ferry** link to Stornoway on Lewis (see p.939) ensures that in high
season it's swamped with visitors. Though busy, Ullapool remains a hugely appealing
place and a good base for exploring the northwest Highlands.

By day, Ullapool's attention focuses on the comings and goings of the ferry, fishing
boats and smaller craft, while in the evening, yachts swing on the current, shops stay
open late, and drinkers line the sea wall. In summer, trips head to the **Summer Isles** –
a cluster of uninhabited islets a couple of miles offshore – to view seabird colonies,
dolphins and porpoises.

The only formal attraction in town is the award-winning **museum**, in the old parish
church on West Argyle Street (April–Oct Mon–Sat 10am–5pm, otherwise call ahead;
☎01854 612987; £3.50), which provides an insight into life in a Highland community,
including crofting, fishing, local religion and emigration.

ARRIVAL AND DEPARTURE   ULLAPOOL

By bus Buses stop near Ullapool's ferry terminal and run to
Durness (May, June & Sept Mon–Sat 1 daily, July & Aug 1
daily; 3hr) and Inverness (1–3 daily; 1hr 30min).

By ferry From the ferry dock along Shore Street, CalMac
(☎0870 565 0000, ⓦcalmac.co.uk) sails to Stornoway and
Lewis (Mon–Sat 2 daily, Sun 1 daily; 2hr 45min).

ACCOMMODATION

Broomfield Holiday Park West Shore St ☎01854
612020, ⓦbroomfieldhp.com. Large, good value
campsite, conveniently located within walking distance of
the harbour. It's exposed to the wind off Loch Broom, but
offers great views and warm showers. Pitches **£15**

★**The Ceilidh Place** 14 West Argyle St ☎01854
612103, ⓦtheceilidhplace.com. Each bedroom comes

with its own handpicked selection of books at this
charismatic place, renowned for its live music and
ceilidhs. Food is served in the excellent café-bar (see
p.914) and there's a bookshop specializing in Scottish
literature, history and art. You can also reserve a bed in
its small bunkhouse across the road. Bunkhouse **£21**,
doubles **£116**

23

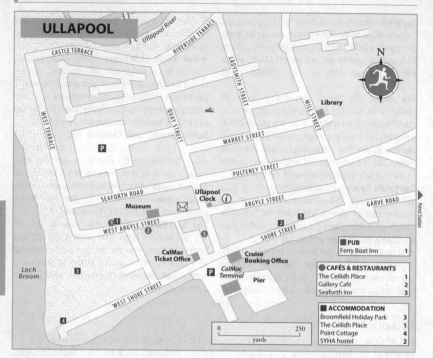

■ PUB	
Ferry Boat Inn	1

● CAFÉS & RESTAURANTS	
The Ceilidh Place	1
Gallery Café	2
Seaforth Inn	3

■ ACCOMMODATION	
Broomfield Holiday Park	3
The Ceilidh Place	1
Point Cottage	4
SYHA hostel	2

Point Cottage 22 West Shore St ☎01854 335062, ⓦpointcottagebandb.co.uk. Watch the ferries sail in from the comfort of this bright, seafront B&B in a quiet part of the centre. Rooms are decorated with subtle hints of tartan, and there's free wi-fi. **£75**

SYHA Hostel Shore St ☎01854 612254, ⓦsyha.org.uk.

Busy but well-kept, this SYHA hostel on the main road running along the waterfront has a cheery maritime theme plus internet access, laundry facilities and lots of good information about local walks. Open March–Oct. Dorms **£20**, doubles **£45**

EATING, DRINKING AND ENTERTAINMENT

The Ceilidh Place 14 West Argyle St ☎01854 612103, ⓦtheceilidhplace.com. A popular spot for lunch, snacks and dinners (their lovely, earthy, venison casserole costs £15.50) in a pleasant bistro. They also hold regular ceilidhs and music nights. Daily 8am–1am.

Ferry Boat Inn Shore St ☎01854 612366, ⓦfbiulla pool.com. You can enjoy a pint of real ale at the "FBI" on the lochside – midges permitting – as well as live Scottish folk music. The pub also has a bistro-style restaurant serving locally sourced seafood (langoustines £17.95). Mon–Thurs noon–10pm, Fri & Sat 11am–10.30pm, Sun noon–9pm.

Gallery Café West Argyle Street ☎01854 613769. Framed photos of the local area adorn the walls of this big, independent café hidden away above a shop selling outdoor equipment. A full cooked breakfast (with haggis and tattie scones) costs around £5.50. Daily 9am–4.30pm.

Seaforth Inn Quay St ☎01854 612122, ⓦtheseaforth .com. Though the interior is hardly intimate, this busy bar/ restaurant serves terrific-value mains (around £10) and starters, including a scrumptious fish pie. They also host regular live music performances. Mon–Sat 9am–1am, Sun noon–midnight.

Assynt

If you've travelled to the northwest of Scotland and come as far as Ullapool, it's worth continuing further north into the ever more dramatic, remote and highly distinctive hills of **Assynt**, which marks the transition from Wester Ross into Sutherland. One of the least populated areas in Europe, this is a landscape not of mountain ranges but of extraordinary peaks rising from the moorland.

Achiltibuie

North of Loch Broom and accessible via a slow, winding singletrack road off the A835 is **ACHILTIBUIE**. This old crofting village is the main settlement on the **Coigach Peninsula**, a narrow spit of land that juts out into the sea just north of Ullapool. The village is scattered across the hillside above a series of white-sand coves and rocks, from where a fleet of small fishing boats carries sheep, and tourists, to the enticing pastures of the **Summer Isles**, lying a little way offshore. The largest, Tanera Mòr, made news in 2013 when it was put up for sale at £2.5m. Though by late 2014, with the price slashed to less than £2m, no buyer had been found.

ARRIVAL AND ACCOMMODATION | ACHILTIBUIE

By bus Scotbus #811 connects Ullapool's ferry terminal with Achiltibuie (Mon–Sat 2 daily, Sun 1 daily; 1hr 10min). Cruises to the Summer Isles (Mon–Sat; summer only) run from the waterfront in Ullapool. See ⓦsummerqueen .co.uk for details.

Summer Isles Hotel Achiltibuie ☎01854 622282, ⓦsummerisleshotel.co.uk. This smart hotel enjoys a perfect setting with views over the islands. It's also a memorable, if pricey, spot for dinner (the set menu, which changes daily and costs £59/person, is published online each morning). April–Oct. **£155**

Lochinver and around

Sixteen miles north of Ullapool (although more than thirty by road), **LOCHINVER** is one of the busiest fishing harbours in Scotland, from where large trucks head off for the continent. The potholed and narrow road that leads there from Achiltibuie, passing through Inverkirkaig on the way, is unremittingly spectacular. It threads its way through a tumultuous landscape of heaving valleys, moorland and bare rock, past the distinctive, mound-shaped **Suilven** (2398ft).

The first village worthy of a detour on the road north is **ACHMELVICH**, three miles northwest of Lochinver, where a tiny bay cradles a stunning white-sand beach lapped by startlingly turquoise water. However, for total peace and quiet, head to other, equally seductive beaches beyond the headlands.

ARRIVAL AND DEPARTURE | LOCHINVER AND AROUND

By bus Lochinver has connections with Inverness (May, June & Sept Mon–Sat 1 daily, July & Aug 1 daily; 2hr 45min) and Ullapool (July & Aug 1–3 daily, Sept–June Mon–Sat 1–3 daily; 1hr).

The north coast

Though a constant stream of sponsored walkers, caravans and tour groups makes it to the dull town of **John O'Groats**, surprisingly few visitors travel the whole length of the Highlands' wild **north coast**. Those that do, however, rarely return disappointed. Pounded by one of the world's most ferocious seaways, Scotland's rugged northern shore is backed by barren mountains in the west, and in the east by lochs and open rolling grasslands. Between its far ends, miles of crumbling cliffs and sheer rocky headlands shelter bays whose perfect white beaches are nearly always deserted, even in the height of summer – though, somewhat incongruously, they're also home to Scotland's best **surfing** waves.

Durness is a good jumping-off point for nearby **Balnakiel beach**, one of the area's most beautiful sandy strands, and for rugged **Cape Wrath**, the windswept promontory at Scotland's northwest tip. **Thurso**, the largest town on the north coast, is really only visited by those en route to Orkney. More enticing are the huge seabird colonies clustered in clefts and on remote stacks at **Dunnet Head** and **Duncansby Head**, to the east of Thurso.

23

Durness and around

Scattered around a string of sheltered sandy coves and grassy clifftops, **DURNESS** is the most northwesterly village on the British mainland. It straddles the turning point on the main A838 road as it swings east from the inland peat bogs of the interior to the north coast's fertile strip of limestone machair. Durness village sits above its own sandy bay, Sango Sands, while half a mile to the east is **SMOO**, formerly an RAF station. In between Durness and Smoo is the village hall, whose windblown and rather forlorn community garden harbours a memorial commemorating the Beatle **John Lennon**, who used to come to Durness on family holidays as a child (and revisited the place in the 1960s with Yoko). It's worth pausing at Smoo to see the 200ft-long **Smoo Cave** (free to access; though tours deeper into the cave run during summer; £4), a gaping hole in a sheer limestone cliff formed partly by the action of the sea and partly by the small burn that flows through it.

ARRIVAL AND ACCOMMODATION

DURNESS

23

By bus Public transport to Durness is sparse; the key service is the D&E Coaches link (May, June & Sept Mon–Sat 1 daily; July & Aug Mon–Sun 1 daily; 5hr 20min) from Inverness via Ullapool and Lochinver.

★ **Lazy Crofter Bunkhouse** At the western edge of the village ☎01971 511202, ⓦvisitdurness.com. Run by the proprietors of *Mackay's* next door, this attractive bunkhouse is brightly furnished and has its own snug,

wood-panelled living room, along with a well-equipped kitchen. **£17.50**

★ **Mackay's** At the western edge of the village ☎01971 511202, ⓦvisitdurness.com. Vintage furnishings and subtle touches of tartan make this B&B a rewarding place to spend the night. The same people run a couple of slick, ecofriendly cottages nearby (min stay one week). Doubles **£110**, cottage **£1500**

Cape Wrath

Two miles southwest of Durness at **KEOLDALE**, a foot-passenger **ferry** (May 2 daily; June–Sept several daily; ☎01971 511246; £6 return) crosses the spectacular Kyle of Durness estuary. The ferry, which only runs when the tides allow, links with a **minibus** (May–Sept; ☎01971 511284; £10–12, depending on the month) that runs the eleven miles out to **Cape Wrath**, mainland Britain's most northwesterly point. Note that nearby Garvie Island (An Garbh-eilean) is an air bombing range, and the military regularly closes the road to Cape Wrath. The headland takes its name not from the stormy seas that crash against it for most of the year, but from the Norse word *hvarf*, meaning "turning place" – a throwback to the days when Viking warships used it as a navigation point during raids on the Scottish coast.

Tongue and around

Arriving from the west, the road to the pretty crofting village of **TONGUE** takes a wonderfully slow and circuitous route around Loch Eriboll and east over the top of A' Mhoine moor. The village is dominated by the ruins of **Castle Varrich** (Caisteal Bharraich), a medieval stronghold of the Mackay clan – it's a three-mile return walk from the centre.

Tongue itself is strewn above the east shore of the **Kyle of Tongue**, which you can either cross via a new causeway or by following the longer and more scenic singletrack road around its southern side. When the tide recedes, this shallow estuary becomes a mass of golden sand flats, superb on sunny days, with the sharp profiles of **Ben Hope** (3040ft), the most northerly Munro, and **Ben Loyal** (2509ft) looming like twin sentinels to the south.

ARRIVAL AND ACCOMMODATION

TONGUE AND AROUND

By bus Stagecoach bus #73 connects Tongue with Thurso (Mon–Fri 1 daily, Sat 2 daily; 1hr 50min) and Bettyhill

(Mon–Sat 2 daily; 35min). The buses pull up outside the *Tongue Hotel*, on the A838.

Kyle of Tongue Hostel Beside the causeway, a mile north of the village centre on the Kyle's eastern shore ☎01847 611 789, ⓦtonguehostelandholidaypark.co .uk. Former SYHA hostel in a nice old stone lodge with big windows that let the light flood in. Some rooms have views over the Kyle; the dorms are single-sex only, with high ceilings and wide bunks. There's also a tidy living area with sofas to crash out on after a hard day's exploring. Dorms £18, doubles £46

Tongue Hotel On the A838, close to the junction with Loyal Terrace ☎01847 611206, ⓦtonguehotel.co.uk. The best accommodation in Tongue is this nineteen-bedroom hotel, the former hunting lodge of the Duke of Sutherland, which is warmed by open fires and decorated with antique furnishings. £90

Bettyhill and around

BETTYHILL is a major crofting village set among rocky green hills, 25 miles east of Tongue. The village's splendid, sheltered **Farr beach** forms an unbroken arc of pure white sand between the Naver and Borgie rivers. Even more visually impressive is the River Naver's narrow tidal estuary, to the west of Bettyhill, and **Torrisdale beach**, which ends in a smooth white spit that forms part of the **Invernaver Nature Reserve**.

The Flow Country

At a junction around fifteen miles west of Thurso you can head forty miles or so south towards Helmsdale on the A897, through the fascinating blanket bog of the **Flow Country**, whose name comes from *flói*, an Old Norse word meaning "marshy ground". At the train station at **FORSINARD**, fourteen miles south of Melvich and easily accessible from Thurso, Wick and the south, there is an **RSPB visitor centre** (Easter–Oct daily 9am–5pm; ☎01641 571225l; free), which acts as the gateway to the so-called Forsinard Flows – a surprisingly rich and diverse nature reserve covering vast tracts of boggy peatland. Here you have a good chance of spotting dunlin, dippers and wading greenshanks, who use the boggy environment as a breeding ground.

Thurso

Approached from the isolation of the west, **THURSO** feels like a metropolis. In reality, it's a relatively small service centre visited mostly by people passing through to the adjoining port of **Scrabster** to catch the ferry to Orkney, or by increasing numbers of surfers attracted to the waves on the north coast. There's little to see, but the grid-plan streets have some rather handsome Victorian architecture in the local, greyish sandstone. If you're coming to **surf**, want a lesson or need to hire a board and wet suit (£20/day), head for Tempest Surf on Riverside Road (see p.918).

Caithness Horizons

High St • Mon–Sat 10am–6pm, Sun 11am–4pm • ☎01847 896508, ⓦcaithnesshorizons.co.uk
Caithness Horizons, housed in a revamped Victorian town hall, comprises a museum, tourist office and café (see p.918). The well-run and informative museum uses interactive technology and evocative old photos to explore local geology, history, farming and fishing, with treasures including a Bronze Age beaker and a Viking brooch.

ARRIVAL AND DEPARTURE	THURSO
By train Thurso station is near the town centre on Princes St. Destinations Dingwall (Mon–Sat 4 daily, Sun 1 daily; 3hr); Inverness (Mon–Sat 4 daily, Sun 1 daily; 3hr 40min); Lairg (Mon–Sat 4 daily, Sun 1 daily; 2hr); Wick (Mon–Sat 4 daily, Sun 1 daily; 35min). **By bus** Buses pass through the middle of town, stopping on the A9.	Destinations Inverness (up to 8 daily; 3–4hr); John O' Groats (Mon–Sat every 1–2hr; 1hr); Wick (Mon–Sat 1–2 hourly, Sun 5; 35min). **By ferry** Buses run from the A9 in the centre of town to the Scrabster ferry terminal, roughly 2 miles northwest of town, every hour or so. From there, ferries cross to Stromness on Orkney Mainland (2–3 daily; 90min).

23

ACCOMMODATION AND EATING

Captain's Galley The Harbour, Scrabster ☎ 01847 894999, ⓦ captainsgalley.co.uk. A former ice-house and salmon bothy close to the check-in for ferry departures which serves the best seafood in the area; a four-course dinner, with mains including hake with saffron potatoes, costs £49. Wed–Sat 7–9pm.

Gallery Café Caithness Horizons, High St ☎ 01847 896508, ⓦ caithnesshorizons.wordpress.com/cafe. The museum's cheerful daytime café serves sandwiches and soup (chicken broth £3.50). There's also home-baked goods, milkshakes and a special menu for kids. Mon–Sat 10am–6pm, Sun 11am–4pm.

The Marine 38 Shore Street ☎ 01847 890676, ⓦ themarinethurso.co.uk. You might not think it at first glance but the pebbledash facade of this B&B hides a row of modern rooms with gleaming en-suite bathrooms. Some have views across the water. **£99**

Murray House 1 Campbell St ☎ 01847 895759, ⓦ murrayhousebb.com. Central, comfortable and friendly guesthouse with five en-suite rooms, one of which is suitable for four people (£100). Two-night minimum stay may apply in high season. **£75**

Tempest Surf Café Riverside Rd ☎ 01847 892500, ⓦ cafetempest.co.uk. Inexpensive snacks by the harbour, and a great place to warm up after a play in the waves. Grab a bowl of steaming hot soup and a baguette (£7.45) and dig into some of the free-to-borrow books. Daily 10am–5pm.

Dunnet Head

Despite the publicity that John O'Groats customarily receives, mainland Britain's most northerly point is in fact **Dunnet Head**. It lies north of Dunnet along the B855, which runs for four miles over bleak heather and bog to the tip of the headland, crowned with a Stevenson lighthouse, at 344ft above sea level. On a clear day you can see the whole northern coastline from Cape Wrath to Duncansby Head, and across the treacherous Pentland Firth to Orkney.

Even if the weather isn't perfect, Dunnet Bay's vast golden beach, backed by huge dunes, is a great place to sink your toes into sand. The bay is enormously popular with surfers, too – even in the winter you can usually spot intrepid figures far out in the Pentland Firth's breakers. To reach **Dunnet Bay** from Thurso, head five miles east along the A836.

ARRIVAL AND INFORMATION   DUNNET HEAD

By bus Bus #80 between Thurso and John O'Groats passes through Dunnet and Mey (Mon–Fri 8 daily, Sat 5 daily).

Tourist information At the northeast end of the bay is an unmanned information centre (Sun–Fri: April, May & Sept 2–5.30pm, July & Aug 10.30am–5.30pm; free) where you can pick up information on local history and nature walks.

The Castle of Mey

15 miles east of Thurso, just off the A836 • May–July & mid-Aug to Sept daily 10.20am–4pm • £11; grounds only £6.50 • ☎ 01847 851473, ⓦ castleofmey.org.uk • Buses run to the A836, a short walk from the castle, from Sir George's Street Church in Thurso (Mon–Fri 8 daily, Sat 5 daily; 30min)

The Queen Mother's former Scottish home, the **Castle of Mey**, is the most northerly castle on the UK mainland. It's a modest little place, hidden behind high flagstone walls, with great views north to Orkney, and a herd of the Queen Mother's beloved Aberdeen Angus grazing out front. She used to spend every August here, and unusually for a royal palace, it's remarkably unstuffy inside, the walls hung with works by local amateur artists (and watercolours by Prince Charles).

John O'Groats and around

From Olrig Street in Thurso, frequent buses (Mon–Fri 10 daily, Sat 5 daily; 50min) run to John O'Groats, stopping at the car park on the A99.

Romantics expecting to find a magical meeting of land and water at **JOHN O'GROATS** are invariably disenchanted – sadly it remains an uninspiring tourist trap.

The views north to Orkney are fine enough, but the village offers little more than a string of souvenir shops and cafés thronged with coach parties. A number of **boat trips** set off from here, with some operators offering whitewater rafting and others heading out to Duncansby Head and local seal colonies. The village gets its name from the Dutchman Jan de Groot, who obtained the ferry contract for the hazardous crossing to Orkney in 1496.

Duncansby Head

Duncansby Head, with its lighthouse, dramatic cliffs and well-worn coastal path, is a much more stimulating place to visit than dreary John O'Groats, which lies a couple of miles to the west. The birdlife around Duncansby Head is prolific, and south of the headland lie some spectacular 200ft cliffs, cut by sheer-sided clefts known locally as *geos*, and several impressive sea stacks.

The east coast

23

The **east coast** of the Highlands, between Inverness and Wick, is nowhere near as spectacular as the west, with gently undulating moors, grassland and low cliffs where you might otherwise expect to find sea lochs and mountains. While many visitors speed up the main A9 road through this region in a headlong rush to the Orkneys' prehistoric sites, those who choose to dally will find a wealth of brochs, cairns and standing stones, many in remarkable condition. The area around the Black Isle and the Tain was a Pictish heartland, and has yielded many important finds. Further north, from around the ninth century AD onwards, the **Norse** influence was more keenly felt than in any other part of mainland Britain, and dozens of Scandinavian-sounding names recall the era when this was a Viking kingdom.

The fishing heritage is a recurring theme along this coast, though there are only a handful of working boats scattered around the harbours today; the area remains one of the country's poorest, reliant on relatively thin pickings from sheep farming, fishing and tourism. The one stretch of the east coast that's always been relatively rich, however, is the **Black Isle** just over the Kessock Bridge heading north out of Inverness, whose main village, **Cromarty**, is the region's undisputed highlight. Beyond the golfing resort of **Dornoch**, the ersatz-Loire chateau **Dunrobin Castle** is the main tourist attraction, a monument as much to the iniquities of the Clearances as to the eccentricities of Victorian taste.

The Black Isle

Sandwiched between the Cromarty Firth to the north and, to the south, the Moray and Beauly firths which separate it from Inverness, the **Black Isle** is not an island at all, but a fertile peninsula whose rolling hills, prosperous farms and stands of deciduous woodland make it more reminiscent of Dorset or Sussex than the Highlands. It probably gained its name because of its mild climate: there's rarely frost, which leaves the fields "black" all winter; another explanation is that the name derives from the Gaelic word for black, *dubh* – a possible corruption of St Duthus. On the south side of the Black Isle, near Fortrose, **Chanonry Point** juts into a narrow channel in the Moray Firth and is an excellent place to look for **dolphins** (see box, p.895).

Cromarty

An ancient legend recalls that the twin headlands flanking the entrance to the **Cromarty Firth**, known as The Sutors (from the Gaelic word for shoemaker), were once a pair of giant cobblers who used to protect the Black Isle from pirates. Nowadays, however, the only giants in the area are the colossal oil rigs marooned in the estuary off Nigg and Invergordon like metal monsters marching out to sea. They form a surreal counterpoint to the web of tiny streets and charming workers' cottages of **CROMARTY**. The Black Isle's main settlement, Cromarty was an ancient ferry-crossing point on the pilgrimage trail to St Duthus's shrine in Tain, but lost much of its trade during the nineteenth century to places served by the railway; a branch line to the town was begun but never completed. Cromarty became a prominent port in 1772 when an entrepreneurial local landlord, George Ross, founded a hemp mill here, fuelling a period of prosperity during which Cromarty acquired some of Scotland's finest Georgian houses: these, together with the terraced fishers' cottages of the nineteenth-century herring boom, have left the town with a wonderfully well-preserved concentration of Scottish domestic architecture.

The **museum**, housed in the old **Courthouse** on Church Street (Easter–June & Sept–Oct Sun–Thurs noon–4pm, July & Aug daily noon–4pm; free), tells the history of the town using audiovisuals and animated figures. Dolphin- and other wildlife-spotting trips (£26; 2hr) are offered locally by EcoVentures (☎01381 600323, ⓦecoventures.co.uk), who travel out through the Sutors to the Moray Firth in a powerful RIB.

ARRIVAL AND DEPARTURE   CROMARTY

By bus Frequent services link the bus station in Inverness with Cromarty, stopping near the Victoria Hall on the High Street (Mon–Sat every 30min, Sun 4 daily; 1hr).
By ferry The tiny four-car Nigg–Cromarty ferry (every

30min: June & Sept Mon–Sat 8am–6.10pm, Sun 9am–6.10pm; July & Aug Mon–Sat 8am–7.10pm, Sun 9am–7.10pm; £4, £9 with a car) is one of Britain's smallest. Embark from the jetty near the lighthouse.

ACCOMMODATION AND EATING

★**Sutor Creek** 21 Bank St ☎01381 600855, ⓦsutorcreek.co.uk. There are few more down-to-earth but satisfying restaurants in the Highlands than this. It serves organic wines, delicious seafood and fresh pizza cooked in a wood-fired oven. Mains £8–22. Wed–Sun 11am–9pm.

Sydney House High St ☎01381 600451, ⓦsydney house.co.uk. A grand red-brick place that once had the distinction of being a temperance hotel, and now serves as a welcoming B&B with wrought-iron bedsteads and smart wooden furniture. **£70**

The Dornoch Firth and around

North of the Cromarty Firth, the hammer-shaped **Fearn peninsula** can still be approached from the south by the ancient ferry crossing from Cromarty to Nigg, though to the north the link is a causeway over the **Dornoch Firth**, the inlet that marks the northern boundary of the peninsula. On the southern edge of the Dornoch Firth the A9 bypasses the quiet town of **TAIN**, an attractive, old-fashioned small town of grand, whisky-coloured sandstone buildings that was the birthplace of **St Duthus**, an eleventh-century missionary who inspired great devotion in the Middle Ages. Tain's main attraction is the **Glenmorangie whisky distillery** where the highly rated malt is produced (☎01862 892477; tours every 30min–1hr; June–Aug Sat 10am–4pm, Sun noon–4pm; Sept–May Mon–Fri 10am–5pm; £5; booking advised); it lies beside the A9 on the north side of town.

Dornoch

DORNOCH, a genteel and appealing town eight miles north of Tain, lies on a flattish headland overlooking the **Dornoch Firth**. A middle-class holiday resort, with trees and flowers in profusion, solid Edwardian hotels, and miles of sandy beaches giving good views across the estuary to the Fearn peninsula, the town is renowned for its championship **golf course**, Scotland's most northerly first-class course.

ARRIVAL AND DEPARTURE   DORNOCH

By bus From Mon–Fri, buses run from the bus station in Inverness to Cathedral Square in Dornoch (1 daily; 1hr 50min).

ACCOMMODATION

Dornoch Castle Hotel Castle St ☎01862 810216, ⓦdornochcastlehotel.com. This fifteenth-century hotel, in the Bishop's Palace on the Square, has a decent restaurant and a cosy old-fashioned bar with a roaring, 11ft-wide log fire. Rooms range from fairly dull doubles overlooking the gardens to the splendid "Old Courtyard", with its impressive, hand-carved four-poster (£250). **£140**

Golspie

The straggling red-sandstone town of **GOLSPIE**, whose status as an administrative centre does little to relieve its dullness, sits ten miles north of Dornoch on the A9. It is, however, the jumping-off point for some brilliant **mountain biking**: the fabulous Highland Wildcat Trails (ⓦhighlandwildcat.com) are within the forested hills just half a mile to the west. The easy to severe (colour-coded) trails include a huge descent from the summit of Ben Bhraggie to sea level and a ride past the **Sutherland monument**, erected in memory of the landowner who oversaw the eviction of thousands of his tenants in a process known as the **Clearances**.

Dunrobin Castle

A mile north of Golspie • April, May, Sept & Oct Mon–Sat 10.30am–4.30pm, Sun noon–4.30pm; June–Aug daily 10am–5pm • £10.50 • ☎01408 633177, ⓦdunrobincastle.co.uk

Mountain-bikers aside, the main reason to stop at Golspie is to look around **Dunrobin Castle**, overlooking the sea north of town. This fairy-tale confection of turrets and pointed roofs – modelled by the architect Sir Charles Barry (designer of the Houses of Parliament) on a Loire chateau – is the seat of the infamous Sutherland family, at one time Europe's biggest landowners, with a staggering 1.3 million acres, and the principal driving force behind the Clearances in this area. The castle has 189 furnished rooms, but as a visitor you'll only be able to see a fraction of these. Staring up at the pile from its elaborate **formal gardens**, it's worth remembering that such extravagance was paid for by uprooting literally thousands of crofters from the surrounding glens.

Sutherland Monument

It's hard to miss the 100ft **monument** to the first Duke of Sutherland, which peers proprietorially down from the summit of the 1293ft **Beinn a'Bhragaidh** (Ben Bhraggie), immediately behind Golspie. An inscription cut into its base recalls that the statue was erected in 1834 by "a mourning and grateful tenantry [to] a judicious, kind and liberal landlord [who would] open his hands to the distress of the widow, the sick and the traveller". Unsurprisingly, there's no reference to the fact that the duke, widely regarded as Scotland's own Josef Stalin, forcibly evicted fifteen thousand crofters from his million-acre estate. It's worth the stiff **climb** to the top of the hill (round trip 1hr 30min) for the wonderful views south along the coast past Dornoch to the Moray Firth and west towards Lairg and Loch Shin. The path is steep and strenuous in places, however, and there's no view until you're out of the trees, about twenty minutes from the top.

ARRIVAL AND DEPARTURE · GOLSPIE

By bus Buses run to Golspie from Thurso (Mon–Sat 5 daily, Sun 4 daily; 1hr 40min) and Inverness (Mon–Sat 6 daily, Sun 4 daily; 1hr 15min).

By train Dunrobin Castle is a summer stop on the Inverness–Thurso line (April–Oct Mon–Sat 3 daily; 2hr 10min from Inverness, 1hr 35min from Thurso).

Helmsdale

HELMSDALE, eleven scenic miles north along the A9 from Golspie, is an old herring port, founded in the nineteenth century to house the evicted inhabitants of Strath Kildonan, which lies behind it. The Strath was the unlikely location of a gold rush in

23

the 1860s, and a few determined prospectors still pan the Kildonan Burn. The story of the area's gold hunters is told in the **Timespan Heritage Centre**, beside the river (daily 10am–5pm, with reduced hours from Nov–March; £4), along with tales of Viking raids, witch-burning, Clearances and fishing.

Just north of Helmsdale, the A9 begins its long haul up the **Ord of Caithness**, a busy, winding pass. Once over the pass, the landscape changes dramatically as heather-clad moors give way to miles of treeless green grazing lands, peppered with derelict crofts and latticed by long dry-stone walls. As you come over the pass, look out for signs to the ruined village of **Badbea**, a ten-minute walk from the car park at the side of the A9. Built by tenants cleared from nearby Ousdale, the settlement entered a slow decline and is now abandoned, its ruined hovels showing what hardship the crofters had to endure: the cottages stood so near the windy cliff edge that children had to be tethered to prevent them from being blown into the sea.

23

ARRIVAL AND DEPARTURE HELMSDALE

By bus From Golspie, buses run to a stop beside the   (Mon–Fri 3 daily; 30min).
roundabout in the centre of the town, right near the river

Lybster

The planned village of **LYBSTER** (pronounced "libe-ster"), nineteen miles north of the Ord of Caithness, was established at the height of the nineteenth-century herring boom, when 200-odd boats worked out of its harbour; now there are just one or two. The **Water Lines** heritage centre by the harbour (May–Sept daily 11am–5pm; suggested donation £2.50) is an attractive modern display about the "silver darlings" and the fishermen who pursued them; there's a snug café downstairs. There's not much else to see here beyond the harbour area.

ARRIVAL AND DEPARTURE LYBSTER

By bus Buses to and from Wick (Mon–Sat 8–9 daily, Sun 3; 25min) stop outside the post office on Greys Place.

Wick

Originally a Viking settlement named *Vik* (meaning "bay"), **WICK** has been a royal burgh since 1589. It's actually two towns: Wick proper, and **Pulteneytown**, south across the river, a messy, rather run-down community planned by Thomas Telford in 1806 to encourage evicted crofters to take up fishing. Wick's heyday was in the mid-nineteenth century when it was the busiest herring port in Europe, with a fleet of more than 1100 boats exporting tonnes of fish to Russia, Scandinavia and the West Indian slave plantations. Though redevelopment of the harbour is under way, the town still has a down-at-heel air. The area around the harbour in Pulteneytown, lined with rows of fishermen's cottages, is worth a wander, with acres of largely derelict net-mending sheds, stores and cooperages around the harbour giving some idea of the former scale of the fishing trade. The town's story is told in the rambling, cluttered **Wick Heritage Centre** in Bank Row, Pulteneytown (Easter–Oct Mon–Sat 10am–5pm; £4). The only other visitor attraction is the fairly simple **Pulteney Distillery** (May–Sept Mon–Fri 10am–5pm, Sat 10am–4pm; Oct–April Mon–Fri 10am–4pm; tours 11am & 2pm or by arrangement; ☎01955 602371, ⊛www.oldpulteney.com; £6) on nearby Huddart Street, a few blocks from the sea.

ARRIVAL AND DEPARTURE WICK

By plane The airport, just north of town, handles flights   (Mon–Fri 2–3 daily; 35min). Stagecoach bus #82 connects
for Edinburgh (Sun–Fri 1 daily; 1hr 10min) and Aberdeen   the airport with Wick and Thurso.

By train The train station is just north of the town centre. Destinations Dingwall (Mon–Sat 4 daily, Sun 1 daily; 3hr 40min); Inverness (Mon–Sat 4 daily, Sun 1 daily; 4hr); Lairg (Mon–Sat 4 daily, Sun 1 daily; 2hr 20min).

By bus Buses connect Wick's town centre with John O' Groats (Mon–Sat every 1–2 hr; 30min).

ACCOMMODATION AND EATING

The Clachan 13 Randolph Place ☎01955 605384, ⓦtheclachan.co.uk. A large white house on the main road through town with excellent rooms fitted with thick carpets (some tartan), spotless modern bathrooms, and good-quality cotton sheets. Friendly owner. **£65**

Mackay's South side of the river in the centre ☎01955 602323, ⓦmackayshotel.co.uk. Recently refurbished (and a little overpriced), this hotel has small but comfortable doubles and larger superior rooms with higher ceilings. There's a restaurant on the ground floor doing pub food (mains around £10). Daily 10.30am–9pm). **£112**

23

Skye and the Western Isles

CALANAIS STANDING STONES, LEWIS

Skye and the Western Isles

A procession of Hebridean islands, islets and reefs off the northwest shore of Scotland, Skye and the Western Isles between them boast some of the country's most alluring scenery. It's here that the turbulent seas of the Atlantic smash up against an extravagant shoreline hundreds of miles long, a geologically complex terrain whose rough rocks and mighty sea cliffs are interrupted by a thousand sheltered bays and, in the far west, a long line of sweeping sandy beaches. The islands' interiors are equally dramatic, a series of formidable mountain ranges soaring high above great chunks of boggy peat moor, a barren wilderness enclosing a host of lochans, or tiny lakes.

Each island has its own character, though the grouping splits quite neatly into two. **Skye** and the **Small Isles** – the improbably named **Rùm**, **Eigg**, **Muck** and **Canna** – are part of the Inner Hebrides. Beyond Skye, across the unpredictable waters of the Minch, lie the Outer Hebrides or **Western Isles**, a 130-mile-long archipelago stretching from **Lewis** and **Harris** in the north to **Barra** in the south. The whole region has four obvious areas of outstanding natural beauty to aim for: on Skye, the harsh peaks of the **Cuillin** and the bizarre rock formations of the **Trotternish** peninsula; on the Western Isles, the mountains of **North Harris** and the splendid sandy beaches that string along the seaboard of **South Harris** and the **Uists**.

24

Brief history

Skye and the Western Isles were first settled by Neolithic farming peoples in around 4000 BC. They lived along the coast, where they are remembered by scores of remains, most famously at **Callanish** (Calanais) on Lewis. Viking colonization gathered pace from 700 AD onwards and it was only in 1266 that the islands were returned to the Scottish Crown. James VI (James I of England), a Stuart and a Scot, though no Gaelic-speaker, was the first to put forward the idea of clearing the Hebrides. However, it wasn't until after the Jacobite uprisings in the eighteenth century, in which many Highland clans backed the losing side, that the **Clearances** began in earnest.

The isolation of the Hebrides exposed them to the whims and fancies of the various merchants and aristocrats who bought them up. Time and again, from the mid-eighteenth century to the present day, the land and its people were sold to the highest bidder. Some proprietors were well-meaning, others simply forced the inhabitants onto ships bound for North America. Despite this, their language survived, ensuring a degree of cultural continuity, especially in the Western Isles, where even today the first language of the majority remains **Gaelic** (pronounced "gallic").

ARRIVAL AND DEPARTURE   SKYE AND THE WESTERN ISLES

Most visitors reach Skye via the **Skye Bridge**, which sweeps across the sea from Kyle of Lochalsh, itself linked to Inverness by train. The more scenic approach is via **Armadale** on the Sleat peninsula, linked by CalMac car **ferry** (ⓦcalmac.co.uk) with Mallaig, at the end of the train line from Fort William. A third option is to arrive at **Kylerhea**, also on the Sleat peninsula, via the tiny **car ferry** (ⓦskyeferry.co.uk) that leaves from Glenelg, south of Kyle of Lochalsh.

If you're heading for the Western Isles, note that it's 57 miles from Armadale and 49 miles from Kyleakin to **Uig**, from where ferries leave for Tarbert on Harris and Lochmaddy on North Uist.

Bonnie Prince Charlie p.933   **Whisky Galore!** p.946
Gaelic in the Western Isles p.938

GEARRANNAN

Highlights

❶ Skye Cuillin These jagged peaks dominate and define Skye's landscape – they also contain twelve Munros and a challenging eight-mile ridge trail. **See p.930**

❷ Loch Coruisk, Skye Few sights in Scotland prepare you for the drama of this beautiful, remote glacial loch in the Cuillin – the boat ride there from Elgol just adds to the fun. **See p.930**

❸ Kinloch Castle, Rùm Visit or stay at this frankly bonkers Edwardian pile to discover the decadence of the landed gentry of the day. See p.936

❹ Garenin (Gearrannan), Lewis An abandoned crofting village whose thatched blackhouses have been restored as self-catering

cottages and a café – with a couple left as they were when last inhabited. See p.941

❺ Callanish (Calanais), Lewis Scotland's Stonehenge in a serene lochside setting on the west coast of Lewis. **See p.941**

❻ Beaches The western seaboard of the Outer Hebrides, particularly South Harris and the Uists, is scattered with stunning, mostly deserted, golden, sandy beaches backed by flower-strewn machair. **See p.942, p.943 & 945**

❼ Rodel (Roghadal) church, Harris Rodel's pre-Reformation St Clement's Church, at the southernmost tip of Harris, boasts the most ornate sculptural decoration in the Outer Hebrides. **See p.943**

HIGHLIGHTS ARE MARKED ON THE MAP ON P.928

Skye

Jutting out from the mainland like a giant butterfly, the bare and bony promontories of **Skye** fringe a deeply indented coastline. The island's most popular destination is the **Cuillin** ridge, whose jagged peaks dominate the island during clear weather. More accessible and equally dramatic are the rock formations of the **Trotternish** peninsula in the north, from which there are inspirational views across to the Western Isles. Of the two main settlements, **Portree** is the only one with any charm, and a useful base for exploring the Trotternish.

SKYE & THE WESTERN ISLES

0 — 20 miles

N

HIGHLIGHTS

1. Skye Cuillin
2. Loch Coruisk, Skye
3. Kinloch Castle, Rùm
4. Garenin (Gearrannan), Lewis
5. Callanish (Calanais), Lewis
6. Beaches
7. Rodel (Roghadal) Church, Harris

By bus Getting around Skye by bus is tricky. Services peter out in the more remote areas, and many close down on Sundays. If you are depending on buses, however, it may be worth buying a Skye dayrider ticket (£8.25/day). Check ⓦstagecoachbus.com for details of local transportation.

Sleat

Thanks to the CalMac ferries from Mallaig to **ARMADALE** (Armadal), many people's introduction to Skye is the **Sleat** (pronounced "Slate") peninsula, on Skye's southern tip, an uncharacteristically fertile area known as "The Garden of Skye".

Clan Donald Skye

On the A851 • April–Sept daily 9.30am–5.30pm; Oct daily 10am–5.30pm • £8 • ⓣ 01471 844305, ⓦ clandonald.com

Now branded as **Clan Donald Skye**, the ancestral home of the MacDonald clan is centred on the shell of the neo-Gothic **Armadale Castle** which houses a café and a library, for those who want to chase up their ancestral Donald connections. The gardens' slick, purpose-built **Museum of the Isles** has a good section on the Jacobite period and its aftermath and one or two top-notch works of art by Angelika Kaufmann and Henry Raeburn.

By ferry Car ferries run from Glenelg to Kylerhea (daily, frequently; 15min), and CalMac ferries travel from Mallaig to Armadale (Mon–Sat 8 daily, Sun 4–6 daily; 30min), for which reservations are recommended in peak season.
By bus All buses depart/arrive from Armadale Pier.

Destinations Portree (mid-June to early Sept Mon–Sat 5 daily, Sun 3 daily; mid-Sept to early June Mon–Sat 5 daily, 1hr 15min); Sligachan (mid-June to early Sept Mon–Sat 5 daily, Sun 3 daily; mid-Sept to early June Mon–Sat 5 daily; 1hr).

ACCOMMODATION AND EATING

Ardvasar Hotel Ardvasar, half a mile southwest of Armadale ⓣ01471 844223, ⓦardvasarhotel.com. This old-fashioned inn, recently refurbished to create comfortable contemporary accommodation, now has a smart restaurant specializing in local seafood – lobster, scallops and crab, plus Speyside beef, which costs around £14. **£130**
Eilian Iarmain Isleornsay, 6 miles northeast of Armadale ⓣ01471 833332, ⓦeileaniarmain.com. This small hotel is a charmer, romantically furnished with

antiques and pretty fabrics, awesome views and not a TV in sight. The restaurant serves venison with garlic and white truffle mash (mains £18–25), or there's bar food (mains around £13). **£170**
Flora MacDonald Hostel Kilmore, 4 miles north of Armadale ⓣ01471 844272, ⓦskye-hostel.co.uk. A bright, modern, community-run hostel that's definitely not a party destination. There's Eriskay ponies out the back and free wi-fi. Last check-in 8pm. Dorms **£16**, doubles **£42**

Kyleakin

The **Skye Bridge** rendered the ferry crossing from Kyle of Lochalsh redundant, leaving the tiny port of **KYLEAKIN** (Caol Acain – pronounced "Kalakin") well and truly bypassed, but bizarrely it's since become something of a backpackers' hangout. The bridge has been less kind to **Eilean Bàn**, an island from which the bridge leapfrogs to cross Loch Alsh. In 1968, the lighthouse keeper's cottage on the island briefly became the home of writer and naturalist Gavin Maxwell, author of *Ring of Bright Water*. The island now serves as a nature reserve and can be visited on tours booked through the **Bright Water Visitor Centre** (Easter–Sept 10am–4pm; ⓣ01599 530040, ⓦeileanban.org) in Kyleakin.

By bus Buses depart from the Shorefront Bus Shelter. Destinations Broadford (Mon–Sat hourly, Sun 3 daily; 15min); Kyle of Lochalsh (Mon–Sat hourly, Sun 3 daily;

10min); Portree (Mon–Sat 5 daily, Sun 3 daily; 1hr); Uig (Mon–Sat 2 daily; 1hr 20min).
Saucy Mary's Lodge Kyleakin ⓣ01599 534845,

24

ⓦsaucymarys.com. The largest hostel in the village has loch views and is popular with backpackers for its location above the pub – quieter accommodation for families is in an annexe, and the same owners also manage a B&B next door. Dorms £19.50, doubles £50

Isle of Raasay

Despite lying less than a mile offshore, the fourteen-mile long, hilly island of **Raasay** (Ratharsair) sees few visitors. Yet, in many ways, it's the ultimate Skye escape, with plenty of walks and that thrill of being cast away on a small island. For much of its history, Raasay belonged to a branch of the Jacobite MacLeods of Lewis. When the last laird sold up in 1843 and moved to Tasmania, the Clearances began. In 1921, several ex-servicemen and their families from neighbouring **Rona** were imprisoned after they squatted in crofts on Raasay. The public outcry led to both islands being bought by the government, and since then they have remained in state hands. Raasay's population continues to fall and is currently around 160. The ferry docks in Churchton Bay, near **INVERARISH** – the island's tiny village set within thick woods on the southwest coast.

The most obvious spot to head for in the island's interior is the curiously flat-topped volcanic plug of **Dun Caan** (1456ft) – the trail to the top of the peak is fairly easy to follow, a splendid five-mile trek up through the forest and along the burn behind Inverarish.

ARRIVAL AND ACCOMMODATION	ISLE OF RAASAY
By ferry CalMac ferries from Sconser arrive at Churchton Bay (Mon–Sat 8–10 daily, Sun 2 daily; 25min). **Raasay House** ☎ 01478 660300, ⓦraasay-house .co.uk. Accommodation at the MacLeods' rebuilt manor ranges from B&B in simple modern bunkrooms to large rooms with balconies and views to the Cuillin; camping is also available. It's also an outdoor centre – activities on offer (Easter–Oct, weather-dependent other months) range from guided walks and canyoning to coasteering,	kayaking and sailing. Camping per person £6, dorms £25, doubles £125 **Raasay SYHA hostel** ☎ 01478 660240, ⓦsyha.org.uk. A two-mile track from the wharf cuts up behind the village to Raasay's hostel, small and simple throughout – just one loo and one shower – but with beautiful views to the Skye Cuillin and well placed to explore the island. A superb getaway. Late May–Aug. Dorms £17.50, doubles £46

The Cuillin and the Red Hills

For many people, the **Cuillin** (An Cuiltheann), whose sharp peaks rise mirage-like from the flatness of the surrounding terrain, are Skye's raison d'être. When – if – the clouds disperse, they are the dominating feature of the island, visible from every other peninsula.

There are three **approaches** to the Cuillin: by foot or by boat from **Elgol** to the south; from the **Sligachan Hotel** to the north; or from **Glen Brittle** to the west of the mountains. The second route, down Glen Sligachan, divides the granite of the round-topped **Red Hills** (sometimes known as the Red Cuillin) to the east from the dark, coarse-grained, jagged-edged gabbro of the real Cuillin (also known as the Black Cuillin) to the west. With some twenty Munros between them, these are mountains to be taken seriously, and many routes through the Cuillin are for experienced climbers only.

Elgol and Loch Coruisk

The road to **ELGOL** (Ealaghol), at the tip of the Strathaird peninsula, is one of the most dramatic on the island, with a stunning view from the top down to Elgol pier. Weather permitting (April–Oct), you can take a **boat** from Elgol across Loch Scavaig, past a seal colony, to a jetty near the entrance to the glacial **Loch Coruisk**. A needle-like shaft of water nearly two miles long, but only a couple of hundred yards wide, Loch Coruisk lies in the shadow of the highest peaks of the Black Cuillin, a wonderfully overpowering landscape. The journey from Elgol takes about an hour and passengers are dropped to spend time ashore before returning to Elgol. **Walkers** can jump ship and hike amid the Red Hills, or over the pass into **Glen Sligachan**.

Glen Brittle

Six miles along the A863 to Dunvegan from the *Sligachan Hotel*, a turning signed "Carbost and Portnalong" quickly leads to the entrance to stony **Glen Brittle**, edging the most spectacular peaks of the Cuillin; at the end of the glen, idyllically situated by the sea, is the village of **GLENBRITTLE**. Climbers and serious walkers tend to congregate at the SYHA **hostel** or the beautifully situated **campsite**, both of which have the only grocery stores for miles.

From the valley a score of difficult and strenuous trails lead east into the **Black Cuillin**, a rough semicircle of peaks, rising to about 3000ft, which surround Loch Coruisk. One of the easiest walks is the five-mile round-trip (3hr) from the campsite up **Coire Làgan** to a crystal-cold lochan squeezed in among the sternest of rock faces. Above the lochan is Skye's highest peak, **Sgùrr Alasdair** (3258ft), one of the more difficult Munros; while Sgurr na Banachdich (3166ft), to the northwest, is considered the most easily accessible Munro in the Cuillin.

ARRIVAL AND DEPARTURE

By bus Elgol is accessed by bus from Broadford (Mon–Fri 3 daily, Sat 2 daily; 40min); Glenbrittle is connected to Portree (Mon–Fri 2 daily; 50min); Sligachan is a stop on the

THE CUILLIN AND THE RED HILLS

Broadford–Portree route (Mon–Sat 5–10 daily, Sun 3 daily; 40min).

ACCOMMODATION AND EATING

★**Coruisk House** Elgol ☏01471 866330, ⓦcoruiskhouse.com. A taste of Skye on unfussy, super-fresh menus – squat lobster in hazelnut butter, a famous fish pie, Soay lamb or rich Mull beef stews – with two courses from £20. Above are two beautiful cottage rooms of understated luxury: expect a relaxing night and an awesome breakfast. Reservation essential. Feb–Oct. **£110**

Glenbrittle Campsite ☏01478 640404. With sea views and the beach in front and mountains behind, this spacious, natural site is the best of both worlds. The midges are bad (May–Aug) unless there's a breeze. April–Nov. Per person **£7.50**

Glenbrittle SYHA hostel ☏01478 640278, ⓦsyha .org.uk. A recent refurb has had a hugely positive impact on this hostel at the foot of the Cuillin – old wood panelling and new leather sofas combine to form a sort of rugged

Scandi chic. Frozen prepared meals on offer. Easter–Sept. Dorms **£18**, twins **£49**

Sligachan Bunkhouse On A87 ☏01478 650458, ⓦsligachanselfcatering.co.uk. No-frills bunkhouse adjacent to the *Sligachan Hotel*. Within are large dorm rooms with some of the largest bunks you'll see, plus a laundry room, kitchen and lounge with fireplace. **£16**

Sligachan Hotel & Campsite On A87 ☏01478 650204, ⓦsligachan.co.uk. The *Sligachan*, the only hotel for miles and with a stunning location, doesn't have to try very hard. Alongside dated, but comfy enough, en-suite rooms, it maintains the barn-like *Seamus Bar* which serves hearty food to hungry hikers (mains around £10–12). A campsite is over the road – the midges in summer are almost as famous as the view. Hotel March–Oct; campsite all year round. Camping per person **£6**, doubles **£130**

Dunvegan

After the Portnalong and Glen Brittle turning on the A863, the road slips north across bare rounded hills to skirt the bony sea cliffs and -stacks of the west coast. Twenty miles on, it reaches **DUNVEGAN** (Dùn Bheagain), an unimpressive place, but a good base for exploring the interesting Duirinish peninsula.

Dunvegan Castle

April to mid-Oct daily 10am–5.30pm · £10, gardens only £8 · ☏01470 521206, ⓦwww.dunvegancastle.com

Dunvegan's conventional tourist attraction is **Dunvegan Castle**, which sprawls on top of a rocky outcrop, sandwiched between the sea and several acres of beautifully maintained gardens. Seat of the Clan MacLeod since the thirteenth century, the present greying, rectangular fortress dates from the 1840s. Inside, you don't get a lot of castle for your money, and the contents are far from stunning; most intriguing are the battered remnants of the **Fairy Flag** which was allegedly carried back to Skye

24

by Norwegian king Harald Hardrada's Gaelic boatmen after the Battle of Stamford Bridge in 1066.

ARRIVAL AND INFORMATION

DUNVEGAN

By bus Dunvegan sees regular buses from Portree (Mon–Sat 3–4 daily; 45min).

Tourist information St Kilda Shop, Dunvegan Castle (April to mid-Oct daily 10am–5.30pm; ☎ 01470 521206).

ACCOMMODATION

Carter's Rest Glendale, 8 miles west of Dunvegan ☎ 01470 511272, ⓦ cartersrestskye.co.uk. Little touches like a digital radio impress almost as much as furnishings like the wooden sleigh bed in this luxury four-star B&B with astonishing coast views. **£85**

Roskhill House Ose, 3 miles southeast of Dunvegan ☎ 01470 521317, ⓦ roskhillhouse.co.uk. Stone walls, crafts and home-made cake bring charm to this old crofthouse, whose modern oak furnishings and bed throws over crisp white linen lend understated style to your stay. Great breakfasts too. **£80**

EATING AND DRINKING

Jann's Cakes 46 Kilmuir, Dunvegan ☎ 01470 592298. This tiny place on the high street is a Skye legend for its cakes and home-made soups. Not cheap at £5 a slice of cake, but the quality is high and they do great sandwiches and scallop chowder. Mon–Sat 10am–5pm.

★**Stein Inn** Stein, 8 miles north of Dunvegan ☎ 01470 592362, ⓦ steininn.co.uk. A sixteenth-century waterfront inn that's as traditional as you'd hope: local ales, 125 malts and home-made dishes like pork Stroganoff (£12). Above are five cheerful en-suite rooms; simple,

clean, and you wake to sea views. Mon–Sat 11am–11pm/ midnight. **£77**

Three Chimneys 5 miles west of Dunvegan ☎ 01470 511258, ⓦ threechimneys.co.uk. A world-famous gourmet restaurant at the vanguard of Skye's foodie revolution. Lunch is £37 per person and in the evening you can even try the "Seven Courses of Skye" for £90. Reservations essential. Easter–Sept Mon–Sat 12.15–1.45pm & 6.15– 9pm, Sun 12.15–1.45pm; Oct Mon–Sat 12.15–1.45pm & 6.15–9pm; Nov–Easter Mon–Sat 6.15–9pm.

Portree

PORTREE is the only real town on Skye, with a population of around 2500. It's also one of the most attractive fishing ports in northwest Scotland with its deep, cliff-edged harbour filled with fishing boats and circled by multicoloured restaurants and guesthouses. Above the harbour is the spick-and-span town centre, spreading out from **Somerled Square**, which was built in the late eighteenth century and now houses the bus station and car park. The **Royal Hotel** on Bank Street occupies the site of *McNab's Inn* where Bonnie Prince Charlie took leave of Flora MacDonald (see box, opposite), and where, 27 years later, Boswell and Johnson had "a very good dinner, porter, port and punch".

ARRIVAL AND INFORMATION

PORTREE

By bus Portree is the hub of all transport on the island and buses pick up and drop off at Somerled Square.
Destinations Dunvegan (Mon–Sat 3–4 daily; 45min); Glasgow (3 daily; 6hr); Glenbrittle (Mon–Fri 2 daily; 50min); Inverness (3 daily; 3hr 15min); Kyle of Lochalsh (Mon–Sat hourly, Sun 3 daily; 1hr); Staffin (Mon–Sat

4–5 daily; 35min); Uig (Mon–Sat 7–8 daily, Sun 3 daily; 30min).
Tourist information Bayfield Rd (April–Oct Mon–Sat 9am–6pm, Sun 10am–4pm; Nov–March Mon–Fri 9am–5pm, Sat 10am–4pm; ☎ 01478 612137).

ACCOMMODATION

★**Ben Tianavaig** 5 Bosville Terrace ☎ 01478 612152, ⓦ ben-tianavaig.co.uk. The best B&B in the centre of town, run by charming hosts offering cottagey rooms that are modern and bright, with art on the walls and unrestricted views over the harbour for an extra £10. **£75**

Torvaig Campsite 2 miles north of Portree on A855 ☎ 01478 611849, ⓦ portreecampsite.co.uk. Flat pitches and views of the mountains appeal at this family-run site on the road to Staffin. Free hot showers and wi-fi, plus laundry facilities. Easter–Oct. Per person **£7**

★**Viewfield House** ☎ 01478 612217, ⓦ viewfield

house.com. The last word in Scots Baronial style is this MacDonald pile on the southern edge of town. Eccentric Victorian grandeur, with fabulous floral wallpaper, hunting trophies, stuffed polecats and antiques. Easter to mid-Oct. **£150**

EATING AND DRINKING

Café Arriba Quay Brae ☎01478 611830, ⓦcafearriba .co.uk. A local institution that packs in the punters, who come to gossip over coffee or tea served in large china pots, as much as for the global menu of home-made wraps, pastas or lamb kebabs (around £8). Daily 7am–6pm.
Harbour View 7 Bosville Terrace ☎01478 612069, ⓦharbourviewskye.co.uk. As cosy as the fisherman's front room it once was, Portree's most romantic restaurant prepares the likes of seared hake on puy lentils (£17), or

Loch Eihort *moules marinières* on its seafood menu. May–Oct daily noon–2.30pm & 5.30–10pm.
Isles Inn Somerled Square ☎01478 612129, ⓦaccommodationskye.co.uk. With its log fire and flagstone floors, this is the most appealing of Portree's pubs; it also has the occasional ceilidh band. Alongside Skye's ales, it has a no-nonsense menu of fish and chips, venison burgers or local haggis, neeps and tatties (£7–12). Mon–Sat noon–midnight, Sun noon–11pm.

Trotternish

Protruding twenty miles north from Portree, the **Trotternish peninsula** boasts some of the island's most bizarre scenery, particularly on the east coast, where volcanic basalt has pressed down on the softer sandstone and limestone underneath, causing massive landslides. These, in turn, have created pinnacles and pillars, at their most eccentric in the **Quiraing**, above **Staffin Bay**, on the east coast.

The east coast

The first geological eccentricity on the Trotternish peninsula, six miles north of Portree along the A855, is the **Old Man of Storr**, a 165ft column of rock, shaped like a willow

24

BONNIE PRINCE CHARLIE

Prince Charles Edward Stewart – better known as **Bonnie Prince Charlie** or "The Young Pretender" – was born in Rome in 1720 where his father, "The Old Pretender", claimant to the British throne, was living in exile. At the age of 25, having little military experience, no knowledge of Gaelic, an imperfect grasp of English and a strong attachment to the Catholic faith, the prince set out for Scotland with two French ships. He arrived on the Hebridean island of **Eriskay** on July 23, 1745, and went on to raise the royal standard at Glenfinnan, gather a Highland army, win the Battle of Prestonpans, march south into England and reach Derby before finally (and foolishly) agreeing to retreat. Back in Scotland, he won one last victory, at Falkirk, before the final disaster at **Culloden** in April 1746.

The prince spent the following five months in hiding, with a price of £30,000 on his head. He endured his share of cold and hunger while on the run, but the real price was paid by the Highlanders who risked, and sometimes lost, their lives by aiding, abetting, or even simply just supporting him. The most famous of these was 23-year-old **Flora MacDonald**, whom Charles met on South Uist in June 1746. Flora was persuaded – either by his beauty or her relatives, depending on which account you believe – to convey Charles "over the sea to Skye", disguised as a servant. She was arrested later in Portree, and held in the Tower of London until July 1747. She went on to marry a local man, had seven children, and in 1774 emigrated to America, where her husband was taken prisoner during the American War of Independence. Flora returned to Scotland and was reunited with her husband on his release; they resettled in Skye and she died aged 68.

Charles eventually boarded a ship back to France in September 1746, but never returned to Scotland; nor did he see Flora again. After mistreating a string of mistresses, he eventually got married at the age of 52 to the 19-year-old Princess of Stolberg, in an effort to produce a Stewart heir. They had no children, and she eventually fled from his violent drunkenness; in 1788, a none-too-"bonnie" Prince Charles died in the arms of his illegitimate daughter in Rome.

leaf, which, along with its neighbours, is part of a massive landslip. Huge blocks of stone still occasionally break off the cliff face of the Storr (2358ft) above and slide downhill. From the woods beside the car park it's a half-hour trek up a footpath to the foot of the column.

Further north, **Staffin Bay** is spread out before you, dotted with whitewashed and "spotty" houses. A singletrack road cuts across the peninsula from the north end of the bay, allowing access to the **Quiraing**, a spectacular forest of mighty pinnacles and savage rock formations. There are two car parks: from the first, beside a cemetery, it's a steep half-hour climb to the rocks; from the second, on the saddle, it's a longer but more gentle traverse.

Skye Museum of Island Life

Kilmuir • Easter–Oct Mon–Sat 9.30am–5pm • £2.50 • ⓦ skyemuseum.co.uk

The **Skye Museum of Island Life** is an impressive cluster of thatched blackhouses on an exposed hill overlooking the Western Isles. The museum gives a fascinating insight into a way of life that was commonplace on Skye a century ago. Behind the museum, in the cemetery up the hill, are the graves of **Flora MacDonald** and her husband. Thousands turned out for her funeral in 1790, creating a procession a mile long – so widespread was her fame that the original family mausoleum fell victim to souvenir hunters and had to be replaced.

Uig

Skye's chief ferry port for the Western Isles is **UIG** (Uige), which curves its way round a dramatic, horseshoe-shaped bay on the west coast of the Trotternish peninsula. There's a lovely, gentle **walk** up Glen Uig, better known as the **Faerie Glen**, a Hobbity landscape of miniature hills at the east end of the bay.

ARRIVAL AND DEPARTURE   TROTTERNISH

By ferry Uig has connections to Lochmaddy (1–2 daily; 1hr 45min) and Tarbert (1–2 daily; 1hr 40min).

By bus Uig sees services to and from Glasgow (1–2 daily; 6hr 50min) and Portree (Mon–Sat 7–8 daily, Sun 3 daily;

30min). The Flodigarry Circular bus service #57A and #57C gives access to almost all of the coast (Mon–Sat 3 daily). Buses depart from Uig Pier.

ACCOMMODATION AND EATING

Dun Flodigarry Hostel Flodigarry ☎ 01470 552212, ⓦ hostelflodigarry.co.uk. Housed in the old servants' quarters of the *Flodigarry Hotel*, this is a spacious, if dated, hostel with great sea views. You can also camp on the lawn and use the excellent kitchen facilities. Pitches £9, dorms £18, doubles £40

★ **Glenview Hotel** Culnaknock (Culnacnoc), 3 miles south of Staffin ☎ 01470 562248, ⓦ glenviewskye .co.uk. Quirky, vintage-style accommodation – all Bakelite radios, naïve paintings and painted floorboards – and sensational cooking in this restaurant with rooms. Short evening-only menus (two courses £30) created from super-fresh produce might include nettle and parsley soup with scallops, sole with local mussel sauce or venison in red wine

and tarragon. March–Nov. £110

The Sheiling & Ella's Café Idrigill Uig ☎ 01470 542797, ⓦ sheiling.net. Within a former crofters' warehouse behind Uig garage, *Ella's* serves home-made toasted focaccia, smoked salmon and crowdie pâté and delicious baking (£5–8). It doubles as a local crafts outlet that makes it feel like a village hall on fête day. Tues–Sat 10am–5pm.

Woodbine House Uig ☎ 01470 542243, ⓦ skye activities.co.uk. The pick of Uig's accommodation, this B&B is in a tasteful house on the Duntulm road. Front rooms benefit from sea views, and all are en suite. The hugely helpful owners also rent out mountain bikes (£12 half-day, £20 full day). March–Oct. £70

The Small Isles

Seen from Skye or the west coast of Scotland, the **Small Isles** – **Rùm**, **Eigg**, **Muck** and tiny **Canna** – lie scattered in a silver-grey sea like a siren call to adventure. After centuries of being passed between owners, most islands have stabilized into tight-knit communities of crofters and incomers. While Muck is privately owned, Eigg was bought out by the islanders in 1997, and the other two islands have been bequeathed to national agencies: Rùm, by far the largest and most-visited of the group, belongs to Scottish Natural Heritage; Canna is in the hands of the National Trust for Scotland.

Many people come on a day-trip from Mallaig, yet the Small Isles deserve longer. They are an opportunity to experience some off-grid island life while walking, birdwatching or simply admiring the seascapes. Accommodation requires **forward planning** and public transport is nonexistent, but the regular ferry service links all the islands: a boon for those wishing to island-hop.

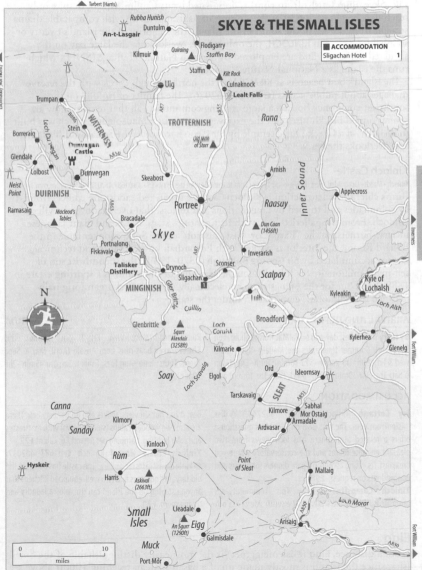

SKYE & THE SMALL ISLES

■ ACCOMMODATION
Sligachan Hotel   1

24

By ferry CalMac ferries sail to the Small Isles from Mallaig (☎ 01687 462403, ⊕ calmac.co.uk; Easter to mid-Oct daily; mid-Oct to Easter Mon–Sat only), although they don't sail to each island every day – day-trips are only possible on Saturdays. The Sheerwater sails from Arisaig (see p.908) to Rùm, Eigg and Muck (☎ 01687 450224, ⊕ arisaig.co.uk; late April to late Sept). The ride doubles as a wildlife cruise, so, while enjoyable, is more expensive than travelling with CalMac.

Rùm

Like Skye, **Rùm** (⊕ isleofrum.com) is dominated by its Cuillin, which, despite only reaching a height of 2663ft at the summit of Askival, rises up with comparable drama straight from the sea in the south of the island. The majority of the island's twenty or so inhabitants live in **KINLOCH**, the only village, overlooking the large bay on the sheltered east coast, and are employed by Scottish Natural Heritage (SNH), which runs the island as a National Nature Reserve.

The island's best beach is at **KILMORY** to the north, though check with the reserve manager about public access (☎ 01687 462026). The hamlet of **HARRIS** on the southwest coast once housed a large crofting community; all that remains now are several ruined blackhouses and the extravagant **Bullough Mausoleum**, which was built in the style of a Greek Doric temple by Sir George to house the remains of his father, and overlooks the sea.

Kinloch Castle

Kinloch • March–Oct guided tours daily around 1pm or 2pm to coincide with the ferry • £9 • ☎ 01687 462037, ⊕ isleofrum.com

Rùm's chief formal attraction is **Kinloch Castle**, a squat, red-sandstone edifice, fronted by colonnades and topped by crenellations and turrets, that overshadows the village of Kinloch. From the galleried hall, with its tiger rugs, stags' heads and giant Japanese incense-burners, to the "Extra Low Fast Cushion" of the Soho snooker table in the Billiard Room, the interior is packed with Edwardian knick-knacks and technical gizmos accumulated by **Sir George Bullough** (1870–1939), the spendthrift son of self-made millionaire Sir John Bullough, who bought the island as a sporting estate in 1888. Look out for the orchestrion, an electrically driven barrel organ (originally destined for Balmoral), crammed in under the stairs.

By ferry The longest day-trip on CalMac from Mallaig is on Sat (11hr). Summer timetables are Mallaig–Rùm (Mon, Wed & Fri– Sun; 1hr 20min–2hr 30min); Rùm–Eigg (Mon & Sat; 1hr–3hr 30min); Rùm–Muck (Sat; 1hr 10min) and Rùm–Canna (Mon, Wed, Fri & Sat; 55min). The **Sheerwater** boat runs from Arisaig (April, May & Sept Tues & Thurs; June–Aug Tues, Thurs & Sat; 1hr 45min–2hr 30min).

ACCOMMODATION

Ivy Cottage Kinloch ☎ 01687 462744, ⊕ fliss @isleofrum.com. The first B&B on Rùm, this guesthouse offers a relaxed atmosphere and loch views from two pleasant en-suite rooms and the conservatory where you breakfast. Its young owners prepare dinners for guests and nonresidents on request. **£90**

Kinloch Campsite Kinloch. This community-run campsite is right by the water on the south side of Kinloch Bay; it has hot showers, toilets and an honesty box. There are also two wooden cabins (sleeping two) with mattresses and solar lighting. Camping per person **£6**, cabins **£22**

Kinloch Castle Hostel Kinloch ☎ 01687 462037, ⊕ kinlochcastle@snh.gov.uk. The castle has dorms in the old servants' quarters and two well-equipped kitchens that anyone staying on the island can use, plus a laundry and drying room. **£20**

Eigg

From a distance, **Eigg** (⊕ isleofeigg.net) is the most easily distinguishable of the Small Isles, since the island is mostly made up of a basalt plateau reaching 1000ft above sea

24

level, and a great stump of columnar pitchstone lava, known as **An Sgurr**, rising 290ft out of the plateau. It's also the most vibrant, populous and welcoming of the Small Isles, with a strong sense of community among its hundred or so residents. With the island's great landmark, An Sgurr (1292ft), watching over you wherever you go, many folk feel duty-bound to climb it, and enjoy the wonderful views over to Muck and Rùm (3–4hr round trip). For a longer, easier stroll, head three miles up the road to the northwest coast and the **Singing Sands**, so called because the quartz grains squeak underfoot.

ARRIVAL AND DEPARTURE EIGG

By ferry CalMac summer timetables are: Mallaig–Eigg (Mon, Tues & Thurs–Sun; 1hr 15min–2hr 25min); Muck–Eigg (Tues & Thurs–Sat; 35min); Rùm–Eigg (Mon & Sat; 1hr–3hr 30min) and Canna–Eigg (Mon & Sat; 2hr 15min). The **Sheerwater** runs from Arisaig (April–Sept daily except Thurs).

ACCOMMODATION AND EATING

Galmisdale Bay Harbour ☎01687 482487, ⓦgalmisdale-bay.com. Eigg's only eating option is a lovely wood-panelled room where island ingredients make home-made soups, quiche, pizza, burgers and blackboard specials such as fishcakes – all for under a tenner. Mon & Tues 10am–5pm, Wed 10am–10pm, Thurs 10am–3pm, Fri & Sat 10am–11pm, Sun 11.30am–5pm.

Glebe Barn Galmisdale ☎01687 315099, ⓦglebebarn .co.uk. Eigg's hostel, in a substantial converted nineteenth-century barn, is above the harbour and has a rather stylish spacious lounge with awesome views of the coast and pleasant, wee dorm rooms. Dorms £17, twins £40

Kildonan House Galmisdale Bay ☎01687 482446, ⓦkildonanhouseeigg.co.uk. A traditional stay in an eighteenth-century farmhouse on the north side of Galmisdale Bay. Marie offers three pleasingly simple pine-panelled rooms, all with sea views and tasty dinners included. £120

★**Lageorna** Cleadale ☎01687 460081, ⓦlageorna .com. Beautiful modern rooms full of contemporary crafts and astonishing views. The owner also prepares good-value dishes such as salmon on spicy puy lentils. Easter–Sept Mon–Wed & Fri noon–4pm; dinner by arrangement. £140

Sue Holland's Croft Cleadale ☎01687 482480, ⓦeiggorganics.co.uk. The island's only campsite is on an organic croft and it's a belter, with views and sunsets to inspire poetry. The old cowshed is now a basic bothy for up to four, or for more comfort choose a yurt. Camping per person £5, bothy/yurt £40

Muck

Smallest and most southerly of the Small Isles, **Muck** (ⓦisleofmuck.com) is low lying, mostly treeless and extremely fertile. You'll arrive at **PORT MÒR**, the village on the southeast corner of the island. A road, a little more than a mile long, connects Port Mór with the island's main farm, **GALLANACH**, which overlooks the rocky seal-strewn skerries on the north side of the island; to the east lies the nicest sandy beach, **Camas na Cairidh**. In the southwest corner of the island, it's worth climbing **Beinn Airein**, despite being only 450ft above sea level, for the 360-degree panoramic view (2hr round trip).

ARRIVAL AND INFORMATION MUCK

By ferry CalMac ferries summer timetables are: Mallaig–Muck (Tues & Thurs–Sun; 1hr 40min–4hr 20min); Eigg–Muck (Tues, Thurs, Sat & Sun; 35min) and Rùm–Muck (Sat; 2hr 45min). The *Sheerwater* boat also sails to Muck from Arisaig (April, May & Sept Mon, Wed & Fri; June–Aug Wed, Fri & Sun).

Tourist information The craft shop in Port Mòr (April–Sept), which springs into life when day-trippers arrive, is a de facto information centre.

ACCOMMODATION AND EATING

The Craft Shop Port Mòr ☎01687 462990, ⓦisleofmuck.com. The only shop on the island prepares daily soups and sandwiches made from fresh home-baked bread, plus afternoon teas and dinners of tasty Scottish home-cooking prepared on request. April, May & Sept hours vary; June–Aug daily 11am–4pm.

Gallanach Lodge Gallanach Bay ☎01687 462365, ⓦisleofmuck.com. A purpose-built luxury lodge that

24

takes full advantage of a superb position above the beach to provide fantastic views of Rùm. The style is island boutique – rustic, handmade beds in rooms with hotel-style mod cons. Full board only. **£170**

Isle of Muck Bunkhouse Port Mòr ☎ 01687 462218, ⓦ isleofmuck.com. Despite the name, the island's characterful, wood-panelled bunkhouse near the port has beds not bunks – two twins and a double – and is heated by an oil-fired Raeburn stove. Not luxurious, but full of character. **£12**

Canna

Measuring just five miles by one, **Canna** (ⓦ theisleofcanna.com) is run as a single farm and bird sanctuary by the National Trust for Scotland (NTS), with a dwindling population now down to single figures. For visitors, the chief pastime is walking – you can circuit the entire island in a long day's hike (twelve miles; 10hr). For a shorter stroll, it's about a mile from the dock across a grassy basalt plateau to the bony sea cliffs of the north shore, which rise to a peak around **Compass Hill** (458ft) – so called because its high metal content distorts compasses – in the northeastern corner of the island, from where you get great views across to Rùm and Skye. The cliffs of the buffeted western half of the island are a breeding ground for Manx shearwater, razorbill and puffin.

ARRIVAL AND ACCOMMODATION CANNA

By ferry Only CalMac sail to Canna, and a day-trip from Mallaig is only possible on Sat (6hr ashore). Mallaig–Canna (Mon, Wed, Fri–Sun; 2hr 30min–3hr 50min), Eigg–Canna (Mon & Sat; 2hr 30min), Muck–Canna (Sat; 1hr 35min); Rùm–Canna (Mon, Wed & Fri–Sun; 55min).

Tighard Half a mile from the jetty ☎ 01687 462474, ⓦ tighard.co.uk. This substantial, red-sandstone, Victorian house is the island's only guesthouse, featuring spacious rooms with glorious views. The Sanday room is the pick of the three twin rooms; they also offer packed lunch and dinner with notice. **£120**

The Western Isles

Beyond Skye, across the unpredictable waters of the Minch, lie the wild and windy Outer Hebrides or **Western Isles**, a 130-mile-long archipelago stretching from Lewis and Harris in the north to the Uists and Barra in the south. An elemental beauty pervades the more than two hundred islands, only a handful of which are inhabited, by a total population of around 28,000 people.

The interior of the northernmost island, **Lewis**, is mostly peat moor, a barren and marshy tract that gives way to the bare peaks of **North Harris**. Across a narrow isthmus lies **South Harris**, presenting some of the finest scenery in Scotland, with wide beaches of golden sand trimming the Atlantic, in full view of a rough boulder-strewn interior. Across the Sound of Harris, to the south, a string of tiny, flatter isles – **North Uist**, **Benbecula**, **South Uist** – linked by causeways, offer breezy beaches whose fine sands front a narrow band of boggy farmland, which, in turn, is mostly bordered by a lower range of hills to the east. Finally, tiny **Barra** contains all these landscapes in one small Hebridean package, and is a great introduction to the region.

GAELIC IN THE WESTERN ISLES

The Outer Hebrides remain the heartland of **Gaelic** culture, with the language spoken by the majority of islanders, though its everyday usage remains under constant threat from the dominance of English. Except in Stornoway, and Balivanich on North Uist, **road signs** in the Western Isles are almost exclusively in Gaelic; the English names can often provide a rough pronunciation guide. Particularly if you're driving, it's a good idea to buy the bilingual Western Isles **map**, available at most tourist offices.

In direct contrast to their wonderful landscapes, villages in the Western Isles are seldom picturesque, and are usually made up of scattered, relatively modern crofthouses dotted about the elementary road system. **Stornoway**, the only real town in the Outer Hebrides, rarely impresses.

GETTING AROUND   **THE WESTERN ISLES**

A series of causeways makes it possible to travel by road from one end of the Western Isles to the other with just two interruptions – the **ferry** from Harris to Berneray, and from Eriskay to Barra. The islands have a decent **bus** service, though there are no buses on Sundays. **Bike rental** is also available, but the wind makes cycling something of a challenge – head south to north to catch the prevailing wind.

Lewis (Leodhas)

Shaped rather like an upside-down ice-cream cone, **Lewis** is the largest and most populous of the Western Isles. Nearly half of the island's inhabitants live in the crofting and fishing villages strung out along the northwest coast, between **Callanish** (Calanais) and **Port of Ness** (Port Nis), in one of the country's most densely populated rural areas. On this coast, you'll also find the best-preserved **prehistoric remains** – including the Callanish standing stones. The landscape is mostly flat peat bog – hence the island's Gaelic name, from *leogach* (marshy) – but the shoreline is more dramatic, especially around the Butt of Lewis in the north. The rest of the island's population live in **Stornoway** on the east coast, the only real town in the Western Isles. In the south, where Lewis is physically joined with Harris, the land rises to just over 1800ft, providing an exhilarating backdrop for the excellent beaches that pepper the isolated west coast.

24

Stornoway (Steornabhagh)

In these parts, **STORNOWAY** is a buzzing metropolis, with around nine thousand inhabitants and all the trappings of a large town. Aesthetics are not its strong point, and the urban pleasures on offer are limited, but in July the town hosts the **Hebridean Celtic Festival** (w hebceltfest.com). Stornoway's best-looking building is the old **Town Hall** on South Beach, a splendid Scots Baronial pile from 1905, its rooftop interspersed with conical towers, above which a central clocktower rises. One block east along South Beach, looking rather like a modern church, you'll find **An Lanntair** – Gaelic for "lantern" – Stornoway's modern cultural centre.

Lews Castle

Castle interior to open 2015 • Free • w stornowaytrust.org.uk

The castellated pomposity of **Lews Castle**, surrounded by mature woodland, was built by Sir James Matheson in 1863 after resettling the crofters who used to live here. As the former laird's pad, it has long been seen as a symbol of oppression by many. However, after lying abandoned for over 25 years, the building is having a £14 million makeover to transform it into the new **Museum nan Eilean**, telling the story of the islands' geology, its Gaelic culture, the struggles of the nineteenth century and the Leverhulme era – the museum is even going to get six Lewis Chessmen on long-term loan from the British Museum.

ARRIVAL AND INFORMATION   **STORNOWAY**

By plane Stornoway Airport (t 01851 707400, w hial.co.uk) is 4 miles east of the town centre: the hourly bus takes 15min (Mon–Sat only), and it's around £5 by taxi.

By ferry CalMac ferries to Ullapool (Mon–Sat 2–3 daily,

Sun 1 daily; 2hr 45min) run from the octagonal CalMac ferry terminal on South Beach, near the bus station.

By bus The bus station (t 01851 704327) is on South Beach in the town centre.

Destinations Callanish (Mon–Sat 4–6 daily; 40min);

Carloway (Mon–Sat 5–6 daily; 45min); Garenin (Mon–Sat 3–4 daily; 1hr); Leverburgh (Mon–Sat 4–5 daily; 2hr); Port of Ness (Mon–Sat 6–8 daily; 1hr); Tarbert (Mon–Sat 5 daily; 1hr).

Tourist information 26 Cromwell St (May–Sept Mon–Sat 9am–6pm, plus open to meet the evening ferry; Oct–April Mon–Fri 9am–5pm; ☎01851 703088, ⓦvisithe brides.com).

ACCOMMODATION

Cairn Dhu 18a Matheson Rd ☎01851 701611, ⓦlewisapartments.co.uk. Plush contemporary apartment, with leather upholstery, a fully equipped modern kitchen and free wi-fi, in a Victorian villa on the town's nicest, leafy residential street. **£140**

Heb Hostel 25 Kenneth St ☎01851 709889, ⓦhebhostel.co.uk. A clean, centrally-located terrace house in salmon pink, converted into a simple hostel, with free wi-fi, laundry and kitchen facilities, and run by a friendly resident warden. **£18**

Jannel 5 Stewart Drive ☎01851 705324, ⓦjannel -stornoway.co.uk. A short walk from the town centre, this B&B is run by a delightful landlady and offers five spacious, immaculate, en-suite rooms. Free wi-fi. **£89**

EATING AND DRINKING

★**An Lanntair** Kenneth St ☎01851 703307, ⓦlanntair.com. Stylish café-restaurant in the arts centre which does decent sandwiches and lighter dishes during the day, as well as more imaginative stuff like black pudding-stuffed chicken wrapped in bacon (mains £8–18) in the evening. Free wi-fi. Food served Mon–Sat 10am–2.30pm & 5.30–8.30pm.

The Criterion 32 Point St ☎01851 701990. A wee, authentic, no-frills Stornoway pub, staging regular informal (music) sessions– if nothing's going down, try nearby *MacNeill's*. Mon–Thurs 11am–11pm, Fri & Sat 11am–1am.

Digby Chick 5 Bank St ☎01851 700026, ⓦdigbychick .co.uk. Smart, modern, buzzy little bistro with a real emphasis on using local produce, such as the famous Stornoway black pudding. Sandwiches available at lunchtimes or two courses for around £13; three-course dinners are under £30. Mon–Sat noon–2pm & 5.30–9pm.

Thai Café 27 Church St ☎01851 701811, ⓦthai-cafe -stornoway.co.uk. Despite the name, this is actually a restaurant, serving authentic Thai food (mains around £8). No licence so bring your own bottle (50p corkage). Mon–Sat noon–2.30pm & 5–11pm.

The road to Port of Ness (Port Nis)

Northwest of Stornoway, the A857 crosses the vast, barren **peat bog** of the interior, an empty, undulating wilderness, riddled with stretchmarks formed by peat cuttings and pockmarked with freshwater lochans. For the people of Lewis the peat continues to serve as a valuable energy resource, its pungent smoke one of the most characteristic smells of the Western Isles.

Twelve miles across the peat bog, near Barvas (Barabhas), the road divides, heading southwest towards Callanish (see opposite), or northeast through a string of scattered settlements to the fishing village of **PORT OF NESS** (Port Nis). Shortly before Port of Ness, a minor road heads two miles northwest to the hamlet of **EUROPIE** (Eoropaidh) – pronounced "yor-erpee". Here, by the road junction that leads to the Butt of Lewis, stands the simple stone structure of **St Moluag's Church** (Teampull Mholuaidh), thought to date from the twelfth century. From Europie a narrow road twists to the blustery northern tip of the island, Rubha Robhanais – known to devotees of the BBC shipping forecast as the **Butt of Lewis** – where a lighthouse sticks up above a series of sheer cliffs and stacks, alive with seabirds and a great place for marine-mammal spotting.

ARRIVAL, ACCOMMODATION & EATING   PORT OF NESS

By bus There's a regular bus service from Stornoway to Port of Ness (Mon–Sat 6–8 daily; 1hr).

Café Sonas Port of Ness (Port Nis) ☎01851 810222. Simple comfort food for the most part, but with a few local specialities thrown in – local fish pie, crab salad and Barra scampi (all under £7). Great views over the bay. Mon noon–5pm, Tues–Sat 10am–7pm.

Galson Farm South Galson (Gabhsann Bho Dheas) ☎01851 850492, ⓦgalsonfarm.co.uk. An attractive converted eighteenth-century farmhouse, which offers generous portions of Aga-cooked meals – dinner, bed and breakfast are all available, and they run a six-bunk bunkhouse close by. Bunkhouse **£18**, doubles **£88**

24

Westside

Heading southwest from the crossroads near Barvas brings you to the **Westside** (An Toabh Siar), an area where several villages meander down towards the sea, and which is home to the **Callanish** stone circle.

Arnol Blackhouse

Arnol • Mon–Sat: April–Sept 9.30am–5.30pm; Oct–March 9.30am–4.30pm • £4.50; HS • ☎ 01851 710395

In **ARNOL**, the remains of numerous blackhouses lie abandoned by the roadside; at the north end of the village, no. 42 has been preserved as the **Arnol Blackhouse**, which shows exactly how a true blackhouse (*taigh dubh*) would have been. The dark interior is lit and heated by a small peat fire, which is kept alight in the central hearth of bare earth, and is usually fairly smoky as there's no chimney; instead, smoke drifts through the thatch, helping to kill any creepy crawlies, keep out the midges and turn the heathery sods and oat-straw thatch itself into next year's fertilizer.

Garenin

May–Sept Mon–Sat 9.30am–5.30pm • £2.50

At Carlabhagh a mile-long road leads off north to the beautifully remote coastal settlement of **GARENIN** (Gearrannan). Here, rather than re-create a single museum-piece blackhouse as at Arnol, a whole cluster of nine thatched crofters' houses – the last of which was abandoned in 1974 – have been restored and put to a variety of uses: a café, a museum and self-catering cottages. As an ensemble, they also give a great impression of what a blackhouse village must have been like.

Dun Carloway (Dùn Charlabhaigh)

Open 24hr • Free

Just beyond Carloway village, **Dun Carloway** (Dùn Charlabhaigh) perches on top of a conspicuous rocky outcrop overlooking the sea. This is one of Scotland's best-preserved brochs (a circular, prehistoric stone fort), its dry-stone circular walls reaching a height of more than 30ft on one side. The broch consists of two concentric walls, the inner one perpendicular, the outer one slanting inwards, the two originally fastened together by roughly hewn flagstones, which also served as lookout galleries reached via a narrow stairwell.

Callanish (Calanais) standing stones

Open 24hr • Free • Callanish Visitor Centre April, May, Sept & Oct Mon–Sat 10am–6pm; June–Aug Mon–Sat 9.30am–8pm; Nov–March Tues–Sat 10am–4pm • £2.50 • ☎ 01851 621422, ⓦ callanishvisitorcentre.co.uk

Overlooking the sheltered, islet-studded waters of Loch Roag (Loch Ròg), on the west coast, are the islands' most dramatic prehistoric ruins, the **Callanish standing stones**. These monoliths – nearly fifty slabs of gnarled and finely grained gneiss up to 15ft high – were transported here between 3000 and 1500 BC, but their exact function remains a mystery. No one knows for certain why the ground plan resembles a colossal Celtic cross, nor why there's a central burial chamber. It's likely that such a massive endeavour was prompted by the desire to predict the seasonal cycle upon which these early farmers were entirely dependent, and indeed many of the stones are aligned with the positions of the sun and the stars. Whatever the reason for their existence, there's certainly no denying the powerful primeval presence, not to mention sheer beauty, of the stones.

ARRIVAL AND ACCOMMODATION
CALLANISH

By bus There are regular buses between Stornoway and Arnol (Mon–Sat 6–8 daily; 30min); Callanish (Mon–Sat 4–6 daily; 40min); Carloway (Mon–Sat 5–6 daily; 45min); and Garenin (Mon–Sat 3–4 daily; 1hr).

Leumadair ☎ 01851 621706, ⓦ leumadair.co.uk. A purpose-built modern guesthouse near the Callanish stones, owned by a very friendly Lewis couple, who cure and smoke their own bacon, keep hens and have a pet hawk. Dinner can be provided on request (£15 for one course, £25 for three courses). **£86**

24

Harris (Na Hearadh)

Harris is much hillier, more dramatic and much more appealing than its northern neighbour, Lewis, its boulder-strewn slopes descending to aquamarine bays of dazzling, white sand. The "island" is clearly divided by a minuscule isthmus into the wild, inhospitable mountains of **North Harris** and the gentler landscape and sandy shores of **South Harris**.

North Harris (Ceann a Tuath na Hearadh)

If you're coming from Stornoway on the A859, mountainous **North Harris** is a spectacular introduction to Harris, its bulging, pyramidal mountains of gneiss looming over the dramatic, fjord-like **Loch Seaforth** (Loch Shìphoirt). You weave your way over a boulder-strewn saddle between mighty **Sgaoth Aird** (1829ft) and **Clisham** (An Cliseam), the highest peak in the Western Isles, at 2619ft. This bitter terrain, littered with debris left behind by retreating glaciers, offers but the barest of vegetation, with an occasional cluster of crofters' houses sitting in the shadow of a host of pointed peaks, anywhere between 1000ft and 2500ft high.

Tarbert (An Tairbeart)

Sheltered in a green valley on the narrow isthmus, **TARBERT** is the largest place on Harris and a wonderful place to arrive by boat. The port's mountainous backdrop is impressive, and the town is attractively laid out on steep terraces sloping up from the dock.

24

ARRIVAL AND INFORMATION   TARBERT

By ferry There are CalMac ferries to and from Uig on Skye (1–2 daily; 1hr 45min).

By bus Tarbert is served by regular buses from Leverburgh via the west coast (Mon–Sat 6–8 daily; 45min–1hr) and via the east coast (Mon–Sat 2–4 daily; 1hr) and Stornoway

(Mon–Sat 5 daily; 1hr). Buses stop at the pier.

Tourist information Tarbert boasts Harris's only tourist office (April, Sept & Oct Mon–Sat 9am–6pm; May–Aug Mon, Wed & Fri 9am–6pm, Tues, Thurs & Sat 9am–8.30pm; ☎0845 225 5121), close to the ferry terminal.

ACCOMMODATION AND EATING

Harris Hotel Scott Rd ☎01859 502154, ⚲harrishotel .com. Just a five-minute walk from the harbour, this is Tarbert's longest-established and largest hotel. It's been refurbished fairly recently so it's a solid choice, with 23 en-suite rooms, some with sea views, and all with free wi-fi – it also serves food, even on a Sunday (bar lunch mains £10–15, restaurant mains £17–23). £100

Isle of Harris Inn Scott Rd ☎01859 502566. Join the locals in this unpretentious pub, next door to the *Harris Hotel*, for fish and chips for under £10, or the occasional seafood special. Mon–Sat noon–11pm; food served noon–9pm.

No. 5 Hostel Dinishader (Drinisiadar) ☎01851 511255, ⚲number5.biz. A converted cottage, 3 miles south of Tarbert, offering bed linen and laundry service along with canoes, kayaks and cycles for hire. There's one dorm and two twins, all with sea views – camping possible, too. March–Oct. Dorms £20, twins £40

Rhenigdale Hostel Rhenigdale (Reinigeadal) ⚲gatliff .org.uk. Simple hostel in an isolated coastal hamlet. There's a request-only bus service or else it's a magnificent six-mile hike (3hr) over the rocky landscape from Tarbert – ask at the tourist office for directions. Camping permitted. No advance booking. Camping £8, dorms £12

South Harris (Ceann a Deas na Hearadh)

The mountains of **South Harris** are less dramatic than in the north, but the scenery is equally breathtaking. There's a choice of routes from Tarbert to the ferry port of **Leverburgh**, which connects with North Uist: the east coast, known as The Bays (Na Baigh), is rugged and seemingly inhospitable, while the **west coast** is endowed with some of the finest stretches of golden sand **beaches** in the whole of the archipelago, buffeted by the Atlantic winds. Most stunning of all is the vast golden strand of **Luskentyre Bay** (Tràigh Losgaintir), with the islet-studded turquoise sea to the west, and even on the dullest day the sand glowing beneath the waves. Paradoxically, most people on South Harris live along the harsh eastern coastline of **Bays** rather than the more fertile west side. But not by choice – they were evicted from their original crofts to make way for sheep-grazing in the nineteenth century.

Leverburgh (An t-Ob)

The west-coast road veers to the southeast to trim the island's south shore, eventually reaching the sprawling settlement of **LEVERBURGH**, named after Lord Leverhulme, who planned to turn the place into the largest fishing port on the west coast of Scotland. The main reason to come here is to catch the CalMac **car ferry** service to Berneray and the Uists (see p.944).

Rodel (Roghadal)

A mile or so from Renish Point (Rubha Reanais), the southern tip of Harris, is the old port of **RODEL** (Roghadal), where a smattering of ancient stone houses lies among the hillocks. On top of one of these grassy humps is **St Clement's Church** ('Tur Chliamainn), burial place of the MacLeods of Harris and Dunvegan in Skye. Dating from the 1520s, the church's bare interior is distinguished by its wall tombs; look out, too, for the *Sheela-na-gig* (a naked pre-Christian fertility goddess) halfway up the south side of the tower. Unusually, she has a brother displaying his genitalia too, below a curving of St Clement on the west face.

ARRIVAL AND DEPARTURE	SOUTH HARRIS

By ferry The CalMac ferry zigzags its way through the shallows between Berneray and Leverburgh (3–4 daily; 1hr).

By bus Buses from Tarbert run to Leverburgh via the west coast (Mon–Sat 6–8 daily; 45min–1hr) and via the east coast (Mon–Sat 2–4 daily; 1hr). Buses stop at the pier.

ACCOMMODATION AND EATING

★**Am Bothan** Ferry Rd, Leverburgh ☎ 01859 520251, ⓦ ambothan.com. Quirky, bright red, timber-clad bunkhouse that makes for a pretty luxurious, very welcoming hostel, close to the ferry. Lovely big kitchen/ living room, plus laundry and drying facilities, too. Dorms **£20**

The Anchorage By the ferry slipway, Leverburgh ☎ 01859 520225. For local venison and beef burgers, langoustines and black pudding with poached egg on muffins (£10–15), head for this lively bar/restaurant by the ferry slipway – great views and occasional live music. Mon–Sat noon–11pm; food served noon–9pm.

★**Lickisto Blackhouse Camping** Lickisto (Liceasto) ☎ 01859 530485, ⓦ freewebs.com/vanvon. A beautiful, rugged spot overlooking the sea where there's fresh bread

and eggs available, a peat fire to warm you in the kitchen blackhouse and toilets in the byres. Yurts also available. March–Oct. Pitches **£24**, yurts **£70**

★**Old School House** Finsbay (Fionnsbhagh) ☎ 01859 530420, ⓦ theoldschoolhousefinsbay.com. A very friendly couple run this nicely converted Victorian former village schoolhouse on the east coast, which comes with free wi fi, good home-cooking and huge portions for breakfast and dinner (£20–30). **£70**

★**Pairc an t-Srath** Borve (Na Buirgh) ☎ 01859 550386, ⓦ paircant-srath.co.uk. A working crofthouse with beautiful Harris Tweed furnishings throughout – there's a superb view across the sea from the dining room and the food is both filling and beautifully prepared (three-course dinners for £35). **£100**

North Uist (Uibhist a Tuath)

Compared to the mountainous scenery of Harris, **North Uist** – seventeen miles long and thirteen miles wide – is much flatter and, for some, comes as something of an anticlimax. More than half the surface area is covered by water, creating a distinctive peaty-brown lochan-studded "drowned landscape". Most visitors are here for the trout and salmon **fishing** and the deerstalking, both of which (along with poaching) are critical to the island's economy. Others come for the smattering of **prehistoric sites**, the **birds**, or the sheer peace of this windy isle, and the solitude of North Uist's vast sandy **beaches**, which extend – almost without interruption – along the north and west coasts.

Lochmaddy

Despite being situated on the east coast, some distance away from any beach, the ferry port of **LOCHMADDY** (Loch nam Madadh, or "Loch of the Dogs") makes a good base for exploring the island. The village itself, occupying a narrow, bumpy promontory, is nothing special, but it does have a tourist office, and the nearby **Taigh Chearsabhagh**.

Taigh Chearsabhagh

July & Aug Mon–Sat 10am–5pm, Sun 10am–2pm; Sept–June Mon–Sat 10am–5pm • Free • ☎ 01870 603970, ⊛ taigh-chearsabhagh.org

A converted eighteenth-century merchant's house, **Taigh Chearsabhagh** is now home to a vibrant community arts centre that houses a café, post office and shop as well as an excellent museum, which puts on innovative exhibitions. The arts centre was one of the prime movers behind the commissioning of a series of seven **sculptures** dotted about the Uists – ask for directions to those in and around Lochmaddy, the most interesting of which is the **Both nam Faileas** (Hut of the Shadow), roughly half a mile north of town.

Berneray (Bhearnaraigh)

The ferry connection with Harris arrives and departs from the southeasternmost point of **Berneray** (⊛ isleofberneray.com), a low-lying island immediately north of North Uist and connected to the latter via a causeway. Two miles by three, with a population of around 140, the island has a superb three-mile-long sandy **beach** on the west and north coast, backed by rabbit-free dunes and machair.

Balranald RSPB Reserve

Open 24hr • Visitor centre April–Aug daily 9am–6pm • Free

North Uist's **Balranald RSPB Reserve**, on the western tip of the island, is best known for its population of corncrakes: there are usually one or two making a loud noise right outside the RSPB **visitor centre**, from which you can pick up a leaflet outlining a two-hour walk along the headland, marked by posts. A wonderful carpet of flowers covers the machair in summer, and there are usually corn buntings and arctic terns inland, and gannets, Manx shearwater and skuas out to sea.

ARRIVAL AND INFORMATION

NORTH UIST

By ferry CalMac car ferries run from Leverburgh to Berneray (3–4 daily; 1hr) and from Uig to Lochmaddy (1–2 daily; 1hr 40min).

By bus There are services between Lochmaddy and Balivanich (Mon–Sat 6–7 daily; 30–45min), Balranald (Mon–Sat 3 daily; 50min), Berneray (Mon–Sat 8 daily; 20min) and Lochboisdale (Mon–Sat 6 daily; 1hr 30min).

Tourist information Pier Rd, Lochmaddy (April–Oct Mon–Sat 9am–5pm; also open to greet the evening ferry; ☎ 01876 500321).

ACCOMMODATION AND EATING

★**Bagh Alluin** 21 Baleshare (Baile Sear) ☎ 01876 580370, ⊛ jacvolbeda.co.uk. A secluded, beautifully designed modern B&B with fantastic views over the island, run by a Dutch artist who is a genuinely warm and friendly host. **£85**

★**Berneray Hostel** Berneray (Bhearnaraigh) ⊛ gatliff.org.uk. Berneray's wonderful hostel, occupying a pair of thatched blackhouses, is located in a lovely beachside spot, beyond the main village on the north side of Bays Loch (Loch a Bhàigh). **£12**

Langass Lodge Loch Eport ☎ 01876 580285, ⊛ langasslodge.co.uk. From the A867, a side road leads off to this old hunting lodge which has a stylish modern extension, and a restaurant and bar that specializes in fresh local seafood dishes (£30 for two courses). **£110**

Moorcroft Holidays Carinish (Cairinis) ☎ 01876 580305, ⊛ moorcroftholidays.co.uk. An exposed, but flat and very well-equipped campsite with sea views; the bunkhouse has just six beds, lovely wooden floors and furnishings and a modern kitchen. April–Oct. Pitches **£8**, bunkhouse **£20**

Westford Inn Claddach Kirkibost (Cladach Chireboist) ☎ 01876 580653, ⊛ 7mis.co.uk/westfordinn. North Uist's only pub is housed in an eighteenth-century factor's house. There's a wood-panelled bar plus several smaller rooms with real fires in bad weather, Skye ales on tap and pub food until 9pm. May–Sept hours vary but theoretically daily noon–11pm.

Benbecula (Beinn na Faoghla)

Blink and you could miss the pancake-flat island of **Benbecula** (stress on the second syllable), sandwiched between Protestant North Uist and Catholic South Uist. Most visitors simply trundle along the main road that cuts across the middle of the island in less than five miles – not such a bad idea, since the island is scarred from the postwar presence of the Royal Artillery who, until recently, made up half the local population.

The legacy of Benbecula's military past is only too evident in barracks-like **BALIVANICH** (Baile a Mhanaich), the grim, grey island capital. The only reason to come here at all is if you happen to be flying into or out of **Benbecula Airport**, need an ATM, the laundrette (behind the bank) or a supermarket.

ARRIVAL AND DEPARTURE   BENBECULA

By plane Benbecula Airport (ⓦhial.co.uk) is just a 10–15min walk north of Balivanich. There's a small café inside the airport building.

By bus Buses en route to and from South or North Uist stop outside the post office.

Destinations Berneray (Mon–Sat 5–7 daily; 1hr 10min); Eriskay (Mon–Sat 5–7 daily; 1hr 30min); Lochboisdale (Mon–Sat 7–8 daily; 1hr); and Lochmaddy (Mon–Sat 6–7 daily; 30min).

South Uist (Uibhist a Deas)

South Uist is the largest and most varied of the southern chain of islands. The west coast boasts some of the region's finest machair and **beaches** – a necklace of gold and grey sand strung twenty miles from one end to the other – while the east coast features a ridge of high mountains rising to 2034ft at the summit of Beinn Mhòr. However, the chief settlement and ferry port, **LOCHBOISDALE**, occupying a narrow, bumpy promontory on the southeast coast, is only worth visiting to catch the ferry.

Howmore (Tobha Mòr)

One of the best places to gain access to the sandy shoreline is at **HOWMORE** (Tobha Mòr), a pretty little crofting settlement with a fair number of restored houses, many still thatched, including one distinctively roofed in brown heather. Close by are the shattered, lichen-encrusted remains of no fewer than four medieval churches and chapels, and a burial ground now harbouring just a few scattered graves. From the village church, it's an easy walk across the flower-strewn machair to the gorgeous **beach**.

Kildonan Museum (Taigh-tasgaidh Chill Donnain)

5 miles south of Howmore • April–Oct daily 10am–5pm • £2 • ☏ 01878 710343, ⓦ kildonanmuseum.co.uk

The **Kildonan Museum** includes mock-ups of Hebridean kitchens through the ages, two lovely box beds and an impressive selection of old photos. Pride of place goes to the sixteenth-century **Clanranald Stone**, carved with the arms of the clan who ruled over South Uist from 1370 to 1839, which used to lie in the church at Howmore. The museum café also has a choice of historical videos for those really wet and windy days.

ARRIVAL AND INFORMATION   SOUTH UIST

By ferry CalMac ferries run to Lochboisdale from Castlebay (Wed, Fri & Sun; 1hr 40min) and Oban (Tues, Thurs & Sat; 5hr 20min–6hr 30min).

By bus There are buses between Lochboisdale and Balivanich (Mon–Sat 7–8 daily; 1hr), Eriskay (Mon–Sat

6–7 daily; 35min) and Lochmaddy (Mon–Sat 6 daily; 1hr 30min).

Tourist information Pier Rd, Lochboisdale (April–Oct Mon–Sat 9am–5pm; open to meet the ferry; ☏ 01878 700286, ⓦ southuist.com).

ACCOMMODATION AND EATING

Howmore Hostel Howmore ⓦ gatliff.org.uk. A simple Gatliff Trust hostel, occupying a lovely thatched crofthouse near

the village church, and just a short walk from the beach. **£12**

Orasay Inn Lochcarnan (Loch a'Charnain), 3 miles west

24

of Lochboisdale ☎01870 610298, ⓦorasayinn.co.uk. A modern, purpose-built hotel off the main road, in the north of the island; rooms are pretty standard, but the location is peaceful and the breakfasts good – if you're looking for a bar meal, it's best to book ahead. **£99**

Polochar Inn Polochar (Poll a' Charra) ☎01878 700215, ⓦpolocharinn.com. One of the best places to hole up in, right on the south coast, overlooking the Sound of Barra, and with its own sandy beach close by. The recently refurbished rooms all have sea views and on the ground floor is a genuine pub, serving decent bar meals, with live music on Sat nights. Mon–Thurs 11am–11pm; Fri & Sat 11am–1am, Sun 12.30–11pm; food served daily 12.30–2.30pm & 5.30–9pm. **£70**

Eriskay (Eiriosgaigh)

Famous for its patterned jerseys and a diminutive breed of pony, the barren, hilly island of **Eriskay** is connected to the south of South Uist by a causeway built in 2001. The island, measuring just two miles by one, shelters a population of about 150, and makes a great day-trip from South Uist; look out for the ponies, who roam free on the hills, but tend to graze around Loch Crakavaig, the island's freshwater source. The island's main beach on the west coast, the **Prince's Cockle Strand** (Coilleag a Phrionnsa), was where **Bonnie Prince Charlie** landed on Scottish soil on July 23, 1745 – the sea bindweed that grows there to this day is said to have sprung from the seeds Charles brought with him from France.

ARRIVAL AND ACCOMMODATION   ERISKAY

By ferry CalMac run a small car ferry between Barra and the southwest coast of Eriskay (4–5 daily; 40min).

By bus There's a regular service between Eriskay and Lochboisdale (Mon–Sat 4–6 daily; 40min).

Am Politician Rubha Ban ☎01878 720246. The island's purpose-built pub, near the two cemeteries on the west coast, offers an extensive bar menu, as well as home-made cakes and coffee, and great sea views from its conservatory.

Easter–Oct Mon–Sat 11am–11pm, Sun noon–11pm; Nov–Easter Sat & Sun 11am–11pm; food served noon–7.45pm.

Oir na Mara 5b Baile ☎01878 720216. This plain, modern, bungalow B&B is better inside than out. It's situated near Eriskay's pub, around a 15-minute walk from the Barra–Eriskay ferry terminal. Only one twin and one double available so book ahead. **£70**

Barra (Barraigh)

Four miles wide and eight miles long, **Barra** is like the Western Isles in miniature: sandy beaches backed by machair, mountains of Lewissian gneiss, prehistoric ruins, Gaelic culture, and a laidback, welcoming, Catholic population of around 1200.

Castlebay

The only settlement of any size on Barra is **CASTLEBAY** (Bàgh a Chaisteil), which curves around the barren rocky hills of a wide bay on the south side of the island. Barra's religious allegiance is immediately announced by the large Catholic church, Our Lady, Star of the Sea, which overlooks the bay; to underline the point, there's a Madonna and Child on the slopes of **Sheabhal** (1260ft), the largest peak on Barra, and a fairly straightforward hike from the bay.

WHISKY GALORE!

Eriskay's greatest claim to fame came in 1941 when the 8000-tonne **SS Politician** – or *Polly* as it's fondly known – sank on its way from Liverpool to Jamaica, along with its cargo of bicycle parts, £3 million in Jamaican currency and 264,000 bottles of whisky, inspiring Compton MacKenzie's book – and the Ealing comedy (filmed here in 1948) – **Whisky Galore!** (released in the US as *Tight Little Island*). The real story was somewhat less romantic, especially for the 36 islanders charged with illegal possession by the Customs and Excise officers, 19 of whom were found guilty and imprisoned in Inverness for helping themselves to the whisky. The ship's stern can still be seen to the northwest of Calvey Island at low tide, and there's a collection of memorabilia on show in the island's modern pub, *Am Politician*, on the west coast.

24

Kisimul Castle

April–Sept daily 9.30am–5.30pm • £5.50; HS • ☎ 01871 810313

As its name suggests, Castlebay has a castle in its bay; the medieval islet-fortress of Caisteal Chiosmuil or **Kisimul Castle**, ancestral home of the MacNeil clan. The castle burned down in the eighteenth century, but in 1937 the 45th MacNeil chief bought the island back and set about restoring Kisimul. There's nothing much to see inside, but the whole experience is fun – head down to the slipway at the bottom of Main Street, where the ferry skipper will take you over (weather permitting).

Cockle Strand

Oddly enough, one of Barra's most interesting sights is its **airport**, on the north side of the island, where planes land and take off from the crunchy shell sands of Tràigh Mhòr, better known as **Cockle Strand**; the exact timing of the flights depends on the tides, since at high tide the beach (and therefore the runway) is covered in water.

ARRIVAL AND INFORMATION   BARRA (BARRAIGH)

By plane Barra Airport (☎ 01871 890212, ⓦ hial.co.uk) has daily direct flights to and from Glasgow (1hr 10min).

By ferry The main ferry terminal on Barra is in Castlebay, where the ferry from Oban arrives: from Eriskay (5 daily; 40min), you arrive at an uninhabited spot on the northeast of the island.

Destinations From Eriskay (5 daily; 40min), you arrive in the northeast of the island; from Oban (1 daily; 4hr 50min),

Lochboisdale (Mon & Tues; 1hr 30min) and Tiree (Thurs; 3hr), you arrive in Castlebay.

By bus Buses run between Castlebay, the airport, and the Eriskay ferry dock (Mon–Sat 4–6 daily, 35–45min).

Tourist information Main St, Castlebay, just round from the pier (April–Oct Mon–Sat 9am–5pm; also open to greet the Oban ferry; ☎ 01871 810336, ⓦ isleofbarra.com).

ACCOMMODATION AND EATING

★ **Café Kisimul** Main St, Castlebay ☎ 01871 810645, ⓦ cafekisimul.co.uk. As well as offering Italian comfort food and great music, the *Kisimul* also cooks up the best curry in northwest Scotland (mains £12–15) – try the unique scallop pakora and book ahead. Daily morning till late.

Castlebay Hotel Castlebay ☎ 01871 810223, ⓦ castlebay-hotel.co.uk. The *Castlebay* is the more welcoming of the town's two hotels – a solid Victorian pile from 1880, with spectacular views from the restaurant and some of the rooms. **£90**

Dunard Hostel Castlebay ☎ 01871 810443, ⓦ dunardhostel.co.uk. A relaxed, family-run place just west of the ferry terminal that has twins, dorm beds and a family room; they also offer sea kayaking. Dorms **£18**, twins **£40**

Tigh-na-Mara Castlebay ☎ 01871 810304, ⓦ tighna mara-barra.co.uk. For value and location – just a few minutes from the pier in Castlebay – you can't beat this simple Victorian guesthouse overlooking the sea. Free wi-fi. April–Oct. **£60**

24

Orkney and Shetland

PUFFINS AT SUMBURGH HEAD

25

Orkney and Shetland

Reaching up towards the Arctic Circle, the Orkney and Shetland islands gather into two distinct and very different clusters. Orkney lies just north of the Scottish mainland, but with the exception of hilly Hoy, its islands are low-lying, gently sloping and richly fertile. Sixty miles further north, Shetland is a complete contrast. Ice-sculpted sea inlets cut deep into the land that rises straight out of the water to rugged, heather-coated hills. With little fertile ground, Shetlanders have traditionally been crofters rather than farmers, scratching an uncertain living in fishing and whaling or the naval and merchant services.

Orkney boasts a bevy of well-preserved Stone Age settlements, such as **Skara Brae**, standing stones and chambered cairns. The Norse heritage is also apparent in Shetland, where there are many unique prehistoric sites, such as **Mousa Broch** and **Jarlshof**. It's impossible to underestimate the influence of the **weather** up here. More often than not, it'll be windy and rainy, though you can have all four seasons in one day. The wind-chill factor is not to be taken lightly, and there's frequently a dampness or drizzle in the air, even when it's not raining.

Orkney

Orkney is a unique and fiercely independent archipelago of seventy or so low-lying islands, with a population of around twenty thousand. For an Orcadian, **Mainland** means the largest island in Orkney rather than the rest of Scotland, and their history is inextricably linked with Scandinavia. Orkney Mainland has two chief settlements: the old port of **Stromness**, an attractive fishing town in the southwest, and the central capital of **Kirkwall**.

Mainland is relatively heavily populated and farmed throughout, and is joined by causeways to a string of southern islands, the largest being **South Ronaldsay**. South of Mainland, **Hoy** presents a superbly dramatic landscape, boasting some of Britain's highest sea cliffs. Hoy, however, is atypical: Orkney's smaller, much quieter **northern islands** are flat, elemental but fertile outcrops of rock and sand, scattered across the ocean.

ARRIVAL AND DEPARTURE   ORKNEY

By car ferry Northlink Ferries (☎0845 600 0449, ⓦnorthlinkferries.co.uk) have services to Stromness from Scrabster (2–3 daily; 1hr 30min), which is connected to nearby Thurso by shuttle bus, and ferries to Kirkwall from Aberdeen (3–4 weekly; 6hr) and Lerwick in Shetland (2–3 weekly; 5hr 30min). Pentland Ferries (☎01856 831226, ⓦpentlandferries.co.uk) run catamarans from Gills Bay, near John O'Groats (linked by bus to Wick and Thurso) to St

Margaret's Hope on South Ronaldsay (3–4 daily; 1hr).
By passenger ferry John O'Groats Ferries (☎01955 611353, ⓦjogferry.co.uk) runs a passenger ferry from John O'Groats to Burwick on South Ronaldsay (May–Sept 2–3 daily; 40min); departures connect with the Orkney Bus from Inverness, and there's a free shuttle service from Thurso train station. The ferry is small and, except in fine weather, is only recommended for travellers with strong stomachs.

Scapa Flow and the Churchill
Barriers p.958

Noss p.966
Mousa Broch p.967

ST MAGNUS CATHEDRAL

Highlights

❶ Maes Howe Europe's finest Neolithic chambered tomb is sealed within a grassy mound in the centre of Orkney's Mainland. **See p.954**

❷ Skara Brae Neolithic village giving a fascinating insight into prehistoric life. **See p.954**

❸ St Magnus Cathedral, Kirkwall Orkney's cathedral is a miniature masterpiece built in red sandstone at Kirkwall by the Vikings. **See p.955**

❹ Rackwick Experience splendid isolation, a rumbling rocky beach and the famous Old Man of Hoy in this remote village on the island of Hoy. **See p.958**

❺ Scapa Flow Visitor Centre & Museum, Lyness Learn about the rich wartime history of

Orkney's natural harbour, Scapa Flow. **See p.958**

❻ Westray Thriving Orkney island with seabird colonies, sandy beaches, a ruined castle, a famous prehistoric fertility symbol and tip-top fish and chips. **See p.959**

❼ Noss Nature reserve island where you're guaranteed seals, puffins and dive-bombing "bonxies". **See p.966**

❽ Mousa Remote Shetland islet with Scotland's finest-preserved 2000-year-old broch and nesting storm petrels (in season) **See p.967**

❾ Jarlshof Impressive archeological site mingling Iron Age, Bronze Age, Pictish, Viking and medieval settlements. **See p.967**

HIGHLIGHTS ARE MARKED ON THE MAP ON P.952 & P963

25

By plane Flybe (ⓦflybe.com) offers direct flights to Kirkwall airport from Sumburgh in Shetland, Inverness, Aberdeen, Edinburgh and Glasgow.

GETTING AROUND

By ferry Getting to the other islands by ferry from the Mainland isn't difficult, but travel between individual islands isn't straightforward. Ask Orkney Ferries (ⓣ01856 872044, ⓦorkneyferries.co.uk) about summer Sunday sailings, which make useful interisland connections. Tickets are expensive and you should book ahead if you've a vehicle.

ORKNEY

0   5 miles

HIGHLIGHTS

1. Maes Howe
2. Skara Brae
3. St Magnus Cathedral, Kirkwall
4. Rackwick
5. Scapa Flow Visitor Centre & Museum, Lyness
6. Westray

By plane Flights from Kirkwall to the outer isles are operated by Loganair (☏ 01856 872494, ⓦ loganair.co.uk), using an eight-seater plane, with discounted fares to North Ronaldsay and Papa Westray and between the islands if you stay over.

By bus Bus services (☏ 01856 870555, ⓦ stagecoachbus .com) on the Mainland are good during the week, but skeletal on Sundays – except in Stromness and Kirkwall,

there are no scheduled bus stops so just stand at a safe visible spot and flag the bus down. On the smaller islands, a minibus usually meets the ferry and will take you to your destination.

By bike Cycling is okay if the weather holds, with few steep hills and modest distances, though the wind can make it hard going.

Stromness

STROMNESS is one of the most enchanting ports at which to arrive by boat, its picturesque waterfront a procession of tiny sandstone jetties and slate roofs. An important harbour town since the eighteenth century, it's well worth a day's exploration, and in many ways is a better base than Kirkwall, especially during the popular four-day **Orkney Folk Festival** (ⓦ orkneyfolkfestival.com) in May.

Pier Arts Centre

Victoria St · Feb to mid June & Sept–Christmas Tues–Sat 10.30am–5pm, mid-June to Aug Mon–Sat 10.30am–5pm · Free
☏ 01856 850209, ⓦ pierartscentre.com

The warehouse on the first of the old jetties on the main street of Stromness now forms half of the **Pier Arts Centre**; the other half is a modern glass-and-steel structure which offers views of the harbour framed like pictures. The gallery features a remarkable collection of twentieth-century British art, including work by Eduardo Paolozzi as well as members of the Cornish school such as Barbara Hepworth, Ben Nicholson, and the self-taught Alfred Wallis. In addition, there are contemporary works, many by northern and Scandinavian artists, which continue the marine themes of the original collection.

Stromness Museum

52 Alfred St · April–Sept daily 10am–5pm; Oct–March Mon–Sat 11am–3.30pm · £4.50 · ☏ 01856 850025

The intriguing **Stromness Museum**, built in 1858, has a wonderfully old-fashioned natural-history collection – don't miss the pull-out drawers of birds' eggs, butterflies and moths – and an early inflatable like the one used by John Rae, the Stromness-born Arctic explorer, whose fiddle, octant and shotgun are also on display. Look out, too, for the barnacle-encrusted crockery from the German High Seas Fleet that was sunk in Scapa Flow in 1919.

ARRIVAL AND INFORMATION   STROMNESS

By ferry Car ferries from Scrabster on the Scottish mainland (2–3 daily; 1hr 30min) arrive in the centre of Stromness. A passenger ferry sails from the old harbour to Moaness Pier on Hoy (Mon–Fri 4–5 daily, Sat & Sun 2 daily; 25min).

By bus Buses depart from Stromness ferry terminal. Destinations Houton (Mon–Fri 2 daily; 20min); Kirkwall

(Mon–Sat hourly, Sun every 2hr; 30min); Skara Brae (Mon, Thurs & Sat 1 daily; 20min).

Tourist information Stromness ferry terminal houses the tourist office (June–Aug daily 9am–5pm; Sept–May Mon–Sat 10am–4pm; ☏ 01856 850716, ⓦ visitorkney .com).

ACCOMMODATION AND EATING

Brinkies Guest House Innertown ☏ 01856 851881. A substantial double-bay-fronted Victorian guesthouse located 10min walk up from the town. Rooms enjoy fantastic views, the residents' lounge has loads of reading matter and there's free wi-fi. **£70**

★**Burnside Farm** North End Rd ☏ 01856 850723, ⓦ burnside-farm.com. A cracking B&B run by a local couple on a working farm about a mile out of town on the road to Kirkwall. The views are great, and the furnishings

and facilities are truly top-notch: en-suite wet-rooms and free wi-fi, plus *bere bannocks* for breakfast. **£75**

Hamnavoe Hostel 10a North End Rd ☏ 01856 851202, ⓦ hamnavoehostel.co.uk. A good 10min walk from the ferry terminal and no beauty from the outside, but inside it's welcoming and well-equipped, with spotlessly clean dorms. **£17**

Hamnavoe Restaurant 35 Graham Place ☏ 01856 850606. Here you'll find the town's most ambitious

25

cooking, concentrating on local produce such as grilled sole or peppered monkfish – mains start at around £15 and booking is essential. May–Sept Tues–Sun 7–10pm.

Julia's Café and Bistro 20 Ferry Rd • ☎01856 850904, ⍟juliascafe.co.uk. Daytime café right opposite the ferry terminal, with a sunny conservatory and tables outside if the weather's good enough. It's comfort food for the most part, but you can get a decent fish pie for under £10. Mon–Sat 9am–5pm, Sun 10am–5pm.

Point of Ness Campsite ☎01856 873535. Busy campsite in a superb (though extremely exposed) setting, a mile south of the ferry terminal, with views over to Hoy. Facilities include a TV lounge and a washing machine. April–Sept. Pitches **£7**

West Mainland

The great bulk of the **West Mainland** – west of Kirkwall, that is – is fertile farmland, fenced off into a patchwork of fields, used for cattle grazing. Fringed by a spectacular western coastline, West Mainland is littered with some of the island's most impressive prehistoric sites, such as the village of **Skara Brae**, the standing **Stones of Stenness** and the chambered tomb of **Maes Howe**.

Ring of Brodgar

Guided tours June–Aug daily 1pm • Free; HS • ☎ 01856 841732

Orkney's most important Neolithic ceremonial complex is centred around the twin lochs of Stenness (which is tidal) and Harray (which is freshwater). On the thin strip of land between the two stands the **Ring of Brodgar**, a wide stone circle dramatically sited on raised ground, originally surrounded by a henge, of which only the ditch survives. Of the 60 stones which once stood in the circle, 27 are currently left standing – the circle dates from before 2000 BC.

Stones of Stenness

Guided tours June–Aug Mon, Wed & Fri 10am • Free; HS • ☎ 01856 841732

The **Stones of Stenness** form part of the same ceremonial complex as the nearby Ring of Brodgar. Originally a circle of twelve rock slabs, four remain standing, the tallest of which is more than 16ft high and remarkable for its incredible thinness. A broken table-top lies within the circle, surrounded by a much-diminished henge (a circular bank of earth and a ditch) with a couple of entrance causeways.

Maes Howe

Daily: April–Sept 9.30am–5pm; Oct–March 9.30am–4pm; guided tours every 45min; timed tickets in summer • £5.50; HS • ☎ 01856 761606

Maes Howe, one of Europe's most impressive Neolithic burial chamber complexes, lies less than a mile from the Stones of Stenness. Dating from around 3000 BC, its excellent state of preservation is partly due to the massive slabs of sandstone it was constructed from, the largest of which weighs more than thirty tonnes. Perhaps its most extraordinary aspect is that the tomb is aligned so that the rays of the winter solstice sun reach right down the passage to the ledge of one of the three cells built into the walls of the tomb. The Vikings entered in the twelfth century, leaving large amounts of runic graffiti, cut into the walls of the main chamber and still clearly visible today.

Skara Brae

Daily: April–Sept 9.30am–5.30pm; Oct–March 9.30am–4.30pm • £6.10–7.10; HS • ☎ 01856 841815

The extensive remains of a small Neolithic fishing and farming village, dating back to 3000 BC, were discovered at **Skara Brae** in 1850 after a fierce storm ripped off the dunes covering them. The village is amazingly well-preserved, its houses huddled together and connected by narrow passages originally covered with turf. The houses themselves consist of a single, spacious living room, filled with domestic detail, including fireplaces, cupboards, beds and boxes, all ingeniously constructed from slabs of stone. The visitor centre houses a good café and an introductory exhibition, while beyond is a full-scale replica of the best-preserved house; it's a bit neat and tidy, but gives you the general idea and makes up for the fact that you can only look down on the village from the outer walls.

Birsay

The parish of **BIRSAY**, in northwest Mainland, was the centre of Norse power in Orkney for several centuries before the earls moved to Kirkwall and built the cathedral. Today a tiny cluster of homes is gathered around the sandstone ruins of the **Earl's Palace**, built in the sixteenth century by Robert Stewart, Earl of Orkney, using the forced labour of the islanders. The palace appears to have lasted barely a century before falling into rack and ruin, though the crumbling walls and turrets retain much of their grandeur.

Brough of Birsay

Accessible 2hr either side of low tide • Tide times available at Stromness and Kirkwall tourist offices (see p.956) and on Radio Orkney (93.7FM; Mon–Fri 7.30–8am) • St Peter's Church Mid-June to Sept daily 9.30am–5.30pm • £4.50

Just over half a mile northwest of Birsay village is the **Brough of Birsay**, a substantial Pictish settlement on a small tidal island. The focus of the village was – and still is – the sandstone built twelfth-century **St Peter's Church**. Close by is a large complex of Viking era buildings, including several houses, a sauna and some sophisticated stone drains.

Broch of Gurness

Evie • April–Oct daily 9.30am–5.30pm • £5.50; HS • ☎ 01856 751414

The **Broch of Gurness** is the best-preserved broch on an archipelago replete with them, and is still surrounded by a remarkable complex of later buildings. As at Birsay, the sea has eaten away half the site, but the broch itself, dating from 100 BC, still stands, its walls up to 12ft in places, its inner cells still intact. The compact group of homes huddled around the broch have also survived amazingly well, with much of their original and ingenious stone shelving and fireplaces still *in situ*.

ACCOMMODATION	WEST MAINLAND
★ **Holland House** Harray ☎ 01856 771400, ⓦ holland houseorkney.co.uk. A beautiful, solidly built manse in Harray, set back from the A986. The house is filled with artworks, there's a peat fire, and the home-cooking, including freshly baked scones for breakfast, is outstanding. **£104**	**Mill of Eyrland** Stenness, off the A964 towards Orphir ☎ 01856 850136, ⓦ millofeyrland.com. Lovingly converted watermill in a delightful spot by a trout-filled stream. Rooms are filled with antiques and the guest lounge is set around the old mill equipment. Free wi-fi and enormous breakfasts. **£80**

Kirkwall

KIRKWALL, Orkney's capital, has one great redeeming feature – its sandstone **cathedral**, the finest medieval building in the north of Scotland. The town itself divides into two main focal points: the old **harbour**, to the north, where interisland ferries come and go, and the flagstoned **main street**, which changes its name four times as it twists its way south from the harbour past the cathedral. Kirkwall's chief cultural bash is the week-long **St Magnus Festival** (ⓦ stmagnusfestival.com), a superb arts festival held in June.

St Magnus Cathedral

Broad St • April–Sept Mon–Sat 9am–6pm, Sun 2–5pm; Oct–March Mon–Sat 9am–1pm & 2–5pm • Free • ⓦ stmagnus.org

Standing at the heart of Kirkwall, **St Magnus Cathedral** is the town's most compelling sight. This beautiful red-sandstone building was begun in 1137 by the Viking Earl

25

Rognvald, who built the cathedral in honour of his uncle Magnus, killed on the orders of his cousin Håkon in 1117. Today much of the detail in the soft sandstone has worn away – the capitals around the main doors are reduced to gnarled stumps – but it's still immensely impressive, its shape and style echoing the great cathedrals of Europe. Inside, the atmosphere is surprisingly intimate, the bulky sandstone columns drawing your eye up to the exposed brickwork arches, while around the walls is a series of mostly seventeenth-century tombstones, many carved with a skull and crossbones and other emblems of mortality.

Bishop's and Earl's palaces

Palace Rd · April–Oct daily 9.30am–5.30pm · £4.50; HS · ☎ 01856 871918

The ruined remains of the **Bishop's Palace**, residence of the Bishop of Orkney since the twelfth century, lie to the south of the cathedral. Most of what you see, however, dates from the time of Bishop Robert Reid, sixteenth-century founder of Edinburgh University. A narrow spiral staircase takes you to the top for a good view over the cathedral and Kirkwall's rooftops.

The **Earl's Palace**, on the other side of Watergate, was built by the infamous Earl Patrick Stewart around 1600, using forced labour. With its grand entrance, fancy oriel windows, dank dungeons, massive fireplaces and magnificent central hall, it's reckoned to be one of the finest examples of Renaissance architecture in Scotland. The roof may be missing, but many domestic details remain, including a set of toilets and the stone shelves used by the clerk.

Orkney Museum

Broad St · Mon–Sat: May–Sept 10.30am–5pm; Oct–April 10.30am–12.30pm & 1.30–5pm · Free · ☎ 01856 873191

The sixteenth-century Tankerness House, a former home for the clergy, opposite the cathedral, is now home to the **Orkney Museum**. A couple of rooms have been restored as they would have been in the 1820s when it was a private house. The rest houses some of the islands' most treasured finds, including a witch's spell box, and a lovely whalebone plaque from a Viking boat grave discovered on Sanday.

ARRIVAL AND INFORMATION   KIRKWALL

By plane Kirkwall Airport (☎ 01851 707400, ⓦ hial.co.uk) is about 3 miles southeast of town on the A960 – take the bus (Mon–Sat every 30min; 15min) or a taxi (£5).

By bus The bus station is behind the Kirkwall Travel Centre, West Castle St.
Destinations Birsay (Mon–Sat 2–3 daily; 45min); Burwick (2–3 daily; 40min); Houton (Mon–Fri 7 daily, Sat 3 daily; 35–40min); Skara Brae (June–Aug Mon, Thurs & Sat 1 daily; 50min); St Margaret's Hope (Mon–Sat hourly, Sun every 2hr; 30min); Stromness (Mon–Sat hourly, Sun every 2hr; 30min); Tingwall (Mon–Sat 4–5 daily; 25min).

By ferry NorthLink ferries from Shetland and Aberdeen (and all cruise ships) dock at the Hatston terminal, a mile or so northwest of town; buses will take you into Kirkwall. Orkney Ferries leave from Kirkwall harbour in the centre of town.
Destinations within Orkney Eday (2–3 daily; 1hr 15min–2hr 25min); North Ronaldsay (Tues & Fri; 2hr 40min); Sanday (2 daily; 1hr 25min); Stronsay (2 daily; 1hr 40min–2hr); Westray (2–3 daily; 1hr 25min).

Tourist information The Kirkwall Travel Centre on West Castle St houses the tourist office (Mon–Sat 9am–5pm, Sun 10am–4pm; ☎ 01856 872856, ⓦ visitorkney.com).

ACCOMMODATION

2 Dundas Crescent ☎ 01856 874805. Run by an Orcadian couple and situated just behind the cathedral, this former manse is a grand and tastefully decorated Victorian house, with four spacious rooms and period fittings. **£75**

Avalon House Carness Rd ☎ 01856 876665, ⓦ avalon-house.co.uk. Don't judge a B&B by its drab, modern exterior; this is a comfortable, purpose-built guesthouse run efficiently by a very welcoming couple, and situated a pleasant 20min coastal walk from the town centre. **£80**

Peedie Hostel 1 Ayre Houses ☎ 01856 875477, ⓦ kirkwallpeediehostel.com. Centrally located overlooking the old harbour and out to sea, this is a clean and comfortable hostel with singles, twins, quads/dorms and a self-catering bothy (min 3 nights). Washing machine and tumble dryer available, plus free wi-fi. April–Oct. Dorms

£15, twins £30, bothy £45
Pickaquoy Campsite Ayre Rd ☎01856 879900, ⓦpickaquoy.net. Central, and well-equipped and

-maintained, Kirkwall's site is behind (and run by) the local leisure centre, but it's not the prettiest of spots. April–Oct. Pitches £10

EATING AND DRINKING

Helgi's 14 Harbour St ☎01856 879293, ⓦhelgis.co.uk. A popular modern pub on the harbourfront, which serves nicely-presented bar food: from burger/fish and chips to fajitas (all under £10). Mon–Wed 11am–midnight, Thurs–Sat 11am–1am, Sun 12.30pm–midnight.
Lucano 31 Victoria Rd ☎01856 875687, ⓦlucano kirkwall.com. A busy, bright, modern and authentic Italian – a real find in Kirkwall – offering pizza, pasta and risotto with an Orcadian angle. It's popular so book ahead. Daily

9am–9pm.
★The Reel 6 Broad St ☎01856 871000, ⓦwrigleyandthereel.com. The old customs house near the cathedral is now a laidback, self-service café run by the musical Wrigley sisters, serving great coffee, sandwiches, pizzas and cake, and offering free wi-fi and regular live music (Wed, Thurs & Sat). Mon–Fri 8.30am–6pm, Sat 9am–1am; in summer also Sun noon–4pm.

South Ronaldsay

At the southern end of the Churchill Barriers (see box, p.958) is **South Ronaldsay**, the largest of the islands linked to the Mainland. Its main settlement is **ST MARGARET'S HOPE** – or "The Hope" – a pleasing little gathering of stone-built houses overlooking a sheltered bay. Once a thriving port, the Hope is now a peaceful place, despite the presence of the **Pentland Ferries terminal**.

Tomb of the Eagles

Liddle • Daily: March 10am–noon; April–Sept 9.30am–5.30pm; Oct 9.30am–12.30pm; Nov–Feb by appointment • £7 • ☎01856 831339, ⓦtomboftheeagles.co.uk

One of the most enjoyable archeological sights on Orkney is the Isbister chambered burial cairn at the southeastern corner of South Ronaldsay, known as the **Tomb of the Eagles**. Discovered, excavated and still owned by local farmer Ronald Simpson, the tomb makes a refreshing change from the usual interpretative centre. First, you get to look round the family's private museum of prehistoric artefacts; then you get a guided tour of a nearby Bronze Age **burnt mound**, which is basically a Neolithic rubbish dump; and finally you walk out to the **chambered cairn** by the cliff's edge, where human remains were found alongside talons and carcasses of sea eagles. To enter the cairn, you must lie on a trolley and pull yourself in using an overhead rope.

ARRIVAL AND DEPARTURE
SOUTH RONALDSAY

By ferry Car ferry catamarans run from Gills Bay, near John O'Groats, to St Margaret's Hope (3–4 daily; 1hr), while passenger ferries run from John O'Groats to Burwick, 7 miles from St Margaret's Hope (2–3 daily; 40min).

ACCOMMODATION AND EATING

The Creel Front Rd, St Margaret's Hope ☎01856 831311, ⓦthecreel.co.uk. The short and seasonal menu regularly features the likes of local beef brisket and hand-dived scallops, with three-course dinners around £40. The rooms are beautifully furnished and breakfasts are among the best on Orkney. Food served April–Oct Tues–Sat 7–9pm. £110
Roeberry House St Margaret's Hope ☎01856 831228, ⓦroeberryhouse.com. Spacious rooms in a beautiful Victorian mansion in Hoxa. There are dogs, cats, chickens and peacocks, spectacular views and a warm welcome, plus a small kitchen for guests' use, a billiard room and free

wi-fi. April–Oct. £110
Skerries Bistro Banks, Cleat ☎01856 831605, ⓦskerriesbistro.co.uk. Fabulous views over the Pentland Firth and Skerries, with local fish and king scallops as big as steaks (mains around £15), plus delicious home-made puddings and cakes. April–Oct 11am–10pm.
Wheems Eastside ☎01856 831537, ⓦwheemsorganic .co.uk. A rambling old crofthouse and organic farm, 1.5 miles east of the main road, with a couple of wooden huts for hire, a sloping field for camping, all the usual facilities plus a communal yurt. April–Oct. Pitches £7, wooden huts £35

25

Hoy

Hoy, Orkney's second-largest island, rises sharply out of the sea to the southwest of the Mainland. Its dramatic landscape is made up of great glacial valleys and mountainous moorland rising to more than 1500ft, dropping into the sea off the red sandstone cliffs of St John's Head.

Rackwick

RACKWICK is an old crofting and fishing settlement squeezed between towering sandstone cliffs on the west coast. A small farm building beside the hostel (see opposite) serves as a tiny **museum** (always open; free), with a few old photos and a brief rundown of Rackwick's rough history. Despite its isolation, Rackwick has a steady stream of walkers and climbers passing through en route to the **Old Man of Hoy**, a sandstone column some 450ft high, perched on an old lava flow protecting it from the erosive power of the sea. The well-trodden footpath from Rackwick is an easy three-mile walk (3hr return). Halfway along the road between Hoy village and Rackwick, duckboards head across the heather to the **Dwarfie Stane**, Orkney's most unusual chambered tomb, cut from a solid block of sandstone and dating back to 3000 BC.

Scapa Flow Visitor Centre & Museum

Lyness, opposite the ferry terminal • Easter hols Mon–Fri 9am–4.30pm; April & Oct Mon–Sat 9am–4.30pm; May–Sept Mon–Sat 9am–4.30pm, Sun from first ferry to last • Free • ☎ 01856 791300, ⦿ scapaflow.co.uk

Hoy played a major role for the Royal Navy during both world wars and the harbour and hills around Lyness are still scarred with the scattered remains of concrete structures that once served as hangars and storehouses during World War II. The old oil pump house has been turned into the **Scapa Flow Visitor Centre & Museum**, a fascinating insight into wartime Orkney. The pump house itself retains much of its old equipment – you can ask for a working demo of one of the oil-fired boilers – used to pump oil off tankers moored at Lyness into sixteen tanks, and from there into underground reservoirs cut into the neighbouring hillside. Even the café has an old NAAFI feel about it.

ARRIVAL, ACCOMMODATION & EATING   HOY

By ferry A passenger ferry runs from Stromness to Moaness pier, by Hoy village (Mon–Fri 4–5 daily, Sat & Sun 2 daily; 25min; ☎ 01856 850624), and a car ferry runs from Houton on the Mainland to Lyness (Mon–Fri 6 daily, Sat & Sun 2–5 daily; 35min–1hr; ☎ 01856 811397). A minibus usually meets the Stromness ferry and will take folk over to Rackwick or further afield. A seasonal Hoy Hopper bus service (mid-May to mid-Sept Wed–Fri only) departs from

---

SCAPA FLOW AND THE CHURCHILL BARRIERS

The presence of a huge naval base in **Scapa Flow** during both world wars presented an irresistible target to the Germans, and protecting the fleet was always a nagging problem for the Allies. During World War I, blockships were sunk to guard the eastern approaches, but just weeks after the outbreak of World War II, a German U-boat managed to manoeuvre past the blockships and torpedo the battleship HMS *Royal Oak*, which sank with the loss of 833 lives.

The sinking of the *Royal Oak* convinced the First Lord of the Admiralty, Winston Churchill, that Scapa Flow needed better protection, and in 1940 work began on a series of barriers – known as the **Churchill Barriers** – to seal the waters between the Mainland and the string of islands to the south. Special camps were built to accommodate the 1700 men involved in the project; their numbers were boosted by the surrender of Italy in 1942, when Italian POWs were sent to work here.

Besides the barriers, the Italians also left behind the beautiful **Italian Chapel** (daily dawn–dusk; free) on the first of the islands, Lamb Holm. This, the so-called "miracle of Camp 60" is made from two Nissen huts, concrete, barbed wire and parts of a rusting blockship. It has a great false facade, and colourful trompe l'oeil decor, lovingly restored by the chapel's principal architect, Domenico Chiocchetti.

Kirkwall Travel Centre and drives onto the ferry to Lyness. **Beneth'hill Café** Moaness ✆ 01856 851116. Friendly, simple café, a short walk from Moaness Pier, serving Cullen Skink, fresh local crab, home-made puddings and proper coffee – they'll even do you a packed lunch and an evening meal on a Friday. May–Sept Mon–Fri 10am–6.30pm.

Rackwick Outdoor Centre ✆ 01856 873535 ext 2417. There's eight dorm beds in Rackwick's tiny little former schoolhouse, but you can also camp behind the hostel, or beside the basic heather-thatched Burnside Bothy

(donations; ✆ 01856 791316) by the beach. Be warned, though, North Hoy is probably the worst place on Orkney for midges. April–Sept. Dorms £13

★ **Wild Heather** Lyness ✆ 01856 791098, ⊕ go-bed andbreakfast.co.uk/wildheatherbandb. The most outstanding accommodation on Hoy lies just beyond the naval cemetery. It's a converted mill with just two en-suite rooms, both with sea views and a lovely breakfast conservatory – they provide evening meals, too, on request. £70

Rousay

The hilly island of **Rousay** is one of the more accessible northern isles and also home to a number of intriguing prehistoric sites. A trio of cairns is spread out on and off the road that leads west from the ferry terminal, and, after four miles, the road passes the most significant and impressive of the island's archeological remains. Approaching from the east, **Midhowe Cairn** comes as something of a surprise, both for its immense size – it's nearly 100ft long and known as "the great ship of death" – and because it's now entirely surrounded by a stone-walled barn with a corrugated roof. Unfortunately, you can't actually explore the roofless communal burial chamber, dating back to 3500 BC, but only look down from the overhead walkway. A couple of hundred yards beyond is Rousay's finest archeological site, **Midhowe Broch**, whose compact layout suggests that it was originally built as a sort of fortified family house, surrounded by a complex series of ditches and ramparts. The interior is divided into two separate rooms, each with their own hearth, water tank and quernstone, all of which date from the final phase of occupation around the second century AD.

ARRIVAL AND GETTING AROUND

ROUSAY

By ferry Rousay makes a good day-trip from the Mainland, with car ferries from Tingwall (5–6 daily; 30min; ✆ 01856 751360).

By bus A bus service runs on request every Thursday

(✆ 01856 821360), and, in season, there are minibus tours available on demand (✆ 01856 821234, ⊕ rousaytours .co.uk; £30), which connect with ferries.

ACCOMMODATION AND EATING

The Pier ✆ 01856 821359, ⊕ pierrestaurantorkney .com. A simple pub, right beside the ferry terminal, that serves bar meals (all under £10) and Orkney beers, and will serve up lobster or make up some fresh crab sandwiches if you phone in advance. May–Sept Mon, Tues, Fri & Sat 11am–11pm, Wed 11am–6pm, Thurs 10am–6pm, Sun 12.30–6pm; shorter hours in winter.

The Taversoe ✆ 01856 821325, ⊕ taversoehotel .co.uk. 3 miles west of the ferry terminal, The Taversoe

offers unpretentious accommodation in three rooms (two with sea views) and does classic pub meals – fish and chips, scampi or burgers (all under £10). £80

Trumland Farm ✆ 01856 821252, ⊖ trumland @btopenworld.com. Just half a mile west of the ferry terminal, this working organic farm has a couple of dorms and a family room – you can also camp here, and they offer bike rental. Camping per person £5, dorms £12

Westray

Although exposed to the full force of the Atlantic weather in the far northwest of Orkney, **Westray** shelters one of the most tightly knit and prosperous island communities. The main village and harbour is **PIEROWALL**, set around a wide bay in the north. The village's **Westray Heritage Centre** (May–Sept Mon 11.30am–5pm, Tues–Sat 10am–noon & 2–5pm, Sun 1.30–5.30pm; £2.50) is a great place to gen up on (and with any luck catch a glimpse of) the Westray Wife or **Orkney Venus**, a remarkable, miniature Neolithic female figurine found in 2009 in the nearby dunes.

25

Above the village to the west is the sandstone hulk of **Noltland Castle**, begun around 1560 by Gilbert Balfour, Master of the Household to Mary, Queen of Scots, who was implicated in the murder of Mary's husband Lord Darnley. To explore, pick up the key at the nearby farm.

The northwestern tip of Westray rises up sharply, culminating in the dramatic sea cliffs of **Noup Head**. In early summer, the guano-covered rock ledges are packed with more than 100,000 nesting seabirds, primarily guillemots, razorbills, kittiwakes and fulmars, with puffins as well – an awesome sight, sound and smell. For a closer view of puffins, head for **Castle o' Burrian**, a sea stack in the southeast of the island.

ARRIVAL AND GETTING AROUND   WESTRAY

By plane You can fly from Kirkwall (Mon–Fri 2 daily, Sat & Sun 1 daily; 15min) and go on the world's shortest scheduled flight between Westray and the neighbouring island of Papa Westray (Mon–Sat 1 daily; 2min).

By ferry Westray is served by car ferry from Kirkwall (2–3 daily; 1hr 25min; ☎01856 872044) and there's a passenger ferry between Pierowall (Westray) and Papa Westray (Mon–Thurs 6 daily, Fri & Sat 4 daily, Sun 3 daily; 25min; ☎01857 8677216).

By bus A minibus (May–Sept; at other times phone ☎01857 677758) meets the ferry and will take you to any point on the island.

ACCOMMODATION AND EATING

★**The Barn** Chalmersquoy, Pierowall ☎01857 677214, ⓦthebarnwestray.co.uk. A converted farm hostel at the southern edge of Pierowall; it's luxurious inside, with family rooms and twin bunks available. It also has a small campsite adjacent to it, a games room and genuinely friendly hosts. Pitches £7, dorms £20, family rooms £45

No. 1 Broughton Pierowall ☎01857 677726, ⓦno1 broughton.co.uk. Top-notch, good-value B&B in a renovated mid-nineteenth-century house with views across the bay, a lovely conservatory and even a small sauna. £60

Pierowall Hotel Pierowall ☎01857 677472, ⓦpierowallhotel.co.uk. Pierowall's social hub is unpretentious and very welcoming – the cheaper rooms have shared facilities. The popular bar has a well-justified reputation for fish and chips, fresh off the boats (much of the catch you're unlikely to have heard of). All mains under £10. £80

Papa Westray

Across Papa Sound from Westray is the island of **Papa Westray**, known locally as "Papay". With a population of around 90, Papay has had to fight hard to keep itself viable over the last couple of decades, helped by a hefty influx of outsiders. With one of Orkney's best-preserved Neolithic settlements, and a large nesting seabird population, the island is worth an overnight stay or a day-trip.

A road leads down from Holland House, in the centre of the island, to the western shore, where the **Knap of Howar** stands. Dating from around 3500 BC, this Neolithic farm building makes a fair claim to being the oldest standing house in Europe. Half a mile north along the coast is **St Boniface Kirk**, a restored pre-Reformation church, with a bare flagstone floor, dry-stone walls, a little wooden gallery and just a couple of surviving box pews.

ARRIVAL AND DEPARTURE   PAPA WESTRAY

By plane You can fly direct from Kirkwall to Papa Westray (Mon–Sat 2–3 daily, Sun 1 daily; 25min) for £21 if you stay overnight. The island is also connected to Westray by the world's shortest scheduled flight (Mon–Sat 1 daily) – two minutes or less with a following wind.

By ferry On Tuesdays, the car ferry goes from Kirkwall to Papa Westray via North Ronaldsay, taking over four hours; on Fridays, the car ferry from Kirkwall to Westray continues to Papa Westray; at other times, you must catch a bus to connect with the Papa Westray ferry from Pierowall. The bus should be booked ahead (ⓦwestraybusservice.com, ☎07789 034289); it accepts a limited number of bicycles.

GETTING AROUND AND ACCOMMODATION

By bus Papa Westray's Community Co-operative (☎01857 644321) has a minibus, which will take you from the pier to wherever you want on the island on request, and can arrange a "Peedie Package" tour including lunch (May–Aug Wed & Sat; £40) – you can even do it from Kirkwall as a 12-hour day-trip.

Beltane House ☎01857 644224, ⑩papawestray.co.uk. The island Co-op offers B&B, a two-room, sixteen-bed hostel, a place to camp, and a shop, within the old estate-workers'

cottages at Beltane, east of Holland House. *Beltane House* opens its "bar cupboard" every Saturday night from 9pm, with bar meals available. Camping per person £5, dorms **£13.50**, doubles **£70**

Eday

A long, thin island, **Eday** (⑩visiteday.com) is dominated by a great block of heather-covered upland, with farmland confined to a narrow strip of coastal ground. The chief points of interest are all in the northern half of the island, beyond the community shop on the main road. Clearly visible from the road is the 15ft **Stone of Setter**, Orkney's most distinctive standing stone, weathered into three thick, lichen-encrusted fingers. From here you can climb the hill to the **Vinquoy Chambered Cairn**, which has a similar structure to that of Maes Howe. You can crawl into the tomb through the narrow entrance: a skylight inside lets light into the main, beehive chamber, now home to some lovely ferns, but not into the four side-cells.

ARRIVAL AND INFORMATION　　　　　　　　　　　　　　EDAY

By plane You can make a day-trip by plane from Kirkwall to Eday on Wednesdays (Mon 1 daily, Wed 2 daily; 10min).
By ferry Eday is served by regular car ferry from Kirkwall (2 daily; 1hr 15min–2hr).
Getting around Eday's ferry terminal is at Backaland pier

in the south; you should be able to get a lift with someone off the ferry. The other option is to contact Eday Minibus Tours (May to mid-Sept Mon, Wed & Fri, or by appointment; £14; ☎01857 622206) who will collect you from the ferry.

ACCOMMODATION AND EATING

Blett B&B ☎01857 622248. A lovely old crofthouse with one double and one single room, near Carrick House, overlooking the bay. They'll provide packed lunches with home-made bread and excellent locally-sourced evening meals are available on request. **£70**
Eday Youth Hostel ☎01857 622283, ⑩syha.org.uk. SYHA-affiliated, community-run barn of a hostel, in an exposed spot just north of the airport – phone ahead, as

there's no resident warden. There's a washing machine and dryer, bike hire and internet access, and you can camp there, too. Per person **£15**
Roadside Pub ☎01857 622303, ⑥anne.cant @hotmail.co.uk. Eday's one and only pub is in a pleasant old building overlooking the ferry terminal, and offers B&B in two en-suite rooms and evening meals on request (mains under £10). **£60**

Stronsay

A beguiling combination of green pastures, white sands and clear turquoise bays, **Stronsay** was a centre for the curing of herring from the 1840s to the 1930s. **WHITEHALL** is the island's only real village, made up of rows of stone-built fishermen's cottages set between two large piers. Wandering along the tranquil harbourfront today, it's hard to believe that the village once supported five thousand people in the fishing industry during the summer, as well as a small army of coopers, coal merchants, butchers, bakers, several Italian ice-cream parlours and a cinema. **Papa Stronsay**, the tiny island that shelters Whitehall from the north, is home to the multimillion-pound **Golgotha Monastery** belonging to the Sons of the Most Holy Redeemer – they're happy to take visitors across to (and around) the island by boat, by prior arrangement (☎01857 616210, ⑩papastronsay.com).

ARRIVAL AND GETTING AROUND　　　　　　　　　　　　STRONSAY

By plane Day-trips are possible from Kirkwall (Mon–Fri 2 daily, Sat 1 daily; 25min) and regular flights depart from Sanday (Mon–Fri 1 daily; 6min).
By ferry Stronsay is served by a regular car ferry from

Kirkwall to Whitehall (2–3 daily; 1hr 40min–2hr).
By taxi/car There's no bus service, but D.S. Peace (☎01857 616335) operates taxis and offers car rental.

25

ACCOMMODATION AND EATING

Storehouse ☎01857 616263, ⓦstorehousestronsay .co.uk. A good alternative to the *Stronsay Hotel* is this welcoming little B&B, also in Whitehall, with en-suite rooms, a guest lounge and full board on request. **£65**

Stronsay Hotel Whitehall ☎01857 616213,

ⓦstronsayhotelorkney.co.uk. Nicely refurbished old hotel, right by the ferry terminal – it once boasted the longest bar in the north of Scotland. The hotel bar serves good pub food (mains under £10) – try the seafood taster. **£80**

Sanday

Despite being the largest of the northern isles, **Sanday** is the least substantial, a great low-lying, drifting dune strung out between several rocky points. The island's sweeping aquamarine bays and vast stretches of clean white sand are the finest in Orkney, and in dry, clear weather it's a superb place to spend a day or two. The coastline offers the opportunity for superb walks, with particularly spectacular sand dunes to the south of Cata Sand. The most impressive archeological sight is **Quoyness Chambered Cairn**, on the fertile farmland of Els Ness peninsula, dating from before 2000 BC, and partially reconstructed to a height of around 13ft.

ARRIVAL AND GETTING AROUND   SANDAY

By plane The airfield is in the centre of the island with regular flights to Kirkwall (Mon–Fri 2 daily; Sat 1 daily; 10min) and a daily connection to Stronsay (Mon–Fri 1 daily; 6min).

By ferry Ferries from Kirkwall (2 daily; 1hr 25min) arrive at Loth Pier, at Sanday's southern tip of the island.

By bus or minibus Visitors are met by the Sanday Bus (☎01857 600438), which will take you to most points on Sanday. The Sanday Ranger (☎01857 600341, ⓦsanday ranger.org) organizes occasional activities, and there's the regular Sanday Experience day-trip (☎01857 600438; May–Sept Wed; £30), both leaving from the ferry port.

ACCOMMODATION AND EATING

Ayre's Rock ☎01857 600410, ⓦayres-rock-sanday -orkney.co.uk. If you're on a budget, this is a great place to stay: there's a well-equipped eight-bed hostel, a caravan, and a small campsite (with several camping pods for hire) overlooking the Bay of Brough, with washing and laundry facilities, a chip shop (every Sat) and bike rental. Pitches **£5**, dorms **£17.50**, pod **£40**

Newquoy Guest House ☎01857 600284, ⓦnewquoy .com. The old school in Burness, in the north of the island, is now a B&B run by an enterprising couple who put on writing courses and storytelling evenings, and, in the summer, run an occasional tea and coffee shop serving snacks and cakes in vintage crockery. **£60**

North Ronaldsay

Measuring just three miles by one and rising only 66ft above sea level, **North Ronaldsay** is almost overwhelmed by the enormity of the sky, the strength of wind and the ferocity of the sea. The island's **sheep** are a unique, tough, goat-like breed, feeding mostly on seaweed, giving their flesh a dark tone and a rich, gamey taste, and making their thick wool highly prized. A high **dry-stone dyke**, running the thirteen miles around the edge of the island, keeps the sheep off the farmland, except during lambing season. The most frequent visitors to the island are ornithologists, who come to catch a glimpse of the rare birds which land here briefly on their spring and autumn migrations. The only features to interrupt the island's flat horizon are two **lighthouses**, in the north of the island, the newer of which you can visit on summer Sundays (noon–5.30pm; £5).

ARRIVAL AND DEPARTURE   NORTH RONALDSAY

By plane Your best bet is to catch a flight from Kirkwall (Mon–Sat 3 daily; Sun 2 daily; 15min): if you stay the night on the island, you're eligible for a bargain £21 return fare.

By ferry The ferry from Kirkwall to North Ronaldsay runs

just once a week (usually Fri; 2hr 40min), though there are also summer sailings via Papa Westray (usually Tues; 3hr 10min), and day-trips are possible on occasional Sundays between late May and early September (☎01856 872044).

ACCOMMODATION AND EATING

Bird Observatory ☎ 01857 633200, ⓦ nrbo.co.uk. You can stay (or camp) at the ecofriendly bird observatory, either in an en-suite guest room or in a hostel bunkbed. The *Obscafé* serves decent evening meals (around £15 for two courses) – obviously try the mutton, washed down with Dark Island beer. Food served daily noon–2pm & evenings by arrangement. Pitches £5, dorms £17.50, doubles £62

Lighthouse ☎ 01857 633297, ⓦ northronaldsay .co.uk. Great little café in the old lightoue-keepers'

SHETLAND

N

Muckle Flugga
Hermaness

Burrafirth

Unst

Haroldswick

Baltasound

Cullivoe

Uyeasound

Sellafirth

Belmont

Gutcher

Yell

Oddsta

Fetlar

Houbie

Funzie

Point of Fethaland

Mid
Yell

Ronas Hill
(1475ft)

Collafirth

Otterswick

Ulsta

Burravoe

Esha Ness

Hillswick

Toft

Out
Skerries

Muckle
Roe

Brae

Ve Skerries

Papa
Stour

Laxo

Vidlin

Whalsay

Vementry

Voe

Symbister

Sandness

West
Burrafirth

Aith

Bixter

Weisdale

Walls

Vaila

Culswick

Tingwall

Bressay

Lerwick

7

Noss

Scalloway

Foula

Hamnavoe

West
Burra

Cunningsburgh

South Havra

Sandwick

8

Mousa

St Ninian's
Isle

Levenwick

Boddam

Quendale

9

Fitful Head

Jarlshof

Sumburgh
Head

Fair Isle

0   10
miles

HIGHLIGHTS

7 Noss

8 Mousa

9 Jarlshof

25

cottages serving snacks and evening meals (by arrangement) – make sure you sample one of their famous

North Ronaldsay mutton pies (£8.50). May–Aug daily 10am–4pm; Sept–April phone ahead.

Shetland

Shetland is surprisingly different from neighbouring Orkney: while Orkney lies within sight of the Scottish mainland, Shetland lies beyond the horizon, closer to Bergen in Norway than Edinburgh, and nearer the Arctic Circle than Manchester. The 23,000 islanders refer to themselves as Shetlanders first, and, with the Shetland flag widely displayed, they regard Scotland as a separate entity. As in Orkney, Mainland is the one in their own archipelago, not the Scottish mainland. And while Shetland experiences occasional spells of dry, sunny weather, it's the **simmer dim** – the twilight which lingers through the small hours at this latitude – which makes Shetland summers so memorable.

The islands' capital, **Lerwick**, is a busy little port and the only town of any size; many parts of Shetland can be reached from here on a day-trip. **South Mainland** is a narrow finger of land that runs some 25 miles from Lerwick to **Sumburgh Head**, an area particularly rich in archeological remains, including the Iron Age **Mousa Broch** and the ancient settlement of **Jarlshof**. A further 25 miles south of Sumburgh Head is the remote but thriving **Fair Isle**, synonymous with knitwear and exceptional birdlife. Even more remote are the distinctive peaks and precipitous cliffs of the island of **Foula**, fourteen miles west of Mainland. Shetland's three **North Isles** bring Britain to a dramatic, windswept end: **Yell** has the largest population of otters in the UK; **Fetlar** is home to the rare red-necked phalarope; and, north of **Unst**, there's nothing until you reach the North Pole.

ARRIVAL AND DEPARTURE   SHETLAND

By plane Flybe (☎0871 7002000, ⌨flybe.com) operate direct flights to Sumburgh Airport, 25 miles south of Lerwick, from Inverness, Aberdeen, Edinburgh, Glasgow and Kirkwall in Orkney, plus summer flights from Bergen in

Norway.
By ferry Northlink run overnight car ferries daily from Aberdeen to Lerwick (1 daily; 12hr), sometimes calling in at Kirkwall in Orkney on the way (3–4 weekly; 6hr).

GETTING AROUND

By plane Directflight (☎01595 840, ⌨directflight.co.uk) run flights from Tingwall Airport (☎01595 745745), 5 miles northwest of Lerwick, to the more remote islands. To reach Tingwall Airport, there's a dial-a-ride taxi service (£1.70), which must be booked a day in advance.
By ferry The council-run interisland ferries

(☎01595 743970, ⌨shetland.gov.uk) are excellent and fares are very low.
By bus The bus network (☎01595 744868, ⌨zettrans .org.uk) is pretty good in Shetland, with buses from Lerwick to every corner of Mainland, and even via ferries across to Yell and Unst.

Lerwick

The focus of Shetland's commercial life, **LERWICK** is home to a third of the islands' population. Its sheltered **harbour** is busy with ferries and fishing boats, and oil-rig supply vessels. In summer, the quayside comes alive with visiting yachts, cruise liners and the occasional tall ship. Behind the old harbour is the compact town centre, made up of one long main street, flagstone-clad **Commercial Street**, whose narrow, winding form, set back from the Esplanade, provides shelter from the elements even on the worst days; from here, narrow lanes, known as **closses**, rise westwards to the Victorian new town.

The northern end of Commercial Street is marked by the towering walls of **Fort Charlotte** (daily: June–Sept 9am–10pm; Oct–May 9am–4pm; free), begun for Charles II in 1665, burnt down by the Dutch fleet in August 1673, and repaired and named in honour of George III's queen in the 1780s.

25

Shetland Museum

Hay's Dock, off Commercial Rd • Mon–Sat 10am–5pm, Sun noon–5pm • Free • ☎ 01595 695057, ⓦ shetland-museum.org.uk

Lerwick's chief tourist sight is the **Shetland Museum**, housed in a stylishly modern waterfront building, off Commercial Road. Exhibits include replicas of a hoard of Pictish silver found locally; the Monk Stone, thought to show the arrival of Christianity in Shetland; and a block of butter, tax payment for the King of Norway, found preserved in a peat bog. Among the boats artistically suspended in the Boat Hall is a sixareen, used, amazingly enough, as a Foula mailboat. The Upper Gallery concentrates on the last two centuries of the islands' social history, from knitting and whaling to the oil industry.

ARRIVAL AND INFORMATION

LERWICK

By bus Buses stop on the Esplanade, very close to the old harbour, or at the Viking bus station on Commercial Rd, north of the town centre.

Destinations Brae (Mon–Fri 5 daily, Sat 3 daily; 45min); Hillswick (Mon–Sat 1–2 daily; 1hr 40min); Levenwick (Mon–Sat 6–8 daily, Sun 4 daily; 30min); Scalloway (Mon–Sat hourly, Sun 2 daily; 25min); Sumburgh Airport (Mon–Sat 5–6 daily, Sun 4 daily; 45min); Tingwall (Mon–Fri 7 daily, Sat 4 daily; 10min); Toft (Mon–Sat 3–4 daily;

45–55min); Voe (Mon–Fri 5 daily, Sat 3 daily; 35min).

By ferry Ferries from Aberdeen and Orkney arrive at Lerwick's ferry terminal, about a mile north of the town centre. Ferries to other islands within Shetland leave from the town harbour.

Tourist information Market Cross, Commercial St (April–Oct Mon–Fri 9am–5pm, Sat & Sun 10am–4pm; Nov–March Mon–Fri 9am–5pm; ☎ 01595 6693434, ⓦ visitshetland.com)

LERWICK

■ ACCOMMODATION	
Alder Lodge	4
Brentham House	1
SYHA Hostel	2
Westhall	5
Woosung	3

● RESTAURANTS, CAFÉS & PUBS	
Hay's Dock	2
The Lounge	4
Mareel	1
Monty's Bistro	5
Peerie Shop Café	3

25

NOSS

Inhabited until World War II, and now a National Nature Reserve, **Noss** is a popular day-trip from Lerwick. Sloping gently into the sea at its western end, and plunging vertically for more than 500ft at its eastern end, the island has the dramatic outline of a half-sunk ocean liner. The cliffed coastline is home to vast colonies of gannets, puffins, guillemots, shags, razorbills and fulmars. As Noss is only one mile wide, it's easy enough to do an entire circumference in one day. If you do, keep close to the coast, since otherwise you're likely to be dive-bombed by the great skuas (locally known as "bonxies"). **Boat trips** from Lerwick to Noss include those run by Seabirds and Seals (mid-April to mid-Sept daily 10am & 2pm; 3hr return; £45; ☎07595 540224, ⓦseabirds-and-seals.com). It's also possible to take a ferry to Maryfield on **Bressay** (every 30min–1hr; 7min; ☎01595 743974); from here it's a three-mile walk to the landing stage where a Scottish Natural Heritage RIB can take you to Noss (May–Aug Tues, Wed & Fri–Sun 11am–5pm; £3 return; phone ☎0800 1077818 before setting off).

ACCOMMODATION

Alder Lodge 6 Clairmont Place ☎01595 695705, ⓦalderlodgeguesthouse.com. *Alder Lodge* is a solid, dependable choice, with eleven rooms, all en suite except the single. Breakfasts are good, with local smoked haddock an option, and there's free wi-fi throughout the building. **£75**

Brentham House 7 Harbour St ☎01950 460201, ⓦbrenthamhouse.com. Spacious, newly furnished rooms in a Victorian, bay-fronted terrace; no reception, and no proper breakfast – you pick the keys up from *Baroc*, the bar a couple of doors down. **£75**

SYHA hostel Islesburgh House, King Harald St ☎01595 692114, ⓦsyha.org.uk. Spacious Victorian building offering unusually comfortable surroundings, family rooms, a café, internet and laundry facilities. April–Sept. Dorms **£20**, family rooms **£60**

★**Westhall** Lower Sound ☎01595 694247, ⓦbedandbreakfastlerwick.co.uk. A splendid Victorian mansion, known as the "Sheriff's Hoose", set in its own grounds a mile southwest of town with fabulous views over to Bressay. Rooms are spacious, the breakfasts are immense and there's free wi-fi. **£110**

Woosung 43 St Olaf St ☎01595 693687, ⓦvisit .shetland.org/woosung. Family-run B&B, up on the hill above the harbour, run by a genuinely friendly, local landlady. The whole place is kept spotlessly clean, but not all rooms are en suite. Free wi-fi. **£60**

EATING AND DRINKING

★**Hay's Dock** Shetland Museum, Hay's Dock ☎01595 741569, ⓣhaysdock.co.uk. Bright, modern, licensed café/restaurant in the museum, with a great view over the north bay. Sandwiches, bagels and simple lunch dishes – from chowder to burgers – are all around £10; the more adventurous evening menu features local salmon and lamb dishes (mains £15–22). Mon 10.30am–4.30pm, Tues–Sat 10.30am–4.30pm & 6.30–9pm, Sun noon–4.30pm.

The Lounge 4 Mounthooly St ☎01595 692231. Lerwick's friendliest pub is this upstairs bar where local musicians often gather for a session – Thursday night is quiz night. Daily 11am–1am.

Mareel North Ness ☎01595 745555, ⓦmareel.org. If you've missed breakfast at your B&B, come to the café-bar in Lerwick's new cultural complex. Sandwiches or baked tatties are available until 4pm and hummus or mackerel ciabatta and nachos after that (all under £5). Mon–Wed & Sun 9am–11pm, Thurs–Sat 9am–1am.

Monty's Bistro 5 Mounthooly St ☎01595 696555, ⓦmontys-shetland.co.uk. Unpretentious place serving sandwiches, pasta, spicy curries and snacks at lunchtimes (under £10); and the likes of pot-roasted local lamb and pan-fried Gressingham duck in the evening (mains £10–22). Tues–Sat noon–2pm & 5–9pm.

Peerie Shop Café Esplanade ☎01595 692817, ⓦpeerieshopcafe.com. Designer shop/gallery/café in an old lodberry, with a good range of cakes, soup and sandwiches (all under £5), and what is probably Britain's northernmost latte. Mon–Sat 9am–6pm.

Scalloway

Once the capital of Shetland, **SCALLOWAY** waned in importance as Lerwick grew. Nowadays Scalloway is fairly sleepy, though its harbour remains busy enough, with a small fishing fleet and the North Atlantic Fisheries College on the far side. The town is dominated by the imposing shell of **Scalloway Castle**, a classic fortified tower-house built using forced labour in 1600 by the infamous Earl Patrick Stewart, who held court in the castle and gained a reputation for cruelty and corruption.

Scalloway Museum

May–Sept Mon–Sat 11am–4pm, Sun 2–4pm • £3 • ☎ 01595 880734, ⓦ scallowaymuseum.org

The **Scalloway Museum**, next to the castle, encompasses everything from Neolithic finds to the impact of modern aquaculture, and there's a replica wheelhouse and a longship for the kids to play with. The most interesting section, however, tells the story of the **Shetland Bus** – the link between Shetland and Norway which helped to sustain the Norwegian resistance in World War II.

ARRIVAL AND ACCOMMODATION   SCALLOWAY

By bus There are regular buses to Scalloway from Lerwick (Mon–Sat hourly, Sun 2 daily; 25min).

Scalloway Hotel Main St ☎ 01595 880444, ⓦ scallowayhotel.com. Well-established hotel on the harbour front, with plain, slightly cramped rooms and a bar that doubles as the local pub. The menu features lots of local fish and seafood – try the platter for around £15.

Food served daily noon–3pm & 5–8.30pm. **£115**

Windward B&B Port Arthur ☎ 01595 880769, ⓦ accommodation-shetland.co.uk. Very comfortable, modern, wood-clad two-room B&B at the far western end of the bay, close to the North Atlantic Fisheries College. Great views from the conservatory and free wi-fi. **£80**

South Mainland

Shetland's **South Mainland** is a long, thin finger of land, three or four miles wide and 25 miles long, ending in the cliffs of **Sumburgh Head** and **Fitful Head**. It's a beautiful area with wild undulating landscapes, lots of good green farmland, fabulous views out to sea and the mother of all brochs on the island of **Mousa**, off the east coast. The most concentrated points of interest are the southern end of the peninsula, where you'll find seabird colonies, a crofting museum, and **Jarlshof**, Shetland's most impressive archeological treasure.

Jarlshof

Daily: April–Sept 9.30am–5.30pm; Oct–March 9.30am to dusk • £5.50; HS • ☎ 01950 460112

Jarlshof is the largest and most impressive of Shetland's archeological sites. Only half of the original broch survives, and its courtyard is now an Iron Age aisled roundhouse, with stone piers. It's difficult to distinguish the original broch from the later Pictish wheelhouses that now surround it, but it's great fun to explore as you're free to roam around the cells, checking out the in-built stone shelving, water tanks, beds and so on. Inland lies the maze of grass-topped foundations marking out the **Viking longhouses**, and towering over the whole complex are the ruins of the laird's house, built by Robert

---

MOUSA BROCH

The island of **Mousa** boasts the most amazingly well-preserved broch in Scotland. Rising to more than 40ft, and looking rather like a Stone Age cooling tower, **Mousa Broch** has a remarkable presence, and even makes an appearance in the Norse sagas. The low entrance-passage leads through two concentric walls to a central courtyard, divided into separate beehive chambers. Between the walls, a rough (very dark) staircase leads to the top parapet; a torch is provided for visitors. Mousa is only a mile wide, but if the weather's not too bad it's easy enough to spend the whole day here. From late May to late July, thousands of **storm petrels** breed in and around the broch walls, fishing out at sea during the day and returning to the nests after dark.

A small **passenger ferry** runs to Mousa from Sandwick (April to mid-Sept; £16 return; ☎ 01950 431367, ⓦ mousa.co.uk). The ferry runs special late-night trips (late May to mid-July Wed & Sat; £20), setting off in the "simmer dim" twilight around 11pm.

25

Stewart, Earl of Orkney and Lord of Shetland, in the late sixteenth century, and the **Old House of Sumburgh**, built by his son, Earl Patrick.

Sumburgh Head

Visitor Centre: May–Aug daily 10am–4pm • £6 • ☎ 0595 694688, ⓦ sumburghhead.com

Shetland's Mainland comes to a dramatic end at **Sumburgh Head** (262ft), with its cliff-top **lighthouse** – now with a brand-new **visitor centre**. The road up to the lighthouse is also the perfect site for watching nesting seabirds such as kittiwakes, fulmars, shags, razorbills and guillemots, not to mention gannets diving for fish. This is also the easiest place in Shetland to get close to **puffins** during the nesting season (May to early Aug).

ARRIVAL AND ACCOMMODATION SOUTH MAINLAND

By bus There are regular buses from Lerwick to Levenwick (Mon–Sat 6–8 daily, Sun 4 daily; 30min); Sandwick (Mon–Fri 8–10 daily, Sat 6 daily, Sun 4 daily; 25min); and Sumburgh (Mon–Sat 5–6 daily, Sun 4 daily; 45min).

Levenwick Campsite Levenwick ☎ 07714 935914, ⓦ levenwick.shetland.co.uk. Small, terraced campsite run by the local community with hot showers, a tennis court, friendly Shetland ponies and a superb view over the east coast. May–Sept. Pitches **£8**

★**Mucklehus** Levenwick ☎ 01950 422370, ⓦ mucklehus.co.uk. A lovely B&B in a former Master

Mariner's house built in 1890 near the beach in Levenwick, 18 miles south of Lerwick; the rooms are small but stylish, and there's free wi-fi. **£80**

Spiggie Hotel ☎ 01950 460409, ⓦ thespiggiehotel .co.uk. Hotel with a popular bar serving real ales and a restaurant with great views (and if you're lucky incredible sunsets). Bar meals are priced around £10, or you can have well-presented dishes such as lobster, or whatever the local catch is, à la carte in the restaurant (mains £12–18). Food served Mon & Tues 6–10pm, Wed–Sun noon–2.30pm & 6–10pm. **£110**

Fair Isle

Fair Isle is marooned in the sea halfway between Shetland and Orkney. By the late 1940s, the population had tumbled from 400 to 44, at which point George Waterston set up a bird observatory and rejuvenation began. Although crofting still takes place in the south of the island, the focus for many visitors remains the **Bird Observatory**, just above the sandy bay of North Haven where the ferry from Shetland arrives. It's one of Europe's major centres for ornithology and its work in watching, trapping, recording and ringing resident and migrant birds goes on all year. Fair Isle is even better known for its **knitting** patterns, still produced with great skill by the local knitwear co-operative – there are samples on display at the island's **museum** (Mon 2–4pm, Wed 10.30am–noon, Fri 2–3.30pm; free; ☎ 01595 760244), next door to the Methodist chapel.

ARRIVAL AND ACCOMMODATION FAIR ISLE

By plane Directflight (☎ 01595 840246, ⓦ directflight .co.uk) flies from Tingwall to Fair Isle (Mon–Sat 1–3 daily) and from Sumburgh (Sat only).

By ferry The passenger ferry connects Fair Isle with either Lerwick (alternate Thurs; 4–5hr) or Grutness in Sumburgh (Tues, alternate Thurs & Sat; 3hr) – it's advisable to book in advance (☎ 01595 760363).

Fair Isle Bird Observatory Lodge ☎ 01595 760258, ⓦ fairislebirdobs.co.uk. Full-board accommodation is

available at the modern observatory in en-suite doubles/ twins and singles. FIBO is the island's social hub and, to guests and visitors alike, the observatory offers tea, coffee and good home-cooking. Late April to Oct. **£130**

South Light House ☎ 07752 566231, ⓦ south lightfairisle.co.uk. A B&B at the southernmost tip of the island, not literally in the lighthouse, but in the adjacent keepers' cottages. Free collection from the ferry/airport and free wi-fi. Full board **£100**

Foula

Foula is without a doubt the most isolated inhabited island in Britain, separated from the nearest point on Mainland Shetland by about fourteen miles of often turbulent ocean. Its western **cliffs**, the second highest in Britain after those of St Kilda, rise at **The Kame** to some 1220ft above sea level; a clear day at The Kame offers a magnificent panorama stretching from Unst to Fair Isle. On a bad day, the exposure is complete and the cliffs generate blasts of wind known as "flans", which rip through the hills with tremendous force. In addition to its forty or so human inhabitants, the island is home to a quarter of a million **birds**, including a colony of **great skuas** or "bonxies", which you can't fail to notice in the breeding season.

ARRIVAL AND ACCOMMODATION   FOULA

By plane A Direct flight (☎01595 840246, �🌐directflight .co.uk) flies from Tingwall (Mon 1 daily, Tues, Wed & Fri 2 daily; 15min).

By ferry Be sure to book and reconfirm your journey by ferry (Tues, Thurs & Sat; 2hr; ☎01595 5840208, �🌐bkmarine.org), which departs from Walls (Tues, Sat & alternate Thurs; 2hr) or Scalloway (alternate Thurs; 3hr 30min). The ferry arrives at

Ham, in the middle of Foula's east coast.

Leraback ☎01595 753226, �🌐originart.eu/leraback /leraback.html. Foula's only accommodation, unless you camp, is a modern croft-house bungalow near Ham. Fortunately, it's a great place to stay; full board only and they'll collect you from the airstrip or pier. **£80**

North Mainland

The **North Mainland**, stretching more than thirty miles north from Lerwick, is wild even for Shetland. The tiny, picturesque fishing port of **VOE** is well worth visiting – not so **BRAE**, built hastily during the 1970s oil boom. **HILLSWICK**, the main settlement in the northwest peninsula of **Northmavine**, was once a centre for deep-sea or haaf fishing, and later a herring station. By the harbour is **Da Böd**, founded by a Hanseatic merchant in 1684, which later became Shetland's oldest pub and is now a seal and wildlife sanctuary (☎01806 503348, �🌐shetlandwildlifesanctuary.com).

A side road leads west to the exposed headland of **Esha Ness** (pronounced "Aysha Ness"), celebrated for its red sandstone cliffs, stacks, blowholes and its lighthouse. A mile or so south off the main road is the **Tangwick Haa Museum** (Easter–Sept daily 11am–5pm; free), which tells the moving story of this remote corner of Shetland and its role in the dangerous trade of deep-sea fishing and whaling.

ARRIVAL AND DEPARTURE   NORTH MAINLAND

By bus From Lerwick there are buses to Brae (Mon–Fri 5 daily, Sat 3 daily; 45min), Hillswick (Mon–Sat 1–2 daily; 1hr 40min) and Voe (Mon–Fri 5 daily, Sat 3 daily; 35min).

ACCOMMODATION AND EATING

★**Busta House** Brae ☎01806 522506, �🌐bustahouse .com. A laird's house with stepped gables that sits across the bay from Brae. Even if you're not staying the night here, it's worth coming for afternoon tea in the Long Room, for a stroll around the wooded grounds, or for a drink and a meal in the hotel's pub-like bar (mains £10–12). **£115**
Frankie's ☎01806 522700, �🌐frankiesfishandchips .com. Brae's best food option, aside from *Busta House*, is this very popular fish-and-chip café with great views over Busta Voe. As well as the usuals, you can get smoked haddock and mussels. Mon–Sat 9.30am–8pm, Sun noon–8pm.

★**Lunna House** Vidlin, 8 miles northeast of Voe down the B9071 ☎01806 577311, �🌐lunnahouse.co.uk. Built in 1660, *Lunna House* is a wonderful place to stay, with spacious bedrooms, lovely views and top-class breakfasts. **£60**
Sail Loft ☎01595 694688, �🌐camping-bods.co.uk. Originally a giant storeroom, this enormous hostel (camping böd) is situated right by the loch and has hot showers, a kitchen and a solid-fuel fire in the smaller of the rooms. April–Oct. Per person **£10**

The North Isles

Many visitors never make it out to Shetland's trio of remote **North Isles**, which is a shame, as the ferry links are frequent and inexpensive, the roads fast, and with Lerwick that much further away, the spirit of independence and self-sufficiency is

25

much more keenly felt. **Yell**, best-known for its otter population, is often overlooked, while **Fetlar**, famed for its phalaropes, is the smallest and most fertile, but it's **Unst** that has the widest appeal, partly because it's the most northerly landmass in the British Isles, and partly for its nesting seabirds.

Yell

The interior of **Yell** features a lot of peat moorland, but the coastline is gentler and greener and provides an ideal habitat for a large population of **otters**. The only sight as such is at **BURRAVOE**, in the island's southeastern corner. Here there's a lovely whitewashed laird's house, dating from 1672, with crow-stepped gables, which now houses the **Old Haa Museum** (April–Sept Tues–Thurs & Sat 10am–4pm, Sun 2–5pm; free). Stuffed with artefacts, the museum has lots of material on the history of the local herring and whaling industry and there's a pleasant wood-panelled café on the ground floor.

ARRIVAL AND DEPARTURE — YELL

By ferry ☎01595 745804, ⓦshetland.gov.uk. Ferries to Ulsta (Yell) from Toft (Mainland) are frequent (every 30min–1hr; 20min).

By bus There's an integrated bus and ferry service from Lerwick that goes all the way to Gutcher (Mon–Sat 1–2 daily; 2hr 10min). On Yell, buses from Ulsta run to Gutcher (Mon–Sat 2–4 daily; 30min).

ACCOMMODATION AND EATING

Gutcher Goose Café Gutcher ☎01957 744382. A café in a prefab at Gutcher offering soup, baked tatties and filled bannocks for those waiting for the ferry to Unst. Mon–Fri 8.30am–4.30pm, Sat 9.30am–4.30pm.

Pinewood House Aywick ☎01957 702092, ⓦpine woodhouseshetland.co.uk. A great option on the east coast of Yell – rooms are plain but comfy, and the guest lounge has a real fire, views over to Fetlar and lots of books on the local area. Full board available. **£70**

Windhouse Lodge Mid Yell ☎01595 694688, ⓦcamping-bods.co.uk. The Windhouse gatehouse, on the main road near Mid Yell, is a hostel (camping böd) with small dorms, a wood- and peat-fired heater and hot showers. April–Oct. **£10**

Fetlar

Fetlar is the most fertile of the North Isles, much of it covered by grassy moorland and lush green meadows with masses of summer flowers. At the main settlement, **HOUBIE**, you can learn more about the island from the welcoming **Fetlar Interpretive Centre** (May–Sept Mon–Sat 11am–4pm, Sun 12.30–4pm; £2; ☎01957 733206, ⓦfetlar .com). Fetlar is also one of the very few places in the UK where you'll see graceful **red-necked phalarope** (late May to early Aug): a hide has been provided overlooking the marshes (or mires) to the east of the **Loch of Funzie** (pronounced "finny").

ARRIVAL AND ACCOMMODATION — FETLAR

By ferry Ferries to Fetlar (Mon–Sat 7–9 daily; 25–40min) depart regularly from both Gutcher (Yell) and Belmont (Unst), and dock at Hamar's Ness, 3 miles northwest of Houbie.

By bus There's a Funzie-to-Hamar's Ness service (Mon–Sat 3 daily), and a dial-a-ride electric minibus service – to use it you must book your journey the day before (☎01595 745745, ⓦfetlar.org).

Aithbank Böd A mile east of Houbie ☎01595 694688, ⓦcamping-bods.com. A cosy wood-panelled cottage with two rooms, sleeping a total of seven. There's hot water, a kitchen and a solid fuel stove. March–Oct. Per person **£10**

Gord Houbie ☎01957 733227, ⓔnicboxall@btinternet .com. The modern house attached to the island shop in Houbie is also a B&B with great sea views from all the rooms. All guests are full board only, and they do meals for nonresidents by arrangement. **£100**

Unst

Much of **Unst** is rolling grassland but the coast is more dramatic: a fringe of cliffs relieved by some beautiful sandy beaches. As Britain's most northerly inhabited island, there is a surfeit of "most northerly" sights. Most visitors head straight for **Hermaness**, to see the seabirds and look out over Muckle Flugga and the northernmost tip of Britain, to the North Pole beyond.

On the south coast of the island, not far from **UYEASOUND**, lie the ruins of **Muness Castle**, a diminutive defensive structure, with matching bulging bastions and corbelled turrets at opposite corners. The castle was built in 1598 by the Scots incomer, Laurence Bruce, stepbrother and chief bullyboy of the infamous Earl Robert Stewart. As you leave Unst's main settlement, **BALTASOUND**, heading north, be sure to look out for **Bobby's bus shelter** (ⓦunstbusshelter.shetland.co.uk), an eccentric, fully furnished, award-winning bus shelter on the edge of the town. The **Keen of Hamar**, east of Baltasound, and signposted from the main road, is one of the largest expanses of serpentine debris in Europe, home to an extraordinary array of plant life.

Haroldswick

Unst Boat Haven & Heritage Centre · May–Sept daily 11am–5pm · £3 each

Near the shore at **HAROLDSWICK**, you'll find the **Unst Boat Haven**, displaying a beautiful collection of historic boats with many tools of the trade and information on fishing. If you want to learn more about Unst's history, head for the nearby **Unst Heritage Centre**, housed in the old school building by the main crossroads, where they also put on activities such as spinning, knitting and potting.

Hermaness Nature Reserve

The bleak headland of **Hermaness**, home to more than 100,000 nesting seabirds (May–Aug), lies northwest from Haroldswick. There's an excellent **visitor centre** in the former lighthouse-keeper's shore station, where you can pick up a leaflet showing the marked routes across the heather to the view over to **Muckle Flugga** lighthouse and **Out Stack**, the most northerly bit of Britain. The views from here are marvellous, as is the birdlife; there's a huge gannetry on one of the stacks, and puffins burrow all along the clifftops.

ARRIVAL AND DEPARTURE   UNST

By ferry ☎01595 745804. Ferries shuttle regularly across Bluemull Sound from Gutcher on Yell over to Belmont on Unst (every 30min 1hr; 10min).

By bus An integrated bus and ferry service goes from Lerwick to Baltasound on Unst (Mon–Sat 1–2 daily) 2hr 40min). From Belmont, Unst's ferry terminal, buses run to Uyeasound (Mon–Sat 2–4 daily; 5min), Baltasound (Mon–Sat 2–3 daily; 15min) and Haroldswick (Mon–Sat 1–2 daily; 30min).

ACCOMMODATION AND EATING

Baltasound Hotel Baltasound ☎01957 711334, ⓦbaltasoundhotel.co.uk. The hotel has a range of rooms available from neat, simple doubles to very plain, but cheap, singles – for evening meals there's no other option than the hotel restaurant (mains £10–18). Food served daily 5–8pm. <u>£90</u>

Gardiesfauld Hostel Uyeasound ☎01957 755279, ⓦgardiesfauld.shetland.co.uk. A clean and modern hostel (no resident warden), with a kitchen and lounge/conservatory near Uyeasound pier, with dorm beds and free wi-fi. You can also camp in one of the fairly sheltered spots around the house, and bike rental is on offer. April–Nov. Camping per person <u>£6</u>, dorms <u>£15</u>

Prestegaard Uyeasound ☎01957 755234, ✉prestegaard@postmaster.co.uk. This attractive, whitewashed Victorian B&B, with just three rooms, is situated in Uyeasound and has great sea views – or, if you're thinking of self-catering, ask about Unst's zero-carbon house. <u>£60</u>

LAURENCE OLIVIER IN SHAKESPEARE'S *HENRY V* (1944)

Contexts

History

Britain's history is long and densely woven, its protagonists influential in western Europe from Anglo-Saxon times, and as leaders of the global British Empire from the eighteenth century onwards. What follows is a necessarily brief introduction.

From the Stone Age to the Bronze Age

Britain has been inhabited for over half a million years. The earliest archeological evidence is scant, but **Old Stone Age (Paleolithic)** bones and flint tools have been found in several different parts of the country. The comings and goings of these migrant peoples were dictated by successive **Ice Ages**, the most recent of which lasted for the ten thousand years up to 5000 BC. Although its final thawing caused the British Isles to separate from the European mainland, the **sea barrier** did little to hinder further influxes of nomadic hunters, drawn by the game that inhabited Britain's forests.

Around 3500 BC, a new wave of colonists reached Britain, probably via Ireland, bringing a **New Stone Age (Neolithic)** culture based on farming and livestock. These tribes were the first to impact upon the environment, clearing forests, enclosing fields and scouring the land for flint for their tools and weapons. Their most profuse relics are **graves**, usually stone-chambered, turf-covered mounds called long barrows, cairns or cromlechs, such as those at Belas Knap in Gloucestershire, Barclodiad y Gawres in Anglesey, and Maes Howe on Orkney.

The next transition, to the **Bronze Age**, began around 2500 BC, with the importation from northern Europe of artefacts attributed to the **Beaker Culture** – named after the distinctive cups found at many burial sites. Spreading along established trade routes, this stimulated the development of a well-organized social structure with an established aristocracy. Many of Britain's **stone and timber circles** were completed at the tail end of the Neolithic period, including **Stonehenge** in Wiltshire and Calanais on the Isle of Lewis, while others belong entirely to the Bronze Age, including the Nine Maidens on Cornwall's Bodmin Moor.

Iron Age progress

From 700 BC, the British **Iron Age** saw the consolidation of a sophisticated farming economy with a social hierarchy dominated by a druidic priesthood. Most farmers grew wheat and barley, and kept cattle, sheep and pigs; chickens arrived later, with the Romans. These early Britons gradually developed better methods of **metal-working**, favouring iron and gold rather than bronze, from which they forged not just weapons but also coins and ornamental works, thus creating the first recognizable indigenous art. A network of **hillforts** or brochs and other defensive works now stretched over the entire country, the greatest being at **Maiden Castle** in Dorset and **Mousa** in the Shetland Islands. These earthworks suggest endemic tribal warfare, a situation further complicated by the appearance of bands of **Celts**, who arrived from central Europe

5000 BC	2500 BC	43 AD
As the ice sheets retreat, the sea floods in, separating Britain from continental Europe.	The start of the Bronze Age – and the construction of dozens of stone and timber circles.	The Roman Emperor Claudius invades Britain – and he means business.

around 600 BC, though some historians dispute the notion of a Celtic "invasion", arguing that change and conflict were triggered by trade rather than conquest.

The Romans

The **Roman** invasion of Britain began hesitantly, when **Julius Caesar** led small cross-Channel incursions in 55 and 54 BC. While Britain's rumoured mineral wealth was a primary motive, the immediate spur to the eventual conquest a century later was anti-Roman collaboration between the Britons of southern England and their Celtic cousins in Gaul (France). The subtext was that the **Emperor Claudius**, who led the invasion, owed his power to the army and needed a military triumph. The death of the British king Cunobelin (the original of Shakespeare's Cymbeline), ruler of southeast England, offered the opportunity Claudius required. In 43 AD, a substantial force landed in Kent, then fanned out to establish a base along the Thames estuary. Joined by elephants and camels for major battles, the Romans soon reached Camulodunum (Colchester), and within four years were dug in on the frontier of south Wales.

By 80 AD the Roman governor, **Agricola**, felt secure enough in the south of Britain to begin an invasion of the **north**, stringing forts across the Clyde–Forth line and defeating the Scottish tribes at Mons Graupius. The long-term effect, however, was slight. In 123 AD, the Emperor Hadrian sealed the frontier against the northern tribes by building **Hadrian's Wall** from the Solway Firth to the Tyne. Twenty years later, the Romans again ventured north and built the **Antonine Wall** between the Clyde and the Forth. Forty years later, however, the Romans, frustrated by the inhospitable terrain of the Highlands, gave up their attempt to subjugate the north, opting instead for containment.

The written history of Britain begins with the Romans, whose rule lasted nigh on four centuries. For the first time, most of England was absorbed into a unified political structure, in which commerce flourished and cities prospered, and **Londinium** assumed a pivotal role in commercial and administrative life. Although Latin became the language of the Romano-British ruling elite, local traditions were allowed to coexist, so that British gods were often worshipped at the same time as Rome's. **Christianity** was introduced during the third century, and became entrenched after its official recognition across the Roman Empire in 313.

The Anglo-Saxons arrive

By the middle of the third century AD, the **Roman Empire** was plagued by frequent collapses of central authority that encouraged its military commanders to act independently. In Britain, the Germanic **Saxons** had begun to raid England's eastern shore. By the end of the fourth century, with Britain irrevocably detached from what remained of the Roman Empire, the **Saxons** – and the **Angles**, also from northern Germany – were settling England and parts of Scotland. Romano-British resistance was led by such semi-mythical figures as **King Arthur**, said to have held court at Caerleon in Wales, but crumbled after the **Battle of Dyrham** (near Bath) in 577. By the end of the sixth century, Romano-British culture was all but eliminated in England, which was divided into the **Anglo-Saxon kingdoms** of Northumbria, Mercia, East Anglia, Kent and Wessex. Even today, some ninety percent of English place names have an

60 AD	313	c. 500
An affronted and enraged Boudicca and her Iceni sack Roman Colchester.	The Emperor Constantine makes Christianity the official religion of the Roman Empire.	St David, the patron saint of Wales, is born on a clifftop during a violent storm.

Anglo-Saxon derivation. Meanwhile, those native Britons who had not been absorbed by the invaders were dispersed into Wales, the far southwest of England, and Scotland, which was a real mix, with Angles on the east coast, Irish-Celtic **Scotti** on the west, the Picts, descended from Iron Age tribes, to the north, and Romano-Britons in between. The Scotti spoke **Goidelic** (or Q-Celtic), the precursor of modern Gaelic, while **Brythonic** (P-Celtic) was spoken in Wales and Cornwall.

Christian epiphany

In England, the revival of Christianity was driven by **St Augustine**, who landed in Kent in 597 at the behest of the pope, accompanied by forty monks. His mission to convert the pagan Anglo-Saxons went relatively smoothly and was continued by a long succession of monkish missionaries; the last part of England to become Christian was Sussex in 680. On what might be called the Celtic fringe, a Christian Church had survived from Roman times, winning new converts and promoting a hermetical vision of holiness exemplified by St David, ultimately Wales's patron saint, and **St Columba**, who founded several Christian outposts in Scotland, including on the island of Iona. Liturgical differences between this "Ionan Church" and the "Roman Church" of St Augustine were resolved when the **Synod of Whitby** determined in 663 that the English Church should follow the rule of Rome.

Arrival of the Vikings

In the eighth century, the kingdom of **Mercia**, occupying what is today the Midlands, became the dominant power in England. Its most talented ruler, Offa, was responsible for **Offa's Dyke**, an earthwork stretching from the River Dee to the Severn, marking the border with Wales. After Offa's death, **Wessex** gained the upper hand; by 825, its King Egbert had conquered or taken allegiance from all the other English kingdoms. Meanwhile, in Scotland, **Kenneth MacAlpine** united the Scotti and the Picts into one kingdom in 843. His successors extended their fiefdoms by marriage and force of arms until, by 1034, almost all of modern Scotland was under their rule. The supremacy of Wessex coincided with the first large-scale **Viking** (or Norse) invasions, which began with coastal raids, like the one that destroyed the great monastery of Lindisfarne in 793, but grew into a migration. By 871, a substantial **Viking (Danish) army** had conquered Northumbria, Mercia and East Anglia. The new king of Wessex, however, **Alfred the Great** (reigned 871–99), successfully resisted the Danes, and signed a truce that fixed an uneasy border between Wessex and Danish territory – the **Danelaw** to the north and east. While the Danes soon succumbed to internal warfare, Alfred modernized his kingdom and strengthened its defences. His successor, **Edward the Elder**, established Saxon supremacy over the Danelaw to become the de facto overlord of all England. The relative calm continued under Edward's son, **Athelstan** (925–40), who extended his sway over much of Scotland and Wales, and his son, **Edgar** (959–75), crowned as the first **king of England** in 973. However, this was but a lull in the Viking storm. Returning in force, the Vikings milked Edgar's son **Ethelred the Unready** (978–1016) for all the money they could, but the ransom (the Danegeld) paid brought only temporary relief and Ethelred hot-footed it to Normandy, leaving the Danes in command.

597	793	796
St Augustine lands in Kent with instructions to convert Britain to Christianity.	In a surprise attack, Viking raiders destroy the monastery at Lindisfarne.	Death of King Offa, the most powerful king in England and long-time ruler of Mercia.

England: Danish dominance and defeat

The first Danish king of England, the shrewd **Canute** (1016–35), constructed an Anglo-Scandinavian empire, but the Saxons regained the initiative from his two disreputable sons, and placed Ethelred's son, **Edward the Confessor** (1042–66), on the throne. It was a poor choice. More suited to be a priest than a king, Edward allowed power to drift into the hands of his most powerful subject, Godwin, Earl of Wessex, and his son Harold. On Edward's death, the Witan – a sort of council of elders – confirmed **Harold** (1066) as king, ignoring several rival claims. That of **William, Duke of Normandy**, was a curious affair, but he always insisted that the childless Edward the Confessor had promised him his crown. Unluckily for Harold, his two main rivals struck at the same time. First to do so was his alienated brother Tostig and his ally King Harald of Norway, reliably reckoned to be seven feet tall. They landed with a Viking army in Yorkshire and Harold hurriedly marched north to meet them. Harold won a crushing victory at **Stamford Bridge**, but then heard that William of Normandy had invaded the south. Rashly, Harold dashed south without mustering more men. William famously routed the Saxons – and killed Harold – at the **Battle of Hastings** in 1066. On Christmas Day, William the Conqueror was installed as king in Westminster Abbey.

England: Normans and Plantagenets (1066–1399)

William I (1066–87) imposed a **Norman** aristocracy on his new subjects, bolstering his rule by constructing such strongholds as the Tower of London. His most effective measure, however, was the compilation of the **Domesday Book** in 1086. Recording land ownership, type of cultivation, the number of inhabitants and their social status, it afforded William an unprecedented body of information, providing the framework for taxation, the judicial structure and feudal obligations. William was succeeded by his son **William Rufus** (1087–1100), an ineffectual ruler who died in mysterious circumstances, killed by an unknown assailant's arrow while hunting in the New Forest. The throne then passed to **Henry I** (1100–35), William I's youngest son, who spent much of his time struggling with his unruly barons, but at least he proved conciliatory in his dealings with his Anglo-Saxon subjects, even marrying into one of their leading families.

A long-winded civil war followed the death of Henry I, ending when **Henry II** (1154–89), the first of the **Plantagenets**, secured the throne. Energetic and far-sighted, Henry kept his barons in check and instigated profound administrative reforms, including the introduction of trial by jury. However, his attempt to subordinate Church to Crown went terribly awry in 1170, when he sanctioned the murder in Canterbury Cathedral of his erstwhile drinking companion **Thomas à Becket**, whose canonization three years later created an enduring Europe-wide cult. Henry had other troubles too: his inheritance had bequeathed him great chunks of France and the struggle to conquer more (or hold on to what they had) was to drain the royal treasury until the fifteenth century. Henry II was succeeded by his eldest son, **Richard I** (or Lionheart; 1189–99), who spent most of his reign crusading in the Holy Land. Neglected, England fell prey to Richard's scheming but inept brother **John** (1199–1216), the villain of the Robin Hood tales, who became king in his own right after Richard's death. John's failure to hold on to many of his French possessions alienated the English barons, who in 1215 forced him to sign a charter guaranteeing their rights and privileges, the **Magna Carta**, at Runnymede, on the Thames.

1066	1085	1102
King Harold, the last Saxon king of England, catches an arrow in the eye at the Battle of Hastings.	The Normans start work on the Domesday Book, detailing who owns what, does what and lives where.	By the terms of the Synod of Westminster, clergy are forbidden to marry.

Edward I to Edward III

Although the power struggle between king and barons continued under **Henry III** (1216–72), Henry's successor, **Edward I** (1272–1307), was much more in control. Also a great law-maker, Edward became obsessed by military matters, spending years subduing Wales and imposing English jurisdiction over Scotland. Fortunately for the Scots, the next king of England, **Edward II** (1307–27), proved completely hopeless. After Robert the Bruce inflicted a huge defeat on his guileless army at the Battle of Bannockburn in 1314 (see p.816), Edward ended up being murdered by his wife Isabella and her lover Roger Mortimer in 1327. After sorting out the Scottish imbroglio, **Edward III** (1327–77) turned his attention to his (essentially specious) claim to the throne of France. Starting in 1337, the ensuing **Hundred Years' War** began with several English victories, principally Crécy in 1346 and Poitiers in 1356, but was interrupted by the outbreak of the **Black Death** in 1349. The plague claimed about a third of the population – and in England the resultant scarcity of labour gave the peasantry great economic clout. Predictably, the landowners attempted to restrict the concomitant rise in wages, provoking widespread rioting that culminated in the **Peasants' Revolt** of 1381. The rebels marched on London hoping to appeal to the king – **Richard II** (1377–99) – for fair treatment. The monarch agreed to meet their spokesman, **Wat Tyler**, but his bodyguards killed Tyler instead and dispersed his followers amid mass slaughter.

THE CONQUEST OF WALES (1272–1415)

William the Conqueror installed a gang of landholding barons, the **Lords Marcher**, along the border with Wales (The Marches) rather than attempting conquest. His successor, **Edward I**, decided to conquer Wales instead, provoked in part by a Welsh chieftain, **Llywelyn the Last**, who failed to attend his coronation and refused to pay him homage. Aided by the skilful use of sea power, Edward had little trouble in forcing Llywelyn into the mountains of Snowdonia, and, by the **Treaty of Aberconwy** in 1277, Llywelyn was robbed of almost all his land and left the hollow title of "Prince of Wales". Five years later, Llywelyn's brother **Dafydd** rose against Edward and Llywelyn felt obliged to help. It was a disaster: Edward crushed the revolt with relative ease and both brothers were killed. The **Treaty of Rhuddlan** in 1284 set down the terms by which the English king was to rule Wales: those parts of the country not given to the Lords Marcher were divided into administrative and legal districts similar to those in England. Often seen as a symbol of English subjugation, the treaty in fact respected much of Welsh law and provided an embryonic basis for civil rights and privileges. Many Welsh accepted Edward's rule, but after he brutally crushed a 1294 rebellion led by **Madog ap Llywelyn**, a number of those privileges were rescinded. Thereafter, the Anglo-Welsh aristocracy took firm hold of Wales, but one of their number, the charismatic Welsh hero **Owain Glyndŵr**, rose in revolt in 1400, declaring himself "Prince of Wales" in defiance of his English overlord, **Henry IV**. The key fortress of Conwy Castle was captured in 1401 and three years later Glyndŵr summoned a parliament in Machynlleth, and had himself crowned. He then demanded independence for the Welsh Church from Canterbury and set about securing alliances with disaffected English noblemen. However, Glyndŵr's allies deserted him, and the rebellion fizzled out, though Glyndŵr was never captured and disappeared into the mountains. It's believed he died in 1415 or 1416, but his body was never found.

1190	1237	1266
King Richard complains that in England it is "cold and always raining", and joins the Third Crusade.	The Treaty of York, signed by Henry III of England and Scotland's Alexander II, sets the Anglo-Scottish border.	Alexander III, the king of Scotland, buys the Western Isles from the Norwegians.

Medieval Scotland (1040–1329)

In 1040, **Macbeth** famously killed King Duncan and usurped the Scottish throne. In 1057, however, Duncan's son, **Malcolm III**, returned to Scotland and defeated Macbeth. His long reign was to transform Scottish society. Malcolm established a secure dynasty – the **Canmores** ("Bigheads") – based on succession through the male line, and replaced the old Gaelic system of blood ties with **feudalism**: the followers of a Gaelic king were his kindred, whereas those of a feudal king were his vassals. While the Canmores successfully feudalized much of southern and eastern Scotland by making grants to their Norman, Breton and Flemish followers, traditional clan-based social relations persisted to the north and west, a division which was to define much of Scotland's later history.

The Canmores also set about reforming the Church. Malcolm III's English wife **Margaret** brought Scottish religious practices into line with the rest of Europe, while **David I** (1124–53) imported monks to found monasteries, principally in the Borders at Kelso, Melrose, Jedburgh and Dryburgh. By 1200 the country was covered by eleven bishoprics, although church organization remained weak within the Highlands. Similarly, the dynasty founded **royal burghs**, recognizing towns such as Edinburgh, Stirling and Berwick as centres of trade. Their charters usually granted a measure of self-government, which the monarchy hoped would encourage loyalty and increase prosperity. Scotland's Gaelic-speaking clans had little influence within the burghs, and by 1550 Scots – a northern version of Anglo-Saxon – had become the main language throughout the Lowlands.

Anglo-Scottish wars

Scotland's progress as an independent nation was threatened by the hotly contested succession that followed the death of **Alexander III** in 1286. Edward I, king of England, muscled in, presiding over a conference in which the rival claimants to the Scottish throne presented their cases. Edward chose John Balliol, in preference to **Robert the Bruce**, and forced John to pay him homage, thus turning Scotland into a vassal kingdom. Bruce's refusal to accept this decision prolonged the conflict, and in 1295 Balliol switched his allegiance from England to **France** – the start of what is known as the "Auld Alliance". In the ensuing warfare, Balliol was defeated and imprisoned, and Edward seized control of almost all of Scotland. However, Edward's cruelty provoked a truly national resistance that focused on **William Wallace**, a man of relatively lowly origins who forged a proto-nationalist army of peasants, lesser knights and townsmen that was determined to expel the English. Yet Wallace never received the support of the nobility and after ten bitter years he was betrayed, captured and executed in London.

Feudal intrigue now resumed. In 1306 **Robert the Bruce** defied Edward and had himself crowned king of Scotland. Edward died the following year, but the turbulence dragged on until 1314, when Bruce decisively defeated an English army under Edward II at the **Battle of Bannockburn**. At last Bruce was firmly in control, and in 1320 the Scots asserted their right to independence in a successful petition to the pope, now known as the **Arbroath Declaration**.

England: the houses of Lancaster and York (1399–1485)

In 1399, **Henry IV** (1399–1413), the first **Lancastrian** king, supplanted the weak and indecisive Richard II. His son and successor, the bellicose **Henry V** (1413–22), promptly

1277	1295	1314	1349
Well-armed and well-organized, Edward I of England embarks upon the conquest of Wales.	France and Scotland sign a treaty of mutual assistance – the start of the "Auld Alliance".	At the Battle of Bannockburn, Robert the Bruce's Scots destroy an English army.	The Black Death reaches England and moves on into Scotland the year after.

renewed the Hundred Years' War. A comprehensive victory at **Agincourt** forced the French king to acknowledge Henry as his heir in the Treaty of Troyes of 1420. However, Henry died just two years later and his son, **Henry VI** (1422–61 & 1470–1471) – or rather his regents – all too easily succumbed to a French counterattack inspired by **Joan of Arc**; by 1454, only Calais was left in English hands. When it became obvious that Henry VI was mentally unstable, two aristocratic factions fought for the throne – the **Yorkists**, whose emblem was the white rose, and the **Lancastrians**, represented by the red rose. At first, in the **Wars of the Roses**, the Lancastrians had the upper hand, but the Yorkist **Edward IV** seized the Crown in 1461. When he imprudently tried to shrug off his most powerful backer, Richard Neville, Earl of Warwick, "Warwick the Kingmaker" returned the favour by switching sides. Edward was driven into exile and **Henry VI** came back for a second term as king – but not for long. In 1471, Edward IV returned, Warwick was killed and Henry captured – and dispatched – when the Yorkists crushed the Lancastrians at the Battle of Tewkesbury.

Edward IV (1461–70 & 1471–83) proved to be a precursor of the great Tudor princes – licentious, cruel and despotic, but also a patron of Renaissance learning. In 1483, his 12-year-old son succeeded as **Edward V** (1483), but his reign was cut short after only two months, when he and his younger brother were murdered in the Tower of London – allegedly by their uncle, the Duke of Gloucester, who was crowned **Richard III** (1483–85). Richard was himself killed at the battle of **Bosworth Field** in 1485 and Henry Tudor, Earl of Richmond, took the throne as **Henry VII**.

England: the Tudors (1485–1603)

The start of the **Tudor** period brought radical transformation. A Lancastrian through his mother's line, **Henry VII** (1485–1509) promptly reconciled the Yorkists by marrying Edward IV's daughter Elizabeth, a shrewd gambit that ended the Wars of the Roses at a stroke. By marrying his daughter off to James IV of Scotland and his son to Catherine, the daughter of Ferdinand and Isabella of Spain, Henry also began to establish England as a major European power.

Henry's son, **Henry VIII** (1509–47) is best remembered for separating Anne Boleyn from her head and the English Church from Rome, thereby establishing the independent Protestant **Church of England**. His schism with the pope was triggered not by doctrinal issues but by the failure of his wife **Catherine of Aragon** – his elder brother's widow – to produce male offspring. When Pope Clement VII refused to grant a decree of nullity, Henry dismissed his chancellor Thomas Wolsey and turned to **Thomas Cromwell**, who helped make the English Church recognize Henry as its head. One consequence, the **Dissolution of the Monasteries**, enabled both king and nobles to get their hands on valuable monastic property. In his later years Henry became a corpulent, syphilitic wreck, six times married but at last furnished with an heir, **Edward VI** (1547–53), who was only nine years old when he ascended the throne. His short reign saw Protestantism established on a firm footing, with churches stripped of their icons and Catholic services banned.

Despite the spread of Protestantism, most of the country accepted **Mary** (1553–58), daughter of Catherine of Aragon and a fervent Catholic, as queen upon Edward's death. Returning England to the papacy, Mary married the future Philip II of Spain, forging an alliance that provoked war with France and the loss of Calais, England's last

1380s	**1485**	**1559**
Geoffrey Chaucer begins work on *The Canterbury Tales* and changes the face of English literature forever.	Battle of Bosworth Field: Richard III deposed and killed, ending the Wars of the Roses.	Religious reformer John Knox returns to Scotland, where he leads the Protestant Reformation.

French possession. The marriage was unpopular and so was Mary's persecution of Protestants: the leading lights of the English Reformation, Hugh Latimer, Nicholas Ridley and Thomas Cranmer, the archbishop of Canterbury, were all executed.

Elizabeth I

When she came to the throne on the death of her half-sister, **Elizabeth I** (1558–1603) looked vulnerable. The country was divided by religion and threatened from abroad by Philip II of Spain, the most powerful man in Europe. Famously, Elizabeth eschewed marriage and, although a Protestant herself, steered a delicate course in relations with the Catholic Church. Her prudence rested well with the burgeoning English merchant class, who were mostly opposed to foreign military entanglements. An exception was, however, made for the piratical activities of English seafarers like Walter Raleigh, Martin Frobisher, John Hawkins and Francis Drake, who made a fortune raiding Spain's American colonies. Inevitably, Philip II's irritation took a warlike turn, but his **Spanish Armada** was defeated in 1588. Elizabeth's reign also saw the efflorescence of a specifically English Renaissance, especially in the field of literature, with **William Shakespeare** (1564–1616) pre-eminent.

Wales under the Tudors

Welsh allegiance during the Wars of the Roses lay broadly with the Lancastrians, who had the support of the ascendant **Tewdwr** (or Tudor) family of northern Wales. Nevertheless, Wales benefited little from the Tudors – at least until a uniform administrative structure was implemented under Henry VIII. The latter also passed two **Acts of Union**, in 1536 and 1543, formalizing English sovereignty. As for the **Church**, Protestantism made rapid headway in Wales, supplanting Catholicism during Henry VIII's reign, and the Bible was translated into Welsh; while new landownership laws hastened the emergence of the **Anglo-Welsh gentry**, eager to claim a Welsh pedigree while promoting the English language and legal system. Landless peasants remained poor, only gaining slightly from the increase in cattle trade with England and the development of mining and ore smelting.

Scotland's Bruces and Stewarts (1329–1603)

After the death of Robert the Bruce in 1329, the Scottish monarchy hit the skids. The last of the Bruce dynasty died in 1371, to be succeeded by the "Stewards", hence **Stewarts** (known as Stuarts in England), though power remained in the hands of the nobility – or at least those nobles who were **regents** during the minority of a series of child kings. **James IV** (1488–1513), the most talented of the early Stewarts, might have restored the authority of the Crown, but his invasion of England ended in a calamitous defeat – and his own death – at the **Battle of Flodden Field** in Northumberland.

The reign of **Mary, Queen of Scots** (1542–87), typified the problems of the Scottish monarchy. Just one week old when she came to the throne, Mary immediately caught the attention of the English king, Henry VIII, who sought, first by persuasion and then by force of arms, to secure her hand in marriage for his 5-year-old son, Edward. The Scottish nobility resisted and turned instead to the **"Auld Alliance"** with the French king

1567	1588	c. 1592	1603
Mary, Queen of Scots, implicated in the murder of her second husband – pandemonium ensues.	Spanish Armada fails to reach England – Elizabeth I relieved.	First performance of Shakespeare's *Henry VI*, Pt 1, at the Rose Theatre, Bankside, London.	King James unites the crowns of Scotland and England.

TOIL AND TROUBLE: THE TRAVAILS OF MARY, QUEEN OF SCOTS

A devout(ish) Catholic, **Mary, Queen of Scots** (1542–87), returned to Scotland in 1561 after the death of Francis, her French husband. It was a country she barely knew and certainly did not understand, although, in fairness, she did try to avoid an open breach with her Protestant subjects. She might have pulled it off too, but for her disastrous second marriage to **Lord Darnley**. A cruel man, Darnley's jealousy led to his involvement in the murder of Mary's favourite, **David Rizzio**, who was dragged from the queen's chambers and stabbed 56 times. Outraged Scottish Protestants were even more horrified when Darnley himself was murdered in 1567, and Mary married the **Earl of Bothwell**, widely believed to be the murderer. The Scots rose in rebellion, driving Mary into exile in England at the age of just 25. The queen's illegitimate half-brother, the **Earl of Moray**, became regent and her son, the infant **James**, was left behind to be raised a Protestant prince. Mary, meanwhile, was such a threat to the English throne that Queen Elizabeth I had little choice but to imprison and ultimately execute her – despite her profound reservations as to the wisdom of executing a fellow royal.

promising military assistance in return for marriage between Mary and the Dauphin Francis. The alliance reaffirmed, the child queen sailed for France in 1548, leaving her loyal nobles and their French allies in control. Six years later, **Mary of Guise**, the French mother of the absent Mary, became regent of Scotland, but although she had some success in keeping the English at bay and quelling her nobles, her French – specifically Catholic – connection was out of sympathy with the times as **Protestantism** took root. In 1557, a group of Protestant nobles banded together to form the **Lords of the Congregation** and they proceeded to depose Mary of Guise with English military backing. In 1560, the Scottish Parliament asserted the primacy of Protestantism, the culmination of the fast-moving **Scottish Reformation**, a complex social process speeded by the weakness of the established Church, the unpopularity of the Catholic Mary of Guise, and the tireless efforts of Protestant reformers like **John Knox** (1514–1572). Protestant proceedings were temporarily interrupted by the return of Mary, Queen of Scots (see box above), but with Mary chased into exile, Knox could concentrate on the organization of the reformed Church, or **Kirk**, which he envisaged as a body empowered by God to intervene in the daily lives of the people. **Andrew Melville** proposed the abolition of all traces of episcopacy – the rule of the bishops in the Church – and suggested instead a **presbyterian** structure, administered by a hierarchy of assemblies, part elected and part appointed. In 1592, the Melvillian party achieved a measure of success when presbyteries and synods were accepted as legal church courts and the office of bishop was suspended.

United Kingdom: 1603–60

James VI of Scotland, the son of Mary, Queen of Scots, succeeded Elizabeth as **James I of England** (1603–25), thereby **uniting** the English and Scottish crowns. James quickly moved to end hostilities with Spain and adopted a policy of toleration to the country's embattled Catholics. Both initiatives offended many Protestants, whose fears were confirmed in 1605 when **Guy Fawkes** and his Catholic co-conspirators were discovered preparing to blow up the Houses of Parliament in the **Gunpowder Plot**: Fawkes was

1605	**1642**	**1660**
Gunpowder Plot: Guy Fawkes plans to blow up the Houses of Parliament, but fails.	The Civil War begins when Charles I raises his standard in Nottingham.	The Restoration: Charles II takes the throne – and digs up the body of Oliver Cromwell to hammer home his point.

tortured and then hung, drawn and quartered for his pains. **Puritan** sentiment and commercial interests converged with the founding of the first permanent **colony in North America**, Virginia, in 1608. Twelve years later, the **Pilgrim Fathers** landed in New England, establishing a colony that absorbed a hundred thousand Puritan immigrants by the middle of the century.

Meanwhile, James restored the Scottish bishops, much to the chagrin of the Presbyterians and assorted Protestants, and alienated England's landed gentry. His absolutist vision of the monarchy – the **divine right of kings** – was out of step with the Protestant leanings of his subjects, and he also relied heavily on court favourites, especially the much reviled George Villiers, Duke of Buckingham. It was a recipe for disaster, but it was his successor, **Charles I** (1625–49), who reaped the whirlwind.

Charles I

Inheriting James's dislike of Protestants and approval of absolutism, **Charles I** ruled without Parliament from 1629 to 1640, but overreached himself when he tried to impose a new Anglican prayer book on the (Scottish) Kirk. Scottish reformers organized the **National Covenant** in religious indignation; lack of finance stopped Charles from responding with an effective military campaign, but the well-financed Covenanters assembled a proficient army under Alexander Leslie. In desperation, Charles summoned the English Parliament hoping it would pay for an army to fight the Scots, but they refused their support. Indeed, the **Long Parliament**, as it became known, impeached several of Charles's allies, and compiled its grievances in the Grand Remonstrance of 1641.

Civil War and Commonwealth

Confronted by this concerted hostility, the king withdrew to Nottingham where, in 1642, he raised his standard, the first act of the **Civil War**. The Royalist forces ("Cavaliers") were initially successful, but in response **Oliver Cromwell** overhauled part of the Parliamentary army ("Roundheads"), to create the formidable, ideologically committed **New Model Army**, which cut its teeth at the battle of Naseby and thereafter simply brushed the Royalists aside. In defeat, Charles surrendered to the Scots, who handed him over to the English Parliament, by whom he was ultimately executed in 1649. The following year, Charles's son, the future Charles II, returned from exile, landing in Scotland. To secure Scottish support, he was obliged to sign the Covenant; however, the New Model Army proved too good for the Royalists and, after several defeats, Charles had to flee into exile yet again.

For the next eleven years the whole of Britain was a **Commonwealth** – at first a true republic, then, after 1653, a **Protectorate** with **Oliver Cromwell** as Lord Protector and commander-in-chief. He reformed the government, secured commercial treaties with foreign nations and put the fear of God into his enemies. After Cromwell died in 1658, his son **Richard Cromwell** ruled briefly and ineffectually until 1660, when **Charles II** (1660–85) regained the throne: the aristocracy and much of the gentry were relieved and delighted.

The Restoration and the later Stuarts (1660–1714)

A Stuart was back on the throne, but **Charles II** had few absolutist illusions – the terms of the **Restoration** were closely negotiated and included a general amnesty for all those

1669	1678	1684
Samuel Pepys gives up his diary, after nine years of detailed jottings.	John Bunyan, the Protestant preacher and reformer, writes his *Pilgrim's Progress*.	Isaac Newton observes gravity – but is probably not hit on the head by an apple.

who had fought against the Stuarts, with the exception of the regicides – those who had signed Charles I's death warrant. Nonetheless, there was a sea change in public life with the re-establishment of a royal court and the foundation of the **Royal Society**, whose scientific endeavours were furthered by Isaac Newton (1642–1727). The low points of Charles's reign were the **Great Plague** of 1665 and the 1666 **Great Fire of London**. Politically, underlying tensions persisted between the monarchy and Parliament, though the latter was more concerned with the struggle between the **Whigs** and **Tories**, factions representing, respectively, the low-church gentry and the high-church aristocracy. There was a degree of religious toleration too, but its brittleness was all too apparent in the anti-Catholic riots of 1678.

The Glorious Revolution

The succession of the Catholic **James II** (1685–88), brother of Charles II, provoked much opposition, though the response was indifferent when the Protestant **Duke of Monmouth**, the favourite among Charles II's illegitimate sons, raised a rebellion in the West Country. Monmouth was defeated at Sedgemoor, in Somerset, in July 1685, nine days later he was beheaded at Tower Hill, and, in the subsequent **Bloody Assizes** of Judge Jeffreys, hundreds of rebels and suspected sympathizers were executed or deported. More important for James's popularity was his **Declaration of Indulgence**, which removed anti-Catholic restrictions, and the birth of his son, which threatened to secure a Catholic succession. Alarmed, powerful Protestants sent for **William of Orange**, the Dutch husband of Mary, the Protestant daughter of James II, to save them from "popery". William landed in Devon and, as James's forces simply melted away, speedily took control of London in the **Glorious Revolution** of 1688. This was the final postscript to the Civil War – although it was another couple of years before James and his remaining Jacobites were finally defeated in Ireland at the **Battle of the Boyne**.

William, Mary and Anne

William and Mary (1688–94) became joint sovereigns after they agreed to a **Bill of Rights** defining the limitations of the monarch's powers and the rights of subjects, thereby making Britain a **constitutional monarchy**, in which the roles of legislature and executive were separate and interdependent. The model was broadly consistent with that outlined by the philosopher and political thinker **John Locke** (1632–1704), whose essentially Whig doctrines of toleration and social contract were gradually embraced as the new orthodoxy.

After Mary's death, **William** (1694–1702) ruled alone; during his reign the **Act of Settlement of 1701** barred Catholics, or anyone married to one, from succession to the English throne. This Act did not, however, apply in Scotland, and the English feared that the Scots would invite James II's son, **James Edward Stuart**, back from France to be their king. These fears were allayed when Scotland passed the **Act of Union** uniting the English and Scottish parliaments in 1707, though neither the Scottish legal system nor the Presbyterian Kirk were merged with their English equivalents.

After William's death the crown passed to Mary's sister **Anne** (1702–14). A string of British military victories on the continent now began with the Duke of Marlborough's triumph at Blenheim in 1704, followed the next year by the capture of Gibraltar, establishing a British presence in the Mediterranean. These military escapades were part of the Europe-wide **War of the Spanish Succession**, a long-winded dynastic squabble

1703	1707	1715
"The Great Storm", a week-long hurricane, blasts through southern England.	The Act of Union merges the Scottish Parliament into the English Parliament.	First Jacobite Rebellion: James Stuart ("The Old Pretender") raises a Scottish army, but is defeated.

that rumbled on until the **Treaty of Utrecht** in 1713 all but settled the European balance of power for the rest of the century.

The Hanoverians (1714–1815)

On Anne's death, the crown passed to the Protestant Elector of Hanover, who became **George I** (1714–27). During his lacklustre reign, power leached into the hands of a Whig oligarchy led by a chief minister – or prime minister – the longest serving of which was **Robert Walpole** (1676–1745). In the meantime, plans were being hatched for a **Jacobite Rebellion** in support of **James Edward Stuart**, the "Old Pretender". Its timing appeared perfect: Scottish opinion was moving against the Union, which had failed to bring Scotland tangible economic benefits, and many English Catholics supported the Jacobite cause too, toasting the "king across the water". In 1715, the Earl of Mar raised the Stuart standard at Braemar Castle, and just eight days later he captured Perth, where he gathered an army of more than ten thousand men. Mar's rebellion took the government by surprise. They had only four thousand soldiers in Scotland, but Mar dithered until he lost the military advantage. There was an indecisive battle at Sheriffmuir, but by the time the Old Pretender landed in Scotland in December 1715, six thousand veteran Dutch troops had reinforced government forces. The rebellion disintegrated rapidly and James slunk back to exile in France. Thirty years later, with **George II** (1727–60) on the throne and England embroiled in yet another dynastic squabble, the War of the Austrian Succession (1740–48), the Jacobites tried again – this time led by the **Young Pretender**, **Charles Stuart** (Bonnie Prince Charlie) – but the Stuarts were defeated once more. With the rebellion crushed, it was back to normal in London, where the political tussles between king and Parliament were enlivened by **John Wilkes**, the first of an increasingly vociferous line of parliamentary radicals.

Empire and colonies

At the tail end of George II's reign, the **Seven Years' War** (1756–63) harvested England yet more overseas territory in India and Canada at the expense of France; and, in 1768, with **George III** (1760–1820) now on the throne, **Captain James Cook** stumbled upon New Zealand and Australia, thereby extending Britain's empire still further. The fly in the ointment was the deteriorating relationship with the thirteen colonies of North America, which came to a head with the **American Declaration of Independence** and Britain's subsequent defeat in the **Revolutionary War** (1775–83). The British government was not, however, directly involved in the momentous events across the Channel, where the **French Revolution** convulsed Britain's most consistent foe. Out of the turmoil emerged one of Britain's most daunting enemies, **Napoleon** (1769–1821), whose stunning military progress was interrupted by Nelson at **Trafalgar** in 1805 and finally halted in 1815 by the Duke of Wellington (and the Prussians) at **Waterloo**.

The Industrial Revolution

Britain's triumph over Napoleon was fuelled by its financial strength, born out of the **Industrial Revolution**. This switch from an agricultural to a manufacturing economy transformed Britain within a century. The earliest mechanized production was in the

1745	1781	1783
Second Jacobite Rebellion: Charles Stuart (Bonnie Prince Charlie) invades England with a Scots army, but is defeated at Culloden.	Opening of the Iron Bridge – the first iron bridge the world has ever seen – over the River Severn.	End of the American War of Independence – the American colonies break from Britain.

Lancashire **cotton mills**, where cotton spinning progressed from a cottage industry to a highly productive factory-based system. Initially, the cotton mills were powered by water, but in 1781 James Watt patented his **steam engine**. As Watt's engines needed **coal**, the population shifted towards the Midlands, central Scotland and the north of England, where the great coal reserves were mined. The industrial economy boomed and diversified, and regional towns mushroomed at an extraordinary rate. Sheffield was a steel town, Manchester possessed huge cotton warehouses, and Liverpool had the docks, where raw materials from India and the Americas flowed in and manufactured goods went out. Commerce and industry were also served by improving transport facilities, such as the construction of **canals**. A second major leap forward arrived with the **railway**, heralded by the Stockton–Darlington line in 1825, followed five years later by the Liverpool–Manchester railway, where George Stephenson's *Rocket* made its first outing.

Boosted by a vast influx of Jewish, Irish, French and Dutch workers, the country's **population** rose from eight and a half million to more than fifteen million during George III's reign.

The Chartists – and social reform

In their hundreds, workers threatened by mechanization joined the **Chartist movement**, which demanded parliamentary reform – the most important industrial boom towns remained unrepresented in Parliament – and the repeal of the **Corn Laws**, which kept the price of bread artificially high. In 1819, during a mass demonstration in support of parliamentary reform in Manchester, protestors were hacked down by troops in the so-called **Peterloo Massacre**. Social tensions ran high throughout the 1820s, but judicious parliamentary acts helped quieten things down: the **Reform Act** of 1832 established the principle (if not always the practice) of popular representation; the **Poor Law** of 1834 improved the condition of the most destitute; and the **Corn Laws** were repealed in 1846. Significant sections of the middle class supported progressive reform, as evidenced by the immense popularity of **Charles Dickens** (1812–70), whose novels railed against poverty and injustice. **John Wesley** (1703–91) and his **Methodists** had pre-empted these social concerns by leading the anti-slavery campaign. As a result of their efforts, **slavery** was banned in Britain in 1772 and throughout the British Empire in 1833.

Victorian Britain

In 1820, a blind and insane George III died. His two sons, **George IV** (1820–30) and **William IV** (1830–37), were succeeded in turn by his niece, **Victoria** (1837–1901), whose long reign witnessed the zenith of British power. The economy boomed, and the British trading fleet was easily the mightiest in the world. Victoria became the symbol of both the nation's success and the imperial ideal. There were extraordinary intellectual achievements too – as typified by the publication of **Charles Darwin**'s *On the Origin of Species* in 1859. Britain's industrial and commercial prowess was embodied by the engineering feats of **Isambard Kingdom Brunel** (1806–1859) and by the **Great Exhibition** of 1851, a display of manufacturing achievements without compare. During the last third of the century, Parliament was dominated by the duel between **Disraeli** and the Liberal leader **Gladstone**. While Disraeli eventually passed the Second Reform

1819	1824	1858
Peterloo Massacre: in Manchester, the cavalry wade into a huge crowd who are demanding parliamentary reform. Many are killed.	Charles Dickens' father is imprisoned as a debtor; his son never forgets.	English engineer Isambard Kingdom Brunel builds the iron-hulled SS *Great Eastern*, the largest ship in the world.

Bill in 1867, further extending the electoral franchise, Gladstone's first ministry of 1868–74 created such far-reaching legislation as compulsory education, and the full legalization of trade unions.

As for foreign entanglements, troops were sent in 1854 to protect the Ottoman Empire against the Russians in the **Crimea**, an inglorious debacle whose horrors reached the public via the first-ever press coverage of a military campaign, and the revelations of **Florence Nightingale** (1820–1910), who was appalled by the lack of medical care for the soldiers. The **Indian Mutiny** of 1857 exposed the fragility of Britain's hold over the Asian subcontinent, though the imperial status quo was brutally restored and Victoria took the title Empress of India after 1876. Thereafter, the British army fought various minor wars against poorly armed Asian and African opponents, but came unstuck when it faced the better armed Dutch settlers of South Africa in the **Boer War** (1899–1902). The British ultimately fought their way to a sort of victory, but the discreditable conduct of the war prompted a military shake-up at home that proved significant in the coming European war.

World War I and its aftermath (1914–39)

Victoria was succeeded by her son, **Edward VII** (1901–10), whose leisurely lifestyle has often been seen as the epitome of the complacent era to which he gave his name. It wasn't to last. On August 4, 1914, with **George V** (1910–36) now on the throne, the Liberal government declared war on Germany, thereby honouring the Entente Cordiale signed with France in 1904. Hundreds of thousands volunteered for the army, but their enthusiastic nationalism could not ensure a quick victory, and **World War I** dragged on for four miserable years. Britain and her allies eventually prevailed, but the number of dead beggared belief, undermining deference for the ruling class, whose generals had displayed a startling combination of incompetence and indifference to the plight of their men. Many Britons looked admiringly towards the Soviet Union, where Lenin and his Bolsheviks had rid themselves of the Tsar and seized control in 1917. After the war ended in 1918, the sheer weight of public opinion pushed Parliament into extending the **vote** to all men 21 and over and to women over 30. The liberalization of women's rights owed much to the efforts of the radical **Suffragettes**, led by Emmeline Pankhurst and her daughters Sylvia and Christabel, but the process was only completed in 1929 when women were at last granted the vote at 21. The royal family itself was shaken in 1936 by the **abdication** of **Edward VIII** (1936), following his decision to marry a twice-divorced American, Wallis Simpson, but in the event, the succession passed smoothly to his brother **George VI**.

Hard times

During this period, the **Labour Party** supplanted the Liberals as the main force on the left of British politics, its strength founded on an alliance between the working-class trade unions and middle-class radicals. Labour formed its first government in 1923 under **Ramsay MacDonald**, but the publication of the Zinoviev Letter, a forgery in which the Soviets supposedly urged British leftists to promote revolution, undermined his position and the Conservatives were returned with a large parliamentary majority in 1924. Two years later, a bitter dispute between coal miners and mine-owners escalated into a **General Strike**, which quickly spread to the railways, the newspapers and the iron

1865	1888	1909	1912
William Booth from Nottingham founds the Salvation Army, in the East End of London.	First football game between Celtic and Rangers in Glasgow.	Lord Baden-Powell forms the "British Boy Scouts".	Bad news: the *Titanic* sinks and Captain Scott and his men die on the ice in the Antarctic.

and steel industries. Involving half a million workers, the strike lasted nine days before it was broken when the government called in the army. The economic situation deteriorated further after the **crash** of the New York Stock Exchange in 1929 precipitated a worldwide depression. Unemployment topped 2.8 million in 1931, generating mass demonstrations that peaked with the 1936 **Jarrow March** from the Northeast of England to London.

The Empire reorganizes

Abroad, the structure of the **British Empire** was undergoing profound changes. After the cack-handed way the British had dealt with Dublin's 1916 Easter Rising, the status of **Ireland** was bound to change. There was a partial resolution in 1922 with the establishment of the Irish Free State, but the six counties of the mainly Protestant North (two-thirds of the ancient province of **Ulster**) chose to "contract out" and stay part of the United Kingdom – and this was to cause endless problems later. Four years later, the **Imperial Conference** recognized the autonomy of the British dominions, comprising all the major countries that had previously been part of the Empire. This agreement was formalized in the 1931 Statute of Westminster: each dominion was given an equal footing in a **Commonwealth of Nations**, though each still recognized the British monarch.

World War II

When Hitler set about militarizing Germany in the mid-1930s, the British government adopted a policy of appeasement. Consequently, when Britain declared war on Germany after Hitler's invasion of Poland in September 1939, she was poorly prepared. After embarrassing military failures during the first months of **World War II**, the discredited government was replaced in May 1940 by a national coalition headed by the charismatic **Winston Churchill** (1874–1965). Partly through Churchill's manoeuvrings, the United States started supplying food and munitions to Britain. In response to the Japanese bombing of Pearl Harbor in December, 1941, the US joined the war, and its intervention, combined with the enormous sacrifice of the Soviet Red Army, swung the military balance. In terms of casualties, World War II was not as calamitous as World War I, but its impact upon British civilians was much greater. In its first wave of **bombing** of the UK, the Luftwaffe caused massive damage to industrial and supply centres such as London, Glasgow, Swansea, Coventry, Manchester, Liverpool, Southampton and Plymouth. Later raids, intended to shatter morale rather than factories and docks, battered the cathedral cities of Canterbury, Exeter, Bath, Norwich and York. Germany surrendered in May 1945 and Japan followed in September, but although the British were overjoyed by the Allied victory, the country's finances were in a parlous state and its infrastructure had been badly damaged.

Postwar Britain: from Attlee to Callaghan (1945–79)

Hungry for change (and demobilization), voters in 1945's immediate postwar election replaced Churchill with the Labour Party under **Clement Attlee** (1883–1967), who set about a radical programme to **nationalize** the coal, gas, electricity, iron and steel industries, as well as the inland transport services. The early passage of the **National Insurance Act** and

1926	1950	1962	1985
Britain's first-ever General Strike: a nine-day walkout in support of the coal miners. The workers lose (again).	Soap rationing ends in Britain – a general clean-up follows.	The Beatles hit the big time with their first single, *Love Me Do*.	The bitter, year-long miners' strike is crushed by Margaret Thatcher.

the **National Health Service Act** gave birth to what became known as the **welfare state**. Despite substantial American aid, the huge problems of rebuilding the economy made austerity the keynote, and food and fuel rationing endured for many years.

Meanwhile, Britain, the US, Canada, France and the Benelux countries defined their postwar international commitments in 1949's **North Atlantic Treaty**, a counterbalance to Soviet power in Eastern Europe. Continuing confusion over Britain's imperial – or rather post-imperial – role, however, bubbled to the surface in the **Suez Crisis** of 1956, when Anglo-French and Israeli forces invaded Egypt to secure control of the Suez Canal, only to be hastily recalled following international (American) condemnation. This shoddy fiasco laid bare the limitations on Britain's capacity for independent action and the Conservative prime minister, **Anthony Eden** (1897–1977), whose judgement had been so appalling, was forced to resign. His replacement, the pragmatic, silky-tongued **Harold Macmillan** (1894–1986), accepted the end of empire, but was still eager for Britain to play a leading international role – and the country kept its nuclear arms, despite the best efforts of the Campaign for Nuclear Disarmament (CND).

The dominant political figure in the 1960s was **Harold Wilson** (1916–95), a witty speaker and skilled tactician who was Labour prime minister from 1964 to 1970 – and again from 1974 to 1976. The 1960s saw a boom in consumer spending, pioneering social legislation (primarily on homosexuality and abortion), and a corresponding cultural upswing, with London becoming the hippest city on the planet. But the good times lasted barely a decade: the Conservatives returned to office in 1970 and although the new prime minister, the ungainly **Edward Heath**, led Britain into the brave new world of the **European Economic Community (ECC)**, the 1970s were a decade of recession and industrial strife. In 1975, with Labour back in power, Heath was usurped by **Margaret Thatcher** (1925–2013). Four years later, to the amazement of many pundits, Thatcher defeated **James Callaghan**'s Labour Party in the general election; as events proved, she was primed and ready to break the unions and anyone else who crossed her path.

Thatcher and Major (1979–97)

Thatcher pushed the UK towards sharp social polarization. While taxation policies and easy credit fuelled a consumer boom for the professional classes, the erosion of manufacturing and the weakening of the welfare state impoverished a great swathe of the population. With the enthusiastic backing of most of the national press, Thatcher won a second term of office in 1983, partly thanks to the recapture of the **Falkland Islands**, a remote British dependency in the South Atlantic, retrieved from Argentine occupiers in 1982. Social and political tensions surfaced in sporadic urban rioting and also in the year-long **miners' strike** (1984–85) against colliery closures, a bitter dispute in which the police were given unprecedented powers to restrict the movement of citizens. Violence in Northern Ireland also intensified, and in 1984 IRA bombers almost blew up the entire Cabinet, who were staying in a Brighton hotel during the Conservatives' annual conference.

The divisive politics of Thatcherism reached their apogee when the desperately unpopular **Poll Tax** led to her overthrow by Conservative colleagues who feared defeat if she led them into another election. Her uninspiring successor, **John Major**, somehow managed to win the Conservatives a fourth term of office in 1992, with a much

1994	1999	2009
The Channel Tunnel opens to traffic.	The Scottish Parliament and the national assemblies for Wales and Northern Ireland take on devolved powers.	Economic crisis prompts the Bank of England to reduce interest rates to a record low of 0.5%: misery for savers; pleasure for spenders.

reduced majority. While his government presided over steady economic growth, they gained little credit amid allegations of corruption and feckless leadership.

The return of Labour

Wracked by factionalism in the 1980s, the **Labour Party** regrouped under Neil Kinnock and then John Smith. The political rewards, however, dropped into the lap of a new and dynamic young leader, **Tony Blair**, whose cloak of idealistic, media-friendly populism swept Labour to power in 1997, on a wave of genuine popular optimism. There were immediate rewards in enhanced relations with Europe and progress in the Irish peace talks, but Blair's re-election in 2001 was accompanied by little of the previous optimism. Few voters fully trusted Blair, and his administration had by then developed a reputation for "**spin**" – laundering events to present the government in the best possible light.

The terrorist attacks of **September 11, 2001** downgraded Blair's domestic agenda in favour of a rush to support President Bush in his assaults on Afghanistan and then **Iraq**, in 2003. In the event, Saddam Hussein was deposed with relative ease, but neither Bush nor Blair had a coherent exit strategy, and back home Blair was widely seen as having "spun" Britain into the war by exaggerating the danger presented by Saddam. Even so, Blair managed to win a third general election in 2005, though not before he had promised to step down before the next election. He was succeeded in June 2007 by his arch-rival, the Chancellor of the Exchequer, **Gordon Brown**.

The obsessive Brown proved to be a clumsy prime minister with a tin ear for the public mood. Failing to create a coherent narrative for either himself or his government, he even failed to secure credit for his one major achievement, staving off a banking collapse during the worldwide **financial crisis** that hit the UK hard in the autumn of 2007.

Back to the future – Britain today

In the build-up to the **general election of 2010**, all three main political parties – the Liberal Democrats, Conservatives and Labour – spoke of the need to cut public spending more or less drastically, manoeuvring the electorate away from blaming the bankers, if not indeed capitalism per se, for the financial crash of 2007. Although no party managed to secure a majority, an impasse was avoided when the Liberal Democrats swapped principles for power to join a **Conservative–Liberal Democrat coalition**, which took office in May 2010 with the Conservative **David Cameron** as prime minister. An old Etonian with a PR background, Cameron made a confident and sure-footed start, keeping his ideological cards well hidden (if indeed he has any), while his government limbered up in the background for a prolonged attack on the public sector under the guise of reducing the national debt and recovering from the crash – with "austerity" as the watch word. The principal threat to the political class came from **Alex Salmond**, the wily leader of the **Scottish Nationalists**, who galvanized support for his vision of an independent Scotland in the **referendum of September 18, 2014**. The Nationalists came within a hair's breadth of victory – and of breaking up the United Kingdom – but the most remarkable feature of the referendum was the high turnout, an astounding 84 percent.

2012	2013	2014
London hosts the Olympic Games.	Same-sex marriage legalized in England and Wales; Scotland follows in 2014.	By a pip and a squeak, the Scots reject independence and remain part of the United Kingdom in the Scottish referendum.

Books

The bibliography we've given here is necessarily selective, and entirely subjective. Most of the books reviewed are currently in print, though if your local bookshops can't help, then Amazon almost certainly can (ⓦamazon .co.uk; ⓦamazon.com). The ★symbol indicates titles that are especially recommended.

TRAVEL AND JOURNALS

★Bill Bryson *Notes from a Small Island*. Bryson's best-selling and highly amusing account of an extended journey around Britain in the 1990s.

William Cobbett *Rural Rides*. First published in 1830, Cobbett's account of his various fact-finding tours bemoaned the death of the old rural England and its customs, while decrying both the growth of cities and the iniquities suffered by the exploited urban poor.

David Craig *On the Crofter's Trail*. Using anecdotes and interviews with descendants, Craig conveys the hardship and tragedy of the Highland Clearances without being mawkish.

★Jan Morris *The Matter of Wales*. Prolific half-Welsh travel writer Jan Morris immerses herself in the country that she evidently loves. Highly partisan and fiercely nationalistic, the book combs over the origins of the Welsh character, and describes the people and places of Wales with precision and affection. Published in the mid-1980s.

J.B. Priestley *English Journey*. Quirky account of the Bradford-born author's travels around England in the 1930s.

GUIDEBOOKS

★Simon Jenkins *England's Thousand Best Churches* and *England's Thousand Best Houses*. These two superb, heavyweight books from a well-known UK journalist describe the pick of England's churches and houses in lucid detail. Wittily written, they're divided into counties with a star system to indicate the best. Sales were so good that Jenkins has had another stab at the same format in 2013 with *England's 100 Best Views*.

A. Wainwright *A Coast to Coast Walk*. Beautiful palm-sized guide by acclaimed English hiker and Lake District expert. Printed from his handwritten notes and sketched maps. Also in the series are seven authoritative books covering a variety of walks and climbs in the Lake District.

★Ben Weinreb and Christopher Hibbert *The London Encyclopaedia*. More than a thousand pages of concisely presented and well-illustrated information on London past and present – the most fascinating single book on the capital.

HISTORY, SOCIETY AND POLITICS

John Campbell *The Iron Lady: Margaret Thatcher*. Campbell has been mining the Thatcher seam for several years now and this abridged paperback version, published in 2012, hits many political nails right on the head. By the same author, and equally engaging, is his 1987 *Aneurin Bevan and the Mirage of British Socialism* as well as his latest work, a biography of *Roy Jenkins*.

Christopher Hill *The World Turned Upside-Down; God's Englishman: Oliver Cromwell and the English Revolution*. A pioneering Marxist historian, Hill (1912–2003) transformed the way the story of the English Civil War and the Commonwealth was related in a string of superbly researched, well-written texts – among which these are two of the best.

★Eric Hobsbawm *Industry and Empire*. Ostensibly an economic history of Britain from 1750 to the late 1960s, charting Britain's decline and fall as a world power, this book's great skill lies in its detailed analysis of the effects on ordinary people. By the same author, *Captain Swing* focuses on the labourers' uprisings of nineteenth-century England, while his magnificent trilogy, *The Age of Revolution 1789–1848*, *The Age of Capital 1848–1875* and *The Age of Extremes 1914–1991* simply can't be bettered.

Philip Jenkins *A History of Modern Wales 1536–1990*. Splendidly thorough book, placing Welsh history in its British and European contexts. Unbiased and rational appraisal of events and the struggle to preserve Welsh consciousness.

★David Kynaston *Austerity Britain 1945–51*. Comprehensive vox pop that gives the real flavour of postwar England. Everything is here, from the skill of a Dennis Compton cricket innings through to the dangers of hewing coal down the pit. Also recommended are Kynaston's follow-up volumes *Family Britain, 1951–1957* and *Modernity Britain, 1957–59*.

Michael Lynch (ed) *The Oxford Companion to Scottish History*. Recently updated, this heavyweight (768pp) volume covers pretty much everything and anything

Scottish you can think of – folklore, biographies, art, towns and cities – all arranged alphabetically. Lynch also wrote the authoritative *Scotland: A New History*, which remains the best book on its subject, though it needs an update – it was published in 1992.

Andrew Rawnsley *The End of the Party*. Arguably Britain's most acute political journalist, Rawnsley cross-examines and dissects New Labour under Blair and Brown to withering effect.

Simon Schama *A History of Britain* (3 vols). British history, from 3000 BC to 2000 AD, delivered by the country's major TV historical popularizer (the books followed the series).

Schama's the best at this kind of stuff, writing in a clear and lucid style.

★ **E.P. Thompson** *The Making of the English Working Class*. A seminal text – essential reading for anyone who wants to understand the fabric of English society – tracing the trials and tribulations of England's emergent working-class between 1780 and 1832.

Wynford Vaughan-Thomas *Wales – a History*. Working chronologically from the pre-Celtic dawn to the aftermath of the 1979 devolution vote, this masterpiece is a warm and spirited history of Wales, offering perhaps the clearest explanation of the evolution of Welsh culture.

ART, ARCHITECTURE AND ARCHEOLOGY

Owen Hatherley *A Guide to the New Ruins of Great Britain*. No good news here from this angry rant of a book, which rails against – and describes in detail – the 1990s architectural desecration of a string of British cities in the name of speculation masquerading as modernization.

★ **Duncan MacMillan** *Scottish Art 1460–2000* and *Scottish Art in the Twentieth Century*. The former is a lavish overview of Scottish painting with good sections on landscape, portraiture and the Glasgow Boys, while the

latter covers its period (till 2001) in splendid detail.

Francis Pryor *Home: A Time Traveller's Tales from Britain's Prehistory*. The often arcane discoveries of working archeologists are given fascinating new exposure in Pryor's lively archeological histories of Britain. This latest book concentrates on prehistoric family life, but other Pryor titles include *Britain in the Middle Ages*; *Britain BC* and *Britain AD: A Quest for Arthur, England and the Anglo-Saxons*.

FICTION BEFORE 1900

★ **Jane Austen** *Pride and Prejudice; Sense and Sensibility; Emma; Persuasion*. All-time classics on manners, society and provincial life; laced with bathos and ever-so-subtle twists of plot.

R.D. Blackmore *Lorna Doone*. Blackmore's swashbuckling, melodramatic romance, set on Exmoor, has done more for West Country tourism than any other book.

James Boswell *The Life of Samuel Johnson*. England's most famous man of letters and pioneer dictionary-maker displayed – warts and all – by his engagingly low-life Scottish biographer.

★ **Emily Brontë** *Wuthering Heights*. Set on the Yorkshire Moors, this is the ultimate English melodrama, complete with volcanic passions, craggy landscapes, ghostly presences and gloomy Yorkshire villagers/villages.

John Bunyan *Pilgrim's Progress*. Simple, allegorical tale of hero Christian's struggle to achieve salvation. Prepare to feel guilty.

Thomas De Quincey *Confessions of an English Opium-Eater*. Tripping out with the most famous literary drug-taker after Coleridge – *Fear and Loathing in Las Vegas* it isn't, but neither is this a simple cautionary tale.

Charles Dickens *Bleak House; David Copperfield; Little Dorrit; Oliver Twist; Hard Times*. Many of Dickens' novels are set in London, including *Bleak House, Oliver Twist* and *Little Dorrit*, and these contain some of his most trenchant pieces of social analysis; *Hard Times*, however, is set in a Lancashire mill town, while *David Copperfield* draws on Dickens' own unhappy experiences as a boy,

with much of the action taking place in Kent and Norfolk.

George Eliot *Scenes of Clerical Life; Middlemarch; Mill on the Floss*. Eliot (real name Mary Ann Evans) wrote mostly about the county of her birth, Warwickshire, the setting for the three searing tales that comprise her fictional debut, *Scenes of Clerical Life*. *Middlemarch* is a gargantuan portrayal of English provincial life prior to the Reform Act of 1832, while the exquisite *Mill on the Floss* is based on her own childhood experiences.

Thomas Hardy *Far from the Madding Crowd; The Mayor of Casterbridge; Tess of the D'Urbervilles; Jude the Obscure*. Hardy's novels contain some famously evocative descriptions of his native Dorset, but originally it was Hardy's defiance of conventional pieties that attracted most attention: *Tess*, in which the heroine has a baby out of wedlock and commits murder, shocked his contemporaries, while his bleakest novel, the Oxford-set *Jude the Obscure*, provoked such a violent response that Hardy gave up novel-writing altogether.

Walter Scott *Waverley*. Swirl the tartan, blow the pipes, this is the first of the books by Scott that did much to create a highly romanticized version of Scottish life and history. Others include *Rob Roy*, a rich and ripping yarn that transformed the diminutive brigand into a national hero.

Lawrence Sterne *Tristram Shandy*. Anarchic, picaresque eighteenth-century ramblings based on life in a small English village; full of bizarre textual devices – like an all-black page in mourning for one of the characters.

★**Robert Louis Stevenson** *Dr Jekyll and Mr Hyde; Kidnapped; The Master of Ballantrae; Treasure Island; Weir of Hermiston*. Superbly imagined and pacily written nineteenth-century tales of intrigue and derring-do.

Anthony Trollope *Barchester Towers*. Trollope was an astonishingly prolific novelist who also, in his capacity as a postal surveyor, found time to invent the letterbox. The "Barsetshire" novels, of which *Barchester Towers* is the best known, are set in and around a fictional version of Salisbury.

TWENTIETH-CENTURY CLASSICS

John Buchan *The Complete Richard Hannay*. This one volume includes *The 39 Steps, Greenmantle, Mr Standfast, The Three Hostages* and *The Island of Sheep*. Good gung-ho stories with a great feel for the Scottish landscape.

Joseph Conrad *The Secret Agent*. Spy story based on the 1906 anarchist bombing of Greenwich Observatory, exposing the hypocrisies of both the police and anarchists.

E.M. Forster *Howards End*. Bourgeois angst in Hertfordshire and Shropshire, by one of the country's best-loved modern novelists.

Lewis Grassic Gibbon *A Scots Quair*. A landmark trilogy, set in northeast Scotland during and after World War I, the events are seen through the eyes of Chris Guthrie, "torn between her love for the land and her desire to escape a peasant culture". Strong, seminal work.

Robert Graves *Goodbye to All That*. Horrific and humorous memoirs of public school and World War I trenches, followed by postwar trauma (Graves had been badly wounded). Graves hit the literary big time in 1934 with a scholarly Roman soap opera, *I, Claudius*.

D.H. Lawrence *Sons and Lovers; Lady Chatterley's Lover*. Lawrence's less-than-flattering take on working-class life in a Nottinghamshire pit village never went down well with the locals. His *Sons and Lovers*, a fraught, autobiographical novel, contains some of his finest writing, as does the infamous *Lady Chatterley's Lover*, which pushes sex and class hard (and harder) together.

Laurie Lee *Cider with Rosie*. Beautifully written reminiscences of adolescent frolics in the rural Cotswolds of the 1920s.

Richard Llewellyn *How Green Was My Valley; Up into the Singing Mountain; Down Where the Moon is Small; Green, Green My Valley Now*. Vital tetralogy in eloquent and passionate prose, following the life of Huw Morgan from his youth in a South Wales mining valley through emigration to the Welsh community in Patagonia and back to 1970s Wales. The pick, *How Green Was My Valley*, captured a longing for a simple if tough life, and steered clear of cloying sentimentality.

Daphne du Maurier *Rebecca*. Long derided in many quarters as a popular piece of fluff, this darkly romantic novel has come to be appreciated as a Gothic meditation on sexual inequality and obsession, focused around the brooding mansion of Manderley, on du Maurier's beloved Cornish coast. See also the same author's *Frenchman's Creek* and *Jamaica Inn*.

George Orwell *Down and Out in Paris and London; The Road to Wigan Pier*. Famous more than anything else for *1984*, which was published in 1949, Orwell had warmed up in the 1930s with these angry denunciations of inequity, giving respectively a tramp's-eye view of the world and the brutal effects of the Great Depression on the industrial communities of Lancashire and Yorkshire.

Alan Sillitoe *Saturday Night and Sunday Morning*. Gritty account of factory life and sexual shenanigans in Nottingham in the late 1950s.

★**Dylan Thomas** *Under Milk Wood; Collected Stories; Collected Poems: 1934–1953*. *Under Milk Wood* is Thomas's most popular play, telling the story of a microcosmic Welsh seaside town over a 24-hour period. *Collected Stories* contains all of Thomas's classic prose pieces, including the compulsive, crackling autobiography, *Portrait of the Artist as a Young Dog*. Thomas's beautifully wrought and inventive poems carry a deep, pained concern with mortality and the nature of humanity.

Evelyn Waugh *The Sword of Honour* trilogy. A brilliant satire of the World War I officer class laced with some of Waugh's funniest set pieces. The best-selling *Brideshead Revisited* is possibly his worst book, rank with snobbery, nostalgia and love of money.

P.G. Wodehouse *Thank You, Jeeves; A Damsel in Distress*. For many, Wodehouse (1881–1975) is the quintessential English humorist and his deftly crafted tales – with their familiar cast of characters, primarily Bertie Wooster and Jeeves – have remained popular for decades.

CONTEMPORARY FICTION

Peter Ackroyd *English Music*. A typical Ackroyd novel, constructing parallels between interwar London and distant epochs to conjure a kaleidoscopic vision of English culture. His other novels, such as *Chatterton, Hawksmoor* and *The House of Doctor Dee*, are variations on his preoccupation with the English psyche's darker depths.

★**Julian Barnes** *The Sense of an Ending; Levels of Life*. One of the UK's most versatile writers, Barnes seems to be able to turn his hand to just about anything. These two novels, his latest, touch on themes of sex and inhibition, regret and false recollection, but most of all death and bereavement.

George Mackay Brown *Beside the Ocean of Time*. A child's journey through the history of an Orkney island, and an adult's effort to make sense of the place's secrets in the late twentieth century.

John Fowles *The Collector; The French Lieutenant's Woman; Daniel Martin*. The Collector, Fowles' first novel, is a psychological thriller in which the heroine is kidnapped by a psychotic pools-winner, the story being told once by each protagonist. *The French Lieutenant's Woman*, set in Lyme Regis on the Dorset coast, is a tricksy neo-Victorian novel with a famous DIY ending, while *Daniel Martin* is a dense (very dense), realistic novel set in postwar Britain.

★**William Golding** *The Spire*. Atmospheric albeit complex novel centred on the building of a cathedral spire, taking place in a thinly disguised medieval Salisbury. Also, if you ever wondered what it was like to be at sea in an early nineteenth-century British ship, try the splendid *Rites of Passage* trilogy.

Alasdair Gray *Lanark*. Gray's first novel was twenty-five years in the writing and remains his most influential, leading Anthony Burgess to hail him as "the most important Scottish writer since Sir Walter Scott". This challenging, loosely autobiographical work – part science fiction, part *bildungsroman* – relates, in sometimes hallucinatory style, the journey of a man who hankers to create great art.

Alan Hollinghurst *The Stranger's Child*. Hollinghurst excels in pin-sharp and often very funny observations of British society. This particular work, from 2011, starts with a pre-World War I encounter in a country house, by turns bucolic, edgy and romantic. The focus of attention is a young poet who is killed in the war, and the narrative that follows develops into a satire on the uncertain art of biography.

★**P.D. James** *Original Sin*. James writes skilful tales of murder and mystery; of her umpteen novels featuring Police Commander/poet Adam Dalgliesh, this is one of the best. The novels *An Unsuitable Job for a Woman* and *The Skull Beneath the Skin* are also worth reading, featuring London private detective Cordelia Gray.

James Kelman *The Busconductor Hines; How Late It Was, how late*. The first is a wildly funny story of a young Glasgow bus conductor with an intensely boring job and a limitless imagination. *How Late It Was* is Kelman's award-winning and controversial look at life from the perspective of a blind Glaswegian drunk. A disturbing study of personal and political violence, with language to match.

Olivia Laing *To the River*. This acclaimed account of the author's midsummer walk along the River Ouse in Sussex from source to sea is beautifully written and observed, interweaving nature writing, history and folklore with plenty on Virginia Woolf, who drowned herself in the river in 1941.

Hilary Mantel *Wolf Hall; Bring up The Bodies*. Best-selling Mantel has made an enormous literary splash with her sharply observed, superbly crafted historical novels – and these are two of the best, set in the troubled days of Henry VIII and focused on his loyal enforcer, Thomas Cromwell.

★**Ian McEwan** *Atonement; On Chesil Beach*. One of Britain's finest contemporary novelists, McEwan's dark and brooding works are punctuated by the unforeseen and the accidental. *Atonement* is possibly his most masterful book, tracing the course of three lives from a sweltering country garden in 1935 to absolution in the new century, while *On Chesil Beach* is a tale of innocence and loss, misunderstanding and tenderness between two newlyweds in a hotel on the Dorset coast in the early 1960s.

Ian Rankin *Knots and Crosses; The Falls*. Britain's best-selling crime author introduced John Rebus in 1987 and since then the hard-drinking, anti-authoritarian, emotionally scarred detective has featured in almost twenty novels. He inhabits the mean streets of Edinburgh – streets the tourists rarely see – though visitors can rub shoulders with him in cherished locations like the *Oxford Bar*.

Ruth Rendell/Barbara Vine *From Doon With Death; Gallowglass, King Solomon's Carpet; Grasshopper; The Birthday Present*. Rendell writes brilliantly and disturbingly of contemporary dysfunction in all its guises. Her long-standing Inspector Wexford series is set in the fictional West Sussex town of Kingsmarkham, but it's when writing as Barbara Vine that Rendell excels in creating memorable fictions and a sense of place, namely London.

Sarah Waters Waters is a consummate storyteller, specializing in subtly psychological and sexually charged historical novels that have a very strong sense of place – that is, London and Southeast England. *Tipping the Velvet*, *Affinity* and *Fingersmith* are set in Victorian times; *The Night Watch* in World War II; *The Little Stranger*, an eerie ghost story, takes place in the postwar period; and *The Paying Guests* back to London in the 1920s.

Film

Britain has produced a wealth of great films as well as some of the world's finest actors, producers and directors. The films reviewed below all depict a particular aspect of British life, whether reflecting the experience of immigrant communities, investigating its rippling class tensions or having a self-deprecatory laugh. The ★ symbol indicates films that are especially recommended.

THE 1930S AND 1940S

The 39 Steps (Alfred Hitchcock, 1935). Hitchcock's best-loved British movie, full of wit and bold acts of derring-do. Robert Donat stars as innocent Richard Hannay, inadvertently caught up in a mysterious spy ring and forced to flee both spies and Scotland Yard. In a typically perverse Hitchcock touch, he spends a generous amount of time handcuffed to Madeleine Carroll – before the action returns to London for the film's great music-hall conclusion.

★ **Brief Encounter** (David Lean, 1945). Wonderful weepie in which Trevor Howard and Celia Johnson teeter on the edge of adultery after a chance encounter at a railway station. Noël Coward wrote the clipped dialogue; the flushed, dreamy soundtrack features Rachmaninov's *Piano Concerto No. 2*.

Brighton Rock (John Boulting, 1947). A fine adaptation of Graham Greene's novel, featuring a young, scary Richard Attenborough as the psychopathic Pinkie, who marries a witness to one of his crimes to ensure her silence. Beautiful cinematography and good performances, with a real sense of film noir menace.

★ **Great Expectations** (David Lean, 1946). An early film by one of Britain's finest directors – also responsible for *Lawrence of Arabia* and *Bridge on the River Kwai* – this superb rendition of the Dickens novel features magnificent performances by John Mills (as Pip) and Finlay Currie (as Abel Magwitch). The scene in the graveyard will (should) make your hair stand on end.

Henry V (Laurence Olivier, 1944). With dreamlike Technicolor backdrops, this rousing piece of wartime propaganda is emphatically cinematic rather than "theatrical", the action spiralling out from the Globe Theatre itself. Olivier is a brilliantly charismatic king, and the atmospheric pre-battle scene where he goes disguised amongst his men is heartachingly muted.

I Know Where I'm Going! (Michael Powell and Emeric Pressburger, 1945). Powell and Pressburger made some of the finest British films of all time (see also *The Life and Death of Colonel Blimp*, *Black Narcissus* and *The Red Shoes*), all of which expose the peculiarities of the British character. In this delightful romance, Wendy Hiller's modern young woman, who knows what she wants and how to get it, is stymied in her goals by the mysterious romanticism of the Scottish islands and their inhabitants.

Jane Eyre (Robert Stevenson, 1943). Joan Fontaine does a fine job of portraying Jane, and Orson Welles is a suavely sardonic Rochester – the scene where he is thrown from his horse in the mist hits the perfect melodramatic pitch. With the unlikely tagline "A Love Story Every Woman Would Die a Thousand Deaths to Live!", it briefly features a young Elizabeth Taylor as a dying Helen Burns.

★ **Rebecca** (Alfred Hitchcock, 1940). Hitchcock does du Maurier: Laurence Olivier is wonderfully enigmatic as Maxim de Winter, and Joan Fontaine glows as his meek second wife, living in the shadow of her mysterious predecessor.

★ **Wuthering Heights** (William Wyler, 1939). The version of Emily Brontë's novel that everyone remembers, with Laurence Olivier as the dysfunctional Heathcliff and Merle Oberon as Cathy. It's tense, passionate and wild, and lays proper emphasis on the Yorkshire landscape, the best of all possible places for doomed lovers.

1950 TO 1970

Billy Liar! (John Schlesinger, 1963). Tom Courtenay is Billy, stuck in a dire job as an undertaker's clerk in a northern town, spending his time creating extravagant fantasies. His life is lit up by the appearance of Julie Christie, who holds out the glamour and promise of swinging London.

Carry On Screaming (Gerald Thomas, 1966). One of the best from the Carry On crew, with many of the usual suspects (Kenneth Williams, Charles Hawtrey, Joan Sims) hamming it up with the usual nudge-nudge merriment in a Hammer Horror spoof. Great one-liners too, but not the best – for this you have to watch *Carry on Cleo* (as in Cleopatra; 1964) with Julius Caesar (Kenneth Williams) announcing "Infamy, infamy...they've all got it in for me".

Far From the Madding Crowd (John Schlesinger, 1967). An imaginative adaptation of Hardy's doom-laden tale of the desires and ambitions of wilful/wishful Bathsheba Everdene. Julie Christie is a radiant and spirited Bathsheba,

Terence Stamp flashes his blade to dynamic effect, Alan Bates is quietly charismatic as dependable Gabriel Oak, and the West Country setting is sparsely beautiful.

★ **Kes** (Kenneth Loach, 1969). The unforgettable story of a neglected Yorkshire schoolboy who finds solace and liberation in training his kestrel. As a still-pertinent commentary on poverty and an impoverished school system, it's bleak but idealistic. Pale and pinched David Bradley, who plays Billy Casper, is hugely affecting. Loach at the top of his game.

★ **The Ladykillers** (Alexander Mackendrick, 1955). Alec Guinness is fabulously toothy and malevolent as "Professor Marcus", a murderous con man who lodges with a sweet little old lady, Mrs Wilberforce (Katie Johnson), in this skewed Ealing comedy.

A Man for All Seasons (Fred Zinnemann, 1966). Sir Thomas More takes on Henry VIII in one of British history's great moral confrontations. Robert Bolt's wry screenplay, muted visuals and a heavenly host of theatrical talent (including Orson Welles as Cardinal Wolsey) add to the spectacle if not the tension, which is where the film dithers.

★ **Night and the City** (Jules Dassin, 1950). Great film noir, with Richard Widmark as an anxious nightclub hustler on the run. It's gripping and convincingly sleazy, and the London streetscapes have an Expressionist edge of horror.

Saturday Night and Sunday Morning (Karel Reisz, 1960). Reisz's monochrome captures all the grit and dead-end grind of Albert Finney's life working in a Nottingham bicycle factory – and his anarchic rejection of pretty much everything that surrounds him. The way out: heavy drinking and heavy petting (if not more).

★ **This Sporting Life** (Lindsay Anderson, 1963). One of the key British films of the 1960s, and a classic of the gritty "kitchen sink" genre. It's the story of a Northern miner turned Rugby League star with the young Richard Harris giving a great (and singularly muscular) performance as the inarticulate antihero, able only to express himself through physical violence.

THE 1970S AND 1980S

★ **Babylon** (Franco Rosso, 1980). A moving account of black working-class London life. We follow the experiences of young Blue through a series of encounters that reveal the nation's insidious racism. Good performances and a great reggae soundtrack: an all too rare example of Black Britain taking centre stage in a British movie.

Distant Voices, Still Lives (Terence Davies, 1988). Beautifully realized autobiographical tale of growing up in Liverpool in the 1940s and 1950s. The mesmeric pace is punctuated by astonishing moments of drama, and the whole is a very moving account of how a family survives and triumphs, in small ways, against the odds.

★ **Get Carter** (Mike Hodges, 1971). Vivid British gangster movie, featuring a hard-nosed, hard-case Michael Caine as the eponymous hero-villain, returning to his native Newcastle to avenge his brother's death. Great use of its Northeastern locations and a fine turn by playwright John Osborne as the local godfather.

The Last of England (Derek Jarman, 1987). Jarman was a genuine maverick in Eighties Britain and this is his most abstract account of the state of the nation. Composed of apparently unrelated shots of decaying London landscapes, rent boys, and references to emblematic national events such as the Falklands War, this may not be to all tastes, but it is a fitting testament to Jarman's unique talent.

My Beautiful Laundrette (Stephen Frears, 1985). A slice of Thatcher's Britain, with a young, on-the-make Asian, Omar, opening a ritzy laundrette in London. His lover, Johnny (Daniel Day-Lewis), is an ex-National Front glamour boy, angry and inarticulate when forced by the acquisitive Omar into a menial role in the laundrette. The racial, sexual and class dynamics of their relationship mirror the tensions in the city itself.

Withnail and I (Bruce Robinson, 1986). Richard E. Grant is superb as the raddled, drunken Withnail, a "resting" actor with a penchant for drinking lighter fluid. Paul McGann is the "I" of the title – a bemused spectator of Withnail's wild excesses, as they abandon their grotty London flat for a remote country cottage, and the attentions of Withnail's randy Uncle Monty (Richard Griffiths).

THE 1990S

Bhaji on the Beach (Gurinder Chadha, 1993). An Asian women's group takes a day-trip to Blackpool in this issue-laden but enjoyable picture. A lot of fun is had contrasting the seamier side of British life with the mores of the Asian aunties, though the male characters are cartoon villains.

Braveheart (Mel Gibson, 1995). Enjoyable cod-Highland camp, with a shaggy-haired Mel Gibson wielding his claymore as thirteenth-century Scottish nationalist William Wallace. The English are thieving effete scum, the Scots all warm-blooded noble savages, and history takes a back seat. Filmed largely in Ireland.

Breaking the Waves (Lars von Trier, 1996). A lyrical, moving drama set in a devout community in the north of Scotland. An innocent young woman, Bess (Emily Watson), falls in love with Danish oil-rig worker Jan (Stellan Skarsgaard). Blaming herself for the injury that cripples him, she embarks on a masochistic sexual odyssey, which rapidly takes her into uncharted waters.

East is East (Damien O'Donnell, 1999). Seventies Salford is the setting for this lively tragi-comedy, with a Pakistani chip-shop owner struggling to keep control of his seven children as they rail against the strictures of Islam and arranged marriages. Inventively made, and with some delightful performances.

Elizabeth (Shekhar Kapur, 1998). Cate Blanchett is stunning in this visually beautiful, Gothic production, where the young, innocent Elizabeth slowly adapts to the role of the "Virgin Queen" to secure her survival. It's better than its sequel *Elizabeth: The Golden Age* (2007), which also stars Blanchett, and focuses on the defeat of the Spanish Armada. But don't take it all as historical gospel.

The Full Monty (Peter Cattaneo, 1997). Set in Sheffield, where six unemployed steel-workers throw caution to the wind and become male strippers, their boast being that all will be revealed in the "full monty". Unpromising physical specimens all, they score an unlikely hit with the local lasses. The film was itself an unlikely hit worldwide and the long-awaited striptease is a joy to behold (well almost).

Howards End (James Ivory, 1992). A superb Anthony Hopkins leads the way in this touching re-creation of E.M. Forster's celebrated novel. From the prolific Merchant Ivory team, who produced a string of exquisite period films, renowned for their elegiac settings.

Lock, Stock and Two Smoking Barrels (Guy Ritchie, 1998). Ritchie may be much derided for his marriage to Madonna and his mock Cockney (mockney) accent, but this – his breakout film – was a witty and inventive comedy-meets-heist movie that gave gangland heavies a "geezer" reboot.

The Madness of King George (Nicholas Hytner, 1994). Adapted from a witty Alan Bennett play, this royal romp is handsomely staged, with the king's loopy antics (a wonderfully nuanced performance from Nigel Hawthorne) played out against a cartoon-like court and its acolytes. Rupert Everett is superb as Prince Regent.

★**Nil by Mouth** (Gary Oldman, 1997). With strong performances by Ray Winstone as a brutish South Londoner and Kathy Burke as his battered wife, this brave and bleak picture delves deep into domestic violence and drug/drink addiction. Brace yourself.

The Remains of the Day (James Ivory, 1993). Kazuo Ishiguro's masterly novel of social and personal repression translates beautifully to the big screen. Anthony Hopkins is the overly decorous butler who gradually becomes aware of his master's fascist connections, Emma Thompson the housekeeper who struggles to bring his deeply suppressed feelings to the surface. Call a counsellor.

Richard III (Richard Loncraine, 1995). A splendid film version of a renowned National Theatre production, which brilliantly transposed the action to a fascist state in the 1930s. The infernal political machinations of a snarling Ian McKellen as Richard are heightened by Nazi associations, and the style of the period imbues the film with the requisite glamour, as does languorously drugged Kristin Scott-Thomas as Lady Anne.

Secrets and Lies (Mike Leigh, 1996). Serious-minded, slice-of-life ensemble drama charting a dysfunctional family's hidden secrets, from infidelity to reconciliation – and all seen through the prism of class. Mike Leigh at his most penetrating.

Sense and Sensibility (Ang Lee, 1995). Ah, the English and their period dramas. They are all here – Rickman, Winslett, Thompson, Grant, Robert Hardy et al – in this tone-perfect re-creation of Jane Austen's sprightly story of love, money and, of course, manners.

Small Faces (Gillies MacKinnon, 1995). A moving little saga about the lives of three brothers growing up in 1960s Glasgow amid feuding gangs of local teenagers. We follow the rough education of young Lex, torn between the excitement and real danger of a life of fighting, and the alternative artistic ambitions of his older brother.

★**Trainspotting** (Danny Boyle, 1996). High-octane dip into the heroin-scarred world of a group of young Scotsmen both at home and in London; includes what might be the best cinematic representation of a heroin fix ever.

Wonderland (Michael Winterbottom, 1999). One Bonfire Night in London as experienced by three unhappy sisters. Winterbottom's use of real locations, natural light and 16mm film gives it a naturalistic air that's also dreamlike, an effect heightened by Michael Nyman's haunting score.

2000 TO 2010

24 Hour Party People (Michael Winterbottom, 2002). Steve Coogan plays the entrepreneurial/inspirational Tony Wilson (1950–2007) – the man of many quotes – in this fast-moving re-creation of the early days of Manchester's Factory Records (late 1970s/80s). Stunning soundtrack too.

Atonement (Joe Wright, 2007). This adaptation of Ian McEwan's highly literary novel of misunderstanding and regret benefits from strong performances from Keira Knightley and James McAvoy and fluent plotting, though the set-piece/one-take Dunkirk scene, while clever, comes across as a tad showy.

Bend It Like Beckham (Gurinder Chadha, 2003). Immensely successful film focusing on the coming of age of a football-loving Punjabi girl in a suburb of London. Both socially acute and comic.

★**Bronson** (Nicolas Winding Refn, 2009). The subject matter may seem unappetizing – Welsh criminal Bronson (Tom Hardy) is reputed to be the most violent man ever locked up in a British prison – and it's not easy viewing, but Refn's take on this unusual antihero is inventive, creative and insightful. Notable also for the appearance of a Rough Guide author as an extra – but blink and you'll miss him.

Control (Anton Corbijn, 2007). Ian Curtis, the lead singer of Joy Division, committed suicide in 1980 at the age of 23. This biopic tracks his life in and around Manchester, based on the account provided by his wife, Deborah. Some have raved over Sam Riley's portrayal of Curtis, others have been less convinced, but as an evocation of the early days of Factory Records it's hard to beat.

Dirty Pretty Things (Stephen Frears, 2003). A tumbling mix of melodrama, social criticism and black comedy, this forceful, thought-provoking film explores the world of Britain's illegal migrants.

Gosford Park (Robert Altman, 2001). Astutely observed upstairs-downstairs murder mystery set in class-ridden 1930s England. The multilayered plot is typical of the director; the script, from Julian Fellowes, is more nuanced than some of his later TV work; and the who's who of great British actors is led by the superb Maggie Smith.

Harry Potter and the Philosopher's Stone (Chris Columbus, 2001). The first film in a series about hero Harry Potter's life at wizard school did wonders for the English tourist industry with its use of places such as Alnwick Castle as locations. The subsequent films are also darkly enjoyable, with excellent ensemble casts – Spall, Gambon, Rickman et al.

In the Loop (Armando Iannucci, 2009). Look what we have to put up with from our politicians, screams Iannucci, in this satire on the opaque and corrupt meanderings of our leaders and their assorted advisors.

The Navigators (Ken Loach, 2001). Feel the fury in Loach's cinematic rant against the privatization of Britain's railway network – and its dreadful effects on five Sheffield railway workers.

The Queen (Stephen Frears, 2006). Dame Helen Mirren became an official national treasure after taking on the role of Her Majesty in this PR movie for the palace, which covers the crisis in the monarchy after the death of Princess Diana. Michael Sheen does a great Tony Blair impression, while Sylvia Syms brings a dash of humour to the role of Queen Mum.

Sexy Beast (Jonathan Glazer, 2000). Gangster thriller distinguished by the performances of Ray Winstone and more especially Ben Kingsley, who plays one of the hardest, meanest criminals ever. Delightful cameos by an evil Ian McShane and a debauched James Fox, too.

Shaun of the Dead (Edgar Wright, 2004). Shuffling and shambolic zombies roam and groan the streets of London in this zom-com, horror-romp that made a name for Simon Pegg. Follow up films in the same vein – The World's End (2013) – have, however, been notably unfunny, making critics wonder if Pegg has anything left in his crypt/locker.

★**This is England** (Shane Meadows, 2006). British cinema rarely ventures into the East Midlands, but this is where Shane Meadows is at home. Set in the early 1980s, this thoughtful film deals with a young working-class lad who falls in with skinheads – the good-hearted ones to begin with, the racists thereafter. If it gives you a taste for Meadows, see also his Dead Man's Shoes (2004), a searing tale of revenge for the cruel murder of the protagonist's brother; again, there's a Midlands setting.

★**Vera Drake** (Mike Leigh, 2004). Moving story of a 1950s working-class woman, who performs illegal abortions from the goodness of her heart and without thought for either money or the legal consequences, which eventually threatens to destroy her and her close-knit family. A powerful counterblast to the anti-abortion lobby.

2010 ONWARDS

The King's Speech (Tom Hooper, 2010). Oscar-scooping hit hinting at the rotten core at the heart of the monarchy without demonizing the royals. Colin Firth is suitably repressed as the vocally challenged King George VI who is given the confidence to become king by Geoffrey Rush's exuberant Australian speech therapist.

Made in Dagenham (Nigel Cole, 2010). Good-hearted, good-natured film about the struggle for equal pay in the car industry in 1960s Britain. Sweet packaging for a tough industrial message.

Mr Nice (Bernard Rose, 2010). Picaresque tale of one-time drug king and (supposedly) very good egg, Howard Marks (Mr Nice himself) from baffled beginnings to stoned (very stoned) fame and fortune via imprisonment and hostile drug cartels. Rhys Ifans is perfect as the drug-addled hero, Chloe Stevens Sevigny as his wife.

Philomena (Stephen Frears, 2013). Coogan and Dench, cynic and innocent, take the high road to find a long lost child taken from Philomena (Dench), once a single, unmarried mother. Thumbs down to the Ireland of the 1950s in general and the Catholic Church in particular. Heartwarming stuff.

★**Sightseers** (Ben Wheatley, 2012). Murder, mayhem, sadism and psychosis on a caravan holiday in the Midlands and the North. Never, but never before, has Crich Tramway Village seemed so dangerous. This is horror with ironic flair – so avert your eyes strategically or prepare to grimace.

Wuthering Heights (Andrea Arnold, 2011). Arnold, whose breakthrough movies were set on urban council estates – Red Road (2006), which used CCTV to tell a story of obsession in Glasgow, and Fish Tank (2009), a searing coming-of-age tale – demonstrates a lyrical eye for the natural world in her arty, elemental reworking of Emily Brontë's romantic tragedy. The emotions are bruisingly raw.

Small print and index

ACKNOWLEDGEMENTS

Tim Burford Thanks as ever to Freddie and Robbie in Haverfordwest, to Jane Harris at Visit Wales and Sara Whines at Four bgb, to Katy and Norm, and to all at Castell Rough Guides.

Samantha Cook Thanks to Rob Humphreys and Claire Saunders, co-authors on my chapters, who made it all easy and loads of fun; Rachel Mills, for an excellent editorial experience; and Greg Ward for everything, always.

Keith Drew Thanks to Tanya Miller, Mani Ramaswamy and Rachel Mills, and especially to Kate, Maisie, Joe and Lilah.

Matthew Hancock and Amanda Tomlin Thanks go to Melissa and Rachel for their excellent editing; Sue Emerson at the Isle of Wight tourist board; Wightlink ferries; *Into the Woods* shepherd's hut and treehouse; all at the very friendly staff at *The Pig*; the National Trust; English Heritage; and to Alex and Olivia for their patience and enthusiasm.

Emma Harrison Thanks to Visit Isle of Man, the guard at Douglas Station and Rachel Mills for excellent guidance.

Phil Lee would like to thank editor, Rachel Mills, for all the help she has given during the preparation of this new edition. Special thanks also to Tom Marlow at Marketing Birmingham; Michelle Marriott-Lodge at the *Castle Hotel*, Hereford; Delysia Hart and Daniella White for their Birmingham tips and hints; Dave Robson for his hospitality in Shrewsbury; and Emma Rees and Marnie Darling Rees for always cheering me up.

Norm Longley would like to thank Greg for diligent and patient editing. A very special thanks to Sara Whines at Four bgb and Jane Harris at Visit Wales for their invaluable assistance. Thanks are also due to Tim, and most importantly, to Christian, Luka, Patrick and Anna.

Claire Saunders Thanks and love to Ian, Tom and Mia.

Ann-Marie Shaw would like to thank Andy Parkinson and Joe Keggin at Marketing Manchester and Liverpool respectively for pointing me in the most interesting directions; Mary Colston, Martin Jones and Katie Bentley for their warm hospitality; Rachel Mills for her flexible and patient editing; and, above all, Mike, George, Ruby, Lily and Cracks for putting up with all the gallivanting.

Jos Simon Thanks to Welcome to Yorkshire, the National Trust, English Heritage and the YHA for information, and to Melissa Graham and Rachel Mills for sympathetic editing.

Helena Smith Thanks to David Brookbranks at NewcastleGateshead, Roger Domeneghetti at Visit County Durham and Natalie Wood at Northumberland Tourism.

Steve Vickers would like to thank the team at Rough Guides, especially Natasha Foges, Rachel Mills and Mani Ramaswamy. Thanks also to Melissa Graham for her careful editing. Research wouldn't have been possible without help from Leanne and Dan at Bunk Campers. Finally, thanks to Kev, Dan and Cara for the laughs along the way.

Rough Guide credits

Editors: Rachel Mills, Greg Dickinson, Kerry Higgins, Melissa Graham
Layout: Pradeep Thapliyal
Cartography: Animesh Pathak, James Macdonald
Picture editor: Raffaella Morini
Proofreader: Diane Margolis
Managing editors: Mani Ramaswamy, Andy Turner
Senior editors: Natasha Foges, Emma Gibbs
Assistant editor: Payal Sharotri

Production: Janis Griffith
Cover design: Nicole Newman, Michelle Bhatia, Pradeep Thapliyal
Editorial assistant: Rebecca Hallett
Senior pre-press designer: Dan May
Programme manager: Gareth Lowe
Publisher: Joanna Kirby
Publishing director: Georgina Dee

Publishing information

This ninth edition published June 2015 by
Rough Guides Ltd,
80 Strand, London WC2R 0RL
11, Community Centre, Panchsheel Park,
New Delhi 110017, India
Distributed by Penguin Random House
Penguin Books Ltd,
80 Strand, London WC2R 0RL
Penguin Group (USA)
345 Hudson Street, NY 10014, USA
Penguin Group (Australia)
250 Camberwell Road, Camberwell,
Victoria 3124, Australia
Penguin Group (NZ)
67 Apollo Drive, Mairangi Bay, Auckland 1310,
New Zealand
Penguin Group (South Africa)
Block D, Rosebank Office Park, 181 Jan Smuts Avenue,
Parktown North, Gauteng, South Africa 2193
Rough Guides is represented in Canada by Tourmaline
Editions Inc. 662 King Street West, Suite 304, Toronto,
Ontario M5V 1M7
Printed in Singapore
© Rough Guides 2015

Maps © Rough Guides
Contains Ordnance Survey data © Crown copyright and
database rights 2015
No part of this book may be reproduced in any form
without permission from the publisher except for the
quotation of brief passages in reviews.
1016pp includes index
A catalogue record for this book is available from the
British Library
ISBN: 978-1-40937-089-5
The publishers and authors have done their best to ensure
the accuracy and currency of all the information in **The
Rough Guide to Great Britain**, however, they can accept
no responsibility for any loss, injury, or inconvenience
sustained by any traveller as a result of information or
advice contained in the guide.
3 5 7 9 8 6 4 2

Help us update

We've gone to a lot of effort to ensure that the ninth edition of **The Rough Guide to Great Britain** is accurate and up-to-date. However, things change – places get "discovered", opening hours are notoriously fickle, restaurants and rooms raise prices or lower standards. If you feel we've got it wrong or left something out, we'd like to know, and if you can remember the address, the price, the hours, the phone number, so much the better.

Please send your comments with the subject line **"Rough Guide Great Britain Update"** to mail @uk.roughguides.com. We'll credit all contributions and send a copy of the next edition (or any other Rough Guide if you prefer) for the very best emails.

Find more travel information, connect with fellow travellers and plan your trip on roughguides.com.

Readers' updates

Thanks to all the readers who have taken the time to write in with comments and suggestions (and apologies if we've inadvertently omitted or misspelt anyone's name):

Belinda Archer, Fleur Ball, Silvia Barbantani, Roger & Lesley Barnett, Ali Bell, John Benjamin, Andy Bennetts, Edward Braisher, Zoe Bremer, Jacky Bright, Richard Brock, Andrew Cameron, Sally Chesters, Patti Collins, Stephen Cook, Cat Coombes, David Cronshaw, Ian Davies, Dalan de Brí, Hilary Fender, Colleen Foggo, Annabella Forbes, Emma Forbes, Mike Foster, Anne Fowler, William Fraatz, Ben Goodhall, Frank Gordon, Murray Grant, Helen Hale, Robert Harding, Nick Hart, Jennie Harvey, Sally Holden, Caroline and John Horder, Ed Hutchings, John Kemp, Harry Kretchmer, Kirsty Laifa, Stefanie Lüdtke, Colm Magee, John Matthews, Lucy Mellor, Adrian Moorman, Celli Moriarty, Kenneth Nichol, Laura Norton, Martin Peters, Richard Reast, Keith Resnick, Rebecca Reynolds, Mitchell Sandler, Rhiannon Scutt, Claire Shirlaw, Simon Sleight, Adrian Smith, David Stubbs, David Walsh, Chris Williamson, Jennifer Wood, Mark Woodall, Tim Woods, Rachel and Martin Wright and Grace Wylie.

ABOUT THE AUTHORS

Jules Brown has written for Rough Guides since 1986 and is the author of the *Rough Guide to the Lake District*.

Tim Burford studied languages at Oxford University and worked briefly in publishing. In 1991 he began writing hiking guides to east-central Europe and then Latin America. He also works on the Rough Guides to Romania, Alaska and Wales, and leads hiking groups in Europe's mountains.

Samantha Cook is a writer and editor born and based in London. She is the co-author of the Rough Guides to London, Vintage London and Kent, Sussex & Surrey, the sole author of the Rough Guides to New Orleans and Chick Flicks, and a contributor to many others.

Keith Drew grew up on the edge of the Mendips and spent his Saturday afternoons at the Rec in Bath, which he fondly recalls, and his Saturday evenings on Park Street in Bristol, which he can't really remember at all. A Managing Editor at Rough Guides, he is also co-author of the *Rough Guide to Bath, Bristol and Somerset*.

Matthew Hancock and Amanda Tomlin are authors of the *Rough Guide to England* and the *Rough Guide to Hampshire, Dorset and the Isle of Wight*. Matthew Hancock is also the author of the Rough Guides to Portugal, Madeira, Lisbon and the Algarve.

Emma Harrison is a writer and editor based in Liverpool. She is Editor of The Independent Map Company and a keen traveller, with a particular interest in the Northwest of England.

Rob Humphreys has lived in London for over twenty years. He has travelled extensively in Scotland and Central Europe writing books for Rough Guides. He is a qualified City of London Tour Guide and spends his spare time directing shows on the Puppet Theatre Barge.

Phil Lee has been writing for Rough Guides for well over twenty years. His other books in the series include Canada, Norway, Belgium & Luxembourg, Bruges, Amsterdam, and Mallorca & Menorca. He lives in Nottingham, where he was born and raised.

Norm Longley spent years writing Rough Guides to countries in Eastern Europe and the Balkans. He has now turned his hand to the UK, having researched guides to Scotland, Wales and Ireland. He lives in Bath and can occasionally be seen erecting marquees on the Rec.

Keith Munro has been a freelance writer since 2010 after a stretch working in London's music industry as a record label manager. A keen traveller, he spent a year in the French Pyrenees before returning to his childhood home of Edinburgh, and has since contributed to the Rough Guides to France, Scotland and other travel related publications.

Claire Saunders grew up in Brighton. After almost ten years of working as an editor and then Managing Editor at Rough Guides in London, she moved back down to Sussex, where she now lives in Lewes and works as a freelance writer and editor.

Ann-Marie Shaw has edited countless Rough Guides, contributed to several others – most recently *Make the Most of Your Time on Earth* – and written for publications including *The Big Issue in the North*. She lives in Cheshire with her partner and three children.

Jos Simon was raised on the Llŷn Peninsula and settled in Yorkshire after teaching in various other parts of the country. He fulfilled a long-held ambition to describe his adopted home county by writing the *Rough Guide to Yorkshire*, and contributing to the Rough Guides to England and Great Britain.

James Stewart researched the North Wales chapter by campervan, tent and hiking trail. A freelance travel journalist specialising in activities and remote destinations for the likes of the *Guardian, Sunday Times, Telegraph* and *Wanderlust*, he is the author of around fifteen guidebooks. James tweets on @itsjamesstewart.

Helena Smith comes from Scotland and lives in Hackney, east London. When she isn't travelling, Helena blogs about food and community at eathackney.com.

Matthew Teller (matthewteller.com) is a journalist, broadcaster and travel writer living tantalisingly close to the unfashionable northeastern fringes of the Cotswolds. He has written for Rough Guides for almost twenty years, and tries to keep his blog QuiteAlone.com up to date. He tweets @matthewteller.

Steve Vickers is a freelance journalist and guidebook author. He's contributed to more than a dozen Rough Guides titles and has worked for BBC Radio 4, the *Independent*, the *Washington Post* and the *Observer*, among others. You can follow him on Twitter @stevenjvickers.

Photo credits

All photos © Rough Guides except the following:
(Key: t-top, c-centre; b bottom; l-left; r-right)

p.1 Getty Images: John Warburton-Lee/AWL Images
p.2 Getty Images: Sylvain Sonnet
p.4 Corbis: Jane Sweeney (tl). Dorling Kindersley: (tc)
p.5 AWL Images: Travel Pix Collection
p.9 Getty Images: Paul Harris/AWL Images (t). Corbis: Frank Krahmer (b)
p.10 Getty Images: cescassawin/Moment Open
p.11 Alamy: BANANA PANCAKE (tr); Duncan Soar (c); Vanda Ralevska (br)
p.12 Getty Images: Duncan Shaw
p.13 4Corners: Olimpio Fantuz/SIME
p.15 AWL Images: David Bank (bl)
p.16 Photolibrary
p.17 Getty Images: Mike Copeland/Gallo Images (t). Corbis: Meinrad Riedo/imageBROKER (c). AWL Images: Travel Pix Collection (b)
p.18 Alamy: Arch White (t). NHPA/Photoshot: Karen van der Zijden (c)
p.19 Corbis: Peter Giovannini/imagebroker (tl). Alamy: Pawel Libera Images (tr). Getty Images: Jeff J Mitchell (br)
p.20 Corbis: Eric Nathan/Loop Images (tl). Alamy: Tony Wright/earthscapes (tr); Steve Vidler (bl)
p.21 Corbis: Alan Copson/JAI (t). Alamy: Imagestate Media Partners Limited - Impact Photos (c); Adrian Sherratt (b)
p.22 Alamy: David Pick (t); Joanne Moyes (c). AWL Images: Travel Pix Collection (b)
p.23 Alamy: Tim E White (tl); Michael Jenner (tr); TravelStockCollection - Homer Sykes (bl). Getty Images: Matt Cardy (br)
p.24 AWL Images: Travel Pix Collection (t). Corbis: Chris Warren/Loop Images (c). Alamy: Loop Images Ltd (b)
p.25 Corbis: Mark Sykes/JAI (tr). Alamy: Premier (b)
p.28 Alamy: LOOK Die Bildagentur der Fotografen GmbH
p.55 Getty Images: EIGHTFISH
pp.132–133 Corbis: John Miller/Robert Harding World Imagery
p.135 Getty Images: Ivan Vdovin/AWL Images
p.151 Alamy: TTL Images (tr)
p.177 Corbis: Jason Hawkes (t)
p.195 Corbis: Paul Seheult/Eye Ubiquitous (t)
p.261 Alamy: London Entertainment
pp.288–289 Corbis: Roy Rainford/Robert Harding World Imagery
p.309 Corbis: Frank Krahmer (tl)

pp.380–381 Corbis: Neale Clarke/Robert Harding World Imagery
p.403 Royal Shakespeare Company: Keith Pattison (t). Getty Images: Neale Clarke/Robert Harding World Imagery (b)
pp.422–423 Photolibrary
pp.450–451 Getty Images: Steve Allen
p.453 Alamy: eye35.com
p.475 AWL Images: Carlos Sanchez Pereyra (tr). Photolibrary (b)
pp.492–493 Corbis: John Short/Design Pics
p.495 Alamy: The National Trust Photolibrary
pp.518–519 Corbis: Wig Worland
p.521 Alamy: Wildscape
pp.570–571 Corbis: Neale Clark/Robert Harding World Imagery
p.573 Corbis: Roy Rainford/Robert Harding World Imagery
p.599 Getty Images: Daniel Bosma (t). Corbis: Ocean (b)
pp.610–611 Corbis: Chris Warren/Loop Images
pp.656–657 Corbis: David Williams/145/Photographer's Choice RF/Ocean
p.693 Alamy: ImageState
p.709 SuperStock: Chris Warren (c)
pp.760–761 SuperStock: Travel Library Limited
p.763 Alamy: Stephen Miller
pp.782–783 Getty Images: Jeff J Mitchell
p.811 Corbis: Peter Adams/JAI
pp.838–839 Corbis: Patrick Dieudonne/Robert Harding World Imagery
pp.862–863 Corbis: Jan Holm/Loop Images
p.865 Alamy: Louisa Macdonell
pp.886–887 SuperStock: Alan Majchrowicz
p.889 Alamy: Gary Cook
p.905 Corbis: Kathy Collins/Robert Harding World Imagery
pp.924–925 SuperStock: Cody Duncan
pp.948–949 SuperStock: Minden Pictures
p.972 Corbis: Bettmann

Front cover & spine Telephone box on roadside, Orkney Islands © Getty Images: Brian Doben
Back cover Tower Bridge and the Thames © AWL Images: Alex Robinson (t), Inner Hebrides, the cliffs of Neist point © AWL Images: Fortunato Gatto (bl); Angel of the North, Gateshead © Robert Lazenby (br)

Index

Maps are marked in **grey**

Y

Z

Map symbols

The symbols below are used on maps throughout the book

✈ Airport	⚜ Vineyard/winery	🎿 Ski area	Minor road
★ Bus stop	⊠ Gate	Beach	Pedestrian road
⊖ London underground station	∴ Ruin	Swamp	Steps
Ⓤ Glasgow subway station	✡ Synagogue	Bridge	Path
Ⓜ Metro station	⊙ Memorial/statue	Waterfall	Wall
Boat	Mosque	▲ Mountain peak	Ferry
P Parking	Stately home/historic house	Mountain range	Funicular railway
@ Internet café/access	Abbey	Cave	Railway
ⓘ Information office	Church (regional maps)	Castle	Cable car
⊞ Hospital	Monument	Museum	Building
⊠ Post office	Viewpoint	Rocks	Church (town maps)
Public gardens	Lighthouse	Hill	Stadium
Spring/spa	Swimming pool	Gorge	Market
Battlefield	Tower	Standing stones	Beach
Point of interest	Campsite	Motorway	Park
Golf course	Whisky distillery	Main road	Cemetery

Listings key

- ■ Accommodation
- ● Restaurant/café
- ■ Pub/club/live music venue/nightlife
- ● Shop